THE ROUTLEDGE HANDBOOK OF POVERTY IN THE UNITED STATES

In the United States, the causes and even the meanings of poverty are disconnected from the causes and meanings of global poverty. *The Routledge Handbook of Poverty in the United States* provides an authoritative overview of the relationship of poverty with the rise of neoliberal capitalism in the context of globalization.

Reorienting its national economy towards a global logic, United States domestic policies have promoted a market-based strategy of economic development and growth as the obvious solution to alleviating poverty, affecting approaches to the problem discursively, politically, economically, culturally, and experientially. However, the handbook explores how, rather than alleviating poverty, it has instead exacerbated poverty and pre-existing inequalities—privatizing the services of social welfare and educational institutions, transforming the state from a benevolent to a punitive state, and criminalizing poor women, racial and ethnic minorities, and immigrants.

Key issues examined by the international selection of leading scholars in this volume include: income distribution, employment, health, hunger, housing, and urbanization. With parts focusing on the lived experience of the poor, social justice and human rights frameworks—as opposed to welfare rights models—and the role of helping professions such as social work, health, and education, this comprehensive handbook is a vital reference for anyone working with those in poverty, whether directly or at a macro level.

Stephen Nathan Haymes, Ph.D., is an Associate Professor in the College of Education and an affiliated faculty member of the Department of Peace, Justice and Conflict Studies Program and the Department of International Studies at DePaul University, Chicago. Professor Haymes' areas of research interest are Africana philosophy, postcolonial theory, forced migration, and education, conflict, and development. Currently, he is working on a project related to place-based education and eco-justice with displaced Afro-descendent communities and a Colombian Human Rights NGO. He serves as the co-editor of *The Journal of Poverty: Innovations on Social, Political and Economic Inequalities*, a quarterly peer review publication of the Taylor & Francis Group.

María Vidal de Haymes, Ph.D., is a Professor in the School of Social Work and Director of the Institute for Migration and International Social Work at Loyola University Chicago. She is the co-editor of *The Journal of Poverty: Innovations on Social, Political and Economic Inequalities*. She teaches courses in areas of social welfare policy and migration studies and her research addresses the economic and political incorporation of Latino immigrants in the United States; the impact of migration on family relationships, roles, and functioning; forced migration; the role of faith-based organizations in the pastoral and social accompaniment of migrants; child welfare; and social work education.

Reuben Jonathan Miller, Ph.D., is an Assistant Professor of Social Work at the University of Michigan. His research, writing, and advocacy work focus on the well-being of former prisoners living in large urban settings and the ways in which criminal justice and social welfare policy is experienced daily by urban poor populations.

THE ROUTLEDGE HANDBOOK OF POVERTY IN THE UNITED STATES

Edited by Stephen Nathan Haymes,
María Vidal de Haymes, and Reuben Jonathan Miller

Routledge
Taylor & Francis Group

LONDON AND NEW YORK

First published 2015
by Routledge
2 Park Square, Milton Park, Abingdon, Oxon OX14 4RN

and by Routledge
711 Third Avenue, New York, NY 10017

Routledge is an imprint of the Taylor & Francis Group, an informa business

British Library Cataloguing in Publication Data
A catalogue record for this book is available from the British Library

Library of Congress Cataloging in Publication Data
The Routledge Handbook of Poverty in the United States / edited by Stephen
Haymes, Maria Vidal de Haymes and Reuben Miller.
pages cm
1. Poverty—United States. 2. United States—Economic conditions. 3. United
States—Social conditions. 4. United States—Economic policy. 5. United States—
Social policy. I. Haymes, Stephen Nathan. II. De Haymes, Maria Vidal. III. Miller,
Reuben Jonathan.
HC110.P6R68 2014
362.50973—dc23
2014009636

ISBN: 978 0 41 567344 0 (hbk)
ISBN: 978 1 31 575551 9 (ebk)

Typeset in Bembo
by GreenGate Publishing Services, Tonbridge, Kent

Printed and bound by CPI Group (UK) Ltd, Croydon, CR0 4YY

This book is dedicated to the memory of our dear friend and colleague, Alfred L. Joseph.

'This Handbook is a treasure trove. Yes, it marshals the data on U.S. poverty, providing an indispensable reference guide. Even more valuably, it theorizes U.S. poverty anew, demonstrating how U.S. destitution and its "surplus populations" are shaped by neoliberalism's global projects and logics, its economic mandates and powers of enforcement. The Handbook is thus also a compendium of knowledge for all who fight to end poverty. This is the book I want my students to have as they work in impoverished communities. It is also the book that all scholars of poverty and globalization will need to keep ready to hand.'

Mark Lewis Taylor, Religion and Society, Princeton Theological Seminary

CONTENTS

Contents

FIGURES

TABLES

APPENDICES

EDITOR BIOGRAPHIES

Stephen Nathan Haymes, Ph.D., is an Associate Professor in the College of Education and is an affiliated faculty member of the Department of Peace, Justice and Conflict Studies Program and the Department of International Studies at DePaul University. Professor Haymes' areas of research interests are Africana philosophy, postcolonial theory, forced migration, and education, conflict, and development. Currently, he is working on a project related to place-based education and eco-justice with displaced Afro-descendent communities and a Colombian Human Rights NGO. He serves as the co-editor of *The Journal of Poverty: Innovations on Social, Political and Economic Inequalities*, a quarterly peer review publication of the Taylor & Francis Group.

María Vidal De Haymes, Ph.D., is a Professor in the School of Social Work and Director of the Institute for Migration and International Social Work at Loyola University Chicago. She is the co-editor of *The Journal of Poverty: Innovations on Social, Political and Economic Inequalities*. She teaches courses in areas of social welfare policy and migration studies and her research addresses the economic and political incorporation of Latino immigrants in the United States; the impact of migration on family relationships, roles, and functioning; forced migration; the role of faith-based organizations in the pastoral and social accompaniment of migrants; child welfare; and social work education.

Reuben Jonathan Miller, Ph.D., is an Assistant Professor of Social Work at the University of Michigan. His research, writing, and advocacy work focus on the well-being of former prisoners living in large urban settings and the ways in which criminal justice and social welfare policy is daily experienced by urban poor populations.

CONTRIBUTORS

Ali A. Abdi is a Professor and Co-Director of the Centre for Global Citizenship Education and Research (CGCER) in the Department of Educational Policy Studies at the University of Alberta. His areas of research include citizenship and human rights education, social and cultural foundations of education, and postcolonial studies in education.

Kimya Barden is an Assistant Professor at Northeastern Illinois University's Inner City Studies Education Program. Dr. Barden earned her Ph.D. in social work at Loyola University Chicago's School of Social Work. A Chicago native, she is a youth program developer and qualitative scholar. Her research interests include African American young adult development, racial socialization processes, and youth violence management.

John R. Barner, MSW, Ph.D., is a Lecturer in the Department of Sociology and Human Services at the University of North Georgia. He has written, presented, and published internationally across many topics, including law and violence, social work education, globalization, immigration, and emergent social movements. His work has appeared in the *British Journal of Social Work*, the *Journal of Policy Practice*, *Qualitative Social Work*, *Social Work Education*, the *Journal of Family Violence*, and *Mortality*.

David Becerra, MSW, Ph.D., is an Assistant Professor in the School of Social Work at Arizona State University. His research focuses on the adverse effects of poverty and inequality among Latinos.

Katherine Beckett is a Professor in the Department of Sociology and the Law, Societies, and Justice Program at the University of Washington. Her recent research projects have explored the consequences of criminal justice expansion for social inequality, the role of race in drug law enforcement, and the transformation of urban social control practices in the United States. She is the author of numerous articles and three books on these topics, including, most recently, *Banished: The New Social Control in Urban America*, published in 2010 by Oxford University Press and a finalist for the C. Wright Mills Book Award.

Lawren E. Bercaw is a Ph.D. candidate at Brandeis University's Heller School for Social Policy and Management and serves as a research analyst within the Aging, Disability, and Long-Term Care division at RTI International. Her primary research interests center around the intersection between housing policy and aging issues.

Kathryn Berg is a doctoral candidate at the University of Buffalo's Social Welfare Program. She has a Master's in Social Work in Women's and Gender Studies from Loyola University Chicago.

Pamela Blackmon is an Assistant Professor at the Department of Political Science, Pennsylvania State University, Altoona. Her research focuses on the policies of the international financial institutions, and she is currently examining the role of export credit agencies in international trade and finance. Her articles have been published in *Third World Quarterly, International Studies Review, Women's Studies*, and *Central Asian Survey*. She has contributed previously to edited volumes that address the policies of the financial institutions in *The International Studies Compendium Project* (2010) and most recently as a contributor to *The Handbook of Global Companies* (2013).

Kevin D. Blair is a Professor of Social Work at Niagara University where he teaches courses in social work methods and poverty. Dr. Blair directs the Vincentian Poverty Studies minor at Niagara. His current research focuses on improving undergraduate poverty education at American universities.

T. Jameson Brewer is a Ph.D. student in the Department of Educational Policy, Organization and Leadership at the University of Illinois at Urbana-Champaign where he studies the implications of educational policies that seek to privatize and commercialize public education and the impacts that those policies have on the profession of teaching and disadvantaged students. Prior to his studies, he taught high school social studies in the inner city Atlanta Public Schools.

Victoria Brockett is an Academic Advisor in the Department of Education at Valparaiso University. Her research interests include racial justice, public sociology, and the intersection of inequality.

Enora R. Brown is an Associate Professor in the Department of Educational Policy Studies and Research in the College of Education at DePaul University. Her publications include the co-edited volume *The Critical Middle School Reader* and a range of articles and book chapters on critical studies in human development, educational policy reform, and youth identity. Her current research focuses on critical discourse analyses of youth in school culture, with an emphasis on identity, race, and social class.

Jessica K. Camp, Ph.D., LMSW, is a recent graduate from the Wayne State University Social Work Doctoral Program. She works as an Assistant Professor of Social Work at the University of Michigan—Flint. Her research focuses on challenging poverty and inequality in the United States, especially among working-age adults in recovery from mental health and substance abuse disorders.

Richard K. Caputo, Ph.D., is a Professor of Social Policy and Research, Wurzweiler School of Social Work, Yeshiva University, New York City. He has authored six books and edited two, including *Policy Analysis for Social Workers* (Thousand Oaks, CA: Sage, 2014), *Basic Income Guarantee and Politics: International Experiences and Perspectives on the Viability of Income Guarantee* (New York:

Palgrave, 2012), and *U.S. Social Welfare Reform: Policy Transitions from 1981 to the Present* (New York: Springer, 2011). He has many peer-reviewed journal articles and serves as an Associate Editor for the *Journal of Family and Economic Issues*. Dr. Caputo also serves on the editorial boards of the *Journal of Poverty*, the *Journal of Sociology and Social Welfare*, *Families in Society*, and *Marriage and Family Review*.

Colleen Casey, Ph.D., is an Associate Professor in the School of Urban and Public Affairs at the University of Texas at Arlington. She has a Ph.D. in Public Policy Analysis and Administration, with an emphasis on urban and community development policy. Her research focus is on urban community and economic development policy, with a particular focus on access to credit, social capital, and social networks.

Shawn Cassiman is an Associate Professor of Social Work at the University of Dayton. Her research, community activism and teaching are concerned with oppression and resistance. She is currently working with the United States BIG (Basic Income) group, as she conceptualizes policy as a form of resistance. Her articles can be found in journals, such as *The Journal of Poverty*, and *Lo Squaderno* among others. For more information: https://udayton.academia.edu/ShawnCassiman

An Chih Cheng, Ph.D., received degrees in Educational Psychology (Ph.D.) and Program Evaluation (MA) from the University of Texas at Austin, and Applied Neuroscience (MS) from the University of Texas at Dallas. He is currently an Assistant Professor of Educational Policy Studies at DePaul University. His work focuses on young children's multimodal literacies and assessment of the efficacy of online education.

Monit Cheung, MA, MSW, Ph.D., LCSW, is a Professor and Chair, Clinical Practice Concentration, and Principal Investigator of the Child Welfare Education Project at the Graduate College of Social Work, University of Houston. Dr. Cheung has been teaching at the graduate level since 1986 after she received her doctoral degree from the Ohio State University. She has been a practitioner in clinical social work for 37 years and has published extensively in the field of child sexual abuse and child protection. She also wrote an article about her experience as a sponsored child which was published in the *Journal of Poverty*.

Brenda Crawley is an Associate Professor Emerita in the School of Social Work at Loyola University Chicago. She is a Fulbright Scholar. Her areas of interest include policy analysis, structural causes of poverty, and international social work.

Elena Delavega, Ph.D., MSW, is an Assistant Professor of Social Work at the University of Memphis. Her research focus centers on understanding and eliminating poverty through policy analysis and interventions grounded in critical theory and French post-structuralism.

Michael P. Dentato, Ph.D., is an Assistant Professor in the School of Social Work at Loyola University Chicago. Dr. Dentato's research centers around sexual minority health disparities and risk behavior attitudes, substance use and addiction disorders, and LGBTQ lifespan development.

Dwanda Farmer, Ph.D., is the Principal Consultant at The CED Doctor, LLC, in Baltimore, Maryland. The firm specializes in community economic development projects including affordable housing, commercial development, and small business enterprise. Dr. Farmer has extensive experience in developing programs and projects in low-income communities with government funding including: New Market Tax Credits, Low Income Housing Tax Credits, and Housing and Urban Development and Community Development Block Grants. She has worked as a CED practitioner for nearly 20 years and has attracted more than $40M to community development projects in low-income communities. She is one of a dozen individuals to obtain a doctorate in Community Economic Development from Southern New Hampshire University.

Richard C. Fording is a Professor and Chair of the Department of Political Science at the University of Alabama. He is the author or co-author of articles appearing in a variety of journals, including *American Political Science Review, American Sociological Review, American Journal of Political Science*, and the *Journal of Politics*. He is the co-author of *Disciplining the Poor: Neoliberal Paternalism and the Persistent Power of Race* (University of Chicago Press).

James C. Fraser is an Associate Professor at Vanderbilt University in the Department of Human and Organizational Development.

Joby Gardner, Ph.D., is an Associate Professor in DePaul University's College of Education and Director of the Program in Curriculum Studies. His research interests include youth cultures, youth development, the institutional experiences of incarcerated and non-dominant youth, and the preparation and support of teachers as change agents. Currently, he is working on a project on re-enrolling youth in Chicago Public Schools after incarceration.

Brendan M. Gaughan completed his Bachelor of Arts in Sociology at Rutgers University in Camden, New Jersey, in 2012. He worked with Dr. Joan Maya Mazelis as a teaching assistant and research assistant during college and has continued as a research collaborator after graduation. His research interests include poverty, inequality, social capital, and social stigmatization.

Christine George, Ph.D., is a Research Associate Professor, Loyola University Chicago, Center for Urban Research and Learning. Dr. George's research, which is primarily within the context of community–university participatory collaborations, focuses on homelessness, domestic violence, and the delivery of social welfare services. She teaches social policy and urban sociology at the undergraduate and graduate levels. She has also been involved in research in the area of women and poverty for many years.

Leigh Graham is an Assistant Professor of Urban Policy at John Jay College of Criminal Justice and on the Doctoral Faculty in Environmental Psychology at the Graduate Center at the City University of New York. Her scholarship on community development conflict and change is grounded in practice in New Orleans, New York City, and Boston, and has been published in *The Journal of the American Planning Association, Housing Policy Debate*, and *Economic Development Quarterly*.

Susan Grossman, Ph.D., is an Associate Dean and Professor, Loyola University Chicago, School of Social Work. Dr. Grossman joined the faculty of the School of Social Work in 1997. She teaches social policy and research in the undergraduate, graduate, and doctoral programs. In addition, she is an Associate Faculty Member of the Women's Studies/Gender Studies Program and the Center for Urban Research and Learning at Loyola. Dr. Grossman's research focuses on the needs and service use of victims of domestic violence and sexual assault and abuse. She has also been involved in research on homelessness for many years and is interested in the area of women and poverty.

Efe Can Gürcan is a Ph.D. candidate in Sociology at Simon Fraser University. His research interests lie in the areas of political sociology, development and food studies, Latin America, and Middle East. His works have been or will be published in journals such as *Rural Sociology*, *Dialectical Anthropology*, *Latin American Perspectives*, *Capital & Class*, *Review of Radical Political Economics*, and *Socialism & Democracy*. His book, *Challenging Neoliberalism at Turkey's Gezi Park*, will be published in January 2015 by Palgrave Macmillan.

Deborah A. Harris is an Associate Professor of Sociology at Texas State University. Her research interests include poverty and social inequality, rural sociology, and the sociology of food. Her newest book, *Taking the Heat Women Chefs and Gender Inequality in the Professional Kitchen*, will come out in 2015 Rutgers University Press..

Spencer Headworth is a Ph.D. candidate in Sociology at Northwestern University and Graduate Research Coordinator at the American Bar Foundation. His research interests include crime and social control, law, inequality, organizations, and professions. His dissertation examines the emergence and development of specialized units tasked with controlling fraud in public benefit programs.

Colleen M. Heflin is an Associate Professor at the Truman School of Public Affairs at the University of Missouri. Her interdisciplinary research program focuses on understanding the survival strategies employed by low-income households to make ends meet, the implications of these strategies on individual and household well-being, and how federal program participation influences well-being. A central focus of her work has been on understanding the causes and consequences of material hardship.

Kasey Henricks is a Law and Social Science Fellow at the American Bar Foundation and Ph.D. Student of Sociology at Loyola University Chicago. His research interests lie in understanding how race and class inequalities are reproduced over time through institutional arrangements sponsored by state fiscal policy.

Steve Herbert is a Professor of Law, Societies, and Justice and Geography at the University of Washington. He is the author of *Policing Space: Territoriality and the Los Angeles Police Department*, *Citizens, Cops and Power: Recognizing the Limits of Community*, and (with Katherine Beckett) *Banished: The New Social Control in Urban America*.

Michael J. Holosko, Ph.D., MSW, is the Pauline M. Berger Professor of Family and Child Welfare at the University of Georgia School of Social Work. He has published extensively in the areas of evaluation, research methods, social work practice, child family services, and gerontology. He has taught in schools of social work (primarily), nursing, and public administration in many countries of the world including: the United States, China, Hong Kong, Sweden, Canada, Australia, New Zealand, and in the U.S. Virgin Islands.

Philip Young P. Hong, Ph.D., is an Associate Professor in the School of Social Work and a faculty associate of the Center for Social Development (CSD) at Washington University in St. Louis. His main academic interest is in poverty and workforce development. He is currently partnering with local workforce development initiatives to develop bottom-up strategies for empowering low-income individuals and families in their quest to achieve self-sufficiency. Findings from his study on psychological self-sufficiency promises to inform empowerment-based workforce development interventions and policy development.

Linda Houser is an Assistant Professor and Ph.D. Program Director at Widener University's Center for Social Work Education, an Affiliate Fellow at the Center for Women and Work at Rutgers University, and a policy practitioner in the areas of employment, caregiving, and health. Her research and practice focus is on financial, workplace, and caregiving security for women and families.

Anupama Jacob, Ph.D., is an Assistant Professor in the Department of Social Work at Azusa Pacific University. Her Ph.D. dissertation was on poverty measurement in the United States at the University of California, Berkeley.

Phyllis Jeroslow is a doctoral candidate in the School of Social Welfare at the University of California, Berkeley, where she researches comparative welfare state policies and government investments in early childhood. She has taught public policy topics related to children and youth in the Department of Child and Adolescent Development at San Francisco State University, and has served for many years as a training and curriculum specialist at the California Social Work Education Center, University of California, Berkeley.

Jennifer R. Jewell co-founded Women in Transition (WIT), a grassroots organization run by and for poor people, when she was homeless and living on welfare. Learning to make the system work for her, she completed her degree in social work and eventually earned her Ph.D. She is an Associate Professor and the Director of the Undergraduate Program at Salisbury University. Her areas of interest focus on privilege and oppression, community organizing, and contemporary poor people's movements. She is the proud mother of three children.

Pascale Joassart-Marcelli is an Associate Professor of Geography at San Diego State University where she teaches and conducts research on immigrant and refugee integration, community, and urban governance. Her current research focuses on the relationship between food, ethnicity, and place, with an emphasis on food justice and alternative food practices in immigrant communities and low-income neighborhoods.

Monique S. Johnson is a Senior Loan Officer with Virginia Community Capital where she manages relationships with developers and community partners, and structures financing transactions that produce social and economic impact across the state. She has been recognized locally and statewide as a "Top 40 Under 40" community leader and nationally as a Young Leader of Affordable Housing by *Affordable Housing Finance Magazine*. Monique serves on numerous non-profit boards and committees. She is an adjunct professor at Virginia Commonwealth University and expects to complete her Ph.D. in Public Policy and Administration with an Urban Policy Concentration in 2014.

Howard Karger, Ph.D., is a Professor and Chairperson, Department of Family Studies and Social Work, Miami University. He has published widely in national and international journals. His books include *Shortchanged: Life and Debt in the Fringe Economy* (winner of the 2006 Independent Publishers Award in Investment/Finance/Economics); (with D. Stoesz) *American Social Welfare Policy*; (with D. Stoesz and L. Costin) *The Politics of Child Abuse and Neglect in America*; (with R. Fisher) *Social Work and Community in a Private World*; and (with D. Stoesz and T. Carrilio) *A Dream Deferred: How Social Work Education Lost Its Way and What Can Be Done*.

Jin Kim is currently an Assistant Professor and Policy Curriculum Specialist in the Social Work Department in the social work program at Northeastern Illinois University. He received a Ph.D. in social welfare and a minor certificate in applied economics from the University of Wisconsin-Madison.

Shveta Kumaria is a doctoral candidate in the School of Social Work, Loyola University Chicago. She holds a M.Phil degree in Clinical Psychology from the National Institute of Mental Health and Neurosciences, Bangalore, India. Her research interests include psychotherapy research, psychotherapy integration, and training and supervision in therapy.

Jacob Lesniewski is an Assistant Professor of Social Work at Dominican University's Graduate School of Social Work. His research focuses on worker centers and their role in improving the conditions of work for low-wage workers through organizing, policy advocacy, and individual service delivery. He teaches in the areas of community practice, history of the welfare state, and social policy analysis. He also gives leadership to the University's West Side Collaborative, which seeks to build lasting and sustained partnerships with organizations and agencies on Chicago's West Side.

Sara Lichtenwalter, LSW, Ph.D., is an Associate Professor with Gannon University's Social Work Program. Her scholarship has focused on the structural factors that contribute to the unyielding and enduring relationship between marginalized women and poverty, with a particular emphasis on mothers and caregivers, as well as women with disabilities.

Michael Lloyd, MSW, LSW, CADC, completed his Bachelor's Degree from DePaul University and his Master's Degree in Social Work and Certification for Alcohol and Drug Counseling at Loyola University Chicago in 2012. Mr. Lloyd has been a research fellow for Dr. María Vidal de Haymes in the Institute on Migration and International Social Work at Loyola for the last two years. He is currently a research assistant for Dr. Michael Dentato focusing on LGBTQ treatment and practice issues. His areas of interest include HIV/AIDS, addiction research, LGBTQ issues, and co-occurring disorders. Mr. Lloyd is currently enrolled in the Loyola University Chicago School of Social Work Ph.D. Program and is pursuing his LCSW certification.

Margaret Lombe, Ph.D., is an associate professor at the Boston College Graduate School of Social Work. She is also a faculty associate at the Center for Social Development at Washington University in St. Louis. Her area of expertise is international social development with an emphasis on social inclusion/exclusion and capacity building. Lombe has provided consultation to the United Nations and has participated in a number of Experts Group Meetings on inclusion/exclusion. She has also published extensively in peer-reviewed journals as well as book chapters.

Christopher Magno is an Assistant Professor in the Criminal Justice Program at Gannon University. He earned his Ph.D. in Criminal Justice at Indiana University, Bloomington, and is the 2013 recipient of Gannon's three-year Cooney-Jackman Endowed Professorship. He is the author of the forthcoming book *Corruption and Revolution in the Philippines* and, as co-author, is writing a book entitled *Radical Criminology for Everyday Life*. His teaching and research specializations include political crime, white-collar crime, terrorism, genocide, law and society, environmental justice, restorative justice, alternative social control, and cross-cultural and comparative criminology.

Erin Malcolm holds a Bachelor and Master of Social Work from Loyola University Chicago. She has worked as an Editorial Associate for the *Journal of Poverty* and the *Routledge Handbook of Poverty*. Her research interests surround immigration and migration.

Nina Martin is an Assistant Professor in the Department of Geography at the University of North Carolina at Chapel Hill. She conducts research on immigration and local political conflicts, urban labor markets, and the management of non-profit organizations. Her work has been widely published in Geography and Urban Planning journals, including *Mobilities, Gender, Place and Culture*, and *Environment and Planning A*.

Jessica Martone, Ph.D., is a graduate of Loyola University Chicago's School of Social Work Ph.D. Program. Jessica is currently adjunct faculty in Loyola's School of Social Work and is a field liaison for the social work field program. Jessica held the Arthur J. Schmitt dissertation fellowship from 2012 to 2013 and was a doctoral research fellow through the Institute for Migration and International Social Work from 2009 to 2012. Jessica completed her Masters in Social Work at Loyola University Chicago in May 2009 with a focus in migration studies. Jessica has been involved with immigration-related research projects and her dissertation focused on Latino student academic achievement in the United States, specifically looking at the transition to higher education.

Joan Maya Mazelis, Ph.D., is an Assistant Professor of Sociology in the Department of Sociology, Anthropology and Criminal Justice and an affiliated scholar at the Center for Urban Research and Education at Rutgers University in Camden, New Jersey. Her teaching and scholarship focus on urban poverty, inequality, stigma, social ties, and reciprocity.

Jennifer Miller holds a Master of Social Work and a Master of Arts in Women's Studies and Gender Studies from Loyola University Chicago. Her professional and academic interests include immigrants and refugees, community organizing, and global health. Jenn has nearly ten years of experience working in the government and non-profit sectors, and currently serves as the Immigrant Family Resource Program Manager at the Illinois Coalition for Immigrant and Refugee Rights.

Joya Misra is a Professor of Sociology and Public Policy at the University of Massachusetts, Amherst, and editor of the journal *Gender and Society*. Much of her research explores how social policies affect inequalities in employment, wages, income, and poverty cross-nationally.

Karen Monkman, Ph.D. (University of Southern California), is a Professor at DePaul University. Her research interests relate to education and social justice; gender, class, ethnicity, and race; and international/comparative education policy, migration, and globalization. She is co-editor of *Globalization & Education: Integration and Contestation across Cultures*, 2nd edition (2014).

Paul S. Myers is a Ph.D. student in the Department of Educational Policy, Organization and Leadership at the University of Illinois at Urbana-Champaign. His research interests include educational governance and the schooling experiences of marginalized persons in light of the involvement of markets in education; specifically, he is interested in the spread and effects of education-related policy across contexts and other considerations therein.

Von E. Nebbitt, Ph.D., is an Associate Professor at the Jane Addams College of Social Work at the University of Illinois at Chicago. He holds a BA, MSW, and Ph.D. Dr. Nebbitt's scholarship and practice is on health-risk behaviors, violence, and mental health in African American youth living in urban public housing. His research has been published in health, psychology, and other social science journals.

Deidre Oakley, Ph.D., is an Associate Professor in the Sociology Department at Georgia State University. Her research, which has been widely published in both academic and applied venues, focuses primarily on how social disadvantages concerning education, housing, homelessness, and redevelopment are often compounded by geographic space. Since 2008 she has been collaborating with Drs. Lesley Reid and Erin Ruel (both from Georgia State University) on two complementary National Institutes of Health (NIH) and National Science Foundation (NSF)-funded projects examining the impact of public housing elimination and forced relocation in Atlanta. Dr. Oakley provided Congressional Testimony concerning public housing preservation and the Neighborhood Choice initiative to the Financial Services Committee in 2010. She also guest edited, along with Drs. Jim Fraser (Vanderbilt University) and Diane Levy (The Urban Institute), a symposium for *Cityscape* concerning public housing transformation and mixed-income initiatives on both sides of the Atlantic, which was published in the July 2013 issue.

John Orwat, Ph.D., is an Associate Professor at Loyola University Chicago. Dr. Orwat teaches and conducts research pertaining to health care policy. Dr. Orwat has several years of experience as a clinical social worker as well as directing health services research regarding the impact of benefit design, the cost effectiveness of interventions, the impact of federal policy changes, and other delivery system issues. He holds a Master of Arts from the School of Social Services at the University of Chicago and a Ph.D. from the Heller School for Social Policy and Management at Brandeis University.

Shaun Ossei-Owusu is a JD/Ph.D. candidate at the University of California, Berkeley. He is from the Bronx, New York, and received his undergraduate degree from Northwestern University and his master's degree from the University of Pennsylvania. He has also been an Exchange Scholar at the University of Chicago. His research interests include race, class, and gender, poverty and urban inequality, law and society, the criminal justice system, and legal history. His dissertation research explores the historical development of legal aid organizations in the United States. This research has been supported by the National Science Foundation, the Law and Society Association, the American Bar Foundation, and the American Society of Criminology.

Gerardo Otero, Ph.D., is a Professor of Sociology and International Studies at Simon Fraser University. He has published numerous scholarly articles, chapters, and books about the political economy of agriculture and food, civil society, and the state in Mexico and Latin America. His latest edited book is *Food for the Few: Neoliberal Globalism and Biotechnology in Latin America* (University of Texas Press, 2008; reissued in paperback in 2010), which is forthcoming in Spanish as *La dieta neoliberal*.

Rubin Patterson is a Professor and Chair of Sociology and Anthropology at Howard University in Washington, DC. He is also a Research Associate in the Department of Sociology at The University of the Witwatersrand in Johannesburg, South Africa. His chief academic and professional areas of interest are social inequality; environmental inequality and sustainable socioeconomic development. He is the author of the 2014 book (published by Temple University Press) titled *Greening Africana Studies: Linking Environmental Studies with Transforming Black Experiences*. Patterson also served for ten years as the founding editor of *Perspectives on Global Development and Technology*.

Gabriela Pechlaner is a sociology instructor in the sociology faculty at the University of the Fraser Valley in Abbotsford, British Columbia. Her research interests include environmental sociology and the sociology of agriculture and food, with a particular emphasis on the legal and regulatory aspects of new technologies. She has published a number of solo and co-authored articles in scholarly journals such as *Anthropologica*, *Rural Sociology*, *Sociologia Ruralis*, and *The Canadian Journal of Sociology*. Her book *Corporate Crops: Biotechnology, Agriculture, and the Struggle for Control* was released by the University of Texas Press in December 2013.

Amira Proweller is an Associate Professor in the Department of Educational Policy Studies and Research in the College of Education at DePaul University. Her research interests are in the cultural politics of urban education; youth culture and identity; gender/race/class in education; social justice education; and qualitative research methods. She has published articles and book chapters exploring youth culture and identity in education, with a particular focus on gender. Her current research is a youth participatory action research project exploring intersections of power and privilege among Jewish teen girls.

Andrew Reynolds, MSW, M.Ed, is a doctoral student in Social Work at Boston College researching youth and adolescence, parent involvement in schools, social vulnerability in youth, and poverty and food security issues.

Susan Roll, MSW, Ph.D., is an Assistant Professor in the School of Social Work at California State University, Chico. She teaches courses on multiculturalism, policy, and community practice. Susan is currently researching how we teach and learn about poverty.

Cesraéa Rumpf is an Assistant Professor in the Department of Criminal Justice at Fayetteville State University. Her research investigates the nature of formerly incarcerated women's interactions with the state and speaks to scholarship on punishment, poverty management, and gender-based violence.

Kenneth J. Saltman is a Professor in the Department of Educational Leadership at University of Massachusetts–Dartmouth. He is the author most recently of *The Failure of Corporate School Reform* (Paradigm, 2013) and *The Politics of Education: A Critical Introduction* (Paradigm, 2014), and co-author of *Toward a New Common School Movement* (Paradigm, 2014).

Celeste Sánchez recently returned to the United States after several years of direct service work with children and adolescents in Central America. She is currently pursuing an MSW at Loyola University Chicago with a sub-specialization in migration studies. Her work in Latin America and in the United States with unaccompanied minors have prompted her interest in resiliency and migration.

Gabriel A. Santos is an Associate Professor and Chair of Sociology and Criminology at Lynchburg College. Dr. Santos regularly engages in community-based research that aims to incorporate sociological tools of analysis into grassroots efforts that engage homelessness, racism, food deserts, and prisoner re-entry. He is the author of *Redeeming the Broken Body: Church and State After Disasters* (Cascade Books, 2009).

Sanford F. Schram teaches at Hunter College, CUNY, in the Political Science Department and the Public Policy Program at Roosevelt House. He is the author of *Words of Welfare: The Poverty of Social Science and the Social Science of Poverty* (1995) and co-author of *Disciplining the Poor: Neoliberal Paternalism and the Persistent Power of Race* (2011).

Andrew Seligsohn is President of Campus Compact, a national coalition of 1,100 colleges and universities promoting civic engagement in higher education. He holds a BA in Modern Intellectual History from Williams College and a Ph.D. in Political Science from the University of Minnesota. He has published articles and chapters on political theory, constitutional law, and youth civic engagement.

Emily Shayman, MSW, is a Doctoral Fellow within the Institute on Migration and International Social Work at Loyola University Chicago and works as an Editorial Associate for the *Journal of Poverty*. She also provides direct service as a school social worker. Her research surrounds immigrant and refugee students within the public school system.

Alexis Silvers holds a Master of Public Policy from Loyola University Chicago. Her research interests include political inequities and urban gentrification. She is Finance Director for the Indiana Senate Democratic Caucus.

Ashish Singh has a Ph.D. in economics and is based in India. His areas of interest primarily include economics of distribution, discrimination, social exclusion, and intergenerational mobility. He also works on nutrition and child health-related issues. He is based at the Indian Institute of Technology Bombay in Mumbai, India.

Shweta Singh is a research and teaching faculty at Loyola University Chicago. Singh teaches in the MSW and WSGS programs in areas of evaluation research, global feminism, social policy, and social media. She examines the concepts of identity and empowerment in her research on women and girls from Asia. She has recently published *Social Work and Social Development: Perspectives from India and the United States*.

Aakanksha Sinha, MSW, is a doctoral student at the Graduate School of Social Work, Boston College, researching access to the basic needs of vulnerable children and low-income families globally.

Kimberly Skobba is an Assistant Professor in Housing and Consumer Economics at the University of Georgia. Her research focuses on the long-term residential mobility patterns, also known as housing careers, of low-income households and the impact of rental assistance programs on household and residential stability. She earned a Ph.D. and MA, both in Housing Studies, from the University of Minnesota's College of Design.

Michael Sosin, Ph.D., is the Emily Klein Gidwitz Professor in the School of Social Service Administration at the University of Chicago. He is an affiliate of the Institute for Research on Poverty at the University of Wisconsin-Madison and the Population Studies Center at the

University of Chicago. His fields of special interest include social welfare institutions, social policy, social administration, substance abuse services, urban poverty, and homelessness. In addition to his faculty appointments, Professor Sosin served as editor of *Social Service Review*, a leading professional journal in the field of social welfare until 2014.

Joe Soss is the inaugural Cowles Chair for the Study of Public Service at the University of Minnesota, where he holds faculty positions in the Hubert H. Humphrey School of Public Affairs, the Department of Political Science, and the Department of Sociology. His research and teaching explore the interplay of democratic politics, societal inequalities, and public policy. His most recent book, co-authored with Richard Fording and Sanford Schram, is *Disciplining the Poor: Neoliberal Paternalism and the Persistent Power of Race* (2011).

Sue Steiner, MSW, Ph.D., is a Professor in the School of Social Work at California State University, Chico. She teaches courses on policy and community practice. Sue is the co-founder of the Northern California Counties Time Bank.

Eiko Strader is a Ph.D. student in the Department of Sociology at the University of Massachusetts, Amherst. She conducts research on gender inequality in labor markets, welfare states, and population control policies across Western industrialized nations and in East Asia.

Giselle Thompson is a doctoral student in the Department of Sociology at York University in Toronto. She completed a Masters in Sociology from the University of Toledo in 2014 with a thesis entitled "IMF-induced Fiscal Austerity and Education in Jamaica." Her research interests include the sociologies of development, education and economics. She is particularly interested in IMF structural adjustment programs, fiscal austerity and social spending in Jamaica, as well as domestic

Darrick Tovar-Murray, Ph.D., is a full-time Associate Professor at DePaul University. He teaches counseling courses for the Department of Counseling and Special Education in the College of Education. His scholarly work focuses on multiculturalism, identity development, vocational counseling, spirituality, and poverty.

Eileen Trzcinski, MSW, Ph.D., was a Full Professor at the Wayne State University School of Social Work and a Research Professor at the DIW (German Institute for Economic Research) until she passed away in March of 2013. With a dual Ph.D. in both social work and economics from the University of Michigan, Dr. Trzcinski worked tirelessly during her lifetime to explore the ways that policy can be used to challenge economic and labor market inequality. Best known for her contribution to family and medical leave, she has left a permanent handprint on the policies that defend the well-being of working families, women, and mothers.

Eduardo Vargas holds a BSW from Goshen College and a MSW from Loyola University Chicago. He has worked in faith-based not-for-profit agencies as a city director and as a grant writer. His research interests are: practice issues with Internally Displaced People (IDP), resiliency, and theodicy with populations that have experienced violent trauma.

Rebecca Vonderlack-Navarro holds a Ph.D. from the University of Chicago, where she focused on immigrant political incorporation. Her current work identifies policy supports to bolster teacher preparation to meet the needs of Illinois' diverse English language learners.

Rebecca also worked in community development in Tegucigalpa, Honduras, where she was awarded a Fulbright scholarship to support research on microfinance programming.

David Wagner, Ph.D., is a Professor of Social Work and Sociology and an author of eight books including *Confronting Homelessness: Poverty, Politics, and the Failure of Social Welfare.*

Pete White is the Founder and Co-Director of the Los Angeles Community Action Network, a grassroots organization working to ensure the rights to housing, health, and security are upheld in Los Angeles. A lifetime resident of South Central Los Angeles, he is committed to fight for a Los Angeles that does not tolerate racial injustice, promotes an equitable distribution of resources, and includes everyone. Pete believes that organizing and leadership development are essential tools needed to achieve social change and racial justice.

Stanley Wilkerson is a native of Los Angeles. He relocated to Chicago to pursue his passion of educating and cultivating the minds of youth. After multiple years of mentoring young adults, he decided to pursue his Master's Degree in Education with a concentration in School Counseling. Stanley graduated with his M.Ed in School Counseling in June of 2013. He currently works as a Dean of Students at Urban Prep Charter Academy.

Judith Wittner, Ph.D., is a Professor of Sociology at Loyola University Chicago and an ethnographer specializing in gender studies. She studied anthropology at Columbia University for two years, but left after the birth of her first child. Drawn back to school by the student movements of the 1960s, she enrolled in Roosevelt University where she taught some of the first women's studies courses offered in Chicago. She received a Ph.D. from Northwestern University in 1977.

Lakshman Yapa is a Professor of Geography at Pennsylvania State University. He teaches courses on poverty and economic development. In 2008 he received the C. Peter Magrath University Community Engagement Award. The award was made by the National Association of State Universities and Land-Grant Colleges for contributions to engagement scholarship through the course, "Rethinking Urban Poverty: The Philadelphia Field Project."

Intae Yoon, MSW, Ph.D., is an Associate Professor in the School of Social Work at East Carolina University. Yoon's research interests include economic justice and financial assets building for low-income families.

Mansoo Yu, MSW, Ph.D., is an Assistant Professor in the School of Social Work and the Master of Public Health Program at the University of Missouri-Columbia. His research interests include health-risk behaviors, healthy and positive living, and health disparity across various segments of the population. He teaches epidemiology, research methods, and health disparity.

Jamilatu Zakari received her Master of Arts degree in Sociology from Texas State University in 2012. During her graduate studies, Jamilatu conducted research comparing the perceptions of food choice from clients who received aid from both client choice food pantries and prepackaged food pantries. Other areas of research include: food insecurity, sustainability, poverty, and the sociology of food.

GENERAL INTRODUCTION

Stephen Nathan Haymes, María Vidal de Haymes,
and Reuben Jonathan Miller

In the study of poverty in the United States, the causes and even the meanings of poverty are disconnected from the causes and meanings of "global poverty" in the "Global South." The analysis of poverty has been exclusively domestic with little or no understanding of how the integration of the U.S. political economy and culture into the global economy has shaped the meaning and character of poverty in the United States. In other words, mainstream studies of U.S. poverty assume that the sources of poverty as well as the "discourses of poverty" (a system of statements made about poverty) are uniquely "American." In which case, little or no attention is given to how globalization, referring specifically to global capitalism and its institutions, both cause and construct the meaning of poverty in the United States and throughout the world.

Rarely, if ever, is poverty in the United States understood in relation to global poverty, and its association with the economic growth and development policies of global capitalism and its global financial institutions. For example, the structural adjustment policies of the World Bank and International Monetary Fund (IMF) assume that poverty reduction is linked to economic growth and economic integration. The structural adjustment economic policies which nations of the Global South must follow in order to qualify for new World Bank and IMF loans to help them make debt repayments have common guiding principles which include export-led growth; privatization and liberalization; lifting import and export restrictions; balancing their budgets; cutting domestic social expenditures; and removal of price controls and state subsidies. By following such a strategy, debt repayment and economic restructuring is insured at the expense of reduced social spending on items such as health, nutrition, and education. In effect, the neoliberal economic integration policies of the IMF and World Bank have demanded that poorer nations lower the standard of living of their people.

Similarly, reorienting its national economy towards a global logic, U.S. domestic economic policies have promoted a neoliberal market-based strategy of economic development and growth as the obvious solution to alleviating poverty. The domestic strategy has followed a similar path towards global economic integration, sharing many of the same elements of a structural adjustment strategy, including privatization and liberalization, the lifting of import and export restrictions, deregulation, and cuts in domestic social expenditures, while providing tax cuts to the rich and corporate subsidies in the name of increasing economic investment, development, and growth.

Developed and implemented through its global financial institutions, such as the World Bank and the IMF, global capitalism's prescriptive policy solutions assume that capitalism, as a social and economic system, is able to reduce global poverty. This is promoted in spite of the fact that contemporary global capitalism is unable to explain the persistence of poverty and its failure to redress inequality. Intended to create jobs and improve income distribution, the neoliberal ideology that guides global capitalism's solutions to global poverty have mostly contributed to creating, producing, and exacerbating poverty in the Global South. More specifically, neoliberal economic development and economic growth policies—cut backs in government expenditure, economic stabilization structural adjustment, efficiency of markets, economic liberalization, limited state intervention in the economy, the importance of a knowledge economy, and human capital development—are viewed to be the solution to alleviating poverty. Political economists critical of the neoliberal policies of globalization point out that poverty does not emerge because of exclusion but because of poor people's incorporation into global political and economic processes. Paradoxically, with the rise of economic globalization and incorporation of poor people, there has emerged a global human rights social movement, and as such, a global moral community in the Global South, to redress the injustices and undemocratic politics of global capitalism.

The Handbook of Poverty addresses the relationship of poverty to the rise of neoliberal capitalism in the United States in the context of globalization. That is, it explores how the logic of globalization and its drive towards neoliberal market-oriented economic development and growth are profoundly reshaping our understanding of poverty in the United States discursively, politically, economically, culturally, and experientially. In Territory, Authority, Rights (2006), Saskia Sassen describes globalization as an epochal transformative process that is "taking place inside the national." The national is "one of the key enablers and enactors of the micro-processes of globalization—whether policies, capital, political subjectivities, urban space, temporal frames, or other of a variety of dynamics and domains." These processes, says Sassen, "reorient particular components of institutions and practices—both private and public—towards global logics and away from the historically shaped national logics" (p. 2). It is in the context of this reorientation that The Handbook of Poverty examines poverty in the United States as part of the epochal phenomenon of globalization and global poverty.

Bringing together a number of scholars in the professional and interdisciplinary fields as well as the social sciences and humanities, The Handbook of Poverty explores how globalization in the context of the U.S. political economy, rather than alleviating poverty, has instead exacerbated U.S. poverty and pre-existing inequalities. Furthermore, The Handbook of Poverty looks at how neoliberal economic reforms in the United States have privatized the services of social welfare and educational institutions, transformed the state from a benevolent to a punitive state, and criminalized the poor, women, racial, ethnic, and sexual minorities, and immigrants. Of particular interest here is also the unique way in which, within the context of the United States, the ideologies of neoliberalism and neoconservatism discursively converge in dominant statements or discourses about poverty and therefore policies to reduce poverty. In fact, what The Handbook of Poverty contributes to the debate about poverty in the United States is that the converging of both neoliberal and neoconservative ideologies has given rise to policies whose objectives are not to alleviate poverty but to control and punish the poor. Other related issues The Handbook of Poverty examines in the context of neoliberal globalization in the United States are, for example, income distribution, employment, health, education, imprisonment, hunger, housing, and the processes of urbanization of the poor. While academic accounts of U.S. poverty have generally focused on issues related to inequality and access, the framework that The Handbook of Poverty will use to address these issues is that of emerging new forms of poverty that are associated with the globalization of the U.S. economy. These are new forms of poverty that render poor communities as destitute and, as such, "surplus populations" in need of control and punishment. Another issue addressed is related to the globalization and localization of human rights discourse in the United States. In this regard, The Handbook of Poverty explores how and why poor communities in the United

States, and the NGOs that support them, have increasingly redefined their struggles for social justice from a welfare rights to a human rights social movement.

The chapters in Part I of *The Handbook of Poverty*, "From the Production of Inequality to the Production of Destitution: The U.S. Political Economy of Poverty in the Era of Globalization," examine how the reorientation of the U.S. economy towards the economic logic of neoliberal global capitalism has restructured the political economy of poverty. The chapters in this part explore the particular way in which poor communities under neoliberal economic policies are incorporated into the U.S. political economy in contrast to earlier periods. Particular attention is given to how neoliberal restructuring dispossesses populations of people and produces forms of destitution through uneven geographical development and the deterritorialization and reterritorialization of geographically defined poor communities. The chapters in this part will examine new emerging forms of "destitute poverty" experienced by the poor communities in the United States. The chapters will show how this emerging form of poverty in the United States is more consistent with the global processes and dynamics of the political economy of global poverty.

The chapters in Part II, "Discourses of Poverty: From the 'Culture of Poverty' to 'Surplus Population,'" examine how the globalizing of the U.S. political economy contributed significantly to the conditions that shifted the discourse about poverty in the United States from a "culture of poverty" discourse to one of "surplus population." The chapters in this part investigate the discursive practices or the family of ideas, beliefs, and concepts that constitute discourses about U.S. poverty, their corresponding policies, as well as the historical circumstances and genealogical conditions that have given rise to the shift from a "culture of poverty" discourse to a discourse of "surplus population." With the globalization of the U.S. economy new forms of poverty are emerging that render poor communities destitute and, as such, "surplus" or "redundant" populations. The term "surplus population" or similar terms like it to describe "destitute poverty" signify a change in the condition and experience of poverty and in particular how it is politically and ideologically represented in the United States. In which case, the chapters in this part are also attentive to the ways in which the ideologies of neoliberalism and neoconservatism converged in the United States to discursively and politically structure and facilitate this shift in the discourse about poverty.

In Part III, "From the Welfare State to the Neoliberal State—From Regulating to Imprisoning the Poor," the chapters examine how globalization and its transformation of the state into a neoliberal state created the conditions for the dismantling of the welfare state in the United States. The chapters in Part III are divided into Section I: "Transformation of the Welfare State: Education"; Section II: "Transformation of the Welfare State: Cash Transfers, Housing, Nutrition, and Health"; and Section III: "Transformation of the Welfare State: Criminalizing the Poor." Each of the chapters investigates how neoliberal globalization in the United States has restructured the state from a "benevolent" welfare state to a post-welfare punitive state. Particular attention will be given to how the disciplining functions of the state are being challenged and transformed, from *regulating*—that is, by expanding relief programs to absorb and control enough of the poor to restore order—to *confining*—by punishing and expanding the criminal justice system into every aspect of poor people's lives or by disciplining the poor by inserting them into the market.

While poverty may be a universal phenomenon, its experiences vary and are often conditioned by race, ethnicity, gender, age, disability, and health and immigrant status. The chapters in Part IV, "Global Poverty and the Lived Experiences of Poor Communities in the United States," explore the diverse experiences of poverty in the United States. Particular attention is given to how that diversity is part of the political, economic, and cultural processes of globalization and global poverty. It is in this context that chapters in this part explore broader ecological and health issues related to poverty such as, for example, hunger, violence, displacement and homelessness, environmental destruction, and environmental racism and sexism, and how these issues shape the experiences of poverty in the United States.

The helping professions, such as education, social work, health, and law, have been those professions that have defined their work as providing services and advocating for the poor in relationship to notions of social justice. In Part V, "Organizing to Resist Neoliberal Policies and Poverty: Activism and Advocacy," the chapters examine the limitations of the concept of social justice as conventionally advanced by the helping professions in the United States, particularly in the era of neoliberal globalization, global poverty, and human rights. The neoliberal structural adjustment policies of the United States, the dominance of global financial institutions, and the transformation of the welfare state into a post-welfare state have given rise to extreme forms of poverty, or what some have called "destitute poverty" in the United States. These neoliberal policies have led to the emergence of forms of advocacy and activism that is focused on social and economic rights of the poor. The poverty experienced today in the United States is rendering more and more people and communities as surplus or redundant populations, which is necessitating a shifting of rights-based discourse from civil or welfare rights to human rights, but a human rights discourse and forms of advocacy and activism that address the inherent structural violence of neoliberal global capitalism in the context of the United States.

Alternatives to the characteristic structural violence of the current neoliberal economic order are proposed by the authors included in Part VI, "Reframing Poverty in the Era of Globalization: Alternatives to a Neoliberal Economic Order." Collectively, the authors call for a replacement of the self-reliance ideology and the values and practices associated with market fundamentalism with: a human rights, approach that strengthens the welfare rights-claims of U.S. citizens; community-based options of support outside of the formal market-based system; and a shift towards a post capitalist basic needs economy.

References

Sassen, Saskia. (2006) *Territory, Authority, Rights: From Medieval to Global Assemblages.* New Jersey: Princeton University Press.

PART I

From the production of inequality to the production of destitution

The U.S. political economy of poverty in the era of globalization

INTRODUCTION

María Vidal de Haymes, Stephen Nathan Haymes, and Michael Lloyd

Neoliberalism represents a reassertion of the liberal political economic beliefs of the 19th century in the contemporary era (Clark, 2005). In the United States, the dominant neoliberal public philosophy that has emerged in recent decades is that of Market Fundamentalism, which Block (2007) defines as "a vastly exaggerated belief in the ability of self regulating markets to solve social problems." Such a philosophy replaces a notion of society with the marketplace and supports deregulation, tax cuts, and a retrenchment of public services (Block, 2007). The authors in this part trace the reassertion of liberal economic beliefs, globalization, and the rise of Market Fundamentalism in the United States through analysis of policies regarding debt, austerity, taxation, employment, and the privatization of public services, an agenda that has resulted in the deepening of poverty and economic inequalities in the United States.

In "Transnational Factors Driving U.S. Inequality and Poverty," Rubin Patterson and Giselle Thompson call attention to the growing poverty in the U.S. and a reversal of the more than 150-year trend of generational gains in income and social mobility. They indicate that approximately one hundred million Americans, one-third of the U.S. population, are poor or nearly poor. They attribute these trends in inequality and poverty to the convergence of a number of factors: the financialization of the economy, the transnationalization of capitalism, deindustrialization, the automation of production, the deunionization of the workforce, rising consumer debt, the democratization of higher education, and the racialization of people of color for the purposes of electoral politics.

In "The Discursive Axis of Neoliberalism: Debt, Deficits, and Austerity," Shawn Cassiman continues the analysis of neoliberal globalization by examining the discursive constructions of debt, deficits, and austerity within and in support of this system. Using Europe as an illustrative example, she discusses the relatively recent turn toward austerity driven by the European Commission, IMF, and European Central Bank. She extends her discussion to the United States' debt crisis and argues that it is an outcome of global capitalism—thus the response needs to come from outside of that logic—and offers the Occupy Wall Street movement's debt refusal campaign as an alternative to the neoliberal austerity discourse.

Similarly, in "Beyond Coincidence: How Neoliberal Policy Initiatives in the IMF and World Bank Affected U.S. Poverty Levels," Pamela Blackmon discusses the rise of neoliberal policies of the IMF and the World Bank during the 1980s. These policies were advanced on global and domestic levels by Margaret Thatcher and Ronald Reagan in the United Kingdom and the United States respectively. On a global level, Blackmon argues that such policies resulted in increased poverty in the countries that followed these policies. Blackmon explores the degree to which a neoliberal shift occurred in U.S. domestic policies during the Reagan administration. She concludes that the decreased funding and deregulation of education, changes in transfer programs for the poor, and the decreases to top marginal income tax rates that characterized the Reagan-era policies contributed to increases in income inequality and poverty in the United States.

Recognizing taxation as a political practice, Kasey Henricks and Victoria Brockett argue that it is a vehicle of social control that organizes, maintains, and supports inequality over time. In "The House Always Wins: How State Lotteries Displace American Tax Burdens by Class and Race," they focus on the role of lotteries in the United States and its social consequences for public finance. In their analysis, they detail the fiscal trends, particularly those induced by neoliberal policies, that created optimal conditions for lotteries to emerge as an alternative tax strategy to finance public services. They conclude that a lottery-based taxation scheme shifts the financial burden of public services away from elite interests to the racially and economically marginalized populations that play the lottery the most, replacing more progressive sources of state income, such as corporate and property taxes.

Similar to other authors in this part, Intae Yoon argues that the election of Ronald Reagan to the presidency in 1981 heralded in an era of neoliberal policies that resulted in increased income inequality and economic injustice. In "Consumer Credits as a Quasi-Welfare System for Failed Neoliberals' Trickle-down Policies Between the 1980s and 2000s," Yoon focuses on the deregulation of financial institutions, the dismantling of anti-trust laws, and deregulation of consumer credit markets, which he argues resulted in the increased vulnerability of low- and middle-income families and widening income gaps. The confluence of these policies and trends created a context in which low- and middle-income families turned to consumer credit as a quasi-safety net, while deregulated financial institutions expanded consumer credits to all income strata for more profits. Also focusing on consumer credit and financial institutions, Howard Karger examines how the poor are often steered towards fringe services, such as short-term loans, check cashing, car loans, and tax refund services offered by peripheral financial institutions. These financial services are characterized by high user fees and extortionate interest rates, which Karger concludes are predatory in nature since they further impoverish borrowers, rather than provide financial products that help to build assets and increase household wealth. In this chapter, Karger provides an overview of some fringe economy services and the impact of neoliberal ideas on predatory lending, and concludes with possible approaches to restrain the depletion of resources from the already poor.

The chapters in this part contributed by Ashish Singh and Andrew Seligsohn and Joan Maya Mazelis examine the effects of globalization and neoliberal policies on their analysis of trends of employment and public service provision at national and local levels. In "Globalization and the Trends in Inequality of Poverty in the United States in the Last Decade," Singh examines inequality and poverty in the United States within the context of globalization, through an analysis of changes in the unemployment–population ratio, unemployment rate, loss of employment (and subsequent re-employment), and average weeks of unemployment. The findings of her analyses indicate increases in poverty for all racial and ethnic groups and family types, as well as native and foreign born, in all regions. While Singh's analysis indicates rising rates of poverty for all racial and ethnic groups, as well as family types, she found that the gap in poverty between Blacks and Whites, as well as across family types, significantly increased during 2002–2011. Furthermore, she found that all of the unemployment indicators included in her analysis increased considerably for the same time period, with the exception of re-employment of displaced workers, which significantly decreased.

In "Deindustrialized Small Cities and Poverty: The View from Camden," Andrew Seligsohn and Joan Maya Mazelis provide a case study of the rise and collapse of Camden, New Jersey, to reveal the relationship between processes of globalization and what they term as the "immiseration in the emerging neoliberal order." As a small, successful economic industrial city in the first half of the 20th century, Camden has been experiencing a serious decline since the 1980s, marked by a significant loss in population, jobs, and tax-base. Seligsohn and Mazelis note that precisely at the moment that unemployment generated demand for city services, the government capacity to respond had deteriorated. They characterize Camden city government as privatizing most services through outsourcing nearly all of its key functions to a non-profit development entity that is driven by powerful interests in the city and region. This is a move that challenges democratic processes by shifting control of the city away from public institutions under popular control to private institutions dominated by regional business and political elites.

References

Block, F. (2007) "Confronting market fundamentalism: Doing 'Public Economic Sociology.'" *Socioeconomic Review* 5(2), 326–334.

Clarke, S. (2005) "The neoliberal theory of society." In A. Saad-Filho and D. Johnston (eds) *Neoliberalism: A critical reader*, London, Pluto Press, pp. 50–59.

1

BEYOND COINCIDENCE

How neoliberal policy initiatives in the IMF and World Bank affected U.S. poverty levels[1]

Pamela Blackmon

Introduction

The dramatic increase in poverty levels in the developing countries from the 1980s to the 1990s has been well documented by economists and social scientists (Wheeler, 1984; Stewart, 1995; Huber, 2005). Scholars have also found that much of the increase in poverty in developing countries was due to changes in policies at the IMF and the World Bank (Edwards and Dornbusch, 1994; Edwards, 1995; Haggard et al., 1995;). These new policy directives for developing countries focused on structural adjustment initiatives broadly defined to include privatization, deregulation, and overall measures for these countries to embrace more market-oriented reforms as opposed to relying on governmental programs.

The policy shift at the institutions has also been attributed to the rise of Ronald Reagan in the United States and the concurrent rise of Margaret Thatcher in the United Kingdom. What has been little addressed is how policy changes at the IMF and the World Bank might also be reflected in similar U.S. governmental policies toward poverty. For example, many socio-economic indicators in the United States have declined over the last 20 years, especially following the 1980s. Data in a recent paper show that for the country's least-educated whites, life expectancy has fallen by four years since 1990 (Olshansky et al., 2012). To what degree were shifts toward neoliberal policies of the international financial institutions of the IMF and the World Bank also seen in shifts in U.S. domestic policies? This chapter will explore the relationship between changes in U.S. domestic policies regarding poverty and the role of the United States as a powerful actor in the development and implementation of policies in the IMF and the World Bank.

The chapter will be organized as follows. The first section will review the ways in which structural adjustment policies resulted in increases in poverty for the countries that followed them, especially in the developing countries. The next sections address the relationship between similar policies implemented in the United States and subsequent rises in U.S. poverty as seen in an analysis of specific policies that are believed to have contributed to the increases in U.S. poverty and growing income inequality. These policies include the 1982 Educational Consolidation and Improvement Act, reduced federal spending for and deregulation of education, changes to transfer programs, and the Tax Reform Act of 1986. The final section provides some concluding remarks about the policy changes that have contributed to higher levels of poverty in the United States.

Problems with structural adjustment policies

The underlying framework of structural adjustment policies (SAPs) included a focus on policies such as privatization, deregulation, and an overall decrease in the level of governmental involvement in the economic realm. These were policies required by the IMF and the World Bank in return for loans and debt restructuring agreements for most of the countries in Africa and Latin America during the 1980s. As part of austerity measures, countries also reduced money for social expenditures in areas such as health, education, and welfare (Huber, 2005, p. 79). However, during the 1980s poverty rose dramatically in Africa and Latin America, whereas prior to this timeframe, poverty had been gradually decreasing in these regions. From 1985 to 1989 the number of people in poverty in sub-Saharan Africa rose from 191 million to 228 million; in Latin America and the Caribbean the number of people in poverty rose from 91 million in 1980 to 133 million in 1989 (Stewart, 1995, p. 1). Thus, the implementation of these types of structural adjustment and austerity policies was deemed at least partly responsible for the rising poverty and inequality in these regions by the end of the 1980s (Stewart, 1995; Huber, 2005, pp. 79–81; Blackmon, 2009).

These types of structural adjustment policies have also been referred to as the "Washington Consensus," a phrase coined by John Williamson because these policies were developed as a consensus based on "the political Washington of Congress and senior members of the administration and the technocratic Washington of the international financial institutions, the economic agencies of the U.S. government, the Federal Reserve Board, and the think tanks" (Williamson, 1990, p. 7). Williamson (1990, p. 11) even noted that expenditures on health and education as proper objects of government expenditure "fell under a cloud during the early years of the Reagan administration." Thus, the political support for the implementation of these types of free-market neoliberal policies came from the leadership change in two of the more powerful member states of the IMF and the World Bank: Ronald Reagan as U.S. president in 1980 and Margaret Thatcher as Prime Minister of the United Kingdom in May 1979 (Blackmon, 2010, p. 4023). Indeed, these leaders came to power promising these types of free market economic policy reforms in their own countries as well as for countries that would need loans from the IMF and the World Bank (Stiglitz, 2003, p. 13; Sachs, 2005, pp. 81–82).

The United States is arguably the most influential member state of the IMF and the World Bank based on its larger voting percentages which translate into influence in policy decision making in the institutions (Woods, 2003; Blackmon, 2008). Indeed, Joseph Stiglitz has asserted that there was a "purge" at the World Bank during Reagan's tenure to oust a distinguished group of development economists including Hollis Chenery, who did not share Reagan's focus on free market ideology as the proper framework for developing countries (Stiglitz, 2003, p. 13). The following section explains how similar neoliberal free market-style policies were implemented in the United States and how these policies also contributed to growing levels of U.S. poverty, through the deregulation and defunding of the U.S. educational system, decreases in funding for transfer programs, and changes to income tax rates.

Structural adjustment: U.S. style

Terrel Bell, as the first Secretary of Education under Ronald Reagan, described Reagan's goals for education during his term as follows: reduce "substantially" federal spending for education; strengthen local and state control of education; and encourage the establishment of laws and rules that would offer greatly expanded parental choice and that would increase competition for students among schools in a newly created public and private structure patterned after the free market system that motivates and disciplines U.S. business and industry.

(Bell, 1986, p. 488)

Bell also noted that Reagan wanted to end the Department of Education and replace it with a new agency that would have less power within the federal government.

While the Department of Education was not disbanded (largely due to push back from the U.S. Congress), there were many policies enacted that would fundamentally change the U.S. educational system to make it more "competitive and accountable" and thus more similar to that of the free market system. David Clark and Mary Anne Amiot (1981, p. 258) explained that the basic education policies of the Reagan administration were derived from the overall goals of the administration's domestic policy platform which was designed to cut taxes, deregulate federal programs, reallocate budget priorities, and reduce expenditures. The following sections will describe how the policy initiatives under the 1982 Educational Consolidation and Improvement Act and the 1983 publication of *A Nation at Risk* were used to achieve the administration's goals of substantial reductions in federal funding for education. Specific reductions in federal spending for education and data indicating changes in high school graduation rates during these time periods will also be reviewed.

The 1982 Educational Consolidation and Improvement Act (ECIA) decreased the amount of federal aid to schools and reduced the power of the federal government by giving states more control over how money was spent on education through providing block grants to states.[2] This 1982 Act was also a distinct change from the original Elementary and Secondary Education Act (ESEA) passed in 1965 under President Johnson which was designed to increase federal funding to school districts in addition to promoting the desegregation of schools. In fact, two years after ESEA was passed, the amount of money that the federal government provided to school districts through the U.S. Office of Education's Annual Budget increased from $1.5 billion to $4 billion (Hanna, 2005).

The block grant and consolidation program was part of the Reagan administration's "decentralization" policy (Clark and Amiot, 1981, p. 258). The change to block grants outlined in Chapter 2 of the ECIA was designed to allow states to decide which areas needed the most funding. The reasoning behind this change was that states could make these decisions better than the federal government because the states were more familiar with the needs of their students. However, even though states could receive larger Chapter 2 grants by having urban schools with larger enrollments of higher-cost students, urban school districts received comparatively smaller grants under Chapter 2 because state education agencies directed more resources to suburban areas for political (higher voting areas) and economic (higher tax paying) reasons.[3] Other problems that were projected with the block grant approach in providing more flexibility for states included the belief that resources would probably be reduced for the disabled and disadvantaged: the primary groups that had been protected by the government through federal funding. To quote the Urban Institute's Report of the first 18 months of policy and program changes in federal education policy under Reagan, "the federal government would not be providing a significant proportion of funds for elementary and secondary education, nor would it have a clear purpose in its funding" (Lewis, 1982, p. 157).

Second, the 1983 publication of *A Nation at Risk: The Imperative of Educational Reform* from Reagan's National Commission on Excellence in Education decreed that the U.S. educational system was failing because public schools were no longer focused on pushing students to excel. The publication relied on comparing standardized testing results (SAT scores) to show that the average scores of students had fallen from 1963 to 1980. Recommendations included introducing a nationwide system of standardized tests which would now determine whether schools would continue to receive federal aid. If schools did not increase their scores, they would lose federal aid.[4] This line of reasoning is very much in line with the context of the free market system in its framework to both motivate and discipline educators and school administrators by setting up a system of rewards and punishments designed to be the motivating factors in order to achieve the goals. Also in 1983, the federal contract for administering the ever-increasing rounds of testing was given to the Educational Testing Service (ETS) and taken away from the Educational Commission of the States (ECS).[5]

Impacts of decreases in educational revenue

Proposed reductions in federal spending for education by Reagan for 1981 and 1982 were already described as "unprecedented" in that the Reagan administration was able to redirect 12 percent of the fiscal year 1981 education budget, and proposed cutting 6 percent from the fiscal year 1982 budget (Clark and Amiot, 1981, p. 258). This was a strategy used throughout Reagan's tenure in that he consistently requested less money for the Department of Education than Congress had allocated or appropriated in the previous year (Verstegen and Clark, 1988). For example, in 1981 Congress had approved $14.8 billion for the Department of Education (DE) while Reagan requested only $13.5 billion; in 1982 Congress approved $14.8 billion for DE, while Reagan requested $12.4 billion; and in 1983 Reagan's budget request for DE was the lowest of his presidency at $9.95 billion, and this amount was almost 33 percent below the previous year's spending total (Verstegen and Clark, 1988, p. 135). During the Reagan administration, real funds for education declined by nearly $15 billion from 1981 to 1988 (Verstegen and Clark, 1988, p. 136).

Programs in elementary and secondary education from 1981 to 1988 saw some of the biggest percentage declines: special programs (−76 percent); bilingual education (−54 percent); and impact aid (−63 percent). The subtotal in declines for elementary/secondary was −28 percent from 1981 to 1988. Higher education registered the highest percentage losses in educational research (−70 percent) and in the office for civil rights (−33 percent). However, programs in higher education that were geared toward a "market and business system" registered percentage increases from 1981 to 1988: programs such as guaranteed student loans (+29 percent) and loans and construction (+81 percent) (Verstegen and Clark, 1988, p. 137). Educational research fell by 70 percent during this time period, and only declines in "special programs" (−76 percent) at the elementary and secondary levels fell by larger percentages. Verstegen and Clark (1988, p. 136) note that this decline in research was unprecedented and that in some ways it was in conflict with the goals of an administration that had argued that the federal government should be involved in collecting data, conducting research, and providing "reliable information about the condition of education." This seemed to be the main point of the 1983 publication *A Nation at Risk*. After examining the program decreases under the Reagan administration, the authors of this study conclude that "when programs had weak or negligible groups of constituents or when the programs had minimal yearly continuation costs" their budgets were reduced (Verstegen and Clark, 1988, p. 136). Apparently the study area of dropouts and delinquencies fell into this category because this area received no new funds at all for collection of data in 1985, although previously, in 1980, 33 awards had been set aside for areas of research into "school problems" (U.S. GAO Report, 1987, pp. 3, 31–36). The following section reviews the findings of a recent article on high school graduation rates from 1946 to 1985 and compares the changes in these rates with changes in funding for education during the time period.

Data on U.S. graduation rates differ widely depending on whether the high school status completion rate is used or whether the 17-year-old graduation ratio is used, and both are compiled by the National Center for Educational Statistics (NCES). Heckman and LaFontaine (2010) reconcile the differences between these estimates and present some very interesting results about the trends in U.S. high school graduation rates. Using multiple sources of data they track high school graduation rates in four-year intervals from 1946 to 1985. First, they illustrate that from 1966 to 1970 high school graduation rates increased from previous levels in 1961–1965. Their data also show steady increases in the graduation rate for the years 1971–1975. In fact, they conclude that the graduation rate "peaked in the early 1970s" (Heckman and LaFontaine, 2010, p. 254). Recall that the ESEA passed in 1965 under President Johnson was designed to increase federal funding provided to school districts in addition to ending desegregation. From 1966 to 1970, the graduation of Blacks increased to 69.2 percent, up from 63.9 percent from 1961 to 1965 (Heckman and LaFontaine, 2010, p. 254, Table 3). Thus, there appears to be at least some positive relationship between federal funding for education and high school graduation rates.

Graduation rates decline from 1976 to 1980 and the rates stay at about the same levels for 1981–1985 data (Heckman and LaFontaine, 2010, p. 256, Figure 4). What explains the decline in graduation rates, especially during the 1980s? One explanation is that more students opted to earn their GED instead of completing high school. Indeed, Heckman and LaFontaine (2010, p. 260) cite studies that "link high-stakes testing and stiffer educational standards to increased GED test taking." It is highly probable that the "high-stakes testing" involves at least in part the standardized tests adopted based on *A Nation at Risk*.

The decline in high school graduation rates is especially disturbing since increasing education is one of the best tools against falling into poverty in addition to the fact that education is one of the primary paths out of poverty, especially for minorities. Indeed, declining high school graduation rates lead to smaller college attendance and completion rates and further declines in the skills of the U.S. work force (Heckman and LaFontaine, 2010). The following section will review income inequality and the changes in household income in the United States during the Reagan administration to illustrate how fiscal policy changes, specifically the Tax Reform Act of 1986, also contributed to growing levels of U.S. poverty and income inequality since the 1970s.

Poverty and income inequality rises

Wage inequality, income inequality, and poverty increased in the United States during the 1980s (Hanratty and Blank, 1992; Katz and Murphy, 1992; Piketty and Saez, 2004).[6] In many cases, policy changes during the Reagan administration provide at least part of the explanation for the increases in these socio-economic indicators. First, poverty rates in the United States had been falling during the 1970s. Using the U.S. definition of poverty, poverty rates for nonelderly families fell from 10.1 percent in 1970 to 9 percent in 1979 but increased to 11.6 percent in 1986 (Hanratty and Blank, 1992, fn. 1). The female-headed family poverty rate was at about 38 percent in 1979 (and had been decreasing since 1976 from about 40 percent) but reached a high of about 42 percent in 1984, before leveling off at 41 percent in 1985–1986 (Hanratty and Blank, 1992, p. 239). Factors believed to have contributed to increases in U.S. poverty during the 1980s include an increase in wage inequality (which will be addressed below) and changes to transfer programs such as Unemployment Insurance, Food Stamp Programs, and Aid to Families with Dependent Children (AFDC) (Hanratty and Blank, 1992, pp. 245–246). Specific changes implemented in 1981 reduced the eligibility of the poor for these programs by requiring states to include the income of step-parents against AFDC eligibility (Omnibus Budget Reconciliation Act of 1981). This tax legislation also required that welfare agencies consider that persons eligible for both the Earned Income Tax Credit (EITC) and AFDC receive the EITC throughout the year (as opposed to the end of the year), thereby reducing benefits from AFDC and food stamps (Hotz and Scholz, 2003, pp. 151–152).

An additional factor that is believed to have contributed to the increase in U.S. poverty during the 1980s is the increase in wage inequality (Hanratty and Blank, 1992). Specifically, that increased wage inequality is due to changes in the demand for more educated and more skilled workers over jobs requiring physical labor in the United States, resulting in changes in the U.S. wage structure (Katz and Murphy, 1992, p. 36). This trend is likely to lead to higher levels of poverty for less-skilled workers, especially given data showing the decline in high school graduate rates, thus diminishing the probability that non-high school graduates (or GED earners) would continue on to college (Heckman and LaFontaine, 2010). Indeed, the wage differential seems to operate in a cyclical effect since an additional explanation for the decline in graduation rates is that during the 1980s the real wages of both those completing high school and those dropping out of high school declined (Autor et al., 2005).

Wage inequality certainly plays a role in overall rising income inequality and increases in poverty, all of which are impacted by education level. Piketty and Saez (2004) examine trends in income inequality in the United States in order to understand increases in income inequality since the 1970s. They present some interesting findings from their data, especially concerning changes in wage inequality measured by top wage shares. They find that "a significant part of the gain (of top income shares) is concentrated in 1987 and 1988 just after the Tax Reform Act of 1986 which sharply cut the top marginal income tax rates" (Piketty and Saez, 2004, p. 7). Their analysis of the data shows that, from 1970 to 1984, the top 1 percent share of wage earners increased from 5 percent to 7.5 percent but, from 1986 to 1988, the top shares of wage earners increased substantially from 7.5 percent to 9.5 percent (Piketty and Saez, 2004, p. 21). Again, they attribute at least part of this "sharp increase" to the large top marginal tax rate cuts of the Tax Reform Act of 1986 (Piketty and Saez, 2004, p. 21). The stated purpose of the Tax Reform Act was to make the tax system more equitable; however, the equity component was limited, "as considerable efforts were devoted to keeping the reform from altering the distribution of the tax burden across broad income classes" (Auerbach and Slemrod, 1997, p. 589).

The cumulative effects of the policies during the Reagan administration can be seen in the differences in life expectancy between groups of the U.S. population based on level of education and its socio-economic status correlates of income and wealth. Indeed, a recent study that examined trends in these disparities from 1990 to 2008 found widening differences in life expectancy due to race and educational differences. Specifically, the study found that having fewer than 12 years of education has a "dramatic negative effect" on the life expectancy of Whites, and that among all racial and ethnic groups "an additional four years of education beyond high school yields a pronounced longevity advantage" (Olshansky et al., 2012, p. 1807). While education is crucial to upward mobility through higher-paying jobs requiring more skills, education has direct benefits on health through the ability to cope better with stress and the adoption of healthier lifestyles (Olshansky et al., 2012, p. 1808). Indirect benefits of education include easier access to social positions, and leading a more privileged life (Olshansky et al., 2012, p. 1808). Thus, more years of education or income also leads to longer life and fewer negative health events (Crimmins and Saito, 2001).

Conclusion

Many studies have found a relationship between structural adjustment or neoliberal policies advocated by the IMF and the World Bank during the 1980s and increasing poverty in the countries that followed those policies. The United States as the most powerful member state of the IMF and the World Bank was instrumental in making changes at the institutions to ensure that these types of market-oriented policies would be implemented. This chapter has provided evidence to show that similar types of market-oriented policies were also implemented in the United States during the Reagan administration and that they had similar impacts in increasing poverty levels. Education funding was decreased substantially during the Reagan administration, and the only programs that did not register percent decreases were those with market incentives such as student loans. The 1982 Educational Consolidation and Improvement Act decreased federal aid for education in addition to a change to provide block grants to states, thereby reducing the role of the federal government in determining how money would be spent.

Most of these policy changes affect outcomes in other areas, which makes them even more problematic. Decreased funding for and deregulation of education has at least in part contributed to lower high school graduation rates, which lead to lower college completion rates. These trends have contributed to higher levels of poverty since higher-paying jobs in the United States require more years of education, thus contributing to increases in wage inequality. Growing disparities in income inequality are also related to the latter phenomenon, but a significant part of the gain for the high-income earners was followed by the Tax Reform Act of 1986.

Finally, the importance of education as seen in greater longevity and a healthier life for U.S. citizens should provide the impetus for policy makers to focus on policies designed to increase the years of education for U.S. citizens. Indeed, it seems clear that increasing the educational levels of U.S. citizens is a key component in the path out of poverty.

Notes

1 I would like to thank Makayla Zonfrilli for research assistance.
2 The Reagan Years: Block Grants and Local Control—accessed at http://www.archives.nysed.gov/edpolicy/research/res_essay_reagan_achvmnt_gap.shtml, November 9, 2012.
3 The Reagan Years: Block Grants and Local Control—accessed at http://www.archives.nysed.gov/edpolicy/research/res_essay_reagan_achvmnt_gap.shtml, November 9, 2012.
4 The Reagan Years: Federal Aid and Test Scores—accessed at http://www.archives.nysed.gov/edpolicy/research/res_essay_reagan_anational_risk.shtml, November 12, 2012.
5 The Reagan Years: Testing and Dropouts—accessed at http://www.archives.nysed.gov/edpolicy/research/res_essay_reagan_testing_dropouts.shtml, November 12, 2012.
6 Buss (2010) concludes that while the rich got richer from 1987 to 2007, the relative status of the poor worsened during the same time period.

References

Auerbach, A., and Slemrod, J. (1997). The Economic Effects of the Tax Reform Act of 1986. *Journal of Economic Literature* 35(2): 589–632.

Autor, D., Katz, L., and Kearney, M. (2005). Rising Wage Inequality: The Role of Composition and Prices. *NBER Technical Working Paper 11625*.

Bell, T. (1986). Education Policy Development in the Reagan Administration. *Phi Delta Kappan* 37(7): 487–493.

Blackmon, P. (2008). Rethinking Poverty through the Eyes of the International Monetary Fund and the World Bank. *International Studies Review* 10(2): 179–202.

Blackmon, P. (2009). Factoring Gender into Economic Development: Changing the Policies of the International Monetary Fund and the World Bank. *Women's Studies* 38(2): 213–237.

Blackmon, P. (2010). International Economic Institutions and Global Justice. In Robert Denemark et al., eds. *The International Studies Compendium Project*. Oxford: Wiley-Blackwell.

Buss, J. (2010). Have the Poor Gotten Poorer? The American Experience from 1987 to 2007. *The Journal of Poverty* 14(2): 183–196.

Clark, D., and Amiot, M. (1981). The Impact of the Reagan Administration on Federal Education Policy. *Phi Delta Kappan* 63(4): 258–262.

Crimmins, E., and Saito, Y. (2001). Trends in Healthy Life Expectancy in the United States, 1970–1990: Gender, Racial, and Educational Differences. *Social Science and Medicine* 52: 1629–1641.

Edwards, S. (1995). *Crisis and Reform in Latin America: From Despair to Hope*. Oxford: Oxford University Press for the World Bank.

Edwards, S., and Dornbusch, R. (1994). *Stabilization, Adjustment and Growth*. Chicago: University of Chicago Press.

Haggard, S., Lafay, J.D., and Morrison, C. (1995). *The Political Feasibility of Adjustment in Developing Countries*. Paris: Organisation for Economic Co-operation and Development.

Hanna, J. (2005). The Elementary and Secondary Education Act: 40 Years Later. *Harvard Graduate School of Education*. Retrieved November 12, 2012, from http://www.gse.harvard.edu/news/2005/0819_esea.html

Hanratty, M., and Blank, R. (1992) Down and Out in North America: Recent Trends in Poverty Rates in the United States and Canada. *The Quarterly Journal of Economics* 107(1): 233–254.

Heckman, J., and LaFontaine, P. (2010). The American High School Graduation Rate: Trends and Levels. *The Review of Economics and Statistics* 92(2): 244–262.

Hotz, J., and Scholz, J. (2003). The Earned Income Tax Credit. In Robert A. Moffitt, ed. *Means Tested Programs in the United States*. Chicago: University of Chicago Press.

Huber, E. (2005). Globalization and Social Policy Developments in Latin America. In Miguel Glatzer and Dietrich Rueschemeyer, eds. *Globalization and the Future of the Welfare State*. Pittsburgh: University of Pittsburgh Press.

Katz, L., and Murphy, K. (1992). Changes in Relative Wages, 1963–1987: Supply and Demand Factors. *The Quarterly Journal of Economics* 107(1): 35–78.

Lewis, A. (1982). Reagan and Critics Exchange Salvos in First Round of War of Statistics. *Phi Delta Kappan* 65(2): 83–85.

Olshansky, J., Antonucci, T., Berkman, L., Binstock, R., Boersch-Supan, A., Cacioppo, J., Carnes, B., Carstensen, L., Fried, L., Goldman, D., Jackson, J., Kohli, M., Rother, J., Zheng, Y., and Rowe, J. (2012). Differences in Life Expectancy Due to Race and Educational Difference are Widening and Many May Not Catch Up. *Health Affairs* 31(8): 1803–1813.

Piketty, T., and Saez, E. (2004). Income Inequality in the United States, 1913–2002. Retrieved November 2, 2012, from http://elsa.berkeley.edu/~saez/piketty-saezOUP04US.pdf

Sachs, J. (2005). *Ending Poverty: Possibilities for Our Time*. New York: The Penguin Press.

Stewart, F. (1995). *Adjustment and Poverty*. London: Routledge.

Stiglitz, J. (2003). *Globalization and Its Discontents*. New York: W.W. Norton.

U.S. General Accounting Office (GAO) Report (1987). *Education Information: Changes in Funds and Priorities Have Affected Production and Quality*. Washington, DC: GAO, PEMD-88-4, November.

Verstegen, D., and Clark, D. (1988). The Diminution in Federal Expenditures for Education during the Reagan Administration. *Phi Delta Kappan* 70(2): 134–138.

Wheeler, D. (1984). Sources of Stagnation in Sub-Saharan Africa. *World Development* 12(1): 1–23.

Williamson, J. (1990). What Washington Means by Policy Reform. In John Williamson, ed. *Latin American Adjustment: How Much has Happened?* Washington, DC: Institute for International Economics.

Woods, N. (2003). The United States and the International Financial Institutions: Power and Influence within the World Bank and the IMF. In R. Foot, S.N. MacFarlane, and M. Mastanduno, eds. *U.S. Hegemony and International Organizations*. Oxford: Oxford University Press.

2

THE DISCURSIVE AXIS OF NEOLIBERALISM

Debt, deficits, and austerity

Shawn Cassiman

"Remember, you are not a loan!" *Debt Resistors Manual*

Debt and deficits

Discourse shapes our worldview, imparts meaning, and helps make understandable the intuited, the incoherent. Discourse is ideological, as are all utterances, perhaps none more so than those described as "neutral" (Schiller, 1973). The neoliberal globalization discourse, following the market crashes of 2008/9, has been primarily concerned with the ills of debt and deficits, prescribing austerity as the cure. This "economic crisis" has been used to promote what Naomi Klein (2008) describes as the neoliberal "shock doctrine" of the Chicago School economists, a doctrine that utilizes crisis/shocks (or fabricates them) in order to impose extreme austerity and privatization programs. The most recent example she provides in the United States is New Orleans following Katrina, where minimum wage laws were "suspended" and school privatization became an "experiment" in charter school education.

Neoliberal globalization is the application of neoliberal capitalism on the global stage (Chossudovsky and Marshall, 2012). Tabb (2001) argues that neoliberalism has replaced Keynesianism as the national and global economic project. He suggests:

> Where national Keynesianism reflected the capacity of working people (in the United States and Europe) to resist the domination of corporate interests, neoliberalism can be seen as the imposition of the most powerful state—the United States—to overcome this resistance and impose its will on others.
>
> (p. 61)

Tabb defines globalization as the imperialism of finance, which is not too far from McNally's (2011) description of globalization as the crisis of capitalism or Harman's (2010) "Zombie" capitalism.

In the United States, the deficit discourse of 2011 became, in post-election 2012, the "Fiscal Cliff" discourse, thus reanimating the specter of debt as a disaster to be avoided at all costs. This debt/deficit logic follows upon a similar discourse to that being employed against populations in Europe. The U.S. discourse even manages to hold up the ghostly European comparisons as a warning: "We don't want to be like Greece," indebted, in danger, and (dis) credited. However, in the United States the "debt equals moral panic" discourse began soon after the spectacular pop of the housing bubble brought consumers/citizens to their knees and is firmly rooted in the welfare queen, deserving or undeserving discourse. It came as no surprise to scholars of welfare reform that the same discourse that had been leveled against welfare claimants was now being directed at "greedy" public sector workers, including teachers (Abramobitz, 2012). The discursive construction of public sector workers became policy recommendations, including union-busting policies or "Right to Work" laws. Calls for TANF recipients and the unemployed to be drug tested occurred (and continue) in many states, and TANF recipients are being drug tested in Florida.

Brooks (2009), a conservative columnist for the *New York Times*, reinforces this "debt as morality" position by arguing that a failure to pay debts is evidence of moral failure. He suggests that this failure exists at both the national and personal level and is a result of profligate spending at the government level, and living beyond one's means at the individual level. In fact, he coins the term "economic morality" in order to argue that we, as a nation, have lost our moral compass. However, his "economic morality" is simply the monster of economic orthodoxy, which is neoliberalism, clad as personal responsibility. "Morality plays" are frequently dusted off and trotted out as needed by free marketers for their functional value. For instance, in an article published soon after the financial crisis, White (2010) notes that when faced with the "rational economic" choice of engaging in strategic default, most homeowners continue to pay on their underwater homes. When White's research was publicized (and later published), he was quickly attacked for "encouraging" irresponsibility and immorality among homeowners (Harney, 2009).

The moral hazard discourse is part and parcel of the devolution revolution, that positions not just welfare receipt as personal responsibility, but increasingly features all care (broadly conceptualized to include care of the environment as well) and morality devolved to the individual level. In other words, while banks "get bailed out," average citizens "get sold out."

Austerity as the cure

Austerity is not a new phenomenon, as it is featured in the Reagonomics and Thatcherism of the 1980s; however, since 2008/9 the potency and the geography of austerity have shifted from International Monetary Fund (IMF) policies addressing austerity at the periphery, to the imposition of Structural Adjustment Policies (SAPs) in the Global North, for instance, Ireland, Spain, Greece, Italy, Portugal, etc., or as in the United States, structurally adjusting ourselves preemptively (McNally, 2011). The IMF's influence in Europe does have a precedent, as Britain was forced to retreat from "innovative" policy responses as a condition for IMF loans in the 1970s in order to pave the way for austerity in the United States (Panitch and Gindin, 2012).

Features of austerity, and SAPs in particular, share a focus on debt reduction at the expense of social welfare programs, as well as privatization of public goods. McNally (2011) describes debt as "a weapon of dispossession" (p. 131). On the ground this means lack, or withdrawal, of support for education, healthcare, pensions, and other programs that benefit those most marginalized and contributes to the production of the Precariat (Standing, 2011). In the United States, the deficit and debt discussions continue to dominate the discourse, though the Occupy Wall Street Movement has done much to draw attention to the crisis of capitalism (Abney-Korn et al., 2013; Butler, 2011; Chomsky, 2000), providing a much-needed counterpoint to the naturalization of austerity, in which neoliberal capitalism seems as natural "as rain" (Makwana, 2006).

This devolution, or what Clarke and Newman (2012) describe as the "shape changing" nature of the austerity discourse, is "the alchemy of austerity" that shifts attention from the private to the public, and the financial to a fiscal crisis. They also are cognizant of the "magical thinking" required to argue markets will provide and austerity is the cure. McNally (2012) reminds us:

> Capitalism is both monstrous and magical. Crucially, its magic consists in concealing the occult economy—the obscure transactions between human bodies and capital—on which it rests. Entranced by this sorcery, the equivalent of magic-caps pulled over our eyes and ears, bourgeois common sense vigorously denies the monsters in our mids.
>
> (p. 113)

The policy discourse, rather than focusing upon structural contributions to worklessness (Wiggan, 2012) or the rise of the Precariat (Standing, 2011), has redoubled its focus on individual deficit explanations rooted in the welfare queen discourse (Cassiman, 2008), expanded to include attacks on "greedy" public sector workers and the unemployed themselves, as "Neoliberal theory conveniently holds that unemployment is always voluntary" (Harvey, 2007, p. 10). The attacks on entitlements, like the social safety net, pensions, and social security, and even work itself, are in sharp contrast to the entitlement to bailouts expressed by the financial sector and a part of the magical thinking associated with neoliberalism. Giroux (2012) discusses the features of neoliberal discourse as a "culture of cruelty":

> ...government supports for the poor, unemployed, low-skilled workers, and elderly are derided because they either contribute to an increase in the growing deficit or undermine the market-driven notion of individual responsibility. And yet, the same critics defend without irony government support for the ultra-wealthy, the bankers, the permanent war economy or any number of subsidies for corporations as essential to the life of the nation, which is simply an argument that benefits the rich and powerful and legitimizes the deregulated Wild West of casino capitalism.
>
> (p. 96)

The cruelty is disappeared through magical thinking as the alchemy of austerity fuels the neoliberal agendas of economic deregulation, welfare state retrenchment, the trope of "individual responsibility," and an expansive penal apparatus (Wacquant, 2009). Enforced by the "troika" of the European Commission, IMF, and European Central Bank, these goals are met as we witness country after country in Europe buckle under the assault of austerity. The refusal to question such policy over the past several decades, in meaningful ways, is a result of the primacy of the "there is no alternative" (TINA) of Thatcherism and Reaganomics discourse, or a sense of the "end of history" (Fukuyama, 1992).

One country, Iceland, is a lone outlier resisting the austerity discourse and insistent upon an alternative. Rather than suggest the citizens of the country bear the burden of the elite banking policies, Iceland refused the debt, going against IMF imperatives, and even going so far as to put bankers and politicians on trial (Lamrani, 2012). These radical policy responses were drafted by the citizens of Iceland and upset the alchemy of austerity, exposing the monster of neoliberalism and the monstrously cruel nature of austerity. Recently, as Lamrani notes, the IMF has praised Iceland's rebound, but "the IMF omitted the information that these results were only possible because Iceland refused its neoliberal shock therapy and developed a program to encourage an economic and efficient alternative" (n.p.).

Occupy Wall Street and the debt strike

It is my contention that the Occupy Wall Street (OWS) Strike Debt group initiatives, while not precisely a stake through the heart of the neoliberal beast (and certainly no Icelandic response), do provide an opportunity to rupture the magical thinking that prevails in the United States, while challenging the disciplinary nature of debt (Schram, 2013). Since this magical thinking is a prerequisite to compliance with capital, this rupture exposes the monster of neoliberalism.

The Strike Debt group of OWS has managed to conceptualize programs that are both functional and educational, as illustrated by *The Debt Resistors' Operations Manual* (Strike Debt Assembly, 2012a), that lays bare the mechanizations of debt, while allowing space and opportunities for individuals and coalitions to challenge and resist the austerity discourse:

> The fact is, most debtors dare not reveal their names nor show their faces. Those who struggle to stay afloat or who have fallen into default are told that they are failures, inadequate and abject, and so they do not speak out. There are literally millions of people who cannot pay the enormous sums that the financial elites claim they owe. They are the Invisible Army of Defaulters. Instead of a personal failure, refusing to pay under our current system is an act of profound moral courage. We see our situation as connected, and we can look for ways to step out of the shadows together. *The Debt Resistors' Operations Manual* is an attempt to assist this invisible army and all other debt resistors in this struggle.
>
> (p. 2)

Conceptualizing default as "an act of profound moral courage" or an act of resistance to the "there is no alternative" discourse at the individual level allows us to draw similarities to Iceland's state response.

The manual begins with a discussion of credit scores and the role they play in even the most basic of human interactions, such as when searching for a job. The authors discuss our increasing reliance upon credit cards, or "the plastic safety net," as real wages fail to keep pace with the cost of living. The manual also focuses upon medical debt, responsible for approximately 62 percent of personal bankruptcies in the United States. The discussion of student loan debt is highly relevant as it is what some experts are predicting to be the next financial "bubble" to burst. The manual also features a strong discussion of housing debt and "the ownership society." The authors also illuminate an often invisible but increasingly problematic municipal debt or, what they term, "the silent killer." The manual manages to document, in one location, the extent, rationale, and consequences of debt in the United States. It incorporates discussions that are obscured or ignored by mainstream media accounts. In addition, each chapter includes ways in which individuals and/or communities can mount resistance strategies, thereby educating while offering opportunities for resistance.

Some scholars insist:

> A solution to the economic crisis requires tackling issues of debt by fundamentally modifying the relationship between creditors and debtors, controlling interest rates, and *erasing certain categories of debt* [emphasis added] and ultimately challenging the overriding power of the creditors to dictate macroeconomic policy.
>
> (Chossudovsky and Marshall, 2012)

One program of the Debt Strike group is called the "Rolling Jubilee" and proposes just such a partial solution. Rolling Jubilee is a Strike Debt project that buys debt for pennies on the dollar, but instead of collecting it, abolishes it.

Together we can liberate debtors at random through a campaign of mutual support, good will, and collective refusal. Debt resistance is just the beginning. Join us as we imagine and create a new world based on the common good, not Wall Street profits.

(Strike Debt Assembly, 2013)

Modeled on practices of many faith traditions and documented in the Bible, the Rolling Jubilee is informed by the historical precedent of debt erasure (Graeber, 2011). This program serves several functions: it draws attention to the one-sided nature of the debt as morality discourse and draws a clear distinction between capitalism and democracy. It also encourages an examination of the marked differences between mutual aid and charity, as it encourages engaging with "strangers" in meaningful ways, by erasing their debt. Finally, it also illuminates the predatory nature of neoliberal capitalism.

The debt discourse, as posited by the Strike Debt group, also allows us to critically examine the ways in which financial debt is similar or different from interdependence among human beings. The debt economy, or market discourse, has moved into such common usage that it is associated with reciprocity or gifts—for instance, being indebted to someone for some assistance, or owing a debt of gratitude (Graeber, 2011). Such common usage contributes to the ease with which we accept the larger discourse of the debt economy. Everyone's a debtor, everyone's in debt, it's natural, like neoliberalism, and just like the discourse of neoliberalism, "there is no alternative."

Whether or not society adopts the attitude that "ubiquity equals natural" and so precludes change, we everywhere find evidence of everyday resistance to the debtor identity. One might go so far as to suggest that the argument for liberty (and even U.S. iterations of libertarianism) is a rejection of the debtor identity essentialism. Indeed, the vilification of welfare claimants, the unemployed, or the retired for their need might imply a desire to reject *their* indebtedness lest we recognize our own.

In addition to Strike Debt, the recent successful action by Quebec students in response to proposed increases in tuition, that later exploded in solidarity actions throughout Canada and the globe (identified by the red square of fabric pinned to clothing denoting "We're All in the Red")[1] and the student debt organizing in the United States as well as the International Student Movement (ISM),[2] raise awareness of the human costs of debt and the toll the austerity discourse and policies are likely to take, not only in our present, but long into our future. However, these movements of moments (Hughes et al., 2010) provide an opportunity to educate and organize across boundaries and borders, an antidote to the "welfare queen," entitlement discourse, and to resist neoliberalism's plan to marketize and privatize the welfare state, including education, in other words, an opportunity to Occupy Precarity (Schram, 2012, 2013). *The Debt Resistors' Organizing Kit* (Strike Debt Assembly, 2012b) reminds us that the ubiquity of debt itself can be a force to be reckoned with, for "You are not a loan, but we are united."

Notes

1 We're all in the red: http://allinthered.org.
2 International Student Movement: http://www.emancipating-education-for-all.org.

References

Abney-Korn, K., Cassiman, S. A., and Fleetham, D. (2013). While we were sleeping: From dystopia to global awakening. *Perspectives on Global Development and Technology*, 12, 1–2, 80–97.
Abramovitz, M. (2012). The feminization of austerity. *New Labor Forum*, 21, 1, 32–41.
Brooks, D. (2009). The next culture war. *New York Times*, September 29, 2009, http://www.nytimes.com/2009/09/29/opinion/29brooks.html?module=Search&mabReward=relbias%3Ar%2C{%222%22%3A%22RI%3A12%22}. Accessed November 11, 2014.
Butler, J. (2011). For and against precarity. *Tidal: Occupy Theory, Occupy Strategy*, 1, 12–13.
Cassiman, S. A. (2008). Resisting the neo-liberal poverty discourse: On constructing deadbeat dads and welfare queens. *Sociology Compass*, 2/5 (2008), 1690–1700, 10.1111/j.1751-9020.2008.00159.x
Chomsky, N. (2000). Globalization: The new face of capitalism. *Democracy Now*, http://www.democracynow.org/2000/2/3/noam_chomsky_globalization_the_new_face. Accessed January 8, 2013.
Chossudovsky, M. and Marshall, A. G. (eds). (2012). *The global economic crisis: The great depression of the XXI century*. Montreal: Global Research Publishers. Centre for Research on Globalization.
Clarke, J. and Newman, J. (2012). The alchemy of austerity. *Critical Social Policy*. 32, 299–319.
Fukuyama, F. (1992). *The end of history and the last man*. Washington, DC: Free Press.
Giroux, H. A. (2012). *Twilight of the social: Resurgent politics in the age of disposability*. Boulder, CO: Paradigm Publishers.
Graeber, D. (2011). *Debt: The first 5000 years*. New York: Melville House Publishing.
Harman, C. (2010). *Zombie capitalism: Global crisis and the relevance of Marx*. Chicago, IL: Haymarket Books.
Harney, K. R. (2009). Professor advises underwater homeowners to walk away from mortgages. *Los Angeles Times*, November 29, 2009, http://articles.latimes.com/2009/nov/29/business/la-fi-harney29-2009nov29. Accessed December 12, 2012.
Harvey, D. (2007). *A brief history of neoliberalism*. New York: Oxford University Press.
Hughes, C., Peace, S., and Van Meter, K. (eds). (2010). *Uses of a whirlwind: Movement, movements, and contemporary radical currents in the United States*. Oakland, CA: AK Press.
Klein, N. (2008). *The shock doctrine: The rise of disaster capitalism*. New York: Picador.
Lamrani, S. (2012). Iceland shows the way: Reject austerity. *Pravda.ru*, http://english.pravda.ru/world/americas/28-11-2012/122952-iceland_reject_austerity-0/. Accessed November 18, 2012.
Makwana, R. (2006). Neoliberalism and economic globalization. *Share the world's resources: Sustainable economics to end global poverty*, http://www.stwr.org/globalization/neoliberalism-and-economic-globalization.html. Accessed June 18, 2010.
McNally, D. (2011). *Global slump: The economics and politics of crisis and resistance*. Oakland, CA: PM Press.
McNally, D. (2012). *Monsters of the market: Zombies, vampires and global capitalism*. Chicago: Haymarket Books.
Panitch, L. and Gindin, S. (2012). *The making of global capitalism: The political economy of American empire*. New York: Verso.
Schiller, H. (1973). *The mind managers*. Boston: Beacon Press.
Schram, S. (2012). *Now time for neoliberalism: Resisting Plan B from below*, http://www.brynmawr.edu/socialwork/GSSW/schram/. Accessed August 15, 2014.
Schram, S. (2013). *Middle-class melancholia: Self-sufficiency after the demise of Christianized capitalism (U.S. style)*, https://www.academia.edu/5888949/Middle-Class_Melancholia_Self-Sufficiency_after_the_Demise_of_Christianized_Capitalism_U.S._Style_. Accessed August 15, 2014.
Standing, G. (2011). *The precariat: The new dangerous class*. New York: Bloomsbury.
Strike Debt Assembly. (2012a). Occupy Wall Street, Common Notions, Antumbra Designs, *The debt resistors' operations manual*. Available for download or read online, http://strikedebt.org/drom/#toc. Accessed January 14, 2013.
Strike Debt Assembly. (2012b). *Debt Resistors' Organizing Kit*, http://strikedebt.org/drom/#toc. Accessed January 14, 2013.
Strike Debt Assembly. (2013). *Rolling Jubilee*, http://strikedebt.org/rjupdate-2/. Accessed June 12, 2013.
Tabb, W. K. (2001). *The amoral elephant: Globalization and the struggle for social justice in the twenty-first century*. New York: Monthly Review Press.

Wacquant, L. (2009). *Punishing the poor: The neoliberal government of social insecurity.* Durham, NC: Duke University Press.

White, B. T. (2010). Underwater and not walking away: Shame, fear and social management of the housing crisis. *Wake Forest Law Review*, 45, 971–1023.

Wiggan, J. (2012). Telling stories of 21st century welfare: The UK coalition government and the neo-liberal discourse of worklessness and dependency. *Critical Social Policy*, 32, 3, pp. 383–405.

3

DEINDUSTRIALIZED SMALL CITIES AND POVERTY

The view from Camden

Andrew Seligsohn and Joan Maya Mazelis

Introduction

Camden, NJ, has achieved infamy as an emblem of urban failure. Long the poorest *small* city in the United States and now simply the nation's poorest city, Camden is also the nation's most dangerous city (CQ Press, 2012; Vargas, 2012). In nearly every dimension of social, economic, and civic experience, the evidence of dysfunction is overwhelming. Poverty saturates Camden. Virtually every resident of the city is poor or nearly poor. The city government itself is starved for cash. Almost without exception, Camden's residential neighborhoods are poor neighborhoods. Unlike most other cities facing high rates of poverty, Camden does not contain concentrated wealth and concentrated poverty. It contains only concentrated poverty.

The State of New Jersey has spent enormous sums of public money in Camden in recent decades without apparent impact on the social problems plaguing the city. In the domain of education, the story begins in 1985 with the first of the Abbott decisions, a series of decisions by the State Supreme Court holding that the New Jersey Constitution requires roughly equal funding of public schools (Walker, 2005). As a consequence, the Camden City Public School District receives a healthy per-pupil allocation, very little of which comes from taxes paid by Camden residents. The same pattern manifests in other areas. Under special legislation passed in 2002 and extended in 2007, the state allocated roughly $175 million for capital projects to rebuild Camden (Katz, 2009). Under its current transitional aid program, the State of New Jersey directs tens of millions of dollars to Camden each year to help it close its gaping structural budget gap (DeMarco, 2011). Federal grants for projects such as Hope VI, special allocations for economic development from the Delaware River Port Authority, and a variety of other public expenditures add to the accumulated public investment over the last three decades (Mulvihill, 2011; U.S. Department of Housing and Urban Development, 2004).

And yet, Camden's problems persist. More than 42 percent of its residents live below the poverty line, including more than half of all Camden children (U.S. Census Bureau, 2011). In 2012, Camden's murder rate of more than 80 per 100,000 residents was 16 times higher than the national average (Laday, 2013a; Tucker, 2012). When New Jersey identified the lowest-performing 1 percent of schools statewide, 23 of Camden's 26 district schools were on the list (Giordano, 2012; New Jersey Department of Education, 2012). Camden's dismal economy compounds these problems. Nearly one quarter of parcels in Camden are officially vacant or have an assessed value of $0, typically an indicator of abandonment (CamConnect, 2009). A great many of those are locked in tortuous legal complexities that make it nearly impossible for even the most courageous entrepreneur to launch a business in the city (Vargas, 2011). Without a functioning private sector, Camden faces an enormous structural deficit. The city can raise just $30 million annually through local taxes but requires roughly $600 million to provide essential services (CamConnect, 2010a).

In the face of hundreds of millions of dollars of public expenditures, Camden's distress is resilient. In light of its history of corruption and the presence in the city of a thriving drug trade, it is easy to see Camden's problems as emanating from within, while sincere but naïve and ultimately doomed efforts to solve those problems come from without (Gillette, 2005). But in Camden, as in other impoverished small cities facing economic and social collapse, a closer examination reveals a different picture. This chapter argues that the story of the city's economic rise and collapse reveals a great deal about the relationship between processes of globalization and immiseration against the backdrop of the emerging neoliberal order. We best understand Camden's ongoing crisis not as a manifestation of characteristics inherent in the city but as a manifestation of global historical processes with profoundly local consequences. Those consequences include not only the suffering of individuals and communities in Camden but also the occlusion of democracy in governing the city's affairs.

Camden's rise

Camden emerged as a small economic powerhouse as industrialization took off nationally in the first half of the twentieth century. Between 1900 and the early 1950s, Camden's population grew from about 75,000 to roughly 125,000 (Gillette, 2005). Through a combination of major industrial producers, smaller manufacturers, and ancillary businesses, Camden was home to 180,000 jobs at its peak in 1955 (Annie E. Casey Foundation, 2001). The local economy grew in direct relationship to the increasing projection of economic, political, and military power by the United States on a global scale.

The histories of Camden's three main employers during its industrial period, New York Shipbuilding (based in Camden, despite its name), RCA Victor, and Campbell's Soup, capture the link between Camden's prosperity and the changing geo-political context. New York Shipbuilding (New York Ship), founded in 1898, became a major contractor for the Department of Defense. The company employed tens of thousands of workers building some of the largest ships in the world, including aircraft carriers. Both world wars represented important growth opportunities for the company, as the United States relied on New York Ship and other large-scale producers to create a military no other country could challenge (Gillette, 2005).

RCA Victor benefited both directly and indirectly from the military and economic aspects of globalization. RCA Victor's Camden origins lie in the founding of the Victor Talking Machine Company in 1901. Victor merged with the Radio Corporation of America to form RCA Victor in 1929. While it is best remembered for entertainment technologies, RCA Victor made a good deal of its money as a defense contractor, supplying communications equipment to the military. Like New York Ship, it benefited from U.S. involvement in World War II, and, as a marketer of consumer products, RCA Victor benefited from the increasing access to global markets guaranteed by the prominence of the United States on the world stage (Cowie, 1999).

Even Campbell's Soup benefited significantly from World War II. Best known as a provider of nutritious meals to America's families, Campbell's supplied non-perishable meals for soldiers during both world wars, a growth opportunity that supported a massive expansion in its productive capacity and gave it experience in global supply-chain development. Campbell's recognized the opportunity for its non-perishable products in global markets and took advantage of the increasing reach of the United States' influence and transportation capacity to extend its sales globally (Sidorick, 2009).

All three of these companies capitalized on Camden's inherent advantages and contributed to making Camden a magnet for migrants and immigrants. Camden is situated in the nation's most densely populated corridor, with road and rail links in all directions and a port of its own. New York Ship benefited directly from Camden's ocean access through the Delaware River, while Campbell's relied for decades on Camden's access to South Jersey's rich agricultural land, especially its tomato crop (Sidorick, 2009). Camden's companies connected local assets to global opportunities in the first half of the twentieth century, which positioned them to shape local life in Camden. Whole neighborhoods in Camden emerged to provide housing to the booming population, notably Yorkship Village, a federally funded planned community of 1,000 homes built during World War I to house new employees at New York Ship (Childs, 1918). The entire local economy stood on the shoulders of these towering pioneers of global industry. In 1955, Camden was the beating heart of South Jersey (Annie E. Casey Foundation, 2001).

Camden's fall

If 1955 was Camden's high-water mark, the next decade revealed the impermanence of Camden's strength. By the early 1960s, employment in Camden was declining, as the same forces that helped it succeed began to engineer its failure. While the particulars varied among Camden's employers, the direction of change was the same for all—sharply down.

Increasing global competition, the demand for ever-larger ships, and the decline in contracts from the U.S. Navy hampered and ultimately felled New York Ship. As new producers entered the shipbuilding business during and after World War II, older producers did not have the facilities to build the increasingly large ships that were in demand (Broadbridge, 1965; Palmer, 1988). The development of enormous new factories with updated technology left New York Ship at a disadvantage from which it could not recover. New York Ship's contracts began to decline in the late 1950s, and the company shut its doors in 1967 (Gillette, 2005).

During this same period, RCA and Campbell's began moving production out of Camden to low-wage areas, first in the United States and then abroad (Cowie, 1999; Sidorick, 2009). These developments accelerated as both companies felt the pressure of global competition, forcing them to build new, more efficient factories and hold wages down. As the major employers contracted, small businesses failed for lack of customers. New business creation moved to the suburbs, where land was cheap. In the 25 years between 1955 and 1980, Camden lost nearly 50,000 residents, and tens of thousands of jobs.[1] Population loss led to a precipitous decline in property values, eroding the wealth of those who continued to own houses in the city. The city's tax base evaporated and, just as joblessness created increasing need for city services, government capacity deteriorated (Gillette, 2005).

Not surprisingly, Camden's out-migration was racially determined. White and middle-class flight was a common component of residential mobility and suburbanization in the post-World War II era (see, for example, Wilson, 1987, 1996). Many non-white families could not even consider leaving the city as the jobs disappeared. Decades of wage discrimination and over-exposure to layoffs in down times had prevented them from accumulating the wealth necessary to buy houses in the suburbs (Cowie, 1999; Sidorick, 2009). Housing discrimination in the emerging suburbs made it difficult for Camden's African-American and Latino populations to find housing in the suburbs if they could afford it (for discussions of these issues on a national scale, see Jackson, 1985; Massey and

Denton, 1993). By the time federal regulation began to reduce housing discrimination in the late 1960s, the decline in Camden property values had trapped African-American and Latino residents in houses whose sale would not yield enough money for a down payment on a suburban house. When riots tore through Camden in 1971, they further damaged a very troubled city. By the time the crack epidemic engulfed Camden in the 1980s, the city's population was already overwhelmingly black or brown and poor (Gillette, 2005; Sidorick, 2009).

If the enmeshment of the United States in the global political economy spurred Camden's prosperity in the first half of the twentieth century, it also caused Camden's misery in the second half. As the rest of the country experienced the boom of the late 1990s, Camden emerged as a paradox: How could a city so favorably positioned be unable to take advantage of the prosperity all around it? As a small municipality that had been fully drained of its wealth, Camden lacked the capacity to take advantage of the apparent opportunities presented by national and regional economic growth. Without even the pockets of wealth that saved larger cities, Camden had nothing to build from. Its small size made it easy to bypass. A victim of the ups and downs of globalization, Camden found itself disconnected from larger economic forces, stripped of the elements that allow a city to link itself to favorable processes in its region.

Neoliberalism as the solution?

Having surfed and then crashed on the wave of globalization, Camden became, in the final decades of the twentieth century, unable to control its destiny. As a consequence, a coalition of regional political and economic elites has driven policy in and for Camden since the 1980s (Gillette, 2005; Knoche, 2005). While the intentions of this coalition with regard to Camden have changed dramatically over that period, a consistent theme has emerged: The privatization of government functions has replaced residents' democratic control of their city. The reality of poverty in Camden is the nearly literal disfranchisement of its residents by the removal of all important matters from the control of those directly affected. With diminished numbers and virtually no wealth, Camden's residents have lost the tools to win political battles and maintain control of their city.

The political foundation for the imposition of a regional neoliberal order is the Democratic Party machine that emerged in Camden County in the 1980s and came to control much of South Jersey politics and policy in subsequent decades. As Camden City's population declined, it became a relatively small fraction of Camden County's population. County politicians no longer depended on city votes for election and no longer concerned themselves with the city's interests. Camden County began to view Camden City as a dumping ground. As the Camden County Democratic Party developed into a sophisticated machine, with control of employment and contracting for nearly all regional public agencies, its leaders acted on the changing political dynamic by siting waste facilities and prisons in the city, accelerating its downward spiral. With access to enormous reserves of political money, the county machine began to control Camden City politics directly, funding the campaigns of favored candidates to a degree that made competition impossible and providing paying jobs to many elected city officials (Annie E. Casey Foundation, 2001; Gillette, 2005; Knoche, 2005; PhillyMag, 2006).

Lacking democratic accountability, city institutions became increasingly dysfunctional. By the turn of the century, a consensus had emerged that Camden City could not govern itself, leading to the special recovery legislation that created a chief operating officer for the city, appointed by the governor, and gave effective control of the Board of Education to the state (Gillette, 2005; Katz, 2009; Knoche, 2005). Not surprisingly, participation in local elections declined rapidly as the pointlessness of action became evident (Camden Churches Organized for People, 2009). By the time local control was restored in 2010, the local electorate had effectively disappeared (CamConnect, 2010b).

In this environment, a broad range of traditional government functions has been withdrawn from democratic control by city residents. Nearly all planning work in the city is carried out by a non-profit organization called Cooper's Ferry Partnership (CFP), whose board consists of leaders of the major institutions and corporations in the city. CFP planned the waterfront development that, beginning in the 1980s, has brought several entertainment and business venues to the city, but has not effectively spurred revitalization. Currently, CFP leads downtown and neighborhood planning efforts. Organizations connected to CFP are well positioned to take advantage of state, federal, and foundation funding. While CFP arguably operates in the interests of Camden's residents, it is controlled not by those residents but by the regional elites who compose its board and give it access to funding streams (Gillette, 2005; Knoche, 2005; Lindsay, 2012).

Public education is following the same path as planning. To begin with, ever fewer school-age students attend schools operated by the Camden City Public Schools; the district enrolled 16,955 students in 2003–04 and just 12,767 in 2011–12—a 25 percent decline (CamConnect, 2008; Camden City Public Schools, 2012). With support from the county Democratic Party machine and major institutions such as Rutgers University and Cooper Hospital, charter schools and a new category known as renaissance schools are beginning to dominate the city's education landscape, with nine charter schools already in existence and additional charter and renaissance schools in the works (Friedman, 2011; Mooney, 2012; New Jersey Department of Education, n.d.; Vargas, 2013a). While the failure of the Camden City public schools is evident to all, these new forms of school organization remove control of education from residents most affected by that failure. Many of the new schools are funded directly by wealthy individuals active in county and regional politics. Thus far, they have not demonstrated their ability to improve academic performance, but they retain the support of regional elites. In May of 2013, the Camden school district itself was formally taken over by the State of New Jersey Department of Education, removing the last vestige of local democratic control over education in the city. The two school board members who voted against approving the state takeover were subsequently replaced by new mayoral appointees as the board shifted to a strictly advisory role (Vargas, 2013b).

The same pattern is evident in public safety and policing. In April 2013, the Camden Police Department was disbanded, and policing in the city was taken on by the Metro Division of a new Camden County police force. Camden City is, oddly, the only municipality of the 37 in the county to choose to participate in this force (Economist, 2013; Zernike, 2012). So the police force that governs only Camden City is entirely under the control of Camden County. The change was made primarily in order to terminate the contract between the city and the police union (Laday, 2013b). While the change will result—at least initially—in a substantial increase in the number of officers policing the city, it will also create an even greater distance between city residents and the police who exercise great power over their daily lives.

Camden's poverty in the new global order

Camden thrived as globalization pumped wealth into America's growing industrial cities. It collapsed as the logic of globalization punished the city for its generous wages and hulking but aging industrial infrastructure. It is now experiencing significant reinvestment, guided by the very regional elites who used the city as an outlet for the negative byproducts—chemical, biological, and human—of late industrial capitalism (Gillette, 2005; Knoche, 2005; Osborne, 2011). Those same elites have concluded that the region in which their financial interests are located cannot succeed with Camden as a weight. So they are attracting public and private money for new development and infrastructure improvements as they seek to fix the education and public safety problems that have made the city deeply unattractive to investors and individuals. While many of these developments hold the potential to benefit Camden's residents—by restoring a tax base to fund city services, improving education, and providing better police protection—they are entirely out of the control of Camden's overwhelmingly poor and minority population. With a lag of several decades, Camden's deindustrialization has ultimately produced its de-democratization.

Note

1 Exact numbers are disputed. Gillette (2005) cites a high of 62,564 jobs in Camden at its peak, but the Annie E. Casey Foundation (2001) estimates Camden had 180,000 jobs at its peak. Currently there are between 23,000 and 30,000 jobs in Camden.

References

Annie E. Casey Foundation (2001). *A path forward for Camden*. Baltimore: Annie E. Casey Foundation.

Broadbridge, S. (1965). Technological progress and state support in the Japanese shipbuilding industry. *Journal of Development Studies*, 1, 142–75.

CamConnect (2008). *Camden facts 2008: education. Education and child welfare*. Retrieved August 15, 2014, from http://www.camconnect.org/datalogue/Camden_Facts_08_3-20-08_education.pdf.

CamConnect (2009). *Vacancy in Camden*. Retrieved August 15, 2014, from http://www.camconnect.org/datalogue/AbandonedProp.pdf.

CamConnect (2010a). *Camden's municipal revenues*. Retrieved August 15, 2014, from http://www.camconnect.org/datalogue/budget_revenues.pdf.

CamConnect (2010b). *Camden voter participation in 2009 elections*. Retrieved August 15, 2014, from http://www.camconnect.org/datalogue/2009VoterParticipation_CamConnect.pdf.

Camden Churches Organized for People (2009). *The survey on Camden's recovery: 2009*. Retrieved August 15, 2014, from http://www.camconnect.org/datalogue/2009%20CCOP%20Report.pdf.

Camden City Public Schools (2012). *User friendly budget*. Retrieved August 15, 2014, from http://www.camden.k12.nj.us/pdf/2012%20-%202013%20Budget.pdf.

Childs, R. (1918). The first war emergency government towns for shipyard workers. I. "Yorkship Village" at Camden, N. J. *Journal of the American Institute of Architects*, 6, 237–244, 249–251. Retrieved August 15, 2014, from http://www.yorkshipvillage.com/article/childs-1918/index.php.

Cowie, J. (1999). *Capital moves: RCA's seventy-year quest for cheap labor*. Ithaca, NY: Cornell University Press.

CQ Press (2012). *City crime rankings 2012*. Retrieved August 15, 2014, from http://os.cqpress.com/citycrime/2012/CityCrime2013_CityCrimeRateRankings.pdf.

DeMarco, M. (2011, December 16). *N.J. legislature passes measure to restore $139M in transitional city aid*. nj.com. Retrieved August 15, 2014, from http://www.nj.com/news/index.ssf/2011/12/nj_legislature_passes_measure.html.

Economist, The (2013, May 11). *Starting from scratch: a crime-ridden city disbands its police department*. Retrieved August 15, 2014, from http://www.economist.com/news/united-states/21577409-crime-ridden-city-disbands-its-police-department-starting-scratch.

Friedman, M. (2011, October 5). *N.J. Democratic leader George Norcross calls for more charter schools, change to teacher tenure*. nj.com. Retrieved August 15, 2014, from http://www.nj.com/news/index.ssf/2011/10/nj_democratic_leader_george_no.html.

Gillette, H. (2005). *Camden after the fall: decline and renewal in a post-industrial city*. Philadelphia: University of Pennsylvania Press.

Giordano, R. (2012, April 12). 23 of 26 Camden schools rated among worst in N.J. *Philadelphia Inquirer*. Retrieved August 15, 2014, from http://mobile.philly.com/news/?wss=/philly/news/new_jersey/&id=147094535.

Jackson, K. T. (1985). *Crabgrass frontier: the suburbanization of the United States*. New York: Oxford University Press.

Katz, M. (2009, November 8). Camden rebirth: a promise still unfulfilled. The promise and the price: how the biggest municipal takeover in U.S. history—$175 million—cost residents their rights for little in return. *Philadelphia Inquirer*. Retrieved August 15, 2014, from http://www.philly.com/philly/news/special_packages/inquirer/20091108_Camden_Rebirth__A.html.

Knoche, T. (2005). *Common sense for Camden: taking back our city*. Camden: Leavenhouse.

Laday, J. (2013a, January 30). *Camden group points to poverty as source of violence*. nj.com. Retrieved August 15, 2014, from http://www.nj.com/camden/index.ssf/2013/01/camden_group_points_to_poverty.html.

Laday, J. (2013b, January 15). *Camden FOP leaders reviewing offer from freeholders on regional police department*. nj.com. Retrieved August 15, 2014, from http://www.nj.com/gloucester-county/index.ssf/2013/01/camden_fop_leaders_reviewing_o.html.

Lindsay, M. (2012, August 15). *Delivering Camden from the brink*. Next City. Retrieved August 15, 2014, from http://nextcity.org/daily/entry/delivering-camden-from-the-brink.

Massey, D. S., and N. A. Denton (1993). *American apartheid: segregation and the making of the underclass*. Cambridge, MA: Harvard University Press.

Mooney, J. (2012, November 29). *"Renaissance Schools" get board's go-ahead in Camden*. NJSpotlight. Retrieved August 15, 2014, from http://www.njspotlight.com/stories/12/11/28/renaissance-schools-get-board-s-go-ahead-in-camden/.

Mulvihill, G. (2011, December 14). *DRPA spends last of its economic development money*. 6abc.com. Retrieved August 15, 2014, from http://abclocal.go.com/wpvi/story?section=news/local&id=8467379.

New Jersey Department of Education (2012, April 11). *Christie administration moves forward to turn around lowest-performing schools in the state, provide targeted support for improvement, and to reward successful schools*. Retrieved August 15, 2014, from http://www.nj.gov/education/news/2012/0411rac.htm.

New Jersey Department of Education (n.d.). *Approved charter schools*. Retrieved August 15, 2014, from http://www.nj.gov/cgi-bin/education/charter/charter3.pl?string=agencycode&maxhits=1000.

Osborne, J. (2011, August 22). Puzzling moves from N.J. political boss George E. Norcross III. *Philadelphia Inquirer*. Retrieved August 15, 2014, from http://articles.philly.com/2011-08-22/news/29914840_1_camden-county-political-decision-largest-teachers.

Palmer, D. (1988). *Organizing the shipyards: union strategy in three Northeast ports, 1933–1945*. Ithaca, NY: Cornell University Press.

PhillyMag (2006). They have no choice. *Philadelphia Magazine*, September. Retrieved August 15, 2014, from http://www.phillymag.com/articles/feature-they-have-no-choice/.

Sidorick, D. (2009). *Condensed capitalism: Campbell soup and the pursuit of cheap production in the twentieth century*. Ithaca: ILR Press/Cornell University Press.

Tucker, N. (2012, December 19). Mass killings up, homicide rate down. *Washington Post*. Retrieved August 15, 2014, from http://articles.washingtonpost.com/2012-12-19/lifestyle/35929227_1_homicide-rate-randolph-roth-gun-control.

U.S. Census Bureau (2011). *American Community Survey: selected economic characteristics*. Retrieved August 15, 2014, from http://factfinder2.census.gov/faces/tableservices/jsf/pages/productview.xhtml?pid=ACS_11_1YR_DP03&prodType=table.

U.S. Department of Housing and Urban Development (2004, June 3). *HUD awards $20 million Hope VI grant to Camden to transform housing, help residents*. Retrieved August 15, 2014, from http://archives.hud.gov/local/nj/news/pr2004-06-03.cfm.

Vargas, C. (2011, April 17). Camden belated in blight offensive. *Philadelphia Inquirer*. Retrieved August 15, 2014, from http://articles.philly.com/2011-04-17/news/29428003_1_cramer-hill-property-values-vacant-properties.

Vargas, C. (2012, September 22). New Census statistics paint grim picture of Camden. *Philadelphia Inquirer*. Retrieved August 15, 2014, from http://www.philly.com/philly/blogs/camden_flow/170812236.html.

Vargas, C. (2013a, January 17). Camden School Board needs KIPP's final numbers pronto. *Philadelphia Inquirer*. Retrieved August 15, 2014, from http://www.philly.com/philly/blogs/camden_flow/187399402.html.

Vargas, C. (2013b, May 3). *Camden schools now in state's hands*. Retrieved August 15, 2014, from http://articles.philly.com/2013-05-03/news/38986182_1_camden-board-camden-school-system-state-board.

Walker, E. M. (2005). *Educational adequacy and the courts: a reference handbook*. Santa Barbara: ABC-CLIO Inc.

Wilson, W. J. (1987). *The truly disadvantaged: the inner city, the underclass, and public policy*. Chicago, IL: University of Chicago Press.

Wilson, W. J. (1996). *When work disappears: the world of the new urban poor*. New York: Vintage Books.

Zernike, K. (2012). To fight crime, Camden will trade in its police. *New York Times*, September 29, A1.

4

TRANSNATIONAL FACTORS DRIVING U.S. INEQUALITY AND POVERTY

Rubin Patterson and Giselle Thompson

Introduction

Approximately one hundred million Americans, one-third of the U.S. population, are poor or nearly poor.[1] Trend lines today point to a gap in take-home income and living income that is both deepening and being experienced by more Americans. Growing poverty in the United States runs counter to the 150-year trend of continually rising real wages for [white] workers between 1820 and 1970 (Wolff, 2012). As a result, about six successive generations could count on rising incomes and upward social mobility, both intra-generationally and inter-generationally. The growing individual prosperity was linked with economic nationalism (Patterson, 2013). Nineteenth-century America was a land of nearly sequestered agriculturally based communities. By the mid-twentieth century it transformed into an organically linked and complex industrial economy. This phenomenon provided a source of wealth production for robber-barons and upward mobility for individual workers and their families. That model of economic nationalism—which, to paraphrase General Motors' Roger Smith, exemplified the concept "what's good for American industry is automatically good for American workers"—is over (Mizruchi, 2013; Robinson, 2004). Mizruchi, who writes from the perspective of traditional business literature, and Robinson, from the critical transnational capitalist school, arrive at much the same conclusion about how "American corporations" are no longer able to serve the interests of American labor and civil society. Rising inequality and the attendant rise in poverty in America are the partial result of the transformation from economic nationalism to economic transnationalism. The U.S. state that managed to simultaneously serve the interests of capital and labor up to the 1970s has lost that capacity as the U.S. state is now being absorbed into a more complex institutional structure that increasingly serves the needs of transnational capital, often at the expense of labor (Robinson, 2004). During the lifetime of Rudolf Hilferding (2006)—the late 1870s to early 1940s author of the classic *Finance Capital*—national capitalism required state assistance to dominate international markets, whereas today's transnational capitalism requires the state to dominate national economic interests. The transformation between these two eras of capitalism is contributing to growing levels of inequality and poverty.

We, the authors of this chapter, will leave it to others to delve deeper into the analysis of the data concerning inequality and poverty in America. Our research shows that some scholars have discussed, and others, no doubt, will continue to discuss, the dissection of data on historical trends as well as the dissection of data on how various social groups (based, for example, on factors such as racial/ethnic, gender, geographic, age, and origin of birth) are faring in this age of growing socioeconomic inequality. Similarly, some scholars have documented, through micro-level studies, the ways in which inequality is played out in the lives of individuals, families, communities, and specific social groups. Coverage of those areas of inequality and poverty in America is comprehensively presented in other chapters of this handbook and also in other scholarly publications. What we have attempted to do in this chapter is to distill the universe of factors contributing to this unprecedented and sustained rise in social inequality and poverty as well as to the termination of broad upward social mobility in America; thus, our goal is to better understand causes of these trends and recommend plausible solutions. The factors covered in this chapter are: financialization and transnationalization of the economy (Robinson and Harris, 2000; Tomaskovic-Devey and Lin, 2011), automation of production (Brynjolfsson and McAfee, 2011; Ford, 2009), deindustrialization of America (Wilson, 1996), deunionization of the workforce (Western and Rosenfeld, 2011), democratization of global higher education (Brown et al., 2011), and racialization of people of color (Martinot, 2010).

Financialization and transnationalization of the economy

The financialization of the economy (Hacker and Pierson, 2010) and the transnationalization of capitalism (Robinson, 2014; Sassen, 2012) are at the heart of the rise of inequality and poverty in the United States. Financialization of the economy refers to the growing share of income and profits—nationally and globally—being dominated by the financial sector. We see financialization increasing in two ways: first, the growing importance of financial services firms vis-à-vis all firms and, second, nonfinancial services firms' increasing involvement in financial activity (Tomaskovic-Devey and Lin, 2011). As an example, in 1980 when Ronald Reagan was first elected president, General Electric (GE) received 92% of its profits from manufacturing and only 8% from finance. However, by 2007, GE earned more than half of its profits from finance (Hacker and Pierson, 2010). Similar financialization transformation stories were unfolding in the retail space, too, such as Sears, which gains most of its profits from finance rather than from sales (Sweeney, 2012). Why were financial services firms moving so deeply into financialization and nonfinancial services firms moving so swiftly into the financial services sector? These trends were happening for the same reason that the notorious bank robber Willie Sutton cited in response to the question of why he robbed banks: "Because that is where the money is!" The share of total corporate profits between 1980 and 2007, dominated by the financial services companies, expanded from 13% to 27%, even though employment in that sector declined (Hacker and Pierson, 2010). Donald Tomaskovic-Devey and Ken-Hou Lin (2011:556) note that "nonfinancial firms paid increasing portions of their incomes to the finance sector, and household wages were restricted by their employers' … payments of fees and interest to a financial sector … more clever at extracting income from other actors in the economy."

Financialization and consumer debt

Financialization was also emphasized over the past generation due to the fact that wages were not keeping pace with rising costs in housing, energy, transportation, education, healthcare, and daycare. American workers have had to finance more and more of their needs through loans and fees as opposed to rising wages and salaries as experienced during previous decades. For instance, during the decade before the 2008 banking crisis, the bottom 80% was consuming about 110% of their income (Stiglitz, 2013). In other words, Americans were financing an extra 10% of their consumption just to stay afloat. The Fordist model of paying American workers increasingly higher salaries so that they could buy company products worked well when both the owners and consumer-base were American. However, over the past generation, Americans, decreasingly, have been the owners and the consumer-base of the companies founded in America. Capitalization of transnational corporations that were founded and registered in the United States is now increasingly globally sourced. Additionally, membership on the boards of directors, the customer-base, employees, and assets are also increasingly global and decreasingly American. In other words, as Sklar (2000) and Sassen (2012) note, the ownership and consumer-base of corporations, historically viewed as American, have increasingly become denationalized. To gain an edge over competitors, corporations in America by the 1970s accelerated the arbitraging of labor costs by moving sections of their production activities abroad to low-skill, low-wage industrial producing nations. Forerunners of this practice had a price advantage over other companies that were either late-comers or resistant to this practice. As labor arbitraging increased and subsequently became the norm in industry after industry, wage increases began and have been sustained in areas that were known as third world nations, while wages had begun to stagnate and decline in America. Companies could worry less about American workers not having rising wages to purchase products as market opportunities were growing in other parts of the global marketplace where production has been moved overseas. And as stated earlier, American workers could finance their needs through loans and fees from financial services and nonfinancial firms (Patterson, 2013).

Automation of production

Financialization of the economy and the transnationalization of capitalism have contributed to the rise of inequality and poverty in America, but so too has automation. Autor and Dorn (2009) note that the process of the automating routine, codifiable job tasks is primed to accelerate as the cost of this activity continues to fall. In general, companies are eager to automate the jobs that have the highest salaries—which can be difficult to automate—but they are also keen on automating massive numbers of low-wage jobs that may be easier to complete (Brynjolfsson and McAfee, 2011). In the early stages of workplace automation, the technology made it much more feasible to automate jobs associated with routine physical movement of objects and routine decision-making within delimited parameters. However, with today's confluence of software automation algorithms, artificial intelligence, and information technology, cerebral jobs in legal, academic, medical, engineering, and other such professions are also amenable to automation. These advancing automating tools encroach on more territory formerly reserved for human abstract thinking and discretion. And when we combine those tools with the ongoing advancements in robotics, we can see that the impact on employment opportunities is potentially devastating to the livelihoods of millions (Ford, 2009).

Martin Ford's *Lights in the Tunnel* (2009) and Erik Brynjolfsson and Andrew McAfee's *Race Against the Machine* (2011) are two major works from an important body of literature on technology and its impact on employment. Ford takes more of a dystopian view while Brynjolfsson and McAfee entertain a range of possible outcomes, some of them quite devastating for many who will not be working due to the implementation of automation technology. American economists have primarily remained confident that automation-engendered job losses would always result in new job opportunities due to the formation of new occupations and entirely new industries—a sort of rolling creative destruction. But economists such as Brynjolfsson and McAfee are not so sure, in light of this accelerating twenty-first-century form of automation, which is efficiently destroying far more jobs than are being created. Should these radical innovation breakthroughs in automation continue, let alone accelerate, the drive that nearly all governments are pursuing to create and attract manufacturing jobs to their countries, states/provinces, and municipalities will be ill-fated. As Rifkin (2011) notes, while there are 163 million manufacturing jobs in the world today, by 2040 there may only be a few million. The loss of manufacturing jobs in America ignited inequality and poverty, first in inner cities but later spread to all geographical regions. There is obviously no way of knowing today if Rifkin, the technology futurist, is correct in his projections about the global collapse of manufacturing jobs, but what is clear, based on recent manufacturing transformations, is that sharp declines in employment will accompany sharp increases in production output.

The deindustrialization of America

The globalization and automation of production contributed to the deindustrialization of America and the attendant growth in inequality, poverty, family dissolution, and the devastation of inner cities across America. In his classic book *When Work Disappears: The World of the New Urban Poor*, William Julius Wilson (1996) describes the unfolding impact of this process. Ford Motor Company's River Rouge production complex with its more than 120,000 employees by the late 1920s was a metaphor of the huge labor needs in manufacturing as well as the significantly higher than average wages. Non-high school graduates held these jobs, in large part, and their wages supported jobs through secondary economic activity in local communities. Today, the River Rouge automotive production complex employs approximately 6,000 workers, about 5% of its number of workers in the past (Henry Ford, 2013). Area businesses that thrived on providing services to the automotive employees and subcontracting work to the Fords of the economy also collapsed, thereby rippling and amplifying unemployment in the broader community. Between 2001 and the banking crisis of 2008, the United States lost 42,400 factories, including 36% of factories that employed more than 1,000 employees (McCormack, 2009). Since manufacturing wages are as much as 20% higher than wages in other sectors for workers of similar skills and credentials, the loss of these jobs contributes to growing inequality and poverty. During the middle of the twentieth century, the largest employers included General Motors, Ford, and United States Steel, which all paid high wages, whereas by the beginning of the twenty-first century the largest employers included Walmart, McDonald's, and Kroger that all pay low wages.

Transformation of the American economy through financialization, transnationalization, automation, and deindustrialization was not inevitable. Instead, the transformation was the result of public policy choices and corporate decisions made over decades. These policy choices and decisions were, on the whole, neither good for American corporations nor American workers. However, they were good for transnational oligopoplist clusters, or what the aforementioned authors Robinson and Sasson, in addition to Sklar (2000) and others, call the transnational capitalist class (TCC). Larry Bartels (2008) in *Unequal Democracy: The Political Economy of the New Gilded Age* chronicles the collusion between plutocrats and politicians to rig the political and economic systems to their advantage against society's general welfare. The transnational capitalist class has employed and mobilized a sophisticated network of media outlets, lobbyists, and politicians to get desired public policies legislated and executed in the interest of financialization, transnationalization, automation, and, as a byproduct, deindustrialization. As Brown et al. (2011:10) state, "It makes less and less sense to think in terms of a national economy or average household income when talking about the fate of individuals and families because it misses what is important about ... [contemporary transnational] capitalism." Continuing their observations, Brown and colleagues note that "some American, Chinese, and Indian workers and companies have economic interests more in common with those living on the other side of the world than with those living on the opposite side of the street" (p.11).

Deunionization of the workforce

One powerful reason why the transnational capitalist class has been able to push through the public policy choices that served their ends instead of the ends of workers and the broader society was due to the deunionization of the workforce since the Reagan era. Private sector unionization between 1973 and 2007 declined from 34% to 8% (Western and Rosenfeld, 2011). Prior to the 1970s, "Unions emerged as the interest groups with the most consistent and widespread tendency to share the policy preferences of low- and middle-income Americans" (Gilens, 2012:161). Western and Rosenfeld (2011:517) were even more explicit as they assert that "Unions are pillars of the moral economy in modern labor markets. ... The moral economy consists of norms prescribing fair distribution that are institutionalized in the market's formal rules and customs." In the end, these social scientists contend that deunionization marks an erosion of the moral economy and its underlying distributional norms.

Just as transformation of the American economy was partly driven by public policy choices and corporate decisions, so, too, was deunionization the partial product of such choices and decisions. Of course, ill-advised strategies of union leaders also contributed to the demise of unions, as they once existed. Union leadership, as it remained, has not been able to develop and implement the strategies and tactics to overcome the challenges of offshoring production and the shift in production from manufacturing to services. But outcomes such as "Right to Work" laws were designed to weaken unions so that they could not be an effective countervailing force to transnational capital in America. Among the ways unions are weakened by such public policy is that they will not have the financial wherewithal to counter the spending by billionaires to protect their global private investments and priorities. As reported in *The Economist* (2013), now that unions of manufacturing workers have been weakened, leading to real wages declining by 2.2% since 2005 while they have risen by 19% *per year* in India and China, companies are beginning to "reshore" in America. In 2012, a survey of "American companies" with sales of over $10 billion reported that 48% of them have begun or have plans to reshore more manufacturing in the United States.

The democratization of higher education

Yet another factor often overlooked in analyzing growing inequality and poverty in America is the democratization of global higher education, which has set up a global skills race. In the post-Great Depression world economy, college-educated Americans and Western Europeans performed the overwhelming majority of the high-skilled, high-salaried managerial, technical, and professional (MTP) work of the transnational corporations and other major institutions. The MTP universe of jobs is expanding; however, that expansion pales in comparison to the rate at which college graduates are emerging around the world, no longer limited to America and Western Europe. There simply aren't enough MTP employment opportunities to go around. In China, for instance, college graduates are four times more likely to be unemployed than their elementary school-educated contemporaries (Bradsher, 2013). In addition to the Chinese, since the democratization of global higher education, Indians, South Koreans, Brazilians, South Africans, and many, many others have gained the MTP expertise, credentials, and the investment from transnational corporations, which has put them in direct competition for a strata of coveted high-end jobs that used to be reserved primarily for Americans and Western Europeans. Over the past decade, global college enrollment has doubled. Americans' disproportionate share of high-skilled, high-salaried jobs has peaked and is largely now in decline. Transnational corporations based in the United States or Western Europe are now hiring elite professional services workers in dynamic markets throughout the world rather than just hiring Americans or Western Europeans for such positions. Additionally, over the past 15 years there has been an upsurge in the number of large and major transnational corporations that are based outside of Western economies, such as China's Huawei (electronics), India's Tata Group (information technology, engineering, automobiles, etc.), Brazil's Embraer (aircraft), and South Africa's Aspen Pharmacare (pharmaceuticals). They are eating into the market share of Western-based transnational corporations (TNCs), and the elite managerial, professional, and technical workers are primarily hired from their respective societies, rather than appointed from Western societies.

The democratization of global higher education has ended the near automatic upward social mobility of college graduates in America. As a result, the master's degree has become the new bachelor's degree and the bachelor's degree has become the new high school diploma. Despite the college degree's declining ability to launch individuals into the middle class and sustain them in this class status, it still prevents individuals with the requisite credential from experiencing the type of sustained grinding poverty experienced often by those without it. For instance, in the United States, the average incomes for individuals with a master's degree, bachelor's degree, a high school diploma, and no high school diploma were $73,000; $56,665; $30,637; and $20,241, respectively (U.S. Census Bureau, 2012). Additionally, unemployment figures for those groups were 4.7%, 8.4%, 10.3%, and 14.9% (U.S. Census Bureau, 2012).

Escape from poverty and general upward social mobility for college-educated Americans was based on selling brain labor power that was in limited supply, but that option is becoming more constricted as "the global labor market is congested with well-educated, low-cost workers" (Brown et al., 2011:12). These authors also note that

> titles such as accountant, professor, engineer, lawyer, and computer analyst no longer tell us as much as they once did about income, job security, or career opportunities because they are characterized by increasingly "winner-take-all" competitions. … how people are positioned in the global auction is of paramount importance. If they are not defined as top talent, they are likely to find themselves in a bidding war with high-skilled workers from emerging economies.

(p.11)

The racialization of people of color

The final factor affecting growing inequality and poverty in America that we cover in this chapter is the racialization of people of color. Our emphasis here is on the racialization of people of color for the purposes of electing politicians to control the organs of the state for the benefit of transnational capital. The transnational capitalist class is different in its interests, composition, and outlook in comparison to the American capitalist class as late as the 1950s, when economic nationalism reigned. At that time, building interstate highways and other colossal infrastructural projects served the needs of capital and workers. For example, the 50,000-mile highway system employed a great number of Americans to construct, and as a result, it enhanced economic vitality and productivity and, therefore, it has indirectly contributed to trillions of dollars in profits for corporations and tens of millions of jobs for citizens over the past half century. Similar mutual benefits for profits and general welfare exist with the G.I. Bill, the Federal Housing Administration, the Social Security Act, and the Pell Grant, among others. However, since the transition from the nation-state phase of world capitalism to a transnational phase, marked by an increasing proportion of world production and commerce being transnational rather than national (Robinson, 2004), there has been a growing discord between the profits of major corporations and the general welfare of American workers (Mizruchi, 2013). And since major transnational corporations that were founded and registered in America have increasing shares of their revenue, assets, employees, and board membership in countries outside of the United States, these global companies have demanded and have won the near elimination of their taxes. For instance, in the 1950s taxes paid by corporations constituted approximately one-third of the federal revenue, but by 2009 it was only 6.6% (Livingston, 2013).

As the transnational capitalist class sees it, taxes on American workers should be more limited to defense, the judiciary and the rule of law, subsidies or incentives to corporations, and the barest of general welfare provisions. The sprawling general welfare state, which is already mea-ger by Western standards, should be sharply scaled back according to important sections of the transnational capitalist class in the United States. This class wants to protect rent-seeking, their preferred method of wealth acquisition, which is "getting income not as a reward to creating wealth but by grabbing a larger share of the wealth that would otherwise have been produced without their effort" (Stiglitz, 2013). Rent-seeking was instrumental in 2010, which allowed the top 1% to take home 93% of the income growth (Stiglitz, 2013). To carry out their rent-seeking interests, key political agents, judges, and appointees must be installed at various levels of state power. Racialization of people of color is a major means to this end.

Patterson (2013) explains how this racialization has been effectively utilized to get working-class whites to vote primarily for Republicans and for those Democrats who were driven to disassemble America's welfare state apparatus. Of course, such measures were not revealed as their platform or agenda; rather, these politicians have typically run on conservative ideas of "lower taxes and strong defense." More important, these conservative politicians have often had a subtle yet effective subtext of exploiting racial and ethnic discord—for example, run-ning against "welfare queens"; "liberal judges" who voted for civil rights; "affirmative action"; abortion rights; school busing; and "law and order," meaning heavy incarceration of blacks and Latinos. This Southern Strategy was skillfully used by conservative politicians to exploit the fears and anxieties of white workers who had "historically enjoyed caste privilege within racially and ethnically segmented labor markets ..." (Robinson and Barrera, 2012:18). Throughout the periods of slavery and Jim Crow in America, white Americans have primarily voted for the party and the politicians they saw as preserving their racial advantages over African Americans. When Republicans presided over the ending of slavery, the white working class of the South moved in droves to the Democratic Party; and when Democrats presided over the ending of Jim Crow, the white working class of the South moved in droves to the Republican Party. Ever since Democratic president Lyndon Johnson signed the Civil Rights Act of 1964, which ended the state's de jure and official measures of preventing blacks from exercising their full freedoms and competing for upward social mobility, white workers have primarily voted Republican in every presidential election. Conservative think tanks such as the American Enterprise Institute; the "grassroots" and conservative political mobilization efforts such as the Christian Coalition and Americans for Prosperity; media outlets such as Fox, *Wall Street Journal* opinion pages, and the *National Review*; and conservative lobbying organizations such as the American Conservative Union and the American Family Association have all worked collectively to support conserva-tive politicians who often referenced racial subtexts as cited above. Volscho and Kelly (2012) put a fine point on the connection between the wealth of the top 1% and the Republican Party:

> The impact of one percentage point in the share of seats held by Democrats in Congress decreases the top income share by .08. ... These numbers at first seemed quite small, but given that national income in 2008 ... was more than $7.8 trillion, an increase of only 1

percent in Democratic seats share (just over five seats), would decrease the income of the 1 percent by nearly $6.6 billion.

(p.692)

Two major reasons why Ronald Reagan is revered by conservatives is that he presided over the tax reduction on the wealthy from 70% to 28% and illustrated how the Southern Strategy could be utilized effectively in the Midwest and the Northeast to get even more conservative politicians in office to eliminate even more of the welfare state, reduce the taxes of the wealthy further, remove regulations on corporations, and provide those corporations with more subsidies. Changes in the demographic makeup will make it much more difficult for the transnational capitalist class to get their political agents in office so as to execute their agenda. For instance, Mitt Romney in 2012 won the same share of the white vote as Ronald Reagan in 1980, that is, by 20 points over their Democratic opponents, but the outcome was dramatically different because, whereas whites con-stituted 88% of the electorate in 1980, 32 years later that share was down to 73%. And given that most children under five in America today are of color, the ability of the transnational capitalist class to utilize racialization against the future majority of the electorate as a means to enact public poli-cies that will drive up inequality and poverty will be severely limited. Since Reagan's presidency, America has become 30% more unequal, at least according to the Gini index. Between 1979 and 2007, real disposable income after taxes of the top 1% more than quadrupled. Meanwhile the middle class shrank as a percentage of the population: "Only 40 percent of American neighborhoods now have an average income within 20 percent of the national median, compared with 60 percent in the 1970s" (*The Economist*, 2012:13). Reaganomics would have remained "voodoo economic theory" if whites had not dominated the electorate in 1980 and 1984.

We can expect one or some combination of three outcomes from the accelerating structural changes in the global economy. The demographic shift over the next three decades, when whites become only a plurality in the population rather than a majority, will usher in an end to racialized politics and all voters will finally be able to vote in their economic interests, which would mean more social welfare state programs and antipoverty programs. Even today, Americans, according to a recent survey, where an economist showed income distributions in countries that were not labeled and asked randomly selected Americans which income distribution they favored, preferred a more equitable society. The surveyed Americans overwhelmingly selected Sweden's system of income distribution (92% to 8%) (Ariely, 2012). Another outcome could be that, while racial-ized politics would end, the transnational capitalist class could reinvent its style of conservatism, thereby making it attractive to voters of color who would vote for policy choices of ending the welfare state and antipoverty programs just as whites have done. The final scenario could be that the transnational capitalist class—recognizing the poor prospects of people of color voting consist-ently to end the welfare state as whites have done historically in the face of the end of racialized politics due to the monumental demographic shift—will engage in a form of fascism to try to protect their wealth. Presumably, Robinson and Barrera (2012) see fascism as potentially escalat-ing as opposed to a full-blown case of fascism. Bertram Gross (1980) discussed such escalation in *Friendly Fascism: The New Face of Power in America*. The oxymoronic title might capture what Stiglitz (2012) calls "disenfranchisement by stealth," which captures machinations on the part of plutocrats and conservative politicians engaging in the dark arts of democratic statecraft such as voter machine fraud; disenfranchisement of felons; *Citizens United*'s unlimited campaign funding without attribution; and changing rules for counting and awarding Electoral College votes, which takes gerrymandering to a whole new level.

Conclusion

It may be noted:

> If more than 200 years of expansion and growth are over, and if the U.S. is looking toward a future of less, a logical strategy for the haves may be to preserve and protect property, income, and assets from the demands of others.
>
> (Edsall, 2012:149)

Working-class whites may recognize that their world "is in crisis and collapsing around them. Their race/ethnic-based social privileges no longer provide against the ravages of global capitalism ..." (Robinson and Barrera, 2012:36). Robinson and Barrera underscore the point that fascism is one possible means for the world of capitalism to protect its wealth and the rent-seeking means of its acquisition from efforts to pay for a broad-scale social welfare state. Essentially:

> Capitalism is an institution. It's like your public school system or like your health care delivery system. We as a nation think it's appropriate to question and debate whether our schools and health care system are working adequately, meeting our needs. Why in the world has it been taboo to ask, is the capitalist system, the way we organize the production and distribution of goods and services, working to meet our needs or not?
>
> (Wolff, 2012:21–22)

To that end, in this chapter, we have examined six macro-economic and macro-social factors, namely financialization and transnationalization of the economy, automation of production, deindustrialization of America, deunionization of the workforce, democratization of global higher education, and, last but not least, racialization of people of color. The factors presented in this chapter provide a framework for critiquing the way in which transnational capitalism is skyrocketing inequality and poverty in America and throughout the world.

Note

1 The "near poor" are those individuals who are less than 50% above the official poverty line.

References

Ariely, Dan. 2012. "Americans Want to Live in a Much More Equal Country (They Just Don't Realize It)." *The Atlantic*. Retrieved January 22, 2013, from http://www.theatlantic.com/business/archive/2012/08/americans-want-to-live-in-a-much-more-equal-country-they-just-dont-realize-it/260639/.

Autor, David H. and David Dorn. 2009. "The Growth of Low Skill Service Jobs and the Polarization of the U.S. Labor Market." Working Paper No. 15150, National Bureau of Economic Research, Chicago, IL.

Bartels, Larry. 2008. *Unequal Democracy: The Political Economy of the New Gilded Age*. Princeton, NJ: Princeton University Press.

Bradsher, Keith. 2013. "In China, Families Bet It All on College for Their Children." *New York Times*. Retrieved November 16, 2013 from http://www.nytimes.com/2013/02/17/business/in-china-families-bet-it-all-on-a-child-in-college.html?pagewanted=all&_r=0.

Brown, Phillip, Hugh Lauder, and David Ashton. 2011. *The Global Auction: The Broken Promises of Education, Jobs, and Incomes*. New York: Oxford University Press.

Brynjolfsson, Erik and Andrew McAfee. 2011. *Race Against the Machine: How the Digital Revolution is Accelerating Innovation, Driving Productivity, and Irreversibly Transforming Employment and the Economy*. Sarasota, FL: Digital Frontier Press.

Economist, The. 2012. "For Richer, For Poorer." *The Economist*, October 13, 3–6.

Economist, The. 2013. "Reshoring Manufacturing: Coming Home." *The Economist*, January 19, 6–9.

Edsall, Thomas Byrne. 2012. *The Age of Austerity: How Scarcity Will Remake American Politics*. New York: Anchor Books.

Ford, Martin. 2009. *Lights in the Tunnel: Automation, Accelerating Technology and the Economy of the Future*. Wayne, PA: Acculant Publishing.

Gilens, Martin. 2012. *Affluence and Influence: Economic Inequality and Political Power in America*. Princeton, NJ: Princeton University Press.

Gross, Bertram. 1980. *Friendly Fascism: The New Face of Power in America*. Boston: South End Press.

Hacker, Jacob and Pierson, Paul. 2010. *Winner-Take-All Politics: How Washington Made the Rich Richer—and Turned Its Back on the Middle Class*. New York: Simon & Schuster.

Henry Ford, The. 2013. "The History of Rouge." Retrieved January 22, 2013, from http://www.thehenryford.org/rouge/historyofrouge3.aspx.

Hilferding, Rudolph. 2006. *Finance Capital: A Study in the Latest Phase of Capitalist Development*. New York: Routledge.

Livingston, James. 2013. "If Companies are People…" *New York Times*. Retrieved May 21, 2013, from http://www.nytimes.com/2013/04/15/opinion/a-fairer-corporate-tax.html.

Martinot, Steve. 2010. *The Machinery of Whiteness: Studies in the Structure of Racialization*. Philadelphia: Temple University Press.

McCormack, Richard. 2009. "The Plight of American Manufacturing." *The American Prospect*, December 21. Retrieved January 22, 2013, from http://prospect.org/article/plight-american-manufacturing.

Mizruchi, Mark. 2013. *The Fracturing of the American Corporate Elite*. Cambridge, MA: Harvard University Press.

Patterson, Rubin. 2013. "The Transnational Capitalist Class: What's Race Got to Do With It? Everything!" *Globalizations* 10(5): 673–690.

Rifkin, Jeremy. 2011. *The Third Industrial Revolution: How Lateral Power is Transforming Energy, the Economy, and the World*. New York: Palgrave Macmillan.

Robinson, William. 2004. *A Theory of Global Capitalism: Production, Class, and State in a Transnational World*. Baltimore, MD: The Johns Hopkins University Press.

Robinson, William. 2014. *Globalization and the Crisis of Humanity*. New York: Cambridge University Press.

Robinson, William and Mario Barrera. 2012. "Global Capitalism and 21st Century Fascism: A U.S. Case Study." *Race and Class* 53: 4–29.

Robinson, William and Jerry Harris. 2000. "Towards a Global Ruling Class? Globalization and the Transnational Capitalist Class." *Science and Society* 64: 11–54.

Sassen, Saskia. 2012. *Cities in a World Economy*. Thousand Oaks, CA: Sage Publications.

Sklar, Leslie. 2000. *The Transnational Capitalist Class*. Hoboken, NJ: Wiley-Blackwell.

Stiglitz Joseph. 2012. *The Price of Inequality: How Today's Divided Society Endangers Our Future*. New York: W.W. Norton & Co.

Stiglitz, Joe. 2013. "Inequality Is Holding Back the Recovery." *New York Times*. Retrieved January 20, 2013, from http://opinionator.blogs.nytimes.com/2013/01/19/inequality-is-holding-back-the-recovery/.

Sweeney, Brigid. 2012. "Sears—Where America Shopped." *Chicago Business*. Retrieved May 20, 2013, from http://www.chicagobusiness.com/article/20120421/ISSUE01/304219970/sears-where-america-shopped.

Tomaskovic-Devey, Donald and Ken-Hou Lin. 2011. "Income Dynamics, Economic Rents, and the Financialization of the U.S. Economy." *American Sociological Review* 76: 538–555.

U.S. Census Bureau. 2012. *Statistical Abstract of the United States*.

Volscho, Thomas and Nathan Kelly. 2012. "The Rise of the Super-rich: Power Resources, Taxes, Financial Markets, and the Dynamics of the Top 1%, 1949 to 2008." *American Sociological Review* 77: 679–699.

Western, Brue and Jake Rosenfeld. 2011. "Unions, Norms, and the Rise in U.S. Wage Inequality." *American Sociological Review* 76: 513–537.

Wilson, William Julius. 1996. *When Work Disappears: The World of the New Urban Poor*. New York: Random House.

Wolff, Richard. 2012. *Occupy the Economy: Challenging Capitalism*. San Francisco, CA: City Lights Books.

5

GLOBALIZATION AND THE TRENDS IN INEQUALITY OF POVERTY IN THE UNITED STATES IN THE LAST DECADE

Ashish Singh[1]

The poverty rate in the United States increased from 11.3% in 2000 to 15.1% in 2010.[2] The increase in poverty during 2000–10 is in exact contrast to the previous decade, where poverty systematically reduced from a peak of 15.1% in 1993 to 11.3% in 2000. In 2011, 46.2 million persons were estimated to have income below the official poverty line. Since 2006, when the poverty rate stood at 12.3% (most recent low), the number of poor has increased by 9.7 million. Also, the 46.2 million persons counted as poor in both 2010 and 2011 are the largest numbers counted in the measure's recorded history, going as far back as 1959 (Gabe, 2012). Though the rise in poverty during the last decade is a phenomenon in itself which needs to be investigated, a more interesting and pressing enquiry would be to look into how poverty among different socio–economic groups has changed during the past decade and the associated reasons behind the changes. Just to make a case: poverty rates for Blacks and Hispanics greatly exceed the national average; in 2011, 27.6% of Blacks and 25.3% of Hispanics were poor, compared to only 9.8% of the non-Hispanic Whites and 12.3% of Asians.

This chapter investigates the second question, that is, how inequality in poverty across different groups has changed in the United States in the past decade (2002–11). To this end, we primarily use data from the Current Population Survey Annual Social and Economic Supplements (CPS ASEC). We also relate the changes in the inequality in the distribution of poverty across groups to the process of globalization. To be specific, we examine how the unemployment–population ratio, unemployment rate, loss of employment (and subsequent re-employment), and average weeks of unemployment among different socio-economic groups have changed due to the rise of neoliberal capitalism in the context of globalization, with a special focus on the increasing disparity in the above indicators. Though globalization is a very broad term, it can be used to refer to changes leading to the free flow of goods, services, and factors of production between countries (Jaffee, 2008). There are primarily two reasons for choosing the period 2002–11 for this study. First, beginning in 2002, CPS respondents could identify themselves as being of more than one race; consequently, the racial data for 2002 and after are not comparable to earlier years (Gabe, 2012). Second, many scholars, for example Thomas L. Friedman, divide the history of globalization into three periods, "Globalization 1" (1492–1800), "Globalization 2" (1800–2000), and "Globalization 3" (2000–present), with each period substantially different from the others (Friedman, 2005). Globalization 1 was marked by countries globalizing for resources and imperial conquest whereas Globalization 2 was spearheaded by companies globalizing for labor and markets. Globalization 3 on the other hand is shrinking the world very fast and is flattening the playing field for all. The unique thing about Globalization 3 is that of the globalization of individuals and small groups (Friedman, 2005). This era of globalization has also seen an increased amount of offshoring and outsourcing of jobs from the developed countries of the West to the developing countries of (mostly) Asia. Globalization 3 further differs from Globalization 1 and 2 in the sense that Globalization 1 and 2 were driven mainly by the European and the American countries and companies but Globalization 3 is also driven by very diverse non-Western companies and groups of individuals. We therefore, in this chapter, focus on the third period of globalization which has seen an accelerating pace of globalization throughout the world.

Trends in poverty by race and ethnicity, region, family-type, and nativity

We first look at the trends in poverty by race (and ethnicity), region, family-type, and nativity, which are presented in Figure 5.1.[3] A few observations from the figure are as follows. First, poverty has increased in all racial (and ethnic) groups, with the gap in poverty between the groups with the highest poverty (Blacks) and the lowest poverty (non-Hispanic Whites) increasing from about 16 percentage points in 2002 to 18 percentage points in 2011. Second, poverty has also increased in all the regions, with the region of the South consistently having the highest poverty. Interestingly, in 2002, the Midwest region had the least poverty, but in 2011 it is the region of the Northeast with the least poverty. Third, poverty has increased in all family-types, but perhaps the most alarming disparity in poverty is visible in the case of poverty by family-types. In 2010, the poverty in female householders was 31.6% compared to only 6.2% in married-couple families and 11.7% in male householders. The gap in poverty between female householders and married-couple families has increased from 21.2 percentage points in 2002 to 25.4 percentage points in 2010. Finally, though poverty has increased in both natives as well as foreign born, the difference in poverty rate between the two has remained at about 5 percentage points during the past decade.

Trends in inequality of poverty

As the extent of poverty is different among different groups with poverty being very high in some groups and very low in some others, it is important to look into the disparity/inequality in the levels of poverty among different groups. Therefore, turning to inequality in the distribution of poverty across groups, we construct two simple measures to investigate the extent and the changes in the extent of intergroup disparity in poverty in the last decade.

Measures of inequality of poverty

Out of the two constructed measures of inequality of poverty, the first—which we call the "Intergroup Disparity Index of Poverty"—is a summary and a representational measure similar to the "Distributional Fairness Index" proposed by Villemez and Rowe (1975). Our index in some sense is also related to the "Society-wide Index of Inter-group Disparity" (aggregate of the "Group-specific Index of Relative Disadvantage") proposed in Jayaraj and Subramanian (2006). The second measure which we use, the "Disparity Indicator," simply captures the difference between the poverty rates of the groups with the highest and the lowest poverty rates.

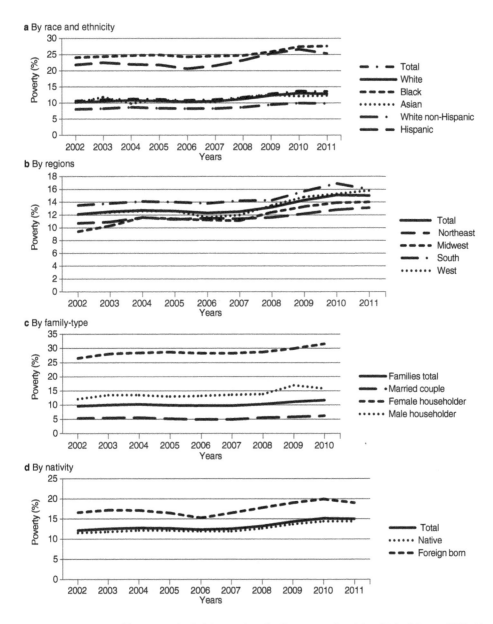

Figure 5.1 Poverty trend by race and ethnicity, region, family-type, and nativity: United States, 2002–11

Source: Current Population Report Series, 2002 to 2011 (Income, Poverty, and Health Insurance Coverage in the United States). Based on Current Population Surveys–Annual Social and Economic Supplements (CPS ASEC) conducted by U.S. Census Bureau (U.S. Census Bureau, 2003–12).

Notes: The terms White, Black and Asian mean of white race alone, black race alone and Asian alone, respectively. Hispanics can be of any race. The term non-Hispanic White refers to people who are not Hispanic and who reported White and no other race. About 2.6% of people have reported more than one race in the 2000 Census (U.S. Census Bureau, 2003). Female householder means female householder with no husband present and male householder means male householder with no wife present.

(1) Intergroup Disparity Index of Poverty

Let us consider a partition of a population of n persons into K (>2) mutually exclusive and exhaustive groups (for example, based on the basis of race, ethnicity, region, etc.), denoted by the running index $j = 1,..., K$. Also, the total number of the poor and the average poverty in the population is denoted by n^p and $\bar{p}$. For every $j \in \{1,..., K\}$, n_j, n_j^p, and p_j will stand for the number of persons, number of poor persons, and the average poverty in the *jth* group, respectively. Also, for every group j, α_j and β_j will stand for the *jth* group's population share and

poverty share, with $\alpha_j = \dfrac{n_j}{n}$ and $\beta_j = \dfrac{n_j^p}{n^p} = \alpha_j . \dfrac{p_j}{\bar{p}}$.

Intuitively any group-specific measure of relative disadvantage (say poverty) must be some function of how large the group's share in total population is in relation to the group's share in total poverty. Therefore a simple specification of relative disadvantage for any group, d_j, can be expressed as the proportionate difference between the group's poverty and population shares:

$$d_j = \left(\frac{\beta_j - \alpha_j}{\alpha_j} \right) \tag{1}$$

Clearly, for a given population share (α_j), relative disadvantage of a group increases with an increase in its poverty share (β_j). Also, group j is relatively advantaged, neither advantaged nor disadvantaged, or relatively disadvantaged according to whether d_j is negative, zero, or positive. That is, group j is relatively advantaged, neither advantaged nor disadvantaged, or relatively disadvantaged according to whether the group's poverty share is less than its population share, equal to its population share, or greater than its population share, respectively.

A simple summary (and representational) aggregate index of intergroup disparity in poverty for the society, D, can be constructed by taking the population-share weighted average of the absolute values of d_j and is given by:

$$D = \frac{1}{2} \sum_{k=1}^{K} \alpha_j \left| d_j \right| = \frac{1}{2} \sum_{k=1}^{K} \alpha_j \left| \left(\frac{\beta_j - \alpha_j}{\alpha_j} \right) \right| \tag{2}$$

This Intergroup Disparity Index of Poverty (D) has a particularly simple interpretation. That is, in a corresponding (or hypothetical) equal population situation (each of the K groups have the same population), a fraction "D" of all the groups (and hence of the total population) has

no poverty at all and the remaining groups will each have a poverty of $\dfrac{\bar{p}}{(1-D)}$.[4] The index

will vary between "0" and "1" (or 0 to 100 in percentage terms). In a case of perfect equality, the index will have a value of zero and will tend to the maximum value of one when all the individuals who are poor are in one particular group (with everybody poor in this group) and the size of this particular group tends to zero (very small).

(2) Disparity Indicator

Our second measure, which we call "Disparity Indicator," can be simply expressed as:

$$DI = \max \left(p_j \right) - \min \left(p_j \right) \tag{3}$$

It is nothing but the difference between the poverty rates of the groups having the highest and the lowest prevalence of poverty, respectively.

Estimates of inequality of poverty

We use data provided in Current Population Report Series: 2002–11 (Income, Poverty, and Health Insurance Coverage in the United States) based on Current Population Survey Annual Social and Economic Supplements conducted by the U.S. Census Bureau to estimate the above-mentioned indices (U.S. Census Bureau, 2003–12). We first estimate the Intergroup Disparity Index and Disparity Indicator for groups based on race. To this effect, we partition the whole population into four groups—White, Black, Asian, and "Others." By White, Black, and Asian, we mean of white race alone, black race alone, and Asian alone, respectively. These three groups include the individuals who have reported only one of the above three races and no other race. Only about 2.6% of people have reported more than one race in the 2000 U.S. Census (U.S. Census Bureau, 2003–12). Also, the proportion of "Others" in the overall population is quite small and varies from about 2.7% in 2002 to 3.7% in 2011. Table 5.1 reports the results for inequality in the distribution of poverty across groups based on race.

In 2011, the Intergroup Disparity Index (in this case we call it the Inter-racial Disparity Index) stood at about 12.4% (substantial), that is, in a corresponding hypothetically equal population situation, 12.4% of all the groups (and hence of the total population) have no poverty at all and the remaining groups (or the remaining population) will each have a poverty of 17%. This is in some sense the lower bound estimate because our partitioning of population into races is very conservative (only four groups); a finer division of population

Table 5.1 Inter-racial disparity in distribution of poverty: United States, 2002–11

Year	Inter-racial Disparity Index (%)	Difference in poverty between groups with highest and lowest poverty (percentage point)	Poverty difference between Blacks and Whites (percentage point)
2002	13.4	14.0	13.9
2003	13.1	12.6	13.9
2004	13.0	14.9	13.9
2005	13.2	13.8	14.3
2006	13.7	14.0	14.0
2007	13.7	14.3	14.0
2008	12.6	12.9	13.5
2009	11.7	13.3	13.5
2010	12.0	15.3	14.4
2011	12.4	15.3	14.8

Source: Author's computations based on data provided in Current Population Report Series: 2002–11 (Income, Poverty, and Health Insurance Coverage in the United States), based on Current Population Survey Annual Social and Economic Supplements (CPS ASEC) conducted by the U.S. Census Bureau (U.S. Census Bureau, 2003–12).

Notes: The race-based groups are White, Black, Asian, and "Others." The terms White, Black, and Asian mean of white race alone, black race alone, and Asian alone, respectively. Hispanics can be of any race. The proportion of "Others" in the overall population is extremely small and varies from about 2.7% in 2002 to 3.7% in 2011. In every year the highest poverty rate was for the Black population.

into races (for example, further partitioning of others into multiple groups) might raise
the estimate. There is a decrease of one percentage point in the index during the period
2002–11. But we should note that the index takes into account the disparity based on all
the groups, and there can always be a case where the difference in poverty between the
extreme groups (groups with the highest and the lowest prevalence of poverty, respectively) has increased but the index takes a lower value because the in-between groups have
come closer to each other in some way. Indeed, if we observe the Disparity Indicator, we
find that the difference in poverty between groups with the highest and lowest poverty has
increased from 14 percentage points to 15.3 percentage points. Also, if we just consider
Blacks and Whites, we find that the difference in their poverty rates has increased from
about 14 percentage points to 15 percentage points and is substantial.

The disparities in poverty based on region, family-type, and nativity are presented in Table 5.2.
The results indicate that the disparities in poverty based on region and nativity have decreased over
time but that the disparity based on family-type is very high and has increased during 2002–11.

We now turn from relating the changes in inequality in distribution of poverty across
groups to the patterns in unemployment, job losses (and re-employment), and average weeks
of unemployment. In doing so, we will focus on race-based disparities and particularly disparities between Blacks and Whites. We do so primarily because of the following three

Table 5.2 Inequality in distribution of poverty by region, family-type, and nativity: United States, 2002–11

Year	Based on region		Based on family-type		Based on nativity
	Inter-region Disparity Index (%)	Difference in poverty between regions with highest and lowest poverty (percentage point)	Inter-family-type Disparity Index (%)	Difference in poverty between family-types with highest and lowest poverty (percentage point)	Difference in poverty between foreign born and natives (percentage point)
2002	5.6	4.1	33.6	21.2	5.1
2003	5.1	3.5	34.4	22.6	5.4
2004	3.9	2.5	34.6	22.9	5.0
2005	4.0	2.7	36.0	23.6	4.4
2006	4.5	2.6	37.7	23.4	3.3
2007	5.0	3.1	37.0	23.4	4.6
2008	3.6	2.7	35.0	23.2	6.4
2009	4.3	3.5	35.6	24.1	4.1
2010	4.6	4.1	34.9	25.4	5.5
2011	3.7	2.9	---	---	4.6

Source: Author's computations based on data provided in Current Population Report Series: 2002–11
(Income, Poverty, and Health Insurance Coverage in the United States), based on Current Population
Survey Annual Social and Economic Supplements (CPS ASEC) conducted by the U.S. Census Bureau
(U.S. Census Bureau, 2003–12).

Notes: The four regions are the Northeast, Midwest, South, and West. In every year, poverty was highest
in the region of the South. The three family-types are Married Couple, Female Households, and Male
Households. Female householder means female householder with no husband present, and male householder means male householder with no wife present. Analysis based on family-type is at the family level,
whereas those based on regions and nativity are at the individual level.

reasons: historical background; increase in the (substantial) poverty difference between Blacks and Whites over time; and the possibility of race-based discrimination in the labor markets.

The changing structure of unemployment and disparities

Table 5.3 documents the unemployment–population ratio (%), unemployment rate (as a percentage of labor force), estimates of job losers (individuals who lost jobs or completed temporary jobs as a percentage of labor force), and average weeks of unemployment among the non-institutional civilian population aged 16 years or older.

Table 5.3 Characteristics of unemployment: United States, 2002–11

Year	Total (1)	White (2)	Black (3)	Difference (4)=(3)−(2)	Total (5)	White (6)	Black (7)	Difference (8)=(7)−(6)
	Unemployment–population ratio (%)				*Unemployment rate (% of labor force)*			
2002	37.3	36.6	41.9	5.3	5.8	5.1	10.2	5.1
2003	37.7	37.0	42.6	5.6	6.0	5.2	10.8	5.6
2004	37.7	36.9	42.8	5.9	5.5	4.8	10.4	5.6
2005	37.3	36.6	42.3	5.7	5.1	4.4	10.0	5.6
2006	36.9	36.2	41.6	5.4	4.6	4.0	8.9	4.9
2007	37.0	36.4	41.6	5.2	4.6	4.1	8.3	4.2
2008	37.8	37.2	42.7	5.5	5.8	5.2	10.1	4.9
2009	40.7	39.8	46.8	7.0	9.3	8.5	14.8	6.3
2010	41.5	40.6	47.7	7.1	9.6	8.7	16.0	7.3
2011	41.6	40.6	48.3	7.7	8.9	7.9	15.8	7.9
	Job losers (as a percentage of labor force)				*Average weeks of unemployment*			
2002	3.2	2.9	5.1	2.2	16.9	15.6	19.6	4.0
2003	3.3	3.0	5.3	2.3	19.2	18.0	22.7	4.7
2004	2.8	2.6	5.0	2.4	19.6	18.5	23.0	4.5
2005	2.5	2.2	4.5	2.3	18.4	16.9	22.6	5.7
2006	2.2	2.0	3.8	1.8	16.8	15.6	20.4	4.8
2007	2.3	2.1	3.6	1.5	16.8	15.7	20.7	5.0
2008	3.1	2.8	5.1	2.3	17.9	16.7	21.7	5.0
2009	5.9	5.6	8.6	3.0	24.4	23.3	28.9	5.6
2010	6.0	5.6	9.0	3.4	33.0	32.0	36.6	4.6
2011	5.3	4.8	8.7	3.9	39.3	37.8	43.3	5.5

Sources: Employment and Earning Series: 2002–11 (U.S. Bureau of Labor Statistics, 2003–12) and Labor Force Characteristics by Race and Ethnicity 2011 for the Unemployment–population ratios (U.S. Department of Labor, 2012b).

Notes: Estimates based on non-institutional civilian population (16 years or older). Job losers are the individuals who lost jobs or completed temporary jobs. Total refers not only to the sum of Whites and Blacks but covers all (non-institutional civilian population 16 years or older).

The main observations from the table are that all the above-considered indicators have increased substantially for both Blacks and Whites and for the considered population as a whole: the unemployment–population ratio increased from 37.3% to 41.6% overall, 41.9% to 48.3% for Blacks, and 36.6% to 40.6% for Whites, respectively; the unemployment rate increased from 5.8% to 8.9% overall, 10.2% to 15.8% for Blacks, and 5.1% to 7.9% for Whites, respectively; job losers increased from 3.2% to 5.3% overall, 5.1% to 8.7% among Blacks, and 2.9% to 4.8% among Whites, respectively; and finally, average weeks of unemployment increased from 16.9 weeks to 39.3 weeks overall, 19.6 weeks to 43.3 weeks for Blacks, and 15.6 weeks to 37.8 weeks for Whites, respectively. Though individuals of both groups have suffered considerably in terms of unemployment (and job losses) on account of globalization and the recent economic recession, it is the Blacks who have borne the greater brunt. To see a more clear and dynamic picture of the race-based disparities in the above indicators we have plotted the difference (between Blacks and Whites) in the above four indicators and have presented them in Figure 5.2.

It can be observed from Figure 5.2 that the difference between Blacks and Whites in all the four indicators shows an upward trend. The Black–White difference in unemployment–population ratio, unemployment rate, job losers, and average weeks of unemployment has increased from 5.3 percentage points to 7.7 percentage points, 5.1 percentage points to 7.9 percentage points, 2.2 percentage points to 3.9 percentage points, and 4 weeks to 5.5 weeks, respectively.[5]

Though we have analyzed the changes in various characteristics of unemployment in this section, we now explore in detail the extent of people having lost their jobs due to reasons which can be related to globalization, their re-employment, and the persistence in unemployment in order to relate the changing welfare of the people to the process of globalization. The details are presented in the next section.

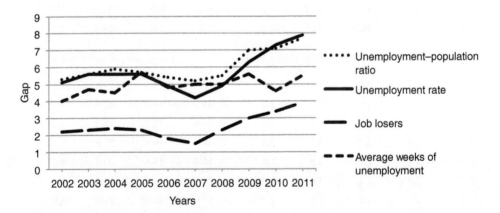

Figure 5.2 Gap between Blacks and Whites in unemployment–population ratio, unemployment rate, job losers, and average weeks of unemployment: United States, 2002–11

Source: Employment and Earning Series, 2002 to 2011 (U.S. Bureau of Labor Statistics, 2003–12) and Labor Force Characteristics by Race and Ethnicity 2011 for Unemployment–Population ratios (U.S. Department of Labor, 2012b).

Notes: All estimates are for individuals 16 years or older (non-institutional civilian). Except for average weeks of unemployment, the gaps in other indicators are in percentage points. Unemployment–population ratio is expressed as a percentage of population. Unemployment rate is expressed as a percentage of labor force. Job losers are the individuals who lost jobs or completed temporary jobs as a percentage of labor force.

Displacement, re-employment, and persistence of unemployment in displaced workers and disparities

We begin by presenting the trend of total displaced workers (with no tenure restriction), that is, the total number of persons (in millions) 20 years of age and older who lost or left jobs (regardless of how long they had held their jobs), because their plant or company closed or moved, there was insufficient work for them to do, or their position or shift was abolished (Figure 5.3).

Figure 5.3 shows an overall upward trend in the total displaced workers where the total number of displaced workers increased from 11.4 million in 2001–03 to 12.9 million in 2009–11.[6]

To further investigate the extent of re-employment and the persistence in unemployment of the displaced workers (with a focus on the Black–White gap), we pay attention to the long-tenured displaced workers because detailed information is available only for this set of displaced workers. The Bureau of Labor Statistics of the United States defines long-tenured displaced workers as persons 20 years of age and older who had three or more years of tenure on a job they had lost or left during the reference period because of the plant or company closing or moving, insufficient work, or the abolishment of their positions or shifts (U.S. Department of Labor, 2012a).

Table 5.4 presents the figures for the long-tenured displaced workers for each three-year reference period from 2001 to 2011, that is, it reports the extent of re-employment (as a percentage of total displaced) in January of the year following the reference period and the extent of unemployed long-tenured displaced workers (as a percentage of total displaced) in January of the year following the reference period for Blacks and Whites and overall.

A few points are worth noting from Table 5.4. First, the total number of long-tenured displaced workers has increased during the 2001–11 period. Second, the extent of re-employment has decreased from 66.4% in 2001–03 to 56% in 2009–11 for the overall population. Third, there is a substantial difference between Whites and Blacks in re-employment and the difference has increased from 8.2 percentage points in 2001–03 to 11.3 percentage points in 2009–11. Fourth, the persistence in unemployment (unemployed in January of the year following the reference period as

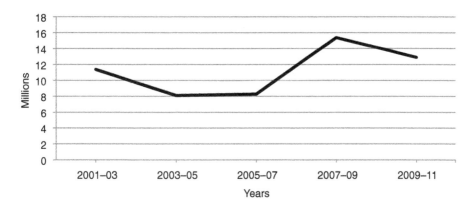

Figure 5.3 Number of workers displaced in millions: United States, 2001–11

Source: Workers Displacement Series: 2001–3 to 2009–11 (U.S. Department of Labor, 2004, 2006, 2008, 2010, 2012a).

Notes: All estimates are for individuals 20 years or older (non-institutional civilian). The total number of workers who lost or left jobs (regardless of how long they had held their jobs), because their plant or company closed or moved, there was insufficient work for them to do, or their position or shift was abolished.

Table 5.4 Characteristics of long-tenured displaced workers: United States, 2001–11

Year	Employed in January of the year following the reference period (%, of total displaced)				Unemployed in January of the year following the reference period (%, of total displaced)				Total number of long-tenured displaced workers
	Total (5)	White (6)	Black (7)	Difference (8)=(7)–(6)	Total (9)	White (10)	Black (11)	Difference (12)=(11)–(10)	(in thousands)
2001–03	66.4	68.2	60.0	–8.2	20.3	18.7	28.8	10.1	5,329
2003–05	69.9	70.0	71.2	1.2	13.4	13.2	13.4	0.2	3,815
2005–07	67.1	67.9	58.6	–9.3	18.0	16.8	28.2	11.4	3,641
2007–09	48.8	50.3	42.9	–7.4	36.1	35.0	41.2	6.2	6,938
2009–11	56.0	57.4	46.1	–11.3	26.7	26.1	31.2	5.1	6,121

Source: Workers Displacement Series: 2001–03 to 2009–11 (U.S. Department of Labor, 2004, 2006, 2008, 2010, 2012a).

Notes: Estimates based on non-institutional civilian population (20 years or older). Estimates refer to displaced individuals, that is, individuals (20 years and older) who had three or more years of tenure on a job they had lost or left during the reference period because of the plant or company closing or moving, insufficient work, or the abolishment of their positions or shifts. Total refers not only to the sum of Whites and Blacks but covers all (non-institutional civilians 20 years or older).

a percentage of total long-tenured displaced) is considerable and has increased from 20.3% to 26.7% during the 2001–11 period for the overall population.[7] Finally, there is also a large Black–White divide in persistence of unemployment as far as long-tenured displaced workers are concerned; for example, in January 2012, out of the total long-tenured Black displaced workers (during 2009–11) about 31% were unemployed, while the corresponding figure for Whites was only 26%.[8]

Concluding remarks

The present chapter examines inequality in poverty in the United States during the past decade and also relates the changes in poverty and inequality of poverty to the process of globalization by analyzing the changes in unemployment–population ratio, unemployment rate, loss of employment (and subsequent re-employment), and average weeks of unemployment. The findings, in essence, add up to a picture which looks dismal. Poverty has increased for all racial and ethnic groups, for all family-types—both natives as well as foreign born—and in all regions. The inequality of poverty in the United States is substantial, and the gap in poverty between Blacks and Whites has increased during 2002–11. Also, the inequality of poverty based on family-type (which is extremely high) has increased during the same period. Further, the unemployment–population ratio, unemployment rate, loss of employment, and average weeks of unemployment have all increased considerably, but the extent of re-employment of displaced workers has decreased enormously during the past decade. Moreover, there are huge gaps between Blacks and Whites in all of the above indicators, with the Blacks on the receiving end. Last but not least, this Black–White divide has increased extensively during the last decade.

Overall, then, this chapter's findings are in conformity with a pessimistic view rather than otherwise about the record of economic development in the United States during the third phase of globalization (2000–present).

Notes

1 The author would like to thank two anonymous reviewers for their valuable comments and suggestions on an earlier draft.
2 In 2011, the poverty rate was 15.0%, statistically tied with the 2011 rate and the highest seen in the past 18 years (Gabe, 2012).
3 All poverty estimates presented are based on U.S. official poverty line and CPS ASEC. Also, we are following the current population survey's categorization (CPS ASEC reports) on race, ethnicity, region, family-type, and nativity. Further, throughout the chapter, poverty should be read as poverty rate (head-count ratio).
4 For details of properties of this index, please see Jayaraj and Subramanian (2006), which develops a similar index but in a different context. Like other such indices, this index is also not perfect but, together with the other indicators used, it suffices for our arguments.
5 We have also obtained the median weekly earnings (for full-time as well as part-time wage and salary workers; annual averages) by race for the years 2002–11 and found that the Black–White difference in median weekly earnings has also increased for both the full-time as well as the part-time wage and salary workers (Appendix 5.2). The details of the unemployment rate, average weeks of unemployment, and median weekly earnings for the period 2002–11 for Hispanics and Asians are presented in Appendix 5.1.
6 The Bureau of Labor Statistics of the United States provides these estimates for three-year periods each.
7 The employment and unemployment rates among the long-tenured displaced workers (in January of the year following the reference period) will not sum to 100 because of some displaced workers leaving the labor force.
8 The details of re-employment and persistence in unemployment of Hispanic as well as Asian long-tenured displaced workers are presented in Appendix 5.3.

References

Friedman, T.L. (2005). It's a flat world, after all. *New York Times* magazine, April 3.

Gabe, T. (2012). *Poverty in the United States: 2011*. Congressional Research Report for Congress 7–5700 (RL33069). Washington, DC: Congressional Research Service.

Jaffee, D.M. (2008). Globalization, offshoring, and economic convergence: A survey. In B. Crawford and E.A. Fogarty (eds.), *The Impact of Globalization on the United States* (pp. 55–77). Westport, CT: Praeger Publishers.

Jayaraj, D., and Subramanian, S. (2006). Horizontal and vertical inequality: Some interconnections and indicators. *Social Indicators Research*, 75, 123–39.

U.S. Bureau of Labor Statistics (2003–12). *Employment and Earnings Series, 2002–11*. Bureau of Labor Statistics, Department of Labor, U.S.. Washington, DC: Bureau of Labor Statistics.

U.S. Census Bureau (2003–12). *Current Population Reports: Income, Poverty and Health Insurance Coverage in the United States Series 2002–11*. United States Census Bureau. Washington, DC: U.S. Census Bureau.

U.S. Department of Labor (2004). *Worker Displacement, 2001–03*. U.S. Department of Labor Document No. USDL 04–1381. Washington, DC: Department of Labor.

U.S. Department of Labor (2006). *Worker Displacement, 2003–05*. U.S. Department of Labor Document No. USDL 06–1454. Washington, DC: Department of Labor.

U.S. Department of Labor (2008). *Worker Displacement, 2005–07*. U.S. Department of Labor Document No. USDL 08–1183. Washington, DC: Department of Labor.

U.S. Department of Labor (2010). *Worker Displacement, 2007–09*. U.S. Department of Labor Document No. USDL 10–1174. Washington, DC: Department of Labor.

U.S. Department of Labor (2012a). *Worker Displacement, 2009–11*. U.S. Department of Labor Document No. USDL 12–1719. Washington, DC: Department of Labor.

U.S. Department of Labor (2012b). *Labor Force Characteristics by Race and Ethnicity, 2011*. U.S. Department of Labor Report 1005. Washington, DC: Department of Labor.

Villemez, W.J., and Rowe, A.R. (1975). Black economic gains in the sixties: A methodological critique and reassessment. *Social Forces*, 54, 181–93.

Appendix 5.1

Table 5.5 Unemployment rate, average weeks of unemployment, and median weekly earnings for Hispanics and Asians: United States, 2002–11

Year	Hispanics				Asians			
	Unemployment rate (%, of labor force)	Average weeks of unemployment	Median weekly earnings ($), full-time	Median weekly earnings ($), part-time	Unemployment rate (%, of labor force)	Average weeks of unemployment	Median weekly earnings ($) full-time	Median weekly earnings ($), part-time
2002	7.5	14.7	424	185	5.9	–	658	193
2003	7.7	15.9	440	190	6.0	23.9	693	212
2004	7.0	17.3	456	192	4.4	23.0	708	203
2005	6.0	16.0	471	198	4.0	23.3	753	204
2006	5.2	14.5	486	202	3.0	21.3	784	216
2007	5.6	14.9	503	206	3.2	17.5	830	222
2008	7.6	16.0	529	222	4.0	20.4	861	235
2009	12.1	22.6	541	225	7.3	26.9	880	253
2010	12.5	30.5	535	229	7.5	36.7	855	251
2011	11.5	36.4	549	229	7.0	47.6	866	255

Source: Employment and Earning Series: 2002–11 (U.S. Bureau of Labor Statistics, 2003–12).

Notes: Individuals identified as Hispanics can be of any race. Estimates based on non-institutional civilian population (16 years or older). Median weekly earnings are annual averages.

Appendix 5.2

Table 5.6 Median weekly earnings by race: United States, 2002–11

Year	Full-time wage and salary workers ($)				Part-time wage and salary workers ($)			
	Total (1)	White (2)	Black (3)	Difference (4)=(2)−(3)	Total (5)	White (6)	Black (7)	Difference (8)=(6)−(7)
2002	609	624	498	126	188	189	178	11
2003	620	636	514	122	192	197	182	15
2004	638	657	525	132	195	196	190	6
2005	651	672	520	152	201	202	197	5
2006	671	690	554	136	206	208	191	17
2007	695	716	569	147	213	214	202	12
2008	722	742	589	153	219	220	210	10
2009	739	757	601	156	226	227	219	8
2010	747	765	611	154	229	230	219	11
2011	756	775	615	160	232	233	220	13

Source: Employment and Earning Series: 2002–11 (U.S. Bureau of Labor Statistics, 2003–12).

Notes: Estimates based on non-institutional civilian population (16 years or older). Median weekly earnings are annual averages. Total refers not only to the sum of Whites and Blacks but covers all (non-institutional civilians, 16 years or older).

Appendix 5.3

Table 5.7 Characteristics of long-tenured displaced workers—Hispanics and Asians: United States, 2001–11

Year	Hispanics		Asians	
	Employed in January of the year following the reference period (%, of total displaced)	Unemployed in January of the year following the reference period (%, of total displaced)	Employed in January of the year following the reference period (%, of total displaced)	Unemployed in January of the year following the reference period (%, of total displaced)
2001–03	68.1	20.0	57.3	24.0
2003–05	65.6	20.7	69.0	16.2
2005–07	67.0	19.6	62.9	14.4
2007–09	49.7	36.6	43.6	39.2
2009–11	54.8	30.5	54.1	29.7

Source: Workers Displacement Series: 2001–03 to 2009–11 (U.S. Department of Labor, 2004, 2006, 2008, 2010, 2012a).

Notes: Individuals identified as Hispanics can be of any race. Estimates based on non-institutional civilian population (20 years or older). Estimates refer to long-tenured displaced individuals, that is, individuals (20 years and older) who had three or more years of tenure on a job they had lost or left during the reference period because of the plant or company closing or moving, insufficient work, or the abolishment of their positions or shifts.

6

THE HOUSE ALWAYS WINS

How state lotteries displace American tax burdens by class and race

Kasey Henricks and Victoria Brockett

No government-sponsored lottery existed in the United States 50 years ago. Today 44 lotteries operate in the United States, and in 2011 alone, they generated over $55 billion in revenues (U.S. Census Bureau, 2011). After accounting for prize winnings and administration fees, about $18.4 billion of this money was allotted to public services. Though lotteries are often adopted on the political promise to provide additional funds, in reality they marginally increase the money available for public services (Miller and Pierce, 1997; Pantuosco et al., 2007). In many cases, lottery money simply alters the composition of taxation and supplants other sources of state revenue like corporate, property, and income taxes (Borg and Mason, 1988, 1990). Fiscal policy restructured in this way has the potential to shift the tax obligations of who pays for infrastructure investment that mostly everyone enjoys.

The lottery is an anomalous form of taxation. Because of its unimposing nature and reliance on voluntary participation, some have labeled it a "painless tax" (Clotfelter and Cook, 1989, p. 215). Unlike conventional conceptions that define taxation as an "obligation to contribute money or goods to the state" (Martin et al., 2009, p. 3), people purchase lottery tickets as consumer products out of their own volition. The state then implicitly retains a fraction of the proceeds, all the while avoiding potential political backlash associated with other mandatory taxes. Regardless of how lottery revenues are collected, however, they carry the same value for the state as do any other taxes. For these reasons, we along with others (e.g., Clotfelter and Cook, 1989; Nibert, 2000) define the lottery as a form of taxation.

To discern how lotteries have reorganized the composition of American taxation, we take up three analytic goals. First, we outline historical fiscal trends that created the conditions for the emergence of lotteries. Then, we detail how lotteries distribute prize winnings, pay operating costs, and, most importantly, finance public services. Lastly, we determine who this money comes from. Overall, this three-pronged strategy augments understandings of the role lotteries play in matters of taxation and what social consequences this may cause. We find that lottery implementation is part of an infrastructural redesign of taxation, whereby financial responsibility of who pays for the state is shifting and being unequally redistributed across social groups by race and socioeconomic status.

National fiscal crises and the emergence of state lotteries

Neoliberalism can be conceptualized as social, political, cultural, and social transformations that incorporate the principles of rugged individualism, open markets, and maximized profits. Though its origins are debated,[1] its consequences are quite clear. Its rise is among the markers of an end to America's unprecedented growth, not to mention fundamental changes in the political economy. Neoliberal-inspired changes have: further concentrated capital through state withdrawal from certain sectors of private industry (Harvey, 2005), deindustrialized many manufacturing-based cities by corporate abandonment (Wilson, 1996), globalized markets that know no borders and frequently leave nation-bound peoples jobless in their wake (Sassen, 1998), divested from the welfare state and enhanced regulation of the poor (Piven and Cloward, 1982), displaced high-paying industrial jobs with low-paying, service-sector ones that are less stable in the long term (Fischer and Hout, 2006), and instituted increasingly regressive tax structures that thwart capital redistribution (Prasad, 2006). Altogether these factors have eroded the tax base and curtailed the ability of federal, state, and local governments to generate money.

The proliferation of state lotteries is a part of these larger neoliberal trends, particularly when it concerns the changing arrangement of American tax codes. Journalists Barlett and Steele (1994) contend that since the 1970s a number of legal reforms began shifting tax obligations:

- From corporations to individuals.
- From foreign corporations to domestic corporations.
- From foreign investors to American workers.
- From multinational companies to medium-sized and small businesses.
- From the federal government to state and local governments, whose taxes already fall most heavily on those in the middle and at the bottom.

(p. 14)

While it can be argued these trends began before 1970, the notion that tax obligations have shifted from elite interests onto those least able to pay is generally correct.

Through a series of reforms federal tax codes have replaced progressive taxes with regressive ones. Let us consider some data from the Office of Management and Budget (2010). Since corporate taxes peaked in 1947 at 7.2 percent of Gross Domestic Product (GDP), these revenues have gradually declined to levels comparable to before the New Deal era (see Figure 6.1). In 2009, corporate taxes comprised only 1.0 percent of GDP. Meanwhile social insurance taxes have steadily risen over time from 1.5 percent of GDP in 1947 to 6.3 percent in 2009. Individual taxes have fluctuated over time, and their fraction of GDP has ranged anywhere between a low of 5.7 in 1947 to a high of 10.2 in 2000. As of 2009, the combined individual income and social insurance taxes generate more than 12 times the revenue derived from corporate income taxes.

Shifts in the federal tax composition foreshadowed and shaped what would later occur in state and local governments. Under the Reagan Administration, states were delegated more responsibility in administering and financing welfare programs (Piven and Cloward, 1982). This ultimately meant that states played a larger role in satisfying services like Medicare and Medicaid, not to mention infrastructure upkeep like highway maintenance. Given these public services cannot be provided without sufficient funds, states were positioned to revise their tax codes and collect levels of unprecedented revenue. All the while, economic insecurity caused by neoliberal shifts in the political economy left many Americans feeling financially pinched, especially as real incomes stagnated and increasing tax debts loomed.

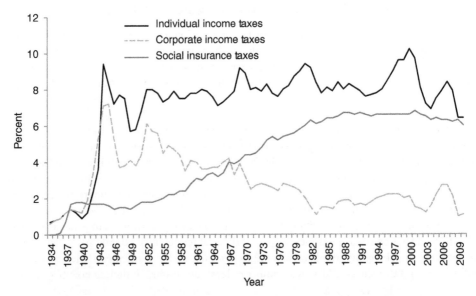

Figure 6.1 Individual, corporate, and social insurance taxes as a share of GDP, 1934–2009

Source: Office of Management and Budget (2010).

Personal matters of how much money government took from people's paychecks increasingly became political matters, and people reacted in backlash by organizing tax revolts that began in California and spread throughout the country (Lo, 1990; Martin, 2008). It was the efforts of these populist-style social movements that spurred a number of state reforms on property, personal income, and sales taxes during the late 1970s and 1980s (see Table 6.1). Between 1978 and 1981, 104 state reforms either limited property taxes or provided property tax relief, 30 reforms reduced personal income taxes, and 28 reforms decreased sales taxes (Peterson, 1982). The consequences of these reforms help explain why property taxes comprised 25.6 percent of all local and state government revenue in 1972 but only 16.6 in 2005 (see Table 6.2). Meanwhile miscellaneous general revenue, which includes net lottery proceeds among other revenues, went from 4.6 percent in 1972 to about 10 percent throughout the 1990s and 8.8 percent in 2005.

Though money is needed to make public services possible, tax rebellions represent a serious disconnect between general demand for these services and the willingness to pay for them. Even amongst those who participated in California's 1970s property tax revolts, most still held favorable views of infrastructure investments like public education, roads and highways, hospitals, and so on (Sears and Citrin, 1982). In a political climate where potential backlash is likely at the sheer mention of the "t-word," lottery adoption can be understood as a viable funding strategy to alleviate state treasuries pinched for cash. Their political feasibility and ability to generate millions and billions of dollars yield reasons, Nibert (2000) and Peppard (1987) argue, for why they proliferated across America at this particular historical juncture (see Figure 6.2).[2]

How states spend their lottery jackpots

Though some scholars (e.g., Mikesell and Zorn, 1986, 1988) label lotteries a "fickle form of finance,"[3] we caution against dismissing what they offer. Lotteries by no means pay a majority of public services, but they do generate more cash than all other forms of gambling combined

Table 6.1 Number of state tax reforms throughout the United States, 1978–1981

Tax action	1978	1979	1980	1981
Property tax				
New statewide limitation				
On levies, rates, or				
assessment growth	7	9	7	4
New property tax relief	20	21	19	17
Total major measures	27	30	26	21
Personal income tax				
Reductions				
Indexation	3	4	2	0
General rates	4	6	2	3
Specific rates	3	3	0	0
Total major measures	10	13	4	3
Increases				
Indexation	0	0	0	1
General rates	2	0	0	0
Specific rates	0	0	0	1
Total major measures	2	0	0	2
Sales tax				
Reductions				
Across-the-board	1	0	0	1
Base contraction				
(food, drugs, or				
medical-exemption				
or reduced rates)	9	12	2	3
Total major measures	10	12	2	4
Increases				
Across-the-board, permanent	0	0	1	3
Temporary and extension				
of temporary	1	1	3	3
Base expansion	3	1	0	3
Total major measures	4	2	4	9

Source: Peterson (1982).

Table 6.2 Sources of local and state revenue: selected years, 1972–2005 (in percentages)

Composition of revenue	1972	1977	1982	1987	1992	1997	2002	2005
Transfers from federal gov't	18.7	21.9	19.1	16.7	18.3	19.0	21.4	21.7
Own sources	81.3	78.1	80.9	83.3	81.7	81.0	78.6	78.3
Charges for services	11.3	10.9	12.4	12.7	14.1	14.8	15.0	15.3
Miscellaneous general revenue[a]	4.6	5.5	10.3	11.6	10.4	9.7	9.9	8.8
Total taxes	65.3	61.7	58.2	58.9	57.1	56.4	53.7	54.2
Property tax	25.6	21.9	17.9	17.6	18.4	17.0	16.6	16.6
General sales tax	12.1	12.8	13.2	14.1	13.5	13.8	13.2	13.0
Select sales tax	10.2	8.5	7.2	6.9	6.7	6.4	6.0	6.0
Individual income tax	9.1	10.3	11.1	12.2	11.8	12.3	12.0	11.9
Corporate net income tax	2.6	3.2	3.3	3.3	2.4	2.6	1.7	2.1
Other taxes	5.7	5.0	5.5	4.8	4.3	4.3	4.2	4.6

Source: U.S. Census Bureau, State and Local Government Finances.

[a] Miscellaneous general revenue includes local and state revenues from interest earnings, net lottery revenues, assessments, sale of property, fines and forfeitures, rents and royalties, gifts of cash or securities from private individuals or corporations, and other revenues received that are unclassified as a tax, intergovernmental revenue, or a current charge.

(Clotfelter and Cook, 1989). They are more profitable than any other public enterprise operated by state governments, and their contributions are larger than most excise taxes (Clotfelter and Cook, 1989). Nearly half of all lottery revenues are returned to players through prize winnings, and the remaining one-third is returned to taxpayers through public finance (see Figure 6.3).[4] Throughout the 2000s in Illinois, for example, lottery sales annually contributed about $600 million to K-12 public education, an amount that represents nearly 10 percent of state spending on public education (Henricks, 2014). These revenues may not be in the same class as income and property taxes, but politicians would be hard-pressed to replace lottery money with another source or reject their contribution as insignificant.

How are lottery revenues spent across the country? Findings remain inconclusive when we visit the academic literature. Largely, this is because the question has long been ignored (Borg et al., 1991). Of the exceptions available, most are limited to case studies of particular states or large metropolitan areas (e.g., Borg et al., 1991; Henricks, 2014; McCrary and Pavlak, 2002; Stranahan and Borg, 2004). No study answers this question, to our knowledge, on a grander scale.[5] To provide a national overview of lotteries, we synthesize a host of legal documents audited from all 44 government-sponsored lotteries as well as the Annual Survey of State Governments, 2011. Given that most states have adopted freedom of information or "sunshine" laws, virtually all of this information is readily available online or through formal request. Government agencies provide documents, like budgets or annual reports, which contain information pertinent to this study.[6]

We audited the appropriate documents to determine each state's lottery status, how much money each generated, the portion of revenues earmarked for public services, and which services were funded in 2011 (see Tables 6.3 and 6.4).[7] Even though many states share a common reporting structure, many definitional inconsistencies are evident among their accounting

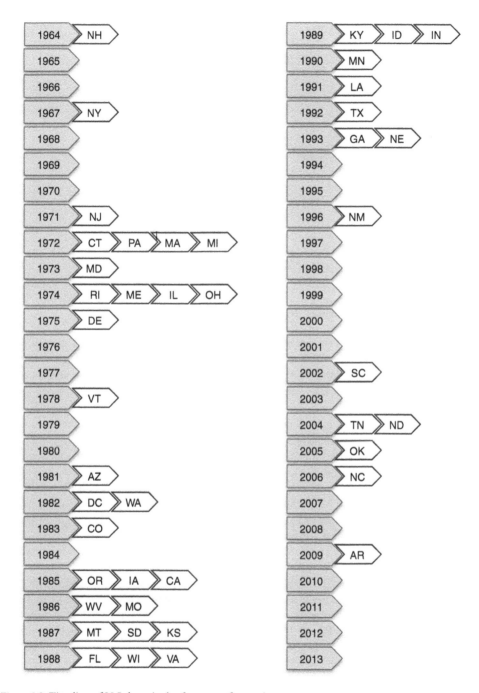

Figure 6.2 Timeline of U.S. lotteries by first year of operation

Source: Authors' tabulations.

Note: ★ The first year of operation is designated by the first year of lottery ticket sales. States having the same first year of operation are listed chronologically according to the month and date of the first sale.

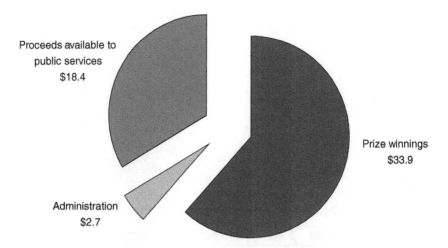

Figure 6.3 Expenditure breakdown of lottery revenues, fiscal year 2011 (in billions)★

Note: ★ Lottery revenues include ticket sales and exclude commissions. Prizes reflect the amount won by ticket buyers, and available proceeds reflect income less prizes and administration costs (U.S. Census Bureau, 2011; District of Columbia, 2011).

practices. For example, when looking at statements of revenues, expenses, and changes in net assets, Arkansas includes prize expenses under total operating costs, while California excludes prize expenses from operating costs. It lists this line item under operating revenues to reflect income generated by ticket sales after prize funds have been dispersed. Due to these inconsistencies, we turn to the Annual Survey of State Governments to standardize our analysis.[8]

Total sales amounted to $55 billion in fiscal year 2011. To put this into perspective, consider what this means in terms of per capita sales. Of the roughly 222 million gaming state and district residents legally permitted to gamble in 2010, each person would have had to spend approximately $248 during fiscal year 2011 to produce this amount of income on the national scale.[9] Empirically, however, lottery revenues were not generated evenly across states. Massachusetts held the highest lottery sales rate per capita at $813 while North Dakota had the lowest at $42. In terms of total sales, New York sold the most tickets totaling an amount of nearly $7 billion, or 13 percent of the national total. Meanwhile North Dakota also generated the least at nearly $22 million.

Much of the revenues generated were reinvested into the lottery to pay for operating costs. About 62 percent of lottery revenues counted toward prize winnings, while nearly 5 percent was spent on administration fees. The state with the highest payout rate was Massachusetts, with nearly 77 percent of its lottery sales being returned to players through prize winnings. West Virginia, on the other hand, had the lowest payout rate of approximately 16 percent. For administrative costs, the most efficient state was Rhode Island with about 1 percent of its sales for operating upkeep while North Dakota spent the largest share of sales on administration at 18 percent.

Most of all the remaining lottery revenues were appropriated for just about every public service imaginable. State lotteries generated nearly $18 billion in tax revenues in 2011. On the whole, these funds were transferred to states as specific earmarked proceeds or pooled in a state's general fund. When proceeds are transferred to general funds, they can be dispersed to hundreds of public services generally determined by state legislatures and governors. For example, Connecticut allocates funds for chronic gambling and the state's general fund. Once there, the state delivers these funds for services like higher education, health and hospitals, corrections, and Medicaid, to name a few. Although not exhaustive, in Tables 6.5 and 6.6 we list the range

Table 6.3 National overview of lottery states A–M: total revenues, sales per capita, prizes, administrative costs, and available proceeds to public services, fiscal year 2011*

	Available to public services[d]		Total prize winnings[a]		Administrative costs[a][c]		Proceeds	
	Total lottery revenues ($)[a]	Sales per capita ($)[b]	($)	(% of total revenues ($))	($)	(% of total revenues ($))	($)	(% of total revenues ($))
Arizona	544,290	122	360,491	(66.2)	39,023	(7.2)	144,776	(26.6)
Arkansas	437,801	199	307,455	(70.2)	37,863	(8.6)	92,483	(21.1)
California	3,483,578	125	1,904,788	(54.7)	193,526	(5.6)	1,385,264	(39.8)
Colorado	479,337	126	326,624	(68.1)	40,904	(8.5)	111,809	(23.3)
Connecticut	959,650	348	620,134	(64.6)	41,218	(4.3)	298,298	(31.1)
Delaware	451,142	652	75,846	(16.8)	49,060	(10.9)	326,236	(72.3)
D.C.	231,749	463	125,860	(54.3)	11,767	(5.1)	94,122	(40.6)
Florida	3,781,550	256	2,460,219	(65.1)	134,339	(3.6)	1,186,992	(31.4)
Georgia	3,109,295	432	2,120,835	(68.2)	140,388	(4.5)	848,072	(27.3)
Idaho	135,379	119	90,230	(66.6)	8,669	(6.4)	36,480	(26.9)
Illinois	2,264,685	233	1,368,472	(60.4)	232,767	(10.3)	663,446	(29.3)
Indiana	735,206	151	494,516	(67.3)	48,202	(6.6)	192,488	(26.2)
Iowa	271,535	125	158,961	(64.3)	40,299	(14.8)	72,275	(26.6)
Kansas	218,590	103	132,332	(60.5)	20,175	(9.2)	66,083	(30.2)
Kentucky	672,069	203	422,410	(62.9)	35,154	(5.2)	214,505	(31.9)
Louisiana	362,222	113	202,902	(56.0)	24,351	(6.7)	134,969	(37.3)
Maine	202,314	192	135,587	(67.0)	15,710	(7.8)	51,017	(25.2)
Maryland	1,600,716	362	1,029,041	(64.3)	103,989	(6.5)	467,686	(29.2)

Continued

Table 6.3 National overview of lottery states A–M: total revenues, sales per capita, prizes, administrative costs, and available proceeds to public services, fiscal year 2011* (continued)

	Available to public services[a d]		Total prize winnings[a]	Administrative costs[a c]	Proceeds
	Total lottery revenues ($)[a]	Sales per capita ($)[b]	(% of total revenues ($))	(% of total revenues ($))	(% of total revenues ($))
Massachusetts	4,167,142	813	3,199,444 (76.8)	88,634 (2.1)	879,064 (21.1)
Michigan	2,139,205	284	1,368,238 (64.0)	70,740 (3.3)	700,227 (32.7)
Minnesota	474,178	118	327,546 (69.1)	23,953 (5.1)	122,679 (25.9)
Missouri	981,542	215	639,011 (65.1)	42,234 (4.3)	300,297 (30.6)
Montana	43,322	57	24,778 (57.2)	7,616 (17.6)	10,928 (25.2)

*All figures reported, aside from percentage values, are rounded to the nearest thousand.

[a] Total lottery revenues is calculated as ticket sales minus commissions (U.S. Census Bureau, 2011; District of Columbia Lottery, 2011).

[b] Sales per capita is calculated as total lottery revenues divided by 2010 Census records of total state populations who are legally permitted, as determined by age, to purchase a lottery ticket. Tickets can be purchased in a majority of states and in the District of Columbia by those 18 years of age and older, though some outliers deviate from this trend. The minimum age in Arizona, Iowa, and Louisiana is 21 years, while the minimum age in Nebraska is 19 years.

[c] Administrative costs reflect the costs associated with operating and maintaining lotteries (U.S. Census Bureau, 2011; District of Columbia Lottery, 2011).

[d] Proceeds available to public services reflect total lottery revenues less prize winnings and administration costs (U.S. Census Bureau, 2011; District of Columbia Lottery, 2011).

Table 6.4 National overview of lottery states N–W: total revenues, sales per capita, prizes, administrative costs, and available proceeds to public services, fiscal year 2011*

	Available to public services[a d]		Total prize winnings[a]		Administrative costs[a c]		Proceeds	
	Total lottery revenues ($)[a]	Sales per capita ($)[b]	(% of total revenues ($))		(% of total revenues ($))		(% of total revenues ($))	
Nebraska	123,711	90	76,871	(62.1)	16,546	(13.4)	30,294	(24.5)
New Hampshire	216,229	210	139,262	(64.4)	14,552	(6.7)	62,415	(28.9)
New Jersey	2,489,474	370	1,505,220	(60.5)	53,118	(2.1)	931,136	(37.4)
New Mexico	129,756	84	76,699	(59.1)	11,636	(9.0)	41,421	(31.9)
New York	6,986,288	464	3,967,672	(56.8)	323,119	(4.6)	2,695,497	(38.6)
North Carolina	1,358,387	187	861,469	(63.4)	59,848	(4.4)	437,070	(32.2)
North Dakota	21,906	42	11,941	(54.5)	3,949	(18.0)	6,016	(27.5)
Ohio	2,439,667	277	1,603,054	(65.7)	89,232	(3.7)	747,381	(30.6)
Oklahoma	211,373	75	106,601	(50.4)	12,391	(5.9)	92,381	(43.7)
Oregon	838,595	283	208,673	(24.9)	75,156	(9.0)	554,766	(66.2)
Pennsylvania	2,905,632	293	1,958,432	(67.4)	69,238	(2.4)	877,962	(30.2)
Rhode Island	505,574	610	142,324	(28.2)	6,919	(1.4)	356,331	(70.5)
South Carolina	973,013	274	667,637	(68.6)	37,300	(3.8)	268,076	(27.6)
South Dakota	140,484	230	27,175	(19.3)	6,664	(4.7)	106,645	(75.9)
Tennessee	1,108,861	229	611,171	(55.1)	51,989	(4.7)	445,701	(40.2)
Texas	3,599,037	197	2,387,244	(66.3)	205,463	(5.7)	1,006,330	(28.0)
Vermont	89,935	181	50,613	(56.7)	7,943	(8.8)	31,379	(34.9)

Continued

Table 6.4 National overview of lottery states N–W: total revenues, sales per capita, prizes, administrative costs, and available proceeds to public services, fiscal year 2011* *(continued)*

| | Available to public services[a][d] | | Total prize winnings[a] | | Administrative costs[a][c] | | Proceeds | |
	Total lottery revenues ($)[a]	Sales per capita ($)[b]	(% of total revenues ($))		(% of total revenues ($))		(% of total revenues ($))	
Virginia	1,398,843	228	881,026	(63.0)	72,134	(5.2)	445,683	(31.9)
Washington	478,516	93	295,155	(61.7)	44,383	(9.3)	138,978	(29.0)
West Virginia	746,738	510	120,707	(16.2)	39,337	(5.3)	586,694	(78.6)
Wisconsin	502,654	116	290,459	(57.8)	33,765	(6.7)	178,430	(35.5)

* All figures reported, aside from percentage values, are rounded to the nearest thousand.

[a] Total lottery revenues is calculated as ticket sales minus commissions (U.S. Census Bureau, 2011; District of Columbia Lottery, 2011).

[b] Sales per capita is calculated as total lottery revenues divided by 2010 Census records of total state populations who are legally permitted, as determined by age, to purchase a lottery ticket. Tickets can be purchased in a majority of states and in the District of Columbia by those 18 years of age and older, though some outliers deviate from this trend. The minimum age in Arizona, Iowa, and Louisiana is 21 years, while the minimum age in Nebraska is 19 years.

[c] Administrative costs reflect the costs associated with operating and maintaining lotteries (U.S. Census Bureau, 2011; District of Columbia Lottery, 2011).

[d] Proceeds available to public services reflect total lottery revenues less prize winnings and administration costs (U.S. Census Bureau, 2011; District of Columbia Lottery, 2011).

Table 6.5 National overview of states A–M: lottery-funded public services, fiscal year 2011

Arizona	Economic and business development; environment; health and public welfare; K-12 and higher education
Arkansas	Higher education financial aid
California	K-12 and higher education
Colorado	Conservation education; environmental conservation; parks and recreation; school health and safety
Connecticut	Chronic gamblers' fund; corrections; conservation and development; debt service; general government; grant payments to local governments; health and hospitals; human services; judicial, regulation and protection; K-12 and higher education; legislative; libraries and education services; Medicaid; mental health; public health; state service
Delaware	Child, youth, and family services; health and social services; judicial and corrections; K-12 and higher education; natural resources and environmental control; public safety
D.C.	Child services; K-12 education; parks and recreation; public housing; public safety; senior services
Florida	Higher education financial aid; K-12 and higher education
Georgia	Higher education financial aid; pre-K-12 education
Idaho	Construction and preservation; K-12 and higher education; public building
Illinois	Breast cancer research and education; HIV/AIDS awareness and support initiatives; K-12 education; multiple sclerosis research; veterans' support programs
Indiana	Offsetting motor vehicle excise taxes; public servants' pension and retirement
Iowa	K-12 education; public building construction and preservation; tourism; veteran support
Kansas	Economic development; gambling treatment; juvenile detention facilities; prison construction and maintenance
Kentucky	Early childhood reading; higher education financial aid; literacy
Louisiana	Gambling treatment; K-12 education
Maine	General fund; wildlife preservation
Maryland	Environment; K-12 and higher education; public health; public safety; stadium authority
Massachusetts	Arts and culture; gambling treatment; unearmarked local aid
Michigan	Gambling treatment; K-12 education
Minnesota	Environmental conservation; gambling treatment; parks and recreation; wildlife preservation
Missouri	K-12 and higher education
Montana	Health; K-12 education; public safety

Table 6.6 National overview of states N–W: lottery-funded public services, fiscal year 2011

Nebraska	Environmental conservation; gambling treatment; K-12 and higher education; state fair; wildlife preservation
New Hampshire	K-12 education
New Jersey	Human services; K-12 and higher education; military and veterans' affairs
New Mexico	Higher education
New York	K-12 education
North Carolina	Gambling treatment; pre-K-12 and higher education
North Dakota	Drug task force; gambling treatment
Ohio	K-12 education
Oklahoma	Gambling treatment; K-12 and higher education
Oregon	Environmental conservation; gambling treatment; job creation and economic development; K-12 and higher education; parks and recreation; wildlife preservation
Pennsylvania	Senior services (rent/tax subsidies, free/reduced transit, prescription drug assistance, living services, senior community centers)
Rhode Island	General government; human services; K-12 education; public safety; natural resources; transportation
South Carolina	Gambling treatment; K-12 and higher education; libraries
South Dakota	Capital construction (water and environment fund, ethanol fuel fund, state highway fund); human services; property tax deduction
Tennessee	Business creation and economic development (diversity and minority business participation); pre-K-12 and higher education
Texas	K-12 education; veterans' support programs
Vermont	K-12 education
Washington	Economic development; gambling treatment; King County (Safeco Field); pre-K-12 and higher education; public debt from sports forums and exhibition centers
West Virginia	K-12 and higher education; racetrack reinvestment and modernization; senior services; tourism
Wisconsin	Gambling treatment; law enforcement; property tax relief

of public services funded by lottery proceeds by state, including the District of Columbia, for 2011. Wide-ranging public services include gambling treatment, economic development, construction initiatives, recreational facilities, libraries, education, environmental conservation, health and human services, law enforcement, military and veterans' affairs, research, public servants' pension and retirement, as well as general tax relief.

As the long list of public services implies, lottery revenues have become pervasively entrenched within the American tax system. Lottery revenues are generated with the purpose of paying for a variety of public services mostly everyone is entitled to. Even those who do not play the lottery are affected by lotteries in some way. Whether they are a Floridian family who sends their children to public school, a Coloradoan skier who enjoys recreation at state parks, or a Pennsylvanian senior citizen who requires state medical assistance, lottery funds help make all these possible. Since these services will likely remain a staple of states and governments will undoubtedly continue to collect lottery revenues, a lingering question remains: From whom does this money come?

Who plays, who pays?

Common knowledge may lead many to believe that those who play are too poor to be playing in the first place. Much evidence is available to support this conclusion, but not all studies corroborate this finding. Many scholars report low-income individuals spend higher proportions of their income on tickets compared to high-income individuals (Brinner and Clotfelter, 1975; Clotfelter and Cook, 1989; Hansen et al., 2000; Miyazaki et al., 1998; Pirog-Good and Mikesell, 1995). Education may also play a factor in determining lottery participation, as those with lower education attainment levels tend to play the lottery more than those with higher levels (Brown et al., 1992; Price and Novak, 1999). Other scholars emphasize how race plays a factor, and measure how lottery money disproportionately comes from people of color (Cook and Clotfelter, 1993; Hansen, 1995; Price and Novak, 1999; Stranahan and Borg, 1998). Though these studies tend to confirm a general pattern, not all analysts report the lottery to be a regressive source of revenue.

Quite the opposite in fact. In Illinois, Mikesell (1989) finds income has a proportional relationship to lottery play at all levels. Oster (2004) confirms similar findings for Powerball lotteries that offer larger jackpots. These have broad appeal and attract more general participation. Clotfelter and Cook (1989) observe a national trend of middle-income groups spending more money on lottery tickets than all other income groups, whereas Stranahan and Borg (1998) surveyed three states to find that middle-income groups play the lottery more than their peers but they do not spend more. In Colorado, Hansen (1995) shows that people with higher education attainment purchase comparably more lottery tickets than their counterparts. A national Gallup poll confirms these observations. Ludwig (1999) provides evidence that the lottery is a progressive tax structure in which groups with higher income and education levels play the lottery at higher rates compared to other groups. All these findings complicate, and in some instances directly challenge, straightforward interpretations that lotteries are socioeconomically regressive sources of revenue.

Inconsistencies linger when matters of race and ethnicity are reconsidered. Some identify no differences among groups in the frequency of lottery play (McCrary and Pavlak, 2002; Stranahan and Borg, 1998). These same studies do show, however, that blacks disproportionately spend more money on lottery products. When it comes to Latinas/os, considerably less research documents their spending habits.[10] Some suggest Latinas/os spend more money on lottery tickets that cost less and yield smaller rewards (Hansen, 1995; Price and Novak, 1999). Aside from whites, blacks, and Latinas/os, other groups remain absent from the literature or are subsumed under umbrella categories of nonblack or nonwhite (Henricks, 2014), which oversimplifies the presence of multiple groups. In reality the presence of multiple racial groups complicates how symbolic and material resources are distributed (Bonilla-Silva et al., 2003).

In light of these findings, more research needs to measure exactly from whom lottery revenues are generated. We explore this question by relying upon a dataset derived from the *Gambling Impact and Behavior Study, 1997–1999*.[11] The survey yields the most comprehensive American dataset available for public use to date. While it includes a number of variables that measure behavioral and attitudinal attributes associated with the lottery, and gambling in general, our focus is limited to describing who plays the lottery and how often. We sketch a general picture by relying upon descriptive statistics that measure what have arguably been the most central variables across the academic literature: indicators of race and socioeconomic status.

Of the 2,947 people surveyed, 75 percent reported having played the lottery at some point in life. Their frequencies of play and amounts of money they reported losing, however, varied significantly (see Table 6.7). About 74.6 percent of those who had ever played said they also purchased a ticket in the past year. Another 15.5 percent said they played in the past month, while an additional 30.0 percent reported playing within the past week. We label those who reported purchasing a ticket during the past week frequent lottery players. It is worth noting that a statistically significant correlation beyond the 0.01 level is confirmed between frequent players and those who reported a net loss in lottery play. What this likely means is that these players are more likely to be "in the red" and suffer a net loss compared to those who play infrequently. Table 6.7 further illustrates that these players are not only more likely to lose given their high frequency of play, but their reported net losses indicate they lost considerably more money than those who play on a monthly or yearly basis.

Table 6.7 Ever played the lottery, frequency of play, and outcomes of net loss

Played lottery during lifetime		
Answer	*Frequency*	*Percent*
Yes	2,210	75.0
No	737	25.0
Total	2,947	100.0

	Last time person played lottery (in percent)		
Net outcome	*Past week (%)*	*Past month (%)*	*Past year (%)*
Ahead	11.1	8.7	8.6
Behind	78.2	82.5	83.3
Broke even	10.8	8.7	8.1
Total	100.0	100.0	100.0
	(660)	(343)	(1,648)

	Last time person played lottery (in percent)		
Amount behind	*Past week*	*Past month*	*Past year*
Under $100	47.5	80.4	73.2
$100 to 500	39.7	18.8	21.6
$501 to 1,000	7.6	0.4	3.1
$1,101 to 5,000	4.6	0.4	1.9
$5,001 to 10,000	0.2	0.0	0.1
$10,001 to 50,000	0.4	0.0	0.2
Total	100.0	100.0	100.0
	(474)	(250)	(1,294)

Source: GIBS, 1997–1999.

When we crosstabulate between frequent players and other socio-demographic variables, it becomes apparent that certain groups are more likely to play than others (see Table 6.8). Nearly a 20-point gap separates blacks (58.2 percent) from whites (42.1 percent) and Latinas/os (40.0 percent), as blacks are more likely to be frequent players compared to their peers. In terms of household income, those in higher-income brackets are less likely to play compared to their lower-income peers. About 69.7 percent of those earning less than $10,000 are frequent lottery players, for example, compared to 42.5 percent of those earning more than $100,000. Consistent with this trend is that higher education attainment levels correspond to lower reported rates of being a frequent lottery player. Only 36.9 percent of those with a graduate or professional degree report frequent play, whereas 64.0 percent of those who did not complete high school are frequent players. Building a profile of who frequently plays helps to answer who ultimately pays when state governments opt to finance public services in this way. Our analysis lends evidence as to who carries this tax burden: black, low-income, and less educated communities.

Table 6.8 Outcomes of frequent lottery play, by race and socioeconomic status

	Played last week		Total (%)	N
	Yes (%)	No (%)		
Race/ethnicity				
White	42.1	57.9	100.0	(1,098)
Black	58.2	41.8	100.0	(201)
Latina/o	40.0	60.0	100.0	(110)
Household income				
Less than $10k	69.7	30.3	100.0	(76)
$10k–24k	57.2	42.8	100.0	(166)
$25k–49k	44.8	55.2	100.0	(366)
$50–99k	43.6	56.4		(383)
$100k or more	42.5	57.5	100.0	(113)
Education attainment				
1st–11th grade	64.0	36.0	100.0	(172)
12th grade	50.6	49.4	100.0	(451)
Some college/tech. school	38.9	61.1	100.0	(491)
4 years of college	33.8	66.2	100.0	(234)
Grad./prof. school	36.9	63.1	100.0	(157)

Source: GIBS 1997–1999.

Concluding thoughts on lotteries as a vehicle for public finance

Budgets provide a window for seeing how states preserve inequitable distributions of capital. They document how resources are circulated and detail answers as to who benefits, prospers, and ultimately pays. Neoliberal-induced transformations in the political economy have severely tested tax systems, leaving many states to devise new means of generating revenue to pay for public services. Given this context, it is no mystery why most if not all states in the union adopted lotteries. They are politically feasible forms of discrete taxation that eschew mandatory tax imposition, all the while generating millions and billions for state treasuries. What remains less understood and understudied, however, is the obscured role of lotteries in the changing composition of American taxation and the social consequences that arise from paying for public services in this way.

In true anti-Robin Hood style, lotteries offer a vehicle for institutionally swindling marginal groups while enriching everyone else. They have partially substituted for other forms of taxation that represent dwindling portions of state budgets, like corporate and property taxes that are inherently more progressive. The regressive nature of lotteries means they generate money from those who occupy marginalized positions of race, income, and education attainment. This money is then distributed to finance public services available to mostly everyone. Altogether, it represents a neoliberal infrastructural redesign that frees elite interests of fiscal responsibility for public finance, all the while displacing the tax burden of public services, ones that help make capital accumulation possible, onto those who play the lottery the most. It is, in many ways, a process in which "the house wins."

Notes

1 While scholars like Harvey (2005) attribute the neoliberal turn to powerful business interests who organized concerted efforts to reduce state intervention in the market, others like Prasad (2012) contend that these policies came in response to public hostility toward "big government."
2 See Chapter 3 of Clotfelter and Cook (1989) for a detailed discussion regarding the historical roots of lotteries in America.
3 According to such a view, lotteries contribute little to state treasuries because administrative costs subsume leftover profits, there are yearly fluctuations in sales, and earmarked returns pale in comparison to other tax revenues.
4 Given lottery winnings (but not losses) are considered "income," federal, state, and local levels of government subject many jackpots, especially larger ones, to taxation. This frequently reduces net income from lottery winnings to about half the original amount (Nibert, 2000). In light of these indirect taxes, the estimate that lotteries transfer a third of their gross revenues to state treasuries is highly conservative.
5 One exception includes Clotfelter and Cook's (1989) *Selling Hope*, which is perhaps the gold standard of lottery studies. It was the first of its kind, and at the time of publication it was a fairly exhaustive analysis of American state lotteries. That said, its analysis is now out of date as most data analyzed were collected between the mid-1970s and 1980s. Since then the number of state lotteries has nearly doubled, and the historical, social, economic, and political contexts have changed considerably.
6 For those interested in learning of where these data were derived, please email the primary author for a detailed listing of the original sources. The information is omitted here due to space constraints.
7 The fiscal year for most states, including the District of Columbia, ends on June 30. New York (March 31), Texas (August 31), and Michigan (September 30) are the only exceptions.
8 For an in-depth summary of the research design, see *2011 State Government Finances Methodology*, available at http://www2.census.gov/govs/state/11_methodology.pdf.
9 The legal age to purchase lottery tickets in the majority of states and the District of Columbia is 18 years. In Arizona, Iowa, and Louisiana the minimum age is 21, and in Nebraska it is 19.
10 Much of the literature privileges the term "Hispanic" over "Latina/o" or treats the terms as interchangeable. Throughout the chapter, we employ the term "Latina/o" as an alternative to "Hispanic"

for political reasons. The latter pan-ethnic label is intricately intertwined with historical European oppression because it refers to those who are of Spanish origin but is broadly imposed onto anyone of Latin American ancestry (Sáenz and Murga, 2011). Thus, the term is a symbolic imposition directly rooted in conquest and colonization.

11 For a much more in-depth summary of the study's research design, see the formal report (National Gambling Impact Study Commission, [2002] 2007).

References

Barlett, D.L. and Steele, J.B. (1994). *America: Who really pays the taxes?* New York: Simon and Schuster.

Bonilla-Silva, E., Forman, T.A., Lewis, A.E., and Embrick, D.G. (2003). "It wasn't me!" How will race and racism work in 21st century America? *Political Sociology for the 21st Century*, 12, 111–134.

Borg, M.O. and Mason, P.M. (1988). The budgetary incidence of a lottery to support education. *The National Tax Journal*, 41(1), 75–86.

Borg, M.O. and Mason, P.M. (1990). Earmarked lottery revenues: Positive windfalls or concealed redistribution mechanisms? *Journal of Education Finance*, 15(3), 289–301.

Borg, M.O., Mason, P.M., and Shapiro, S.L. (1991). *The economic consequences of state lotteries*. New York: Praeger.

Brinner, R.E. and Clotfelter, C.T. (1975). An economic appraisal of state lotteries. *National Tax Journal*, 28(4), 395–404.

Brown, D.J., Kaldenberg, D.O., and Browne, B.A. (1992). Socioeconomic status and playing the lotteries. *Sociology and Social Research*, 76, 161–167.

Clotfelter, C.T. and Cook, P.J. (1989). *Selling hope: State lotteries in America*. Cambridge, Massachusetts: Harvard University Press.

Cook, P.J. and Clotfelter, C.T. (1993). The peculiar scale economics of lotto. *American Economic Review*, 83(3), 634–643.

District of Columbia Lottery. (2011). *Fiscal year 2011 annual report*. Retrieved January 1, 2013, from http://dclottery.com/2011-annual-report/index.html.

Fischer, C.S. and Hout, M. (2006). *Century of difference: How America changed in the last one hundred years*. New York: Russell Sage.

Gambling Impact and Behavior Study, 1997–1999. (1999). *Codebook for the Gambling Impact and Behavior Study—Adult Surveys*. Ann Arbor, Michigan: Inter-University Consortium for Political and Social Research.

Hansen, A. (1995). The tax incidence of the Colorado state Instant Lottery Game. *Public Finance Quarterly*, 23(3), 385–398.

Hansen, A., Miyazaki, A.D., and Sprott, D.E. (2000). The tax incidence of lotteries: Evidence from five states. *The Journal of Consumer Affairs*, 34(2), 182–203.

Harvey, D. (2005). *A brief history of neoliberalism*. New York: Oxford University Press.

Henricks, K. (2014). Who plays? Who pays? Education finance policy that supplants tax burdens along lines of race and class. *Race Ethnicity and Education*, 1, 1–26 (doi:10.1080/13613324.2013.868343).

Lo, C.Y.H. (1990). *Small property versus big government: Social origins of the property tax revolt*. Berkeley: University of California Press.

Ludwig, J. (1999). Charge that gambling industry preys on the poor not borne out in Gallup Survey: High-income and high-education Americans play heavily. *Gallup Inc.* Retrieved November 18, 2009, from http://www.gallup.com/poll/3733/Charge-Gambling-Industry-Preys-Poor-Borne-Gallup-Survey.aspx.

Martin, I.W. (2008). *The permanent tax revolt: How the property tax transformed American politics*. Stanford, California: Stanford University Press.

Martin, I.W., Mehrotra, A.K., and Prasad, M. (eds). (2009). *The new fiscal sociology: Taxation in comparative and historical perspective*. Cambridge, England: Cambridge University Press.

McCrary, J.L. and Pavlak, T.J. (2002). *Who plays the Georgia Lottery? Results of a statewide survey*. Athens, Georgia: University of Georgia, Carl Vinson Institute of Government.

Mikesell, J.L. (1989). A note on the changing incidence of state lottery finance. *Social Science Quarterly*, 70(2), 513–521.

Mikesell, J.L. and Zorn, K.C. (1986). State lotteries as fiscal savior or fiscal fraud: A look at the evidence. *Public Administration Review*, 46(4), 311–320.

Mikesell, J.L. and Zorn, K.C. (1988). State lotteries for public revenue. *Public Budgeting and Finance*, 8(1), 38–47.

Miller, D.E. and Pierce, P.A. (1997). Lotteries for education: Windfall or hoax? *State and Local Government Review*, 29(1), 34–42.

Miyazaki, A.D., Hansen, A., and Sprott, D.E. (1998). A longitudinal analysis of income-based tax regressivity of state-sponsored lotteries. *Journal of Public Policy and Marketing*, 17(2), 161–172.

National Gambling Impact Study Commission. [2002] (2007). Gambling Impact and Behavioral Study, 1997-1999. Nibert, D. (2000). *Hitting the lottery jackpot: Government and the taxing of dreams*. New York: Monthly Review.

Office of Management and Budget. (2010). *Budget of the U.S. government: Fiscal year 2011*. Washington DC: U.S. Government Printing Office.

Oster, E. (2004). Are all lotteries regressive? Evidence from the Powerball. *National Tax Journal*, 57(2), 179–187.

Pantuosco, L., Seyfried, W., and Stonebreaker, R. (2007). The impact of lotteries on state education expenditures: Does earmarking matter? *The Review of Regional Studies*, 37(2), 169–185.

Peppard, Jr., D.M. (1987). Government as bookie: Explaining the rise of lotteries for revenue. *Review of Radical Political Economics*, 19(3), 56–68.

Peterson, G.E. (1982). The state and local sectors. Pp. 157–217 in *The Reagan experiment*, edited by Palmer, J.L. and Sawhill, I.V. Washington DC: The Urban Institute.

Pirog-Good, M. and Mikesell, J.L. (1995). Longitudinal evidence of the changing socio-economic profile of a state lottery market. *Policy Studies Journal*, 23(3), 451–465.

Piven, F.F. and Cloward, R.A. (1982). *The new class war*. New York: Pantheon Books.

Prasad, M. (2006). *The politics of free markets: The rise of neoliberal economic policies in Britain, France, Germany, and the United States*. Chicago: University of Chicago Press.

Prasad, M. (2012). The popular origins of neoliberalism in the Reagan tax cut of 1981. *Journal of Policy History*, 24(3), 351–383.

Price, D.I. and Novak, E.S. (1999). The tax incidence of the three Texas lottery games: Regressivity, race, and education. *National Tax Journal*, 52(4), 741–751.

Sáenz, R. and Murga, A.L. (2011). *Latino issues: A reference handbook*. San Diego, California: ABC-CLIO.

Sassen, S. (1998). *Globalization and its discontents: Essays on the new mobility of people and money*. New York: The Free Press.

Sears, D.O. and Citrin, J. (1982). *Tax revolt: Something for nothing in California*. Cambridge, Massachusetts: Harvard University Press.

Stranahan, H.A. and Borg, M.O. (1998). Separating the decisions of lottery expenditures and participation: A truncated Tobit approach. *Public Finance Review*, 26(2), 99–117.

Stranahan, H.A. and Borg, M.O. (2004). Some futures are brighter than others: The net benefits received by Florida Bright Futures Scholarship recipients. *Public Finance Review*, 32(1), 105–126.

U.S. Census Bureau. (2011). *State government finances: 2011 annual survey of state government finances*. Retrieved January 2, 2013, from http://www.census.gov/govs/state/.

Wilson, W.J. (1996). *When work disappears: The world of the new urban poor*. New York: Alfred A. Knopf.

7

PREDATORY FINANCIAL SERVICES

The high cost of being poor in America

Howard Karger

The global financial crisis and the meltdown of the subprime lending sector have left greater numbers of the poor without mainstream credit and hence more vulnerable to the predations of a wide range of fringe economic services, including pawnshops, payday lenders, dodgy used car lots, and check-cashers, to name a few. The predatory lending industry has grown due to a lack of regulation, the free movement of capital across political borders, and the internationalization of the industry. The limitation of this chapter only permits an examination of a few large sectors of the fringe economy.

Unbanked individuals and families who have no relationship with a mainstream financial institution make up much of the clientele of fringe economic services. According to the Federal Deposit Insurance Corporation (FDIC), 8.2 percent of U.S. households (10.2 million) are totally unbanked, while 20 percent (24 million) are underbanked. Almost one-third of U.S. households do not have a savings account. One-quarter of all households used at least one fringe economy service in 2011, while almost 10 percent used two or more (FDIC, 2012).

The unbanked may forego a checking or savings account for several reasons, including not writing enough checks to warrant one, having insufficient month-to-month savings to justify an account, they cannot afford bank fees nor maintain a high enough minimum bank balance, they desire to keep their financial records private, and/or they experience discomfort when dealing with banks (Booz-Allen and Shugoll Research, 1997; Caskey, 1997; Karger, 2005). Others may have had their bank accounts involuntarily closed due to too many overdrawn checks or other credit problems.

Credit and the poor

Credit is the cornerstone of the modern economy, and it functions as a cushion for emergencies or for purchasing goods and services that a consumer does not want to defer. It is the bridge between real household earnings and consumption decisions, offering relief during periods of economic distress and uncertainty (Manning, 2000). Credit card payment options are flexible for those with a good credit score, and collateral is not required for a purchase or cash advance. As such, the middle class can borrow cash or purchase goods without parting with any of their possessions. The repayment of the loan is secured by the borrower's fiscal probity and their desire to maintain good credit.

Historically, the credit needs of the poor were partly met by loan sharks who were often backed by organized crime. Interest rates were high and the failure to repay frequently resulted in physical injury or even death. Taking their cues from the illegal street economy, American entrepreneurs soon realized that money could be made by providing legal financial services to those outside the economic mainstream. In some cases, the same mainstream banks that denied credit to the poor financed fringe lenders or owned subsidiaries that lent money to low-income individuals and families (DiStefano, 2002; Hudson, 1996; Mortgage Bankers Association of America, 2001).

Legal "quick cash" loans targeted at the poor serve a similar purpose as credit card advances for the middle class. Namely, they provide cash for an emergency or when income is insufficient to make ends meet. These loans are not designed as a long-term financial solution. Quick cash loans can be divided into two categories: non-secured or promissory loans and secured collateral-based loans. In an unsecured loan, the borrower promises to repay the lender and no collateral is required. Interest rates and fees tend to be extremely high for all quick cash loans, and cash advances on credit cards can accrue an annual percentage rate (APR) of 21 percent or more. In secured loans, the borrower provides collateral (either property or guaranteed future income) that is worth as much or more than the loan. While the middle class can generally access non-secured loans, they are often denied to the poor or those with bad credit.

Pawnshops

Pawnshops provide collateral-based loans and do well in economic downturns. In 2011 the 11,000 pawnshops across the United States generated $14.5 billion in revenues; in 2009 the pawn industry served 35 million customers who borrowed an average loan amount of $100 (PRWEB, 2012).

Pawnshop loans are relatively simple transactions. A pawnbroker makes a fixed-term (usually for 30 days) loan to a customer who leaves behind collateral as a guarantee. The customer receives a pawn ticket that includes a description of the item, the amount lent, the maturity date, and how much will be needed to reclaim the property. If the loan is not repaid by the agreed-upon date the collateral becomes the property of the pawnbroker and the customer's debt is extinguished. The pawnshop will often allow the loan to be renewed once the interest is paid. The industry claims an 80 percent retrieval rate for customer collateral (National Pawnbrokers Association, 2009).

Pawnshops are typically regulated by state and sometimes local ordinances, and interest rates can range from 1.5 percent to 25 percent a month, depending on the state. For instance, North Carolina pawnshops charge 2 percent a month for interest and an additional 20 percent in fees (a 264 percent APR).

Like all fringe economy transactions there is a catch. Appraisals for jewelry, guns, gold, and appliances are typically extremely low since they are based on wholesale prices. On average, pawnshops lend only a small percent of the value of an item. Some pawnshops have a maximum loan limit regardless of an item's value. For instance, a pawnshop may only lend $500 or $1,000 for an item that is worth $2,000. Interest rates are also high. Houston pawnshops charge $75 for the first month on a $500 loan. At the end of the first 30 days it will cost $575 to redeem the item; after 60 days it will cost $650; and at the end of a 90-day period it would be $725 or 45 percent of the item's value. Some borrowers will renew their loans for a year or more (Karger, 2005). While some states cap interest rates, loopholes can allow "lease back" agreements to add fees, sometimes effectively doubling the cost (Karger, 2005).

The big three publicly traded pawnshop chains, Cash America (2011 revenues of $1.54 billion), EZCorp (2011 revenues of $869 million), and First Cash Financial (2011 revenues of $521 million), control 20 percent of the pawnshop market. They do not operate in states, such as New York and New Jersey, where monthly interest rates on pawn loans are capped at 10 percent or less (PRWEB, 2012). One characteristic of neoliberalism is open trading borders, and U.S.-based corporations like Cash America and EZ Corp operate in Germany, while First Cash Financial Services has offices in Mexico, Germany, and the United Kingdom.

Although costly to borrowers, pawnshop transactions are relatively safe since in the event of loan forfeiture the collateral simply passes to the pawnshop owner and the debt is cancelled. On the other hand, payday loans are riskier since they can easily lead to a spiraling debt trap.

Payday loans

In 2010 the traditional payday loan industry claimed $40 billion in revenues by serving 19 million customers in 20,000 storefronts. The average payday loan in 2011 was $400 (Community Financial Services Association of America, n.d.; Dougherty, 2012). Payday lending is an important and robust segment of the fringe economy due to the growth in consumers with poor credit and the refusal of mainstream financial institutions to provide small consumer loans. While growth in the bricks and mortar payday lending industry has stabilized, the more expensive offshore and unregulated Internet lending sector is growing rapidly and is expected to claim 60 percent of the payday market by 2016 (Sandman, 2012).

To qualify for a payday loan, customers must have a bank account from which the loan and fees can be withdrawn. Many payday lenders consider governmental benefits as income and extend loans to those on public assistance, recipients of child support or alimony, and Social Security beneficiaries (Fox and Mierzwinski, 2001). Credit checks are normally not required.

Interest rates on a two-week payday loan can range from 391 percent to 521 percent. In a typical 14-day $300 payday loan, a customer might pay $45 in fees and interest and receive $255 in cash. After 14 days the borrower can let the lender deposit the $300 check or renew (or roll over) the loan by taking out another one. In this transaction, the borrower gets no "new" money and pays another $45 in fees to cover their overdue loan. This triggers a spiral of debt whereby borrowers are forced to initiate new loans to cover the pre-existing ones. Unlike pawnshops where collateral is simply forfeited, a payday loan default can result in aggressive collection agency actions, including contacting employers and adding extra recovery fees to the loan. In some states, the lender can prosecute the borrower for writing a "hot check" (Karger, 2005).

The lucrativeness of payday lending has captured the interest of some commercial banks struggling with profitability in the wake of the global financial crisis. Wells Fargo, Bank of America, U.S. Bank, J.P. Morgan Bank, and National City (PNC Financial Services Group) not only lend money to large payday loan corporations, but some are also making short-term payday loans to their checking account customers based on a deposit paycheck. The loan is repaid once the paycheck is directly deposited into the borrower's account. The fees and interest on short-term bank payday loans rival those of the storefront payday sector, and like their industry counterparts, bank payday loans force some customers into a destructive cycle of borrowing to repay existing loans. The Center for Responsible Lending (2011) found that average bank payday borrowers were indebted for 175 days a year and 44 percent of their next paycheck went toward repaying the loan, forcing them into a new loan to make it to their next payday.

Cars and the fringe economy: car title loans and high-cost services

Car title lenders operate similarly to pawnshops. Instead of using a television or stereo as collateral, a customer uses their vehicle title. In most cases, that substantially increases the loan amount since vehicles have more value than many other pawned goods. Unlike a pawnshop transaction, the customer can continue to use their collateral during the course of the loan, although it is now technically owned by the lender until the loan is repaid. Signing over a vehicle for a risky high-interest loan has serious consequences since in many places the use of a car is critical for getting to work, picking up children, shopping, and medical visits. For many low-income workers a vehicle loss may translate into a loss of employment, especially if the vehicle is used for transportation to their place of employment.

Car title pawns are relatively simple transactions. The borrower provides the lender with a free and clear vehicle title and an extra set of keys. In return, the borrower signs over the title or agrees to a lien on the car. Vehicles are generally appraised at the lowest possible value, which is the wholesale price in a poor condition. According to the Center for Responsible Lending (2010), the largest car title lenders loan on average about 25 percent of the vehicle's retail value. There is no credit check and only minimum employment verification.

Vehicle title loans are usually for 30 days and often involve an APR of around 300 percent. In addition to high interest rates, these loans can include processing and document fees, late fees, origination fees, mandatory comprehensive insurance, and a costly roadside assistance policy. All told, these fees can add from $80 to $115 on a $500 loan (Neiger, 2008). Borrowers may be able to extend or roll over loans for an additional 30 days or more. In that instance, the customer pays only the interest until a certain date, after which they have to repay the principal. For example, a borrower may owe $250 in interest charges and fees on a 30-day $1,000 car title loan. If the loan is extended for an additional month, the costs will rise to $500 or almost half the loan amount. By the fifth month the interest payments will exceed the loan amount.

Title lenders may repossess a vehicle if just one payment is missed. Moreover, depending upon the state, borrowers whose vehicles are repossessed will not receive any proceeds from the resale, even if the vehicle sells for more than the loan amount. Since car title loans are oversecured, it is sometimes more lucrative for lenders if the borrower actually defaults.

What makes car loans so risky is that they are based on the value of the collateral rather than on the ability of the borrower to repay the loan. Writing in the *Baltimore Sun*, Eileen Ambrose (2011) observes: "Car-title loans, which allow you to borrow against the value of your vehicle, are such bad deals that more than half of the states, including Maryland, basically don't allow them" (p. B8).

Low-income borrowers or those with bad credit face other vehicle-related minefields, including Buy-Here, Pay-Here (BHPH) used car lots that finance their own over-priced cars and fold high interest rates into weekly or monthly payments. Since dealers self-finance they can set prices unrelated to any real Blue Book value. Not surprisingly, BHPH cars are often high-mileage clunkers bought cheaply at car auctions (Karger, 2005). The draw for borrowers is the absence of a credit check.

The transaction is straightforward. A customer puts down a cash deposit toward a used car and agrees to make a weekly, bi-weekly, or monthly payment for two to four years. If even one payment is missed, the car is promptly repossessed, sold to another customer, and the buyer forfeits their deposit and the previous payments.

BHPH used car lots are big business. There are approximately 33,000 BHPH lots nationally (compared to 20,000 that sell new cars) and each year dealers make $80 billion in loans. In 2010 BHPH lots sold nearly 2.4 million cars, almost double the number in 2000. Although one in four customers will default on their loan, profit margins remain high (nearly 40 percent) partly due to "churning" (reselling cars again and again after a repossession). By 2011 BHPH used car loans accounted for more than one-fifth of all used car loans (Bensinger, 2011).

Tax refund anticipation loans (RALs and RACs)

RALs are expensive (from a 50 percent to 500 percent effective APR) short-term loans secured by an expected tax refund. The loans are repaid within two weeks after a tax refund deposit made by the IRS. On average, the fees for a $1,500 RAL in 2009 was $61.22 (149 percent APR). Nearly 7.2 million people received RALs in 2009, 87 percent of whom were low income. Almost two-thirds (64 percent) of RAL borrowers are working poor families that receive the Earned Income Tax Credit (EITC) refunds (the largest federal anti-poverty program) which are distributed through the tax system. RALs drained about $900 million in loan fees from 8.67 million taxpayers in 2007 (Center for Responsible Lending, 2012; Fox, 2009). These loans are risky, since if the tax refund or credits are denied or reduced, the borrower owes the loan balance and may face late fees, debt collection harassment, and a damaged credit history.

Many low-income families use commercial tax preparers and RALs for several reasons: tax preparers are ubiquitous in low-income neighborhoods; the tax code (especially EITC and Child Tax Credit regulations) is complex and not easily understood; the receipt of fast cash is alluring; the scarcity of free tax assistance drives the poor into neighborhood tax preparers; and the poor often lack the cash to pay commercial tax preparers (all fees are automatically deducted from the available refund). The high cost of tax preparation and RAL services hurt the poor and diminish the impact of the EITC (Karger, 2005).

Although RALs still exist in some venues, most major banks have now shied away from them. Instead, tax preparers are opening up accounts for customers into which their tax refunds are deposited. The rub is the high fees they charge to set up those accounts.

Check-cashing and other services

There are limited choices for the unbanked in terms of cashing employment or other checks. Many banks will not cash checks for non-customers, even if the check is drawn from that bank. Low-income people living from hand-to-mouth often cannot wait the eight days or so it takes for a check to clear the commercial banking system. Some of the unbanked—or those who cannot wait for the cash—will often turn to check-cashers. Many larger check-cashing outlets, such as Ace Cash Express (1,700 locations), are one-stop financial service centers that provide check-cashing, payday loans, installment loans, car title loans, prepaid debit cards, auto insurance, bill payments, money transfers, and RALs (Ace Cash Express, 2012).

The cost of cashing a check ranges from around 2 to 6 percent of the face value, depending upon the check. Even at the lower end of the cost spectrum, a consumer would pay $360 a year to cash 12 paychecks, considerably more than the service costs of maintaining a bank account. One study found that it cost $396 a year for a family of four with a $24,000 annual income to buy six money orders a month and cash paychecks or government checks at a 1.5 percent fee (Caskey, 1997).

Check-cashing and financial services are so profitable that large corporations like Walmart have entered the field. Walmart stores charge $3.00 to cash a $1,000 check and $6.00 to cash one up to $5,000 (the maximum amount they will cash) (Walmart Check Cashing, 2012).

Check-cashers have added a new business strategy in the form of prepaid debit cards. Prepaid debit cards are largely targeted at the unbanked or those who cannot get a credit card because of poor credit. Check-cashers like Walmart and Ace Cash Express try to convince customers to put the cash they receive onto a prepaid debit card. While this may sound like a good idea, the customer must be wary in all fringe economy transactions. For instance, ACE Cash Express's (2012) pay-as-you-go debit card has no monthly fee but costs $1.00 for each signature transaction, $2.00 for each pin purchase transaction, $2.50 for each ATM cash withdrawal (excluding any charges by the ATM owner), and 50 cent ATM balance inquiry fee. Their monthly plan costs $9.95 a month plus $2.50 for each cash withdrawal. Even with the monthly plan, consumers would pay $119.00 a year for the debit card plus another $60.00 a year if they had only two ATM withdrawals a month. This would increase the cost to $174.40 a year, or several times more than most annual fees for a credit card. Walmart prepaid debit cards include a $3.00 monthly maintenance fee plus a $3.00 reload fee (Walmart Check Cashing, 2012).

Conclusion

The fringe economy is a shadow economy that closely mirrors mainstream economic services, albeit at an outrageous cost. It is allowed to exist in a largely unregulated form because it fits within the neoliberal ideology of a free, open, and competitive marketplace. This market framework is based on the assumption that increased competition will eventually drive down the costs of payday loans and other fringe economy services. Moreover, neoliberalism assumes a priori that virtually any regulatory activity is detrimental to a healthy marketplace.

Because of space limitations, this chapter was not able to examine other fringe economy services, such as rent-to-own stores, prepaid telecommunication services, and for-profit debt counseling agencies. There are no simple answers to predatory lending practices. The fringe economy exists because it addresses a real need. If it were outlawed, the poor would be forced to return to illegal loan sharks and risk serious injury if they were unable to repay their debt.

In effect, the fringe economy fills the void left by mainstream banks that have written off the poor as a non-profitable market sector. The mainstream banking sector must come to realize what fringe businesses already know: Low-income communities can be a profitable market. Moreover, mainstream banks could learn from fringe lenders' expertise in marketing, packaging, and bundling vital economic services in one-stop shopping. Banks could offer similar one-stop financial services for low-income customers. At the same time, larger financial institutions can employ economies of scale to help reduce the costs of financial services for low-income households. Mainstream banks that enter this market may also reap the rewards of fostering new, full-service customers as the incomes of those consumers increase (Caskey, 2002).

Banks can develop innovative programs to help low-income households build savings and improve their credit profiles, lower their cost of financial services, and gain access to lower-cost credit. Caskey (2002) suggests that banks can open special, conveniently located branch offices or outlets targeted at low-income households. In addition to traditional banking products, the outlets could offer services such as low fee-based check-cashing, basic low-cost savings accounts that include access to money orders, deposit accounts designed to encourage savings, deposit-secured loans to those whose credit histories would make them ineligible for mainstream credit, and budget-management and credit-repair seminars.

Regardless of whether the poor use check-cashers or banks, they are further impoverished by paying more than the middle class for financial services in both absolute dollars and relative to their income. These costs are exacerbated by the neoliberal opposition to regulations, leading to the bifurcation of financial services whereby there is one financial system for the poor and another for the non-poor. This bifurcation also leads to greater inequality: banks for the middle class and check-cashers for the poor; access to savings for the middle class and barriers to savings for the poor; and low-cost financial services for the middle class and high fee-based services for the poor. The regulation of the fringe economy is an economic justice issue that should be a central focus of any progressive agenda.

References

Ace Cash Express (2012). Ace Cash Express. Retrieved October 2012 from https://www.acecashexpress.com/.

Ambrose, E. (2011). Marylanders can't go to Virginia to take out high-cost car-title loans, but Virginia lawmakers may change that. *The Baltimore Sun*, February 6, p. B8.

Bensinger, K. (2011). A vicious cycle in the used-car business. *Los Angeles Times*, October 30, p. A9.

Booz-Allen and Hamilton Shugoll Research (1997). *Mandatory EFT demographic study: A report prepared for the U.S. Department of Treasury*, September 15. Washington, DC: U.S. Department of the Treasury.

Caskey, J. (1997). *Lower income American, higher cost financial services*. Madison, WI: Filene Research Institute.

Caskey, J. (2002). Bringing unbanked households into the banking system. *Capitol Xchange*, The Brookings Institution, January. Retrieved August 15, 2014, from http://www.cfsinnovation.com/sites/default/files/imported/managed_documents/caskey_jan2002.pdf.

Center for Responsible Lending (2010). Title loan: Don't risk losing your car. Retrieved December 2012 from http://www.responsiblelending.org/other-consumer-loans/car-title-loans/.

Center for Responsible Lending (2011). Big bank payday loans, high-interest loans through checking accounts keep customers in long-term debt, July 21. Retrieved November 2012 from http://www.responsiblelending.org/payday-lending/research-analysis/big-bank-payday-loans.html.

Center for Responsible Lending (2012). Rapid refunds: Instant trouble. Retrieved December 2012 from http://www.responsiblelending.org/other-consumer-loans/refund-anticipation-loans/tools-resources/fast-facts.html.

Community Financial Services Association of America (CFSAA) (n.d.). About the payday advance industry. Retrieved August 15, 2014, from http://cfsaa.com/about-the-payday-advance-industry/myth-vs-reality.aspx.

DiStefano, J.N. (2002). Bank to refund fees in "predatory-lending" cases. *The Philadelphia Inquirer*, April 26, p. A6.

Dougherty, C. (2012). Consumer Bureau focuses on payday lending. *Bloomberg News*, January 20. Retrieved November 2012 from http://www.bloomberg.com/news/2012-01-19/payday-lending-is-focus-of-consumer-bureau-alabama-field-hearing.html.

FDIC (2012). 2011 FDIC national survey of unbanked and underbanked households, September 1, 2012. Retrieved December 2012 from http://www.fdic.gov/householdsurvey.

Fox, J. (2009). Research findings illustrate the high risk of high-cost short-term loans for consumers. *Consumer Federation of America*, February 18. Retrieved August 2012 from http://www.paydayloaninfo.org/facts#8.

Fox, J. and Mierzwinski, E. (2001). *Rent-a-bank payday lending: How banks help payday lenders evade state consumer protections*. Consumer Federation of America and the U.S. Public Interest Research Group, November. Washington, DC: Consumer Federation of America.

Hudson, M. (ed.) (1996). *Merchants of misery*. Monroe, ME: Common Courage Press.

Karger, H. (2005). *Shortchanged: Life and debt in the fringe economy*. San Francisco, CA: Berrett-Koehler.

Manning, R.D. (2000). *Credit card nation*. New York: Basic Books.

Mortgage Bankers Association of America (2001). FTC charges one of nation's largest subprime lenders with abusive lending practices: Associates First Capital Corporation and its successors Citigroup Inc. and CitiFinancial Credit Company named in complaint, March 7. Retrieved August 15, 2014, from http://www.ftc.gov/news-events/press-releases/2001/03/ftc-charges-one-nations-largest-subprime-lenders-abusive-lending.

National Pawnbrokers Association (2009). The real story about the pawn industry, May 18. Retrieved August 15, 2014, from https://www.facebook.com/permalink.php?id=268396053187498&story_fbid=614795381880895.

Neiger, C. (2008). Why car title loans are a bad idea. *CNN News*, October 8. Retrieved August 15, 2014, from http://articles.cnn.com/2008-10-08/living/aa.car.title.loans_1_car-title-loan-interest-rates-responsible-lending-for-title-loans?_s=PM:LIVING.

PRWEB (2012). U.S. pawn shops industry sails through the recession: Gold prices, cash hungry consumers fuel demand, says market data. Tampa, FL, May 22. Retrieved December 2012 from http://www.prweb.com/releases/2012/5/prweb9529413.htm.

Sandman, J. (2012). Is the payday loan business on the ropes? *Reuters*, September 21. Retrieved November 2012 from http://blogs.reuters.com/great-debate/2012/09/21/is-the-payday-loan-business-on-the-ropes/.

Walmart Check Cashing (2012). Retrieved December 2012 from http://www.walmart.com/cp/Check-Cashing/632047.

8

CONSUMER CREDITS AS A QUASI-WELFARE SYSTEM FOR FAILED NEOLIBERALS' TRICKLE-DOWN POLICIES BETWEEN THE 1980s AND 2000s

Intae Yoon

The recent Great Recession and its recovery process shed light on income inequality and economic injustice built into American public policies. The progenitors of these policies were neoliberal scholars, including Milton Friedman and his colleagues in the Chicago School of Economics. Neoliberal economists supported the trickle-down effects and supply-side economics. Their major doctrines include a free market, flexible labor market, financial deregulations, and easy domestic and international capital flow through financial deregulations (Chang, 2010). These academic discourses became translated into public policies in the late 1970s and were fully adopted in the early 1980s with the election of Ronald Reagan as the 40th president of the United States.

In his inaugural speech, Reagan proclaimed that "government is not the solution to our problem; government is the problem," and that the growth of government should be reversed (1981, pp. 1–2). To cure the economic ills of the time, such as high inflation and unemployment rates, "removing the roadblocks that have slowed our economy and reduced productivity" was delineated as one of the top priorities during his presidency. It did not take long for him to remove the roadblocks by implementing deregulations through public policies and his executive powers. Even after his presidency, the neoliberals' agendas were promoted as the president's legacy and have continued to this date.

The primary goal of this writing is to establish connections between those policies and the expansion of consumer credits as a quasi-welfare system in the United States. As there are wide ranges of deregulation policies, financial deregulations are the focus of the connection. It is equally as important in this chapter to suggest a solution to the social injustice contributed to by the neoliberal public policies.

Deregulating boundaries among financial institutions

The recent epoch in financial deregulation happened in 1999 with the enactment of the Financial Services Modernization Act, commonly known as the Gramm-Leach-Bliley Act (GLBA). The Act removed barriers between commercial banking, securities, and insurance companies. As it allowed those companies to consolidate and engage in riskier financial transactions, the Act is criticized as one of the main contributors to the recent financial meltdown and the subsequent Great Recession (Bunch, 2009; Kleinknecht, 2009). As its formal name implies,

GLBA was introduced to modernize financial markets in the United States by repealing the Glass-Steagall Act of 1933 (GSA), which set restrictions on the affiliations among commercial banks, savings and loan associations (known as thrifts), and securities firms.

The enactment of GLBA did not happen in a day. Rather, it was the result of two decades of tenacious efforts of neoliberals to deregulate the financial markets through intentionally ignoring GSA or the administrative or judicial interpretations of GSA (Carpenter and Murphy, 2010). For example, with the belief in the trickle-down effect, President Reagan appointed Donald Regan as the Secretary of the Treasury in 1981. The new Secretary had been a chairperson of the investment company Merrill Lynch. Serving in that position in 1977, he made a concession for customers to have quasi-checking accounts so that they could write a check against their investment portfolio (Kleinknecht, 2009). This allowance violated the GSA, as the Act prohibited security firms' banking activities and vice versa. When commercial banks took the case to federal regulatory agencies, President Reagan and his appointed regulators interpreted that such a business activity seemed not to violate GSA and supported Merrill Lynch.

Again in 1986, the Federal Reserve Board, which was mostly operated by Reagan's appointees, interpreted the GSA from deregulatory perspectives, and commercial banks were allowed to step into securities transactions, as long as the transactions did not account for 5% or more of each bank's gross revenues. The 5% ceiling continued to rise until it reached 25% in 1996. Thus, even before the 1999 official repeal of the GSA, neoliberal policy makers and administrators deregulated financial markets without approval by the U.S. Congress (Kleinknecht, 2009).

Financial deregulations also happened in a form of enactments of statute during the same period. In 1982, the Garn-St. Germain Depository Institutions Act freed saving and loan institutions (known as thrifts) to expand their identity from mortgage lenders to investment institutions (Federal Deposit Insurance Corporation, n.d.). Thus, traditional mortgage industries began to engage in more profitable, yet risky, investment business. The Act also removed the minimum 400-shareholder requirement for a saving and loan institution. Therefore, a single individual could be the owner of the institution and engage in risky investments at his or her own whims, even into another company of his or hers.

Deregulating consumer credit markets

On the surface, neoliberal policy makers and administrators insisted that these measures were necessary responses to high inflation rates. But those measures were to protect the well-being of financial institutions, not that of consumers. After the Vietnam War, the U.S. economy experienced double-digit inflation in the late 1970s and the early 1980s. While the inflation rate was high, usury laws of individual states specified the maximum interest rates on commercial lending. Thus, the profits of lending institutions were curtailed. Free-market believers demanded that existing caps on interest rates should be abolished. As a result, in 1978 the more conservative U.S. Supreme Court ruled in Marquette National Bank vs. First of Omaha Serve Corp that national banks could charge any interest rates to consumer credit borrowers as long as their rates are within the legal caps set by the states where the national banks' headquarters are located, not by the states where actual customers are located (Map, 2004, November 23). As a result, eight out of ten major credit card companies began to relocate to those states with no state cap on credit card interest (Yoon, 2009).

In 1980, the Depository Institutions Deregulation and Monetary Control Act (DIDMCA) mandated gradual elimination of individual states' various ceilings on deposits in thrifts and commercial banks, including credit card interest rates (Federal Reserve Bank of Boston, n.d.).

DIDMCA also increased the federally insured deposit amount in thrifts to $100,000 from $40,000. Thus, this made it easier for large institutional investors to break down their fund into multiple $100,000 accounts, and these investors began to exert their influence on mortgage markets and mortgage issuers began not to rely on local deposits as their funding sources (Kleinknecht, 2009).

The combination of the 1978 Supreme Court ruling and the deregulation in 1980 ignited competitions among states to bring financial institutions to create jobs and tax revenues for the states. For example, Delaware changed its laws to bring banks from the Empire State and other states by offering

> the ability to charge interest rates not subject to any legal ceiling, to raise interest rates retroactively, to charge variable interest rates, to levy unlimited fees for credit card usage and to foreclose on a home in the event of default for credit card debts.
>
> (Gerth, 1981, March 17)

As another response to high inflation, the previously mentioned Garn-St. Germain Depository Institutions Act in 1982 was enacted to create adjustable rate mortgages (ARMs) and other interest-only mortgages, and President Reagan called the creation a jackpot (1982). During Reagan's presidency, asset-based securitization expanded to non-housing assets (Comptroller of the Currency, 1997), and Alan Greenspan, a strong follower of Milton Friedman and the president's appointee for the Federal Reserve, drastically expanded mortgage-backed security as a financial innovation (Kleinknecht, 2009).

Widening income gaps

Dismantling anti-trust laws

During the neoliberals' prevalence in the executive, judiciary, and/or legislative branches between the late 1970s and the 1990s, most of the financial practices that brought the financial meltdown, the Great Recession, and subsequent federal bailouts were created to promote the well-being of financial institutions, rather than consumers of the financial institutions. Such pro-business deregulation measures were not limited to financial industries. Deregulations in anti-trust laws preventing hostile takeover were another achievement of neoliberal policies that planted seeds of labor instability and income polarization.

Business mergers and hostile takeovers did happen before the dominance of neoliberal doctrines in the last two decades of the 20th century. However, the practice was not common until the Reagan administration. There were 1,565 business mergers in 1980. The number skyrocketed to 4,323 in 1986 (Kleinknecht, 2009). During Reagan's presidency, more than 10,000 mergers and acquisitions happened in the United States. To expedite those business transactions, Reagan appointed deregulators as the administrators of the Securities and Exchange Commission (SEC), the Federal Trade Commission (FTC), and the Antitrust Division of the Justice Department and thus weakened the regulatory agencies (Kleinknecht, 2009). Only 26 merger requests were challenged by the Antitrust Division among 10,723 mergers that were brought to the Division between 1981 and 1987.

Those business mergers appeared to be innocuous to the American public. However, mergers created another fatal component of income polarization in the United States. Once acquisition of a company was completed, hostile takers tended to resell the company to another company with a goal of quick profits. For quick profits, the new owner sold the assets of the company and/or ruthlessly laid off the employees of the company (Chang, 2010). Laying off employees was challenging with a strong labor union's presence. Reagan was a formidable anti-labor union figure. Thus, these business acquisitions and mergers became relatively easy and accelerated labor instability in the United States. During the widely accepted economic boom in the 1980s, up to 1.8 million manufacturing jobs were eliminated (Bunch, 2009). Not only blue-collar jobs but also white-collar jobs became subject to job insecurity (Sullivan et al., 2000).

Shareholder value maximization

On the contrary, during Reagan's presidency, the income levels of CEOs and financial assets holders began to experience an increase unprecedented in recent American history. The increase was supported by the idea of shareholder value maximization (Chang, 2010). In a nutshell, professional managers of companies need to be rewarded based on how much monetary value they return to the *shareholders*, not stakeholders, of the companies. Therefore, the professional manager was expected to generate maximum short-term profits for his or her company, increase the value of the company's stocks, and distribute the profit back to the shareholders of the company.

To the professional managers, generating profits by cutting costs was an easier option than by defeating competitors. The profits were redistributed to shareholders and used to buy back shares of the company so that the value of each share could stay high. This brought a windfall to shareholders. Shareholders in return increased the compensation packages for their professional managers. This reciprocity between professional managers and shareholders decreased the portion of profits that could have been reinvested for the company's future market competitiveness (Chang, 2010; Kleinknecht, 2009). This short-term profit-oriented management by CEOs and their shareholders pushed companies to lose global market advantages in the long term, while their income surged at the cost of further labor instability.

Tax code changes

Another contributing factor to widening the income gap from the 1980s was the enactment of pro-business tax codes with the expectation of the trickle-down effect. For example, the Economic Recovery Tax Act of 1981 was the biggest tax cut during the last three decades of the 20th century (Tempalski, 2006). The Act lowered the tax rate of the top-income bracket to 50% from 70%, and the rate was lowered once again in 1986 by the Tax Reform Act to 28%. During the same period, the income tax for the lowest tax bracket increased to 15% from 14%. The Act of 1986 also reduced top corporations' income tax rates. Corporations with more than $100,000 income had a tax rate of 46% in 1981, and the rate went down to 35% at the end of Reagan's presidency (Tax Foundation, n.d.). When he left the Oval Office, capital gains tax was also depressed to 20% from 28% (Bunch, 2009).

The change added another windfall for those who owned financial assets. According to the U.S. Bureau of Economic Analysis' data (n.d.), the income based on the total salary and other compensations from employment in the United States grew approximately five times, from about $1.76 trillion in January of 1981 to about $8.73 trillion at the end of 2012 (of course, these included the salaries of CEOs and high-income earners), while income among dividend recipients increased 15.5 times (from $67.4 billion to over $1 trillion) during the same period.

Due to tax preferences, shareholder value maximization, and deregulations in financial markets, the gap between the top-income earners and the rest of Americans began to widen. In 1978, the earnings ratio between CEOs in major U.S. companies and the average workers in the United States was 29:1 (Mishel and Sabadish, 2012). The ratio increased to 58.5:1 in 1989 and peaked to 411.3:1 in 2000. In 2007, the CEOs of major U.S. companies earned about 355 times more than the average American worker. Yet, the ratio in other developed countries did not show similar drastic income gap increases (Chang, 2010).

While top-income earners experienced unprecedented income increases, actual infla-tion-adjusted household income for low- and middle-income families has not changed that much in the last three decades (Congressional Budget Office, 2011; DeNavas-Walt et al., 2012). The stagnant *household* income in the last three decades would have been impossible without female members joining the labor force, as the inflation-adjusted income for males actually decreased. Even the federal minimum wage became stagnant at $3.35 between 1981 and 1990 (U.S. Department of Labor, n.d.). Subsequent changes in minimum wages were below the inflation rate and contributed to the depressed income for low- and mid-dle-income families, while health insurance premiums (Kaiser Family Foundation, 2009) and college education costs (Yoon, 2012) outpaced the inflation rate. Thus, low- and middle-income families became financially squeezed and more vulnerable to interruption in employment.

Rise of consumer credits as a quasi-welfare system

During this Great Divergence era in income in the last three decades (Krugman, 2007), families needed other sources of money to ease the financial pressure or stay afloat. Due to previously described financial deregulations, financial institutions expanded consumer credits to all income strata for more profits. Then, consumer credits emerged as a quasi-safety net for the financially vulnerable. As shown in Figure 8.1, the consumer credit debt began to increase sharply. The outstanding consumer credit debt was almost $2.8 trillion by the end of 2012, while it was $353 billion in January of 1981 (Federal Reserve, 2013). It is a 798% growth in three decades. Especially, consumer credit among the low- or middle-income families outgrew that of the high-income families during the last decade of the 20th century (Retsinas and Belsky, 2005, p. ix).

The growth was due not to reckless spending beyond means, but to supplement insuf-ficient income. A bankruptcy study in 1991 reports that 82.5% of bankruptcy debtors who incurred credit card debt had experienced interruptions in their jobs during the two years before filing for bankruptcy (Sullivan et al., 2000). Another example would be credit card usage to cover higher education costs. A study reports that more than a quarter of college students used credit cards to pay for tuition in the 1990s (Baum and Saunders, 1998). The National Association of College and University Business Officers (2004) reported that about 18% of college tuition and fees were paid by credit cards in 2003 to its member institutions. This trend went up as various university fees and tuitions increased. A recent federal National Postsecondary Student Aid Study reports that the average college edu-cational debt was $23,200 for the class of 2008 (Institute for College Access and Success, 2009). In the aftermath of the Great Recession, credit cards were reported to be the most common *private* loan to cover graduate education (Yoon, 2012). Surprisingly, the largest percentage of debt increase between 2000 and 2011 occurred among people 65 or older because medical costs have drastically increased and retirement funds were reduced due to the Great Recession (Vornovytskyy et al., 2013). Consumer credits have been helping many of them weather the economic downturn. These statistics suggest that consumer credits have been a quasi-social safety net since the 1980s.

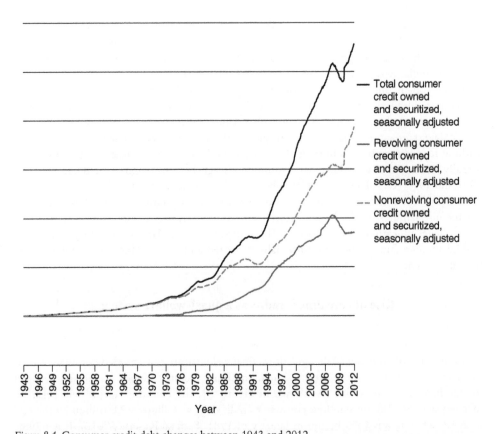

Figure 8.1 Consumer credit debt changes between 1943 and 2012

Note: the currency unit in the column is $1 million (Multiply $1,000,000). Based on the Federal Reserve's G. 19-Consumer credit data.

It is not a new phenomenon for consumer credits to be a safety net for vulnerable Americans. New settlers in early cities in the East and pioneers in new frontiers in the West used consumer credits for their survival (Gelpi and Julien-Labruyère, 2000). Just as low-income farmers in the antebellum American society borrowed for their survival during the winter or after a poor harvest, middle- and low-income families in the last three decades have used credit cards as a lifebuoy for survival during the increase in living expenses and decrease in the real wage.

One major difference between now and 100 years ago is that the current financial institutions exploited their consumers, rather than improving their consumers' well-being while making a profit. In 2003, the average credit card debt snowballed to about $8,000 per household, and credit card companies enjoyed a net profit of $30 billion from interest and various fees (Introduction, 2004, November 23). By the end of 2008, the total amount of credit card debt in the United States jumped to $972.73 billion and the average balance of outstanding credit card debt among households with at least one credit card was $10,679 (Woolsey and Schulz, 2009). According to the Joint Congress Economic Committee (May, 2009), about 13.9% of disposable income from October through December in 2008 went for payments or service fees from using mostly credit cards and other revolving consumer debt. The fees and monthly payments significantly reduced disposable incomes and led low- and middle-income families to file bankruptcy petitions (Sullivan et al., 2000).

A solution: investing in social overhead capital

Zealots of neoliberalism prevailed in the last three decades in the executive, legislative, and/ or judicial branches of the U.S. government. Even though President Clinton was a Democrat, neoliberal agendas continued to be promoted as Congress was controlled by free-market supporters. Neoliberals claimed that tax benefits for high-income earners, deregulations for financial systems, and a flexible labor market would increase the income of the wealthy. The wealthy, in return, were expected to trickle down their wealth to the rest of American society. Yet, while the former part of the trickle-down effects happened, the latter did not happen. Middle- and low-income families became more financially squeezed under the policy. Millions of Americans lost their home due to deregulations in financial industries.

Since the Reagan Administration, neoliberals have been demanding a smaller government and disinvestment in social safety nets. Under the banner of fiscal discipline, the voices again argue that tax increases among the wealthy will hurt our economy and that cutting spending for social overhead capital (SOC) is the way to revive our economy. Their political power is strong enough to revive federal budget sequestration in 2013.

Now is the time to learn from this failed approach of the trickle-down effects. Governmental investment for SOC needs to be expanded. Investment in our infrastructures will give jobs back to the unemployed. Disinvestment in social safety nets should be reversed in this fragile labor market. When unemployment insurance is intact, displaced workers are less likely to rely on credit cards for their survival even after losing their jobs. Pushing them to use high-interest credit cards by cutting the safety net is a real threat to our future, including our children's. As college students swipe their credit cards at their registrar's office, they pawn their future. When senior citizens pass away with consumer debt due to daily expenses and medical costs, the failed debt will eventually haunt financial institutions. Breaking down our SOC is a real threat to the future of all of us.

Thus, the multiplier effects through enhancing social safety nets and investing in SOC should be sought. Interestingly, European workers are reported to have less resistance than American workers toward industrial restructuring as they have better unemployment insurance programs (Chang, 2010). That suggests that having better social safety nets can create a flexible labor market, which is what neoliberals are eager to create. If a government dismantles the social safety net for its people while enabling financial institutions to exploit their customers, lets the people rely on consumer credit as a quasi-welfare system, and thus benefits only financial institutions, the government is indeed a problem. It is that kind of government and its political leaders which should be recalled, not the ones who try to expand the social safety net.

References

Baum, S., and Saunders, D. (1998). *Life after Debt: Results of the National Student Loan Survey* (Final Report). Braintree, MA: Nellie Mae.

Bunch, W. (2009). *Tear Down This Myth: How the Reagan Legacy has Distorted Our Politics and Haunts Our Future.* New York: Free Press.

Carpenter, D. H., and Murphy, M. M. (2010, April 12). *Permissible Securities Activities of Commercial Banks Under the Glass-Steagall Act (GSA) and the Gramm-Leach-Bliley Act (GLBA).* Washington, DC: Congressional Research Service. Retrieved August 15, 2014, from http://assets.opencrs.com/rpts/R41181_20100412.pdf.

Chang, H. (2010). *23 Things They Don't Tell You about Capitalism.* New York: Bloomsbury Press.

Comptroller of the Currency. (1997, November). *Asset Securitization: Comptroller's Handbook.* Retrieved August 15, 2014, from http://www.occ.gov/publications/publications-by-type/comptrollers-handbook/assetsec.pdf.

Congressional Budget Office. (2011, October). *Trends in the Distribution of Household Income Between 1979 and 2007*. Retrieved August 15, 2014, from http://www.cbo.gov/sites/default/files/cbofiles/attachments/10-25-HouseholdIncome.pdf.

DeNavas-Walt, C., Proctor, B., and Smith, J. C. (2012, September). *Income, Poverty, and Health Insurance Coverage in the United States: 2011*. U.S. Census Bureau. Retrieved August 16, 2014, from http://www.census.gov/prod/2012pubs/p60-243.pdf.

Federal Deposit Insurance Corporation. (n.d.). *Garn-St Germain Depository Institutions Act of 1982*. Retrieved August 16, 2014, from http://www.fdic.gov/regulations/laws/rules/8000-4100.html.

Federal Reserve. (2013, March 6). *G.19-Consumer Credit*. Retrieved March 6, 2013, from http://www.federalreserve.gov/datadownload/Download.aspx?rel=G19&series=58a4544d23ef4c8fac2452a8b64b451c&lastObs=&from=&to=&filetype=csv&label=include&layout=seriescolumn&type=package.

Federal Reserve Bank of Boston. (n.d.). *Depository Institutions Deregulation and Monetary Control Act of 1980*. Retrieved March 28, 2013, from http://www.bos.frb.org/about/pubs/deposito.pdf.

Gelpi, R., and Julien-Labruyère, F. (2000). *The History of Consumer Credit: Doctrines and Practices* (translated by Mn Liam Gavin). New York: St. Martin's Press.

Gerth, J. (1981, March 17). New York Banks Urged Delaware to Lure Bankers. *New York Times*. Retrieved August 16, 2014, from http://www.nytimes.com/1981/03/17/business/19810317BANK.html?ei=5087anden=c010543948675c8bandex=1103259600andadxnnl=1andadxnnlx=1193245204-ckO1ZDcs60vgSJZA7pDANw.

Institute for College Access and Success. (2009, December). *Student Debt and the Class of 2008*. Retrieved August 16, 2014, from http://projectonstudentdebt.org/files/pub/classof2008.pdf.

Introduction. (2004, November 23). Secret History of the Credit Card. *PBS Frontline*. Retrieved August 16, 2014, from http://www.pbs.org/wgbh/pages/frontline/shows/credit/etc/synopsis.html.

The Joint Congress Economic Committee. (2009, May 12). *Vicious Cycle: How Unfair Credit Card Practices are Squeezing Consumers and Undermining the Recovery*. Retrieved August 17, 2014, from http://www.jec.senate.gov/public/?a=Files.Serve&File_id=42840b23-fed8-447b-a029-e977c0a25544.

Kaiser Family Foundation. (2009, March). *Trends in Health Care Costs and Spending*. Retrieved August 17, 2014, from http://kff.org/health-costs/fact-sheet/trends-in-health-care-costs-and-spending.

Kleinknecht, W. (2009). *The Man who Sold the World: Ronald Reagan and the Betrayal of Main Street America*. New York: Nation Books.

Krugman, P. (2007). *The Conscience of a Liberal*. New York: W. W. Norton and Company.

Map: Snap Shot of the Industry. (2004, November 23). Secret History of the Credit Card. *PBS Frontline*. Retrieved August 17, 2014, from http://www.pbs.org/wgbh/pages/frontline/shows/credit/more/map.html.

Mishel, L., and Sabadish, N. (2012, May 2). CEO Pay and the Top 1%: How Executive Compensation and Financial-sector Pay have Fueled Income Inequality. *Economic Policy Institute*. Retrieved August 17, 2014, from http://www.epi.org/files/2012/ib331-ceo-pay-top-1-percent.pdf.

National Association of College and University Business Officers. (2004, August). *Paying with Plastic: Analyzing the Results of the 2003 NACUBO Tuition Payment by Credit Card Survey*. Retrieved August 17, 2014, from http://www.nacubo.org/documents/research/Paying%20with%20Plastic.pdf.

Reagan, R. (1981, January 20). *Inaugural Address*. Retrieved August 17, 2014, from http://www.reaganfoundation.org/pdf/Inaugural_Address_012081.pdf.

Reagan, R. (1982, October 15). *Remarks on Signing the Garn-St Germain Depository Institutions Act of 1982*. Retrieved August 17, 2014, from http://www.reagan.utexas.edu/archives/speeches/1982/101582b.htm.

Retsinas, P., and Belsky, E. S. (2005). *Building Assets, Building Credit: Creating Wealth in Low-income Communities*. Washington, DC: Brookings Institution.

Sullivan, T. A., Warren, E., and Westbrook, J. A. (2000). *The Fragile Middle Class: Americans in Debt*. New Haven, CT: Yale University Press.

Tax Foundation. (n.d.). *Federal Corporate Income Tax Rates, Income Years 1909–2012*. Retrieved March 31, 2013, from http://taxfoundation.org/article/federal-corporate-income-tax-rates-income-years-1909-2012.

Tempalski, J. (2006, September). Revenue Effects of Major Tax Bills. *U.S. Department of the Treasury, Office of Tax Analysis*. Retrieved August 17, 2014, from http://www.treasury.gov/resource-center/tax-policy/tax-analysis/Documents/ota81.pdf.

U.S. Bureau of Economic Analysis. (n.d.). *National Income and Product Accounts Table*. Retrieved June 17, 2014, from http://www.bea.gov/iTable/iTable.cfm?ReqID=9&step=1#reqid=9&step=3&isuri=1and910=X&911=0&903=58&904=1950&905=2012&906=Q.

U.S. Department of Labor. (n.d.). *History of Federal Minimum Wage Rates under the Fair Labor Standards Act, 1938–2009*. Retrieved August 17, 2014, from http://www.dol.gov/whd/minwage/chart.htm.

Vornovytskyy, M., Gottschalck, A., and Smith, A. (2013, March 21). *Household Debt in the U.S.: 2000–2011*. Retrieved April 4, 2013, from http://www.census.gov/people/wealth/files/Debt%20 Highlights%202011.pdf.

Woolsey, B., and Schulz, M. (2009, September 10). *Credit Card Statistics, Industry Facts, Debt Statistics*. Retrieved November 14, 2009, from http://www.creditcards.com/credit-card-news/credit-card-industry-facts-personal-debt-statistics-1276.php.

Yoon, I. (2009). Securing Economic Justice and Sustainability from Structural Deviances: Recommendations for Consumer Credit Policy Changes. *Journal of Poverty*, 13(1), 40–54.

Yoon, I. (2012). Debt Burdens among MSW Graduates: A National Cross-sectional Study. *Journal of Social Work Education*, 48(1), 1–21.

PART II

Discourses of poverty

From the "culture of poverty" to "surplus population"

INTRODUCTION

Stephen Nathan Haymes and Eduardo Vargas

Modern social institutions deploy discourses of poverty as technologies of governance that produce and manage the poor vis-à-vis the non-poor. Broadly speaking, discourses are normalized or regulated ways of speaking that define and produce objects of knowledge (e.g., the poor, poverty). In doing so, the discourses produced by modern institutions govern the way something is talked about and how related practices are conducted. In *The Archaeology of Knowledge and the Discourse on Language*, Foucault maintains that it is in discourse or a family of concepts that power relations are inscribed. Discourses are made up of discursive practices. These practices are the rules by which discourses are formed, rules that determine what can be said and what must remain unsaid, and who can speak with authority and who must listen (Foucault, 1972). Thus, modern institutions exercise power by governing through discursive practices. Says Foucault:

> Discursive practices are not purely and simply ways of producing discourse. They are embodied in technical processes, in institutions, in patterns for general behavior, in forms of transmission and diffusion, and pedagogical forms which, at once, impose and maintain them.
>
> (1997:200)

For those modern institutions responsible or charged with alleviating or reducing poverty, discourses can be described as a "regulated system of statements" that establish differences between the poor and non-poor.

In this regard, modern institutional discourses of poverty are discourses of power that produce "subjects who fit into, constitute and reproduce a social order" (Baker and Galasiński, 2001:13). Discourses of power are social technologies that are inseparable from the way modern institutions attempt to control populations through the governing of mentalities. Foucault refers to this mode of governing populations by modern institutions as "governmentality" (2001:13). It is through this way of governing that modern institutions regulate or "police" societies and subject populations to bureaucratic regimes and modes of discipline (2001:13). Discourses of "poverty" are therefore social technologies that link the production of knowledge about the "poor" with forms of institutional power and intervention that represent and produce "poor people." More generally, discourses of power do not only represent populations of people, but also represent those populations in relation to categories of difference. To explain this further let's turn to gender discourses. In *Technologies of Gender*, Teresa de Lauretis explains that gender is not only a representation that refers to an object but is "a representation of a relation, that of belonging to a class, a group, a category" (1987:4). De Lauretis goes on to say that as a relation

> [g]ender constructs a relation between one entity and other entities, which are previously constituted as a class, and that relation is one of belonging; thus gender assigns to one entity, say an individual, a position within a class, and therefore also a position vis-à-vis other preconstituted classes. [...] So gender represents not an individual but a relation, and a social relation; in other words, it represents an individual for a class.
>
> (1987:4–5)

Extrapolating from de Lauretis' point that gender is a representation of a social relation we can say too that discourses of poverty represent a social relation. As discourses of modern institutional power, discourses of poverty represent poverty by constructing knowledge about populations of people considered "poor" in relation to populations of people not poor. In other words, modern institutions through discourses of power construct relations of belonging that regulate and manage how populations of people classify themselves and others as poor or non-poor. Modern institutions do this by sanctioning who can speak authoritatively about poverty and who cannot, which is related to how institutions produce knowledge about the poor and intervene to eliminate poverty.

For example, through policy interventions modern institutions intervene to reduce the incidence of material deprivation experienced by people living in poverty. The dominant definition of poverty given by modern institutions defines it "as a state in which individuals lack the financial resources to satisfy their basic needs and/or reach a minimum standard of living." The main emphasis is on income, expenditure, or nutritional deficits, each of which goes well with the concept of the "poverty line," which offers a "distinct and measurable cut-off between the poor and the non-poor." Lakshman Yapa argues that "in poverty/development discourses the subject–object binary appears in the form of a statistical construction of a 'poverty sector'" (1996:712). This sector "usually [consists of] a set of households that fall below a given income criterion," which, according to Yapa, "is the most popular approach to poverty used by the World Bank, the U.S. Census, United Nations' agencies and national governments" (1996:712).

Yapa identifies three steps used in official approaches to alleviating poverty. The first involves the collecting of data "on the extent and the geographical location of poverty"; the second, gathering "information on 'causative' variables such as race, gender and employment that can be correlated with poverty"; and third, "information on the incidence of poverty and correlated variables is used in models to help formulate appropriate policy and action" (1996:712). Yapa concludes that by constructing a "poverty sector" the discourses of poverty of modern institutions neutrally position the authors of poverty studies as subjects and poor people in the poverty sector as objects. For Yapa, the binary subject–object logic of the "poverty sector" in official discourses of poverty constructs the poor people as a problem. He writes:

> The subject–object binary in the definition of poverty sector goes to the heart of epistemology. According to official approaches, the poverty sector is where poor people are located, and therefore, the locus of the "poverty problem." By viewing the poor (the object) as the problem, then non-poor (the subject) are automatically situated in the realm of the non-problem. The non-poor subject thus becomes the source of intellect, analysis, policy, resources, and solutions. [...] According to the "dividing practices" of the official

methodology on poverty, the subject emerges as a rational, compassionate, moral agent—the embodiment of self that possesses the intellectual and the material resources to solve the poverty problem. The poor emerge as the needy other—the object of study and compassion—in need of development. The status of the discourse, with its statistical profiles of poverty along with data on correlated variables, is unproblematic.

(1996:713)

Within the context of neoliberalism, the chapters in this part examine the power of words, of discourse, upon poverty policy and those living in poverty. Each of the chapters, whether directly or indirectly, is uniquely attentive to how neoliberal discourses of poverty are socially constituted, and how these discourses have serious implications for policy and its effects on those living in poverty. In different ways, the chapters in this part encourage readers to make a distinction between poverty as a material condition experienced by the "poor" and its representations in academic literature and media, and in political, economic, cultural, and social institutions, within the contemporary context of neoliberalism.

The chapters examine in a variety of ways how contemporary neoliberal discourses of poverty construct a hyper-individualized or privatized discourse of the causes of poverty that shifts the blame of poverty onto the individual behavior of people living in poverty. The chapters also reflect on how neoliberal discourse obscures the structural sources of poverty away from neoliberal market fundamentalism and the shift from welfarism, a formal commitment to distributive justice, to postwelfarism, in which the formal commitment is now to market democracy and competitive individualism. In Chapter 9, "The Problematic Conceptualizations and Constructions of Poverty: Select Global Analysis," Ali Abdi argues that neoliberal "institutional constructions of poverty in the United States and surely elsewhere fit the general thesis of institutionalization of social life, where the problematic intersections of highly uneven power relations could de-subjectify the complex daily lives of people." Abdi examines how "the widespread objectification of the lives of the poor [become] conceptualized and discursively [...] mathematicized into numerical silos that de facto become the prerogative of the bureaucrats and institutions that design and control their lives." Abdi epistemologically links the discursive production of these institutional constructions of poverty to "the Western-driven pathologization of poverty," which he suggests "is not a common ontology in the rest of the world."

In Chapter 10, "Neoliberal Economics and Undergraduate Poverty Education," Kevin Blair and Gabriel Santos propose that the privatizing of poverty in neoliberal discourses is implicitly dominating poverty education within the university curriculum. Amongst undergraduate students in particular, this is reinforcing the common sense belief that living in poverty is the consequence of individual choice. The authors, reflecting on their class discussions, write: "The majority position was that in the United States people are free to choose, a phrase directly used by one of the students and echoed by many others." Elaborating further they write:

> Class discussion generally indicates that students view the global poor as being poor through little or no fault of their own, while they tend to view the U.S. poor as failing to meet the challenges and to take advantage of the opportunities inherent in the market.

Blair and Santos argue that the implicit neoliberal influences on the university curriculum help students cultivate a sense of "sympathy" but not necessarily a "social empathy" in relation to the poor. Analyzing course syllabi on the internet regarding this distinction, Blair and Santos identify two competing categories of pedagogical approaches to the teaching of poverty: "strongly academic" and "strongly experimental." These approaches, Blair and Santos claim, are limited pedagogically because both do not provide undergraduates with a critical theoretical analysis of poverty and thus do not enable undergraduates to challenge the prevailing neoliberal discourse nor cultivate through their studies a sense of "social empathy" with people living in poverty.

In Chapter 11, "The Importance of Context to the Social Processes Around Material Hardship," Colleen Heflin contends that household-level measures of well-being such as food hardships, bill-paying hardships, and home hardships are better indicators of the impact of neo-liberal economic and post-welfare policies on people living in poverty. This is because household well-being provides a social context in contrast to state-level measures of economic growth, such as employment, per capita gross state product, and the unemployment rate. Heflin's focus on household well-being better captures in social context the distinctiveness of the vulnerability experienced by people living in poverty within a neoliberal political economy. Thus, household well-being is more appropriate than indicators that were meant to measure the economic growth of local and national states. This properly shifts the attention of discourses of poverty away from the economic growth policies of the neoliberal state, which support market democracy and com-petitive individualism, to focusing on the actual impact of these policies on the poor.

In Chapter 12, "Welfare Dependency and Poverty: Neoliberal Rhetoric or Evidence-Informed Choice?," Phillip Hong and Brenda Crawley trace how the discourse of poverty has changed from the problem of too little income to a problem of dependency, and how depend-ency became the neoliberal post-welfare goal of self-sufficiency in the United States. Hong and Crawley challenge the premise of the neoliberal post-welfare goal that "penalties or sticks will move people from dependency to independence or self-sufficiency."

In Chapter 13, "Babies as Barriers: Welfare Policy Discourse in an Era of Neoliberalism," Linda Houser and colleagues examine the emergence of the "barriers discourse" in the Temporary Assistance for Needy Families (TANF) program. The authors look at how under neoliberal logic "public assistance programs have been redesigned to prod people into whatever jobs the changing economy provides." In these programs paid work "has been enshrined as the chief responsibility of citizenship." Thus, access to the TANF public assistance program is dependent on individual compliance with work and other behavioral requirements. Non-compliance to requirements due to disparate conditions such as parenting young children, having an active substance addiction, having limited access to public transportation, or living with intimate partner violence is considered as "having barriers," which is grounds for dismissal from the TANF program. The authors critically analyze the "barriers discourse" within the neoliberal poverty discourse of the TANF public assistance program.

Finally, in Chapter 14, "We are the 99 Percent: The Rise of Poverty and the Decline of Poverty Stigma," Joan Maya Mazelis and Brendan Gaughan illustrate how in 2008 neolib-eral discourses on poverty were disrupted by the counter-discourses of anti-poverty protest in the United States. The authors argue that while neoliberal capitalism has increased economic inequality and poverty in the United States, poverty stigma has decreased. In an analysis of public opinion data from the General Social Survey and the Pew Research Center, and data on poverty, unemployment, and food stamp participation, the authors propose a decline in poverty stigma among people in the United States. They argue that anti-poverty protest may have con-tributed to the decrease in stigma. This chapter considers the importance of economic context, public attitudes about poverty, and the role of the Occupy Wall Street Movement (OWS) in explaining the effects of the Great Recession on poverty stigma.

References

Baker, Chris and Dariusz Galasiński (2001). *Cultural Studies and Discourse Analysis: A Dialogue on Language and Identity*, New York and London: Sage Publications.

de Lauretis, Teresa (1987). *Technologies of Gender: Essays on Theory, Film, and Fiction*, Bloomington and Indianapolis: Indiana University Press.

Foucault, Michel (1972). *The Archaeology of Knowledge and the Discourse on Language*, translated by A.M. Sheridan Smith, New York: Pantheon Books.

Foucault, Michel (1997). *Power/Knowledge: Selected Interviews on Other Writings 1972–1977*, edited by Colin Gordon and translated by Colin Gordon, Leo Marshall, John Mepham, and Kate Soper, New York: Pantheon Books.

Yapa, Lakshman (1996). What Causes Poverty? A Postmodern Perspective. *Annals of the Association of American Geographers*, 86(4): 707–728.

9

THE PROBLEMATIC CONCEPTUALIZATIONS AND CONSTRUCTIONS OF POVERTY

Select global analysis

Ali A. Abdi

Introduction

In today's globalizing, extensively networked, and, by extension, complexly interconnected world, our reading and analysis of poverty should be more complicated than the simple assumption that, because one is deprived of certain countable things that others have, such a person should be depicted as poor. Throughout history, different societies have had diverse qualitatively but more so quantitatively attached realities of poverty, and those understandings and/or measurements have been revised based on the unofficial continuum of the gap between the haves and have-nots. This is indeed the case of developed countries vis-à-vis the developing world, which itself is no longer as descriptively tenable as it used to be. While historically Western Europe, Mexico-less North America, and Japan used to be known as the developing world, now we are not only dealing with many potential candidates for this category (South Korea, Singapore, Taiwan, and selectively China and Malaysia), but we certainly see the need to redo the meaning of developed, developing, and underdeveloped. In actual fact, what we are dealing with is a world in which all three categories could exist in one country (e.g., China). Even in the United States of America, the gap between the well to do and the poor is more complicated than ever, and especially with this last recession, complemented by the problematic notions of how much individuals and families need to live viable lives. So the simplistic assumption of quantifying poverty and from there defining effectively is more complicated than ever. Still, one distinction which seems to hold ground in defining the claim to be a developed country could be the size of a nation's middle class in relation to the total population.

The contention of who is in the middle class is also murky, and difficult to measure, which again complicates the need to understand poverty and its causes and outcomes. If, for example, 15 percent of Americans are classified as poor, which out of a total population of 313 million totals about 47 million, then one might also heed Newman and Chen's call in their book, *The Missing Class* (2008), where over 50 million, although they are classified as middle class, are actually quantifiably (i.e., in money terms) poor. Needless to add that with Newman and Chen's data covering pre-2008 events, surely things have gotten worse in America, and it may not be an observational hazard to add millions to the ranks of the poor in early 2013. So how many people are poor in the United States? The right answer from my reading should be, it depends on how you define poverty. This difficulty of definitively parametering what I might dub "scientific" poverty, where via institutional analysis we quantify poverty, also begs another inquiry: Are the monetary numbers (i.e., minimum/maximum income) which either associate or dissociate one with poverty or its absence reliable to the point where these define and represent the real lives of people? If, for example, the Federal government's poverty guideline is about $23,000 for a family of four, what needs does this amount cover? And in a country like the United States, what categories of poverty are counted? Perhaps food, shelter, and medication, but the concern with this actually becomes two-pronged. First, is the number itself ($23,000) actually enough for those basic needs? This question should also be attached to the extra point where, by only numerically quantifying poverty, one could miss so much that defines poverty including self-perception, social status, self-esteem, and all the packages that come with these. But even if one stays within institutional and para-institutional quantifications, the amount that defines poverty will only have meaning when it is contextualized to given situations where it fulfills certain expectations, needs, and potential outcomes. With this understanding, it is clear that the meanings of poverty, indeed their conceptual and attached discursive locations, are institutionally perceived phenomena that are then constructed through policy platforms which are supposedly depersonalized, for, as far as I can discern, the policy makers do not belong to the social class of poverty, and as such are neither emotionally nor pragmatically conscious of the lives of the poor.

Referring to the Foucauldian perspective, the institutional constructions of poverty in the United States and surely elsewhere fit the general thesis of the institutionalization of social life, where the problematic intersections of highly uneven power relations could de-subjectify the complex daily lives of people. Here, the apparent quasi-post-structuralist analysis of the case should refute the problematic a priori assumptions about the lives of the poor, which by being institutionalized are posed as afflicted with not normal conditions that should be dissipated, or even cured. That leads to the hardly discussed but widespread objectification of the lives of the poor who basically, because they are conceptualized and discursively located as lacking certain measurable resources for bargain and exchange, are mathematicized into numerical silos that de facto become the prerogative of the bureaucrats and institutions that design and control their lives. For me also, this involves an extra-subjective systematic depersonalization where presumptions about the powerlessness of the materially deprived somehow justifies their en masse de-agentification and, I submit, it gets even more dangerous with respect to the desired de-pauperizations of the poor.

Critical readings of systemic poverty constructions

With the quasi-pathologization of poverty as a not normal condition that should be overcome when, in actuality, some people attaining less means that others should be seen as a natural outcome of historical formations, cultural realities, inherent individual situations, and perennially uneven resource distributions, there seems to occur wide implications of the poor being systemically (by the system) misrecognized. This misrecognition, according to Taylor (1995), could befall any group who, through their demerited power locations, are defined by others. Here, the issue extends into the complex terrains of imposed and authentic identities where, by and large, the former is externally constructed while the latter is internally ascertained and achieved. That is, the source of authentic identity is the subject of such identity, basically free people telling us who they are, while imposed identity assumes differential power relations where those who have some control over the lives of others deconstruct or refuse to recognize an oppressed group's primordial personhoods and characteristics, thus subjecting them to arbitrarily constructed clusters of false identities that are, more often than otherwise, designed to perpetuate a system of physical or psychological controls over the lives of the disempowered.

As Taylor notes (I agree with him), such impositions negatively impact the well-being of marginalized populations, thus spawning active fragments of depressed ontologies that, due to their lowered self-perceptions, accord them less than effective domains of self-efficacy for social and personal well-being.

As Bandura (2006) noted, what makes us fully developed human beings is in large measure related to people's capacities to effect change in the contexts in which they live. Such capacity is a function of the level as well as the quality of our agentic being where we have the freedom as well as the means to independently, but within prescribed boundaries, make decisions that directly affect our lives, and to have some influence on those that indirectly touch our existentialities. Bandura, in his extensive study of self-efficacy, identifies several aspects of human agency which we must acquire to achieve our full humanity. These include *intentionality*, or our capacity to design our objectives and undertake them; and *forethought*, which he describes as our ability to foresee the outcomes of the actions we take. In addition, Bandura talks about what he calls *self-reactiveness*, which speaks about our subjective power to create actions and be in control of those actions; then there is *self-reflectiveness*, which may encompass all the other categories but is intended here to depict our conscientized location in relation to our personal efficacies and the meanings we attach to these activities, complemented by our possibilities of correcting those activities so that they fit our changing socio-economic and political conditions while still serving our interests and needs.

In bringing together Taylor and Bandura in my analysis of poverty conceptualizations, I intend to show the arbitrary discursive constructions that locate, indeed proscribe, the lives of the institutionalized poor. Those constructed as such become dependent for their daily survival upon externally imposed identities that misrecognize their complex realities and reduce them to a monolithic descriptive and practical block. Such a block is again socio-economically and politically institutionalized and re-institutionalized, and by extension marginalized, but also subjected to onto-existential onslaughts that apply a high number of demerit points on their identities, self-esteem, and certainly self-efficacy. From there, it shouldn't be difficult to see the impediments that continually hinder the social well-being aspirations of the poor. Indeed, the problematic naturalization of the phrase "the chronically poor" creates a perception where some of us are infected by a non-curable "poverty virus" that, although not necessarily fatal (although it can be), cannot be cured with available remedies, and can only be selectively controlled so we can live with it longer. This totally problematic biologization of poverty hides a bigger issue, namely the institutional failure to deal with institutionally created poverty. Basically, therefore, the depiction of poor people and their condition (i.e., poverty) in the United States and elsewhere requires new lines of counter-hegemonic analysis that start with headlong challenges to the conceptual institutionalizations of poverty, and bring back well-organized critical pointers and counter-pointers that change the language and the policy representations of poor people as numerically economizable elements that can be produced and reproduced via countable (not accountable), externally monetarized mechanisms. These mechanisms, in turn, facilitate the control of the poor as forlorn figures in deprived urban and rural landscapes that should be discursively and practically separated from the rest of society and benevolently cared for with straight-line solutions that many times miss the complete person's historical needs, actualities, and expectations.

Depersonalizing and re-socializing (re-politicizing poverty)

The world of public institutions is a complex but selectively problematic one. In liberal democracies such as the United States and Canada where I work, the essence of public institutions has never been delinked from the fundamentals of capitalist competition where their primary raison d'être is to mediate the actions of individuals who should freely compete in the national public space. This reality posits a situation where an underlying assumption dictates a priori adherence to a world of winners and losers. More often than otherwise, the winner–loser rules are created by those defined by the brilliant late sociologist C. Wright Mills (2000) as the power elite, and while the United States was his focus, the analysis applies to almost all so-called Western democracies and surely to other countries in the world. The reign of the power elite is still in vigour, for, as Wedel (2009) cogently noted, admission into the power elite is based on institutional controls of the world where, with a quasi-inherited situation, once you are admitted into the circles of those wonderful exclusive power clubs, you stay there for good, and would continually have a sizable say in who is admitted during your tenure and even after your tenure. With this understanding, with the top-down lines of public policy and the increasing interconnectedness of the global power elite (Wedel) as the controlling block of what to do with the world's resources, all complemented by the savagely wide and increasing gap between the poor and the have-lots, one need not be that challenged to know that global poverty, or American poverty for that matter, is anything but an isolated personal affliction. It is a globally institutionalized platform of socio-politically deprived lives that have been systematically (by the system) imprisoned in the "non-competitive" corners of the democratic promise that serves the interests of the elite and those who can serve the elite loyally and more effectively.

At the global level, the wrongly personalized story reflects upon the continuing problematic conceptual and theoretical constructions of poverty. But in the developing world especially, the case has the extra dimension of extra-national impositions that are mostly driven by neoliberal globalization, which rhetorically talks about the expansion of wealth while in reality it has led to the pauperization of hundreds of millions of people (Abdi, 2006). Indeed, with the inception of these extensive and intensive forms of globalization, the gap between the have-nots and have-lots has increased to the extent where, in 2012, it was at a 20-year high (Save the Children, 2012). Certainly, therefore, this dominant global system has not only created more poverty in the way we have been taught to measure the phenomenon, but, for me at least, it has also heavily contributed to the discursive fabrications of poverty in communities where social well-being was never measured by the amount of coins one possesses but by the collective livelihood possibilities people achieve. Here, the poverty charts created by the main drivers of neoliberal globalization, mainly the World Bank and International Monetary Fund (IMF), among other international financial institutions (IFIs), were suddenly applicable to people in many countries and zones where the capitalist system itself was highly underdeveloped and where materialistic ownership was so limited that one could see them as quasi-egalitarian societies that didn't demonstrate that much of wealth–poverty gaps or divisions. Certainly, the externally imposed measures, which at a different level are comparable to the extra-subjective identity impositions discussed above, totally ignored the complex primordial meanings of the poor and non-poor and their socio-cultural and inter-global implications, and should be problematized, especially with respect to people who have different life views, experiences, and expectations.

Indeed, the dreadful numericalizations of the way people live in simplistic, collaborative locales were not actually invented by neoliberal globalization, but were certainly perfected by it. The first constructions of problematic global poverty conceptualizations and policy implications actually started with the birth of the extensive global industry we call today "international development." With the inception of the American Marshall Plan for the reconstruction of post-war Europe, it was President Harry Truman who first spoke about the expansion of such development projects into the world's poor corners (Black, 2007). Suddenly, over millennia developed life systems were depicted as lacking with respect to Western schemes of deprivation measurements, and from there rendered in need of palliative development care. Such an attitude of poverty deconstructions and reconstructions was not created via an analytical or discursive vacuum; it was actually attached to the enlightenment-driven rationalist perspectives that scientifically viewed and measured the world. Such a rationalist analysis of life was continued by prominent theorists of modernity including Huntington (1971) and Rostow (1990).

Modernist pragmatics and global poverty

In his analysis of human well-being, Huntington followed a highly Eurocentric line on modernity where, with its assumptions as the globally prescribed main development platform, it advances efficient resource management systems that were not only good for Western progress, but were to be adopted by everyone else in the world. To his thinking, the dichotomy between modern man[/woman] and traditional man[/woman] was a divide created by the efficiency with which the former exploits the time/space/resource triads that are accorded to him[/her], and the absence of such efficiency in the lands of backward populations. Rostow, on the other hand, advanced in his book, *Stages of Economic Growth: A Non-Communist Manifesto* (1990), an escalator-like progression of economic development that, as implicated in his sub-title, should be completely de-socialized and de-communalized. What both of these men didn't extensively discuss is how modernist schemes of development are actually achieved via expansive practices of exploitation where poverty is actually deliberately manufactured via the delinking of whole populations who supposedly reside in countries certified as modern (the United States, Canada, Western Europe), but are pauperized by low wages and the absence of any escape from ongoing inter-generational economic alienations. Here, we can talk about the so-called underclass, the unemployed and the working poor, who, as was indicated above, should be close to or even above the 100 million mark in the United States alone. Add the hundreds of millions who have been economically thrown overboard by the current modernity-produced recession in Western Europe where in some countries such as Spain youth unemployment is over 50 percent, with modernist economists telling us to see these extensively deprived humanscapes as the new normal.

In reality, with the inception of the relatively new neoliberal globalizations which more than all other previous globalizations are distinguished by their intensities and extensities (Held and McGrew, 2004), the situation is so much worse in many places. For experiential privilege, let us consider the example of Africa, where modernist development importations didn't develop anybody (Ake, 1996), but actually led to what I may call the double jeopardy of socio-economic and political mal-being. Let me start with the latter; the political mal-being was an outcome of Africa's loss of sovereign public policy making via the draconian loan conditionalities that were imposed by Western IFIs, and with that came the socio-economic problems, where the disjuncture between people's communal ways of living and the perforce individual-istic economization of life was in full vigor. This has resulted in what we habitually see today as Africa's celebrated status as the world's perennial poor zone. Looking at the history of how this happened, though, one can clearly and actually follow the lines of how this reality was under construction in the past few decades, culminating in a situation where those described as poor are estimated to be around 80 percent of the continent's people.

With Africa now incorporated into the hegemonic numericalizations of the global paradigm of poverty, the inescapable numbers are very bad and do not bode well for Africans. Indeed, while we speak about the problem of a 7.6 percent unemployment rate in the United States (surely it is for those affected by this), the numbers in many post-Western development, post-neoliberal globalization countries in Africa are, for all pragmatic undertakings, tragic. The case is especially so in these post-facto times where this ancient continent is so incorporated into the global capitalist system it cannot, even if it wanted (which is most unlikely), withdraw from the heavily numericalized realities and relationships of global privilege or lack thereof. Quickly looking through available data, one finds some unemployment rates that are not at first look believable, including an unemployment rate of 51 percent in Namibia, 48 percent in Senegal, and 40 percent in Kenya. For those of us who have worked and researched in these contexts, the numbers are not actually surprising and one need not read this chapter to get them. In most urban centers in Africa today (say Nairobi in Kenya or Dakar in Senegal), one can simply walk the streets and see the sea of young people who are either unemployed or involved in what is euphemistically called the informal market, generally meaning that youth and many middle-aged people are selling anything they can find to earn their daily bread and soup, and nothing more. Indeed, when one hears the now Western media popularized expression that 80 percent of the population lives on less than one U.S. dollar per day, the story is again about the post-numericalization of poverty where, this time, the psychology of believing in such realities and numbers has been implanted, the need has been created, and the numbers are, per system imperatives, believed and acted upon.

Certainly, the conceptual constructions as well as the discursive operationalizations of the one U.S. dollar per day story are at least interesting. Here again, the numbers reign supreme and actually represent a higher analytical status in the minds of external agents than what directly affects the lives of people. Usually the simple question of what U.S.$1/day means in the lives of the concerned people is hardly raised. If and when it is ever raised, the hegemonic calculations usually minimize the real impacts of the situation, with the modernist dichotomies kicking in with the false claims that, over there, that should be enough. Actually, it is not enough, but with no recourse, people have precariously adjusted to the number-based rules of global pluto-crats, who have freely decided to label the systematically constructed conditions of the world's poor as the global precariat. To very briefly explain the post-facto point I have deployed a few times above, I only need to say that with the historical, psycho-cultural, and by extension socio-economic deconstructions of so-called developing countries, and their perforce incor-poration into global systems where they lack the primary industrial or financial capacities to compete in free zone globalizations, their value as nations, more or less, becomes a source of raw materials and cheap labor when and if those are needed. This is fully complemented by the information technology-conveyed possibilities of overseas lifestyles in the developed world that are not attainable, but must be strived for, and from there, everything is measured on artificial numericalizations that are perceived (quite problematically) as either helping or hindering such possibilities. Needless to add that the promise of development which usually derides simple and locally sustainable forms of subsistent living (Rahnema, 1997) that might not descriptively be based on countable categories of poverty, as instances of underdevelopment that should be shunned by all, practically represents a shallow misreading of effective livelihood contexts that have a unique and respected place in many simple living world communities.

Concluding remarks

Certainly, it is high time to recast the meanings as well as the practice-driven constructions of poverty. It is surely the right epoch to disavow the tendency to evaluate conditions of poverty only on one's economic liquidity, which itself should have a lot to do with what defines and creates such conditions. It is an opportune moment, indeed, to apply multiple and new dis-cursive formations to the way we explain, analyze, and pragmatically locate the ideas as well as the practices of poverty, where via a multicentric reading of our world we realize that the Western-driven pathologization of poverty is not a common ontology in the rest of the world. In addition, the location of poor people is not necessarily on the precarious margins of society, but can be re-positioned, in fact is already positioned in many non-Western contexts, at the center of most communities where respect and full social, cultural, and political endowments are bestowed upon all, irrespective of their contemporary financial conjecture and measurable monetary liquidities.

References

Abdi, A.A. (2006). Culture of Education, Social Development and Globalization: Historical and Current Analyses of Africa. In A. Abdi, K.P. Puplampu, and G.J.S. Dei (eds), *African Education and Globalization: Critical Perspectives*. Lanham, MD: Rowman and Littlefield.

Ake, C. (1996). *Democracy and Development in Africa*. Washington, DC: The Brookings Institution.

Bandura, A. (2006). Toward a Psychology of Human Agency. *Perspectives on Psychological Science*, 2(1), 164–180. Retrieved June 18, 2012, from http://wexler.free.fr/library/files/bandura%20%282006%29%20towards%20a%20psychology%20of%20human%20agency.pdf.

Black, M. (2007). *No-nonsense Guide to International Development*. Toronto: Between the Lines.

Held, D. and McGrew, A. (2004). *The Global Transformations Reader: An Introduction to the Globalization Debate*. Cambridge: Polity.

Huntington, S. (1971). The Change to Change: Modernization, Development and Politics. *Comparative Politics*, 3(3), 283–322.

Mills, C.W. (2000). *The Power Elite*. New York: Oxford University Press.

Newman, K. and V.T. Chen (2008). *The Missing Class: Portraits of the Near Poor in America*. Boston: Beacon Press.

Rahnema, M. (1997). Introduction. In M. Rahnema and V. Bowtree (eds), *The Post-development Reader*. London: Zed Books.

Rostow, W.W. (1990). *The Stages of Economic Growth: A Non-Communist Manifesto*. Cambridge: Cambridge University Press.

Save the Children (2012). Global Inequality Highest in 20 Years. Retrieved April 15, 2012, from http://www.salon.com/2012/11/01/global_inequality_highest_in_20_years/.

Taylor, C. (1995). *Philosophical Arguments*. Cambridge, MA: Harvard University Press.

Wedel, J. (2009). *Shadow Elite: How the World's New Power Brokers Undermine Democracy, Government, and the Free Market*. New York: Basic Books.

10

NEOLIBERAL ECONOMICS AND UNDERGRADUATE POVERTY EDUCATION

Kevin D. Blair and Gabriel A. Santos.

Introduction

Educating undergraduates at American universities about poverty via an integrated series of courses leading to a minor is a small, but steadily growing, phenomenon. These efforts to strengthen undergraduate poverty education stem from a desire to aid the poor, but also from the need to provide students with the tools they need to develop an ethical orientation that can challenge the basic assumptions of neoliberal economics and policies that tend to dominate undergraduate education in the areas of business and economics on American campuses. As noted by Craig Murphy (2001, p. 354) amongst others (Stiglitz, 2012), it is vital that we educate undergraduate students on the consequences likely to arise "in a world in which some of us are so relatively rich and others so relatively poor." Echoing Murphy's concerns, Krian and Shadle (2006, p. 52) note:

> Very few undergraduates have more than a basic understanding of this global crisis, and very few college courses deal adequately with that knowledge gap. The issue can seem very abstract to college students, particularly those in the developed world who are surrounded by all-you-can-eat dining options and an endless array of fast-food delivery services. To help bridge the gap between the reality of poverty, inequality, and hunger, and that of the average college student, innovative pedagogical techniques must be used.

However, few universities offer more than a course here or there about poverty (most often a sociology course in social stratification) and thus fail to offer an integrated approach to teaching students about poverty (Blair, 2011) and, in turn, "because of its complexity, [poverty] can be addressed throughout the curriculum (e.g., policy, practice, theory, research, diversity, and/or specialization courses) or nowhere in the curriculum, that is, 'everybody's business becomes nobody's business'" (Austin, 2007).

This chapter examines current approaches to teaching students about poverty, with a focus on undergraduate students at American universities and in particular on what we view as the pervasiveness of neoliberal economics within the overall implicit curriculum of American higher education. By this we mean that without ever taking an actual course in economics, students are exposed to the general idea that markets are the best way to organize the economy, that minimal—if any—market failure exists, that free markets are the natural form of commerce, and that market outcomes—including who lives in poverty and who does not—are fairly determined and thus do not need to be addressed.

Review of relevant literature in the teaching of poverty to undergraduates

The literature on the teaching of poverty to undergraduates is limited, but it is growing as the movement to create undergraduate poverty education courses and minors progresses. However, in contrast to the roughly 20 American universities that now offer a minor in poverty studies, the majority of American colleges and universities generally provide one or maybe two courses that focus on poverty (e.g., Sociology of Poverty, Social Stratification, and The Economics of Poverty and Discrimination are common course titles) and no minor or integrated approach to educating their students about poverty. It is unlikely that these scattered course offerings produce students who possess an in-depth understanding of poverty and of the complexities in crafting solutions, let alone a lifelong commitment to aiding those in need and to alleviating poverty (Blair, 2011; Mulroy and Austin, 2004).

Clark (2007) points to the body of research, especially in relation to social work students, that underpins the essential position of the authors: the more students learn about those in poverty and why they are in poverty, the more likely they are to develop a positive view of those living in poverty. Having a positive view of those in poverty is linked to a willingness to work with the poor, to supporting efforts to improve the lives of the poor and to efforts to eradicate poverty (Blair, 2011). Segal (2007) refers to this as the development of social empathy and questions the use of teaching and related materials that create sympathy rather than empathy for the poor. Segal's concerns are also expressed by Carr and Sloan (2003) in their book *Poverty and Psychology: From Global Perspective to Local Practice*. Carr and Sloan, along with Lehning et al. (2007), who examined the most common theories of poverty to be found in social work textbooks, express concern that psychological theories that focus on the individual explanation as the underlying cause of poverty have come to dominate and may emphasize "negative personal characteristics of those living in poverty" (p. 7). Carr and Sloan (2003) note that in recent years the focus on the negative characteristics of those in poverty have been augmented by theories that emphasize resiliency and human capabilities, but the focus remains on the individual and not on the other structural explanations for the existence of poverty. Segal (2007) concludes that such efforts will not lead to students developing a commitment to ending poverty, but instead to a desire to be helpful through charity that enables the giver to feel better about themselves, but that has no long-lasting impact because the efforts are not directed at the true underlying structural causes of poverty.

Examining the implicit poverty/neoliberal curriculum: the need to cultivate a new political subjectivity

In the following sections we explore the implicit curriculum in relation to neoliberal economics and by implication the impact on students' understanding of poverty—an understanding, no doubt, that bears directly upon the formulation of what kinds of actions are necessary for social change. By implicit curriculum we refer to student learning not only from the formal course of instruction (i.e., courses that meet general education requirements and courses that meet major requirements) but also to the pedagogical approach to teaching contained within courses and to the policies and procedures that govern conduct and guide social interaction within the educational setting. Stated more bluntly: students are not granted the tools to develop an ethical orientation to challenge the basic assumptions and teachings of neoliberal policies. In fact, we argue the opposite occurs, primarily via the implicit curriculum: students are given to understand that neoliberal policies and approaches are the norm and the correct approach, and that they should resist efforts to be taught otherwise.

The comprehensive permeation of neoliberal doctrine is most evident, within the context of higher education, to the degree that it allows for a distinction that would be disallowed by a properly comprehensive program of poverty education: that between political education and political subjectivity. Undoubtedly, students at colleges and universities are informed about the organization and history of partisan politics in the United States, even of the origins and nature of social movements of various kinds that have challenged the political status quo. They are very often not taught, however, to be *political*, to be immersed in the life and destiny of a people with whom they share life and for whom they must attain and exercise their critical and imaginative faculties. Indeed, it is virtually axiomatic among contemporary American students that to be marketable is to be mobile. Career seeking is itself entrenched in the fluid logic of global capitalist speculation and, as a result, detracts from dedication to a place and its political and economic histories, aspirations, and struggles. Consequently, students know about economics and politics in their respective maneuvering and rules and are encouraged to envision their own participation in this system of debating, voting, and consuming, but are not taught to develop a critical, creative consciousness with respect to the "rules of the game." The consequent loose and often cynical attitude to prevailing political processes is a fundamental cause of the lack of alternative thought with respect to neoliberalism and hence, as Hayek, Friedman, and Greenspan avow in their own ways, the "pure" market becomes the benchmark by which governmental activity is determined or judged. Hayek (1988) militantly claims that extreme individualism alone adequately reflects the human call to flourish, with unbridled competition in all spheres of life as the best possible condition for the maximization of human expression. Any form of governmental intervention or overt commitment to altruism or collective enterprise is deemed a regression from the already realized, and growing, potential of human rationality. In emphasizing what is essentially global American cultural hegemony, Thomas Friedman (2005) asserts that if India and China were to become full-fledged free-market democracies, then the world would be all the more prosperous because "[t]hree United States are better than one" (p. 150). The Chair of the Federal Reserve of the United States from 1987 to 2006, Alan Greenspan (2008), is perhaps the most enthusiastic in this description of the economic state of affairs since the early 1970s:

> The *spreading* of a commercial rule of law and especially the protection of the rights of property has fostered a worldwide entrepreneurial stirring. This in turn has led to the creation of institutions that now anonymously guide an *ever-increasing* share of human activity—an international version of Adam Smith's "invisible hand."
>
> (p. 15; emphasis added)

In pondering the implications of these positions, from the contradictions inherent in the arrogant stance with respect to other global cultures and governments to the perplexing disavowal of the altruistic virtues, it is both unsurprising and unsettling to observe the deficient (and acquiescent) political subjectivity of American students. But the problem runs deeper still: the very composition of ethical–analytical skills and creativity is minimal with respect to economic policy and practice, thereby demonstrating that neoliberal socialization is a multi-layered affair, spanning the interlaced cultural, religious, emotional, social, and political spheres of the life-world. This complexity is due, of course, to neoliberalism's mythical or world-historical status.

Indeed, whatever students are taught about commerce and the political conditions that facilitate or hinder trade, it is beholden to the apparently natural or even divinely approved qualities of a "free" market. Part of the ethically impoverished status of economic education in higher education in the West is not simply due to academic fragmentation and specialization or the fear of confrontation between disciplines, but the sheer weight of association—perhaps even identification—between the virtues of civilization and neoliberalism. The opposite side of this "blessed" union of civilizational advance and neoliberalism is the blunting of moral orientation and ethical commitment that looks across class experiences. Regular or deliberate contact between members of different classes, and especially between the privileged and those often socio-economically invisible, may result in the evocation of an activist impulse and with it the refusal to allow responses of compassion and solidarity to be subsumed by a putatively more important goal or market logic often stated thus:

> This is the best of all the possible economic arrangements, so don't interfere, especially if the workings of the market cannot be understood. The "losers" in this affair don't want to cooperate, aren't willing to make their contribution, or are hypocrites that seek to bite the hand that feeds them.

Even if human knowledge is incapable of grasping all of the factors that attend to the exchange of human goods for the sustenance or betterment of life, this does not mean, as Hayek asserted in his Nobel Prize speech, that the work of the market ought to continue unhindered from external or governmental regulation (1974). Instead of prioritizing the presumably dynamic and beneficent workings of the market, and thus render the ongoing presence of rampant global and local inequalities as simply "necessary" costs of the system or the result of "faulty consumers," a student of poverty in its present complexities prioritizes alternative human relations from a perspective of open-eyed engagement that allows the exigencies of economic reality to make demands on the student. Seeing and meeting this demand must emerge from a multidisciplinary and interdisciplinary conversation that situates ethics and social analysis as daily, intertwined processes that are constitutive of the democratic political subject.

The opening claims of this section suggest, then, some of the most deleterious, institutionalized aspects of neoliberalism that a robust poverty education curriculum could definitively address—namely, its (1) un-democratic processes of enactment, (2) tendency to abstract from the local, particular, and singular, and (3) historical amnesia regarding human loss, helplessness, and suffering. These factors, in turn, reinforce students' notions that poverty is a normal condition of those who fail to act correctly within the market and who are receiving the consequences of their own poor decisions. The implicit curriculum reinforces the ideas that those in poverty potentially deserve sympathy and charity, but not political action geared toward addressing structural obstacles and market failure. That is, the curriculum in question turns a blind eye to the structural factors inherent in the process of capital accumulation that compel financial actors to suffer no limits whatever but, as David Harvey (2010) aptly put it, consider an economic crisis (a "limit") to be a mere obstacle to be circumvented. Financial innovation persists within a well-protected sphere of elitist conservatism that keeps the system going in isolation from the lives of the poor and precariously employed. Institutionally, American higher education has not been immune to the influence of this sort of conservative isolationism or abstraction from the lives of struggling people.

Indeed, in the context of higher education, which is heralded as an open-space of inquiry, examination, and refinement, the apparent domination of economic thought and practice that favors neoliberal trade doctrine and policies is evident in the all-too-common chasm that separates the campus from the surrounding community that actually provides the material and communal conditions that make the life of the institution possible. In light of neoliberal economic practices that abstract from localized commitments in pursuit of greater opportunities for expansion, which depend upon the reduction of labor costs and concomitant rise in precarious labor, this is hardly surprising. This is especially true in the case of the many people and products used in the operations of the educational institution that often come, as it were, rather cheaply. The triad of service learning, action research, and community-based research, therefore, becomes a prospective site for the analysis of concrete social situations that can provoke the development of joint ethico-political and economic praxes that are able to furnish the questions to think creatively about poverty (more about this below). From a more political standpoint, encouraging research and action that places a student—quite often from a privileged background—within a concrete social context that calls them to respond to the economic quandaries of poverty and the actual human toll they exact is also to *practice democracy*. It is this sort of education that cultivates and enhances democracy, especially of a more *ordinary* and *radical* kind. If students are placed in a position to be tested at the point at which poverty, ethics, and economics meet in concrete life, then quotidian democracy can be nurtured. By contrast, interested faculty must beware: service learning and related activities may fail to generate more than sympathy for those in poverty because these are short-term activities that are disconnected from an *integrated* approach centered on praxis.

The global liberalization of trade, on the other hand, has historically been associated with a violation of democratic involvement and expression. Take note, for example, of the momentous demonstration of large-scale democratic education and participation against the anti-democratic nature of neoliberal trade policies in Brazil's National Plebiscite on the External Debt Jubilee Campaign for a debt-free millennium. This effort was the result of a large and sufficiently well-coordinated effort among a network of local civic organizations, churches, and other local groups that spanned the entire country and aimed at garnering a response to national economic matters with respect to which ordinary citizens and residents had not been allowed a voice. Chief among their concerns was Brazil's relationship with the International Monetary Fund (IMF), which was viewed by many citizens as a recipe for economic disaster over the long haul. The citizen plebiscite voted on several basic questions about the economic state of the nation and submitted the results to the government. This entire effort encapsulates some of the more critically important goals of poverty education: encouraging a change in the political subjectivity of students in contemporary universities in the West and doing so in such a way that eliminates the hard and fast distinction between the supposed experts on economy and the people not situated within privileged circles of economic policymaking. Brazil's plebiscite assumed that citizens can inform the process of democracy from beginning to end, without privileging one group of participants to such a degree that the views of others ceased to matter. Poverty education can enact, by means of direct community involvement, internships, and action-oriented inquiry, a student political culture that seeks to identify and align itself to the cumulative wisdom of the people of the community.

Poverty education: countering the implicit neoliberal curriculum and forming the student subject

Poverty education as we propose it here intends to address this dearth of ethical and analytical tools, paired with embodied experience, which in concert prepare the student for concrete democratic engagement. Radical and ordinary democratic engagement, beyond that noted above, also refers to a movement across ethnic groups within the working class and greater attention to how lack of solidarity between working-class whites and blacks has undermined working-class activism. College students are in a prime position to support such a movement by virtue of the intersubjective transformations that cross-cultural and service-learning student cultures may engender. To be sure, some colleges and universities foster collaborative student initiatives directed at issues beyond intra-campus life better than others. Such capacity must be directed toward the proverbial elephant in the room: the enduring race and class structure of the United States. After steady gains during the beginning of the 20th century (workplace conditions, health insurance, pensions), the working class has, by and large, abdicated its interests. Higher learning, with too few exceptions, has largely abandoned the working class and aided the demise of its political potency in a context of aggressive globalization of financial markets, labor outsourcing, diminished buying power, and a growing gap between the wealthy and the poor. Slavoj Zizek (2009) and Miguez et al. (2009) have both offered cogent arguments regarding a perplexing trend: small business owners and members of the working class continue to vote against their own economic welfare.

In light of the abiding class-fractured polity of the United States, the mutual alienation of multiple registers of academic work are found to be rather illusory because students come to realize that a citizen cannot deal with economic matters as if politics resides in a separate epistemic or practical sphere. Ethics, for that matter, is evidently important to both spheres because both concern the nature of the flesh-and-blood existence of fellow human beings upon whom one depends. As the forthcoming section demonstrates, among the various combinations and permutations of poverty education programs, there are common threads that bind them all to one another. These commonalities amount to a set of analytical orientations and ethical commitments that provide the basis for a critical response to neoliberal economic thought and practice, a response that also furnishes the basis of alternative courses of economic practice.

Among the commonalities that will receive treatment below by means of an account of the personal experiences of the authors include (1) an appreciation of the qualities of political subjectivity most in need of explicit address among students, which encompass both ethical–existential and analytical commitments, and (2) the necessity of embodied engagement at the local level as a basis for broader economic reflection and action. These elements are, in turn, basic to the development of a radical democratic revival in American institutions of higher learning such that students embrace the promise of a critical consciousness in service of the community. In what follows we articulate these constructive commitments and practices more fully such that they address the deleterious institutional aspects of neoliberalism noted above. While it may at first seem strange that local democratic immersion is claimed to be absolutely integral to the task of assembling an effective critique of neoliberalism in its global dimensions, it is our hope that an elaboration of this aspect of poverty education at its most robust will convince readers of just that claim.

A poverty education program that straddles multiple disciplines and that is firmly embedded in the real political and economic demands of the place in which the institution resides—as exemplified in Spelman College's initiative to enhance the community contained within a 1.7-mile radius surrounding its campus—must include an understanding of the actual qualities of the acting subject. The experiences of the authors have enabled some of the characteristics essential to the formation of a certain political subjectivity to become more well defined and recognizable, both in their requirements and challenges. As a result of attempting to carry out multiple community-based projects of solidarity concerning, for instance, prisoner re-entry, urban farming, homelessness, and job creation, we have learned that the central interlaced ethical commitments of a subjectivity that challenges the seeming validity of neoliberalism are (1) the cultivation of a memory of loss, (2) the willingness to accept the demands of unjust

113

suffering, and (3) the resolve to continue learning from the people of a historical community until economic development is achieved by means of radical democratic processes. We will address these in turn and elaborate upon the constituent praxes of such commitments. A brief prefatory remark is in order. Each of the orienting elements to be reviewed in the initial section is the result of, and prompts further, historical actions. The social–ethical particularity of these orienting elements is simply part and parcel of the theory–praxis hermeneutic that we have learned to embrace during the course of teaching students about poverty. It is a crucial antidote to the abstracting tendencies of neoliberal frameworks of thought and its aggravation of working-class impotence and racial animosity in the United States. Perhaps echoing a well-known indigenous epistemology, orthopraxis and orthodoxy must form a unity; the dichotomy of believing/doing is not adequate to the dynamics of the subjectivity under consideration. Again, as many an indigene would say, beliefs *are* actions. This sort of "grounded" and self-critical subjectivity is a necessary condition for developing a sufficiently "exterior" perspective on the regnant economic and political institutions for which self-preservation, especially in service of established neoliberal practices, is a priority over against the quality and structure of actual human relations (see Miguez et al., 2009, Chap. 4).

The cultivation of a memory of loss, and with it a new historical consciousness, emerges initially from any well-informed research about the profound debt and social instability that neoliberal trade agreements have brought upon a host of nations, such as Mexico after the passage of NAFTA. It becomes virtually impossible for us to carry on research regarding the consequences of such trade policies without, as the Frankfurt School theorist Walter Benjamin (1969) would assert, acknowledging the claim of the dead on the present. In taking note of the extraordinary range of loss tied to these agreements and policies, including the loss of once-viable independent businesses, it became clear that much of the loss was the result of well-established social, economic, and political structures that deemed certain people and ecologically protective habitats as disposable, untrustworthy, dangerous, and even worthy of sacrifice in service of the status quo. Benjamin, however, rattles our sociological sensibilities in that he argued for a changed relationship with the dead and the past. He argues for a new historical orientation that seeks to recognize the moments during which a constellation can be formed that links a present struggle for economic justice with a similar struggle in the past so that, as in a flash, the two (or more) causes compress time and make exceedingly clear that the voices of the forgotten are still seeking vindication. The present has yet to answer them. This perspective, in other words, instills a particular historical answerability and affection within the subject; it asserts that there is an indefatigable continuity—even if tragically misshapen or disregarded—with the persons of the past. Simply because they are not alive, as Horkheimer and Adorno (2007) argue in their fragment *On the Theory of Ghosts*, does not mean that no important link with these past persons exists. Indeed, this is more than simple memorialization. It is an active historical attitude that assumes the existence of a community of persons that, even if comprised of alive and dead, does not tolerate the fact that many of the members of such a community had their demands for redemptive action denied. With this, we now realize that any community-based research must take up the task of connecting with the history of struggle and loss in that place and must take up the importance of giving priority to the memories of the most mature members that live as custodians of community memories.

The second commitment is linked to the first. The cultivation of a memory of loss is bound up with a willingness to respond to the demands of unjust suffering. Again, in discussing such occurrences, students must combat a certain set of established norms and habits that are peculiar to our class situation that is largely given to historical amnesia. A sense of powerlessness, guilt, and "compassion fatigue" seem to mark the thought-life of those similarly situated in privilege.

It occurred to us, as a result of failed attempts to generate certain programs for job creation (ink cartridge recycling and small cafés or kiosks operated by formerly homeless persons), that such efforts cannot be so much about trying to save others or initiate feel-good charitable deeds, but as an effort of mutual risk and liberation. The amount of effort and time required to think through the options, opportunities, and complexities of the matters under consideration actually entail loss for us and the student, just as the fellow community members squarely face actual or potential loss on a regular basis. As sociologists, it is evident that if we enter the memories of a place, and acknowledge the injustices of their reality, that we then cannot simply live as a spectator in a sealed room, comfortably isolated from harm, disappointment, and loss of reputation. Hence, as Mark Lewis Taylor (2003) argues, we are not sure how we can speak for or to a people of loss or victims of enduring oppression or inequality, but we do know that we must learn to accept potentially significant failure and pain in an effort to share in their life. Admittedly, it is hard to discern how much solidarity of this kind has been generated as a result of the poverty education programs of universities and colleges, and perhaps for that reason it behooves educators to ask: What of our poverty education (across every discipline) must change in order to garner trust among community partners that are convinced we are willing to win and lose with them?

The last component is perhaps the most troubling for the person of middle-class and upper-middle-class persuasion. A certain fixation on expert knowledge and specialization originally holds many captive to the presumed superiority of neoliberal doctrines, generating ever-greater levels of frustration in light of the many disregarded failures. The main catalyst of change in this regard is the formation of friendships—singularly *political* friendships—by virtue of which a certain pedagogy is impressed upon the student subject: We are simply one of many members of this community, all of whom have gifts and talents, joined by scars and wounds, that must be brought together in order to overcome the prevailing race and class-based boundaries of the city and the historical amnesia that forgets the claims that the victims of the past make on the present. The forgetfulness that must be avoided became a crucial concern in the second to third year of work in the community. The work of Walter Benjamin noted above featured prominently in attempts to understand that none of our efforts for fellow citizens of the city could be carried out in a historical vacuum, a quality that is more than evident in standard, one-time charitable efforts. Once a person is historically informed, it is almost impossible to not discover the failures in answering the cries of the unfulfilled aspirations of past movements. Indeed, the fact that these "cries" were heard by us simply reinforced not only the notion that a certain political subjectivity hears what other subjectivities disregard but also Benjamin's contention that these cries from the past amount to claims on the present that seek to re-surface in "now-time" (p. 263). The "now-time," or *kairos* moment, is a veritable event during which some miscarriage of justice, glaring impairment to the process of communication and accountability, or severe deprivation stemming from economic and political irresponsibility becomes manifest. It is an event that demands and prompts action, the suppression of which significantly blunts the relationship between the affective and critical capacities of the political subject. This kind of moment grounded in a distinct ethical and socio-economic kind of commitment, and the profound challenge it poses to a human being as a whole, is rarely possible in most forms of classroom instruction. Pedagogy that privileges these solidaristic moments therefore demands to be prioritized, without excluding other pedagogical methods, within a creative multi-dimensional poverty education program (see the next section about pedagogical options).

A personal account should suffice in portraying what can be engendered when students directly engage local matters of economic import, thereby initiating a process of subject refinement by which a number of connections between different institutional spheres become identifiable. In spring 2012, when canvassing the streets of a working-class neighborhood in a small city in a mid-Atlantic state in the United States, which was a veritable food desert by most standards (lowest car ownership in the city, low median family income, and no super-market within three miles), one of the authors and several students made it a point to converse with residents as they distributed student-made pamphlets. These pamphlets addressed a lack of transparency and concerns about watershed pollution associated with a local chemical com-pany. This firm produced chemical substrates for use among many larger cosmetic and personal hygiene corporations, but had not informed the neighborhood from which it drew the majority of its employees what chemicals had periodically entered its local water supply (the laboratory is a mere 1.2 miles from a major river). This storyline is all-too-common in an era of neoliberal expansion. Even so, distributing information about the situation was difficult for students. Most compelling, however, was the fruit that sustained discussion could yield even in a relatively ephemeral encounter. These encounters, the students learned, could be quite transformative if carried out many times over. In said neighborhood, the students initiated a conversation with a city employee who at first was not pleased with our calls for corporate honesty or transparency regarding the seepage that had turned a local creek into a suds-covered, raspberry aroma-infused waterway. However, by means of honest, back-and-forth disputation, we were able to arrive at a point that made it clear to all parties involved that only action could resolve our concerns. At one point we asked, "If you are convinced that water-testing would reveal inadequacies, then what about the standards that constitute adequacy—are they in flux?" He conceded, "Maybe they are." The resident almost immediately relayed a story concerning his encounter with city workers who, for a number of years, had washed off road paint from their trucks above a drainage ditch that emptied into a local creek. Once he had completed his retelling, we knew that further efforts were needed because the degree of mystification and ignorance was too pronounced to leave unaddressed. In other words, the irruption into our horizon of potentially unjust damage, albeit hidden, was a sort of event that demanded a response. He assured us that he would do his part to make sure that such practices would be discontinued.

This kind of action, in conjunction with classroom education, research, and discussion, ena-bles the student to palpably connect neoliberalism, urban marginalization, and even ecological degradation. The strong interrelationship of the first two phenomena mentioned are astutely formulated in the work of Loic Wacquant, for whom the "penalization of poverty," expressed chiefly in "get-tough" criminal justice policy, works hand-in-hand with the rise of neoliberalism (Wacquant, 2001, p. 402). This student involvement is one that embeds the student in a process of subject formation that situates concrete participation as a fount from which ideas and questions may emerge in service of still-greater refinement of action that aims at challenging the institution-alized patterns of conduct and perception tied to neoliberal policies. In what follows, we place the aforementioned concerns and claims regarding the student subject and political subjectivity within the framework of a pedagogy and curriculum design that has poverty at its center.

Pedagogical approaches, experiential learning, and other challenges to poverty education

Segal (2007, p. 72) and others (Lang, 2007; Schiller, 2008) have suggested that there are essen-tially four explanations used to explain both the existence and intransience of poverty in the United States. These explanations are (Segal, 2007, p. 72):

poverty as a result of capitalism; poverty as a consequence of individual behaviors; or poverty as a consequence of structural conditions. A fourth perspective suggests that the differences and gaps between those who are well-off and those who are poor perpetuates poverty and keeps society from addressing the problems.

Segal also notes that the fourth explanation, which seeks to address the us/them split and cognitive distancing, is the least likely to be taught and used as a way of getting students to engage in the process of alleviating poverty.

As noted by Blair (2011), a range of approaches to teaching about poverty exist, but they can be broadly grouped into two basic categories: strongly academic or strongly experiential. Also, instructors must determine the balance they seek between a focus on poverty in the United States and a focus on global poverty. Our experience has been that students tend to have a more favorable view of those in poverty outside of the United States than they do of the poor who reside in the United States. Class discussion generally indicates that students view the global poor as being poor through little to no fault of their own, while they tend to view the U.S. poor as failing to meet the challenges and to take advantage of the opportunities inherent in the market.

Strongly academic

These approaches emphasize empirical data, census reports, and a scholarly approach, usually with an emphasis on political and economic policy as it affects those living in poverty. A collection of course syllabi that is posted on the internet appears to show that Bradley Schiller's (2008) *The Economics of Poverty and Discrimination, 10th Edition* is the most widely used text for these types of undergraduate courses on poverty. Other commonly used texts include: Amartya Sen's (1999) *Development as Freedom*, Kevin Lang's (2007) *Poverty and Discrimination*, John Iceland's (2006) *Poverty in America*, Rebecca Blank's (1998) *It Takes a Nation: A New Agenda for Fighting Poverty*, and a handful of others. In addition, many instructors create a "course pack" of selected readings, pulling together chapters from some or all of the above books in combination with articles from scholarly journals, "think tanks" such as the Urban Institute and the Heritage Foundation, and newspapers, magazines, and other popular sources.

Assignments in these academically focused courses show an emphasis on research, analysis of data, analysis of the impact of policy changes (e.g., analysis of a change in minimum wage laws on the income of those living in poverty), and similar typically academic assignments.

Strongly experiential or service learning

These approaches emphasize service by students and direct exposure to those living in poverty via volunteering in soup kitchens, food pantries, and similar service programs and agencies. Readings for courses with this emphasis tend toward ethnographies such as Judith Goode and Jeff Maskovsky's (2002) *The New Poverty Studies*, popular books that show life in poverty such as Barbara Ehrenreich's (2008) *Nickel and Dimed: On (Not) getting by in America* and David K. Shipler's (2005) *The Working Poor: Invisible in America*, popular literature such as Betty Smith's (1943) *A Tree Grows in Brooklyn*, along with readings from the Bible, short stories, and other firsthand accounts of what it is like to live in poverty.

Assignments in these courses typically involve hours of volunteering and the keeping of journals, reflection papers, on-line discussions with classmates and others about the experiences, and a general emphasis on development of one's self in relation to understanding and empathizing with those living in poverty.

While the experiential learning may help the development of prosocial behaviors, greater empathy toward those in poverty, and a willingness to do more to help (see Brandenberger and Trozzolo, 2001; Eyler and Giles, 1999; and Twenge, et al., 2007), it may also undermine efforts to develop the in-depth knowledge and skills needed to critically analyze and counter the permeation of neoliberal thinking. Thus ultimately we return to the need for an integrated series of courses that provide a coordinated effort to balance both academic/theoretical learning about poverty with experiential learning that is designed to lessen cognitive distancing and increase social solidarity and localized economic commitment.

Conclusion

In a recent class on social stratification taught by one of the authors, discussion centered on why some people live in poverty and some live in abundance. The majority position was that in the United States people are free to choose, a phrase directly used by one of the students and echoed by many others. When the instructor asked if the student had read Friedman and Friedman's (1990) book by that title, the student indicated that he didn't know such a book existed. And while indicating that some of them had heard of Milton Friedman, none of the students had read any of his writings, including two that had taken a year-long course in macro and microeconomics. In his essay assessing neoliberalism Clarke (2013) offers the following observation:

> However, to argue that the neoliberal model is unrealistic is somewhat to miss the point, since the neoliberal model does not purport so much to describe the world as it is, but the world as it should be. The point for neoliberalism is not to make a model that is more adequate to the real world, but to make the real world more adequate to its model. This is not merely an intellectual fantasy, it is a very real political project, to realize which neoliberalism has conquered the commanding heights of global intellectual, political and economic power, all of which are mobilized to realize the neoliberal project of subjecting the whole world's population to the judgment and morality of capital.

This class discussion, and many more like it over the years, suggests to the authors that the desire to remake the world into a neoliberal world as described by Clarke is succeeding. Only those students who take a series of courses designed to broaden and sharpen their thinking in relation to neoliberalism, growing social and economic inequality, poverty, and concrete political action are in a position to objectively analyze the value of neoliberal approaches and to offer alternatives. We thus seek the expansion of undergraduate poverty education and specifically the creation of minors in poverty that can provide the integrated theoretical and experiential education that is needed to counter the neoliberal efforts on American campuses.

References

Austin, M. (2007). Understanding Poverty: Multiple Social Science Perspectives. *Journal of Human Behavior in the Social Environment*, 16(1/2), 1–4.

Benjamin, W. (1969). *Illuminations: Essays and Reflections*. New York: Schocken Books.

Blair, K. (2011). Developing an Understanding of Best Practices for Teaching Undergraduate Students About Poverty, in Paul Kriese and Robert Osborne, eds: *Social Justice, Poverty and Race: Normative and Empirical Points of View*. Amsterdam, Netherlands: Rodopi.

Blank, R. (1998). *It Takes a Nation: A New Agenda for Fighting Poverty*. Princeton, NJ: Princeton University Press.

Brandenberger, J. and Trozzolo, T. (2001). *Religious Commitment and Prosocial Behavior: A Study of Undergraduates at the University of Notre Dame*. Center for Social Concerns: Report 2.

Carr, S. and Sloan, T. (eds) (2003). *Poverty and Psychology: From Global Perspective to Local Practice*. New York: Kluwer Academic.

Clark, S. (2007). Social Work Students' Perceptions of Poverty. *Journal of Human Behavior in the Social Environment*, 16(1/2), 149–166.

Clarke, S. (2013). The Neoliberal Theory of Society: The Ideological Foundations of Neoliberalism. Retrieved January 28, 2013, from http://homepages.warwick.ac.uk/~syrbe/pubs/Neoliberalism.pdf.

Ehrenreich, B. (2008). *Nickel and Dimed: On (Not) getting by in America*. New York: Henry Holt and Company.

Eyler, J. and Giles, D.E. (1999). *Where's the Learning in Service Learning?* San Francisco: Jossey-Bass.

Friedman, M. and Friedman, R. (1990). *Free to Choose: A Personal Statement*. New York: Harcourt, Inc.

Friedman, T. (2005). *The World is Flat: A Brief History of the 21st Century*. New York: Farrar, Straus, and Giroux.

Goode, J. and Maskovsky, J., eds (2002). *The New Poverty Studies: The Ethnography of Power, Politics, and Impoverished People in the United States*. New York: New York University Press.

Greenspan, A. (2008). *The Age of Turbulence: Adventures in a New World*. New York: Penguin Books.

Harvey, David. (2010). *The Crisis of Capitalism*. RSA Lecture Series. Retrieved January 21, 2013, from http://www.thersa.org/__data/assets/pdf_file/0011/558929/RSA-Lecture-David-Harvey-transcript.pdf.

Hayek, F.A. von. (1974). "The Pretence of Knowledge." Acceptance Speech Upon Reception of Nobel Prize in Economics. Retrieved January 12, 2013, from http://www.nobelprize.org/nobel_prizes/economics/laureates/1974/hayek-lecture.html.

Hayek, F.A. von. (1988). *The Fatal Conceit: The Errors of Socialism*. Chicago: University of Chicago Press.

Horkheimer, M. and Adorno, T.W. (2007). *Dialectic of Enlightenment*. Stanford: Stanford University Press.

Iceland, J. (2006). *Poverty in America*. Berkeley: University of California Press.

Krain, M. and Shadle, C. (2006). Starving for Knowledge: An Active Learning Approach to Teaching About World Hunger. *International Studies Perspectives*, 7, 51–66.

Lang, K. (2007). *Poverty and Discrimination*. Princeton, NJ: Princeton University Press.

Lehning, A., Vu, C., and Pintak, I. (2007). Theories of Poverty: Findings from Textbooks on Human Behavior and the Social Environment. *Journal of Human Behavior in the Social Environment*, 10(3), 5–19.

Miguez, N., Rieger, J., and Sung, J.M. (2009). *Beyond the Spirit of Empire: Theology and Politics in a New Key*. London, UK: SCM Press.

Mulroy, E. and Austin, M.J. (2004). Towards a Comprehensive Framework for Understanding the Social Environment: In Search of Theory for Practice. *Journal of Human Behavior in the Social Environment*, 10(3), 61–84.

Murphy, C.N. (2001). Political Consequences of the New Inequality. *International Studies Quarterly*, 45, 347–356.

Schiller, B. (2008). *The Economics of Poverty and Discrimination, 10th edition*. Upper Saddle River, NJ: Pearson/Prentice Hall Publishers.

Segal, E. (2007). Social Empathy: A New Paradigm to Address Poverty. *Journal of Poverty*, 11(3), 65–81.

Sen, A. (1999). *Development as Freedom*. Oxford: Oxford University Press.

Shipler, D.K. (2005). *The Working Poor: Invisible in America*. New York: Vintage Books.

Smith, Betty. (1943). *A Tree Grows in Brooklyn*. New York: Perennial Classics; 1st Perennial Classics Edition (September 1, 1998).

Stiglitz, J. (2012). *The Price of Inequality*. New York: W.W. Norton and Company.

Taylor, M.L. (2003). *Opting for the Margins: Postmodernity and Liberation in Christian Theology*, ed. Joerg Rieger. New York: Oxford University Press.

Twenge, J., Baumeister, R., DeWall, D., Ciarocco, N., and Bartels, J. (2007). Social Exclusion Decreases Prosocial Behavior. *Journal of Personality and Social Psychology*, 92(1), 56–66.

Wacquant, L. (2001). The Penalisation of Poverty and the Rise of Neo-Liberalism. *European Journal of Criminal Policy and Research*, 9, 401–412.

Zizek, S. (2009). *First as Tragedy, Then as Farce*. New York: Verso Books.

11

THE IMPORTANCE OF CONTEXT TO THE SOCIAL PROCESSES AROUND MATERIAL HARDSHIP

Colleen M. Heflin

Scholarly research into the causes and consequences of social stratification often conceptualize the stratification process as either resulting from individual choices regarding education, employment, or family formation, or as dominated by structural forces outside the individual's control, such as the neoliberal market-oriented drive towards economic growth. While a focus on one side of the equation can increase our understanding of the stratification process while holding the other side of the equation constant, in reality both individual and structural factors are at play. Therefore, this chapter will examine the role of both individual and state-level factors in predicting household-level measures of well-being—food insufficiency, bill-paying hardships, and home hardships.

While there is a growing literature describing the patterns and correlates of material hardship (Mayer and Jencks, 1989; Edin and Lein, 1997; Bauman, 1999; Boushey and Gundersen, 2001; Heflin, 2006), prior work has tended to focus on individual determinants of material hardship and largely ignored the role of the structure of the welfare state. This is surprising in light of the body of research indicating that state economic and policy characteristics are important determinants of risk for income poverty and, to some extent, food security.

This chapter combines nationally representative data from five panels of the Survey of Income and Program Participation (SIPP) on food insufficiency, bill-paying hardships, and home hardships to explore the extent to which observed variation in reports of material hardship is influenced by state-level economic conditions, social policy, political conditions, and the physical climate. Results suggest that food insufficiency, bill-paying hardships, and home hardships are sensitive to the context in which the household is embedded.

Past research on state-level determinants of well-being

Prior research on state-level determinants of the well-being of low-income populations has focused almost exclusively on measures of poverty. Empirical studies are united in their characterization of the relationship between macroeconomic performance and poverty over the 1960–1980 time period (Cutler and Katz, 1991; Haveman and Schwabish, 2000). Time series analyses over the 1960–1970 period describe a consistent pattern in which poverty declines during periods of economic expansion and increases during economic recessions. After the early 1982–1983 recession, however, the tight relationship between economic conditions and poverty loosened, partly as a result of growing income inequality. Thus, the truism used to describe the early years of the War on Poverty, "A rising tide lifts all boats," became questionable in its applicability after the 1980s.

Research on the 1990s to the present is much less consistent, and findings vary depending on the analytic technique employed. Haveman and Schwabish (2000) examine the 1959–1998 period and report that poverty in the 1992–1998 period does appear to be sensitive to the per capita GDP growth. Iceland et al. (2005) examine the change in poverty over the 1980–1982 and 2000–2002 periods and look separately at three different components of economic growth—employment, per capita gross state product, and the unemployment rate. They find that while poverty was influenced by employment and per capita gross state product, unemployment had little effect on poverty.

Arguably the best study of the post-1980 time period is that by Gundersen and Ziliak (2004). In a time series analysis using the 1981–2000 Current Population Survey, Gundersen and Ziliak find that a strong macroeconomy was associated with reductions in poverty but that effects varied across household types. Changes in the unemployment rate and the employment growth rate reduced poverty among married-couple households and those headed by a white person. However, female-headed households and those headed by black persons experienced substantial reductions in poverty as a result of increases in median wages.

While there is a body of literature providing a strong theoretical basis for the relationship between the shape of neoliberal policies and well-being (Larner, 2000; Hartman, 2005; Coburn, 2006), only one prior study examines the role of state-level characteristics on measures of well-being besides the federal poverty measure. Using 1998–2001 data from the Current Population Survey, Bartfeld and Dunifon (2006) explore the role of economic, policy, and social conditions in determining state-level variation in one form of material hardship—food insecurity. After controlling for household demographic characteristics, and indicators of state-level federal food programs, economic policies, and economic conditions, they report a positive relationship between the state unemployment rate and median rent and a negative relationship between the average wage per job and the probability of being food insecure.

This chapter builds upon the prior literature on state-level predictors of well-being to provide several important contributions to the extant literature. 1) By examining three types of material hardship (food sufficiency, bill hardship, and home hardship), our knowledge base is moved beyond the realm of food security or income poverty alone and a multidimensional picture of well-being can be achieved. 2) Prior work that examined multiple types of material hardship either used data that was not nationally representative (Heflin, 2006) or presented mostly descriptive or reduced form models of correlates with hardship (Bauman, 1999; Beverly, 2001). This chapter utilizes nationally representative data from the 1992–2004 SIPP and thus presents the most comprehensive and representative picture of material hardship possible with current data sources. 3) This chapter continues in the Durkheimian (1897) tradition of considering the role of context in the study of social events by directly modeling the relative contribution of household characteristics and state characteristics to the risk of experiencing material hardship. This is an important methodological advancement that will inform the process by which two households with similar household characteristics have different risks of material hardship due to their location.

Data

Data are from the 1992–2004 panels of the SIPP. Specifically, data are merged from the eighth wave of the 2004 SIPP panel (n = 11,457); the eighth wave of the 2001 SIPP panel (n = 6,013); the eighth wave of the 1996 SIPP panel (n = 9,553); the ninth wave of the 1993

SIPP panel (n = 5,491); and the third wave of the 1992 SIPP panel (n = 6,243). My analytic sample includes only households with completed interviews with children; the total sample size is 38,757. When survey weights are used, the SIPP is designed to be representative of the civilian non-institutionalized population in the United States.

Measures

Bill-paying hardship: Survey respondents were asked if in the last 12 months there was a time when they did not pay the full amount of the electric, gas, or oil bill, when the telephone company disconnected the service because payments were not made, when they did not meet the household's essential expenses, or when they did not pay the full amount of rent or mortgage. Approximately 17 percent of all households report a bill-paying hardship.

Housing hardship: Six items are used to indicate housing hardship. The first measure is an indicator for whether or not survey respondents said the household had a problem with pests such as rats, mice, roaches, or other insects. The second and third measures indicate respondent reports of problems concerning a leaky roof or ceiling and broken windows, respectively. The fourth measure indicates a problem in the household with a toilet, hot water heater, or other plumbing that did not work. The fifth and sixth measure indicates whether respondents said there was a problem in their household with either open cracks or holes in the walls or ceiling, or holes in the floor big enough for someone to catch their foot on. If two or more of these problems are present, a home hardship is indicated. On average, 2.5 percent of all households meet this definition.

Food hardship: The food hardship measure is constructed based on the question "Which of the following statements best describes the food eaten in your household in the last 12 months: enough to eat, sometimes not enough to eat, or often not enough to eat?" Those answering "sometimes" or "often not enough to eat" were coded as food insufficient for this measure. On average, 2.8 percent of the population meets the criteria for food insufficiency.

State-level characteristics come from a variety of sources. The University of Kentucky Center for Poverty Research compiles annual state-level data on a variety of measures that were used here including the unemployment rate, gross state product, minimum wage levels, Temporary Assistance for Need Families (TANF) and food stamp benefit levels for a family of three, and the state Earned Income Tax credit rate. The measure of the physical climate used here is the number of heating degree days, defined as the difference between a reference value of 65°F (18°C) and the average outside temperature for that day (NOAA, 2008). The state median wage is computed using the three-year moving average of the ratio of labor market earnings to annual hours of work for the family head from the Current Population Survey. Finally, I use a measure of state government liberalism, designed by Berry et al. (1998).

Household-level characteristics, like the outcome measures, come directly from the SIPP. Each household is defined in terms of the characteristics of the head and their demographic membership (black, Hispanic, female), education level (less than high school, high school graduate, some college, or bachelor's degree or more), marital status (married, never married, or divorced, widowed, or separated), if the household lives in a metropolitan area, the number of children in the household, the household's income-to-needs ratio, and if the head is employed, disabled, or elderly.

Methods

This chapter examines the importance of the state environment in determining the household risk of food insufficiency, bill hardships, and home hardships. Model 1 includes both state-level and household-level characteristics. Results for fixed effect linear probability models are also presented in Model 2. The main advantage of fixed effect models is that time-invariant unmeasured characteristics at the state level are captured by the state fixed effect, rendering the fixed effect model the strongest model for causal inference.

Results

Food insufficiency

In Table 11.1 we begin by presenting results for our models of food insufficiency. Starting with Model 1, the risk of food insufficiency increases as the unemployment rate increases and decreases as the per capita gross state product increases. Policy conditions are less clear drivers of the risk of food insufficiency. We find a positive relationship between the generosity of the TANF + food stamp benefit and food insufficiency but are unable to reject the null hypothesis of no relationship in the case of the minimum wage and the state EITC rate. In terms of the political environment, we find that state government liberalism is positively associated with household food insufficiency, while a more severe physical climate is associated with less food insufficiency.

Individual-level characteristics are consistent with prior research in all cases. Blacks, Hispanics, and females all face higher levels of risk of food insufficiency relative to whites and males. A negative monotonic relationship between education level and food insufficiency is found. The risk of food insufficiency increases with the number of children in the household, and the risk is higher for never married or divorced, widowed, or separated households (compared to married households). A negative relationship is found with the income-to-needs ratio. However, disabled household heads and those living in metropolitan areas face higher risks; the elderly face lower risks of food insufficiency.

Fixed effect models shown in Model 2 indicate the within-state variation in food insufficiency. State EITC rates are positively associated with food insufficiency, while other economic, social, political, and physical conditions are found to be unrelated to the risk of food insufficiency after controlling for unobserved time-invariant heterogeneity at the state level. Individual characteristics, however, are shown to be the primary drivers of within-state variation in food insufficiency.

Bill hardship

Models of bill hardship are shown in Table 11.2. Beginning with Model 1, economic factors are important predictors of bill-paying hardships but in ways that differ from models of food insufficiency. The state median wage is negatively associated with bill-paying hardships and there is no evidence in Model 1 of a relationship between the state unemployment rate and bill-paying hardships. In terms of state policy conditions, the EITC is protective in Model 2 as expected, since higher state EITC rates puts more money in the hands of low-wage earners. Once again, high levels of state government liberalism are associated with lower levels of bill-paying hardships and physical climate is unrelated. Among individual-level characteristics, being black or female is associated with higher levels of bill-paying hardships. Hispanics, however, are not shown to face a differential probability based on ethnicity of reporting a bill-paying hardship in Model 2. Similar to models of food insufficiency, married households face an advantage over never married or

Table 11.1 Determinants of food insufficiency

	Model (1)			Model (2)		
	Beta	Sig.	(SE)	Beta	Sig.	(SE)
Economic environment						
Unemployment rate	0.0687	★★★	(0.0169)	0.0008		(0.0010)
Gross state product	−22.4907	★★★	(8.2387)	−0.4502		(0.4952)
Median wage	0.0058		(0.0082)	0.0069		(0.0061)
Policy environment						
Minimum wage	0.0167		(0.3949)	0.0085		(0.0099)
TANF + food stamp benefit	0.3903	★★	(0.1536)	−0.0080		(0.0172)
State EITC rate	−0.1453		(0.3735)	0.0447	★	(0.0268)
Political and physical environment						
State government liberalism	0.0028	★★	(0.0012)	0.0000		(0.0000)
Physical climate	−0.0003	★★★	(0.0001)	0.0000		(0.0000)
Demographic characteristics of head						
Black	0.1159	★	(0.0674)	0.0121	★★★	(0.0019)
Hispanic	0.2661	★★★	(0.0518)	0.0156	★★★	(0.0026)
Female	0.1734	★★★	(0.0384)	0.0053	★★★	(0.0012)
Education level of head						
High school graduate	−0.2775	★★★	(0.0538)	−0.0158	★★★	(0.0018)
Some college	−0.3142	★★★	(0.0696)	−0.0192	★★★	(0.0019)
Bachelor's degree or higher	−1.0842	★★★	(0.0875)	−0.0293	★★★	(0.0020)
Marital status						
Never married	0.7142	★★★	(0.0630)	0.0271	★★★	(0.0017)
Divorced/widowed/separated	0.6704	★★★	(0.0647)	0.0211	★★★	(0.0014)
Number of children	0.1337	★★★	(0.0188)	0.0090	★★★	(0.0006)
Income-to-needs ratio	−0.4223	★★★	(0.0359)	−0.0020	★★★	(0.0002)
Employed head	−0.0550		(0.0587)	−0.0178	★★★	(0.0015)
Disabled head	0.8176	★★★	(0.0605)	0.0436	★★★	(0.0019)
Elderly head	−1.3541	★★★	(0.0932)	−0.0333	★★★	(0.0018)
Metropolitan residence	0.1377	★	(0.0758)	0.0048	★★★	(0.0015)

Note: $p<.10$=★; $p<.05$=★★; $p<.01$=★★★

Table 11.2 Determinants of bill hardship

	Model (1)			Model (2)		
	Beta	Sig.	(SE)	Beta	Sig.	(SE)
Economic environment						
Unemployment rate	0.0199		(0.0123)	0.0057	★★★	(0.0022)
Gross state product	3.7838		(4.4421)	0.8186		(1.0749)
Median wage	0.0124	★★★	(0.0041)	−0.0039		(0.0013)
Policy environment						
Minimum wage	0.0629		(0.2706)	−0.0407	★	(0.0215)
TANF + food stamp benefit	0.1319		(0.1027)	0.0493		(0.0372)
State EITC rate	−0.2994	★	(0.1540)	0.0163		(0.0580)
Political and physical environment						
State government liberalism	−0.0019	★★	(0.0008)	−0.0003	★★★	(0.0001)
Physical climate	−0.0001		(0.0001)	0.0000		(0.0000)
Demographic characteristics of head						
Black	0.5522	★★★	(0.0453)	0.1105	★★★	(0.0041)
Hispanic	0.0496		(0.0467)	0.0262	★★★	(0.0056)
Female	0.2761	★★★	(0.0274)	0.0288	★★★	(0.0026)
Education level of head						
High school graduate	−0.0830	★★	(0.0369)	−0.0192	★★★	(0.0040)
Some college	−0.0353		(0.0415)	−0.0228	★★★	(0.0041)
Bachelor's degree or higher	−0.5836	★★★	(0.0538)	−0.0836	★★★	(0.0044)
Marital status						
Never married	0.3564	★★★	(0.0293)	0.0716	★★★	(0.0036)
Divorced/widowed/separated	0.4297	★★★	(0.0304)	0.0669	★★★	(0.0030)
Number of children	0.1964	★★★	(0.0113)	0.0444	★★★	(0.0013)
Income-to-needs ratio	−0.3025	★★★	(0.0102)	−0.0123	★★★	(0.0004)
Employed head	0.1427	★★★	(0.0271)	−0.0233	★★★	(0.0034)
Disabled head	0.7275	★★★	(0.0324)	0.1353	★★★	(0.0041)
Elderly head	−1.2831	★★★	(0.0451)	−0.1324	★★★	(0.0039)
Metropolitan residence	0.0374		(0.0413)	0.0004		(0.0033)

Note: p<.10=★; p<.05=★★; p<.01=★★★

ever married households. The risk of bill-paying hardship increases with the number of children present in the household but decreases with the household's income-to-needs ratio. Households who are disabled or employed face a higher risk of bill hardships while the elderly face lower risks. Metropolitan residence has no effect on the risk of bill-paying hardships.

Fixed effect results presented in Model 2 reveal the drivers of within-state differences in levels of predicted bill-paying hardships. Beginning with economic conditions, after controlling unobserved state-level factors associated with bill-paying hardships, increases in the state unemployment rate are associated with increases in household-level prediction of bill-paying hardship. State gross product and median wage are unrelated to bill-paying hardships in fixed effect models. In terms of social policies, households living in states with higher minimum wage levels have lower predicted levels of bill-paying hardships relative to households in the same state with lower minimum wage levels, suggesting that minimum wage policies may help low-income populations make ends meet. Social welfare generosity and the state EITC rate are unrelated to within-state differences in bill-paying hardships. All individual-level characteristics are found to be related to within-state differences in bill-paying hardships with the exception of metropolitan residence.

Home hardship

Models examining home hardships are shown in Table 11.3. Beginning with Model 1, per capita gross state product is negatively related to home hardships, suggesting that the strength of the state economy is an important component of the risk of home hardships. The minimum wage level is found to be protective for home hardships in Model 1, while the state EITC rate is positively correlated with home hardships. State government liberalism, our measure of the political environment, is positively associated with home hardships.

Individual-level covariates are as expected. Blacks and Hispanics have a higher probability of reporting housing hardships but the risk is evenly distributed with respect to gender. Education is protective and the relationship is monotonic, indicating that the higher the level of education, the lower the risk of home hardships. As with the other hardships examined, both never married and ever married (divorced, separated, or widowed) households have higher predicted levels of home hardships than married households. Once again, the probability of home hardships increases with the number of children present but decreases with the household's income-to-needs ratio. The disabled face higher levels of home hardship and the elderly lower levels, as with other forms of hardships. Living in a metropolitan area reduces the probability of home hardships, however, suggesting that home hardships are unique among the hardships examined here for being more prevalent in non-metropolitan residence. Finally, as with food insufficiency, household-head employment status is unrelated to the risk of home hardships in Model 2.

Fixed effect models for the within-state difference in levels of home hardship suggest that differences in economic conditions are related to the household probability of home hardships. This finding is consistent with that for food insufficiency. In terms of state policy conditions, only the state EITC rate is found to be related to the within-state household probability of home hardships. The positive relationship between the state EITC rate and home hardships was found in each of the models shown in Table 11.3, suggesting that the relationship is strong enough to remain consistent to different model specifications. The positive relationship is consistent with the finding of Gundersen and Ziliak (2004) in their analysis of state determinants of poverty levels. Finally, within-state differences in the physical climate around the time of the survey may be related to the probability of home hardships, although the substantive effect is very weak.

Table 11.3 Determinants of home hardship

	Model (1)			Model (2)		
	Beta	*Sig.*	*(SE)*	*Beta*	*Sig.*	*(SE)*
Economic environment						
Unemployment rate	0.0373		(0.0343)	−0.0016		(0.0011)
Gross state product	−25.6762	★★★	(9.6477)	0.3308		(0.5476)
Median wage	−0.0089		(0.0136)	−0.0012		(0.0064)
Policy environment						
Minimum wage	−0.6421	★	(0.3489)	0.0081		(0.0103)
TANF + food stamp benefit	−0.4426		(0.3646)	−0.0338		(0.0180)
State EITC	1.1328	★★★	(0.3001)	0.0813	★★★	(0.0294)
Political and physical environment						
State government liberalism	−0.0005		(0.0018)	0.0000		(0.0000)
Physical climate	0.0001		(0.0001)	0.0000	★★	(0.0000)
Demographic characteristics of head						
Black	0.3678	★★★	(0.1013)	0.0153	★★★	(0.0020)
Hispanic	0.4670	★★★	(0.1420)	0.0133	★★★	(0.0028)
Female	0.0368		(0.0590)	0.0016		(0.0013)
Education level of head						
High school graduate	−0.2994	★★★	(0.0941)	−0.0132	★★★	(0.0020)
Some college	−0.3129	★★★	(0.0767)	−0.0153	★★★	(0.0020)
Bachelor's degree or higher	−0.4939	★★★	(0.0816)	−0.0181	★★★	(0.0022)
Marital status						
Never married	0.4332	★★★	(0.0862)	0.0142	★★★	(0.0018)
Divorced/widowed/separated	0.4595	★★★	(0.0736)	0.0132	★★★	(0.0015)
Number of children	0.1986	★★★	(0.0222)	0.0085	★★★	(0.0006)
Income-to-needs ratio	−0.1807	★★★	(0.0192)	−0.0011	★★★	(0.0002)
Employed head	−0.0351		(0.0639)	−0.0069	★★★	(0.0016)
Disabled head	0.7903	★★★	(0.0832)	0.0319	★★★	(0.0020)
Elderly head	−0.5756	★★★	(0.9957)	−0.0137	★★★	(0.0019)
Metropolitan residence	−0.2650	★★★	(0.1010)	−0.0063	★★★	(0.0016)

Note: p<.10=★; p<.05=★★; p<.01=★★★

Discussion

Neoliberalism influences both household characteristics, such as household formation, educational attainment, labor market behavior, and health, as well as state economic and policy conditions (Larner, 2000; Hartman, 2005; Coburn, 2006). This chapter documents the different pathways that neoliberalism influences the well-being of poor people in the United States. While previous estimates of cross-state variation in poverty rates indicate that economic conditions are strong determinants of poverty, results here suggest that measures of well-being that are not tied to income show a much weaker relationship to the state economy. The structure of the welfare state does offer some buffer against material hardship, particularly the generosity of the TANF and food stamp benefit package, although there is also evidence to suggest that increases in the state EITC rate is associated with increases in home hardships and food insufficiency. Finally, at the state level, the political and the physical environment are not strongly related to probability of reporting food insufficiency, bill-paying hardships, or home hardships. Consistent with prior research on correlates of material hardship (Beverly, 2001; Iceland and Bauman, 2007), I find strong support for the role of household characteristics in determining the risk of material hardship. Thus, I conclude that the context in which households face financial difficulties does influence their probability of food insufficiency, bill-paying hardships, and home hardships, but that the indicators considered here are insufficient measures of how the local context matters.

One important limitation of this work is the reliance on the state as the geographic unit of analysis. The state is not the ideal geographic level to conduct this analysis as all of the factors examined here have a great deal of within-state heterogeneity. Preferably, this analysis could be conducted at the county, community, or neighborhood level in order to really identify how different facets of the external world constrain a household's ability to cover their basic needs. However, as a first approximation, and given the current data constraints on the availability of representative data on material hardship, it provides an important first step forward towards the consideration of contextual factors in social processes underlying the production of food insufficiency, bill-paying hardships, and home hardships.

In conclusion, this chapter suggests that the risk of experiencing food insufficiency, bill-paying hardships, or home hardships does vary by the context in which the household is embedded but that standard measures of economic conditions, policy conditions, and the political and physical environment are only partially able to identify the mechanisms at work. Household-level characteristics remain strong determinants of experiencing hardship. Future work that seeks to unpack the social processes by which neoliberalism impacts family well-being will have to look to other measures of the social context.

References

Bartfeld, Judi and Rachel Dunifon. 2006. "State-Level Predictors of Food Insecurity Among Households With Children." *Journal of Policy Analysis and Management*, 25(4): 921–942.

Bauman, Kurt J. 1999. "Extended Measures of Well-Being: Living Conditions in the United States: 1995." *Current Population Reports, Series P70-67*. Washington, DC: U.S. Government Printing Office.

Berry, William D., Evan J. Ringquist, Richard C. Fording, and Russell L. Hanson. 1998. "Measuring Citizen and Government Ideology in the American States, 1960–93." *American Journal of Political Science*, 42(1) (January): 327–348.

Beverly, Sondra. 2001. "Measures of Material Hardship: Rationale and Recommendations." *Journal of Poverty*, 5(1): 23–41.

Boushey, Heather and Bethney Gundersen. 2001. "When Work Just Isn't Enough: Measuring Hardships Faced by Families after Moving from Welfare to Work." *Briefing Paper No. 107*. Economic Policy Institute, Washington, DC.

Coburn, D. 2006. "Income Inequality, Social Cohesion and the Health Status of Populations: The Role of Neo-Liberalism." *Social Science and Medicine*, 51(1): 135–146.

Cutler, D.M. and Larry Katz. 1991. "Macroeconomic Performance and the Disadvantaged." *Brookings Papers on Economic Activity*, 2: 1–61.

Durkheim, E. 1897. *Suicide* (reprinted 1997). New York: The Free Press.

Edin, Kathryn and Laura Lein. 1997. *Making Ends Meet: How Single Mothers Survive Welfare and Low-Wage Work*. New York: Russell Sage Foundation.

Gundersen, Craig and James P. Ziliak. 2004. "Poverty and Macroeconomic Performance across Space, Race, and Family Structure." *Demography*, 41(1): 61–86.

Hartman, Y. 2005. "In Bed with the Enemy: Some Ideas on the Connections between Neoliberalism and the Welfare State." *Current Sociology*, 53(1): 57–73.

Haveman, Robert and Jonathan Schwabish. 2000. "Has Macroeconomic Performance Regained Its Antipoverty Bite?" *Contemporary Economic Policy*, 18(4) (October): 415–427.

Heflin, Colleen. 2006. "Dynamics of Different Forms of Material Hardship in the Women's Employment Survey." *Social Service Review*, 80(3): 377–397.

Iceland, John and Kurt J. Bauman. 2007. "Income Poverty and Material Hardship." *The Journal of Socio-Economics*, 36(3): 376–396.

Iceland, John, Lane Kenworthy, and Melissa Scopilliti. 2005. "Macroeconomic Performance and Poverty in the 1980s and 1990s: A State-Level Analysis." Institute for Research on Poverty, University of Wisconsin–Madison, Discussion Paper, DP # 1299-05.

Larner, W. 2000. "Neo-Liberalism: Policy, Ideology, Governmentality." *Studies in Political Economy*, 63: 5–25.

Mayer, Susan E. and Christopher Jencks. 1989. "Poverty and the Distribution of Material Hardship." *Journal of Human Resources*, 24(1): 88–114.

12

WELFARE DEPENDENCY AND POVERTY

Neoliberal rhetoric or evidence-informed choice?

Philip Young P. Hong and Brenda Crawley

Introduction

The United States has seen its sovereignty on welfare rights challenged by the neoliberal rhetoric of ending welfare as we know it. The prevailing political argument was that social policies create work disincentives and this in turn traps many people in the state of dependency that exacerbates poverty. At the individual level, the argument was such that long-term welfare recipients have psychological barriers that put them in weak positions vis-à-vis the labor market. Unable to secure stable employment, they end up settling for welfare checks and government subsidies and continue to abuse the system by staying in the state of welfare dependency.

Reflecting this problem definition, ending welfare dependency has surfaced as one of the four explicitly stated goals in the Personal Responsibility and Work Opportunity Reconciliation Act of 1996 (PRWORA; P.L. 104–193). This welfare reform legislation created the Temporary Assistance to Needy Families (TANF) that replaced the 60-year-old federal assistance program, Aid to Families with Dependent Children (AFDC). The reluctant welfare state has made a strong statement about removing the role of government in providing the safety net for its citizenry. Evidence from comparative welfare suggests that the United States is one of the least generous welfare states with the highest poverty rate (Smeeding, 2005; Brady, 2009a, 2009b). With weak left party politics in a highly globalized economy, the United States fits the conditions that contribute to its inability to protect its most vulnerable members.

The focus on labor force attachment (LFA) and human capital development (HCD) as market-based solutions for people to escape poverty has continued to maintain dominant status in the push to end welfare dependency and promote economic self-sufficiency (Gueron and Hamilton, 2002; Hong and Pandey, 2008; Kim, 2010). Under the assumption that the psychological barriers that breed welfare dependency would be remedied by working, able-bodied welfare recipients have been recategorized as the dependent "undeserving" poor. These policy choices based on the change of heart have been too quick to penalize the target population by intensifying mandatory work participation. In this regard, the purpose of this chapter is to revisit the U.S. data from a period soon after the implementation of welfare reform during the welfare state retrenchment era and validate the extent to which welfare dependency explains various aspects of poverty—welfare status, employment, poverty, and working poverty.

Background literature

In a brilliant genealogy of the construct known as dependency, Fraser and Gordon (1994) reveal that at various historical times being dependent has been a virtue and has even been required by society in certain types of relationships. For example, women have been expected to be dependent on men as "breadwinners" for the home. As Fraser and Gordon (1994) note:

> ... people were supposed to be organized into heterosexual, male-headed nuclear families, which lived principally from the man's labor market earnings. The male head of the household would be paid a family wage, sufficient to support children and a wife and mother, who performed domestic labor without pay.
>
> (p. 591)

It is not only women who have been expected to assume a dependent role in society, but other groups, such as indentured servants, sharecroppers, and the disabled, were forced into dependent status by the structure of society's labor market arrangements and economic system (Luhman, 2002; Robinson, 2000). Hence, groups were proscribed dependency status without necessarily being ascribed negative social sanction for such a status. Increasingly, however, women who are poor and those with children who use public assistance programs have been and are negatively labeled for their "dependency" status.

In more recent times, individuals and groups from communities that experience chronic conditions of unemployment, underemployment, severely restricted labor market opportunities, persistently underperforming schools, and non-existent or extremely low levels of affordable housing have been labeled as part of the *welfare dependent* class (Mincy et al., 1990; Niskanen, 1996). In (re)constructing the genealogy, Fraser and Gordon (1994) question the underlying and tacit assumptions regarding current constructions of *welfare dependency*.

> If we can step back from this discourse, however, we can interrogate some of its underlying presuppositions. Why are debates about poverty and inequality in the U.S. now being framed in terms of welfare dependency? How did the receipt of public assistance become associated with dependency...?
>
> (p. 310)

They offer the useful perspective that (U.S.) society's modern emphasis on the individual personality paves the way for the "moral/psychological register" to reflect itself in viewing both independence and dependence in previously unconsidered ways. This perspective opens the door to viewing the individual as solely responsible for the things that accrue in one's life. As such, structural forces such as economic recessions and depressions, plant closings, job outsourcing, discrimination, and the like have no place in determining responsibility for (welfare) dependency and poverty (Hong, 2013a). Subsequently, issues surrounding the "isms" such as sexism, racism, ageism, and able-ism remain in the person's purview for resolution.

Previous research suggests that former welfare experience has an impact each on the likelihood of being on welfare (Cancian et al., 1998; Ellwood, 1986; Zedlewski, 1999) and on employment and earnings (Cancian and Meyer, 2000; Hershey and Pavetti, 1997; Pindus et al., 2000). Caputo (1997) reports that the number of years respondents made use of public assistance programs was the best predictor of becoming self-sufficient. Gottschalk et al. (1994) found that the majority of poor people remain poor for only short periods of time and welfare recipients benefit from welfare for only a few years. Some do, however, go through long-term poverty and welfare dependency.

Human capital has traditionally been found to be a strong predictor of individuals' economic well-being—educational attainment (Bane and Ellwood, 1994; Cancian et al., 1998; Danziger et al., 1998; Duncan and Hoffman, 1988; Holzer, 1996; Hong and Wernet, 2007; Zahn and Pandey, 2004a, 2004b), job training (Brodsky and Ovwigho, 2002; Hong and Pandey, 2007), and physical health (Beverly and Sherraden, 1997; Hong and Pandey, 2007). Other demographic variables that are found to be associated with poverty are: age, race, gender, marital status, the number of children, and additional household earners (Hong and Pandey, 2007, 2008; Hong and Wernet, 2007).

Based on the review of the literature, this chapter combines the three theoretical perspectives—human capital (Model 1), welfare dependency (Model 2), and demographic characteristics (Model 3)—to explain what welfare reform is designed to accomplish, having former welfare recipients successfully leave welfare, find jobs, and subsequently get out of poverty. The research question being investigated is: Given one's human capital and demographic characteristics, how does welfare dependency contribute to welfare status, employment, poverty, and working poverty?

Methods

Sample

This chapter uses data from the Core and Topical Module files of the 1996 panel of the Survey of Income and Program Participation (SIPP). Wave 8 (August–November 1998) of the 1996 panel is used because it includes the welfare reform module questions. Data regarding work, job training, health conditions, and welfare history were extracted from Topical Modules 1, 2, and 5. The sample consisted of those who had once received AFDC prior to the 1996 welfare reform. A total of 5,497 observations were found in the sample, which consisted of individuals surveyed in 1998 who were on AFDC at some point before the 1996 welfare reform.

Variables

Welfare status, employment, poverty, and working poverty are dichotomous dependent variables that capture economic well-being outcomes with the value of 1 indicating receipt of AFDC, having a paid job, having total household income less than the official poverty line, and working and living in poverty at the time of the survey in August 1998. The remaining individuals were coded as 0.

Total years on welfare is a dichotomous independent variable that captures whether one has been on AFDC for less than 5 years (=1).[1] *Number of welfare spells* is a continuous independent variable that measures the number of times a respondent has received AFDC.[2] For human capital variables, low education is a dichotomous variable that reflects whether a respondent has completed less than (=1) or more than or equal to high school education (=0). Job training is a dichotomous variable that captures whether a respondent has received any job training (=1) or not received any job training (=0) in the past. Health is a dichotomous independent variable that captures whether a respondent had work-preventing health conditions (=1).

The demographic control variables examined are respondent's age, race, gender, marital status, number of children under 18 living in the household, and additional earners. The respondent's age and number of children under 18 living in the household are continuous variables, while the remaining ones are categorical. *Race* (non-White=1, White=0), *gender* (female=1, male=0), and *marital status* (1 for married and 0 for non-married) are included as factors associated with being poor. A second earner needs to provide about $2,000–$3,700 in earnings in order to offset the increase in family needs required by the additional person

(Lerman, 2002), based on which *additional household earner* is coded 1 if other earner(s) with more than $2,000 annual income is present in the household and 0 if not.

Analyses

This section uses multivariate logistic regression analyses of a set of dichotomous dependent variables—welfare status, employment, poverty, and working poverty—on welfare dependency controlling for human capital and other demographic control variables. Estimation of each dependent variable is conducted by performing a series of empirical tests that compares the effects of human capital, welfare dependency, and demographic control variables. First, the impact of individual models—human capital (Model 1), welfare dependency (Model 2), and demographic control variables (Model 3)—are assessed separately (see Table 12.3). Second, holding Model 1 and Model 3 constant, Model 2 is added to form the combined Full Model (Model 1 + 2 + 3) and to observe whether this yields a statistically significant increase in the log likelihood (see Table 12.4).

Findings

Univariate analyses

As shown in Table 12.1, about 3 percent of the sample (n=145) were recipients of AFDC in August 1998. Approximately 78 percent (n=4,263) reported to be working in a paid job in

Table 12.1 Descriptive statistics of dependent variables

Dependent variables	N	%
Past-welfare use sample		
Welfare status[a]	5,497	
(0) No welfare	5,352	97.36
(1) Welfare	145	2.64
Employment status	5,497	
(0) Not working	1,234	22.45
(1) Working	4,263	77.55
Poverty	5,497	
(0) Non-poor	4,883	88.83
(1) Poor	614	11.17
Working poverty[b]	4,263	
(0) Work, non-poor	3,960	92.89
(1) Work, poor	303	7.11
Valid N	5,497	

[a] As a percentage of people who were on AFDC at some point in the past before the 1996 welfare reform.
[b] As a percentage of people who were on AFDC at some point in the past before the 1996 welfare reform and were working without receiving AFDC in August 1998.

August 1998. An estimated 11 percent (n=614) had total household incomes at or below the poverty level. The proportion of working poor in the sub-sample of working individuals was 7.11 percent, and slightly less than 93 percent (n=3,960) were working non-poor.

Table 12.2 shows variability in respondents' characteristics in the sample. Examining the human capital variables, about 14 percent of the respondents had lower than high school education. Having some type of job training was reported at a lower percentage, of about 12 percent. About 20 percent of individuals in the sample reported having health conditions that prevent working.

As for the welfare dependency variables, out of those interviewed in both Wave 1 and Wave 8 (n=1,123), about 85 percent had less than five total years on welfare. On average, past welfare recipients had experienced more than one welfare spell.

The demographic characteristics of past welfare recipients indicated that the average age was about 35 and about 80 percent were White. The sample was 58 percent female and 44 percent married. The average number of children was about 0.7, and slightly higher than 80 percent had other earner(s) in the household with more than $2,000 in annual income.

Table 12.2 Descriptive statistics of independent variables

Independent variables	N	Min	Max	Mean	Std. deviation
Human capital variables					
Education < 12 years	5,497	0	1	0.14	0.34
Job training	5,497	0	1	0.12	0.33
Health conditions that prevent working	5,497	0	1	0.20	0.40
Welfare dependency variables					
Total years on welfare < 5 years[a]	1,123	0	1	0.85	0.36
Number of welfare spells (revised)[b]	1,113	0	17	1.49	1.20
Demographic characteristics					
Age (years)	5,497	18	65	34.93	11.71
Race (1=non-White)	5,497	0	1	0.19	0.40
Gender (1=female)	5,497	0	1	0.58	0.49
Marital status (1=married)	5,497	0	1	0.44	0.50
Number of children	5,497	0	8	0.66	1.07
Additional household earner	5,497	0	1	0.82	0.39
Valid N	5,497				

[a] As a percentage of people interviewed in both Wave 1 and Wave 8, who were on AFDC at some point in the past before the 1996 welfare reform and who had reported the number of years on AFDC.
[b] As a percentage of people interviewed in both Wave 1 and Wave 8, who were on AFDC at some point in the past before the 1996 welfare reform after dropping 10 extreme cases.

Multivariate logistic regression (LR) analysis

Welfare status. Logistic regression models explaining welfare status were examined (see Table 12.3). Two individual models were found to have good fits between the model and the data—Model 1 ($\chi^2(3)$=49.17, p<.001) and Model 3 ($\chi^2(6)$=151.97, p<.001). Model 2 was not found to have a good fit. The model fit in the combined perspective was significant—Model 1 + 2 + control ($\chi^2(11)$=39.21, p<.001; see Table 12.4). The LR test results in the combined model suggested that adding Model 2 to Model 1 + control did not significantly increase the log likelihood value ($\chi^2(2)$=.05).

Employment status. A series of logistic regression analyses of employment status on three sets of independent variables were examined (see Table 12.3). Two individual models—Model 1 ($\chi^2(3)$=458.65, p<.001) and Model 3 ($\chi^2(6)$=213.38, p<.001)—were found to have good fits between the model and the data. Model 2 once again did not yield significant results. The combined perspective displayed a significant model fit—Model 1 + 2 + control ($\chi^2(11)$=133.26, p<.001; see Table 12.4). The LR test result for adding Model 2 to Model 1 + control was not significant ($\chi^2(2)$=1.35).

Poverty. Logistic regression models explaining poverty were examined in sequence (see Table 12.3). All three individual models had good fits between the model and the data—Model 1 ($\chi^2(3)$=154.20, p<.001), Model 2 ($\chi^2(2)$=7.00, p<.05), and Model 3 ($\chi^2(6)$=751.14, p<.001). The combined model was also found to have a significant model fit—Model 1 + 2 + control ($\chi^2(11)$=238.84, p<.001). The LR test result did not yield a significant increase in the log likelihood value after adding Model 2 to Model 1 + control ($\chi^2(2)$=1.05).

Working poverty. The final column of Table 12.3 presents a series of individual logistic regression models explaining working poverty. Model 1 ($\chi^2(3)$=75.21, p<.001) and Model 3 ($\chi^2(6)$=376.37, p<.001) were significant, while Model 2 was not significant. The model fit in the combined perspective was significant—Model 1 + 2 + control ($\chi^2(11)$=146.44, p<.001). The LR test results revealed that adding Model 2 to Model 1 + control did not significantly increase the log likelihood value ($\chi^2(2)$=.86).

Discussion and conclusion

This chapter provided empirical evidence of past welfare recipients in 1998 from the SIPP data that both the human capital perspective (Model 1) and demographic characteristics (Model 3) explain significantly the likelihood of all four dependent variables throughout the analyses in individual and combined models. Welfare dependency, however, was found to be significant only in the individual model explaining poverty but not with those explaining welfare status, employment, and working poverty. The number of welfare spells was one welfare dependency variable that significantly affected the likelihood of living in poverty. Further, no significant effects were found of any of the welfare dependency variables in the combined model. Therefore, there is weak evidence as to whether welfare dependency—the length of welfare experience and the number of welfare spells—contributes to the various dimensions of poverty.

It is interesting to find that the null findings on welfare dependency further confirmed what the framers of the welfare reform had envisioned—to exchange welfare payment with salaries. Siding with the political rhetoric rather than relying on comprehensive evidence-informed policy making, America seem to have embarked on a vast experiment, much of it based on the premise that penalties or sticks will move people from dependency to independence or self-sufficiency, and eventually from poverty to economic security and financial stability (Hong, 2013b). In fact, this problem definition has been effectively mobilized in the political arena to reaffirm the government's position to turn its back on people living in poverty.

Table 12.3 Individual logistic regression models explaining various aspects of poverty

Independent variables	Welfare status[a]			Employment[b]			Poverty[c]			Working poverty[d]		
	$\hat{\beta}(se(\hat{\beta}))$	Sig.	Odds ratio	$\hat{\beta}(se(\hat{\beta}))$	Sig.	Odds ratio	$\hat{\beta}(se(\hat{\beta}))$	Sig.	Odds ratio	$\hat{\beta}(se(\hat{\beta}))$	Sig.	Odds ratio
Human capital (Model 1)												
Education < 12 years	.80 (.20)	***	2.23	−.77 (.09)	***	.46	.94 (.10)	***	2.56	.93 (.15)	***	2.52
Job training	.77 (.21)	***	2.17	.50 (.12)	***	1.65	.49 (.12)	***	1.63	.75 (.15)	***	2.11
Work-preventing health conditions	.79 (.18)	***	2.21	−1.32 (.07)	***	.27	.67 (.10)	***	1.96	.65 (.14)	***	1.92
Constant	−4.12 (.12)	***		1.65 (.04)	***		−2.49 (.06)	***		−2.96 (.08)	***	
	N=5,497			N=5,497			N=5,497			N=4,263		
	LL=1291.18			LL=5395.96			LL=3694.24			LL=2110.99		
	$\chi^2(3)$=49.17***			$\chi^2(3)$=458.65***			$\chi^2(3)$=154.20***			$\chi^2(3)$=75.21***		
Welfare dependency (Model 2)												
Total years on welfare < 5 years	−.20 (.33)			−.20 (.19)			−.17 (.20)			−.15 (.25)		
Number of welfare spells	.06 (.09)			.04 (.06)			.13 (.05)	**	1.14	.12 (.06)		
Constant	−2.65 (.34)	***		−.90 (.20)	***		−1.28 (.20)	***		−1.65 (.26)	***	
	N=1,113			N=1,113			N=1,113			N=840		
	LL=511.15			LL=511.15			LL=1186.16			LL=759.63		
	$\chi^2(2)$=.77			$\chi^2(2)$=1.43			$\chi^2(2)$=7.00*			$\chi^2(2)$=3.71		

Independent variables	Welfare status[a]			Employment[b]			Poverty[c]			Working poverty[d]		
	$\hat{\beta}(se(\hat{\beta}))$	Sig.	Odds ratio	$\hat{\beta}(se(\hat{\beta}))$	Sig.	Odds ratio	$\hat{\beta}(se(\hat{\beta}))$	Sig.	Odds ratio	$\hat{\beta}(se(\hat{\beta}))$	Sig.	Odds ratio
Demographic characteristics (Model 3)												
Age (years)	-.02 (.008)	*	.98	-.02 (.003)	***	.98	-.03 (.004)	***	.97	-.04 (.01)	***	.96
Non-White	.74 (.18)	***	2.10	-.31 (.08)	***	.74	.32 (.11)	**	1.38	.29 (.15)	*	1.34
Female	1.60 (.27)	***	4.96	-.71 (.07)	***	.49	.33 (.10)	***	1.40	.37 (.14)	**	1.44
Married	-.75 (.21)	***	.47	-.03 (.07)			-.17 (.10)			-.25 (.15)		
Number of children	.26 (.07)	***	1.30	.002 (.03)			.38 (.04)	***	1.46	.46 (.05)	***	1.58
Additional household earner	-.69 (.19)	***	.50	.28 (.08)	***	1.32	-1.91 (.10)	***	.15	-1.83 (.14)	***	.16
Constant	-3.94 (.42)	***		2.26 (.15)	***		-.20 (.20)			-.45 (.29)		
	N=5,497			N=5,497			N=5,497			N=4,263		
	LL=1188.39			LL=5638.23			LL=623.16			LL=1809.83		
	$\chi^2(6)=151.97$***			$\chi^2(6)=213.38$***			$\chi^2(6)=751.14$***			$\chi^2(6)=376.37$***		

Note: * indicates p<.05, ** indicates p<.01, and *** indicates p<.001.
[a] Dependent variable (Welfare status) = (0) no welfare, (1) welfare.
[b] Dependent variable (Employment) = (0) no welfare, (1) welfare.
[c] Dependent variable (Poverty) = (0) no welfare, (1) welfare.
[d] Dependent variable (Working poverty) = (0) no welfare, (1) welfare.

Table 12.4 Full logistic regression models explaining various aspects of poverty

Independent variables	Welfare status[a]			Employment[b]			Poverty[c]			Working poverty[d]		
	$\hat{\beta}(se(\hat{\beta}))$	Sig.	Odds ratio	$\hat{\beta}(se(\hat{\beta}))$	Sig.	Odds ratio	$\hat{\beta}(se(\hat{\beta}))$	Sig.	Odds ratio	$\hat{\beta}(se(\hat{\beta}))$	Sig.	Odds ratio
Human capital (Model 1)												
Education < 12 years	.56 (.31)			−.86 (.18)	***	.42	.81 (.20)	***	2.25	.63 (.27)	★	1.87
Job training	.09 (.27)			.58 (.16)	***	1.79	−.43 (.17)	**	.65	−.29 (.21)		
Work-preventing health conditions	.62 (.27)	★	1.86	−1.16 (.16)	***	.31	.69 (.18)	***	2.00	.49 (.24)	★	1.64
Welfare dependency (Model 2)												
Total years on welfare < 5 years	−.08 (.35)			.18 (.21)			−.15 (.23)			−.23 (.29)		
Number of welfare spells	−.0003 (.10)			.05 (.07)			.04 (.06)			.04 (.07)		
Demographic characteristics (Model 3)												
Age (years)	−.02 (.02)			−.01 (.01)			−.04 (.01)	***	.96	−.06 (.02)	***	.94
Non-White	.47 (.27)			.08 (.18)			.38 (.18)	★	1.46	.32 (.22)		
Female	−1.30 (.68)			.58 (.61)			−.40 (.61)			.77 (1.08)		
Married	−.11 (.32)			−.73 (.18)	***	.48	−.11 (.20)			−.16 (.26)		
Number of children	.07 (.11)			−.03 (.06)			.32 (.07)	***	1.38	.33 (.09)	***	1.39
Additional household earner	−1.04 (.30)	***	.35	.05 (.18)			−1.83 (.19)	***	.16	−1.85 (.25)	***	.16

Independent variables	Welfare status[a]			Employment[b]			Poverty[c]			Working poverty[d]		
	$\hat{\beta}(se(\hat{\beta}))$	Sig.	Odds ratio	$\hat{\beta}(se(\hat{\beta}))$	Sig.	Odds ratio	$\hat{\beta}(se(\hat{\beta}))$	Sig.	Odds ratio	$\hat{\beta}(se(\hat{\beta}))$	Sig.	Odds ratio
Constant	-.66 (1.10)			1.47 (.80)			1.01 (.83)			.04 (1.29)		
	N=1,113			N=1,113			N=1,113			N=840		
	LL=472.72			LL=1106.83			LL=954.32			LL=616.75		
	$\chi^2(11)=39.21$***			$\chi^2(11)=133.26$***			$\chi^2(11)=238.84$***			$\chi^2(11)=146.44$***		
	AIC=.45			AIC=1.02			AIC=.88			AIC=.76		
	LR test: $\chi^2(2)=.05$			LR test: $\chi^2(2)=1.35$			LR test: $\chi^2(2)=1.05$			LR test: $\chi^2(2)=.86$		

Note: * indicates $p<.05$, ** indicates $p<.01$, and *** indicates $p<.001$.
[a] Dependent variable (Welfare status) = (0) no welfare, (1) welfare.
[b] Dependent variable (Employment) = (0) not working, (1) working.
[c] Dependent variable (Poverty) = (0) poor, (1) non-poor.
[d] Dependent variable (Working poverty) = (0) working and non-poor, (1) working poor.

Every conceivable human characteristic, trait, and status has been implicated in the label and condition of welfare dependency. Additionally, numerous societal institutions, such as family, education, the economy, and government, have been plugged into the huge net of explanations, rationales, causes, and reasons for the "condition" of welfare dependency. Certainly no single factor can be tagged as fully responsible for this condition. However, the political rhetoric has subscribed to micro-level, psychological, attitudinal, behavioral, and cultural explanations, often overlapping with each other (Bartholomae et al., 2004; Fraser and Gordon, 1994; Niskanen, 1996). Micro-level explanations have been met with a victim-blaming approach to social engineering of individuals as policy choices—whether moral, ethical, character-altering, and/or behavioral in nature—intended to remedy welfare dependency (Niskanen, 1996).

Some contending views posit at the mezzo level that welfare dependency can best be understood by examining family structure and dynamics (Antel, 1992; McLanahan, 1988; Taylor and Barusch, 2004). Others at this level turn attention to the nature and structure of communities and how these impact the life chances for individuals (Wilson, 1996). At the macro level, the structural vulnerability thesis implicates human capital as a manifestation of low-wage workers' weak positions in societal institutions such as but not limited to the economy, labor market, education, and wages/salaries (Crew and Eyerman, 2001; Hong and Pandey, 2007; Rank, 2004). However, these views were incapable of withstanding the dominant individually based problem definition of welfare dependency.

It is apparent that welfare dependency was tagged with a negative image and fell prey to the political rhetoric as a tool to support welfare reform. Subsequently, it was transformed into self-sufficiency by putting a positive spin on the "old" welfare dependency that was deemed to be plaguing the welfare system. The triumphant neoliberal rhetoric has set the tone for poverty politics in the United States. Therefore, this chapter contributes to the redefinition of how poverty is viewed in the U.S. policy-making process. According to DiNitto and Cummins (2007), "poverty has gone from being a problem of too little income to a problem of dependency" (p. 118). Then, the problem of dependency became the goal of self-sufficiency in a new policy reality post-welfare reform.

This reality is too real to do away with as the United States continues to downsize its welfare state within the context of its government being structurally dependent on global capitalism and market performance (Hong, 2008). This chapter proposes to transform the global welfare state crisis into an opportunity for organizing bottom-up strategies for invigorating workforce development and nudging the local labor market to become an inclusive system. While one can critique the concept of self-sufficiency for its lack of clarity, therefore making it difficult to measure and evaluate its success outcome, it opens the opportunities for social investment for empowering low-income jobseekers—not only in their "personal responsibility" but also their "work opportunities" to sustain their individual efforts (Cooney, 2006; Hong, 2013b; Hong et al., 2009; Sandlin, 2004).

If the negative image of welfare dependency has been effectively used by the political rhetoric to individualize the issue of poverty and dismantle the welfare system as we know it, self-sufficiency could present a positive opportunity. Reclaiming power and ownership of the concept of self-sufficiency by reframing it as personal empowerment could open the doors to transforming the often-blamed "debilitating" individual deficiencies into positive motivations, work-readiness, and economic success among low-income jobseekers (Hong et al., 2009). This transformation demands structural matching of the local labor market system and other social institutions to nurture human development and sustainability (Hong, 2013b).

While the approaches offered by the policy reality may have stayed individualistic in nature, the anticipated community-based, bottom-up change could bring about macro social change if the resources are capitalized on comprehensively to maximize the potential social investment from both the private and public sectors. Without doubt, empowerment-based workforce development programs need to be encouraged and transitional employment planning would need to break away from *labor market dependency*—relying on the demand side of the labor market—and tailor labor market development to the needs and efforts of low-income jobseekers.

Notes

1 This variable is equivalent to Indicator 7 (Dependence Spell Duration) examined by the U.S. Department of Health and Human Services (2001), which was designed to tap into the dynamics of welfare receipt and welfare dependence. The issue of spell duration is particularly important in light of the time limits that have been enacted under state TANF programs.
2 This measurement is consistent with Indicator 10 (Long-Term Receipt) of those identified by the U.S. Department of Health and Human Services (2001). Indicator 10 focuses on individuals who leave welfare programs and cycle back on after an absence of several months. It was calculated to examine the cumulative amount of time individuals receive assistance over a period of several years.

References

Antel, J.J. (1992). The Intergenerational Transfer of Welfare Dependency: Some Statistical Evidence. *The Review of Economics and Statistics*, 74(3), 467–473.

Bane, M., and Ellwood, D. (1994). *Welfare Realities: From Rhetoric to Reform*. Cambridge, MA: Harvard University Press.

Bartholomae, S., Fox, J.J., and McKenry, P.C. (2004). The Legacy of Welfare. *Journal of Family Issues*, 25(6), 783–810.

Beverly, S., and Sherraden, M. (1997). *Human Capital and Social Work* (Working Paper 92–2). Saint Louis, MO: Washington University, Center for Social Development.

Brady, D. (2009a). Putting Poverty in Political Context: A Multi-Level Analysis of Adult Poverty Across 18 Affluent Democracies. *Social Forces*, 88(1), 271–299.

Brady, D. (2009b). *Rich Democracies, Poor People: How Politics Explain Poverty*. Oxford: Oxford University Press.

Brodsky, A.E., and Ovwigho, P.C. (2002). Swimming Against the Tide: Connecting Low-Income Women to Living Wage Jobs. *Journal of Poverty*, 6(3), 63–87.

Cancian, M., and Meyer, D. (2000). Work After Welfare: Women's Work Effort, Occupation, and Economic Well-Being. *Social Work Research*, 24(2), 69–86.

Cancian, M., Haveman, R., Kaplan, T., and Wolfe, B. (1998). *Post-Exit Earnings and Benefits Receipt among Those Who Left AFDC in Wisconsin*. Madison, WI: University of Wisconsin-Madison, Institute for Research on Poverty.

Caputo, R. (1997). Escaping Poverty and Becoming Self-Sufficient. *Journal of Sociology and Social Welfare*, 26(3), 5–23.

Cooney, K. (2006). Mothers First, Not Work First: Listening to Welfare Clients in Job Training. *Qualitative Social Work*, 2, 217–235.

Crew, R.E., Jr., and Eyerman, J. (2001). Finding Employment and Staying Employed After Leaving Welfare. *Journal of Poverty*, 5(4), 67–91.

Danziger, S., Kalil, A., and Anderson, N. (1998). Human Capital, Health and Mental Health of Welfare Recipients: Co-Occurrence and Correlates. *Journal of Social Issues*, 54(4), 637–656.

DiNitto, D.M., and Cummins, L.K. (2007). *Social Welfare: Politics and Public Policy*. Boston, MA: Pearson Allyn and Bacon.

Duncan, G., and Hoffman, S. (1988). The Use and Effects of Welfare: A Survey of Recent Evidence. *Social Service Review*, 62, 238–257.

Ellwood, D. (1986). *Working Off of Welfare: Prospects and Policies for Self-Sufficiency of Women Heading Families* (Discussion Paper 803-86). Madison, WI: University of Wisconsin-Madison, Institute for Research on Poverty.

Fraser, N., and Gordon, L. (1994). A Genealogy of Dependency: Tracing a Keyword of the U.S. Welfare State. *Signs: Journal of Women in Culture and Society*, 19(2), 309–336.

Gottschalk, P., McLanahan, S., and Sandefur, G.D. (1994). The Dynamics and Intergenerational Transmission of Poverty and Welfare Participation. In S.H. Danziger, G.D. Sandefur, and D.H. Weinberg (eds.), *Confronting Poverty: Prescription for Change* (pp. 85–108). Cambridge, MA: Harvard University Press.

Gueron, J.M., and Hamilton, G. (2002). *The Role of Education and Training in Welfare Reform* (Policy Brief No. 20). Washington, DC: Brookings Institution.

Hershey, A., and Pavetti, L. (1997). Turning Job Finders into Job Keepers: The Challenge of Sustaining Employment. *The Future of Children*, 7(1), 74–86.

Holzer, H. (1996). *What Employers Want: Job Prospects for Less-Educated Workers*. New York: Russell Sage Foundation.

Hong, P.Y.P. (2008). Globalizing Structural Poverty: Reclaiming Hope for Children and Families. *Illinois Child Welfare*, 4(1), 23–38.

Hong, P.Y.P. (2013a). Planning Development in the United States. In S. Singh (ed.), *Social Work and Social Development: Perspectives from India and the United States* (pp. 64–77). Chicago, IL: Lyceum Books.

Hong, P.Y.P. (2013b). Toward a Client-Centered Benchmark for Self-Sufficiency: Evaluating the "Process" of Becoming Job Ready. *Journal of Community Practice*, 21(4), 356–378.

Hong, P.Y.P., and Pandey, S. (2007). Human Capital as Structural Vulnerability of U.S. Poverty. *Equal Opportunities International*, 26(1), 18–43.

Hong, P.Y.P., and Pandey, S. (2008). Differential Effects of Human Capital on the Poor and the Near Poor: Evidence of Social Exclusion. *Journal of Poverty*, 12, 456–480.

Hong, P.Y.P., Sheriff, V., and Naeger, S. (2009). A Bottom-Up Definition of Self-Sufficiency: Voices from Low-Income Jobseekers. *Qualitative Social Work*, 8(3), 357–376.

Hong, P.Y.P., and Wernet, S.P. (2007). Structural Reinterpretation of Poverty by Examining Working Poverty: Implications for Community and Policy Practice. *Families in Society*, 88(3), 361–373.

Kim, J. (2010). Welfare-to-Work Programs and the Dynamics of TANF Use. *Journal of Family and Economic Issues*, 31, 198–211.

Lerman, R. (2002). *How do Marriage, Cohabitation, and Single Parenthood affect the Material Hardships of Families with Children?* Washington, DC: The Urban Institute.

Luhman, R. (2002). *Race and Ethnicity in the United States: Our Differences and Our Roots*. Fort Worth: Harcourt College Publishers.

McLanahan, S.S. (1988). Family Structure and Dependency: Early Transitions to Female Household Headship. *Demography*, 25(1), 1–16.

Mincy, R.B., Sawhill, I.V., and Wolf, D.A. (1990). The Underclass: Definition and Measurement. *Science*, 248, 450–453.

Niskanen, W.A. (1996). Welfare and the Culture of Poverty. *Cato Journal*, 16(1), 1–15.

Pindus, N., Koralek, R., Martinson, K., and Trutko, J. (2000). *Coordination and Integration of Welfare and Workforce Development System*. Washington, DC: The Urban Institute.

Rank, M.R. (2004). *One Nation Underprivileged: Why American Poverty Affects Us All*. New York: Oxford University Press.

Robinson, R. (2000). *The Debt: What America Owes to Blacks*. New York: Dutton.

Sandlin, J.A. (2004). "It's All up to You": How Welfare-to-Work Educational Programs Construct Workforce Success. *Adult Education Quarterly*, 54(2), 89–104.

Smeeding, T. (2005). Public Policy, Economic Inequality, and Poverty: The United States in Comparative Perspective. *Social Science Quarterly*, 86, 955–983.

Taylor, M.J., and Barusch, A.S. (2004). Personal, Family, and Multiple Barriers of Long-Term Welfare Recipients. *Social Work*, 49(2), 175–183.

U.S. Department of Health and Human Services (2001). *Indicators of Welfare Dependence: Annual Report to Congress*. Washington, DC.

Wilson, W.J. (1996). *When Work Disappears: The World of the New Urban Poor*. New York: Knopf.

Zedlewski, S. (1999). *Work-Related Activities and Limitations of Current Welfare Recipients: Assessing the New Federalism* (Discussion Paper 99-06). Washington, DC: The Urban Institute.

Zhan, M., and Pandey, S. (2004a). Postsecondary Education and Economic Well-Being of Single Mothers and Single Fathers. *Journal of Marriage and Family*, 66, 661–673.

Zhan, M., and Pandey, S. (2004b). Economic Well-Being of Single Mothers: Work First or Postsecondary Education? *Journal of Sociology and Social Welfare*, 31(3), 87–112.

13

BABIES AS BARRIERS

Welfare policy discourse in an era of neoliberalism

Linda Houser, Sanford F. Schram, Joe Soss, and Richard C. Fording

Over the past four decades, shifting labor markets have severely diminished the work and income prospects for low-skilled Americans. Partly as a response, public assistance programs have been redesigned to prod people into whatever jobs the changing economy provides (Peck, 2001). Under the neoliberal logic that guides these programs, paid work has been enshrined as the chief responsibility of citizenship (Soss et al., 2011). Activities that were once seen as societal contributions in their own right (e.g., care of children or aging adults) are now widely viewed as impediments to paid work (Stone, 2007). In the process, a remarkable variety of life conditions have come to be known by a simple term: barriers.

In this chapter, we analyze the historical origins of the barriers discourse and explore its contemporary deployment in the Temporary Assistance for Needy Families (TANF) program. TANF was created by federal legislation in 1996 that abolished the entitlement-based Aid to Families with Dependent Children (AFDC) program. It operates today as a federally funded cash assistance program administered at the state and county levels. Most TANF beneficiaries are poor families headed by single mothers who must comply with work and other behavioral requirements to be eligible for benefits.

TANF was widely hailed as a success during its first decade, primarily because it appeared to move welfare-reliant women into the workforce. Caseload reductions have varied by state (Pavetti et al., 2011), but their effect has been to produce historically small caseloads disproportionately populated with mothers who struggle to find consistent paid employment. In the parlance of welfare reform, these "hard-to-serve" mothers are said to "have barriers," which may include such disparate conditions as young children, an active substance addiction, limited access to transportation, or intimate partner violence.

The result is one of the more troubling paradoxes of contemporary welfare provision. Given the meager size of cash benefits and the high bar for program compliance, only those with the most complex and desperate needs tend to opt into the program. On the other hand, work-centered performance benchmarks in the TANF program have become more stringent over time, making the remaining "hard-to-serve" clients ever-more undesirable. Their work-participation failures become the performance failures of case managers (and thus, of welfare agencies and state governments), with serious financial consequences (Soss et al., 2011).

It should come as no surprise, then, that factors impeding employment are of deep concern to actors throughout the TANF system. We argue, however, that the barriers discourse does far more than just label such impediments. It organizes understandings and practices in welfare administration, and does so in ways that accomplish important political and emotional work (Schram, 2012). The barriers discourse averts attention from the structural forces that marginalize and subjugate low-income families by assimilating them into a personalized roster of the individual market actor's characteristics. Many of these forces can be traced to durable forms of privilege and subordination in relations of gender, race, and class. Others arise more directly from labor market conditions and public disinvestments that have undermined the life prospects for lower-skilled Americans. Regardless, such external conditions are recast as problems that individuals "have" and must overcome.

The "barriers" concept migrated to public assistance from discussions of disability accommodations and health access long before welfare reform in 1996. Nationally, it came to prominence alongside rising calls to incentivize work among the poor, gathering into its orbit a wide variety of physical and mental impairments, social relations and obligations, and conditions in community environments (see U.S. GAO, 1971). "Barriers talk" is pervasive today in discussions of public assistance, whether one looks in governance settings or in relevant areas of scholarship. Yet it has largely escaped critical analysis. We know little about how the barriers discourse arose, how it matters for politics and administration, how workers themselves understand and use this term, or how it affects their work with clients.

To advance such an analysis, we begin by exploring the "pre-history" of the barriers discourse in public aid programs from the 1930s through the 1960s. Although workforce participation was not yet the norm for most U.S. women, we suggest that *for welfare recipients* the 1930s–60s era marked a key period of change in the gender balance of caregiving and labor market roles. Indeed, by 1970 conditions were ripe for the emergence of the barriers discourse, which was already starting to appear in its contemporary form. We then turn to the contemporary period to pursue an analysis of how the barriers discourse operates in practice. We examine how the barriers discourse has entered into the lexicon of frontline welfare administrators, when the term is used, how it is deployed, and, most importantly, what political and practical work the barriers discourse accomplishes.

To pursue these questions, we draw on in-depth interviews with fifty Welfare Transition (WT) case managers and administrators that were conducted as part of a larger project on TANF service delivery in the state of Florida (for a full description of our methodology, see Soss et al., 2011). We find that barrier categories and scales provide rubrics for assessments of client needs and employment prospects. Understandings of barriers structure decisions about whether and how to penalize client noncompliance. They shape moral judgments of clients, ideals regarding service provision, and beliefs about how to improve welfare systems in practice.

The barriers discourse reverberates beyond the practical activities of street-level bureaucrats to frame perceptions and shape understandings in poverty governance. The discourse converts diverse circumstances, from the conventionally celebrated (e.g., giving birth) to the deeply traumatic (e.g., being abused and violated), into roadblocks to the normative destination of paid work. In the process, it rewrites the boundaries of the problematic: It normalizes life conditions that, however difficult, do not seem to impede work, just as it suggests that persistent hardships are unproblematic (and thus, undeserving of public concern and remediation) once paid employment has been obtained.

As it is deployed today, the barriers discourse collapses the distinction between internal characteristics and external conditions, rendering both as traits of individuals who are expected to change their behaviors and become "self-sufficient." In so doing, it constructs a population defined and classified according to its enumerated work impediments, such that each additional barrier indicates a more problematic subject of governance. By making populations legible in this manner, the barriers discourse produces more knowable and governable targets for state interventions. In these ways, the barriers discourse is not merely indicative but constitutive of neoliberal shifts in U.S. employment and poverty policy.

A pre-history of the barriers discourse: 1930s–1960s

To illuminate the significance of the barriers discourse in poverty governance today, it is helpful to begin by clarifying its historical origins. Dominant discourses are typically experienced as natural and unremarkable. They narrow the field of possible thoughts and actions, in part, because we find it hard to imagine the world otherwise. By interrogating the history of a dominant discourse, it is possible to expose its taken-for-granted terms as particular, contestable framings. In the discussion that follows, we attempt to open a space for critical analysis by revealing that the rise of the barriers discourse was far from inevitable or politically neutral. We do not aim to provide a comprehensive account of the frames in play during any particular period. Rather, we aim to clarify how discourses of welfare and work intersected from the 1930s to the 1960s and how hierarchical relations of gender, race, and class shaped these developments. Because the destination of our analysis is the TANF program, we begin with the creation of its first federal precursor during the New Deal, the Aid to Dependent Children (ADC) program.

The Great Depression of the 1930s brought on a crisis of confidence in market institutions and solutions, as the harsh realities of unemployment and deprivation clashed with established free market ideologies (Hacker and Pierson, 2002). The sheer number of those thrust into the ranks of the poor made it hard to portray poverty as an individual failure or as a local community problem, and activists and reformers seized the opportunity to reframe poverty as a societal problem with structural causes and national solutions (Gordon, 1994). Under the New Deal, the federal government took on a far greater role in setting employment and public assistance policies and providing citizens with income and jobs outside the market. Cash relief programs for the poor, such as ADC, emerged alongside public jobs programs such as the Works Progress Administration (WPA) as federal initiatives for the first time.

The new programs quickly revealed the political ambiguities of "workfare" and the powerful ways that race, gender, and class shape its meanings and practices. By supplying the pay and dignity of a job, the WPA aimed to shield unemployed family breadwinners from the degradations of poor relief. To appease business interests, however, the WPA was designed to follow the same doctrine of "less eligibility" that kept cash relief programs from offering benefits high enough to provide adults with an alternative to the worst jobs at the worst wages (Piven and Cloward, 1993). Congress forbid the WPA from offering jobs that might be competitive with private industry and required WPA applicants to file for need-based public relief first so as to reinforce the idea that support, even if work-based, should be seen as temporary "relief as an antecedent to a job" (Goldberg, 2005, p. 345). As a result, public jobs were often viewed as low-paid "make-work," hard to distinguish from the handouts offered to the undeserving poor. The relationship of work to relief, and the status of WPA beneficiaries as workers or welfare recipients, would remain the subjects of a bitter "classification struggle" throughout the course of the program (Goldberg, 2005).

The discursive relationship between work and relief during the New Deal was deeply rooted in gender ideology and a "family-wage model" built around male breadwinners (Gordon, 1994). WPA administrators, for example, sought to avoid "public criticisms for employing 'too many women'" and largely achieved this goal by limiting enrollment to one member of each family and by limiting women enrollees to "gender-appropriate" work such as sewing and filing (Noble, 1997; Goldberg, 2005, pp. 343–4). The ADC program, by contrast, reflected maternalist interests and ideals, often rooted in a race-specific discourse of Republican Motherhood that identified white women as the holders of a special civic duty (and right) to raise and care for the next generation of citizens (Skocpol, 1992; Gordon, 1994).[1] Under the prevailing terms of discourse, men fulfilled their roles as citizens and family members by earning wages; women did so as mothers and homemakers (Mink, 1995). As former Children's Bureau director Grace Abbott explained in 1937:

Employment of mothers with dependent children [in federal work programs] is to be deplored, as experience shows that unless the mothers' earnings are sufficient to enable them to employ competent assistance in the home, the children will be neglected and the mothers' health will break under the double burden of serving as wage-earners and homemakers.

(Quoted in Mink, 1995, p. 123)

Although some maternalists argued for better work opportunities and wages for women, employment was generally understood as a secondary role to be put aside in favor of caregiving as mothers. Occupational exclusions (such as those applied to domestic and charitable workers) in laws such as the Social Security Act of 1935 and the Fair Labor Standards Act of 1938 institutionalized the aberrational status of work for women – at best a temporary and less virtuous state preceding the familial roles of wife and mother (Mettler, 1998). In these ways, the New Deal charted vastly different economic courses for men and women (Gordon, 1994). For men, the impediments to employment security were varied and often framed in structural terms. For women, babies were not seen as barriers to work so much as work was seen as an undesirable impediment to having babies and fulfilling the roles of wife and mother.

The gendered discourse of the time, however, did not apply consistently to "men" and "women" *tout court*; it applied variously to groups of men and women who were subjected to vastly different social norms and experiences of governance depending (among other things) on their race and class positions. White women who could afford the services of mostly non-white, working-class domestic assistants were morally free to pursue work outside the home (Mink, 1995). At the same time, *expectations* of work attached to women of color, and especially black women, far more than white women. To maintain racially exploitative labor relations, southern elites successfully excluded agricultural and domestic workers from coverage under social insurance programs and made sure federally funded public aid programs would be subject to local control (Lieberman, 1998). Almost from the outset of the ADC program, southern states began to institutionalize work expectation for black women by creating "employable mothers" rules in ADC programs "in areas where seasonal employment was almost exclusively performed by nonwhite families" (Bell, 1965, p. 46).

The ADC program's discourse of "employable" black mothers, which drew on racial understandings dating back to slavery, differed markedly from the discourse of work for male WPA beneficiaries. Yet as both flourished in the gray areas between welfare and work, neither incorporated a barriers frame. Neither framed poor people as market actors who carried with them a roster of employment-impeding problems in need of resolution.

In the 1940s, white women were repositioned in discourses of welfare and work, as the war effort created powerful labor market needs and the new patriotic role of "Rosie the Riveter." Maternalists pushed back by promoting a carefully crafted public awareness campaign that became the official policy of the War Manpower Commission of 1942: the patriotic duty of wives and mothers was to do "the home job better" (quoted in Mink, 1995, p. 163). Even so, the war effort continued to pull women into the workplace. In response, maternalists fought employer discrimination toward women with children but also resisted the idea that decisions to pursue paid work should be left to women's individual judgment. Stationed at job training and recruitment centers, "day care counselors" maintained a regulatory stance in determining whether a mother's work was justified by the extent of her family's economic need. Mothers seeking employment "merely" to improve their lives were often asked to reflect on whether this desire was worth the risks of turning their children over to day nurseries. With strength of conviction that is almost inconceivable today, counselors resisted the pull of labor market demands and directed many (mostly white) mothers toward public assistance (Mink, 1995).

The economically prosperous years following World War II were marked by a reinvigoration of New Deal liberals' desires to expand social insurance coverage in a way that would allow public aid programs to wither away. Successive efforts to do so, however, were defeated in the 1940s by Congressional conservatives and state officials loathe to cede power to the federal level. In the wake of these defeats, liberals shifted their efforts toward making public assistance programs more "comprehensive."

As they did so in the 1950s, gendered discourses of welfare and work moved toward new terms that connected images of the "lone mother" with nascent conceptions of "social disability." From the earliest days of state mothers' pensions, maternalists pursued shifting strategies in response to discourses that stigmatized single mothers. Early narratives, which portrayed single mothers as innocent victims of husbands who had deserted their families, proved too vulnerable to the idea that women's immorality or incompetence may have driven their men away (Gordon, 2001). In addition to suggesting that deserted mothers were undeserving, this counter-narrative raised the specter of perverse incentive effects: By providing public benefits to lone mothers, officials might encourage husbands to desert their families and, more broadly, encourage women to engage in sexual promiscuity, illegitimacy, and generalized "immorality."

In response, welfare advocates shifted their focus to depictions of widowed women—i.e., a group of innocents victimized by an event (death) unlikely to be seen as resulting from perverse incentives. As "widow discourse" portrayed some lone mothers as blameless, however, it did so through a contrast with other mothers who were not. This feature of the discourse proved critical when the passage of Survivor's Insurance in 1939 moved so-called "worthy widows" out of ADC and into the superior Social Security channel of the welfare state. It was now quite easy to see the ADC program as a repository for groups of women who were less deserving than "worthy widows"—an image reinforced by the fact that the women left behind were disproportionately never-married mothers and nonwhite women (Mittelstadt, 2005).

As these developments strengthened images of ADC recipients as a deficient group, they converged with a second discursive shift that, like the widow discourse, originated in liberal reformers' efforts to protect public aid programs. During World War II, military institutions developed medical and vocational approaches that were widely viewed as successful in mobilizing less than able-bodied troops. In the 1950s, welfare officials sought to connect their programs to these well-regarded models and, toward this end, adopted "social disability" as an umbrella term for factors that kept poor people out of the labor market. Chief among these were the combined "handicaps" of lack of work experience and job training (Higgins, 1953, as cited in Mittelstadt, 2005, p. 52). But as a 1959 study of Boston ADC recipients demonstrated, such disabilities could also include problems of "disordered behavior"—a nonspecific category thought to include a broad range of maladjustments such as "personal insecurity," "feeblemindedness," "low mentality," and "illegitimacy" (Mittelstadt, 2005, p. 54).

The liberal strategy of linking program expansion to rehabilitation soon produced tangible results. The Social Security Amendments of 1956 extended ADC coverage to needy dependent children living with extended family members and increased federal matching maximums for cash assistance. The votes needed for passage were secured, in part, through provisions that devoted federal funds to maintaining and improving family life and encouraging "self-support" among recipient families. The dual rehabilitative goals—stronger families and self-support—marked a new iteration of "the double burden" Grace Abbott had named two decades earlier. Indeed, welfare leaders themselves remained ambivalent on this point. In demonstration projects, they recommended work for some single mothers but not others, with no clear logic beyond the old dividing line of racialized work expectations (Mittelstadt, 2005).

In addition to embracing social disability and rehabilitation, liberal reformers in the 1950s and early 1960s sought to build consensus through two additional discursive strategies. The first reframed ADC recipients as *families* rather than morally suspect individuals (i.e., unmarried women and their "illegitimate" children). The second sought to protect ADC by "erasing race" from the public image of the program (Mittelstadt, 2005, p. 77). Both strategies responded to the erosion of consensus on the idea "that women with children were properly unemployable" (Kondratas, 1986, p. 231). With larger numbers of middle-income women starting to work outside the home, critics began to highlight the inequity of working women's taxes being used to support the non-work of other mothers—and did so in ways designed to fuel white outrage by portraying the non-working mothers as disproportionately black (Kondratas, 1986).

Against this backdrop, attempts to shift the focus from mothers to families found symbolic expression in the 1962 change of the ADC program's name to Aid to Families with Dependent Children (AFDC). Welfare officials also initiated public-awareness campaigns that stressed the normality of recipient families. When a New York City study placed infants in need of foster home care with AFDC recipient families, for example, unmarried women headed 19 of the 22 families initially selected for the program. Publicity for the program lauded these families as warm and loving, deeply integrated in strong communities, and headed by eminently capable mothers. Tellingly, published reports of the study omitted any mention of the fact that 20 of these 22 families were African American (Mittelstadt, 2005).

Indeed, with some notable exceptions,[2] most public welfare studies of the era avoided mentioning family racial characteristics or problems of race-based discrimination. Although this strategy may have provided some political cover for a time, Mittelstadt (2005) concludes that it ultimately left liberals less able to respond to racist attacks on welfare that emerged in various media and government venues over the course of the 1960s. As the media publicized public welfare scandals and Congressional investigations focused attention on welfare fraud in 1962 and 1963, several localities engaged in racially targeted purges of welfare caseloads (Mittelstadt, 2005). By the middle of the decade, the ineffectiveness of liberal attempts to position AFDC as a deracialized "family" service had become clear. Increasingly, liberals now turned to work-based rhetoric to protect welfare programs, defending them on terms that cast mothers as workers and state supports as rehabilitative labor market interventions.

Indeed, by the mid-1960s—prior to the period when women in the workforce became a normative feature of the American landscape—the uneasy balance between caregiving and labor market roles in welfare discourse was tipping decidedly in favor of the latter. The 1962 Public Welfare Amendments identified women in AFDC as targets for work and training programs and created both limited work incentives via earnings disregards and limited funding for child care and other work-related expenses (Rose, 1995; Mittelstadt, 2005). To support these changes, the Amendments also funded rehabilitation-focused research, with particular emphasis on fostering self-support among women in AFDC (Mittelstadt, 2005). Two years earlier, in 1960, an American Public Welfare Association study titled *The American Dependency Challenge* had already begun to set the tone for this new body of research by enumerating a litany of family problems contributing to welfare dependency, such as single parenthood, promiscuity/prostitution, desertion/abandonment, marital conflict,[3] intergenerational patterns of illegitimacy, lack of job skills or training, physical and mental health problems, and "inadequate housekeeping or neatness" (Mittelstadt, 2005, p. 74). The political conditions of possibility for the neoliberal barriers discourse were now falling into place.

Indeed, by the end of the decade, policy analysts would group these sorts of life conditions under the label "barriers to employment." Prior to this time, the term appeared in discussions of "barriers to access" for people with disabilities or in need of healthcare but was largely absent from discussions of public aid. Outside the mainstream of welfare discourse, welfare rights advocates in the 1950s used the term to suggest that a society that erected unjust "barriers" to work and adequate life conditions took on obligations to support those who suffered the consequences (Ten Broek and Wilson, 1954, pp. 248–9). It was during the 1960s, as work roles took on a greater value in aid programs for poor women with children, that "barriers" began to acquire its current meaning. By 1965, researchers were deploying the term "barriers" in a manner that listed individual characteristics—including racial patterns of "dependency psychology"—alongside environmental obstacles to work (e.g., Stone and Schlamp, 1965). By 1970, welfare researchers were asking, "How employable are AFDC women?," and seeking answers in "employment barriers" defined as "the conditions that could keep an AFDC woman from even applying for a job: poor health, lack of day care facilities, high unemployment or lack of jobs for which she is qualified, psychological problems, and the like" (Levinson, 1970, p. 12).

By this time, the turn to work that would come to fruition with welfare reform in 1996 was well underway. The federal Work Incentive (WIN) program, which combined work expectations with earnings disregards and promises of work supports, was created as a voluntary option in 1967 and then mandated in 1971. As WIN failed to produce what its creators promised, calls for tougher modes of work enforcement grew and successive legislative interventions paved the way for work-first welfare reform in 1996 (Rose, 1995; Soss et al., 2011).

The pervasiveness of the barriers discourse in the era of welfare reform

Conditionality lies at the heart of contemporary welfare provision. Across a wide array of programs, poverty and need no longer suffice to establish eligibility for public assistance. Deservingness must be established through documented behaviors. Thus, sobriety is required before housing (Dordick, 2002), a negative drug screen before food (National Conference of State Legislatures, 2013), and proof of employment before child care, job training, and cash assistance (Houser et al., 2014). In the TANF program that replaced AFDC in 1996, recipients must adhere to a variety of behavioral standards—first and foremost in areas such as work participation and paternity establishment but also in some locales in areas such as parenting practices (e.g., children's school attendance). Under federal guidelines, welfare administrators must impose sanctions (i.e., reductions or eliminations of cash and benefits) when clients fall out of compliance with behavioral requirements.

Federal welfare reform produced roughly a decade of rapid caseload decline. Evidence suggests that the adults who remain on the rolls are mostly women who face substantial difficulties meeting employment and other behavioral requirements (Butler et al., 2008). As time has gone on, however, federal officials have steadily raised their expectations. Thus, as state welfare agencies and contracted service providers have been pressured to move ever-greater proportions of their caseloads into employment, the clients on their caseloads have become ever-less employable. Not surprisingly, evidence suggests that the vast majority of clients who exit the TANF program do not wind up in stable jobs that allow them to escape poverty (Anderson et al., 2000; Frogner et al., 2010).

Against this backdrop, the concept of "barriers to employment"—which maintained a modest profile in the era between WIN and TANF—has come to play a dominant role in welfare discourse.[4] Among researchers and policy experts, just as among elected officials and program officials, one finds the term "barriers" applied to conditions as diverse as low educational attainment, lack of work experience, low functional literacy, physical or mental health problems, substance abuse and addictions, a child who is young, a child with a serious disability, domestic violence experiences, lack of access to transportation, difficulties obtaining child care, inadequate or inconsistent housing, recent release from a correctional institution, involvement with the child welfare system, lack of English proficiency, obesity, being subjected to the negative attitudes of co-workers, work-related stress, spatial mismatch between available work and available workers, and neighborhood disorder (Burt, 2002; Loprest, 2002; Allard et al., 2003; Coulton, 2003; Siegel et al., 2004; Cawley and Danziger, 2005; Haney, 2013).

Measures of barriers are routinely used today to delineate subgroups of welfare recipients and explain why they vary in their odds of exiting and returning to welfare programs (Smith et al., 2002; Gutman et al., 2003; Nadel et al., 2003; Taylor and Barusch, 2004). In addition to analyzing barriers separately and adding them up to create indexes, scholars have devised numerous frameworks of "barrier domains" to capture the ways that co-occurring barriers cluster together and affect employment opportunity and retention (cf. Danziger et al., 2000; Kalil et al., 2001; Hasenfeld et al., 2004).

Federal agencies now make extensive use of the term to bring order to the complicated challenges that surround poor people's lives. The U.S. General Accounting Office (GAO) offered a typical example in its 2000 report on state sanction policies: "Among families under sanctions, 76 percent had at least one barrier to compliance [with work requirements] and 39 percent had multiple barriers, more than double the rates among all TANF families." The language of "multiple barriers," here and elsewhere, collapses and erases vast differences between actual life conditions. Such conditions (perhaps all conditions) in the lives of aid recipients now derive their policy-relevant meanings from the end goal of work placement.

The language of "barrier reduction" plays an increasingly important political role in unifying those who seek to expand services for the poor and those who seek to speed the poor into low-wage labor markets. The term's meaning is broadly understood to encompass forms of treatment, rehabilitation, or support (desired by the first group) in order to make individuals available for employment (desired by the second group). Yet the terms of this discursive bargain are far from equal. Work promotion is the trump determining which policy actions are legitimate and how they should be pursued. Moreover, while the term "barriers" is applied to all manner of conditions external to the individual, *practices* of identifying and reducing barriers focus mostly on the individual alone. Consider, for example, Burt's (2002) enumeration of ways that employment barriers are identified: through an initial screening; through a standardized formal assessment; and through behavioral evidence that an individual has failed to find a job, received sanctions, or returned to welfare.

As this list suggests, the barriers discourse is a language of case-level intervention. It frames structural conditions confronted by individuals as characteristics of individuals. Welfare clients are said to *have* barriers as if they were possessions or traits carried within. Thus, they *have* psychological trauma from an experience of violent sexual abuse just as they *have* limited access to reliable public transportation. Such barriers are diagnosed and enumerated at the individual level. They are used to classify individuals in relation to relevant populations and program goals. They are addressed through individual interventions designed to modify behavior and, ultimately, provide a form of therapeutic rehabilitation. To understand what the barriers discourse is and does, then, one must look to the ways it is put into practice in individual cases.

The barriers discourse on the frontlines of welfare reform

While it is important to understand how "barriers" are conceived and operationalized in policy research, a different kind of analysis is needed to understand how the barriers discourse matters for the daily operations of welfare systems. For the latter, we turn to field interviews with welfare case managers in the Florida WT program (see Soss et al., 2011). We focus on Florida because, by many estimates, it has been a leader in pursuing the core priorities of welfare reform: in devolving policy control to local actors, in privatizing welfare services, in placing service provision on a performance footing, and in shifting to what management explicitly calls a "business model" of service delivery (Soss et al., 2011).

Government services, of course, are not legislative words on a page; they emerge through the interactions of street-level workers and citizens (Lipsky, 1980). "Insofar as the state is an actor," Korteweg (2003, p. 453) reminds us, "it acts through these representatives whose discourses are proscribed but not completely determined by the policies they implement." Thus, to understand how policy discourses shape poverty governance, we must study and listen to its agents. In the present case, we must learn how frontline workers deploy "barriers" as a term of art in administrative practice and how their uses of the barriers discourse matter for governance.

In his 1977 monograph *Political Language*, Edelman describes how simple phrases evoke webs of politically consequential meanings. To speak of "training programs" for the unemployed, for example, is to partake in a language that implicitly suggests "job training is efficacious in solving the unemployment problem, that workers are unemployed because they lack necessary skills, [and] that jobs are available for those trained to take them" (p. 16). Though each alone may be a questionable assertion, the term "training programs" condenses them in routine usage and, thus, allows them to structure thought and action in ways more likely to go unnoticed and unchallenged. Like "training programs," the term "barriers" provides a prime example of how "strange talk," to use Becker's (1998, p. 151) formulation, can point "right to the heart of how a complex social activity is organized and carried out."

Indeed, the Florida WT program is an organizational world filled with the strange talk of neoliberal welfare reform. Commitments to the business model are expressed through a host of renaming practices. Caseworkers are referred to as "job coaches" and "career managers." They work alongside "job developers" and are overseen by "quality assurance managers" as they interact with clients now designated as "job candidates" or "customers." The barriers discourse fits easily into this linguistic milieu, and is easily assimilated into the actuarial ethos of the business model. Like the work participation hours logged for each client each week, like the agency's required performance indicators, and like a litany of work-relevant traits monitored for each client, barriers can be itemized, quantified, aggregated, and tracked. Discrete steps of remediation can be assessed for cost (and expected benefit), prescribed, and written into the client's welfare-to-work contract. Indeed, providers attentive to the bottom line can estimate per-client service costs given a particular barriers profile, much as an employer might calculate a salary based on factors such as experience and education.

As the concept of barriers turns complex and various life situations into enumerated client characteristics, it paves the way for policy implementers and analysts to exercise clinical authority. As Stone (1993) explains, clinical authority is a form of political power exercised by actors who (a) treat their external observations of individual traits as objective and, thus, superior to the person's own subjective reports, (b) enumerate and aggregate individual observations into population distributions, (c) diagnose and categorize the individual via their location in these distributions, and (d) present their preferred remedial actions as expert technical prescriptions rather than contestable moral and political claims on others. Through the logic of clinical authority, citizens' private characteristics are subjected to the gaze of public officialdom and legitimated as objects of state remediation and control. Clinical authority, one might say, is where the actuarial ethos of the business model meets and meshes with aspirations to scientific objectivity, the exigencies of state social control, and the therapeutic culture of client transformation that is the signature of contemporary welfare reform. Through objective diagnosis, classification, and treatment, policy actors can judiciously apply state power to bring clients into the right relationship with society as independent, wage-earning citizens.

The world of practice, however, is considerably more complicated than this logic. The women who sit across the desk from welfare case managers are visibly (and sometimes vocally) more than the sum total of a barriers checklist. As Soss et al. (2011, p. 202) explain, "case managers spend their days with clients whose problems are real and deep, who are anxious for their children, who long to escape poverty, and who have come to them for help. They want their difficult daily work to have a purpose and to mean something more than the numbers on a balance sheet." At the administrative frontlines, case managers deploy the barriers discourse on a complex terrain where work-first performance pressures and professional investments in clinical authority run up against desires to be "sympathetic counselors who provide much-needed social services and help people solve their problems" (Soss et al., 2011, p. 202).

Use at the frontlines

Roughly 90 percent of the case managers we interviewed were women, and nearly the same proportion was non-white. About one-third of those we interviewed were single mothers who had experienced spells of welfare receipt. Many others alluded to histories of poverty or financial hardship in childhood or adulthood.

Interviews revealed that these case managers, their supervisors, and senior administrators made regular use of the barriers discourse in ways that assumed tacit agreement on its content and meaning. All referred to clients as "having barriers," typically without any felt need to specify the referent for the phrase (i.e., barriers to *work*) or the nature of the barriers in a particular case.

When asked to describe their meetings with new clients, case managers almost universally reported that the first step is to "go over their barriers." "Barriers assessment" emerged as an essential step in initiating program participation and getting a fix on the client. Yet case managers varied considerably in the ways they understood the norms and boundaries of barriers assessment, with some describing detailed, searching discussions of clients' circumstances and others stating that they were not permitted to ask highly "personal" questions.

Once clients are established in the program, barriers remain central to daily case management. Case managers routinely begin their work days by "checking [their] alerts," using a regional tracking system that identifies clients who are out of compliance with their welfare-to-work contracts. To make sense of these alerts and infer appropriate responses, case managers compare reported infractions with the information they have about a client's barriers. Assessing the two together, they make decisions about whether a sanction or some course of remedial action is warranted. Actors at all levels of the WT program also relied heavily on the concept of barriers when evaluating the current system. While very few questioned the normative goal of work promotion, many called for greater efforts to accommodate clients' barriers and said that more suitable "activities" were needed for clients with multiple serious barriers—i.e., activities such clients could complete in fulfillment of their contracts and, thus, avoid being sanctioned.

Putting work first

In the WT program, as in neoliberal poverty governance in general, work functions as the primary goal, normative standard, and interpretive anchor. A key feature of the barriers discourse is that it folds this non-negotiable imperative into a more ambiguous language that evokes images of needs and problems, caregiving and solutions. "Barriers" are barriers *to work*, of course, but this fact – and the power-laden act of reframing that it entails—is generally left implicit and cloaked in the taken-for-granted. The dialogue between case manager and client pivots on questions of how the former can help the latter deal with her barriers (which are ultimately *her* responsibility) so she does not have to be sanctioned (the ubiquitous backdrop of coercion) and can succeed in meeting her goals (an equation of low-wage work with success, and program goals with personal goals).

At the same time, the barriers discourse at the frontlines flattens differences between life problems and reframes some hardships as unproblematic. Diverse conditions, from childbirth to child abuse, from a learning disability to a substance addiction, and from a lack of job skills to a rotten labor market, are designated and tallied as equivalent problems because, from a work promotion perspective, they are instances of the same thing: impediments to work. Thus, a WT client experiencing post-traumatic stress disorder, substance addiction, and domestic abuse is grouped with a client who lacks transportation, lives in an area of high unemployment, and has very limited job skills. Both are deemed clients with "multiple barriers" and treated accordingly.

On the other side of the ledger, a host of problems experienced and described by clients are kept off the agenda because they cannot be officially interpreted as limiting work. These conditions, in effect, cease to be "problems" within the social-service context. In this manner, the barriers discourse functions as a mechanism for the construction of social problems: It frames some hardships as authentic problems, while pushing others to the margins. In the process, it constrains case managers just as it provides them with a powerful tool for controlling the scope and terms of interactions with clients.

To be deemed an official problem within this discourse, however, it is not enough for a life condition to impede work. As case managers often emphasized in interviews, the threshold is reached, not when circumstances make it difficult for a client to work, but when the resulting limitation on work can be formally documented in a manner that conforms to program categories. One case manager (who was also a former recipient) explained this dynamic in recalling cases where she felt compelled to keep her personal and emotional response separate from actions as a policy implementer.

> *I follow the policy regardless of whoever it is. Because I've had people that was on chemotherapy … but their doctor was saying that they can still participate in some form of participation. I have very well sympathized with them, but if I have a documentation in my file, if a monitor comes in, and they see that this doctor said that this person can do this, I got to have backup as to why this person can't. So, what I would do in that situation is tell them, "You need to go back to your doctor; if you are having these certain circumstances where right now your body's weak where you can't do this, you need to give me updated information." […] So, when we're talking about the sanctioning process, it's a process in place, and everybody follows the process.*

In gauging the "true" extent of a client's barriers to work, and thus their legitimate need for public services and supports, case managers often relied on a litmus test: a WT policy known as "diversion." Under a diversion plan, Florida families otherwise eligible for TANF may accept an up-front payment of $1,000 in exchange for giving up program eligibility for three months. According to Florida's TANF State Plan Renewal (2011), case managers are required to take steps to obviate the need for even this one-time payment, including screening for employment barriers, connecting the applicant to a job opportunity, offering services such as transportation and child care, and responding to emergency needs.

In interviews, case managers were united in applauding this option as a successful deterrent to TANF enrollment for those who could do something else. A decision to "go on" TANF, with its tough requirements and penalties for noncompliance, was viewed as signifying an inability to achieve employment without help and, thus, as an indicator of genuine need. In a kind of catch-22, however, many case managers also saw the client's act of choosing to enter the WT program—with its clear emphasis on the client's obligations to overcome barriers—as a contractual declaration of personal responsibility. In bypassing diversion, the client signifies she is unable to make it on her own and needs assistance, but in entering the WT program instead, she affirms her responsibility for overcoming her own problems.

> *Case Manager (CM): The case manager assesses the barriers that are holding the customer back, like if they are dealing with domestic abuse, not to get too personal, but we need to know these things. Then we can give them the alternatives and get them some help. I think it's just taking responsibility, and when they come into the program it is on the client at that point.*

Interviewer (I): Because they had the choice of up-front diversion and they chose to enter the program?

CM: Yes, they have made a conscious decision to open up the cash, and they know that when they make the conscious decision they are expected to get a job or go to school or do some community service work. [...] And we're offering them the opportunity to get the skills that will help them, so I think yes at that point it is their responsibility.

Individualizing need

Consistent with its uses in policy research, "barriers" is used at the frontlines to frame a host of structural and environmental conditions as if they were the properties of individuals. In interviews, case managers routinely spoke of clients as having barriers that they needed to personally identify, figure out, confront, address, take responsibility for, work on, overcome, and so on. Most case managers described their role as enforcing WT program rules and providing clients with services and supports in order to help *them* overcome *their* barriers and reach *their* employment goals.

The individualizing nature of this discourse facilitates its assimilation into age-old moral distinctions between the deserving and undeserving poor. Even as case managers expressed sympathy for their clients with barriers, they continued to distinguish sharply between those who made an effort and those who did not. Indeed, personal lack of effort was sometimes cited as a barrier in its own right, just as "barrier" was sometimes used as a euphemism for lack of self-discipline. One case manager illustrated this tendency in distinguishing between complacent clients and those who are "seriously looking for work opportunities." When asked about clients with barriers, she responded without hesitation as if the term referred to a culturally rooted lack of individual resilience, a failure to be "mind-strong."

I: So you notice that people with more barriers get sanctioned a lot while other folks don't get sanctioned as much?

CM: That is correct. Because you have to be mind-strong to accomplish the activities. I don't know if it is a cultural thing or what, but some people don't understand the consequences.

As the barriers discourse framed clients as individuals with deficits (or in some cases, as deficient individuals), it also framed the ways case managers thought about the possibilities and limits of the welfare-to-work system. On one side, critiques of the program cited its failure to confront the depth of individual barriers and provide case managers with flexible-enough rules and adequate tools of intervention. As one case manager put it: "Never mind that Deborah can't read, and she's got a 6th grade education, but you want [her to] go out and get a job at ten bucks an hour. Or, my candidate, who has a substance abuse problem, you know, he keeps drinking on the job, that's why he can't *keep* his job." Another case manager concluded: "The program regulations need to be looked at immediately [at the] highest level and [they need to] give us the tools to help clients to a better outcome."

On the other side, critiques of the current system frequently focused on its failure to motivate clients to remediate their own barriers. In these instances, case managers deployed hard-to-overcome barriers as justifications for tougher approaches. Outcomes would improve, they suggested, if the rules required clients to demonstrate more significant effort "up front" in the program entry process. Some argued that the WT program should do a better job of mirroring "the real world" (i.e., conditions in low-wage jobs) where individuals receive no pay until *after* they work and there are few, if any, second chances for failing at a job. Few clients will overcome their barriers, they argued, if the program structure allows them to sidestep personal responsibility. In this sense, program accommodations for barriers were seen as a design flaw that provided clients with openings to "play the system." A male case manager who described his role as "quality assurance" echoed others in this discussion of clients with multiple barriers.

> CM: *I think that to some extent some of the welfare clients have to be manipulative to maintain the lifestyle they are accustomed to, which in our minds might not be a good lifestyle, but that is all that they have. [...]*
>
> I: So, how will they manipulate?
>
> CM: *Usually in talking about their problems and telling the case managers that they should not have to do requirements because they are different and that they have too many children or something. They will say that they have too much sickness in the family or that they don't have any transportation and things like that.*
>
> I: So are those largely emotional appeals for sympathy?
>
> CM: *That, and I think some of the customers want to get out of doing what they are supposed to do. My question is always: Why are they trying to get out when they knew from the beginning that they are required to do these things? Why do they not want to go to GED classes when they are free and we will give them gas-cards and childcare if they attend? Do they not care about their future? [...] Often customers are afraid to put forth the effort to achieve their goals because people told them they will always fail, so they may as well not try. They are often not brought up in effective family environments or may be the children of welfare recipients, so that is the model that they have.*

Case managers frequently expressed sympathy for clients with serious life challenges. Many identified with clients as having similar poverty histories, and some wished they could offer more help. The most common assumption, however, was that clients who wanted to succeed and made an effort to succeed could do so. It is the individual who has the barrier—it resides within her—and thus its eradication depends on individual change.

Conferring and complicating clinical authority

By construing individuals as carriers of work impediments (that vary in number), the barriers discourse produces a rationally ordered target population for state intervention. As the individual becomes a client, a kind of subjectification occurs: the "client with barriers" emerges as one who is principally defined by, and who must be helped to overcome, one or more of a checklist of negative traits. Unruly differences in life problems, many of which actually occur in only a small percentage of cases, are replaced by "barriers," which nearly all clients have. The category "clients with barriers" condenses diverse conditions and anticipations to constitute a population in need—a population of clients who vary in the extent to which they are "hard to serve" but who all require active state governance to achieve the "normal" condition of paid employment.

As described earlier, this process confers a kind of "clinical authority" on policy actors, who are positioned in relation to the target population as practitioners of objective, technical modes of observation, diagnosis, and remediation (Stone, 1993). The barriers discourse operates to confer clinical authority, and thus obscure the workings of power, in administrators' discussions of local operating procedures as much as in scholars' discussions of policy analysis. At the frontlines of service provision, however, the countervailing realities and understandings of the case manager role complicate this aspect of the barriers discourse.

The case manager is positioned as a therapeutic agent in two distinct senses, which are often hard to reconcile. On one side, they are invested with clinical authority, joining others in the welfare domain as practitioners of objective diagnosis and remediation. On the other, they are positioned as "recovery" role models for their clients: people who have personally walked the hard road from degradation and despair to respectability, people who have earned their knowledge through life experience and who bring this perspective to bear in the manner that "sponsors" do in addiction recovery programs.

Over the past two decades, case management has been recast as a deskilled, low-wage position. Case managers today are increasingly likely to share community backgrounds and social character-istics with their clients. Few if any case managers can lay claim to formal credentials of expertise as sources of legitimacy and credibility. To fill the gap, they draw on their own lives and lay claim to a kind of wisdom that, for many, is more profound than professional expertise and more deserving of client attention. In so doing, however, they appeal to a deeply subjective source of authority that lies in tension with the appeal to objective diagnosis and prescription that underpins clinical authority.

Case managers routinely express these discursive contradictions as uncertainties about their own role and authority. In official terms, they have the power to identify and diagnose barri-ers with an objective gaze that trumps clients' own interpretations of their life conditions. Yet many felt uncomfortable with the idea that they were qualified to "diagnose" individual barri-ers. As one case manager put it, "We're not psychiatrists and I'm sure you've heard that from other people." In reality, they suggested, they were not observing and diagnosing barriers, like a doctor who can see symptoms more fully, accurately, and knowledgably than the patient. They were mostly dependent on clients to disclose barriers, which they documented and then used as a basis for applying program rules and trying to motivate the client. Indeed, interviews with case managers often revealed a strong sense that—contrary to the classic doctor–patient relationship of clinical authority—*it is up to the client* to identify the barrier and overcome it. One case manager explained:

> We [case managers] set it all down ... their barriers and their needs and what they want to do in the future ... and we go from there. If you [the client] want to get the ball and run with it, great. Some people don't. Some people, I'm not sure they know how to take the ball and run with it. Something's always jumped up in their life and [...] If they have a drug problem, they're not going to ... you know. [...] I can't badger them. They have to be upfront with me in all this.

In response to this disjuncture (between images of objective clinical authority and more mod-est self-conceptions), case managers often assimilated the barriers discourse into the "recovery model" they felt more comfortable appealing to for credibility. "Barriers," in this guise, become part of a narrative that aligns the case manager with the client and justifies the latter's deference and cooperation. This sort of appeal to personal determination in overcoming barriers—which broadly takes the form of "I did it, so you can do it if you listen to me"—was well illustrated by a female case manager who was also a former welfare recipient:

> I know it's really hard but I know you just have to get out there and do it and not use it as an excuse. Because I myself got out there and did it myself, and within a month I was re-employed, and I had some pretty big barriers. In terms of housing, I had to find my own place. I had to get enough money to get my own place and child-care assistance. So I get angered with clients who play the victim role. It's okay to have barriers but don't use them as an excuse. Overcome them.

Most case managers know well that some clients have barriers that make it difficult, or even impossible, for them to hold jobs. Yet they also maintain that barriers are the client's responsibility and that they can and should be overcome. The apparent paradox becomes easier to understand when one considers the severe limits that case managers work under. It is exceptionally rare for a case manager to have the resources, tools, or forms of rule flexibility needed to address a client's barriers in a meaningful way. To shift responsibility for the barrier away from the client would, in many cases, be to acknowledge that little will be done. In this respect, the barriers discourse is an example of what Joel Handler (1995) calls "myth and ceremony" in the welfare office—a ritual that expresses policy aspirations but ultimately does little for the client. One female case manager spoke for many when she complained that her clients "are individuals [who] have different needs, who have different barriers, and [the system is] forcing us to put them in the same type of process." A male case manager described the situation in animated terms, juxtaposing the seriousness of clients' situations with the limits of what he has to offer:

I had a customer that … had issues with depression, major breakdown, you know, so I'm like … by the way could not read very well either. So I'm like, oh my gosh, I just got her in school, and now she's out for two weeks in the hospital. But then they'll tell you, "Oh well, okay, when she gets out have her make up her hours." And you're like "But she's in the hospital; she's depressed, she doesn't want to make up [anything]" and they don't wanna hear it [laughs]. So, it's just that kind of thing, you know?

Thus, even as case managers deploy the barriers discourse for a variety of purposes, the type of authority it suggests rests uneasily on their shoulders. As they lay claim to forms of credibility based on subjective life experiences, case managers unsettle the discourse's pretensions to formal expertise and objectivity. Daily experiences make it clear that, although they have the power to override clients' accounts and substitute their own assessments, they have limited abilities to diagnose conditions that clients do not disclose. And perhaps above all, they experience the frustration of lacking the tools and resources needed to "remediate" the barriers their clients confront. One case manager reflected on the contradictions of her job:

You're working with people who have needs, who have barriers. […] It's hard for me to sit with an individual there telling me that they've been evicted from their apartment, they don't have any place to live, they don't have any food, they don't have any clothes. And then here I am as a case manager: "You have to participate at 40 hours a week." You know, it's just kind of … it's crazy!

Conclusion

Today's welfare recipients are said to *have* barriers, rather than having barriers imposed upon them. While "barriers" seemingly denote factors outside of the individual, and perhaps even outside of her control, our interviews with Florida's welfare-to-work case managers suggest that barriers have come to be treated as the properties of individuals. Thus, people must be rehabilitated from, cured of, and/or take responsibility for their barriers, much as, in the past, they did for their deviances, social disabilities, and misguided choices.

Most case managers we interviewed discussed clients' employment barriers within a highly individual frame of personal responsibility. They sympathized with the severity of clients' barriers—even, in a few cases, openly grieved their limited ability to help—but ultimately differentiated clients based on assessments of their individual efforts. As has been well documented in previous work on Florida (Soss et al., 2011), TANF administrators, supervisors, and case managers face tremendous performance pressures which are often passed along to their clients. Under these conditions, client success may take on a more proximal meaning for case managers, equated to completing and submitting evidence of work hours; receiving, in exchange, some combination of cash, child care, and transportation assistance; and exiting TANF with a job. The resources of a case manager are so limited, and her clients' needs are so extensive, that there may be a degree of comfort to be derived from the formulaic and observable nature of individual clients demonstrating personal responsibility by acting in compliance within the welfare-to-work system.

In this sense, perhaps the term "barriers" does not *contain* babies and addictions, mental health problems and car troubles, as much as it *proxies* for them. A few case managers—some in their frustration and grief and one other by repurposing the term and applying it to systems— seemed to challenge the notion that conditions such as a serious and persistent mental illness or a lengthy history of violence and abuse could be addressed within a short time span of two years and with a piecemeal series of training and volunteer opportunities. Addressing or overcoming barriers, then, does not mean finding long-term (or even perhaps short-term) solutions to the conditions which make finding and keeping paid employment difficult, but rather doing in ritualistic fashion what the TANF system asks of you despite these things. Barriers become something case managers need to "work around" in order to be able to claim that they are moving their recipients in the direction the system expects. Under these conditions, case management becomes a series of "work arounds," or makeshift practices designed to enable clients to be seen as succeeding in the short run even if they will not in the long run.

The barriers discourse, as practiced on the frontlines of welfare reform, lumps together the conditions of life and packages them as things that keep people from making progress in moving from welfare to work. Employment remains the goal as the civic ideal, and all other societal contributions are positioned as secondary. Indeed, some things that had historically been seen as contributory, such as parenting and caring for others in need, are now viewed as barriers to the one thing that denotes citizenship. This is certainly at a minimum disconcerting to those who would like concerns about caregiving to have a place in a calculus of the rights and responsibilities of citizenship.

Yet, even in the context of a focus on paid work, evidence from studies of income shocks, underground economies, and secondary labor markets has consistently shown us that paid work does not mean economic security. Case managers and others who work with welfare clients know this all too well. Nonetheless, the barriers discourse provides cover for continuing to approach welfare-to-work programs as sufficient to address the problems welfare recipients confront. It encourages people inside and outside the welfare system, and on both sides of the case manager's desk, to internalize the idea that if recipients could only overcome their barriers to employment, their road to the middle class would be assured. In this way, it does important political and emotional labor, distracting many from a more critical gaze into the problems confronting low-income families. The barriers discourse operates as an ideological mystification to rationalize neoliberal policies that incentivize work at wages so low that families cannot but remain poor.

Notes

1 Maternalist reformers of the Progressive and New Deal era sought to draw attention to the significance of motherhood in social policy and politics, the civic contributions of mothers in childrearing, and the role that "private" familial interests can and should play in public policy (see Gordon, 1994; Mink, 1995).
2 Among these were important studies by Josephine Williams and Winifred Bell. Williams found that while low-income black women generally had more work experience than their white counterparts, they had greater difficulty finding jobs. Winifred Bell noted that not only were employers refusing to hire qualified black women, these women also could not find day care centers willing to accept their children (Mittelstadt, 2005).
3 "Marital conflict" would now likely be classified as domestic or intimate partner violence.
4 As an illustration, consider the results of a Google Scholar search for works containing the terms "barriers to employment" and "welfare" (performed January 9, 2014). The search produces 778 results for the period from 1974 to 1993. By contrast, it yields 8,840 for the period from 1994 to 2013.

References

Allard, S. W., Tolman, R. M., and Rosen, D. (2003). The geography of need: Spatial distribution of barriers to employment in metropolitan Detroit. *Policy Studies Journal*, 31, 293–307.

Anderson, S. G., Halter, A. P., Julnes, G., and Schuldt, R. (2000). Job stability and wage progression patterns among early TANF leavers. *Journal of Sociology and Social Welfare*, 27(4), 39–61.

Becker, H. S. (1998). *Tricks of the trade: How to think about your research while you're doing it.* Chicago: University of Chicago Press.

Bell, W. (1965). *Aid to families with dependent children.* New York: Columbia University Press.

Burt, M. R. (2002). The "hard-to-serve": Definitions and implications. In A. Weil and K. Finegold (eds.), *Welfare reform: The next act* (pp. 163–178). Washington, DC: The Urban Institute Press.

Butler, S. S., Corbett, J., Bond, C., and Hastedt, C. (2008). Long-term TANF participants and barriers to employment: A qualitative study in Maine. *Journal of Sociology and Social Welfare*, 35(3), 49.

Cawley, J., and Danziger, S. (2005). Morbid obesity and the transition from welfare to work. *Journal of Policy Analysis and Management*, 24(4), 727–743.

Coulton, C. J. (2003). Metropolitan inequities and the ecology of work: Implications for welfare reform. *Social Service Review*, 77, 159–190.

Danziger, S. K., Kalil, A., and Anderson, N. J. (2000). Human capital, physical health, and mental health of welfare recipients: Co-occurrence and correlates. *Journal of Social Issues*, 56, 635–654.

Dordick, G. A. (2002). Recovering from homelessness: Determining the "Quality of Sobriety" in a transitional housing program. *Qualitative Sociology*, 25(1), 7–32.

Edelman, M. (1977). *Political language: Words that succeed and policies that fail.* Institute for Research on Poverty Monograph Series, Academic Press Inc.

Florida Department of Children and Families (F-DCF). (2011). Temporary Assistance for Needy Families State Plan Renewal: October 1, 2011, to September 30, 2014.

Frogner, B., Moffitt, R., and Ribar, D. (2010). Leaving welfare: Long-term evidence from three cities. Working Paper 10-01. Retrieved January 13, 2014, from https://orchid.hosts.jhmi.edu/wfp/files/WP10-01_Leaving%20Welfare.pdf.

Goldberg, C. A. (2005). Contesting the status of relief workers during the New Deal: The Workers Alliance of America and the Works Progress Administration, 1935–1941. *Social Science History*, 29(3), 337–371.

Gordon, L. (1994). *Pitied but not entitled: Single mothers and the history of welfare.* Cambridge, MA: Harvard University Press.

Gordon, L. (2001). Who deserves help? Who must provide? *Annals*, 577, 12–25.

Gutman, M. A., McKay, J., Ketterlinus, R. D., and McLellan, A. T. (2003). Potential barriers to work for substance-abusing women on welfare: Findings from the CASAWORKS for Families pilot demonstration. *Evaluation Review*, 27, 681–706.

Hacker, J. S., and Pierson, P. (2002). Business power and social policy: Employers and the formation of the American welfare state. *Politics & Society*, 30(2), 277–325.

Handler, J. (1995). *The poverty of welfare reform.* New Haven, CT: Yale University Press.

Haney, T. J. (2013). Off to market: Neighborhood and individual employment barriers for women in 21st century American cities. *Journal of Urban Affairs*, 35(3), 303–325.

Hasenfeld, Y., Ghose, T., and Larson, K. (2004). The logic of sanctioning welfare recipients: An empirical assessment. *The Social Service Review*, 78, 304–319.

Houser, L., Schram, S. F., Soss, J., and Fording, R. C. (2014). From work support to work motivator: Child care subsidies and caseworker discretion in the post-welfare reform era. *Journal of Women, Politics, and Policy*, 35, 174–193.

Kalil, A., Schweingruber, H. A., and Seefeldt, K. S. (2001). Correlates of employment among welfare recipients: Do psychological characteristics and attitudes matter? *American Journal of Community Psychology*, 29, 701–722.

Kondratas, A. S. (1986). The political economy of work-for-welfare. *Cato Journal*, 6, 229–243.

Korteweg, A. C. (2003). Welfare reform and the subject of the working mother: "Get a job, a better job, then a career." *Theory and Society*, 32(4), 445–480.

Levinson, P. (1970). How employable are AFDC women? *Welfare in Review*, 8, 12–16.

Lieberman, R. C. (1998). *Shifting the color line: Race and the American welfare state.* Cambridge, MA: Harvard University Press.

Lipsky, M. (1980). *Street-level bureaucracy: Dilemmas of the individual in public services.* New York: Russell Sage.

Loprest, P. J. (2002). Making the transition from welfare to work: Successes by continuing concerns. In A. Weil and K. Finegold (eds.), *Welfare reform: The next act* (pp. 17–31). Washington, DC: The Urban Institute Press.

Mettler, S. (1998). *Dividing citizens: Gender and federalism in New Deal public policy.* New York: Cornell University Press.

Mink, G. (1995). *The wages of motherhood: Inequality in the welfare state, 1917–1942.* Ithaca: Cornell University Press.

Mittelstadt, J. (2005). *From welfare to work: The unintended consequences of liberal reform, 1945–1965.* New Jersey: Johns Hopkins University Press.

Nadel, M., Wamhoff, S., and Wiseman, M. (2003). Disability, welfare reform, and Supplemental Security Income. *Social Security Bulletin,* 65, 1–23.

National Conference of State Legislatures. (2013, April 17). Drug testing and public assistance. Retrieved January 13, 2014, from http://www.ncsl.org/issues-research/human-services/drug-testing-and-public-assistance.aspx.

Noble, C. (1997). *Welfare as we knew it: A political history of the American welfare state.* New York: Oxford University Press.

Pavetti, L., Trisi, D., and Schott, L. (2011). *TANF responded unevenly to increase in need during downturn.* Washington, DC: Center on Budget and Policy Priorities. Retrieved January 13, 2014, from http://www.cbpp.org/files/1-25-11tanf.pdf.

Peck, J. (2001). *Workfare states.* New York: Guilford Press.

Piven, F. F., and Cloward, R. (1993). *Regulating the poor: The functions of public welfare* (2nd updated ed.). New York: Vintage Books.

Rose, N. E. (1995). *Workfare or fair work: Women, welfare, and government work programs.* New Brunswick, NJ: Rutgers University Press.

Schram, S. F. (2012). The deep semiotic structure of deservingness: Discourse and identity in welfare policy. In Frank Fischer and Hebert Gottweis (eds.), *The Argumentative Turn in Policy Analysis (Revisited)* (pp. 236–268). Durham: Duke University Press.

Siegel, D., Green, J., Abbott, A., Mogul, M., and Patacsil, M. (2004). Barriers to employment, returners to welfare, and those who have left the welfare and employment rolls. *Social Policy Journal,* 3(4), 19–39.

Skocpol, T. (1992). *Protecting soldiers and mothers: The political origins of social policy in the United States.* Cambridge, MA: The Belknap Press of Harvard University Press.

Smith, L. A., Romero, D., Wood, P. R., Wampler, N. S., Chavkin, W., and Wise, P. H. (2002). Employment barriers among welfare recipients and applicants with chronically ill children. *American Journal of Public Health,* 92, 1453–1457.

Soss, J., Fording, R. C., and Schram, S. F. (2011). *Disciplining the poor: Neoliberalism and the persistent power of race.* Chicago: University of Chicago Press.

Stone, D. A. (1993). Clinical authority in the construction of citizenship. In H. Ingram and S. R. Smith (eds.), *Public Policy for Democracy* (pp. 45–67). Washington DC: Brookings Institution.

Stone, D. A. (2007). Welfare policy and the transformation of care. In J. Soss, J. S. Hacker, and S. Mettler (eds.), *Remaking America: Democracy and Public Policy in an Age of Inequality* (pp. 183–202). New York: Russell Sage Foundation.

Stone, R. C., and Schlamp, F. T. (1965). Characteristics associated with receipt or nonreceipt of financial aid from welfare agencies: An exploratory study. *Welfare Review,* 3, 1–11.

Taylor, M. J., and Barusch, A. S. (2004). Personal, family, and multiple barriers of long-term welfare recipients. *Social Work,* 49, 175–184.

Ten Broek, J., and Wilson, R. B. (1954). Public assistance and social insurance—a normative evaluation. *UCLA Law Review,* 3, 237–306.

U.S. General Accounting Office. (1971). *Problems in accomplishing objectives of the Work Incentive Program (WIN).* B-164031(3). http://www.gao.gov/assets/230/228975.pdf.

U.S. General Accounting Office. (2000). *Welfare reform: State sanction policies and number of families affected.* GAO/HES-00-44. Washington, DC: U.S. Government Printing Office.

14

WE ARE THE 99 PERCENT

The rise of poverty and the decline of poverty stigma

Joan Maya Mazelis and Brendan M. Gaughan

Stigma about being poor compounds the material struggles of the poor. In a society focused on individual responsibility and financial success as a life goal, it's easy, and common, for poor people to feel like failures, and to blame themselves for their disadvantaged position. Yet the Occupy Wall Street (OWS) movement reflected a shift in perceptions about poor people—and may have also helped to shape it. OWS began on September 17, 2011 in Lower Manhattan's Financial District. Soon after the movement solidified in New York City's Zuccotti Park, the rest of the country, and even the world, saw the formation of new Occupy protests in cities, towns, and college campuses. Within the days following the initial protests and subsequent encampments on Wall Street, an Occupy encampment was established in Chicago on September 23, 2011, and in Boston on September 30, 2011. Between October 1 and October 6, 2011, encampments sprung up in an almost routine fashion across the United States, with Los Angeles and Wichita joining the ranks of the protests, followed by cities like Philadelphia, Seattle, and Houston. By October 15, 2011, the Occupy Movement had spread to over 951 cities in 82 countries, from Washington DC to Madrid, and from Ann Arbor to Sydney. Protestors in nearly every corner of the globe exclaimed the movement's characteristic slogan "we are the 99 percent" (Weigel and Hepler, 2011). Images of demonstrators announcing their poverty, and citing structural factors as the cause, saturated news coverage. OWS directly responded to the influence of banks and multinational corporations on the democratic process. The influence of the protestors is apparent in news coverage and in shifting popular perceptions about inequality (Milkman et al., 2012).

Widespread sympathy with the OWS movement was surprising given that the majority of the American public has negative attitudes toward welfare and welfare recipients, as well as toward the poor more generally (Fraser and Gordon, 1994; Gilens, 1999; Katz, 1986, 1989). Since 1973 inequality has been rising, with the top 20 percent gaining ground and the bottom 80 percent falling behind. Rising contempt for the poor combined with political rhetoric and a long-existing individualist ethos to facilitate punitive welfare reforms in the 1990s (Wilson, 2000).

Americans blame the persistence of poverty on poor individuals (Edelman, 2012; Gans, 1995; Handler and Hasenfeld, 1997; Jencks, 1992; Katz, 1983, 1986; Wilson, 2000). Wilson (2000) asserts that the belief that poverty results from individuals' moral fabric rather than the social structure accounts partially for public support of cuts in welfare. Americans believe that the poor are generally lazy and undeserving and don't value work the way the non-poor do (Garin et al., 1994; Gilens, 1999; Jencks, 1992; Wilson, 2000).

As Goffman states, the "stigmatized individual tends to hold the same beliefs about identity that we do" (1963:7). The poor differentiate themselves from other poor people by asserting their values of hard work, responsibility, and morality. They define themselves in opposition to and see themselves as better than others in similar economic positions. They separate themselves as good and deserving from others who they define (or whose definition by the media and politicians they accept) as essentially bad and undeserving. They gain self-worth by distinguishing themselves from other poor people (Cohen, 1997). In *Promises I Can Keep* (2005), Edin and Kefalas note that many of the poor mothers they interviewed set themselves apart from others in, or close to, their situations. In *A Place on the Corner* (1976), Anderson illustrates how people define themselves partly by whom they oppose by using sets of discursive oppositions; thus, the regulars set themselves apart from the hoodlums, and the wineheads struggle to set themselves apart from other wineheads. Snow and Anderson (1993) also found this distancing among the homeless people they studied. Investigating rhetoric and practices at welfare-to-work agencies, Chad Broughton found this attribution paradox among the clients: they subscribed to the ideology about welfare recipients' faults and failings, but did not apply those understandings to themselves. Broughton refers to this process of "othering," "by which, in this case, welfare recipients shift the stigma that welfare receipt carries from themselves to other welfare recipients" (2001:109). In some ways, OWS represented a departure from a near-ubiquitous othering, spurring those who had never previously identified as poor to see their commonalities with those at the bottom. The phrase "the 99 percent" articulated a unity among all those not in the most privileged category of the American populace.

OWS represented a change in political rhetoric as well, which has historically divided the poor into those who are "deserving" and those who are "undeserving" (Cohen, 1997; Katz, 1989). Women made widows by the Civil War once represented the "deserving" poor (Katz, 1989), yet twenty-first-century society expects women to work outside the home if their financial situation necessitates it. The "deserving" poor is now a virtually empty category in a generally healthy economy; society expects people to have sole responsibility for their skills and educational and occupational attainment. However, in a struggling economy, non-individualized reasons for poverty become more apparent. Evidence suggests the wider economic context influences the degree of stigmatization poor people feel; widespread unemployment may point to external factors at work and make it easier to see the process as larger than any one individual's personal failings. The Great Recession seems to have had an effect on the rhetoric about class and poverty and unemployment, just as stigma decreased during the Great Depression (Katz, 1989; Zastrow, 2010).

People typically view those who are chronically unemployed as victims of their own poor decisions, such as the decision to cut education short. Those faced with such circumstances themselves tend to focus on what they might have done differently. However, on an individual level, a man who is laid off from his factory job after many years of employment and consequently suffers from financial difficulties may say to himself, "If only the company didn't close, I'd have my job and my income." Whether he sees root causes leading to corporate closings, downsizing, and outsourcing in an era of deindustrialization and neoliberal capitalism or not, he may find reasons other than personal failure to point to for his poverty, if a plant closing precipitates his status. When *many* plants close, poverty stigma may decline in general and pave the way for a cultural shift like OWS. During the Great Depression of the 1930s, poverty rates were very high, and historians assert that the stigma connected to poverty lessened.

Although there was no official poverty measure during the Great Depression, historians estimate that about one-third of American families, more than double the poverty rate in 2010, were poor at that time (Barrington, 1997). The President's Committee on Economic Security estimated that the number of unemployed went from under half a million to over four million people in the time between October 1929 and January 1930 (Piven, 1977). In *The Undeserving Poor*, Michael Katz noted, "Poverty lost much of its moral censure as unemployment reached catastrophic levels, but the idea of relief remained pejorative and degrading" (Katz, 1989:15). There was still a distinction between the deserving and undeserving poor, and still a stigma against receiving governmental assistance. However, high unemployment mitigated stigma. Zastrow states:

> Americans, until the Great Depression, believed in the myth of individualism—that is, each individual is master of his or her own fate. Those in need were viewed as lazy, as unintelligent, or as justly punished for their sinful ways. The Great Depression of the 1930s called into question the individualism myth. ... With large numbers of people out of work, including those from the middle class, a new view of relief applicants developed: These people were not essentially different from others who were caught up in circumstances beyond their control.
>
> (Zastrow, 2010:116)

Current trends in public perceptions and stigmatization of the poor in the wake of the Great Recession mirror those during the Great Depression, with America once again in the midst of another economic crisis. The 18-month period between 2007 and 2009 proved to be the worst since the Great Depression (Roberts et al., 2011). According to the U.S. Census Bureau, the poverty rate climbed to a staggering 46.2 million people, or 15.1 percent, by the year after the recession officially ended (2010), the highest rate since 1993 (DeNavas-Walt et al., 2011). By contrast, in 2000, during better economic times, 11.3 percent of the population was in poverty (U.S. Census Bureau, 2001). In 2010, the unemployment rate was at a high of 9.6 percent, more than double the rate in the year 2000, when it was only 4 percent (U.S. Department of Labor, U.S. Bureau of Labor Statistics, 2014). The U.S. Department of Agriculture's (USDA) national average of food stamp (Supplemental Nutritional Assistance Program, or SNAP) participation also followed a similar trend. At the end of the recession in 2010, food stamp participation was at an all-time high of over 40 million individuals (U.S. Department of Agriculture, 2013), and it increased by nearly five million more people in 2011 (see Edelman, 2012). The level of participation more than doubled from 2000 according to the USDA, when food stamp participation was just over 17 million people (U.S. Department of Agriculture, 2013).

The years during the Great Recession also gave way to an era of increased income inequality. In 2009, the top quintile of household income earners in the United States. increased their share of the total income distribution from 42.9 to 49.4 percent, while the bottom quintile's share fell to an abysmal 3.4 percent (Smeeding, 2012). This disparity became even more amplified in the years that followed, with the lowest-quintile share dropping even further to 3.2 percent, and the highest-quintile share rising to 51.1 percent in 2011 (Smeeding, 2012).

Americans' opinions about welfare spending have an ebb and flow that correlates with times of economic boom and bust. Disdain for poor people shifts slightly when unemployment and poverty are more palpable. The percentage of people responding that welfare spending was too high peaked in or around years when the U.S. economy was doing relatively well. During 1976 and 1996, the percentage of respondents who considered welfare spending to be too high peaked at around 64 percent (Smith et al., 2011). On the other hand, when the economy was not doing as well, during recession, or in the midst of a recovery, such as in 1974, 1975, 1984, and 1991, more respondents thought welfare spending was too *low*. The percentage peaked at around 25 percent (Smith et al., 2011).

The Pew Research Center's report titled *Trends in Political Values and Core Attitudes* shows a similar connection between public opinion and the state of the economy. According to surveys conducted between 1987 and 2007, the public's view of the social safety net has shifted along with good and bad economic times. Since the mid-1990s, when the economy was relatively stable, Americans have responded in greater percentages that the government has the responsibility to take care of the poor. The shift in Americans' perception of the widening gap between the rich and the poor has followed a similar trajectory, and reached its highest points during times of economic hardship, such as 1991, when 80 percent of respondents thought the gap between the rich and the poor was too wide, and in 2007 when 73 percent of respondents thought the gap between rich and poor was growing (Pew Research Center, 2007).

OWS reflected, and perhaps helped to shape, a shift in Americans' perception of poor people. OWS consisted of people rejecting poverty stigma and joining with others in disadvantaged economic positions. In addition, OWS began during bad economic times; as in the Great Depression, economic context may have played a role in decreasing poverty stigma and thereby making OWS possible. Indicators of public opinion about poverty, economic trend data, and changed media and political rhetoric about poverty during recessions all suggest a potential relationship between economic context and poverty stigma. OWS used powerful slogans that captured our attention and entered the lexicon:

> Two out of three Americans now perceive strong social conflicts over the income gap—up sharply from two years ago. Paul Taylor of the Pew Research Center has an idea what's behind the increase. "The Occupy Wall Street movement kind of crystallized the issue: 1 versus 99. [It's] arguably the most successful slogan since 'Hell no, we won't go,' going back to the Vietnam era … [It] certainly triggered a lot of coverage about economic inequality."
>
> (Horsley, 2012)

OWS transformed, at least for a time, the way Americans talk about class in the popular media. Numerous articles and editorials in *The New York Times* and other popular media sources covered these issues; by discussing the issues and noting how the national rhetoric seemed to have changed as a result of OWS, the coverage itself further changed the rhetoric. The title of one *New York Times* article, "Camps Are Cleared, But '99 Percent' Still Occupies the Lexicon" evidences the change (Stelter, 2011). Stelter states:

> Within weeks of the first encampment in Zuccotti Park in New York, politicians seized on the phrase. Democrats in Congress began to invoke the "99 percent" to press for passage of President Obama's jobs act—but also to pursue action on mine safety, Internet access rules and voter identification laws, among others. Republicans pushed back, accusing protesters and their supporters of class warfare; Newt Gingrich this week called the "concept of the 99 and the 1" both divisive and "un-American."
>
> (2011)

"We are the 99 percent" is a direct reference to class and economic inequality; it invokes the fact that the top 1 percent of the population in the United States holds the majority of wealth and influence, and that almost all people are in the group of have-nots. It identifies the massive disparity in wealth in the United States, and spurred some to join OWS and speak out against their own disadvantaged economic position, and has allowed them to openly announce their fall into poverty as well; they held up signs at protests and, on a website (http://wearethe99per-cent.tumblr.com) for all to see, broadcast that they were unemployed, poor, in debt, and they blamed the system, not themselves as individuals.

OWS brought these issues to the center of public discourse, at least for a brief time. A simple internet search reveals news items and editorials published in January 2012 asserting that the OWS movement influenced national rhetoric, with titles like "The Occupy effect" (*The Nation*); "Occupy Wall Street has changed the national conversation" (*Chicago Tribune*); and "Obama's speech echoes Occupy movement themes" (*San Francisco Chronicle*). As scholar Peter Dreier states in a popular press piece:

> The Occupy Wall Street (OWS) movement has changed our national conversation. At kitchen tables, in coffee shops, in offices and factories, and in newsrooms, Americans are now talking about economic inequality, corporate greed, and how America's super-rich have damaged our economy and our democracy. The wide gulf between the richest one percent and the rest of Americans hasn't changed over the past year, but in the past month OWS has made it the dominant topic of discussion across the nation. Even the GOP presidential candidates, while first criticizing the occupiers as a radical fringe, have had to do an about-face when they saw that the protesters had, in fact, captured the national mood.
>
> (Dreier, 2011)

Dreier presents data showing that U.S. newspapers published three times the number of stories with the word "inequality" in the month after the OWS protests began, and even more stark rises for the phrases "greed" and "richest one percent." He states:

> Of course, not every story with the words "inequality," "greed" and "richest one percent" was about the issues that Occupy Wall Street is raising. But the pattern is clear. The protest movement that burst onto the scene has shaken up our daily discourse and our political system.
>
> (Dreier, 2011)

As a report released by the Pew Research Center states:

> The Occupy Wall Street movement no longer occupies Wall Street, but the issue of class conflict has captured a growing share of the national consciousness. A new Pew survey of 2,048 adults finds that about two-thirds of the public (66%) believes there are "very strong" or "strong" conflicts between the rich and the poor—an increase of 19 percentage points since 2009.
>
> (Morin, 2012)

In discussing this poll, Noam Chomsky noted:

> It's not that the poll measured income inequality itself, but the degree to which public recognition, comprehension and understanding of the issue has gone up. That's a tribute to the Occupy movement, which put this strikingly critical fact of modern life on the agenda so that people who may have known of it from their own personal experience see that they are not alone, that this is all of us.
>
> (Chomsky, 2012)

The Spring 2012 issue of *Contexts*, a quarterly magazine published by the American Sociological Association, contained a feature article in which several scholars comment on the significance of the OWS movement. Their assessments provide further evidence for our assertion that OWS has had an effect on public opinion. William Julius Wilson argues, "The Occupy movement has accomplished one very important goal—it has raised public awareness of the growing economic inequality in the United States" (Milkman et al., 2012).

Ruth Milkman states:

> OWS captured the imagination of the wider public. Its deceptively simple slogan, "We are the 99 percent!" raised popular awareness of the issue of economic inequality, stoking the moral outrage of ordinary citizens and transforming the national political conversation. The movement also deserves credit for a flurry of modest policy concessions: for example, extending the New York "millionaires' tax," which had been set to expire at the end of 2011.
>
> (Milkman et al., 2012)

And Dana Williams affirms:

> Occupy has already enjoyed many victories, convincing countless people of the potential for radical social change. The mass media is now running stories on capitalism, social inequality, and direct democracy. Someone ought to thank Occupy for accomplishing in a few short months what sociologists have been unable to achieve over decades.
>
> (Milkman et al., 2012)

These scholars argue that OWS has changed political and media rhetoric about economic inequality, raised public awareness, and even occasioned policy changes. As people become angrier about economic inequality and their recognition of systemic, structural causes increases, the stigma experienced by the poor may indeed change.

Just as historians identify economic context as a factor in the rejection of poverty stigma during the Great Depression, the Great Recession—and the underlying neoliberal policies that created it—may be a factor in OWS's rejection of poverty stigma. When the economy is doing well, poverty rates are lower, and people tend to blame poverty on individual shortcomings and lack of hard work, rather than on structural causes. Prosperity during times of economic boom tends to obscure these structural causes, yielding a greater stigmatization of poverty. On the other hand, elevated poverty rates lead to a re-labeling of those in poverty as people who have simply fallen on bad times, and a corresponding lessening of poverty stigma.

Americans do not generally have the language to talk about poverty as rooted in structural factors; OWS gave people the language to talk about their poverty and non-individual reasons and causes for it. The Great Recession allowed ideas challenging the legitimacy of inequality to enter the public discourse. OWS bestowed a sense of pride and community on the "99 percent," in opposition to the out of touch, undeserving, and even originators of the economic crisis, who occupy the "1 percent."

While "we are all" the 99 percent, poverty stigma affects the poor directly. People who receive public assistance often share general public attitudes as well, and are ashamed about their situations (Burton et al., 1998; Cherlin et al., n.d.). The poor accept widespread stereotypes of poor people and seek to distinguish themselves from other poor people. They tend not to discuss societal responsibility to address poverty, but rather, focus on the importance of personal responsibility (Cohen, 1997). Of course, the poor are not a monolithic group; there is variation among the poor in how they respond to their poverty (Small, 2004). Small also found cohort effects, that different groups of people will respond differently given their own experiences, perspectives, and ways of seeing the world.

In the case of OWS, a large number of people at a variety of income levels embraced a positive rhetoric against poverty stigma, symptomatic of the environment created by increasing inequality. The cause and effect relationships between the wider economic context, OWS, and poverty stigma are not simple. However, the rhetorical changes OWS prompted demonstrate that poverty stigma has changed, regardless of whether the rhetoric caused the change in stigma or the change in stigma came first. When our bumper stickers claim "We Are the 99 Percent," we signal where we stand: with the majority, and with the poorest. The 1 percent at the top of the socioeconomic hierarchy, not the 1 percent at the bottom, becomes the Other.

Change may prove fleeting; in better economic times we may once again redraw boundaries, taking individual credit for our relative successes and blaming the poor for continuing to fail. But for now, many people claim membership in the 99 percent, signaling a lessening of poverty stigma. Regardless of the degree or direction of causation, changes in national rhetoric signal meaningful and significant changes in perceptions about poverty.

These changes may be temporary, but the poor may remember their one-time inclusion in the deserving majority. The symbolic power of the 99 percent may have lasting effects just as other changes seemed temporary, but really did change public opinion in the long term. Rosie the Riveter had to go back home when her male counterpart returned from the War to resume his factory job, but she forever changed our understanding of what women could do, given the right context. For a time, it undoubtedly seemed as if middle-class working women's time had come and gone, but the effects became more apparent in the decades that followed, and Rosie continues to be an icon for women's rights. Similarly, Bill Clinton's first presidential campaign promised meaningful change on the military's policy on gay servicemen and women, but Don't Ask, Don't Tell (DADT) represented a devastation of high hopes. Yet, while DADT may have been a setback, it was not the end of the story. In 2010 it was repealed (Stolberg, 2010) and the military began allowing gays and lesbians to serve openly for the first time, arguably in part as an eventual outgrowth of the attention Clinton brought to the issue. Therefore, a longer historical perspective on women's rights and gay rights reveals an uneven road but a steady march to equal rights. Similarly, scholars and pundits might now assess that OWS lost its chance at making an impact (Sorkin, 2012; Tangel, 2012). But we may see renewed calls for financial reform and decreased income inequality in the years to come, made possible in part by decreased poverty stigma and a persistent, if latent, impact of Occupy Wall Street.

References

Anderson, E. (1976). *A Place on the Corner*. Chicago, IL: University of Chicago Press.

Barrington, L. (1997). Estimating Earnings Poverty in 1939: A Comparison of Orshansky-Method and Price-Indexed Definitions of Poverty. *The Review of Economics and Statistics*, 79, 406–414.

Broughton, C. (2001). *Reforming Poor Women: The Cultural Politics and Practices of Welfare Reform*. Ph.D. dissertation, Department of Sociology. Chicago, IL: University of Chicago.

Burton, L., Cherlin, A. J., Francis, J., Jarrett, R., Quane, J., Williams, C., and Cook, N. M. S. (1998). *What Welfare Recipients and the Fathers of Their Children Are Saying about Welfare Reform: A Report on 15 Focus Group Discussions in Baltimore, Boston, and Chicago*. Retrieved August 8, 2014, from http://web.jhu.edu/threecitystudy/Publications/index_old.html.

Cherlin, A., Winston, P., Angel, R., Burton, L., Chase-Lansdale, P. L., Moffitt, R., Wilson, W. J., Coley, R. L., and Quane, J. (n.d.). *Welfare, Children and Families: A Three City Study. What Welfare Recipients Know about the New Rules and What They Have to Say about Them, Policy Brief 00-1*. Retrieved August 8, 2014, from http://web.jhu.edu/threecitystudy/Publications/index_old.html.

Chomsky, N. (2012). What Next for Occupy? *The Guardian*, April 30. Retrieved May 16, 2012, from http://www.guardian.co.uk/world/2012/apr/30/noam-chomsky-what-next-occupy. See http://www.chomsky.info/interviews/20120530.htm, retrieved August 15, 2014, and Chomsky, Noam. 2012. *Occupy*. Westfield, NJ: Zuccotti Park Press. This article is no longer available in this location because the copyright has expired.

Cohen, J. R. (1997). Poverty: Talk, Identity, and Action (Nature of Poverty Revealed by the Conversations of the Poor). *Qualitative Inquiry*, 3, 71–92.

DeNavas-Walt, C., Proctor, B. D., and Smith, J. C. (2011). U.S. Census Bureau, Current Population Reports, P60-239, *Income, Poverty, and Health Insurance Coverage in the United States: 2010*. Washington, DC: U.S. Government Printing Office.

Dreier, P. (2011). Occupy Wall Street: Changing the Topic. *The Huffington Post*, November 1. Retrieved August 15, 2014, from http://www.huffingtonpost.com/peter-dreier/occupy-wall-street-media_b_1069250.html.

Edelman, P. (2012). *So Rich, So Poor: Why It's So Hard to End Poverty in America*. New York: The New Press.

Edin, K., and Kefalas, M. (2005). *Promises I Can Keep: Why Poor Women Put Motherhood before Marriage*. Berkeley, CA: University of California Press.

Fraser, N., and Gordon, L. (1994). A Genealogy of Dependency: Tracing a Keyword of the U.S. Welfare State. *Signs*, 19, 309–336.

Gans, H. J. (1995). *The War Against the Poor: The Underclass and Antipoverty Policy*. New York: Basic Books.

Garin, G., Molyneux, G., and DiVall, L. (1994). Public Attitudes Toward Welfare Reform. *Social Policy*, 25, 44–49.

Gilens, M. (1999). *Why Americans Hate Welfare: Race, Media, and the Politics of Antipoverty Policy*. Chicago, IL: University of Chicago Press.

Goffman, E. (1963). *Stigma: Notes on the Management of Spoiled Identity*. New York: Simon and Schuster Inc.

Handler, J. F., and Hasenfeld, Y. (1997). *We the Poor People: Work, Poverty, and Welfare*. New Haven, CT: Yale University Press.

Horsley, S. (2012). The Income Gap: Unfair, Or Are We Just Jealous? *Weekend Edition*, January 14, 2012. Retrieved August 15, 2014, from http://www.npr.org/2012/01/14/145213421/the-income-gap-unfair-or-are-we-just-jealous%20.

Jencks, C. (1992). *Rethinking Social Policy: Race, Poverty, and the Underclass*. New York: Harper Perennial.

Katz, M. B. (1983). *Poverty and Policy in American History*. New York: Academic Press.

Katz, M. B. (1986). *In the Shadow of the Poorhouse: A Social History of Welfare in America*. New York: Basic Books.

Katz, M. B. (1989). *The Undeserving Poor: From the War on Poverty to the War on Welfare*. New York: Pantheon Books.

Milkman, R., Barber, B., Bamyeh, M. A., Wilson, W. J., Williams, D., and Gould, D. B. (2012). Understanding "Occupy." *Contexts*, 11(2). Retrieved May 16, 2012, from http://contexts.org/articles/spring-2012/understanding-occupy.

Morin, R. (2012). Rising Share of Americans See Rising Conflict Between Rich and Poor. *Pew Research Center Social and Demographic Trends*. Washington, D.C. Retrieved May 16, 2012, from http://www.pewsocialtrends.org/2012/01/11/rising-share-of-americans-see-conflict-between-rich-and-poor.

Pew Research Center for the People and Press. (2007). *Trends in Political Values and Core Attitudes: 1987–2007 Political Landscape More Favorable to Democrats*, March 22. Retrieved June 25, 2012, from http://www.people-press.org/files/legacy-pdf/312.pdf.

Piven, F. F. (1977). *Poor People's Movements: Why They Succeed, How They Fail*. New York: Pantheon Books.

Roberts, B., Povich, D., and Mather, M. (2011). Overlooked and Underpaid: Number of Low-Income Working Families Increases to 10.2 Million. *The Working Poor Families Project Policy Brief Winter 2011–2012*. Retrieved June 14, 2012, from http://www.workingpoorfamilies.org/pdfs/Overlooked_Dec2011.pdf.

Small, M. L. (2004). *Villa Victoria: The Transformation of Social Capital in a Boston Barrio*. Chicago and London: University of Chicago Press.

Smeeding, T. (2012). *Income Wealth and Debt and the Great Recession*. Stanford, CA: Stanford Center on Poverty and Inequality. Retrieved August 15, 2014, from https://www.stanford.edu/group/recessiontrends/cgi-bin/web/research-areas/income-wealth-and-debt.

Smith, T. W., Marsden, P., Hout, M., and Kim, J. (2011). *General Social Surveys, 1972–2010* (National Data Program for the Social Sciences, No. 2).

Snow, D. A. and Anderson, L. (1993). *Down on their Luck: A Study of Homeless People.* Berkeley, CA: University of California Press.

Sorkin, A. R. (2012). Occupy Wall Street: A Frenzy That Fizzled. *The New York Times*, September 17, 2012. Retrieved January 8, 2012, from http://dealbook.nytimes.com/2012/09/17/occupy-wall-street-a-frenzy-that-fizzled/.

Stelter, B. (2011). Camps Are Cleared, but "99 Percent" Still Occupies the Lexicon. *The New York Times*, November 30, 2011. Retrieved February 10, 2012, from http://www.nytimes.com/2011/12/01/us/we-are-the-99-percent-joins-the-cultural-and-political-lexicon.html.

Stolberg, S. G. (2010). Obama Signs Away "Don't Ask, Don't Tell." *The New York Times*, December 22, 2010. Retrieved January 8, 2012, from http://www.nytimes.com/2010/12/23/us/politics/23military.html.

Tangel, A. (2012). Occupy Movement Turns 1 Year Old, Its Effect Still Hard to Define. *Los Angeles Times*, September 15, 2012. Retrieved January 8, 2012, from http://articles.latimes.com/2012/sep/15/business/la-fi-occupy-anniversary-20120915.

U.S. Census Bureau. (2001). Poverty in the United States: 2000. Current Population Reports: Consumer Income. *U.S. Department of Commerce, Economics and Statistics Administration.* Retrieved August 20, 2014, from http://www.census.gov/prod/2001pubs/p60-214.pdf.

U.S. Department of Agriculture, Food and Nutrition Service. (2013). *Program Data.* Retrieved May 25, 2013, from http://www.fns.usda.gov/pd/snapmain.htm.

U.S. Department of Labor, U.S. Bureau of Labor Statistics. (2014). *Labor Force Statistics from the Current Population Survey: Household Data Annual Averages, Employment Status of the Civilian Noninstitutional Population, 1943 to Date.* Modified February 26, 2014. Retrieved August 20, 2014, from http://www.bls.gov/cps/cpsaat01.htm.

Weigel, D., and Hepler, L. (2011). Everything You Need to Know About Occupy Wall Street—Entry 3: A Timeline of the Movement from February to Today. *Slate*, November 18, 2011. Retrieved January 4, 2013, from http://www.slate.com/articles/news_and_politics/politics/features/2011/occupy_wall_street/what_is_ows_a_complete_timeline.html.

Wilson, W. J. (2000). *Welfare, Children and Families: The Impact of Welfare Reform in the New Economy.* The Beth and Richard Sackler Lecture, University of Pennsylvania, October 6, Philadelphia, PA.

Zastrow, C. (2010). *Introduction to Social Work and Social Welfare, Tenth Edition.* Belmont, CA: Brooks/Cole.

PART III

From the welfare state to the neoliberal state

From regulating to imprisoning the poor

SECTION I

Transformation of the welfare state
Education

INTRODUCTION

Stephen Nathan Haymes and Emily Shayman

Neoliberalism not only dissolves the bonds of sociality and reciprocity, it also undermines the nature of social obligations by defining civil society exclusively through an appeal to market-driven values.

(Giroux, 2005:7)

Market fundamentalism—a vastly exaggerated belief in the ability of self-regulating markets to solve problems—has become firmly entrenched as the reigning public philosophy in the USA.

(Block, 2007:327)

Giroux and Block's remarks are discussed in the context of their broader argument that the destruction of public life, of civic life, in the United States is attributed to the hegemonic dominance of the corporate neoliberal ideology of market fundamentalism. This hegemonic ideology is committed to "privatizing property, utilities, and social programs, to reducing state expenditures and bureaucracy, increasing efficiencies, and to individual freedom from state regulation" (Goldberg, 2009). The commitments of this hegemonic ideology to the privatization or marketization of public life is now part of the common sense. Promoted by market fundamentalism is the belief that "there is no society," no civic or public life and responsibility, that all that exists is an "enormous marketplace, peopled by rational actors pursuing their self-interest with the potential to create" (Block, 2007) the highest levels of consumption and economic growth in human history.

The hegemonic dominance of neoliberal ideology has resulted in the marketization of education, its privatization, and reduction to a service delivery. In this regard and more generally, market fundamentalism has reconfigured the relationship between the state and its citizens. It has reorganized that relationship from a political to an economic relationship. As Gert Biesta explains:

This relationship is less a political relationship—that is, a relationship between government and citizen, who together are concerned about the common good—and more an economic relationship—that is, a relationship between the state as a provider and the taxpayer as consumer of a public service.

(Biesta, 2010)

In this regard, education has been seen less as a public good or part of the public domain and more as a tradable public service or commodity, diminishing citizens to consumers or citizen-consumers. In the more recent past, as a public good, the role of education was to create political citizens that could govern and collectively define through struggle, argument, debate, and negotiation the public interest and produce public goods (Biesta, 2010). Or as others have put it, education is now viewed as a commodity and not as a consciousness–raising experience. In fact, the dominant values that had once sustained education as a public good were not the values of self-interest but of collective interest. In neoliberal discourse, "a public is depicted as consumers who relate to their government on the basis of an economic, rather than a social, contract—through the logic of consumption—getting value for their dollars" (Hall, 2005).

This shift in values is traceable to the transformation of the welfare state into a post-welfare state. In the prior welfare state, there was a characteristic commitment to "professional standards and values such as care and social justice; and an emphasis, on cooperation" (Biesta, 2010). In his analysis of the neoliberal or post-welfare state, Stephen Ball writes: "Perhaps most significantly, the role of schooling in facilitating such societal values as inclusivity and social justice in society of politically engaged 'critical citizens' is being eroded" (Ball, 1998). In contrast, the post-welfare state and its related new approach to management is characterized by a "consumer-oriented ethos, decisions are driven by efficiency and cost-effectiveness, and there is an emphasis on competition, especially, free-market competition" (Biesta, 2010). Similarly, Hall comments that

> the political imaginary of the "social state" [welfare state] has been usurped by the notion of the "enabling state" [post-welfare state]. Instead of providing for the public's needs "from the cradle to the grave," the state's role in the era of "advanced liberalism" is to enable citizen-consumers to take responsibility for their own well-being. The responsibility of the state is to insure the quality of services that will enable citizens through acts of consumption to secure a better life.
>
> (Hall, 2005)

In the context of the post-welfare state, the responsibility for securing a better life has now shifted onto individuals and less so onto institutions. For what is most important is the capability of individuals to make the most of their assets to improve their situation. The lack of capabilities, like in education or health care, results in a low level of income and of consumption (Hall, 2005:155).

The shifting of responsibility for a better life onto the capability of individuals, and not institutions, is conterminous with how, within the post-welfare state, the hegemonic social practices of neoliberal market fundamentalism have privatized race, and accommodated racial discrimination in the private realm. In this way, racism has been a central technology in the restructuring of the welfare state into a neoliberal or post-welfare state. In *The Threat of Race: Reflections on Racial Neoliberalism*, David Theo Goldberg explains that neoliberal commitment to the marketization or privatization of public life became, for white neoconservatives, an important racial technology for responding to what these critics perceived as a state that directly identified with advancing black interests, at the expense of whites, through social programs, anti-discrimination legislation, and affirmative action programs (2009). To quote Goldberg fully regarding this point:

As the state was seen increasingly to support black employment, to increase expenditures on black education, and to increase regulations to force compliance, white neoconservatives found neoliberal commitments increasingly relevant to their interests. [...] It was but a short step from privatizing property to privatizing race, removing conception and categorization in racial terms from the public to the private realm. It does not follow that the state purges racism from its domain. Rather, the state is restructured to support the privatizing of race and the protection of racially driven exclusions in the private sphere where they are set off-limits to state interventions.

(Goldberg, 2009:337)

Neoliberal market fundamentalism de-historicizes racism; it renders racism a matter of individual preference, and is without any institutional consequence; in other words, racism is absent of any structural effects. Racial inequality is therefore the outcome of the lack of capability of individuals, who just so happen to be nonwhite, to not make something of their assets. In *Racism without Racists: Color-Blind Racism and Racial Inequality in Contemporary America*, Eduardo Bonilla-Silva maintains that the de-historicizing of racism as an institutional phenomenon that structures inequality has given way to what he calls "color-blind racism." According to Bonilla-Silva (2009), "color-blind racism has rearticulated elements of traditional liberalism (work ethic, rewards by merit, equal opportunity, individualism, etc.), for racially illiberal goals" (p. 27). Bonilla-Silva concludes that "neoliberal raceless racism" or color-blind racism relies more on cultural rather than biological tropes to explain the inequality between whites and nonwhites in the United States.

The chapters in Section I, "Transformation of the Welfare State: Education," address the presumption of neoliberal education reforms that marketization or commodification is a color-blind process that improves the quality of public education. Instead it is argued that neoliberal education reform has deepened racial and class inequality in U.S. education. In Chapter 20, "The New Two-Tiered Education System in the United States: Expanding and Commodifying Poverty and Inequality," Kenneth Saltman examines how neoliberal school reform reduces education to job preparation, consequently structuring schooling to serve the economic priorities and interests of global capitalism. For Saltman, the commodification of education, and its transformation from a public good to private interest, has given rise to a new two-tiered educational system that privatizes poverty and inequality. In Chapter 16, "How Neoliberalism Subverts Equality and Perpetuates Poverty in Our Nation's Schools," T. Jameson Brewer and Paul Myers call attention to how the inculcation of business terminology into schooling not only has exacerbated racial and class stratification but legitimates inequality through what the authors refer to as a "merit-based version of social justice."

In Chapter 18, "Poverty Reduction Through Education: An Analytical Framework for Cash Transfers for Education," Elena Delavega and Monit Cheung analyze the ideological underpinnings of neoliberal educational policies that use economic incentives, specifically conditional cash transfers, to promote improvement in individual student school achievement. They further examine how conditional cash transfers maintain the status quo by blaming the marginalized for their 'lack of effort' and their inability to comply. In Chapter 19, "Students that Lag or a System that Fails? A Contemporary Look at the Academic Trajectory of Latino Students," Jessica Martone examines how neoliberal education reform policies transfer the blame for Latino educational inequality onto Latino students and their families. Martone analyzes how the restructuring of public schooling by these policies divests schools of resources that promote Latino student academic success. For example, Latino students are placed in lower-track courses; attend schools that are without college preparatory classes; and there is a lack of programs that socialize Latino students into the cultural capital of academic culture.

In Chapter 17, "Invisible Students and the Issues of Online Education," An Chih Cheng discusses how the trend towards online education in urban school systems is driven not by pedagogical considerations, but by neoliberal market logic, whose institutional practices support the commercialization and privatization of K-12 education. Using a social constructivist frame of analysis, Cheng challenges the neoliberal rhetoric that the privatization and commercialization of education through online education democratizes learning and promotes educational equality via innovative online pedagogies. Cheng argues that the efforts of urban school systems and online businesses to promote virtual classrooms contribute not only to race and class educational inequality, but also makes invisible certain student populations adversely impacted by this inequality. In Chapter 15, "Neoliberalism and African Americans in Higher Education," Kimya Barden provides an historical analysis of how U.S. economic policies "historically and contemporarily shape[d] African American collective higher education experiences." Barden examines how the shift from Keynesian to neoliberal policies in student higher education funding has had damaging repercussions especially for the African American collegiate. Barden addresses how this economic policy shift in student funding has dramatically impacted African American matriculation and graduation rates in higher education. Barden's analysis suggests that, unlike neoliberalism, Keynesianism promoted a vision of higher education as a public good and site for critical inquiry and democratic pluralism.

References

Ball, Stephen J. (1998). Performativity and Fragmentation in Postmodern Schooling, in J. Carter (ed.) *Postmodernity and the Fragmentation of Welfare*, London: Routledge.

Biesta, Gert J.J. (2010). *Good Education in an Age of Measurement: Ethics, Politics and Democracy*, Boulder: Paradigm Publishers.

Block, Fred (2007). Confronting Market Fundamentalism: Doing "Public Economic Sociology," *Socio-Economic Review*, 5(2): 319–367.

Bonilla-Silva, Eduardo (2009). *Racism without Racists: Color-Blind Racism and Racial Inequality in Contemporary America* (Third Edition), Lanham: Rowman and Littlefield Publishers.

Giroux, Henry (2005). Resisting Market Fundamentalism and the New Authoritarianism: A New Task for Cultural Studies, *Journal of Rhetoric, Culture, and Politics*, 25(1): 1–29.

Goldberg, David Theo. (2009). *The Threat of Race: Reflections on Racial Neoliberalism*, Malden: Wiley-Blackwell.

Hall, Kathleen D. (2005). Science, Globalization, and Educational Governance: The Political Rationalities of the New Managerialism, *Indiana Journal of Global Legal Studies*, 12(1): 153–182.

15

NEOLIBERALISM AND AFRICAN AMERICANS IN HIGHER EDUCATION

Kimya Barden

Introduction

From 1976 to 2010, African American enrollment in institutions of higher education increased from 9 to 14 percent (U.S. Department of Education, 2012). There are currently 3.7 million African Americans enrolled in U.S. colleges and universities (Red and Black Inc., 2014). Despite these gains, scholars agree that given the increase in both employability and earnings potential that come with an earned college degree, enrollment rates for African Americans should be even higher in these institutions.

For African Americans, like most social groups, higher education experiences and outcomes are deeply influenced by economic policy, the interrelationships of state and federal budgets, and international trade, laws, and taxation. Thus, key features of America's economic policies both historically and contemporarily shape African American collective higher education experiences. America's recent economic policy trend, *neoliberalism*, which emphasizes the freedom of markets, privatization, competition, and deregulation (Harvey, 2005), offers a considerable insight into the ways in which contemporary economic policy intersects with African American higher education experiences.

Hence, this chapter will address African Americans' higher education experiences within the context of neoliberal economic policy. Although there is a vast literature on either African Americans in higher education (Fleming, 1984; Freeman, 1998; Gurin and Epps, 1975) or neoliberalism (Baez, 2007; Harvey, 2005), few articles seek to discuss the enrollment, academic, and post-graduation experiences of African Americans as a function of neoliberal policy. Thus, little is known about the implications of a neoliberal agenda within African American higher education experiences. In light of this gap in the literature, this chapter illuminates African American higher educational experiences within a neoliberal context. To achieve this end, the chapter will: describe the historical context of African American higher education experiences, linking them to relevant economic policies; describe African Americans' contemporary experiences in higher education given the modern neoliberal agenda; and describe how the two interface to impact African Americans enrolled in institutions of higher learning.

African Americans and higher education: a historical framework

African American contemporary higher education experiences have been shaped by a series of economic policies spanning from the colonial American era to today. More specifically, changes in the nation's approach to economic policy beginning with the shift from colonial mercantilism to antebellum classical liberalism, and again from the ascendance of Keynesian economic policy to neoliberalism, were particularly important for African Americans' experiences of higher education. In the following sections, I will examine each of these approaches in turn to locate neoliberal higher education policy within a broader historic context. I will conclude by discussing the implications of neoliberal economic and education policies for African Americans in higher education in the twenty-first century and beyond.

First phase: mercantilism (1492 to 1777)

In 1619, during the early stages of colonialism, Africans were brought as slaves by the Dutch to Virginia, an American colony economically beholden to "mother" England (Bennett, 1988). This early African presence throughout the colonial period coincided with a budding economic policy, mercantilism (Bennett, 1988). Mercantilism is based on the theory that wealth is inextricably linked to trade surplus whereby a nation's exports are greater than its imports (Vaggi and Groenewegen, 2003). The success of a mercantile economy was thus contingent on an individual nation's independence from other national markets, as well as its ability to be self-sufficient and produce its own manufactured goods. Such economic independence was thought to be a protection from international competition as a means to ensure a nation's economic growth.

The mercantile economy was particularly important in isolating enslaved Africans' labor as part of the "transatlantic" process of producing export goods to maximize Great Britain's wealth (Anderson, 1994). Beginning in the mid-1600s, Great Britain initiated the triangular, transatlantic trade system of crops, goods, and people between England, the American colonies, and Africa (Franklin, 2000). The latter continent was particularly important as coastal African women and men were sold as commodities to perform free labor as slaves, cultivating crops such as tobacco, cotton, and sugar in newly forming American colonies (Berlin et al., 1998). American colonies were responsible for shipping raw goods to Great Britain. These goods were then manufactured into products exported back to the American colonies.

The mercantile economic system, fueled by the transatlantic slave trade, supported a structure of African American learning rooted primarily at the whims of white benevolence. An enslaved African American was legally deemed "property" devoid of human rights, much like land and animals. Consequently, education, in the form of reading and writing, was primarily contingent on the intentions of the private, religious sector. Motivated by the Great Awakening, a religious movement with the goal of spreading the Christian "gospel," groups such as the Louisiana French Catholics, Pennsylvania Quakers, and Church of England clergy sought to teach enslaved African American women, men, and children to read, specifically bible scriptures (Woodson, 1919). While these groups encouraged the reading of scriptures in the mid-1700s, state legislatures, mainly in the American South, began to pass laws prohibiting "slave education"—particularly the teaching of enslaved African Americans to write. The criminalization of writing was principally legislated to restrict enslaved African Americans' ability to communicate with each other about abolitionism and other acts of resistance against the slave system. As such, the formal training of African Americans was restricted. Mercantilism would set the tone for African American higher educational experiences and reflect the valuation of their free labor within the broader American economy (Anderson, 1994).

Second phase: classical economic liberalism (1770s to 1860s)

The decline of the mercantile economy in the late 1770s coincided with both colonial America's sovereignty from Great Britain and the emergence of classical liberalism as an economic framework. Undergirded by a series of scholarly interventions, like Adam Smith's *Wealth of Nations* originally published in 1776, economic liberalism promoted ideals pertinent to sustaining "free market" economies with limited government intervention. Eschewing the tenets of mercantilism, Smith advocated for the following competitive conditions to ensure a nation's economic development: no restrictions on manufacturing, no tariffs, and no barriers to international trade (Smith, 1937). In short, Smith argued for the "invisible hand" of a free market economy of goods and services exchanged internationally, absent government regulation and control.

Much like the mercantile economic system, African American free slave labor was an essential component of classical liberalism. Slavery, at the time of classical liberalism's implementation, was contingent on the human cultivation of "cash" crops such as cotton (Bennett, 1988). Thus, the enslavement of Africans and their descendants provided the foundation of America's "liberal" economy as their free labor was both the "good" and the "service" used to increase America's budding wealth. Classical liberalism, the precursor of contemporary neoliberalism, impacted enslaved African American learning as education became an act of criminality, punishable by the law (Woodson, 1919). Since education was largely disseminated by white men and women with access to power—philanthropists, religious leaders, and planters—both the enslaved African American seeking education *and* his/her white educator were in violation of statutory law. For enslaved African Americans, penalties such as fines and six-month prison stints would be given (Bennett, 1988). However, education-seeking African Americans were often subjected to corporal punishment sanctioned by slave codes (Franklin, 2000).

Slave codes were statutory laws which further defined the status of enslaved African Americans. More importantly, slave codes deemed African American behaviors pertinent to acquiring freedom from indefinite, institutionalized bondage as illegal.

In addition to escape, reading and writing were outlawed by the slave codes of many U.S. states. Enslaved African Americans who violated these codes were subject to punishment by severe beatings and even death. For example, an 1830s Alabama slave code mandated "Any slave who shall write for any other slave, upon conviction, shall receive, on his or her back, one hundred lashes for the first offence, and seven hundred lashes for every offence thereafter ..." (Leary, 2005). Consequently, of the 4.5 million enslaved African Americans from 1850 to 1856, only 5% were literate, possessing the ability to read and write (Fleming, 1984). Like mercantilism, the success of the American economy during this time, guided by the tenets of classical liberalism, isolated African American learning as an overall threat to its wealth and economic development. Thus, it would take the post-American Civil War policy efforts of the 1860s to support African Americans' quest for higher learning.

Third phase: HBCUs and Keynesianism (1860s to 1970s)

The demise of classical liberalism coincided with African American manumission and eventually made room for the emergence of Keynesian economic policy nearly 60 years later. Beginning in 1865, the Freedmen's Bureau, a federal agency aimed at restoring civil and educational liberties to recently manumitted African Americans, was enacted to encourage their attendance at Historically Black Colleges and Universities (HBCUs) (Lomax, 2006). Much like the educational initiatives exhibited during the mercantile era, HBCUs were initially instituted by the white, private religious sector. Although the first HBCU, Cheney

University, was established in 1837, HBCUs like Fisk University (1865), Morehouse College (1867), and Howard University (1867) were each created under the leadership of white clergy and missionaries for the purposes of academic training used to enter the labor market in the fields of teaching, law, and religion (Harper, 2007). In addition, the Second Morrill Act (1890), a federal higher educational policy, was enacted to establish 16 "black land-grant colleges" (Harper, 2007). HBCUs such as Tuskegee University, Tennessee State University, and North Carolina A & T each supported African American higher learning experiences steeped in biological sciences, agriculture, and research. Notables such as George Washington Carver would benefit from the Second Morrill Act and thus contribute to the ingenuity of agricultural science as he developed over 100 household and farming inventions using the peanut.

In the early 1900s, African American higher education experiences were primarily prescribed to HBCUs due to segregationist, "separate but equal" policies like *Plessy vs. Ferguson, 1896* (Fleming, 1984). However, African Americans began to attend colleges and universities that were not HBCUs in larger numbers in the 1930s, with the emergence of Keynesian economic policy. Named after economist John Maynard Keynes, this policy sought to ameliorate the staggering economic conditions that characterized the Great Depression of the 1930s, namely a 25% unemployment rate and the loss of millions in household savings. Focused less on minimalist governmental policies, Keynesian policies advocated for government spending to increase demand for goods and services; this helped America recover from the ten-year economic slump. More importantly, Keynesianism created a policy context supportive of higher education initiatives for African Americans.

Keynesian economic policy emphasizes the government's ability to tax, borrow, and spend to ensure economic stability. For higher education, this resulted in a litany of policies, both targeted toward African Americans and policies that were written to be "race-neutral." These policies were designed to address racial segregation and increase African American access to *all* colleges and universities (Fleming, 1984). Policies such as the Servicemen's Readjustment Act of 1944 (G.I. Bill) provided World War II veterans, including African American soldiers, grants and tuition assistance. The Higher Education Act (HEA) of 1965, part of the legislation born out of the Civil Rights Act, focused on equality among groups and established the first need-based federal grant and loan program. Specifically, Title III of the Higher Education Act of 1965 authorized direct federal aid, grants, and matching endowments for enhancing HBCUs (Harper, 2007). In addition, the Federal Pell Grant initiative (1972) was established to provide financial grants based on household income. Both HEA and the Federal Pell Grant shaped African American experiences in higher education, as their college enrollment doubled between 1965 and 1980 (Fleming, 1984).

African Americans and higher education today: the implications for costs, choice, and culture

African Americans' intergenerational experiences in higher education reflect the historic changes in economic policy (Wilson, 1998). The educational gains in the Keynesian era, for both African American collegiates and other college-aspiring Americans such as veterans and working-class families, have been lost in the current era of neoliberalism (Morey, 2004). Since the 1980s, in part initiated by the politically conservative leadership of President Ronald Reagan, America's trend toward "liberal" economic enterprise has resulted in an economic framework reminiscent of the late eighteenth- and early nineteenth-century economic policy of classical liberalism (Harvey, 2005).

Labeled neoliberalism by critics of these policies, and neo-classical economic policy by its supporters (Peck, 2010), neoliberalism is focused on ideals and principles pertinent to "free" enterprise (Harvey, 2005). Like its classical predecessor, neoliberalism is predicated on minimal government intervention, believing that regulation by the state impedes competition, international trade, and investment. Contemporary trends such as the re-regulation of markets to favor free trade, the privatization of essential goods and services, the retrenchment of the state in both the social and economic arena, and the erosion of unions and other interest group activities that could impact capital accumulation have been associated with neoliberal economic policies (Harvey, 2005). Neoliberal education policy is focused on privatizing services and goods historically deemed public (e.g., public colleges) funded through tax dollars. Last, neoliberalism's aim of small government has resulted in decreased public funds generated through taxation for public services like higher education. The combination of these factors suggest that neoliberalism's primary aim is to adopt a "business-model" with the goal of profit maximization in industries historically supported by the public sector, like higher education (Morey, 2004; Ruch, 2001). In doing so, the corporatized neoliberal framework appears to shape higher education experiences in three key areas: cost, choice, and culture. Tuition is rising at a higher rate than in previous generations as the government rescinds funding for institutions of higher education, forcing colleges and universities to become more entrepreneurial, emphasizing scholarly activity that contributes to economic growth, such as the acquisition of patents and federal, state, and private grants, and places a greater emphasis on the philanthropy of alumni (cost). In addition to this assault on universalist education, states have begun to embrace competition through the emergence of for-profit higher education institutions alongside public and private colleges (choice). Finally, neoliberal policy impacts educational curriculum and structure reflective of neoliberal principles (culture). Accordingly, contemporary African American collegiates' higher education experiences appear to be inextricably linked to this trinity (costs, choice, and culture).

Costs

Since the 1980s, higher education costs have dramatically risen. According to the U.S. Department of Education (2012), for the 2010–2011 academic school year, the average cost to attend two- and four-year college institutions—including tuition, room, and board—is approximately $18,000. This is a $15,000 increase from the 1980–1981 school year (U.S. Department of Education, 2012). When comparing costs of public schools to for-profit or private schools, the former averages $13,000 while the latter is more than double, totaling $32,000. These numbers have also grown since the implementation of neoliberal policy, with public and private costs averaging $2,300 and $5,470 for the 1980–1981 school year respectively (U.S. Department of Education, 2012).

Higher education costs, specifically for public universities, are due to one main factor: decreased state and federal expenditures (Ruch, 2001). During the Keynesian economic period, the federal government's commitment to equity for all its citizens, regardless of ethnic status and/or socioeconomic status, trickled down into policies and budgets reflective of affordable tuition through grants, scholarships, and endowments. This resulted in federal spending increasing exponentially over a ten-year period from $655 million in 1956 to $3.5 billion in 1966 (Diener, 1976). The National Association of State Budget Officers (2013) examined per capita spending for higher education from 1987 to 2011. Their report shows that per capita spending for higher education has steadily decreased for the past 25 years. In 2011, approximately 10% of state budget expenditures supported public colleges and universities. This is a decrease from 1987, 1991, and 2001 state budget expenditures of 12.3%, 11.5%, and 11.3%, respectively.

The increase of higher education costs has implications for potential African American students in pursuit of a college degree. A key factor of college attendance is an individual's or family's ability to pay the costs of tuition, board, fees, and other related expenses (St. John et al., 2005). African Americans have a median income of approximately $33,321 (Red and Black Inc., 2014), while 27% of all African American families live at or below the poverty line (Red and Black Inc., 2014). With rising college costs, many aspiring African American students lack financial means to pay for college completion. To do so, African Americans need to borrow a greater share of their tuition than other ethnic groups. This translates into 81% of all African American students graduating with student loan debt, compared to 67% and 64% of Latinos and whites, respectively (Johnson et al., 2012).

Hence, the presumed higher education benefits of moving into the middle and upper class are often compromised, as African American graduates have a monthly expense in the form of loan repayment that, unlike credit card debt, can never be litigated in bankruptcy court. This is particularly salient as African American unemployment rates have consistently remained higher than the national average. In 2012, African American unemployment reached 13.7% (Bureau of Labor Statistics, 2012). For African American young, college graduates aged 21 to 24, the unemployment rate is nearly 12%, compared to 9.1% and 8% for Latino and white college graduates respectively (Economic Policy Institute, 2013). Taken together, these statistics suggest an urgency to re-institute federal measures to ensure not only African American enrollment, but also affordability devoid of debt in a labor market that disproportionately fails to hire African Americans.

Choice

The ever-increasing cost of higher education has contributed in important ways to how African American college aspirants make decisions about which colleges to attend. Prior to the 1980s, college aspirants primarily decided between public or private, non-profit universities. Not only does recent data suggest African American students are dissuaded from enrolling in more prestigious institutions they would likely be admitted to due to increased tuition and associated fees, but neoliberal education and economic policy has resulted in the ascendance of a third "type" of higher education—for-profit schools.

According to *The Project on Student Debt* (2011), 7% of earned bachelor's degrees were awarded from for-profit colleges and universities. African Americans disproportionately enroll in for-profit colleges and universities, with 19% of African American men and 23% of African American women enrolling in these universities (National Center for Educational Statistics, 2012). While public and private schools seek to educate the broader community and/or self-identified groups (e.g., religious, gender, race/ethnicity) respectively, for-profit schools seek to simultaneously educate students and generate a financial return for their corporate owners. Born out of 1770s colonial America, for-profit schools are primarily focused on the dissemination of "career"-oriented skills or trades (Ruch, 2001). In addition, for-profit schools seek to engage in "non-traditional" education for working adult students by providing on-line classes, weekend and evening hours, and abbreviated course terms.

The structure of for-profit schools is notably desirable for some non-traditional students who may lack the time and/or energy commensurate with traditional public and private schools of higher education. Thus, for some, choosing for-profit schools appears to be a natural choice. However, for African Americans, "choosing" to enroll in for-profit schools may be purposefully guided by for-profit schools themselves. For-profit schools adhere to principles echoed in classical liberal economic thought implemented by other capitalist corporations, namely profit generation. Their structure, model, and marketing plans target a particular kind of audience, seeking to acquire skills directly related to the needs of the current labor market. Rather than foster critical thinking skills, or a well-rounded, "universalist" education associated with the traditional goals of higher education, these institutions provide training programs geared toward specific entry-level jobs. By focusing on jobs rather than careers, and saturating underemployed markets, schools like the University of Phoenix, Westwood College, and Everest College appear to be a rational option. This is due as much to the structure and content of their educational initiatives as it is to the billions of dollars these universities spend to court underemployed and disadvantaged populations. For example, the University of Phoenix, the largest for-profit university, spends $400,000 a day towards on-line and televised advertisements. The latter is particularly culpable in attracting African Americans—particularly young, single mothers.

The high rate of African American unemployment, particularly of those with minimal education and skills in the form of high school diplomas or GED, often creates the opportunity of viewing daily television programs such as talk shows, court shows, and local news programs. For-profit schools appear to capitalize on this viewing demographic and thus appeal to it using actors who are either African American, female, mothers, or some combination of all three, urging the viewer to enroll on the promise to "get a better life ... 'cause I did and you can too." Such advertisements appear to impact African Americans' choice, as public universities are often void of the capital needed to advertise their educational curriculum; and private schools may advertise, but appeal to a demographic less representative of African Americans. The effect of for-profit advertisement is seen as African American growth in the for-profit higher education sector has grown 218% between 2004 and 2010 (Wright, 2013). Of those African Americans, women are increasingly enrolling in greater numbers than men. More importantly, 16% of African American students who attended a four-year private for-profit college began and completed a Bachelor's degree within six years (Baum et al., 2010). This is comparably less than white, Hispanic, and Asian students, each of whom have for-profit graduation rates of 26%, 28%, and 36% respectively. This is especially notable as African American college graduation rates from four-year institutions in both private non-profit and public sectors are 45% and 39% respectively—double the aforesaid for-profit rate. The data suggests that, despite targeted advertising efforts, African American collegiates are more likely to be successful and timely graduates in "traditional" private, non-profit, and public colleges and universities than from for-profit schools of higher education.

Culture

Neoliberal economic policy too impacts the culture of higher education. Ogbu (1978) defines culture as "a way of life shared by members of a population." Accordingly, higher education culture appears to reflect college students as both consumer driven and cost/benefit oriented. Modern collegiates perform a constant assessment of their "bottom line" pertinent to higher education attainment. They seek the best "return" on their tuition costs in the form of inflated grades, multiple career-focused internships, and immediate post-graduation job procurement.

It is not to suggest that these three higher education "benefits" are faulty. A major motivation for attending college is to academically succeed in preparation for joining the labor market with a choice job. However, neoliberal policy, particularly in for-profit schools, has co-opted career-oriented majors like criminal justice, business, education, and health care, all the while undermining humanities-oriented majors like history, foreign language, fine art, and performing art (Morey, 2004). Thus, contemporary American college students are often devoid of the self-exploration, appreciation for diversity of culture, and critical inquiry that often comes with another type of education—"liberal arts" education.

Since the 1980s, there has been a notable shift away from liberal arts education toward models geared toward the acquisition of more rationalized, practical skill sets applicable to entry-level positions within the labor market. This shift has resulted in some promising initiatives, such as what some would argue to be the democratization of higher education through the emergence of massive open on-line courses (MOOCs), and changes in the structure and curriculum of higher education to cater toward the needs of non-traditional students. At the same time, there has been increased pressure to rationalize education, demonstrating its direct applicability to the current labor market, and for college and university systems to generate funds through patents, grant-funded research, and tuition. The federal government has decreased its funding of liberal arts education and emphasized training in STEM. For the former, $135 million was allocated for Fiscal Year 2012 (National Endowment for the Arts, 2013). Conversely, for Fiscal Year 2014, the federal government has allocated $3.1 billion towards science and technology (Office of Science and Technology Policy Executive Office of the President, 2013).

In addition, there is public pressure to increase the likelihood that college graduates will secure employment. These pressures have contributed to the closure of "less critical" departments within even long-standing and well-ranked institutions of higher education. Administrators have pushed departments to slash their budgets, eliminating positions, or subsuming departments within other units within a given university system, limiting or eliminating altogether the very majors that attract many African Americans to higher education in the first place. These trends have been most severe in the humanist disciplines, with humanities departments, social sciences, and education being most affected. Since African Americans overwhelmingly specialize in these majors, they are arguably restricted from pursuing their educational and career interests in meaningful ways.

The rationalization of education associated with this period has resulted in what some have called the "adjunctification" of college and university systems. A general focus on funded research and a reluctance to fill tenure-track positions has taken full-time, tenured, and tenure-track professors out of the classroom, replacing them with adjuncts. According to Figlio et al. (2013), the granting of tenure has dramatically decreased in recent decades. In 1975, 57% of faculty was in the tenure system; by 2009 it had dropped to 30%. Adjunct faculty now represents 70% of the professorate (June, 2012). These positions are often under-funded, lack employee benefits, and have been shown to diminish the overall quality of education for students.

The increased focus on vocation specialty has implications for not only African American college students, but the broader African American community. African American political, religious, and artistic leaders have historically come from traditional colleges and universities— both public and private, non-profit. Much of this leadership is largely due to processes that supported academic, social, and emotional development. Students enrolled in both public and private universities are exposed to culturally sensitive programming such as "Black Cultural Centers" (Hefner, 2002). These centers seek to affirm African American identity and interests through exposure to experiential trips, African American speakers and guest lectures, and community projects supportive of a healthy African American development. More importantly, these centers often provide African American students with caring models of excellence in the form of African American professors and other staff committed to mentoring, tutoring, and providing informal resources such as job and internship leads.

Higher education as a site instrumental to the affirmation and validation of African American collegiate worth is particularly noteworthy as there is a lack of ethnic diversity among higher education faculty. According to the National Science Foundation (2011), African American-earned doctorates from 2001 to 2011 have yet to make any steady gains and average around

2,300 earned for the past 11 years. Recently, the number of African Americans who earned doctorates decreased from 2,708 to 2,489 to 2,383 in 2009, 2010, and 2011, respectively. Of the 49,000 doctorates awarded in 2011, 2,383 were earned by African Americans compared to 26,488, 12,434, and 2,975 by whites, Asians, and Hispanics, respectively (National Science Foundation, 2011). Of all ethnic groups, African Americans are least likely to earn doctorates (there was no data on Native American doctorate recipients).

Neoliberal policy in higher education thus has implications for African American social capital. Social capital refers to the network of social relationships which impact a group's access to power and self-determination (Putnam, 2000). Higher education's current proclivity toward efficiency in the form of vocational training, on-line courses, and decreased face-to-face access to professors may compromise African American collective economic, political, and social development.

Conclusion

For the past 400 years, changes in African American higher educational experiences have reflected changes in American economic policy. For nearly 250 years, during the era of systematic African American enslavement, the prevailing sentiment of American lawmakers regarding African American learning was expressed as "education was antithetical to slavery" (Lomax, 2006). Consequently, from the 1600s to 1865, economic policies such as mercantilism and classical liberalism depended on enslaved African American laborers being denied access to education to ensure America's wealth building. Attempting to redress the wrongs of pre-Civil War educational policies, Historically Black Colleges and Universities were born out of both the public and private sector. Keynesian policy of the 1930s to 1970s, too, sought federal initiatives supportive of African American higher learning, particularly in the form of federal grants and scholarships awarded to African Americans. From the era of mercantilism to Keynesian economic policy, higher educational experiences represented an opportunity to defy systematic racism through the acquisition of not only a college degree, but an opportunity to support African Americans' quest to fulfill their American Dream efforts in the face of race-based oppression and inequality.

Today, with the ascendance of a neoliberal economic agenda proven to dismantle the gains of educational policy during the Keynesian economic era, African Americans appear to be regressing with regard to higher education experiences. Since its rebirth, neoliberalism has had deleterious implications for African American collegiates in particular. When compared to other ethnic groups, African Americans are more likely to enroll in expensive, for-profit schools, amass inordinate amounts of college debt, drop out of college and/or prolong graduation, and, if lucky enough to graduate, be the first in the unemployment line.

These somber trends suggest that as African Americans continue to matriculate at institutions of higher learning, neoliberal economic policy must be altered to reflect their specific needs. Policies reminiscent of Keyensianism, which focused on state and federal expenditures earmarked for "debt free" scholarships and grants, must be reinstituted to ensure African Americans have access to higher education. Policies which emphasize greater federal expenditures toward public education will yield an increase in African American enrollment, devoid of insurmountable debt. This in turn will result in a greater number of African Americans pursuing master's degrees and doctorates so that they can provide living examples of African American excellence in both the academy and the broader community.

References

Anderson, C. (1994). *Black labor, white wealth*. Maryland: PowerNomics Corporation of America.

Baez, B. (2007, November). *Neoliberalism in higher education*. Paper presented at the meeting of the Association for the Study of Higher Education, Louisville, KY.

Baum, S., Ma, J., and Payea, K. (2010). Education Pays 2010: The benefits of higher education for individuals and society. Retrieved from: http://trends.collegeboard.org/sites/default/files/education-pays-2010-full-report.pdf. Accessed June 23, 2013.

Bennett, L. (1988). *Before the Mayflower*. Chicago: Johnson Publishing Company.

Berlin, I., Favreau, M., and Miller, S.F. (1998). *Remembering slavery*. New York: The New Press.

Bureau of Labor Statistics. (2012). Unemployment rate demographic: September 2012. Retrieved from: http://www.bls.gov/opub/ted/2012/ted_20121010.htm. Accessed January 6, 2013.

Diener, T. (1976). Growth of an American invention: A documentary history of the junior and community college movement. In Lawrence E. Gladieux and Thomas R. Wolanin (eds), *Congress and the colleges*, pp. 1–14. Lexington: Lexington Books.

Economic Policy Institute. (2013). *Young graduates still face dim job prospects*. Retrieved from: http://www.epi.org/publication/class-of-2013-graduates-job-prospects. Accessed June 25, 2013.

Figlio, D.N., Schapiro, M.O., and Soter, K.B. (September 2013). *Are tenure track professors better teachers?* NBER Working Paper No. w19406. Retrieved from: http://ssrn.com/abstract=2321458. Accessed June 26, 2013.

Fleming, J. (1984). *Blacks in college*. San Francisco: Jossey-Bass.

Franklin, J.H. (2000). *Up from slavery*. New York: McGraw-Hill, Inc.

Freeman, K. (1998). *African American Culture and Heritage in Higher Education Research and Practice*. Westport, CT: Praeger.

Gurin, P. and Epps, E.G. (1975). *Black consciousness, identity, and achievement*. New York: John Wiley and Sons.

Harper, B. (2007). African American access to higher education: The evolving role of historically black colleges and universities. *American Academic*, 3, 109–127.

Harvey, D. (2005). *A brief history of neoliberalism*. Oxford: Oxford University Press.

Hefner, D. (2002). Black cultural centers: Standing on shaky ground. *Black Issues in Higher Education*, 17, 22–29.

Johnson, A., Osterm, T.A., and White, A. (2012). *Student debt crisis*. Retrieved from: http://www.americanprogress.org/issues/higher-education/report/2012/10/25/42905/the-student-debt-crisis/. Accessed June 24, 2013.

June, A.W. (2012). Adjuncts build strengths in numbers. *The Chronicle of Higher Education*. Retrieved from: http://chronicle.com/article/Adjuncts-Build-Strength-in/135520. Accessed June 26, 2013.

Leary, J. (2005). *Post traumatic slave syndrome*. Milwaukee: Uptone Press.

Lomax, M.L. (2006). Historically black colleges and universities: Bringing a tradition of engagement into the twenty-first century. *Journal of Higher Education Outreach and Engagement*, 11(3), 5–13.

Morey, A.I. (2004). Globalization and the emergence of for-profit higher education. *Higher Education*, 48, 131–150.

National Association of State Budget Officers. (Spring 2013). *Improving post-secondary education through the budget process: Challenges and opportunities*. Retrieved from: http://www.nasbo.org/higher-education-report-2013. Accessed June 27, 2013.

National Center for Educational Statistics. (2012). *National post-secondary student aid study*. Retrieved from: http://nces.ed.gov/surveys/npsas/. Accessed June 27, 2013.

National Endowment of the Arts. (2013). *National endowment of the arts: Annual report 2012*. Retrieved from: http://arts.gov/sites/default/files/2012-NEA-Annual-Report.pdf. Accessed June 26, 2013.

National Science Foundation. (2011). *Science and engineering doctorates: Doctorate recipients, race/ethnicity and citizenship, 2001–11*. Retrieved from: http://www.nsf.gov/statistics/sed/2011/data_table.cfm. Accessed June 26, 2013.

Office of Science and Technology Policy Executive Office of the President. (2013). *The fiscal year 2014 science and technology R and D budget*. Retrieved from: http://www.whitehouse.gov/sites/default/files/microsites/ostp/2014_R&Dbudget_Release.pdf. Accessed June 26, 2013.

Ogbu, J.U. (1978). Cultural diversity and human development. In D.T. Slaughter (ed.), *Black children and poverty: A developmental perspective*. San Francisco: Jossey-Bass.

Peck, J. (2010). *Constructions of neoliberal reason*. Oxford: Oxford University Press.

Putnam, R. (2000). *Bowling alone: The collapse and revival of American community.* New York: Simon and Schuster.

Red and Black Inc, (2014). Black history short story of the week: census facts about African Americans. Retrieved from: http: //http://myemail.constantcontact.com/Short-Story-of-the-Week---Census-Facts-about-African-Americans.html?. Accessed November 11, 2014.

Ruch, R. (2001). *Higher Ed, Inc.: The rise of the for-profit university.* Maryland: The Johns Hopkins Press.

Smith, A. (1937). *An inquiry into the nature and causes of the wealth of nations.* New York: The Modern Library.

St. John, E., Paulsen, M.B., and Carter, D. (2005). Diversity, college costs, and postsecondary opportunity: An examination of the financial nexus between college choice and persistence for African Americans and whites. *The Journal of Higher Education,* 76, 545–569.

The Project on Student Debt. (2012). *Student debt and the class of 2011.* Retrieved from: http://www. projectonstudentdebt.org. Accessed June 24, 2013.

U.S. Department of Education, National Center for Education Statistics. (2012). *Digest of education statistics, 2011* (NCES 2012–001). Retrieved from: http://nces.ed.gov/fastfacts/display.asp?id=372. Accessed June 27, 2013.

Wilson, R. (1998). Overview: African American participation in higher education. In Kassie Freeman (ed.), *African American culture and heritage in higher education research and practice,* pp. 195–206. Westport: Praeger.

Woodson, C.G. (1919). *The education of the Negro prior to 1861: A history of the education of the colored people of the United States from the beginning of slavery to the civil war.* Whitefish, Montana: Kessinger Publishing.

Vaggi, G. and Groenewegen, P. (2003). *A concise history of economic thought: From mercantilism to monetarism.* New York: Palgrave Macmillan.

Wright, Kai (2013). Preying on Black ambition. Retrieved from: http://colorlines.com/archives/2013/06/predatory_lending_and_black_education.html. Accessed June 25, 2013.

16

HOW NEOLIBERALISM SUBVERTS EQUALITY AND PERPETUATES POVERTY IN OUR NATION'S SCHOOLS

T. Jameson Brewer and Paul S. Myers

Introduction

Poverty, by way of social stratification, is a unique characteristic of economies operating within the realm of capitalism. Under this system, individual players engage with their surroundings and with others under the guise of meritocracy, which leads to the social creation of the "other," the "wealthy," and the "poor." But how do some achieve the highest status associated with wealth and living the good life? Despite the myth of meritocracy, what will be argued here are that the reasons so few achieve the most while the most end up with the least is nothing less than a concerted effort to perpetuate the stratification that we find ourselves in as a society (Massey, 2007). This effort is reflected in many spheres of daily life and is highly evident in the practice of schooling and the policies which regulate education.

Drawing on literature that examines the increased role of neoliberal thought in education, this chapter will examine the impact of such practices on our nation's schools. Building on the work of Bowles and Gintis's seminal work, we argue that schools are still the institution of choice to reproduce economic inequalities. Neoliberal practices in education have increasingly taken on the form of privatization, competition, school "choice," and the deprofessionalization of teaching. Neoliberal pedagogy is employed to replicate social control rather than perpetuate democracy and freedom. All of this is done under the guise of competition and rugged individualism which has resulted in reducing the curriculum down to testable units to be used for quantifiable comparison, mass production of standards to the benefit of textbook and test publishers, and subverting social programs designed to aid the poor. Accordingly, the United States continues to promote socioeconomic principles that shift further away from ensuring equal opportunity for all while protecting and legitimizing methods of increasing wealth for a privileged few.

As former middle and high school teachers, we have seen firsthand the onslaught of neoliberal policies that seek to exacerbate the reproduction of class and inequality. At the core of neoliberalism is competitive capitalism. As is the case, schools are seen as the foundational building block of a meritocratic society. They are seen as the "great equalizer." This colloquialism is an acknowledgement that we currently live in an unequal society. If the contrary were true, we would not need an "equalizer," great or otherwise. Nevertheless, those advocating for competition and meritocracy continue to insist that all students have the same opportunity to pull themselves out of poverty through education. Our contention, along with decades of research literature, is that schools do not provide equitable experiences. At best, schools serve as a mechanism for the reproduction of the haves and have nots through systemic sorting, the dumbing down of the curriculum, and the insistence that students compete with each other as individuals. What is more, attempts to further entrench educational policies that aid the reproduction of poverty by neoliberals while ignoring larger systemic causes of poverty will only further exacerbate generational poverty in the United States. What follows is a brief review of the literature surrounding reproduction theory, neoliberalism as the practice of undermining the collective good for the sake of the individual, and the increasing presence of neoliberalism in our nation's schools. In short, this chapter will suggest that social stratification is perpetuated generationally by pro-choice, pro-market, competitive structures that are characteristic of neoliberalism. What is more, these neoliberal practices have found root in our nation's schools.

Literature then and now

Schools, largely idealized as democratic and public, have increasingly become more engaged in the language of "business methods" (Bowles and Gintis, 1976, p. 44) through the use of neoliberal market competition schemes. Rooted in Milton Friedman's assertion that the federal government is the least-desired provider of services (2002), schools—especially in the decades following Bowles and Gintis's initial work (1976)—are fashioned to adhere to capitalist principles including competition, privatization, and managerialism (e.g., vouchers, charters, deprofessionalization of teachers, etc.). For Friedman and his followers, this type of education reform is described as innovative as it engages new stakeholders and offers families and students a choice in their schooling and opposes the status quo of attending the local public school. Friedman's legacy can be seen in the work of "reformers" such as Michelle Rhee and Joel Klein, think-tanks like the American Legislative Exchange Council and the Center for Education Reform, but also in the legislative agendas of Presidents Obama, Bush, Clinton, and Reagan. However, capitalism and competition, by definition, require the existence of winners and losers. And while we are not arguing that, historically, schooling in the United States was any more egalitarian before the increase of business and neoliberal practices, we argue that the present and aggressive injection of market competition into what should be public and democratic exacerbates inequalities, namely poverty.

Historically, schools have been the site where systemic inequalities have been reproduced for generations (Bowles and Gintis, 1976). Seeing schools as an equalizer while ignoring systemic inequalities within society and schools allows for the justification of continued systemic inequalities. According to Brown (1995), merit is conceived as the sum of ability and effort with the assumption of an equality of opportunity. Because schooling is seen by many as the remedy for the continued perpetuation of poverty, poor students who are given the opportunity to "better themselves" in school but remain in poverty should blame themselves for a lack of effort or be pitied for a lack of intellectual gifts. From this perspective, it is the teachers and schools who are responsible for providing the "equality of opportunity" to students to learn and gain the wherewithal to climb the socioeconomic ladder. But there exists a more sinister purpose of schooling in the United States. This sinister purpose, as Jean Anyon points out, lies within the curriculum, so that working-class children's

> present school work is appropriate preparation for future wage labor that is mechanical and routine. Such work, insofar as it denies the human capacities for creativity and planning, is degrading; moreover, when performed in industry, such work is a source of profit to others.
>
> (Anyon, 1990, p. 434)

Anyon's thesis, possibly in need of updating for the post-industrialization of many Western economies where the factory floor has been replaced by service industries, points out that schools are not the great equalizer. Rather, schools exist to reproduce a stratified economy as students are prepared for their future working conditions. To achieve these ends, Carnoy (1990) argues that schools are organized to imbue students with the "skills, values, and ideology" that most prepare them for legitimizing and being controlled by capitalist "relations" and "systems" of production. But, how is it that the parents and families of these students do not generally challenge the type of reproductive schooling that takes place causing, for those at the lower end of the economic spectrum, generational poverty? Swartz (1990) calls attention to the fact that "students' academic performance is strongly related to parents' cultural background. Bourdieu claims that education contributes to the maintenance of an unequal social system by allowing inherited cultural differences to shape academic achievement and occupational attainment" (p. 71).

This hypothesis has been studied and concluded to be true by many (Coleman et al., 1966; Sacks, 2007; Willis, 1977). In fact, studies continue to show that parental education attainment, family income, and the home environment are the most significant factors in determining student outcomes (D'Arcy, 2012). And while theorists like Bourdieu argued "that working-class students can succeed academically ... he goes on to note that they pick up a stilted, formal academic style that is very different from the easy, eloquent style of successful upper class students" (Swartz, 1990, p. 71). As a society we have collectively bought into the ideology of a meritocratic system whereby education is the leveling mechanism. However, this type of ideology consists more of indoctrination (namely through schooling—do good work, get good grades) rather than true equality. Michael Apple points out:

> Manufacturing baron Abram Hewitt said it best when, in the latter part of the nineteenth century, he claimed that the task of social science and education was to find ways of making "men who are equal in liberty [content with the] inequality in distribution inevitable in modern society." Not only the rich, but the middle class in general as well, believed that one's inability to advance in society was simply evidence of a lack of "character."
>
> (2001, p. 21)

The ideology of blaming one's character for one's socioeconomic status is a key tenet of capitalist competition within global neoliberalism. The myth of meritocracy can only be continued through hegemonic indoctrination by convincing students and parents that poor performance is not an indication of systemic inequalities; rather, a telltale sign of laziness (e.g., the recent discussion of makers vs. takers and "the 47%" in our national political and electoral dialogue) or lack of motivation.

A more contemporary perspective on how neoliberal conceptions of competition, the free market, and meritocracy have been injected into education policy and practice has been the remaking of schooling in the urban centers of Chicago and New Orleans. In each of these locations, urban, predominantly black-serving schools have been deemed in need of repair: Chicago, after successive plans for school improvement, did not provide the desired results, nor did New Orleans after Hurricane Katrina. Yet, as Lipman notes with respect to Chicago, while the "reform " agenda surrounding schools (specifically the Arne Duncan-initiated Renaissance 2010 initiative) appears rhetorically democratic and altruistic:

> These policies discursively shift public policy from economic redistribution to behavior modification, obligating the state to do nothing about root causes of poverty, racism,

substandard and scarce affordable housing, and failing schools. They mask the network of public policy and investment decisions that produced deindustrialization, disinvestment, unemployment, and degradation of public health, the built environment, and education in urban neighborhoods and schools over the past 30 years and laid the groundwork for a new round of investment.

(Lipman, 2009, p. 23)

In the neoliberal paradigm, concerns of general welfare and equity are no longer handled singularly by the state, but instead through market arrangements and mechanisms which do not legitimate collective issues and often operate with blatant ahistoricism. In Chicago, this is not only true of Renaissance 2010, but also in the 2013 closure of 49 Chicago Public Schools which overwhelmingly served poorer, African American communities (Ahmed-Ullah et al., 2013).

Despite the business adage that the market solves problems, what is most true is that the market capitalizes on problems. Ball (2012) effectively argues that, in the neoliberal age, this capitalization, and the actors and policies which validate it, exists in a complex relationship with the state where it concurrently relies upon, demonizes, and reshapes state systems of government. This is evidenced in what Milton Friedman (2005) wrote in the aftermath of Hurricane Katrina: "The children are now scattered all over the country. This is a tragedy. It is also an opportunity to radically reform the educational system." Following Hurricane Katrina, New Orleans schools were taken over by the state of Louisiana. The state aggressively opened the process of creating charter schools to corporations. As an outgrowth of this takeover, a massive restructuring of the teacher workforce as well as a reformulation of the curriculum occurred. In attempting to create "the first school district in the nation that is 100% choice" (Dixson, 2011, p. 146), the choice has been turned over, in actuality, to charter schools, which are allowed to restrict and select students based on slapdash criteria.

Neoliberalism

Michael Peters asserts that neoliberalism is a struggle between "opposing and highly charged ideological metaphors of 'individualism' and 'community'" (2011, p. 1). More to the point, Giroux posits that "[w]edded to the belief that the market should be the organizing principle for all political, social, and economic decisions, neoliberalism wages an incessant attack on democracy, public goods, and noncommodified values" (1980, p. xiii). It is through this understanding of the world that neoliberalism seeks to undermine teacher professionalism. For those interested in shaping educational policy, traditional teacher training and traditional teachers are seen as a noncommodified value, whereas a privately trained and privately controlled group of teachers constitutes a commodified value. This reinforces the conflict between the individual and the community. Dispositions towards education are then characterized by what is best for the individual rather than the collective good. In fact:

Arguing that an unfettered free-market is the best, if not only, path to progress, equality and a … merit-based version of social justice, public institutions are viewed through the lens of neoliberalism as, at best, social distractions and, at worst, antiquated seeds of Bolshevism. For the advocate of neoliberalism, anything that operates outside the free-market model, whether a public school, a library, or a post office, is actually counterproductive to human progress.

(Elmore, 2013, p. 109)

Such a view of the world and how it ought to look has found its way into the minds of policy makers and otherwise influential individuals. In what amounts to social engineering, the involvement of business moguls (e.g., Broad, Gates, Walton, Kramer, etc.) has exacerbated the privatization of public schools by way of charters, vouchers, and alternative certification programs like Teach For America (TFA) (Glass, 2008; Kovacs, 2011; Saltman, 2010, 2011). With such involvement, corporate donors have inculcated business terminology into our schools. It is largely because of these individuals/corporations that we now expect our schools to perform "better" on state standardized tests. For the venture philanthropists, and those who peddle their "reforms," equal outcomes on state standardized tests proves equality. For these individuals, the goal of increasing student test scores, namely of the non-white and poor students, will close the so-called achievement gap and prove that we are a country of equality and that schools are the great equalizer. These neoliberal reformers have also commandeered the language of political and social liberalism as they call their actions part of the "rights" issue of our time (Thomas, 2011, p. 59). In fact, within TFA, the reproduction of social stratification is tied to the misdirection that is testing. Accordingly, TFA's sole focus is

> on student assessment, raising test scores, and the standards. All to pass along the "value" to students that their best option in life is to ace a series of tests so that they can go to college and get a "good" job that is starkly different than their present lives.
>
> (Cody, 2013, p. 70)

Unfortunate, however, is the fact that teaching students how to pass tests does not provide them with the real opportunities to develop the necessary cultural capital that is required to stay in college and get a job—and most importantly, end generational poverty. However, even if students are able to do well in K-12 education, and then either do well at presenting themselves as a viable candidate for a job or go to college, they will still find themselves facing obstacles within our stratified society. In fact, the research indicates that the ability to get a job can be hindered based not only on race but also on geographic location (Moss and Tilly, 2001). In essence, a well-educated black male who happens to live in what is seen as an unsafe neighborhood will have vastly less job options than his identical counterpart who lives in a "nicer" neighborhood. And unfortunately, a white male would still have a better chance of employment than both aforementioned men based on nothing more than the complexion of his skin. The argument, so it goes, is that in order to close the achievement gap and create equal opportunity for all students, manifested in academic outcomes, our schools must create more rigorous standards. Kathryn McDermott points out that it is

> common to hear that maintaining high standards and closing achievement gaps are civil rights issues (for examples, see Dobbs 2004; and Bruni 2001). In this view, insisting that all students meet challenging academic standards is in itself an antiracist intervention. Some standards advocates go even further and insist that calling any attention to the greater challenges that face low-income students and students of color constitutes making excuses for failure. By defining equity in terms of a common educational threshold for all students, the performance-based understanding of educational equity shifts to a universal definition of equity and away from understandings of equity that target specific disadvantaged groups such as low-income students, students of color, or girls.
>
> (McDermott, 2011, p. 167)

Students are seen as passive recipients of culture and knowledge. Paulo Freire coined the term *banking* to describe the relationship of the teachers giving information to obedient students and the empty deposits/withdrawals made at a later time (Freire, 1992). From the liberal perspective, the act of treating students as empty vessels and supplanting any semblance of student agency, teachers, schooling administration, and the prescribed set of knowledge and behaviors becomes absolutism. Moreover, in the recent decade, schools and those who seek to reform them insist that what is most important are equal academic outcomes. For the reformers, equal academic outcomes denote equal educational opportunity.

Neoliberalism's manifestation in schooling

The emergence of neoliberalism within our nation's schools coincides with the growing rhetoric of "no excuses" (Thernstrom and Thernstrom, 2003). Organizations like TFA and the charter network Knowledge is Power Program (KIPP) insist that considering a student's socioeconomic background as a factor in outcomes can be regarded as "excuses." In fact, TFA teaches its corps members that: (1) poverty is not an inhibitor of education (Farr, 2010); and (2) helping poor students do well on standardized tests will end generational poverty as it will open doors to college acceptance. Moreover, programs like TFA are a factor in the perpetuation of poverty via schools as such programs deprofessionalize teaching and destabilize the ability of unions to resist reform with the insistence that (1) anyone can teach; and (2) that 18 hours of preparation are equal to or better than a traditional educator program (Brewer, 2014). Many TFA corps members and KIPP participants engage in drill and kill test-prep pedagogy under the guise that what is most needed to remedy poverty are higher test scores and not systemic changes to who has access to affordable housing, healthcare, jobs, food, etc. Such myopic reforms intentionally ignore the larger and more casuistic foundations of generational poverty.

As stated previously, the venture philanthropists of today are not only injecting millions of dollars into education reforms, they also seek to play an active role in policy decisions that often highlight the desire to reproduce a stratified socioeconomic society. For example, the second author of this writing worked in a charter school in a blighted section of Northwest Indiana that was heavily funded by the Walton Foundation, the family behind Wal-Mart. One thing noticed rather late into the first semester at this school was student uniforms bearing a striking resemblance to the ones worn by Wal-Mart employees. While it could be argued that this was merely coincidence, this subtle part of the official culture of school, along with regimented training the students had received in earlier grades, suggested an overt attempt at class reproduction. Students acknowledged this resemblance and the intentions behind such a choice in uniform. However, they were less cognizant of other forms of socially hegemonic actions within the charter network. Furthermore, a lack of union representation and an open contract with Teach For America led to high teacher turnover. Students felt there were few adults in the building who could be trusted. This message was relayed to parents, who understood that the uncertainty of high turnover and inability to attend to the community ultimately placed their children further behind.

As schools "dumb down" (Gatto, 1992) the curriculum to make way for more standardized prescribed lessons and standardized tests, teachers are teaching more to tests rather than utilizing a holistic and qualitative approach to curriculum as seen outside of the States (Brewer, 2012). The result of this dumbed-down education will only further serve the benefit of the wealthy class while exacerbating the non-education of the middle- and lower-class student. The growth of the testing industry, despite research suggesting the ineffectiveness of test scores accurately reporting student growth and teacher effectiveness (Papay, 2011), suggests the extent of the influence that the testing corporations have in education policy. Moreover, the rampant rise of using standardized tests for competitive comparison is indicative of the larger neoliberal marketization of schools (Sacks, 1999). What is more, the genesis of standardized tests was rooted in the eugenics movement in the early twentieth century in an effort to create stratification within American society (Sacks, 1999). And while testing no longer has the overt goal of reproducing inequality, the modern hype surrounding testing and standards-based education is being promoted outside of the walls of the classroom. This is indicative of the increasing involvement of businesses in the funding and policy making of schooling.

Because schools that serve the neediest of students usually perform on the lower-achieving end when it comes to standardized testing, they are the students who are most likely to experience having their schools closed as one of the more insidious parts of the No Child Left Behind Act (NCLB) passed during the George W. Bush presidential administration. There is a great deal of scholarship rebuking this law as well as the Race to the Top legislation passed during Barack Obama's first presidential term. Each of these laws infused a false sense of competition required in the neoliberal governance strategies. In this schema, government recuses itself of responsibility as it simultaneously creates space for the marketization and capitalization of sectors formerly under its legislative domain (Dale, 1997). For parents and students in or near poverty, the false illusion of preference and choice are presented in the form of vouchers and charter schools (Linkow, 2011) which may do more to exacerbate social stratification if administrated without proper regulation (Cobb and Glass, 2009). As Gary Orfield notes, "Both choice and the other currently preferred interventions ... are applied most extensively in poor nonwhite communities with schools highly segregated by race and poverty" (Orfield and Frankenberg, 2013, p. 9). With the lack of political will and resources, ghettos and impoverished rural areas are seen as ripe for educational experimentation; without the ammunition of poor test scores or accusations of a culture of poverty (Ladson-Billings, 2006), affluent communities are left to privileged positions.

Conclusions

What can be said of the decades following Bowles and Gintis's seminal work positing that schools were society's mechanism for the reproduction of class? Unfortunately, with the increase of venture philanthropists (the haves) and their influence on education policy, the problem has only gotten worse. And while researchers continue to conclude that poverty and the predispositions that it can create are the greatest factors in determining educational outcomes, reforms continue to focus on the myopic (e.g., replacing traditionally trained and veteran teachers with TFA novices, dressing students in Wal-Mart attire to psychologically prepare them for a life of sub-livable wage work, increasing standardized testing, and so on). All the while, the hegemonic message of schooling as being meritocratic (thus suggesting that our society is also meritocratic) continues to reinforce to those in power that they arrived there from their hard work and others who do not are simply lazy. If society continues to ignore the systemic causes of poverty (access to quality schools, teachers, healthcare, housing, jobs, etc.) we will only reproduce them. If schools continue to remain in the power of those who have a vested interest in the reproduction of systemic inequality, schools will continue to be the mechanism of choice for offering false hope in a game where the deck is stacked against those who began life in an impoverished circumstance through no fault of their own.

In short, the practice of capitalism and its governmental and ideological offshoot of neoliberalism create an environment where individuals are pitted against one another to clamor for the few resources left available to the middle and lower classes. And despite schools being marketed as the great equalizer, they are in effect the exact site where such myths of meritocracy are perpetuated. Students are forced to compete with one another—the same goes for the teachers—all while they are being conditioned to enter the hyper-competitive world that is capitalism and neoliberalism. Accordingly, such preparation situates students into predetermined positions within society that strikingly resemble the socioeconomic predispositions of their parents (Willis, 1977). The use of TFA novice teachers who practice a pedagogy that insists that testing is the way to end economic disparity only further entrenches poor students deeper into generational poverty. In this way, those individuals seeking to aid poor students are in fact causing more harm than good. Even if meritocracy and competition were viable mechanisms within our society, the increasing segregation of students by race and socioeconomic status in our schools constitutes an unfair advantage for students who have better access than their poorer counterparts, namely in the inner-city.

As has been pointed out in the literature discussed above, capitalism requires the existence of a stratified economy. When taken to the extreme levels of market-based solutions, neoliberalism feeds off of this stratification while exacerbating generational reproduction of the haves and the have nots. And while there have been incredible gains towards equality and justice over the last half century, unless neoliberalism's unfettered power in our society—and namely in our nation's schools—is not kept in check, we may find ourselves regressing towards even less equality. Presently, the continued practice of replacing public institutions with market-based solutions will only further reproduce social stratification and the inequality and injustice that comes with such a society.

References

Ahmed-Ullah, N., Chase, J., and Secter, B. (2013). CPS approves largest school closure in Chicago's history. *The Chicago Tribune*. Retrieved August 17, 2014, from http://www.chicagotribune.com/news/local/breaking/chi-chicago-school-closings-20130522,0,4746227.story.

Anyon, J. (1990). Social class and the hidden curriculum of work. In K. J. Dougherty and F. M. Hammack (eds), *Education and society: A reader* (pp. 424–437). San Diego, CA: Harcourt Brace Jovanovich.

Apple, M. W. (2001). *Educating the "right" way: Markets, standards, god, and inequality*. New York, NY: RoutledgeFalmer.

Ball, S. J. (2012). *Global Education Inc.: New policy networks from the neo-liberal imaginary*. New York, NY: Routledge.

Bowles, S., and Gintis, H. (1976). *Schooling in capitalist America*. New York: HarperCollins.

Brewer, T. J. (2012). Rousseau plays outside in Norway: How Norwegian outdoor kindergartens employ notions of play. *International Journal of Play*, 1(3), 231–241.

Brewer, T. J. (2014). Accelerated burnout: How Teach For America's "academic impact model" and theoretical culture of hyper-accountability can foster disillusionment among its corps members. *Educational Studies*, 50(3), 246–263.

Brown, P. (1997). Cultural capital and social exclusion: Some observations on recent trends in education, employment, and the labour market. In A. H. Halsey, H. Lauder, P. Brown, and A. S. Wells (eds), *Education: Culture, economy, and society* (pp. 736–749). Oxford, UK: Oxford University Press.

Carnoy, M. (1990). Marxism in education. In K. J. Dougherty and F. M. Hammack (eds), *Education and society: A reader* (pp. 60–69). San Diego, CA: Harcourt Brace Jovanovich.

Cobb, C. D., and Glass, G. V. (2009). School choice in a post-desegregation world. *Peabody Journal of Education*, 84(2), 262–278.

Cody, A. (2013). Learning to teach: Values in action. In P. L. Thomas (ed.), *Becoming and being a teacher: Confronting traditional norms to create new democratic realities* (pp. 63–73). New York, NY: Peter Lang.

Coleman, J. S., Campbell, E. Q., Hobson, C. J., McPartland, J., Mood, A. M., Weinfeld, F. D., and York, R. L. (1966). *Equality of educational opportunity*. Washington, DC: U.S. Department of Health, Education, and Welfare.

D'Arcy, J. (2012). *Does a parent's education and income affect how a child's brain develops?* Retrieved August 17, 2014, from http://www.washingtonpost.com/blogs/on-parenting/post/does-a-parents-education-and-income-affect-how-a-childs-brain-develops/2012/10/17/8715e348-187c-11e2-a55c-39408fbe6a4b_blog.html.

Dale, R. (1997). The state and the governance of education: An analysis of the restructuring of the state–education relationship. In A. H. Halsey, H. Lauder, P. Brown, and A. S. Wells (eds), *Education: Culture, economy, and society* (pp. 274–282). Oxford, UK: Oxford University Press.

Dixson, A. (2011). Whose choice? A critical race perspective on charter schools. In C. Johnson (ed.), *The neoliberal deluge*. Minneapolis, MN: University of Minnesota Press.

Elmore, J. M. (2013). Neoliberalism and teacher preparation: Systematic barriers to critical democratic education. In P. L. Thomas (ed.), *Becoming and being a teacher: Confronting traditional norms to create new democratic realities* (pp. 107–118). New York, NY: Peter Lang.

Farr, S. (2010). *Teaching as leadership: The highly effective teacher's guide to closing the achievement gap*. San Francisco, CA: Jossey-Bass.

Freire, P. (1992). *Pedagogy of the oppressed*. New York, NY: The Continuum Publishing Company.

Friedman, M. (2002). *Capitalism and freedom*. Chicago, IL: University of Chicago Press.

Friedman, M. (2005). The promise of vouchers. *The Wall Street Journal*. Retrieved August 17, 2014, from http://online.wsj.com/article/SB113374845791113764.html.

Gatto, J. T. (1992). *Dumbing us down: The hidden curriculum of compulsory schooling*. Philadelphia, PA: New Society Publishers.

Giroux, H. (1980). Beyond the correspondence theory: Notes on the dynamics of educational reproduction and transformation. *Curriculum Inquiry*, 10(3), 225–247.

Glass, G. V. (2008). *Fertilizers, pills, and magnet strips: The fate of public education in America*. Charlotte, NC: Information Age Publishing.

Kovacs, P. (ed.) (2011). *The Gates Foundation and the future of U.S. "public" schools*. New York, NY: Routledge.

Ladson-Billings, G. (2006). It's not the culture of poverty, it's the poverty of culture: The problem with teacher education. *Anthropology and Education Quarterly*, 37(2), 104–109.

Linkow, T. W. (2011). Disconnected reform: The proliferation of school choice options in U.S. school districts. *Journal of School Choice*, 5(4), 414–443.

Lipman, P. (2009). *Making sense of Renaissance 2010 school policy in Chicago: Race, class, and the cultural politics of neoliberal urban restructuring*. Chicago, IL: Great Cities Institute.

Massey, D. (2007). *Categorically unequal: The American stratification system*. New York, NY: Russell Sage Foundation.

McDermott, K. A. (2011). *High-stakes reform: The politics of educational accountability*. Washington, DC: Georgetown University Press.

Moss, P., and Tilly, C. (2001). *Stories employers tell: Race, skill, and hiring in America*. New York, NY: Russell Sage Foundation.

Orfield, G., and Frankenberg, E. (2013). *Educational delusions? Why choice can deepen inequality and how to make schools fair*. London, UK: University of California Press.

Papay, J. P. (2011). Different tests, different answers: The stability of teacher value-added estimates across outcome measures. *American Educational Research Journal*, 48(1), 163–193.

Peters, M. (2011). *Neoliberalism and after? Education, social policy, and the crisis of Western capitalism*. New York, NY: Peter Lang.

Sacks, P. (1999). *Standardized minds: The high price of America's testing culture and what we can do to change it*. Cambridge, MA: Da Capo Press.

Sacks, P. (2007). *Tearing down the gates: Confronting the class divide in American education*. Los Angeles: University of California Press.

Saltman, K. J. (2010). *The gift of education: Public education and venture philanthropy*. New York, NY: Palgrave Macmillan.

Saltman, K. J. (2011). From Carnegie to Gates: The Bill and Melinda Gates Foundation and the venture philanthropy agenda for public education. In P. E. Kovacs (ed.), *The Gates Foundation and the future of U.S. "public" schools* (pp. 1–20). New York, NY: Routledge.

Swartz, D. (1990). Pierre Bourdieu: Culture, education, and social inequality. In K. J. Dougherty and F. M. Hammack (eds), *Education and society: A reader* (pp. 70–80). San Diego, CA: Harcourt Brace Jovanovich.

Thernstrom, A., and Thernstrom, S. (2003). *No excuses: Closing the racial gap in learning*. New York, NY: Simon and Schuster.

Thomas, P. L. (2011). Educational hope ignored under Obama: The persistent failure of crisis discourse and utopian expectations. In P. R. Carr and B. J. Porfilio (eds), *The phenomenon of Obama and the agenda for education: Can hope audaciously trump neoliberalism?* (pp. 49–72). Charlotte, NC: Information Age.

Willis, P. (1977). *Learning to labor: How working class kids get working class jobs*. New York, NY: Columbia University Press.

17

INVISIBLE STUDENTS AND THE ISSUES OF ONLINE EDUCATION

An Chih Cheng

The essence of this critique is to deconstruct how the recent trend of online education is fueled by a neoliberal ideology, rather than based on pedagogical consideration. It first illustrates how the neoliberal market logic has led to institutional practices of the commercialization and privatization of education. The analysis will shatter common myths such as "anytime, anywhere learning," or that "online courses bring quality education and are cost-effective." The last part of this chapter addresses the discriminatory impact online education may have on minority students and its potential threat to democratic education.

Institutional practices

Online learning is gaining currency at all educational levels, from K-12 to postgraduate. In the context of higher education, a recent survey reported that about six million students (approximately 31.3% of all student populations) took at least one online course in the fall of 2010 (Allen and Seaman, 2011). Furthermore, *The Chronicle of Higher Education* projected that 3.97 million students will enroll in at least one fully online course in 2014 (Parry, 2010).

The move to online education however is not based on pedagogical principles, and so far there is no clear evidence supporting the benefit of online education. Advocates for online education frequently cite a Department of Education report (Means et al., 2010) to claim online learning is academically effective and that student performance "proved" to be better than traditional face-to-face classroom teaching. Yet the document states that although positive outcomes were found in online/face-to-face blended courses, the results were due to the additional support students received, not because of the online platform. Means et al.'s caution of how the results should be interpreted was often omitted from the citation. Here is the quote from the abstract:

> The meta-analysis found that, on average, students in online learning conditions performed modestly better than those receiving face-to-face instruction … Analysts noted that these blended conditions often included additional learning time and instructional elements not received by students in control conditions. This finding suggests that the positive effects associated with blended learning should not be attributed to the media, per se.
>
> (p. 11)

Rather than rooted in pedagogical considerations, online education is driven by economic principles following the logic of neoliberal policy, which is represented in a report by the Department of Education (Bakia et al., 2012):

> The need to do more with less is an imperative for decision makers in nearly every economic sector. Education is no exception … Educational systems are under increasing pressure to reduce costs while maintaining or improving outcomes for students. To improve educational *productivity*, many school districts and states are turning to online learning.
>
> (emphasis in original, pp. 1, 7)

Though the promise of maintaining or improving education is not supported by empirical evidence, the privatization and commercialization of public good through online education is what is actually taking place.

With schools facing massive budget cuts across the country and personnel costs commonly representing more than half of the budget, administrators look to technology to reduce labor costs and draw in revenue, at the expense of educational quality. Online education fits this business purpose well, often justified on the grounds of economic efficiency. Touted as "anytime, anywhere learning," online education is marketed to cater to individual needs and promises cost-efficiency for both students and institutions. Boasting the promise to transform educational experience and shape the future, as *Educause* claims, the once-failed business model of distance education has been resurrected, only this time in the guise of digital revolution and school reform. Under this commercially driven model, courses are regarded as a source of income and are packaged as products to be sold to consumers from both near and far-off locales in the increasingly competitive education market. Class notes and lectures are replicated online ready to be downloaded in a "pay-per-view," "course-on-demand" business-type model. As the online move is pushed from the top administrators and policy makers, online courses also hold great potential for strengthening bureaucratic controls, deskilling faculty, and infringing on academic freedom and autonomy (Giroux, 2002).

In the past couple of years, the blind faith in mass markets as educational mechanisms has ushered in an unprecedented wave in the level of investment and scale of online education, the Massive Open Online Courses (MOOCs) (DeSantis, 2012). Elite universities from coast to coast have rushed to contract with major players, start-ups such as Coursera (for-profit), Udacity (for-profit), and edX (nonprofit), to deliver online courses. The pressure of joining in online education has become so intense that in June 2012 the University of Virginia's Board of Visitors fired its president, Teresa A. Sullivan, for her slowness to jump on the MOOCs bandwagon (Vaidhyanathan, 2012). Course enrollments in MOOCs are massive. For example, a Stanford course on artificial intelligence enrolled more than 160,000 students from 190 countries. Yet, underlying the alleged democratic access to higher education in MOOCs is a crowded environment insensitive to individual needs and cultural differences. With the advent of MOOCs, the lowest-quality education and highest student–teacher ratio nightmare has become a reality. Yet such massification has received a warm welcome and is celebrated by university administrators and private vendors. Class experience is reduced to watching pre-recorded class lectures, studying means mouse-clicking, and feedback is given in the form of quizzes and peer-grading. Authentic learning environments are non-existent and social interaction is buried in a mass of thousands of online messages—all in the name of economic efficiency and maximum revenue generation. Although MOOCs are offered for free, universities charge fees for proctored exams and certificates of completion. In early 2013 Udacity and San Jose State University announced a joint offer for for-credit online classes at the price of $150 for each three-unit course, even though these start-ups are non-accredited.

Higher education institutions are not alone in adopting online education models. In K-12, a growing number of online courses began in the 1990s. A recent National Center for Education Statistics survey (Queen and Lewis, 2011) of 2,150 districts reports 1,816,400 course enrollments in distance education (90% of them are internet-based) during the school year 2009–10. These courses serve purposes such as credit recovery, advanced placement, enriched experience, alternative instruction, or the ability to avoid issues like limited space or schedule conflicts. In the name of school reform, offering educational options and improving educational quality, virtual schools are growing exponentially and have joined the mainstream education efforts. This becomes possible as state boards and legislators with joint lobbying efforts have made it easy for virtual charter schools to operate.

Unlike higher education where faculty tends to develop online courses in-house, a growing trend in K-12 schools is to join multi-district consortia or purchase content and contract services from large private companies. Cash-strapped school districts in particular want to open their own virtual schools in order to draw new pupils, address overcrowding and scheduling conflicts, and deter students from transferring to other districts (pupils are typically allowed to enroll in virtual school across districts). Ironically, these schools are precisely the ones that lack the expertise in teaching online and can least afford the expensive cost involved in the development and maintenance of virtual schools. The solution is to outsource. Consequently an increasing number of pupils are enrolling in full-time virtual charter schools run by private vendors, such as K12 Inc. (cofounded by investor Michael Milken and former education secretary William Bennett), Insight Schools (once owned by the Apollo Group Inc. and by Kaplan Inc. but now by K12 Inc.), Connections Academy, etc. These multi-district charter schools currently serve about 275,000 pupils across all grade levels, and operate in 31 states and the District of Columbia. While securing state dollars and costing millions to local government for the operation of virtual schools, these vendors receive little oversight.

A more pressing question is how students perform in those virtual schools. Emerging evidence indicates that students enrolled in virtual schools are more likely to fall behind than their counterparts in brick-and-mortar schools and have high dropout rates. A Stanford study of Pennsylvania charter schools found that students enrolled in online charter schools made significantly less learning gains, in both reading and math, and were more likely to repeat a grade even though they entered virtual schools with significant higher test scores (CREDO, 2011). Similarly, the National Education Policy Center (Miron and Urschel, 2012) reports that only 27% of schools managed by K12 Inc. met adequate yearly progress in reading and math. Despite such gloomy academic results, K12 Inc. stock prices continue to rise and draw investment.

Issues of online learning

The myth of anytime, anywhere learning

The biggest selling point of online learning is "anytime, anywhere learning" or "learn at your own pace." Under a neoliberal framework individuals are in need of improvement, and thus need to constantly learn more so that they can live up to the media-defined lifestyle and stay competitive in the fierce job market. The problems here are perpetuating self-interested individuals and equating learning to access of information. According to John Dewey, learning is an engaging and expanding social experience. And contemporary learning and teaching theories (e.g., social constructivism) stress that knowledge is constructed based on prior understanding in a socially meaningful way (Bandura, 1986; Prawat and Floden, 1994; Vygotsky, 1978). Thus an optimal pedagogical environment is a classroom where students come to understand more about themselves, develop critical thinking skills, have hands-on experience with scientific inquiry and experiments, and engage in intellectual dialogues about the democratic society in a socially meaningful way. Computer-based learning environments, however, are mechanical and prescriptive and disregard individual experience and social context. They are essentially a behaviorist's dream come true, reducing experiential learning to a mode of conditioning, like a Skinner's box where a mouse learns to push the lever to receive a food reward or to avoid punishment. Behaviorism sees learning as the product of stimuli, not a process of thinking; therefore these online courses are focused on narrow and fragmented information presented in a predictive and mechanical fashion. As such, they are devoid of a substantive curriculum based on humanistic approaches to authentic learning. This type of learning model puts students in a passive role, memorizing and reproducing factual knowledge, doing drill and practice exercises, and filling in prescriptive worksheets and being instantly rewarded for "right" answers or punished in standardized quizzes. Developed by remote vendors, these quizzes and materials leave no room for students to bring their intrinsic subjectivity to the classroom.

As Dakers (2005) argues, teachers who employ behaviorist paradigms will produce unthinking students, who then reinforce behaviorist fundamentalist values, and this "hegemonic behaviorist cycle" continues. Even under a behaviorist paradigm students may not retain much information as it is well known that students often skip the content and instead jump to the quizzes to complete the online course. These inflexible, primitive exercises and uninspiring technicized content also diminish teachers' role and their control of the curriculum, restricting them from contributing their rich knowledge of subjects in guiding students' learning experiences. The consequence of a behaviorist paradigm with instrumental rationality is that it will dehumanize education, fostering a condition for obedience and nonresistance of existing social hegemony, rather than promoting civic responsibility and educational liberalization. Given their poor course design and narrow teaching focus, behaviorist models at best suit informal learning or job training, but they are not the same as attaining an education. The long-term effects of such impoverished learning conditions are especially of concern for children who are enrolled full time in a virtual school and are expected to spend hours a day in front of a computer.

Specifically, online courses are currently built upon course management software (CMS), such as Blackboard, Desire2Learn, eCollege, Instructure, and Moodle. Historically these programs are used to sequence content and provide instructors with a means to manage student records for the purpose of the automation of routine work. In order to tap into the online learning market, venders now prefer CMS to be called a learning management system (LMS). The issue here is that the sellers and devotees of CMSs and MOOCs mistake a site of material distribution as a classroom and equate access of information to education. The design of CMS emphasizes static content, sequential modularization, and micro management—thus learning in a CMS is passive, linear, and inflexible. As learning objectives are pre-determined and learning takes place in largely text-based environments, online courses effectively strip the lively interactive experience and co-construction of knowledge between teachers and students. They also make it impossible for a teacher to build complex and authentic tasks into the curriculum or to affirm students' identity and agency in the learning process in an authentic and meaningful way.

In the 21st century when scholars and educators have long repudiated behavioral paradigms or the use of the once-popular Bloom's taxonomy for assessment that assumes learning is sequential and hierarchical, these outdated models see a resurrection in online course design (e.g., Chyung and Stepich, 2003; Friend and Johnston, 2005), and are embraced by special interest groups such as the Southern Regional Education Board, International Association for

K-12 Online Learning, and Quality Matters Program. The result is that teaching and curriculum are reduced to a set of numerical indicators and meaningless matrices to meet hierarchical objectives and standards. Test and objective-driven online courses essentially fragment complex knowledge into modules, disregard controversial topics and complex epistemology, conceal the social prejudices and ideologies behind these artificial constructs, deliver only simple and easily implemented curricula, and treat students as empty vessels to be filled with factual knowledge, what Freire (2007) called the banking model of education.

False individualized curriculum

The claim of individualized curriculum and personal attention is a false advertisement and can be dangerous to students. The common practice of preparing online courses in higher education, especially MOOCs, is simply moving materials from traditional classrooms to online platforms. Thus online courses are but a repository of static course materials. This practice embraces a linear, teacher-centered, and one-size-fits-all teaching approach. The online lecture addresses no one. Instead of constructing new understanding and developing critical thinking, students become duplicators of declarative knowledge. In order to maximize economic efficiency, online courses are designed with minimum cost on curriculum development but aim to reach maximum customers. The results are then severely watered-down standardized content with some interchangeable modules indifferent to individual needs. What is marketed as individualized curriculum is in fact pre-packaged generic material with recycled modules optimized for automatic computer operation such as the scoring of multiple-choice tests. This extremely narrow and reductive content formatted for screen display bears no resemblance to the substantive curriculum found in traditional classrooms. Students enrolled in online courses are of diverse bodies: Blacks, Hispanics, Asians, Whites, Native Americans, men, women, as well as LGBT; a standardized content does not know them or their names, languages, and cultures. Refusing to acknowledge the differences but treating everyone with the same materials, standardized contents effectively bury identity, silence voice, and exacerbate inequality between members of majority and minority populations.

Certain courses claim the ability to differentiate students. Yet the algorithms used to select "individualized" lessons are based on questionable criteria. For example, one question used by Connections Academy is "What is your learning style?" And students are asked to choose visual, aural, read/write, or kinesthetic. Misleading questions like this have no basis in learning research (Pashler et al., 2008) or neuroscience (Goswami, 2006), no practical meaning in an online context, and when ethnographic information is used it can run the risk of profiling students. Even if vendors are willing to invest and build an adaptive learning system (National Institute of Standard and Technology, 2005; Schwartz et al., 1999), the initial norm reference will inevitably be based on limited middle-class standards, thus lacking ecological validity in the broader context where students from a wide variety of school districts and socioeconomic backgrounds are served. Before less-biased measurements, algorithms, and a massive database can be established, students enrolled in these courses essentially become uninformed "experimental subjects."

The critique of economic efficiency

Despite the lack of sound research and empirical evidence supporting the pedagogical value of online education and the growing evidence suggesting students' low academic performance in K-12 virtual schools, the use of online education is justified on the grounds of economic efficiency under neoliberal ideology. Proponents argue that online courses and virtual schools are cost-effective because they bring quality education but cost less than traditional schools. Not only does this essentially turn complex education into a simple per-pupil cost formula, its economic value is falsified in that online education does not bring quality education nor does it save money. In fact, it has huge hidden costs.

First, a market and technology-driven business model is unrealizable in education because quality education is labor intensive. This so-called economic efficiency is achieved by sacrificing the most important asset of quality education: the teacher. Despite extensive research showing that high-quality teaching is at the heart of student achievement (Darling-Hammond, 2000), proponents of online education hope to use computer automation to replace "routine" teaching jobs. Under a neoliberal discourse, faculty and teachers are reduced to facilitators and portrayed as expensive and inefficient; thus they are the subjects of the elimination of dispensable labor and students are treated as consumers and a source of income. The close relationship between teachers and students is replaced with computer automation and is defined in marketing terms as minimum labor cost (on teacher) but maximum client (of student).

This neoliberal ideal of economic consideration and diminishing faculty is well reflected in a report from the Thomas B. Fordham Institute (Battaglino et al., 2012) that argues "[b]y significantly reducing school-operations costs, a virtual school can potentially save approximately $3,600 per student, a savings of more than a third over a traditional school." A closer look at Battaglino et al.'s document reveals that the "saving" is done mostly by cutting the expenses on faculty. This is achieved by reducing payout, eliminating faculty or replacing them with adjuncts, assistants, and a "learning coach," which is a euphemism for parental home schooling.

Second, online education can induce a major catastrophe in school finance. With neoliberalist reluctance to fund public education, online education is used as a convenient way for conservative forces to curtail spending on public goods, and is perceived as an easy budget fix. Hence, funding to public education is cut but is interpreted as a cost-efficiency. Yet as virtual schools try to avidly recruit students across districts, online education further tightens the budgets of small school districts, which in turn are forced to open their own virtual schools that are contracted and operated by major private vendors. In their vision of "transforming education," corporations offer the infrastructure of virtual schools in exchange for state dollars and gaining control of public education at public expense. In order to keep the withdraw rate low and retain government funds, virtual schools take low requirement for attendance and grade inflation becomes commonplace. While securing state dollars and costing millions to local government for the operation of virtual schools, virtual schools receive little oversight and spend a large amount of money for advertising and lobbying, making "excessive profits." Thus the money actually spent on pupils is even less.

Invisible students

Over a decade ago Press and Washburn (2001) cautioned that "far from democratizing education, many critics argue, online learning could facilitate the rise of a two-tiered educational system—prestigious campus-based diplomas for the children of elites, mass-marketed online degrees for those less fortunate." This premonition, unfortunately, has come true. Currently, for-profit schools in post-secondary education serve a large proportion of students from disadvantaged backgrounds. Seeing technology as a good way to minimize labor and curriculum cost and to reach a broad student population, as well as the relaxation of regulations to allow more government funding for distance education, these for-profit schools have increasingly offered online courses over the past decade. These schools, for example the University of Phoenix, see the majority of their revenue coming from government-funded student aid. They are eligible for up to 90% of their total revenue from Title IV funds and have received billions in government funding each year. Yet students enrolled in these schools have high dropout rates, twice as high debt levels, high default rates, higher unemployment, and lower earnings than students in traditional non-profit schools (Deming et al., 2012). Critics have pointed out that these schools have specifically targeted low-income and minority students who are eligible for student aid. As online degrees are less welcomed in the jobs market, the employment situation and high cost of education make the higher levels of debt even harder to repay.

If what is happening in higher education can be any indicator, the trend in K-12 education is of serious concern, as K-12 virtual schools have the greatest potential for pushing students from the most disadvantaged backgrounds to become invisible in society. K-12 virtual schools are designed based on a neoliberal standard: a romanticized "Western tradition" and an affluent family model. Virtual schools require the family to have broadband to access the internet, as well as computer equipment, and have one parent who serves as a tutor, or "learning coach," at home. This neo-conservative ideal, a traditional White male heterosexual norm, is well illustrated in the following excerpt depicting a "Day in the Life" of a 6th-grade virtual student, from Greenway and Vanourek (2006):

7:00 a.m.	Wakes up, gets dressed, and eats breakfast
8:15	Logs on to his personalized school page and reviews his lessons scheduled for the day
8:40	American History: reviews notes on the French and Indian War; writes a diary entry in his history journal from the perspective of an officer in the Virginia militia serving with General Washington; reads chapter 3 on the role of the Iroquois Indians
10:00	Language Arts: reviews words for today's spelling test; completes lesson on revising and proofreading an essay; completes grammar, usage, and mechanics lesson on the use of irregular verbs; completes vocabulary lesson on root words
11:45	Break/free time
12:00 p.m.	Lunch with mom and younger sister

This middle-to-upper-class-based model is consistent with existing reports (CREDO, 2011; Sturgis et al., 2010) that virtual schools currently enroll more White students who are ineligible for free and reduced lunches (not provided by virtual schools). Tailoring teaching to the majority with the neoliberal personal-responsibility-and-family-values discourse, virtual public schools essentially discriminate against the "non-traditional" family and fail to fulfill their obligation to provide equal educational opportunities.

Like the privatization in higher education, in seeking a new market "niche" and revenue, virtual schools have started to target low-income districts, which receive more subsidies. While couched in the language of improving educational quality and the promise of alternatives for pupils who may not perform well in traditional schools, the likely results of online education will be driving the most disadvantaged students off of the class roster faster, denying them needed resources, and causing even more damage to the already highly stratified system. In the name of accountability, teachers are replaced with computer automation, resources spent on public education continue to be curtailed, and low-performing schools are increasingly being closed in poor neighborhoods. The adverse impact of online education will be greater for poor and minority families, who have lower income to spend on new technology and have less resources to meet the expectations of online schooling. When vouchers and online schools become the only options in these areas, online education will lead to serious discriminatory results and open other social issues such as no more school lunch, the early diagnosis and intervention of learning disabilities becoming impossible, etc.

It is crucial to recognize the danger of online education, on top of its low pedagogical value. Education cannot be reduced to technology and controlled by private companies. A market mechanism cannot meet the great social needs and human development in education. The ongoing European sovereign-debt crisis, the global economic crisis of 2007–2008, the Asian financial crisis of 1997, and the Latin American economic emergency have shown that unrestricted markets do not create the conditions for success but are chaotic and inefficient, and can produce unintended consequences. Although developmental economists have started to recognize the limits and failures of the neoliberal model and have introduced the appropriate regulation, the business metaphor and neoliberal threat are becoming prevalent in educational discourses. Educators should be critical of the free market as the mechanism for education and the discourse of defining education in capitalist terms, and should not unquestioningly accept unfounded claims made by researchers, vendors, politicians, and special-interest groups.

Driven by the neoliberal market but in the name of education reform and school choice, online education is used as an excuse to curtail further public education while funding corporatization and subsidizing home schooling. At a time when educators are trying hard to eradicate the scholastic achievement gap between rich and poor students, the pedagogy of poverty (Haberman, 1991; see also Darling-Hammond, 1998) that dominates the stratified education system is only strengthened through online education. The poor are further disadvantaged, stripped of rich educational opportunity and getting low-cost and low-quality education in the form of online worksheets. When the father of American public education Horace Mann wrote that education was "the great equalizer" in 1848 he would never have imagined that education could deteriorate into a virtual form yet exert a real disparate impact on the poor, perpetuating old discriminations and making them invisible in school and in society.

The implication of this is that policymakers, practitioners, and researchers should be mindful of the threats that online education poses to the equality of education; that the design of online courses and the assessment of student and school performance must involve an awareness of the unique affordances and limitations of an online environment (Cheng et al., 2013; CREDO, 2011); and that there is no "best practice" in online teaching but rather identifying some of the issues that make this area problematic that is critical for future research and discussion.

References

Allen, I. E., and Seaman, J. (2011). *Going the distance: Online education in the United States.* Needham, MA: Sloan Consortium and Babson Research Group. Retrieved January 10, 2014, from http://www.onlinelearningsurvey.com/reports/goingthedistance.pdf.

Bakia, M., Shear, L., Toyama, Y., and Lasseter, A. (2012). *Understanding the implications of online learning for educational productivity.* Washington, DC: U.S. Department of Education.

Bandura, A. (1986). *Social foundations of thought and action: A social cognitive theory.* Englewood Cliffs, NJ: Prentice-Hall.

Battaglino, T. B., Haldeman, M., and Laurans, E. (2012). *The Costs of Online Learning. Creating Sound Policy for Digital Learning: A Working Paper Series from the Thomas B. Fordham Institute.* Washington, DC: Thomas B. Fordham Institute.

Cheng, A.-C., Jordan, M. E., and Schallert, D. L. (2013). Reconsidering assessment in online/hybrid courses: Knowing versus learning. *Computers and Education,* 68, 51–59.

Chyung, S.-Y., and Stepich, D. (2003). Applying the congruence principle of Bloom's taxonomy to designing online instruction. *Quarterly Review of Distance Education,* 4(3), 317–330.

CREDO. (2011). *Charter school performance in Pennsylvania.* Standford, CA: Center for Research on Education Outcomes (CREDO), Stanford University. Retrieved December 20, 2013, from http://credo.stanford.edu/reports/PA State Report_20110404_FINAL.pdf.

Dakers, J. R. (2005). The hegemonic behaviorist cycle. *International Journal of Technology and Design Education*, 15(2), 111–126.

Darling-Hammond, L. (1998). New standards, old inequalities: The current challenge for African-American education. In L. A. Daniels (ed.), *The state of Black America* (pp. 109–171). New York, NY: National Urban League.

Darling-Hammond, L. (2000). Teacher quality and student achievement. A review of state policy evidence. *Education Policy Analysis Archives*, 15(1), 1–44

Deming, D., Goldin, C., and Katz, L. F. (2012). The for-profit post secondary school sector. *Journal of Economic Perspectives*, 26(1), 139–164.

DeSantis, N. (2012, April 18). Online-education start-up teams with top-ranked universities to offer free courses. *The Chronicle of Higher Education*.

Freire, P. (2007). *Pedagogy of the oppressed*. New York: Continuum.

Friend, B., and Johnston, S. (2005). Florida virtual school: A choice for all students. In Z. L. Berge and T. Clark (eds), *Virtual schools: Planning for success* (pp. 97–117). New York, NY: Teachers College Press.

Giroux, H. (2002). Neoliberalism, corporate culture, and the promise of higher education: The university as a democratic public sphere. *Harvard Educational Review*, 72(4), 425–464.

Goswami, U. (2006). Neuroscience and education: From research to practice? *Nature Reviews Neuroscience*, 7(5), 406–411.

Greenway, R., and Vanourek, G. (2006). The virtual revolution: Understanding online schools. *Education Next*, 6(2), 34–41.

Haberman, M. (1991). The pedagogy of poverty versus good teaching. *Phi Delta Kappan*, 7(3), 290–294.

Means, B., Toyama, Y., Murphy, R., Bakia, M., and Jones, K. (2010). *Evaluation of evidence-based practices in online learning: A meta-analysis and review of online-learning studies*. Washington, DC: U.S. Department of Education.

Miron, G., and Urschel, J. L. (2012). *Understanding and improving full-time virtual schools: A study of student characteristics, school finance, and school performance in schools operated by K12 Inc.* Boulder, CO: National Education Policy Center.

National Institute of Standard and Technology. (2005). *Adaptive learning systems*. Retrieved January 10, 2014, from http://www.atp.nist.gov/atp/97wp-lt.htm.

Parry, M. (2010, October 31). Tomorrow's college. *The Chronicle of Higher Education*. Retrieved January 10, 2014, from http://chronicle.com/article/Tomorrows-College/125120.

Pashler, H., McDaniel, M., Rohrer, D., and Bjork, R. (2008). Learning styles: Concepts and evidence. *Psychological Science in the Public Interest*, 9(3), 105–119.

Prawat, R. S., and Floden, R. E. (1994). Philosophical perspectives on constructivist views of learning. *Educational Psychologist*, 29(1), 37–48.

Press, E., and Washburn, J. (2001). Digital diplomas. *Mother Jones*, 26(1), 34–41.

Queen, B., and Lewis, L. (2011). *Distance education courses for public elementary and secondary school students: 2009–10* (NCES 2012-008). U.S. Department of Education, National Center for Education Statistics. Washington, DC: Government Printing Office.

Schwartz, D. L., Lin, X., Brophy, S., and Bransford, J. D. (1999). Toward the development of flexibly adaptive instructional designs. In C. M. Reigeluth (ed.), *Instructional design theories and models* (Vol. 2, pp. 183–213). Hillsdale, NJ: Lawrence Erlbaum Associates.

Sturgis, C., Rath, B., Weisstein, E., and Patrick, S. (2010). *An evaluation: Virtual charter schools*. Madison, WI: Wisconsin Department of Public Instruction.

Vaidhyanathan, S. (2012). What's the matter with MOOCs? *The Chronicle of Higher Education*. Retrieved December 10, 2013, from http://chronicle.com/blogs/innovations/whats-the-matter-with-moocs/33289.

Vygotsky, L. (1978). *Mind in society: The development of higher psychological process*. Cambridge, MA: Harvard University Press.

18

POVERTY REDUCTION THROUGH EDUCATION

An analytical framework for cash transfers for education

Elena Delavega and Monit Cheung

The first of the UN Millennium Development Goals is the reduction of global poverty by half by 2015 (Kanbur, 2005). Among the many approaches to reduce poverty, education has been shown to promote economic well-being (Bauer and Chytilová, 2010; Figlio, 2007–2008). With the globalization of technological advances, education is fundamental to economic development (United Nations Educational, Scientific and Cultural Organization [UNESCO], 2005). The positive effect of education on the income and well-being of each individual is not questionable (Kawachi et al., 2010; UNESCO, 2005), but the question is how to increase the education levels of the entire population in order to extend the intended benefits and promote well-being to the entire nation. To this effect, countries have implemented innovative policy initiatives consisting of an array of laws and regulations aimed at achieving the goals of universal education, including conditional cash transfers.

Conditional cash transfers for education

Conditional cash transfers are designed to both immediately provide needed economic support to poor people, and to reduce poverty in the long term through the promotion of desired behaviors in exchange for economic incentives (Fiszbein et al., 2009). These transfers consist of regular direct subsidies for low-income families with children in exchange for pre-determined activities, such as school attendance or regular health care (Attanasio et al., 2005; Borraz and González, 2009; Dugger, 2004; Fernald et al., 2009; Ferro and Nicollela, 2007; Fiszbein et al., 2009; Hodges et al., 2007; Rawlings and Rubio, 2005; Reimers et al., 2006; Skoufias and Parker, 2001; Son, 2008). Conditional cash transfers for education have focused on promoting enrollment in primary and secondary school, and in some cases the completion of high school, but the results in this respect have been inconclusive (Attanasio et al., 2005; Bourguignon et al., 2002; Reimers et al., 2006; Son, 2008). The authors of this chapter found in 2010 that 33 countries, mostly in Latin America and Southeast Asia, had implemented some form of conditional cash transfer program for education. The most well-known programs are *Bolsa Familia* in Brazil and *Oportunidades* in Mexico, but programs exist in Bangladesh, Colombia, Mongolia, Turkey, and other countries (Fiszbein et al., 2009). Conditional cash transfers are promoted to a great extent by the World Bank and the International Monetary Fund (IMF), which have required developing countries to adopt neoliberal policies as a prerequisite for economic assistance and loans (Kanbur, 2005). World Bank policies have tended to ignore structural inequalities and systemic oppression (Bexley, 2007; Siisiäinen, 2000; Sobel, 2002), but conditional cash transfers appear to be a genuinely compassionate idea that recognizes that the very poor need assistance (Williamson, 2000).

Conditional cash transfers as incentives

Governments that implement transfer policies aim to reduce poverty, but most of these poli-cies provide only a temporary fix as the recipients may return to poverty as soon as the transfer ends (Ferro and Nicollela, 2007). The idea behind conditional welfare policy is to promote behaviors that result in long-term poverty reduction. Because it has long been known that education results in increased human capital (Ferro and Nicollela, 2007), and this in turn results in increased income (Bauer and Chytilová, 2010; Rawlings and Rubio, 2005), it is thought that promoting education is a good long-term policy (Barrientos and DeJong, 2004; Ferro and Nicollela, 2007). Under these assumptions, increasing the utilization of education is a desir-able national goal, which can be achieved through "certain but contingent funding" (Sperling, 2008, p. 10), commonly known as conditional cash transfers.

The basic assumption behind conditional cash transfers is that demand-side incentives encourage people to purchase more of a good or service by making it more attractive or by reducing the cost or opportunity cost of forgoing alternative options (Sexton, 2005). An example is the immediate gratification of putting a child to work, as the law allows for income-gaining rather than educating the child for the future. Parents in this scenario do not see how not working as an alternative can allow the child to gain more income in the future. When the opportunity cost is calculated, the present may be preferred at the expense of the future, with the result that human capital accumulation for the child may be forsaken (Hodges et al., 2007; Nguyen, 2008). Poor families may simply not have the resources to send their children to school, or parents may not realize that investing in education has long-term benefits, and thus poor families may prefer to avoid the opportunity cost of sending their children to school (Bils and Klenow, 2000; Jensen, 2007).

A policy that funds or rewards people for going to school is thus a demand-side incentive that enhances the value of going to school and reduces the opportunity cost of other alternatives such as employment (Hodges et al., 2007). It also promotes increased enrollment in school and graduation rates for very poor children (Jensen, 2007; Rawlings and Rubio, 2005; Tooley and Dixon, 2006). In his theory of capital, Pierre Bourdieu (1986/2001/2011) calls cultural capital the human infrastructure needed for development. Cultural capital is the human capital of skills and knowledge, but in Bourdieu's conceptualization, it includes also the reputation and prestige of the school attended, and the symbolic value attached to it.

Are conditional cash transfers effective?

Conditional cash transfers represent a favorite idea of neoliberal policy-makers (Dammert, 2009; Williamson, 2000), but research does not show consistent positive results on education and economic development. At best, conditional cash transfers have been deemed ineffective (Lomelí, 2009; Ponce and Bedi, 2010; Reimers et al., 2006; Son, 2008), and at worst, they are considered cruel and punitive (Freeland, 2007; Ruckert, 2009). The examination of 19 out of 33 countries that had implemented conditional cash transfers and individual development accounts to serve at least 10% of their children conducted by the authors in 2010 failed to pro-vide enough evidence to support the widespread use of conditional cash transfers (Cheung and

Delavega, 2012). A trend-analysis with data from the World Bank and the IMF suggests that while it is still too early to determine whether conditional cash transfers promote development through improved literacy and enrollment rates in primary and secondary school, they may have limited impacts (Cheung and Delavega, 2012). This is consistent with the findings of other research throughout the world (Attanasio et al., 2005; Ferro and Nicollela, 2007; Fiszbein et al., 2009; Rawlings and Rubio, 2005; Son, 2008). More recently, Dubois et al. (2012) examined the *Oportunidades* program in Mexico and found that, while enrollment rates increased, academic outcomes were unsatisfactory. In 2009, Dammert found that the effects are inconsistent and may not hold from one year to the next, casting doubt on the effectiveness of conditional cash transfers as poverty reduction strategies.

Bourdieu's capital model

Bourdieu's model is applied in this chapter to analyze the effectiveness of conditional cash transfer policies. This model suggests that capital exists in many interchangeable forms, including economic, social, and cultural. Capital is thus basically any resources needed to produce more resources (Granovetter and Swedberg, 2001), referred to as "a stock of wealth" used for the production of more wealth (Fisher, 1918/2007, p. 38). Although originally defined in purely economic terms (Marx, 1978), the concept of capital has been expanded to include social and other forms of capital (Berkes and Folke, 1998; Bourdieu, 1972/1977, 1986/2001/2011; Coleman, 1988; Fisher, 1918/2007; Putnam, 1995). The importance of Bourdieu's work, in particular for the practice of social work, is in his recognition of the impact of non-economic elements for resource distribution and allocation (Fram, 2004).

Bourdieu (1986/2001/2011) conceptualizes a typology consisting of economic capital, social capital, and cultural capital. Economic capital is the money, land, and tangible economic resources recognized as such. Social capital is defined as networks to which an actor has access, the relationships, and the reciprocity that this entails. Bourdieu's conceptualization is used for this analysis because it considers the economic dimensions of social capital as well as the power dimensions in hierarchical social structures and the different opportunities inherent in social stratification (Bexley, 2007; Gamarnikow and Green, 1999; Siisiäinen, 2000; Sobel, 2002). Bourdieu rejects the idea that other forms of capital are disinterested or unrelated to economic pursuits, and posits that social capital involves access to the resources of a given social group. Bourdieu also defines cultural capital as the skills, knowledge, and abilities that a person may acquire over time. Note that cultural capital does not refer to the understanding of culture as defined by cultural anthropology, the distinctive set of values and customs that are shared by a particular human group (Cheung and Leung, 2008). Although education is the vehicle for transmission of cultural capital, class differentials produce differential educational outcomes (Roy et al., 2005). Cultural capital is directly related to the amount of social capital and economic capital of one's family of origin, for its acquisition takes time, effort, and money. Bourdieu states that it is through the investment in cultural capital that members of the elite hide and transmit economic and social capital to the next generation and reproduce the existing social structure. Capital takes the different forms in order to assure the hidden reproducibility of social class segmentation and intergenerational transmission of capital for the maintenance of existing social structures (Bourdieu, 1986/2001/2011).

Education as the formation of cultural capital is particularly suitable to the maintenance of social inequalities in that it allows for the hidden transfer of wealth from one generation to the next (Bourdieu, 1986/2001/2011). Because education permits economic elites to transfer wealth to the next generation in a way that belies the reality of the reproduction of wealth and social class, education is seen as the means out of poverty. Evidence suggests that it is indeed the case, as mechanisms for exclusion are seldom perfect, but this mechanism has worked well to reproduce social class because poor families are often disinclined to make the long-term investments in education required due to the import of short-term challenges (Jensen, 2007; Nguyen, 2008). In other instances, poor families simply do not have the necessary economic or social capital required to educate their children (Rahman and Uddin, 2009). All forms of capital are intimately tied to social class (Turner, 2003). For Bourdieu, class is the major constraint on any form of capital, despite the reducibility of other forms of capital to economic capital.

The formation of cultural capital and the neoliberal agenda

Capital is further analyzed within the neoliberal agenda. Neoliberalism is defined here as an economic approach to social policy that ultimately depends on market-based structures and leads to the individualization of social problems. The neoliberal ideology stems from a fear of collective action and governments operationalized by Hayek (1944/1994). Neoliberal policies emphasize privatization, deregulation, trade liberalization, the protection of property rights and lower taxation, and an aversion to welfare transfers for the poor unless absolutely necessary (Williamson, 2000). Neoliberalism is, in short, the set of "policy reforms that reduce the role of government" (Williamson, 2000, p. 255). Neoliberal policies, also called the *Washington Consensus*, have been favored by the World Bank and the IMF (Williamson, 2000), and given the power these organizations have on developing countries, it is not surprising that these policies have been adopted in some form or another by Latin American and other countries in the global South (Delgado Wise and Covarrubias, 2012). Under the neoliberal ideology, private firms and market-based provision of services are seen as preferable to collective action, and social problems are the result of individual deficits (Williamson, 2000). Thus the way to help the poor is to help them overcome their inadequacies. A key element in neoliberal policy consists of "build[ing] the human capital of the poor" rather than providing income supports and redistribution (Williamson, 2000, p. 257). It is essentially an economic conservative approach to social policy. It purports to be kinder than strict conservatism in that it recognizes that, without governmental supports, the poor do not have the bootstraps from which to pull themselves up (Williamson, 2000).

Given the increasing levels of inequality between the rich and poor, the degradation of living conditions for the vast majority of people throughout the world, as well as increasing inequalities between nations (Delgado Wise and Covarrubias, 2012), conditional cash transfers provide a very useful cover to a scheme that depends on concealing the system of unequal exchange and distortion to maintain itself (Delgado Wise and Covarrubias, 2012). Neoliberal conditional cash transfers appear to help the poor while at the same time denying help, maintaining social inequalities, and reproducing socioeconomic statuses. It is a model that pretends that conditioning any public assistance or welfare transfers to proactive or productive attitudes and behaviors among the poor is the way to help people escape poverty. When programs fail to produce their ostensible goal results (see, for instance, Freeland, 2007; Reimers et al., 2006), the poor are blamed for their lack of initiative, ability, talent, or skill. They are presumed to have been provided ample means for success, so when they fail, they are blamed absolutely, either because the poor have failed to maintain the necessary conditions to receive the assistance they need to survive, or because they have failed to convert their education, or cultural capital, into cash (Ruckert, 2009). Conditional cash transfers brush aside the importance of possessing enough of all forms of capital to meet the conditions, and ignore the barriers posed by structural inequality while presenting the problem of poverty as simply one of motivation.

Education is not equal to all

Bourdieu (1986/2001/2011) posited that it is not only education but the quality of said education and the status and prestige attached to the educational institution itself that drive the reproduction of social class and create a wealthy next generation. At the most fundamental level, basic education is not enough for poverty remediation, as a high school diploma is becoming the bare minimum necessary to obtain a decent job (Hall, 2007). It is not enough that children are enrolled in school, but they should also complete the educational cycle as well, since the positive effects of education require that, globally, students graduate from high school (Alliance for Excellent Education, 2010, 2011; Hall, 2007). Even then, graduation may not be sufficient and may belie the fact that not all education is created equal. Conditional cash transfers are designed to incentivize primary or secondary education (Cheung and Delavega, 2012), but it is higher education that is associated with increased well-being, status, and freedom of choice (Kawachi et al., 2010; Wolbers, 2000). Another potential failure of conditional cash transfers stems from the fact that school attendance does not guarantee knowledge acquisition (Jenson, 2010). If educational systems are not rigorous or current enough, they may not prepare students for the labor market of the 21st century, regardless of completion of grades (ECOSOC, 2011). As Bourdieu predicted (1986/2001/2011), the children of wealthy parents, who provide sufficient amounts of all forms of capital, have better outcomes resulting from education (Grinstein-Weiss et al., 2009; Williams, 2004). Furthermore, graduates of private schools, which the poor cannot afford, are often perceived as better educated, more valuable people (Dronkers and Avram, 2009). This places even the most dedicated poor children from much less prestigious schools at a disadvantage in the labor market (Bourdieu and Champagne, 1993/1999). Even within the same school, rankings and perceived achievement serve to mark the students as more or less capable, as more or less deserving as a result of their own efforts and qualifications rather than those inherent in a system that is designed to produce asymmetrical outcomes (Bourdieu and Champagne, 1993/1999). Consequently, conditional cash transfers have not successfully helped the poor leave poverty even when they behave exactly as required by the transfers. The poor are placed in the double bind of experiencing barriers to success while being blamed for failure to achieve success. Social class reproduction is thus assured.

Coercion and exclusion

While conditional cash transfers may not result in the elimination of poverty, they are an effective means to exclude people from receiving transfers in the first place. Clearly, the conditioning of transfers contains coercive elements that may be used to support the policies or politics of certain groups (Ruckert, 2009), resulting in the possible exclusion of marginalized people in punitive ways. Second, the conditions may be too difficult for certain people to meet, and as a result become ineligible for benefits, regardless of need (Lund et al., 2009). The conditional cash transfer program implemented in the city of New York in 2007 initially failed due to the complexity of the requirements which made it difficult for the participants to meet them (Figlio, 2007–2008). Thus the conditionality of the transfers may be utilized to deny economic support to poor children (Barrientos and DeJong, 2004; Lund et al., 2009). These are important considerations in view of the basic premise of Bourdieu's theory that the principal function of education is the reproduction of social class and the maintenance of social inequalities across class lines. Furthermore, consistent with Bourdieu's model, these latent functions of conditional cash transfers remain hidden.

Conditional cash transfers can also be perverted in ways that are not immediately apparent, but which visibly expose their inherent exclusionary and punitive foundations. Senator Stacey Campfield of the Tennessee General Assembly introduced SB 0132 designed to move the state toward "breaking the cycle of poverty" and based on the idea of conditional cash transfers as implemented in Latin America (Humphrey, 2013). Senator Campfield proposed to motivate the poor by cutting welfare benefits for families whose children failed to make "satisfactory academic progress" (Humphrey, 2013). However, herein lies the extraordinary brilliancy of the conditional cash transfer idea as a means to reproduce social class in covert ways: Senator Campfield's bill was so obviously punitive that the community was outraged (Humphrey, 2013), whereas conditional cash transfers amounting to essentially the same concept are praised as a helping hand for the poor. Senator Campfield missed the point entirely that the reproduction of social class through education requires much more subtlety. It is precisely the hidden nature of the conversion of economic capital into cultural capital and back into economic capital through the educational choices and opportunities that the rich provide to their children that social class can be reproduced with the full acquiescence of the lower economic classes (Bourdieu, 1986/2001/2011). It is the perception that social problems are merely the result of individual faults that focuses the attention of the poor away from the system of oppression and onto themselves and allows the system to continue unabated and inequalities to persist.

Non-conditional universal support

Conditional cash transfers have gained popularity for poverty remediation, but are by no means the only or most effective poverty reduction strategy (Lund et al., 2009). Their appeal to neoliberal policy-makers lies in the increased economic prosperity and reduced corruption resulting from an educated population (Uslaner and Rothstein, 2012) while simultaneously perceiving the problem of poverty as one of lack of motivation and effort on the part of the poor (Delgado Wise and Covarrubias, 2012; Williamson, 2000). This view ignores the role of structural inequalities and the inadequacies of the system to provide a just standard of life for all people. In contrast, the Nordic model of universal provision of services has consistently delivered the lowest poverty rates and most widely shared well-being among developed countries through an infrastructure of universal service provision (Lister, 2009), which contributes to social solidarity (Lund et al., 2009). Education provided through the welfare state has been shown to be of high quality and has achieved the greatest success (Uslaner and Rothstein, 2012). When good universal services are provided with a minimum of barriers to access, the poor utilize them effectively (Lund et al., 2009) and do not need to be punished.

Macro-economic implications to poverty reduction

This analysis supports the view that development is an important concern for social work. Social workers have an imperative to promote social justice (Clark, 2007), but they have left the work of development to economists and political scientists, with the resulting focus on economic growth rather than human well-being (Szostak, 2009). A major criticism of the research on social capital conducted by the World Bank is that it ignores the work of Bourdieu without discussing the implications on how to fund the developing world (Bexley, 2007; Grootaert et al., 2004; Siisiäinen, 2000; Sobel, 2002) in non-punitive ways that recognize the structural failings of the current system and challenge it.

The World Bank and the IMF are proponents of conditional cash transfers because the conditionality elements individualize social problems (Ruckert, 2009). The very conditionality that makes the policy attractive to policy-makers and funders may present insurmountable barriers to those intended beneficiaries who most need the assistance, however. Conditionality may be a way to limit and deny aid, and reduce expenses for social welfare programs. Universal programs such as those in common in Nordic countries may be more effective in reaching the entire population and eliminating structural poverty; but these stand in direct contradiction of neoliberal policies.

As much as neoliberalism proclaims to want to end poverty and recognize hard work, it is ultimately a pro-rich, pro-economic elite ideology that despises workers, in particular when they utilize their joint social capital, from a union (Delgado Wise and Covarrubias, 2012; Williamson, 2000). It is the old *don't worry about dividing the pie fairly, let's grow the pie* school of thought dressed in the mantle of concern. Williamson (2000) calls these policies potentially "pro-poor" (p. 258) with the expectation the poor will become rich. These policies deliberately jettison redistribution (Williamson, 2000). While the World Bank is not allowed by its constitution to get involved in politics (Williamson, 2000), neoliberal policies and the implementation of such economic policies as a condition for assistance have provided a very clear way to dictate the political direction of countries. Economic policy lies at the heart of politics.

Conclusion

Bourdieu provides a model with which it is possible to explain the emphasis of the World Bank and the IMF on conditional cash transfers. This model provides a way to analyze the effects of class and economic oppression, and how the hidden and symbolic elements central to the transmission of wealth and reproduction of social class inherent in education operate in the context of conditional cash transfers. Development interventions favored by the World Bank support the neoliberal agenda and maintain the interests of dominant countries over exploited countries (Bebbington, 2007; Delgado Wise and Covarrubias, 2012). Bourdieu empowers us to see behind the benign façade of conditional cash transfers into the hidden mechanism supporting a system that may benefit the rich at the expense of the poor.

It is only when the issues of class stratification and economic oppression are brought to light that they can be addressed. Only then will the world begin to solve the gross injustices inherent in economic inequality. Thus, while it has been suggested that education is the most effective way to end poverty, a number of structural barriers may prevent the realization of this goal. Then the question that emerges from Bourdieu is: If we educate the entire population, will that eliminate poverty? Many factors may contribute to the success or failure of an educational program vis-à-vis development, and, as Bourdieu suggests, these may not necessarily be related to positive behaviors or education *per se*. Conditional cash transfers for education support a main component in neoliberal policy and restrict transfers to investment only. Given the very conservative and *marketist* view of economics imbued in neoliberal policies, conditional cash transfers become an acceptable form of transfer because they are seen as investments with expected returns. Social justice becomes invisible as a concept because social issues are re-transformed into private problems, to be solved by the individual, and unintentionally the hand extended to the poor hides within itself the very injustice it purports to eliminate.

References

Alliance for Excellent Education. (2010). *The economic benefits of halving the dropout rate*. Retrieved January 22, 2013, from http://all4ed.org/wp-content/uploads/2010/01/EconBeneCityCardBooklet011210.pdf.
Alliance for Excellent Education. (2011). *The high cost of high school dropouts: What the nation pays for inadequate high schools*. Issue Brief. Retrieved January 11, 2013, from http://www.all4ed.org/files/HighCost.pdf.

Attanasio, O., Battistin, E., Fitzsimons, E., Mesnard, A., and Vera-Hernández, M. (2005). How effective are conditional cash transfers? Evidence from Colombia. *The Institute for Fiscal Studies, Briefing Note 54.*

Barrientos, A., and DeJong, J. (2004). *Child poverty and cash transfers. CHIP Report No. 4.* London: Childhood Poverty Research and Policy Centre.

Bauer, M., and Chytilová, J. (2010). The impact of education on the subjective discount rate in Ugandan villages. *Economic Development and Cultural Change*, 58(4), 643–669.

Bebbington, A. (2007). Social movements and the politicization of chronic poverty. *Development and Change*, 38(5), 793–818.

Berkes, F., and Folke, C. (1998). Linking social and ecological systems for resiliency and sustainability. In F. Berkes and C. Folke (eds), *Linking social and ecological systems: Management practices and social mechanisms for building resilience* (pp. 1–26). Cambridge, UK: Cambridge University Press.

Bexley, E. (2007, Nov.). *Social capital in theory and practice: The contribution of Victorian tertiary education in the "new economy" disciplines of business studies and IT.* Melbourne: The University of Melbourne, Centre for the Study of Higher Education.

Bils, M., and Klenow, P. (2000). Does schooling cause growth? *American Economic Review*, 90(5), 1160–1183.

Borraz, F., and González, N. (2009). Impact of the Uruguayan conditional cash transfer program. *Cuadernos de Economía*, 46(134), 243–271.

Bourdieu, P. (1972/1977). *Outline of a theory of practice.* Cambridge, UK: Cambridge University Press. (Original work published 1972.)

Bourdieu, P. (1986). The forms of capital. In J. Richardson (ed.), *Handbook of theory and research for the sociology of education.* New York, NY: Greenwood Press.

Bourdieu, P. (2001/2011). The forms of capital. In M. Granovetter and R. Swedberg (eds), *The sociology of economic life* (2nd and 3rd eds). Boulder, CO: Westview Press.

Bourdieu, P., and Champagne, P. (1993/1999). Outcasts on the inside. In P. Bourdieu et al., *The weight of the world: Social suffering in contemporary society.* Stanford, CA: Stanford University Press. (Original work published 1993.)

Bourguignon, F., Ferreira, F., and Leite, P. (2002). *Ex-ante evaluation of conditional cash transfer programs: The case of Bolsa Escola.* William Davidson Institute Working Papers Series 516. Michigan: William Davidson Institute at the University of Michigan.

Cheung, M., and Delavega, E. (2012). Child savings accounts: Learning from poverty reduction policies in the world. *International Social Work*, 55(1), 71–94.

Cheung, M., and Leung, P. (2008). *Multicultural practice and evaluation: A case approach to evidence-based practice.* Denver, CO: Love Publishing Co.

Clark, E. (2007, July). Advocacy: Profession's cornerstone. *NASW News*, 52(7). Retrieved July 17, 2010, from http://www.socialworkers.org/pubs/news/2007/07/clark.asp.

Coleman, J. S. (1988). Social capital in the creation of human capital. *American Journal of Sociology*, 94, 95–120.

Dammert, A. C. (2009). Heterogeneous impacts of conditional cash transfers: Evidence from Nicaragua. *Economic Development and Cultural Change*, 58(1), 53–83.

Delgado Wise, R., and Covarrubias, H. (2012). Strategic dimensions of neoliberal globalization: The exporting of labor force and unequal exchange. *Advances in Applied Sociology*, 2(2), 127–134.

Dronkers, J., and Avram, S. (2009). Choice and effectiveness of private and public schools: A new approach. *Zeitschrift für Pädagogik*, 55(6), 895–909.

Dubois, P., de Janvry, A., and Sadoulet, E. (2012). Effects on school enrollment and performance of a conditional cash transfer program in Mexico. *Journal of Labor Economics*, 30(3), 555–589.

Dugger, C. W. (2004). To help poor be pupils, not wage earners, Brazil pays parents. *The New York Times.* Retrieved August 15, 2014, from http://www.nytimes.com/2004/01/03/world/to-help-poor-be-pupils-not-wage-earners-brazil-pays-parents.html.

ECOSOC. (2011). The education for all agenda. *United Nations.* Retrieved January 22, 2013, from http://www.un.org/en/ecosoc/docs/book2011/05_Dialogues%20at%20ECOSOC%202011_A_The%20Education%20for%20All%20Agenda.pdf.

Fernald, L., Gertler, P., and Neufeld, L. (2009). 10-year effect of Oportunidades, Mexico's conditional cash transfer programme, on child growth, cognition, language, and behaviour: A longitudinal follow-up study. *The Lancet*, 374(9706), 1997–2005.

Ferro, A. R., and Nicollela, A. C. (2007). *The impact of conditional cash transfer programs on household work decisions in Brazil.* FEA-ARP Working Paper Series.

Figlio, D. N. (2007–2008). Improving educational outcomes for disadvantaged children. *Focus*, 25(2), 13–19.

Fisher, I. (1918/2007). *Elementary principles of economics*. New York, NY: Cosimo, Inc.

Fiszbein, A., Schady, N., Ferreira, F. H. G., Grosh, M., Kelleher, N., Olinto, P., and Skoufias, E. (2009). *Conditional cash transfers: Reducing present and future poverty*. Washington, DC: The World Bank.

Fram, M. S. (2004). Research for progressive change: Bourdieu and social work. *Social Service Review*, 78(4), 553–576.

Freeland, N. (2007). Superfluous, pernicious, atrocious and abominable? The case against conditional cash transfers. *Institute of Development Studies Bulletin*, 38(3), 75–78.

Gamarnikow, E., and Green, A. (1999). Social capital and the educated citizen. *The School Field*, 10(3/4), 103–126.

Granovetter, M., and Swedberg, R. (2001). *The sociology of economic life* (2nd ed.). Boulder, CO: Westview Press.

Grinstein-Weiss, M., Yeo, Y. H., Irish, K., and Zhan, M. (2009). Parental assets: A pathway to positive child educational outcomes. *Journal of Sociology and Social Welfare*, 36(1), 61–85.

Grootaert, C., Narayan, D., Jones, V. N., and Woolcock, M. (2004). *Measuring social capital: An integrated questionnaire*. World Bank Working Paper No. 18.

Hall, D. (2007). Graduation matters: Improving accountability for high school graduation. *The Education Trust*. Retrieved August 15, 2014, from http://files.eric.ed.gov/fulltext/ED497689.pdf.

Hayek, F. A. (1944/1994). *The road to serfdom*. Chicago, IL: University of Chicago Press.

Hodges, A., Dashdorj, K., Jong, K. Y., Dufay, A. C., Budragchaa, U., and Mungun, T. (2007). *Child benefits and poverty reduction: Evidence from Mongolia's child money programme*. New York, NY: United Nations Children's Fund (UNICEF).

Humphrey, T. (2013, Jan. 26). Campfield bill would tie benefits to report cards. *The Knoxville News Sentinel*. Retrieved February 5, 2013, from http://www.knoxnews.com/news/2013/jan/25/campfield-bill-would-tie-welfare-benefits-to/.

Jensen, R. (2007). *The perceived returns to education and the demand for schooling*. Mimeo, Brown University.

Jenson, J. (2010). Diffusing ideas after neoliberalism: The social investment perspective in Europe and Latin America. *Global Social Policy*, 10(1), 59–84.

Kanbur, R. (2005). Growth, inequality and poverty: Some hard questions. *Journal of International Affairs*, 58(2), 223–232.

Kawachi, I., Adler, N. E., and Dow, W. H. (2010). Money, schooling, and health: Mechanisms and causal evidence. *Annals of the New York Academy of Sciences*, 1186(1), 56–68.

Lister, R. (2009). A Nordic nirvana? Gender, citizenship, and social justice in the Nordic welfare states. *Social Politics: International Studies in Gender, State and Society*, 16(2), 242–278.

Lomelí, E. V. (2009). Conditional cash transfer programs: Achievements and illusions. *Global Social Policy*, 9(2), 167–171.

Lund, F., Noble, M., Barnes, H., and Wright, G. (2009). Is there a rationale for conditional cash transfers for children in South Africa? *Transformation: Critical Perspectives on Southern Africa*, 70, 70–91.

Marx, K. (1978). Wage labour and capital. In R. C. Tucker (ed.), *The Marx and Engels reader* (2nd ed.). New York, NY: W. W. Norton and Company, Inc.

Nguyen, T. (2008). *Information, role models and perceived returns to education: Experimental evidence from Madagascar*. Working Paper, Dept. of Economics (Cambridge, MA: Massachusetts Institute of Technology). Retrieved February 2, 2013, from http://www.povertyactionlab.org/sites/default/files/documents/Nguyen%202008.pdf.

Ponce, J., and Bedi, A. S. (2010). The impact of a cash transfer program on cognitive achievement: The Bono de Desarrollo Humano of Ecuador. *Economics of Education Review*, 29(1), 116–125.

Putnam, R. D. (1995). Bowling alone: America's declining social capital. *Journal of Democracy*, 6, 65–78.

Rahman, A. U., and Uddin, S. (2009). Statistical analysis of the different socioeconomic factors affecting the education of N-W.F.P. (Pakistan). *Journal of Applied Quantitative Methods*, 4(1), 88–94.

Rawlings, L. B., and Rubio, G. M. (2005). Evaluating the impact of conditional cash transfer programmes. *The World Bank Research Observer*, 20(1), 29–55.

Reimers, F., DeShano da Silva, C., and Trevino, E. (2006). *Where is the "education" in conditional cash transfers in education?* Retrieved from UNESCO Institute for Statistics.

Roy, J., Allegretto, S., and Fungard, Y. (2005, Oct. 12). *Low income hinders college attendance for even the highest achieving students*. Economic Policy Institute Snapshot. Retrieved November 4, 2009, from http://www.epi.org/economic_snapshots/entry/webfeatures_snapshots_20051012/.

Ruckert, A. (2009). A decade of poverty reduction strategies in Latin America: Empowering or disciplining the poor? *Labour, Capital and Society*, 42(1/2), 56–81.

Sexton, R. L. (2005). *Exploring macro-economics* (3rd ed.). Mason, OH: Thomson-South Western.

Siisiäinen, M. (2000). *Two concepts of social capital: Bourdieu vs. Putnam*. Paper presented at ISTR Conference, July 5–8, Trinity College, Dublin, Ireland.

Skoufias, E., and Parker, S. W. (2001). *Conditional cash transfers and their impact on child work and schooling*. Paper provided by International Food Policy Research Institute (IFPRI) in its series FCND Discussion Papers No. 123.

Sobel, J. (2002). Can we trust social capital? *Journal of Economic Literature*, 40, 139–154.

Son, H. H. (2008). *Conditional cash transfer programs: An effective tool for poverty alleviation?* Economics and Research Department Policy Brief Series No. 51. Manila, Philippines: Asia Development Bank.

Sperling, G. (2008). *A global education fund: Toward a true global compact on universal education*. CUE Working Paper. Council on Foreign Relations Press. Retrieved October 23, 2009, from http://www.cfr.org/publication/18051#.

Szostak, R. (2009). *The causes of economic growth: Interdisciplinary perspectives*. Berlin: Springer-Verlag.

Tooley, J., and Dixon, P. (2006). "*De facto*" privatisation of education and the poor: Implications of a study from sub-Saharan Africa and India. *Compare*, 36(4), 443–462.

Turner, J. (2003). *The structure of sociological theory*. New York, NY: Wadsworth Thomson.

United Nations Educational, Scientific and Cultural Organization [UNESCO]. (2005). *Higher education*. Retrieved August 15, 2014, from http://www.unesco.org/new/en/education/themes/strengthening-education-systems/higher-education.

Uslaner, E. M., and Rothstein, B. (2012). *Mass education, state-building, and equality: Searching for the roots of corruption*. Gothenburg: University of Gothenburg, The Quality of Government Institute Working Paper Series, 2012:5.

Williams, T. R. (2004). *The impacts of household wealth on child development* (Working Paper No. 04-07). St. Louis, MO: Center for Social Development, Washington University in St. Louis.

Williamson, J. (2000). What should the World Bank think about the Washington Consensus? *The World Bank Research Observer*, 15(2), 251–264.

Wolbers, M. H. J. (2000). The effects of level of education on mobility between employment and unemployment in the Netherlands. *European Sociological Review*, 16(2), 185–200.

19

STUDENTS THAT LAG OR A SYSTEM THAT FAILS?

A contemporary look at the academic trajectory of Latino students

Jessica Martone

Introduction

Neoliberal and poverty concepts have been introduced to the discourse on schools, school policy, school achievement, and school transitions. What in fact does this mean in the framework of the educational system in the United States? What are schools doing that result in poor academic achievement, disproportionate dropout rates, and low college enrollment rates for minority and low-income students? These are the questions that we must consider to understand what is happening within our school systems. Poverty is conceptualized in a multitude of ways and it is important that we understand unequal access to education and disproportionate educational outcomes as a form of poverty for the Latino population.

Lipman (2003) looks at inequalities within the school system and in the labor market, taking a close look at Latino and African-American students. The author largely attributes the differential opportunities and treatment as a result of education policy. She states that students bear the blame for their educational outcome, following the belief that education is a personal responsibility, not a collective responsibility. Students are considered to be the cause for educational discrepancies, which further removes responsibility from the school systems that have already created a structure of large-scale inequality. Regarding the influence of neoliberal practices in the school system, Lopez (2000) states:

> Neoliberalism assumes that students, teachers, and principals need incentives and sanctions in order to bring about radical changes in the school system. Competition in schools is seen as conducive to teaching and learning. Accordingly, schools should mimic mini-businesses, as parents and students "shop" for the best deals among the winners and losers of the marketplace.
>
> (p. 55)

Lopez describes a system in which students again bear the responsibility for their academic success, arguing that students should not have to compete for a quality education. In a report on Latinos in academia, Schmidt (2003) states that there is a problem in the pipeline for Latino students and describes them as getting stuck or leaked out. Contreras (2011) also describes a leaking pipeline, and Gandara and Contreras (2009) describe the educational pipeline as much narrower and more tenuous than it was in the past (p. 40). Students are being funneled into certain channels within school systems, causing differential outcomes in academic achievement.

Literature on academic achievement and the tracking of students within school systems introduce us to the idea that schools have a structure in place which both creates and perpetuates unequal outcomes. This chapter focuses specifically on the academic trajectories of Latino students in the United States with the goal of understanding the structures and systems that impact academic achievement rather than the deficit and personal responsibility discourse which focuses on students and individual-level factors that contribute to poor performance.

The high dropout percentage and low college enrollment for Latinos has changed little over the last decades, suggesting that it is a persistent social issue. Stafford and Warr (1985) and Manis (1974) explain that something moves from being a private trouble to a public issue by the degree of concern, the numbers affected, the injustice, frequency of a problem, and the damage it has caused. Additionally, they explain that something has become a social problem and issue when there is a discrepancy between the norm for society and the actual conditions for a group. The statistics that follow demonstrate that there is a discrepancy in educational outcomes for students of different ethnic/racial groups, namely for Latino students. The frequency of the problem is evident in that Latino students continue to have the highest dropout rates from high school and there has been little change in the numbers of students enrolling in college. As the number of Latinos in the United States continues to rise and the discourse that removes responsibility from school systems continues to gain momentum, a critical analysis of the educational system and educational structures is needed.

Background on Latino students in education

Latino students in the United States have consistently had the highest dropout rate of all ethnic groups as reported from 1990 to 2012. The latest statistics indicate a 13% dropout rate for youth between the ages of 16 and 24 (U.S. Department of Education, 2014). This figure has decreased by just over half since 2000 (Pew Hispanic Center, 2013a), and the gap between Latino students and White, Black, and Asian students continues to decrease (Pew Hispanic Center, 2013b). The most recent census data indicate that the Latino population in the United States totals just over 53 million people (U.S. Census, 2013), an increase of 17.7 million people since 2000 (U.S. Census, 2000). These numbers indicate a large and rising Latino population in the United States and the importance of looking at the Latino experience in education.

In a comparison of national school enrollment by race and ethnicity between 2000 and 2009, the Pew Hispanic Center[1] (2011a) reported an increase of 2,695,046 Latinos. According to the figures, 21% of all students enrolled in schools in 2009 were Latino between the ages of 5 and 17. This figure increased, with new reports showing that 23.9% of public K-12 students are Latino (Pew Hispanic Center, 2012). Additionally, the report shows that 24.7% of public elementary school students are Latino and that 25.2% of 18–24-year-olds who are enrolled in two-year colleges are Latino (Pew Hispanic Center, 2012). Not only are more Latino students attending high school but, between 2010 and 2011, the number of Latino students who earned their high school diploma or GED increased by close to 4% (from 72.8% to 76.3%). With Latinos as one of the fastest-growing segments of the U.S. school population, more attention is needed from researchers and policy makers.

The Pew Hispanic Center (2011b) found an increase in the number of Latino students attending college, with the majority enrolling in community colleges. They found that 2011 resulted in Latino students being the nation's largest minority group enrolled in four-year colleges and universities. Of importance, the number of Latino students enrolled in college increased by 15% from 2010 to 2011 (Pew Hispanic Center, 2012). A report prepared for the National Center for Education Statistics indicates that 23% of the 22.3 million undergraduate students in the United States were immigrants or second-generation students. Of this group, Asian students represented the largest number of first-generation immigrants and Latinos the largest number of second-generation students (Staklis and Horn, 2012). Although there has been a significant increase in college enrollment among Latinos, it has not kept pace with the growth of the Latino population. Despite increases, Latinos remain less likely to enroll in college than their Asian and White counterparts, though their enrollment in four-year colleges surpassed that of Black students in 2011 (Pew Hispanic Center, 2012). Additionally, Latinos are less likely than their counterparts to receive associate and bachelor's degrees; however, the numbers have increased among Latinos (Pew Hispanic Center, 2012).

School structure and sorting

Noguera (2003) discusses the many factors that youth cannot control in their lives, and often failure is not for a lack of trying. He states, "Due largely to circumstances beyond their control, their dreams and those of their parents were never realized, not because of a lack of effort, but because of a lack of luck and opportunity" (p. 12). He goes on to state that the terrible conditions of urban schools are known and "that America simply does not care that large numbers of children from inner-city schools and neighborhoods are not properly educated" (p. 14). In 2001, President Bush signed an executive order, which created the President's Advisory Commission on Educational Excellence for Hispanic Americans. This Commission called for more research on Latino students. Lauro F. Cavazos, a former secretary of education, explained that no more reports were needed—the problem is known: what is lacking is a will to do the work that is needed (Schmidt, 2003). Similarly, Gandara and Contreras (2009) issue a call to action in their book, stating that the educational crisis in the United States has a Latino face. The authors explain that to better understand the Latino educational trajectory more than individual factors need to be considered; group factors as well as social and schooling conditions and community contexts and resources must be taken into account. Contreras (2011) adds that there is unequal investment in schools and that this must be addressed in order to change the educational discrepancies among students. She discusses unequal access, which begins early, in preschool, and persists. Elsewhere, Noguera (2004) states that what is missing from earlier research on the education of immigrants is a discussion of how the socialization and sorting of students play a role in their academic outcomes. Noguera discusses research that introduces the idea of social capital and its influence on the performance of immigrant students. He states that a consideration of structure in the education process is needed.

Much of the literature on academic achievement fails to consider important structural factors that play a role in academic success both within school systems and the successful transitions between school systems. Students' academic trajectories, with consideration given to the transition to higher education, can be influenced by the information they are given in school, programming to which they have access, mentorship, and classes they are permitted to take. The division of students into classes or programs based on levels of achievement is known as tracking (Oakes, 1986). Specifically, when students are divided into pathways for those who are college bound, those who will go into the workforce, and those who are in the general pool, the term is *curriculum tracking*, and when students are divided into different levels for specific academic classes (such as math and English) the term is *ability grouping* (Oakes, 1986, 1987). Oakes has written extensively on the tracking of students within schools, discussing the underlying philosophy, which states that students who perform at the same level should be educated together and those who are lower performing might suffer emotionally if placed in classes with higher-performing students (Oakes, 1986). However, she states that there is much evidence to the contrary and posits that tracking within schools is not effective and perpetuates inequalities (Oakes, 1986, 1987). Students who are in the high-performing tracks may have access to more information, resources, and higher-quality teachers, and often those teachers have higher expectations of the students in the higher-performing tracks (Gamoran, 1992; Oakes, 1987). Minority and low-income students are generally not placed in the high-achieving classes, nor the track for college-bound students (Oakes and Guiton, 1995).

Schools make choices about which students will be given priority access to resources likely to promote success, but as suggested by Werblow et al. (2013), the sorting of students within school systems is not frequently discussed with regard to school reform. Given the results of their study and others like it, tracking should be closely considered with regard to reforming school policies. In an analysis of a nationally representative dataset, Werblow et al. examined whether academic tracking and school climate have an impact on the dropout rates of high school students. Their bivariate results show that Latino students have the most disproportionate rates of enrollment in the college preparatory track. Using data for 16,081 students, they found that those who were in the college preparatory track experience a 24% dropout rate as compared to those students placed in the lower tracks (general and vocational) which have a 76% dropout rate. Using hierarchical generalized linear modeling (HGLM), which allows for the consideration of data at multiple levels, they found that students who were not placed in the college preparatory track were 60% more likely to drop out of high school. These findings highlight Noguera's (2003, 2004) conclusion that school structure in fact plays a critical role in the success of students. With minority students so seriously underrepresented in college preparatory programming, his critique of the school system becomes understood in a new manner.

Some schools are found to have racial stratification in the course offerings, with Latino and African-American students enrolled in lower-level math courses often resulting in a lower senior-year GPA and lower enrollment in four-year colleges (Miller et al., 2010). In addition to Latino and other minority students, tracking has also been found to have a significant impact on students who are English-language learners (Callahan, 2005). While not all Latino students are necessarily English-language learners, 89% (of 355) of the high school students used in Callahan's study were Spanish-speakers, which calls attention to the placement of this segment of students within the school system. Ninety-eight percent of the students in her sample had not taken the necessary courses to transition to a four-year college. She argues that the problem moves beyond language, again calling attention to tracking and how decisions get made about which students can be exposed to certain curricula.

A number of qualitative research studies have shown that there are structural barriers in the way of Latino students' academic success (Campa, 2010; Gonzales, 2010; Kimura-Walsh et al., 2009), and offer that the cultural, economic, historic, and political structures of schools are often left out of the discussion (Campa, 2010). Kimura-Walsh et al. (2009) found that students used teachers and college counselors as their primary source for college information. Some students—those with high rankings—indicated they benefited from using the College Corner at their school; however, those with lower rankings expressed difficulty accessing college resources. The authors found that students were given certain types of college information depending on how they were tracked within the school. Some students indicated that they sought college information at programs offered outside of their school. Gonzales (2010), like Kimura-Walsh et al., also discusses the tracking of students and the effect this has on the knowledge they are able to obtain regarding college, as well as the relationships they are able to form with teachers within the school. He describes that "positively tracked" students had beneficial experiences with respect to gaining access to college information and teachers. He explains that students' educational trajectory is influenced by their position in the school hierarchy.

In addition to students being sorted within educational systems, there is also the phenomenon of teacher sorting. In essence this has the same effect on certain groups of students, typically minority and low-income, where their access to resources, information, and high-quality teachers may be limited. According to Kalogrides et al. (2013), the research in this area is limited, though necessary, to better understand the process by which teachers are assigned to students and what that means for educational outcomes. In their research they look at elementary, middle, and high schools in Miami/Dade County to better understand the types of teachers that are assigned to high- and low-achieving students, with achievement defined by prior year school success. Their results demonstrate that female and minority teachers tend to be assigned to lower-achieving students as compared to male and white teachers. Also, the Black, Hispanic, and low-income students in their sample were more often in classrooms with inexperienced teachers. In addition, those teachers who studied at what the authors call "more selective" undergraduate institutions and had leadership positions within the school tended to teach in classrooms with higher-achieving students. The authors are clear in their explanation that minority teachers working with minority students is not a relationship that should be portrayed as negative, but rather one in which students may thrive given that they may relate to the teacher's racial background. The bigger concern with teacher sorting is the pairing of inexperienced teachers with classrooms that may be more difficult, or with minority and low-income students, groups that may require additional support (Kalogrides et al., 2013). The structural issues within schools have important implications for the academic success of students and their ability to transition to new school systems. The research on school structure and school policies fits well with the work of Henry Trueba, an educational anthropologist who looks closely at minority education.

Structure as a function of culture within school systems

Trueba (1988) emphasizes that culture is often omitted from the discussion on the academic success of minority students. In describing an appropriate theoretical and practical approach to understanding the academic achievement of minority students, Trueba (1988) states that there are five essential components: (1) recognize the significance of culture in specific instructional settings; (2) prevent stereotyping of minorities; (3) help resolve cultural conflicts in school; (4) integrate the home and the school cultures; and (5) stimulate the development of communicative and other skills that children need in order to participate meaningfully in the instructional process (p. 270).

Trueba (1999) addresses the drastic changes in the racial makeup of the school system over a 40-year period, pointing out that White students are no longer the majority. He comments that the United States is not equipped to meet the growing needs of Latinos, who are quickly becoming the majority group. In his many books on education, Trueba discusses several themes related to the educational experiences of Latino students. His stance on the classroom focuses on preparing teachers to be ready to meet the cultural and linguistic needs of the children (Trueba, 1989, 1999). He states that teachers need to be re-trained in how to think about their students and how to engage them in the classroom. He argues for the creation of a classroom where no group is made to feel superior. Trueba (1989, 1993) and Delgado-Gaitan and Trueba (1991) also focus attention on the schools themselves, stating that policies that incorporate students' native language and culture need to be implemented by schools, and argue that the lack of policies contributes to school dropout. With regard to academic failure, Trueba (1989) states that it can be "fully understandable only in its macro-historical, social, economic, and political context" (p. 28). Trueba indicates that the educational experience is not just the result of the individual student, but also a function of their environment. In order to better understand the academic phenomenon, he is interested in the exchange of resources among families in addition to the school context and economic and political environment.

Trueba has written extensively on culture and minority education and some of the literature included dates back over 20 years. In 1989, Trueba wrote that teachers should be prepared to meet the diverse cultural and linguistic needs of students. A decade later (1999), he wrote that the racial makeup of schools was changing and that Latinos were quickly becoming the majority. It has been over 20 years since he introduced these concepts and, in 2011, the Initiative on Educational Excellence for Hispanic Students echoed these same ideas and recommendations. With the large and growing U.S. Latino population, Trueba's vision is even more relevant in achieving these goals.

Policies and recommendations that address academic achievement

Looking forward, previous reports and recommendations need to be closely considered in programmatic and policy changes focused on improving educational trajectories and outcomes. Suarez-Orozco and Suarez-Orozco (2009) have contributed principles and recommendations they see as necessary for the Obama administration to follow in order to address the educational issues of Latino students. The authors describe several key factors that must be examined: poverty, segregation, parental education, language, documentation status, school factors, English-language learning, teacher preparation/expectations, individual socio-emotional and engagement factors, generational factors, and social supports. Among their recommendations they include increased opportunities for preschool education, refocused and revitalized teacher training, rethinking language education, increased after-school programs, supporting community mentorship programs, and developing college-pathway information. Contreras (2011) also offers recommendations to address the educational inequalities, some of which include a focus on resources, parental support, teacher support and certification, and eliminating high school exit exams. She also describes a model with four components that are necessary for students to do well in school and prepare for college: peer networks, community networks and infrastructure, access to adult human resources, and access to infrastructure courses.

In 2011 the White House launched an Initiative on Educational Excellence for Hispanic Students, with an agenda to diminish the disparity, expand the educational opportunities, and improve the academic achievement of Latino students (U.S. Department of Education, 2011a, 2011b). The policy recommendations of these agencies and other organizations call for increasing access to culturally and linguistically appropriate educational services, including parent-education programming; employing bilingual teachers and administrators with expertise in working with Latino communities; supporting early childhood education; promoting parent involvement; and expanding educational services to full-day programming. Obama's proposal states that new approaches to teaching and learning are needed, including teacher preparation, support for community colleges, strengthening Hispanic-serving institutions, and improving the affordability of college, among others (U.S. Department of Education, 2011b). The time and money invested in producing these reports indicates an acknowledgement of the issue. What remains to be seen is how the results of these reports and their recommendations will continue to be implemented.

In the fields of social work and education, understanding why Latinos, one of the largest minority groups in the United States, have lower performance outcomes when compared to other students is of importance. While many policy recommendations have been put in place, it is crucial that we continue to critically analyze the structure of the school system, looking at the tracking of both students and teachers. The tracking of students has been in place for many years and seems to be a system people are comfortable with and one that in theory should function properly. However, research shows that tracking is in fact not optimal, especially when it comes to minority and low-income students. The inequalities with regard to access and educational outcomes need to be understood as a form of poverty and one that has a solution. As we continue to analyze the disproportionate educational outcomes among Latino students, we must keep our dialogue focused on questioning the current educational systems and structures. A neoliberal lens allows us to view education as a system where resources are limited and ever more privatized, organized around a market logic, and where responsibility for outcomes is increasingly shifted from the state to the individual.

Note

1 The Pew Hispanic Center is a research organization that studies the impact of Latinos on the nation and aims to better understand the U.S. Hispanic population.

References

Callahan, R.M. (2005). Tracking and high school English learners: Limiting opportunity to learn. *American Educational Research Journal*, 42(2), 305–328.

Campa, B. (2010). Critical resilience, schooling processes, and the academic success of Mexican Americans in a community college. *Hispanic Journal of Behavioral Sciences*, 32(3), 429–455.

Contreras, F. (2011). *Achieving equity for Latino students: Expanding the pathway to higher education through public policy*. New York, NY: Teachers College, Columbia University.

Delgado-Gaitan, C., and Trueba, H. (1991). *Crossing cultural borders: Education for immigrant families in America*. Washington, DC: The Falmer Press.

Gamoran, A. (1992). The variable effects of high school tracking. *American Sociological Review*, 57(6), 812–828.

Gandara, P., and Contreras, F. (2009). *The Latino education crisis: The consequences of failed social policies*. Cambridge, MA: Harvard University Press.

Gonzales, R.G. (2010). On the wrong side of the tracks: Understanding the effects of school structure and social capital in the educational pursuits of undocumented immigrant students. *Peabody Journal of Education*, 85(4), 469–485.

Kalogrides, D., Loeb, S., and Beteille, T. (2013). Systematic sorting: Teacher characteristics and class assignments. *Sociology of Education*, 86(2), 103–123.

Kimura-Walsh, E., Yamamura, E.K., Griffin, K.A., and Allen, W.R. (2009). Achieving the college dream?: Examining disparities in access to college information among high achieving and non-high achieving Latina students. *Journal of Hispanic Higher Education*, 8(3), 298–315.

Lipman, P. (2003). Chicago school policy: Regulating Black and Latino youth in the global city. *Race, Ethnicity and Education*, 6(4), 331–355.

Lopez, N. (2000). The missing link: Latinos and educational opportunity programs. *Equity and Excellence in Education*, 33(3), 53–58.

Manis, J.G. (1974). Assessing the seriousness of social problems. *Social Problems*, 22(1), 1–15.

Miller, C., Riegle-Crumb, C., Schiller, K.S., Wilkinson, L., and Frank, K.A. (2010). Race and academic achievement in racially diverse high schools: Opportunity and stratification. *Teachers College Record*, 112(4), 1038–1063.

Noguera, P.A. (2003). *City schools and the American dream: Reclaiming the promise of public education*. New York, NY: Teachers College Press.

Noguera, P.A. (2004). Social capital and the education of immigrant students: Categories and generalizations. *Sociology of Education*, 77(2), 180–183.

Oakes, J. (1986). Keeping track, part 1: The policy and practice of curriculum inequality. *Phi Delta Kappan*, 68(1), 12–17.

Oakes, J. (1987). Tracking in secondary schools: A contextual perspective. *Educational Psychologist*, 22(2), 129–153.

Oakes, J., and Guiton, G. (1995). Matchmaking: The dynamics of high school tracking decisions. *American Education Research Journal*, 32(1), 3–33.

Pew Hispanic Center. (2011a). *Statistical portrait of Hispanics in the United States, 2009, Table 24*. Retrieved July 5, 2011, from http://pewhispanic.org/files/factsheets/hispanics2009/Table%2024.pdf.

Pew Hispanic Center. (2011b). *Hispanic college enrollment spikes, narrowing gaps with other groups*. Retrieved December 8, 2011, from http://www.pewhispanic.org/2011/08/25/hispanic-college-enrollment-spikes-narrowing-gaps-with-other-groups/.

Pew Hispanic Center. (2012). *Hispanic student enrollments reach new highs in 2011*. Retrieved August 21, 2012, from http://www.pewhispanic.org/files/2012/08/Hispanic-Student-Enrollments-Reach-New-Highs-in-2011_FINAL.pdf.

Pew Hispanic Center. (2013a). *Hispanic high school graduates pass Whites in rate of college enrollment*. Retrieved February 7, 2014, from http://www.pewhispanic.org/2013/05/09/hispanic-high-school-graduates-pass-whites-in-rate-of-college-enrollment/.

Pew Hispanic Center. (2013b). *Among recent high school grads, Hispanic college enrollment rate surpasses that of Whites*. Retrieved November 1, 2013, from http://www.pewresearch.org/fact-tank/2013/09/04/hispanic-college-enrollment-rate-surpasses-whites-for-the-first-time/.

Schmidt, P. (2003, November 28). Academe's Hispanic future. Retrieved from http://chronicle.com/article/Academes-Hispanic-Future/20497/

Stafford, M.C., and Warr, M. (1985). Public perceptions of social problems: Some propositions and a test. *The Journal of Applied Behavioral Science*, 21(3), 307–316.

Staklis, S., and Horn, L. (2012, July). *New Americans in postsecondary education: A profile of immigrant and second-generation American undergraduates*. Retrieved August 20, 2012, from http://nces.ed.gov/pubs2012/2012213.pdf.

Suarez-Orozco, C., and Suarez-Orozco, M. (2009). Educating Latino immigrant students in the twenty-first century: Principles for the Obama administration. *Harvard Educational Review*, 79(2), 327–340.

Trueba, H.T. (1988). Culturally based explanations of minority students' academic achievement. *Anthropology and Education Quarterly*, 19(3), 270–287.

Trueba, H.T. (1989). Rethinking dropouts: Culture and literacy for minority student empowerment. In H.T. Trueba, G. Spindler, and L. Spindler (eds), *What do anthropologists have to say about dropouts?* (pp. 27–49). Bristol, PA: The Falmer Press.

Trueba, H.T. (1993). Culture and language: The ethnographic approach to the study of learning environments. In B.J. Merino, H.T. Trueba, and F.A. Samaniego (eds), *Language and culture in learning: Teaching Spanish to native speakers of Spanish* (pp. 26–44). Washington, DC: The Falmer Press.

Trueba, H.T. (1999). *Latinos unidos: From cultural discontinuity to the politics of solidarity*. Oxford, UK: Rowman and Littlefield Publishers, Inc.

U.S. Census. (2000). *The Hispanic population*. Retrieved February 7, 2014, from https://www.census.gov/prod/2001pubs/c2kbr01-3.pdf.

U.S. Census. (2013). *Asians fastest-growing race or ethnic group in 2012, Census Bureau reports*. Retrieved November 1, 2013, from http://www.census.gov/newsroom/press-releases/2013/cb13-112.html#.

U.S. Department of Education. (2011a). *White House Initiative on Educational Excellence for Hispanics*. Retrieved December 8, 2011, from http://ed.gov/about/inits/list/hispanic-initiative/index.html.

U.S. Department of Education. (2011b). *Winning the future: Improving education for the Latino community*. Retrieved January 18, 2012, from http://www.whitehouse.gov/sites/default/files/rss_viewer/WinningTheFutureImprovingLatinoEducation.pdf.

U.S. Department of Education. (2014). *Fast facts*. Retrieved February 7, 2014, from http://nces.ed.gov/fastfacts/display.asp?id=16.

Werblow, J., Urick, A., and Duesbery, L. (2013). On the wrong track: How tracking is associated with dropping out of school. *Equity and Excellence in Education*, 46(2), 270–284.

20

THE NEW TWO-TIERED EDUCATION SYSTEM IN THE UNITED STATES

Expanding and commodifying poverty and inequality

Kenneth J. Saltman

In the 1970s and 1980s scholars from the critical perspective raised a number of crucial questions about the relationship between education and the economy. In the U.S. context, theorists of social and cultural reproduction Samuel Bowles and Herbert Gintis, in *Schooling in Capitalist America*, challenged the meritocratic ideology of both liberals and conservatives who presumed schooling to be an equality-promoting device (Bowles and Gintis, 2010). Instead, Bowles and Gintis explained that schooling largely functioned to deepen and entrench the racialized class order under the guise of merit. They empirically demonstrated that the determinant of students' future wealth and income is a student's class position and family wealth and income rather than either intelligence or amount of schooling. Liberals and conservatives have largely ignored the insights of reproduction theory with regard to the relationship between schooling and poverty. Rather than recognize the extent to which schooling has been and continues to be implicated in the recreation of the class hierarchy across the political spectrum, a simple yet false connection is made in which more schooling is equated with greater inclusion into the capitalist economy. Following the economic crisis of 2008 President Barack Obama, Federal Reserve Chairman Ben Bernanke, and Thomas Friedman all insisted that the solution to the unemployment crisis was better education, more effective teachers, and so on. "Better" under the Obama administration would turn out to mean even more aggressive expansion of the neo-liberal restructuring of education promoted by his predecessor — privatization, union-busting, testing to punish teachers and students, and the expansion of corporate culture into all realms of education. Displacement of the destruction of the capitalist economic system onto teachers and children is shared by conservatives and liberals alike. Conservative economists of education such as the prominent Hoover Fellow Erik Hanushek argue that radically unequal educational spending should not be remedied but that better teaching methods and more privatization will increase the "quality" of education and that this will yield higher incomes and greater prosperity (Hanushek and Woessmann, 2010). Such a view is refuted by nations that have high levels of educational attainment but high levels of unemployment among these graduates. Liberal policy scholar Linda Darling-Hammond argues for equalizing educational resources on the basis that the United States. will be better able to compete in the global economy and the American empire will be able to maintain its global economic and military dominance which will translate into greater upward mobility for American students (Darling-Hammond, 2010). Darling-Hammond says little about the global race to the bottom for cheap labor in the neoliberal context nor how expanded capitalist production produces poverty and labor exploitation in the places receiving industrial production. While she recognizes that the United States has become a knowledge economy, she, nor Hanushek for that matter, has no explanation for how these jobs too will not be outsourced to India, Jamaica, and other nations with highly educated super-exploited and underemployed populations. The liberal defense of public schooling amidst the neoliberal onslaught is inadequate because it fails to address what reproduction theory makes central. That is, while liberals and conservatives disagree as to teaching methods, investment in schooling, and equality of educational resources, they share a false assumption that education is responsible for ameliorating poverty and they remain silent on capitalism's necessary production of poverty to make profits for owners, class antagonism, and the crises of overproduction, not to mention the ecological unsustainability of capitalist growth, the fostering of anti-democratic social relationships, and the corrupting effects to ethics and non-market values such as care, compassion, equality, and justice. In what follows here I revisit the insights of reproduction theorists during Fordism and what needs to be understood about reproduction and the dominant educational reform trends in the current post-Fordist economy.

Reproduction in Fordism

In *Schooling in Capitalist America* Bowles and Gintis elaborated on the "correspondence principle" between schools and the economy.[1] They sought to explain how schools are centrally involved in making workers for capitalism. Particularly, they described how schools educate students not just with the job skills and knowledge useful for business owners but also for hierarchical social relationships conducive to future domination by a boss. Bowles and Gintis offer five key points about correspondence: (1) economic inequality in society is mostly a function of markets and the broader economy, not of the education system; (2) schooling educates students to understand inequality as natural and deserved and to accept social hierarchy in forms that are useful for owners in the economy; (3) the reproduction of the economy is accomplished to a large extent by educating students into hierarchical relationships that correspond to the hierarchical relationships of the workplace; (4) education is contradictory and complex, with school producing not just docile and disciplined workers but also misfits and rebels; and (5) the form of schooling corresponds to the particular historical moment of the economy and to popular struggles associated with efforts for capital accumulation.

Reproduction theorists from Europe, particularly Louis Althusser and Pierre Bourdieu, similarly contended that schooling largely serves to reproduce social relationships for capitalism. Bourdieu focused on how schools added to the cultural capital of privileged classes while punishing those students who don't already bring cultural capital with them (Bourdieu, 1973, 1986). That is, mechanisms such as testing reward the knowledge, tastes, and dispositions as well as the tools for appropriating class-specific knowledge, all of which begins in the home. Testing and other sorting and sifting techniques naturalize and disguise the unequal distribution of cultural capital and life chances. Althusser explained how the school functions as the principal Ideological State Apparatus (ISA) (Althusser, 1994). As an ISA, the school is the site where students are formed as ideological subjects or interpellated. That is, they are "called in" or hailed to the place that the state has already reserved for them, and only by answering this call do they become subjects. Though subjects were historically formed through the call of the church, for Althusser the school has replaced the church as the principal site where subjects are called into relation with the plans of the state. Through the rituals and practices of the school, ideology most often succeeds—that is, students come to recognize themselves as "good subjects" of those in positions of authority. For Althusser the making of particular kinds of subjects ultimately came back to the reproduction of the capitalist economy and social organization.

Reproduction theorists emphasized that the principal way for profit to be made in a capitalist economy is by exploiting workers—paying them less than their time and labor power is worth. The economy can only be ongoingly recreated in this view if workers learn to take their place and play their role in the production process. The reproduction theorists emphasize that the hierarchical arrangement of the capitalist economy is not necessarily the most efficient form of production, but it is the most efficient in terms of maintaining a hierarchical control over the production process and its workers. In order for a tiny portion of the population to retain control and ownership over industry, a highly anti-democratic form of relating to other people must be taught and learned.

Working-class and professional-class schools reproduce the stratified labor force while making such unequal sorting and sifting appear as a matter of either merit or natural talent. Working-class schools in working-class communities are subject to punitive, rigid, disciplinary reforms that are designed to instill in students submission to hierarchical control. Scripted lessons, direct instruction, strict bodily codes demanding students keep their feet on the floor and their hands on the desk and their eyes on the teacher, uniforms, strict speaking codes, uniform lessons—the celebrated though not necessarily good school reforms targeting working-class and poor students aim to make docile disciplined subjects who will submit to the authority of the teacher to later submit to the authority of the boss and ever-worsening work conditions of low-skill, low-pay work in a deregulated globalizing economy. Such ideological preparation for the labor force also functions to teach submission to relative exclusion from the levers of power of the state.

From Fordist to post-Fordist reproduction

Writing in the 1970s, the critics of social and cultural reproduction were describing the relationship between education and the economy of the Fordist era. In the era of the industrial "Fordist" economy dominant throughout most of the 20th century, public schools played an economic role of not just preparing workers and ideologically forming them but also of creating a "reserve army of labor." As an economic strategy for capital and ruling-class people, schooling in the industrial economy had the public absorb the training costs for business while flooding the labor market to keep labor costs cheap for owners.

The Fordist economy was defined by industrial production and a post-World War II boom in unionized factory jobs, a compact between capital and labor, and a social arrangement characterized by time-intensive forms of social control such as not just schooling but also psychotherapy, rehabilitative incarceration, social work, and a growing safety net for the expanding middle class. Schools in the Fordist era, while reproducing a two-tiered workforce, were seen as making the workforce by providing a long-term investment in the knowledge and skills of future workers.

The post-Fordist economy from the early 1970s was marked by the replacement of unionized industrial work with low-paying, low-skill, and deunionized service work, the suppression of real wages accompanying the expansion of women and immigrants into the workforce, the advent of computer automation and steady increases in productivity, increasing consumer debt, an individualized sense of economic responsibility, and the whittling away of the safety net. With the departure of industrial production to nations with cheap labor, the shift to the post-industrial service economy, and the expansion of neoliberal ideology, public schools are seen by capitalists as playing a new role in contributing to the wealth of the owners of industry. By the early 1980s an ideological push had begun in which educational "improvement" was framed as responsible for global economic competition and individual upward mobility within the capitalist economy. The neoliberal restructuring picked up speed in education in the 1990s with the push by the political right for privatizing the public schools, reimagining public schooling as a private industry, and installing the framing assumptions of corporate culture into the public system. The possibilities for profit through public schooling expanded from the Fordist era in which the public subsidized private industry to create workers educated to take their place in the economy.

By the late 1990s business discovered public education as a roughly $600 billion a year sector to privatize. There are strong financial incentives for corporations and rich investors to attempt to seize one of the few remaining public sectors. As well, the standardized testing push of the 2000s was interwoven with the financial interests of test makers and textbook publishers, curriculum producers, and contracting companies including technology firms. With neoliberal restructuring, short-term profit can be made by treating students as commodities, as public schools are subject to contracting and privatization. Working-class and poor schools in urban and rural areas are targeted by for-profit school management by educational management organizations (EMOs) and special educational service remediation schemes (SES), test contracting, and database tracking contracts (Saltman, 2012). The charter school and "turnaround" movement is playing a central role in closing unionized public schools and opening de-unionized schools ready for contracting. The for-profit management companies cannot get a foot in the door in the well-funded public schools in rich suburbs that often spend three times the amount spent in urban districts. After all, why would a rich district spending $25,000 per pupil accept the model of a for-profit management company that spends about $7,000 per pupil while being given $7,800 per pupil by the urban district contracting it? Urban school districts have a long legacy of shortchanging working-class and poor citizens when it comes to education. Yet now predominantly African American and Latino urban poor students and rural White poor students are being targeted by business to capture public tax dollars. A crucial strategic aspect of the charter school movement is not just privatization but also the de-unionization of schools that removes organized opposition to the decreased pay and worsened conditions facing teachers. Chartering is an interim strategy of the privatization movement. The broad strategy is to replace universal public schooling with a system of contracting organized by the principle of "churn" or "creative destruction" (Saltman, 2012). This involves the remaking of the historical two-tiered system into a new two-tiered system that is privatized at the bottom. The implications include worsened racial segregation, worse funding inequalities, and the expansion of rigid and repressive pedagogies for working-class and poor racial and ethnic minorities. The inevitable result of this will not be the official rhetoric of more competition resulting in higher quality but rather more skimming out of public resources for investors and the consolidation of the for-profit management industry. Indeed the large for-profit school management sector is consolidating (Miron et al., 2011), and the model for the education industry is the corporate media sector which has seen consolidation to just seven massive companies. Edison Learning creator Chris Whittle predicts as much, and sees the trend of for-profit education companies consolidating going global (Whittle, 2009). Right-wing think tanks are now taking this a step further and want to see public schooling dis-bundled with every part of the school and school day potentially for sale—that is, contracted out to for-profit contractors.

The standardization of knowledge through standardized testing and standardization of curriculum not only expands anti-intellectual and anti-critical positivism—that is, a prohibition on thinking.[2] It also lends itself to the financial pursuits of fiscal conservatives or neoliberals who want to treat knowledge as an industrial commodity and use private sector methods for "delivery." Such standardization makes cultural conservative common core approaches to knowledge especially attractive to fiscal conservatives as they can be mass produced (this convergence is neatly exemplified by K12, Inc., which is a for-profit online charter and homeschool company with a culturally conservative curriculum) (Apple, 2001). As Bertell Ollmann contends, heavy emphasis on standardized testing in the past 15 years can be understood as a way of instilling in students a number of implicit values designed to further the interests of the owners of businesses (Ollmann, 2002). The emphasis on student discipline and docility through the enforcement of standardized regimes reveals what Ollmann calls the real lessons of testing: obeying authority, understanding truth to reside with those in power, and preparation for work speedups. Such discipline becomes crucial in the context of a steadily worsening economy in the United States as factories and unionized and secure jobs have been shipped overseas in the past few decades under the economic dictates of neoliberal globalization—particularly public sector privatization, trade liberalization, and deregulation of state controls over capital and labor.

It is crucial today to debunk the myth that more schooling or reformed schooling equates to economic equality or poverty eradication. The making of poverty is a function of capitalist accumulation and it is only ameliorated within capitalism through authoritative action designed to reduce it. The myth of improving schooling for better competition in the global economy simply aims to redistribute poverty to the global south and the "losers" of the economic race to the bottom for cheap deregulated labor. Moreover the current neoliberal restructuring of public education through privatization and corporate culture expands the poverty-producing effects of capitalism by exacerbating wealth-based unequal access. Changes to schooling can challenge poverty but not in the ways that have become common sense among liberals and conservatives. Material investments in working-class and poor schools coordinated with desegregation efforts would raise the material standards of living for children in those schools. The United States could follow the rest of the industrialized world and equalize per pupil funding on a federal basis. Challenging poverty requires the expansion of critical pedagogies that link knowledge to power and develop in students collective forms of political agency such that students can theorize and act on the institutional and structural forces that produce poverty and other forms of oppression.[3] That is, schools can foster the knowledge, tastes, and dispositions for cultural, political, and economic democracy rather than the knowledge, tastes, and dispositions for submission to the hierarchical and authoritarian regimes of capital accumulation. However, the democratization of schools and their cultures through critical educational practices, while necessary, must be joined with social movements outside of schools to democratize the economy, political system, and culture.

Notes

1 For a crucial discussion of the limitations of the correspondence principles and reproduction theories, see Henry Giroux's *Theory and Resistance in Education* (1983). While I agree with Giroux about these theoretical limitations for theorizing agency and mediation, reproduction theory needs to be addressed anew for its insights as to the relationships between education and labor in a neoliberal context characterized by a new form of surplus value—that is, profit taking in which students are commodified and public schooling is pillaged for short-term profit rather than used for long-term making of a disciplined labor force.
2 I elaborate on what I call the New Market Positivism—that is, the way that positivism has been reinvigorated in post-Fordist reproduction in the neoliberal context—in Chapter 3, "White Collar, Red Tape," of Saltman (2012).
3 See the abundant writings of Henry Giroux on this such as *On Critical Pedagogy* (2010).

References

Althusser, Louis. (1994 (original 1970)) "Ideology and Ideological State Apparatuses (Notes Towards an Investigation)," pp. 100–140 in *Mapping Ideology*, Slavoj Zizek (ed.). New York: Verso.

Apple, Michael. (2001) *Educating the Right Way*. New York: Routledge.

Bourdieu, Pierre. (1973) "Cultural Reproduction and Social Reproduction," pp. 71–112 in *Knowledge, Education, and Cultural Change*, Richard Brown (ed.). London: Tavistock.

Bourdieu, Pierre. (1986) "The Forms of Capital," pp. 46–58 in *Handbook for Theory and Research for the Sociology of Education*, J. Richardson (ed.) and Richard Nice (trans.). New York: Greenwood.

Bowles, Samuel and Herbert Gintis. (2010) *Schooling in Capitalist America*. Chicago: Haymarket Books.

Darling-Hammond, Linda. (2010) *The Flat World and Education*. New York: Teachers College Press.

Giroux, Henry. (1983) *Theory and Resistance in Education*. Westport: Bergin and Garvey.

Giroux, Henry. (2010) *On Critical Pedagogy*. New York: Continuum.

Hanushek, Erik and Ludger Woessmann. (2010) "Education and Economic Growth," pp. 60–69 in *Economics of Education*, Dominic J. Brewer and Patrick J. McEwen (eds). Amsterdam: Elsevier.

Miron, Gary, Jessica Urschel, Mayra A. Yat Aguilar, and Breanna Dailey. (2011) *Profiles of For Profit and Non Profit Educational Management Organizations*, Thirteenth Annual Report 2010–2011, National Education Policy Center. Available online at http://nepc.colorado.edu/publication/EMO-profiles-10-11. Accessed August 15, 2013.

Ollmann, Bertell. (2002) "Why So Many Exams? A Marxist Response," *Z Magazine* 15 (October 2002). Available online at http://www.nyu.edu/projects/ollman/docs/why_exams.php. Accessed August 15, 2013.

Saltman, Kenneth J. (2012) *The Failure of Corporate School Reform*. Boulder: Paradigm Publishers.

Whittle, Christopher. (2009) "The Rise of Global Schooling." Talk at the American Enterprise Institute Conference *More Than Just Schools: Rethinking the Demand for Educational Entrepreneurship*, December 7, 2009. Available online at http://www.aei.org/event/100146. Accessed August 15, 2013.

Transformation of the welfare state

Cash transfers, housing, nutrition, and health

SECTION II

Transformation of the welfare state

Cash transfers, housing, nutrition and health

INTRODUCTION

María Vidal de Haymes, Erin Malcolm and Celeste Sánchez

In the opening chapter of Section II, entitled "Neoliberal Globalization: Social Welfare Policy and Institutions," Michael Holosko and John Barner argue that neoliberal globalization has been the guiding paradigm for the U.S. social welfare regime for the last 15 years. This paradigm is characterized by a supraterritorial organization of social relations and transactions across political and geographical regions and networks that are best handled by privatized and deregulated markets, decentralized governance, global capitalism, and elite global networks. Holosko and Barner conclude that neoliberal globalization presents a turn away from the traditional model of state-supported interventions towards market-based interventions focused on efficiency and material welfare, often at the expense of cultural, ecological, economic, political, and social benefits. This turn, they continue, is incongruent with the customary ethical stance advocated by social welfare professionals because it has contributed to human insecurity, income inequality, poverty, and precarious labor.

Holosko and Barner identify neoliberal globalization as a catalyst for policies such as the Personal Responsibility and Work Opportunity Reconciliation Act of 1996 (PRWORA), which enacted the Temporary Assistance for Needy Families (TANF) program. Richard Caputo's contribution to this section (Chapter 22) examines the political impacts and effects of PRWORA on low-income women's employment, and includes a historical background and description of political trends. PRWORA was designed to establish requirements for those enrolled in welfare programs to influence labor force participation. He compares the TANF program created under Title I of the Act with the program that it replaced, Aid to Families with Dependent Children (AFDC). TANF implemented strict requirements for both recipients and states. Under the new program, recipients are required to meet specific eligibility guidelines, and punishments and rewards are administered on the basis of the achievement of policy goals. Caputo outlines these requirements with an emphasis on how PRWORA contributed to the increase of low-wage workers and massive decreases in welfare caseloads in the years immediately following its enactment, only to rise again in 2008 with the U.S. economic crisis.

In "Anti-Poverty Policies and the Structure of Inequality" (Chapter 23) Eiko Strader and Joya Misra draw linkages between U.S. social policies, neoliberal ideology, and the structure of inequality. In their analysis of six major federal means-tested programs, they argue that a general concern that cash-transfer programs promote dependency has led to policies that focus on individual self-sufficiency and labor force participation. They note that the enactment of

PRWORA in 1996 sparked a sharp decline in direct cash-transfer programs by restricting the eligibility criteria to limit recipients to those experiencing deep poverty. Supplemental Security Income (SSI) on the other hand saw a steady increase in recipients during this time. Strader and Misra say that SSI is based on outdated criteria; therefore many recipients are still living below the poverty threshold.

Because of the neoliberal ideology that fuels the country, the United States leans away from cash benefit programs such as TANF and SSI, and puts greater emphasis on programs such as Medicaid, the Supplemental Nutrition Assistance Program (SNAP), and Earned Income Tax Credit (EITC), regardless of the fact that the research on in-kind benefit programming has been "inconclusive, contradictory, and mixed at best." While a few of these programs in some cases assist in alleviating the depth of poverty, according to the authors, they create more barriers for extra-vulnerable populations such as lawful immigrants; none are sufficient to pull people out of poverty completely; and concurrently they do not form an effective safety net. Noting that the United States has one of the highest rates of inequality among wealthy nations, Strader and Misra discuss how federal poverty programs contribute to this growing gap. They conclude that the United States should allocate more funding for social programs and offer more universal programs to shore up economic inequality.

The other chapters in this section support these observations and claims as they review the impact of neoliberal globalization on housing, health, and nutrition programs. Several of the chapters in this section highlight the transformation of housing support programs over the last two decades, which has been marked by a dramatic move from the provision of public housing to various private market housing schemes. In "Mixed-Income Communities and Poverty Amelioration" (Chapter 24), James Fraser and Deirdre Oakley argue that residential concentration of poverty increased over the last decade. The high-poverty neighborhoods are characterized by heightened isolation and racial segregation, and are disproportionately occupied by African Americans due to the mass suburbanization of whites and racial zoning codes.

Fraser and Oakley argue that the negative portrayal of these communities in the media contributed to the creation of poverty de-concentration housing policies, such as the Department of Housing and Urban Development (HUD) Reform Act of 1989, which created the National Commission on Severely Distressed Public Housing. This Commission identified and assessed problems in severely distressed public housing developments and created the Homeownership Opportunities for People Everywhere (HOPE VI) program in 1993. The initial aim of the program was not neighborhood transformation, but rather intervention in the most severely distressed public housing developments. However, programmatic changes expanded the sites qualified for the funds to include most public housing. While some claim that the HOPE VI program was a success, Fraser and Oakley argue that the poverty de-concentration goal was not achieved; rather it resulted in the displacement of public housing residents to private sector housing in other highly distressed neighborhoods. Furthermore, they argue that the sense of community decreased in mixed-income areas due to a loss of commonality and that the goals of the program are contradictory in that they allow for more discrimination and contributed to further displacement of the poor.

In "Countering Urban Poverty Concentration in the United States: The People versus Place Debate in Housing Policy" (Chapter 25), Anupama Jacob discusses shifts in federal housing policy during the late 1960s and 1970s that were premised on the belief that increasing the socio-economic diversity of neighborhoods would lead to a decrease in the social problems associated with concentrated poverty. She identifies people-based and place-based policy approaches to de-concentrating residential poverty, reflected in the HUD Housing Choice Voucher Program and Mixed-Income Housing Development programs respectively. While distinct, both of these approaches reflect the neoliberal elements of increased reliance on market-based programs.

The housing voucher approach provides rent subsidies to low-income families for units that fulfill minimum-quality criteria set forth by HUD. After an initial success of the program in Chicago, HUD launched the Moving to Opportunity (MTO) social experiment in 1993 to study the long-term (10 to 15 years) effects of the program on participants, finding improved social networks, gender differences in crime, better mental health, and increased perceptions of safety overall, but no significant changes in employment or income-related networks, as well as no significant differences in the educational outcomes for children. The second approach, the mixed-income housing development approach, aimed to decrease the social isolation of the urban poor by residentially integrating families with varying income levels. Jacob notes that this is a strategy that has grown in popularity since the mid-1990s, and is reflected in HUD programs such as HOPE VI, but has not yielded improvements in social networks, employment opportunities, or educational benefits for program participants.

Monique Johnson also focuses on housing policy aimed at residential poverty de-concentration. In "Poverty De-Concentration Priorities in Low-Income Housing Tax Credit Allocation Policy: A Content Analysis of Qualified Allocation Plans" (Chapter 27), Johnson examines the federal Low-Income Housing Tax Credit (LIHTC) initiated in 1996. This neoliberal market-based policy encouraged private sector provision of low-income housing through tax credit incentives for private investors to stimulate affordable housing production. Johnson provides evidence to support her claim that, prior to the initiation of LIHTC, most public and subsidized housing was constructed by the federal government through HUD. In a multi-state longitudinal analysis, Johnson examines how states have prioritized poverty de-concentration within their plan design and finds mixed results of the program's effectiveness in meeting this goal as implemented from 2000 to 2010. Johnson concludes with a summary of policy implications and recommendations to enhance the strategic outcomes of locational equity within the program.

In "Privatizing the Housing Safety Net: HOPE VI and the Transformation of Public Housing in the United States" (Chapter 26), Kimberly Skobba, Deirdre Oakley, and Dwanda Farmer provide an overview of federal housing policies from the 1930s to the contemporary period. In this overview, they examine how various policies have contributed to racial and class-level segregation, white flight, and mass suburbanization, leaving public housing as the only option left for the urban poor. They trace how federal policies have shifted over time to market-based housing and voucher programs which have generated an ever-shrinking pool of affordable housing options for the poor.

Theorizing that the motivations of present-day public housing programs have more to do with stimulating the economy than with altruism, Skobba, Oakley, and Farmer argue that current federal housing policies benefit higher-income residents and the private real estate industry rather than the poor populations which they initially intended to serve. They argue that contemporary housing initiatives such as HOPE VI have effectively dismantled public housing and displaced residents, privatized low-income housing options, and generally weakened the housing safety net. They conclude with a case study of public housing in Atlanta, which exemplifies the neoliberal shift in public housing described by these authors.

In "Neo-Liberalism and Private Emergency Food Networks" (Chapter 28), Deborah Harris and Jamilatu Zakari examine the growth of private emergency food networks as a result of the neoliberal turn in social services in the United States. They discuss the emergence of food banks and pantries as a response to the retrenchment of social welfare and food assistance programs available to low-income individuals and families. These private emergency networks aim to address hunger and food insecurity through local forms of private assistance that shore up the gap created by the government divestiture in social welfare programs. In addition, the authors discuss the ideological and discursive practices of neoliberalism that privilege notions of individualism and personal responsibility at the expense of the recognition of structural social, economic, and spatial inequality. The authors argue that this maneuver stigmatizes the poor, leaving them less likely to advocate for their rights. In response, they conclude that an approach that positions food as a human right should be promoted to strengthen communities and empower individuals who experience food insecurity.

Similarly, in "Examining Food Security Among Children in Households Participating in the Supplemental Nutrition Assistance Program (SNAP): Implications for Human Rights" (Chapter 29), Margaret Lombe and colleagues call for a human rights approach, rather than a neoliberal one, to food insecurity. Building on previous research, these authors analyze data from the Current Population Survey Food Security Supplement for 2010 to examine the effects of SNAP participation and the moderating effects of informal support, both community non-food support and food assistance, on food security among children in vulnerable households. The study suggests that race/ethnicity, immigrant status, and household composition are related to child food insecurity. Informal food assistance was negatively associated with child food security, while an interaction effect between household food security and informal food assistance was indicated.

Lombe and her co-authors conclude with a call to a rights-based perspective to address the persistence of child hunger in the United States. This perspective, informed by the UN Declaration of Human Rights and the Convention on the Rights of the Child, is offered as an alternative to the existing neoliberal framework that advances a program of reductions in state mediations and market-driven interventions to hunger and food insecurity. The adoption of such a perspective would shift from a paradigm of food security as a charity provision to a right, a move that would actively seek to ensure that all children are guaranteed adequate nutrition.

Finally, in "The Influence of a Neoliberal World View on Health Care Policy" (Chapter 30), John Orwat, Michael Dentato, and Michael Lloyd argue that there is a national consensus that rising health care costs, without increases in quality and access, should be addressed through policy reforms, but note that there is a chasm in thinking regarding the type of reforms that should be pursued. Proponents of neoliberal reforms, which have greatly influenced recent policy directions, posit that government intervention is inefficient and advocate for private market solutions that include decentralization, de-regulation, privatization of public health systems and public insurance (e.g., Medicare Advantage and the prescription drug benefit), use of tax breaks to reduce the "cost" of insurance and health services, increased cost sharing with patients, and promotion of individual decision making. The authors argue that recent health care policy changes have favored such private market-based programs that treat health care as a commodity. They conclude that market-based policies have resulted in the corporate consolidation of small family practices, the "mechanizing" of physician and nursing practice, a focus on profit over the provision of health care services, and reductions in public input into decision-making regarding resource allocation. They close with a call for research that addresses the impact of such policies on the most vulnerable, including those living in poverty.

21

NEOLIBERAL GLOBALIZATION

Social welfare policy and institutions

Michael J. Holosko and John R. Barner

This chapter presents an overview of neoliberal globalization and its impact on employment-based social welfare policies in the United States. We conclude by highlighting how this paradigm has challenged the ability for social welfare workers to provide ethical practice to their clients within this rather unjust economic reality.

Over the past 40 years, social welfare networks and institutions have become instrumental players in the move toward globalization, reaching beyond national borders to provide the material means to offer the promise of sustainable change for the impoverished around the globe. In light of the current downturn in the global economy and efforts at "economic recovery" posed by major Western nations, social welfare professionals (including social workers, public and private welfare advocates, and policy analysts) who combat poverty are seeing the development of programs that are no longer consistent with their prior commitments to welfare state entitlements, and necessitate a response that requires a significant shift away from a state-centric, or commercially supported (i.e., philanthropic), perspective of social welfare provision.

Neoliberalism, globalization, and social welfare

Harvey (2006) defined neoliberalism as a "theory of political economic practices which proposes that human well-being can best be advanced by the maximization of entrepreneurial freedoms within an institutional framework characterized by private property rights, individual liberty, free markets and free trade" (p. 145). The salient aspects of this definition highlight both political and economic social welfare realities by clearly defining a neoliberal conception of the state which can facilitate social welfare, but cannot control it outright, since it is viewed as radically outside of both social networks and economic markets. However, the definition is still dependent upon the state as arbiter of whether personal welfare and the freedom to pursue well-being are effectively maximized.

Over 25 years ago, neoliberalism as a term in the critical social sciences had already usurped the labels referring to specific political initiatives (i.e., Thatcherism, Reaganomics, etc.), and was more widely used than its counterparts such as: economic rationalism, monetarism, neo-conservatism, managerialism, and contractualization (Hindess, 1997). Given that it relates to the

239

post-welfare states of citizenship regimes, it may be used as a term to describe welfare policy, ideology, or governmentality (Larner, 2000).

Turning to the concept of globalization, Giddens (1990) defined it as the "intensification of worldwide social relations which link distant localities in such a way that local happenings are shaped by events occurring many miles away and vice versa" (p. 64). Held et al. (1999) quantified it as a "process [or set of processes] which embodies a transformation in the spatial organization of social relations and transactions—assessed in terms of their extensity, intensity, velocity and impact—generating transcontinental or inter-regional flows and networks of activity" (p. 16). The neoliberal paradigm elides these two definitions together, in terms of the governance and management of social relations and economics, through processes by which markets monetize those social relations. This has produced a neoliberal perspective that takes a distinctive nation-state market-based approach to the problem of poverty.

As Schram (2008) noted, this "re-inscribes people's subordination by having them included as people who had to accept low-paying jobs. [People] being included in the labor market in this way reinforces the idea that some people are more deserving than others" (p. 2). The shift to a market-supported model of passive governance is reflected by a "deserving" social infrastructure, rendering the ability for nation-state governments to exercise control or oversight of monies to a uniform social welfare system increasingly unstable, particularly in times of economic crises and recovery (Geddes, 2005; Harvey, 2006; Lightman et al., 2008; Lyons, 2006). Thus, the growth and development of a "global economy" can be seen as both an engine driving neoliberal economic policy, and as a shelter from government intervention.

Neoliberal globalization and social welfare policy

Although the concepts of neoliberalism and globalization were presented separately with social welfare policy above, in the past 15 or so years they have become inextricably braided. In short, globalization is the reigning socio-historical reconfiguration of social space, and neoliberalism is a policy approach to it. The current term used to connote their interrelationship is neoliberal globalization. This is based on the following core tenets as posited by Scholte (2005):

1. Globalization is a transformation of social space that occurs with the spread of transplanetary—in contemporary times often also supraterritorial—connections between people.
2. Neoliberalism prescribes that globalization is an economic process that should be managed by markets through privatization, liberalization, and deregulation.
3. Neoliberalism has in various cases promoted gains in efficiency and material welfare but it has also tended to neglect other important issues and to produce or exacerbate a number of cultural, ecological, economic, political, and social harms.
4. Neoliberal policies have been generated by a powerful combination of forces characterized by decentered governance, supraterritorial capitalism, modern economic science, and global elite networks. (p. 24)

However, it appears that the impact and limitations of neoliberal globalization in the areas of social welfare policy have had more negative consequences than positive ones. As a policy framework, it has been shown to have had serious and inherent flaws that have impacted: human security (Standing, 1999), social justice (World Bank, 2001:3), income inequality (Milanovic, 1999, 2001), poverty (Boote and Thugge, 1997; Child Poverty, 2004; Jolly, 1995; World Bank, 2001), and employment (Simai, 1995; Wood, 1994).

U.S. "workfare" policy

Under the Clinton (1993–2001) and Bush (2001–2009) administrations, a growth of neoliberal globalization in public policy and the reliance on temporary, "precarious" labor emerged as a fundamental change in the material conditions of modern work. Nationally, we noted a connection between material (large increases in GDP) and temporal aspects, conditioned by money as *an economy of time*, which culminated in exchange relationships that continually undermined the material conditions of the individual, thus compromising and de-personalizing the individual. Moreover, during this time the focus in the United States rapidly turned to *immaterial labor*, with informational, educational, and cultural productions becoming divorced from their producers—instantaneously caught up and disseminated into the broader media cycle (Wacquant, 2001). Bourdieu (1998, 2001) recognized in the United States the dual relationship of material conditions to aspects of individual identity and well-being, going so far as to note that, within a precarious neoliberal globalized economy, distinctions between classes and societal roles flounder.

In the United States, the material paradox of workforce precariousness was no more evident than in the current instrument for state-employed social welfare professionals to provide aid and assistance to the low-income unemployed, established by the *Personal Responsibility and Work Opportunity Reconciliation Act of 1996* (*PRWORA*), frequently called "welfare reform," or "workfare." In establishing the *Temporary Assistance for Needy Families* (*TANF*) program, the *PRWORA* was conceived as a block grant fund to provide supplementary income for families on a strictly time-limited (i.e., a 5-year cap on lifetime assistance) and means-tested basis, linked primarily to employment needs.

TANF quickly became the centerpiece of the "welfare-to-work" philosophy toward social welfare. The *1996 Act* listed its stated objectives as promoting care for children in the parental home, preventing out-of-wedlock pregnancy, and promoting marriage as "an essential institution of a successful society," which, by creating employable two-parent families, works in the best interest of children (*PRWORA* 1996, P.L. 104–193, 110 Stat. 2110, Sec. 101). In so doing, the Act also set in place several major barriers to employability and benefits, denying aid based on marital, residential, and criminal status, while imposing strict eligibility guidelines on the states with regard to distribution of grant funding.

States required *TANF* recipients to work after two years or risk the loss of their funding. Also, it was up to states to fund any necessary subsidized job training, educational, or childcare programs. While initially heralded a success, many families were dropped by the program for not complying with the rules, or for exceeding the time limits for acquiring employment because of layoffs or the termination of temporary labor. Moreover, social welfare professionals were now in the position of managing "drop-offs" from *TANF* rosters, with states ill-prepared, especially in times of economic recovery, to provide supplementary assistance (Schram et al., 2008). The decade since the initial drops in child poverty rates, unemployment, and welfare eligibility has seen a steady rise in the new millennium, with additional rises in poverty, income inequality, the divorce-rate, and out-of-home foster care placements, all of which contradict the *1996 Act*'s mandate (Cancian et al., 2005; Danielson and Klerman, 2008; Shaefer and Ybarra, 2012).

In the decade following the passage of *PRWORA* and the institution and implementation of *TANF*, a significant criticism of the policy and its implementation has focused on the barriers to employability that existed for *TANF* recipients. As Cancian and colleagues (2005) stated in their review, "many *TANF* recipients now have more barriers to employment than non-recipients; more physical and mental health problems, lower levels of education, less work experience, more children, exposure to domestic violence, and limited access to transportation" (p. 200). There has also been significant difficulty in researching the impact these barriers have had on whether or not families qualified for *TANF* assistance and what impact this has had on the perceived successes or failures of welfare reform in America. Studies have focused on the experiences of underserved or "invisible" populations, and have questioned the effectiveness of the *TANF* in addressing and providing adequately, through screening, assessment, and treatment protocols, for the needs of these specific populations (Dunlap et al., 2003; Morgenstern et al., 2006; Pollack and Reuter, 2006; Wells and Shafran, 2005). Unemployment, underemployment, exclusion of impoverished or immigrant groups, and a nation-state-sanctioned sovereignty of private enterprise at the expense of its citizens are just a few of the specified consequences of providing for the unemployed under the current "workfare" system. In sum, the institutional perspective indicates the adoption of a social welfare program that assumes employment as a condition of benefit receipt.

As Table 21.1 illustrates, this has led to high increases in GDP in the United States, with sporadic rises in unemployment rates, and significant cuts in social welfare institutional budgets seen throughout the Bush Administration (U.S. Bureau of Labor Statistics, 2009). As the table shows, despite the 5-year increase in GDP and social welfare expenditures, the actual per capita percentage spent on social welfare decreased over this same time period. The latter contextual perspective of *TANF* reveals that the fundamental gap between market-based initiatives and employment-based social welfare interventions has created difficult situations for social welfare professionals who have no recourse but to provide services on a stricter needs-based criterion (Cancian et al., 2005), as well as "drop-offs" or rises in welfare ineligibility, without any recourse to supplementary services. This has necessitated additional spending related to unemployment and social welfare interventions as part of the most recent economic recovery stimulus legislation proposed by President Obama in 2009 and subsequently extended in 2012.

Table 21.1 Social welfare expenditures as percentage of U.S. gross domestic product, 2003–2007*

Fiscal year	Gross domestic product (GDP) (in trillions of U.S. dollars)	Social welfare expenditure (in billions of U.S. dollars)	Percent of GDP	Change from previous year
2003	10.4	249.5	2.24	−.05%
2004	10.8	244.3	2.06	−.18%
2005	11.1	252.2	2.00	−.06%
2006	11.4	254.2	1.90	−.10%
2007	11.6	262.1	1.87	−.03%

*Sources: Gross Domestic Product: The World Bank, http://data.worldbank.org/indicator/NY.GDP. MKTP.CD; Social Welfare Expenditures and Percentage of GDP: http://www.usfederalbudget.us.

The faces of poverty meet the institutions of welfare

Given the above neoliberal globalization reality which has significantly impacted social welfare policy, we felt compelled to exemplify more concretely how social welfare policies are meted out at the micro, mezzo, and macro levels in America. Table 21.2 shows how the faces of poverty in America meet the institutions of social welfare. The table presents four levels of impact on a continuum which has transformed from previous social-liberal paradigms into neoliberal globalization ones. We will briefly discuss each of these, highlighting the essence of where the proverbial "rubber meets the road"—or "where the client walks in to a welfare agency"; more specifically, social worker–client interactions—in an effort to "put a face" to the consequences of current welfare policy at the levels outlined in Table 21.2.

Individual: The ubiquitous worldwide trend of more and more people needing more and more welfare services, with less per capita spending on social welfare initiatives, escalates on a daily basis (Holosko, 2000). This notion transcends politics, economies, policies, and governments all over the world. The previous social-liberal paradigm was dominated by a "people-changing/people-sustaining" orientation, and the chief concern of social welfare workers was assisting clients in adjusting to living in poverty. Neoliberal globalization has de-personalized individuals and their needs into requiring more stringent criteria to fit the eligibility status for care. Thus, our welfare institutions are fiscally rewarded for seeing more and more people (people processing) for shorter periods of time—to receive more funds. This has had the rather deleterious effects of promoting the rhetoric of prevention, in that if people do not receive services, agencies do not receive funding (Holosko et al., 1998). Second, fitting poor people into narrow eligibility slots allows a shift in client–worker relationships from the focus of adjusting to poverty, to one of just being poor. In this paradigm, the poor are relegated, categorized, and ascribed a variety of judgmental labels to their stigmatization, e.g., "deserving poor," "undeserving poor," "rebellious poor," "entitled poor," "criminal poor," "economy-draining poor," etc.

Organizational: A main organizational area exemplifying the impact of neoliberal globalization is privatization. In countries with no national health and/or social welfare insurance, people with money pay fees for services, and those with no money go without services. For those who have more money, privatization opens up options both within their own country and in other countries—to receive timelier, specialized, or better-quality care. In countries with national health insurance (e.g., the United Kingdom, Canada, Australia), the "privatization creep" has invasively infringed on national policy and has supplemented more and more of the public system (Forbes and Tsang, 2012).

Table 21.2 Comparison of key tenets of social liberal and neoliberal paradigms

Levels of impact	Traditional social-liberal paradigm	Neoliberal globalization paradigm
Individual	"People changing/people sustaining"	"People processing"
Organizational	Organizational robustness and proliferation	Privatization and "devolution revolution"
National	Bureaucratization	Corporatization
International	Collaborative and interconnected	Complex interconnectedness

In Canada, for example, the universal Medicare system launched in 1967 ensures that all citizens have access to good-quality health care across the country. However, "universal care" is not "universal" across the provinces. Drug insurance coverage, home care, dental care, and eye care vary considerably across the country, as the federal government subsidizes provinces for the necessary health care specified in the *Canada Health Act* (Department of Justice, 1985), and such disbursements are based on provincial population differences. In many of the wealthier provinces (e.g., British Columbia, Ontario, Alberta, and Quebec) private clinics are offered for those willing to pay for out-of-pocket expenses to avoid lengthy public system waiting times (Forbes and Tsang, 2012). In addition, those citizens having better health and welfare pension plans from employment tend to have access to better-quality services with higher co-payments within the two-tiered system. In terms of worker–client interactions, most Canadians resent the insidious "privatization creep" and feel that their citizenship birthright has been trodden upon. Further, more bureaucracy, regulation, and eligibility criteria driven by for-profit motives have spawned a burgeoning "health care paperwork" cottage industry of its own. For instance, Skowronski (2009) noted that:

> Prior to the introduction of market elements [from 2002 to 2008] into the UK's health care system, administrative costs in the National Health Services averaged around 4% of the budget. Now, the cost of paperwork and record keeping is between 12% and 15% within the "reformed" health system.
>
> (p. 1)

The second feature related to privatization is the "devolution revolution" (Dunlap, 2009). That is, national services have devolved to state services, which have devolved to local services. Thus, the "YTI-YTO" syndrome ("You Touch It—You Own It") has gained considerable traction. Nation-state governments have pushed the responsibility for financing, administration, accountability, and policy down to their local "communities of care," where higher levels of accountability for health and social services have become the province of local community organizations (Dunlap, 2009; Holosko et al., 2009). Many countries, including Canada, Germany, India, Spain, Sweden, Switzerland, the United Kingdom, and the United States, to name but a few, have been content to devolve health and social services without figuring out how it really translates at local levels (Holosko, 2000; Rodden, 2002). Thus, the community one resides in determines the care offered to their citizens. So, if an individual needs services in their community, and there are no services, they relocate to the community in their country that has the services they need. Our so-called "communities of care," then, have now evolved to "communities with care." Such devolution has faced other challenges, namely: financing vs. authority/accountability, discretion and decision-making, evaluation complexities, developing informal care networks to offset limited formal services, and voluntary vs. mandatory collaboration (Holosko et al., 2009).

In regard to client–worker implications: (a) clients migrate to where they can find partial or full services for their needs, depending on service availability and eligibility; (b) informal networks of care have popped up as viable avenues of service otherwise not provided by formal care arrangements; (c) care provision has shifted more to individual responsibility; and (d) client self-determination and autonomy have taken a back seat to seeking and obtaining those care arrangements that clients may avail themselves of, while worker advocacy for clients is directed to seeking and networking with available care arrangements.

National: As seen within a country's social welfare organizational framework, nations have responded to the influx of neoliberal globalization through reform efforts and shifts in both infrastructure and governance. As Haque (2000) noted:

Under this new global approach based on neoliberal reforms, public governance has undergone significant changes in terms of its objectives, norms, structures, roles, and service recipients. These contemporary changes in governance—toward efficiency, outcome, competition, value-for-money, catalytic role, autonomy, partnership, and customer orientation—have critical implications for its public accountability.

(p. 600)

From the perspective of client–worker relationships within a changing infrastructural and policy-level national paradigm, the mode of service provision radically changes, as Noordegraaf and Schinkel (2011) noted, from the traditional bureaucratic conception of professional assistance to a conception of corporate management and oversight. Within the new paradigm, as long as service quotas are being met, the quality, availability, or accessibility of that service does not factor into the definition of "well-managed" social welfare provision. Indeed, the privileging of efficiency of provision has been central to corporatization's reception as somehow more "evidence-based" and "better" than the traditional bureaucratic conception and its evolution within the United States as the guiding managerial model of service provision (Noordegraaf and Schinkel, 2011; Stoesz and Karger, 1991). As the paradigm persists and more corporatized infrastructural changes have been wedded to policies (e.g., *TANF*), the loudest critical voices have come not from workers in the United States or similar economies in Europe or North America, but rather smaller economies and nation-states looking to the United States for workable models of service provision.

International: Among the most salient literature from around the globe are instances in which, contrary to policy decisions made at the highest echelons of state and corporate power, individuals and professionals are united to find "bottom-up" or "counter-hegemonic" approaches to neoliberal reforms of social welfare provision throughout the world, from Westernized democracies like England, Denmark, and Australia to the poorest areas of the world, including Latin America and the Middle East (Lightman et al., 2008; Malmberg-Heimonen and Julkunen, 2006; McDonald and Reisch, 2008; Morgen and Gonzales, 2008; Munck, 2003; Ong, 2006; Sawpaul, 2007; Strier et al., 2008). This may mean a complete re-working of the conception of social welfare from a radically different perspective, one which functions outside of typical conceptions of a "modernized" economy and beyond the reach of institutional frameworks of social welfare provision altogether. As Ong (2006) suggested, neoliberal globalization can be viewed as presenting either seemingly insurmountable barriers to public welfare, or as a means of providing individuals committed to social justice with the tools to galvanize the public, creating "new kinds of borderless ... identifications enabled by technologies and forums of opinion making" (p. 63).

In examining the shifting nature of public opinions, and changes necessitated within the social work profession, Krumer-Nevo (2008) explored how social welfare practitioners are coming to terms with the societal impact of welfare reform in Israel:

Social workers did not agree with their clients' definition of needs, nor with their idea of the way to fulfill their needs, that is, to acquire money. In the social workers' view the people's need for money was supposed to be fulfilled through work. But work means giving up income security [i.e., welfare] benefits, and people were not willing to do this. Responding to the people's voice meant, therefore, accepting their need for money, and offering them assistance in acquiring money without giving up their benefits.

(p. 561)

From the perspective of client–worker relationships, the juxtaposition of both top-down policy directives and the bottom-up counter-narratives that critique the encroachment of the neoliberal paradigm have contributed to what Baldock (2011) termed the "complex inter-connectedness" within social welfare provision. Drawing from the work of sociologist Beck, Baldock (2011) outlined the "organized irresponsibility in which many leading social institutions, including private companies, large government bureaucracies, and the legal system, produce risks of harm or disadvantage against which individuals have little power to protect themselves" (p. 15; see also Beck, 1992). Clients, and the workers who serve them, may not, in many circumstances, understand the changes that occur as a result of adopting a globalized, neoliberal paradigm, or what circumstances necessitated them. Mobilization and organization around countering perceived negative impacts may require education on the policies and initiatives themselves, as well as adjustment to practices and a return to the traditional social-liberal conception of collaboration between worker and client, despite what the neoliberal paradigm considers as inefficiencies within the provision of service (Haque, 2008; Krumer-Nevo, 2008; Noordegraaf and Schinkel, 2011; Stoesz and Karger, 1991).

Concluding remarks

Contextually, neoliberal globalization has changed how social welfare professionals (e.g., social workers, union organizers, public and private welfare advocates, and policy analysts) provide services as well as delimiting eligibility to those they serve. This shift away from a traditional model of state-supported interventions to market-supported non-intervention has caused significant concern for scholars in terms of incongruence with the traditional ethical stance advocated by social welfare professionals (Ferguson and Lavalette, 2006; Midgley, 2007; Rotabi et al., 2007). This contradictory relationship between neoliberal globalization and the ethics of social welfare professionals can clearly be seen in the examples noted previously in this chapter. The real challenge facing social welfare professionals is to consider the influence of neoliberal globalization which declares that the existing traditional social policies of the welfare state long championed by social workers and other professionals are, in fact, doing more harm than good.

As Strier et al. (2008) noted, the need for social welfare professionals of all varieties, including clinicians, policy analysts, and community organizers, to unite in giving voice to those they are committed to serving is of the utmost importance; in particular, "when public discourse is based on stigmas that tag the poor as lazy and parasitic, there is great importance to collecting and presenting data that refute this tagging" (p. 506). For social welfare professionals to continue to support the philosophical foundations, the need to unite all of the aspects of its influence, to be mindful of the (social, political, and economic) context of the field, and to promote service provision outside of institutional constraints will do much to strengthen and maintain professional integrity against the pressures of neoliberalism in an increasingly globalized world. Given the potential these pressures have to resonate throughout the global economy, more research is needed to address *all facets* of this phenomenon—economic, social, cultural, and personal.

References

Baldock, J. (2011). Social policy, social welfare, and the welfare state. In J. Baldock, L. Mitton, N. Manning, and S. Vickerstaff (eds). *Social policy* (4th ed.). Oxford, UK: Oxford University Press.
Beck, U. (1992). *Risk society: Towards a new modernity*. London, UK: Sage.
Boote, A. R., and Thugge, K. (1997). Debt-relief for low-income countries: The HIPC initiative. Pamphlet Series No. 51. Washington, DC: IMF Reports.
Bourdieu, P. (1998). *Acts of resistance: Against the tyranny of the market* (R. Nice, trans.). New York: The New Press.
Bourdieu, P. (2001). *Firing back: Against the tyranny of the market 2* (L. Wacquant, trans.). New York: The New Press.

Cancian, M., Meyer, D., and Wu, C-F. (2005). After the revolution: Welfare patterns since TANF implementation. *Social Work Research*, 29(4), 210–212.

Child Poverty. (2004, June 17). We're united for change: Campaign against child poverty. *The Globe and Mail*, p. 3.

Danielson, C., and Klerman, J. A. (2008). Did welfare reform cause the caseload decline? *Social Service Review*, 82(4), 703–730.

Department of Justice. (1985). *Canada Health Act R.S.C., 1985, c. C-6.* Retrieved December 13, 2012, from http://laws-lois.justice.gc.ca/eng/acts/C-6/.

Dunlap, E., Golub, A., and Johnson, B. D. (2003). Lived experience of welfare reform in drug-using welfare-needy households in inner-city New York. *Journal of Sociology and Social Welfare*, 30(3), 39–58.

Dunlap, J. (2009). Social policy devolution: An historical review of Canada, the United Kingdom, and the United States (1834–1999). *Social Work in Public Health*, 24(3), 160–178.

Ferguson, I., and Lavalette, M. (2006). Globalization and social justice: Toward a social work of resistance. *International Social Work*, 49(3), 309–318.

Forbes, C., and Tsang, E. (2012). Healthcare in Canada: Privatization and how to contain it. *University of British Columbia Medical Journal*, 4(1), 4–5.

Geddes, M. (2005). Neoliberalism and local governance: Cross-national perspectives and speculations. *Policy Studies*, 26(3/4), 359–377.

Giddens, A. (1990). *The consequences of modernity.* Stanford, CA: Stanford University Press.

Haque, M. S. (2000). Significance of accountability under the new approach to public governance. *International Review of Administrative Sciences*, 66(4), 599–617.

Haque, M. S. (2008). Global rise of neoliberal state and its impact on citizenship: Experiences in developing nations. *Asian Journal of Social Science*, 36(1), 11–34.

Harvey, D. (2006). Neo-liberalism as creative destruction. *Geografiska Annaler*, 88(2), Series B,145–158.

Held, D., McGrew, A., Goldblatt, D., and Perraton, J. (1999). *Global transformations: Politics, economics and culture.* Cambridge: Polity Press.

Hindess, B. (1997). A society governed by contract? In G. Davis, B. Sullivan, and A. Yeatman (eds). *The new contractualism?* Melbourne, AU: Macmillan Publishing.

Holosko, M. (2000). The churches' response to welfare reform in America. In L. Nackerud and M. Robinson (eds). *Early implications of welfare reform in the Southeast.* Huntington, NY: Nova Sciences Publishers, Inc.

Holosko, M., Feit, M. D., and Bulcke, G. (1998). Health care prevention: Real or rhetoric? *Journal of Health and Social Policy*, 10(1), 101–104.

Holosko, M., Holosko, D. A., and Spencer, K. (2009). Social services in Sweden: An overview of policy issues, devolution and collaboration. *Social Work in Public Health*, 24(3), 210–235.

Jolly, R. (1995). *Remarks by the acting director of UNICEF.* Presented at the World Summit for Social Development, March 5–12, 1995, Copenhagen, Denmark. New York: United Nations Department of Economic and Social Affairs.

Krumer-Nevo, M. (2008). From noise to voice: How social work can benefit from the knowledge of people living in poverty. *International Social Work*, 51(4), 556–565.

Larner, W. (2000). Neo-liberalism: Policy, ideology, governmentality. *Studies in Political Economy*, Autumn, 63, 5–25.

Lightman, E., Mitchell, A., and Herd, D. (2008). Globalization, precarious work, and the food bank. *Journal of Sociology and Social Welfare*, 35(2), 9–28.

Lyons, K. (2006). Globalization and social work: International and local implications. *British Journal of Social Work*, 36(3), 365–380.

Malmberg-Heimonen, I., and Julkunen, I. (2006). Out of unemployment? A comparative analysis of the risks and opportunities longer-term unemployed immigrant youth face when entering the labour market. *Journal of Youth Studies*, 9(5), 575–592.

McDonald, C., and Reisch, M. (2008). Social work in the workfare regime: A comparison of the U.S. and Australia. *Journal of Sociology and Social Welfare*, 35(1), 43–74.

Midgley, J. (2007). Perspectives on globalization, social justice, and welfare. *Journal of Sociology and Social Welfare*, 34(2), 17–36.

Milanovic, B. (1999). *True world income distribution, 1988 and 1993: First calculations, based on household surveys alone.* World Bank Policy Research Working Paper No. 2244. Washington, DC: World Bank. Retrieved December 13, 2012, from http://www-wds.worldbank.org/external/default/WDSContentServer/IW3P/IB/1999/12/30/000094946_99121105392984/Rendered/PDF/multi_page.pdf.

Milanovic, B. (2001). *World income inequality in the second half of the 20th century*. Washington, DC: World Bank. Retrieved December 14, 2012, from http://info.worldbank.org/etools/docs/voddocs/89/177/Maksense.pdf.

Morgen, S., and Gonzales, L. (2008). Neoliberal American dream as daydream: Counter-hegemonic perspectives on welfare restructuring in the United States. *Critique of Anthropology*, 28(2), 219–236.

Morgenstern, J., Blanchard, K. A., McCrady, B. S., McVeigh, K. H., Morgan, T. J., and Pandina, R. J. (2006). Effectiveness of intensive case management for substance-dependent women receiving Temporary Assistance for Needy Families. *American Journal of Public Health*, 96(11), 2016–2023.

Munck, R. (2003). Neoliberalism, necessitarianism and alternatives in Latin America: There is no alternative? *Third World Quarterly*, 24(3), 495–511.

Noordegraaf, M., and Schinkel, W. (2011). Professional capital contested: A Bourdieusian analysis of conflicts between professionals and managers. *Comparative Sociology*, 10(1), 97–125.

Ong, A. (2006). *Neoliberalism as exception: Mutations in citizenship and sovereignty*. Durham, NC: Duke University Press.

Personal Responsibility and Work Opportunity Reconciliation Act of 1996, 42 U.S.C. § 1305 note. Retrieved December 13, 2012, from the Cornell University Law School Legal Information Institute Website: http://www.law.cornell.edu/uscode/.

Pollack, H. A., and Reuter, P. (2006). Welfare receipt and substance-abuse treatment among low-income mothers: The impact of welfare reform. *American Journal of Public Health*, 96 (11), 2025–2031.

Rodden, J. (2002). The dilemma of fiscal federalism: Grants and fiscal performance around the world. *American Journal of Political Science*, 46(3), 670–687.

Rotabi, K., Gammonley, D., Gamble, D., and Weil, M. (2007). Integrating globalization into the social work curriculum. *Journal of Sociology and Social Welfare*, 34(2), 165–185.

Sawpaul, V. (2007). Challenging East–West value dichotomies and essentialising discourse on culture and social work. *International Journal of Social Welfare*, 16(4), 398–407.

Scholte, J. A. (2005). *The sources of neoliberal globalization*. United Nations Research Institute for Social Development, Programme Paper No. 8, 6E. 05-02689. Geneva, Switzerland.

Schram, S. (2008, August). *Neoliberal poverty governance: U.S. welfare policy in an era of globalization*. Paper presented at "The New Poverty Agenda: Reshaping Policies in the 21st Century," Queen's University, International Institute on Social Policy, Kingston, Ontario.

Schram, S., Fording, R., and Soss, J. (2008). Neoliberal poverty governance: Race, place and the punitive turn in U.S. welfare policy. *Cambridge Journal on Regions, Economy and Society*, 1(1), 17–36.

Shaefer, H. L., and Ybarra, M. (2012). The welfare reforms of the 1990s and the stratification of material well-being among low-income households with children. *Children and Youth Services Review*, 34(9), 1810–1817.

Simai, M. (ed.). (1995). *Global employment: An international investigation into the future of work*. London, UK: Zed Books, Inc.

Skowronski, L. (2009, January 1). *Two-tier or not two-tier? That is the health care question!* Alberta Social Credit Policy Newsletter, 1. Retrieved December 14, 2012, from http://www.socialcredit.com/newsletters/2tier_article.htm.

Standing, G. (1999). *Global labour flexibility: Seeking redistributive justice*. Basingstoke, UK: Macmillan.

Stoesz, D., and Karger, H. (1991). The corporatization of the United States welfare state. *Journal of Social Policy*, 20(2), 157–171.

Strier, R., Surkis, T., and Biran, D. (2008). Neo-liberalism: Bottom-up counter-narratives. *International Social Work*, 51(4), 493–508.

U.S. Bureau of Labor Statistics (2009). *Employment situation summary*. Retrieved August 15, 2014, from http://www.bls.gov/news.release/archives/empsit_01082010.pdf.

Wacquant, L. (2001). The penalisation of poverty and the rise of neo-liberalism. *European Journal on Criminal Policy and Research*, 9(4), 401–411.

Wells, K., and Shafran, R. (2005). Obstacles to employment among mothers of children in foster care. *Child Welfare*, 74(1), 67–96.

Wood, A. (1994). *North–south trade, employment, and inequality*. Oxford, UK: Clarendon Publishing.

World Bank. (2001). *World development report 2000/2001: Attacking poverty*. New York: Oxford University Press.

22

THE PERSONAL RESPONSIBILITY AND WORK OPPORTUNITY RECONCILIATION ACT OF 1996 (PRWORA)

Richard K. Caputo

Ending public assistance as it was known

President Bill Clinton signed the Personal Responsibility and Work Opportunity Reconciliation Act of 1996 (PRWORA, P.L. 104-193) on August 22. PRWORA fulfilled President Clinton's campaign promise to end public assistance as it was known, but in a way that neither he nor his administration's key welfare reform architects, including David Ellwood, Mary Jo Bane, Peter Edelman, and Wendell Primus, had intended. Rather, many of the provisions mirrored what U.S. Congressional House Republicans had promised two years earlier in their *Contract with America*, whose ten legislative goals included the contemporary mantra of cutting taxes, balancing the federal budget, and reducing the federal role in social welfare provision. In 1994 the *Contract* helped shift the terms of public debate to the right side of the political spectrum in the United States, taking the Clinton administration along with it (Heclo, 2001, pp. 190–191). As such, PRWORA provided incentives to shape the behavior of recipients of cash assistance and other benefits to meet public ends, some of which related directly to labor force participation, and others to meet a variety of social concerns such as abortion and teenage pregnancy, and the standing of undocumented or illegal immigrants.

Among other things, PRWORA capped federal welfare spending to the states, limited federal cash assistance for welfare recipients to five years maximum while permitting states to end it sooner (which 17 did; see Farrell et al., 2008), set labor force participation targets for recipients of cash and other public benefits such as vouchers for food, awarded bonuses to states demonstrating decreased out-of-wedlock births and abortions from a prior two-year period (reflecting the social concerns of the Christian right; see Reed, 1996), and restricted welfare and other public benefits for illegal immigrants. By ending the entitlement aspect of the Aid to Families with Dependent Children (AFDC) program and creating the Temporary Assistance Program for Needy Families (TANF), PRWORA in effect increased the supply of low-wage workers in the United States. An original component of the Social Security Act of 1935, AFDC had made available federal cash assistance to low-income mothers and their dependent children based on state-determined eligibility of financial need independent of their attachment to the labor force. Ellwood (1996) clearly indicated that "two years and you're off [welfare]," a mantra Clinton had used while campaigning for president, had come to imply "no help at all after two years," although this was "never what was intended." To underscore what they perceived as the pernicious nature of PRWORA, Bane, Edelman, and Primus resigned their positions with the Clinton administration within a month from its signing (Acts of Principle, 1996).

Provisions of the Personal Responsibility and Work Opportunity Act of 1996 (PRWORA)

Title I: creation of TANF

PRWORA encompassed nine titles that departed markedly from prior law and went beyond the AFDC population (Congressional Research Service, 1996; Haskins and Blank, 2001, Table 1-1, pp. 8–11; Comparison of Prior Law and the Personal Responsibility and Work Opportunity Reconciliation Act, 1996). Title I replaced AFDC with the Temporary Assistance for Needy Families (TANF) program. The AFDC, Emergency Assistance (EA), and JOBS programs were combined into a single capped entitlement to states. The total cash assistance block grant was estimated at $16.4 billion for each year from FY 1996 to FY 2003, with states receiving a fixed amount based on a formula that took into account prior expenditures for AFDC, EA, and JOBS. States were permitted to carry over unused grant funds to subsequent fiscal years and they were mandated to maintain 80 percent of FY 1994 state funding on AFDC and related programs including JOBS, EA, and child care. TANF programs had to be operational by July 1, 1996. In striking contrast to AFDC which guaranteed benefits to eligible individuals for as long as they were deemed eligible by their respective states, PRWORA made no provisions for the individual guarantee of benefits. It deemed ineligible for federally funded cash assistance families who had received such assistance for five cumulative years or less at state option.

Work requirements

Title I of PRWORA required states to demonstrate that they will require families to work after two years on assistance and set work participation rates for single-parent families at 25 percent in FY 1997, increasing to 50 percent by FY 2000, and for two-parent families from 75 percent to 90 percent by FY 1999. Work hours were also specified for single-parent and two-parent families, 20 and 35 hours per week respectively, with some exemptions for single parents with children under six years old who could not find child care. Work activities included unsubsidized or subsidized employment, OJT, work experience, community service, up to 12 months of vocational training, or providing child care services to individuals who were participating in community service. Up to six weeks of job search were also permitted, although states with unemployment rates 50 percent above the national average could count up to 12 weeks. No more than 20 percent of the caseload was permitted to count vocational training toward meeting the work requirement. Unlike AFDC which had no provisions for persons convicted of drug-related crimes, those so convicted after the date of enactment were prohibited for life from receiving benefits under the TANF and Food Stamp programs. States were penalized with a percentage reduction of their block grants for, among other things, failure to meet work participation rates, to submit required reports, for misuse of funds, and poor performance with respect to child support enforcement. Unmarried minor parents were required to live with an adult or in an adult-supervised setting and participate in educational and training activities in order to receive federal assistance. Bonuses were provided to states which exceeded work requirement provisions. Title I made no provision for family caps which by default was left to the states to impose if they chose to do so.

Provisions reflecting the political clout of the Christian right

Other provisions in Title I included bonuses to states demonstrating decreased out-of-wed-lock births and abortions from a prior two-year period, Medicaid retention, and transitional Medicaid coverage when earnings would have resulted in loss of coverage under the prior law. President Clinton (1995), the politically active Christian right (Heclo, 2001; Reed, 1996; Watson, 1997), and other social conservative intellectuals (e.g., Murray, 1993) advanced the idea that family-value issues such as out-of-wedlock births in general and among teens in particular were major social problems that welfare reform should address. Family formation, however, never received the programmatic attention that states gave to work requirements, in part because of public ambivalence about the matter and lack of known successful programs to address the issue (Mead, 2001; Weaver, 2000). Also reflecting the political clout of the Christian right, Section 104 of Title I required states and local governments to include faith-based organi-zations when purchasing services from non-governmental sources. This "charitable choice" provision signified a new formal relationship or partnership between religious organizations and public welfare. Local church groups would no longer be denied access to government funds simply because of their association with religious activities (Carlson-Thies, 2001; Heclo, 2001; Wineberg et al., 2008).

Title II: Supplemental Security Income program provisions

Title II provided a new definition of disability for children to determine eligibility for the Supplemental Security Income (SSI) program. SSI was created in 1972 and had removed such children from the AFDC rolls. Title II suspended SSI for ten years to individuals found to have fraudulently misrepresented residence in order to obtain benefits simultaneously in two or more states. It also denied SSI for fugitive felons and probation and parole violators.

Title III: child support enforcement provisions

Title III mandated states to operate a child support enforcement (CSE) program meeting fed-eral requirements in order to be eligible for TANF. Recipients were required to sign rights to child support and cooperate with paternity establishment efforts, penalizing those who refused by reducing their cash assistance by at least 25 percent. Title III also mandated states to set up automated registry data systems for the purposes of the collection and disbursement of support payments. States were also required to establish a directory of newly employed persons contain-ing prescribed information to employers, thereby enabling wages to be garnished for support purposes when necessary. Information about new employees was to be transferred to the Health and Human Services director to maintain a National Directory of New Hires and a Federal Parent Locator Service. Title III also required states to devise a plan enabling a determination as to whether a program recipient cooperates in good faith to establish paternity and secure support.

Title IV: restricting public benefits and other programs to aliens

Title IV defined "qualified aliens" and restricted welfare and other public benefits, such as Food Stamps and Medicaid, accordingly. This was done for the purported purposes of assur-ing self-reliance by aliens in accordance with national immigration policy and of removing the incentive for illegal immigration thought to be encouraged by the availability of public benefits. Qualified immigrants or aliens included lawful permanent residents, asylees, refugees, parolees, those held under deportation, and others granted conditional entry. Title IV prohibited federal public benefits to non-qualified aliens except for emergency medical services, certain disaster relief, public health immunizations and treatment of communicable diseases, housing assistance, specified in-kind community services, and specified provisions of the Social Security Act. It made qualified aliens ineligible (with limited exceptions for refugees, asylees, certain permanent residents, veterans and active duty personnel, aliens whose deportation is withheld, and aliens then receiving benefits) for SSI, food stamps, TANF, social services block grants, and Medicaid (the program that makes medical care provisions and services available to low-income persons and their families).

Title V: child protection

Title V contained child protection provisions in regard to foster care, abuse, and neglect. It provided for kinship care, requiring states to consider giving preference to adult relatives over non-relative caregivers when determining child placement.

Title VI: child care

Title VI provided a separate allocation specifically for child care, but eliminated the child care guarantee for working AFDC recipients, those participating in JOBS or state-approved job-training or education programs, as well as for up to one year during transition off welfare due to employment. Single parents with children under six years of age who could not find child care were exempt from engaging in work activities.

Title VII: child nutrition programs

Title VII availed child nutrition programs to individuals eligible for free public education benefits under state or local law regardless of citizenship or immigrant status. It also gave states the option to determine whether to provide WIC (for mothers with infants) and other nutritional benefits to illegal immigrants.

Title VIII: Food Stamps and commodity distribution

Title VIII denied Food Stamps to most legal immigrants until citizenship. It increased penalties for specified food stamp voucher violations and permanently disqualified individuals convicted of specified voucher violations. Fleeing felons were disqualified from program participation. Title VIII also established a new work requirement under which non-exempt 18–50-year-olds with no dependent children responsibilities were ineligible to receive Food Stamps after three months within a 36-month period unless they were working or participating in a workfare, work, or employment and training program. The emergency food assistance program was merged with the soup kitchen–food bank program and repealed the food-bank demonstration project that had been authorized by the Charitable Assistance and Food Bank Act of 1987 (P.L. 100-232, 101 Stat. 1566).

Title IX: miscellaneous

Title IX contained several miscellaneous provisions: (a) one establishing spending levels for the Social Services Block Grant, (b) another allowing states to perform drug tests on recipients and to sanction those testing positive, and (c) the third providing funds for states to provide abstinence education with the option of targeting the funds to high-risk groups; that is, those most likely to bear out-of-wedlock children. PRWORA had an expiration date of October 1, 2002 (Comparison of Prior Law and the Personal Responsibility and Work Opportunity Reconciliation Act, 1996).

The impact of PRWORA on welfare caseloads

Reductions in welfare caseloads were immediate and steep. By July 1997 full implementation of TANF provisions under PRWORA began to exacerbate the gradual decrease in AFDC caseloads that started in 1994. At the end of fiscal year 2001, the average monthly number of TANF recipients was 5.5 million, or 56 percent lower than the AFDC caseload in 1996 (U.S. Department of Health and Human Services Administration for Children and Families, 2002). By 2006, the average monthly number of TANF recipients had dropped further, to 4.2 million (U.S. Department of Health and Human Services Administration for Children and Families, 2008a). From its peak of 14.4 million in March 1994, the number dropped by 63.2 percent to 5.3 million in September 2001. As a percentage of the U.S. population, the caseload had reached its lowest point, about 2 percent, since the 1960s. Caseloads dropped by more than 70 percent between fiscal years 1996 and 2001 in eight states (Colorado, Florida, Idaho, Illinois, Louisiana, Mississippi, Wisconsin, and Wyoming) and between 40 and 70 percent in 35 states. A robust economy with relatively low unemployment rates, ranging from 5.6 percent in 1996 to 4.0 percent in 2000 before increasing to 4.7 percent in 2001, and expansion of the Earned Income Tax Credit (EITC) program, contributed to the decline in TANF caseloads, with 7.2 million persons having left the welfare rolls between fiscal years 1996 and 2001. Also contributing to the decline was a U.S. Department of Health and Human Services Administration for Children and Families (1999) ruling that permitted states to use TANF funds for certain types of assistance without time limits and other strictures under the TANF block grants (Gais and Nathan, 2001). Of 23 states that provided these "diversion benefits" for short-term assistance, such as emergency needs for car repairs or long-term assistance for child care or education and training, 15 did not count this assistance toward the TANF time limits (Kassabian et al., 2014).

Caseload reduction was initially accompanied by a decline in child poverty and an increase in single-mother employment. The child poverty rate dropped from 40.3 percent in 1995 to 35.7 percent in 2000, with the related number of children decreasing from 14 million to 11 million, respectively. The percentage of single-mother employment increased from 64 percent in 1995 to 75.5 percent in 2000. Caseloads continued to decline until reported notable increases in 2008, with unemployment rates ranging from a low of 4.6 in 2006 and 2007 to highs of 6.0 in 2003 and 5.8 in 2003 and 2008 (As Economy Slides, 2008; U.S. Census Bureau, 2014; U.S. Department of Labor, Bureau of Labor Statistics, n.d.).

As the Center on Budget and Policy Priorities (2012) shows, however, such early gains masked the decline in the number of families receiving AFDC/TANF benefits for every 100 families with children in poverty, from 68 in 1996 to 27 in 2011. Further, the role of TANF in providing income support to poor families declined dramatically during the Great Recession of 2008–2009 through 2011. The uptick in caseloads during this time from about 1.8 million to 2 million was less than the increase in families with children in poverty, which jumped from about 6 million to 7 million, and in families with children in deep poverty (income below half the poverty line), from about 2.8 million to 3.2 million. Finally, the value of TANF benefits has declined in most states since 1996: benefits did not keep pace with inflation, such that in

2011 they were below the poverty line in half the states; in addition, 7 states had value declines of 10–20 percent, 28 states of 20–30 percent, and 6 states above 30 percent.

The Earned Income Tax Credit

The Earned Income Tax Credit (EITC) was enacted provisionally in 1975 as part of the Tax Reduction Act (P.L. 94-12, 89 Stat. 34) during the Gerald Ford administration to offset the burden of the Social Security payroll tax on low-income working parents. P.L. 94-12 allowed a credit of 10 percent of earned income that did not exceed $4,000 (that is, a maximum credit of $400), with a phase-out rate also of 10 percent range that ended at $8,000. The EITC became permanent during the Jimmy Carter administration as part of the Revenue Act of 1978 (P.L. 95-600, 92 Stat. 2763). The congressional mindset favoring the EITC in the 1970s coalesced in the context of debates about unsuccessful welfare reform initiatives that had embodied pro-work, pro-growth, and low-cost policies, notably the Family Assistance Plan (FAP) of the Richard Nixon administration and the Program for Better Jobs and Income (PBJI) of the Carter administration (Caputo, 1994). The EITC matured as an anti-poverty strategy during the Ronald Reagan administration as part of the Tax Reform Act of 1986 (P.L. 99-514, 100 Stat. 2085) when Congress raised the maximum EITC benefit, which had fallen by 35 percent in real terms, to the 1975 level, increased the phase-out level to near the 1975 level, and most importantly guaranteed the future integrity of the EITC by indexing it for inflation (U.S. Joint Committee on Taxation, 1987; Ventry, 2000). As Ozawa (1995) and Lang (1999) noted, the EITC was preferred to raising the minimum wage as an anti-poverty strategy in part because it better targeted low-income household heads rather than low-wage-earning students or teenagers, and it accounted for family size (Caputo, 2011).

The EITC generally equals a specified percentage of wages up to a maximum dollar amount. The credit rates, maximum credit amounts, phase-out ranges, and number of qualifying children have changed over the years (Tax Policy Center, 2012). For tax year 2012, earned income and adjusted gross income (AGI) must each be less than $45,060 ($50,270 married filing jointly) with three or more qualifying children, $41,952 ($47,162 married filing jointly) with two qualifying children, $36,920 ($42,130 married filing jointly) with one qualifying child, and $13,980 ($19,190 married filing jointly) with no qualifying children. Maximum credits were $5,891 with three or more qualifying children, $5,236 with two qualifying children, $3,169 with one qualifying child, and $475 with no qualifying children. Additionally, investment income must be $3,200 or less for the year (Internal Revenue Service, 2012).

From 1975 through 1987 the number of EITC claimants ranged between 6,000 and 9,000; in 1988 more than 11,100 individuals claimed the credit (Hotz and Scholtz, 2003). By 2010, the most recent year of data available at the time of this writing, nearly 27.8 million returns were filed claiming the credit, representing nearly 19.5 percent of all tax returns filed for that tax year and $60.9 billion in revenue lost to the U.S. Treasury Department (Internal Revenue Service, n.d.). By contrast, for fiscal year 2006, net federal expenditures for TANF amounted to $13.6 billion, less than one third of revenue lost in calendar year 2006 due to the EITC (U.S. Department of Health and Human Services Administration for Children and Families, 2008b). Total claimants climbed to 27.4 million in 2009, surpassing the 24.8 million in 2008, with total costs increasing from $50.7 billion to $60.4 billion, respectively (de Rugy, 2014; Internal Revenue Service, n.d.).

TANF, EITC, and women's labor force participation

Trends in women's employment

In 1996, after expansion of the EITC and passage of PRWORA, 61.9 million women 16 years of age or over constituted the female labor force, with a participation rate reaching a high of 59.3 percent. The proportion of female labor force participants who were married declined slightly to 54.3 percent from 54.7 percent in the late 1980s, with their labor force participation rate increasing to 61.2 percent from 56.7 percent. The proportion of female labor force participants who were single also declined slightly to 25.6 percent from 26.0 percent in the late 1980s, with a labor force participation rate increasing even further to 67.1 percent from 66.7 percent. The proportion of female labor force participants who were widowed, divorced, or separated increased to 48.1 percent from 46.2 percent in the late 1980s (*Statistical Abstract of the United States*, 1997a).

By 1996, the labor force participation rate of married women with children between the ages of 6 and 17 had further increased to 76.7 percent from 61.7 percent in 1980 and to 62.7 percent from 45.1 percent for those with children under the age of 6. The labor force participation rate of single women with children between the ages of 6 and 17 in 1996 increased to 71.8 percent from 67.6 percent in 1980 and to 55.1 percent from 44.1 percent for those with children under the age of 6. The labor force participation rate of widowed, divorced, or separated women with children between the ages of 6 and 17 in 1996 increased to 80.6 percent from 74.6 percent in 1980 and to 69.2 percent from 60.3 percent for those with children under the age of 6 (*Statistical Abstract of the United States*, 1997b).

One of the more pronounced increases in women's labor force participation occurred among those with children under the age of three. In March 1975, the first year of available national-level data, the labor force participation rate of women with children under three years of age was 34.3 percent (U.S. Department of Labor, Bureau of Labor Statistics, n.d.). By 1980, it had increased to 41.9 percent, by 1988 to 52.4 percent, and by 1996 to 59.0 percent. The labor force participation rate of women with children under three years of age peaked at 62.2 percent in 1998, and it stood at 60.1 percent in 2007.

Effects of TANF and EITC

As previously noted, the early employment gains correlated with full implementation of TANF by July 1, 1997 were buttressed by a strong labor market and expansion of EITC, in addition to state policies that mandated work and provided supports such as child care assistance (Center on Budget and Policy Priorities, 2012). Employment rates increased significantly for single mothers, including those with less than a high school education, and modest work-related income gains were reported, although family income gains were more likely due to increased labor force participation among other family or household members (Blank, 2002; Schoeni and Blank, 2003). Economist Jeffrey Grogger (2003) estimated that welfare reform accounted for 13 percent of the total rise in employment among single mothers in the 1990s; the EITC, about 34 percent; and the strong economy, about 21 percent. The economic downturns of 2000 and of 2008–2009 quickly eroded these gains. Since 2000, employment among never-married mothers with a high school education or less, which had peaked at about 75 percent in the late 1990s from about 50 percent in the early 1990s, has been about the same as for single women *without* children with the same education level, which had hovered between 75 and 80 percent throughout the 1990s. Both groups of women had precipitous declines in employment rates to less than 65 percent by 2010.

Early state-related studies of welfare leavers suggested that about 50–60 percent of mothers who left welfare and stayed off worked regularly (at least almost full time for a long period of time, generally 6 months or longer over a 12-month period) and about 30–40 percent reported no work (Acs and Loprest with Roberts, 2001; Besharov and Germanis, 2002). Leavers who worked most or all of the time reported higher levels of family income than those working only some of the time and much higher than the relatively small percentage (< 10 percent) of those who did not work. Nonetheless the income of about 40 percent of those who worked most or all of the time fell below the poverty line, and the poverty rates of those who worked only some of the time or not at all were 60 and 80 percent respectively. Material hardships reflected leavers' economic and work-related circumstances: about 30 percent of those who reported no or some work also reported insufficient food compared to 16 percent for those who worked most of the time and 19 percent for those who worked all the time.

Conclusion

As programmatic responses to poverty and low-income workers, TANF and EITC signified the resurgent triumph of liberal or free market economic ideology in political discourse and public policy. Sidelined from mainstream political economic thought after the Great Depression of 1935, liberal economic ideology staged a comeback from the 1970s onwards as public debates in the United States, but also elsewhere such as in the European Union (e.g., the United Kingdom and Germany) and in Latin America (e.g., Chile and Peru) (Gane, 2012), were permeated with assumptions that workings of the free market should be protected from government interventions (Burgin, 2012) and by extension that government should rely more on market-based incentives as the basis for social welfare policies and programs (Sumner, 2013). As such, increasing income and asset inequality were viewed less as a social problem to be addressed and more as a natural byproduct of market forces, signifying the presence of human agency (freedom of individual action). Low-income parents with young children and adolescents were now "free" to negotiate the labor market, knowing that federal cash assistance was time-limited and that, although the EITC rewarded work, its incentives were little comfort during recessions, as those of 2000 and 2008–2009 bore out as job creation faltered, employers laid off more and hired fewer workers, unemployment rates rose, and the early gains of TANF and EITC eroded.

TANF and EITC also signified the government's attempt to "mainstream" able-bodied non-working, low-income parents into the economy and society, with labor force participation (either employment or seeking work) as the common denominator. Earlier efforts during the Nixon administration to link able-bodied non-working, low-income parents and low-income workers—that is, to nationalize the AFDC program and provide an income floor below which no family in the United States would fall—had failed in part because of the prospect of adding 11 million low-income workers to the 10 million or so able-bodied non-working, low-income parents already on welfare rolls. With the passage of PRWORA and the creation of TANF, Congress in effect made the able-bodied non-working poor look and act like the working poor, namely having to face the vicissitudes of the labor market with all its inherent uncertainties and fluctuations come what may. To many low-income working persons this may seem fair—to them providing cash assistance to able-bodied persons unwilling to participate in the labor force is a hard sell when millions of them are willing to do so. Yet one cannot help but think that this is a rather mean-spirited approach to achieving social justice.

References

Acs, G., and Loprest, P., with Roberts, T. (2001). *Final synthesis report of findings from ASPE's "Leavers" grants*. Washington, DC: The Urban Institute. Retrieved August 15, 2014 from http://www.urban.org/UploadedPDF/410809_welfare_leavers_synthesis.pdf.

Acts of Principle. (1996, September 13). *New York Times*. Opinion. Retrieved August 15, 2014 from http://www.nytimes.com/1996/09/13/opinion/acts-of-principle.html.

As Economy Slides, More People Seek Assistance. (2008, December 17). *The Washington Post*, p. A10.

Besharov, D.J., and Germanis, P. (2002). Welfare reform update. In D.J. Besharov (ed.), *Family well-being after welfare reform* (2-1–2-45). Baltimore, MD: Welfare Reform Academy, Maryland School of Public Affairs.

Blank, R.M. (2002). Evaluating welfare reform in the United States. *Journal of Economic Literature*, 40(4), 1105–1166.

Burgin, A. (2012). *The great persuasion: Reinventing free markets since the Depression*. Cambridge, MA: Harvard University Press.

Caputo, R.K. (1994). *Welfare and freedom American style: The role of the federal government, 1941–1980*. Lanham, MD: University Press of America.

Caputo, R.K. (2011). *U.S. social welfare reform: Policy transitions from 1980 to the present*. New York: Springer.

Carlson-Thies, S. (2001). Charitable choice: Bringing religion back into American welfare. *Journal of Political History*, 13(1), 109–132.

Center on Budget and Policy Priorities. (2012). *Chart Book: TANF at 16*. Washington, DC. Retrieved August 15, 2014 from http://www.cbpp.org/files/8-22-12tanf.pdf.

Comparison of Prior Law and the Personal Responsibility and Work Opportunity Reconciliation Act. (1996). (P.L. 104-193). Retrieved November 12, 2014 from http://aspe.hhs.gov/hsp/isp/Reform.htm.

Congressional Research Service. (1996). *Bill summary & status: H.R.3734*. Retrieved August 15, 2014 from http://thomas.loc.gov/cgi-bin/bdquery/z?d104:HR03734:@@@D&summ2=m&.

de Rugy, V. (2014). *Trends in EITC spending and numbers of beneficiaries*. George Mason University, Mercatus Center. Retrieved August 15, 2014 from http://mercatus.org/publication/trends-eitc-spending-and-numbers-beneficiaries.

Ellwood, D.T. (1996). Welfare reform as I knew it: When bad things happen to good policies. *The American Prospect*, 7(6), 22–27.

Farrell, M., Rich, S., Turner, L., Sieth, D., and Bloom, D. (2008). *Welfare time limits: An update on state policies, implementation, and effects on families*. Falls Church, VA: The Lewin Group; New York: MDRC. Retrieved August 15, 2014 from http://www.acf.hhs.gov/programs/opre/resource/welfare-time-limits-an-update-on-state-policies-implementation-and-effects.

Gais, T., and Nathan, R. (2001). *Status report on the occasion of the 5th anniversary of the 1996 Personal Responsibility Welfare-Reform Act*. Albany, NY: The Rockefeller Institute of Government. Retrieved August 15, 2014 from http://www.rockinst.org/pdf/workforce_welfare_and_social_services/2001-08-17-status_report_on_the_occasion_of_the_5th_anniversary_of_the_1996_personal_responsibility_welfare-reform_act.pdf.

Gane, N. (2012). [Review of the book *The road from Mont Pèlerin: The making of the neoliberal thought collective* by D.S. Jones]. *Sociological Review*, 60, 777–780.

Grogger, J. (2003). The effects of time-limits, the EITC, and other policy changes on welfare use, work, and income among female-headed families. *The Review of Economics and Statistics*, 85(2), 394–408.

Haskins, R., and Blank, R.M. (2001). Welfare reform: An agenda for reauthorization. In R.M. Blank and R. Haskins (eds), *The new world of welfare* (pp. 3–32). Washington, DC: Brookings Institution Press.

Heclo, H. (2001). The politics of welfare reform. In R.M. Blank and R. Haskins (eds), *The new world of welfare* (pp. 169–200). Washington, DC: Brookings Institution Press.

Hotz, V.J., and Scholtz, J.K. (2003). The Earned Income Tax Credit. In R.A. Moffitt (ed.), *Means-tested transfer programs in the United States* (pp. 141–197). Chicago: University of Chicago Press.

Internal Revenue Service. (2012). *EITC income limits, maximum credit amounts and tax law updates*. Retrieved August 15, 2014 from http://www.irs.gov/Individuals/2012-EITC-Income-Limits,-Maximum-Credit--Amounts-and-Tax-Law-Updates.

Internal Revenue Service. (n.d.). [Historical tables]. *Table 1. Individual tax returns: Selected income and tax items for tax years 1999–2012*. Retrieved August 15, 2014 from http://www.irs.gov/pub/irs-soi/histab1.xls.

Kassabian, D., Huber, E., Cohen, E., and Giannarelli, L.; The Urban Institute. (2013). *Welfare rules data book: State TANF policies as of July 2012.* Retrieved August 15, 2014 from http://www.urban.org/publications/412973.html.

Lang, S.S. (1999). Income tax credits, not minimum wage hike, will benefit the working poor. *Human Ecology Forum,* 27(4), 3.

Mead, L.M. (2001). The politics of conservative welfare reform. In R.M. Blank and R. Haskins (eds), *The new world of welfare* (pp. 201–220). Washington, DC: Brookings Institution Press.

Murray, C. (1993). Welfare and the family: The U.S. experience. *Journal of Labor Economics,* 11(1, Part 2), S224–S262.

Ozawa, M.N. (1995). The Earned Income Tax Credit: Its effects and significance. *Social Service Review,* 69(4), 563–582.

Reed, R. (1996). *Active faith: How Christians are changing the soul of American politics.* New York: The Free Press.

Schoeni, R.F., and Blank, R.M. (2003). *What has welfare reform accomplished? Impacts on welfare participation, employment, income, poverty, and family structure.* Ann Arbor: University of Michigan, Population Studies Center. Retrieved August 15, 2014 from http://www.psc.isr.umich.edu/pubs/pdf/rr03-544.pdf.

Statistical Abstract of the United States. (1997a). *No. 630 Marital status of women in the civilian labor force: 1960 to 1996.* Retrieved August 15, 2014 from http://www.census.gov/prod/3/97pubs/97statab/labor.pdf.

Statistical Abstract of the United States. (1997b). *No. 631 Employment status of women, by marital status and presence and age of children: 1960 to 1996.* Retrieved August 15, 2014 from http://www.census.gov/prod/3/97pubs/97statab/labor.pdf.

Sumner, S. (2013). The neoliberal revolution. [Review of the book *Masters of the universe: Hayek, Friedman, and the birth of neoliberal politics* by D.S. Jones.] *Reason,* 44(9), 56–59.

Tax Policy Center. (2012). *Earned Income Tax Credit parameters, 1975–2014.* Retrieved August 15, 2014 from http://www.taxpolicycenter.org/taxfacts/Content/PDF/historical_eitc_parameters.pdf.

U.S. Census Bureau. (2014). *Historical Tables People. Table 15. Age distribution of the poor.* Retrieved August 15, 2014 from http://www.census.gov/hhes/www/poverty/data/historical/people.html.

U.S. Department of Health and Human Services Administration for Children and Families. (1999, April 12). *Temporary Assistance for Needy Families (TANF) Program: Final rule.* Part II. Federal Register, 64(69), 17720–17931. Retrieved August 15, 2014 from http://www.gpo.gov/fdsys/pkg/FR-1999-04-12/content-detail.html.

U.S. Department of Health and Human Services Administration for Children and Families. (2002). *Temporary Assistance for Needy Families (TANF) Program: Fourth annual report to Congress.* Retrieved August 15, 2014 from http://archive.acf.hhs.gov/programs/ofa/data-reports/ar2001/indexar.htm.

U.S. Department of Health and Human Services Administration for Children and Families. (2008a). *Temporary Assistance for Needy Families (TANF) Program: Eighth annual report to Congress.* Retrieved August 15, 2014 from http://archive.acf.hhs.gov/programs/ofa/data-reports/annualreport8/ar8index.htm.

U.S. Department of Health and Human Services Administration for Children and Families. (2008b). *Indicators of welfare dependence: Annual report to Congress.* Retrieved August 15, 2014 from http://aspe.hhs.gov/hsp/indicators08/index.shtml.

U.S. Department of Labor, Bureau of Labor Statistics. (n.d.). *Labor force participation rate of women by age of youngest child, March 1975–2007.* Retrieved August 15, 2014 from http://www.bls.gov/opub/ted/2009/jan/wk1/art04.txt.

U.S. Joint Committee on Taxation. (1987). *General explanation of the Tax Reform Act of 1986.* Washington, DC: GPO. Retrieved August 15, 2014 from http://www.house.gov/jct/jcs-10-87.pdf.

Ventry, D.J. (2000). The collision of tax and welfare politics: The political history of the Earned Income Tax Credit, 1969–1999. *National Tax Journal,* 53(4, Part 2), 983–1026.

Watson, J. (1997). *The Christian coalition: Dreams of restoration, demands for recognition.* New York: St. Martin's Press.

Weaver, R.K. (2000). *Ending welfare as we know it.* Washington, DC: Brookings Institution Press.

Wineberg, R.J., Coleman, B.L., Broddie, S.C., and Cnaan, R.A. (2008). Leveling the playing field: Epitomizing devolution through faith-based organizations. *Journal of Sociology and Social Welfare,* 35(1), 17–42.

23

ANTI-POVERTY POLICIES AND THE STRUCTURE OF INEQUALITY

Eiko Strader and Joya Misra

Characteristics of the poor in the United States

Poverty in the United States reflects larger societal inequalities, based on race, ethnicity, nativity, age, gender, disability status, and family structure. Figure 23.1 summarizes these trends, using 2011 data from the Current Population Survey (U.S. Census Bureau, 2012). While women are only slightly more likely to be poor than men, more than one quarter of Blacks and Hispanics are poor, as compared to less than 10% of Whites and 12% of Asians. By nativity and citizenship status, foreign-born citizens have the lowest rates of poverty, followed by native-born citizens and foreign-born

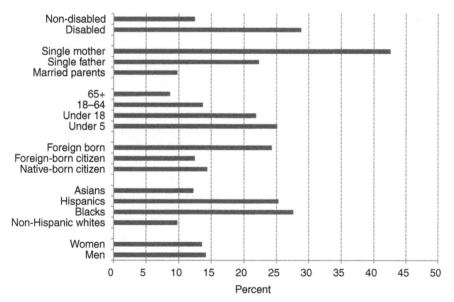

Figure 23.1 Poverty status for groups in the United States, 2011
Source: U.S. Census Bureau, 2012.

immigrants. Poverty varies a great deal by age, with children most likely to experience poverty. Families with children headed by single mothers experience the highest levels of poverty, compared to single-father families and families headed by two parents. Poverty also varies by disability status.

As a whole, single parents, racial minorities, migrants, people with disabilities, children, and women face higher rates of poverty in the United States (Browne and Misra, 2003; Danziger and Haveman, 2001; Lichter and Jayakody, 2002; McLanahan and Percheski, 2008; Western et al., 2012). While programs such as Social Security and Medicare have helped reduce poverty among the aged in the United States, many other groups remain vulnerable. The U.S. welfare state is premised on the notion that households should provide for themselves; yet this requires access to jobs—and often more than one earner. Indeed, while only 2.5% of families with two or more workers fall into poverty, 16.5% of families with one worker live in poverty (U.S. Census Bureau, 2012). Given the low level of the minimum wage in the United States, poverty occurs among many working families. In the following sections, we provide a brief review of U.S. anti-poverty policies and assess their effectiveness in mitigating poverty.

U.S. anti-poverty policy

Anti-poverty policies aim to correct disparities by promoting a more equitable distribution of opportunity through the provision of cash and non-cash supports for structurally vulnerable sub-groups of the population. The U.S. welfare state is premised on a neoliberal ideology. In this context, individuals are expected to support themselves through work, and anti-poverty programs are designed to complement labor force participation. Universal social programs are nearly non-existent in the United States, and means-tested programs are not very generous. Unlike universal social insurance schemes available to all citizens, means-tested programs only provide benefits to individuals who qualify for them based on need and certain eligibility criteria. Currently, there are over 80 means-tested programs, though health care-related services account for almost half of the federal expenditure for means-tested programs, and Medicaid alone accounts for 40% of the federal spending (Congressional Research Service, 2012; Spar, 2011).

Table 23.1 summarizes the current levels of expenditures and caseloads of the six leading means-tested programs, which account for more than 75% of the federal spending on anti-poverty policies. Programs that provide in-kind benefits, such as Medicaid and the Supplemental Nutrition Assistance Program (SNAP; formerly food stamps), have much higher caseloads and total expenditures, whereas programs that provide cash assistance, such as Supplemental Security Income (SSI) and Temporary Assistance for Needy Families (TANF), have lesser expenditures and caseloads. This reflects a concern in the United States that providing cash benefits may help create dependency; programs such as the Earned Income Tax Credit (EITC), in which benefits are provided only to working parents whose incomes fall beneath a certain level, receive more support. However, even programs with relatively high popular support, such as EITC and SNAP, are based on much lower levels of government spending than Medicaid.

There has been a sharp decline of direct cash transfer programs and rise in in-kind benefits since the passage of the Personal Responsibility and Work Opportunity Act (PRWORA) in 1996. While some see the decrease in TANF caseloads as the direct success of the welfare reform, the decline in TANF caseloads has not necessarily translated into a decrease in the rate or depth of poverty (Danziger, 2010; Lichter and Jayakody, 2002). Even though the recent recession has witnessed modest increases in caseloads since 2007, the caseload is still lower than it was in 2005 (Loprest, 2012), yet a record number of Americans are in poverty (U.S. Census Bureau, 2012).

PRWORA created a number of changes in U.S. anti-poverty policy, based on its "work-first" neoliberal assumptions. For example, the reform mandated welfare recipients (including

Table 23.1 Annual expenditures and caseloads of six major programs, 2010

		Expenditures (millions)	Caseloads[a] (thousands)	Average per recipient
Medicaid (total)		$358,500	52,900	$6,775
	Children	$72,800	26,800	$2,717
	Adults	$51,400	11,900	$4,314
	Disabled	$160,700	9,500	$16,963
	Aged	$73,700	4,800	$15,495
SNAP		$68,316	40,302	$1,605[b]
EITC		$58,620	26,170[c]	$2,240
SSI		$47,800	7,600	$5,712[d]
Pell Grants		$32,295	8,355	$3,865
TANF		$18,064	4,402[e]	$4,103

Sources: IRS, 2012; SSA, 2011; USDA, 2012; USDHHS, 2012a, 2012b, 2012c.
Notes:
[a] Number of individual recipients unless otherwise noted.
[b] Based on an average monthly payment of $133.70 in 2010.
[c] Number of tax unit caseloads.
[d] Based on an average monthly payment of $476 in January 2010.
[e] Average monthly number of recipients based on January to September data (total of adults and children, where children make up roughly 75% of the total recipients).

those with young children) to engage in work activities, imposed a five-year time limit, and sanctioned those who "refuse" to be employed. While TANF was meant to include child-care and transportation support, restricted funding for these programs mean that many who are eligible do not receive these services (Parisi et al., 2005). Many states have implemented their own policies and additional eligibility criteria to discourage new applicants, and thus the reform successfully restricted the TANF recipients to the "truly needy" in deep poverty (Ellwood, 2000; Gonzales et al., 2007). Another central change was the use of block grants, which incentivized regional governments to cut caseloads so that they can appropriate the funds for other expenses (Besharov and Germanis, 2007). The reform also excluded newly arrived legal immigrants from cash assistance, job training, childcare, and transportation for at least five years, and signaled the resurgence of nativism and racism in American welfare politics (Graefe et al., 2008; Reese and Ramirez, 2002).

SSI on the other hand has witnessed a steady increase in the number of recipients, and provides direct cash support to people with disabilities and the elderly with very limited incomes. Yet SSI benefit rates are not adjusted according to different needs at different life stages. In addition, benefits are based on outdated criteria, and remain lower than the poverty threshold for most families (Wiseman, 2011). Therefore, receipt of SSI remains reserved for relatively few very poor families, and thus should be seen more as a last-resort resource than a viable social safety net program.

Rather than relying on direct cash transfer programs such as TANF and SSI, the United States emphasizes other approaches. In 2011 alone, an estimated average of 56 million people were enrolled in Medicaid, a monthly average of 45 million people received food stamps, and over 27 million workers received EITC (Internal Revenue Service, 2014; U.S. Department of Agriculture,

2012; U.S. Department of Health and Human Services, 2012a). Yet research on the effectiveness of in-kind benefits in reducing poverty has been inconclusive, contradictory, and mixed at best.

EITC was created in 1975 to provide sizable refunds in the form of tax credits for low-income households as a part of "welfare-to-work" initiatives, and aims to decrease the number of people on welfare by encouraging continual labor force participation (Mendenhall, 2006). While EITC prioritizes more vulnerable subgroups including single mothers, young parents, and the extreme poor, Kim (2001) points out that the program does not effectively reduce the risk of poverty by tying benefits to employment. Other shortcomings include a lack of outreach to non-English-speaking and illiterate populations, the insufficiency of credit amounts to the extreme poor and the households with three or more children, high rates of noncompliance, and use of non-inflation-adjusted minimum wage figures (Eamon et al., 2009; Lim et al., 2010; Mendenhall, 2006). While EITC clearly provides some families with much-needed support, its design limits its potential to reduce poverty.

A number of studies show that food stamps reduce depth of poverty by providing monetary assistance for the purchase of food (Ratcliffe et al., 2011). Yet the program is less effective in pulling people out of poverty. Many poor and near-poor families do not participate in the program, while those that receive sizable food stamp support require additional support—beyond food—to move out of poverty (Jolliffe et al., 2005). Food stamps are supposed to be supplemental, and therefore each participant must partially pay for their groceries out of their own pocket (Jilcott et al., 2011; Teters and Weber, 2007). Faced with limited options and resources, many participants make unhealthy choices for the sake of volume, calorie, and convenience (Kupillas and Nies, 2007). Overall, SNAP provides important support for low-income families, but cannot substitute for a substantial income transfer program aimed at limiting poverty.

Medicaid makes very important contributions, by providing health care coverage for the poor. Yet, despite the centrality of this program, Medicaid falls short on the coverage of working-age adults (Cornelius, 2003) and immigrants (Kim et al., 2006). Several structural conditions create these gaps in coverage. Without a universal health care program, and before the adoption of the Affordable Care Act (ACA), those in the United States have been largely dependent on employer-funded private insurance programs for their health care. In addition, the PRWORA reform limited the access of lawful immigrants and their families to public benefit programs by granting states authority to define their own eligibility criteria, which has increased the number of uninsured children of immigrant families (Kim et al., 2006). At the same time, Medicaid reimbursements are relatively low; for physicians and health clinics that primarily treat residents covered by Medicaid, the quality of care may be compromised by a lack of resources (Reschovsky and O'Malley, 2008). Therefore, even though Medicaid constitutes the largest portion of the social welfare expenditures, it still falls short on safeguarding structurally disadvantaged subgroups from falling into poverty. While still speculative, studies estimate that the ACA may strengthen the effectiveness of Medicaid by decreasing the number of uninsured and underinsured adults (Schoen et al., 2011) and by promoting the use of preventative care (Koh and Sebelius, 2010).

The aforementioned studies have examined the effectiveness of the existing anti-poverty programs by analyzing how monetary and non-monetary redistributive policies safeguard structurally vulnerable groups from falling into poverty, and these studies agree that U.S. social programs do not yet form an effective safety net. There are two major flaws in U.S. social programs—inadequate levels of cash and non-cash transfers, and the exclusion of groups of poor through program designs. How does the United States compare to other countries?

U.S. poverty in comparative context

Welfare state scholars have long documented the cross-national variation in poverty rates, and many have paid attention to the peculiarly high level of poverty in the United States. Despite being one of the richest nations on earth, the United States reports one of the highest levels of inequality among wealthy nations, and the magnitude of inequality is steadily increasing for the last couple of decades (OECD, 2011). Figure 23.2 compares relative pre- and post-tax and transfer poverty rates for 21 developed countries using the Luxembourg Income Studies micro-data. While the United States has one of the lowest poverty rates based on market income, it reports one of the highest poverty rates based on post-tax and transfer income (income after taxes and welfare program benefits are included). As the figure makes clear, the high poverty rate in the United States reflects a welfare and taxation system that exacerbates inequality, rather than mediating it. Furthermore, when analyzing one of the most structurally vulnerable groups—single-mother-headed households—the United States lags behind many of the industrialized nations (OECD, 2008). What explains America's higher-than-average poverty rates and in what ways does the United States differ from other industrialized nations?

Cross-national research suggests that these differences are not simply due to the characteristics of the population. While controlling for differences in the educational attainment or the household structure helps explain some of the cross-national variation in poverty (McLanahan, 2004), there remains significant variation once we control for these factors (Heuveline and Weinshenker, 2008; Misra et al., 2012; Rainwater and Smeeding, 2003; Wiepking and Maas, 2005).

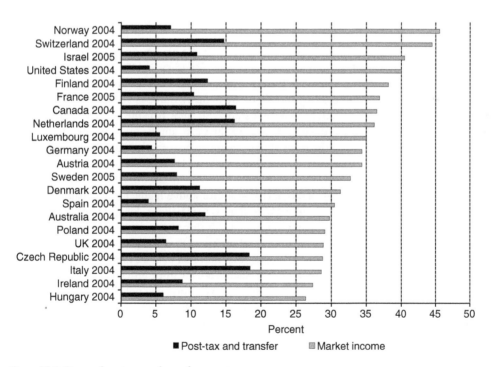

Figure 23.2 Pre- and post-tax and transfer poverty rates

Source: Compiled by authors using Wave VI data collected around 2004 from http://www.lisdatacenter.org/our-data/lis-database/.

Many attribute the source of high-income inequality in the United States to its low levels of social expenditure (Brady et al., 2009; Christopher, 2002; Huber et al., 2009; Moller et al., 2003). Not counting employer-provided benefits, the United States spends much less on social welfare programs and directs the least amount of budget towards direct cash transfer programs (Brandolini and Smeeding, 2009; Osberg, et al., 2004; Smeeding, 2004). The share of social benefits relative to total household income is 27.3% in Sweden and only 7.7% in the United States, indicating the small role which public transfers play in the U.S. context (Mahler and Jesuit, 2006). This reflects the difference between universal programs versus targeted anti-poverty programs that redistribute income to a very limited segment of the population.

While targeted programs like TANF may somewhat reduce inequality (Moller et al., 2009), comprehensive universal cash assistance programs are superior in reducing the overall income inequality (Brady and Burroway, 2012; Christopher, 2002; Christopher et al., 2002; Kenworthy, 1999; Misra et al., 2012; Smeeding, 2005). Korpi and Palme (1998) theorize that the more targeted benefits are at the poor, the less effective they are in actually reducing poverty, because targeted redistributive processes involve more welfare state institutions and different interest groups. Indeed, recent cross-national studies have shown that not only the size of the welfare state matters but how social transfers are distributed matters greatly. For example, while EITC is only available in the form of tax credits for qualified low-income households with children in the United States many European countries offer universal family allowances, which substantially alleviate poverty by subsidizing the costs of raising children (Christopher, 2002; Christopher et al., 2002; Kenworthy, 1999; Misra et al., 2012; Smeeding, 2005).

Another cross-national difference can be found in the variety and the availability of family policies financed by taxation. For example, infant and toddler child care is usually purchased out of pocket in countries like the United States, whereas many European countries have high-quality public child care systems in place (Misra et al., 2012). Estimates vary between studies and survey years, but only about 4% to 15% of eligible low-income working families received the Child Care Development Fund subsidies (Boushey and Wright, 2004; Crawford, 2006; Meyers et al., 2002), while much larger portions of the overall population are enrolled in publicly provided infant, toddler, and child care in many European countries (Gornick and Meyers, 2003; Misra et al., 2012). A recent study also finds that the work requirements of TANF significantly increased the overall costs of child care among low-income single mothers after the reform, negating the possibility of reducing poverty through child care subsidies (Ahn, 2012). Yet again, studies show that universally available child care programs are more effective in reducing poverty.

In summary, our brief survey of recent cross-national studies highlights two major issues surrounding the effectiveness of the current U.S. anti-poverty policies. First, studies agree that the more generous the welfare state, the fewer households that remain in poverty. Yet the United States allocates much less of its budget on social programs than many other developed nations do. Second, despite ample evidence suggesting that universal benefits more effectively alleviate poverty than targeted programs, the United States abstains from providing universal benefits and maintains strict eligibility criteria and neoliberal work-oriented policies for its low-income programs. These two points mirror what the aforementioned studies on the U.S. anti-poverty programs have shown: inadequate levels of cash and non-cash transfers and exclusion of structurally vulnerable groups from the redistributive process.

References

Ahn, Haksoon. 2012. "Child Care Subsidy, Child Care Costs, and Employment of Low-Income Single Mothers." *Children and Youth Services Review*, 34: 379–387.

Besharov, Douglas J., and Peter Germanis. 2007. "Welfare Reform and the Caseload Decline." *Gender Issues*, 24(1): 32–58.

Boushey, Heather, and Joseph Wright. 2004. *Working Moms and Child Care*. CEPR Data Brief No. 3. Washington, DC: Center for Economic and Policy Research.

Brady, David, and Rebekah Burroway. 2012. "Targeting, Universalism, and Single-Mother Poverty: A Multilevel Analysis across 18 Affluent Democracies." *Demography*, 49: 719–746.

Brady, David, Andrew S. Fullerton, and Jennifer Moren Cross. 2009. "Putting Poverty in Political Context: A Multi-Level Analysis of Adult Poverty across 18 Affluent Democracies." *Social Forces*, 88(1): 271–299.

Brandolini, Andrea, and Timothy Smeeding. 2009. "Income Inequality in Richer and OECD Countries." Pp. 71–100 in *Oxford Handbook of Economic Inequality*, edited by Wiemer Salverda, Brian Nolan, and Tim Smeeding. Oxford, UK: Oxford University Press.

Browne, Irene, and Joya Misra. 2003. "The Intersection of Gender and Race in the Labor Market." *Annual Review of Sociology*, 29: 487–513.

Christopher, Karen. 2002. "Welfare State Regimes and Mothers' Poverty." *Social Politics*, 9: 60–86.

Christopher, Karen, Paula England, Timothy M. Smeeding, and K. R. Phillips. 2002. "The Gender Gap in Poverty in Modern Nations: Single Motherhood, the Market, and the State." *Sociological Perspectives*, 45: 219–242.

Congressional Research Service. 2012. *Spending for Federal Benefits and Services for People with Low Income, FY2008–FY2011: An Update of Table B-1 from CRS Report R41625, Modified to Remove Programs for Veterans* (CRS-2012-CRS-0005). Washington, DC: Author.

Cornelius, Llewellyn J. 2003. "Fixing that Great Hodgepodge: Health Care for the Poor in the U.S." *Journal of Poverty*, 7(1/2): 7–21.

Crawford, April. 2006. "The Impact of Child Care Subsidies on Single Mothers' Work Effort." *Review of Policy Research*, 23(3): 699–711.

Danziger, Sandra K. 2010. "The Decline of Cash Welfare and Implications for Social Policy and Poverty." *Annual Review of Sociology*, 36: 523–545.

Danziger, Sheldon H. and Robert H. Haveman. 2001. *Understanding Poverty*. Cambridge, MA: Harvard University Press.

Eamon, Mary Keegan, Chi-Fang Wu, and Saijun Zhang. 2009. "Effectiveness and Limitations of the Earned Income Tax Credit for Reducing Child Poverty in the United States." *Children and Youth Services Review*, 31(8): 919–926.

Ellwood, David T. 2000. "Anti-Poverty Policy for Families in the Next Century: From Welfare to Work—and Worries." *Journal of Economic Perspectives*, 14(1): 187–198.

Gonzales, Lisa, Kenneth Hudson, and Joan Acker. 2007. "Diverting Dependency: The Effects of Diversion on the Short Term Outcomes of TANF Applicants." *Journal of Poverty*, 11(1): 83–105.

Gornick, Janet C. and Marcia K. Meyers. 2003. *Families That Work: Policies for Reconciling Parenthood and Employment*, New York: Russell Sage.

Graefe, Deborah R., Gordon F. De Jong, Matthew Hall, Samuel Sturgeon, and Julie VanEerden. 2008. "Immigrants' TANF Eligibility, 1996–2003: What Explains the New Across-State Inequalities?" *International Migration Review*, 42(1): 89–133.

Heuveline, Patrick, and Matthew Weinshenker. 2008. "The International Child Poverty Gap: Does Demography Matter?" *Demography*, 45(1): 173–191.

Huber, Evelyne, John D. Stephens, David Bradley, Stephanie Moller, and Francois Nielsen. 2009. "The Politics of Women's Economic Independence." *Social Politics*, 16(1): 1–39.

Internal Revenue Service. 2014. *Statistics for 2011 Tax Year Returns with EITC*. Retrieved August 15, 2014. http://www.eitc.irs.gov/EITC-Central/eitcstats/2011stats.

Jilcott, Stephanie B., Elizabeth D. Wall-Bassett, Soane C. Burke, and Justin B. Moore. 2011. "Associations between Food Insecurity, Supplemental Nutrition Assistance Program (SNAP) Benefits, and Body Mass Index among Adult Females." *Journal of the American Dietetic Association*, 111(11): 1741–1745.

Jolliffe, Dean, Craig Gundersen, Laura Tiehen, and Joshua Winicki. 2005. "Food Stamp Benefits and Child Poverty." *American Journal of Agricultural Economics*, 87(3): 569–581.

Kenworthy, Lane. 1999. "Do Social-Welfare Policies Reduce Poverty? A Cross-National Assessment." *Social Forces*, 77: 1119–1139.

Kim, Rebecca Y. 2001. "The Effects of the Earned Income Tax Credit on Children's Income and Poverty: Who Fares Better?" *Journal of Poverty*, 5(1): 1–22.

Kim, Rebecca Y., Younghee Lim, and Wonik Lee. 2006. "A Study of Health Care Coverage Among Children in Immigrant Families in the Post Welfare-Reform Era." *Journal of Poverty*, 10(3): 93–118.

Koh, Howard K., and Kathleen G. Sebelius. 2010. "Promoting Prevention through the Affordable Care Act." *New England Journal of Medicine*, 363: 1296–1299.

Korpi, Walter, and Joakim Palme. 1998. "The Paradox of Redistribution and Strategies of Equality: Welfare State Institutions, Inequality, and Poverty in the Western Countries." *American Sociological Review*, 63(5): 661–687.

Kupillas, Lauren M., and Mary A. Nies. 2007. "Obesity and Poverty: Are Food Stamps to Blame?" *Home Health Care Management Practice*, 20(1): 41–49.

Lichter, Daniel T., and Rukamalie Jayakody. 2002. "Welfare Reform: How Do We Measure Success?" *Annual Review of Sociology*, 28: 117–141.

Lim, Younghee, Michelle Livermore, and Belinda Creel Davis. 2010. "Material Hardship Among Banked and Unbanked Earned Income Tax Credit-Eligible Families." *Journal of Poverty*, 14(3): 266–284.

Loprest, Pamela J. 2012. "How Has the TANF Caseload Changed Over Time?" *Urban Institute Research Synthesis Brief*, March 8, 2012.

Mahler, Vincent A., and David K. Jesuit. 2006. "Fiscal Redistribution in the Developed Countries: New Insights from the Luxembourg Income Study." *Socio-Economic Review*, 4: 483–511.

McLanahan, Sara. 2004. "Diverging Destinies: How Children Fare Under the Second Demographic Transition." *Demography*, 41(4): 607–627.

McLanahan, Sara, and Christine Percheski. 2008. "Family Structure and the Reproduction of Inequalities." *Annual Review of Sociology*, 34: 257–276.

Mendenhall, Amy N. 2006. "A Guide to the Earned Income Tax Credit: What Everyone Should Know About the EITC." *Journal of Poverty*, 10(3): 51–68.

Meyers, Marcia K., Theresa Heintze, and Douglas A. Wolf. 2002. "Child Care Subsidies and the Employment of Welfare Recipients." *Demography*, 39(1): 165–179.

Misra, Joya, Stephanie Moller, and Michelle J. Budig. 2007. "Work-Family Policies and Poverty for Partnered and Single Women in Europe and North America." *Gender and Society*, 21: 804–827.

Misra, Joya, Stephanie Moller, Eiko Strader, and Elizabeth Wemlinger. 2012. "Family Policies, Employment and Poverty Among Partnered and Single Mothers." *Research in Social Stratification and Mobility*, 30(1): 113–128.

Moller, Stephanie, Arthur Alderson, and François Nielsen. 2009. "Changing Patterns of Income Inequality in U.S. Counties." *American Journal of Sociology*, 114: 1037–1101.

Moller, Stephanie, David Bradley, Evelyne Huber, Francois Nielsen, and John D. Stephens. 2003. "Determinants of Relative Poverty in Advanced Capitalist Democracies." *American Sociological Review*, 68(1): 22–51.

Organisation for Economic Co-operation and Development (OECD). 2008. *Growing Unequal? Income Distribution and Poverty in OECD Countries*, Paris: OECD Press.

Organisation for Economic Co-operation and Development (OECD). 2011. *Growing Income Inequality in OECD Countries: What Drives it and How Can Policy Tackle it?* Retrieved December 10, 2012. http://www.oecd.org/social/socialpoliciesanddata/47723414.pdf.

Osberg, Lars, Timothy M. Smeeding, and Jonathan Schwabish. 2004. "Income distribution and public social expenditure: Theories, effects, and evidence." Pp. 821–859 in *Social Inequality*, edited by Kathryn M. Neckerman. New York: Russell Sage Foundation.

Parisi, Domenico, Deborah A. Harris, Steven Michael Grice, Michael Taquino, and Duane A. Gill. 2005. "Does the TANF Work-First Initiative Help Low-Income Families Make Successful Welfare-to-Work Transitions?" *Journal of Poverty*, 9(1): 65–81.

Rainwater, Lee, and Timothy M. Smeeding. 2003. *Poor Kids in a Rich Country*. New York: Russell Sage Foundation.

Ratcliffe, Caroline, Signe-Mary McKernan, and Sisi Zhang. 2011. "How Much Does the Supplemental Nutrition Assistance Program Reduce Food Insecurity?" *American Journal of Agricultural Economics*, 93(4): 1082–1098.

Reese, Ellen, and Elvia Ramirez. 2002. "The New Ethnic Politics of Welfare: Struggles Over Legal Immigrants' Rights to Welfare in California." *Journal of Poverty*, 6(3): 29–62.

Reschovsky, James D., and Ann S. O'Malley. 2008. "Do Primary Care Physicians Treating Minority Patients Report Problems Delivering High-Quality Care?" *Health Affairs*, 27(3): 222–231.

Schoen, Cathy, Michelle M. Doty, Ruth H. Robertson, and Sara R. Collins. 2011. "Affordable Care Act Reforms Could Reduce the Number of Underinsured U.S. Adults by 70 Percent." *Health Affairs*, 9: 1762–1771.

Smeeding, Timothy M. 2004. "Twenty Years of Research on Income Inequality, Poverty, and Redistribution in the Developed World." *Socio-Economic Review*, 2(2): 149–163.

Smeeding, Timothy M. 2005. "Public Policy, Economic Inequality, and Poverty: The United States in Comparative Perspective." *Social Science Quarterly*, 86: 955–983.

Social Security Administration (SSA). 2011. *Annual Report of the Supplemental Security Income Program.* Washington, DC: Government Printing Office.

Spar, Karen. 2011. *Federal Benefits and Services for People with Low Income: Programs, Policy, and Spending, FY2008–FY2009.* Washington, DC: Congressional Research Service.

Teters, Jennifer, and Jennifer Weber. 2007. "The Challenge with Food Stamps." *The Journal of the American Dietetic Association*, 107(9): 1489–1490.

U.S. Census Bureau. 2012. *Current Population Survey: 2011 Poverty Table of Contents.* Retrieved November 3, 2012. http://www.census.gov/hhes/www/cpstables/032012/pov/toc.htm.

U.S. Department of Agriculture (USDA). 2012. *Supplemental Nutrition Assistance Program Participation and Costs.* Retrieved November 24, 2012. http://www.fns.usda.gov/pd/SNAPsummary.htm.

U.S. Department of Health and Human Services (USDHHS). 2012a. *2011 Actuarial Report on the Financial Outlook for Medicaid*, Washington, DC: Government Printing Office.

U.S. Department of Health and Human Services (USDHHS). 2012b. *Office of Family Assistance: Caseload Data 2010.* Retrieved November 24, 2012. http://www.acf.hhs.gov/programs/ofa/resource/caseload-data-2010.

U.S. Department of Health and Human Services (USDHHS). 2012c. *Office of Family Assistance: TANF Financial Data—FY 2010.* Retrieved November 24, 2012. http://www.acf.hhs.gov/programs/ofa/resource/tanf-financial-data-fy-2010.

Western, Bruce, Deirdre Bloome, Benjamin Sosnaud, and Laura Tach. 2012. "Economic Insecurity and Social Stratification." *Annual Review of Sociology*, 38: 341–359.

Wiepking, Pamala, and Ineke Maas. 2005. "Gender Differences in Poverty: A Cross-National Study." *European Sociological Review*, 21(3): 187–200.

Wiseman, Michael. 2011. "Supplemental Security Income for the Second Decade." *Poverty and Public Policy*, 3(1): 1–18.

24

MIXED-INCOME COMMUNITIES AND POVERTY AMELIORATION

James C. Fraser and Deirdre Oakley

Over the twentieth century studies have shown that poverty in U.S. cities has become more concentrated, forming neighborhoods that are largely disconnected from the amenities that other places take for granted (i.e., grocery, other retail, and banks), and that these places are typically occupied by African-Americans (Massey and Denton, 1993). These trends and the disinvestment in many inner-city neighborhoods did not happen overnight. The story of mass suburbanization of whites from cities, as well as the de jure and de facto discrimination against racial minority group members through redlining and planning codes such as racial zoning to keep them from accessing these new housing markets, has had a lasting legacy (ibid.). Between the 1960s and the 1980s many of these areas were considered "no-go zones" and several have been home to project-based public housing developments.

The media often represented these places as dysfunctional, for example in films like *New Jack City* where drug cartels were pictured as running entire public housing developments (Fraser et al., 2012). And the academic literature also vacillated between describing the roots of this spatialized poverty as caused by structural and cultural factors (O'Connor, 2002). During the late 1980s William Julius Wilson (Wilson, 1987) wrote *The Truly Disadvantaged*, positing that, for the poor, living in hyper-segregated and impoverished neighborhoods exponentially cut people off from mainstream institutions as well as opportunity structures that could assist them in achieving a higher socioeconomic status. Arguably, this set the stage for mixed-income housing policies to be implemented under the umbrella of de-concentrating poverty in order to assist low-income families economically and with their quality of life.

Mixed-income housing certainly occurs in a variety of contexts, but the majority of studies on it focus on the HUD's Homeownership Opportunities for People Everywhere (HOPE VI) program. The HUD Reform Act of 1989 called for the creation of the National Commission on Severely Distressed Public Housing. The Commission was charged with identifying severely distressed public housing developments nationwide, assessing strategies for addressing the problems of these developments, and formulating a plan of action (National Housing Law Project, 2002).[1] The Commission issued its final report in 1992, estimating that of the approximately 1.3 million public housing units in the country, 86,000 were severely distressed (National Commission on Severely Distressed Public Housing (U.S.), 1992). In response to the Commission's findings, the HOPE VI program was initiated in 1993.

The HOPE VI program did not begin as a mechanism for neighborhood transformation but rather as an initiative targeting the most severely distressed public housing developments in the country. The program had five key objectives: (1) changing the physical shape of public housing by replacing the worst developments with apartments or townhouses; (2) reducing concentrations of poverty by encouraging a greater income mix among public housing residents; (3) establishing support services to help public housing residents get and keep jobs; (4) establishing and enforcing high standards of personal and community responsibility; and (5) forging broad-based partnerships in planning and implementing improvements in public housing (Pitcoff, 1999). However, for its first six years, HOPE VI operated under a number of evolving laws, regulations, and HUD legal opinions that increasingly gave local housing authorities more latitude (Salama, 1999, p. 96).

According to Salama (1999) such measures included: (1) elimination of federal preferences emphasizing the lowest-income household for admissions to public housing; (2) the elimination of the one-for-one replacement requirement for demolished public housing units; and (3) authorization allowing housing authorities to utilize housing development funds and operating subsidies for projects owned by private housing organizations. One of the outcomes was a shift in focus away from the "most" severely distressed public housing sites, towards sites with the greatest potential to attract private investment for HOPE VI (National Housing Law Project, 2002).

Such changes were codified in 1998 under the Quality Housing and Work Responsibility Act. In addition, this legislature included amendments to the Housing Act of 1937, which authorized further deregulation of local housing authorities in an effort to de-concentrate poverty and develop mixed-income communities (Hunt et al., 1998). Thus, the program was recast as a poverty dispersal initiative that replaces poverty-concentrated public housing developments with new mixed-income housing (Goetz, 2013; Smith, 2002). This policy shift was firmly grounded in the theory that former public housing neighborhoods would attract economic investment and that former public housing residents would benefit from greater exposure to higher-income residents (Joseph et al., 2007; Vale, 2007).

These legislative changes meant that nearly any public housing site could now qualify for HOPE VI funds regardless of the condition of the housing stock (National Housing Law Project, 2002). Despite concerns about the loss of low-income units and displacement, HOPE VI has since expanded into a $6.1 billion effort involving 254 local housing authorities throughout the country (Nguyen et al., 2012). Although touted as one of the most important and innovative inner city revitalization programs, critics assert that a major flaw continually overlooked in policy circles is HOPE VI's inability to accommodate public housing residents who are displaced, as well as those at the lowest end of the income scale (Buron et al., 2007). In other words, explicit to the structure and aims of HOPE VI is the relocation of public housing residents, many of whom do not get the opportunity to return to the redevelopments because, on average, only about 20 percent of the new units are set aside at the former residents' income levels (Clampet-Lundquist, 2004; Goetz and Chapple, 2010; Oakley and Burchfield, 2009). Instead, through the use of Housing Choice Voucher (HCV) subsidies (formerly Section 8), qualified public housing residents are relocated to the private rental market (Oakley and Burchfield, 2009). Ironically, concerns about displacement in particular are reminiscent of the slum clearance efforts authorized by the 1949 Housing Act (Hirsch, 1998).

Many in academic and policy circles consider HOPE VI a success: public–private partnerships have been forged, blighted housing has been replaced with attractive mixed-income developments, and poverty has been reduced at the redeveloped sites (Stoloff, 2004). Yet, the proverbial elephant in the room is the fact that because there is no one-for-one replacement requirement, there has not only been a net loss of housing units affordable to very low-income households, but congressional allocations of voucher subsidies have not increased at a level to meet the gap caused by this loss as well (Fraser and DeFilippis, 2012; Goetz and Chapple, 2010). To situate this crisis in the broader perspective of unmet need, in 1970 there were 130 affordable units for every 100 low-income households in the country, whereas today there are only 38 (Urban Academic Scholars in Opposition to PETRA, 2010). In addition, the elimination of one-for-one replacement has meant further reliance on the private rental market. While research indicates that many former public housing residents who receive vouchers end up in somewhat less poor neighborhoods than public housing, tight rental markets, as well as racial and economic segregation, have left almost 40 percent living in other highly distressed neighborhoods (Popkin, 2004).[2] Likewise, family situations, health issues, and place-dependent considerations, such as proximity to kin and public transportation, shaped relocation preferences, possibly resulting in the varying quality of destination neighborhoods (Goetz and Chapple, 2010; Kleit and Carnegie, 2011; Popkin et al., 2004).

Reflections: HOPE VI and beyond

Many studies on HOPE VI stress empirical findings about how people have experienced the profound changes occurring in the transformation of public housing. Our sense is that there are two broad literatures that could be parsed out. Numerous "evidence-based" studies have been conducted that largely take the stated goals of HOPE VI and mixed-income housing at face value. In this realm people enumerate the effects of poverty de-concentration on economic and social measures applied to former public housing residents. It is fair to say that virtually all of these studies found that former public housing residents and those returning to HOPE VI developments reported that they lived in improved environments but that their actual wages were no better due to this intervention (Goetz and Chapple, 2010). Other than that, these empirical studies leave the theorizing of mixed-income housing to others. This is pretty evident in that much of what these studies conclude is that there was imperfect implementation of HOPE VI and that people faced multiple barriers to employment such as childcare, health issues, and transportation (Popkin, 2004).

This work motivated DeFilippis and Fraser (2010) to pose the rhetorical question "Why do we want mixed-income housing and neighborhoods?" as a way to suggest that the hegemony of mixed-income housing has been so strong that many of us took it for granted. In other words, of course, social mix is desirable. This is not to say everyone supports HOPE VI. Many people have been very critical of the displacement of public housing residents and the razing of developments in lieu of repairing what was there. In this vein Ed Goetz stands out as a very thoughtful scholar who has demonstrated in multiple studies that HOPE VI has a deleterious effect on many former residents, as well as on the provision of low-income housing itself (Goetz, 2013).

Alternatively, to "evidence-based" studies of mixed-income housing there has been a body of work that is oftentimes empirically light but strong on thinking through what HOPE VI, and really mixed-income policies more broadly, means in relation to changes in state, market, and societal arrangements. Here we are thinking about a group of scholars who have drawn on neoliberalism as the theoretical scaffolding to make the claims that both public housing is being privatized and that mixed-income interventions in low-income neighborhoods is tantamount to gentrification (Hackworth, 2005; Rose et al., 2012). Loretta Lees (2008) has made a compelling case that social mixing (i.e., bringing the middle class to impoverished neighborhoods) may actually be a technique of gentrification.

In many of these treatments we see more scholars turning toward an explicitly socio-spatial frame. Joanna Duke (2009) draws on the work of Henri Lefebvre in her analysis of mixed-income housing and low-income people's rights to appropriate and participate in the production of neighborhood space (e.g., drawing from Lefebvre's "right to the city"). Similarly, Lucio and Wolfersteig (2012) deploy "right to the city," suggesting that effective community and social support programs could assist in building effective structures for public housing residents in HOPE VI developments to participate in the governance of their new developments.

At times our own work on mixed-income development, HOPE VI and otherwise, has focused on the production of space and examining the ways in which people claim the right to inhabit or create neighborhoods. In a ten-year study conducted in Chattanooga, Tennessee, part of our project focused on the differential ways in which people performed their belonging through performative acts and how these signifiers of having a right to be in a neighborhood shifted as the mixed-income development strategy began to gentrify the target neighborhood (Fraser et al., 2003). At first low-income residents were enrolled in a community-building effort that transformed into a mixed-income development project when the funders of the initiative met a consultant for the NeighborWorks who suggested that higher-income homeowners would stabilize the neighborhood. As housing prices shot up and higher-income people began moving into the neighborhood, low-income residents' performance of belonging to the neighborhood through their participation in the community-building portion of the project was no longer effective. In this case, mixed-income development was what Gary Bridge, Tim Butler, and Loretta Lees refer to as "gentrification by stealth" (Bridge et al., 2012).

On that note, we have noticed in some treatments of mixed-income housing a consistent theoretical interest in what we call a politics of inclusion. In particular, a recent article, "Participation, Deliberation, and Decision Making: The Dynamics of Inclusion and Exclusion in Mixed-Income Developments" (Chaskin et al., 2012), suggests that participatory governance structures where public housing residents can play a meaningful role in the everyday activities that reproduce development/neighborhood space are largely non-existent. And in "'Positive' Gentrification, Social Control and the 'Right to the City' in Mixed-Income Communities: Uses and Expectations of Space and Place" (Chaskin and Joseph, 2013), the spatial turn is taken further into what many consider to be seminal work in urban geography. Likewise Fraser et al. (2013), in "HOPE VI, Colonization, and the Production of Difference," document the spatial politics that unfold between different income and tenure groups. All of these studies question the foundational tenet of mixed-income policy; that is, how can mixed-income neighborhoods (and developments) be advantageous for low-income residents when relationships between groups are oftentimes characterized by benign neglect, apathy, or by various levels of hostility and distrust?

If income and tenure mixing in HOPE VI developments is not unfolding in lock step with the more optimistic proponents of mixed-income housing, then how do we account for this? We see HOPE VI as having at least four somewhat contradictory sets of goals. The first is a mechanism to improve housing conditions by providing for reinvestment in the public housing stock. In order to maintain this objective, Public Housing Associations (PHAs) have to be vigorous in protecting their units from unruly, damaging tenants—in other words, tenants who are not perceived as being good citizens. The second is to provide safe, decent housing for people who cannot provide for themselves, which necessitates meeting the needs of a diverse and vulnerable population. The third is to move people away from dependence and towards independence through facilitating entry into private job and housing markets. To meet this goal, PHAs must carefully choose tenants who seem amenable to a self-improvement project. They also must provide a range of resources and incentives for people to succeed, carefully monitor their progress through the program, and reward success and punish failure. The fourth and final goal fueling HOPE VI is to stabilize and improve the neighborhoods in which the complexes exist in a way that demonstrates a secure investment. Ultimately, this goal seeks to encourage private real estate developers to rediscover neighborhoods that they had previously abandoned by withdrawing their invested capital.

Consequently, HOPE VI serves as a vehicle for a second circuit of capital, where economic activity is focused, not just on production through labor, but on the cycling of capital through trade. It represents an effort to make visible those neighborhoods not yet touched by general processes of gentrification (Hackworth and Smith, 2001; Smith, 2002). It is a remaking of place, by moving the "problem" of low-income housing from something dangerous and indicative of government failure to something safe and representative of the promise of private investment and public–private partnerships (Engels, 1948[1887]; Kipfer and Petrunia, 2009; Lefebvre, 1978).

But mixed-income policies have gone well beyond public housing redevelopment. City officials, seeking ways to revitalize low-income inner-city neighborhoods, have turned toward an ever-increasing set of organizations and their consultants espousing the virtues of mixed-income, in order to legitimate public–private ventures that oftentimes seek to gentrify neighborhoods (Dutton, 2007; Fraser et al., 2003; Lees, 2008; Rose et al., 2012; Skirtz, 2012). However, while this may be the case in some mixed-income housing initiatives, it would be premature and suspect to write off mixed-income housing as simply a way to displace lower-income people from neighborhoods cities want to redevelop.

Mixed-income policies and programs have become dominant urban planning strategies even as hypotheses about what mixed income can achieve continue to change and questions remain about the model's purpose and actual impact. Core questions debated since the reemergence of the mixed-income model in the 1990s have evolved and broadened as empirical studies have shed light on the models in practice.

While the hypothesized benefits of such initiatives have included the assumed socioeconomic advantages of poverty alleviation, the reduction of racial and income-based segregation, and the benefits of homeownership, the realities of living in these reconfigured spaces do not necessarily map well onto the original goals associated with them. This has led some scholars to suggest that such "mixing" strategies boil down to state-implemented strategies to prepare neighborhoods for capital investment through the regulation, marginalization, and displacement of the poor. Such suggestions raise more fundamental questions about when and how society, and its government leaders, should house the least advantaged.

Notes

1 Severely distressed refers to dilapidated, often largely vacant buildings that show the effects of poor construction, managerial neglect, inadequate maintenance, and rampant vandalism. These developments typically have huge backlogs of repairs, including non-working elevators, leaky pipes, old electric wiring, unstable walls, and pest infestations that create a poor and often unsafe living environment for residents. However, it is important to note that the HOPE VI legislation did not codify this definition as a program requirement (National Housing Law Project, 2002).

2 Likewise, according to the written Congressional testimony submitted by the Urban Academic Scholars in Opposition to PETRA, the reduction in public housing stock is paralleled by the loss of 360,000 mostly project-based Section 8 units, as private owners have opted out when their 20-year contracts came to an end, and another 335,000 are coming up for renewal in the next few years (2010). These reductions are compounded by the fact that the majority of former public housing residents have never benefited from the HOPE VI redevelopments (Oakley and Burchfield, 2009). The evidence is also unclear concerning how these redevelopments influence the spatial distribution of poverty throughout the urban core and whether former public housing residents relocated with vouchers end up in substantively better neighborhoods (Goetz and Chapple, 2010).

References

Bridge, G., Butler, T., and Lees, L. (2012). *Mixed communities: Gentrification by stealth?* Bristol: Policy Press.

Buron, Larry, Diane K. Levy, and Megan Gallagher. 2007. *Housing choice vouchers: How HOPE VI families fared in the private market.* HOPE VI: Where Do We Go from Here? Brief 3. Washington, DC: Urban Institute Press.

Chaskin, R., and Joseph, M. (2013). "Positive" gentrification, social control and the "right to the city" in mixed-income communities: uses and expectations of space and place. *International Journal of Urban and Regional Research*, 37(2), 480–502.

Chaskin, R., Khare, A., and Joseph, M. (2013). Participation, deliberation, and decision making: the dynamics of inclusion and exclusion in mixed-income developments. *Urban Affairs Review*, 48(6), 863–906.

Clampet-Lundquist, S. (2004). HOPE VI relocation: Moving to new neighborhoods and building new ties. *Housing Policy Debate*, 15(2), 415–447.

DeFilippis, J., and Fraser, James. (eds.). (2010). *Why do we want mixed-income housing and neighborhoods?* New York: SUNY Press.

Duke, J. (2009). Mixed income housing policy and public housing residents, "right to the city." *Critical Social Policy*, 29(1), 100–120.

Dutton, T.A. (2007). Colony Over-the-Rhine. *The Black Scholar*, 37(3), 14–27.

Engels, F. (1948[1887]). *Zur Wohnungsfrage.* Berlin: Dietz Verlag.

Fraser, J., and DeFilippis, J. (2012). HOPE VI: Calling for modesty in its claims. In G. Bridge, T. Butler, and L. Less (eds), *Mixed communities: Gentrification by stealth?* Bristol: Policy Press.

Fraser, J., Lepofsky, J., Kick, E., and Williams, P. (2003). The construction of the local and the limits of contemporary community-building in the United States. *Urban Affairs Review*, 38(3), 417–445.

Fraser, J., Oakley, D., and Bazuin, J. (2012). Public ownership and private profit in housing. *Cambridge Journal of Regions, Economy and Society*, 5(3), 397–412.

Fraser, James Curtis, Burns, Ashley Brown, Bazuin, Joshua Theodore, and Oakley, Deirdre Áine. (2013). HOPE VI, colonization, and the production of difference. *Urban Affairs Review*, 49(4), 525–556.

Goetz, E.G. (2013). The audacity of HOPE VI: Discourse and the dismantling of public housing. *Cities*, 35, 342–348.

Goetz, E.G., and Chapple, K. (2010). You gotta move: Advancing the debate on the record of dispersal. *Housing Policy Debate*, 20(2), 209–236.

Hackworth, J. (2005). Progressive activism in a neoliberal context: The case of efforts to retain public housing in the United States. *Studies in Political Economy*, 75, 29–51.

Hackworth, J., and Smith, N. (2001). The changing state of gentrification. *Journal of Economic and Social Geography*, 92(4), 464–477.

Hirsch, A.R. (1998). *Making the second ghetto: Race and housing in Chicago 1940–1960.* Chicago: University of Chicago Press.

Hunt, L., Schulhof, M., and Holmquist, S. (1998). Summary of the Quality Housing and Work Responsibility Act of 1998 (Title V of P.L. 105–276). *Washington, DC Office of Policy, Program and Legislative Initiatives, U.S. Department of Housing and Urban Development (HUD).*

Joseph, M.L., Chaskin, R.J., and Webber, H.S. (2007). The theoretical basis for addressing poverty through mixed-income development. *Urban Affairs Review*, 42(3), 369–409.

Kipfer, S., and Petrunia, J. (2009). "Recolonization" and public housing: A Toronto case study. *Studies in Political Economy*, 83, 111–139.

Kleit, R.G., and Carnegie, N.B. (2011). Integrated or isolated? The impact of public housing redevelopment on social network homophily. *Social Networks*, 33(2), 152–165.

Lees, L. (2008). Gentrification and social mixing: Towards an inclusive urban renaissance? *Urban Studies*, 45(12), 2449–2470.

Lefebvre, H. (1978). *De L'Etat Volume 4.* Paris: Union Générale des Editions.

Lucio, J., and Wolfersteig, W. (2012). Political and social incorporation of public housing residents: Challenges in HOPE VI community development. *Journal of Community Development*, 43(4), 476–491.

Massey, Douglas S., and Denton, Nancy A. (1993). *American apartheid: Segregation and the making of the underclass.* Cambridge, MA: Harvard University Press.

National Commission on Severely Distressed Public Housing (U.S.) (1992). *The final report of the National Commission on Severely Distressed Public Housing: A report to the Congress and the Secretary of Housing and Urban Development. Washington, DC: NCSDPH.*

National Housing Law Project. (2002). *False HOPE: A critical assessment of the HOPE VI Public Housing Redevelopment Program.*

Nguyen, M.T., Rohe, W.M., and Cowan, S.M. (2012). Entrenched hybridity in public housing agencies in the USA. *Housing Studies*, 27(4), 457–475.

O'Connor, A. (2002). *Poverty knowledge: Social science, social policy, and the poor in twentieth-century U.S. history*: Princeton University Press.

Oakley, D., and Burchfield, K. (2009). Out of the projects, still in the hood: The spatial constraints on public-housing residents' relocation in Chicago. *Journal of Urban Affairs*, 31(5), 589–614.

Pitcoff, W. (1999). New hope for public housing. *Shelterforce Magazine*, 21(2), 18–22.

Popkin, S.J. (2004). A decade of HOPE VI: Research findings and policy challenges. *Urban Institute Report.*

Popkin, S.J., Levy, D.K., Harris, L.E., Comey, J., Cunningham, M.K., and Buron, L.F. (2004). The HOPE VI program: What about the residents? *Housing Policy Debate*, 15(2), 385–414.

Rose, D., Germain, A., Bacque, M., Bridge, G., Fijalkow, Y., and Slater, T. (2012). "Social mix" and neighbourhood revitalization in a transatlantic perspective: Comparing local policy discourses and expectations in Paris (France), Bristol (UK) and Montréal (Canada). *International Journal of Urban and Regional Research*, 37(2), 430–450.

Salama, J.J. (1999). The redevelopment of distressed public housing: early results from HOPE VI projects in Atlanta, Chicago, and San Antonio. *Housing Policy Debate*, 10(1), 95–142.

Skirtz, A. (2012). *Econocide: Elimination of the urban poor.* Washington, DC: NASW Press.

Smith, N. (2002). New globalism, new urbanism: Gentrification as global urban strategy. *Antipode*, 34(3), 427–450.

Stoloff, J.A. (2004). *A brief history of public housing.* Paper presented at the annual meeting of the American Sociological Association, San Francisco, CA.

Urban Academic Scholars in Opposition to PETRA. (2010). *Written testimony submitted to the U.S. House of Representatives Financial Services Committee: The Administration's proposal to preserve and transform public and assisted housing.* Washington, DC.

Vale, L.J. (2007). *From the puritans to the projects: Public housing and public neighbors.* Cambridge, MA: Harvard University Press.

Wilson, W.J. (1987). *The truly disadvantaged.* Chicago: University of Chicago Press.

25

COUNTERING URBAN POVERTY CONCENTRATION IN THE UNITED STATES

The people versus place debate in housing policy

Anupama Jacob

Title 42 of the U.S. Code states that "the future welfare of the Nation and the well-being of its citizens" requires "systematic and sustained action by Federal, State, and local governments to … improve the living environment of low- and moderate-income families, and to develop new centers of population growth and economic activity" (U.S. Department of Housing and Urban Development [HUD], n.d.(a)). Policymakers and researchers are increasingly recognizing the importance of economic, social, cultural, and political features of a neighborhood in influencing the short- and long-term opportunities available to its residents (Brooks-Gunn et al., 1997; Ellen and Turner, 2003; Sampson et al., 2002).

One major obstacle to the government's goal of building viable urban communities is the spatial concentration of poverty. Neighborhoods in which at least 40% of the residents live below the federal poverty line are considered high-poverty areas. Kneebone et al. (2011) find that, after falling in the 1990s, the number of people living in high-poverty neighborhoods increased by a third from 2000 to 2005–2009. In fact, in 2005–2009, 10.5% of the poor population lived in such pockets of extreme poverty. The economic recession is believed to have intensified the re-concentration of poverty into high-poverty neighborhoods.

The spatial concentration of poverty has been linked with economic and social maladies such as fewer employment opportunities, poorer health outcomes, and lower levels of academic achievement compared to residents of more advantaged neighborhoods (Duncan and Raudenbush, 1999; Galster, 2003; Wilson, 1987, 1996). These findings emphasize the need to focus on strategies that promote the economic and social well-being of residents in deprived neighborhoods. It is not just poor residents who stand to benefit from targeted policies, but as Congress noted, the very welfare of the nation depends on providing a "suitable living environment for every American family" (Preamble to 1949 Housing Act, in Schwartz, 2010).

Housing policy responses have typically centered on the debate between people-based and place-based strategies. People-based strategies focus on social mobility by providing individuals with the opportunity to move to "better" neighborhoods, while place-based strategies focus on revitalizing areas of concentrated poverty. This chapter critically assesses two housing programs that exemplify these two approaches to countering the spatial segregation of neighborhoods of concentrated poverty: the Department of Housing and Urban Development (HUD) Housing Choice Voucher Program (people-based) and Mixed-Income Housing Developments (place-based). Both strategies reflect a neoliberal orientation through an increasing reliance on consumer choice and the privatization of public housing combined with a general "rolling back" of the state (Peck and Tickell, 2002). The chapter also discusses the implications for research and policy.

Vouchers and mixed-income housing development: policy tools to counter the concentration of poverty?

The late 1960s and 1970s saw a marked shift in federal housing policy. The state's ability to counter poverty concentration was questioned, with the growing recognition that the public housing developments that had formed the basis of federal intervention for over 30 years had in effect created pockets of concentrated poverty with attendant social problems such as high rates of unemployment, crime, and school drop-outs (Massey and Denton, 1993; Wilson, 1987). Researchers began to highlight the vital role more socio-economically diverse neighborhoods could play in providing individuals with opportunities to become economically self-sufficient and productive citizens (Goetz and Chapple, 2010). Joseph et al. (2007) highlight four propositions to explain how such neighborhoods might specifically promote the overall well-being of low-income families:

Social networks: Social interaction among families of different income levels is assumed to provide low-income families, in particular, with valuable contacts and access to resources, information, and employment opportunities.

Social control: The presence of higher-income residents is presumed to naturally produce informal social control by fostering accountability to shared norms and rules.

Culture and behavior: Linked to the highly controversial discussion on the "culture of poverty" thesis, higher-income families are viewed as role models who can encourage behavioral changes and an enhanced sense of self-efficacy among low-income families through increased labor market participation, educational achievements, and the permeation of norms that encourage upward mobility.

Political economy of place: In contrast to the other three propositions, the political economy of place focuses on the relationship between residents and external actors. The main argument here is that higher-income residents engender new market demand and political pressures that secure a higher quality of services and goods for the entire neighborhood.

Using the four propositions as a general framework, this chapter presents an overview of the background and key research findings on the economic and social outcomes of the two housing policy approaches.

The housing voucher approach

Background

Housing vouchers became part of official federal housing policy with the passing of the Housing and Community Development Act of 1974. The program initially provided rental certificates to families with incomes up to 80% of the area median income. Recipients paid around 30% of their household income in rent, and the remaining amount was subsidized by the federal government. To determine the maximum permissible rent, the area median income was used to calculate the Fair Market Rent in over 2,600 local housing markets, accounting for unit size. The program enabled low-income families to obtain rental housing that fulfilled HUD's minimum-quality criteria in the private market (Schwartz, 2010).

The rental certificate program was modified in 1983 to a freestanding voucher program. Households could choose to spend more than 30% of their income on rent; however, the additional amount would not be subsidized by the government. The 1998 Housing Choice Voucher program allows participants to spend no more than 40% of their income on rent and transfer their vouchers to any part of the country. The program also requires that at least 75% of all annually issued vouchers be set aside for households earning less than 30% of the area's median family income. Vouchers have become the main rental support program since their inception, assisting more than 2.2 million households by the year 2009 (Schwartz, 2010).

Economic and social outcomes of the voucher approach

The Gautreaux program in Chicago provided the earliest support for the voucher program. The program grew out of a class action lawsuit levied against the Chicago Housing Authority and HUD in 1966 and ran from 1976 to 1998. In response to the claim that African American house-holds were being intentionally segregated in less desirable neighborhoods, the U.S. Supreme Court decreed that vouchers be provided to around 7,000 families either living in or waiting for public housing units so they could find private rental units in predominantly white suburban areas or other parts of the city. Eligible families entered a lottery system voluntarily, and counselors helped winners find appropriate housing (Schwartz, 2010; Varady and Walker, 2003).

Research found that (1) families who moved to suburban areas were more likely to realize better employment outcomes, although not necessarily higher wages, (2) children of families who moved to suburban areas were more likely to graduate from high school and enter college, and (3) families who relocated to higher socio-economic neighborhoods experienced a greater sense of safety (Goering, 2003; Rosenbaum et al., 2002). Examining the long-term residential outcomes of the Gautreaux program, a more recent study found that, approximately 14 years later, around 57% of participating families continued to reside in the suburban areas they had relocated to under the program, while nearly 30% returned to the city, and the remaining roughly 13% resided outside the Chicago metropolitan area. Furthermore, the participants were found to reside in areas that had similar rates of poverty, education, and male unemployment as their original placement neighborhoods (DeLuca and Rosenbaum, 2003).

It is questionable whether the encouraging findings of the Gautreaux program can be gen-eralized to the larger voucher program because of the self-selection of participants, screening process, counseling, and small scale of the program. However, the findings still provided the stimulus for the Moving to Opportunity (MTO) demonstration launched by HUD in 1993. MTO was conceived as a randomized social experiment to explore the effects of housing mobility on public housing residents. Covering five metropolitan areas (Baltimore, Boston, Chicago, Los Angeles, and New York City) and running from September 1994 to July 1998, the program randomly assigned around 4,600 eligible volunteers to one of three groups: (1) a treatment group that received vouchers who could reside only in neighborhoods with poverty rates less than 10% for a minimum of one year and received mobility counseling; (2) a com-parison group that received open choice vouchers but no counseling services; and (3) a control group that received no vouchers (Goetz and Chapple, 2010; Schwartz, 2010).

Congress mandated that the impact of the MTO be studied over a 10-year period. The final impact evaluation assesses the long-term (10- to 15-year) effects of the program (Sanbonmatsu et al., 2011). Researchers found that, compared to the control group, families in both the treatment and comparison groups lived in neighborhoods with lower rates of poverty. Families that moved with vouchers were also more likely to see significant improvements in the quality of housing, neighborhood environment, and perceptions of safety.

Social networks and employment opportunities

The final report suggests improvements in social interactions and social networks. MTO appeared to have enabled families to move to neighborhoods where residents encouraged the building of shared norms. However, the researchers found no significant differences in employment rates, types of employment, or income among the three different groups. In fact employment trends mirrored shifts in policy and the general economy. One explanation might be that more diverse social networks do not automatically provide access to employment opportunities that match the skills of the movers. Another might be that education, skill development, and employment services might influence labor market outcomes more directly than a simple change in neighborhood location.

Culture and behavior

The long-term MTO assessment did not find any significant effects on educational outcomes for children. There were no major differences in average reading or math achievement test scores, grades, or grade retention across the three groups. The lack of significant educational improvements may be attributed to the fact that a majority of MTO children still attended predominantly low-income public schools where the "quality" of schooling remains questionable. The report noted gender differences in crime and risky behavior among youth. Compared to the control group, male MTO youth appeared to engage in more risky behavior such as smoking, while female youth showed waning in risky behavior such as drinking.

In terms of health and mental health outcomes, the study found reduced obesity, diabetes, depression, and psychological distress rates among adults who relocated. While girls experienced improvements in mental health outcomes in the form of lower rates of anxiety and distress, this did not hold true among boys who moved to low-poverty neighborhoods. On the whole, better mental health and increased perception of safety seem to be the most consistent positive outcomes of relocation. It is likely that these two outcomes are strongly associated (Goering, 2003; Kling et al., 2007; Orr et al., 2003).

The mixed-income approach
Background

The mixed-income approach to poverty deconcentration and urban renewal has gained increasing prominence in policy circles since the mid-1990s. As the name suggests, this approach focuses on the economic integration of families with varying income levels within the same housing development or residential area. Mixed-income housing ranges from public housing authority developments that cater exclusively to low- to moderate-income families to private housing developments with certain portions reserved for low-income households (Joseph et al., 2007; Schwartz and Tajbakhsh, 1997). The federal government's HOPE VI program to redevelop distressed public housing and create diverse, revitalized communities has drawn much of the national interest in the mixed-income approach (Goetz and Chapple, 2010; Joseph, 2006).

Mixed-income developments are envisioned as a tool to counter the social isolation of the urban poor and encourage upward social mobility. A revived public interest in urban living and revitalization of valuable inner-city land provides opportunities to unite otherwise conflicting political groups and generate needed financial resources, making the mixed-income approach also appear as both a politically and economically beneficial strategy (Joseph et al., 2007).

Economic and social outcomes of the mixed-income approach

This section presents evidence from the limited research on the proposed economic and social benefits or the viability of the mixed-income approach.

Social networks and employment opportunities

Studies have generally found little support for the proposition that mixed-income developments promote social interaction and increase access to social networks that are beneficial to low-income families. For example, in their study of seven mixed-income developments, Brophy and Smith (1997) found that upper-income residents (typically White and childless) had very limited interaction with lower-income residents who were typically African-American or Latino families with children. Rosenbaum et al. (1998) conducted a comprehensive study of Lake Parc Place, a mixed-income development in Chicago. They found that while low- and moderate-income families engaged in more superficial forms of interaction such as greeting one's neighbors or chatting for a few minutes, more involved interaction such as sharing a meal or watching a neighbor's child was far less common. Residents of this development did not experience any increase in employment.

Kleit's (2005) study of the Seattle-based New Holly HOPE VI redevelopment found that although there appeared to be more social interaction among the residents, proximity and attributes of neighbors (e.g., ethnicity, language, education) appeared to be linked with higher levels of social connections. No employment gains were found in other studies on HOPE VI developments, calling into question the idea that social networks will somehow automatically translate into access to better jobs and higher earnings (Clampet-Lundquist, 2004; Goetz, 2010; Levy and Woolley, 2007).

Social control

Support for the social control proposition is also mixed. Rosenbaum and colleagues (1998) found that 26.8% of the low-income residents felt that Lake Parc Place had too many rules in contrast to 5.4% of the moderate-income residents. Based on a survey of residents from eight HOPE VI sites, Buron and colleagues (2002) found no reported difference in levels of social control among residents of the HOPE VI sites, voucher program, unsubsidized housing, or public housing. Smith (2002) reported that "the ability to manage negative social behaviors appears to have far more to do with the practices of the management than the income mix of the tenants" (p. 22).

Culture and behavior

The highly controversial nature of the notion that higher-income groups serve as role models to low-income households and thereby induce positive behavioral changes makes it extremely challenging to conduct empirical research. There is evidence to suggest that low-income children and youth benefit from role modeling of more affluent neighbors in terms of aspirations and the value of education, work, and civility (Briggs, 1997; Ellen and Turner, 2003). Nevertheless, the processes behind these benefits remain unclear, and the limited research cannot unequivocally say if role modeling takes place or has any positive effects in mixed-income developments. For example, studies have not found any positive effects on educational engagement or outcomes among children across various HOPE VI sites (Gallagher and Bajaj, 2007; Jacob, 2004).

Rosenbaum and colleagues (1998) found that low-income residents found the idea of other residents serving as role models insulting because it implied that they were somehow inferior and in need of improvement. Joseph (2006) notes that although the idea of middle-class residents role modeling acceptable "mainstream" behavior has become an inherent part of the motivation for mixed-income developments, the relative significance of this proposition remains open to discussion. A key question may be whether low-income residents have access to mainstream opportunities rather than whether they are detached from mainstream values.

Political economy of place

No research exists on what influence higher-income residents have in securing external resources. Smith (2002) conducted interviews with the property managers and developers of mixed-income developments and found market pressures help maintain high development and maintenance standards. The presence of higher-income residents itself is believed to elicit responses from market actors in the form of greater investments and services.

In summary, the housing voucher and mixed-income approaches to housing policy are both based on the fundamental assumption that deconcentration of poverty results in better outcomes for low-income families. Assisted housing mobility appears to have enabled families to move to safer and more secure environments, where they are able to live with less fear for their safety and risk of victimization (Turner and Briggs, 2008). However, these policies do not appear to have had any significant impact on employment, earnings, or educational outcomes.

Research findings on the benefits of the mixed-income approach have not been very persuasive either. There is limited evidence supporting the proposition regarding social networking and social interaction across income levels, particularly in the short term. Joseph (2006) notes that the level of residential stability and investment in relationship-building activities may positively influence family outcomes in the long run. There is also little evidence to support the idea of moderate- to higher-income families acting as role models and inducing behavioral change among lower-income families. However, the possibility of adult role modeling and the neighborhood environment influencing children and youth appears to hold more promise. The most compelling evidence seems to be in favor of the social control and political economy of place propositions. Research suggests that the presence of higher-income residents leads to stricter rule enforcement, better property management, and a greater ability to secure more external resources and higher-quality services for the community as a whole.

Research and policy implications

This chapter highlighted two dominant housing policy approaches to countering urban poverty concentration in the past 40-plus years in the United States. The first, housing vouchers, was a people-focused strategy that sought to help individuals move out of distressed neighborhoods into low-poverty neighborhoods with opportunities to become self-sufficient, productive citizens. The second, mixed-income developments, took a place-based approach by seeking to transform distressed neighborhoods into neighborhoods of opportunity. So, which of these two approaches is better?

Research indicates that both people-based and place-based approaches to housing policy have had limited success in achieving the goal of the deconcentration of poverty. The question then is why these two approaches continue to direct low-income housing policy. The advance of private actors and state retrenchment in addressing the housing needs of poor households is a clear hallmark of the ascendency of neoliberalism in housing policy. Given that neoliberalism may continue to dominate as the overarching framework for social policy, it is likely that these two approaches will remain as the principal tools of housing intervention in the United States. It is therefore constructive to consider some ways in which these two approaches could better achieve the goal of improved life outcomes for low-income individuals.

Turner and Briggs (2008) note that it is hard to unequivocally label experimental programs as a "success" or "failure" based on research findings. Goetz and Chapple (2010) point out that although "there is a compelling body of evidence that neighborhood context affects poverty, it is less clear which factors matter most and which, if addressed, will improve community and individual outcomes most effectively" (p. 225). They also question whether neighborhood features such as quality of schools or access to entry-level jobs might more effectively capture neighborhood quality than poverty rates alone.

Examining the relationship of underlying social and structural factors with place can provide a multi-level framework for understanding the outcomes of dispersal programs. Turner and Briggs (2008) suggest that researchers focus on the short-term effects of whether low-income families have access to transportation, child care, employment, and good schools in their new neighborhoods, and the long-term effects on employment, earnings, and educational outcomes. More detailed studies can better inform the design of policy targeted at improving the life chances of low-income families. It is difficult to ascertain whether the limited success of deconcentration policies should be attributed to faulty policies, underlying structural factors, political context, individual and neighborhood dynamics, or multiple overlapping dimensions. The research to date influences the scope of policy and program development from the micro- to the macro-level.

On the micro-level, Turner and Briggs (2008) stress the importance of providing counseling services that enable families to find affordable housing and adjust to their new neighborhoods. Pre- and post-move counseling can address parental concerns regarding issues such as safety, quality of schools, and employment opportunities. Counseling services should also be distinguished from informational services. While counseling services could be customized and focused on addressing individual needs, informational services could focus on providing general information and addressing common concerns. Some mobility programs, for example, ask former participants to host informational sessions for prospective movers, providing an opportunity for families to learn more about the potential neighborhood and meet other residents at the same time. Such meetings may also support the building of social ties in the neighborhood and increase social interaction.

To make mobility programs more effective, meso-level interventions could focus on improving coordination among landlords, tenants, housing agencies, and other stakeholders. Accountability and the setting of clear performance management systems should also be key elements. Turner and Briggs (2008) note that this part of the country's mobility agenda is especially susceptible to the "strong-idea-weakly-implemented problem" (p. 8). As such, they call for the setting of clearly articulated goals in terms of *inputs* (e.g., counseling staff, transportation support), *process* (e.g., screening and enrollment process), and *outputs* (e.g., placement).

Another meso-level goal could be the adequate provision of affordable housing. Local authorities can ensure that private developers reserve a certain number of affordable units for low-income families. Although this is currently already happening, the demand for affordable housing far exceeds the available supply. The housing market (availability of rental units), number of landlords willing to take on the additional bureaucracy (paperwork and supervision) related to the voucher program, and program requirements add to the challenge of finding affordable housing (Goetz and Chapple, 2010).

At the macro-level, it is important to note that a mere change of address cannot offset the structural barriers that low-income families face. Turner and Briggs (2008) assert that policymakers should take a "mobility plus" approach to the extent possible. To do so, they recommend the linking of housing assistance to "workforce development, reliable transportation (through 'car voucher' programs), and reliable childcare" as tools to strengthen the mobility approach (p. 9). Workforce development could include human capital building (through education and training) as well as recruitment programs (linking employers with potential workers). Such an approach would likely require coordination of action among federal, state, and local agencies in the public and private sector.

Mobility programs should carefully consider the criteria used to identify neighborhoods of opportunity. President Obama's Choice Neighborhood Initiative is a policy example that seeks to transform distressed neighborhoods into viable mixed-income neighborhoods "by linking housing improvements with appropriate services, schools, public assets, transportation, and access to jobs" (HUD, n.d.(b)). Ultimately, the seeming dichotomy between people-based and place-based approaches to poverty deconcentration might be misplaced. After all, people are part of a place and a place is part of people. As the preceding discussion suggests, a comprehensive strategy that focuses on more than just housing is needed to counteract the concentration of poverty. It may well be that alternative strategies can be more effective in the amelioration of poverty. Urban policies that support community economic development, neighborhood revitalization, public investments in the community, asset-building, and workforce development hold much greater promise in terms of countering the spatial concentration of poverty (Goetz and Chapple, 2010). As Turner and Briggs (2008) note, "it's time to expand housing mobility as part of a larger opportunity agenda for the nation" (p. 9).

In closing, the shift in federal housing policy toward the use of housing vouchers and mixed-income developments as the main form of social provision in publicly subsidized housing directly reflects the neoliberal orientation toward privatization, consumer choice, and individual responsibility. Neil Smith (1996) refers to this as "revanchist urbanism" where the state's regulatory role diminishes, and the state instead becomes an instrument of the market. Both housing policy approaches further exhibit what Harvey (2008) notes as "new systems of governance" through the merging of "state and corporate interests" (p. 38). This merging of what might otherwise be considered conflicting interests is a manifestation of what appears to be a continuing trend in neoliberal housing policy. While we debate people vs. place, perhaps it is also time to debate the merits of neoliberalism as an underlying framework for low-income housing policy.

References

Briggs, X. (1997). Moving up versus moving out: Neighborhood effects in housing mobility programs. *Housing Policy Debate*, 8(1), 195–234.
Brooks-Gunn, J., Duncan, G. J., Leventhal, T., and Aber, J. L. (1997). Lessons learned and future directions for research on the neighborhoods in which children live. In J. Brooks-Gunn, G. J. Duncan, and J. L. Aber (eds), *Neighborhood poverty. Volume 1: Context and consequences for children*. Newark, NJ: Russell Sage Foundation.
Brophy, P. C., and Smith, R. N. (1997). Mixed-income housing: Factors for success. *Cityscape: A Journal of Policy Development and Research*, 3(2), 3–31.

Buron, L., Popkin, S., Levy, D., Harris, L., and Khadduri, J. (2002). *The HOPE VI resident tracking study: A snapshot of the current living situation of original residents from eight sites.* Washington, DC: The Urban Institute.

Clampet-Lundquist, S. (2004). HOPE VI relocation: Moving to new neighborhoods and building new ties. *Housing Policy Debate*, 15(2), 415–447.

DeLuca, S., and Rosenbaum, J. E. (2003). If low-income Blacks are given a chance to live in White neighborhoods, will they stay? Examining mobility patterns in a quasi-experimental program with administrative data. *Housing Policy Debate*, 14(3), 305–345.

Duncan, G., and Raudenbush, S. (1999). Assessing the effects of context in studies of child and youth development. *Educational Psychologist*, 34(1), 29–41.

Ellen, I. G., and Turner, M. A. (2003). Do neighborhoods matter and why? In J. Goering and J. Feins (eds), *Choosing a better life? Evaluating the Moving to Opportunity experiment* (pp. 313–338). Washington, D.C.: Urban Institute Press.

Gallagher, M., and Bajaj, B. (2007). *Moving on: Benefits and challenges of HOPE VI for children* (Brief No. 4). Washington, DC: The Urban Institute.

Galster, G. (2003). Investigating behavioral impacts of poor neighborhoods: Towards new data and analytical strategies. *Housing Studies*, 18(6), 893–914.

Goering, J. (2003). Place-based poverty, social experimentation, and child outcomes: A report of mixed effects. *Children, Youth, and Environments*, 13(2), 31–61.

Goetz, E. (2010). Better neighborhoods, better outcomes? Explaining relocation outcomes in Hope VI. *Cityscape: A Journal of Policy Development and Research*, 12(1), 5–31.

Goetz, E., and Chapple, K. (2010). You gotta move: Advancing the debate on the record of dispersal. *Housing Policy Debate*, 20(2), 209–236.

Harvey, D. (2008). The right to the city. *New Left Review*, 53 (September–October), 23–40.

Jacob, B. A. (2004). Public housing, housing vouchers, and student achievement: Evidence from public housing demolitions in Chicago. *The American Economic Review*, 94(1), 233–258.

Joseph, M. L. (2006). Is mixed-income development an antidote to urban poverty? *Housing Policy Debate*, 17(2), 209–234.

Joseph, M. L., Chaskin, R. J., and Webber, H. S. (2007). The theoretical basis for addressing poverty through mixed-income development. *Urban Affairs Review*, 42(3), 369–409.

Kleit R. G. (2005). HOPE VI new communities: Neighborhood relationships in mixed-income housing. *Environment and Planning*, 37(8), 1413–1441.

Kling, J., Liebman, J., and Katz, L. (2007). Experimental analysis of neighborhood effects. *Econometrica*, 75(1), 83–119.

Kneebone, E., Nadeau, C., and Berube, A. (2011, November). *The re-emergence of concentrated poverty: Metropolitan trends in the 2000s.* Washington, DC: Metropolitan Policy Program at Brookings.

Levy, D. K., and Woolley, M. (2007). *Relocation is not enough: Employment barriers among HOPE VI families* (Brief No. 6). Washington, DC: The Urban Institute.

Massey, D., and Denton, N. (1993). *American apartheid.* Cambridge, MA: Harvard University Press.

Orr, L., Feins, J. D., Jacob, R., Beecroft, E., Sanbonmatsu, L., Katz, L. K., Lieman, J. B., and Kling, J. R. (2003). *Moving to opportunity for fair housing demonstration: Interim impacts evaluation.* Washington, DC: U.S. Department of Housing and Urban Development.

Peck, J., and Tickell, A. (2002). Neoliberalizing space. *Antipode*, 34(3), 380–404.

Rosenbaum, J., Reynolds, L., and DeLuca, S. (2002). How do places matter? The geography of opportunity, self-efficacy and a look inside the black box of residential opportunity. *Housing Studies*, 17(1), 71–82.

Rosenbaum, J., Stroh, L., and Flynn, C. (1998). Lake Parc Place: A study of mixed-income housing. *Housing Policy Debate*, 9(4), 703–740.

Sampson, R. J., Morenoff, J. D., and Gannon-Rowley, T. (2002). Assessing "neighborhood effects": Social processes and new directions in research. *Annual Review of Sociology*, 28, 443–478.

Sanbonmatsu, L., Ludwig, J., Katz, L. F., Gennetian, L. A., Duncan, G. J., Kessler, R. C., Adam, E., McDade, T. W., and Lindau, S. T. (2011). *Moving to Opportunity for fair housing demonstration program: Final impacts evaluation.* Washington, D. C.: Office of Policy Development and Research, U.S. Department of Housing and Urban Development.

Schwartz, A. (2010). *Housing policy in the United States: An introduction.* New York, NY: Routledge.

Schwartz, A., and Tajbakhsh, K. (1997). Mixed-income housing: Unanswered questions. *Cityscape*, 3(2), 71–88.

Smith, A. (2002). *Mixed-income housing developments: Promise and reality*. Cambridge, MA: Harvard Joint Center on Housing Studies.

Smith, N. (1996). *The new urban frontier: Gentrification and the revanchist city*. New York, NY: Routledge.

Turner, M. A., and Briggs, X. (2008). *Assisted housing mobility and the success of low-income minority families: Lessons for policy, practice, and future research* (Brief No. 5). Washington, DC: The Urban Institute.

U.S. Department of Housing and Urban Development [HUD]. (n.d.(a)). Sec. 5301.★ Congressional Findings and Declaration of Purpose [★Section 101 of the Act]. Retrieved December 1, 2010, from http://portal.hud.gov/hudportal/HUD?src=/program_offices/comm_planning/communitydevelopment/rulesandregs/laws/sec5301.

U.S. Department of Housing and Urban Development [HUD]. (n.d.(b)). Choice neighborhoods. Retrieved December 1, 2010, from http://portal.hud.gov/hudportal/HUD?src=/program_offices/public_indian_housing/programs/ph/cn.

Varady, D. P., and Walker, C. C. (2003). Housing vouchers and residential mobility. *Journal of Planning Literature*, 18(1), 17–30.

Wilson, W. J. (1987). *The truly disadvantaged: The inner city, the underclass, and public policy*. Chicago, IL: The University of Chicago Press.

Wilson, W. J. (1996). *When work disappears: The world of the new urban poor*. New York, NY: Alfred A. Knopf, Inc.

26

PRIVATIZING THE HOUSING SAFETY NET

HOPE VI and the transformation of public housing in the United States

Kimberly Skobba, Deirdre Oakley, and Dwanda Farmer

Introduction

The interests of the private real estate industry have been a predominant force throughout its history, though the effort has largely been to influence policy in a way that has kept the government from providing direct competition in the housing market. For many decades, the private sector had no direct role in developing or managing housing for the poor. Housing for the poor was the responsibility of the government. Yet housing policies, including policies about housing the nation's low-income households, are often about something other than housing. While public housing in the United States has a history of serving the very poorest and most vulnerable households, the policy intentions have never been entirely altruistic. As a large part of the U.S. economy, the stimulation of housing activity has often been used as an economic driver.

Changes over the past few decades have shifted the safety net from a stock of publicly owned and managed housing to a market-based approach utilizing public–private partnerships. This shift has both blurred the lines between the formerly dual housing policy approaches that provided limited rental housing subsidies for low-income households while generously subsidizing higher-income homeowners. In the era of neoliberal federal housing policy, this dual approach plays out on a grander scale, with increasingly fewer subsidies for the poor and significantly more subsidies for the private sector in the building of a privately owned public housing (Hanlon, 2010). The net result is a decreased supply of affordable units and fewer households receiving the deep subsidies needed to maintain housing in the private market (Ruel et al., 2012).

In other words, we contend that policies such as Housing Opportunities for People Everywhere (HOPE VI) and other neoliberal housing initiatives have led to a privatization of low-income housing that has weakened the housing safety net and dismantled the institution of public housing. This chapter outlines the rise and fall of public housing in the United States and the way in which neoliberal housing policies have transformed low-income housing programs, using Atlanta and its housing authority as a case example. Weaving in the experiences of public housing in Atlanta is fitting. Atlanta is where public housing began and exemplifies how public housing is, in many ways, coming to an end. We discuss the implications of these trends for the provision of affordable housing for low-income households.

The housing safety net of the past: public housing for the poor

Since the 1930s, the government has played a significant role in providing housing for the nation's poorest households. Public housing was originated in the midst of the Great Depression, when the nation faced high levels of unemployment and poverty and a large portion of the population was unable to find adequate, affordable housing (Wright, 1981). The conditions during this time led Senator Robert F. Wagner, who would go on to author public housing legislation, to declare that there was a portion of the population whose housing needs would not be met by the private market (Wagner, 1936). Over the next few decades, the government would take on an expanded role by providing deeply subsidized public housing for poor households (Hunt, 2009). Legislation enacted in the 1930s put in place a two-tiered housing policy: one tier benefiting the real estate industry and middle- and upper-income households by subsidizing homeownership through the insured mortgages and later the mortgage interest deduction, and a lower tier that offered reluctant support for the poor through the public housing program (Radford, 2000). The private sector had no direct role in developing or managing housing for the poor.

Rooted in the environmental determinism, the foundation of public housing was based on the belief that improving housing conditions would result in social betterment for the poor (von Hoffman, 1996). Concerned over the persistence of urban slum conditions, early housing advocates championed a European-inspired large-scale rental housing program (Radford, 1996). Supported by the federal government, this new form of rental housing would house poor, unskilled workers as well as the working and middle classes (von Hoffman, 2000). Bauer, one of the early housing reformers, advocated for government development of housing that was of high quality, offered a mix of housing types, integrated individual housing units with townhouses and smaller-scale apartment buildings, and provided open space for nearby parks and playgrounds and access to amenities needed for a variety of age groups (Bauer, 1934). These design concepts, along with the idea of providing housing that incorporates both poor and middle-class households, would reappear decades later with HOPE VI's new urbanist redevelopment of public housing into mixed-income neighborhoods.

The early housing reformers' vision of government housing was never fully realized; however, their ideas about design and community life heavily influenced the New Deal housing program that would serve as a precursor to public housing (Radford, 2000). Implemented through the Housing Division of the Public Works Administration (PWA), the legislation was primarily a job creation bill that included provisions for both the development of low-income housing and slum clearance (McDonnell, 1957; von Hoffman, 1996). As a result, 51 publicly funded housing developments including nearly 21,800 units across the country were approved between 1936 and 1937 (McDonnell, 1957). Techwood Homes in Atlanta, Georgia, is credited as the first public housing development in the United States and was one of the New Deal-funded programs that served as a model for the 1937 legislation (Keating, 2000a and b; Radford, 2000).

Created as part of the Housing Act of 1937, the public housing program was shaped by the acute need to resolve both the shortage of affordable housing and improve poor housing conditions. However, it was the need to reduce unemployment that likely spurred legislative action (Bratt, 1989; Schwartz, 2010). This dual purpose is evident in the description of the Wagner-Steagall Housing Act of 1937, which marked the beginning of the public housing system in the United States.

> To provide financial assistance to the States and political subdivisions thereof for the elimination of unsafe and insanitary housing conditions, for the eradication of slums, for the

provision of decent, safe, and sanitary dwellings for families of low income, and for the reduction of unemployment and the stimulation of business activity, to create a United States Housing Authority, and for other purposes.

(U.S. Housing Act of 1937)

The 1937 legislation gave local public housing authorities the ability to use federal funding to finance the costs of building public housing; the operating costs would be covered by tenants' rent (Schwartz, 2010). The Housing Act of 1937 provided for capital to produce public housing, leaving maintenance and operating costs largely the responsibility of local housing authorities for many decades (Stoloff, 2004). The legislation provided housing authorities with funding to fill the gap between rents and operating expenses but did not address the need for maintenance of the now-aging stock of public housing. Over time, the poor-quality construction, inadequate federal funding, and in some cases poor management left these developments with huge backlogs of repairs, in some cases creating hazardous conditions that placed residents at risk for injury or disease (Keating, 2000a and b; Stoloff, 2004). Tenant selection policies targeted households with incomes 10 percent lower than the income needed to afford private-market housing so that public housing would not interfere with the real estate industry (Marcuse, 1998). The poor tenant population, combined with later legislation that capped rents, would make it difficult for housing authorities to achieve financial sustainability (Bratt, 1989).

The shift to local-level decision-making ensured that segregation by race and class would be an outcome of public housing legislation (Radford, 2000). Discriminatory siting of public housing led to concentrated development on land cleared through urban renewal in or near poor neighborhoods, often blocks from original residences (Bickford and Massey, 1991). The ability to decide at the local level allowed affluent suburban communities to opt out; as a result, nearly two-thirds of the public housing stock was located in central cities and less than one-fifth in the suburbs (Schwartz, 2010). This introduced federal involvement in linking the general wealth and overall health of the country to housing at the local level (Goetz, 2003).

The 1949 Housing Act, which reauthorized the 1937 legislation, declared that every American has the right to "a decent home and a suitable living environment" (Lang and Sohmer, 2000, p. 291). Thus, the spatial arrangements of federally sponsored housing programs should have provided access to neighborhoods where poverty, crime, and poor public-education opportunities would not constrain children's opportunities for upward mobility (Freeman, 2004; Newman and Schnare, 1997). However, the 1949 Act had contradictory consequences. White flight from the cities, fueled in part by provisions in the Act that expanded federal mortgage insurance, caused rapid suburbanization and market disinvestment in the urban core. At the same time, discriminatory mortgage practices kept minority households out of the suburbs (Massey and Denton, 1993). Finally, urban renewal initiatives razed inner-city neighborhoods, displacing minority families and shrinking the supply of affordable housing in cities across the country (Teaford, 2000). Public housing became the only option for the urban poor (Freeman, 2004).

Shift to a market-based housing safety net

The private sector had influenced government policies since the inception of public housing. However, it had not been instrumental in owning and operating housing for the poor (Fraser et al., 2012a). This changed in the 1960s when the federal government introduced a variety of public financing programs that launched an era of public subsidies for privately owned housing. The Housing and Development Act of 1968, which established a goal of building six million units of housing over ten years for low-income families, redefined the government's role in affordable housing (Mallach, 2009). The shift to privately developed low-income housing began with several programs enacted in the mid- to late 1960s to encourage real estate developers, owners, and managers to build and operate low-income housing. These programs included mortgage subsidies to lower the financing costs for developers and rental subsidies to cover the gap between operating costs and the rent paid by low-income tenants (Oakley et al., 2013; Stoloff, 2004). Over the past four decades, the stock of privately owned, federally subsidized affordable housing has grown to 1.6 million units, surpassing the highpoint of the public housing units (Schwartz, 2010).

The Brooke Amendments to the U.S. Department of Housing and Urban Development (HUD) Acts of 1969, 1970, and 1971 shifted federally sponsored low-income housing construction to rent supplements and capital-cost subsidies to private-market landlords. According to Hartman (1975), these amendments capped the amount of rent that residents could pay as a portion of their income (typically 30 percent), and introduced an operating subsidy so that housing authorities could increase rental revenue. These amendments led to the passage of the Housing and Community Development Act in 1974. Including funding for a new program, Section 8, the Act subsidized private-market initiatives to rehabilitate existing housing and limited privately sponsored new construction (Freeman, 2004). By the early 1980s, all construction of federally subsidized low-income housing ceased; Section 8 was recast as a demand-side subsidy for existing private-market housing through vouchers to qualified tenants (Burchell and Listokin, 1995). Although existing public housing continued to be widely used for low-income housing along with voucher subsidies to private-market housing, federal devolution and funding cuts resulted in a rapidly deteriorating public housing stock (Goetz, 2003; Stone, 1993).

Though the voucher program has evolved over the last two decades, the conversion from physical public housing units to the use of tenant-based rental subsidies combined with government-subsidized financing for housing development and tax incentives is the public–private formula for affordable housing that continues to this day (Goetz, 2012). This transfer from a low-income housing policy based on a stock of public housing units to one based on vouchers, which require renewed funding and are subject to funding cuts, and a privately owned, publicly subsidized stock of housing that is time-limited, has generated concern over a vulnerable and shrinking set of housing options for the poor (Vale and Freemark, 2012).

HOPE VI: the latest step in privatizing the housing safety net

The HUD Reform Act of 1989 created the National Commission on Severely Distressed Public Housing to identify severely distressed public housing developments nationwide, assess strategies to address their problems, and formulate a plan of action (National Housing Law Project, 2002). The Housing Opportunities for People Everywhere (HOPE VI) program was initiated several years later in response to the estimate that of the more than 1 million public housing units in the country, 86,000 of them were severely distressed (National Commission on Severely Distressed Public Housing, 1992; Turbov and Piper, 2005).

HOPE VI represents the most dramatic change of direction in the history of U.S. public housing policy. HOPE VI promised nothing less than a full transformation of the nation's most distressed public housing projects (Holin et al., 2003). With the goals of deconcentrating poverty, improving deteriorating neighborhood conditions and increasing self-sufficiency among public housing residents, HOPE VI includes the demolition of distressed public housing projects and replacement with new smaller-scale, mixed-income housing developments, and the dispersal of the poor to private-market rental housing in lower-poverty areas through the use of Housing Choice Vouchers (Goetz, 2002; Hanlon, 2010). Since 1993, HUD has awarded more than $6 billion in HOPE VI grants to 190 housing authorities across the country (Castells, 2010).

Interestingly, the components of HOPE VI are reminiscent of the ideals espoused by Catherine Bauer and other housing advocates in the 1930s. The mixed-income communities developed through HOPE VI redevelop formerly poor neighborhoods using New Urbanist principles that include traditional neighborhood design with a mix of housing types in pedestrian-friendly communities that offer access to local amenities (Neary, 2011). HOPE VI also includes other aspects of former efforts to transform the provision of housing for low-income households, including a version of slum clearance, and the imposition of punitive rules and moralistic control over the poor (Fraser et al., 2012b).

Yet, unlike the public housing of the past, which created a program, albeit an imperfect one, to support the poor, HOPE VI has led to a privatization of low-income housing that has weakened the housing safety net and dismantled the institution of public housing. To be sure, in order for HOPE VI to meet its goals, the majority of public housing residents need to be relocated. Because only 20 to 40 percent of the redevelopment units are earmarked for low-income residents, most former public housing residents do not get the opportunity to return (Goetz, 2010). In other words, by the very definition of mixed income, the majority of the public housing units are not replaced (Keene and Geronimus, 2011). Instead, through the use of Housing Choice Voucher (HCV) subsidies (formerly Section 8), public housing residents are relocated to the private rental market (Oakley and Burchfield, 2009).

Destination neighborhood characteristics have led to policy debates. While many former residents have been relocated to somewhat safer neighborhoods with moderately lower poverty levels, moves tend to be short distances and destinations just as racially segregated as public housing (see, for example, Fraser and Nelson, 2008; Goetz, 2010; Kleit and Galvez, 2011; Oakley et al., 2011; Varady and Walker, 2000). According to Oakley et al. (2013), these findings are similar in Atlanta. Thus, many housing researchers have questioned whether HOPE VI has really met its stated goals. The program has also been harshly criticized for displacing residents, eliminating units of public housing without developing replacement units, and failing to provide supportive services to residents who no longer live in public housing (Keating, 2000a; Oakley and Burchfield, 2009). Despite this, however, HOPE VI is typically lauded in policy circles as turning around conditions in public housing neighborhoods with improvements in educational attainment levels, average household income, and percentage of people in poverty (U.S. GAO, 2007).

The Atlanta model

The experience of the Atlanta Housing Authority (AHA) serves as bookends in the history of public housing, offering a case study on U.S. low-income housing policy and the shift to privatization through neoliberal reforms. The transformation of public housing in Atlanta offers a rags to riches story for what was formerly one of the nation's poorest-performing housing authorities. The story of Atlanta is important for understanding the shift towards low-income housing policies that favor privatization. Atlanta marks the beginning and end of public housing as it was once known.

According to Farmer (2012), the AHA is the fifth-largest housing authority in the United States, and is credited with building the first public housing community in 1935. The Atlanta Housing Authority owned and operated almost 14,300 apartments during public housing's pinnacle year in 1994. These 14,300 units were in 43 housing developments, including 26 large buildings for families and the remainder being smaller buildings reserved for the elderly and disabled (Husock, 2010). In 1993, the AHA was one of the poorest-performing housing authorities in the country and at risk of being taken over or put into receivership by the U.S. Department of Housing and Urban Development (HUD). At the same time, the federal government was also rethinking public housing based on the findings of the 1992 Commission on Severely Distressed Public Housing.

In 1990 Atlanta was chosen for the 1996 Summer Olympic Games, providing the city with the unprecedented opportunity for revitalization. City officials quickly moved into action, designating the area where two public housing communities (Techwood and Clark Howell Homes) were located as the site for the Olympic Village. These communities were centrally located and adjacent to the campus of Georgia Institute of Technology, as well as Coca-Cola's headquarters (Newman, 2002). However, according to Keating (2000a, 2000b), business and political leaders began to ask whether Atlanta could host athletes from all over the world in a high-poverty area. Thus, one of the key actors involved in preparing the city for the Olympics was the AHA. During the early 1990s, a series of taskforces and planning committees were formed to determine how to redevelop the Techwood and Clark Howell Homes communities, but none of these plans were feasible (Keating and Flores, 2000). Then the AHA formed the Olympic Legacy Program with an eye toward demolishing and redeveloping these properties along with two others in the city (Newman, 2002).

In addition, two important policy changes at the federal level allowed AHA to take a new approach. First, Congress eliminated the one-for-one replacement rule that required public housing authorities (PHAs) to provide a new replacement unit before demolishing an old unit. The second important change was the advent of the public housing mixed-finance program that allowed housing authorities to create mixed-income developments that could be owned and operated by private development partners (Turbov and Piper, 2005). During this period a new Executive Director, Renee Glover, took control of the AHA. Plans to raze and redevelop these properties in preparation for the Olympic Games coincided with the new HOPE VI legislation. This meant strong support for public housing demolition and redevelopment from both city officials and HUD. Therefore, despite opposition from advocacy and public housing resident groups, these plans were approved. The AHA successfully secured more than $200 million in HOPE VI funding to partner with private developers to build mixed-income replacement properties (Keating and Flores, 2000; Shalhoup, 2007; White, 1997). Under Glover's leadership, the AHA also leveraged what was seen among policymakers as an innovative plan to reinvent public housing to get approval and additional funding from HUD to demolish and redevelop ten more public housing complexes scattered across the city (Boston, 2005; Husock, 2010; Newman, 2002).

The initial redevelopment phase of Techwood and Clark Howell Homes in preparation for the Olympics was completed by 1995, and the area was subsequently fully redeveloped by 1997. Redevelopment was completed on East Lake Meadows in 1997 and on John Hope Homes in 1998. Demolition was completed on Carver, Harris, John Eagan, and Perry Homes, as well as Kimberly Courts, between 1997 and 1998. While relocation was completed at Capitol Homes by 1998, demolition and redevelopment did not begin until 2001. In the early 2000s, three more public housing communities, John O'Chiles, McDaniel Glenn, and University Homes, were demolished. Redevelopment was completed at these communities by 2006. Figure 26.1 shows the location of the HOPE VI redevelopment sites, all of which were renamed, as well as the remaining public housing as of 2007.

As plans for demolition and redevelopment began in the early 1990s, about half of the tenants in the Techwood and Clark Howell Homes communities had either moved on their own or been evicted (Keating, 2000b). No attempt to track these residents was made, although it

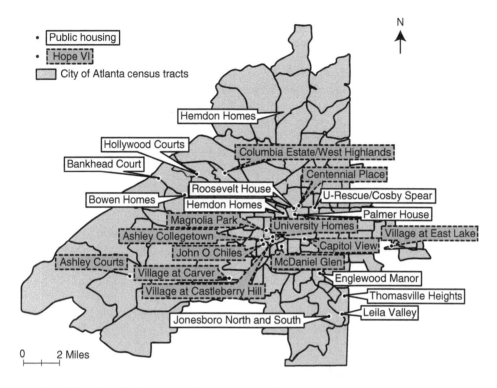

Figure 26.1 Atlanta's public housing and HOPE VI redevelopments as of 2007
Source: Developed by Deirdre Oakley using data from the Atlanta Housing Authority.

is believed that most remained within the city limits in private unsubsidized rental housing (Creighton and Keating, 1999; Keating, 2000b; Newman, 2002).

Qualified public housing residents were given a choice to either move to one of the other public housing communities not slated for redevelopment or receive a voucher for private-market rental housing. About one-third chose to move to another public housing community (Boston, 2005). Most of these residents, whether they moved with a voucher or to another public housing community, remained within the city limits (Newman, 2002). Residents who moved with assistance were initially given an option to return to the redevelopments. Yet, by the early 2000s, only 17 percent of the original public housing residents were able to return to the new HOPE VI developments (Newman, 2002; Oakley et al., 2008).

A Georgia Institute of Technology study conducted on the residential outcomes of residents who received a voucher compared to those who either relocated to, or remained in, other traditional public housing concluded that the voucher households experienced significant improvements in socioeconomic status and neighborhood quality (Boston, 2005). Bulent et al. (2010) found improvements in employment among Atlanta's relocated former public housing residents as well. Rich et al. (2010) found that residents relocated with vouchers from Atlanta's McDaniel Glen public housing community experienced improvements in education quality. None of these findings are consistent with the broader literature: *little* socioeconomic or educational improvements. In fact, a subsequent examination of Boston's (2005) findings by other housing researchers concluded that *significant improvements* were overstated (Goetz, 2005). Still, what is now known as the "Atlanta Model" for public housing transformation was deemed a success by local officials, as well as by those in national policy circles, leading to the 2007 decision to demolish the remaining public housing.

While Atlanta has since demolished all of its family, project-based traditional public housing, as well as five senior high-rises, only seven of these developments were awarded HOPE VI
funds. The last round of demolitions was not done under HOPE VI; rather, it was completed
under Section 18 of the 1937 Housing Act, which, unlike HOPE VI, requires no immediate
replacement of any units. About 10,000 former public housing residents have been relocated
since 2007, bringing the grand total since 1994 to 50,000 (Oakley et al., 2013). For the last
round of demolitions, the only relocation option residents were given was to move to private
rental-market housing with a voucher. Therefore the city has experienced a dramatic decrease
in housing stock affordable to very low-income residents, and the waiting list for vouchers has
been closed for the past seven years (AHA, 2012).

Figure 26.2 shows the mix of units through HOPE VI redevelopment. According to Farmer
(2012), the mix of units delivered drastically reduced the availability of public housing units,
resulting in a loss of 85 percent of public housing units available in the Atlanta market. Since
qualified public-housing residents were relocated with voucher subsidies, the long-term impact
may not be known for some time. Yet the bottom line is that the affordable housing safety net
has been severely compromised by the elimination of public housing. How can the city ensure
the availability of housing at all income levels for newcomers to Atlanta communities as they
will not have access to housing choice vouchers? Will an inclusionary zoning policy that would
require new developments to include a small percentage of affordable housing be an opportunity to increase available affordable units?

Implications and conclusions

This chapter has sought to chronicle how the housing safety net was gradually weakened
through increasingly privatizing the provision of housing for low-income households and the
dismantling of public housing through HOPE VI redevelopment, which is a public–private
venture. We used Atlanta as a case example as the city has eliminated all of its project-based
public housing. The most obvious implication of this weakening is that there is now far less
housing out there that is affordable to low-income households. The original public housing

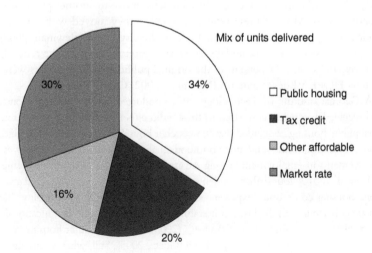

Figure 26.2 Unit type through HOPE VI redevelopment in Atlanta
Source: Atlanta Housing Authority.

legislation was based on a market-failure premise, that is, the private market could not meet the housing needs of low- and moderate-income households (Hunt, 2009). While public housing has been associated with an array of problems, it has served its purpose in providing housing to households who are not served by the private market. For several decades, public housing provided a source of affordable housing for very low-income households who were unable to secure private-market housing. Over the past 25 years, nearly 260,000 public housing units have been demolished; replacing these units are tenant-based subsidies and mixed-income communities that benefit higher-income households (Goetz, 2012). According to Urban Academic Scholars in Opposition to PETRA (2010), the decrease in affordable units has been dramatic: in 1970 there were 130 affordable units for every 100 low-income households in the country, but now there are only 38. This increases the likelihood that the housing situation for low-income households who do not have access to a voucher subsidy or a subsidized unit is precarious and perhaps unstable.

The transformation of public housing, the replacement of poor neighborhoods with new urbanist housing communities, appears to harken back to the ideas of the early housing reformers. Yet neoliberal housing policy is not a return to an old idea (Schram et al., 2008). The low-income housing policy supported by Catherine Bauer and the early housing reformers included a long-term federal program that provided adequate housing for low-income families. The policy approach that has emerged since the 1990s has replaced the social welfare model of housing with one that benefits higher-income residents and the private real estate industry (Goetz, 2012). Federal housing policies once served as a safety net for people whom the private sector could not serve. Today, federal housing policies serve to publicly subsidize a housing safety net for the private sector.

References

Atlanta Housing Authority (AHA). (2012). *Annual Implementation Report*. Atlanta, GA: Atlanta Housing Authority.

Bauer, C. (1934). *Modern Housing*. Boston, MA: Houghton Mifflin.

Bickford, A., and Massey, D. (1991). Segregation in the second ghetto: Racial and ethnic segregation in American public housing, *Social Forces*, 69(4), 1011–1036.

Boston, T. (2005). The effects of revitalization on public housing residents: A case study of the Atlanta Housing Authority. *Journal of the American Planning Association*, 71(4), 393–406.

Bratt, R. (1989). *Rebuilding a Low-Income Housing Policy*. Philadelphia, PA: Temple University Press.

Bulent, A., Sjoquist, D., and Wallace, S. (2010). The effect of a program-based housing move on employment: HOPE VI in Atlanta. *Southern Economic Journal*, 77(1), 138–160.

Burchell, R., and Listokin, D. (1995). Influences on United States housing policy. *Housing Policy Debate*, 6(3), 559–617.

Castells, N. (2010). HOPE VI neighborhood spillover effects in Baltimore. *Cityscape*, 12(1), 65–98.

Creighton, M., and Keating, L. (1999). *Inventory of Assisted Housing: A Report to the City of Atlanta Commissioner of Planning, Development and Neighborhood Conservation*. Atlanta, GA: City Hall.

Farmer, D. (2012). *Exploring the Impacts of the HOPE VI Program on Residents and Surrounding Neighborhoods in the City of Atlanta*. Manchester, NH: A dissertation submitted to the School of Community Economic Development of Southern New Hampshire University.

Fraser, J., and Nelson, M. (2008). Can mixed-income housing ameliorate concentrated poverty? The significance of a geographically informed sense of community. *Geographic Compass*, 2(6), 2127–2144.

Fraser, J., Oakley, D., and Bazuin, J. (2012a). Public ownership and private profit in housing. *Cambridge Journal of Regions, Economy and Society*, 5(3), 397–412.

Fraser, J., Brown-Burns, A., Bazuin, J., and Oakley, D. (2012b). In the neighborhood: HOPE VI and the production of difference. *Urban Affairs Review*. (First online: DOI: 12/17/12, 10.1177/1078087412465582.)

Freeman, L. (2004). *Siting Affordable Housing: Location and Neighborhood Trends of Low Income Housing Tax Credit Developments in the 1990s*. Washington, DC: Brookings Institution, Census 2000 Survey Series.

Goetz, E.G. (2002). Forced relocations vs. voluntary mobility: The effects of dispersal programmes on households. *Housing Studies*, 17(1), 107–123.

Goetz, E.G. (2003). *Clearing the Way*. Washington, DC: Urban Institute Press.

Goetz, E.G. (2005). Comment: Public housing demolition and the benefits to low-income families, *Journal of the American Planning Association*, 71(4), 407–409.

Goetz, E.G. (2010). Better neighborhoods, better outcomes? Explaining relocation outcomes in HOPE VI. *Cityscape*, 12(1), 5–32.

Goetz, E.G. (2012). The transformation of public housing policy, 1985–2011. *Journal of American Planning Association*, 78(4), 452–463.

Hanlon, J. (2010). Success by design: HOPE VI, new urbanism, and the neoliberal transformation of public housing in the United States. *Environment and Planning A*, 42, 80–98.

Hartman, C. (1975). *Housing and Social. Policy* Englewood Cliffs, NJ: Prentice Hall.

Holin, M.J., Buron, L., Locke, G., and Cortes, A. (2003). *Interim Assessment of the HOPE VI Program Cross-Site Report*. Prepared by ABT Associates for the U.S. Department of Housing and Urban Development, Washington, DC.

Hunt, D.B. (2009). *Blueprint for Disaster*. Chicago, IL: The University of Chicago Press.

Husock, H. (2010). *Reinventing Public Housing: Is the Atlanta Model Right for Your City?* New York, NY: The Manhattan Institute for Policy Research.

Keating, L. (2000a). *Atlanta: Race, Class, and Urban Expansion*. Philadelphia, PA: Temple University Press.

Keating, L. (2000b). Redeveloping public housing: Relearning urban renewal's immutable lessons, *Journal of the American Planning Association*, 66(4), 384–397.

Keating L., and Flores, C. (2000). Sixty and out: Techwood Homes transformed by enemies and friends. *Journal of Urban History*, 26(3), 275–311.

Keene, D., and Geronimus, A. (2011). "Weathering" HOPE VI: The importance of evaluating the population health impact of public housing demolition and displacement. *Journal of Urban Health*, 88(3), 417–435.

Kleit, R., and Galvez, M. (2011). The location choices of public housing residents displaced by redevelopment: Market constraints, personal preferences, or social information? *Journal of Urban Affairs*, 33(4), 375–407.

Lang, R., and Sohmer, R. (2000). Legacy of the Housing Act of 1949: The past, present, and future of federal housing and urban policy. *Housing Policy Debate*, 11(2), 291–298.

Mallach, A. (2009). *A Decent Home: Planning, Building and Preserving Affordable Housing*. Chicago, IL: American Planning Association Planners Press.

Marcuse, P. (1998). Mainstreaming public housing: A proposal for a comprehensive approach to housing policy. In *New Directions in Housing Policy*, ed. David P. Varady. New Brunswick, NJ: Center for Urban Policy Research.

Massey, D., and Denton, N. (1993). *American Apartheid: Segregation and the Making of the Underclass*. Cambridge, MA: Harvard University Press.

McDonnell, T.L. (1957). *The Wagner Housing Act: A Case Study of the Legislative Process*. Chicago, IL: Loyola University Press.

National Commission on Severely Distressed Public Housing. (1992). *The Final Report of the National Commission on Severely Distressed Public Housing: A Report to the Congress and the Secretary of Housing and Urban Development*. Washington, DC: Author.

National Housing Law Project. (2002). *False HOPE: A Critical Assessment of the HOPE VI Public Housing Redevelopment Program*. Washington, DC: Author.

Neary, B.U. (2011). Black women coping with HOPE IV in Spartanburg, South Carolina. *Journal of African American Studies*, 15, 524–54.

Newman, H. (2002). *The Atlanta Housing Authority's Olympic Legacy Program: Public Housing Projects to Mixed Income Communities*. Atlanta: Research Atlanta.

Newman, S., and Schnare, A. (1997). "… And a suitable living environment": The failure of housing programs to deliver on neighborhood quality. *Housing Policy Debate*, 8(4), 703–741.

Oakley, D., and Burchfield, K. (2009). Out of the projects, still in the hood: The spatial constraints on public housing residents' relocation in Chicago. *Journal of Urban Affairs*, 31(5), 589–614.

Oakley, D., Ruel, E., and Reid, L. (2013). 'It was really hard… it was alright…it was easy.' Public housing relocation experiences and destination satisfaction in Atlanta. *Cityscape: A Journal of Policy Development and Research*, 15(2), 173–192.

Oakley, D., Ruel, E., and Wilson, E. (2008). *A Choice with No Options: Atlanta Public Housing Residents' Lived Experiences in the Face of Relocation.* Atlanta: Georgia State University.

Oakley, D., Ward, C., Reid, L., and Ruel, E. (2011). The poverty deconcentration imperative and public housing transformation. *Sociology Compass,* 5(9), 824–833.

Radford, G. (1996). *Modern Housing for America.* Chicago, IL: The University of Chicago Press.

Radford, G. (2000). The federal government and housing during the Great Depression. In *From Tenements to the Taylor Homes,* eds J.F. Bauman, R. Biles, and K.M. Szylvian. University Park, PA: The Pennsylvania State University Press.

Rich, M., Owens, M., Griffiths, M., Haspel, M., Hill, K., Smith, A., and Stigers, K. (2010). *Evaluation of the McDaniel Glenn HOPE VI Revitalization: Final Report.* Atlanta, GA: Emory University, Office of University-Community Partnerships.

Ruel, E., Oakley, D.A., Ward, C., Alston, R., and Reid, L.W. (2012). Public housing relocations in Atlanta: Documenting residents' attitudes, concerns and experiences. *J. Cities.* Available at http://dx.doi.org/10.1016/j.cities.2012.07.010. Accessed 10/7/2012.

Schram, S.F., Fording, R.C., and Soss, J. (2008). Neo-liberal poverty governance: Race, place and the punitive turn in U.S. welfare policy. *Cambridge Journal of Regions, Economy and Society,* 1, 17–36.

Schwartz, A.F. (2010). *Housing policy in the United States.* New York, NY: Routledge.

Shalhoup, M. (2007). Public housing on the chopping block. *Creative Loafing,* September 20. Available at http://clatl.com/atlanta/public-housing-on-the-chopping-block/Content?oid=1269735. Accessed 1/20/13.

Stoloff, J. (2004). *A Brief History of Public Housing* Paper presented at the annual meeting of the American Sociological Association, San Francisco, CA, August 14, 2004.

Stone, M. (1993). *Shelter Poverty: New Ideas on Housing Affordability.* Philadelphia: Temple University Press.

Teaford, J. (2000). Urban renewal and its aftermath. *Housing Policy Debate,* 11(2), 443–465.

Turbov, M., and Piper, V. (2005). *HOPE VI and Mixed-Finance Redevelopments: A Catalyst for Neighborhood Renewal.* Washington, DC: Brookings Institution Metropolitan Policy Program.

Urban Academic Scholars in Opposition to PETRA. (2010). *Written Testimony Submitted to the U.S. House of Representatives Financial Services Committee: The Administration's Proposal to Preserve and Transform Public and Assisted Housing.* Washington, DC.

U.S. General Accounting Office. (U.S. GAO). (2007). *Information on the Financing, Oversight, and Effects of the HOPE VI Program.* Washington, DC: Author.

U.S. Housing Act of 1937 (Wagner-Steagall Act), Pub. L. No. 93-383, 88 Stat.653, 42 U.S.C. § 1437.

Vale, L., and Freemark, Y. (2012). From public housing to public–private housing. *Journal of the American Planning Association,* 78(4), 379–402.

Varady, D., and Walker, C. (2000). Vouchering out distressed subsidized developments: Does moving lead to improvements in housing and neighborhood conditions? *Housing Policy Debate.* 11(1), 115–159.

von Hoffman, A. (1996). High ambitions: The past and future of American low-income housing policy. *Housing Policy Debate,* 7(3), 423–446.

von Hoffman, A. (2000). A study in contradictions: The origins and legacy of the Housing Act of 1949. *Housing Policy Debate,* 11(2), 299–326.

Wagner, R.F. (1936). Should the administration's housing policy be continued? *Congressional Digest,* 15(4), 112–118.

White, R. (1997). Reinventing public housing: The Atlanta experience. *Journal of Housing and Community Development,* 4(July/August), 1–5.

Wright, G. (1981). *Building the Dream: A Social History of Housing in America.* New York, NY: Pantheon Books.

27

POVERTY DE-CONCENTRATION PRIORITIES IN LOW-INCOME HOUSING TAX CREDIT ALLOCATION POLICY

A content analysis of qualified allocation plans

Monique S. Johnson

Although U.S. housing markets may soon reach stabilization, structural shifts within the social and economic environment will continue to have impacts on the housing conditions of the poor. Those impacts include persistent marginalization by swelling housing cost burdens, growing shelter insufficiency, and socio-spatial restriction to the lowest-income communities (Pelletiere, 2009). Socio-spatial isolation is an outgrowth of historic patterns that overwhelmingly located subsidized housing within low-income neighborhoods—contributing to the concentration of low-income minority households in communities shut off from economic opportunities, access to adequate services, and quality education (Belsky and Drew, 2007; Erickson et al., 2008). Research examining the longitudinal trends of poverty concentration shows increases between the 1970s and 1990s in response to "school desegregation, deindustrialization and the exodus of white and eventually middle class blacks to the suburbs" (Jargowsky, 2003, p. 6). During the 1990s socio-economic divides decreased due to "economic growth, changes in federal policy and bank lending practices and the revitalization of downtowns" (p. 7), encouraging investment and decreasing geographic isolation. However, this research suggests that, since 2000, concentrated poverty may again be increasing (Jargowsky, 2003, 2008).

Often overlooked in this cyclical analysis of poverty concentration is the underlying influence of neoliberal housing policy on socio-economic stratification within metropolitan areas (Hackworth, 2007). Over the past 30 years the built environment has become "a quasi-autonomous vehicle for economic development in cities," encouraged by a growing reliance on private capital markets to stimulate growth (Hackworth, 2007, p. 77). These trends have shifted housing funding methods toward approaches that encourage public–private partnership and globally diversified capital sources. All of which have contributed to the dismantling of mainstay housing approaches, replacing them with policy approaches designed to insert capital market "discipline" into low-income housing provision.

The most prominent neoliberal housing policy mechanism created was the low-income housing tax credit (LIHTC). While the program created an alternative source of capital to support low-income housing production, it discounted the consequences of prioritizing market efficiency in low-income housing provision. Market-based approaches tend not to consider equity measures, more specifically housing placement patterns, thereby contributing to low-income housing saturation within low-income communities. The subsequent consequences are that the poor continue to be confined to communities of limited opportunity and maintained within a cycle of poverty. This research contributes an alternative perspective on the LIHTC—the primary neoliberal mechanism supporting the development of low-income housing across the United States. It explores the flagship program by analyzing its priorities at the state level and the policy design's intersection with poverty de-concentration.

Background: the low-income housing tax credit

The advent of the LIHTC program was the beginning of a housing policy revolution (Erickson, 2006). Prior to 1978, the federal government, through the Department of Housing and Urban Development (HUD), constructed a majority of low-income public housing and subsidized housing units. For instance, in 1976, the federal government had constructed 248,000 units of low-income housing; however, by 1996 that number had drastically decreased to 18,000 units (Erickson, 2009, p. xi). These changes were spawned by neoliberal housing policy shifts that encouraged private sector provision of low-income housing through the LIHTC.

Amid the various federal low-income housing programs, the LIHTC serves as the flagship model for low-income housing provision nationally. The program has received broad support from a diverse coalition of policy and practitioner advocates since its enactment within the Tax Act of 1986—becoming the dominant mechanism for low-income housing development and preservation (Cummings and DiPasquale, 1999; Erickson, 2006). The LIHTC was designed to stimulate affordable housing production through the provision of federal tax incentives for the acquisition, rehabilitation, or construction of affordable rental housing (Khadduri and Wilkins, 2007). The LIHTC provides incentives for private investment in low-income housing, allowing investors to use the credits to reduce their federal tax liability; in turn, property owners are able to offer reduced rents to low-income tenants (Usowski and Hollar, 2008). These incentives were created upon recognition that the private sector may not otherwise generate sufficient rental income from low-income development to adequately "cover the costs of developing and operating the project" or "provide a return to investors sufficient to attract the equity investment needed for development" (Department of Treasury, 1999, p. 11). The program is jointly administered by the Internal Revenue Service and state tax credit allocation agencies under enabling legislation that authorizes states, within defined parameters, to design an allocation strategy and qualify rental housing developments. States are expected to consider the diversity of housing needs in these requirements. More specifically, allocation agencies create and implement a qualified allocation plan (QAP) each year that identifies the states' housing priorities and also includes the selection criteria for tax credit awards (Khadduri and Rodda, 2004).

Each state interprets federal guidelines through its own unique environmental frame to craft allocating criteria (Khadduri and Rodda, 2004). However, the LIHTC program is under increasing scrutiny regarding state policies governing allocation. This study seeks to provide insight into the following research questions: How have state housing agencies characterized socio-spatial goals in their low-income housing tax credit allocation plans? Do these socio-spatial goals emphasize poverty de-concentration? How have these priorities changed over time? What similarities and differences exist between the states?

Poverty concentration inherently assumes that a high number of households are contained within a defined area and that a statistically significant number of those households are economically disadvantaged. That being so, there was an expectation that the study's outcomes would highlight positive correlations between the presence of high poverty concentration MSAs within a state and the state's emphasis of poverty de-concentration goals within its LIHTC QAP. By examining states' scoring priorities, this study analyzed how the distribution of low-income populations is considered within the plans. The research explored whether strides have been made to encourage poverty de-concentration—actively considering the socio-spatial needs of low-income households within the LIHTC policy design—or whether additional emphasis needs to be directed toward incorporating approaches that contribute to locational equity within program allocation plans.

Theoretical framework: policy design theory's intersection with socio-spatial segmentation

Policies contain a structural framework comprised of both empirical elements and value-laden content defining how resources are allocated (Schneider and Ingram, 1997). Dahl and Lindblom (1953) were among the first policy scholars to recognize the integral importance of policy's architecture on policy analysis. Schneider and Ingram's (1997) seminal work built upon this framework by defining a set of categories to describe policy content and to also illuminate the underlying logic and social constructs that influence policy design. These elements together led to policy design theory, suggesting that policy text and practices contain a design that can be described and evaluated across a myriad of dimensions (Schneider and Sidney, 2009). The theory has made space for scholarly research that uses empirical data to analyze the technical aspects of policy while also exploring policy's implicit ideas relative to the distribution of costs and benefits. This theory asserts that the multi-dimensional nature of policy is best understood through a systematic evaluation of policy content illuminating the relationship between design and the "underlying understanding of the social world that places meaning-making at the center" (Schneider and Sidney, 2009, p. 106).

This research study will use policy design theory as an underlying framework to analyze how socio-spatial justice is (or is not) emphasized within the low-income housing tax credit policy design. Based upon social construction theory, the demands and/or requirements of advantaged and contender target groups are usually elevated above those of dependent and deviant social groups (Schneider and Ingram, 1997). If this theory holds relative to low-income housing tax credit policy design and its intersection with poverty concentration, then the policy is less likely to encourage poverty de-concentration since this could be perceived as burdensome to advantaged groups.

Integral to this research premise is socio-spatial theory—a guiding framework cementing the relationship between geographic location and advantage. Socio-spatial theory is rooted in the understanding that "equity, equality or social justice is spatially constituted" (Fincher and Iveson, 2008). Geographic segmentation within housing markets creates barriers to entry based upon the socio-economic characteristics of an environment (Harsman and Quigley, 1995). In addition, the means by which space is used and defined, and the way that social groups are defined and segmented, are central to the manifestation of inequality (O'Sullivan and Gibb, 2003). Ultimately spatial location impacts access to resources and affects well being. Therefore, advantage and disadvantage are embedded into how space is produced and organized.

Literature review: poverty de-concentration and the LIHTC

Concentrated poverty is defined as "the confinement of the poor to a subset of neighborhood locations rather than their dispersion across all parts of an urban area" (Greene, 1991, p. 1).

Concentration often leads to social disorder and economic disparities (Fellowes, 2006; Schwartz et al., 2006). The concentration effect has led to the creation of a locationally ostracized underclass where "certain social pathologies among the poor are ascribed to their geographic confinement and social isolation from the mainstream" (Greene, 1991, p. 1).

As one of the few surviving housing programs, the LIHTC has assumed an increasingly responsible role for mediating the complex intersection between socio-spatial outcomes and housing need. While poverty concentration has been a factor in the program's design since its inception, how it has been addressed at both the federal and state level has evolved over the life of the program. For instance, a defining feature of the LIHTC program has been its incentive to locate developments in qualified census tracts (QCTs).[1] This provision was designed to encourage investment within economically depressed housing markets. However, it has also been credited with encouraging development patterns that further contribute to poverty concentration in communities with a high volume of existing low-income households. Hence, in 2000, federal guidelines were amended, directing states to encourage "projects which are located in qualified census tracts ... and the development of which contributes to a concentrated community revitalization plan" (Inland Revenue Code Section 42, 2011). The intent of this amendment along with the inclusion of criteria to encourage locational patterns outside of high poverty areas was intended to temper the program's contribution to poverty concentration in communities with a high volume of existing low-income households (Abt Associates, Inc., 2006).

Nevertheless, the outcomes of poverty de-concentration goals with the LIHTC program have been mixed. While LIHTC developments are increasingly located in favorable economic environments, a body of literature exploring the program's impact on poverty de-concentration and its extension of housing opportunities within socio-economically diverse communities shows LIHTC developments continued locational patterns in racially segregated and poverty-concentrated communities (Baum-Snow and Marion, 2009; Ellen et al., 2009; Gustafson and Walker, 2002; Oakley, 2008; Williamson et al., 2009). In particular, the U.S. Department of Housing and Urban Development's sample assessment of the economic and social characteristics of LIHTC residents and neighborhoods found that LIHTC properties are primarily located in city neighborhoods with a high concentration of rental units and with a high concentration of poor, minority residents (Jackson, 2007). A study by Williamson et al. (2009) assessing the intersection of rental housing subsidies (housing choice vouchers) and low-income housing tax credit developments found that LIHTC developments in low-income communities house a high proportion of housing choice voucher holders, doing little to reverse poverty concentration. While studies show that the program has done a better job of de-concentrating poverty than its predecessors, there is also evidence that more needs to be done (Freeman, 2004; Funderberg and Macdonald, 2010; Voicu et al., 2009).

Methodology

This study is a content analysis of LIHTC qualified allocation plans in Virginia, Ohio, and Illinois from 2000 to 2010—examining the presence of specific preferences. Each state designs a system that ranks low-income housing development proposals according to criteria defined within its qualified allocation plan. The content of each plan's scoring system was used to identify, classify, and tabulate scoring priorities. This longitudinal analysis is designed to capture changes over time, showing how these preferences are classified and how they are quantified relative to poverty de-concentration goals. Although there are various means of geographic delineation, the literature commonly analyzes poverty concentration using metropolitan statistical areas as the geographic unit. The conventional measure of poverty concentration adopted in the leading studies measures the proportion of poor people that live in a census tract (Jargowsky, 2003, 2008; Jargowsky and Bane, 1990; Kneebone et al., 2011). Poverty concentration literature substantiates that the nation's most populous metro areas house a disproportionate share of the nation's extreme poverty neighborhoods and retain the highest-concentrated poverty rates.[2] This data contextualizes patterns per findings from this study.

Research design

The policy documents serve as the unit of analysis for assessing priorities within the point allocation system. The QAP typically stipulates priorities and requirements in a specific manner to minimize ambiguity—a critical element of the design given the program's goal of allocating a scarce and competitive resource. By classifying these priorities according to defined categories and capturing the points associated with each, the analysis seeks to minimize threats to reliability. By virtue of this approach, the researcher is less likely to misinterpret the emphasis assigned to defined criteria.[3]

A two-tier plan evaluation matrix was designed to collect, categorize, and analyze the scoring criteria. Priorities with associate point allocations were recorded and consolidated using this instrument. The first tier of the instrument matrix assessed how priorities were classified according to broad program and housing goals.[4] The second tier of the plan evaluation matrix specifically analyzed spatial priorities according to their encouragement of poverty de-concentration. Those criteria designed to encourage poverty de-concentration were proportionally analyzed relative to overall spatial priorities. This research codifies these priorities and uses regression analysis to demonstrate the degree and significance of change over time.

Results and analysis of socio-spatial priorities

The overarching goal of the program is to support affordable housing provision for low- to moderate-income households. In addition to affordability, qualified allocation plans incorporate goals designed to encourage the efficient use of these resources and to influence both the property and spatial characteristics of the developments. Those criteria include the following:

Spatial priorities describe locational incentives within the qualified allocation plans. These criteria included the characteristics of the physical environment relative to tenant characteristics and need. They are designed to discourage locational patterns that do not contribute to the physical, social, economic or environmental well-being of LIHTC tenants.

Affordability. These criteria are intended to expand the depth and width of income targeting within developments.

Unit and property characteristics. There is an emphasis on the physical design of the units and the development site. These characteristics are intended to encourage specific characteristics within the controlled environment of the development.

Efficiency. This emphasizes the efficient use of time and financial resources. Efficiency relative to time is designed to encourage proposals that have initiated adequate due diligence by securing necessary government approvals and performing sufficient demand analysis so that tax credits are allocated to housing developments prepared to execute a project plan upon allocation. Efficiency also addresses the efficient use of financial resources, analyzing tax credit requests relative to development characteristics.

Prior to 2001, qualified allocation plans generally encouraged development location in high-poverty census tracts. In 2000, a federal amendment to the program was enacted discouraging locational patterns within qualified census tracts when the development did not contribute to comprehensive revitalization. For example, Virginia's 2000 QAP provided incentives to "proposed developments located in a qualified census tract or such other locally identified revitalization area" (VHDA, 2000, p. 10). The language suggests that "qualified census tract" and "revitalization area" were perceived as synonymous. It also suggested that placement approaches in low-income areas would create beneficial community outcomes. Encouraging locational patterns within low-income areas was likely a consequence of the policy's intent to promote development within depressed markets. What may have been underestimated was the market's tendency to travel the path of least resistance—maintaining or exacerbating current conditions unless policy is deliberately designed to induce alternative behavior.

In 2001, there was a shift, and federal directives governing the administration of the program discouraged states from incentivizing these locational patterns. Since this policy shift, incentives for locating in poverty-concentrated communities are awarded when developments are "located in a revitalization area and … an integral part of the local government's plan for revitalization of the area" (IHDA, 2005, p. 36). This policy shift suggests a realization that isolated approaches to low-income housing placement patterns would not produce beneficial outcomes for low-income households in poverty-concentrated communities. Rather, housing placement in high-poverty communities would only contribute to beneficial outcomes if and when these developments and their characteristics were considered within the context of comprehensive community needs.

In addition to a focus on strategic placement within high-poverty communities, criteria were also designed to locate developments within moderate-income communities. The 2008 Illinois QAP awarded points to developments within neighborhoods where "less than 10% of its housing stock was deemed as affordable" based on Census data (IHDA, 2008, p. 44). In addition, an expanded emphasis on the connection between housing, services, transportation , and jobs was the impetus for criteria that encouraged the

> availability of and access to appropriate public services, including: public transportation; public safety (police/fire department); schools; day care/after school programs; library; community center. The area and population to be served will be considered in the evaluation of the site … Availability of and access to appropriate community services, including: shopping (gas, grocery, banking, pharmacy, etc.); restaurants; parks; recreational facilities; hospital; health care facilities.
>
> (OHFA, 2009, p. 19)

These criteria were designed to address the complex intersection of physical, social, and economic needs among low-income households.

While the policy language suggests a focus on spatial and poverty de-concentration goals, the scoring analysis shows that these criteria generally represent a relatively small proportion of the scoring.

Table 27.1 shows that an overall emphasis of spatial criteria increased in Ohio and Illinois and decreased in Virginia over the decade. However, Table 27.2 highlights that poverty de-concentration's emphasis within these spatial priorities decreased in Ohio while increasing in Illinois and Virginia over the study period. To determine the strength of the relationship between spatial priorities and poverty de-concentration, inferential analysis was performed. The regression analysis showed a statistically significant relationship for Illinois—suggesting that increasing emphasis of spatial priorities was correlated with an increasing emphasis of poverty de-concentration goals. The relationship between Illinois' spatial criteria and poverty de-concentration resulted in an R squared factor of 0.782 and a t-value of 5.68. These results were statistically significant at $p<0.001$. However, neither Ohio nor Virginia's results showed a statistical significant relationship between the qualified allocation plan's emphasis of spatial priorities and poverty de-concentration goals—therefore the null hypothesis, that there was no relationship between these variables, could not be rejected.

When these results are superimposed over poverty concentration statistics, based upon 2000 and 2005–2009 census data, there are some interesting findings (Kneebone et al., 2011). The Kneebone et al., 2011 study, entitled *The Re-emergence of Poverty Concentration*, shows that the Midwest regions experienced some of the largest increases in poverty concentration, with the poor in these areas almost doubling over the decade. Chicago experienced a 13 percent increase in the number of poor living in extreme-poverty tracts, while in Ohio, poverty concentration increased in Toledo (15.3), Youngstown (14.3), and Dayton (11.9) and was among the highest in the nation (Kneebone et al., 2011). In stark contrast, the Virginia Beach–Norfolk metropolitan areas of Virginia experienced some of the greatest declines in poverty concentration at 6.7 percent, while Richmond, VA, experienced a 1.8 percent increase (Kneebone et al., 2011). Virginia's decreasing emphasis of poverty de-concentration goals relative to spatial priorities within the QAP can be correlated with the decline in poverty concentration within one of its high-poverty MSAs. However, Richmond has an extreme level of poverty concentration, ranking 39th among the 100 highest poverty MSAs across the country (Kneebone et al., 2011). The challenge presented in Virginia's policy design is that the decreased emphasis of poverty de-concentration within the QAP subsequently deflates the focus on poverty de-concentration within other high-poverty metropolitan statistical areas.

In Ohio, the results reflected in Table 27.1 and 27.2 show an increase in spatial priorities but a decrease in poverty de-concentration goals. This contradicts the expected findings—given the presence of seven high-poverty MSAs in the state with a total of 194 extreme poverty tracts (Kneebone et al., 2011). These findings suggest that there may be a shift in Ohio's approaches to consider the diversity of need within high-poverty communities. More specifically, if the broader goal of de-concentration is difficult to achieve, then ancillary goals related to access "to appropriate goods and services" (2009 Ohio QAP, p. 19) become prioritized. However, apart from poverty de-concentration goals, broader spatial goals are a

Table 27.1 Proportion of spatial criteria relative to overall LIHTC scoring criteria in qualified allocation plans

	2000	2001	2002	2003	2004	2005	2006	2007	2008	2009	2010
Ohio	0.0503	0.0497	0.0552	0.0570	0.0506	0.0229	0.0221	0	0.0244	0.3043	0.2919
Illinois	0.1053	0	0.0886	0.0805	0.0886	0.0843	0.1807	0.1807	0.1868	0.1868	0.1753
Virginia	0.1193	0.1211	0.0308	0.0518	0.0359	0.0456	0.0742	0.0748	0.0769	0.0753	0.0755

Table 27.2 Proportion of poverty de-concentration criteria relative to spatial criteria in LIHTC qualified allocation plans

	2000	2001	2002	2003	2004	2005	2006	2007	2008	2009	2010
Ohio	0.4444	0.4444	0.4444	0.4444	0.5000	0	0	0	0.5000	0.2000	0.2000
Illinois	0	0	0	0	0	0	0.2000	0.2000	0.2941	0.2941	0.2727
Virginia	0	0	0	0	0	0	0.3846	0.3846	0.3846	0.3571	0.3571

challenge to sustain within economically desolate communities—making it difficult to create benefit beyond marginal change.

Illinois' QAP's statistically significant correlation between spatial and poverty de-concentration goals shows a positive relationship between these variables within QAP scoring priorities. As the weight of spatial priorities increased within Illinois' qualified allocation plan design, Table 27.2 shows there was also an increasing emphasis of poverty de-concentration within the plan design. There were 175 extreme high-poverty tracks within Illinois' largest metropolitan statistical areas (Kneebone et al., 2011). Over 80 percent of those extreme poverty tracks are within the Chicago MSA. Since Chicago has served as the testing ground for poverty de-concentration through public housing redevelopment programs like HOPE VI and Moving to Work (MTW), there has likely been some degree of coordination between de-concentration goals within this MSA and the LIHTC qualified allocation plan design.

Policy implications

Over the past 25 years, the LIHTC program has addressed critical and diverse housing needs where unique public–private partnerships, broad accountability, and economic motivation are frequently cited as the primary reasons for its success (Serlin, 2011). However, this research questions whether this mechanism can do more to encourage socio-spatial patterns that aid in ameliorating the isolation of the poor. When low-income housing developments are located in communities with quality education, adequate public transportation, and diverse economic opportunities, then these developments contribute to beneficial outcomes for low-income households (Fletcher, 2008). Given those correlations, the design of the allocation plans should encourage innovative development approaches that address the spatial needs of marginalized individuals. Often, the dissension surrounding locational patterns of subsidized housing is heavily influence by NIMBY sentiments at the jurisdictional level.[5] These sentiments subsequently erect barriers that influence land-use policies (including land affordability and zoning regulations) and impact outcomes. However, strategic enhancements within the qualified allocation plan that expand the influence of socio-spatial priorities may lead to incremental improvements at the local level with beneficial long-term implications.

Second, if the allocation plan design does not broaden its approach to promoting socio-spatial equity, then the program cannot adequately respond to the isolation that produces undesirable social and economic implications.[6] These results indicate that more concerted policy approaches may be necessary to influence the socio-spatial outcomes of LIHTC developments. An alternative socio-spatial policy approach would require an evaluation of evolving housing needs relative to existing scoring priorities in addition to evaluating development outcomes within diverse geographies. Analyzing the existing environment and the policy design allows policymakers to assess the degree of success achieved and (1) the type of developments located in diverse regions, (2) their access to sustainable goods and services, and (3) the surrounding depth of educational and employment opportunities relative to the community demographic mix. Recasting how these outcomes are analyzed provides insight to support alternative approaches and enhance decision making. In addition, designing both the allocation policy and its process to encourage input from diverse coalitions enhances understanding and ultimately impacts outcomes. Specifically, households served by the program have perspectives that can improve the design of the allocating mechanism. Social policy must transition from models that assume socially constructed advantaged groups can speak for dependent groups (Schneider and Ingram, 1997). In the case of the LIHTC, those whose life experiences are directly impacted by the program's design should be extended a platform for participation.

Finally, a state's low-income housing tax credit policy is designed to widely address diverse housing needs. Although developing overarching goals and subsequently allowing developer decision and local regulations to guide specific features is a rational policy approach, there is value in encouraging geographically targeted characteristics designed to promote socio-spatial equity. While these types of goals are difficult to implement without local governments setting a complementary framework, it does not negate the importance and potential influence that changes in the allocation priorities could have on local outcomes. Given the unique needs of urban, suburban, and rural communities within a national environment which portents a growing dependence upon the low-income housing tax credit, strategic logic may need to shift to encourage enhanced coordination between state allocation priorities and regional interests—addressing the diverse socio-spatial needs of low-income households.

Conclusion

"Matters of location, design, standards … are central to the experience and interpretation of housing, and very much determined by policies and the policy process" (Franklin, 2001, p. 80). Structural elements embedded into the LIHTC allocation plan consistently elevate specific priorities in response to institutional and environmental conditions. However, as communities become increasingly socio-economically segmented, the program should respond to the growing spatial divides that disproportionately disadvantage marginalized groups. In part, this can be achieved through an integral allocation plan tailored to address the diverse spatial needs of diverse communities and by encouraging end-user participation in the allocation prioritization planning process.

Analysis of both the program structure and its implications can mitigate the potential for designing programs and "constructing housing according to narrowly held perspectives, thereby producing errors of the previous decades" (Franklin, 2001, p. 80). As state LIHTC allocating agencies assume the growing pressure of allocating scarce resources amid expanding housing needs, it is important that program administrators critically analyze how the program and its guiding policies can be enhanced. This study identifies opportunities to enhance outcomes within the LIHTC program by exploring how policy design powers held by the state represent levers for change. Doing so could prove to be a small but important step toward improving the well-being of low-income households.

Notes

1 The Department of Housing and Urban Development (HUD) defines a QCT as a census tract where 50 percent or more of households have incomes less than 60 percent of the gross area median income or that have a poverty rate of at least 25 percent (Khadduri and Rodda, 2004).
2 Kneebone et al.'s (2011) findings show that 66.7 percent of extreme poverty neighborhoods are located in large MSAs, 10.9 percent in small MSAs, and 6.3 percent in non-MSAs. MSAs are "geographic entities used by Federal statistical agencies in collecting, tabulating and publishing Federal statistics" (U.S. Census Bureau, 2013). Metropolitan statistical areas are geographic areas that contain urban areas of 50,000 or more, while micropolitan areas contain an urban core of at least 10,000 but less than 50,000.
3 Researchers have used similar research designs to analyze comprehensive plans and zoning codes. These studies measured various attributes and scored policy documents for the frequency and strength of specific items (Burby and May, 1997; Norton, 2005; Talen and Knaap, 2003). For example, Norton's (2008) study of master plans determined the influence of multiple items by assessing a given concept of interest or category and then summing or averaging the items to produce a standardized measure of a particular concept. This research study employs a similar methodological approach to categorize allocation preferences. Each category with point allocations will be recorded and captured. Once coded, the points associated with each category will be proportionally analyzed for each state and study year.

4 The method used in Brody's (2003) study examining the degree to which the quality of local plans changed over time relative to natural hazard mitigation.
5 NIMBY is an acronym for the phrase "not in my back yard". It is used to describe the opposition of residents to a proposal for a new development within their neighborhood.
6 For example, although public housing provides needed shelter for a growing number of poor families, its value has been deflated due to the model's correlation with social ills associated with poverty concentration and community disinvestment. In direct contrast, the low-income housing tax credit was designed to be flexible and more responsive to both the diverse housing needs within a community and the environmental conditions that impact need. However, research shows that while concentration patterns are not comparable to public housing, the existence of tax credit developments within a community are a predictor of subsequent developments within a community (Oakley, 2008).

References

Abt Associates, Inc. (2006). *Are States Using the Low Income Housing Tax Credit to Enable Families with Children to Live in Low Poverty and Racially Integrated Neighborhoods?* Cambridge: Poverty and Race Research Action Council and National Fair Housing Alliance.

Baum-Snow, N., and Marion, J. (2009). The Effects of Low Income Housing Tax Credit Developments on Neighborhoods. *Journal of Public Economics*, 93, 654–666.

Belsky, E., and Drew, R. (2007). *Taking Stock of the Nation's Rental Housing Challenges and a Half Century of Public Policy Responses.* Cambridge: Joint Center for Housing Studies of Harvard University.

Brody, S. D. (2003). *Are we learning to make better plans? A longitudinal analysis of plan quality associated with natural hazards* (Technical Report No. 02-08-R). College Station, TX: Texas A&M University Hazard Reduction and Recovery Center.

Burby, R.J., and May, P.J. (1997). Making Plans that Matter: Citizen Involvement and Government Action. *Journal of the American Planning Association*, 69(1), 33–49.

Cummings, J., and DiPasquale, D. (1999). The Low-Income Housing Tax Credit: An Analysis of the First Ten Years. *Housing Policy Debate*, 10(2), 251–307.

Dahl, R., and Lindblom, C. (1953). *Politics, Economics and Welfare.* New York: Harper.

Department of Treasury. (1999). *The Low Income Housing Tax Credit.* Washington, DC. Retrieved September 2012 from http://unclefed.com/SurviveIRS/MSSP/lihc.pdf.

Ellen, I., O'Regan, K., and Voicu, I. (2009). Siting, Spillovers, and Segregation: A Re-examination of the Low-Income Housing Tax Credit Program. In E. Glaeser and J. Quigley (eds), *Housing Markets and the Economy: Risk, Regulation, and Policy* (pp. 233–267). Cambridge: Lincoln Institute of Land Policy.

Erickson, D. (2006). Community Capitalism: How Housing Advocates, the Private Sector and Government Forged New Low-Income Housing Policy, 1968–1996. *The Journal of Policy History*, 18(2), 167–204.

Erickson, D. (2009). *The Housing Policy Revolution: Networks and Neighborhoods.* Washington, DC: The Urban Institute.

Erickson, D., Reid, C., Nelson, L., O'Shaughnessy, A., and Berube, A. (2008). *The Enduring Challenge of Concentrated Poverty in America.* Richmond: Federal Reserve Bank.

Fellowes, M. (2006). *From Poverty, Opportunity: Putting the Market to Work for Lower-Income Families.* Washington, DC: Brookings Institution.

Fincher, R., and Iveson, K. (2008). *Planning and Diversity in the City: Redistribution, Recognition and Encounter.* New York: Palgrave Macmillan.

Fletcher, N. (2008). Poverty Concentration and De-concentration: A Literature Review. *LBJ Journal of Public Affairs, Poverty and Social Enterprise*, 19, 69–81.

Franklin, S. (2001). Discourses of Design: Perspectives on the Meaning of Housing Quality and Good Design. *Housing, Theory and Society*, 18(1–2), 79–92.

Freeman, L. (2004). *Siting Affordable Housing: Location and Neighborhood Trends of Low Income Housing Tax Credit Developments in the 1990s.* Washington, DC: Brookings Institute.

Funderberg, R., and MacDonald, H. (2010). Neighborhood Valuation Effects from New Construction of Low-Income Housing Tax Credit Projects in Iowa: A Natural Experiment. *Urban Studies*, 47(8), 1745–1770.

Greene, R. (1991). Poverty Concentration Measures and the Urban Underclass. *Economic Geography*, 67(3), 240–252.

Gustafson, J., and Walker, J. (2002). *Analysis of State Qualified Allocation Plans for the Low-Income Housing Tax Credit Program.* Washington, DC: Urban Institute.

Hackworth, J. (2007). *The Neoliberal City: Governance, Ideology and Development in American Urbanism.* Ithaca, NY: Cornell University Press.

Harsman, B., and Quigley, J.M. (1995). The Spatial Segregation of Ethnic and Demographic Groups: Comparative Evidence from Stockholm and San Francisco. *Journal of Urban Economics*, 37(1), 1–16.

Illinois Housing Development Authority (IHDA). (2005). *Low Income Housing Tax Credit Qualified Allocation Plan for the State of Illinois*. Retrieved from: http://www.novoco.com/low_income_housing/lihtc/qap_2005.php

Illinois Housing Development Authority (IHDA). (2008). *Low Income Housing Tax Credit Qualified Allocation Plan for the State of Illinois*. Retrieved from: http://www.novoco.com/low_income_housing/lihtc/qap_2005.php

Internal Revenue Code (2011). *Low Income Housing, 26 U.S.C. § 42*. Retrieved from http://www.gpo.gov/fdsys/pkg/USCODE-2011-title26/html/USCODE-2011-title26-subtitleA-chap1-subchapA-partIV-subpartD-sec42.htm.

Jackson, P. (2007). *The Low-Income Housing Tax Credit: A Framework for Evaluation*. Washington, DC: Congressional Research Service Report for Congress.

Jargowsky, P. (2003). *Stunning Progress, Hidden Problems: The Dramatic Decline of Concentrated Poverty in the 1990s*. Washington, DC: Brookings Institute.

Jargowsky, P. (2008). *The Enduring Challenge of Concentrated Poverty in America: Case Studies from Communities across the U.S.* Washington, DC: Community Affairs Offices of the Federal Reserve System and the Brookings Institution.

Jargowsky, P., and Bane, M. (1990). Ghetto Poverty: Basic Questions. In L.E. Lynn and M.G.H. McGeary (eds), *Inner City Poverty in the United States* (pp. 16–67). Washington, DC: National Academy Press, 1990.

Khadduri, J., and Rodda, D. (2004). *Making the Best Use of Your LIHTC Dollars: A Planning Paper for State Policy Makers*. Bethesda: Abt Associates.

Khadduri, J., and Wilkins, C. (2007). Designing Subsidized Rental Housing Programs: What Have We Learned? In N. Retsinas and E. Belsky (eds), *Revisiting Rental Housing Policies, Programs and Priorities* (pp. 161–190). Washington, DC: Brookings Institution Press.

Kneebone, E., Nadeau, C., and Berube, A. (2011). *The Re-emergence of Concentrated Poverty*. Washington, DC: The Brookings Institute.

Norton, R.K. (2005). More and Better Planning: State-Mandated Local Planning in Coastal North Carolina. *Journal of the American Planning Association*, 13(4), 241–259.

Norton, R.K. (2008). Using Content Analysis to Evaluate Local Master Plans and Zoning Codes. *Land Use Policy*, 25, 432–454.

Oakley, D. (2008). Locational Patterns of Low-Income Housing Tax Credit Developments: A Sociospatial Analysis of Four Metropolitan Areas. *Urban Affairs Review*, 43, 599–629.

Ohio Housing Finance Agency (OHFA). (2009). *Housing Credit Program Qualified Allocation Plan*. Retreived from: http://www.novoco.com/low_income_housing/lihtc/qap_2009.php

O'Sullivan, A., and Gibb, K. (2003). *Housing Economics and Public Policy*. Oxford: Blackwell Science Ltd.

Pelletiere, D. (2009). *Preliminary Assessment of American Community Survey Data Shows Housing Affordability Gap Worsening for Lowest Income Households from 2007 to 2008*. Washington, DC: National Low Income Housing Coalition.

Schneider, A.L., and Ingram, H. (1997). *Policy Design for Democracy*. Lawrence, KS: University Press of Kansas.

Schneider, A.L., and Sidney, M. (2009). What is Next for Policy Design and Social Construction Theory? *The Policy Studies Journal*, 37(1), 103–119.

Schwartz, A., Ellen, I., Voicu, I., and Schill, M. (2006). The External Effects of Place-Based Subsidized Housing. *Regional Science and Urban Economics*, 36(6), 679–707.

Serlin, C. (2011, June). The LIHTC at 25. *Affordable Housing Finance*. Retrieved June 2011 from http://housingfinance.com/ahf/articles/2011/june/0611-specialfocus-The-LIHTC-At-25.htm.

Talen, E., and Knaap, G. (2003). Legalizing Smart Growth: An Empirical Study of Land Use Regulation in Illinois. *Journal of Planning Education and Research*, 22(4), 345–359.

U.S. Census Bureau. (2013). Metropolitan and micropolitan statistical areas main. U. S. Department of Commerce, Washington, DC. Retrieved from http://www.census.gov/population/metro/

Usowski, K., and Hollar, M. (2008). Social Policy and the U.S. Tax Code: The Curious Case of the Low-Income Housing Tax Credit. *National Tax Journal*, 61(3), 519–529.

Virginia Housing Development Authority (VHDA). (2000). *The Plan of the Virginia Housing Development Authority for the Allocation of Low Income Housing Tax Credits*. Retrieved from: http://www.novoco.com/low_income_housing/lihtc/qap_2000.php

Voicu, I., O'Reagan, K., and Ellen, I. (2009). Sitting, spillovers, and segregation: A re-examination of the low-income housing tax credit program. In E. Glaeser, and J. M. Quigley (eds.), *Housing markets and the economy: Risk, regulation, and policy* (pp. 233–267). Cambridge, MA: Lincoln Institute of Land Policy.

Williamson, A., Smith, M., and Strambi-Kramer, M. (2009). Housing Choice Vouchers, the Low-Income Housing Tax Credit, and the Federal Poverty Deconcentration Goal. *Urban Affairs Review*, 45(1), 119–132.

28

NEO-LIBERALISM AND PRIVATE EMERGENCY FOOD NETWORKS

Deborah A. Harris and Jamilatu Zakari

Introduction

Hunger and food insecurity in the United States are significant social problems that have gained substantial political and media attention (Berberoglu, 2011; Bruening et al., 2012). In 2011, 14.9 percent of American households experienced food insecurity, and almost one-third of these households were classified as having very low food security characterized by reduced food intake and disrupted eating patterns (Coleman-Jensen, 2012). Nord and Golla (2009) state that the increase in food insecurity and hunger within the United States is a reflection of the recent economic downturn. Within the United States, periods of economic turmoil are character- ized by drastic changes within government-funded food entitlement programs and increasing growth of private emergency food networks (Daponte and Bade, 2006; Poppendieck, 1998; Scanlan, 2009; Vartanian et al., 2011). As a result of the recession, rising rates of unemploy- ment and food insecurity have increased demands on the largest federal food assistance program, the Supplemental Nutrition Assistance Program (SNAP), formerly known as the Food Stamp Program (USDA, 2012).

While many of the food insecure may turn to federal programs such as SNAP, private sources of aid, including local food banks and pantries, are increasingly called upon to provide supple- mental food assistance. As a result, private food networks that were originally created to provide temporary, emergency food assistance have now become permanent fixtures in the social ser- vices arena (Daponte and Bade, 2006; Poppendieck, 1998). According to a study conducted by the U.S. Department of Agriculture (USDA), in 2011, approximately six million people received food aid from one of the nation's food banks or pantries (Coleman-Jensen et al., 2012). As the nationwide economic recovery slowly progresses, private emergency food networks are expected to continue their role as a social safety net for the food insecure. Furthermore, recent legislation proposing funding reductions to SNAP could lead to even more pressure on pri- vate emergency food networks to fill in the gaps left by decreased federal funding (New York Times, 2012).

Private emergency food networks undoubtedly provide an important service to their local communities. However, their increasing importance in the greater food assistance landscape suggests a shift in both regard and response to the poor. These trends include localizing and privatizing social service delivery as well as reorienting codes of citizenship to align more with the market agenda. All of these changes are related to the larger neo-liberalization of social welfare. We argue in this chapter that neo-liberal ideologies have fundamentally changed how food assistance is provided in the United States often to the detriment of those served by private emergency food networks. To illustrate this, we first provide an overview of the rise of private emergency food networks. This is followed by a description of the emergence of neo-liberal doctrines that have shaped the public assistance landscape for the past several decades. We pay particular attention to how increased localization and privatization has affected emergency food assistance as well as how the concepts of "personal responsibility" and "empowerment" have been used to delegitimize the food needs of the poor. Finally, we discuss the movement toward redefining food as a basic human right and compare this to the current neo-liberal discourse on food security.

The rise and growth of emergency food networks

Private emergency food networks arose as a response to periods of economic turmoil and a lack of adequate government assistance (Daponte and Bade, 2006; Poppendieck, 1998; Scanlan, 2009; Vartanian et al., 2011). The category of "private emergency food networks" encompasses several different models including food banks, food pantries, soup kitchens, and food and meal delivery services (Berner et al., 2008). For several decades, private emergency food networks have filled gaps left from low food stamp benefits and provided for those who eschewed government assistance due to concerns over stigma and program bureaucracy (Daponte and Bade, 2006; Poppendieck, 1998; Riches, 2002). When federal budget cuts significantly reduced the food assistance safety net for millions of Americans during the recession of the 1980s, food banks began to grow to help supplement decreasing government assistance. Later in that decade, the federal government began to encourage the growth of private emergency food networks in earnest (Biggerstaff et al., 2002; Poppendieck, 1998; St. Mary's Food Bank Alliance, 2012).

Founded in 1967, St. Mary's Food Bank in Phoenix is considered to be the first official food bank in the United States (Poppendieck, 1998). The Emergency Food and Medical Program, created during Johnson's War on Poverty, encouraged the creation of food pantries as a way to increase the national safety net and help low-income populations gain access to food resources (Poppendieck, 1998). In 1976, the government gave St. Mary's a grant to educate other cities on how to establish and create food banks as part of a project called Second Harvest (Poppendieck, 1998). The organization eventually changed its name to America's Second Harvest and took on the role of umbrella organization. Food banks would join the organization and, in return, America's Second Harvest would certify the food bank, stating that it was a nonprofit organization, served a particular geographic area, was able to warehouse food donations, met standards for sanitation and safety, and was financially stable (Daponte and Bade, 2006). The entry of America's Second Harvest into the emergency food environment greatly changed the nature of private food assistance. Corporate sector food producers were able to donate to food banks in large quantities. Elements of the tax code allowed businesses to claim deductions for these donations, and the certification process by America's Second Harvest helped assuage business owners' fears that improper storage or other mishandling could lead to food-borne illnesses and lawsuits against their companies (Berner et al., 2008; Daponte and Bade, 2006).

Since the 1980s, food banks have been the fastest-growing charitable industry in the United States (Riches, 2002). Today, America's Second Harvest is one of the largest government-funded organizations aimed at alleviating hunger in America. Some recent growth in private emergency food networks can be attributed to Charitable Choice provisions that were part of the 1996 Welfare Reform Act. Under Charitable Choice, states were no longer allowed to discriminate against religious organizations in awarding grants and contracts to provide social services (Cashwell et al., 2004). The national organization Feeding America has calculated that, as of 2010, over 200 food banks have provided food to 33,500 food pantries, serving approximately 33.9 million pantry users (Mabli et al., 2010).

Overview of neo-liberalization of social welfare

The neo-liberalization of social welfare provisions accelerated during the 1980s Reagan and Thatcher-era administrations and was firmly entrenched in the political sphere by the 1990s (Harvey, 2005). The process of neo-liberalism came during a time of economic and social "crisis" and represents a major turning point in how nations relate to the poor (Mudge, 2008; Peck et al., 2009). The process of neo-liberalization does away with Keynesian notions of the state and market regulation and prioritizes the market and its ability to meet human needs (Harvey, 2005). Due to competition, market-based solutions are believed to be more efficient and innovative than government programs that are depicted as being bloated in cost and staff, overly bureaucratized, and stagnant regarding their mission and approach (Allen and Guthman, 2006).

Under neo-liberalism, social welfare provisions are rolled back with the assumption that market-based solutions to problems such as poverty would be more appropriate (Harvey, 2005). During this process, aspects of the for-profit world come to dominate the social services field through increasing privatization of social services. Private companies, local communities, and nonprofits compete for government contracts frequently promising innovation and ways to control spending (Connell, 2010). As localities compete for and gain projects, corporate metrics for determining success and "profitability" are applied to providing services to the poor (Connell, 2010; Peck and Tickell, 2002).

As Allen and Guthman (2006) argue, "The process of neoliberalism thus leaves many gaps in services, regulations and social protections in its wake" (p. 402). Yet, it is hard to fight the entrenchment of neo-liberal ideology in social service provisions. Collaboration between intellectual, bureaucratic, and political spheres has transformed the tenets of neo-liberalism into the guiding forces for much of social policy in recent decades (Centeno and Cohen, 2012; Mudge, 2008). Even though these spheres were integral in *establishing* neo-liberalism in social policy, they were also *transformed* by neo-liberalism. According to Peck et al. (2009), neo-liberalism has changed the relations between these spheres, including their "logics of action, institutional routines, and political projects" (p. 112).

Perhaps no facet of neo-liberalism has so altered the food assistance landscape as the movement towards localism and privatization and the overall focus on individual responsibility as the defining principle of citizenhood. Both of these changes have helped rewrite the social contract vis-à-vis food assistance. As Daponte and Bade (2006) argue, private emergency food networks are no longer a temporary source of aid, but actually act as a private system that runs parallel to government assistance programs. By firmly linking food assistance to market-based processes, these changes also undermine the concept of food and protection from hunger as a basic human right, ultimately making more people food insecure.

Going local and moving private

Major changes to social welfare programs under neo-liberalism include the movement away from government sources of aid and a push towards more local entities. It was suggested that, by devolving programmatic responsibility to more local levels, new initiatives could be formed that drew from community strengths and better fit the needs of local vulnerable populations (Allen and Guthman, 2006; Peck and Tickell, 2002). While this devolution of responsibility was often accompanied by funds, there were also frequently limits on how much control localities had over program design and implementation. This was particularly true regarding food assistance. While other social welfare programs, such as Temporary Assistance for Needy Families (TANF), were devolved to the state level through a block grant system, the Food Stamp Program, after much debate, remained a federal program. Instead, much of the focus on local communities regarding food assistance involved greater funding (often through grants or private donors) for food banks and pantries.

The movement toward localizing responses to food insecurity does not take into account the varying levels of resources across communities (Allen and Guthman, 2006). Not all communities have the ability to create and administer such programs, which often require a population with high levels of human and social capital (Johnston and Baker, 2005). This not only sets some communities up for failure, but even successful local food assistance efforts can have negative consequences. As Alkon and Mares (2012) point out, community groups have arisen to "fill holes left by a shrinking state" and this has "implicitly impl[ied] that it is their role, and not the state's, to provide such services" (p. 349). By moving responsibility to local jurisdictions, the overall responsibility of the federal government for preventing hunger could be diminished (Allen and Guthman, 2006).

This devolution of food assistance was often accompanied by the privatization of programs. It fit within the overarching neo-liberal paradigm that encouraged the privatization of services, which would eventually extend to areas of corrections, education, and job training among others (see Alkon and Mares, 2012). This process served to commodify social services—entities that had never been seen as commodities before (Connell, 2010; Mudge, 2008). Connell (2010) describes how, through the process of privatization, "Needs formerly met by public agencies on the principle of citizen rights, or through personal relationships in communities and families, are now to be met by companies selling services in the market" (p. 23).

In some cases, there is an out-and-out privatization of services, in which services once provided by government programs are delivered by private companies. In others, there is what is known as public–private partnerships and the government provides funding or other forms of assistance for social programs that are eventually run by private entities (Allen and Guthman, 2006). An example of public–private partnerships involves food pantries tied to religious organizations that were granted federal monies through Charitable Choice partnerships (Cashwell et al., 2004).

Issues that can arise through these partnerships involve meshing the task of providing social services, including food assistance, with the types of arrangements usually reserved for the for-profit world. Grants or other partnership agreements may be tied to performance measures (Allen and Guthman, 2006; Connell, 2010; Peck and Tickell, 2002). However, in the area of emergency food assistance, how would such measures be created? While metrics such as numbers of households served or how many pounds of food are distributed per month exist, these statistics say nothing about how food pantries actually address the issue of hunger prevention.

Privatization of social services has also brought business practices such as managerialism to providers and added extra layers of employees and bureaucracy—the very conditions privatization was supposed to end (Connell, 2010). Federal and state monies may require implementing additional accounting measures, which may mean hiring more staff and further eroding the resources of small organizations. These agreements may also request more information from clients in order to assure those receiving food assistance are "truly" needy, diminishing the entire point behind "neighbor helping neighbor" sources of aid (Daponte and Bade, 2006). In addition, grants and contracts ultimately end, leaving community organizations to find funding to replace lost monies or else end programming (Allen and Guthman, 2006).

Redefining citizenship

According to Ferguson (2009), earlier Keynesian ideas about social welfare centered on the concept of the citizen as a worker—an individual who, through their participation in the workforce, was able to take care of themselves. Those who were unable to work, such as children or the elderly, were acknowledged as needing, and being deserving of, economic assistance. With the shift toward neo-liberal social policies, people's relationship to the market became primary and those unable to further the ends of the market were seen as having failed in their role as citizen (Centeno and Cohen, 2012; Piven and Cloward, 1993; Riches, 1999). The entrenchment of this ideology speaks to the power of neo-liberalism to shape culture by drawing from long-held values of individualism and self-responsibility and remolding them to become the dominant ideals of citizenhood (Alkon and Mares, 2012; Busch, 2010; Harvey, 2005). Individuals who need help are stigmatized for being unable to support themselves and their families. If all their efforts of self-help are ineffectual, they are encouraged to seek assistance from their extended family or local communities, with government aid being the last resort of the most desperate (Luxton, 2010). Even then, it is acknowledged that such assistance should be for the shortest time frame possible (Harvey, 2005).

The successful redefinition of citizenship to market-based arrangements and reduction of the state's role in providing assistance speaks to the powerful rhetoric used by policymakers. Politicians and policymakers reiterated buzzwords such as "ending dependency" and "giving empowerment" and argued that it was in the best interest of the poor and food insecure to roll back assistance programs (Alkon and Mares, 2012; Luxton, 2010). Evidence suggests the poor have internalized these views. Luxton's (2010) study of low-income individuals found that many were reluctant to ask for help and did not expect it from the government. Research on rural clients of a food assistance program similarly described the need for personal responsibility and expressed gratitude for the food they were given rather than suggesting the government had any duty to provide for its citizens (Gross and Rosenberger, 2010).

Food, rights, emergency food assistance, and avoiding the neo-liberal trap

Concerns over food insecurity have led to a variety of efforts to ensure access to healthy, affordable food to the poor. These efforts include reclassifying food as a human right (Allen, 1999). Riches (1999) argues hunger in Western nations is not just about economic resources, it is about the failure to acknowledge food as a basic human right. Food was named as a human right in the 1948 Universal Declaration of Human Rights (United Nations, 1998). The United States, while claiming support for its inclusion, points to the Constitution for not recognizing food as a human right (Messer and Cohen, 2007). In addition, the United States continues to vote against Right to Food Resolutions proposed by the United Nations. Allen (1999) suggests that part of the reluctance to label food a human right is that doing so would make the government responsible for providing food if it was unavailable elsewhere.

Despite lack of government acknowledgement that food is a human right, there is a growing movement to address issues of hunger and food access within the United States. According to Levkoe (2006), the food justice movement is geared toward redefining people as citizens rather than consumers. Such a movement would focus on providing food security in a way that "all people have access to adequate amounts of safe, nutritious, culturally appropriate food produced in an environmentally sustainable way and provided in a manner that promotes human dignity" (Levkoe, 2006, p. 91).

Some have tried to implement these principles at a local scale. These community food security advocates seek to reorient the approach to food access "as a social, rather than individual, concern ... [and] emphasize the role of the built environment and longstanding patterns of racial and class-based inequalities in producing inadequate access to healthy food" (Alkon and Mares, 2012, p. 350). Still, issues of inequality make changes difficult to implement. Among these constraints are patterns of class, race, and spatial inequality (Centeno and Cohen, 2012). Not all communities share the same resources and ability to come together to address issues like hunger (Johnston and Baker, 2005). Even within these communities, it is unlikely that everyone would be able to participate equally, suggesting that important stakeholders may be left out of public action (Allen, 1999; Johnston and Baker, 2005).

More troubling is when these local food security programs actually uphold neo-liberal ideals through the focus on self-help and self-determination and cast those with low income as a group that needs to be transformed (Alkon and Mares, 2012; Allen and Guthman, 2006; Guthman, 2011). Also, because many community food security programs pride themselves on being better able to provide food than the government, these beliefs can further erode the concept of government responsibility (Levkoe, 2006). Advocates may view providing food to the food insecure as "empowering" rather than fostering "dependence" on state aid, yet this orientation still does not cast food as a human right but rather as a form of charity from one group to another (Alkon and Mares, 2012; Allen, 1999).

It is important for community food security organizations to realize that, although they may measure success at the local level, the issue of food insecurity still intersects with extra local forces such as nationwide food policy (Allen, 1999; Johnston and Baker, 2005). Allen (1999) reminds us that large-scale attacks on inequality and injustice have traditionally come from the federal level. For this reason, researchers have suggested that community food security organizations focus on both "scaling out" and "scaling up." Scaling out refers to expanding coverage areas, whereas scaling up calls for linking issues of food insecurity to other neo-liberal trends in wealth and income inequality (Johnston and Baker, 2005). This scaling out can also refer to involvement in pressing for more government responsibility for addressing the issues of food security, including advocating for food to be considered a right. This way, community food security advocates can simultaneously work toward building local community infrastructure for food growth and delivery while also insisting the government provide a more stable social safety net for the poor (Levkoe, 2006).

Community food initiatives, while not a panacea for alleviating food insecurity, can still provide valuable resources for community members. In Johnston and Baker's (2005) study of one such program in Toronto, they detailed how the program was able to provide educational and community development components to help clients become aware of both their rights and responsibilities as community members. Such arrangements can transform "clients"—or people in need of assistance—to "collaborators"—individuals with a sense of ownership and even leadership in the local food security community. Research finds that when volunteers participate in food programs as a means to "earn" their food benefits (even when not required by programs), this may make them feel less stigmatized about needing assistance (Gross and Rosenberger, 2010). By involving clients, programs can help identify new leaders who are able to draw from their own experiences in order to design programs that are applicable to the lives of the food insecure. Community food security programs can also focus on food's place as a universal human need and draw attention to some of the larger, neo-liberal projects that impact food security (Allen, 1999; Johnston and Baker, 2005). Doing so may help encourage clients to think about alternative arrangements and be better able to advocate for their rights at both the local and national levels.

Conclusion

On the surface, private emergency food networks, particularly in the form of community food banks and pantries, seem an unquestionable social good. However, further reflection requires us to ask why these networks have been necessary. The answer to this question is complex and relates to large economic, political, and social shifts toward a neo-liberal revision of the state's responsibility to the poor. Through increased privatization, social services have been transformed into commodities. Local communities are tasked with solving massive social problems, often with few resources or guidance (Levkoe, 2006). This process serves to further increase social inequality as communities with vastly different levels of resources must compete for much of the same funding that used to be passed on by the government. In the meantime, the emphasis on local may lead to smaller organizations being disadvantaged in funding scenarios while simultaneously being called upon more and more to service their local communities. The end result of this process is that tremendous responsibilities may be shifted to the private sector, allowing the government to reduce its responsibility and investment regarding food security. This also prevents the government from having to entertain difficult conversations regarding what exactly are the rights of citizens and if food security should be considered a right.

Neo-liberalization also helps redefine what citizens believe they can expect from their government. Under the neo-liberal paradigm, failure to be able to feed one's family is regarded as a failure of the individual. At its heart, the neo-liberalization of social services rewrites the social safety net in a way that "rights" and "entitlements" disappear and are replaced by calls for "personal responsibility" and "empowerment." This focus on the individual directs attention away from larger social structures and provides participation in the market as the only true remedy to poverty and hunger.

In the current recessionary economic climate, food security becomes an even more pressing issue (Nord and Golla, 2009). Ironically, such conditions may also serve to benefit those wishing to redefine the nature of food security in this country. Due to recent economic restructuring and the current economic downturn, more and more educated, able-bodied people are unable to support their families (Ferguson, 2009). When poverty issues filter up to the middle class, they have the opportunity to highlight common causes between groups and shift attention to larger structural inequalities. As more people gain awareness of larger social forces impacting their family's food security, this creates room for resistance to the insertion of neo-liberal doctrine in the provision of food, the most primary of human needs. This, combined with the work being done by community food advocates to redefine food security as a right, can provide a platform from which collective action can begin.

References

Alkon, A.H., and Mares, T.M. (2012). Food sovereignty in U.S. food movements: Radical visions and neoliberal constraints. *Agriculture and Human Values*, 29(3), 347–359. Retrieved on October 31, 2012 (doi:10.1007/s10460-012-9356-z).

Allen, P. (1999). Reweaving the food security safety net: Mediating entitlement and entrepreneurship. *Agriculture and Human Values*, 16(2), 117–129. Retrieved on June 16, 2012 (http://cgirs.ucsc.edu/research/environment/afsrg/publications/Allen_1999.pdf).

Allen, P., and Guthman, J. (2006). From "old school" to "farm-to-school": Neoliberalization from the ground up. *Agriculture and Human Values*, 23(4), 401–415. Retrieved on April 1, 2012 (doi:10.1007/s10460-006-9019-z).

Berberoglu, B. (2011). The global capitalist crisis: Its origins, dynamics and impact on the United States. *International Review of Modern Sociology*, 37(2), 159–184. Retrieved on October 6, 2012 (http://www.e-history.eu/files/uploads/Paper_-_2012.03.19.pdf).

Berner, M., Ozer, T., and Paynter, S. (2008). A portrait of hunger, the social safety net, and the working poor. *The Policy Studies Journal*, 26(3), 403–420. Retrieved on June 16, 2012 (doi: 10.1111/j.1541-0072.2008.00274.x).

Biggerstaff, M.A., Morris, P.M., and Nichols-Casebolt, A. (2002). Living on the edge: Examination of people attending food pantries and soup kitchens. *Social Work*, 47(3), 267–277. Retreived on June 16, 2012 (doi: 10.1093/sw/47.3.267).

Bruening, M., MacLehose, R., Loth, K., Story, M., and Newmark-Sztainer, D. (2012). Feeding a family in a recession: Food insecurity among Minnesota parents. *American Journal of Public Health*, 102(3), 520–526. Retrieved on October 31, 2012 (http://www.ncbi.nlm.nih.gov/pubmed/22390517).

Busch, L. (2010). Can fairy tales come true? The surprising story of neoliberalism and world agriculture. *Sociologia Ruralis*, 50(4), 331–351. Retrieved on August 27, 2012 (doi: 10.1111/j.1467-9523.2010.00511.x).

Cashwell, S.T., Bartowski, J.P., Duffy, P.A., Casanova, V., Molnar, J.J., and Irimia-Vladu, M. (2004). Private food assistance in the deep south: Assessing agency directors' knowledge of charitable choice. *Journal of Sociology and Social Welfare*, 31(2), 157–177. Retrieved on August 27, 2012 (http://srdc.msstate.edu/ridge/projects/recipients/01_cashwell_final.pdf).

Centeno, M.A., and Cohen, J.N. (2012). The arc of neoliberalism. *Annual Review of Sociology*, 38, 317–340. Retrieved on October 6, 2012 (doi: 10.1146/annurev-soc-081309-150235).

Coleman-Jensen, A. (2012). Predictors of U.S. food insecurity across nonmetropolitan, suburban, and principal city residence during the great recession. *Journal of Poverty*, 16(4), 392–411. Retrieved on November 17, 2012 (doi:10.1080/10875549.2012.720657).

Coleman-Jensen, A., Nord, M., Andrews, M., and Carlson, S. (2012). *Household food security in the United States in 2011 U.S. Department of Agriculture*, Economic Research Service Report No. 141. Retrieved on October 31, 2012 (http://www.ers.usda.gov/media/884525/err141.pdf).

Connell, R. (2010). Understanding neoliberalism. In S. Braedley and M. Luxton (eds), *Neoliberalism and everyday life* (pp. 22–36). Montreal, Quebec: McGill-Queen's University Press.

Daponte, B.O., and Bade, S. (2006). How the private food assistance network evolved: Interactions between public and private responses to hunger. *Nonprofit and Voluntary Sector Quarterly*, 35(4), 668–690. Retrieved on August 27, 2012 (http://nvs.sagepub.com/content/35/4/668.abstract).

Ferguson, J. (2009). The uses of neoliberalism. *Antipode*, 41(S1), 166–184.

Gross, J., and Rosenberger, N. (2010). The double binds of getting food among the poor in rural Oregon. *Food, Culture and Society*, 13(1), 47–70. Retrieved on July 2, 2012 (http://www.ingentaconnect.com/content/bloomsbury/fcs/2010/00000013/00000001/art00003?crawler=true).

Guthman, J. (2011). *Weighing in: Obesity, food justice, and the limits of capitalism*. Berkeley, CA: University of California Press.

Harvey, D. (2005). *A brief history of neoliberalism*. New York: Oxford University Press.

Johnston, J., and Baker, L. (2005). Eating outside the box: Foodshare's good food box and the challenge of scale. *Agriculture and Human Values*, 22(3), 313–325. Retrieved on June 16, 2012 (doi: 10.1007/s10460-005-6048-y).

Levkoe, C.Z. (2006). Learning democracy through food justice movements. *Agriculture and Human Values*, 23(1), 89–98. Retrieved on June 16, 2012 (http://link.springer.com/article/10.1007/s10460-005-5871-5).

Luxton, M. (2010). Doing neoliberalism: Perverse individualism in personal life. In S. Braedley and M. Luxton (eds), *Neoliberalism and everyday life* (pp. 163–183). Montreal, Quebec: McGill-Queen's University Press.

Mabli, J., Cohen, R., Potter, F., and Zhao, Z. (2010). *Hunger in America 2010: Local report prepared for the Capital Area Food Bank of Texas, Inc (4408)*. Retrieved on April 1, 2012 (http://cafbtx.convio.net/site/DocServer/4408.pdf?docID=601).

Messer, E. and Cohen, M. (2007). *The human right to food as a U.S. nutrition concern, 1976–2000*. IFPRI Discussion Paper. Washington, D.C., International Food Policy Research Institute.

Mudge, S.L. (2008). What is neo-liberalism? *Socio-Economic Review*, 6, 703–731.

New York Times. (2012). *Food Stamps and the Farm Bill*. Retrieved on January 29, 2013 (http://www.nytimes.com/2012/06/13/opinion/food-stamps-and-the-farm-bill.html).

Nord, M., and Golla, A.M. (2009). *Does SNAP decrease food insecurity? Untangling the self-selection effect*. U.S. Department of Agriculture, Economic Research Service Report No. 85. Retrieved on June 16, 2012 (http://www.ers.usda.gov/media/184824/err85_1_.pdf).

Peck, J., Theodore, N., and Brenner, N. (2009). Postneoliberalism and its malcontents. *Antipode*, 41(S1), 94–116.

Peck, J., and Tickell, A. (2002). Neoliberalizing space. *Antipode*, 34, 380–404. Retrieved on August 27, 2012 (doi: 10.1111/1467-8330.00247).

Piven, F., and Cloward, R. (1993). *Regulating the poor: The functions of public welfare*. New York: Vintage.

Poppendieck, J. (1998). *Sweet charity? Emergency food and the end of entitlement*. New York: Penguin.

Riches, G. (1999). Advancing the human right to food in Canada: Social policy and the politics of hunger, welfare, and food security. *Agriculture and Human Values*, 16, 203–211.

Riches, G. (2002). Food banks and food security: Welfare reform, human rights and social policy. Lessons from Canada? *Social Policy & Administration*, 36(6), 648–663. Retrieved on April 1, 2012 (doi: 10.1111/1467-9515.00309).

Scanlan, S. (2009). New direction and discovery on the hunger front: Toward a sociology of food security/insecurity. *Humanity & Society*, 33(4), 292–316. Retrieved on June 16, 2012 (http://has.sagepub.com/content/33/4/292.abstract).

St. Mary's Food Bank Alliance. (2012). *Our history*. Retrieved on December 3, 2012 (http://www.firstfoodbank.org/learn-more/our-history).

United Nations. (1998). *Fiftieth anniversary of the Universal Declaration of Human Rights*. Retrieved on November 17, 2012 (http://www.un.org/rights/50/decla.htm).

U.S. Department of Agriculture (USDA). (2012). *Supplemental nutrition assistance program: A short history of SNAP*. Washington, DC. Retrieved on October 6, 2012 (http://www.fns.usda.gov/snap/rules/Legislation/about.htm).

Vartanian, T. P., Houser, L., and Harkness, J. (2011, December). Food stamps and dependency: Disentangling the short-term and long-term economic effects of food stamp receipt and low income for young mothers. *Journal of Sociology & Social Welfare*, 38(4), 101–122. Retrieved on April 1, 2012 (http://www.wmich.edu/hhs/newsletters_journals/jssw_institutional/institutional_subscribers/38.4.Vartanian.pdf).

29

EXAMINING FOOD SECURITY AMONG CHILDREN IN HOUSEHOLDS PARTICIPATING IN THE SUPPLEMENTAL NUTRITION ASSISTANCE PROGRAM (SNAP)

Implications for human rights

Margaret Lombe, Von E. Nebbitt, Mansoo Yu, Andrew Reynolds, and Aakanksha Sinha

Introduction: background to the study

Right to food is an internationally recognized human right that every individual should enjoy. Despite being one of the richest nations in the world, a significant proportion of the population within the United States does not enjoy this right and suffers from hunger and food insecurity (USDA, 2012). Food insecurity is the lack of consistent access to adequate food (Nord, 2003). In order to tackle issues of hunger and food insecurity, formal food assistance mechanisms have been put in place. Primary among these is SNAP, the largest food assistance program in the United States. The program's primary objective is to safeguard the health and wellbeing of low-income households (Borjas, 2004; C-SNAP, 2007; Jolliffe et al., 2005). Indeed the federal government continues to spend a significant amount of resources on the program. Between 2007 and 2011 SNAP spending increased from approximately $30 billion to $72 billion (CBO, 2012). In 2012 approximately $81 billion was spent on SNAP (Rosenbaum, 2013). There has also been a significant increase in the number of households participating in the program. The number of people receiving SNAP benefits increased significantly between 2007 and 2011. According to the 2011 Congressional Budget, SNAP-participating households peaked at 45 million (CBO, 2012). Furthermore, current estimates are that the number of people participating in SNAP will continue to rise from fiscal year 2012 through fiscal year 2014 (CBO, 2012); the noted rise is largely attributed to the economic downturn.

Despite this, food insecurity continues to be a concern. There is some data to suggest that in 2011 a total of 17.9 million households were food insecure (USDA, 2012). Specifically, an estimated 50.1 million people lived in food insecure households; 16.7 million of these were children, while 33.5 million were adults. This figure has remained consistent since 2008 and 2009, a period when the economic downturn was at its peak (Schutter, 2008; USDA, 2012).

Households with children, female-headed households, minority households, and immigrant households are more likely to be food insecure compared to other household types (Gundersen and Kreider, 2007; Lombe et al., 2009a). In recent years, as a result of laws introduced to tighten SNAP take-up, food insecurity is particularly prevalent in the immigrant households (Borjas, 2004; Hook and Balistreri, 2006).

Food insecure households employ a number of methods to gain access to food. The Food Stamp Program (renamed as the Supplemental Nutrition Assistance Program on October 1, 2008) is the first line of defense against hunger (C-SNAP, 2007). Yet even with assistance received from SNAP, a significant proportion of households, particularly those with children, continue to be food insecure (Bhattacharya et al., 2004; Borjas, 2004; Gundersen and Kreider, 2007; Hofferth, 2004; Hook and Balistreri, 2006; Lombe et al., 2009a; Nord, 2003; Yu et al., 2010). When threatened by food insecurity, households typically seek additional support from informal food assistance sources (Biggerstaff et al., 2002; Kicinski, 2012). For many individuals food pantries and other private food assistance programs provide short-term relief when household resources are depleted.

Over the years, a plethora of research has focused on understanding the relationship between individual characteristics and use of SNAP. Research has also examined program effects on the welfare of participants (Bartlett and Burstein, 2004; Gundersen and Oliveira, 2001; Kostova and Jensen, 2002; Wilde and Nord, 2005). These studies have produced new insights on the program and its effect. Still, systematic assessment of multiple factors that may influence food security among children in vulnerable households is rarely undertaken. Moreover, little is known about the role of informal support (community-based food assistance) in mitigating food insecurity among children in poor households. It seems likely that the relationship between SNAP take-up and household food sufficiency may depend on the level of informal support that a household can draw upon. Indeed, for many individuals and households in poverty, these networks constitute the main locus of support—providing short-term relief during times when personal circumstances are strained (Collier, 1998; Gundersen and Oliveira, 2001; Lombe and Ssewamala, 2007).

As a contribution to ongoing efforts to understand predictors of food security among children in vulnerable households (children in households below 185% of the poverty line), this study investigates the effects of SNAP take-up on child food security as well as the moderating effects, if any, of informal food assistance networks on this relationship. Understanding these relationships is important because hunger has adverse effects on all affected, but particularly children. It impedes growth and development, and is a significant predictor of adverse health conditions. It is also associated with behavioral problems and poor academic performance among school-aged children (Oberholser and Tuttle, 2004; Vozoris and Tarasuk, 2003; Zekeri, 2006). Moreover, each year, significant federal resources continue to be allocated to the program.

Literature review

The Supplemental Nutrition Assistance Program (SNAP) and child food security

Available data on SNAP participation suggests that about 72% of program participants live in households with children. In general, research evidence indicates that the program has helped to reduce hunger and food insecurity among children (Child Trends Data Bank, 2013; Jolliffe et al., 2005; Lee and Mackey-Bilaver, 2007; Lombe et al., 2009a). Further, SNAP take-up is said to have positive long-term effects on the health and developmental outcomes of children (Jyoti et al., 2005; Lee and Mackey-Bilaver, 2007). Existing evidence on the nutritional benefits of the program indicates that the program, for the most part, has been effective in providing essential nutrients to children (Bhattacharya et al., 2004; Jyoti et al., 2005; Lee and Mackey-Bilaver, 2007). Despite these positive observations, there is also some evidence to suggest persistent food insecurity and hunger among both adults and children in vulnerable households, even with participation in food assistance programs (Gorman et al.., 2006; Gundersen and Kreider, 2007; Oberholser and Tuttle, 2004). This is especially true for children in single-parent households (Hofferth, 2004; Lombe et al., 2009a) and children in low-income minority households (Gundersen and Kreider, 2007; Hook and Balistreri, 2006).

Further, due to the enactment of the Personal Responsibility and Work Opportunity Reconciliation Act of 1996 (PRWORA), many households are no longer eligible for food assistance (Hook and Balistreri, 2006; Nord, 2003). The Act specified that Food Stamp allotments be reduced in proportion to the number of non-citizens living in the household (Hook and Balistreri, 2006). This led to the reduction in the number of children of non-citizen parents that were eligible recipients of Food Stamps, heightening the possibility for children of immigrants to experience higher levels of food insecurity (Hook and Balistreri, 2006). This may have important welfare implications as the children of immigrants comprise the fastest-growing population in the United States (Gundersen and Kreider, 2007; Hook and Balistreri, 2006). In addition, there is evidence to suggest that a significant proportion of households that are eligible for SNAP do not participate in the program for various reasons, including stigma, lack of information, lack of transportation, language barriers, and high transaction costs (Hook and Balistreri, 2006). It is likely that households that fall through the cracks end up utilizing informal food assistance programs to meet their food needs. It is also likely that households on SNAP turn to these programs to supplement their food needs.

Use of informal food assistance networks and child food security

Past research indicates that most low-income households that are food insecure rely on public food assistance programs as well as informal food assistance networks to meet their needs (Bhattarai et al., 2005; Daponte and Bade, 2000; Kicinski, 2012; Lombe et al., 2009b). The use of informal food support has risen since the Reagan Administration, when eligibility for public food assistance programs was tightened (Daponte and Bade, 2000). Although there is limited research on the use of informal food assistance, evidence suggests that informal assistance in the form of food banks, food pantries, community food kitchens, and meals on wheels programs may be important in understanding food security. Indeed, emergency food support is no longer restricted to remediation of chronic short-term food insecurity but also provides for long-term household food security (Kicinski, 2012).

Moreover, participation in informal food assistance is associated with a number of factors including female headship of a household, lower levels of education, lower disposable income, residency in rural areas, and unemployment (Bhattarai et al., 2005; Lombe et al., 2009b). According to available evidence, about 52% of food pantry clients are households with children; a significant number of these are single-parent households (Kicinski, 2012). Furthermore, about one-third of the people who rely on food pantries to meet their food needs are children (Daponte and Bade, 2000).

The evidence reviewed in the foregoing discussion provides a sound framework for investigating the relationship between SNAP take-up and child food security. It also provides a platform from which to assess the moderating effect, if any, of community-based informal food assistance on the relationship indicated. More specifically, we developed an integrated model (see Figure 29.1) which posits that participating in SNAP will positively influence child food security and that the influence of SNAP take-up, if any, on child food security will be influenced by the level of informal food assistance utilized by the household.

Research questions

Using data from the Current Population Survey and Food Security Supplement (CPS-FSS) for 2010, the study builds upon previous research (Lombe et al., 2009b; Yu et al., 2010) and advances the following questions:

- What are the effects of formal (SNAP) and informal food supports on child food security (among children in households below 185% of the poverty line)?
- What are the moderating effects of informal food assistance networks on child food security when controlling for socioeconomic characteristics?

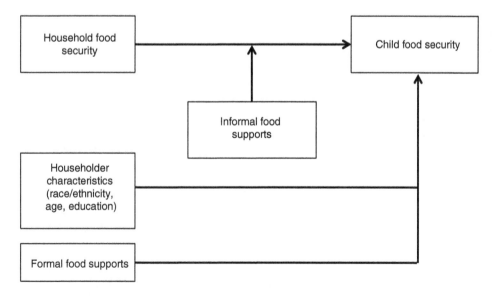

Figure 29.1 Conceptual model showing influence of SNAP on food security
Source: Adapted from Lombe et al., 2009, p. 304; Yu et al., 2010, p. 769.

Study sample

The study sample includes householders who completed both the Current Population Survey (CPS) and the Food Security Supplement (FSS) in December of 2010. The December 2010 CPS (N=152,384) provides data on labor force participation and examines the prevalence of hunger in American households. The Food Security Supplement also includes data on the use of formal (SNAP) and informal (e.g., food banks, soup kitchens, etc.) community food assistance networks. Both surveys were made available in English and Spanish. The sample for this study was narrowed down to include only survey participants who met the following three conditions: (1) is head of household, (2) is below 185% of the poverty line, and (3) answered specified food security questions for the household and children (N=1,186). About 71% of respondents were Caucasian, 19% were African American, and 11% defined themselves as other/mixed race. Respondents were further classified as Latino (24%), immigrant (21%), and female-headed households (47%). Table 29.1 provides an overview of the sample's demographic characteristics.

Measures

Child Food Security (CFS) (Dependent Variable) was measured on an eight-item scale based on a 12-month recall (Hamilton et al., 1997; Nord, 2012). Respondents were asked to state whether or not they experienced the following during the past 12 months: (1) the use of low-cost food, (2) a lack of balanced meals, and (3) an inability to afford food. Response categories provided were often (=2), sometimes (=1) or never (=0). Respondents were also asked to indicate whether or not they experienced the following: (4) meal size reduction, (5) child experiences of hunger, (6) skipping meals, and (7) child forgoing food for an entire day. Response options provided were yes (=1) or no (=0). Respondents who answered yes to skipping meals were asked to report (8) the frequency of meals skipped (1–2 months=1, >1–2 months=2). Items were reverse-summed to create a discrete interval measure such that a score of 8=food secure and a score of 0=very food insecure.

Household Food Security (HFS) was measured on a ten-item scale based on a 12-month recall. Examples of questions include "We couldn't afford to eat balanced meals. Was that often, sometimes, or never true for you in the last 12 months?" and "In the last 12 months, were you ever hungry, but didn't eat, because there wasn't enough money for food?" (Yes/No). Items were organized into four categories: high, marginal, low, and very low food security. High food security households indicated no problems or anxiety about accessing adequate food, and marginal food security households indicated some anxiety about access to food but no reduction in food intake (Coleman-Jensen and Nord, 2013). Low food security households reported reduced food quality, variety, and desirability of food, and very low food security households indicated that the eating patterns of one or more household members was disrupted and food intake was reduced (Coleman-Jensen and Nord, 2013). Results were dichotomized such that 1 denoted high and marginal household food security (HFS=1) and 0 low and very low food security (HFS=0). Both the HFS and CFS scales have been rigorously examined and are known to have high internal validity (Hamilton et al., 1997; Nord, 2012).

Participation in the SNAP (Food Stamp Participation, or FSP) is measured by a single item. Respondents were asked whether anyone in their household had participated in SNAP in the past 12 months (USDA-ERS, 2011). Responses are dichotomized, with 1 indicating program participation and 0 indicating non-participation.

Use of informal food supports reflects whether or not anyone in a respondent's household received any meals delivered to the home from community programs (e.g., Meals on Wheels), went to a community program/senior center to eat prepared meals, ever got emergency food from a church, food pantry, or food bank, or received food from a soup kitchen or shelter in the past 12 months (USDA-ERS, 2011). Responses were dichotomized, with 1 indicating use of informal assistance and 0 indicating non-use of informal assistance.

Data analysis procedures

Data screening of individual variables was conducted to access normality among ratio and interval-level variables such as age, child food security, hours worked, household income, and number of children in the household. Chi-square and independent sample t-tests were conducted to examine differences in study variables by race/ethnicity, immigrant status, and household status. A zero-order Pearson correlation was obtained to examine relationships among study variables. Two OLS regression analyses were conducted, first with all study variables and second with all study variables and the interaction term between household food security and informal food supports to examine the moderation effects (if any) of informal food supports on child security. All analyses were conducted using Stata 12.

Results

Sample demographic characteristics

Sample demographic characteristics are presented in Table 29.1 and indicate that the age of respondents ranged from 16 to 85, with a mean age of 44 years [SD=15.19]. With respect to the level of education attained by the head of the household, the following was observed: less than high school (28%), high school or equivalent (37%), and some college or beyond (35%). Respondents averaged 13.82 hours of work per week [SD=18.67], though the majority of householders reported not working (61.05%). Income ranged from less than $5,000 to $99,999, with a mean of $24,999. The majority of households report having two children or fewer (77%). Roughly half (53%) of the respondents participate in SNAP. About two-thirds make use of informal food supports (69%), and just over half (57%) are food secure households. A significant percentage of respondents (48%) reported child food security.

Bi-variate relationships between key study variables

Differences among racial/ethnic groups, immigration status, and household type were also examined. African American respondents reported fewer work hours (t=2.56, p=.011), lower household income (t=5.09, p<.001), higher levels of SNAP participation (χ^2=13.41, p<.001), and lower levels of child food security (t=2.23, p=.026) in comparison to non-African Americans. Latino respondents reported younger age (t=2.28, p=.023), lower levels of education (χ^2=131.53, p<.001), more work hours (t=−2.68, p=.008), higher numbers of children in the household (t=−3.32, p<.001), and lower levels of child food security (t=2.11, p=.036) in comparison to non-Latinos. Respondents included in the "Other" category (signifying non-Caucasian and non-African American) reported higher levels of education (χ^2=11.48, p=.003) and lower levels of participation in informal food supports (χ^2=5.54, p=.019) in comparison with Caucasian and African American groups.

Table 29.1 Demographic characteristics of SNAP and informal food support users. Descriptive information (n=1,186)

	Mean	SD	%	Min	Max
Household characteristics					
Age of householder	44.07	15.19		16	85
African American			18.38%		
Other			10.71%		
Latino			24.03%		
Immigrant			20.74%		
Female-headed households			46.96%		
Number of children	1.54	1.30		0	7
Education, employment, and income					
Less than high school degree or equivalent			28.33%		
High school degree or equivalent			37.10%		
Some college or beyond			34.57%		
Hours worked (weekly)	13.82	18.67		0	99
Household income	6.44	3.31		1	14
Food security					
SNAP participation (1=Yes)			53.04%		
Informal food supports (1=Yes)			68.97%		
Household food security (1=Secure)			56.75%		
Child food security (8=Secure)	6.76	1.63		0	8

Immigrant households reported lower levels of education (χ^2=88.92, p<.001), more hours worked (t=−4.24, p<.001), higher household income (t=−3.21, p=.001), higher numbers of children in the household (t=−3.72, p<.001), lower participation in informal food supports (χ^2=21.10, p<.001), lower SNAP participation (χ^2=23.06, p<.001), and lower child food security (t=3.52, p<.001) in comparison to non-immigrants. Female heads of household reported younger age (t=2.74, p=.006), fewer work hours (t=4.56, p<.001), lower household income (t=12.75, p<.001), lower numbers of children in the household (t=2.90, p=.004), greater participation in informal food supports (t=36.19, p<.001), higher levels of SNAP participation (χ^2=83.95, p<.001), lower household food security (t=20.90, p<.001), and lower child food security (t=4.49, p<.001).

Correlations of study variables

As presented in Table 29.2, zero-order correlations of study variables (n=1,186) were examined. Child food security was positively associated with age, high school education, household income, and household food security, and negatively associated with being African American and Latino, immigration status, female-headed households, number of children, informal food supports, and SNAP participation.

Table 29.2 Correlations of SNAP and informal food support study variables. Correlations among study variables (n=1,186)

	1	2	3	4	5	6	7	8	9	10	11	12	13	14	15
1 Age	1														
2 African Am.	0	1													
3 Other	.03	-.16***	1												
4 Latino	-.07*	-.21***	-.13***	1											
5 Immigrant	.02	-.11***	.14***	.52***	1										
6 Ed—HS or Eq	-.04	.05	-.02	-.18***	-.14***	1									
7 Ed—College	.05	-.03	.09**	-.19***	-.12***	-.56***	1								
8 Female HH	-.08**	.16***	0	-.05	-.17***	-.02	0	1							
9 Work Hrs	-.15***	.077*	.04	.08**	.12***	0	.05	-.13***	1						
10 HH inc.	.24***	-.15***	.03	-.02	.09**	0	.15***	-.35***	.29***	1					
11 Num child	-.52***	-.04	.02	.01***	.11***	-.01	0	-.08**	.15***	-.01	1				
12 IFS	-.53***	.02	-.07*	.01	-.13***	0	-.06*	.17***	0	-.39***	.36***	1			
13 SNAP	-.28***	.11***	-.02	-.04	-.14***	.02	-.11***	.27***	-.20***	-.47***	.13***	.37***	1		
14 HFS	.28***	-.04	.03	-.04	-.03	.05	.03	-.13***	-.01	.20***	-.21***	-.42***	-.23***	1	
15 CFS	.15***	-.06*	0	-.06*	-.10***	.06*	.03	-.13***	-.02	.13***	-.20***	-.31***	-.14***	.59***	1

*p < .05, **p < .01, ***p < .001

Household food security was positively associated with age and household income. Household food security was negatively associated with being African American and Latino, immigration status, female-headed households, number of children in the household, informal food supports, SNAP participation, and child food security.

SNAP participation was positively associated with being African American, female-headed households, number of children, and informal food supports, and negatively associated with age, immigration status, college education, hours worked, and household income. Finally, use of informal food supports was positively associated with female-headed households and number of children, and negatively associated with age, being non-Caucasian or African American, immigration status, college education, and household income.

Predicting Child Food Security (CFS)

Tables 29.3 and 29.4 present two regression models used to predict child food security, the first without and the second with the interaction term IFS★HFS. The first model was significant [F (14,1171)=52.46; p<.001], and explained 39% of the variance in the dependent variable. Examination of regression coefficients indicates that age, being African American, being an immigrant, being a female-headed household, having fewer children, lower use of informal food supports, and greater household food security significantly predicted child food security.

The second model [F (15,1170)=50.27; p<.001] included the same predictors as the first model with the addition of the interaction term IFS★HFS.

There was no difference in child food security in households with high or marginal levels of food security with respect to whether or not the household received informal food supports. However, variations were observed in child food security among households with low or very low levels of food security in relation to whether or not the household received informal food supports (CFS mean = 5.82) or did not receive informal supports (CFS mean = 6.49).

Limitations

A number of study limitations are noted. First, responses utilized were based on a 12-month recall of the responses provided by household heads on behalf of their children, and may not accurately reflect the experience of food security in the previous year. Moreover, recall responses are also mediated by individual perception of "enough" or "lacking" with respect to food and may vary across socioeconomic groups. Third, the variables used in this study may not include all factors important to food security, including participation in other government assistance programs (public housing, TANF, etc.) or the degree to which families access food supports. Finally, an examination of residuals of some study variables revealed minor violation of the assumptions of OLS regression (e.g., heteroscedasticity and normality). Notwithstanding such limitations of the measures of food security used in this study have been validated (Nord, 2012).

Discussion

This study set out to examine factors that may be related to food security among children in vulnerable households and examined the moderation effects of informal food assistance on this relationship (see Figure 29.1). As observed by others (see for example Yu et al., 2010), respondent demographic characteristics such as age, being African American, being an immigrant, being a female-headed household, and having fewer children were related to food security among children. Further, SNAP participation did not significantly predict

Table 29.3 Multivariate regression models predicting child food security

	B	SE	β	SR²
Constant	7.26***	.27		
Age	−.01***	.00	−.12	.01
African American	−.22*	.10	−.05	.00
Other	−.08	.13	−.02	.00
Latino	.03	.11	.01	.00
Immigrant	−.42***	.12	−.10	.01
High school or GED	.06	.10	.02	.00
College	.03	.10	.01	.00
Female HH	−.22**	.08	−.07	.00
Work hours	.00	.00	−.01	.00
HH Inc.	−.01	.01	−.01	.00
Number of children	−.12**	.04	−.10	.00
IFS	−.44***	.11	−.12	.01
SNAP	.03	.09	.01	.01
HFS	1.79***	.08	.54	.00

$r2 = .39$, *p < .05, **p < .01, ***p < .001

Table 29.4 Multivariate regression models predicting child food security with the interaction term

	B	2 SE	β	SR²
Constant	7.57***	.28		
Age	−.01***	.00	−.11	.01
African American	−.22*	.10	−.05	.00
Other	−.08	.13	−.01	.00
Latino	.05	.11	.01	.00
Immigrant	−.44***	.11	−.11	.01
High school or GED	.06	.10	.02	.00
College	.03	.10	.01	.00
Female HH	−.23**	.08	−.07	.00
Work hours	.00	.00	−.01	.00
HH Inc.	.00	.01	−.01	.00
Number of children	−.12**	.04	−.09	.01
IFS	−.82***	.15	−.23	.01
SNAP	.01	.09	.00	.00
HFS	1.33***	.15	.41	.04
HFS*IFS	.64***	.18	.16	.01

$r2 = .39$, *p < .05, **p < .01, ***p < .001

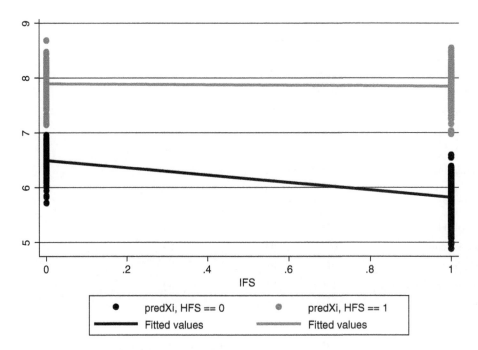

Figure 29.2 Interaction of IFS and HFS in predicting CFS
Source: Compiled by the authors.

child food security in this sample. Further, unlike expected, informal food assistance was negatively related to child food security. Moreover, we observed that access to informal food assistance moderates the relationship between household food security and child food security. In addition, we observed that African Americans, immigrants, and female-headed households were at increased risk for child food insecurity. Below we discuss these findings in the context of a rights-based approach to food informed by the Convention on the Rights of the Child.

The fact that low-income minority households, immigrant households, and female-headed households are at increased risk for child food security has been indicated by previous research (Gundersen and Kreider, 2007; Lombe et al., 2009b). Yet, while each of these groups share the experience of increased food insecurity among children, there remain important differences among them. For example, despite working more hours and having a higher income than non-immigrant households in the study sample, immigrant households reported lower levels of SNAP take-up as well as lower rates of utilizing informal food assistance programs. This disparity is particularly problematic given that food is a basic human rights guarantee to all, especially children, by international instruments such as the United Nations Declaration of Human Rights (UNDHR) and the Convention on the Rights of the Child (CRC) (UNHCR, 1946, 1989). The prevalence of food insecurity indicated by children in immigrant households may be interpreted as a violation of this fundamental right.

Conversely, low-income African American households reported working fewer hours per week, had lower incomes, and had higher levels of SNAP utilization. This observation is consistent with the results of previous research (Daponte and Bade, 2000). A similar pattern emerges with respect to female-headed households who, generally, reported greater participation in both informal and formal food supports as well as higher degrees of food insecurity among children. As observed earlier, this might mean that the state is not adequately fulfilling its obligation to guarantee the right to food to children in vulnerable households. It could also be that the SNAP program is providing much-needed assistance but that utilization of this resource may be much more complex than previously understood.

Unlike previous research, use of informal food assistance, in this sample, predicted lower food security among children (Yu et al., 2010). This result is noteworthy. It could be that the decision to access informal food assistance may be taken when the food supply commanded by the household is very low. Moreover, these results appear to contradict claims of abuse of food assistance programs. Indeed, households using informal supports seem to be those who experience low food security.

The relationship between household food security and child food security as moderated by informal food assistance highlights the risks faced by households with low food security and their reliance on informal food assistance. We noted that food insecure households that accessed informal food supports had lower child food security compared to households that did not. While this finding may seem counter-intuitive, it may indicate that informal food supports may be a significant form of assistance for food insecure households, particularly ones with children. Informal food assistance programs may either (1) help to make up for what may be lacking in the SNAP program, or (2) are accessed only by families in greatest need and with fewest outside supports.

Despite the other benefits of SNAP participation, this study suggests that the program, representing the primary duty bearer, the state, may be failing in its obligation to guarantee food and nutritional needs of the right holder, children in vulnerable households. The Convention on the Rights of the Child explicitly states that state parties, as duty bearers, have the responsibility to respect, protect, and fulfill basic human rights by taking appropriate actions to ensure that the child, the right holder, enjoys a high standard of living and health (UNHCR, 1989). The right to adequate food for every child falls under this category. Moreover, the fact that both informal and formal food assistance programs remain insufficient in addressing the needs of child hunger challenges prevailing neoliberal frameworks of limited state intervention, and calls for a rights-based perspective that recognizes and guarantees food security as a fundamental human right. Indeed, devolving the responsibility for tackling child food insecurity to local/community-based actors may not be a viable option in that the primary duty bearer, from a rights-based framework, is the state. Further, informal actors, despite their proximity to the problem, often lack the resources to intervene adequately.

Study implications

A number of implications may be suggested drawing upon findings from this study. We highlight only a few. Food insecurity is a serious impediment to the overall well-being and development of children. Successful amelioration of food insecurity among children in vulnerable households may require a consolidated effort from civil society, focusing specifically on advocating for food as a fundamental human right. Alongside this, effort may need to be devoted to enhancing the cultural competency of formal and informal service providers to ensure sensitivity to the unique needs presented by vulnerable groups. For example, consideration could be given to constraints of single parenthood and work limitations that affect individuals and households in this group. Another area of focus may be exploration of barriers experienced by low-resource households and testing interventions with greater potential to mitigate challenges associated with food insecurity. Future research might also examine the link between formal and informal food assistance providers and how these could work together to reduce food insecurity among children in vulnerable households. This research might examine both service-provision and client access from multiple service levels. In addition, continued examination of the degree to which formal food supports are reaching vulnerable populations, particularly immigrants who may lack the social and human capital necessary to navigate programs like SNAP, may be warranted.

The persistence of child hunger in the United States poses a significant challenge to the existing neoliberal frameworks that encourage market-driven approaches and decreased state interventions. Recognizing that access to food is a fundamental human right, state providers may need to exercise their roles as duty bearers and engage in more substantial and effective interventions to address the concern of child hunger. Additionally, states need to shift from a paradigm of food security as a safety net or charity provision to a rights-based perspective that actively seeks to ensure that all children are guaranteed the right to adequate food.

References

Bartlett, S. and Burstein, N. (2004). *Food Stamps Program Access Study: Eligible Non-Participants*. Washington, DC: U.S. Department of Agriculture Economic Research Service EFAN-03-013-2.

Bhattacharya, J., Currie, J., and Haider, S. (2004). Poverty, Food Insecurity, and Nutritional Outcomes in Children and Adults. *Journal of Health Economics*, 23(4), 839–862.

Bhattarai, G.R., Duffy, P.A., and Raymond, J. (2005). Use of Food Pantries and Food Stamps in Low-Income Households in the United States. *Journal of Consumer Affairs*, 39(2), 276–298.

Biggerstaff, M.A., Morris, P.M., and Nichols-Casebolt, A. (2002). Living on the Edge: Examination of People Attending Food Pantries and Soup Kitchens. *Social Work*, 47(3), 267–277.

Borjas, G. (2004). Food Insecurity and Public Assistance. *Journal of Public Economics*, 88, 1421–1443.

Child Trends Data Bank (2013). *Food Stamps Receipt: Indicators on Children and Youth*. Retrieved August 2014 from http://www.childtrends.org/?indicators=food-stamp-receipt.

Coleman-Jensen, A., and Nord, M. (2013). Food Security in the U.S.: Survey Tools. *USDA*. Retrieved April 2013 from http://www.ers.usda.gov/topics/food-nutrition-assistance/food-security-in-the-us/survey-tools.aspx#.UUeCrltATWY.

Collier, P. (1998). *Social Capital and Poverty. Social Capital Initiative Working Paper No. 4*. Washington, DC: World Bank, Social Development Department.

Congressional Budget Office, CBO (2012). *The Supplemental Nutrition Assistance Program*. Retrieved April 2013 from http://www.cbo.gov/sites/default/files/cbofiles/attachments/04-19-SNAP.pdf.

C-SNAP (2007). *Food Stamps as Medicine: A New Perspective on Children's Health*. Retrieved April 2013 from http://www.centerforhungerfreecommunities.org/sites/default/files/pdfs/food_stamps_as_medicine_Feb07.pdf.

Daponte, B., and Bade, S. (2000). *The Evolution, Cost, and Operation of Informal Food Assistance Network*. Institute of Research on Poverty Discussion Paper 121. Retrieved April 2013 from http://www.irp.wisc.edu/publications/dps/pdfs/dp121100.pdf.

Gorman, K.S., Horton, K.D. and Houser, R.F. (2006). Food Security, Hunger, and Food Stamp Participation among Low Income Working Families in Rhode Island. *Journal of Hunger & Environmental*.

Gorman, K., Horton, K., and Houser, R. (2006). Food Security, Hunger, and Food Stamp Participation Among Low-Income Working Families in Rhode Island. *Journal of Hunger & Environmental Nutrition*, 1(1), 105–125.

Gundersen, C., and Kreider. B. (2007). *Food Stamps and Food Insecurity among Families with Children: What Can be Learned in the Presence of Nonclassical Measurement Error?* Institute for Research on Poverty, University of Wisconsin-Madison, Research Center.

Gundersen, C., and Oliveira, V. (2001). The Food Stamp Program and Food Insufficiency. *American Journal of Agriculture*, 83(4), 875–887.

Hamilton, W.L., Cook, J.T., Thompson, W.W., Buron, L.F., Frongillo, Jr. E.A., Olson, C.M., and Wehler, CA. (1997). *Household Food Security in the United States*. Technical Report on the Food Security Measurement Project. Washington, DC: Food and Consumer Service, U.S. Department of Agriculture.

Hofferth, S.L. (2004). *Persistence and Change in the Food Security of Families with Children, 1997–1999*. Washington, DC: U.S. Department of Agriculture.

Hook, J.V., and Balistreri, K. (2006). Ineligible Parents, Eligible Children: Food Stamps Receipt, Allotments, and Food Insecurity Among Children of Immigrants. *Social Science Research*, 35, 228–251.

Jolliffe, D., Gundersen, C., Tiehen, L., and Winicki, J. (2005). Food Stamp Benefits and Child Poverty. *American Journal of Agricultural Economics*, 87(3), 569–581.

Jyoti, D.F., Frongillo, E.A., and Jones, J.S. (2005). Food Insecurity Affects School Children's Academic Performance, Weight Gain and Social Skills. *American Society for Nutrition*, 135(12), 2831–2839.

Kicinski, L.R. (2012). Characteristics of Short and Long-Term Food Pantry Users. *Michigan Sociological Review* 26, 58–74.

Kostova, S., and Jensen, H. (2002). *An Empirical Analysis of the Effects of Joint Decisions on Food Stamp Program, Temporary Aid to Needy Families, and Labor Force Participation.* Working Paper No. 02-WP 314, Center for Agricultural and Rural Development Service, U.S. Department of Agriculture.

Lee, B.J., and Mackey-Bilaver, L. (2007). Effects of WIC and Food Stamp Program Participation on Child Outcomes. *Children and Youth Services Review*, 29, 501–517.

Lombe, M., and Ssewamala, F.M. (2007). The Role of Informal Social Networks in Micro-Savings Mobilization. *Journal of Sociology & Social Work*, 37(3), 37–52.

Lombe, M., Yu, M., and Nebbitt, V.E. (2009a). Assessing Effects of Food Stamp Program Participation on Food Security in Female-Headed Households: Do Informal Supports Matter? *Journal of Policy Practice*, 8(4), 301–316.

Lombe, M., Yu, M., and Nebbitt, V.E. (2009b). Assessing Effects of Food Stamp Program Participation on Child Food Security in Vulnerable Households: Do Informal Supports Matter? *Families in Society*, 90(4), 353–358.

Nord, M. (2003). Food Insecurity in Households with Children. *Food Assistance and Nutrition Research Report No. (FANRR) 34–13.* USDA, Economic Research Service, Washington, DC.

Nord, M. (2012). Assessing Potential Technical Enhancements to the U.S. Household Food Security Measures. *USDA-ERS Technical Bulletin* (1936), 124.

Oberholser, C.A., and Tuttle, C.R. (2004). Assessment of Household Food Security among Food Stamp Recipients in Maryland. *American Journal of Public Health*, 94(5), 790–795.

Rosenbaum, D. (2013). Snap Is Effective and Efficient. *Center on Budget and Policy Priorities.* Retrieved April 2013 from http://www.cbpp.org/cms/index.cfm?fa=view&id=3239.

Schutter, O.D. (2008). Building Resilience: A Human Rights Framework for World Food and Nutrition Security. *United Nations Human Rights Council.* Retrieved April 2013 from http://www.unhcr.org/refworld/pdfid/48cf71dd2.pdf.

UNHCR (1946). *Universal Declaration of Human Rights.* Retrieved April 2013 from http://www.un.org/en/documents/udhr/index.shtml.

UNHCR (1989). *Convention on the Rights of the Child.* Retrieved April 2013 from http://www.ohchr.org/EN/ProfessionalInterest/Pages/CRC.aspx.

USDA (2012). *Characteristics of Supplemental Nutrition Assistance Program Households: Fiscal Year 2011—Summary.* Retrieved Nov 2014 from http://www.fns.usda.gov/sites/default/files/2011Characteristic sSummary.pdf.

USDA-ERS (2011). *Current Population Survey, December 2010: Food Security Supplement.* Washington, DC. doi:10.3886/ICPSR32241.v1. Accessed April 2013.

Vozoris, N., and Tarasuk, V. (2003). Household Food Insufficiency is Associated with Poor Health. *The Journal of Nutrition*, 133, 120–126.

Wilde, P., and Nord, M. (2005). The Effects of Food Stamps on Food Security: A Panel Data Approach. *Review of Agricultural Economics*, 27(3), 425–432.

Yu, M., Lombe, M., and Nebbitt, V.E. (2010). Food Stamp Program Participation, Informal Supports, Household Food Security and Child Food Security: A Comparison of African American and Caucasian Households in Poverty. *Children and Youth Services Review*, 32(5), 767–773.

Zekeri, A. (2006). *Food Insecurity in Poor, Female-Headed Families in Five of Alabama's Black Belt Counties.* Research Center: Southern Rural Development Center, Mississippi State University.

30

THE INFLUENCE OF A NEOLIBERAL WORLD VIEW ON HEALTH CARE POLICY

John Orwat, Michael P. Dentato, and Michael Lloyd

Neoliberalism: background

Neoliberalism is a world view that supports economic liberalization, or freedom from government intervention, as the best way to maximize the effect of trade, or economic efficiency. Liberalism was the most influential economic theory until the Great Depression in the 1930s, when Keynesian economics was introduced and quickly became influential. Keynesian economics also supports the notion that private markets maximize economic efficiency; however, it acknowledges the role of public sector interventions when private sector decisions result in inefficient macroeconomic outcomes. Keynesian economics was very influential from the 1930s until the 1970s; the manifestations may be seen in increased government intervention in everything from monetary policy to public assistance, such as income support for those out of the labor market such as the elderly or those that are temporarily unemployed. Two of the most popular and influential programs in the United States are Social Security, which provides income support to seniors, and Medicare, which provides health benefits.

In the early 1970s, economic liberalization was reintroduced in the form of neoliberalism as a general global shift toward *market-oriented* neoliberalism, which was readily embraced to explain the economic stagnation of the time. Neoliberalism continues to influence policy choices by favoring market forces to create equilibrium and views government interventions as worsening problems. Although there is little consensus on the definition of neoliberalism, the contemporary neoliberal world view emphasizes the wisdom of markets through a strong private sector with open markets through privatization and deregulation, individualism, and decentralization (McGregor, 2001). The overall goal is to maximize economic efficiency through "governance at a distance" and asserts a strong role for the private sector (Gibbon, 2012). This supports the three major tenets of neoliberalism: (1) markets are the best allocators of resources with regard to production and distribution; (2) societies consist of individuals whose main motivators are material and economic success; and (3) competition in markets propels innovation (Coburn, 2000, p. 138).

The overall impact of the rise of neoliberalism is the continued decline of the welfare state and an ongoing shift to a market orientation. The neoliberal world view acknowledges the inequalities produced by free markets; however, it challenges the Keynesian notion that they are best "prevented" by the public sector (through labor market policies) or ameliorated (through social welfare measures or the "decommodification" of education, health, and welfare) (Coburn, 2000, p. 139). Instead, the neoliberal view advocates for market-based solutions to inequalities and the restriction of public sector intervention to include the elimination of discretionary public spending. Such free market policies ultimately impact the disenfranchised, poor, and vulnerable disproportionately. Wilkinson (1989) focuses on mortality differences by social class in Britain from 1921 to 1981, arguing that mortality rates decrease rapidly when the income differential is narrow. Nazroo (2003) supports this idea, stating that a large body of convincing evidence now supports the possibility that ethnic inequalities in health are largely a consequence of socioeconomic differentials (p. 282). McGregor (2001) notes that within neoliberalism there is no legitimate role for the welfare of people, communities or societies, or for the state, except to ensure that government enforces the rules and logic of the free market—economic profit, technological progress, and growth and development (p. 84). Further, questions remain about the restrictions on consumer power that may result from the market-dominant approach in neoliberal policies (Varmin and Vikas, 2007).

The application of the neoliberal template to health care has had a significant influence on the framing of the health care debate in the United States and has influenced health care policies as a strategy to solve problems in the health care system. These problems include rapidly rising costs, access to care by the insured and uninsured, safety and quality, low satisfaction, and poor outcomes. Advocates for neoliberalism maintain that the resolution of these problems is dependent on freeing up the private market through decentralization, de-regulation, and promoting individual decision making. Critics contend, however, that the promotion of free markets may not resolve these problems, but will lead to winners and losers among consumers of health care. In this chapter, we review neoliberalism and the health care policies that result, provide a context in the field of health care, and examine some of the implications for consumers.

Neoliberalism and health care policy

As with most policy, understanding health care policy is complicated and elicits passion in most Americans. Health care policy is a complex web of stakeholders that includes providers (e.g., physicians, hospitals), payers (e.g., private insurance companies, Medicare, Medicaid), purchasers (e.g., employers, individuals), and others such as device and pharmaceutical manufacturers. Further, comprising almost 18% of GDP, it is one of the most important aspects and drivers of the U.S. economy. Despite all of these stakeholders, many agree that there are three important problems and ongoing challenges: cost, access, and quality. In this section, each of these problems is reviewed and, in the next section, we discuss proposed solutions, which is the source of most disagreement.

U.S. health care costs

Health care spending in the United States approached $2.6 trillion in 2010, making up 17.9% of GDP (Centers for Medicare and Medicaid, 2012; Martin et al., 2012). Americans spend more on health care than on any other basic necessity; in fact, the United States spends a greater percentage of gross domestic product on health care than most other countries (Larson and Dettmann, 2005). Over half of these costs are associated with providers—hospital care (31%) and physician/clinical services (20%)—and approximately 7% may be attributed to the administrative costs of government programs (1%) and the net cost of health insurance (6%) (Martin et al., 2012).

Although costs have slowed slightly in recent years, expenditures are expected to increase in the coming years. The drivers of current expenditures and growing costs are the subject of debate; however, they are most often attributed to changes in the population, demand for technology, and administrative costs. *Changes in the population* refers to an ageing population, increasing rates of chronic illness due to longer life spans, and lifestyle issues (e.g., obesity-related diabetes). Treatment for chronic illness has been estimated at 75% of all health care expenditures (Centers for Disease Control and Prevention. Rising Health Care Costs Are Unsustainable, April 2011). Much of this is a manifestation of success in the health care system: people are living longer due to advances in health care, including the treatment of chronic illness. As a result, recent efforts have focused on improving and incentivizing preventive care. A second driver of rising health care costs is the *demand for the most state-of-the-art technology and medications*, which increases with availability regardless of medical or cost-effectiveness (Centers for Medicare and Medicaid, 2012). Finally, the third driver of health care costs results from *inefficiencies and the administration of health care* to include the cost of unnecessary duplicated services as well as gaps in care due to the fragmented health care system; high administrative costs and overheads as a result of a mixed private/public system; and gaps in health care quality and safety.

Access to health care in the United States

Access to health care in the United States means something different to everyone. However, access to care is often hampered by a variety of factors unrelated to need, such as difficulty paying for services, the supply of providers, etc. Health insurance is an important factor associated with accessing health care. Overall, health insurance reduces the cost of expected and unexpected health care services (e.g., well vs. emergency visits) and develops a delivery system for health care (e.g., by contracting with providers). Individuals obtain health insurance through employers, government, covering the cost themselves, or doing without (uninsured).

In 2011, just over half of Americans were covered by employment-based insurance (55%), 16.5% were covered by Medicaid, and 15.2% by Medicare (coverage for elderly and people with disabilities who have paid into the system), up from 14.6% due to the aging baby boomer population (DeNavas-Walt et al., 2012). Over 15% of Americans did not have health insurance in 2011, most of them living in poverty (DeNavas-Walt et al., 2012). The number of underinsured, or those that do not have adequate coverage to protect against high medical expenses, continues to dramatically rise—particularly among members of the middle class, with estimates that the underinsured make up about 10% of all Americans covered by private insurance.

The uninsured have significant barriers to accessing health care. Uninsurance has a negative impact on health and presents a significant financial strain, to include decreased utilization of preventive care; delaying or forgoing necessary medical care to include prescription drugs; and financial hardship that often negatively impacts other basic necessities such as housing and food (Institute of Medicine, 2009; Kaiser Commission on Medicaid and the Uninsured, 2012). The uninsured pay higher prices for health care since they do not have access to the discounted rates negotiated by health plans. Most rely on overwhelmed and underpaid safety net providers, who take on cases complicated by delayed treatment, with low levels of supplemental payment by government that rarely covers the full cost of care. It has been estimated that 45,000 deaths per year are associated with not having health insurance among non-elderly adults (Wilper et al., 2009). Underinsurance also results in financial hardship, increased debt, delays, and/or forgoing needed care to include prescription drugs (Schoen et al., 2008).

Quality/outcomes

The Institute of Medicine (IOM) has defined quality as the degree to which health services for individuals and populations increase the likelihood of desired health outcomes and are consistent with current professional knowledge (Institute of Medicine, 2001). The IOM further defines six dimensions of health care quality that includes access to care that is: (1) safe, (2) timely, (3) effective, (4) efficient, (5) equitable, and (6) patient-centered (Institute of Medicine, 2001). Recent efforts to manage reduced variations in health care quality include better measurement of quality as well as public reporting.

Each year, the Agency for Healthcare Research and Quality (AHRQ) publishes a report of the state of health care quality in the United States as well as progress towards reducing disparities. AHRQ's recent report finds continued quality and access problems in the United States, particularly for minority populations and those living in poverty (2012). Efforts to improve quality have been somewhat successful, with 30% of Americans failing to receive services appropriate for their needs in 2009, down from 34% in 2005 (AHRQ, 2012). Difficulty with access to health care, however, has increased, with 26% of Americans reporting problems with access in 2009, up from 24% in 2005 (AHRQ, 2005).

Several reasons for gaps in quality and outcomes are frequently cited in the literature. The fee for service reimbursement system in the United States has led to misaligned incentives whereby the financing system rewards volume over outcome or receipt of recommended services (quality). Access to care is impeded by a lack of health insurance as covered in the previous section, which has a particular impact on minority populations and those living in poverty.

Neoliberal solutions

As mentioned earlier, despite vast agreement that health care costs, quality, and access are problems in the United States, there is wide divergence on policy recommendations, most often related to the role of government. Government intervention is seen by those with a neoliberal view as inefficient, thus the cause of these problems, and advocate for private market solutions. As a result, recent health care policy changes have favored private market solutions with a limited role for government. Critiques of privatization and corporatization focus on the problems with treating health care as a commodity, resulting in concerns related to the corporate consolidation of small family doctor practices, the "mechanizing" of physician and nursing practice, making health care less local, the focus on profit by private equity firms over the provision of health care services, and reducing public input into decision making about resource allocation. Although the full range of possible solutions is beyond the scope of this chapter, some examples include the privatization of public health systems and public insurance (e.g., Medicare Advantage and the prescription drug benefit), using tax breaks to reduce the "cost" of insurance and health services, and increased cost sharing with patients.

Cost sharing is when a portion of health expenditures are shared with the patient. Cost sharing is one of many tools used to influence the individual's behavior, either in the quantity of health care services utilized (cost sharing in the form of copayments or coinsurance) or the value of those services (e.g., higher cost sharing for services that have lower value). In economic terms, cost sharing is important since health insurance dramatically reduces the price of care for

333

the individuals who demand the care. Economic theory leads us to theorize that, as a result of lower-cost services, the quantity of the service used increases (at least for those with insurance), much of it with little marginal value. Cost sharing gives individual patients "skin in the game" as they make decisions about care, so the likelihood is that higher-quality and lower-cost services are more likely to be chosen (e.g., higher cost for out-of-network providers, lower cost for generic medications). The high deductible health plan is one example of cost sharing. This is a health plan with a very high deductible coupled with a tax-exempt health savings account that may be used to fill the deductible. We now describe this insurance scheme and review the related impact, with a particular focus on those living in poverty.

Consumer-directed health plans

Consumer-directed health plans are health insurance plans with a high deductible coupled with a health savings account (HSA). HSAs, as authorized in the 2003 Medicare Prescription Drug Improvement and Modernization Act, are medical savings accounts with a double tax benefit, i.e., contributions are tax deductible going in, and distributions are tax free going out (Larson and Dettmann, 2005). Eligibility for an HSA in 2012 required that an individual must be enrolled in a health plan with a minimum deductible of at least $1,200 and a cap on out-of-pocket expenses of $6,050; family deductibles are $2,400 with a $12,200 cap. Maximum allowable contributions to an HSA in 2012 are $3,100 for individuals and $6,250 for families. Funds for contribution to the HSA may come from the individual or the employer. The full rules that apply to HSAs may be found at the Resource Center of the U.S. Treasury (http://www.treasury.gov/resource-center/faqs/Taxes/Pages/Health-Savings-Accounts.aspx).

HSA disbursements may be used to cover eligible health care services during the deductible period as well as other cost sharing once the deductible is met and the health plan kicks in (e.g., copayments). However, some health plans may cover preventive care during the deductible period. Services may be purchased at the rate negotiated by the health plan. HSAs have three overall goals: (1) to provide incentives to save for future health care expenses; (2) to encourage individuals to make cost-conscious decisions and participate more actively in their health care, including the tracking of physician care; and (3) to increase the overall number of individuals with health insurance (Steinorth, 2011).

HSAs provide an incentive for saving for future medical expenses by allowing consumers to roll balances from year to year, between jobs, and into retirement (Reed et al., 2012). This is unlike previous medical spending accounts, in which unused funds were lost to the consumer at the end of the year. Additionally, consumers may invest the balances of these accounts to maximize return. Based on market principles, therefore, consumers will make more rational choices about health care services by considering cost, necessity, and quality. To help consumers, decision-making tools have been developed, including tools that provide cost information (Bundorf, 2012). Since consumers have access to the prices negotiated by the health plan, the price paid is also lower. Access to health insurance will also increase, since price-conscious consumers will use only the health care they need and shop around for the lowest prices, thus lowering premiums, and making such plans more affordable. As a result, problems with price and quality in the health care delivery system will be corrected by these private market forces.

The high deductible health plan attempts to create a true market by giving consumers financial clout for services up to a catastrophic amount, consistent with an understanding of insurance as pooled risk against an unpredictable, rare, and financially catastrophic event. As a result, such an insurance scheme separates the "catastrophic" component of health insurance from the predictable, such as routine health care, and reduces the likelihood of overuse of un-needed services, yet providing consumers with choices. Advocates of consumer-directed care argue for the elimination of provider-based monopolies, simplified insurance plans, clarificaton of cost/quality options, and care directed by decision making that is influenced by financial incentives and will result in higher consumer satisfaction, greater choice, and lower costs since financial clout is actually at the level of the consumer rather than the physician or health plan (Brennan and Reisman, 2007).

In such a health plan, the role of the individual, or patient, is shifted to that of a "consumer" of health care services. Now an agent in an economic market, the consumer is the vehicle for improving the health care market. This is done by giving the consumer financial clout, who will use such clout in making economically rational choices. Consistent with neoliberal economic theory, the role of the consumer will then maximize their satisfaction with health care choices by pursuing their own individualistic interests and manage their own unlimited demands for health care within a limited supply, thus driving down prices and increasing qual-ity. It also assumes that the consumer, as they make choices between providers, has adequate information to make this rational choice, with the capacity to discriminate between the cost and quality of various providers, the financial and health consequences of choosing one health care provider over another, etc.

However, critics contend that such schemes have a differential effect based on several factors that, most often, predispose individuals to obtain care. The use of such an insurance scheme raises many questions, to include the effect on vulnerable populations. Next, we examine the literature on the potential impact of high deductible health plans.

Access, cost, and utilization

Impact on utilization and spending

There is growing evidence that consumer-directed plans such as HSAs have varied levels of impact on health care, from spending (Buntin et al., 2011) to utilization and cost, among other areas.

Enrollment

There remains limited research with regard to HSA contributions or the overall impact on patient care as well as care seeking (Reed et al., 2012). Recent studies find that enrollment in HSAs has slowly been increasing. One report illustrates growth from 4% in 2006 to 13% in 2010 (Kaiser Family Foundation, 2010), while the number of employers offering HSAs or planning to offer them has grown as well (Haviland et al., 2012). Other work demonstrates a rise from 8% to 17% of covered workers between 2009 and 2011 (Bundorf, 2012; Claxton et al., 2011) enrolled in HSAs. The annual census conducted by America's Health Insurance Plans (AHIP) of U.S. health insurance carriers evidences that the number of individuals cov-ered by HSAs totaled 13.5 million in January of 2012, an increase from 11.4 million in 2011 (Buck, 2012). The number of people covered has been increasing by roughly 2 million per year beginning with 6.1 million in 2008 (Buck, 2012). Furthermore, implementation of the Affordable Health Care Act of 2010 might also continue the expansion of growth associated with enrollments and employer provision of HSAs, while providing additional incentives and potential penalties for not offering coverage (Haviland et al., 2012). The Act requires comprehensive health benefits and specific actuarial values. HSAs, and consumer-directed health care plans in general, include such comprehensive benefits, and their actuarial values are above the minimum required by the Act (Haviland et al., 2012).

There are a certain number of inherent assumptions present in any discussion surrounding HSAs. The first common assumption regarding these accounts is the price-point benefit. HSAs are promoted by proponents as a less expensive option for persons with high deductible health care plans. However, the question remains that if such health care premiums are cheaper, the likelihood is greater that more individuals will purchase them. Previous research predicted HSAs would attract a large number of individuals, especially those without health insurance (Feldman et al., 2005); provide limited tax deductions for those with lower incomes (Hoffman and Tolbert, 2006; Remler and Glied, 2005); provide an increase in cost sharing in health care (Remler and Glied, 2006); may lead to higher deductibles and copayments (Cardon and Showalter, 2007); or influence savings behavior over the course of a lifetime (Steinorth, 2011). In a ten-year review of the literature surrounding consumer-driven health care, Bundorf (2012) found that proponents of HSAs emphasized the promotion of greater value in health care spending and the accommodation of diverse consumer preferences (Baicker, 2006; Cogan et al., 2005; Feldstein, 2006). Critics raise the concern that, while consumers may react to high deductibles with less care, they may not differentiate valuable care, thus reducing quality of care, and greater cost sharing creates an excessive financial burden on low-income and/or less healthy individuals (Davis, 2004; Woolhandler and Himmelstein, 2007). Others point to the potential for greater risk segmentation in health insurance markets if HSAs disproportionately attract favorable risks due to their lower premiums and higher cost sharing (Robinson, 2004; Rosenthal and Daniels, 2006).

Research suggests that the primary savings associated with HSAs occur through the reduction of outpatient costs and pharmaceutical expenditures. (Lo Sasso et al., 2010; Parente et al., 2008). In her meta-analysis, Bundorf (2012) found no significant difference regarding inpatient utilization of health services between consumer-directed health plans and traditional HMO insurance plans. Regarding preventive services, Wharam et al. (2008) found no evident reductions in preventive screening measures, including breast, colorectal, or cervical cancer screening, when comparing consumer-directed plans and traditional HMOs.

Sociodemographic factors

Examination of the impact of consumer-directed health care plans upon impoverished, uninsured, or underinsured populations is essential. The likelihood for disparities is greatly associated with access to HSA accounts, or especially with regard to the ability to contribute on an ongoing basis. Similarly, it is important to examine the impact of factors including, but not limited to, age, rural vs. urban location, race/ethnicity, socioeconomic status, employer contributions, and tax exemptions. Ultimately, continued growth in consumer-directed health plans and enrollments holds a multitude of practice and policy implications related to the overall costs of care, use of preventative care, the health care decision-making process, and choice of plans (Haviland et al., 2012).

There are several factors that may likely impact an individual's ability to participate in an HSA including race/ethnicity, age, gender, and employment, among others. Additionally, the challenge of maintaining some form of economic security may enable or inhibit an individual from participating in and contributing to an HSA. Such predisposing factors provide a unique lens through which to examine neoliberalism and health care. Three categories of impact specifically draw attention to this issue and include: (1) the consumer-directed care's effect on the numbers and composition of the uninsured; (2) the impact on the quality of care provided to the less well-off and minority groups; and (3) its potential to widen disparities in wealth (Bloche, 2007). When reviewing the concepts of access to care and quality of care, previous studies have found that patients who are older; racial/ethnic minorities; female; lower socioeconomic status; less educated; underinsured; or uninsured are less likely to receive care, typically due to a lack of access rather than a deficiency in the quality of care (Asch et al., 2006; Smedley et al., 2003).

Socioeconomic status

Adoption of the consumer-directed model might also widen socioeconomic disparities in care and redistribute wealth from the working poor and middle classes to the upper class, as well as worsen racial and ethnic disparities (Bloche, 2007) in care. Disparities in the quality of care received by poor and high-income Americans are rising according to the 2006 National Healthcare Disparities Report. The authors monitored 12 "core measures" of quality over varying periods of several years, all between 1999 and 2004. On eight of these measures, income disparities worsened, while poor people received worse care than their high-income counterparts on all 12 measures (AHRQ, 2006). Early studies of consumer-directed plans have found some adverse selection: subscribers tend to be healthier and have higher incomes than enrollees in other kinds of plans (Bloche, 2007). While HSAs do decrease insurance costs, provided the beneficiary can pay for preventive care and can afford out-of-pocket costs that do not exceed what's saved in the HSA, these plans were not any more affordable for low-income families than the more traditional plans (Moser, 2005). The likely consequences for the less well-off include diminished provision of high-value preventive care, as well as poorer outpatient management of such chronic conditions as hypertension, diabetes, asthma, and schizophrenia. Socioeconomic disparities in outpatient care are likely to widen, at least along the lower end of the income spectrum, as consumer-directed plans increase their market share (Bloche, 2007).

Race/ethnicity

The National Healthcare Disparities Report's 22 "core measures" were assessed for members of disadvantaged minority groups. Blacks fared worse than Whites on 16 of the 22 measures; Hispanics fared worse than non-Hispanic Whites on 17 out of 22 (AHRQ, 2006) measures. Not only do Blacks, Hispanics, and members of some other minority groups take home lower incomes, on average, than Whites, they also have less wealth, and thus less out-of-pocket health care purchasing power, even after one controls for income (Bloche, 2007).

Age/gender

According to America's Health Insurance Plans' Center for Policy and Research, 49% of all HSA enrollees in the individual market were age 40 or over, 51% were under age 40, while gender distribution was evenly split with 50% male and 50% female (Buck, 2012). When employers offer an HSA in addition to offering alternative health care plans, HSAs are typically favored based on age, health status, or both (Bundorf, 2012).

The RAND Health Insurance Experiment of the 1970s and 1980s provides additional insight with regard to disparities among various communities. The RAND study examined the effects of different cost-sharing levels on use of medical services, cost, and health outcomes among families.

The study found that families with a high deductible plan used fewer services and generated lower overall health care costs than families in the free plan. For most families in the high deductible plan, the effects on health status were minimal to none compared with families in the free plan. However, for persons who were both poor and sick, the reductions in health utilization in the high deductible plan were harmful by comparison. While the RAND study occurred in the pre-managed care era and did not have a pure health spending account component, these findings are informative and predictive of the cost, utilization, and health outcome consequences of HSAs (Moser, 2005). These findings are consistent with hundreds of studies, performed over many years, showing that disparities by class, race, and ethnicity are pervasive in U.S. health care related to structural challenges in the delivery system (Bach et al., 2004), while underscoring the impact of access and utilization of HSA among minority populations. Ultimately, those least able to navigate through fragmented systems, which are typically the least educated and the least prosperous, will probably fare the worst in the HSA environment. Those most marginalized by language and cultural barriers, geographic separation, and persisting racial and ethnic bias will have greater difficulties than others with similar incomes (Bloche, 2007). Therefore such a discussion surrounding cost, access, utilization, and quality of care related to such diverse populations is relevant with regard to the impact of HSAs and other types of health care reform.

Options and choice

An additional and relevant component of consumer-directed health care programs relates to whether individuals have adequate options, availability, and choice. Preliminary studies indicate that options and choice are both difficult to discern. The EBRI/Commonwealth Fund survey found that the majority of people enrolled in any type of health plan lack information regarding these plans and coverage options. Survey participants acknowledged the "yawning gap" (Collins et al., 2006) between cost and quality of information which is necessary to make health care decisions, as well as to discern what is available. The percentage of adults enrolled in comprehensive or high deductible plans who acknowledge awareness of the quality of care provided by their doctors and hospitals was marked at a mere 14% to 16%. Subsequently, 12% to 16% of insured adults identified awareness of cost-of-care information for their doctors and hospitals (Collins et al., 2006). The information obtained in the Commonwealth Fund report would support the idea that, in general, few Americans have the information necessary to make health insurance decisions. In their report card of consumer-directed health care plans, Rosenthal et al. (2005) challenge the success of such plans in effectively promoting informed consumer choice, while calling for enrollees to have greater access to detailed information related to efficiency of costs and overall quality. The authors continue that such transparency is lacking across the consumer-directed market, while other models do not claim to promote consumerism or to leverage consumer choice for value improvement (2005).

Data collected by the Center for Policy and Research (Buck, 2012) found that online access to HSA information, along with health education, personal health records, and physician-specific information, was offered to online members in order to make better health decisions. However, Haviland et al. (2012) report findings which illustrate a lack of consumer information in relation to preventive health care and found inadequate support tools and information technology available to consumers regarding health care information. This is concerning, as use of information technology was a strong component and vital argument supporting the consumer-directed model of care. Van Deursen (2012) studied internet skills in relation to accessing online health information and found that the general public lacks strategic internet skills in relation to finding and processing health information. Much of the information available on HSAs provided by insurance providers is disseminated online, yet online literacy can often prove to be a significant barrier to the information-seeking process. Van Deursen recommends the formation of policies which specifically address the varied levels of internet skills among consumers, as well as a need for greater understanding of competency related to information technology across diverse communities.

Conclusion

In this chapter, we examined neoliberalism and health care in the United States Neoliberal solutions to the problems of access, cost, and quality focus on private market interventions that reduce the role of government and free private markets through decentralization, deregulation, and promotion of individual decision making. We discussed neoliberalism in health care followed by a review of the literature focused on the potential impact of high deductibles on different populations. Attention to the impact of such policies on the most vulnerable, to include those living in poverty, should be the attention of future research.

References

Agency for Healthcare Research and Quality (AHRQ). (2005). National Healthcare Quality Report. June 2005. Agency for Healthcare Research and Quality, Rockville, MD.

Agency for Healthcare Research and Quality (AHRQ). (2006). National Healthcare Disparities Report. Retrieved January 10 , 2014, from http://www.ahrq.gov/qual/nhdr06/nhdr06.htm

Agency for Healthcare Research and Quality (AHRQ). (2012). National Healthcare Disparities Report. Retrieved June 15, 2013, from http://www.ahrq.gov/research/findings/nhqrdr/nhdr12/index.html

Asch, S.M., Kerr, E.A., Keesey, J., Adams, J.L., Setodji, C.M., Malik, S., and McGlynn, E.A. (2006). Who is at greatest risk for receiving poor-quality health care? *New England Journal of Medicine*, 354(11): 1147–1156.

Bach, P.B., Pham, H.H., Schrag, D., Tate, R.C., and Hargraves, J.L. (2004). Primary care physicians who treat blacks and whites. *New England Journal of Medicine*, 351, 575–584.

Baicker, K. (2006). Improving incentives in health care spending. *Business Economics*, 41(2): 21–25.

Bloche, M.G. (2007). Consumer-directed health care and the disadvantaged. *Health Affairs (Project Hope)*, 26(5): 1315–1327.

Brennan, T., and Reisman, L. (2007). Value-based insurance design and the next generation of consumer-driven health care. *Health Affairs*, 26(2): w204–w207.

Buck, K. (2012). January 2012 census shows 13.5 million people covered by health savings account/high-deductible health plans (HAS/HDHPs). *American Health Insurance Plans, Center for Policy and Research*, 1–11.

Bundorf, M.K. (2012). *Consumer-directed health plans: Do they deliver?* Research Synthesis Report, Robert Wood Johnson Foundation, 24, 1–28.

Buntin, M.B., Haviland, A., McDevitt, R., and Sood, N. (2011). Health care spending and preventative care in high-deductible and consumer-directed health plans. *American Journal of Managed Care*, 17(3): 222–230.

Cardon, J. H., and Showalter, M. H. (2007). Insurance choice and tax-preferred health savings accounts. *Journal of Health Economics*, 26(2): 373–399.

Centers for Disease Control and Prevention. Rising Health Care Costs are Unsustainable. Retrieved April 2011 from http://www.cdc.gov/workplacehealthpromotion/businesscase/reasons/rising.html.

Centers for Medicare and Medicaid. (2012). *National health care expenditures data*, January 2012. Office of the Actuary, National Health Statistics Group.

Claxton, G., Rae, M., Panchal, N., Lundy, J., and Damico, A. (2011). *Employer Health Benefits 2011 Annual survey*. Menlo Park, CA. Henry J. Kaiser Foundation, and Chicago: Health Research and Educational Trust.

Coburn, D. (2000). Income inequality, social cohesion and the health status of populations: The role of neo-liberalism. *Social Science and Medicine*, 51(1): 135–146.

Cogan, J.F., Hubbard, R.G., and Kessler, D.P. (2005). *Healthy, wealthy and wise: Five steps to a better health care system*. Washington, DC: American Enterprise Institute for Public Policy Research.

Collins, S.R., Kriss, J.L, Davis, K., Doty, M.M., and Holmgren, A.L. (2006). "Squeezed: Why rising exposure to health care costs threatens the health and financial well-being of American families. *Commonwealth Fund Survey*, 1–34.

Davis, K. (2004). Consumer-directed health care: Will it improve health system performance? *Health Services Research*, 39(4): 1219–1234.

DeNavas-Walt, Carmen, Proctor, Bernadette D., and Smith, Jessica C. (2012). *Income, poverty, and health insurance coverage in the United States: 2011*. U.S. Census Bureau, Current Population Reports, P60-243. Washington, DC: U.S. Government Printing Office.

Feldman, R., Parente, S.T., Abraham, J., Christianson, J.B., and Taylor, R. (2005). Health savings accounts: Early estimates of national take-up. *Health Affairs (Project Hope)*, 24(6): 1582–1591

Feldstein, M. (2006). *Balancing the goals of health care provision*. NBER Working Paper 12279. Cambridge, MA: National Bureau of Economic Research.

Gibbon, P. (2012). A standard fit for neoliberalism. *Comparative Studies in Society and History*, 54(2): 275307.

Haviland, A.M., Marquis, M.S., McDevitt, R.D., and Sood, N. (2012). Growth of consumer-directed health plans to one-half of all employer-sponsored insurance could save $57 billion annually. *Health Affairs (Project Hope)*, 31(5): 1009–1015.

Hoffman, C., and Tolbert, J. (2006). *Health savings accounts and high deductible health plans: Are they an option for low-income families?* Issue paper 7568, The Henry Kaiser Foundation.

Institute of Medicine (IOM). (2001). *Crossing the quality chasm: A new health system for the 21st century*. Washington, DC: National Academy Press.

Institute of Medicine (IOM). (2009). *America's uninsured crisis: Consequences for health and health care*. Washington, DC: The National Academies Press.

Kaiser Commission on Medicaid and the Uninsured. (2012). *The uninsured and the difference health insurance makes*. Washington, DC: Kaiser Commission on Medicaid and the Uninsured.

Kaiser Family Foundation, *Employer health benefits: 2010 annual survey*. Menlo Park. Retrieved June 15, 2013, from http://kaiserfamilyfoundation.files.wordpress.com/2013/04/8085.pdf

Larson, E.J., and Dettmann, M. (2005). The impact of HSAs on health care reform: Preliminary results after one year. *Wake Forest Law Review*, 40(4): 1087–1124.

Lo Sasso, A.T., Shah, M., and Frogner, B. (2010). Health savings accounts and health care spending. *Health Services Research*, 45(4): 1041–1060.

Martin, A.B., Lassman, D., Washington, B., and Catlin, A. (2012). Growth in U.S. health spending remained slow in 2010; health share of gross domestic product was unchanged from 2009. *Health Affairs*, 31(1): 208–219.

McGregor, S. (2001). Neoliberalism and health care. *International Journal of Consumer Studies*, 25(2): 82–89.

Moser, J. (2005). Health savings accounts: Description, analysis, and implications. *Journal of the American College of Radiology*, 2(12): 1008–1015.

Nazroo, J.Y. (2003). The structuring of ethnic inequalities in health: Economic position, racial discrimination, and racism. *American Journal of Public Health*, 93(2): 277–284.

Parente, S.T., Feldman, R., and Chen, S. (2008). Effects of a consumer-driven health plan on pharmaceutical spending and utilization. *Health Services Research*, 43(5): 1542–1556.

Reed, M., Graetz, I., Wang, H., Fung, V., Newhouse, J.P., and Hsu, J. (2012). Consumer-directed health plans with health savings accounts: Whose skin is in the game and how do costs affect care seeking? *Medical Care*, 50(7): 585–590.

Remler, D., and Glied, S. (2005). *The effect of health savings accounts on health insurance coverage*. Issue Brief. The Commonwealth Fund Publication No. 811.

Remler, D., and Glied, S. (2006). How much more cost sharing will health savings accounts bring? *Health Affairs*, 25(4): 1070–1078.

Robinson, J.C. (2004). Reinvention of health insurance in the consumer era. *Journal of the American Medical Association*, 291(15): 1880–1886.

Rosenthal, M. and Daniels, N. (2006). Beyond competition: The normative implications of consumer-driven health plans. *Journal of Health Politics, Policy and Law*, 31 (3): 671–685.

Rosenthal, M., Hsuan, C., and Milstein, A. (2005). A report card on the freshman class of consumer-directed health plans. *Health Affairs*, 24(6): 1592–1600.

Schoen, C., Collins, S.R., Kriss, J.L., and Doty, M.M. (2008). How many are underinsured? Trends among U.S. adults, 2003 and 2007, *Health Affairs Web Exclusive*, June 10, 2008, w298–w309. (Data: 2007 Commonwealth Fund Biennial Health Insurance Survey.)

Smedley, B.D., Stith, A.Y., and Nelson, A.R. (eds) (2003). *Unequal treatment: Confronting racial and ethnic disparities in health care*. Washington, DC: National Academy Press.

Steinorth, P. (2011). Impact of health savings accounts on precautionary savings, demand for health insurance and prevention effort. *Journal of Health Economics*, 30(2): 458–465.

van Deursen, A.J. (2012). Internet skill-related problems in accessing online health information. *International Journal of Medical Informatics*, 81(1): 61–72.

Varmin, R., and Vikas, R.M. (2007). Rising markets and failing health: An inquiry into subaltern health care consumption under neoliberalism. *Journal of Macromarketing*, 27(2): 162–172.

Wharam, J.F., Galbraith, A.A., Kleinman, K.P., Soumerai, S.B., Ross-Degnan, D., and Landon, B.E. (2008). Cancer screening before and after switching to a high-deductible health plan. *Annals of Internal Medicine*, 148(9): 647–655.

Wilkinson, R.G. (1989). Class mortality differentials, income distribution and trends in poverty 1921–1981. *Journal of Social Policy*, 18(3): 307–335.

Wilper, A.P., Woolhandler, S., Lasser, K.E., McCormick, D., Bor, D.H., and Himmelstein, D.U. (2009). Health insurance and mortality in U.S. adults. *American Journal of Public Health*, 99(12): 2289–2295.

Woolhandler, S., and Himmelstein, D.U. (2007). Consumer directed healthcare: Except for the healthy and wealthy it's unwise. *Journal of General Internal Medicine*, 22 (6): 879–881.

SECTION III

Transformation of the welfare state
Criminalizing of the poor

INTRODUCTION

Reuben Jonathan Miller and Emily Shayman

The criminalization of poverty has been central to the rise of mass incarceration in the United States. Due to its size, scope, and most likely target population, carceral expansion has been alternatively labeled mass imprisonment, racialized mass incarceration, hyper-incarceration, the prison industrial complex, the new Jim Crow, or neoliberal penality. The carceral techniques of the current age, however, are not new. Since the birth of the prison, penal institutions have been used to manage poverty (Wacquant, 2009). From its humble origins as the Poor House, Work House, and the House of Corrections in Europe, to the development of its more magisterial, if foreboding, structures erected to ensure the penitence of dishonored and criminalized populations, the penal state has attempted to correct the "rogues," "sturdy beggars," and "hardened criminals" it houses. These stigmatized groups were believed to have bypassed the formal economy, choosing to live a life of crime, vice, and dependence. Mirroring contemporary practices, there are long-standing racial disparities in the arrest and incarceration of supposed "offenders" even with the helping institutions of the welfare state imbricated in the punishment of these groups (Miller, 2013).

W.E.B. DuBois was among the first scholars to explore the relationship between punishment, poverty, and social welfare policy (DuBois, 1935). Turning his lens toward reconstruction in America, DuBois (1901 and 1935) highlights the importance of the U.S. Bureau of Refugees, Freedmen, and Abandoned Lands (The Freedmen's Bureau) in the lives of former slaves. As the first federally administered social welfare institution (Goldberg, 2008), the bureau expanded the civil rights of former slaves by appointing specialized courts to mitigate disputes, registering Black voters, opening some of the first public schools in the south, and providing for the basic human needs of former slaves and poor, dispossessed Whites (DuBois, 1935; Goldberg, 2008). At the same time, Black freedmen and women were expected to take the most "immediate and available jobs" at the threat of being labeled a vagrant by local constables and agents of the Bureau. Subsequently many emancipated former slaves were forced into long-term sharecropping relationships on the plantations they just left (Farmer-Kaiser, 2004).

The expectation of labor and peonage (working in harsh conditions to pay off debt) crossed genders and was indeed hostile to the entrepreneurial initiatives of freedmen and women who often sought to establish their own farms and businesses (DuBois, 1935; Taylor, 2009). Refusal to work the fields of the plantation was policed at the threat of the vagrancy conviction. These practices foreshadowed the stigma of the "welfare queen" for poor mothers who "refused" to work low-wage jobs, and "deadbeat" to Black fathers who were not "formally" employed. They raise important questions about the similarities of this period with the current one, given the draconian work requirements of welfare reform.

Conviction as a vagrant meant lengthy terms of confinement and forced labor under the chain gangs and convict leasing system of the "new" south. As a result, by the end of the 19th century, Blacks comprised more than 90 percent of all leased convicts in the United States (Gorman, 1997). The southern prison system rapidly expanded in just under a generation. Prisoners were sentenced at younger ages for longer periods of time and in exponentially greater volume. For example, between 1865 and 1890, Georgia's prison census increased tenfold, while Mississippi's quadrupled and Alabama's more than tripled (Mancini, 1978). We can therefore see that a kind of "mass incarceration" was well underway during the post-bellum period, mirroring many of the carceral techniques rolled out in the neoliberal age to discipline, manage, and contain the dispossessed (i.e., the hyper policing of poor people of color, racial disproportionality in arrest and sentencing, and a disciplinary logic in welfare administration). What then do we make of neoliberal penality? What makes it novel? How can we distinguish it from previous penal forms?

While there is significant continuity between old and new forms of penal governance, neoliberal social and economic policy has more deeply embedded the carceral state within the lives of the poor, transforming what it means to be poor in America (Miller, 2014). The contributions that follow capture fundamental changes in the ways in which poor people are managed by state-sanctioned institutions, the novel forms of social life that have emerged in the wake of neoliberal penality, and the consequence of carceral expansion for poor people across categories of difference. Katherine Beckett and Steve Herbert's chapter, "Managing the Neoliberal City," examines the ways in which ordinances and the stigma of criminality have been deployed to effectively "banish" former prisoners from full participation in social, civic, and economic life. Jessica Camp and Eileen Trzcinski's contribution walk us through a brief history of de-institutionalization in "The Rise of Incarceration Among the Poor with Mental Illnesses," while shedding light on the scale and consequence of incarceration in the current age.

Turning our attention to the dual-sided nature of neoliberal penality, Spencer Headworth's chapter, "Class, Crime, and Social Control in the Contemporary United States," highlights the regulatory mechanisms that facilitate the overpolicing of "crime in the streets" and the simultaneous underpolicing of "crime in the suites." Furthermore, Shaun Ossei-Owusu's chapter, "A People's History of Legal Aid," demonstrates the contribution of the legal aid society to race, gender, and ethnic relations, and contemporary modes of citizenship. Cesraéa Rumpf's chapter, "Surviving Gender-Based Violence in the Neoliberal Era," exhibits a paradox: the state often plays dual roles, to protect and to punish, in the lives of domestic violence survivors caught in the penal dragnet. Enora Brown's chapter, "Systematic and Symbolic Violence as Virtue: The Carceral Punishment of Adolescent Girls" examines the racialization and symbolic dimensions of "girl violence," displaying it as an instrument of symbolic violence that pathologizes and dehumanizes black girls in the United States, justifying their over-incarceration and substantiating longstanding tropes of their aggressive natures. We conclude with Colleen Casey's interrogation of entrepreneurship's underside. In "The Paradox of Entrepreneurship as a Policy Tool for Economic Inclusion in Neoliberal Policy Environments," Casey argues that the promotion of entrepreneurship, in its current form, exacerbates inequality. Taken together, these chapters help us to think carefully and critically about neoliberal penality, drawing our attention to the ways in which it has radically changed the daily lives of poor and marginalized populations.

References

DuBois, W.E.B. (1901). The Freedman's Bureau. *The Atlantic Monthly: Digital Edition*. Retrieved from https://www.theatlantic.com/past/docs/issues/01mar/dubois.htm.

DuBois, W.E.B. [1935] 1999. *Black Reconstruction in America, 1860–1880*. Durham, NC: Duke University Press.

Farmer-Kaiser, M. (2004). "Are They Not in Some Sorts Vagrants?" Gender and the Efforts of the Freedmen's Bureau to Combat Vagrancy in the Reconstruction South. *Georgia Historical Quarterly*, 88(1), 25–49.

Goldberg, C.A. (2008). *Citizens and Paupers: Relief, Rights, and Race, from the Freedmen's Bureau to Workfare*. Chicago and London: University of Chicago Press.

Gorman, T.M. (1997). Back on the Chain Gang: Why the Eighth Amendment and the History of Slavery Proscribe the Resurgence of Chain Gangs. *California Law Review*, 85(2) :441–478.

Mancini, Matthew J. (1978). Race, Economics, and The Abandonment of Convict Leasing. *The Journal of Negro History*, 63(4), 339–352.

Miller, R. (2013). Race, Hyper Incarceration, and U.S. Poverty Policy in Historic Perspective. *Sociology Compass*, 7(7), 573–589.

Miller, R. (2014). Devolving the Carceral State: Race, Prisoner Reentry and the Micropolitics of Urban Poverty Management. *Punishment and Society*, 16, 305–335.

Taylor, K.Y. (2009). W.E.B. Du Bois: Black Reconstruction in America. *International Socialist Review*, 57.

Wacquant, L. (2009). *Punishing the Poor: The Neoliberal Government of Social Insecurity*. Durham, NC: Duke University Press.

31

MANAGING THE NEOLIBERAL CITY

"Quality of life" policing in
the twenty-first century

Katherine Beckett and Steve Herbert

Introduction

The politics of urban social control are frequently contentious, and often focus on the proper way to police those considered undesirable. In the contemporary era, "quality of life" policing—often referred to as "zero tolerance" and "broken windows" policing—has become increasingly popular in cities in the United States and elsewhere (Harcourt, 2001; Herbert, 2001; Wacquant, 2003). Originally articulated by James Q. Wilson and George Kelling in 1982, this approach rests on the assumption that street-level behaviors engaged in by the homeless and other ostensibly disreputable people generate more serious criminality. For Wilson and colleagues, "broken windows" and other manifestations of "disorder" symbolize a neighborhood that does not care about itself; this serves as a cue for those seeking to engage in more serious criminal acts (Kelling and Coles, 1996; Wilson and Kelling, 1982).

This theory suggests that rather than waiting for serious crime to occur and trying to apprehend suspects, urban police departments should instead proactively address the conditions in which crime allegedly incubates. Advocates of broken windows policing therefore call for city governments to give the police broad and flexible means of regulating public spaces and removing those deemed "disorderly." Indeed, although the theory ostensibly concentrates on the built environment, it principally focuses upon unwanted human behavior—particularly that which is engaged in by "disreputable or obstreperous or unpredictable people: panhandlers, drunks, addicts, rowdy teenagers, prostitutes, loiterers, the mentally disturbed"—as a cause of serious crime (Wilson and Kelling, 1982: 32). The police are therefore encouraged to consider misdemeanor offenses such as public drunkenness, panhandling, and drug possession as very serious matters.

The spread of this theory has fueled the use of police practices that treat various behaviors and conditions as crimes rather than as medical or social matters. This trend has also coincided with the ascendance of neoliberal, global capitalism, raising the question of how the embrace of "quality of life" policing may be related to the broader socio-economic context.

These developments deserve critical scrutiny. We use this chapter as a component of that larger project. In the chapter's first part, we briefly describe the rise of "quality of life" policing in the United States and elsewhere. We show that although police efforts to employ criminal law to manage social marginality are not new, they now involve the use of novel control tactics. These include the use of social control tools that entail banishment, as well as the devotion of an unprecedented degree of police attention to the use and distribution of illegal drugs. In the second part of the chapter, we assess whether and how these policing practices are related to the rise of neoliberalism. We argue that the dynamics set in motion by global neoliberalism help to explain both the popularity of "quality of life" policing and its geography. Yet we also suggest that the connection between economic dynamics and particular policing practices is not a functional one; the former does not *require* the latter. Rather, the turn to the police to solve social problems is a resolutely political one, and must be resisted in precisely those terms. It will hence require a shift in the political discourses about crime and policing before more humane and effective social control practices become common.

Part I. "Quality of life" policing in the 21st century

The police have long played a central role in the regulation and management of social marginality. And particularly since the 19th century, the police also engaged in ambitious projects aimed at "moral regulation" in cities across the country (Adler, 1989; Hunt, 1999; Novak, 1996). "Quality of life" policing thus represents the continuation of a well-established historical pattern.

Historically, the police were able to regulate the movement of "disreputable" people through invocation of vagrancy laws. For hundreds of years, vagrancy and loitering laws in the United Kingdom and United States made it a crime to wander without destination or visible means of support (Feldman, 2004). A number of events shaped the emergence and implementation of these laws, including the enclosure movement, the dissolution of monasteries, and the shift toward industrialized production and associated migratory processes. Early vagrancy legislation thus sought to control a new kind of poverty, that experienced by "masterless men" (Beier, 1985). Similarly, vagrancy laws were used by Southern authorities in the United States to control the black population and to prevent the collapse of the sharecropping system following the abolition of slavery. Mississippi's "Black Code," for example, defined vagrants as "runaways, drunkards, pilferers; lewd, wanton, or lascivious persons ...; those who neglect their employment, misspend their earnings, and fail to support their families; and ... all other idle and disorderly persons" (Stewart, 1998; see also Adamson, 1983). Under the Black Codes, those without work contracts were then prosecuted as vagrants and sentenced to hard labor.

Vagrancy laws were also an important weapon in urban battles against immorality and disorder (Adler, 1989; Novak, 1996). As adapted and implemented in the United States, these laws reflected deeply held concerns about idleness; they primarily penalized those who did not appear to work. Indeed, those arrested for vagrancy were often given the option of leaving town in lieu of jail time, a modified version of granting a pardon to those willing to submit to banishment (Armstrong, 1963). Vagrancy and related laws thus helped to punish and regulate vice, and to maintain race, power, and property relations.

Yet these laws came under disabling scrutiny in the 1960s and 1970s as part of the U.S. courts' short-lived "rights revolution." In a series of well-known decisions, the courts ruled that the vagueness and breadth of the vagrancy and loitering statutes enabled unjustifiable police discretion. For example, in one key Supreme Court case, *Papchristou vs. City of Jacksonville*, a unanimous court ruled that a Florida loitering law: "Furnishes a convenient tool for harsh and discriminatory enforcement by displeasure. It results in a regime in which the poor and unpopular are permitted to stand on a public sidewalk only at the whim of any police officer" (Stewart, 1998: 2259). The vagueness of vagrancy and loitering laws, in other words, granted the street officer too much discretion in deciding whom to arrest, and were therefore rejected by the courts.

Dissatisfied with this restriction on police power, many cities began in the 1990s to pass "civility codes." Like the vagrancy laws, these ordinances criminalized behaviors deemed "disorderly," and were used to deal with nuisances rather than serious crime. Unlike vagrancy laws, however, these criminal laws proscribe specific behaviors (e.g., sitting) rather than status (being transient or homeless). The most widely adopted "civility" laws made it a crime to sit or lie on sidewalks or in bus shelters, sleep in parks and other public spaces, place one's personal possessions on public property for more than a short period of time, drink alcohol in public, engage in public elimination, sell newspapers and other written materials in public spaces, and panhandle aggressively (Feldman, 2004).

Because they criminalized many common behaviors (such as sleeping, lying down, sitting, and urinating) *when those behaviors occur outdoors*, the homeless and unstably housed bore the brunt of the civility codes (Foscarinis, 1996; Harcourt, 2001). Despite the significance of civility laws, the behavioral specificity they outlined meant that they did not re-create the broad police discretion afforded by vagrancy and loitering laws. They were, moreover, subject to sometimes-successful legal challenges.

In light of these limitations, many cities developed an even more potent arsenal of new legal tools. These new tools banish their targets from contested urban spaces for extended periods of time, and rest on an innovative blend of civil, criminal, and administrative law. Indeed, in many U.S. cities, legally hybrid exclusion orders that make mere presence in public space a crime are regularly imposed. Increasing swaths of urban space are delimited as zones of exclusion from which the undesirable are banned. The uniformed police are marshaled to enforce and often to delineate these boundaries; they use their powers to monitor and arrest in an attempt to clear the streets of those considered unsightly or "disorderly." Examples of the new tactics include civil gang injunctions (Stewart, 1998), no contact orders (Suk, 2006), off-limits orders, and innovations in trespass law that authorize officials to spatially exclude those perceived as disorderly from urban spaces (Beckett and Herbert, 2008, 2010).

Although it is not well known, New York City, Los Angeles, Portland, Cincinnati, Honolulu, and many other municipalities across the United States employ one or more banishment strategies. Similar measures are in use in many other cities of the global North, particularly in Western Europe and Canada (Belina, 2007; von Mahs, 2005). In the United Kingdom, for example, new control measures are increasingly employed to reduce "anti-social" behavior and thereby to enhance "security." In particular, Anti-Social Behavioural Contracts and Anti-Social Behavioural Orders cover a wide range of unwanted behaviors, fuse civil and criminal law, and quite often lead to the imposition of place-based restrictions (Burney, 1999, 2005; Crawford and Lister, 2007; Flint and Nixon, 2006; Millie, 2008; Raco, 2003).

In short, although vagrancy laws remain unconstitutional in the United States, new legal tools that entail banishment increasingly function as their 21st-century replacement. Other cities of the global North deploy similar tactics. And as many analysts have noted, fences, gates, walls, and armed security personnel are also increasingly used to channel the socially undesirable away from sites of luxury living in cities from Sao Paulo to London and Los Angeles (Caldeira, 2000; Davis, 1992; Lynch, 2001).

In the United States, the embrace of "quality of life" or "broken windows" policing coincided with the unprecedented ratcheting up of the nation's drug war. FBI data indicate that the number of annual drug arrests more than tripled between 1980 and 2010, from about one-half of a million to over 1.6 million. Although early studies indicated that these arrests were concentrated in residential minority neighborhoods, more recent research indicates that, at least in some cities, drug arrests are concentrated in contested downtown areas that are linked to redevelopment strategies. In Seattle and San Francisco, for example, drug arrests are concentrated in areas undergoing significant gentrification (Beckett, 2008, 2012; Lynch et al., 2013). Indeed, racial disproportionality in drug arrests has been particularly acute in these ostensibly liberal,

West Coast cities (ibid.). Thus, particularly in global "consumer cities" like San Francisco, Seattle, and New York, it appears that aggressive, racialized drug policing is also part of an effort to segregate the socially marginal from contested urban spaces, and thereby enhance the "quality of life" of other urban residents.

Part II. Neoliberalism and "quality of life" policing: understanding the connection

Policing tactics in the contemporary era, then, continue long-standing practices of attempting to regulate those labeled undesirable, particularly the poor. Yet the particular form of current policing tactics—and the vigor with which they are promoted and practiced—is undeniably connected to recent economic changes; the rise of neoliberalism helps to explain the rise of broken windows policing. However, these two developments are not causally connected, but instead are mediated through wider and culturally entrenched political discourses.

Certainly, the adoption of broken windows policing—and new social control tools that enable its implementation—coincided with the dramatic uptick in homelessness. The rise of homelessness is, in turn, inextricably connected to certain economic transformations, most notably the shift to a post-industrial economy, as well as the adoption of neoliberal social policies (Barak, 1992; Burt, 1992; Wolch and Dear, 1993). As the manufacturing sector declined in the United States, so did the factory jobs that once provided a reasonably comfortable existence for low-skilled workers. Service jobs became more prominent, but these were bifurcated. Those who worked largely with information—in the finance and high-tech sectors, for example—drew hefty salaries, while those who worked in the lower rungs of the service sector—in retail or restaurants—labored for minimum wages. In the 1980s, more than three-quarters of new jobs paid the minimum wage (Wolch and Dear, 1993). This wage level typically fails to generate sufficient income to escape poverty (Morris and Western, 1999).

This dynamic generated the "great U-turn" in the American income structure: the numbers at the higher and lower ends of the income spectrum grew, while the middle class declined. As joblessness and reduced earnings increased inequality, changes in the housing market made acquiring inexpensive shelter more and more difficult. A key dynamic in many urban housing markets was the rise of gentrification. In this process, older, deteriorating city neighborhoods witnessed infusions of capital for remodeling and thereby attracted young professionals as residents (Hackworth, 2007; Lees et al., 2008; Smith, 1996; Wyly and Hammel, 1999).

Gentrification often works to deplete the stock of affordable housing. Single Resident Only (SRO) hotels are an important example of this. Indeed, the loss of SROs decreased the stock of inexpensive housing by about one million units in urban America between 1970 and 1982 (Wolch and Dear, 1993). Often, they were replaced by apartments or condominiums that typically lay beyond the means of the urban poor. This process generated a shortfall of affordable housing that persists today.

Economic shifts thus helped to generate a dearth of affordable housing by both limiting living wage jobs and fueling urban real estate redevelopment. Yet neoliberal government policies were also complicit in generating the housing crunch. Most significantly, federal government involvement in providing housing assistance dropped precipitously in the 1980s, as did funding for other forms of social support. In the three-year period from 1982 to 1985 alone, federal programs targeted to the poor were cut by $57 billion (Wolch and Dear, 1993). The resulting decline in government-built public housing was dramatic. This withdrawal of the federal government from an active role in providing housing for low-income people is arguably the single-greatest factor in the growth of homelessness.

The decline of governmental support for low-income housing was part of a broader movement to lessen government obligations to those at the bottom of the economic ladder. The derogation of welfare is one of the components of the rise of neoliberalism. But it is a mistake to conclude that federal assistance for housing declined across the board. For those who can afford to purchase a home, federal assistance is robust. Government support for downtown redevelopment has also been substantial (Gibson, 2004).

By adopting neoliberal policies, then, governments at multiple scales abandoned the goal of providing affordable housing even as they continued to make it easier for wealthier individuals to purchase homes and to shop at attractive upscale downtown stores. Homelessness and inequality skyrocketed, as did municipal governments' interest in excluding the disorderly and disreputable from urban landscapes.

In short, the spread of homelessness, the intensification of gentrification, and the increased importance of tourism and retail in rising "consumer" cities help to explain the appeal of "quality of life" policing in those urban areas, even where ostensibly liberal politics are firmly entrenched. In linking these forces, our argument appears to be compatible with studies that attribute the rise of hyper-penal practices to the recent ascendance of neoliberal governance, that is, national and transnational policies that limit state responsibility for the provision of social welfare, facilitate private economic transactions, and favor corporate interests and established hierarchies of wealth. Although we recognize the important connections between social control practices and socio-economic dynamics, we suggest that these connections are better understood as historical and political than as causal.

Perhaps the best known and most powerful articulation of the relationship between penal developments and neoliberalism is found in the work of Loic Wacquant. He argues that the growth of penal populations in "advanced" societies is a consequence of the replacement of the welfare apparatus with the penal system as the "instrument for managing social insecurity and containing the social disorders created at the bottom of the class structure by neoliberal policies of economic deregulation and social-welfare retrenchment" (Wacquant, 2001: 401). For Wacquant, then, the "penalization of poverty" is "designed to manage the effects of neoliberal policies at the lower end of the social structure of advanced societies" (p. 401).

From this perspective, practices such as "zero tolerance" policing are functional and necessary counterparts to neoliberal social policies. Indeed, the deregulation of the economy is necessarily accompanied by hyper-penality, as elites seek to manage the social consequences of rising inequality caused by neoliberalism. Wacquant also argues that, symbolically, get-tough policies dramatize political elites' "new-found commitment to slay the monster of urban crime and because they readily fit the negative stereotypes of the poor who are everywhere portrayed as the main source of street deviance and violence" (2003: 198).

Urban geographers and sociologists working from a political-economic perspective offer a similar account of the relationship between intensified urban policing efforts and neoliberalism. As Passavant suggests, "cities are at the center of the story of neoliberal transformation" (2012: 743). These scholars stress the simultaneous emergence of "fortress cities," punitive anti-crime policies, and neoliberal transformation, particularly at the urban level. For example, critics such as Mike Davis (1992) thus argue that architectural and policing techniques are used to "contain" the socially undesirable in one area of the city and to enhance and protect the social insulation of the middle and upper classes who seek to "revitalize" the city (see also Caldeira, 2000; Lynch, 2001).

From this perspective, the transformation of the global economy explains the need for aesthetically pleasing urban landscapes and the immense popularity of zero tolerance policing among urban elites. In particular, the increased mobility of industry and finance associated with deindustrialization and deregulation has led many cities to attempt to create the most hospitable environment for investors and to aggressively promote tourism and retail operations (Gibson, 2004; Peck and Tickell, 2002; Sassen, 2002). Particularly in cities that depend on tourists and shoppers for their economic well-being, the "environment" on city streets has become the subject of much official attention. In this context, municipal governments often engage in what Timothy Gibson (2004) calls "projects of reassurance": efforts to counter widespread images of cities as sites of decay and danger with sanitized images of urban consumer (and investment) utopias. Broken windows policing appeals to urban developers and city officials because it seems to promise to help the "revitalization" of urban downtowns; this appeal is especially pronounced in "global" cities characterized by robust retail and tourist sectors.

In short, this body of scholarship suggests that the implementation of neoliberal social policies necessitates hyper-penal practices at both the national and local levels. Whether by "disciplining" the disruptive elements of the working class through incarceration or by creating urban, "bourgeois playgrounds," hyper-punitive policies are, from this perspective, functionally integral to global neoliberalism.

While this theoretical framework has much to commend it, the *processes* by which neoliberalism generates "tough" responses to crime require further explication. The argument that neoliberalism *necessitates* hyper-penality in order to manage and contain the "disorders spawned by the deregulation of the economy, the desocialization of wage labor, and the relative and absolute immiseration of large sections of the urban proletariat" (Wacquant, 2003: 200) does not shed light on the *process* by which crime-related problems assume political ascendance. Neither does it account for popular receptivity to calls to get tough on crime and implement "quality of life" policing. Political dynamics are the crucial medium through which concerns about crime and disorder are named, framed, and channeled; popular perceptions of these issues and policy options do not spring "naturally" from some element of the globalized or neoliberal social condition.

In addition, Wacquant's argument overstates the extent to which hyper-punitive policies and practices reduce social conflict and ameliorate the effects of neoliberalism. It is not clear that "tough" penal policies actually manage the social disruptions caused by neoliberalism other than sometimes achieving "containment" and spatial segregation at the local level. Indeed, Wacquant himself emphasizes that the implementation of hyper-penality in Brazil and other Latin American countries "promises to produce a social catastrophe of historic proportions" (2003: 197). The adoption of these policies cannot be explained in terms of a function they do not serve.

Conclusion

The rise of "quality of life" policing, the adoption of tactics that entail banishment, and the intensification of drug policing in contested urban areas are not historical accidents. The shift toward a post-industrial economy and away from a strong welfare state increased levels of poverty. Extensive gentrification coupled with a decline in public housing made affordable shelter increasingly scarce. Together, these structural dynamics generated a sizeable increase in the number of urban residents who are visibly homeless or otherwise marginalized. Their presence in downtown public spaces caused widespread concern about the effects of "disorder." This concern was particularly acute for commercial establishments reliant upon shoppers and tourists, many of whom abhor visible evidence of social disadvantage. For those seeking to "revive" downtowns, and improve downtown aesthetics, the broken window theory was a boon. The popularity of this theory legitimized various "civility codes" that targeted the everyday behaviors of those deemed disorderly.

Yet the civility codes did not make homelessness disappear. This is not surprising, since these codes left the underlying dynamics of homelessness untouched. The persistence of homelessness meant that municipal governments continued to face ongoing pressures to "clean up" contested downtown areas. New control tools significantly increase the power of the police to place pressure upon those who spend a considerable amount of time in public space, and to otherwise extend the net of surveillance and control.

The rise of neoliberalism and the transformation of rising, global "consumer" cities thus created fertile soil for the spread and implementation of "quality of life" policing and control tactics intended to enable the police to effectively regulate urban space. Yet it would be a mistake to interpret shifts in policing as the functional and inevitable consequence of the rise of neoliberalism. The idea that the police can use any control tactics to remake urban landscapes is a political one, and may already be discredited in cities that have tried this approach and found it to be less than effective. In the end, these processes are best understood as political and historically contingent rather than functional and determined. Transformation of these processes is possible, and will need to occur through a shift in the political discourse about crime, security, and policing.

References

Adamson, Christopher R. (1983) "Punishment After Slavery," *Social Problems* 30, 5 (June): 493–507.

Adler, Jeffrey S. (1989) "A Historical Analysis of the Law of Vagrancy," *Criminology* 27, 2: 209–229.

Armstrong, Michael F. (1963) "Banishment: Cruel and Unusual Punishment," *University of Pennsylvania Law Review* 111, 6 (April): 758–786.

Barak, Gregg. (1992) *Gimme Shelter: A Social History of Homelessness in Contemporary America*. Westport, CT: Praeger.

Beckett, Katherine. (2008) *Race and Drug Law Enforcement in Seattle*. Report commissioned by the Racial Disparity Project and the ACLU Drug Law Reform Project. Available online: http://www.aclu.org/criminal-law-reform/race-and-drug-law-enforcement-seattle. Accessed August 14, 2014.

Beckett, Katherine. (2012) "Race, Drugs and Law Enforcement: Toward Equitable Policing," *Criminology and Public Policy* 11, 4: 641–653.

Beckett, Katherine and Steve Herbert. (2008) "Dealing with Disorder: Social Control in the Post-Industrial City," *Theoretical Criminology* 12: 5–30.

Beckett, Katherine and Steve Herbert. (2010) *Banished: The New Social Control in Urban America*. Oxford, UK: Oxford University Press.

Beier, A.L. (1985) *Masterless Men: The Vagrancy Problem in England 1560–1640*. New York: Methuen.

Belina, Bernd. (2007) "From Disciplining to Dislocation: Area Bans in Recent Urban Policing in Germany," *European Urban and Regional Studies* 14: 321–336.

Burney, Elizabeth. (1999) *Crime and Banishment: Nuisance and Exclusion in Social Housing*. Winchester, UK: Waterside Press.

Burney, Elizabeth. (2005) *Making People Behave: Anti-Social Behaviour, Politics, and Policy*. Cullompton, UK: Willan.

Burt, Martha. (1992) *Over the Edge: The Growth of Homelessness in the 1980s*. New York: Russell Sage Foundation.

Caldeira, Teresa P.R. (2000) *City of Walls: Crime, Segregation, and Citizenship in São Paulo*. Berkeley: University of California Press.

Crawford, Adam and Stuart Lister. (2007) *The Use and Impact of Dispersal Orders*. Bristol, UK: Polity Press.

Davis, Mike. (1992) *City of Quartz: Excavating the Future in Los Angeles*. New York: Vintage Books.

Feldman, Leonard C. (2004) *Citizens Without Shelter: Homelessness, Democracy and Political Exclusion*. Ithaca: Cornell University Press.

Flint John and Judy Nixon. (2006) "Governing Neighbours: Anti-Social Behaviour Orders and New Forms of Regulating Conduct in the UK," *Urban Studies* 43: 939–956.

Foscarinis, Maria. (1996) "Downward Spiral: Homelessness and its Criminalization," *Yale Law and Policy Review* 14: 1–63.

Gibson, Timothy. (2004) *Securing the Spectacular City: The Politics of Revitalization and Homelessness in Downtown Seattle*. Lanham, MD: Lexington Books.

Hackworth, Jason. (2007) *The Neoliberal City: Governance, Ideology, and Development in American Urbanism.* Ithaca, NY: Cornell University Press.

Harcourt, Bernard E. (2001) *The Illusion of Order: The False Promise of Broken Windows Policing.* Cambridge, MA: Harvard University Press.

Herbert, Steve. (2001) "Policing the Contemporary City: Fixing Broken Windows or Shoring up Neo-liberalism?" *Theoretical Criminology* 5: 445–466.

Hunt, Alan. (1999) *Governing Morals: A Social History of Moral Regulation.* Cambridge, UK: Cambridge University Press.

Kelling, George L. and Catherine M. Coles. (1996) *Fixing Broken Windows: Restoring Order and Reducing Crime in Our Communities.* New York: The Free Press.

Lees, Loretta, Tom Slater, and Elvin Wyly. (2008) *Gentrification.* New York: Routledge.

Lynch, Mona. (2001) "From the Punitive City to the Gated Community: Security and Segregation across the Social and Penal Landscape," *University of Miami Law Review* 56: 89–112.

Lynch, Mona, Marisa Omori, Aaron Roussell, and Matthew Valasik. (2013) "Policing the 'Progressive' City: The Racialized Geography of Drug Law Enforcement." *Theoretical Criminology* 17: 283–313.

Millie, Andrew. (2008) "Anti-Social Behaviour, Behavioural Expectations and an Urban Aesthetic," *British Journal of Criminology* 48: 379–394.

Morris, Martina and Bruce Western. (1999) "Inequality in Earnings at the Close of the Twentieth Century," *Annual Review of Sociology* 25: 623–652.

Novak, William J. (1996) *The People's Welfare: Law and Regulation in Nineteenth Century America.* Chapel Hill, NC: The University of North Carolina Press.

Passavant, Paul A. (2012) "American Cities and American Political Science," *Perspectives on Politics* 10, 3: 742–747.

Peck, Jamie and Adam Tickell. (2002) "Neoliberalizing Space," *Antipode* 34: 380–404.

Raco, Mike. (2003) "Remaking Place and Securitizing Space: Urban Regeneration and the Strategies, Tactics and Practices of Policing in the UK," *Urban Studies* 40: 1869–1887.

Sassen, Saskia. (2002) *The Global City.* Princeton: Princeton University Press.

Smith, Neil. (1996) *The New Urban Frontier: Gentrification and the Revanchist City.* New York: Routledge.

Stewart, Gary. (1998) "Black Codes and Broken Windows: The Legacy of Racial Hegemony in Anti-Gang Civil Injunctions," *The Yale Law Journal,* 107, 7 (May): 2249–2280.

Suk, Jeannie. (2006) "Criminal Law Comes Home," *The Yale Law Journal* 116, 2: 2–70.

von Mahs, Jurgen. (2005) "The Sociospatial Exclusion of Single Homeless People in Berlin and Los Angeles," *American Behavioral Scientist* 48: 928–960.

Wacquant, Loic. (2001) "The Advent of the Penal State is Not a Destiny," *Social Justice* 28, 3: 81–88.

Wacquant, Loic. (2003) "Toward a Dictatorship over the Poor? Notes on the Penalization of Poverty in Brazil," *Punishment and Society* 5, 2: 197–205.

Wilson, James Q. and George F. Kelling. (1982) "The Police and Neighborhood Safety," *Atlantic Monthly,* May, pp. 28–38.

Wolch, Jennifer and Michael Dear. (1993) *Malign Neglect: Homelessness in an American City.* San Francisco: Jossey-Bass.

Wyly, Elvin and Daniel Hammel. (1999) "Islands of Decay in Seas of Renewal: Urban Policy and the Resurgence of Gentrification," *Housing Policy Debate* 10: 711–777.

32

THE RISE OF INCARCERATION AMONG THE POOR WITH MENTAL ILLNESSES

How neoliberal policies contribute

Jessica K. Camp[1] and Eileen Trzcinski

In the United States, incarceration has often played a major role in the policy towards poor Americans who have mental health disorders. Fluctuations in incarceration rates among those with mental illnesses have historically been framed by changes in capitalism, transformation in the labor market, and public attitudes towards the poor. In the United States, asylums, rather than jails or prisons, were once the primary form of incarceration. The goal of deinstitutionalization, as mandated by the Community Mental Health Centers Act of 1963 and Community Mental Health Centers Act Amendment of 1965, was to move those with mental illnesses out of state-run hospitals and into the community where they could receive adequate treatment and engage in recovery. Unfortunately, as neoliberal policies have expanded, both globally and in the United States, many poor individuals with mental health problems are finding themselves re-incarcerated in jails and prisons. This chapter will discuss the historical context of incarceration among those with mental illnesses and how the expansion of neoliberal globalism contributes to increased incarceration rates of the poor with psychiatric illnesses today.

Neoliberal is defined as a modified form of liberalism that tends to favor free-market capitalism ("Neoliberal," 2013). Neoliberal policies in the United States generally focus on the deregulation of business and finance, both domestically and globally, to allow for the expansion of free-market economies (Kotz, 2009). Neoliberals, or individuals who support neoliberal capitalism, tend to believe that governments should limit their involvement with market forces, protect property rights, and support corporate freedoms (De Vogli, 2011).

The expansion of neoliberal policies that have contributed to increased incarceration for individuals with psychiatric disorders in the United States is not unique, but instead represents a re-emergence of policies towards individuals with mental illnesses that have historical precedence. Capitalistic free-market systems experience tension providing for those who experience poverty and have limited access to the basic needs and the cost of providing support. Due to this, as the underlying structure of the market changes, so do the attitudes towards the disadvantaged. During times that policy has focused on maximizing business and capital profits, the incarceration rates among those with mental illnesses have risen. Alternatively, when policies in the United States have focused on the importance of providing social services, there have been decreases in incarceration rates among those with psychiatric disorders.

The rise of industrial capitalism and incarceration

At the end of the 1700s in the United States, the industrial revolution was contributing to growth in the populations of many major cities. The expansion of industry created a demand for cheap labor that drew immigrants to the United States and farmers to the cities. The changing demographics contributed to communities becoming increasingly unwilling to provide care since most of the newcomers were poor and needy. As the public attitudes towards the poor and disabled became less tolerant, institutions, such as almshouses, became an attractive solution to policy makers as a method to manage the poor. Shifts in civil law centered on aiding economic development which made it important to distinguish between the able-bodied poor and non-able-bodied poor (Brown, 1985). This distinction, between the abled and the disabled, led to communities making decisions about which poor individuals were considered deserving of aid and which were forced to work to receive assistance (Grob, 1994). The poor with mental illnesses were categorized as being members of the non-deserving poor, which meant they were obligated to work to receive any type of assistance. As the capitalist system continued to demand cheap labor, work became compulsory, and the poor who would not, or could not, participate in the workhouses were left unprotected to starve or were placed in jail (Brown, 1985). Foucault (1965) notes that the seventeenth and eighteenth centuries were a critical time for individuals with mental health disorders since incarceration became the punishment reserved for those who were not working. The development of "enormous houses of confinement" and their use on those with mental illnesses was

> the moment when madness was perceived on the social horizon of poverty, of incapacity for work, of inability to integrate with the group; the moment when madness began to rank among the problems of the city. The new meanings assigned to poverty, the importance given to the obligation to work, and all the ethical values that are linked to labor, ultimately determined the experience of madness and inflected its course.
>
> (p. 61)

Instead of individuals with psychiatric disorders being recognized as dissimilar to minor criminals, the poor, the elderly, orphans, and other groups in need of assistance, "society now lumped them together because of their common refusal [or inability] to work" (Midelfort, 1995, p. 120).

Incarceration as treatment

At their inception, psychiatric hospitals focused on using moral treatment, believing that psychiatric illness was caused, in part, by the stresses of the new industrial world and that rest and separation from this world promoted recovery. This approach initially appeared to have high success rates as the few, often well-to-do clients who were hospitalized seemed to recover and were able to return home (Rothman, 1990, p. 128). In reality, the exact rates of recovery during this time are dubious since psychiatrists often exaggerated their successes. Still, believing that doctors had found a way to "cure" mental illnesses encouraged states to rapidly develop mental hospitals across the United States (Rothman, 1990, p. 129).

Between 1863 and 1880, states nearly completely replaced families and communities in the role of caring for "dependents," especially those who were poor and had psychiatric disorders (Grob, 1983). By the end of the 1800s, asylums became overwhelmed by the number of individuals who needed care. As they became increasingly crowded, asylums quickly changed from focusing on treatment to becoming custodial institutions (Grob, 1966). Many of the psychiatric hospitals were little better than jails—a tool of last resort for those who had no other resources and had the most serious psychiatric conditions (Grob, 1983). Since psychiatric hospitals rarely discharged patients, they could no longer claim that they were treatment facilities and their existence became justified in other ways, such as providing a level of protection to society (Grob, 1966). Eugenicists during this time argued that if individuals with mental disabilities were left within the community, they would contribute to the "debasement and deterioration of the American people" and contended that individuals with mental health disorders were unable to function in a competitive industrial economy (Snyder and Mitchell, 2006, p. 69). In this way, incarceration in asylums was rationalized as good for the general public and as a necessary protective factor for individuals with mental illnesses who were framed as being unable to handle the stresses of work and society.

Policy and deinstitutionalization

By the end of World War II, President Truman signed the National Mental Health Act, which for the first time involved the federal government, in conjunction with states, as responsible for the provision of mental health care (Armour, 1981). This Act was crucial because it provided the funding that created the National Institute of Mental Health (NIMH), trained mental health professionals, encouraged mental health research, and extended aid to states to pay for additional psychiatric services (Foley and Sharfstein, 1983). In short, this funding constructed several positive changes in the field of mental health care because it underwrote the research that highlighted the detrimental nature of incarceration on successful recovery from mental illness and provided the resources necessary for scientists to create psychotropic medications (Harcourt, 2011). Also, it allowed for the dissemination of these new scientific findings to mental health professionals, academics, and the general public.

By 1955, asylums became the primary form of incarceration in the United States, housing nearly 560,000 individuals with mental illnesses, most of whom were poor (Mechanic, 1987). Although there were several years of debate about funding and feasibility, in 1963 the Community Mental Health Centers Act was signed into law by President Kennedy (Foley and Sharfstein, 1983). Two years later, President Johnson signed the Community Mental Health Centers Act Amendment into law as a part of the Great Society and the War on Poverty programs. These Acts, in conjunction with the development of several new social welfare programs developed under the Great Society, such as Medicaid and Medicare, promoted a rapid change towards deinstitutionalization and movement of mentally ill persons away from asylums. Between 1955 and 1980 the number of individuals incarcerated in asylums and mental hospitals decreased by 75% (Harcourt, 2011).

Problems with deinstitutionalization

The rapid rate of deinstitutionalization led to many individuals with mental illnesses being placed in nursing homes, general hospitals, and even the street, since little thought had gone into where the former patients would go after having been released from state hospitals (Scull, 1982). States, which had viewed asylums and mental hospitals as a drain on finances and resources, supported the movement towards community treatment and other federally funded alternatives as a way to manage rising costs (Rose, 1979). As stated by Scull (1989), "particularly in the United States the precipitous decline in mental hospital population from the mid-1960s onwards has been matched by an equally dramatic upsurge in the numbers of psychiatrically impaired residents in nursing homes" (p. 319). Since states did not, or were not, able to imme-diately invest needed funds into building the necessary community resources, individuals with mental illness remained without treatment support. Public support for deinstitutionalization wavered as communities began to become concerned with the level of risk and danger of hav-ing the seriously mentally ill untreated and on the streets (Carpenter, 2000).

Re-incarceration of the mentally ill

Incarceration rates of individuals with mental illness in jails and prisons rose following the dein-stitutionalization movement and have remained high. Recent estimates show that nearly three times more mentally ill individuals reside in jails and prisons than receive treatment in hospitals (Treatment Advocacy Center, 2009). Those with mental illness who become incarcerated are also disproportionately poor, uninsured, and members of minority groups (U.S. Department of Health and Human Services, 2005). In 2006, the U.S. Department of Justice reported that about 73% to 75% of incarcerated women and 55% to 63% of incarcerated men were identified as having mental health problems. When examining the relationship between poverty, mental health, and arrests, the U.S. Department of Health and Human Services (2010) reported that approximately 20% of all individuals who end up in jails or prisons experienced both mental health symptoms and homelessness prior to their arrest.

In three main ways the expansion of neoliberal globalism in the 1980s has an effect on the ris-ing rates of incarceration among individuals with mental illnesses. First, neoliberal globalization has contributed to a decrease in employment opportunities for the poor and working class, especially among groups who have historically experienced discrimination in the labor market. Second, the rising unemployment caused by neoliberal globalization has been met with policies that have: (1) focused on the "responsibility" for needy individuals to work to receive social assistance, and (2) been framed as "tough on crime," instituting social control among the working-class unemployed and underemployed in post-industrial urban centers. Lastly, neoliberal policies have pushed for cuts to community treatment programs for poor individuals with mental health disorders. The next section will discuss the emergence of neoliberal globalism and each of the four ways it con-tributes to incarceration of poor individuals with mental health disorders.

Current emergence of neoliberal globalization

Since the late 1970s and 1980s, the rise of neoliberal policies in the United States and interna-tionally has influenced a global push towards the deregulation of trade, investments, and capital markets (De Vogli, 2011). This trend in policy is worrisome because neoliberal policies allow transnational corporations and the extremely wealthy to greatly influence global market forces (De Vogli, 2011; Walby, 2011). This influence is used to further corporate freedoms, often at the direct cost to individual and social freedoms, contributing to rising levels of inequality both within, and between, countries (De Vogli, 2011; Walby, 2011).

Neoliberal policies are not only targeted towards minimizing government regulation of the market, but also focus on the elimination of all systems that have power to challenge corpo-rate control, such as labor unions, social welfare programs, and government-run human service programs (De Vogli, 2011). For example, labor unions have the ability to directly control corpo-rations because they can be used by laborers to bargain for higher wages or better work conditions at a direct cost to profits for large businesses and wealthy business owners (Minor, 2012).

Social welfare and government-run human service programs, on the other hand, can be used to regulate the labor market because they have an indirect ability to control corporations. Social welfare decommodifies basic needs, or allows individuals to access basic needs (food, clothing, shelter) or needed services (health care, mental health services, job training), independent of their participation in the labor market (Esping-Andersen, 1990, p.21–22). Neoliberal policies ensure that welfare only offers the most meager resources, with payments remaining below what is actually needed to provide for the most basic needs. For the working-class poor this means that "any job at any wage" is a preferable alternative to accepting welfare, guaranteeing that there will always be an influx of workers willing to do the "harshest work for the least reward" (Piven and Cloward, 1971, p. xix). Inadequate social protections allow businesses and corporations to keep wages exceedingly low, especially for low-skilled work positions. For individuals who are unwilling to work, refuse to accept meager wages, are limited in their ability to work, or unable to find jobs, incarceration acts as an extreme form of social control that reaches beyond the labor market.

Poverty and unemployment. As corporations in the United States have become increasingly globalized, they have outsourced factory and manufacturing jobs to countries where laborers are not unionized, can be more easily exploited, and can be paid less (Gonzales, 2011). The exodus of jobs from the former manufacturing centers in the United States has been devastating for many cities, as most of the working-class population has been left without the same types of employment opportunities that were common prior to the rise of globalism (Western and Wildeman, 2009).

The reduction of employment opportunities has been especially hard for poor, working-class individuals diagnosed with mental health issues because they face additional discrimination and barriers to employment that are not faced by other poor individuals. The foremost of these challenges is that individuals with mental illnesses continue to experience stigma and discrimination from employers who may fear that such individuals may not be as productive as other employees or that they may be unpredictable or dangerous. Although these eugenics-era beliefs have been substantially rebutted by current medicine and science, discrimination remains (Parry, 1997; Stefan, 2001, 2002). Current employment rates and wages remain much lower for individuals who are disabled when compared to the rest of Americans, while poverty levels remain higher (see Table 32.1). Also, among working-aged women and men with self-reported mental disabilities, the chances of living in poverty are nearly two times higher (see Table 32.2).

Americans with Disabilities Act. During the 1990s, a renewed emphasis was placed on the labor market participation of disabled individuals who experienced exclusion from the labor market. The Americans with Disabilities Act, passed in 1990 and amended in 2008, was intended to remove barriers to labor force participation of those with mental and physical limitations by prohibiting discrimination. The ADA required employers to make reasonable accommodations for individuals with disabilities so long as employers did not face "undue hardship" by doing so. Unfortunately, the ADA has had little effect on reducing the unemployment rate among individuals with mental illnesses or in challenging wage discrimination. In fact, individuals with mental health disabilities continue to be less likely to be employed and tend to receive lower wages in exchange for their labor (see Table 32.3). Additionally, individuals with mental disabilities are less likely to be able to access long-term, year-round employment positions that are frequently paired with higher wages and health insurance (see Table 32.4). As stated by Gates and Akabas (2011), "the employment experience of people with serious mental health conditions continues to be a search for acceptance by and inclusion into the world of work."

Table 32.1 Selected economic characteristics for the civilian noninstitutionalized population by disability status in 2011

Subject	Without a disability	With a disability
Employment status		
Employed	64.4%	21.5%
Not in labor force	28.7%	73.4%
Earnings in past 12 months (in 2009 inflation-adjusted dollars for individuals with earnings)		
Median earnings	30,285	19,735
Poverty status in the last 12 months		
Earnings below 100% of the poverty level	12.8%	21.7%
Earnings between 100% and 149% of the poverty level	8.3%	14.6%
Earnings at or above 150% of the poverty level	78.9%	63.7%

Note: Data from the American Community Survey, retrieved on January 2, 2013 from http://factfinder2.census.gov/, Table S1811. Selected Economic Characteristics for the Civilian Noninstitutionalized Population by Disability Status (U.S. Census Bureau, 2013).

Table 32.2 Predicted percentage of family poverty for working aged individuals (aged 18–61) with mental disabilities in 2010[a,b]

	No disability	CI		Mental disability	CI	
		Lower	Upper		Lower	Upper
Men	13%	13%	14%	25%	24%	27%
Women	16%	16%	16%	30%	28%	31%

[a] Authors' calculations using data from the Survey of Income and Program Participation (SIPP) Core and Functional Limitation Disability Topical Modules 2008–2012 (U.S. Census Bureau, 2010). Estimates conducted using SPSS, Version 20 Complex Samples module.
[b] Only White and Black race categories were included due to underrepresentation in other race categories, particularly among disabled individuals.

Table 32.3 Average monthly income earned among individuals aged 18–61 with mental disabilities in CPI-adjusted dollars in 2010[a,b,c]

	No disability	CI		Mental disability	CI	
		Lower	Upper		Lower	Upper
Men	$3,901	$3,859	$3,943	$2,803	$2,651	$2,955
Women	$2,976	$2,940	$3,013	$2,315	$2,195	$2,435

[a] Authors' calculations using data from the Survey of Income and Program Participation (SIPP) Core and Functional Limitation Disability Topical Modules 2008–2012 (U.S. Census Bureau, 2010). Estimates conducted using SPSS, Version 20 Complex Samples module.
[b] Only White and Black race categories were included due to underrepresentation in other race categories, particularly among disabled individuals.
[c] Analysis conducted examining only individuals who had at least one dollar of earned income.

Table 32.4 Percentage of individuals with mental disabilities aged 18–61 employed at the same job for the past year in 2010[a,b]

	No disability	CI		Mental disability	CI	
		Lower	Upper		Lower	Upper
Men	76%	74%	78%	23%	22%	26%
Women	78%	77%	79%	22%	21%	23%

[a] Authors' calculations using data from the Survey of Income and Program Participation (SIPP) Core and Functional Limitation Disability Topical Modules 2008–2012 (U.S. Census Bureau, 2010). Estimates conducted using SPSS, Version 20 Complex Samples module.
[b] Only White and Black race categories were included due to underrepresentation in other race categories, particularly among disabled individuals.

Criminalization of social unrest. Rising unemployment levels in the 1970s and 1980s were accompanied by rising social unrest, as many working-class individuals became unable to find employment that would allow them to provide for their family's needs (Piven and Cloward, 1971, p. 390). As politicians became increasingly worried that rising unemployment could cause riots and social discontent, such as that which occurred in the 1930s and 1960s, social unrest became increasingly criminalized in the 1980s. The use of "tough on crime" rhetoric to promote new policies, such as the "war on drugs" strategies that were implemented in most urban centers, has resulted in the incarceration of many poor, minority, and working-age individuals (Alexander, 2010; Corva, 2008; Gonzales, 2011). According to the U.S. Bureau of Justice, the number of individuals in jails or prisons in 1974 was relatively small, with only 216,000 people incarcerated (Bonczar, 2003). In 1986, as neoliberal and "tough on crime" policies became increasingly popular, the incarceration rates nearly doubled, with 524,000 incarcerated (Bonczar, 2003). By 2009, 1,613,740 individuals were lodged in state and federal prisons in the United States (Glaze, 2010). Since the 1980s, drug offenses have been among the largest categories of arrests (Lurigio, 2011). Increasingly punitive crime-control policies, coupled with strict drug laws, have been especially detrimental for individuals with psychiatric issues, since there are "high rates of comorbidity between mental health and substance use disorders" (Lurigio, 2011).

Cuts to social programs. One of the main reasons the expansion of neoliberal policies has directly contributed to increased incarceration rates among those who are poor with mental illnesses is due to the drastic reductions in funding for social welfare and public services and the push to privatize mental health services. One of the largest cuts to social welfare programs in the last 20 years is the Personal Responsibility and Work Opportunity Reconciliation Act (PRWORA) of 1996. PRWORA created drastic changes to welfare programs for families in poverty by reducing payments and capping the total time a family could receive assistance to five years. This time limit does not take into account the parent's ability to access viable employment opportunities in the current market. In several ways, PRWORA mimics the policies implemented during the rise of industrial capitalism that created the workhouses because it ensures that for poor families that have run out of welfare, no matter the wage or the tasks required, work is compulsory.

In conjunction with reforms to welfare, reduction of funding for public services, especially following the Great Recession of 2008, have undermined the ability of community mental health systems to provide adequate care to the growing number of poor and uninsured mental health consumers (Harcourt, 2011; Johnson et al., 2011). As community treatment programs struggle with dwindling finances, they must increasingly rely on institutions such as the police and hospitals to fill the growing gap between existing and needed mental health services. The U.S. Department of Health and Human Services (2009) notes that in recent years the police have become the most common first responders in the event of a mental health crisis. Unfortunately, interactions with the police can be especially traumatic for individuals experiencing mental health crises and increase their chances of being incarcerated (Steadman et al., 2000; Teplin, 1992, 2000; Tucker et al., 2008).

Conclusion

In conclusion, in the United States incarceration rates among the poor with mental illnesses have risen during times when there have been changes in the underlying capitalist market system, such as during the rise of industrial capitalism and neoliberal capitalism. This has occurred, in part, because of the capitalist market demands for sources of cheap labor and its need to expand the rights of corporations and businesses to maximize profits. To meet both these goals, the capitalist market must not only exert control over the working-class poor, who are paid the lowest wages for the hardest forms of work, but also outside of the labor market to create disincentives to any alternative other than accepting low-wage labor. This disincentive, especially for poor individuals with mental illness, has historically been and is currently incarceration.

Unlike other poor and disenfranchised groups, individuals with psychiatric disabilities have momentarily benefited from a deinstitutionalisation movement that promoted the de-incarceration of many individuals with mental health disorders from state-run asylums and hospitals (Harcourt, 2011). Unfortunately, the goals of deinstitutionalization have never been fully realized, as these policy changes have been driven mostly by States' financial concerns rather than humanitarian ones. Due to this, incarceration rates among individuals who experience poverty and have psychiatric diagnoses remains high.

Still, a trend has been illuminated that shows that during times that U.S. policy has been focused on the expansion of business and corporate rights, incarceration levels among the poor with mental illnesses have increased, while the times that policy has focused on the provision of needed social programs and services, such as mental health care, incarceration rates have decreased. Currently, neoliberal policies have resulted in the imprisonment of individuals who experience poverty and mental illnesses. The implementation of new policies that are centered on treatment, expand social welfare support, create employment and educational opportunities, and enforce wage equality are crucial for fully realizing de-incarceration for the poor with mental illnesses in the United States.

Note

1 Dr. Jessica K. Camp, Ph.D., LMSW, is an Assistant Professor in Social Work at the University of Michigan-Flint. All correspondence regarding this chapter should be directed to the University of Michigan-Flint, School of Education and Human Services, Social Work Department, 454 David French Hall, 303 E. Kearsley Street, Flint, Michigan 48502 or jkcamp@umflint.edu.

References

Alexander, M. (2010). *The new Jim Crow: Mass incarceration in the age of colorblindness.* New York, NY: The New Press.
Armour, P.K. (1981). *The cycles of social reform.* Washington, DC: University Press of America.

Bonczar, T. (2003). *Prevalence of imprisonment in the U.S. population, 1974–2001.* Bureau of Justice Statistics Bulletin, NCJ 197976. Washington, DC: U.S. Department of Justice, Bureau of Justice Statistics, August 2003.

Brown, P. (1985). *Mental health care and social policy.* Boston, MA: Routledge and Kegan Paul.

Carpenter, M. (2000). "It's a small world": Mental health policy under welfare capitalism since 1945. *Sociology of Health and Illness,* 22(5), 602–620.

Corva, D. (2008). Neoliberal globalization and the war on drugs: Transnationalizing illiberal governance in the Americas. *Political Geography,* 27, 176–193.

De Vogli, R. (2011). Neoliberal globalization and health in a time of economic crisis. *Social Theory and Health,* 9, 311–325.

Esping-Andersen, G. (1990). *The three worlds of welfare capitalism.* Princeton, NJ: Princeton University Press.

Foley, H.A., and Sharfstein, S.S. (1983). *Madness and government: Who cares for the mentally ill?* Washington, DC: American Psychiatric Press.

Foucault, M. (1965). *Madness and civilization: A history of insanity in the age of reason.* New York, NY: Random House.

Gates, L.B., and Akabas, S.H. (2011). Inclusion of people with mental health disabilities into the workplace: Accommodations as a social process. In I.Z. Schultz and E.S. Rogers (eds) *Work accommodation and retention in mental health* (pp. 375–391). New York, NY: Springer.

Glaze, L.E. (2010). *Correctional populations in the United States, 2009.* Bureau of Justice Statistics Bulletin, NCJ 231681. Washington, DC: U.S. Department of Justice, Bureau of Justice Statistics, December 2010.

Gonzales, R. (2011). *Race, money, and power: Racializing crime and the political economy of the U.S. criminal justice system.* Proceedings from the National Conference on Undergraduate Research. New York, NY: Ithaca College.

Grob, G.N. (1966). The state mental hospital in mid-nineteenth-century America: A social analysis. *The American Psychologist,* 21(6), 510–523.

Grob, G.N. (1983). *Mental illness and American society, 1875–1940.* Princeton, NJ: Princeton University Press.

Grob, G.N. (1994). *The mad among us: A history of the care of America's mentally ill.* New York, NY: The Free Press.

Harcourt, B.E. (2011). Reducing mass incarceration: Lessons from the deinstitutionalization of mental hospitals in the 1960s. *John M. Olin Law and Economic Working Paper,* 542.

Johnson, N., Olif, P., and Williams, E. (2011). *An update on state budget cuts: At least 46 states have imposed cuts that hurt vulnerable residents and cause job loss.* Washington, DC: Center on Budget and Policy Priorities. Retrieved on November 27, 2012, from http://www.cbpp.org/files/3-13-08sfp.pdf.

Kotz, D.M. (2009). The financial and economic crisis of 2008: A systemic crisis of neoliberal capitalism. *Review of Radical Political Economics,* 4, 305–317.

Lurigio, A.J. (2011). People with serious mental illness in the criminal justice system: Causes, consequences, and correctives. *The Prison Journal,* 91(3), 66S–86S.

Mechanic, D. (1987). Correcting misconceptions in mental health policy: Strategies for improved care of the seriously mentally ill. *The Milbank Quarterly,* 65(2), 203–230.

Midelfort, E.H.C. (1995). Madness and civilization in early modern Europe: A reappraisal of Michel Foucault. In B. Smart (eds), *Michel Foucault II: Critical Assessments: Rationality, Power and Subjectivity* (pp. 117–133). New York, NY: Routledge.

Minor, D. (2012). Poverty, productivity, and public health: The effects of "Right to Work" laws on key standards of living. *Thought and Action,* 16–29.

Neoliberal. (2013). In Oxford English Dictionary, online. Retrieved January 8, 2012, from http://oxforddictionaries.com/us/definition/american_english/neoliberal?q=neoliberal.

Parry, J.W. (1997). *Mental disabilities and the Americans with Disabilities Act* (2nd ed.). Washington, DC: The American Bar Association.

Piven, F.F., and Cloward, R.A. (1971). *Regulating the poor: The functions of public welfare.* New York, NY: Vintage Books.

Rose, S.M. (1979). Deciphering deinstitutionalization: Complexities in policy and program analysis. *Health and Society,* 54(4), 429–460.

Rothman, D.J. (1990). *The discovery of the asylum: Social order and disorder in the new republic.* New York, NY: Walter de Gruyter, Inc.

Scull, A.T. (1982). The asylum as community or the community as asylum: Paradoxes and contradictions of mental health care. *Mental Illness: Changes and Trends*, 329–350.

Scull, A.T. (1989). The asylum as community or the community as asylum: Paradoxes and the contradictions of mental health care. In A.T. Scull (eds), *Social order/mental disorder: Anglo-American psychiatry in historical perspective* (pp. 300–329). Berkeley, CA: University of California Press.

Snyder, S.L., and Mitchell, D.T. (2006). *Cultural locations of disability*. Chicago, IL: The University of Chicago Press.

Steadman, H.J., Deane, M.W., Borum, R., and Morrissey, J.P. (2000). Comparing outcomes of major models of police responses to mental health emergencies. *Psychiatric Services*, 51(5), 645–649.

Stefan, S. (2001). *Unequal rights: Discrimination against people with mental disabilities and the Americans with Disabilities Act*. Washington, DC: American Psychological Association.

Stefan, S. (2002). *Hollow promises: Employment discrimination against people with mental disabilities*. Washington, DC: American Psychological Association.

Teplin, L.A. (2000). Keeping the peace: Police discretion and mentally ill persons. *National Institute of Justice Journal*, 244, 8–15.

Tepin, L.A., and Pruett, N.S. (1992). Police as street corner psychiatrist: Managing the mentally ill. *International Journal of Law and Psychiatry*, 15, 139–156.

Treatment Advocacy Center. (2009). *Jails and prisons*. Retrieved on February 28, 2011, from http://www.treatmentadvocacycenter.org/resources/consequences-of-lack-of-treatment/jail/1371.

Tucker, A.S., Van Hasselt, V.B., and Russell, S.A. (2008). Law enforcement response to the mentally ill: An evaluative review. *Brief Treatment and Crisis Intervention*, 8(3), 236–250.

U.S. Census Bureau. (2010). *Survey of Income and Program Participation (SIPP)*. Retrieved on December 12, 2012, from http://www.census.gov/programs-surveys/sipp/data.html.

U.S. Census Bureau. (2013). *Selected economic characteristics for the civilian noninstitutionalized population by disability status*. Retrieved on January 2, 2013, from http://factfinder2.census.gov/faces/tableservices/jsf/pages/productview.xhtml?src=bkmk.

U.S. Department of Health and Human Services. (2005). *Building bridges: Consumers and representatives of the mental health and criminal justice systems in dialogue*. Retrieved on August 7, 2014, from http://store.samhsa.gov/product/Consumers-and-Representatives-of-the-Mental-Health-and-Criminal-Justice-Systems-in-Dialogue/SMA05-4067.

U.S. Department of Health and Human Services. (2009). *Practice guidelines: Core elements in responding to mental health crisis*. Rockville, MD: U.S. Department of Health and Human Services..

U.S. Department of Health and Human Services. (2010). *Current statistics on the prevalence and characteristics of people experiencing homelessness in the United States*. Rockville, MD: U.S. Department of Health and Human Services.

U.S. Department of Justice. (2006). *Mental health problems of prison and jail inmates*. Retrieved on December 19, 2011, from http://bjs.ojp.usdoj.gov/content/pub/pdf/mhppji.pdf.

Walby, S. (2011). Globalization and multiple inequalities. In E. Chow, M. Segal, and T. Lin (eds), *Analyzing gender, intersectionality, and multiple inequalities: Global-transnational and local contexts* (pp. 17–33). Bingley, EN: Emerald Group Publishing Limited.

Western, B., and Wildeman, C. (2009). Punishment, inequality, and the future of mass incarceration. *Kansas Law Review*, 27, 851–877.

33

CLASS, CRIME, AND SOCIAL CONTROL IN THE CONTEMPORARY UNITED STATES

Spencer Headworth

Introduction

Since the 1980s, regulatory and law enforcement activity in the United States has steadily polarized. Less effort has been devoted to exerting social control on the potential illegal actions of more advantaged people, and a combination of policy decisions and broader changes in political economy has produced a situation in which social control over the economically advantaged is markedly attenuated. Simultaneously, the state, with substantial aid from third-party policing (Desmond and Valdez, 2013), has carried out a far-reaching campaign to increase social control over the actions of less advantaged people, creating in the process an unprecedented punishment regime.

These trends are in many ways two sides of a single sociopolitical coin. As neoliberal arguments about the virtues of the market took hold, support for efforts to address the social causes of street crimes withered. These movements share a certain ideological core, in which collective responsibility is minimized and individual responsibility championed. The common social vision is atomistic, with individuals understood to be acting in clear separation from each other. The pernicious, often obscured threat of financial crime victimization may be less dramatic than the immediately palpable and politically mobilizable threat of street crime. Members of the upper class are valorized, explicitly and implicitly, as having earned their dominant position, and the unimpeded market action of bankers and traders is billed as necessary for economic prosperity. In this market-first mindset, the poor represent an unproductive, parasitic segment of society, and "tough on crime" policies that demonize the urban poor, especially people of color, provide political pay dirt, even while street crime rates decline, as they did precipitously throughout the 1990s and beyond (Zimring, 2007).

In this chapter, I focus primarily on two populations as representatives of the poles that orient this neoliberal approach to criminal justice: elite traders, bankers, and other financial sector actors whose actions, inactions, and sometimes crimes hold massive implications for the condition of the larger economy and the lives of millions, in the United States and beyond, and the urban poor, who have been the primary focus of punitive policies directed at street crime. After describing the two offending categories of interest, white-collar and street crime, I analyze contemporary trends in regulation and enforcement directed at different ends of the U.S. class structure, drawing comparisons over time and between social groups. I conclude with a discussion of the recent crises related to both sides of this changing picture of social control and a look toward the future.

Conceptualizing white-collar crime and street crime

The pedigree of the idea of white-collar crime makes drawing its precise boundaries a difficult and at times contentious task. The term itself was coined by sociologist and criminologist Edwin Sutherland in the 1930s, and his ([1949] 1983) monograph on the topic in the next decade found a place among the best-known and most influential criminological works of the twentieth century (Geis and Goff, 1983). In *White Collar Crime*, Sutherland defines the subject of his inquiry thusly: "White collar crime may be defined approximately as a crime committed by a person of respectability and high social status in the course of his occupation" ([1949] 1983: 7).

More recently, the Federal Bureau of Investigation defined white-collar crimes as

> those illegal acts which are characterized by deceit, concealment, or violation of trust and which are not dependent upon the application or threat of physical force or violence. Individuals and organizations commit these acts to obtain money, property, or services; to avoid the payment or loss of money or services; or to secure personal or business advantage.
>
> (USDOJ, 1989: 3)

This definition reflects many experts' misgivings about a conceptualization that, like Sutherland's, fundamentally depends on the attributes of the offender—particular occupational or socioeconomic status—and defines the concept instead in terms of the characteristics of the acts involved.

Susan Shapiro (1990) argues that the key attribute of white-collar crime, as the FBI's definition reflects, is the abuse of trust. She says, "[White-collar criminals] have refined the modus operandi of pedestrian property crime" (p. 350). "Ordinary" or street crimes do not depend on established trust relationships. For example, in the property crimes most analogous to white-collar crime, property is illegitimately obtained via force or its threat, stealth, or trespass; however, in place of these techniques, white-collar criminals leverage positions of trust in the pursuit of profit.

The dependence of white-collar crime on agent–principal relationships means that perpetrators are often individuals of elevated social and occupational status, although this is not always the case; crimes like tax and social security fraud are good examples of white-collar offenses whose perpetrators commonly vary widely across the socioeconomic spectrum. The financial sector actors who populate the pole of the contemporary criminal justice orientation I describe are at the very peak of the U.S. socioeconomic structure. They also command a unique agency role in relationship to others, in the United States and beyond. At the immediate level, they operate as agents for the individuals and collectives whose money they hold, transfer, and invest. From a broader perspective, however, they operate as *de facto* agents for a much more encompassing population.

Financial markets have shaped the transition to a post-industrial society since the 1980s. Large manufacturers set the tone and standard for middle-class jobs through the mid-twentieth century, providing stable long-term employment, solid health insurance, and pensions. These corporations also enjoyed considerable influence in the policy arena. Now, the corporate capitalism model has atrophied, giving way to what Gerald Davis (2009) labels "the new financial capitalism." Since the 1950s, the proportion of U.S. households owning stock more than quintupled, from less than 10% to more than half. Mutual fund ownership grew from around one in twenty households in 1980 to around one in two by 2000; this expansion translated into growth in mutual fund companies' assets from $1 trillion to nearly $7 trillion during the 1990s. Meanwhile, savings account ownership dropped precipitously, from more than three-quarters to less than half of households; as Davis puts it, "'savers,' in short, became 'investors'" (p. 18).

This movement has created new and remarkable ties between the state of financial markets and the organization and health of U.S. society. From industry-based corporate capitalism has emerged market-based financial capitalism. Financial market conditions and shareholder value have replaced corporate direction as the underlying motors of large-scale economic events. Advocates for the move toward a finance-centered economy have attached the label of "the ownership society" to the multifaceted trend. And indeed, personal ownership is a central theme of the interrelated changes that have characterized the U.S. economy over the last 30 years, from the overwhelming emphasis on home ownership that helped create the subprime-mortgage-centered economic collapse of 2008 to the transition away from corporate pensions to employee-owned 401(k) retirement accounts. In such a "portfolio society" (Davis, 2009) the domestic implications of financial market action are thoroughgoing, reaching from individual households to the national economy. The 2008 crisis provides a prime example, as the proliferation of subprime-mortgage lending and the construction and sale of complex financial instruments based on these loans forced millions of homes into foreclosure and precipitated the worst economic collapse since the Great Depression (see Angelides et al., 2011; Morgenson and Rosner, 2011).

U.S. financiers' actions also have major global implications. In the second half of the twentieth century, American bankers and their European allies created an unprecedented worldwide economic financial system, built largely on the argument that international economic cooperation among capitalist countries was a necessary bulwark against Soviet influence (Frieden, 1987;,2006). Subsequent technological advances have linked the world in a high-speed network of free-flowing financial exchange powered by electronic trading (see Zaloom, 2006), in which national economic outcomes are profoundly interconnected, as dramatically demonstrated in the swift global diffusion of the effects of the 2008 U.S. mortgage collapse. In portfolio society, thus, elite financial actors are in important ways agents for us all, though most of us may never have explicitly vested trust in them. This situation creates new opportunities for white-collar crime, while at the same time exponentially increasing the potential scope of consequences of such offending.

Street crime, on the contrary, is committed at the individual or interpersonal level. As the term is used here, street crimes constitute the conventional offenses that have been the traditional focus of criminological attention. This class of offenses includes crimes widely considered to be serious, including those involving violence (e.g., homicide, rape, assault, robbery), property (e.g., burglary, larceny, arson), and drugs. The rise of broken-windows and quality-of-life policing strategies has also increased the importance of less serious offenses (e.g., loitering, public intoxication, open container violations) as forms of street crime used selectively in "regulating" particular populations.

In those forms of street crime that involve direct victims, the effects of victimization are just that: direct, immediate, tangible. The consequences of this sort of interpersonal victimization on individuals or families, especially in cases of violent crime, are frequently devastating. The most damaging psychological and physical consequences of victimization are unique to street crime, and are pivotal in the fear of conventional crime as a driver of political action. White-collar victimization has more insidious, less immediately palpable effects. Early on, Sutherland ([1949] 1983: 9) noted that, in addition to costing far more in monetary terms, "white collar crimes violate trust and therefore create distrust, and this lowers social morale and produces social disorganization on a large scale. Ordinary crimes, on the other hand, produce little effect on social institutions or social organization." (See also Shapiro, 1984, 1987.)

There is substantial evidence to suggest that white-collar lawbreakers have historically faced relatively light social consequences compared to their street-crime counterparts (Clinard and Yeager, 1980; Hagan and Parker, 1985; Hagan and Palloni, 1986; Tillman and Pontell, 1992; Kerley and Copes, 2004; Schoepfer et al., 2007; Hagan, 2010).[1] In general, early research linked this pattern of comparatively lax sanctions to a perception that business crimes are not particularly serious, especially when compared to crimes committed directly against individuals (Wheeler et al., 1988). However, more recent studies challenge this view, providing data indicating that both prosecutors (Benson and Cullen, 1998) and ordinary citizens (Holtfreter et al., 2008; Piquero et al., 2008) perceive these different categories of crime as comparably serious and demanding of social control, with the harshest punishments for violent offenders.

As Sutherland ([1949] 1983) pointed out early on, the differential treatment of white-collar lawbreaking is in part a product of the fact that it is often handled by organizations other than mainstream criminal justice agencies. In many cases, these enforcement actions involve coordination across agencies operating at different levels of government (federal, state, and local), and with varying missions and sanctioning authority. Particular characteristics of white-collar crimes relative to street crimes are also important in explaining differences in punishment patterns between the two categories of offenses. The trust inherent to agency relationships creates enormous opportunities for criminal behavior, and the at-a-distance nature of white-collar crimes makes them harder to detect than immediately visible crimes. Crimes of this sort are based on symbolic stand-ins for tangible property—accounting statements, contracts, certificates, and the like—that are easier to manipulate and obfuscate than the resources they represent. They are often carried out within complex organizations, sheltered from the prying eyes of external regulators and enforcement agencies (Shapiro, 1990: 353). Further, effective enforcement in white-collar cases often requires combinations of traditionally separate processes of investigation and prosecution, and conventional criminal justice agencies can be flummoxed by free-wheeling white-collar crimes that transcend jurisdictional boundaries (Schlegel and Weisburd, 1992: 15).

Over recent years, a constellation of social phenomena worked in concert to exacerbate these difficulties of social control, both directly and indirectly. A campaign of deregulation of business in general, and particularly the financial sector, significantly expanded opportunities for committing white-collar crime. Like "tough on crime" measures aimed at increasing social control of the urban poor, these relaxations of social control efforts with regard to financiers enjoyed widespread support from politicians of both major parties. One of the notable early financial deregulations of the neoliberal era was the Depository Institutions Deregulation and Monetary Controls Act (DIDMCA) of 1980. Signed into law by Democratic President Jimmy Carter, this Act began the process of eliminating the caps on interest rates that had been in place since the Great Depression, and aimed to foster competition between banks, savings and loans, and mutual funds. The Garn-St. Germain Act followed shortly after, signed into law by Republican President Ronald Reagan in 1982. This legislation was the centerpiece of an early 1980s initiative to remove restrictions on thrifts, allowing them to engage in new types of transactions and take on new forms of risk. The new latitude provided to thrifts created new opportunities for profits in real estate, creating an early 1980s real estate boom that busted in the mid-1980s (Sherman, 2009).

In 1999, bankers won perhaps their most significant deregulation of the contemporary era, with passage of the Gramm-Leach-Bliley Act. This legislation, sponsored by congressional

Republicans but passed with Democratic support and signed by Democratic President Clinton, repealed crucial portions of the 1933 Glass-Steagall Act. Glass-Steagall was passed in the wake of the Great Depression, and aimed to reduce the risk of economic crisis by prohibiting mergers of investment and commercial banks. Gramm-Leach-Bliley removed these restrictions, permitting the same firms to conduct commercial banking, investment banking, and insurance. This allowed banks to return to the type of speculative, risky financial behaviors that led to the Great Depression, including creating the mortgage-backed securities that precipitated the 2008 crisis. Further exacerbating the climate of risk was the Commodity Futures Modernization Act (CFMA) of 2000. With a similar political pedigree to Gramm-Leach-Bliley, this Act reduced the oversight of federal regulators with regard to these complex debt instruments.

The federal regulators hamstrung by the CFMA, namely the Securities and Exchange Commission (SEC) and the Commodity Futures Trading Commission (CFTC), have historically been at the center of efforts to regulate the financial sector, deterring white-collar crime through policing functions and enforcing the law when violations occurred. In addition to deregulatory policy that reduced their power, these organizations have faced over recent years an exponentially larger and more labyrinthine financial world, without commensurate increases in their own size or capacities. Operating in a globalized banking environment and lubricated by instantaneous electronic trading, traders have rapidly developed financial instruments of truly mind-boggling complexity. Even highly trained enforcement agents are often befuddled by these new products, and find themselves increasingly relying on representatives of the issuing firms to guide them through their intricacies. Clearly, this is less than an ideal scenario for detecting and punishing instances of white-collar crime, and regulators are often at a loss in efforts to do so.

Meanwhile, a systematic campaign directed at the urban poor has focused on tightening social control, with major consequences for the disadvantaged. Driven by "a new collective experience of crime and insecurity" (Garland, 2001: 139), the late modern approach to regulating street crime varies greatly from the emphasis on a liberated marketplace and reduced oversight of market actors that contextualizes contemporary white-collar offending. The approach to street crime is characterized by reductions in efforts to rehabilitate, including rollbacks in mental health, education, and other services for convicted offenders; an emphasis on offender labeling and publicized punishment; and in general harsher, more punitive punishment practices.

Although individuals across the socioeconomic spectrum commit street crimes, regulatory and enforcement policy targeting these offenses has been aimed primarily at the urban poor; in substantial part, the class and racial disparities that characterize prison and jail populations are the product of this orientation. Police, the front-line enforcement figures in street crime contexts, have widely adopted "broken-windows" policing techniques that focus on targeting minor offenses in an effort to instill "law and order" at the neighborhood level. Policing strategies like New York City's infamous "stop and frisk" program and technologically driven initiatives like COMPSTAT are some of the characteristic techniques of this hands-on approach to regulation of the streets.

The primary emblem of the late twentieth- and early twenty-first-century approach to street crime, though, is the prison. The incarcerated population in the United States—overwhelmingly composed of street criminals—began rising precipitously in the mid-1970s, and grew exponentially over subsequent decades. In 1980, 1.8 million U.S. residents were under some form of correctional supervision; by 2007 that number had grown to 7.3 million (Uggen, 2012: 3). The supervised population, then, was about 90% of the size of New York City, and double that of Los Angeles. By the beginning of 2008, more than 1% of U.S. adults were incarcerated in prison or jail—one in 99.1 (Warren, 2008: 5). If the elderly are removed from the calculus, the share of all adults incarcerated grows to around 2% (Gottschalk, 2006: 1). In 2009, 2.3 million people were behind bars—768 out of every 100,000 U.S. residents (Pettit, 2012: 11). These figures make the United States the standalone global leader in incarceration and correctional supervision, both in raw numbers and as a proportion of its total population.

Stark racial/ethnic and class disparities characterize the prison population. African-Americans and Latinos make up two-thirds of those incarcerated in state prisons, and African-American men are eight times more likely to be incarcerated than whites. African-American men are now more likely to serve time in prison than to earn a college degree or serve in the military. Incarceration is also markedly concentrated among the poor and less educated, a trend that translates into shockingly high incarceration rates among the country's most disadvantaged. In 2000, over 11% of all African-American men between 20 and 40—and almost a third of those men who did not complete high school—were in prison or jail (Western, 2006: 15–17). The "cumulative spiral of disadvantage" imposed by incarceration continues after release, with the previously incarcerated facing enormous obstacles to employment, reduced wages, and a wide range of other consequences (Western, 2006). The consequences of mass incarceration extend beyond the individual, and also include major implications for families (Johnson and Waldfogel, 2004; Nurse, 2004; Comfort, 2008; Foster and Hagan, 2009), neighborhoods (Lynch and Sabol, 2004; Massoglia et al., 2013), and democracy (Manza and Uggen, 2008). In total, the mass incarceration regime has played a major role in derailing the promise of the Civil Rights Movement and retarding the movement toward social and economic equality for African-Americans (Pettit, 2012).

Despite the departures in regulatory and enforcement attention to these two polar populations, there are also significant convergences in contemporary efforts to exert social control upon them. The central role of prosecutors is particularly pivotal in both contexts. In their dealings with the state, alleged offenders from both categories are significantly subject to prosecutorial discretion. Prosecutors are the most important actors in determining outcomes in the criminal legal system, and their decisions are enormously consequential in both white-collar and street-crime cases.

Prosecutors have largely unrestricted power in determining whom to charge with crimes and with what crimes to charge them. This discretion has long been significant, but has expanded over recent years as national sentencing guidelines and "tough on crime" legislation like mandatory minimum sentencing laws have reduced judges' authority to make decisions regarding appropriate case outcomes. With judges' hands often tied by sentencing rules, case outcomes depend to a greater degree on the charges prosecutors choose to press. In many cases, prosecutors select charges deliberately, with the intention of offering a lesser charge in exchange for a guilty plea in plea bargaining.

This practice has become essential in the era of broken-windows policing and mass incarceration as hallmark criminal justice strategies used in application to the urban poor. The adversarial legal system of the popular imagination, always to some degree a myth, has further shriveled; now, more than 90% of criminal cases are resolved by plea bargaining, and less than 1% of defendants are ever tried by a jury of their peer. (Alexander, 2010; Devers, 2011). The huge increases in the number of people arrested and charged with street crimes have placed trials to assess guilt completely out of reach as a norm of criminal justice practice. Even with the prevalence of plea bargaining, court dockets around the country are heavily backlogged, and individuals who have not been convicted of any crime spend months in local jails awaiting court appearances (Rabinowitz, 2010). Indeed, contemporary criminal justice practice directly relies on the vast majority of individuals accused of crimes waiving their Sixth Amendment right to a trial in exchange for the promise of relatively lenient treatment; the process would grind to a halt if significant numbers of defendants began demanding their days in court (see Davis, 2007).

Prosecutorial influence and discretion takes a somewhat different form for alleged white-collar offenders. As in cases of alleged street crimes, prosecutors have considerable discretion in deciding whether to charge individuals, and if so, with what to charge them. However, many statutes pertaining to these types of offenses are quite broadly written and open to greater subjectivity in interpretation. This relative indeterminacy in the law gives prosecutors especially wide leeway; they may read the law in different ways, and the exact boundaries of criminality may be fuzzy. Prosecutors—generally locally elected officials—express hesitance to pursue white-collar cases that require particular expertise and disproportionately large investments of time, and which they perceive to carry lower likelihoods of conviction (Benson and Cullen, 1998). A criminal conviction requires meeting the "beyond a reasonable doubt" standard, which generally includes substantiating both *actus reus*—the criminal act itself—and *mens rea*—the purpose, knowledge, recklessness, or negligence necessary for criminal liability (with the exception of a small category of strict liability crimes, for which no demonstration of fault or negligence is required). The blurry lines between legal and illegal actions in many types of white-collar crime make substantiating mens rea particularly crucial, and this element of crime features prominently in these cases much more frequently than in their street-crime counterparts (Strader, 2011: 9–10). When these cases go to trial, most boil down to the effort to prove criminal intent.

Like their street-crime counterparts, most white-collar crime cases end in a plea bargain. When criminal charges are pressed, white-collar cases are more likely to go to trial. In many of these cases, however, the government will often choose to pursue civil rather than criminal charges, or civil and criminal charges simultaneously. Civil charges offer the possibilities of regaining lost money and precluding further harm, either directly through deploying judicial authority to compel or forbid particular actions, or indirectly through deterrence (Strader, 2011: 7). Another noteworthy attraction of civil trials is the lower burden of proof these cases present—civil cases generally require plaintiffs only to meet a less stringent "preponderance of evidence" standard.

Pursuing a civil case has long been an attractive option in instances of detected financial malfeasance. Now, the intersection of increasing sophistication and complexity in financial instruments and rollbacks in limitations and oversight have essentially pushed the potentiality of pressing criminal charges in the largest cases of fraud and theft in human history to the very margins of the possible. In perhaps the most striking example, it now appears unlikely that any criminal charges will be pressed against representatives of the banks and mortgage firms that engaged in predatory lending, mortgage fraud, and the questionable financial dealings that precipitated the 2008 financial collapse. Instead, the nation's largest banks are agreeing to an $8.5 billion settlement with regulators, which they negotiated down from $15 billion (see Silver-Greenberg, 2012, 2013).

While eight and a half billion dollars is undoubtedly an enormous sum of money, it is a relative drop in the bucket for these hugely profitable firms, who now have largely free rein to continue conducting business as they see fit. And, because of the Byzantine character of the contemporary lending market and the immanent uncertainty surrounding the nature and extent of harm done to borrowers, regulators have abandoned efforts to distribute settlement funds according to any calculation of desert based on harm. Instead, the less than half of the total settlement ($3.3 billion) that will be paid to consumers will be spread across all of the roughly four million households with loans in foreclosure, resulting in payments of less than $1,000 each. This settlement, like many paid by powerful firms whose employees have victimized middle- and lower-class Americans, does not require any admission of wrongdoing, but instead essentially reduces to "buying" a clean slate (see Morgenson, 2013; Silver-Greenberg, 2013). Thus, the identification and punishment of offenders so central to criminal justice strategies aimed at street criminals disappear from social control efforts with regard to white-collar offenders, and the need to occasionally "settle up" with government regulators becomes just a cost of doing business.

Conclusion

Every system of production tends to discover punishments which correspond to its productive relationships

(Rusche and Kirchheimer, 1939: 5)

During the post-industrial period and the rise of portfolio society, we have adopted a new set of punishment practices that reflects a changed economic order. While blue-collar manufacturing jobs have steadily disappeared, city centers have decayed, and a regime of mass incarceration has risen to warehouse huge numbers of the associated urban poor. Meanwhile, we have moved away from the Keynesian vision of state involvement in the market that dominated the prosperous mid-century U.S. political economy in favor of a laissez-faire approach that valorizes unrestricted action among the financial elite, increases opportunities for egregiously exploitative behavior, and damages the prospect of prosecuting such acts.

Over the past few years we have witnessed the crises that this approach to social control fosters. Even ignoring the humanitarian and long-term social consequences, the enormous and aging prison population is simply fiscally unsustainable. The U.S. carceral complex currently costs around $70 billion annually, an increase of over 600% from costs in the early 1980s (Bureau of Justice Statistics, 2011a, 2011b). Some politicians have begun to recognize this crisis, and a number of states have passed laws aimed at reducing prison populations. Indeed, the most recent statistics show some evidence of tapering off in the predominance of mass incarceration as a street-crime regulation strategy. Since 2007's high of 7.3 million, the growth of the population under correctional supervision has leveled off, and total numbers have even declined slightly. At year-end 2009, the total supervised population had dropped to around 7.2 million (Glaze, 2010: 1). Between 2007 and 2010, the supervised population dropped about 3.7% (Uggen, 2012: 3). While this decline is relatively small, it is appreciable, especially in comparison to the continuous annual increases in incarceration rates witnessed over the preceding four decades. The average annual growth in the imprisonment rate (adjusted for population growth) between 1975 and 2009 was 4.7%; the total incarceration rate (including jail as well as prison populations) also grew quickly, at 4% per year between 1982 and 2009 (Pettit, 2012: 10). During the 2007–2010 decline in the supervised population, the imprisoned population stayed basically stable at around 1.5 million, while probation and jail populations declined. The number of parolees actually grew, from around 826,000 to close to 841,000—this growth could be the result of early-release programs tied to budgetary belt-tightening (Uggen, 2012: 3).

The consequences of deregulation and failures of oversight in the financial sector are manifest, and have garnered substantial public attention. Yet, there is not much to suggest a significant change in the approach to white-collar crime. Despite the outcry over bankers enriching themselves at the rest of our expense and statements about reining in Wall Street from the Obama administration and other politicians, there has been little in the way of substantial reform of social control policy in this area. Since the 2008 crisis, banks and bankers have grown wealthier and more powerful, and their close relationship with authorities continues.

Note

1 Others, however, have challenged the notion that white-collar lawbreakers are handled with kid gloves by formal social control systems. Critics of the "privileged offenders" hypothesis argue against the notion of systematic advantages for this category of the accused in the operation of the criminal justice system (see Buell, 2013). That white-collar defendants enjoy at least some privilege in terms of legal representation and associated negotiations with prosecuting attorneys, though, is widely acknowledged (Mann, 1985; Weisselberg and Li, 2011; Buell, 2013).

References

Alexander, Michelle. 2010. *The New Jim Crow: Mass Incarceration in the Age of Colorblindness*. New York: New Press.

Angelides, Phil, Brooksley Born, Byron Georgiou, Bob Graham, Heather H. Murren, and John W. Thompson. 2011. *The Financial Crisis Inquiry Report*. Washington, DC: The Financial Crisis Inquiry Commission.

Benson, Michael L., and Francis T. Cullen. 1998. *Combating Corporate Crime: Local Prosecutors at Work*. Boston, MA: Northeastern University Press.

Buell, Samuel W. 2013. "Is the White Collar Offender Privileged?" *Duke Law Journal* 63:1–54.

Bureau of Justice Statistics. 2011a. *Expenditure Trends by Function Chart*. Washington, DC: U.S. Department of Justice.

Bureau of Justice Statistics. 2011b. *Table about Trend Expenditures on Criminal Justice in the United States by Function*. Washington, DC: U.S. Department of Justice.

Clinard, Marshall B., and Peter Yeager. 1980. *Corporate Crime*. New York: Free Press.

Comfort, Megan. 2008. *Doing Time Together: Love and Family in the Shadow of the Prison*. Chicago: University of Chicago Press.

Davis, Angela J. 2007. *Arbitrary Justice: The Power of the American Prosecutor*. New York: Oxford University Press.

Davis, Gerald F. 2009. *Managed by the Markets: How Finance Re-Shaped America*. New York: Oxford University Press.

Desmond, Matthew, and Nicol Valdez. 2013. "Unpolicing the Urban Poor: Consequences of Third-Party Policing for Inner-City Women." *American Sociological Review* 78:117–141.

Devers, Lindsey. 2011. *Plea and Charge Bargaining: Research Summary*. Washington, DC: Bureau of Justice Assistance, U.S. Dept. of Justice.

Foster, Holly, and John Hagan. 2009. "The Mass Incarceration of Parents in America: Issues of Race/Ethnicity, Collateral Damage to Children, and Prisoner Reentry." *Annals of the American Academy of Political and Social Science* 623:179–194.

Frieden, Jeffry A. 1987. *Banking on the World: The Politics of American International Finance*. New York: Harper and Row.

Frieden, Jeffry A. 2006. *Global Capitalism: Its Fall and Rise in the Twentieth Century*. New York: W.W. Norton and Co.

Garland, David. 2001. *The Culture of Control: Crime and Social Order in Contemporary Society*. Chicago: University of Chicago Press.

Geis, Gilbert, and Colin Goff. 1983. "Introduction." In *White Collar Crime: The Uncut Version*. New Haven, CT: Yale University Press.

Glaze, Lauren E. 2010. *Bulletin: Correctional Populations in the United States, 2009*. Washington, DC: U.S. Department of Justice, Bureau of Justice Statistics.

Gottschalk, Marie. 2006. *The Prison and the Gallows: The Politics of Mass Incarceration in America*. New York: Cambridge University Press.

Hagan, John. 2010. *Who Are the Criminals? The Politics of Crime Policy from Roosevelt to the Age of Reagan*. Princeton, NJ: Princeton University Press.

Hagan, John, and Alberto Palloni. 1986. "'Club Fed' and the Sentencing of White-Collar Offenders Before and After Watergate." *Criminology* 24:603–621.

Hagan, John, and Patricia Parker. 1985. "White-Collar Crime and Punishment: The Class Structure and Legal Sanctioning of Securities Violations." *American Sociological Review* 50:302–316.

Holtfreter, Kristy, Shanna Van Slyke, Jason Bratton, and Marc Gertz. 2008. "Public Perceptions of White-Collar Crime and Punishment." *Journal of Criminal Justice* 36:50–60.

Johnson, Elizabeth I., and Jane Waldfogel. 2004. "Children of Incarcerated Parents: Multiple Risks and Children's Living Arrangements." Pp. 97–101 in *Imprisoning America: The Social Effects of Mass Incarceration*, edited by Mary Pattillo, David Weiman, and Bruce Western. New York: Russell Sage Foundation.

Kerley, Kent R., and Heith Copes. 2004. "The Effects of Criminal Justice Contact on Employment Stability for White-Collar and Street-Level Offenders." *International Journal of Offender Therapy and Comparative Criminology* 48:65–84.

Lynch, James P., and William J. Sabol. 2004. "Effects of Incarceration on Informal Social Control in Communities." Pp. 135–164 in *Imprisoning America: The Social Effects of Mass Incarceration*, edited by Mary Pattillo, David Weiman, and Bruce Western. New York: Russell Sage Foundation.

Mann, Kenneth. 1985. *Defending White-Collar Crime: A Portrait of Attorneys at Work*. New Haven, CT: Yale University Press.

Manza, Jeff, and Christopher Uggen. 2008. *Locked Out: Felon Disenfranchisement and American Democracy*. New York: Oxford University Press.

Massoglia, Michael, Glenn Firebaugh, and Cody Warner. 2013. "Racial Variation in the Effect of Incarceration on Neighborhood Attainment." *American Sociological Review* 78:142–165.

Morgenson, Gretchen. 2013. "Surprise, Surprise: The Banks Win." In *The New York Times*.

Morgenson, Gretchen, and Joshua Rosner. 2011. *Reckless Endangerment: How Outsized Ambition, Greed, and Corruption Led to Economic Armageddon*. New York: Holt.

Nurse, Anne M. 2004. "Returning to Strangers: Newly Paroled Young Fathers and Their Children." Pp. 76–96 in *Imprisoning America: The Social Effects of Mass Incarceration*, edited by Mary Pattillo, David Weiman, and Bruce Western. New York: Russell Sage Foundation.

Pettit, Becky. 2012. *Invisible Men: Mass Incarceration and the Myth of Black Progress*. New York: Russell Sage Foundation.

Piquero, Nicole Leeper, Stephanie Carmichael, and Alex R. Piquero. 2008. "Assessing the Perceived Seriousness of White-Collar and Street Crimes." *Crime and Delinquency* 54:291–312.

Rabinowitz, Mikaela. 2010. *Holding Cells: Understanding the Collateral Consequences of Pretrial Detentions*. Unpublished dissertation. Evanston, IL: Northwestern University.

Rusche, Georg, and Otto Kirchheimer. 1939. *Punishment and Social Structure*. New York: Columbia University Press.

Schlegel, Kip, and David Weisburd. 1992. "Introduction." In *White-Collar Crime Reconsidered*, edited by Kip Schlegel and David Weisburd. Boston, MA: Northeastern University Press.

Schoepfer, Andrea, Stephanie Carmichael, and Nicole Leeper Piquero. 2007. "Do Perceptions of Punishment Vary Between White-Collar and Street Crimes?" *Journal of Criminal Justice* 35:151–163.

Shapiro, Susan P. 1984. *Wayward Capitalists: Target of the Securities and Exchange Commission*. New Haven, CT: Yale University Press.

Shapiro, Susan P. 1987. "The Social Control of Impersonal Trust." *American Journal of Sociology* 93:623–658.

Shapiro, Susan P. 1990. "Collaring the Crime, Not the Criminal: Reconsidering the Concept of White-Collar Crime." *American Sociological Review* 55:346–365.

Sherman, Matthew. 2009. *A Short History of Financial Deregulation in the United States*. Washington, DC: Center for Economic and Policy Research.

Silver-Greenberg, Jessica. 2012. "Settlement Expected on Past Abuses in Home Loans." In *The New York Times*.

Silver-Greenberg, Jessica. 2013. "Bank Deal Ends Flawed Reviews of Foreclosures." In *The New York Times*.

Strader, J. Kelly. 2011. *Understanding White Collar Crime*. New Providence, NJ: LexisNexis.

Sutherland, Edwin. [1949] 1983. *White Collar Crime: The Uncut Version*. New Haven, CT: Yale University Press.

Tillman, Robert, and Henry N. Pontell. 1992. "Is Justice 'Collar-Blind'? Punishing Medicaid Provider Fraud." *Criminology* 30:547–574.

Uggen, Christopher. 2012. "Crime and the Great Recession." In *Recession Trends*. Stanford, CA: Stanford Center on Poverty and Inequality.

U.S. Department of Justice, (USDOJ). 1989. *White Collar Crime: A Report to the Public*. Washington, DC: Government Printing Office.

Warren, Jenifer. 2008. *One in 100: Behind Bars in America 2008*. Philadelphia, PA: Pew Charitable Trusts.

Weisselberg, Charles D., and Su Li. 2011. "Big Law's Sixth Amendment: The Rise of Corporate White-Collar Practices in Large U.S. Law Firms." *Arizona Law Review* 53:1221–1299.

Western, Bruce. 2006. *Punishment and Inequality in America*. New York: Russell Sage Foundation.
Wheeler, Stanton, Kenneth Mann, and Austin Sarat. 1988. *Sitting in Judgment: The Sentencing of White-Collar Offenders*. New Haven, CT: Yale University Press.
Zaloom, Caitlin. 2006. *Out of the Pits: Traders and Technology from Chicago to London*. Chicago: University of Chicago Press.
Zimring, Franklin. 2007. *The Great American Crime Decline*. New York: Oxford University Press.

34

A PEOPLE'S HISTORY
OF LEGAL AID

A brief sketch

Shaun Ossei-Owusu

Legal aid typically refers to the organized provision of advice and counseling as it relates to substantive and procedural legal issues for indigent clients. The most influential analyses of legal aid tend to start slightly before the Progressive Era, with the development of the *Der Deutsche Rechtsschutz Verein* (German Law Association) in 1876, which was designed to offer legal aid to German immigrants to New York City (Smith, 1919; Maguire, 1928; Johnson, 1974; McConville and Mirsky, 1987; Rhode, 2004). These immigrants were often susceptible to the chicanery and exploitation that was common of the Gilded Age. The organization's work

> was to protect the immigrant from the thief who took his little hoard for railway tickets that were never delivered, or for property that never existed; or, worse still, who exchanged for him his good German coin into counterfeit American money.
>
> (Loew, 1902: 126)

The association eventually widened its clientele to include other ethnic groups, and in 1896 it changed its name to the Legal Aid Society (LAS). It served as a template for other cities that developed legal aid societies (e.g., Boston in 1900, Philadelphia in 1902, Cleveland in 1905, Cincinnati in 1907). The NYLAS continues to be a major provider of legal services in New York City, and is considered the oldest legal aid organization in the country. Unfortunately, the scholarship on legal aid is imprecise, as there are several instances of organized legal assistance that predate the NYLAS. This short chapter bucks a century of legal aid historiography by pointing to earlier and unrecognized episodes of legal assistance to demonstrate how legal aid is not just about class and indigence, but is deeply woven in the social divisions of race, gender, ethnicity, and citizenship.

One of the earliest institutions to provide legal aid was the Pennsylvania Abolition Society (PAS). The organization was developed in 1773, but its activities were interrupted by the Civil War. The Society's activity resumed in 1784, with Benjamin Franklin serving as president starting in 1787. In the decades leading to the Civil War the courtroom was an important battleground between the North and the South with abolitionist legal aid and slavery serving as undeniably central features to this struggle. The PAS "hired more lawyers and represented more blacks in court at the close of the eighteenth century than any other abolitionist organization," and from 1800 to 1830, a third of the PAS' cases were related to kidnapping (Newman,

2002: 69; 2008: 55). For plaintiffs, abolitionist lawyers investigated violations of the slave-trade (after the national 1808 prohibition) and aided black family members and friends attempting to liberate loved ones who were kidnapped. On the defense side, abolitionist lawyers for the PAS negotiated (and in a few instances outright bought) escaped slaves' freedom or bargained it down to indentured servitude. The PAS bureaucrats also traveled to other states to deliver kidnapped persons' freedom papers and even created a collated master file of indentured contracts to protect black servants from masters who attempted to duplicitously break their agreements (Turner, 1912; Winch, 1987; Newman, 2002). The PAS also held manumission, birth, and marriage certificates of free blacks and paid for the expenses of witnesses who were traveling to testify for blacks attempting to maintain their free status (Wilkinson, 1944). Union Army officer Edward Needles (1848) discusses the precarious situation for indigent fugitive litigants and signals toward the unfavorable socio-political climate abolitionist lawyers encountered:

> In such cases, ignorance or inability to prosecute their claim to freedom, unable to plead for themselves, and perhaps, none to plead for them, their chance for redress was very uncertain. Funds also were requisite, of which they were destitute; legal characters in general were not over forward in pleading for them before magistrates. "They were only negroes"—poor and despised—their cause unpopular, and nothing to be gained by advocating their rights, but the ill-will and malice of their surrounding enemies.

These comments foreshadow the seemingly unenviable labor that indigent lawyers would encounter for the next two centuries. To be sure, the motivations of abolitionist legal aid varied and included: ideological concerns about "slave power" and the threat posed by the powerful, "conspiratorial" Southern slaveholding class; whites' perceived susceptibility to slavery via ambiguous racial categories and kidnappings of "mistaken identity"; investments in the rhetoric of rights; and genuine altruism.

The Freedmen's Bureau, which was established after the Civil War, also provided another form of legal aid that is often overlooked. The federal government assigned the Bureau with the daunting task of providing aid to freedmen and women. The Bureau helped with the provision of food, housing, clothing, and education. It also assisted in the supervision of labor contracts, the family reunification process, and in legal disputes. The types of cases the Bureau supported ranged widely and included debt collection, criminal prosecutions, domestic violence, divorces, and labor contracts. The legal aid offered by the Bureau included assistance for freed peoples as plaintiffs and as defendants. In some locales, Bureau agents "exercised an informal judicial function, acting as arbitrators, mediators, or mere diplomats to dispose of disputes" (Westwood, 1970: 502). In others, Bureau agents observed judicial proceedings and acted as "watchdogs" to ensure that freed people's rights were being upheld. Paul Skeels Peirce (1904: 145) notes that Bureau agents

> acted as counselors and advisers of colored litigants and even appeared in court as free attorneys for such as were unable to procure counsel; in Mississippi and the District of Columbia the Bureau retained a lawyer to defend freedmen in their suits.

There are other documented examples of the Bureau paying for the legal assistance of freedmen and women in Maryland, South Carolina, Florida, and Georgia while also helping bankroll the travel, rent, and clerical expenses of these indigent lawyers in Washington DC (Westwood, 1970).

The short-lived life of the Freedmen's Bureau marks the advent of the federal government's lukewarm commitment to organized legal aid for the impoverished. The lack of resources provided to the Bureau to achieve its legal goals is similar to the federal government's perfunctory dedication to substantive equality as well as its lack of careful thought on how both the transition from slavery to freedom as well as legal aid would be successfully accomplished. At the peak of its existence, the Bureau employed no more than 900 agents throughout the entire South, a figure that made it virtually impossible for the Bureau to address even a majority of freed people's legal needs (Foner, 1988: 143). The Bureau's assistance also offers an early example of how legal aid can be implicated in the same system of class, race, and gender subordination that it seeks to confront. This occurs more insidiously through the common-sense assumptions of bureaucrats and directly through outright complicity. While Bureau agents "varied all the way from unselfish philanthropists to narrow-minded busybodies and thieves," the unfortunate reality is that biased, assumptive proclivities influenced even the most well-intentioned bureaucrats and their legal personnel (Du Bois, 1901: 360). Notwithstanding the Bureau's admittedly sketchy directive of "help," many agents were actively complicit in blacks' conscription into egregious labor arrangements that were undergirded by the threat of criminal prosecution if violated. These arrangements usually took shape through sharecropping, apprenticeship schemes, and the convict-leasing system. Indeed, the prejudiced sensibilities of the Bureau sometimes led them to reify the status quo. These examples of complicity resonate with contemporary commentaries on the collusive nature of plea bargaining in today's legal system as well as the paternalist attitudes that sometimes animate bureaucrat–client relationships in indigent defense, and "helping professions" more generally.

While the aforementioned episodes highlight unacknowledged racial undercurrents, gender has been and continues to be deeply woven into legal aid. While there is a longer history of organized feminist labor activity (Foner, 1979; Dublin, 1981), the post-Civil War era was a particularly formative era. It was during this time that women became more active participants in the industrial workforce, while being excluded by men from most trade unions. The lack of institutional protection created a precarious situation for female workers. Labor movement supporter M.E.J. Kelley (1898: 413) argued that the confluence of women's entrance into the workforce and the changing nature of the economy encouraged exploitation. The "sudden outpouring from the home into the market of women unused to the ways of the business world," she asserted, "was probably too tempting an opportunity to the unscrupulous to be allowed to pass" (Kelley, 1898: 413). This eventually led to the creation of a host of organizations designed to protect women workers' legal and labor interests. One of these groups, the Working Women's Protective Union (WWPU) of New York City, is integral to understanding the gendered dimensions and origins of legal aid.

The WWPU was originally established in 1863 as the Workingwomen's Union. It provided free legal aid to female laborers, acted as an employment agency, lobbied for laws to protect women workers, and dragooned employers into paying women fair wages and maintaining reasonable-hour workloads. The main goals of the WWPU were to

> promote the interests of women who obtain a livelihood by employments other than household service, and *especially to provide them with legal protection from the frauds and impositions of unscrupulous employers*, to assist them in procuring employment, and to open to them such suitable departments of labor as are not occupied by them.
>
> (WWPU, 1868, emphasis added)

Women were not only clients in the WWPU, but also conducted much of the legal work (interviewing clients and witnesses, determining whether women had a viable case, contacting employers) despite being generally excluded from the legal profession (Batlan, 2010).

Subsequently, men's professional demarcation and devaluation of women's legal work, along with females' strategic utilization of the language of maternalism, led to more narrow and conservative ideas about the kind of work lawyers should perform.

The emergence of the German Legal Aid Society in 1876 led it to go into direct competition with the WWPU. After widening its goals and expanding its clientele beyond Germans, it attempted to address the legal issues of working women while disassociating itself with the supposedly feminist practices of charity, philanthropy, and sentimentalism; it essentially deemed much of the labor done by lay female lawyers as marginal and as social work (Batlan, 2010). These ideas resonate today in ways that are unrecognized by individuals in legal aid communities. Heated discussions abound about whether lawyers should focus strictly on legal issues and leave the rest to the putatively feminine domain of social work; or whether they should take a more integrative, "holistic" approach to their work beyond the confines of the court (e.g., Holland, 2005; Steinberg, 2005). Similarly attorneys (male or female) who are "too compassionate" to their clients are often seen as "hand-holders" and not "real trial attorneys." Interlocutors in contemporary legal aid discussions would benefit from having a better understanding of where these gendered ideas emanate from historically.

The Progressive Era and the development of the New York Legal Aid Society is where most scholarship begins, but even assumptions about this time period are inexact. During this time the three major institutional configurations for legal aid included: legal aid societies, public defenders, and the assigned counsel system. The assigned counsel system (ASC), which was in existence in some states, entailed a judge's discretionary appointment of legal counsel for indigent clients. But these assigned attorneys were often inexperienced in the practice of criminal law and inadequately compensated. These factors hindered their ability to effectively investigate cases and offered few incentives for them to zealously and ethically defend their clients. (This is still the case today.) The public defender and legal aid society models were largely successful because of the gross inequalities of the ASC.

The idea of the public defender (PD) was first suggested by Clara Foltz at the 1893 Chicago World's Fair. Foltz was a pioneer female attorney in California, and witnessed the vagaries of the ASC. Espousing social contract rhetoric, Foltz (1893: 250) believed that the government's chief function was to protect the liberty and lives of citizens. "To support them," she argued,

> each citizen surrenders his natural right to defend himself and pays his share for the support of the State, under the implied contract that for such surrender of right and contribution, the government will defend his life and liberty from unlawful invasion.

While Foltz promoted the concept of a PD as a publicly funded, natural opponent in an adversarial legal system, this idea was diluted. Progressives adopted the public defender as a *collaborator*, often expressing the PD as instrumental to court efficiency (Babcock, 2006). Walton J. Wood, who became the first public defender in U.S. history in Los Angeles in 1914, insisted that:

> Reduction of expense to the tax-payers has followed the establishment of the office of public defender ... Figures show that the attorneys in private practice consumed much more time on the average for each trial than did the public defender. *A higher percentage of pleas of guilty was interposed by the public defender thus saving the expense of trial. A lower percentage of appeals was taken by the public defender and a smaller number of demurrers and motions filed.*
> (Wood, 1926: 72, emphasis added)

While contemporary accounts understand plea-bargain compliance and the "McDonaldization" of the penal system as unique to neoliberal poverty management, the reality is that Taylorist efficiency and the often non-adversarial division of labor was hardwired into the design of criminal legal aid.

The Progressive Era LAS model was fairly moderate in historical hindsight. While cities varied in whether they took both civil and criminal cases, their operations cohered around two ideas: that their operations could effectively *Americanize* ethnic white immigrants and curtail poor people's rising discontent with the law. The legal system was sullied by the corruption and bureaucratic malfeasance of the late nineteenth century. Legal reformers were concerned about the threat of anarchism (which often had a southern or eastern European face), communism, and social unrest.[1] Advocates believed the LAS would provide the legal system with legitimacy while improving court operations. In 1919, Boston attorney Reginald Heber Smith published *Justice and the Poor*, an ambitious, but seminal, survey of the national legal aid environment. The book was funded by the Carnegie Foundation and published the same year the organization undertook a ten-volume "Americanization Studies" project. Smith (1919: 10) maintained that the

> denial of justice is the short cut to anarchy ... nothing rankles more in the human heart than the feeling of injustice. It produces a sense of helplessness, then bitterness. It is brooded over. It leads directly to contempt for law, disloyalty to the government, and plants the seeds of anarchy ... A persuasion spreads that there is one law for the rich and another for the poor.

Despite their historically documented monopoly on legal inequality, blacks, Latinos, Asian Americans, and Native Americans were largely out of the purview of legal aid reformers, as evidenced by these groups' conspicuous absence from Progressive Era discourse as well as legal aid archival collections and historiography. Instead these groups relied on a creative mix of voluntary associations, ethnic newspapers, fraternal organizations, mutualistas, local consulates, churches, and various networks of solidarity. Similar to their exclusion from other social welfare imperatives (Lasch-Quinn, 1993; Gordon, 1994; Poole, 2006; Muhammad, 2010; Ward, 2012), racial minorities' exclusion from burgeoning legal aid institutions challenges the historiographical myth that legal aid—specifically assistance offered by charity organizations, the bar, and municipalities—was readily available to everyone.

A few things changed between the 1930s and 1960s. The Immigration Act of 1924, which introduced strict quota limitations on immigration, intensified nativist impulses and led many legal aid institutions to abandon their courting of immigrants. Instead, they emphasized the trope of the "deserving poor." Many legal aid organizations utilized this rhetoric before this time period, but the idea of deservingness became more in vogue with New Deal welfare state developments. Jurisprudentially, a series of cases forced the Supreme Court to deal more squarely with due-process protections and indigent defense (e.g., *Powell v. Alabama* in 1932, *Johnson v. Zerbst* in 1938, and *Betts v. Brady* in 1942). While the Court flip-flopped on the state's responsibility to provide legal counsel, it eventually decided in the landmark case *Gideon v. Wainwright* (1963) that the Sixth and Fourteenth Amendments require that indigent criminal defendants be provided with legal counsel in felony cases. This right was extended to juveniles and misdemeanants in *In re Gault* (1967) and *Argersinger v. Hamlin* (1972). These cases forced states to develop legal aid schemes. No similar extension was made for civil cases. Similar to the Progressive Era, legal aid schemes entailed either PD systems, assigned counsel, or contracts with local law firms. The key difference is that it was no longer optional, and funding came from the state. Poor whites would still be major consumers of legal aid, but the hue of criminal legal assistance became increasingly black and brown with the rise in hyperincarceration in the 1960s and 1970s.

Since *Gideon*, criminal legal aid has emerged as an often-unacknowledged component of the welfare state and an underappreciated component of the penal state. In 2007, $2.3 billion was spent on public defender programs, with state and county-based programs handling 5.5 of the approximately 5.6 million cases nationwide (Langton and Farole 2010; Farole and Langton 2010). Put succinctly, the majority of people who are accused of a crime receive publicly funded legal assistance. The problem with legal aid, like other social welfare services, is that the level of support is sometimes so basic that it is almost perfunctory. A particularly salient issue is the *quality* of defense, which is usually framed under the two-pronged trope of "ineffective counsel." The first form typically deals with egregious cases of incompetent attorneys. In the past 40 years, conservative jurisprudence has disemboweled the spirit of *Gideon* via generous if not ludicrous interpretations of what constitutes "effective counsel." Indeed, there have been a host of cases where counsel has been considered effective despite: sleeping through parts of the trial; using heroin and cocaine during the trial; and coming to trial drunk, with one attorney being arrested for driving to court with a .27 blood alcohol content (Cole, 1999: 76–81). Perhaps less egregiously, but similarly troubling, is the reality that the mere volume of cases can easily induce occupational burnout and compassion fatigue. But liberal opponents of federally funded legal aid predicted this. Brown (1938: 257) warned that, "the defender would become so hardened to the stories of defendants that he might become indifferent to the justice of each case … as the result of indifference and lack of enthusiasm, he would likely recommend pleas of 'guilty' be entered." Autobiographical and journalistic accounts of indigent defense seem to suggest that this is the case (e.g., Feige, 2006; Bach, 2010).

Ineffective counsel is also a result of the financial limitations and organizational constraints legal aid attorneys inherit. These attorneys are often unable to do their job due to the lack of institutional and political independence in indigent defense. Legal aid is often tethered to and regulated by politicians and judges (via tightfisted funding from legislators and judicial control of approval for investigators and expert witnesses). Indigent defense attorneys are overworked (typically exceeding the national standard caseload) and under-resourced (with most offices not having enough attorneys or personnel to meet caseload guidelines). Embarrassingly, even government research confirms this. In the United States, public defense is funded through states (in 22 states) or counties (in 28 states). Department of Justice data show that "More than 7 in 10 county-based offices had an insufficient number of attorneys to meet the professional guidelines," whereas "15 of the 19 reporting state programs exceeded the maximum recommended limit of felony or misdemeanor cases per attorney" (Farole and Langton 2010; Langton and Farole, 2010). As of 2013, the 50-year "anniversary" of *Gideon*, U.S. Attorney General Eric Holder described the pitiful state of indigent defense as "unacceptable" and "unworthy of a legal system that stands as an example for all the world" (Cohen 2013). Across the country from Nevada to New York City, Miami to Missouri, attorneys are carrying more than twice their recommended caseloads on meager budgets, in backlogged criminal bureaucracies where the accused linger in jail for months and years awaiting trial (McAlister, 2009; Dandurand, 2011; Baxter, 2012; Giovanni and Patel, 2013; Glaberson, 2013; Houppert, 2013;).

These organizational restraints often temper the abilities of the many committed, hardworking legal aid attorneys working across the country. Unfortunately, public opinion of indigent defense is not encouraging. Despite majoritarian, abstract support of quality indigent defense, Americans do not want to spend money on legal aid. In response to the query "Do you think the government should be spending more or spending less on legal defense for people who cannot afford a lawyer, or should the government keep the funding about where it is now?," more than half of the respondents in the last notable study on legal aid believed that funding should be the same (Belden Russonello and Stewart Research and Communications, 2001). Although there is an increasingly bipartisan agreement on the need to address our current penal disaster, simultaneous fiscal austerity measures suggest that improving the quality of legal aid might not fit into this endeavor.

Legal aid sheds light on a key intermediary between the criminally accused and the state. If scholars are right about hyperincarceration as a de facto poverty management program (e.g., Beckett and Western, 2001; Wacquant, 2009; Soss et al., 2011), then legal aid attorneys are essential to this equation. But it has not figured prominently into important examinations of the welfare state and poverty and is largely out of the purview of recent scholarship on crime and punishment. Instead, the important discussions on criminal legal assistance are often limited to the intraprofessional dialogue between practitioners and legal scholars. Despite a rich assemblage of historiographical literature, primary sources, and archival data, historians have left the topic virtually untouched for three decades.[2] And even as students of Foucault on the one hand and scholars of race, class, gender, and ethnicity on the other have fruitfully pointed out the thorny issues confronted by bureaucrats and clients in the "helping professions," the role of legal aid for the indigent has continued to be woefully understudied.[3]

But the unacknowledged racial and gendered histories of legal aid highlight how the development of this service is deeply political and tied to crucial social justice movements as well as coercive statecrafting imperatives. As durable inequality continues to persist and various constituents attempt to address the deluge of bodies entering the criminal justice machinery, the role of legal aid attorneys will be crucial, whether they are plea-bargain compliant bureaucrats or zealous champions of the criminally accused. As the only allies of criminal defendants (at least in theory), these advocates, along with their institutional history and empirical context, offer unique insights into incarceration and the management of marginalized populations. At best, their work might offer partial solutions to the country's imprisonment problem, and at least, they provide an alternative institutional and conceptual perspective on our penal status quo—one that differs from the steady chorus of explanations that point to indifferent or callous politicians, hardened criminals, crooked cops, overzealous prosecutors, and discretion-less (or overly discretionary) judges.

Notes

1 Some important events that prompted this anxiety include: the murder of President William McKinley by a Polish-American anarchist in 1901, the dynamiting of the *Los Angeles Times* building in 1910, the torrent of bombings across major cities that were attributed to Galleanist anarchists that are too numerous to mention, the Bolshevik Revolution of 1917, and the bombing of Wall Street in 1920.
2 The last major historical study of institutionalized legal aid is McConville and Mirsky (1987).
3 On the knotty issues faced by female bureaucrats of color in the medical system and welfare system see Watkins-Hayes (2009) and Bridges (2011), respectively. For a similar, but broader, discussion on the intricacies of street-level helping bureaucracies, specifically the police, teachers, and counselors, see Maynard-Moody and Musheno (2003). For Foucauldian takes on the multifarious nature of help, empowerment, and the state see Cruikshank (1999), Li (2007), and Fairbanks (2009).

References

Babcock, Barbara Allen. 2006. "Inventing the Public Defender." *American Criminal Law Review* 43: 1267.
Bach, Amy. 2010. *Ordinary Injustice: How America Holds Court.* New York: Metropolitan Books.
Batlan, Felice. 2010. "The Birth of Legal Aid: Gender Ideologies, Women, and the Bar in New York City, 1863–1910." *Law and History Review* 28(4): 931–971.

Baxter, Heather. 2012. "Too Many Clients, Too Little Time: How States Are Forcing Public Defenders to Violate Their Ethical Obligations." *Federal Sentencing Reporter* 25(2): 91–102.

Beckett, Katherine, and Western, Bruce. 2001. "Governing Social Marginality Welfare, Incarceration, and the Transformation of State Policy." *Punishment and Society* 3(1): 43–59.

Belden Russonello and Stewart Research and Communications. 2001."National Survey on Indigent Defense." August 2001. Available online at http://www.nlada.org/DMS/Documents/1075394127.32/Belden%20Russonello%20Polling%20short%20report.pdf Accessed on April 10, 2013.

Bridges, Khiara M. 2011. *Reproducing Race: An Ethnography of Pregnancy as a Site of Racialization*. Berkeley and Los Angeles: University of California Press.

Brown, Esther Lucille. 1938. *Lawyers and the Promotion of Justice*. New York: Russell Sage Foundation.

Cohen, Andrew. 2013 "Eric Holder: A 'State of Crisis' for the Right to Counsel." *The Atlantic*. March 15, 2013. Available online at http://www.theatlantic.com/national/archive/2013/03/eric-holder-a-state-of-crisis-for-the-right-to-counsel/274074/. Accessed on April 10, 2013.

Cole, David. 1999. *No Equal Justice: Race and Class in the American Criminal Justice System*. New York: The New Press.

Cruikshank, Barbara. 1999. *The Will to Empower: Democratic Citizens and Other Subjects*. Ithaca: Cornell University Press.

Dandurand, Chris. 2011. "Walking Out on the Check: How Missouri Abandoned Its Public Defenders and Left the Poor to Foot the Bill." *Missouri Law Review* 76: 185–212.

Dublin, Thomas. 1981. *Women at Work: The Transformation of Work and Community in Lowell, Massachusetts, 1826–1860*. New York: Columbia University Press.

Du Bois, W. E. B. 1901. "The Freedmen's Bureau." *Atlantic Monthly* 521(87): 354–365.

Farole, Donald. J. and Langton, Lynn. 2010. *County-Based and Local Public Defender Offices, 2007*. Washington, DC: Bureau of Justice Statistics, U.S. Department of Justice.

Fairbanks, Robert. 2009. *How It Works: Recovering Citizens in Post-Welfare Philadelphia*. Chicago: University of Chicago Press.

Feige, David. 2006. *Indefensible: One Lawyer's Journey into the Inferno of American Justice*. New York: Little, Brown and Company.

Foltz, Clara. 1893. "Public Defenders: Rights of Persons Accused of Crime-Abuses Now Existing." *Albany Law Journal* 48: 248–250.

Foner, Eric. 1988. *Reconstruction: America's Unfinished Revolution*. New York: Harper and Row.

Foner, Phillip Sheldon. 1979. *Women and the American Labor Movement: From Colonial Times to the Eve of World War I*. New York: Free Press.

Giovanni, Thomas, and Patel, Roopal. 2013. "Gideon at 50: Three Reforms to Revive the Right to Counsel." Brennan Center for Justice. New York: New York University School of Law.

Glaberson, William. 2013. "Faltering Courts, Mired in Delays." *New York Times*, April 13, 2013. Available online at http://www.nytimes.com/2013/04/14/nyregion/justice-denied-bronx-court-system-mired-in-delays.html?pagewanted=all&_r=0. Accessed on April 15, 2013.

Gordon, Linda. 1994. *Pitied but Not Entitled: Single Mothers and the History of Welfare, 1890–1935*. New York: Free Press.

Holland, Brooks. 2005. "Holistic Advocacy: An Important but Limited Institutional Role." *New York University Review of Law and Social Change* 30: 637–652.

Houppert, Karen. 2013. *Chasing Gideon: The Elusive Quest for Poor People's Justice*. New York: New Press.

Johnson, Earl. 1974. *Justice and Reform: The Formative Years of the American Legal Services Program*. New York: Russell Sage Foundation.

Kelley, M. E. J. 1898. "Women and the Labor Movement." *The North American Review* 166(497): 408–417.

Langton, L., and Farole, D. J. 2010. *State Public Defender Programs, 2007*. Washington, DC: Bureau of Justice Statistics, U.S. Department of Justice.

Lasch-Quinn, Elizabeth. 1993. *Black Neighbors: Race and the Limits of Reform in the American Settlement House Movement, 1890–1945*. Chapel Hill: University of North Carolina.

Li, Tania Murray. 2007. *The Will to Improve: Governmentality, Development, and the Practice of Politics*. Durham: Duke University Press Books.

Loew, Rosalie. 1902. "The Rise and Purposes of the Legal Aid Society." *Central Law Journal* 54: 126.

Maguire, John MacArthur. 1928. *The Lance of Justice: A Semi-Centennial History of the Legal Aid Society, 1876–1926*. Cambridge, MA: Harvard University Press.

Maynard-Moody, Steven, and Musheno, Michael. 2003. *Cops, Teachers, Counselors: Stories from the Front Lines of Public Service*. Ann Arbor: University of Michigan Press.

McAlister, Stephanie L. 2009. "Between South Beach and a Hard Place: The Underfunding of the Miami-Dade Public Defender's Office and the Resulting Ethical Double Standard." *University of Miami Law Review* 64: 1317–1352.

McConville, Michael, and Mirsky, Chester L. 1987. "Criminal Defense of the Poor in New York City." *New York University Review of Law and Social Change* 15: 581–964.

Muhammad, Khalil Gibran. 2010. *The Condemnation of Blackness: Race, Crime, and the Making of Modern Urban America.* Cambridge, MA: Harvard University Press.

Needles, Edward. 1848. *An Historical Memoir of the Pennsylvania Society: For Promoting the Abolition of Slavery; The Relief of Free Negroes Unlawfully Held in Bondage, and for Improving the Condition of the African Race.* Philadelphia: Merrihew and Thompson, Printers.

Newman, Robert S. 2002. *The Transformation of American Abolitionism: Fighting Slavery in the Early Republic.* Chapel Hill: University of North Carolina Press.

Newman, Robert S. 2008. *Freedom's Prophet: Bishop Richard Allen, the AME Church, and the Black Founding Fathers.* New York: New York University Press.

Peirce, Paul Skeels. 1904. *The Freedmen's Bureau: A Chapter in the History of Reconstruction.* Iowa City: The University of Iowa.

Poole, Mary. 2006. *The Segregated Origins of Social Security: African Americans and the Welfare State.* Raleigh: The University of North Carolina Press.

Rhode, Deborah L. 2004. *Access to Justice.* New York: Oxford University Press.

Smith, Reginald Heber. 1919. *Justice and the Poor.* New York: Carnegie Foundation.

Soss, Joe, Fording, Richard C., and Schram, Sanford F. 2011. *Disciplining the Poor: Neoliberal Paternalism and the Persistent Power of Race.* Chicago: University of Chicago Press.

Steinberg, Robin G. 2005. "Beyond Lawyering: How Holistic Representation Makes for Good Policy, Better Lawyers, and More Satisfied Clients." *New York University Review of Law and Social Change* 30: 625–636.

Turner, Edward Raymond. 1912. "The First Abolition Society in the United States." *The Pennsylvania Magazine of History and Biography* 36(1): 92–109.

Wacquant, Loïc. 2009. *Punishing the Poor: The Neoliberal Government of Social Insecurity.* Durham: Duke University Press.

Ward, Geoff K. 2012. *The Black Child-Savers: Racial Democracy and Juvenile Justice.* Chicago: University of Chicago Press.

Watkins-Hayes, Celeste. 2009. *The New Welfare Bureaucrats: Situated Bureaucrats and Entanglements of Race, Class, and Welfare.* Chicago: University of Chicago Press.

Westwood, Howard C. 1970. "Getting Justice for the Freedman." *Howard Law Journal* 16: 492–538.

Wilkinson, Norman B. 1944. "Papers of the Pennsylvania Society for Promoting the Abolition of Slavery." *The Pennsylvania Magazine of History and Biography* 68(3): 286–290.

Winch, Julie. 1987. "Philadelphia and the Other Underground Railroad." *The Pennsylvania Magazine of History and Biography* 111(1): 3–25.

Wood, Walton J. 1926. "The Office of Public Defender." *Annals of the American Academy of Political and Social Science* 124: 69–73.

Working Women's Protective Union (WWPU). 1868. *Fifth Annual Report of the Working Women's Protective Union.* New York: WWPU.

35

SURVIVING GENDER-BASED VIOLENCE IN THE NEOLIBERAL ERA

The role of the state in transforming poor women from victims to survivors

Cesraéa Rumpf

Neoliberalism fundamentally has changed the nature of poverty in the United States, particularly with regard to the state's poverty management efforts. Current research thoroughly examines how neoliberal ideologies and policies have influenced the convergence of the social welfare and criminal justice systems in the United States and the punitive turn both systems have taken since the mid-1970s (Beckett and Western, 2001; Garland, 2001; Haney, 2004, 2010; Wacquant, 2009). While federal and state governments significantly have cut funding for social welfare programs, they have invested increasing amounts of money into the corrections system, thereby contributing to the current era of mass incarceration (Beckett and Western, 2001; Wacquant, 2009). Such explicit shifts represent a coordinated effort by the state to regulate social marginality in new ways (Beckett and Western, 2001; Garland, 2001; Haney, 2004; Wacquant, 2009).

Feminist scholars have begun to examine what the convergence and punitive turn of the social welfare and criminal justice systems mean for poor women who are survivors of violence (Bumiller, 2008; Hays, 2003; Richie, 2012). Drawing on the work of such scholars, this chapter examines how the institutionalization of the mainstream anti-violence movement in the United States has contributed to a discourse of victimization and survivorship that is deeply influenced by neoliberalism. I focus on criminal responses to domestic violence to argue that mainstream responses to gender-based violence seek not only to punish abusive men but also to control victimized women. I develop the concept of "internalized neoliberalism" to show how these mainstream responses encourage women to undergo a process of "responsibilization" (Garland, 1996, 2001; Hannah-Moffat, 2000) in order to transform from victims to survivors. The concept of internalized neoliberalism provides a useful tool to bridge scholarship in three fields that often are not explicitly in conversation: social welfare, criminal justice, and anti-violence. I conclude that integrating scholarship in these fields can deepen our understanding of how the neoliberal state regulates socially marginalized populations and may even promote new strategies to resist the state's punitive interventions. To situate my argument, I first provide a brief description of the neoliberal state, followed by overviews of recent major shifts in the U.S. social welfare and criminal justice systems and the mainstream anti-violence movement.

The neoliberal state

Globalization and deindustrialization have reshaped work, poverty, and inequality around the world. Scholars have shown not only how these processes were brought about and supported by state policies, but also how these processes have influenced the state's governance of poverty and social marginality. A set of key characteristics describes how the neoliberal state operates, particularly in the United States (Bumiller, 2008; Garland, 1996; Haney, 2004; Wacquant, 2009, 2012). First, while promoting market-oriented solutions, the neoliberal state has deregulated the economic market, providing greater flexibility for corporations while eliminating protections for workers. Second, the neoliberal state is a decentralized state. Through a process of devolution, the state increasingly has entered into partnerships with non-profit and private entities to contract out services it once provided. As Haney (2010) explains, "a multiplication of actors now [are] playing the role of the state. Quite often, these actors are disguised as community members, therapists, businessmen, or NGO activists" (p. 16). Additionally, the neoliberal state is a bifurcated state, characterized by social welfare retrenchment, as evidenced by the shrinking and increasingly punitive nature of social welfare and public services, and an expansion of the criminal justice system, as evidenced by pervasive surveillance practices, the increased criminalization of poverty, and the growth of the incarcerated population (Garland, 2001; Wacquant, 2009). Undergirding all of these characteristics is the deeply entrenched rhetoric of personal responsibility, which stresses the duty of individuals to solve personal problems through engaging the market and absolves the state of responsibility to provide for its members.

Social welfare in the neoliberal era

Social welfare policy in the United States underwent a dramatic and conservative shift throughout the 1980s and 1990s, culminating in the 1996 Personal Responsibility and Work Opportunity Reconciliation Act (PRWORA). This federal legislation reflected a policy shift away from entitlement and toward the regulation and punishment of welfare recipients (read: single mothers), particularly through replacing Aid to Families with Dependent Children (AFDC) with Temporary Assistance to Needy Families (TANF) and effectively ending social welfare as an entitlement program (Hays, 2003; Jimenez, 1999; Reese, 2007).

Under AFDC, family heads were eligible to receive modest cash assistance in addition to food stamps and Medicaid coverage for themselves and their families for as long as they needed such assistance. Under TANF, family heads face a lifetime limit of 60 months' cash assistance, regardless of ongoing demonstrated need. The PRWORA also ushered in an explicit focus on moving recipients off of welfare and into work, regardless of the type of work they are able to secure. Within two months of beginning a TANF case, recipients must participate in some type of work activity ("workfare"), such as job training classes and low-wage public service jobs (Hays, 2003). Recipients also must secure paid employment within two years of the start of their TANF cases. States sanction recipients who do not participate in a work activity by decreasing or cutting their cash assistance all together, as the federal government can reduce funding to states that fail to meet these work requirements. Finally, the PRWORA explicitly identifies marriage as a policy goal and dedicates substantial funding to healthy marriage and responsible fatherhood initiatives. The clear message behind this policy focus is that single mothers are not worthy of governmental support. TANF's mandatory paternity establishment and child support enforcement policies further punish women recipients who have children out of wedlock.

Beyond these TANF provisions, the PRWORA also significantly changed the relationship between the federal and state governments with regard to welfare provision. Under AFDC, the federal government matched each state's welfare expenditures. Under TANF, each state receives a fixed "block grant" from the federal government regardless of what its welfare expenditures total. Each state has the authority to set the eligibility requirements and benefit levels for its own TANF program, which results in wide variation in welfare programs from one state to the next. In fact, states can be even more restrictive than the federal guidelines (Reese, 2007). By reorganizing the relationship between the federal and state governments in this way, the PRWORA facilitated the decentralization of the social welfare state, a common trend in the neoliberal era.

The neoliberal rhetoric of personal responsibility fused with race-, gender-, and class-based ideologies to create a particular type of punitive public assistance that is available to single mothers. The rhetoric of the welfare reform debates revealed politicians' and the white, middle-class electorate's concern that single Black mothers had grown financially dependent on the state (Hays, 2003; Jimenez, 1999). In a revival of the culture of poverty thesis, politicians proclaimed that sexually irresponsible women (read: African-American single mothers) who lacked both a work ethic and respect for family values were depleting the state of financial resources through their generational use of public assistance. Research on welfare recipients consistently challenged this rhetoric but had little impact on changing the terms of the welfare reform debate or the popular image of welfare recipients. Key welfare reform provisions, such as the implementation of lifetime limits on TANF, work requirements, and incentives for marriage, reflected an effort by the state to instill poor women of color with family and work values (Hays, 2003; Jimenez, 1999; Reese, 2007).

Poverty and welfare scholarship illuminates how the PRWORA is rooted in a commitment not to end poverty but to end welfare by transforming "dependent" welfare recipients to "independent" workers (although precarious employment in the low-wage service sector hardly ensures independence). The PRWORA exemplifies the neoliberal strategy of policymakers to ignore the structural causes of poverty and instead to engage in "legislating moral prescriptions for work and family life," thereby treating social problems as "private concerns" (Hays, 2003, p. 30). The neoliberal principles of personal responsibility (as named in the Act's title) and market reliance to solve social problems (as evidenced in strict work requirements) structure individuals' experiences of poverty and assistance in the United States today.

Criminal justice in the neoliberal era

The criminal justice system's punitive turn is evident in the sheer number of people the United States presently incarcerates. In just 30 years, the incarcerated population in prisons and jails skyrocketed by 500%, such that the United States currently incarcerates 2.2 million people, more than any other country (The Sentencing Project, n.d.), and holds nearly 7 million people under some form of correctional supervision (Glaze and Perks, 2012). This drastic increase, facilitated by the War on Drugs and tougher sentencing laws, occurred while crime rates were declining (Alexander, 2010; Wacquant, 2009). The 1994 Violent Crime Control and Law Enforcement Act is the pinnacle of the "tough on crime" movement. The Act allocated more than $30 billion to crime control and social programs (Alexander, 2010). In addition to expanding policing and prisons, it influenced sentencing by creating new federal crimes that call for the death penalty and introducing the infamous "three strikes" law, which mandates life in prison for certain third offenses.

Racial bias in arrest, prosecution, and incarceration rates, as well as unprecedented expansion of the criminal justice system, have contributed to the disproportionate incarceration of people of color and of low-income and poor people. The racial and class dynamics of mass incarceration have prompted critical analyses of the carceral state as a racialized form of social control (Alexander, 2010; Davis, 2003; Wacquant, 2009). Alexander (2010) argues that mass incarceration is "the new Jim Crow" in the sense that it supports a racial caste system in the United States not only through incarceration but also through disenfranchisement and the loss of social rights and benefits imposed on individuals post-incarceration.

Similar to the revamping of the social welfare system, the transformation of the U.S. criminal justice system is a decidedly neoliberal project. Neoliberal policies that deregulated the economic market, facilitated deindustrialization, and allowed corporations to exploit a global labor pool contributed to growing wealth inequality and social stratification. The resultant economic and social insecurity felt by the middle class contributed to support for harsh law-and-order approaches to maintain social control (Bumiller, 2008; Davis, 2003; Garland, 2001; Wacquant, 2009, 2012). Given these concerns, it is not surprising that public and private prisons largely have abandoned their past goal of rehabilitation and replaced it with a managerial ethos (Davis, 2003; Haney, 2004; Wacquant, 2009). Importantly, it is not just the number of incarcerated people that has changed, but also the nature and recognized goal of incarceration.

In addition to mass incarceration, Garland (1996, 2001) argues that the state's inability to provide social security pushed federal and state governments to develop new crime control strategies. Drawing on O'Malley's (1992) work, he identifies "responsibilization strategies" as another hallmark of neoliberal crime control. Garland (1996) explains that responsibilization "involves the central government seeking to act upon crime not in a direct fashion through state agencies (police, courts, prisons, social work, etc.) but instead by acting indirectly, seeking to activate action on the part of non-state agencies and organizations" (p. 452). The locus of control moves from the centralized prison, police station, or courthouse into the community as the state administers "coordinated-community response efforts" and contracts out services (and responsibility) to private and non-profit providers to reform offenders and respond to victims (Garland, 1996, 2001; Hannah-Moffat, 2000; Haney, 2010).

Feminist scholars have made important contributions to understanding how responsibilization strategies work by assessing how these strategies extend to the individual offender. In her research on women's prisons in Canada, Hannah-Moffat (2000) describes how despite the use of a feminist/Aboriginal-inspired empowerment strategy, the incarcerated woman, not the state or contracted service providers, is responsible for reform. Prisons offer a series of classes such as life skills, parenting, and anger management that are designed to "empower" incarcerated women as they learn to "conform to a series of normative standards" (Hannah-Moffat, 2000, p. 524). Regardless of the "structural or situational limitations" that contribute to their incarceration, women must accept personal responsibility for their imprisonment. As Hannah-Moffat (2000) concludes, "This individualistic approach contradicts feminist approaches, which place the woman's actions into a wider social, political, and economic context" (p. 525). Haney (2010) reaches a similar conclusion in her study of alternative-to-incarceration programs in the United States. She describes how staff members at one program ignore inmates' repeated requests for "practical help," such as GED classes, employment readiness, and preparation for release, arguing that the program's recovery focus is more transformative and addresses the "real," deep issues and concerns these women face (Haney, 2010, pp. 167–168). As Haney (2010) explains, "The goal was to bracket inmates' social and economic marginalization in order to target their psychologies" (p. 169).

In short, the carceral state has followed a similar trajectory as the social welfare state under neoliberalism. The rhetoric of personal responsibility and state devolution dominate both fields.

Additionally, coercion and containment largely have replaced entitlement and rehabilitation as the state's undergirding philosophical approach to dealing with poverty.

Anti-violence services in the neoliberal era

The social welfare and criminal justice systems target groups at the bottom of the social hierarchy. In a similar fashion, anti-violence services also target a marginalized group. Formalized victim services, such as specialized criminal courts and domestic violence shelters, typically serve poor and low-income women who have survived interpersonal violence. While middle- and upper-class women experience gender-based violence, social capital and access to material recourses often enable them to bypass shelters and the criminal justice system in favor of counseling and civil courts. There is a degree of overlap among the populations the social welfare, criminal justice, and anti-violence systems target, and thus it is important to include considerations of how victim services have fared under neoliberalism alongside analyses of social welfare and criminal justice.

While the social welfare and criminal justice systems underwent the changes described above, the mainstream movement against sexual and domestic violence (commonly referred to as "the anti-violence movement") gained public recognition. Feminist anti-violence activists and advocates largely succeeded in challenging the popular discourse that sexual and domestic violence were personal, private problems and introduced a framework that situated violence against women in the context of gender inequality. This framework provided an important corrective to theories that blamed women for the abuse in their lives and failed to connect women's subordinate social status to the vulnerability they experienced in relationships. Scholarship on the domestic violence movement, in particular, traces the noteworthy legislative and institutional victories won throughout the 1980s and 1990s, such as federal and state funding for domestic violence shelters, hotlines, and other services, as well as criminal remedies to address domestic violence, such as prosecution of abusive partners and orders of protection. Specifically, the 1994 federal Violence Against Women Act (VAWA) institutionalized government funding for domestic violence and sexual assault services, prevention and training, and law enforcement responses to gender-based violence.

While feminist anti-violence scholars widely acknowledge that abuse survivors have several options for help today that did not exist just 30 years ago, a subgroup of these scholars, primarily working from an intersectionality framework that centers the experiences of poor women and women of color, offer important critiques about the costs of the mainstream movement's institutionalization. For one, the movement has foregrounded gender-based oppression as primary while neglecting the development of a comprehensive analysis of how race, class, sexuality, immigration status, and (dis)ability contribute to women's social disadvantage and vulnerability in interpersonal relationships (Coker, 2005; Crenshaw, 1997; Davis, 2000; Hirschmann, 1997; Koyama, 2006; Richie, 2012; Ritchie, 2006). As a result of this oversight, the mainstream movement has prioritized a dual focus on institutionalizing battered women's shelters and criminal justice responses—interventions which often are not safe for and do not meet the needs of many women who experience interpersonal gender-based violence. As Richie (2012) argues, while women with social privilege have benefited from the gains of the anti-violence movement, "Black women who are most vulnerable to male violence remain unprotected, disbelieved, and unsupported by institutionalized programs, unexposed to prevention messages, cut off from the crisis intervention services that the movement had fostered, and marginalized in their communities" (p. 96).

Another strand of criticism analyzes how the mainstream anti-violence movement became complicit with the rise of mass incarceration in the United States (Bumiller, 2008; Ferraro, 1996; Richie, 2012). According to Bumiller (2008):

> Mainstream feminist demands for more certain and severe punishment for crimes against women … resulted in a direct alliance between feminist activists and legislators, prosecutors, and other elected officials promoting the crime control business. Although the feminists' "gender war" did not have the same impact on incarceration rates as the "war on drugs," it still contributed to the symbolic message.
>
> (p. 7)

The convergence of the mainstream anti-violence and "tough on crime" movements crystallized in the VAWA, which Congress passed as part of the Violent Crime Control and Law Enforcement Act (discussed above). According to Richie (2012):

> It is very significant to note that what could be understood as legislative success with the passing of the VAWA came with a cost—a set of harsh laws that disadvantaged some of the same communities that the population of women who are most vulnerable to male violence come from.
>
> (p. 86)

A third strand of criticism of the mainstream anti-violence movement focuses on how it has traded its liberatory potential for a social services model that focuses on individual "empowerment" (Bumiller, 2008; Ferraro, 1996; McDonald, 2005; Richie, 2012). For one, reliance on government funding to run domestic violence services limits organizations' ability to do radical, social justice work from an explicitly feminist perspective. Bumiller (2008) argues that feminist cooperation with the state in the form of government-funded services and shelters contributes to a discourse of dependency that focuses on individual responsibility while silencing the structural violence women also face. When violence survivors engage shelters and the criminal justice system for protection, they must learn to comply with these institutions' rules and policies (see also Dunn, 2002). According to Bumiller (2008):

> This performance of compliance does not prepare women for combating gender hierarchies or confronting injustices in society at large. In this way, clients of the welfare state learn to improve their short-term survival strategies rather than enlarge their life expectations. This is particularly unfortunate because many women soon return to communities where the conditions of poverty and lack of adequate government services will encumber their freedom in ways not so different from the environment of the shelter.
>
> (p. 131)

Like critical social welfare and criminal justice scholarship, domestic violence research identifies a similar neoliberal focus on empowerment rhetoric, personal responsibility, and punitive approaches that is disconnected from an analysis of how structural inequality shapes individual experiences.

Personal responsibility in the criminal domestic violence court

The individual-level focus was evident in my own research with domestic violence survivors who engaged the criminal justice system. Over five months in 2008 and in January 2009, I conducted in-depth, one-on-one interviews with 11 women who turned to the misdemeanor criminal domestic violence court in Chicago following incidents of physical violence perpetrated by intimate partners, all of whom were men. I found that while cooperating with the state to prosecute abusive partners, interviewees learn to "accomplish victimization" (Dunn, 2002; Holstein and Miller, 1990). While in the courtroom and particularly when testifying, women learn they must fit popular notions of victimhood, such as meekness, passivity, fear, and blamelessness, in order for the state's attorneys and judges to recognize them as "worthy" victims deserving of the court's assistance. Court actors, specifically defense attorneys, draw attention to characteristics and behaviors that do not conform to popular notions of victimhood, such as fighting back against abusive partners, to call victims' credibility into question. Importantly, women must exercise self-restraint in the courtroom while attorneys question their victim status, as showing anger would support the attorneys' depiction and undermine their processes of accomplishing victimization.

One way judges show recognition of "worthy" victims is through issuing a criminal order of protection, which mandates an abusive party to follow specified provisions regarding the protected party. The order shows institutional recognition of the abuse and the need for ongoing protection, and it documents the expectations victims and the court should hold for one another going forward. Judges, assistant state attorneys, and victim advocates repeatedly tell women to call the police if the abuser does anything threatening and offer assurance that, in return, the police will recognize these calls as legitimate because an order of protection is in place. Court actors further assure that after police intervene by arresting the abuser, the court will recognize the woman's call for help as legitimate by punishing the abuser for violating the order. The order provides women with a tool to engage and reengage different parts of the criminal justice system, stressing that an appropriate response to future violence is continued reliance on the system.

I argue that as women successfully accomplish victimization, thereby gaining legitimacy with the court and acquiring tools to manage the interpersonal violence in their lives, they also learn to distinguish themselves from "unworthy" victims. Interviewees indicated a perception that their use of the domestic violence court made their responses to abuse distinctive. Importantly, the court became an avenue for them to distinguish themselves from women whom they described as inexplicably putting up with and even enjoying abuse. Thus, one consequence of court engagement is that women can leave the court feeling alienated from other domestic violence victims and with a reinforced understanding that domestic violence is a personal problem they are responsible for ending, primarily through obtaining orders of protection, following the order's provisions, and continuing to engage the criminal justice system in their efforts to end partners' abuse. Even interviewees who expressed the most dissatisfaction with their experiences with the police and the court talked about how they learned to engage the criminal justice system more effectively. As one interviewee reflected:

> [I]t's a learning experience. Now I know. Now I know if a man touch me again, go to the police officers right then and there. Get all evidence. Um, and tell the truth to everybody. Cuz I could have brought other people in if I had told like my family members the truth … I'm sure I could have brought them in. And don't hide from it. And most definitely don't let no man talk down to you for no reason whatsoever.

Not only does this comment indicate that she has been socialized into the domestic violence court system so that she now knows how to use it more effectively, but it also points to how the court encourages women to undergo a process of responsibilization as part of their transformation from "victim" to "survivor." The individual victim, as well as her family and friends, are at least partly, if not primarily, responsible for documenting and regulating the abusive partner's behaviors.

The ambivalent status of the mainstream anti-violence movement

While the mainstream anti-violence movement successfully has created institutional responses that allow some women to access help in dealing with interpersonal violence, the movement has been less successful in addressing structural violence, such as lack of access to living-wage jobs, education, and support for caretaking. Perhaps one of the greatest ironies of the mainstream anti-violence movement's institutionalization is that despite critiquing public discourse that focuses on women's responsibility to end the violence in their lives, many interventions unwittingly reinforce this discourse in direct service work with individuals.

The most helpful feminist critiques of the mainstream anti-violence movement highlight that this movement has been shaped significantly by a "neoliberal, law-and-order-oriented social agenda [that] has supplanted the state's willingness to provide basic material resources and opportunity for self-sufficiency for low-income groups" (Richie, 2012, p. 103). In charting the trajectory of the anti-violence movement, these scholars explicitly situate the movement's shifts within a broader context of neoliberalism. A key factor in understanding anti-violence services today is recognizing that the mainstream anti-violence movement demanded the state accept accountability to intervene in gender-based violence not just during the heyday of the "tough on crime" movement but also at the precise moment when the state was devolving and implementing responsibilization strategies. Thus, when the state acknowledged gender-based violence, most notably and symbolically with the passage of the VAWA, it did so within the context and framework of "devolv[ing] responsibility for crime prevention to agencies, organizations and individuals which are quite outside the state and to persuade them to act appropriately" (Garland, 1996, p. 452). This responsibilization framework contributes to individualized responses to gender-based violence that focus on punishing individual abusers and transforming abused women through individual empowerment. At best, this framework fails to challenge larger systems of inequality; at worst, it supports these systems. According to Gruber (2009), "The feminist movement's continued calls for more and harsher punishment of gendered crimes in this era of vengeance and victims' rights makes it complicit in a neoliberal system that undermines women's equality and economic health and retards equality generally" (p. 625).

Internalized neoliberalism as a unifying concept

To this point, I have provided a brief overview of major recent policy shifts in the U.S. social welfare, criminal justice, and anti-violence systems. Pulling together these subfields contributes to an emerging cross-dialogue among scholarship that investigates how the state intervenes in the lives of groups positioned at the bottom of the social hierarchy under neoliberalism (Wacquant, 2012). This cross-dialogue is fruitful not only because it shows how each system has evolved in accordance with the neoliberal principles of personal responsibility, social welfare retrenchment, penal expansion, market reliance, and state devolution, but also because it shows how each system promotes the internalization of these principles within its target population. I refer to this process as "internalized neoliberalism."

Despite studying different state interventions, scholarship on social welfare, criminal justice, and anti-violence services demonstrates that in order to navigate and in some cases survive each of these systems, individuals must accept, at least outwardly, neoliberal principles. For instance, Hays (2003) shows how the personal responsibility rhetoric of welfare reform diverts attention away from the realities of low-wage work, inadequate childcare, and educational disparities along race and class lines and argues that the "cultural power" of the American "ethos of individualism" encourages us to view poverty and the need for public assistance as the result of individuals' own poor choices (p. 125). She also notes how the single mothers she interviewed adopted this welfare reform rhetoric even after their cases had been sanctioned due to various rule infractions. Despite being harmed by the social welfare system's punitive approach, interviewees defended the system's logic. In a similar way, Haney (2010) documents how the institutional narratives of two alternative-to-incarceration programs for incarcerated mothers discount the social realities of women's lives in favor of focusing on women's personal dependencies and various "addictions." An important consequence in one program was that inmates quickly turned on each other and pointed out others' psychological failings. Rather than collectively organize to address the routine violation of their rights as prisoners, the inmates remained divided as "weak" individuals, in accordance with the institutional narrative's framing of their identities and construction of their problems. Similarly, in my research with victims at a criminal domestic violence court, interviewees engaged in discursive work to separate themselves from "unworthy" victims who failed to leave abusive partners and effectively utilize the criminal justice system.

Taken together, this research shows that, across various systems, the state imposes a framework on marginalized groups that promotes bracketing social problems and inequalities (Haney, 2010), limiting claims on the state to provide assistance, and individual responsibility to personally transform from a stigmatized identity (i.e., welfare recipient, offender, victim) to a redeemed identity (i.e., employed person, ex-offender, survivor). The concept of internalized neoliberalism provides a framework to investigate the occurrence of similar processes across diverse state interventions while focusing on what macro-level shifts mean for individuals who encounter these interventions on the ground. The state's divisive work to discourage marginalized groups from seeing individual circumstances as connected to patterns of social inequality does not *only* encourage internalized racism, sexism, or classism; it encourages *all* of these processes simultaneously and in the historical context of neoliberalism. The concept of internalized neoliberalism foregrounds an intersectional understanding of neoliberalism in theorizing how the state regulates social marginality across a wide range of seemingly disparate systems.

Conclusion

Neoliberalism has been hugely consequential not only for the criminal justice and social welfare systems but also for victim assistance services. Despite the liberatory focus of the early mainstream anti-violence movement, today it is increasingly difficult for women who experience gender-based violence to access services in contexts that articulate a critical social justice framework. As a result, many mainstream responses to gender-based violence operate as yet another arm of the state that seeks to control and reform poor women in the present neoliberal era. Integrating scholarship on criminal justice, social welfare, and anti-violence services can deepen our understanding of how the neoliberal state regulates socially marginalized populations and may even promote new strategies to resist the state's punitive interventions. For instance, by foregrounding neoliberalism in her assessment of the mainstream anti-violence movement, Richie (2012) develops the "violence matrix," which situates women's interpersonal violence within the context of community and state violence, such as the structural harm that results from neoliberal public policies. The violence matrix makes clear that ending gender-based violence necessitates crafting a strong social safety net while reversing the expansion of the criminal justice system. Advocates, activists, and academics no longer can afford to study these fields in isolation.

References

Alexander, M. (2010). *The new Jim Crow: Mass incarceration in the age of colorblindness.* New York, NY: The New Press.

Beckett, K., and Western, B. (2001). Governing social marginality: Welfare, incarceration, and the transformation of state policy. *Punishment and Society*, 3(1), 43–59.

Bumiller, K. (2008). *In an abusive state: How neoliberalism appropriated the feminist movement against sexual violence.* Durham, NC: Duke University Press.

Coker, D. (2005). Shifting power for battered women: Law, material resources, and poor women of color. In N. J. Sokoloff (ed.), *Domestic violence at the margins: Readings on race, class, gender, and culture* (369–388). New Brunswick, NJ: Rutgers University Press.

Crenshaw, K. (1997). Mapping the margins: Intersectionality, identity politics, and violence against women of color. In M.A. Fineman and R. Mykitiuk (eds), *The public nature of private violence: The discovery of domestic abuse* (93–118). New York, NY: Routledge.

Davis, A. (2000). The color of violence against women. *Colorlines: Race, Culture, Action*, 3(3), 4–12.

Davis, A. (2003). *Are prisons obsolete?* New York, NY: Seven Stories Press.

Dunn, J. (2002). *Courting disaster: Intimate stalking, culture, and criminal justice.* New York, NY: Aldine de Gruyter.

Ferraro, K. J. (1996). The dance of dependency: A genealogy of domestic violence discourse. *Hypatia*, 11(4), 77–91.

Garland, D. (1996). The limits of the sovereign state: Strategies of crime control in contemporary society. *British Journal of Criminology*, 36(4), 445–471.

Garland, D. (2001). *The culture of control: Crime and social order in contemporary society.* Chicago, IL: The University of Chicago Press.

Glaze, L.E., and Perks, E. (2012). *Correctional populations in the United States, 2011.* Washington, DC: U.S. Department of Justice.

Gruber, A. (2009). Rape, feminism, and the war on crime. *Washington Law Review*, 84(4), 581–658.

Haney, L. (2004). Introduction: Gender, welfare, and states of punishment. *Social Politics*, 11(3), 333–362.

Haney, L. (2010). *Offending women: Power, punishment, and the regulation of desire.* Berkeley, CA: University of California Press.

Hannah-Moffat, K. (2000). Prisons that empower: Neoliberal governance in Canadian women's prisons. *British Journal of Criminology*, 40(3), 510–531.

Hays, S. (2003). *Flat broke with children: Women in the age of welfare reform.* New York, NY: Oxford University Press.

Hirschmann, N. J. (1997). The theory and practice of freedom: The case of battered women. In M.L. Shanley and U. Narayan (eds), *Reconstructing political theory: Feminist perspectives* (194–210). University Park, PA: The Pennsylvania State University Press.

Holstein, J. A., and Miller, G. (1990). Rethinking victimization: An interactional approach to victimology. *Symbolic Interaction*, 13(1), 103–122.

Jimenez, M. (1999). A feminist analysis of welfare reform: The Personal Responsibility Act of 1996. *AFFILIA*, 14(3), 278–293.

Koyama, E. (2006). Disloyal to feminism: Abuse of survivors within the domestic violence shelter system. In INCITE! Women of Color Against Violence (ed.), *Color of violence: The INCITE! anthology* (208–222). Cambridge, MA: South End Press.

McDonald, J. (2005). Neo-liberalism and the pathologising of public issues: The displacement of feminist service models in domestic violence support services. *Australian Social Work*, 58(3), 275–284.

O'Malley, P. (1992). Risk, power and crime prevention. *Economy and Society*, 21(3), 252–274.

Reese, E. (2007). The causes and consequences of U.S. welfare retrenchment. *Journal of Poverty*, 11(3), 47–63.

Richie, B. E. (2012). *Arrested justice: Black women, violence, and America's prison nation.* New York, NY: New York University Press.

Ritchie, A. J. (2006). Law enforcement violence against women of color. In INCITE! Women of Color Against violence (ed.), *Color of violence: The INCITE! anthology* (138–156). Cambridge, MA: South End Press.

The Sentencing Project. (n.d.). Incarceration. Retrieved March 4, 2013, from http://www.sentencing project.org/template/page.cfm?id=107.

Wacquant, L. (2009). *Punishing the poor: The neoliberal government of social insecurity*. Durham, NC: Duke University Press.

Wacquant, L. (2012). The wedding of workfare and prisonfare in the 21st century. *Journal of Poverty*, 16(3), 236–249.

36

SYSTEMIC AND SYMBOLIC VIOLENCE AS VIRTUE

The carceral punishment of African American girls

Enora R. Brown

For three decades, African American girls have been the fastest-growing group of youth arrested and detained within the juvenile justice system. As the incidence of crime for 10–17-year-old girls rose steadily, from the mid-1980s to mid-1990s, African American girls' violent crime arrests, simple assaults, and subsequent detention rates doubled and tripled, far outstripping rates for African American boys and White girls (Chesney-Lind and Jones, 2010; Puzzanchera and Adams, 2011). As youth arrests and detentions declined from 1995 to 2009, African American girls' descent trailed behind their counterparts. In 2010, they sustained the highest residential detention rate (Morris, 2012). These troubling patterns were flagged as indicators of an upsurge in the new phenomenon, "girl violence," created by a new type of wayward girl.

Though "girl violence" generated an array of explanatory theories, *biopsychological theories* held sway, conceptualizing it as a form of aggression endemic to girlhood (Crick et al., 1998; Simmons, 2002). "Girl violence" is viewed as covert, non-physical expressions of anger, that uniquely emerge in females as relational aggression, e.g., "meanness," or as overt expressions of internalized male aggression, e.g., physical assault, rooted in girls' "masculinization"—an aberrant shift in "the essential female's docile nature" (Chesney-Lind and Shelden, 2004). The rise in detentions and gendered aggression theories bolstered the discourse that "girl violence" and "bad" femininity jeopardized females' "natural" position in society, evoking a "just deserts" backlash against gender equality. *Eugenic/cultural deficit theories* racialized "girl violence," attributed to African Americans' inborn criminality, matriarchal family, and community dysfunction (Brown and Gourdine, 2001; Holsinger and Holsinger, 2005). They reified resurgent views of crime-prone African American girls' "male aggression," and Black youth of *both sexes* as predictable violent threats to societal safety and moral sanctity. Sensational media depictions of *typical* gun-toting urban girls of color, e.g., *For Gold Earrings and Protection*, and *atypical* aggressive suburban White girls, e.g., *Girl Fight: Savagery in Chicago Suburbs*, popularized "violent girls" as poor, Black, and Latino, and "mean girls" as White and middle class (Lee, 1991; Meadows et al., 2002). Racial constructs and rising incarcerations situated Black girls as the force behind the violent surge, sounding a clarion call to stem the tide (Covington, 2010).

This chapter addresses obscurant *structural and attributional* underpinnings of "girl violence," and counters theories that foreground individual pathology and displace systemic origins of social problems. Using Zizek's violence theory and Wacquant's penal state analysis, I argue that *systemic and symbolic violence* embody three prongs of neoliberal reform policy that undergird the construction and incidence of *subjective* "girl violence" and criminalize African American girls. The pronounced visibility of racialized "girl violence" overshadows routine penal state violence, and affirms the "common-sense" logic of the crime-and-punishment box (Wacquant, 2009; Zizek, 2008). *Symbolic and systemic violence* undergird a *dehumanization process* that amplifies historical patterns of racial criminalization and masks current neoliberal aims, as it justifies "violent girls'" detainment as a virtuous societal imperative and fuels resistance in pursuit of democratic visions for a *civil* society (Fromm, 1990).

Conceptual frameworks revision "girl violence": Zizek and Wacquant

Zizek draws on critical theorists' concepts of physical *and* non-physical violence, e.g., structural, symbolic, everyday, political, psychological, decolonizing violence—situated *outside* of aberrant individuals, *endemic* to the state and social institutions, and *organically linked* to sustaining-resisting economic–political relations of domination (Fanon, 1963; Scheper-Hughes and Bourgois, 2004). His triumvirate—*subjective, systemic, symbolic violence*—provides a lens to revision "girl violence" (2008). Most visible is *subjective violence* between subjects—illegitimate acts by "clearly identifiable agents," e.g., domestic violence, rebellions and terror. "Girl violence" constitutes these highly publicized, "everyday" acts, e.g., physical assault and property damage, forming the crime nexus around which the criminal justice system and our collective psyche revolve. Least visible are two forms of *objective violence—symbolic and systemic. Symbolic violence* is embodied in daily language and hegemonic discourses, which forge assaultive meanings about phenomena and social identities, e.g., welfare queens and gangsta girls, and have "precise material effects" on social life, e.g., welfare reform and policing girls. *Systemic violence* embodies "smooth functioning" mechanisms that sustain exploitative systems, e.g., capitalism, via force, threat of repression, and routine institutional policies, e.g., police assault, surveillance, and incarceration. Its "catastrophic consequences," e.g., racism, poverty, are "invisible genocides and small holocausts," that maintain an illusory non-violent society, whose "peace" is disrupted by unruly elements' *subjective violence* (Scheper-Hughes and Bourgois, 2004). Synergistically, the cathexis of *subjective* "girl violence" verifies *symbolic* codified views of "poor-Black-violent girls" and "mean-White-middle-class girls," and rationalizes *systemic* racial profiling and disparate detention rates. Urgent *systemic* responses to violent acts' threat to society's imagined "zero" violence level precipitate inexplicable, seemingly irrational *subjective violence* eruptions, e.g., "wilding" and social protest, that reaffirm *symbolic* notions of "the unruly."

Wacquant's analysis of neoliberalism's rising penal state exposes its twin modalities, *workfare* and *prisonfare,* as mechanisms of *systemic and symbolic violence,* undergirding girls' rising incarcerations (2009). Dispelling the "crime-and-punishment box," he argues that the state's response to pervasive *social insecurity,* produced by deep economic decline, catalyzed mounting detentions, *not* girls' criminality. In the wake of deindustrialization, permanent unemployment, and intensified race–class polarization, the state apparatus reconfigured, by unifying social and penal policies into two strands of punitive poverty policy. Under mantras of "individual responsibility" and market fundamentalism, the retooled state withdrew social goods and expanded retributive discipline, through *workfare*—the constriction of welfare, replaced by obligatory subpar work in exchange for social support—and *prisonfare*—the expansion of non-rehabilitative carceral punishment and surveillance. These state modalities jointly target and punish the poorest, racially stigmatized surplus labor sector—sequestered in depleted African American communities, and most resistant to sustained assault on their lives. I add a *third* complementary modality designed for poor youth, *edufare*—constricted public education, replaced by test-based performance in exchange for tiered schooling. These three modalities embody *systemic and symbolic violence* to manage and demonize African American girls. This *objective violence* is obscured, as dispossessed subjects—failing students, young welfare recipients, and perpetrators of hypervisible *subjective "girl violence"*—are pathologized as parasitic, undeserving, dangerous girls, who need to be sanctioned, detained, and inculcated with a work/achievement ethic, personal restraint, and militarized discipline.

Systematic and symbolic violence: three-pronged policy reform and African American girls' detention

[It] ... deform[s] reality [to] artificially extract delinquent behaviors from the fabric of social relations in which they take root and make sense, deliberately ignoring their causes and ... meanings ...

(Wacquant, 2009, p. xii)

We should ... disentangle ourselves from the fascinating lure of ... directly visible "subjective" violence ... to perceive the contours of the background, which generates such outbursts.

(Zizek, 2008, p. 1)

Zizek and Wacquant urge an examination of shrouded *systemic* and *symbolic* origins of the *subjective violence* underlying the ostensible upsurge in "girl violence" and African American girls' juvenile arrests and detentions. Through their work, I argue that penal state *systemic* assaults on poor youth embody *three prongs* of neoliberal reform policy—the *Personal Responsibility and Work Opportunity Act (PRWORA) (1996)*, *Juvenile Justice Delinquency Prevention Act (JJDPA)(1974/2002)*, and *No Child Left Behind and Race to the Top (NCLB and RTTT) (2001 and 2009)*—that execute *workfare, prisonfare,* and *edufare* and serve corporate interests. Their convergent *symbolic* assaults reify notions of African American girls' *criminality, hypersexuality,* and *irresponsibility*, distort the incidence of "girl violence," and poise these girls as "societal dregs," preparing to fill their maternal forebearers' shoes.

Workfare: As PRWORA (1996) replaced Aid to Families with Dependent Children (AFDC) with Temporary Assistance to Needy Families (TANF), it ended federally guaranteed cash assistance for children. TANF instituted "workfare for girls," mandating school/job training in exchange for constricted support and punitive, surveillant regulations for unwed teen mothers' welfare eligibility, i.e., 5-year life-time limit, residence with adult, family birth caps, and abstinence education. The view that poor girls' deficits caused teen pregnancy and joblessness, framed PRWORA's aim to limit welfare dependence and out-of-wedlock births, and promote work, self-sufficiency, parent responsibility, and "morality." Suffused in gender-blaming racial discourses, its statistics on rising "illegitimacy" rates, criminality in intergenerational single-parent, fatherless homes, and tropes on family dysfunction and sexual promiscuity infused African American girl constructs (Pillow, 2004; Roberts, 2002). Though slight rises in employment affirmed that labor market vagaries, *not* personal irresponsibility, generate joblessness, PRWORA's *systemic and symbolic violence* further impoverished girls, produced images of oversexed, predatory agents of *subjective violence*, i.e., "freeloaders" having babies for money, and enabled "corporate welfare" bailouts, via neoliberal accumulation-by-dispossession (Harvey, 2007; Krugman, 2013). From 1996 to 2011, TANF increased deep poverty by 64%, decreased AFDC's safety net by 300%, and failed to improve girls' education, work, childbearing, and residential status (Acs and Koball, 2003; Trisi and Pavetti, 2012). Its "misery index" soared, as basic needs were rationed, creating conditions for underground economies, policy violations, and incarceration. *One* sensationalized "welfare fraud" case feigned an epidemic, branding girls as emergent criminal, "welfare queens" (Casey, 2013; Coughlin, 1987; Hancock, 2004). *Workfare* assails poor African American girls, populating child welfare and juvenile justice systems, and works in tandem with the second penal state modality, *prisonfare* (Hildebrandt and Stevens, 2009; Monroe, 2005; Roberts, 2002).

Prisonfare: As the *Juvenile Justice Delinquency Prevention Act* of 1974/2002 (JJDPA) protectively de-institutionalized and separated youth from adult offenders, its due process measures formalized the juvenile justice system, aligning the juvenile with the adult criminal court. This structural shift scaffolded the systemic move from *individual rehabilitation*'s discretionary "parens patriae" to uniform *retributive punishment* administrator (Butts and Mears, 2001; Lawrence and Hermens, 2008). JJDPA's infrastructure was convergent with the "law and order" backlash against 1960s radicalized masses, and ripe for 1980s–1990s "get tough" on drugs–crime legislation, e.g., mandatory harsh penalties, criminal court transfers, minimum sentences, and transfer age (Jarecki et al., 2012; Parenti, 1999). This penal campaign targeted poor youth of color, likely to resist deindustrialization's ravages, seek extralegal survival means, and seek equality. *Systemic* assaults forged boys' (60%) and girls' (132%) steady rise in violent crime arrests, a 140% increase in delinquency cases waived to criminal court, and swollen dividends for burgeoning privatized abuse-ridden juvenile prisons (Adams and Addie, 2012; Hall, 2013; Puzzanchera and Adams, 2011). *Symbolically*, the upsurge was attributed to "super-criminals'" increasingly violent nature and deviant Black girls' male aggression, justifying detention and criminal adultification (Friedman, 2003; Graham and Lowery, 2004; Jones, 2010).

Becca's Bill (1995), *prisonfare*'s coup de grace, affirmed JJDPA's juvenile–criminal court alignment, by converting status-to-delinquent offenses. Designed to protect minors, after a 13-year-old chronic runaway, sexual abuse victim was killed, it authorized runaways' detention, erasing the boundary between social support and retribution. It targeted girls, whose minor offenses and sexuality were more heavily policed–sanctioned than boys', e.g., domestic violence and shoplifting, whose running away often belied histories of victimization, and whose "person offenses" in minor family disputes were recalibrated as violent assaults. It enabled zero tolerance policing, catalyzed an 835% rise in Washington State detentions—60% of girls needed support services—and a 98% rise nation-wide—1991 to 2003 (Chesney-Lind and Sheldon, 2004; Roberts, 1999).

African American girls were 50% of female detainees, with a 30% case dismissal rate vs. 70% for White girls. Often, their status offenses were processed criminally vs. White girls' processed as welfare cases with treatment. Courts were intolerant of Black girls' *average offenses*, but punished White girls more harshly for *above average* offenses that violated race–gender expectations. Stereotypes of Black girls' negative personality traits—independent, aggressive, loud, sexual, rude, mature—and of White girls as social environs victims—passive, need protection, non-threatening, rehabilitable, immature—influenced court decisions. Media "techniques of neutralization" disparately ascribed blameworthiness, guilt–innocence, and sanctions deserved to White and Black females (Brennan and Vandenburg, 2009; Nanda, 2012).

Prisonfare policies repositioned youth as adults, relabeled/"bootstrapped" repeat status offenses as court violations with increasingly severe penalties, and "upcrimed" minor into major offenses. The resultant spike in arrests and detentions was a *feigned rise* in girls' violence, a fraudulent epidemic. While girls have *always* been capable of violence, and offense-conversion policy distorted the volume and quality of violent acts, molding gendered and racialized constructs of "girl violence" and "violent girls." The amplified rise in *subjective* "girl violence" obscured *systemic* and *symbolic* assaults from detainment and assertions of male aggression. JJDPA and PRWORA mandated the exchange of metered doses of social support to girls for obligatory detention/protection or work. *Edufare*, the third penal state modality, withdrew public education from girls targeted by *workfare* and *prisonfare*.

Edufare: As *No Child Left Behind (NCLB)*(2001) and *Race to the Top (RTTT)* (2009) standardized, privatized, and dismantled public education, they exchanged test-based performance for tiered, zero-tolerance schooling, withdrew education's democratic possibilities, and provided new corporate investment markets. Ostensibly designed to reduce school failure, close the achievement gap, and improve college-career readiness in safe schools, the policies implemented punitive race–class stratifying "accountability" mandates and business-run charter schools (Saltman, 2012). *Systemic and symbolic violence* entailed pervasive school closings for private appropriation—"a corrective" for failure, "No Excuses" mantra, expansive vs. limited options for "low-need," and motivated, "successful" vs. "high-need," unmotivated "at-risk" youth in "Reward" vs. "Challenge" Schools (USDE, 2009). Gatekeeping lotteries and exams for select school admission vs. guaranteed admission to neighborhood charter schools/"dropout factories" forged codified tracks of engaging inquiry-based learning vs. dull rote-based schooling, and promising life options vs. restricted school-to-prison/military pipelines (Brown, 2010; Fine and Ruglis, 2009; Meiners, 2007).

NCLB/RTTT's *systemic* assaults induced a 40% dropout rate for African American girls, rising to 50%, as schools for pregnant girls closed for mainstreaming (Bosman, 2007; Kain, 2011; Orfield, 2004). Ostensibly, zero-tolerance policies' stringent surveillance and policing would avert underperforming student disruptions (Reyes, 2006). They led to 43% of African American girls' suspensions or expulsions for "upcrimed" behaviors, e.g., profanity, loudness, defiance, precocity, and normalized unconscionable assaults on 5–7-year-olds—terrorized, arrested, booked, and detained for "tantrums" (Herbert, 2007; Skiba, 2002). "Good" middle-class White girls' pregnancy "mistakes" and "mean," "misguided" behavior deserved compassionate care, while "bad" pregnant Black girls' delinquent "irresponsible choices" justified punitive school closures. *Symbolic* assaults placed them at the disparaged hub of "culture of poverty," teen pregnancy, and "girl violence" epidemic discourses. They were viewed as academic failures, who posed the figurative threat of *subjective* violence, i.e., moral contamination of school culture, and castigated for "ungovernable," "unfeminine," so-called "ghetto" behavior, i.e., nonconformity to stereotypic White middle-class gender roles (Luttrell, 2003; Morris, 2012; Pillow, 2004).

Penal state modality-driven policies are complementary: NCLB/RTTT's cost-cutting school closures and pushouts of African American mothers or visibly expectant girls withdrew educational support, setting them up for *workfare* education sanctions under TANF and *prisonfare* truancy sanctions under JJDPA; zero-tolerance policies funnel girls to *prisonfare* school-to-prison pipeline arrests under JJDPA and *workfare* residency sanctions under TANF. Their convergent *systemic* and *symbolic* assaults amplify "girl violence," reify notions of African American girls' *criminality*, *hypersexuality*, and *irresponsibility*, and justify resource withdrawal, discipline, and incarceration. Invisible, normalized violence is silenced—drowned out by the cacophony of African American girls' rising detentions, welfare dependence, and underachievement. This state *violence* engages a long-standing *process of dehumanization.*

Systemic and symbolic violence: dehumanization processes

Dehumanization is a *psychological and sociocultural* process that strips stigmatized groups of their humanity. Through unconscious, affective *animalization, objectification,* and *deindividuation,* it denies "the other" from possessing *unique* qualities, marking indelible boundaries between humans and animals—higher cognition, civility, morality, emotionality, agency, and self-reflection. The dehumanized are reduced to less-evolved animals and machine-like objects—child-like, incompetent, illogical, instinct-driven, uncultured, inert, cold, and exchangeable/disposable (Goff et al., 2008; Haslam, 2006). Dehumanization relies on psychological defenses that enable, excuse, and reframe *systemic, symbolic, and subjective violence* against them.

It intensifies, abates, and morphs relative to specific economic–sociocultural conditions. African Americans' dehumanization began with chattel slavery—the foundation of U.S. capital—and surged during Post-Reconstruction's extralegal, state-sanctioned reign of terror. *Symbolic and systemic violence* animalized and objectified Blacks as "property" and "3/5 of a man" in the Slave Codes and

Constitution. Viewing Blacks as impervious to loss, love, pain, and civility enabled brutality, willful family severance, life-long slavery, and the imposition of Black Codes and Jim Crow Laws (Covington, 2010; Muhammad, 2010; Williams, 2012). Woven throughout the nation's socio-cultural fabric, eugenic discourses defined humanity's "racial boundaries," instantiating African Americans' race–class position. This violence "ebbed" in the post-World War II ascendance of U.S. capitalist democracy's legalized racial equality.

Current economic–social insecurity evoked neoliberalism's vengeful resurgent dehumanization through the rationalized enactment of *workfare, prisonfare,* and *edufare.* Age-old referents to African American girls—inherent violent criminality, hypersexuality, immoral irresponsibility, incivility, laziness, parental incompetence, and sans femininity—indicate their "not-quite-human" status. Insidious gendered *animalization, objectification,* and *deindividuation* construct them as "tough," unbridled "breeding mules," more like Black males' "ape-like savagery" than White females' "genteel femininity" (Eberhardt et al., 2006; Polakow, 2000; Spagnoli, 2009). Paradoxically, Black girls are criminally adultified in welfare, juvenile justice, and school systems, but denied the humanity of sentient youth, who desire education and a decent life, who often childbear as an earnest first-step towards adulthood, sans alternatives, and who relish support and human connectedness. Three-pronged policy sanctions, that feed corporate wealth, are eerily reminiscent of illegal slave education, post-bellum arrests and forced labor of jobless ex-slaves, and 1935's Social Security Act, which prohibited agricultural/domestic workers, i.e., African Americans, from receiving unemployment benefits insured for Whites (Quadagno, 1994). Past–present violence draws on the *racialized pathology of criminality*, presumed guilt, and reassurance that confinement is society's requisite preservative.

Dehumanization obscures the structural roots of poverty's racial feminization, girls' brushes with the law, school failure, and incites moral panic about *subjective "girl violence."* It veils the state's strident, violent efforts to protect capital, amidst chronic, severe economic crises, and justifies *warehousing* "disposable" jobless masses—scapegoated as the cause of social–economic insecurity. Redemptively, penal state modalities impose stringent oversight, sanctions, and confinement, which constrict agency, and ration human needs/rights, for national economic and social solvency. Psychological defenses—*projection, rationalization, denial*—erase others' humanity, reframe violent assaults as "for their own good," and allows hatred to masquerade as virtue. Fromm states: "There is perhaps no phenomenon which contains so much destructive feeling as 'moral indignation,' which permits envy or hate to be acted out under the guise of virtue" (Fromm, 1990, p. 235).

Penality poses as humanity's savior, striving to quell dissent, *but contains seeds of resistance.* Slavery wrought slave rebellions, underground railroads, avid educational pursuits, and perilous efforts to rejoin disrupted families. Three penal state modalities have incurred welfare rights' struggles for money and daycare, activism against incarceration and upcriming, youth movements against school closings and standardized tests, and critical pedagogical work to expose the content–function of false epidemics. Democratic strivings are endemic to the seeming overwhelming nature of penal state violence and dehumanization.

Conclusion

Systemic and symbolic violence embody three convergent neoliberal reform policies that instantiate penal state modalities (*workfare, prisonfare, and edufare*), undergird the construction and incidence of hypervisible *subjective* "girl violence," and criminalize African American girls. Zizek and Wacquant's analyses decenter the pathological origins of *subjective "girl violence,"* expose its systemic roots, and recenter the penal state's obscurant *objective violence* that maintains the social order. State violence engages a long-standing *dehumanization process* that masks current neoliberal aims. It justifies "violent girls'" incarceration as society's virtuous imperative, *and* fuels resistance in pursuit of democratic goals for a *civil* society. Critical examination of the "virtue" of dehumanizing penal state modalities is vital to revision "girl violence" and "violent girls," and target the systemic origins of "social problems."

References

Acs, G. and Koball, H. (2003). TANF and the status of teen mothers under age 18, *New Federalism: Issues and Options for States*, Series A, # A-62, 1–7.

Adams, B. and Addie, S. (2012). *Delinquency cases waived to criminal court, 2009*. Washington, DC: U.S. Department of Justice.

Brennan, P. and Vandenberg, A. (2009). Depictions of female offenders in front-page newspaper stories: The importance of race/ethnicity, *International Journal of Social Inquiry*, 2:2, 141–175.

Bosman, C. (2007, May 24). New York's Schools for pregnant girls will close, *New York Times*.

Brown, A. and Gourdine, R. (2001). Black adolescent females, *Journal of Human Behavior in the Social Environment*, 4:4, 275–298.

Brown, E. (2010). Freedom for some, discipline for "Others": The structure of inequity in education. In K. Saltman and D. Gabbard (eds) *Education as enforcement: The militarization and corporatization of schools*. New York: Routledge.

Butts, J. and Mears, D. (2001) Reviving juvenile justice in a get-tough era, *Youth and Society*, 3:2, 169–198.

Casey, T. (2013). *A TANF Misery Index*. New York: Legal Momentum.

Chesney-Lind, M. and Jones, N. (2010). *Fighting for girls: New perspectives on gender and violence*. Albany, New York: State University of New York.

Chesney-Lind, M. and Shelden, R. (2004). *Girls, delinquency and juvenile justice (3rd ed.)*. Belmont, CA: Wadsworth.

Coughlin, R. (1987). Welfare myths and stereotypes. In R. M. Coughlin (ed.) *Lessons, limits, and choices*, (pp. 79–106). Albuquerque: University of New Mexico Press.

Covington, J. (2010). *Crime and racial constructions: Cultural misinformation about African Americans in media and academia*. New York: Rowman and Littlefield.

Crick, N. R., Werner, N. E., Casas, J. F., O'Brien, K. M., Nelson, D. A., Grotpeter, J. K., and Markon, K. (1998). Childhood aggression and gender: A new look at an old problem, *Nebraska Symposium on Motivation*, 45, 75–141.

Eberhardt, J., Davies, P., Purdie-Vaughn, V., and Johnson, S. (2006). Looking deathworthy: Perceived stereotypicality of Black defendants predicts capital-sentencing outcomes, *Psychological Science*, 17:5, 383–386.

Fanon, F. (1963). *Wretched of the earth*. New York: Grove Press.

Fine, M. and Ruglis, J. (2009). Circuits and consequences of dispossession: The racialized realignment of the public sphere for U.S. youth, *Transforming Anthropology*, 17:1, 20–33.

Friedman, A. (2003). Juvenile crime pays—But at what cost? In T. Herivel and P. Wright (eds) *Prison nation: The warehousing of America's poor*. New York: Routledge.

Fromm, E. (1990). *Man for himself: An inquiry into the psychology of ethics*. New York: Holt Publishers.

Goff, P., Williams, M., Eberhardt, J., and Jackson, M. (2008). Not yet human: Implicit knowledge, historical dehumanization, and contemporary consequences, *Journal of Personality and Social Psychology*, 94:2, 292–306.

Graham, S. and Lowery, B. (2004). Priming unconscious racial stereotypes about adolescent offenders, *Law and Human Behavior*, 28:5, 483–504.

Hall, K. (4/11/2013). CCA Letters reveal private prison industry's tactics, *Huffington Post*. Retrieved from: http://www.huffingtonpost.com/2013/04/11/cca-prison-industry_n_3061115.html

Hancock, A. (2004). *The politics of disgust: The public identity of the welfare queen*. New York: New York University Press.

Harvey, D. (2007). *A brief history of neoliberalism*. Oxford: Oxford University Press.

Haslam, N. (2006). Dehumanization: An integrative review, *Personality and Social Psychology Review*, 10:3, 252–264.

Herbert, B. (2007, April 9). Six-year-olds under arrest, *New York Times*.

Hildebrandt, E. and Stevens, P. (2009). Impoverished women with children and no welfare benefits: The urgency of researching failures of the Temporary Assistance for Needy Families Program, *American Journal of Public Health*, 99:5, 793–801.

Holsinger, K. and Holsinger, A. (2005). Differential pathways to violence and self-injurious behavior: African American and White girls in the juvenile justice system, *Journal of Race in Crime and Delinquency*, 42:2, 211–242.

Jarecki, E., Shopsin, M., and St. John, C. (Producers) and Jarecki, E. (Director) (2012). *The House I Live In* [Documentary]. United States: Charlotte Street Films.

Jones, N. (2010). *Between good and ghetto: African American girls and inner-city violence*. New Brunswick, NJ: Rutgers University Press.

Kain, E. (2011, September 13). Schools for pregnant teens. *Forbes Magazine*.

Krugman, P. (2013, January 27). From welfare queen to disabled "deadbeats." *New York Times*.

Lawrence, R. and Hermens, C. (2008). *Juvenile justice: A Text reader*. New York: Sage.

Lee, F. R. (1991, November 25). For gold earrings and protection, more girls take the road to violence. *New York Times*, pp. A1, B7.

Luttrell, W. (2003). *Pregnant bodies, fertile minds: Gender, race, and the schooling of pregnant teens*. New York: Routledge.

Meadows, S., Johnson, D., and Downey, S. (2002, May 19), Girl fight: Savagery in the Chicago suburbs, *Newsweek*, 141:20, 37.

Meiners, E. (2007). *Right to be hostile: Schools, prisons, and the making of public enemies*. New York: Routledge.

Monroe, A. (2005 Fall/Spring). Women of color and TANF: Issues, barriers, and hindrances, *Human Architecture: Journal of the Sociology of Self-Knowledge*, 4:1 and 2, 165–178.

Morris, M. (2012). *Race, gender and the school-to-prison pipeline: Expanding our discussion to include Black girls*. New York: African American Policy Forum.

Muhammad, K. (2010). *The condemnation of blackness: Race, crime and the making of modern urban America*. Cambridge, MA: Harvard University Press.

Nanda, J. (2012). Blind discretion: Girls of color and delinquency in the juvenile justice system, *UCLA Law Review*, 59, 1502–1539.

Orfield, D. (2004). *Dropouts in America: The graduation rate crisis confrontation*. Cambridge, MA: Harvard Educational Group.

Parenti, C. (1999). *Lockdown America: Policy and prisons in the Age of Crisis*. New York: Verso.

Pillow, W. (2004). *Unfit subjects: Educational policy and the teen mother*. New York: RoutledgeFalmer.

Polakow, V. (2000). *The public assault on America's children: Poverty, violence, and juvenile injustice*. New York: Teachers College Press.

Puzzanchera, C. and Adams, B. (2011, December). *Juvenile arrests, 2009*. Washington, DC: Office of Juvenile Justice and Delinquency Prevention, U.S. Department of Justice.

Quadagno, J. (1994). *The color of welfare: How racism undermined the War on Poverty*. New York: Oxford University Press.

Reyes, A. (2006). *Discipline, achievement, and race: Is zero tolerance the answer?* New York: Race and Education.

Roberts, D. (1999). Foreward: Race, vagueness, and the social meaning of order-maintenance policing, *Supreme Court Review*, 89:3, 775–836.

Roberts, D. (2002). *Shattered bonds: The color of child welfare*. New York: Basic Books.

Saltman, K. (2012). *The failure of corporate school reform*. Boulder, CO: Paradigm Publishers.

Scheper-Hughes, N. and Bourgois, P. (2004). *Violence in war and peace: An anthology*. New York: Blackwell.

Simmons, R. (2002). *Odd girl out: The hidden culture of aggression in girls*. New York: Harcourt.

Skiba, R. (2002). *Zero tolerance: Can suspensions and expulsions keep schools safe?* New York: Jossey Bass.

Spagnoli, F. (2009, December 28). Female animalization: A collection of images [Web blog]. Retrieved October 8, 2013, from: https://filipspagnoli.wordpress.com/tag/female-animalization

Trisi, D. and Pavetti, L. (2012). *TANF weakening as a safety net for poor families*. Washington, DC: Center on Budget and Policy Priorities.

U.S. Department of Education (USDE)(2009). *Executive summary: Race to the Top program*. Washington, DC: USDE.

Wacquant, L. (2009). *Punishing the poor: The neoliberal government of social insecurity*. Durham, NC: Duke University Press.

Williams, H. A. (2012). *Help me find my people: The African American search for family lost in slavery*. Chapel Hill, NC: University of North Carolina Press.

Zizek, S. (2008). *Violence: Six sideways reflections*. New York: Picador Press.

37

THE PARADOX OF ENTREPRENEURSHIP AS A POLICY TOOL FOR ECONOMIC INCLUSION IN NEOLIBERAL POLICY ENVIRONMENTS

Colleen Casey

The viability of entrepreneurship as a policy tool for economic inclusion among the poor is a highly contentious subject. Entrepreneurship itself has emerged as a neoliberal policy tool for economic inclusion; however, it is further complicated when situated in a broader neoliberal policy environment whereby shifts have occurred across major social and economic institutions, transcending political party lines and creating new inequalities and distances between those with and those historically without. To be an effective strategy, entrepreneurship rests heavily upon the assumption that, through social capital, entrepreneurs can overcome these structural barriers. In this chapter, I argue that these reforms have created a paradoxical relationship between entrepreneurship and neoliberal policy environments for economic inclusion. Specifically, I draw upon both qualitative and quantitative secondary data sources to develop three primary lines of thought:

- Socioeconomic or structural barriers do not bind the concept of entrepreneurship; however, when used as a policy tool in the neoliberal agenda, socioeconomic and structural barriers become paramount.
- Entrepreneurship as a policy tool for economic inclusion operates in a broader neoliberal policy environment that privileges wealth and advantage, and deemphasizes access for the disadvantaged to the major social and economic institutions that have been historically associated with social capital formation.
- This combined effect creates a *paradox* that has the potential to foster greater inequality among those most likely to be poor, by not only fostering greater individual inequalities but also by eroding the collective structures necessary to bridge the gaps.

In the remainder of the chapter, I outline the disparities faced by poor entrepreneurs, the policy reforms in the areas of education, labor, and financial markets that threaten to erode the key economic and social institutions that have historically provided opportunity for the poor, and the effects of these reforms.

Entrepreneurship as a policy tool

Entrepreneurship, defined as the creation of new ideas or innovations, can be viewed as a means for community empowerment (Dumas, 2001; Hoselitz, 1952). Conceivably, ideas and innovations are not constrained by socioeconomic or structural factors, and in a perfectly random world, we might expect ideas and innovations to appear and diffuse at the same rate everywhere. However, Gans (1971) suggested that despite the fact that the poor often provide the source of new ideas and innovations, it is those with the social and financial resources that are able to bring the innovations or new trends to market. Data from the Panel Survey of Entrepreneurial Dynamics (I and II) support this notion and suggest that indeed the average successful entrepreneur benefits from a greater level of social and financial resources than the average poor person. In a random survey of individuals interested in pursuing or thinking about pursuing entrepreneurship, Reynolds and Curtin (2008) found that young adults 25–34 years of age are the most active, men are twice as active as women, and African Americans and Hispanics are more active than whites. However, in turning ideas into economic action, those with more education and household income are more likely to be able to move an entrepreneurial idea to actual firm creation.

A challenge all entrepreneurs face is access to formal financial resources for start-up efforts; however, existing research suggests that those with lower levels of wealth or of minority status are more likely to face challenges in accessing resources for start-up activities (Cavalluzzo and Wolken, 2005; Fairlie, 2004; Robb and Fairlie, 2007; Salazar, 2007). The majority of financial resources for entrepreneurial start-up activities come from an entrepreneur's own personal savings or wealth, including that from their job, savings, investments, and real estate, which places low-wealth entrepreneurs, particularly minorities, at a disadvantaged starting point. For example, in the United States, based on 2007 data, the net worth of high-income African Americans was substantially less than the net worth of middle-income whites, and one-quarter of African Americans reported no financial assets or wealth (Shapiro et al., 2010). Based on 2009 data, the median net worth of Hispanic and African American households was $6,325 and $5,677, respectively, compared to the median net worth of white households, $113,149 (Taylor et al., 2011). Hispanics are less likely than whites to own their homes and cars or receive investment income, have overall lower levels of income, and one-third of Hispanics live in poverty (Holguin et al., 2007). Thus, when the conceptualization of entrepreneurship shifts away from the notion of new ideas and innovations that can empower communities or foster collective action (Dumas, 2001) to an explicit focus on the utilization of market mechanisms for private profit, the barriers created by socioeconomic and structural factors become more evident. Some groups become more privileged with the start-up financial resources necessary to pursue, develop, and expand entrepreneurial efforts.

The promise of social capital

In the neoliberal policy environment, social capital is viewed as playing an important role in overcoming disparities. As Tabb argues (2002), neoliberalism, and its emphasis on "the deregulation of the economy, trade liberalization, the dismantling of the public sector, and the predominance of the financial sector of the economy over production and commerce" (p. 7), emphasizes the "privatization of the public provision of goods and services and puts into question all collective structures capable of obstructing the logic of the pure market" (p. 29). A neoliberal policy environment shifts attention to the private arena, and places an emphasis on the importance of private relationships to overcome disadvantage (Fukuyama, 1995). Theories of social capital applied to the entrepreneurial arena suggest that those that are disadvantaged can gain access and participate in the neoliberal policy space by building connections to those that possess these resources necessary to start and expand business efforts (Casey, 2012). Social capital used in this manner is defined as a set of relationships that can lead to more positive economic opportunities.

The operating assumption is that social capital can help poor entrepreneurs overcome their lack of personal financial resources—hence the solution for poor entrepreneurs is to build social relationships. A premise of the promise of a social capital solution to overcoming the challenges faced by poor entrepreneurs is that it is a free resource equally available to everyone. Figure 37.1 illustrates the nature of these relationships, suggesting that social capital can help one to gain greater education, labor, and economic opportunities, which in turn fuels more social capital and the cycle continues. As one accumulates a higher level or value of these indicators, for example a greater level of education or obtaining a more prestigious career, the returns to social capital increase in the form of economic opportunity. Put more simply, as one obtains higher levels of education, career prestige, and professional experience, one builds their social resource base, and the cycle continues.

However, Lin (2001) argued that social capital is embedded in the social resources that one possesses, and often individuals make connections to others with similar social resources as their own. Social resource theory suggests that, through attainment of education and career experience, one accumulates a "stock" of social resources that can be used as a source of emotional, material, and information aid, and can influence economic action, i.e., influencing one's social capital (Lin, 2001). Social resources include one's educational level, professional or management experience, career prestige or status, and diversity of racial and ethnic ties (Lin and Erickson, 2008; Moren

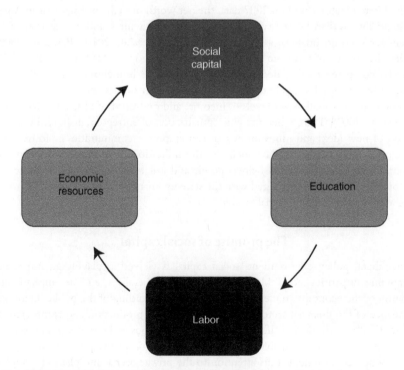

Figure 37.1 The relationship between social capital, education, labor, and economic resources
Source: Compiled by the author.

Cross and Lin, 2008). Moren Cross and Lin (2008) found that gender, race, and ethnicity is correlated with one's individual "stock" of social resources, with members of nondominant groups having lower levels of social resources, and members of nondominant groups often make connections or rely on those with very similar social resources. While there is evidence that these like connections are beneficial to some extent, and often provide great emotional aid, there are also limits to the economic benefits of these connections (Aguilera, 2009; Holguin et al., 2007). Thus, social capital that facilitates economic opportunity may not be equally available to everyone.

The challenge facing poor entrepreneurs, and the potential limit of social capital as a solution, is that one's stock of social resources is often dependent on one's starting place in the social structure. Poor entrepreneurs often have lower levels of education, less career experience or managerial positions, or are concentrated in less prestigious careers. Data from the Panel Survey of Entrepreneurial Dynamics (PSED II) suggests that, after controlling for a number of enterprise and owner characteristics, entrepreneurs in the lowest quintiles of the wealth distribution are at a social resource disadvantage, with typical indicators such as management experience, years of industry experience and career prestige being much lower than that of their wealthier counterparts. This suggests that the cycle in Figure 37.1 starts not with social capital, but with the economic resources available to the entrepreneur, and that individuals may experience very different trajectories, enabling some to spin upwards to generate more social capital through education and labor opportunities, enhancing their economic resources. Conversely, others may spin further down, allowing the gap to grow farther and farther apart. For those lacking financial resources or wealth, social capital is argued to be the solution, but the dark side of the promise of social capital is that it is in fact influenced by one's current level of economic resources, suggesting the already advantaged stand to benefit the most.

Neoliberal policy reforms: education, labor, and financial markets

As neoliberal reforms cut across all social and economic institutions, the poor's ability to generate wealth has been diminished and, concurrently, the poor are further removed from the promise of social capital and opportunities to connect to those with social resources unlike their own. It is as if the marketplace of neoliberal reforms has created a sorting effect, further segmenting the advantaged from the disadvantaged. As Kotz (2002) described it, policies from neoliberalism are concerned mainly with dismantling what remains of the regulated welfare state, emphasizing the deregulation of business, elimination or privatization of social welfare programs, and creating more favorable investment conditions. As the neoliberal agenda knows no bounds, it creates a ripple effect as it diffuses across all social and economic institutions and policy arenas.

For example, education institutions provide opportunity not only through the provision of a certain end, a level of education, but also by providing exposure to a wide range of abilities, cultures, and incomes, expanding one's stock of social resources and potential social capital. However, as argued by Hursh (2007), recent education policy reforms emphasize competitive markets as the panacea for advancing educational achievement, resulting in the heavy involvement of educational management organizations, the introduction of voucher plans, charter schools, and other instruments that influence the privatization of education. As Hill et al. (2008) found, these privatized forms of education tend to be disproportionately beneficial to those in society who can afford to pay for better educational experiences, indirectly enhancing the social capital returns for the advantaged. For example, Reardon (2011) found that the gap in test scores of high- and low-income students has grown by 40 percent. Specifically, by eighth grade, upper-income students are four grades ahead of their low-income counterparts.

Hursh (2007) found that the No Child Left Behind Act (NCLB) and its emphasis on competitive mechanisms and high stakes testing has played a role in fueling and reproducing these gaps. Data from schools in New York suggest test scores are likely to correlate with a student's family income and a school's score is more likely to reflect its students' average family income; as a result, the largest percentage of failing schools are in poor urban school districts (Hursh, 2007). Furthermore, the chase to achieve NCLB's test standards have led to creaming effects, the establishment of lower expectations for disadvantaged students, the retention or mysterious transfer of students out of schools to General Education Development (GED) programs, and the reallocation of resources to reproduce existing patterns of success (Hursh, 2007; Lewin and Medina, 2003; Lipman, 2004; McNeil, 2000). The end result is that the lowest-performing students, those that may stand to seek the most benefit from education, are left behind.

Neoliberal policy reforms also transcend post-secondary education as well. Bailey and Dynarski (2011) found that college completion rates increased by only four percentage points for low-income cohorts born around 1980 relative to cohorts born in the early 1960s, but by 18 percentage points for those who grew up in high-income families. Evidence suggests that these benefits accrue to the wealthier not because of better overall performance on tests or greater intellect, but due to the financial resources they possess. For example, among those that are poor and perform above average on standardized tests, only 26 percent graduate college, compared to 70 percent of the richest students. Conversely, 30 percent of students who are rich but perform below average on test scores complete college, compared to 6 percent of the poor (DeParle, 2012). Factors attributing to this include the experiences and expectations leading into college, and the cumulative effect reforms at all levels have had on concentrating the poor in class-segregated neighborhoods and in lower-quality schools, and higher education reforms that shifted the burden of paying for college to private markets, leaving many poor students buried in debt or unable to purchase an education. These reforms encourage further social exclusion, by limiting the social capital potential of these institutions to those with the financial means.

At the same time neoliberal policy reforms threaten education opportunities, changes in labor market policies have further segmented the workplace as an institution that can build social capital. Labor markets can be thought of as a set of arrangements through which workers learn about jobs, come into contact with others that possess different levels of social resources, and through which employers learn about workers (Spalter-Roth and Lowenthal, 2005). While there is a direct connection between labor markets and the poor in terms of income and earnings potential, labor markets also provide social capital by enhancing one's social resource base.

For example, affirmative action and equal employment laws designed to increase opportunity helped to close the wage gap by building bridges between those in the labor market and those that had been excluded. While these laws had direct effects on reducing the wage gap, by increasing one's income they also had social capital effects—providing the potential for those with lower stocks of social resources to build their own stock of social resources, experience career mobility, and make connections to those with greater social resources. As Spalter-Roth and Lowenthal (2005) argued, adequately enforced policies and programs can equalize labor opportunities in a market; however, without such policies, existing patterns of social networks and connections prevail, diminishing opportunities for those historically excluded.

However, changes in policies during the 1980s began to halt some of the progress of the earlier years. Lax federal enforcement of the new civil rights as well as a deregulation of labor markets had a negative effect, as did corporate downsizing and restructuring (Spalter-Roth and Lowenthal, 2005). The move towards less permanent positions and work arrangements that seek to maximize profit and investment have resulted in the creation of fewer new permanent jobs (Beder, 2009), and has concentrated African American and Hispanic men and women in nonstandard work positions, such as temporary and on-call work, that yield lower pay and benefits (Spalter-Roth and Lowenthal, 2005) and lower prestige. In this new environment of work, corporations focus on external or numerical flexibility, defined as an organization's ability to adjust the size of its work-force to fluctuations in demands by using workers that are not full time or regular, as it allows them to respond more quickly to market forces. As Kalleberg (2003) describes, these new arrange-ments place workers on the company payroll, but provide relatively weak ties to the organization, as employees are only hired for the short term, and often receive no benefits.

These new work arrangements place the poor and the minority at a disadvantage. Based on 2010 CPS data, about 10.5 million people were working but still classified as poor, and 4.2 percent of people working full time were classified as poor (Bureau of Labor Statistics [BLS], 2012). Workers in occupations requiring lower education and characterized by lower earnings were more likely to be classified as the working poor. For example, about one-third of respond-ents classified as the working poor reported a service occupation (BLS, 2012). Not surprisingly, executive, administrative, and managerial occupations and professional specialty jobs had low incidences of poverty, as high earnings and full-time, continual employment often accompany these positions. However, Census 2010 data on the working population indicates that only 20 percent of African American men and 15 percent of Hispanic men are employed in managerial and professional occupations, or jobs with related responsibilities, compared to 34 percent of white men and 46 percent of Asian men (BLS, 2012). About 21 percent of African American men work in service occupations, and 24 percent hold jobs in production, transportation, and material moving occupations. Among Hispanic men, about 21 percent work in service occupations and 26 percent work in natural resources, construction, and maintenance occupa-tions. Among women, a higher percentage of African Americans and Hispanics are employed in lower-paying service occupations, 27 and 29 percent respectively, compared to whites (19 percent) and Asians (20 percent). Thus, the working poor largely hold jobs characterized by few benefits and less career mobility, and minorities are more likely to hold these jobs.

Here again, neoliberal reforms have eroded a second potential source of social capital, reduc-ing the likelihood that disadvantaged groups gain additional social resources to improve their social capital. This has important ramifications for entrepreneurs because often those that are able to turn their ideas into economic opportunity have benefited from the social resources, career longevity and experience, managerial experience, financial resources, greater income, and salary provided through labor institutions characterized by upward mobility.

Neoliberal reforms have not only permeated labor and education institutions, but have also impacted financial markets. Historical practices of discrimination and redlining (refusing to lend to borrowers based on the characteristics of the community in which they live) created institu-tional barriers to access to mainstream lenders—key relationships that are critical in the wealth generation cycle.

Most entrepreneurs rely on their personal savings, equity, and investments, and loans and lines of credit from banks, to expand or grow their business. In essence, they need the abil-ity to obtain credit at a fair price in order to grow and expand business operations as well as access to affordable financial products. However, connections between lenders and the poor are often missing. Twenty-two percent of residents in low-income communities are "unbanked," meaning they do not have access to a bank account (Barr, 2004), and are largely cut-off from mainstream sources of credit for short-term borrowing and for homeownership. Driving through a poor or minority community, it is quite probable one will see signs advertising "payday" loans, "check-cashing," pawn shops, and rent-to-own stores, illustrating the nontra-ditional banking relationships that have historically been available to the poor.

The Community Reinvestment Act (CRA) of 1977 sought to stimulate reinvestment in poor and minority communities by increasing traditional lending activity in poor and minority communities. Likewise, Fair Lending Laws have been implemented to reverse the practices of racial and ethnic discrimination. However, during the mid-1980s, changes in policy at the federal level removed many of the regulations lenders faced, further opening up financial markets to the mechanisms of the private marketplace through the growth of the subprime industry. Whereas prime markets typically serve middle-income borrowers with good credit, defined as credit scores above 650 (Renaurt, 2004), subprime is often viewed as an alternative for "riskier" borrowers, defined as borrowers with a lower credit rating, typically below the mid-600s. Temkin et al. (2000) identified several factors contributing to the industry's growth, including deregulation of the lending industry, federal legislation preempting state restrictions on allowable rates and loan features, and an increase in securitization, packaging pools of loans, and redistributing to investors. The growth of this industry not only had an effect on the cost of homeownership but also the ability of the poor to generate equity.

The Depository Institutions Deregulation and Monetary Control Act (DIDA) of 1980 and the Alternative Mortgage Transaction Parity Act (AMTPA) of 1982 made it possible for lenders to originate mortgages with prices and features previously prohibited by individual states. DIDA preempted state limits on the rate or amount of interest, discount points, finance charges, or other charges (Ernst et al., 2004), providing leeway for lenders to strip home equity through fees. AMTPA gave non-federally chartered housing lenders the ability to offer alternative mortgage transactions on a par with federally chartered institutions. Allowing creditors to extend alternative loan products, AMTPA emerged during a time period of high interest rates when state housing creditors were having a difficult time originating fixed-rate, fixed-term loans. AMTPA also preempted state regulations designed to protect borrowers, hindering the ability of states to provide any additional consumer protections. These changes helped to fuel the growth of private market innovations through mortgage-backed securities (MBS). MBS are pools of mortgages packaged together to sell to the secondary market to be traded in markets, like stocks or other fixed-income securities, and designed to protect private investors from the increased level of credit risk from the underlying subprime mortgage collateral pool.

Additional barriers for lenders were removed in 1999 under the Gramm-Leach-Bliley Act (GLBA), allowing the financial markets to "open-up" further. The Act, otherwise known as the Financial Services Modernization Act of 1999, repealed the Glass-Steagall Act of 1933, which established clear legal boundaries separating retail and commercial banking, insurance, investment banking, and securities. The GLBA created financial holding companies, which are permitted to combine banking, securities, and insurance business under one corporate roof. The deregulation of financial markets had a negative impact on CRA, because it created a whole marketplace of lenders not subject to CRA regulatory requirements.

As financial markets "opened up," access to credit for the poor increased—borrowers and communities that once had a difficult time attracting any private sources of capital received an influx of new private sector capital, but at a higher cost. The subprime market and its focus on serving "high risk" borrowers often places the poor at a disadvantage, as they are more likely to report a lack of credit history or dealing with day-to-day financial emergencies that can wreak havoc on existing credit scores (Anibarro et al., 2008). These market financial innovations provide a very different economic trajectory for poor borrowers, as they are increasingly more likely to be served by alternative financial service providers who offer credit at a higher price. In turn, the poor end up paying more for credit for homeownership or other purposes, eroding their ability to generate equity and create wealth.

Conclusion

Paradoxically, the response to a neoliberal state, the greater reliance on social capital, may generate greater inequalities. Neoliberal policy reforms in the United States have cut across a number of different social and economic institutions, eroding social capital formation where it may be of most benefit, and destroying the collective structures of opportunity. As government increasingly retreats from building the collective structures necessary across all policy domains, the opportunities for individuals to build their social resources to generate social capital that produces economic opportunity becomes contingent upon their wealth.

Public policy rhetoric treats entrepreneurship as a way out of poverty, for those excluded from labor markets or not suitable for advanced education. However, the challenge facing the concept of entrepreneurship as a policy tool for economic inclusion is that social and economic institutions are interconnected, and in the neoliberal policy environment, being poor further distances you from the social resources necessary to overcome "being poor." Being poor in a neoliberal environment means you are less likely to gain access to higher levels of education, less likely to earn employment that provides the opportunity to increase your income to save or invest in future entrepreneurial ventures, and less likely to obtain access to mainstream financial institutions and products. As the neoliberal policy regime further disconnects the poor from the primary institutions that are avenues to economic opportunity, the promise of social capital diminishes and the paradox of entrepreneurship as a policy tool for economic inclusion becomes more apparent.

References

Aguilera, M. (2009). Ethnic enclaves and the earnings of self-employed Latinos. *Small Business Economics*, 33, 413–426.

Alternative Mortgage Transaction Parity Act (AMTPA). (1982). 12 U.S.C. 3801. Text from: United States Code Service. Current through 2/8/07. Available from: LexisNexis Congressional. Accessed: 2/10/2007.

Anibarro, B., Yoo, M., Ganti, A., Jung, S., and Watrus, B. (2008). *The high cost of being poor in Washington.* Retrieved January 4, 2013 from http://www.seattle.gov/civilrights/newsletter/docs/HighCostBeingpoor_FINAL.pdf.

Bailey, M., and Dynarski, S. (2011). *Gains and gaps: Changing inequality in U.S. college entry and completion.* National Bureau of Economic Research, Working Paper Series, 17633. Cambridge, MA.

Barr, M. (2004). Banking the poor. *Yale Journal on Law and Regulation*, 21(1), 121–238.

Beder, S. (2009). Neoliberalism and the global financial crisis. *Social Alternatives*, 8(1), 17–21.

Bureau of Labor Statistics (BLS). (2012). *A profile of the working poor, 2010.* Report 1035. U.S. Department of Labor. Washington, DC. Retrieved March 5, 2013 from http://www.bls.gov/cps/cpswp2010.pdf.

Casey, C. (2012). Low-wealth, minority enterprises and access to financial resources for start-up activities: Do connections matter? *Economic Development Quarterly*, 26, 252–266.

Cavalluzzo, K., and Wolken, J. (2005). Small business loan turndowns, personal wealth, and discrimination. *Journal of Business*, 78, 2153–2177.

Community Reinvestment Act (CRA). (1977). 12 U.S.C. 2901. Text from: United States Code Service. Current through 2/8/07. Available from: LexisNexis Congressional. Accessed: 2/10/2007.

DeParle, J. (2012, December 22). For poor, leap to college often ends in a hard fall. *New York Times.* Retrieved December 28, 2012 from http://www.nytimes.com/2012/12/23/education/poor-students-struggle-as-class-plays-a-greater-role-in-success.html?pagewanted=all.

Depository Institutions Deregulation and Monetary Control Act (DIDA). (1980). 12 U.S.C. 1831d. Text from: United States Code Service. Current through 2/8/07. Available from LexisNexis Congressional. Accessed: 2/10/2007.

Dumas, C. (2001). Evaluating the outcomes of micro-enterprise training for low-income women: A case study. *Journal of Developmental Entrepreneurship*, 6(2), 97–129.

Ernst, K., Goldstein, D., and Richardson, C. (2004). Legal and economic inducements to predatory practices. In G. Squires (ed.), *Why the poor pay more: How to stop predatory lending* (pp. 103–132). Westport, CT: Praeger Publications.

Fairlie, R. (2004). Recent trends in ethnic and racial business ownership. *Small Business Economics*, 23, 203–218.

Fukuyama, F. (1995). *Trust: The social virtues and the creation of prosperity*. Penguin: Auckland.

Gans, H. (1971). The uses of poverty: The poor pay all. *Social Policy*, 20–24.

Glass-Steagall Act. (1933). 12 U.S.C. 377. Text from: United States Code Service. Current through 2/8/07. Available from: LexisNexis Congressional. Accessed 2/10/2007.

Gramm-Leach-Bliley Act of 1999 (PL 106–102, November 12, 1999). Available from: Library of Congress. Accessed August 18, 2014 from https://beta.congress.gov/106/plaws/publ102/PLAW-106publ102.pdf.

Hill, D., Greaves, N., and Maisuria, A. (2008). Does capitalism inevitably increase education inequality? In Holsinger, D.B., and Jacob, W.J. (eds). *Inequality in Education: Comparative and International Perspectives, CERC Studies in Comparative Education*, (Vol. 24, pp. 59–85). Hong Kong, China: Comparative Education Research Centre.

Holguin, J., Gamboa, E., and Hoy, F. (2007). Challenges and opportunities for Hispanic entrepreneurs in the United States. In L. Dana (ed.), *Handbook of research on ethnic minority entrepreneurship: A co-evolutionary view on resource management* (pp. 193–209). Cheltenham, England: Edward Elgar.

Hoselitz, B. (1952). Entrepreneurship and economic growth. *American Journal of Economics and Sociology*, 12(1), 97–110.

Hursh, D. (2007). Assessing No Child Left Behind and the rise of neoliberal education policies. *American Educational Research Journal*, 44, 493–518.

Kalleberg, A. (2003). Flexible firms and labor market segmentation: Effects of workplace restructuring. *Work and Occupations*, 30(2), 154–175.

Kotz, D. (2002). Globalization and neoliberalism. *Rethinking Marxism*, 12(2), 64–79.

Lewin, T., and Medina, J. (2003, July 31). To cut failure schools shed students. *New York Times*, p. A1.

Lin, N. (2001). *Social capital: A theory of social structure and action*. Cambridge, MA: Cambridge University Press.

Lin, N., and Erickson, B. (eds). (2008). *Social capital: An international research program*. New York: Oxford University Press.

Lipman, P. (2004). *High-stakes education: Inequality, globalization and urban school reform*. New York: Routledge.

McNeil, L. (2000). Creating new inequalities: Contradictions of reform. *Phi Delta Kappan*, 81(10), 728–734.

Moren Cross, J., and Lin, N. (2008). Access to social capital and status attainment in the United States: Racial/ ethnic and gender differences. In N. Lin and B. Erickson (eds), *Social capital: An international research program* (pp. 364–379). New York: Oxford University Press.

Reardon, S.F. (2011). The widening academic achievement gap between the rich and the poor: New evidence and possible explanations. In R. Murnane and G. Duncan (eds), *Whither opportunity? Rising inequality and the uncertain life chances of low-income children* (pp. 91–116). New York: Russell Sage Foundation Press.

Renaurt, E. (2004). An overview of the predatory lending process. *Housing Policy Debate*, 15(3), 467–502.

Reynolds, P., and Curtin, R. (2008). Business creation in the United States: Panel Study of Entrepreneurial Dynamics II Initial Assessment. *Foundations and Trends in Entrepreneurship*, 4, 155–307.

Robb, A., and Fairlie, R. (2007). Access to financial capital among U.S. businesses: The case of African American firms. *Annals of the American Academy of Political and Social Science*, 613, 73–94.

Salazar, M. (2007). *The effect of wealth and race on start-up rates*. Washington, DC: Office of Advocacy, Small Business Administration Press.

Shapiro, T., Meschede, T., and Sullivan, L. (2010). *The racial wealth gap increases fourfold* (Research and Policy Brief). Boston, MA: Institute on Assets and Social Policy, The Heller School for Social Policy and Management, Brandeis University and Society, 27, 151–208.

Spalter-Roth, R., and Lowenthal, T.A. (2005). *Race, ethnicity and the American labor market: What's at work?* Sydney S. Spivack Program in Applied Social Research and Social Policy. ASA Series on How Race and Ethnicity Matter. American Sociological Association.

Tabb, W. (2002). *Unequal partners: A primer on globalization*. New York: The New Press.

Taylor, P., Kochhar, R., Fry, R., Velasco, G., and Motel, S. (2011). Wealth gaps rise to record highs between whites, blacks and Hispanics. Pew Research Center, Social and Demographic Trends, Washington, DC. Retrieved January 14, 2013 from http://www.pewsocialtrends.org/2011/07/26/wealth-gaps-rise-to-record-highs-between-whites-blacks-hispanics/.

Temkin, K., Johnson, J., and Levy, D. (2002). *Subprime markets, the role of GSE's, and risk-based pricing*. Washington, DC: Urban Institute and the U.S. Department of Housing and Urban Development, Office of Policy Development and Research.

PART IV

Global poverty and the lived experiences of poor communities in the United States

INTRODUCTION

Reuben Jonathan Miller and Alexis Silvers

I hope we have once again reminded people that man is not free unless government is limited. There's a clear cause and effect here that is as neat and predictable as a law of physics: as government expands, liberty contracts.

(President Ronald Reagan, Farewell Address, 1989)

We have moved past the sterile debate between those who say government is the enemy and those who say government is the answer. My fellow Americans, we have found a third way.

(President William Jefferson Clinton, State of the Union Address, 1998)

Despite assertions from "third way" evangelists that participation in a "free" and "unfettered" labor market restores dignity and ameliorates disparate social conditions, changes in the political economy over the last several decades have had considerable, negative effects on the life chances of poor people across categories of difference. Neoliberalism has in part facilitated the advent of new modes of surveillance to police the "dangerous classes," has resulted in the "hollowing out" of the welfare state and general erosion of the social safety net, signaled the emergence of a new "enemy from within" through harsh immigration policies, and catalyzed the re-regulation of the domestic sphere in ways that privilege markets. This includes the de-regulation of food, labor, housing, and transportation policies that at least rhetorically protected groups considered to be the nation's "deserving poor"—children, the elderly, the "disabled," and the willing but unemployed worker.

Street-level bureaucrats' discretion and authority in the day-to-day lives of impoverished people has increased significantly (Lipski, 1980). New welfare regulations disqualified families struggling with generational poverty from the receipt of continuous welfare benefits (Katz, 2001; Soss et al., 2011). All the while sanctions targeting single mothers and "dead-beat fathers" were used to fleece the welfare rolls and, in effect, privilege "traditional" family forms, all the while policing the reproductive behaviors, leisure, and work patterns of single-parent families that were often non-white, considered "non-traditional," and impoverished (Geva, 2005; Roberts, 1997). With the emergence and "glorification" of "hyper-incarceration"—the selective targeting of unskilled black workers made "redundant" by a changing political economy for criminal justice intervention—poor urban and rural denizens now live under the watchful gaze of an expanded penal state (Eason, 2012; Goffman, 2009; Wacquant, 2009 and 2010), leading sociologist Loic Wacquant to admonish scholars of punishment and poverty to "relink social welfare and penal policies" in order to "grasp the new politics of marginality" (Wacquant,

2009 and 2012a). This "new politic" is not simply the result of a "hollowed-out state," but of a redeployed and reconfigured one (Wacquant, 2012b), significantly expanding the reach of the state into the everyday lives of the poor. To this end, Wacquant writes:

> [T]he police, the courts and the prisons are, upon close examination, the somber and stern face that Leviathan turns everywhere toward the dispossessed and dishonored categories trapped in the hollows of the inferior regions of social and urban space by economic deregulation and the retrenchment schemes of social protection.
>
> (2008: xviii)

These not-so-subtle shifts are the result of *policy decisions* that have effectively pushed families "off the dole" of a comparatively anemic social welfare state and onto the rolls of a flexible labor sector with few benefits and unsustainable wages (Peck, 2001 and 2010; Piven and Cloward, 1993; Wacquant, 2009). Unsurprisingly, neoliberalism has not liberated the poor from the shackles of poverty, but instead concretized their positions in the lower reaches of a de-indus-trialized economy, shaming them along the way for their inability to move up the ladders of economic success. At the same time, these policy shifts have rendered the most vulnerable among the poor voiceless and invisible, hidden within the ranks of the homeless, the impris-oned, the stigmatized, the undocumented, and the otherwise dishonored, utterly transforming the ways in which poverty is experienced in the United States. The contributions in this part examine the experience of poverty in the shadow of U.S. neoliberalization, and the ways in which the "punitive turn" affects the lives of poor people across categories of difference. They demonstrate how changes in U.S. social policy impact poor people's life chances and their daily routines, ossify their social positions, and shape their interactions with organizational, institu-tional, and community actors, their families, and friendship networks.

We begin our journey with a chapter by Mazelis, "Social Ties Among the Poor in a Neoliberal Capitalist Society." Mazelis uses a welfare rights organization as a case study to demonstrate how poor people, in the face of a weakened social safety net, formed "sustainable ties" among each other to address their needs. With an eye toward structural factors, Grossman, Sosin, Wittner, and George uncover the ways in which broader shifts in the economy and rising rates of incarceration have impacted the life circumstances of the housing insecure in their chapter, "Paths into Homelessness." Kim's contribution, "Examining Racial–Ethnic and Gender Disparities in Poverty Among the Elderly," highlights a paradox. Poverty has declined among the elderly over the past decade. The risk of falling into poverty, however, remains more prevalent than ever for elderly women and elderly racial and ethnic minorities, implicat-ing the rollback of essential social safety net programs, such as Social Security Insurance (SSI), in the precarity of this group. While Lichtenwalter and Magno's chapter, "Ableism, Poverty, and the Under-Celebrated Resistance," highlights the ways in which neoliberal policy exacerbates the exclusion of other-abled social actors from key cultural, political, and economic institutions.

In "Breaking the Silence," Wagner and White call our attention to the relative absence of race in the policy discourse on homelessness, coupling this phenomenon with the success of neoliberal reform in rendering issues of economic and racial justice "outdated" and irrelevant to current economic conditions. Tracing the effects of neoliberalism on the push and pull fac-tors associated with immigration, Becerra's' chapter, "The Effects of Neoliberal Capitalism on Immigration and Poverty Among Mexican Immigrants in the United States," exhibits the role of NAFTA (North American Free Trade Agreement) in weakening the Mexican econ-omy, along with the passage of PRWORA (Personal Responsibility and Work Opportunities Reconciliation Act) and acts such as the Bracero program in the creation of a hostile and punitive environment for Mexican migrants. The chapters rounding out this section, Otero, Pechlander, and Gürcan's "The Neoliberal Diet," Bercaw's "Grounding Grandma," and Singh, Kumaria's and Berg's "Poverty, Health, and Asian Non-Linearity" demonstrate how neoliberalism contributes to a decline in poor people's health and wellbeing. Otero, Pechlander and Gürcan link diet, and, more specifically, the disproportionate consumption of "calorie dense" foods, with social inequality and concurrent changes in U.S. social policy, demonstrating how neoliberalism is not only an engine of inequality, but of disparities in population health. Bercaw documents a crisis, the aging of a growing elderly population in communities that are ill equipped to address their needs. Finally, Singh, Kumaria, and Berg push the discourse on immigrant women's health beyond the cultural considerations emergent in the current era that hide the structural factors that contribute to their health outcomes.

The contributions in this part feature the social policy mechanisms that have altered poor people's lives, challenging popular assumptions about choice and decision making among the poor. The chapters demonstrate considerable variation in the effects of neoliberalization across geography and various categories of cultural difference. In doing so, they demonstrate the ways in which social policy contributes to the endurance of longstanding inequalities in the United States, and show how neoliberalism has changed what it means to be poor in America.

Note

1   See Part III, Section III, of this Handbook.

References

Eason, J. (2012). Extending the Hyper Ghetto: Toward a Theory of Punishment, Race, and Rural Disadvantage. *Journal of Poverty: Innovations in Social, Political and Economic Inequalities*, 16(4): 274–295.

Geva, Dorith. (2005). "From Family Preservation to Nuclear Family Governance: Regulating Families Through American Welfare Processes." Unpublished manuscript. Northwestern University RC19.

Goffman, A. (2009). On the Run: Wanted Men in a Philadelphia Ghetto. *American Sociological Review*, 74: 339–357.

Katz, Michael. (2001). *The Price of Citizenship: Redefining the American Welfare State*. New York: Henry Holt and Company.

Lipski, Michael. (1980). *Street Level Bureaucracy: Dilemmas of the Individual in Public Services*. New York: Russell Sage Foundation.

Peck, J. (2001). *Workfare States*. London: Guilford Press.

Peck, J. (2010). *Constructions of Neoliberal Reason*. Oxford: Oxford University Press.

Piven, Francis F., and Cloward, Richard. (1993). *Regulating the Poor: The Functions of Public Welfare*. New York: Vintage Books.

Roberts, D. (1997). *Killing the Black Body: Race, Reproduction, and the Meaning of Liberty*. New York: Vintage Books.

Soss, J., Schram, S., and Fording, R. (2011). *Disciplining the Poor: Neoliberal Paternalism and the Persistent Power of Race*. Chicago, IL: University of Chicago Press.

Wacquant, L.J.D. (2008). *Punishing the Poor: The Neoliberal Government of Social Insecurity*. Durham, NC: Duke University Press.

Wacquant, L.J.D. (2009). *Prisons of Poverty*. Minneapolis, MN: University of Minnesota Press.

Wacquant, L.J.D. (2010). Class, Race and Hyperincarceration in Revanchist America. *Daedalus*, 140(3): 74–90.

Wacquant, L.J.D. (2012a). The Wedding of Workfare and Prisonfare in the 21st Century. *The Journal of Poverty: Innovations on Social, Political and Economic Inequalities* 16 (3): 236–249.

Wacquant, L.J.D. (2012b). Three Steps toward a Historical Anthropology of Actually Existing Neoliberalism. *Social Anthropology*, 19(4): 66–79.

38

SOCIAL TIES AMONG THE POOR IN A NEOLIBERAL CAPITALIST SOCIETY

Joan Maya Mazelis

Social scientists have long documented the importance of social ties. Whether they focus on the power of social networks to further employment opportunities, or on the effectiveness of social capital for support and for leverage, researchers agree that social ties matter, though they do not always reach the same conclusions about who has what sorts of ties, and to whom. Carol Stack, in her seminal work *All Our Kin: Strategies for Survival in a Black Community* (1974), documented the depth of support social ties among kin and fictive kin (friends who refer to each other with kin titles like "cousin" and "sister," and often feel and act as though they are related) can provide. Her work has been immensely influential; an entire generation of sociologists and anthropologists has continued to explore the meanings and mechanisms of social support in various poor communities in the decades since *All Our Kin* appeared.

Research on social support has demonstrated the importance of resources available through social networks (Domínguez and Watkins, 2003; Edin and Lein, 1997; Henly et al., 2005; Mazelis, forthcoming; Newman, 1999; Stack, 1974). Kin and fictive kin provide a variety of kinds of assistance, ranging from free meals to child care to financial support to employment referrals. We all rely on help from others, often from those closest to us; whether it's transportation to the airport, babysitting on date night, or co-signing a loan, stable middle-class people and those above them in the socioeconomic hierarchy get lots of help. For those struggling on the bottom of the socioeconomic ladder, the assistance they get from social ties in paying bills or watching their kids can be crucial for survival, and sometimes provides the only glimmer of hope for upward mobility.

Researchers also describe social ties providing support as social capital:

> Social capital is easiest to "see" in its individual guise, wherein it refers to a resource for individual action that is stored in human relationships. Social capital is what we draw on when we get others, whether acquaintances, friends, or kin, to help us solve problems, seize opportunities, and accomplish other aims that matter to us.
>
> (Briggs, 1998:178)

Briggs distinguishes between social networks that offer support for coping day to day, or bonding social capital, from those that can allow for leverage for upward mobility, or bridging social capital. Coping support usually comes from "strong" ties such as family and friends, whereas leverage more often comes from "weak" ties—acquaintances rather than more intimate others (Briggs, 1998; Granovetter, 1973; Putnam, 2000). Often, poor people who have any social capital have only bonding, not bridging, social capital (Henly et al., 2005).

Researchers have noted that people in disadvantaged areas often lack bridging social capital, due to structural macroeconomic forces such as deindustrialization and middle-class flight from cities. The spatial concentration of poverty creates disadvantaged environments that become progressively isolated socially and economically (Massey and Denton, 1993; Wilson, 1987, 1996).

Portes notes that social capital has two elements: (1) the relationship that allows individuals to claim access to the resources of others in their networks, and (2) the amount and quality of those resources (Portes, 1998). Even when those living in neighborhoods with concentrated poverty have strong social ties to others in their communities, those ties rarely lead to upward mobility. That is, they are bonding ties, but not bridging ties. Stack found "a cooperative lifestyle built upon exchange and reciprocity" (1974:125) in which social networks, and what social capital members *could* tap into even among the very poor, were crucial to their survival (see also: Edin and Lein, 1997; Mazelis and Mykyta, 2011; Seccombe, 1999).

However, not everyone can rely on kin networks for employment referrals, material assistance, or emotional help (Desmond, 2012; Harknett, 2006; Henly, 2002; McDonald and Armstrong, 2001; Roschelle, 1997; Smith, 2007), due to kin's reluctance or inability to help. Many isolate themselves from peers while trying to become upwardly mobile (Portes, 1998). When it is available, support aids daily survival, but also comes with obligations to reciprocate, which recipients may be unable to fulfill (Hansen, 2005; Mazelis, forthcoming; Nelson, 2000, 2005; Offer, 2012). Reciprocal obligations can also serve to hold the poor back; excess claims on group members constitute a potential negative to social capital. Poor people's networks tend to have few resources; with immense need, members may quickly drain those resources (Domínguez and Watkins, 2003; Edin, 2001; Levine, 2013; Nelson, 2005). These circumstances contribute to some people in need seeking assistance outside their kin networks.

While some researchers have discovered a role of kin and other close ties in providing support (Domínguez and Watkins, 2003; Edin and Lein, 1997; Harknett, 2006; Henly et al., 2005; Mazelis and Mykyta, 2011; Stack, 1974), others have documented the ways in which kin sometimes fall short (Desmond, 2012; Edin and Kefalas, 2005; Smith, 2007). Kin may be struggling to survive and therefore without ability or willingness to provide support. This deficiency compounds the struggles of the poor, when it occurs. And yet, the struggles of the poor do not dissipate simply because there are no kin available to provide assistance. Rather, the lack of family members on whom to rely compounds the struggles of the poor.

Desmond details the experiences and strategies of a set of poor individuals encountering a difficult crisis (2012). His ethnographic work provides a compelling illustration of what may happen when people do not rely on kin. Those he studied, after being evicted, often did rely on some limited help from family members, but also faced obstacles in doing so.

> As a result, to meet their most pressing needs, evicted tenants often relied more on *disposable ties* formed with new acquaintances than on a stable network of reliable kin. They established new ties quickly and accelerated their intimacy. Virtual strangers became roommates and "sisters." Once a disposable tie was formed, all kinds of resources flowed through it. But these bonds often were brittle and fleeting, lasting only for short bursts. This strategy of forming, using, and burning disposable ties allowed families caught in a desperate situation to make it from one day to the next, but it also bred instability and fostered misgivings between peers.
>
> (Desmond, 2012:1296–1297)

As Desmond argues, literature to this point has either asserted the importance of kin support or documented its absence:

> There are no stations, then, between kin support and raw individualism, embeddedness and isolation. If kin support has been eroded in poor neighborhoods, then their residents must learn to get by on their own. Yet all the evidence indicates that this is next to impossible.
>
> (2012:1298)

Rather than muddle through alone or piece together assistance from social service agencies, strategies doomed to failure because of their inadequacy to the task, the individuals he studied formed what he calls "disposable ties." In some ways the ties take on the characteristics of kin relationships, due to their intimacy and cooperative exchange nature. Yet, in other ways, they are quite different, because the intimacy is formed in an accelerated way and, as Desmond shows, the relationships are fleeting—indeed, this is what makes them disposable ties.

Such ties provide real support in moments of crisis, enabling Desmond's informants to move forward from one day to the next. Yet when the fragile threads connecting people to their disposable ties break under the weight of heavy burdens, people move on to the next tenuous connections.

Just as Desmond posits that existing literature has presented us with an apparent dichotomy of "embeddedness and isolation," it seems that his addition to the spectrum, while it adds nuances to the meaning of support and social ties, still leaves a theoretical and practical gap between extremes. Existing literature documents two potential realities for poor people: they may have a dense network of closely connected and supportive kin in which members pool resources and help one another survive (though even in this scenario these networks can be fraught with complications due to obligations of reciprocity), or in the absence of a kin network, they establish fleeting relationships with virtual strangers, rife with potential problems arising from misunderstandings, limits on resources, arguments over money or lovers, or competing demands from other disposable ties. Desmond does note that disposable ties vary in their duration; sometimes they may last months or transform into weak ties to be activated later on, but typically they are much more fleeting.

> When tenuous but intense relationships between virtual strangers ended badly—or violently, as they sometimes did—they fostered deep misgivings between peers and neighbors, eroding community and network stability. The memory of having been used or mistreated by a disposable tie encouraged people to be suspicious of others. Relying on disposable ties, then, is both a response to and a source of social instability.
>
> (Desmond, 2012:1322)

I argue there is yet another in-between category of support through social ties, one that, while not common, is more sustainable and does not contribute to social instability. Disposable ties may in fact be an indispensable resource for the poor, but *sustainable ties* would certainly provide many of the same benefits with perhaps fewer of the drawbacks for those who cannot rely on kin.

Stack and Desmond both did ethnographic work, making no claim as to the generalizability of their results, yet many other researchers have reached similar conclusions as did Stack, and Desmond's findings ring true as well. It is quite possible Desmond discovered a common pattern, made more widespread in an era of rising residential mobility and fractured families, particularly in the context of neoliberalism's reduced role of government paving the way for deindustrialization, high unemployment, and an increasingly restrictive public safety net. It would be unsurprising if many of those in the most dire circumstances, without kin on whom to rely, use disposable ties in order to survive. Indeed, Desmond notes that previous researchers, going back to Elliot Liebow's 1967 *Tally's Corner*, have found evidence of disposable ties, although such ties have not been the focus of their analyses (see Desmond, 2012:1322–1323).

However, the research this chapter describes below documents a type of non-kin social tie with greater longevity than disposable ties. The existence of these *sustainable ties* provides clues about other ways in which people form and use social ties and advances our understanding of the ways in which people cope with poverty. Beyond lasting kin ties and fleeting disposable ties, there are, in fact, sustainable non-kin ties. Qualitative research in Philadelphia found non-kin relying on an organization, and its members relying on one another, for various types of support.

Over a period of two years, participant observation and in-depth interviews with 25 members of the Kensington Welfare Rights Union (referred to below as KWRU) demonstrated the importance of the organization as a source of social ties and social support for members. A group of poor women, led by anti-poverty activist Cheri Honkala, started KWRU in April 1991, and its members and activists are poor men and women. It is based in Kensington, a North Philadelphia neighborhood that was once a manufacturing center but is now among the poorest areas in Pennsylvania. Honkala remained active in KWRU even during her 2011 Green Party candidacy for Philadelphia Sheriff and 2012 candidacy for Vice President of the United States (accompanying Jill Stein on the Green Party ticket).

KWRU's activist members deliberately announce their poverty and decry its root causes, sloughing off the self-blame that plagues so many others in their situations. KWRU has also founded an organization called the Poor People's Economic Human Rights Campaign, and leaders and activists travel all over the world speaking about poverty and calling for change. More locally, they engage in protests to obtain housing for their homeless members and they offer informational support and practical assistance to people who are having difficulty getting food stamps or utility assistance. While these calls for political change represent the public face of KWRU, most come to the organization initially for services to help them survive.

KWRU members are mostly women, but there are men active in the organization as well. Interview respondents' ages range from 21 to 59. Nine respondents are African American, eight are Latina, and eight are white. The KWRU office is located right in the heart of one of the highest-poverty areas in Philadelphia, in West Kensington, but members live all over the city.

Norms of reciprocity, the notion that people are obligated to help others because they've been helped, functions as currency within the context of KWRU (see Mazelis, 2015). Members could never pay dues; the organization depends on the time and resources that members provide to satisfy the norms of reciprocity established by the group. KWRU specifically discourages those who seek its help from viewing it as a social service organization, but it does provide aid for people experiencing homelessness or at risk of homelessness, who may be denied welfare benefits, or whose utilities are going to be shut off. KWRU also distributes food for free in poor neighborhoods.

Because KWRU does not consider itself a social service provider, it asks that those it helps provide help in turn. Sometimes this help takes an easy-to-observe, concrete form, such as going to the office and volunteering there, offering assistance to people who come to the office with questions or problems; going to rallies and demonstrations to help KWRU have enough people for a successful protest; or going on food distributions, giving out free food in neighborhoods and trying to organize people to join KWRU. Even if there isn't much going on, KWRU leaders and activists expect members, especially those currently receiving housing assistance from KWRU, to show their faces. Members fulfilling reciprocity obligations sometimes make long journeys to come to the office even at slow times or when the presence of many volunteers means they have little to do.

All the KWRU members I interview speak about mutual aid and obligations. I found that most members of KWRU feel positive about the sustainable ties they build in KWRU—about their involvement and connections with other members of the group. They are very well aware of the resources to which membership in the group gives them access. And yet, *former* members of the group exist—not everyone maintains their commitment to the organization. Even among those involved in current group activities, not everyone sees the social ties that come from KWRU in a positive light. For some, the burdens of membership are too great. Sustainable ties can be broken, but they have more resilience than disposable ties and do not depend on kinship.

Those who have remained involved report long-term help from the organization and sustainable ties with other members that extend beyond the parameters of the group's activities. Jessie considers Cate to be like a mother to her. She relays a story to me:

> Like not too long ago ... I don't have a dryer, I have a washer ... And they were winter clothes in the summertime, so I was just trying to catch up with the laundry. So I washed all the laundry and I had like a big trash bag full of wet clothes. I throw them all in my car. I took 'em to [Cate's] house .... She dries them for me, she folds them for me and puts them back in the bags and I just picked them up. So that's the relationship that I have with [Cate].

Amanda lists other members of the organization as those who may pick up her children at school, telling me, "I think my son is the only person in any preschool that has a list of like ten people that have authorization to pick him up ... all people from the organization that I have like family relationships with." James contrasts KWRU's sustainable ties with his observation of kinship ties: "The only reason [they give help is] because they want something in return." KWRU's sustainable ties arise from relationships built on a mutual understanding of helping one another. Like those Desmond studied, KWRU members often do not feel they have family members on whom they can rely.

Sustainable ties may not always be sustained. Members who leave the group show the effect of forgoing or forsaking sustainable ties. Helen, a woman in her 40s, was at one time a very active member of KWRU, but has become a member in name only by the time I interview her. She lives in a very poor neighborhood in a dilapidated house with no running water. She struggles to pay for even the most basic necessities. Helen works intermittently at one of the Philadelphia stadiums, but her work schedule is inconsistent and so her income is unpredictable. She does not receive cash assistance through welfare, and reports no social ties consistently available to her.

Helen feels that KWRU demanded more of her than it provided in turn, and she decided she was better off fighting her battles alone. Sadly, Helen lives in conditions among the worst I observed, and rather than improve since she reduced her KWRU involvement, they have worsened. I can only speculate that her life might be better if she had maintained KWRU membership and the access to social capital it offered.

KWRU not only provides sustainable ties to those who remain involved; remaining involved is what allows members to sustain those ties, and when they do, the assistance flows more readily. A relatively new member of KWRU living in a house rented by the organization, Rebecca has difficulty letting go of her memories of not getting help in the past, from social ties. Rebecca explains to me that she has given help to many people, and it's been difficult for her to ask for help as she has been turned down in the past: "I ask for help and then I get screwed over. That's why I knew from when I was growing up, you know, you just don't ask people for help ... Because they won't help you ... I can't count on it."

KWRU takes reciprocity norms seriously and enforces them. By our second interview Rebecca has been told by KWRU leaders that she must vacate the house they have been letting her live in, and she isn't sure why, but she admits that she doesn't always attend events as instructed, because when she goes she feels unappreciated. She does not want to do what the organization asks of her because she doesn't trust that they'll help her in turn. It is likely that KWRU withdrew aid from Rebecca in part because of her reluctance to fulfill norms of reciprocity. For both Helen and Rebecca, the norms of reciprocity prevent them from creating sustainable ties through KWRU—yet without these norms, the organization would have few resources, and the sustainable ties they offer would provide scant social capital. People with disposable ties might forgo sustainable ties because of the relatively larger reciprocity requirement—or, if there were more organizations like KWRU, they might take advantage of sustainable ties.

In KWRU, the organization bolsters and strengthens otherwise thin and fragile bonds between people who start off as strangers. If individuals disappear from the group, those to whom they were linked do not lose the benefits of that social bond, for the tie is really to the organization. Individuals can be replaced, with KWRU as the mediator and voucher for new individuals. Poor individuals develop ties to the group, and through the group to other individuals, but the organization acts to strengthen a tenuous strand between them, and the ties become better able to bear the heavy burdens they face, more likely to withstand swift winds of crisis, and therefore more likely to be sustainable.

Desmond explains that in his work, "The environment most conducive to producing disposable ties was that which gathered together people with pressing needs" (Desmond, 2012:1313). This certainly characterizes KWRU and its members, yet something renders those ties sustainable rather than disposable. Desmond notes that institutions geared to the poor were often sites of disposable tie formation: "Welfare offices, food pantries, job centers, Alcoholics Anonymous clubs, methadone clinics, even the waiting areas of eviction court—disposable ties regularly were initiated in such venues" (Desmond, 2012:1313). KWRU is both similar to and different from these sorts of institutions. Because KWRU requires something of its members rather than simply providing services to them, it creates social ties in which it is embedded as an organization, thereby strengthening the tenuous bonds between new acquaintances.

As neoliberalism persists in privatizing public support and reducing the role of government, social ties will continue to shape the poor's ability to survive. Kin ties will be crucial for some poor people; disposable ties will undoubtedly play a large role as well, both for those without kin available and for those who have only limited kin support. As need for a private safety net endures, and perhaps grows, competing possibilities are equally likely: social ties may be forced to bear heavier burdens and therefore fray more frequently, multiplying the need for disposable ties, in order to replace ever-disappearing ones, or they may adapt to new circumstances and become more sustainable, particularly if organizations like KWRU become more prevalent as a means to help people cope with poverty.

Organizations such as KWRU make the poor better able to pool their resources to help one another. It is not clear how replicable KWRU is; founded and run by a charismatic figure with the skill to get foundation funding *and* to whip up passionate outrage among members at protests, KWRU is unusual in important respects. Yet, to the extent that other KWRUs surface and develop over time, they will provide an important piece of the patchwork of help on which the poor rely, a piece different from what social service agencies offer and from family assistance restricted to those with strong and productive kin ties, but a sort of communal assistance people living in poverty can both contribute to and draw on. They provide a source of social capital similar to what disposable ties offer, but with greater stability. Certainly, organizations like KWRU cannot solve the problems neoliberalism creates, but they can help provide a productive, collective response to increasing poverty and deepening challenges to survival.

References

Briggs, X. D. (1998). Brown Kids in White Suburbs: Housing Mobility and the Many Faces of Social Capital. *Housing Policy Debate*, 9, 177–221.

Desmond, M. (2012). Disposable Ties and the Urban Poor. *American Journal of Sociology*, 117, 1295–1335.

Domínguez, S., and Watkins, C. (2003). Creating Networks for Survival and Mobility: Social Capital Among African-American and Latin-American Low-Income Mothers. *Social Problems*, 50, 111–135.

Edin, K. (2001). More than Money: The Role of Assets in the Survival Strategies and Material Well-Being of the Poor. In T. M. Shapiro and E. N. Wolff (eds), *Assets for the Poor: The Benefits of Spreading Asset Ownership*, (pp. 206–231). New York: Russell Sage.

Edin, K., and Kefalas, M. (2005). *Promises I Can Keep: Why Poor Women Put Motherhood before Marriage*. Berkeley, CA: University of California Press.

Edin, K., and Lein, L. (1997). *Making Ends Meet: How Single Mothers Survive Welfare and Low-Wage Work*. New York: Russell Sage.

Granovetter, M. (1973). The Strength of Weak Ties. *American Journal of Sociology*, 78, 1360–1380.

Hansen, K. V. (2004). "The Asking Rules of Reciprocity in Networks of Care for Children." *Qualitative Sociology* 27(4): 421–437.

Hansen, K. V. (2005). *Not-So-Nuclear Families: Class, Gender, and Networks of Care*. New Brunswick, NJ: Rutgers University Press.

Harknett, K. (2006). The Relationship Between Private Safety Nets and Economic Outcomes Among Single Mothers. *Journal of Marriage and Family*, 68, 172–191.

Henly, J. R. (2002). Informal Support Networks and the Maintenance Of Low-Wage Jobs. In F. Munger (Ed.), *Laboring Below the Line: The New Ethnography of Poverty, Low-Wage Work, and Survival in the Global Economy* (pp. 179–203). New York: Russell Sage.

Henly, J. R., Danziger, S. K., and Offer, S. (2005). The Contribution of Social Support to the Material Well-Being of Low-Income Families. *Journal of Marriage and Family*, 67, 122–140.

Levine, L. (2013). *Ain't No Trust: How Bosses, Boyfriends, and Bureaucrats Fail Low-Income Mothers and Why It Matters*. Berkeley, CA: University of California Press

Massey, D. S., and Denton, N. A. (1993). *American Apartheid: Segregation and the Making of the Underclass*. Cambridge, MA: Harvard University Press.

Mazelis, J. M. (forthcoming). I Got to Try to Give Back: How Reciprocity Norms in a Poor People's Organization Influence Members' Social Capital. *Journal of Poverty*, 19(1).

Mazelis, J. M., and Mykyta, L. (2011). Relationship Status and Activated Kin Support: The Role of Need and Norms. *Journal of Marriage and Family*, 73, 430–445.

McDonald, K. B., and Armstrong, E. M. (2001). De-Romanticizing Black Intergenerational Support: The Questionable Expectations of Welfare Reform. *Journal of Marriage and Family*, 63, 213–223.

Nelson, M. K. (2000). "Single Mothers and Social Support: The Commitment to, and Retreat from, Reciprocity." *Qualitative Sociology* 23(3): 291–317.

Nelson, M. K. (2005). *The social economy of single motherhood: Raising Children in Rural America*. New York: Routledge.

Newman, K. S. (1999). *No Shame in My Game: The Working Poor in the Inner City*. New York: Vintage Books.

Offer, S. (2012). "The burden of reciprocity: Processes of exclusion and withdrawal from personal networks among low-income families." *Current Sociology* 60(6): 788–805.

Portes, A. (1998). Social Capital: Its Origins and Applications in Modern Sociology. *Annual Review of Sociology*, 24, 1–24.

Putnam, R. D. (2000). *Bowling Alone: The Collapse and Revival of American Community*. New York: Simon and Schuster.

Roschelle, A. R. (1997). *No More Kin: Exploring Race, Class, and Gender in Family Networks*. Thousand Oaks, CA: Sage.

Seccombe, K. (1999). *So You Think I Drive a Cadillac? Welfare Recipients' Perspectives on the System and Its Reform*. Boston, MA: Allyn and Bacon.

Smith, S. S. (2007). *Lone Pursuit: Distrust and Defensive Individualism Among the Black Poor*. New York: Russell Sage.

Stack, C. B. (1974). *All Our Kin: Strategies for Survival in a Black Community*. New York: Harper and Row.

Wilson, W. J. (1987). *The Truly Disadvantaged: The Inner City, the Underclass, and Public Policy*. Chicago, IL: University of Chicago Press.

Wilson, W. J. (1996). *When Work Disappears: The World of the New Urban Poor*. New York: Vintage Books.

39

PATHS INTO HOMELESSNESS

An examination of structural factors

Christine George, Susan Grossman, Judith Wittner, and Michael Sosin

Introduction

The process of deindustrialization, which began in earnest in the United States in the 1970s, has had a strong impact on working people in the United States. Well-paid industrial jobs for high school graduates and immigrants without language skills have all but disappeared, as industry migrated to the global South, non-industrial regions where workers were paid a small fraction of what the largely unionized American labor force had come to expect (Doussard et al., 2009; Hill and Negry, 1987; Wilson, 1996). A powerful indicator of the transformation of the American economy is easily available to anyone who cares to investigate the place of production of most of the goods available to us. Simply look at the place of manufacture on clothing tags and on other commodity goods.

Beyond deindustrialization, and related to it, are the increasing incarceration rates of people of color in the United States According to the Criminal Justice Fact Sheet (NAACP, n.d.), from 1980 to 2008 the number of people incarcerated in America quadrupled from about 500,000 to 2.3 million. The United States today has 5% of the world's population but 25% of the world's prisoners. There has been a 500% increase over the past 30 years in the number of people currently in the nation's prisons or jails, making the United States "the world's leader in incarceration" (The Sentencing Project, 2013a). Further:

> More than 60% of the people in prison are now racial and ethnic minorities. For Black males in their thirties, 1 in every 10 is in prison or jail on any given day. These trends have been intensified by the disproportionate impact of the "war on drugs," in which two-thirds of all persons in prison for drug offenses are people of color.
>
> (The Sentencing Project, 2013b)

Incarceration is related to rising unemployment, first in the targeting of unemployed youth as criminals and, second, in the restricted hiring of people with criminal records. These realities have had an especially profound effect upon Black men and the urban communities they come from. Western (2007) in particular notes how the increasing incarceration rates of African American men beginning in the 1970s and continuing into the 21st century have destabilized Black families, and depressed the wages and work opportunities of Black men, particularly young Black men. Other works show that there is an interaction between existing racial stratification and incarceration that makes it even harder for formerly incarcerated African American men to find employment (Pager, 2003; Visher et al., 2008).

Concurrent to the changing economy and increasing incarceration rate, homelessness became an issue in the late 1970s and early 1980s. While the reasons for the emergence of homelessness as a new social problem are complex and point to many different factors (Jencks, 1994; Wright et al., 1998), unemployment and underemployment, along with criminal justice involvement are clearly associated with homelessness (National Coalition for the Homeless, 2009; Roman and Travis, 2004). In this chapter, we examine the ways in which changing employment opportunities and incarceration have contributed to and continue to impact the life circumstances of homeless individuals. While these two trends are interrelated, we examine them separately and then discuss overlap. Our analysis and discussion are based on data from two studies done in Chicago between 2000 and 2010. The primary study was a multi-method evaluation of Chicago's Ten Year Plan to End Homelessness (PTEH). It included a longitudinal survey of a representative sample of people in the homeless service system as well as focus group interviews with homeless individuals regarding their experience in the system and paths into homelessness. The second source of information is based on a study of the aging of the homeless population of Chicago and includes data from focus groups with homeless individuals and in-depth life history interviews. Together, these data suggest that some individuals who are homeless can find themselves survivors of a perfect storm. As we will discuss in this chapter, deindustrialization has led to lessening economic opportunities and fewer high-paying, low-skilled jobs. Incarceration rates, in turn, have led to individuals who are much less competitive in the wage market, who experience depressed wages and have less accessibility to any employment.

Methodology

The Plan to End Homelessness (PTEH) evaluation

The first source of data for this chapter comes from a comprehensive evaluation, begun in 2009, of Chicago's Ten Year Plan to End Homelessness (Chicago Continuum of Care, 2000). The Plan was designed around a Housing First approach, which argues for providing housing to clients as soon as possible and does not link access to housing to the use of services (National Alliance to End Homelessness, 2006). The evaluation was intended to determine the effectiveness of the homeless service system in Chicago and to describe its fidelity to the Housing First model.

The evaluation design was extensive, including both quantitative and qualitative methods that complemented and confirmed each other, and provided information from the vantage points of the homeless and providers of housing. The major components of the evaluation included: a longitudinal client survey, an exploration of access to and negotiation of the system based on 16 focus groups of consumers, participant observation of homeless individuals at points of entry into the homeless service system (city social service offices, police stations, and hospital emergency rooms), an assessment of the City of Chicago's 311 City Services system, a program providers survey, and qualitative interviews with homeless youth.

A central part of the evaluation of adults was a longitudinal client survey that included questions about client demographic characteristics, homeless experiences, service needs and utilization, experiences with service providers, client difficulties (including health and mental health challenges and substance abuse problems), housing quality, and social support resources. A total of 554 clients took part in the survey, including both single individuals and heads of families.[1]

As part of an effort to understand the in-depth experience of consumers, focus groups were also conducted. A total of 95 individuals in 15 sites reflecting the different types of housing programs and drop-in centers that comprise the Chicago homeless service system took part in focus group interviews.[2]

Homelessness and older adults

The second data source for this chapter was derived from *Homeless after 50: The Graying of Chicago's Homeless Population*, a study of homelessness among older adults conducted in 2007 (George et al., 2008). The goal of the research was to understand the experiences and needs of homeless individuals who were 50–64 years of age. Specifically, the study looked at the demographic characteristics and population trends of this age group; the service and housing needs and challenges experienced by this age group; and the help-seeking experience of these individuals.

Data was collected from homeless individuals and service provider interviews, focus groups with 53 homeless individuals from 8 sites throughout Chicago and 14 life history interviews with homeless individuals. In addition, we analyzed secondary data from survey of homeless individuals in the metropolitan Chicago areas and a merged administrative data from homeless service and housing agencies in Chicago.

The focus group participants and life history interviewees reflected the diversity of the aging homeless population. They included Vietnam and other veterans, persons with serious problems of physical health, mental health, addiction, and alcoholism, people with disabilities, male and female ex-offenders, many of whom were unemployed, and indigent men and women. It is important to note that the data presented in this chapter are descriptive. They are not meant to imply causality. Indeed, it would be simplistic to argue that unemployment or incarceration in and of themselves cause homelessness, nor is that our intention. Rather, our aim is to illustrate some of the effects and impact of deindustrialization and the changing economy in the lives of homeless people particularly as they struggle to regain employment and deal with criminal histories.

Results

Employment

A consistent theme in both studies was the lack or loss of a stable place in the labor force. Homeless people exist at the center of an economic contradiction. They work, but they cannot find jobs. That is, regular, full-time work with or without benefits is no longer available to them. What is available is casual work—part-time, low-paid, and erratic. Such people make up a permanent underclass available for work but without protections.

The homeless people we met in our focus groups were individuals who worked hard and many had years-long work histories. They had been factory workers and service workers, truck drivers, plumbers, carpenters, electricians, security guards, elevator repairmen in city-owned public housing, printers, artists, and clerks and receptionists in banks, telephone sales, and retail sales. Many of the older workers stated that, in years past, these jobs were easier to find and workers moved among them for a variety of reasons, able to find work when they wanted. Supporting Wilson's (1990) arguments about factors leading to concentrations of poverty within communities, they noted that some of these jobs no longer exist. Other jobs are now too far away in the suburbs (and overseas) to be accessible to inner city residents. Still others have been down-sized into part-time and temporary work. Yet for various reasons—advancing age, stereotypes about homeless people, mental and physical health problems, and criminal records—together with the collapse of the job market for these workers—finding employment has become almost impossible for them.

Data from the longitudinal study further reflects this trend. More than one third or 39.4% of those in the longitudinal study reported that they had lost a job prior to homelessness. When asked about their profession, trade, or skill, slightly less than one third of those in the longitudinal study (32.7%) said they did not have one. Of the 67% who said they had a profession, one third (33.4%) were engaged in unskilled employment such as factory work, janitorial or custodial jobs, or fast food service or unskilled manual labor, while about one quarter (26.3%) were blue collar workers, skilled laborers, or tradesmen (carpenters, welders, machine operators). Another quarter (23.6%) were in clerical positions (11.9% or half of the 23.6%) or jobs that entailed caregiving (nurses' aides, home health aides, or home care; 11.7% or the other half of the 23.6%). Only 14.4% of those who said they had a profession were in fields we could classify as professional (mental health professionals, educators, accountants).

These data indicate that many homeless people are in jobs that have and continue to disappear, including manufacturing jobs. In fact, data from individuals in the longitudinal study related to their most current or recent job showed that almost half of the whole sample (48.8%, N=549) were in low or unskilled jobs, and 20% reported that they were in positions involving skilled manual work, but only 7.4% were in jobs that we could classify as professional. In addition, many of the jobs that they reported as having more recently or currently were part-time or temporary. When asked what their current employment pattern had been over the past year, among all those who reported working (N=188), only 40% worked full-time (more than 35 hours per week) on a regular basis. Another 34% reported working regularly, but less than 35 hours per week, and more than one quarter (26.1%) worked irregularly and part-time. Perhaps reflecting this same pattern, 26.5% of those who reported an employment problem in the 30 days prior to the interview (N=196) reported that they were currently underemployed or not working enough hours. Another 76.8% of those reporting employment problems also noted that they had not been able to find work despite trying in the past 30 days.

The decline of full-time jobs with benefits has hit this group hard. Willie Jones (no real names are used) worked for many years as a maintenance man for a realty company, doing "everything from electrical to plumbing." When the owner of the company moved to Texas in 2004, Mr. Jones was left without work. Soon his savings were gone and he lost his apartment. Terrance Washington worked 22 years and Nathan Brown 11 for the Chicago Housing Authority. When the buildings were put under private stewardship, both men were laid off and soon became homeless.

Individuals who are older regularly discover that they are too old to qualify for jobs and too young to qualify for public assistance. Indeed, people in their 50s are years away from receiving old-age benefits. Few individuals in the study of the older homeless population qualified for Supplemental Security Income (SSI), a Federal income supplement program designed to help those aged, blind, and disabled with little or no income. Homeless and near-homeless people in this age group may therefore see a job as the best and perhaps the only way to obtain the steady income that forestalls or ends homelessness. This reality is painfully clear to homeless and near-homeless people we met in both studies. The hope and ambition of many interviewees was to find a steady, reliable job. Their experience was that such jobs are virtually impossible to find.

Some jobs are too far away. One man took and passed the test for postal workers, but was placed in Willow Springs, 29 miles to the west, although he stated on his job application that he had no transportation. Two participants tried to make the long commute to Hopkins, Illinois, 80 miles from Chicago's South Side. Relying on public transportation proved impossible. One man was up at 1:00 a.m. to make the trip to work. Another described three-hour-long commutes each way. They might have persisted in these commutes, but the pay-off—a full-time job—was very far in the future.

> You know, it's like I say, I was getting up actually three hours ahead of time in order to get to the [job] and I was trying to get out there every day, you know. And you gotta be out there sometimes maybe six, seven, eight years before they even think about making you ... full time.

Still others described regularly waiting two hours after work in the dark and cold for Pace buses to bring them back to the city; all this for part-time and temporary work.

When Carolyn Smith had a car, she worked as a bank teller in Naperville, about 40 miles from home. When her car broke down for good, she started her long commute to work every morning at 4:45 a.m. in order to arrive by 8:30 a.m. at the Des Plaines bank where she was then employed. Her day ended at 8:00 p.m. or 8:30 p.m., when she returned home. According to Ms. Smith, many employers won't hire a person without transportation, because they believe

> that if you're on public transportation then you won't get there on time ... Like, a lot of times when I'm on the internet looking for jobs, and it will ask you do you drive. And it will say, if you don't drive, then don't bother to apply.

These accounts show how some unemployed and homeless workers must extend their working day to its limits (and beyond) in order to take jobs. Having skills or a good work history does not necessarily make finding work easier. One employer told an electrician with over 23 years' experience that he was too old to be hired. Others told him that he had too much experience and was "overqualified for a lot of jobs." The idea that workers are overqualified suggests that such workers are consigned to the lowest levels of work and remuneration regardless of their backgrounds or abilities. They are filling the ranks of the casual labor force. As another respondent noted, "I understand when people tell me I have to crawl before I walk, but I can't go work at McDonald's. Those jobs are for teenagers. I would just end up homeless again."

Another talked about the fact that he runs into people with a lot of skills but nowhere to use them. Further, he lamented, without a job, he felt that it was impossible to get subsidized housing.

Day shelters can be a rich source for employers of casual workers who accept minimum-wage temporary jobs. According to many men we interviewed, employers got access to cheap but often skilled labor by showing up each morning at shelters to hire day laborers on construction and rehab projects. For example, Curtis Moore, a skilled machine operator with years of experience, could only find temporary and part-time work with these companies a few days a week. Pay for this work: $7.50 an hour.

> Because, normally we come here [day shelter] in the morning, because we can get some type of work. Couple of them needs help coming in here. Come in here, they take some of the guys out and we make a little change that way, instead of just being on the street.

Such work provides unemployed and homeless workers with small amounts of cash ("a little change") that helps them to survive on the Chicago streets, providing bus fare, cigarette money, or money enough to rent an inexpensive room on an occasional night. Intentional or not, employers have the advantage. As one respondent noted:

> We have a lot of reputable companies that come here looking for people to work. The problem with that is they come here because they figure if we're homeless, we're vulnerable. Like they can give us anything that they want to give you. It's like we'll put it right here and take it or leave it.

Incarceration and homelessness

While limited job skills in changing economies present challenges to homeless individuals, qualitative data from both the focus groups and interviews suggest that felony convictions make it almost impossible to obtain both housing and employment. As one respondent with a prior felony conviction noted: "People don't take chances on you. I always used to do well in interviews and get by. But now people won't even call me."

Another focus group participant reported that most people do not hire if you have a felony, even if that felony happened 20 years ago. One individual told about a worker at a nursing home who was a good worker, but the background check came and "they show[ed] him the door." A female resident of one program also had this experience. She said several times that she wished more could be done for individuals with criminal backgrounds. She still faced difficulties despite her offense being 15 years in the past and having a clean record ever since. She wished for her current program and other agencies to have a better relationship with experts on criminal backgrounds and for a program or policy that might allow for forgiveness.

Some respondents noted that the jobs that are available are not enough to live on.

> Living-wage jobs, the cost of living is disproportionate to the jobs that are available for people who have made a mistake who are trying to get back to a certain level and, uh, positions offered for someone trying to get back, without an education or any representation from any institutions, you know, to show yourself, to prove that you're trying to get back into society, seem to be just, nonexistent.

More than one third (38.5%) of the individuals in the evaluation of the Plan to End Homelessness had a history of felony convictions; in most cases these included incarceration (92.9%) and, for 75% of these individuals (N=197), more than once. In addition, 19.3% of all those in the longitudinal study report recent discharge from prison and/or merely "getting in trouble with the law" as reasons for their most recent episode of homelessness.

Not surprisingly, given the high incarceration rates of African American men, among our homeless sample, they were the most likely to report a felony conviction (51.7% of African American men reported a felony conviction versus 33.3% of men who were not African American and 20% of White men specifically). However, 27.3% of all women in the sample also had felony convictions.

Nonetheless, despite anecdotal reports that felony convictions make it more difficult to find employment and stable housing, the quantitative data did not clearly show a significant relationship between felonies and moving out of homelessness when controlling for other characteristics including personal problems and family status. This suggests that the relationship between involvement in the criminal justice system and homelessness is complex.

Conclusion and recommendations

The data from these studies demonstrate the bind in which many homeless people find themselves. Given the mis-match between their skills and the changing post-industrial job market, respondents in both studies find their employment status, even when connected to employment agencies, is tenuous at best. Felony convictions, the stigma of homelessness, and the lack of employment mobility create serious barriers to achieving and maintaining work and may in turn affect housing stability. Respondents had several ideas about what might help change their situations. These included good, secure part-time jobs and jobs that paid living wages. For those with felony convictions, amnesty for old convictions was also high on the list. As one respondent noted:

> ... they got legislation to stop us from getting jobs, because of our backgrounds. Why isn't there any legislation to tear that law down? Because, for me, it's unconstitutional. [Other person: It's discrimination really.] And it's discriminatory, because 80–95 percent of the people with backgrounds are Afro-American. You know, and like him [referring to another focus group member with a felony conviction], he's been driving trucks most of his life, me, I've been doing nursing most of my life, then you come up with a law that says I can't work because I did something 30 years ago. A criminal background punishes you the rest of your life.

Another talked about creating jobs or giving residents in programs a first crack at jobs that opened up in the neighborhoods where programs were located:

> ... they build stuff in certain neighborhoods, but they don't hire people in those neighborhoods. That makes no sense to me. Why wouldn't you hire the people in the neighborhoods? That way, everybody would be working. Not only that, it's easier for them to get to the job. And then when they get there, it just cuts out a lot, the middle. They want you to go 40 miles, so you can spend money on gas, on the bus pass, so everybody else is getting something and you ain't getting nothing. And it would help as far as in the homeless situation too. Because I'm not saying that it's going to cure homelessness right then [snaps fingers], but it will help motivate individuals to do the best that they can even if they have to stay in the shelter a little bit longer. [Other person: Right.] We know we have a better opportunity, a better percentage wise of getting a place of our own, a room, an apartment of our own, to build up from that. And we would be able to set the example.

As their recommendations suggest, respondents clearly understand the dynamics that keep them locked out of employment and prevent them from moving up the economic ladder. Further, these data demonstrate that for the portion of the homeless individuals for whom illness (either chronic or acute) does not preclude employment, merely having a job-readiness employment strategy to assist individuals who are unstably housed is not sufficient. It points to the need for a more in-depth examination and exploration of a number of policy strategies including a higher minimum wage (living wage) and the provision of benefits for part-time employment. As noted, laws that make it possible to expunge criminal records for certain crimes are essential. Additional social supports such as affordable and accessible housing are critical as well. Ultimately, in this complex post-industrial global economy, complex solutions are necessary.

Notes

1 The sample for the client survey was selected using a two-stage random sampling approach to ensure that it was representative of individuals in three types of housing. Individuals agreeing to take part in the survey were followed for a year and took part in three interviews at six-month intervals. The interviews were all conducted between October 20, 2009 and April 14, 2011. Questions in the follow-up interviews asked about current homeless status and changes in housing, service needs and use, and status related to areas of client difficulty and support systems.
2 In total, 95 individuals took part, including adults and youth, families, and single individuals. All focus groups were tape recorded, and an additional individual who was part of the research team took notes during the session. Tapes were later transcribed and notes added into one document to capture the content of each focus group. Thematic coding of the content then took place.

References

Chicago Continuum of Care (2000). *Getting Housed, Staying Housed: A Collaborative Plan to End Homelessness (PTEH)*. Chicago, IL: Mimeo.

Doussard, M., Peck, J., and Theodore, N. (2009). After Deindustrialization: Uneven Growth and Economic Inequality in "Postindustrial" Chicago. *Economic Geography*, 85:2, pp. 183–207.

George, C., Krogh, M., Watson, D., and Wittner, J. (2008). *Homeless after 50: The Graying of Chicago's Homeless Population*. Chicago: Loyola University Chicago, Center for Urban Research and Learning. Available online at http://www.luc.edu/media/lucedu/curl/pdfs/FinalTech.pdf. Accessed January 20, 2013.

Hill, P. and Negry, C. (1987). Deindustrialization in the Great Lakes. *Urban Affairs Review*, 22:2, pp. 580–597.

Jencks, C. (1994). *The Homeless*. Cambridge, MA: Harvard University Press.

National Alliance to End Homelessness (2006). *What is Housing First?* Available online at: http://www.endhomelessness.org/library/entry/what-is-housing-first. Accessed February 10, 2013.

National Association for the Advancement of Colored People (NAACP) (n.d.) *Criminal Justice Fact Sheet*. Available online at: http://www.naacp.org/pages/criminal-justice-fact-sheet. Accessed January 9, 2013.

National Coalition for the Homeless (2009, July). *Employment and Homelessness*. Available online at: http://www.nationalhomeless.org/factsheets/employment.html. Accessed April 28, 2013.

Pager, D. (2003). The Mark of a Criminal Record. *American Journal of Sociology*, 108:5, pp. 937–975.

Roman, C.G. and Travis, J. (2004). *Taking Stock: Housing, Homelessness and Prison Re-entry*. Washington, DC: The Urban Institute. Available online at: http://www.urban.org/UploadedPDF/411096_taking_stock.pdf. Accessed April, 28, 2013.

The Sentencing Project (2013a). *Incarceration*. Available online at: http://www.sentencingproject.org/template/page.cfm?id=107. Accessed January 25, 2013.

The Sentencing Project (2013b). *A Black Agenda (Reprinted from the Florida Courier)*. Available online at: http://www.sentencingproject.org/detail/news.cfm?news_id=1449&id=107. Accessed January 25, 2013.

Visher, C., Debus, S. and Yahner, J. (2008). *Employment after Prison: A Longitudinal Study of Releases in Three States: Research Brief*. Washington, DC: Urban Institute.Available online at: http://www.urban.org/UploadedPDF/411778_employment_after_prison.pdf. Accessed April 13, 2013.

Western, B. (2007). *Punishment and Inequality in America*. New York: Russell Sage Foundation.

Wilson, W.J. (1990). *The Truly Disadvantaged: The Inner City, the Underclass and Public Policy*. Chicago: University of Chicago Press.

Wilson, W.J. (1996). *When Work Disappears*. New York: Knof.

Wright, J.D., Rubin, B.A., and Devine, J.A. (1998). *Beside the Golden Door: Policy, Politics and the Homeless*. New York: Aldine de Gruyter.

40

EXAMINING RACIAL–ETHNIC AND GENDER DISPARITIES IN POVERTY AMONG THE ELDERLY

Jin Kim

Background and significance

Over the last ten years, absolute poverty rates in the United States have climbed steadily from 12.1% in 2002 to 15.0% in 2011 according to Current Population Survey estimates (U.S. Bureau of the Census, 2013). Meanwhile, as shown by Table 40.1, absolute poverty rates among those 65 years and over have fallen from 10.4% to 8.7% in the same time span (U.S. Bureau of the Census, 2013). Amidst the decrease in absolute poverty overall among the elderly population, a closer examination of absolute poverty across racial–ethnic and gender lines further underscores the positive gains achieved for those 65 and over even while poverty among the general population continues to rise. Absolute poverty rates, for instance, among both White and Black elderly individuals (6.7% and 17.2%, respectively) currently stand at ten-year lows (U.S. Bureau of the Census, 2013). In a similar vein, absolute poverty rates for both male and female elderly individuals (6.2% and 10.7%, respectively) are also the lowest that the United States has experienced over the past decade (U.S. Bureau of the Census, 2013).

To be sure, our public income maintenance programs designed to mitigate the effects of lost income upon old age have played a substantial role in these declines. Over the ten-year period in question, total annual benefits paid under Social Security (namely, Old Age Survivors Insurance) have increased from $388.1 billion in 2002 to $596.2 billion in 2011, while total annual benefits paid to aged recipients under Supplemental Security Income (the program of last resort for income-poor elderly) have similarly increased from $3.9 billion in 2002 to $4.9 billion in 2011—indeed a modest but significant aggregate sum for those who may face dire economic circumstances (U.S. Social Security Administration, 2013). Yet, while our public policies have been rather generous in protecting against lost income in old age for those with the requisite work history or significant ties to this country (i.e., U.S. citizens), there are still various segments within the elderly population that lag significantly in their levels of economic well-being.

Part of the illusion of prosperous economic circumstances among the elderly stems from the public dissemination of statistics that rely on repeated cross-sections of poverty data. While the absolute poverty rates released annually by the Census Bureau are able to describe the financial situations of those who are in the midst of a spell of poverty in a given year, they do not describe how absolute poverty rates vary as individuals grow older. Thus while on its face absolute poverty appears to have diminished when looking at repeated cross-sections of elderly

Table 40.1 Poverty status of persons 65 years and over, by race, Hispanic origin, and sex: 2002–2011

			Percent below poverty			
	All persons 65 and over	White alone, not Hispanic	Black alone or in combination	Hispanic (of any race)	Male	Female
2011	8.7	6.7	17.2	18.7	6.2	10.7
2010	8.9	6.8	18.1	18.0	6.7	10.7
2009	8.9	6.6	19.2	18.3	6.6	10.7
2008	9.7	7.6	20.0	19.3	6.7	11.9
2007	9.7	7.4	23.3	17.1	6.6	12.0
2006	9.4	7.0	22.7	19.4	6.6	11.5
2005	10.1	7.9	23.2	19.9	7.3	12.3
2004	9.8	7.5	23.8	18.4	7.0	11.9
2003	10.2	8.0	23.5	19.5	7.3	12.5
2002	10.4	8.3	23.6	21.4	7.7	12.4

Source: Adapted from U.S. Bureau of the Census (2013).

Americans over this period, a longitudinal examination of absolute poverty among the elderly along racial–ethnic and gender lines reveals that poverty may be much more prevalent than the cross-sectional data suggest. As such, this study uses longitudinal data from the Rand version of the Health and Retirement Study spanning the years 2002–2010 to examine the risk of falling into poverty in old age and the extent to which these patterns vary along racial–ethnic and gender lines. Accordingly, prior longitudinal research examining transitions to poverty among the elderly reveals that single individuals (i.e., widows) and couples display quite different patterns as it is the initial transition from work to retirement that presents the greatest risk of becoming poor for couples, while the risk of becoming poor is approximately constant over time for widows (Burkhauser et al., 1991). This study extends prior work by examining the changing patterns of risk among various racial–ethnic and gender groupings.

The literature

For many elderly individuals, the later stages of life can be a time of rapid and considerable changes in the areas of income, health and functioning, and living situations (Soldo et al., 1997). Thus, while there are many positive changes that can occur in old age, the effects of negative changes, such as loss of income, declining health and functioning, and loss of a spouse, may accumulate over time to impose significant financial hardship to an aging individual. This points to the importance of examining long-term transitions to absolute poverty among the elderly as opposed to cross-sections, since it is already well established that the majority of poor persons at any time are in the midst of a long spell of poverty (Bane and Ellwood, 1983). The suggestion that cross-sectional data provide limited insight into the changing circumstances of the elderly is certainly not new. The research is replete with studies documenting the effects of potentially significant life changes on the elderly—most notably, in studies examining transitions to poverty in old age (see (Burkhauser et al., 1991; Burkhauser et al., 1988; Holden et al., 1988; Holden and Kuo, 1996; Holden and Smock, 1991; Rank and Hirschl, 1999).

In Burkhauser et al. (1991), the researchers used longitudinal data from the Retirement History Study (RHS) to trace the economic well-being of intact couples and widows[1] spanning a period of ten years. Utilizing a hazard model approach, they examined two dynamic measures of economic well-being (i.e., the risk of a drop into poverty and the risk of a replacement rate drop below 50 percent of preretirement income) and found that, for intact families, the risk of a drop into poverty diminishes over time, while for widows, the risk of a drop dramatically increases following the death of a spouse. They found the same patterns when examining the risk of a drop below 50 percent of preretirement income. Moreover, particularly noteworthy was the finding that, for intact families, it is the initial transition from work to retirement (i.e., the first period) that presents the greatest risk of becoming poor, while for widows, the risk of becoming poor is approximately constant over time.

This line of research examining transitions to poverty in old age provides a number of important lessons and serves as a foundation for the current descriptive study that also uses a ten-year window to detail the risk of falling into absolute poverty. For one, the findings underscore the importance of using a dynamic approach to modeling late-life transitions and the changing circumstances of the elderly. Cross-sectional data on poverty can accurately describe the percentage of the elderly population that is in the midst of a spell of poverty but does not reveal the risk of poverty as individuals grow older. Moreover, the finding that intact couples and widows have different trajectories to poverty highlights the importance of tracking transitions to poverty among disparate groupings of individuals. Thus, this study extends prior work by examining the changing patterns of risk associated with falling into absolute poverty across various combinations of racial–ethnic and gender groupings.

Data and methods

This study uses data from the Rand version (L) of the Health and Retirement Study (HRS) to estimate life tables that describe the risk of falling into absolute poverty during retirement among different racial–ethnic and gender groups. The Rand version of the HRS is a cleaned, processed, and streamlined collection of variables derived from the original HRS. Meanwhile, the HRS itself is a national panel study of persons age 50 and over and their spouses. The HRS survey elicits information about various sources of income, job history, and demographics, among numerous other categories, and is thus well suited for a study estimating absolute (income) poverty during retirement. The full HRS consists of six cohorts representing persons born before 1959 in the United States. The Rand HRS, version L, contains all five cohorts up to the Early Baby Boomer cohort, but does not include data for the new cohort of Mid Baby Boomers that was first interviewed in 2010.

The study draws a sample of individuals age 65 years and over from Waves 6 (2002), 7 (2004), 8 (2006), 9 (2008), and 10 (2010), and follows these individuals over the same years to determine whether and to what extent the risk of falling into absolute poverty during retirement varies across time and across different racial–ethnic and gender groups. Data are drawn beginning with Wave 6 (2002) to establish a ten-year window (2002–2011) over which poverty can be examined.[2] Each individual, then, may be at risk of falling into absolute poverty for a minimum of two years (e.g., in the case of early attrition or death) and a maximum of ten years where Wave 6 (2002) sample members survive through Wave 10 (2010) without target-event occurrence.

The original sample, then, consists of 15,913 individuals who are examined to see if they first transition to retirement.[3] The longitudinal analysis of absolute poverty, then, focuses only on those who make this initial transition to retirement, and hence begins in the first two-year period of retirement, continuing until they first fall into absolute poverty, they die, they reach the end of the study period, or they unretire. Individuals who report transitioning back into the labor force are treated as censored, beginning with the first period in which they report this transition.[4] In sum, the final sample to be used for the longitudinal poverty analysis includes 12,911 individuals who report a retired employment status.

An important part of the poverty estimation, of course, is the derivation of the poverty variable that is used to denote transitions to absolute poverty. One of the many strengths of the Rand HRS data file is that it already includes a measure of poverty that uses the official absolute poverty thresholds from the U.S. Census Bureau. The Rand contributors then use data on family composition to determine the absolute poverty threshold that applies to each individual or family, and then compares the individual's or family's income to the appropriate threshold. In short, there is very little in the derivation of the absolute poverty variable(s) in the Rand HRS that might raise concern over the accuracy of the absolute poverty estimates, given that this is the method used by the U.S. Census Bureau to estimate poverty and since the annual reporting of income in the HRS (as opposed to monthly reporting in other datasets) can be assessed directly against the official Census poverty thresholds which are annual amounts. One concern might be if a researcher used the alternate measure of absolute poverty contained in the Rand HRS that includes the income of institutionalized family members. However, this alternate measure of absolute poverty is not used here.

Results

Below are two life tables describing the number of years at risk of falling into poverty during retirement for persons 65 years and over. Each table is divided into a series of rows indexing time intervals that correspond to the number of years at risk. In period 1, all individuals are in their first two years of retirement. In period 2, all individuals are in their third and fourth years of retirement. In period 3, all individuals are in their fifth and sixth years of retirement, and so on for subsequent periods. The life tables also include information on the conditional probability that an individual will fall into poverty in a given time period (given that he or she did not fall into poverty in an earlier retirement period), i.e., estimated hazard probabilities, the probability that an individual will survive past a given time period, i.e., estimated survivor probabilities, as well as the number of persons who enter the risk set at baseline, i.e., n_1. In short, estimated hazard and survivor probabilities are provided for various racial–ethnic and gender classifications in these two tables.

Table 40.2 tracks the poverty histories of a sample of individuals 65 years and over beginning at retirement until they fall into poverty, they die, or they reach the end of the study period. At the beginning of the first two-year time interval, a total of 12,911 persons age 65 and over were at risk of falling into poverty during retirement. By the end of the ten-year study period, 22.2% of all persons 65 and over had fallen into poverty. As is consistent with the most recent Current Population Survey estimates, Table 40.2 also indicates that the hazard of falling into poverty is highest among Hispanic and female individuals 65 and over. At the beginning of the first two-year time interval, 9,982 White, 1,762 Black, and 944 Hispanic individuals age 65 and over were at risk of falling into poverty during retirement, while 6,046 males and 6,865 females age 65 and over were at similar risk. By the end of the ten-year study period, 14.3% of Whites, 49.9% of Blacks, and 52.3% of Hispanics in the sample had fallen into poverty, while 16.7% of males and 27.6% of females in the sample had fallen into poverty.

Meanwhile, Table 40.3 tracks the poverty histories of a sample of individuals 65 years and over from various combinations of racial–ethnic and gender groups beginning at retirement until they fall into poverty, they die, or they reach the end of the study period. At the beginning

Table 40.2 Life table describing the risk of poverty during retirement for persons aged 65 and over

Two-year period of retirement	All persons 65 and over		White		Black	
	Estimated hazard probability	Estimated survivor probability	Estimated hazard probability	Estimated survivor probability	Estimated hazard probability	Estimated survivor probability
1	0.0874	0.9126	0.0485	0.9515	0.2157	0.7843
2	0.0429	0.8734	0.0265	0.9263	0.1122	0.6963
3	0.0311	0.8463	0.0205	0.9073	0.0812	0.6398
4	0.0359	0.8159	0.0249	0.8847	0.1046	0.5729
5	0.0462	0.7783	0.0361	0.8528	0.1250	0.5013
	$n_1 = 12{,}911$		$n_1 = 9{,}982$		$n_1 = 1{,}762$	

Two-year period of retirement	Hispanic		Male		Female	
	Estimated hazard probability	Estimated survivor probability	Estimated hazard probability	Estimated survivor probability	Estimated hazard probability	Estimated survivor probability
1	0.2468	0.7532	0.0599	0.9401	0.1117	0.8883
2	0.1353	0.6513	0.0321	0.9100	0.0540	0.8403
3	0.0972	0.5880	0.0243	0.8879	0.0387	0.8078
4	0.1053	0.5261	0.0303	0.8610	0.0427	0.7733
5	0.0930	0.4771	0.0324	0.8331	0.0643	0.7236
	$n_1 = 944$		$n_1 = 6{,}046$		$n_1 = 6{,}865$	

of the first two-year time interval, 4,726 White males and 5,256 White females were at risk of falling into poverty during retirement. By the end of the study period, 10.5% of White males and 19.1% of White females in the sample had fallen into poverty. In contrast, Table 40.3 further indicates that the hazard or risk of falling into poverty is exceptionally high among Black and Hispanic females. At the beginning of the first two-year time interval, 744 Black males, 1,018 Black females, 465 Hispanic males, and 479 Hispanic females were at risk of falling into poverty during retirement. By the end of the ten-year study period, 38.1% of Black males and 58.6% of Black females in the sample had fallen into poverty, while 48.7% of Hispanic males and 56.5% of Hispanic females in the sample had fallen into poverty.

Discussion

This study examined racial–ethnic and gender disparities in absolute poverty among the elderly living in the United States, and the long-term risk associated with falling into poverty as elderly individuals enter retirement. Motivated by the 2012 release of official poverty data showing positive gains achieved in the area of financial well-being among the elderly during a time of economic crisis among numerous segments in the population, this research examined poverty among the elderly through a different lens and discovered that while elderly individuals in the United States seemingly enjoy greater economic protection than at any other point in the past

Table 40.3 Life table describing the risk of poverty during retirement for persons aged 65 and over

Two-year period of retirement	White male		White female		Black male	
	Estimated hazard probability	*Estimated survivor probability*	*Estimated hazard probability*	*Estimated survivor probability*	*Estimated hazard probability*	*Estimated survivor probability*
1	0.0281	0.9719	0.0668	0.9332	0.1573	0.8427
2	0.0172	0.9551	0.0362	0.8995	0.0911	0.7660
3	0.0139	0.9419	0.0281	0.8742	0.0688	0.7132
4	0.0221	0.9211	0.0282	0.8495	0.0773	0.6581
5	0.0281	0.8952	0.0469	0.8097	0.0583	0.6197
	n_1=4,726		n_1=5,256		n_1=744	

Two-year period of retirement	Black female		Hispanic male		Hispanic female	
	Estimated hazard probability	*Estimated survivor probability*	*Estimated hazard probability*	*Estimated survivor probability*	*Estimated hazard probability*	*Estimated survivor probability*
1	0.2583	0.7417	0.2151	0.7849	0.2777	0.7223
2	0.1308	0.6447	0.1265	0.6856	0.1466	0.6164
3	0.0924	0.5851	0.0962	0.6197	0.0989	0.5555
4	0.1302	0.5089	0.0947	0.5610	0.1228	0.4873
5	0.1858	0.4143	0.0862	0.5126	0.1071	0.4351
	n_1=1,018		n_1=465		n_1=479	

decade, the long-term risk of poverty is still quite prevalent. Indeed, the official poverty estimates that use repeated cross-sections of the elderly in generating the annual poverty statistics appear to underestimate the true extent of absolute poverty, particularly among racial–ethnic and gender minority groups. To begin, life table analysis revealed a cumulative, ten-year poverty rate of 22.2% among all retired sample members 65 years and over, which is of course well above the current cross-sectional estimate of 8.7% of all elderly using CPS data. In examining disparities across racial–ethnic and gender lines, life table analysis also revealed that ten-year poverty rates were highest among Hispanics (52.3%) and females (27.6%), numbers that would seem staggering amidst the apparent positive gains achieved over the past decade. Moreover, when interacting race–ethnicity and gender, it was revealed that ten-year poverty rates were highest among Black females (58.6%) followed by Hispanic females (56.5%), thus further reinforcing the notion that the long-term risk of falling into poverty among certain groups of elderly is exceedingly high.

The existing disparities in poverty among various racial–ethnic and gender groups may be due, at least in part, to lack of take-up and scaling back of benefits under the program of last resort for income-poor elderly, i.e., Supplemental Security Income (SSI). As of 2010, only 10.3% of Black females reported cash public assistance from the SSI program as an income source, while only 12.0% of Hispanic females reported the same, despite their high rates of poverty (U.S. Social Security Administration, 2013). Further, there is reason to believe that due to recent reductions in SSI state supplementation amounts that characterize the current neoliberal policy environment, cash benefits provided under a combination of SSI and other public programs (i.e., Social Security) may still not be sufficient to lift income-poor elderly individuals above the poverty thresholds (U.S. Social Security Administration, 2013).

One potential limitation in this study is the possibility that the ten-year poverty estimates reflect re-entry into poverty for many sample members, that is, that the numbers may reflect an overabundance of individuals who may have been poor throughout their working years. This possibility is tempered, however, by the fact that only those individuals who transition to retirement were included in the study sample. Thus, the ten-year poverty estimates reported here are not a reflection of unemployment status (which would inflate the degree of poverty) but rather a function of the various sources of income (or lack thereof) that are made available to elderly individuals upon retirement.

In sum, while the most recent estimates provided by the U.S. Census Bureau indicate that poverty continues to decline for elderly individuals overall, the results of this longitudinal study suggest that the true extent of poverty among the elderly is highly understated. Moreover, the existing racial–ethnic and gender disparities in poverty among elderly individuals are magnified when expanding the observation window. This research underscores the critical importance of our public income maintenance programs in buffering against the effects of lost income in old age. Particularly vulnerable even with the protections afforded under our current public programs are elderly individuals who may have come to this country at a relatively later age, and thus do not have the requisite work history (or citizenship status for that matter) to qualify for existing income support programs. All in all, policy advocates should exercise caution in interpreting the annual poverty estimates to gauge any level of progress in combating poverty among the U.S. elderly population.

Notes

1 They also trace the economic well-being of widowers but find little distinction from intact couples.
2 This is also the first year in which poverty variables are derived in the Rand HRS.
3 The Rand HRS includes two questions regarding retirement. One question asks whether the respondent considers himself/herself retired. A second question asks whether the respondent reports a retired employment status. This study uses responses to the second question to determine an individual's retirement status as it contains fewer missing values. Note that respondents may report being either "only retired" or "retired plus other" in response to the question on retired employment status, and thus both response categories are used to indicate a transition to retirement.
4 Alternative treatment of this transition (e.g., allowing individuals to return to the analytic sample if they retire again) does not result in substantially different conclusions.

References

Bane, M. J., and Ellwood, D. T. (1983). *Slipping into and out of poverty: The dynamics of spells*. NBER Working Paper No. 1199. Cambridge, MA: National Bureau of Economic Research.

Burkhauser, R. V., Butler, J. S., and Holden, K. C. (1991). How the death of a spouse affects economic well-being after retirement: A hazard model approach. *Social Science Quarterly*, 72(3), 504–519.

Burkhauser, R. V., Holden, K. C., and Feaster, D. (1988). Incidence, timing, and events associated with poverty: A dynamic view of poverty in retirement. *Journal of Gerontology*, 43(2), S46–S52.

Holden, K. C., Burkhauser, R. V., and Feaster, D. J. (1988). The timing of falls into poverty after retirement and widowhood. *Demography*, 25(3), 405–414.

Holden, K. C., and Kuo, H. H. D. (1996). Complex marital histories and economic well-being: The continuing legacy of divorce and widowhood as the HRS cohort approaches retirement. *The Gerontologist*, 36(3), 383–390.

Holden, K. C., and Smock, P. J. (1991). The economic costs of marital dissolution: Why do women bear a disproportionate cost? *Annual Review of Sociology*, 51–78.

Hurd, M. D. (1990). Research on the elderly: Economic status, retirement, and consumption and saving. *Journal of Economic Literature*, 28(2), 565–637.

Rank, M. R., and Hirschl, T. A. (1999). Estimating the proportion of Americans ever experiencing poverty during their elderly years. *The Journals of Gerontology Series B: Psychological Sciences and Social Sciences*, 54(4), S184.

Soldo, B., Hurd, M., Rodgers, W., and Wallace, R. (1997). Asset and health dynamics among the oldest old: An overview of the AHEAD study. *The Journals of Gerontology*, 52B(Special Issue): 1–20.

U.S. Social Security Administration. (2013). *Research, Statistics, and Policy Analysis*. Washington, DC: U.S. Social Security Administration. Retrieved June 13, 2013 from http://www.ssa.gov/policy/docs/statcomps/index.html.

U.S. Bureau of the Census. (2013). *2012 Census Data*. Washington, DC: U.S. Bureau of the Census. Retrieved June 13, 2013 from http://www.census.gov/hhes/www/poverty/.

41

ABLEISM, POVERTY, AND THE UNDER-CELEBRATED RESISTANCE

Sara Lichtenwalter and Christopher Magno

Disability and ableism

Transportation is a gateway to social inclusion and economic opportunities, so it is not surprising that some of the initial struggles for both African Americans and people with disabilities in the United States involved buses. Rosa Parks is rightly heralded as a courageous heroine for refusing to move to the back of a bus in Montgomery, Alabama. However, decades later Ellen Nuzzi, who defied a bus driver's orders to get herself and her wheelchair off the bus entirely, would be labeled as "selfish" for delaying the other passengers' New York City commute, her act of resistance fading into obscurity (Johnson, 2003). Ellen Nuzzi, along with others in the Disability Rights Movement, have fallen into what disabilities studies scholars refer to as a "profound historical gap," a discursive invisibility through which the struggles and successes of Americans with disabilities have remained largely unknown and unheralded (Bell, 2006; Longmore and Umansky, 2001, p.3; Snyder and Mitchell, 2006, p.5). People with disabilities as a group have lagged behind women, and racial and religious minorities, in their struggle for equality. Ms. Parks was jailed in 1955 for defying racial segregation on the bus, yet it was over 20 years later before many people with disabilities could even board the bus (Fleischer and Zames, 2011).

Ableism and paternalistic attitudes place people with disabilities at a very high risk for living in poverty and dependence, subject to powerlessness and indignities (Charlton, 2006, p.217). National citizenship, race, sexual orientation, and even the type of disability, specifically cognitive and mental disabilities, add to the complex dimensions of disability oppression (Bell, 2006; Davis, 2006; Deal, 2007; Longmore and Umansky, 2001; Trent, 1994). Bell (2006) draws attention to the fact that the "face" of disability has too long been the white, presumably straight, man in a wheelchair. However, some scholars contend that sexism, racism, ethnicism, and other isms can arguably be viewed as driven by, and rooted in, forms of a general ableism (Ford, 2009; Wolbring, 2008).

Ableism is a type of discrimination, like sexism or racism. It emerges from a fear of, or aversion to, people with disabilities (Nielsen, 2012). It is the devaluation of human variation, the differences that exist in "human behavior, appearance, functioning, sensory acuity, and cognitive process" (Linton, 1998, p.2). Ableism results in "societal attitudes that uncritically assert that it is better to walk than roll, speak than sign, read print than Braille"—briefly, that it is best for the disabled to do things in the same manner as the nondisabled (Campbell, 2003, p.94).

Disability discrimination has been present throughout U.S. history, and disability has long been used as a justification for inequality. Attacks against suffragist, abolitionist, and immigration proponents employed disability to discredit claims to citizenship. Purported physical, intellectual, and psychological "flaws" at various times in history have excluded women and minority groups from voting, property ownership, and employment opportunities. Echoing these views, women, African Americans, and immigrants would vehemently reject the association with disability, rather than question the legitimacy of disability as rational for denying rights to political and social equality (Baynton, 2001; Kudlick, 2003).

Even people with disabilities have and often still do reject association with the category of "disabled" (Linton, 1998; Shapiro, 1994) because of the powerful stigma of a spoiled and discredited, inferior identity (Goffman, 1963). There are multiple types and degrees of disability; some are associated with more delimiting stigmas than others both within and outside the disability community (Deal, 2007). These stigmatic differences have served to impede the coalescence of persons with disabilities into a group to pursue common goals. Hooper's wry comment on the U.S. Census head count of 57 million people with disabilities reflects this barrier: "someone better tell those folks that they're part of this group" (Hooper, 1994, p.5). He expresses the fissure beautifully: "If you use a wheelchair, try going up to someone using a hearing aid and explain to them that you're both in the same community. Good luck!" (Hooper, 1994, p.5; see also Fleischer and Zames, 2011). People with disabilities can and do "internalize ableism" (Campbell, 2003; Deal, 2007).

Campbell (2003) contends that ableism is not a system of oppression where a specific enemy can be identified and extracted. She defines ableism as "a convergence of networks that produce exclusionary matrices and ontologies ... players in the government of disability may change; other formations such as the use of regimes of law and medicine remain constant" (Campbell, 2003, p.94). These "regimes of laws" and policies effectively construct environments around people with disabilities that are socially, economically, and physically disabling.

For the purpose of this chapter, the following discussion will be limited to economic barriers and other encumbrance contributing to poverty for people with disabilities. After highlighting the economic disparities experienced by people with disabilities, the authors present a summary of the resistance mounted by the Disability Rights Movement, and an overview of challenges to people with disabilities that are arising within today's frameworks and practices of neoliberalism.

Disability and poverty

Poverty

Disability is a primary cause and consequence of income poverty, although until recently the scrutiny of most statisticians and scholars consistently neglected to examine this link. Nevertheless, approximately 50% of working-age adults experiencing income poverty have a disability, and two thirds of adults experiencing long-term income poverty report having a disability (Fremstad, 2009).

Although the U.S. government expends considerable resources in data collection efforts, which include hundreds of different surveys and sets of administrative records, current disability data is neither comprehensive nor easily accessible. "The range of disability definitions and multiple uses of the term 'disability' in laws, policies, programs and data collection instruments make comprehensive data on people with disabilities extremely difficult to compile" (National Council on Disability, 2008, p.25). For the purposes of this chapter the U.S. Census Bureau's

Survey of Income and Program Participation (SIPP) and Current Population Survey (CPS) were utilized unless otherwise noted.

The number of people with disabilities is estimated to be over 57 million, or 19% of the civilian, non-institutionalized population (U.S. Census Bureau, 2014). This number would increase with the inclusion of people residing in institutional settings, such as prisons, nursing homes, and psychiatric institutions. People with disabilities are the largest minority group in the United States (Davis, 2006; Shapiro, 1994), exceeding the number of Hispanics or African Americans, who in fact have disability rates that exceed those of the White population. The U.S. Census Bureau's SIPP reports the age-adjusted disability rates of 22.2% for the Black population alone, compared to 17.4% and 17.8% for non-Hispanic White and Hispanic/Latino populations, respectively (Brault, 2012).

The most common cause of disability is categorized by the SIPP as the physical domain (80.6%), which is predominantly ambulatory difficulties, and is followed by the mental domain (32.6%), which includes cognitive and emotional difficulties (Brault, 2012). These are trailed by the communicative domain (30.5%), which includes seeing, hearing, and speech limitations (Brault, 2012). More than one third (38.5%) of people with disabilities affiliate with more than one domain. The most common single cause for disability is musculoskeletal disorders, such as arthritis and back/spine problems, followed by heart disease (Centers for Disease Control and Prevention, 2011).

Individuals with disabilities represent the largest group experiencing income poverty; this population exceeds that of any single minority or ethnic group, or all minority ethnic and racial groups in combination (Fremstad, 2009). The Center for Economic Policy and Research reports that people with disabilities account for a larger share of the income poor than even single parents (Fremstad, 2009).

Despite, or perhaps because of, the myriad of fragmented government programs for people with disabilities, the economic conditions for their households have deteriorated over time. A long-term study by the Mathematica Policy Research Center concluded that "Over the past 30 years, people with disabilities have had steadily declining household incomes and rates of employment relative to their peers" (Mann and Stapleton, 2011, p.2).

Employment and income

The statistics on the employment of individuals with disabilities typically report that people with disabilities are approximately half as likely to be employed, and earn significantly less than their non-disabled peers. The U.S. Census Bureau's most recent SIPP data indicates that among the civilian non-institutionalized population 21 to 64 years old with a disability, 4 in 10 (41.1%) were employed compared to 8 in 10 (79.1%) for those without a disability. Furthermore, median monthly earnings were $1,961 and $2,724 for a worker with and without a disability, respectively (Brault, 2012).

Unemployed individuals and low-wage workers are more likely to be in need of government supports. A review of the government expenditures on income-based assistance programs indicates that from among the 19.8% or 46 million people in the civilian non-institutionalized population 18 years and over receiving income-based government assistance, 30.4% (14 million) had one or more disability (Boursiquot and Brault, 2013). Although more than 70% of income-based government assistance is dedicated to people without disabilities, some critics focus on the federal government expenditures of over $357 billion on programs for working-age people with disabilities, which has grown to nearly 12% of total federal expenditures (Brault, 2012).

There has been a decline in the number of working-age people with disabilities in the work force (Stapleton, 2011). Undoubtedly contributing to this are the work disincentives that link earnings to eligibility for over 50 state and federal health care and support services; other factors likely influencing this trend are the poor educational outcomes for people with disabilities, as well as discrimination in the workplace.

According to the most recent American Community Survey, there are significant disparities in the educational outcomes for individuals with disabilities. People with disabilities are twice as likely to lack a high school education compared to people without disabilities. Among individuals with a disability who are 25 years and older, 25.8% have less than a high school graduate education, compared to 11.5% for those without a disability. In addition, only 13.9% have a bachelor's degree compared to 31.7% for individuals without a disability (U.S. Census Bureau, 2014).

According to data from the most recent American Community Survey in 2012, there are significant disparities in the educational outcomes for individuals with disabilities. People with disabilities are twice as likely to lack a high school education compared to people without disabilities. Among non-institutionalized individuals with a disability who are 25 years and older, 22.2% have less than a high school graduate education, compared to 10.2% for those without a disability. In addition, only 12.4% have a bachelor's degree or higher compared to 31.7% for individuals without a disability (Erickson, Lee and von Schrader, 2014). Furthermore, individuals with disabilities were more likely to work part-time than full-time, even when full-time work is their preference. The National Council on Disability reports that two thirds of those with disabilities who are not employed prefer to be working (Mann and Stapleton, 2011).

Impact of recession/recovery

A longitudinal study based on data from the Current Population Survey revealed that the 2007–2009 recession was harsher on workers with disabilities. Overall there was a 9% decline in the presence of workers with disabilities in the employed labor force, which was disproportionately experienced among workers with mobility impairments, and younger persons with disabilities and persons with disabilities without college degrees (Kaye, 2010). The loss of representation among these groups in the workforce was as high as 17.8% (Kaye, 2010).

Although workers without a disability have benefited from the currently slow economic recovery, as evidenced by a reduction in unemployment rates, the unemployment rates for people with disabilities remained the same in 2011 as in 2010 (Bureau of Labor Statistics, 2012).

Disability and civil rights
Defining disability

Within the human species there is a vast diversity of human behavior, appearance, functioning, sensory acuity, and cognitive processing. Most disabilities are acquired during the human life course and in old age, with a relatively smaller number being present at birth. Ironically, rather than reducing the number of people with disabilities, advances in modern medicine have actually "spurred a disability population explosion" by extending the life expectancies of people with disabilities (Shapiro, 1994, p.5). This is most apparent among soldiers, as combatants with the types of injuries that were fatal in WWI survived in WWII. Similarly, soldiers from Desert Storm and Operation Freedom are surviving wounds, head injuries, limb-losses, and other traumas that were more often fatal in earlier conflicts.

Historically disability has been perceived as a tragic matter and viewed as an individual misfortune eliciting pity and charity, or necessitating medical intervention and treated as an "aberration to be eradicated" (Swain et al., 2003, p.52). This outlook locates deficit within the individual, placing limitations on the expectations for the person's performance of ordinary activities, such as attending school, participating in recreational activities, working, or even caring for themselves.

The critical shift in this perspective offered by the Disability Rights Movement has been distinguishing between bodily *impairment*, as a physiological condition such as blindness, deafness, amputation, etc., and *disability*, as the disadvantage or constraint in activities such as work, education, or recreation caused by societal construction and organization which excluded people with impairments from participation (Winter, 2003). This spawned the recognition of disability as a "minority identity that must be addressed not as personal misfortune or individual 'defect' but rather as the product of a disabling socially, economically and physically constructed environment" (Siebers, 2008, p.3).

Within this framework or understanding, an individual may have an impairment such as low vision, but due to the availability of corrective lenses, this individual is not disabled in the way an individual using crutches or a wheelchair is disabled by stairways to the subway. Although *impairment* and *disability* were both of concern to the Disability Rights Movement, their focus was on the elimination of the latter (Winter, 2003).

In the United States, *disability-specific* advocacy efforts would first emerge, followed much later by wider *cross-disability* alliances of what is now called the Disability Rights Movement. This was in large part due to societal compulsions to categorize and medicalize disabilities and to disabled persons' failure to envision common goals. "After the Civil War, segregated insane asylums developed quickly across much of the United States—simultaneously to and part of the trend by which schools for idiots, deaf, and blind people also developed" (Nielsen, 2012, p.92). Different constituencies, including family members, social service professionals, and medical professionals specializing in the particular impairment, as well as individuals with the specific disability, would focus on the support or reform of these institutions in separate, unrelated efforts (Longmore and Umansky, 2001).

Subsequently, medical science's promises of cures led to the "poster child" phenomenon of the mid-1940s and 1950s; the most successful of the early campaigns was the cure for polio (Shapiro, 1994). Disease-specific organizations raising funds for the "cure" would eventually include telephons for Easter Seals, United Cerebral Palsy, and the Muscular Dystrophy Association (Shapiro, 1994). Parent groups often energized and staffed by volunteer mothers "became professional and astute lobbyists: they befriended the female secretaries of male legislators ... took legislative wives on tours of state hospitals" (Nielsen, 2012, p.143) as they competed for limited government dollars to support their "special" schools, institutions, or services.

Civil rights: exclusion of disability

In 1954, the U.S. Supreme Court's *Brown v. the Board of Education* decision struck down the "separate but equal" racial segregation that the Court had established nearly a century earlier in *Plessy v. Ferguson*. While African Americans would be achieving greater integration into society, people with disabilities would remain relegated to "special," meaning segregated, spaces (Johnson, 2003)—special housing, special education, special sheltered workshops, and special buses for conveyance back and forth (Carey, 2009; Johnson, 2003; Shaw, 1994; Shevin, 2007).

More than a decade after *Brown*, Lex Frieden, an advocate for disability rights and independent living, was denied admission to Oral Roberts University despite the university's architectural design that included level and wide doorways, which rendered their buildings wheelchair accessible. Frieden was informed by the university that his "presence in a wheelchair would be an imposition on other students" (Fleischer and Zames, 2011, p.43).

The landmark Civil Rights Act of 1964 afforded civil rights protections to racial and ethnic minorities and women, but the disability activists lacked sufficient power to have disability covered by this legislation. Subsequent efforts to amend the Civil Rights Act to gain the inclusion of people with disabilities were rejected by both other civil rights advocates and legislators (Fleischer and Zames, 2011; Nielsen, 2012). Mainstream civil rights groups feared that the inclusion of individuals with disabilities would "dilute the effectiveness" of the law (Johnson, 2003, p.30).

Prior to the Disability Rights Movement, most federal legislation for people with disabilities had been benefits, rather than rights, orientated. For example, the public response to "joblessness and begging among disabled citizens" was the introduction of vocational rehabilitation programs (Hahn, 2002, p.164). These rehabilitation programs were initially limited to WWI veterans, but by 1920 expanded to include unemployed civilians with disabilities (Hahn, 2002). Disabled veterans benefit programs, which brought together injured veterans with multiple disabilities, served to initiate some early cross-disability alliances (Longmore and Umansky, 2001).

In the prosperity that followed WWII, Congress created a cash benefit program, Social Security Disability Insurance (SSDI), for workers with long-term disabilities, which is accompanied by health care through Medicare. In 1972, Supplemental Security Income (SSI) began providing cash benefits to low-income people with disabilities, regardless of their work history, and was accompanied by health care through Medicaid (Scotch, 2001).

Civil rights: disability legislation

The national Disability Rights Movement "embarked upon a belated mission parallel to other liberation movements" (Charlton, 1998, p.3). Indeed, most disability activists were strongly influenced by the feminist and African American civil rights movements. Disability rights activists enjoyed a series of successes with federal legislation, ranging from the Architectural Barriers Act of 1968 and the Rehabilitation Act of 1973, to the Education for All Handicapped Children Act of 1975, which would culminate in successful passage of the landmark 1990 Americans with Disabilities Act. These federal laws represented a policy shift from *care* to *rights* (Longmore and Umansky, 2001, p.10).

The Architectural Barriers Act of 1968 was the result of a "campaign to make public places and public transportation accessible" (Longmore and Umansky, 2001, p.10). Easter Seals, then called the National Society for Crippled Children and Adults, was a major advocate for this legislation. Although the law was very poorly enforced, it represented the first time access was argued as a "right" of people with disabilities, and the Architectural Barriers Act set the stage for future activism (Nielsen, 2012).

The Rehabilitation Act of 1973 prohibited programs receiving federal funding from discriminating against people with disabilities (Fleischer and Zames, 2011). The regulations to enforce the critical Section 504 of this Act were signed only after people with disabilities conducted sensational sit-ins in New York City, Washington DC, and San Francisco. The San Francisco protest led by Judy Heumann, a polio survivor and quadriplegic, was a powerful cross-disability effort that was sustained for 25 days at the federal building. In addition, this protest received support from individuals from other civil rights groups, including the Black Panthers and the Butterfly Brigade of gay men (Shapiro, 1994). Hahn (2002) identifies the success in winning the enforcement regulations for Section 504 of this Act as the pivotal point in which people with disabilities recognized their power.

The Individuals with Disabilities Education Act in 1975, originally named the Education for All Handicapped Children Act, finally secured the right to attend public school for all children.

This legislation extended to children with disabilities "the principle of equality of educational opportunities underlying the landmark 1954 Supreme Court decision in *Brown v. Board of Education*" (Fleischer and Zames, 2011, p.185) more than two decades later. Interestingly, it was initiated by the African American children's advocate Marian Wright Edelman when she investigated why 750,000 children were not attending school, assuming these were Black students being prevented from enrolling in segregated schools (Shapiro, 1994). Her shocking findings were that nearly all these youth were White kids with disabilities who were being systematically turned away from school districts all over the United States. This law was then passed largely due to the efforts of the parents of children with disabilities. Although Congress pledged to contribute 40% of the costs to educate students with disabilities, the federal government has never contributed more than 19% (Fleischer and Zames, 2011, p.242) and, as of 2008, it has provided only 17% (The Forum for Education and Democracy, 2008).

The 1990 Americans with Disabilities Act (ADA) was modeled after the 1964 Civil Rights Act and "capped a generation of innovative lawmaking regarding Americans with disabilities" (Longmore and Umansky, 2001, p.10). An unprecedented cross-disability alliance was forged on behalf of the ADA's passage. The bill was endorsed by over 180 national organizations ranging from the American Diabetes Association and the Muscular Dystrophy Association to the International Ventilator Users Network. Advocacy efforts were mounted from people with disabilities ranging from multiple sclerosis, deafness, mental illness, and arthritis to relatively newer disabilities like Tourette's syndrome, chronic fatigue syndrome, and AIDS. Joining people with disabilities in the push for the ADA were family members, health care providers, social workers, and rehabilitation professionals (Shapiro, 1994). Due to an onslaught of challenges to the 1990 ADA, which arose after its passage and served to limit its breadth, in 2008 the ADA Amendments Act was added to redress decisions made by the state courts and Supreme Court that had weakened the ADA. "What power the ADA has retained is only due to the constant vigilance and activism of disabled people and their allies" (Nielsen, 2012, p.181).

Disability and neoliberalism

The neoliberal mantras of "free enterprise," "free competition," and "privatization and globalization" now reduce all people to one of two body categories: (1) bodies that create profits and (2) bodies that do not (Connell, 2011). The paid work of human labor threatens to be the principal mode of social inclusion as everyone is "enjoined to seek opportunities for work and manage risk inherent in a labor market in which anything is possible" (McDowell, 2004; Rose, 1999).

Meanwhile, entitlement reforms, eligibility restrictions, and program spending reductions have been the hallmarks of neoliberal, public social welfare policies. These public policies are operating amidst a free market economy of accelerating corporate deregulation and globalization. Therefore, for the bodies in category (2) that do not contribute to corporate profits, the social safety net is becoming dangerously thin and torn.

This neoliberal political economy regulates "who survives and who prospers, who controls and who is controlled" (Charlton, 2006, p.218) through the commodification of its citizens, of which people with disabilities are among the most vulnerable.

Social welfare programs

Mathematica's Center for Studying Disability Policy reports that Social Security Disability Insurance (SSDI) caseloads nearly tripled between 1980 and 2010, which represents an increase that is significantly outpacing the increase in the working-age population (Mann and Stapleton, 2011). The study also warns of the financially unsustainable pace of this rate of increase, reporting that total federal expenditures on support for individuals with disabilities have risen to over 12% of all federal outlays.

As the number of claimants for SSDI and SSI rapidly expanded through the latter half of the twentieth century, efforts at cost containment have resulted in a social security disability program that is fraught with unpredictable variations in eligibility awards. The American Association for Disability Policy Reform (2012) compares the Social Security Administration's application process to entering the "largest and longest-running lottery in the world." It is a "lottery" that can be influenced by such arbitrary factors as the state in which the claim is submitted, the examiner assigned the case, and the claimant's ability to obtain medical care from multiple sources (AADPR, 2012). Work disincentives are embedded in both the SSI and SSDI programs, as earnings exceeding a specific threshold trigger a loss of the recipients' health care and cash benefits. These "paternalistic policies trap many people with disabilities in poverty by devaluing their often considerable ability to contribute to their own support through work" (Stapleton et al., 2006, p.2).

Employment

Repeatedly, disability program reforms are offered up that are labor related. Endeavors focused on transitioning social welfare recipients into the workforce typically make several unsubstantiated assumptions. These assumptions are that there are a sufficient number of jobs and that these jobs provide the necessary flexibility to accommodate workers with disabilities (Wilson and Schuer, 2006). Employment in the neoliberal era is often characterized by insecurity and material hardship as companies continue to gravitate toward transnational ownership of businesses, disinvestment, globalization, and temporary employees or contract workers. It would be unrealistic to expect that the workforce will ever absorb everyone with a disability.

On the other hand, the Bureau of Labor Statistics (2012) announced that employed persons with a disability are more likely to be self-employed than are employed persons without a disability. It could be that, lacking opportunities with existing employers, people with disabilities are more likely to explore entrepreneurial avenues. Advanced technology and globalization have risen as prominent features of the neoliberal age and offer a possible "route to transcend problems of mobility, communication, time and space—fundamental barriers to social participation" for some people with disabilities (Seymour, 2005, p.195). Hafner and Owens (2008) suggest that supported employment or even self-employment opportunities in the areas of e-commerce, e-consignments, online auctions, computer graphics, video or DVD production, and website development may be compatible with the needs and abilities of disabled persons.

Supporting people with disabilities' greater participation in employment and self-employment is consistent with both the desires of people with disabilities and the neoliberal environment. Nevertheless, maintaining effective community-based services to enable disabled people to work and live in the community will also benefit the disabled worker and those with disabilities that are unable to work. These networks of community-based services, as well as institutionalized services, also have their place in the neoliberal economy.

Disability as commodity

"The world economic system inexorably transforms everything it touches into commodities. Most important, the transformation of people into commodities hides their dehumanization and exploitation by other human beings" (Charlton, 1998). Charlton contends that although laborers become commodities as soon as they become employed and sell their work for a paycheck, likewise people with disabilities become commodities the moment their impairment becomes something from which others can profit. He points to the network of services for people with disabilities such as rehabilitation, paratransit, sheltered workshops, and residential facilities like group homes and long-term care institutions, all of which rely on the disabled population for their profits.

A current frontline battle is for the right to live independently and autonomously, retaining the ability to self-direct services that best meet a person's needs, rather than being confined in an institution or nursing home. If home and community-based services were offered on a par with institutional services, people would have greater access to personal attendants and greater opportunity to obtain services in a setting of their choice and by a provider of their choice. Disability activists, often low-income people, are up against powerful professional lobbyists like the Alliance for Quality Nursing Home Care, which spent over $2.9 million in 2012 and over $3 million in both 2010 and 2011 to influence legislators against community options (AAPD, n.d.; Open Secrets, 2014).

Sometimes people with disabilities serve as both profit generators for human services and profit creators for industries. A clear example of a hybrid of the worst of both worlds is the sheltered workshop. There are approximately 420,000 persons with disabilities laboring in sheltered workshops and supported employment settings for subminimum wages (National Council on Disability, 2012). The Fair Labor Standards Act mandates that employers must compensate their employees at rates no lower than the federally mandated minimum wage and some states have laws that set higher minimum wages. Compensation at rates below this minimum is illegal, except for employees with disabilities. Section 14(c) of the Fair Labor Standards Act permits the legal discrimination of people with disabilities in the workplace.

Conclusion

Notwithstanding the great strides that have been made in the past 50 years, the National Council on Disability reports on the continued presence of significant barriers to achieving the goals of independence, inclusion, and empowerment for all people with disabilities. This is evidenced by extraordinarily higher rates of poverty, unemployment, and welfare dependence with simultaneously lower rates of educational achievement. Indeed, the first decade after the ADA passage evidenced no significant improvements, as people with disabilities continued to "endure economic deprivation and social marginalization," with poverty rates ranging from 50% to 300% higher than the general population depending upon the survey's definition of disability (Longmore, 2003, p.19).

Johnson (2003, p.11) described the ADA as a "civil rights act with an economic loop hole built in … if rights cost too much, they didn't have to be granted." Johnson is referring to specific language in the ADA that grants "reasonable accommodation" if it can be accomplished without "undue hardship." The battle continues to be waged by disability advocates to increase choice, control, and self-directed decision making for people with disabilities across a wide spectrum beyond work and benefits. The war is now being waged in the courts as well as the halls of Congress and in our communities. Johnson believes the plethora of court cases is due to the fact that judicial authorities believed the ADA was poorly constructed, in terms of a benefits law, and "they were correct. It was civil rights oriented, not a benefits law, but few understood the objective" (Johnson, 2003, p.xiv).

The ironic aspect of the public's unwillingness to comply with the ADA and the creation of flexible work environments, more affordable housing with universal designs, reforms in health care, and the institutional bias in the health care delivery system, along with a myriad of other sensible changes, is that these things do not *just benefit* people with disabilities. These benefit us all. People without disabilities are temporarily able bodied at best. The aging population, environmental degradation, accidents, tobacco and the vulnerability to disability-causing agents in the food chain, and the proliferation of fire arms and war injuries are leading to the recognition of disability as a universal experience. Accessible physical, political, and economic environments benefit the non-disabled as well as people with disabilities.

The Asthma and Allergy Foundation of America (2005) reports that ADA accommodations made in stores, schools, and workplaces have helped obtain safer, healthier environments for everyone. The Forest Service and State Parks have found that universal designs to the outdoor overlooks, walking trails, beach access, and nature centers facilitates participation, freedom of choice, and integration. It serves to increase the number of visitors, disabled and non-disabled, as well as their engagement level (Kermeen, 2007).

Manufacturers find that accommodations can help all workers and save the business costs. UE reported an instance when a $65 electric screwdriver was all that was required to keep a laborer with carpal tunnel working. Once other workers began using the same tool, the company enjoyed a reduction in their workers' compensation costs (UE, 2013). Showcasing examples from such companies as Cingular and Doritos, Haller (2010, p.195) believes there are signs that corporations have a role in the empowerment and inclusion of disability as it becomes a "profitable undertaking for business."

Accommodations made for people with disabilities have had what Gary Wunder would term the "curb cut effect," indicating that "sidewalks with curb cuts are just better sidewalks" that benefit everyone, not just people with disabilities (Johnson, 2003, p.216). Mothers with strollers, kids on skateboards, and people pushing shopping carts, as well as bikers and roller blade skaters, all appreciate curb cuts. Likewise, subways with elevators are just better subways for everyone as passengers tow baggage or belongings with greater ease and televisions with decoders and closed captions permit people to watch TV in both noisy bars and in bed while their partners are sleeping. Everyone has benefited from the battles waged by the under-celebrated Disability Rights Movement.

References

American Association for Disability Policy Reform (AADPR) (2012). *The Need for Disability Policy Reform.* Retrieved 3-15-13 from http://www.disref.org/page2.html.

American Association of People with Disabilities (AAPD) (n.d.). *Improving Medicaid Home and Community-Based Services to Reduce Institutional Bias.* Retrieved 8-17-14 from http://www.aapd.com/what-we-do/health/aapd-medicaid-hcbs-fact-sheet.pdf.

Asthma and Allergy Foundation of America (AAFA) (2005). *Americans with Disabilities Act.* Accessed 8-15-14 from http://www.aafa.org/display.cfm?id=9&sub=19&cont=255.

Baynton, D.C. (2001). Disability and the justification of inequality in American history. In P.K. Longmore and L. Umansky (eds) *The New Disability History: American Perspectives*, pp.33–57. New York, NY: New York University Press.

Bell, C. (2006). Introducing white disability studies. In L. Davis (ed.) *The Disability Studies Reader* (2nd ed.), pp.275–282. New York, NY: Routledge.

Boursiquot, B.L. and Brault, M.W. (2013). *Disability Characteristics of Income-Based Government Assistance Recipients in the United States: 2011.* Washington, DC: U.S. Census Bureau. Retrieved 8-15-14 from http://www.census.gov/prod/2013pubs/acsbr11-12.pdf.

Brault, M.W. (2012). *Americans with Disabilities: 2010.* Washington, DC: U.S. Census Bureau. Retrieved 8-15-14 from http://www.census.gov/prod/2012pubs/p70-131.pdf.

Bureau of Labor Statistics (2012). *Persons with Disabilities: Labor Force Characteristics—2011.* Economic News Release USDL-12-1125. Retrieved 8-15-14 from http://www.bls.gov/news.release/archives/disabl_06082012.htm.

Campbell, F.A.K. (2003). *The Great Divide: Ableism and Technologies of Disability Production*. Center for Social Change Research, School of Humanities and Human Services, Queensland University of Technology: Brisbane, Australia. Retrieved 10-15-12 from http://eprints.qut.edu.au/15889/.

Carey, A.C. (2009). *On the Margins of Citizenship: Intellectual Disabilities and Civil Rights in Twentieth Century America*. Philadelphia, PA: Temple University Press.

Centers for Disease Control and Prevention (2011). *47.5 Million U.S. Adults Report a Disability; Arthritis Remains Most Common Cause*. Atlanta, GA: National Center for Chronic Disease Prevention and Health Promotion. Retrieved 11-15-12 from http://www.cdc.gov/Features/dsAdultDisabilityCauses/.

Charlton, J.I. (1998). *Nothing About Us Without Us: Disability Oppression and Empowerment*. Berkeley, CA: University of California Press.

Charlton, J.I. (2006). The dimensions of disability oppression: An overview. In L. Davis (ed.) *The Disability Studies Reader* (2nd ed.) pp.217–227. New York, NY: Routledge.

Connell, R. (2011). Southern bodies and disability: Re-thinking concepts. *Third World Quarterly*, 32(8): pp. 1369–1381.

Davis, L. (2006). *The Disability Studies Reader* (2nd ed.) New York, NY: Routledge.

Deal, M. (2007). Disabled people's attitudes toward other impairment groups. *Disability and Society*, 18(7): pp.897–910.

Erickson, W., Lee, C., and von Schrader, S. (2014). *Disability Statistics from the 2012 American Community Survey (ACS)*. Ithaca, NY: Cornell University Employment and Disability Institute (EDI). Retrieved 8-17-14 from http://www.disabilitystatistics.org/reports/acs.cfm?statistic=9#table.

Fleischer, D.Z. and Zames, F. (2011). *The Disability Rights Movement: From Charity to Confrontation*. Philadelphia, PA: Temple University Press.

Ford, A.R. (2009). It's not just about racism, but ableism. *Diverse Issues in Higher Education*, 26(4): pp.16.

Fremstad, S. (2009). *Half in Ten: Why Taking Disability into Account is Essential to Reducing Income Poverty and Expanding Economic Inclusion*. Washington, DC: Center for Economic and Policy Research. Retrieved 8-15-14 from http://www.cepr.net/documents/publications/poverty-disability-2009-09.pdf.

Goffman, E. (1963). *Stigma: Notes on the Management of Spoiled Identity*. New York, NY: Simon and Schuster, Inc.

Hafner, D. and Owens, L.A. (2008). How globalization is changing our workforce: A global vision to job development. *Journal of Vocational Rehabilitation*, 29: pp.15–22.

Hahn, H. (2002). Academic debates and political advocacy. In C. Barnes, M. Oliver, and L. Barton (eds) *Disability Studies Today*. pp.162–187. Cambridge, UK: Polity Press.

Haller, B. (2010). *Representing Disability in an Ableist World: Essays on Mass Media*. Louisville, KY: Avocado Press.

Hooper, E.L. (1994). Seeking the disabled community. In B. Shaw (ed.) *The Ragged Edge: The Disability Experience from Pages of the First Fifteen Years of the Disability Rag*, pp.4–6. Louisville, KY: Avocado Press.

Johnson, M. (2003). *Make Them Go Away: Clint Eastwood, Christopher Reeves and the Case Against Disability Rights*. Louisville, KY: Avocado Press.

Kaye, H.S. (2010, October). The impact of the 2007–09 recession on workers with disabilities. *Monthly Labor Review*, 133(10): pp.19–30.

Kermeen, R.B. (2007). How accessible recreation facilities benefit everyone. National Trails Training Partnership. Retrieved 8-15-14 from http://www.americantrails.org/resources/accessible/BuildDisabl Kermeen.html.

Kudlick, C. (2003). Disability history: Why we need another "other." *American Historical Review*, 108(3): pp.763–793.

Linton, S. (1998). *Claiming Disability: Knowledge and Identity*. New York, NY: New York University.

Longmore, P.K. (2003). *Why I Burned My Books and Other Essays on Disability*. Philadelphia, PA: Temple University Press.

Longmore, P.K. and Umansky, L. (2001). *The New Disability History*. New York, NY: New York University.

Mann, D.R. and Stapleton, D.C. (2011). *Fiscal Austerity and the Transition to Twenty-First Century Disability Policy: A Road Map*. Center for Studying Disability Policy. Princeton, NJ: Mathematica Policy Research. Retrieved 3-3-13 from http://www.mathematica-mpr.com/publications/PDFs/disability/fiscal_austerity.pdf.

McDowell, L. (2004). Work, workfare, work/life balance and an ethic of care. *Progress in Human Geography*, 28(2): 145–163.

National Council on Disability (2008). *Keeping Track: National Disability Status and Program Indicators*. Retrieved 3-7-13 from http://www.ncd.gov/publications/2008/April212008#ExecutiveSummary.

National Council on Disability (2012). *Subminimum Wage and Supported Employment*. Washington, DC: NCD. Retrieved 3-7-13 from http://www.ncd.gov/publications/2012/August232012/.

Nielsen, K.E. (2012). *A Disability History of the United States*. Boston, MA: Beacon Press.

Open Secrets (2014). Annual lobbying by Alliance for Quality Nursing Home Care. Retrieved 8-17-14 from https://www.opensecrets.org/lobby/clientsum.php?id=D000021026&year=2012.

Rose, N.S. (1999). *Powers of Freedom: Reframing Political Thought*. Cambridge, United Kingdom; New York, NY: Cambridge University Press.

Scotch, R.K. (2001). American disability policy in the twentieth century. In P.K. Longmore and L. Umansky (eds) *The New Disability History*, pp. 375–392. New York, NY: New York University.

Seymour, W. (2005). ICTs and disability: Exploring the human dimensions of technological engagement. *Technology and Disability*, 17: pp.195–204.

Shapiro, J.P. (1994). *No Pity: People with Disabilities Forging a new Civil Rights Movement*. New York, NY: Three Rivers Press.

Shaw, B. (ed.) (1994). *The Ragged Edge: The Disability Experience from the Pages of the First Fifteen Years of the Disability Rag*. Louisville, KY: Avocado Press.

Shevin, M.S. (2007). *Widening the Circle: The Power of Inclusive Classrooms*. Boston, MA: Beacon Press.

Siebers, T. (2008). *Disability Theory*. Ann Arbor, MI: University of Michigan.

Snyder, S.L. and Mitchell, D.T. (2006). *Cultural Locations of Disability*. Chicago, IL: The University of Chicago Press.

Stapleton, D.C. (2011). *Bending the Employment, Income, and Cost Curves for People with Disabilities*. Center for Studying Disability Policy. Princeton, NJ: Mathematica Policy Research, Inc. Retrieved 8-15-14 from http://www.mathematica-mpr.com/~/media/publications/pdfs/disability/disability_bendemploy_ib.pdf.

Stapleton, D.C., O'Day, B.L., Livermore, G.A., and Imparato, A.J. (2006). Dismantling the poverty trap: Disability policy for the twenty-first century. *The Milbank Quarterly*, 84(4): pp.701–732.

Swain, J., French, S., and Cameron, C. (2003). *Controversial Issues in a Disabling Society*. Berkshire, UK: Open University Press.

The Forum for Education and Democracy (2008). *Democracy at Risk: The Need for a New Federal Policy in Education*. Retrieved 8-17-14 from http://www.forumforeducation.org/sites/default/files/u48/FED%20FINAL%20REPORT.pdf.

Trent, J.W. (1994). *Inventing the Feeble Mind: A History of Mental Retardation in the United States*. Berkeley and Los Angeles, CA: University of California Press.

UE—United Electrical, Radio and Machine Workers of America (2013). *Worker-Friendly Laws: Using ADA in the Workplace*. Retrieved 2-13-13 from http://ranknfile-ue.org/ic_ada.html.

U.S. Census Bureau (2014). Anniversary of Americans with Disabilities Act: July 26. Retrieved 8-17-14 from https://www.census.gov/newsroom/releases/pdf/cb14ff-15_ada.pdf.

Wilton, R. and Schuer, S. (2006). Towards socio-spatial inclusion? Disabled people, neoliberalism and the contemporary labour market. *Area*, 38(2): 186–195.

Winter, J.A. (2003). The development of the Disabilities Rights Movement as a social problem solver. *Disability Studies Quarterly*, 23(1): pp.33–61. Retrieved 3-3-13 from http://www.dsq-sds.org/article/view/399/545.

Wolbring, G. (2008). The politics of ableism. *Development*, 51(2): pp.252–258.

42

BREAKING THE SILENCE

Homelessness and race[1]

David Wagner and Pete White

Introduction

The current period of homelessness in the United States dates back to approximately 1979 and 1980 when advocates, reporters, social workers, and others began to notice a significant number of people with no place to live in. Despite many thousands of articles in our newspapers, stories on television, and discussions and websites on the Internet, aspects of this issue still remain almost uncommented on. One important silence in most of the literature about homelessness is race.

While figures (see Table 42.1) clearly show evidence that African-Americans are by far over-represented in the homeless population relative to their numbers (Native Americans are also overrepresented), a search of the academic journals and newspapers finds minimal discussion of this fact. When the discussion about race does appear, it is invariably downplayed. Moreover, the minor mentions of race do not include the structural inequities that have plagued African-Americans throughout history—structural inequities that continue to run amuck.

This chapter explores the data about homelessness and the African-American community, speculates on why this issue has not received much attention, and notes the chief causes of the gap between the high rate of homelessness among African-Americans and other racial/ethnic groups.

The discussion is shaped by the success over the last three decades of neoliberal economic and policy changes along with new ideologies that buttress neoliberalism. Prior to these decades, economic and political elites in the United States and other "advanced nations" tolerated greater provisions of social welfare, cooperation with trade unionism, and even some efforts to undo the historic oppression of people of color in order to ensure the social peace. Over the last decades, however, the drive for profits has shaped a new capitalist state that has been able to shed many of the fruits of prior legislation from the New Deal to the 1970s. As part of this change, a major impact has also been the weakened oppositional discourses with particular hostility in the media and even in academia to older discourses about social class and racial justice and inequality. These views are scoffed at as "outdated" and not relevant to the current economy and polity as they are remnants of the previous eras (such as "1960s rhetoric").

Silence about race

To give just several examples of how race and ethnicity has been rather ignored in the homeless crisis, we will use three examples. The newspapers of the National Coalition of the Homeless, the oldest and most established of all the advocacy groups for homeless people, were kindly provided to one of the authors as part of a book project (NCH, 2009b). While at times national and local data was presented on the race and ethnicity of homeless people, at no time was an article or news story addressed to the issue of the overrepresentation of certain races or ethnicities. An even more surprising finding was a review of the National Newspaper Index (Proquest, 2013a) available at most universities. This index covers most major newspapers and magazines. Over a period of nearly three decades only a few articles could be found that addressed racial imbalances in homelessness. One suggestive article in the *Los Angeles Times* (Harris, 1993) explained that charities were concerned about portraying homeless people as other than white and male, finding their contributions went down when other groups were used to portray the homeless. Only two other articles could be found that addressed the issue: one entitled "Race and Homelessness" was in, of all places, an editorial in the *Tulsa World* (1996) citing the large numbers of African-Americans and citing a study by researchers Dennis Culhane and Stephen Metraux; and one article in *The Crisis* in 1995 (which was picked up by some other media outlets) by Tsitsi Wakhisi entitled "Homelessness in Black America." While it is possible our study missed some article here and there, out of many thousands of articles, editorials, commentaries, and other stories discussion of race and homelessness appear almost totally absent.

Academic journals (EBSCO, *Academic Search Complete*, 2013a; EBSCO, *Social Work Abstracts*, 2013b; and Proquest, *Sociological Abstracts*, 2013b) showed the same general pattern; articles at times noted the count of race, but few articles were ever devoted to this issue (with the exception of an article by Whaley and Link, 1998; see below). Even studies about the housing and economic status of African-Americans were often silent on the issue of homelessness. In 2005 the California Legislative Black Caucus (CLBC) released its report, *The State of Black California*. The Housing section showed African-Americans having among the lowest homeownership rates among other racial/ethnic groups and high rates of renters. Not mentioned at all, however, is the issue of homelessness, let alone the racial disparities among those without homes. Actually, when renter and homeowner categories were combined, they conveniently totaled 100%; as if African-Americans and others are all housed—an error of huge omission.

We do not argue that any conspiracy exists to explain this silence. To some degree, many Americans, including liberal writers and activists, do believe we are in a "post racial" society. They may feel discussion of race is fruitless or divisive, particularly where cross-racial advocacy groups exist. Some activists, probably of all races, believe it is of benefit not to talk of race. *This trend, as noted, helps even liberals and advocates maintain legitimacy in a neoliberal environment.* Second, and more concretely, in many advocacy and activist causes, homelessness and poverty included, a rather interesting development has occurred in the last several decades. Because it is better public relations to stress that social problems affect all classes, colors, nationalities, and so forth, we get statements that homeless people "are just like you and me." Such statements have also been made about all sorts of issues such as AIDS, child abuse, crime, domestic violence, drugs, lack of health care, unemployment, and so on (Wagner, 1997).

Classically, we are told social problems "cut across all lines." But in fact this is only literally true, and misrepresents as much as it represents. Homelessness *could* happen to anyone but such presentations as a homeless professor (as captured in the 1980s movie *The Fisher King*) or a homeless heart surgeon (portrayed in the 1980s TV drama *Saint Elsewhere*) are a bit "over the top." More recently Hollywood has produced a few stories about homeless African-Americans, but they too are quite atypical, such as the medical equipment salesman played by Will Smith in *The Pursuit of Happyness* or the Juilliard graduate in *The Soloist*. Those who have ever visited a homeless shelter, or an area of town where homeless people congregate, and have ever talked with homeless people, know there are just a few homeless surgeons, professors, medical equipment salespeople, or Juilliard students. Instead, there are many people who come from working-class or poor families. The style of presentation which advocacy groups and the media have adopted in recent decades not only misleads others by situating the problem among (usually white) middle- or even upper-income people, but for a variety of reasons lead at least some advocates to believe their own characterizations themselves and get angry at those who contradict this image by pointing to persistent class and racial statuses as making up the majority of the homeless.

A third reason for the absence may be a finding in a study by Whaley and Link (1998) which indicated that, among white survey respondents, the greater association of the homeless population with African-Americans, the greater the view that the homeless are dangerous. It may well be that advocates feel that it would not be at all helpful to portray the reality of homeless people being disproportionately persons of color.

The veiled reality behind the public relations and political discourse that "it can happen to anyone" is that middle-class people with a home and large savings can under certain circumstances become homeless, but these are exceptional circumstances, and would take years of losing savings and homes, and failing to secure help from family and friends. What is rare among the white (and other racial and ethnic groups) middle class is a daily experience among African-American working-class and poor people.

At least for the reasons above the presentation of social problems as universals leaves out discussions of class and race when discussing homelessness.

Data about homelessness and race

As with all information about homelessness, notes of skepticism are appropriate about data collection methods and results. Few homeless people jump up to greet census takers or other professionals to say "we are here." For this and other reasons, advocates have challenged the U.S. Census enumerations every ten years. Generally speaking we have the most accurate information about shelter users, but as we get out into the community to people living under bridges, in cars, in abandoned housing, or doubled up with relatives, we have less information. Having said this, it would be a little silly to ignore the growing information collected by better sources, primarily the U.S. Department of Housing and Urban Development's (HUD) annual assessment reports to Congress that began in 2006, and the U.S. Conference of Mayors reports on the homeless which use 25 cities to study homelessness. Though the gross numbers of homeless people may be far from accurate (almost surely understating the numbers), there is less reason to believe the characteristics of homeless people (gender, race, family status, veteran status, and so on) are totally incorrect unless we can prove a certain subpopulation is systematically avoiding counts.

The U.S. Census data available to us (2002, 2012) show that whites (including Hispanics) have been about 74% of the population (over 80% in 1990), African-Americans have ranged narrowly in the 12 to 12.3% range, Asians have moved from 3.9% to 4.4%, Native Americans between 0.8 and 1.2% of the population, and if Hispanics/Latinos are separated from "white" they have increased from 9% of the population in 1990 to over 15% in 2009 estimates. Not surprisingly, the poverty rates defined by the U.S. government (which profoundly underestimate poverty) are quite different for racial and ethnic groups: whites below the poverty level have ranged in the 8% to 9% range over the last decades; African-Americans have stood between 24% and 26% being in poverty; Native Americans also range in the 25% area; and Hispanics have also ranged between 23% to 26%.

What is then so striking in examining about 20 reports on homeless counts including the U.S. Mayors Conference reports, the HUD Assessment reports, and the U.S. Census reports, all

Table 42.1 Racial and ethnic population breakdowns and the racial disparities in homelessness

Race/ethnicity	Estimated % of nation's total population (from U.S. Census data, 1990, 2000, and 2009 estimates)	Estimated % of nation's homeless population (homeless counts/surveys between 1991 and 2009)
African-Americans	12–12.3%	40–56%
Asian/Pacific Islander	3.9–4.4%	1–3%
Hispanic/Latino	9–15%	12–15%
Native American	0.8–1.2%	3–4%
White	59–71%	32–39%

such reports show African-American homelessness at about three and a half times their number in the general population, and well above the expected number by poverty rates.

Table 42.1 shows the racial and ethnic population breakdowns and the racial disparities in homelessness.

These studies clearly show the overwhelming statistical overrepresentation of African-Americans on the streets as well as an overrepresentation of Native American peoples. Surprisingly, Hispanics/Latinos are estimated to be about their numbers in the general population, but far lower in the homeless population than their poverty rate.

Some caveats must always be included with statistics. First, since whites are the majority of the nation's population, the majority of the poor are Caucasian. Raw numbers differ from percentages. Second, these are nationwide statistics, and there are cities and regions with a much higher rate of African-American homeless people, but some regions have a majority of white homeless people and some a majority of Hispanic or Latino homelessness. Nevertheless the national numbers are quite striking in the case of African-Americans being far more present in the homeless population, even with what we might conjecture with the poverty rates.

Race, inequality, and homelessness

In his 1963 letter from a Birmingham, Alabama jail, Dr. Martin Luther King Jr. wrote, "Our people are smothering in an airtight cage of poverty in the midst of an affluent society." Oddly enough poverty, in and of itself, is rarely held up as a leading cause of homelessness. Rarely, if ever, does the conversation of social stratification emerge as a leading cause of homelessness. Yet poverty and stratification, and particularly the disparate impacts of such on African-Americans, must be identified and explored in conversations and analysis of homelessness. Unfortunately the inequality King spoke about has in some ways worsened since the late 1970s between African-Americans and other racial/ethnic groups.

Three factors that are central to the growing numbers of homeless people in the last three decades are considerably worse for African-Americans than others: deindustrialization, gentrification, and the impact of the drug war.

Almost all studies of homelessness cite the impact of deindustrialization (Baxter and Hopper, 1981; Blau, 1992; Hombs and Snyder, 1983; Hopper, 2003; Kozol, 1988; Marcuse, 1988; Rossi, 1989; Snow and Anderson, 1993; Wagner, 1993, 2012; Wright, 1997) on the working class and working poor in America. From the early 1970s to our current recession, tens of millions of manufacturing jobs have vanished from America, some to technology, some to overseas relocation, and some to cheaper work processes. The major jobs that have "replaced" blue collar jobs, often high-wage and high-benefit jobs with more union representation, have been service jobs in hotels and motels, restaurants, convenience stores, fast food, and other low-paid workplaces without unions and often without any fringe benefits. Studies by teams of researchers led by William Julius Wilson and others have shown the dramatic impact deindustrialization has had on African-American communities, especially in America's major cities such as New York, Philadelphia, Washington DC, Chicago, Los Angeles, and elsewhere (Smelser et al., 2001; Wilson, 1996, 2004, 2009; Wilson and Taub, 2006). At the time deindustrialization wiped out a large number of jobs, African-Americans constituted a majority of working-class members of central cities, although of course whites and Latino/Hispanics were affected (for example, in New York City, large numbers of Puerto Ricans suffered from these changes).

The second most cited reason for the growth in homelessness beginning in the late 1970s and 1980s is "gentrification"—the popular term for the dramatic escalating rise in the price of housing in the cities and the conversion of single-room occupancy apartments (SROs) and boarding houses into high-cost condominiums and luxury apartments. Analysts have been able to document the loss of many millions of units of low-cost housing, accelerated as of late by continued destruction of the nation's public housing stock (Blau, 1992; Hoch and Slayton, 1989; Hombs and Snyder, 1983; Hopper, 2003; Kozol, 1988; Marcuse, 1988; NCH, 2009a; Ropers, 1988; Rossi, 1989; Snow and Anderson, 1993; Wagner, 1993, 2012). Although fewer studies have been done on race and ethnicity and the impact of gentrification, it stands to reason that with the destruction of low-income housing units in the central cities, it would again make sense that a stronger impact would have occurred among African-Americans than among other groups, given the demographics of the central cities in these decades.

Finally, indisputably the nation's "war on drugs" and massive increase in the incarceration of African-Americans since 1980 (along with the parole, probation, and other criminal authority over especially black men) have added to the number of homeless people. According to the Pew Center on the States (2009), the rate of correctional control for African-Americans was 1 in 11 overall with even higher rates in some inner-city neighborhoods. The drug war and massive incarceration of African-American men have in the words of Clyde Woods "asset-stripped" these men, cutting off their employment potential and making them often ineligible for housing and social welfare benefits (2011). Like the old Black Codes, the millions of African-American men who have been in prison occupy a nether zone in our society: they are neither free nor slave, but in a legal and civic limbo which is unique in current-day America (see, for example, Alexander and West, 2012). Of course, large numbers of Latinos and lesser numbers of other races and ethnicities have been victims of the drug war and the new movement to incarceration. The impact on communities of each cause is complicated because the effects of policies is not just quantitative but becomes a qualitative difference. So, for example, because far more African-Americans live in areas of high "concentrated poverty" than other groups (see, for example, Wilson, 2009), the impact of policies hostile to poor people have a more dramatic effect on the stability of African-American neighborhoods and communities than do the same policies on for example Caucasians or Asian-Americans. Latino/Hispanic neighborhoods may vary depending on the length of time of immigration and the concentration of poverty.

Conclusion

This chapter has reviewed data which appears to show that homelessness has taken its most dramatic toll on African-Americans. Most academic, advocacy, and even popular writing on homelessness appears to avoid this discussion. We have noted some reasons for this silence, but ultimately we suggest that covering up the truth of homelessness for whatever reason hides the reality of what has happened in America in the last three or more decades. It may not be polite, but the racialization of poverty and homelessness needs discussion. Although poorer people of all groups of Americans have been affected, deindustrialization, gentrification, and the war on drugs has taken a harsh toll particularly on African-American citizens. It is not too late to imagine a world where the human right to housing, work, and basic citizenship rights can be realized for all.

Note

1 An earlier version of this chapter was published in *Freedom Now: Struggles for the Human Right to Housing in LA and Beyond* (Jordan T. Camp and Christina Heatherton, 2012).

References

Alexander, M., and West, C., 2012. *The New Jim Crow*. New York: The New Press.

Baxter, E., and Hopper, K., 1981. *Private Lives/Public Spaces: Homeless Adults on the Streets of New York City*. New York: Community Service Society.

Blau, J., 1992. *The Visible Poor: Homelessness in the United States*. New York: Oxford University Press.

California Legislative Black Caucus (CLBC), 2005. *The State of Black California*. Sacramento: California Legislative Black Caucus.

Camp, J. T. and Heatherton, C. (eds.), (2012) *Freedom Now! Struggles for the Human Right to Housing in LA and Beyond*. Los Angeles: Freedom Now Books.

EBSCO, *Academic Search Complete*, 2013a.

EBSCO, *Social Work Abstracts*, 2013b.

Harris, R., 1993. "Selling an 'Image' of Homelessness to the Charitable." *Los Angeles Times*, November 25, 1993, p.1.

Hoch, C., and Slayton, R., 1989. *New Homeless and Old*. Philadelphia: Temple University Press.

Hombs, M. E., and Snyder, M., 1983. *Homelessness in America: The Forced March to Nowhere*. Washington, DC: Community for Creative Non-Violence.

Hopper, K., 2003. *Reckoning with Homelessness*. Ithaca: Cornell University Press.

Kozol, J., 1988. *Rachel and Her Children*. New York: Fawcett.

Marcuse, P., 1988. "Neutralizing Homelessness." *Socialist Review* 18: 69–96.

National Coalition for the Homeless (NCH), 2009a. Fact sheet, July. Retrieved June 4, 2010 from http://www.nationalhomeless.org/factsheets/why.html.

National Coalition for the Homeless (NCH), 2009b. *Safety Network*. 1983–2009.

Pew Center on the States, 2009. *One in 31: The Long Reach of American Corrections*. Pew Charitable Trusts.

Proquest LLC, 2013a. *National Newspaper Archives*.

Proquest LLC, 2013b. *Sociological Abstracts*.

Ropers, R., 1988. *The Invisible Homeless*. New York: Social Science Press.

Rossi, P., 1989. *Down and Out in America: The Origins of Homelessness*. Chicago: University of Chicago Press.

Smelser, N., Wilson, W. J., and Mitchell, F., eds., 2001. *America Becoming: Racial Trends and Their Consequences*. Commission on Behavioral and Social Sciences and Education, National Research Council. Washington, DC: National Academy Press.

Snow, D., and Anderson, L., 1993. *Down on Their Luck: A Study of Homeless Street People*. Berkeley: University of California Press.

Tulsa World, Editorial, 1996. "Homeless in a Heartless New York City," July 11, 1996, A 15. [Reproduced in *The Economist*, January 18, 1997: pp. 30–31.]

U.S. Census Bureau (September 13, 2002). Table 1. United States—Race and Hispanic Origin: 1790 to 1990. Accessed November 18, 2014. http://www.census.gov/population/www/documentation/twps0056/tab01.pdf

U.S. Census Bureau (2012). Statistical Abstract of the United States: 2012. Table 6. Resident Population by Sex, Race, and Hispanic Origin Status: 2000-2009. Accessed on November 18, 2014 from: http://www.census.gov/compendia/statab/2012/tables/12s0006.pdf

U.S. Conference of Mayors. Sample of Homeless, various years.

U.S. Department of Housing and Urban Development (HUD), 2006–2010. Annual Assessment Data.

Wagner, D., 1993. *Checkerboard Square: Culture and Resistance in a Homeless Community*. Boulder, CO: Westview.

Wagner, D., 1997. "Universalization of Social Problems: Some Radical Explanations," *Critical Sociology* 23(1): 3–24.

Wagner, D., 2012. *Confronting Homelessness: Poverty, Politics, and the Failure of Social Policy*. Boulder, CO: Lynne Rienner Publishers.

Wakhisi, T., 1995. "Homelessness in Black America." *Crisis*. 102(8) (November/December): 14–19.

Whaley, A., and Link, B., 1998. "Racial Categorization and Stereotype-Based Judgments About Homeless People." *Journal of Applied Psychology* 28(3): 189–205.

Wilson, W. J., 1996. *When Work Disappears: The World of the New Urban Poor*. New York: Knopf.

Wilson, W. J., 2004. *Race, Class, and the Postindustrial City: William Julius Wilson and the Promise of Sociology*. Albany, NY: State University of New York Press.

Wilson, W. J., 2009. *More Than Just Race: Being Black and Poor in the Inner City*. New York: Norton.

Wilson, W. J., and Taub, R., 2006. *There Goes the Neighborhood: Racial, Ethnic, and Class Tensions in Four Chicago Neighborhoods and Their Meaning for America*. New York: Knopf.

Woods, C., 2011. "Traps, Skid Row and Katrina," in *Downtown Blues: A Skid Row Reader*, pp. 50–55. Los Angeles, CA: Freedom Now Book.

Wright, T., 1997. *Out of Place: Homeless Mobilizations, Subcities, and Contested Landscapes*. Albany: State University of New York Press.

43

THE EFFECTS OF NEOLIBERAL CAPITALISM ON IMMIGRATION AND POVERTY AMONG MEXICAN IMMIGRANTS IN THE UNITED STATES

David Becerra

Introduction

Neoliberal policies have had devastating effects on developing countries and people living in poverty. Under the guise of expanding economic opportunity for all, globalization through neoliberal capitalistic policies have served to primarily benefit wealthy nations and the wealthy individuals within those nations. Neoliberal capitalism operates under the belief that a free and unregulated market is able to provide more efficient and fair outcomes for individuals than the government (Ossei-Owusu, 2012). Neoliberal economic policies promote the idea that a free market is essential for sustained economic growth and prosperity (Haque, 1999). Therefore, policies push for privatization of government services, liberalization of trade practices, deregulation of the marketplace, a reduction in social welfare programs, and a greater emphasis on individual self-interest over the interests of the greater society (Coburn, 2004). Neoliberal policies often involve a shift in the role of the federal government and its responsibilities to state and local governments and ultimately the people, and promote privatization of public services under the assumption that more localized control and privatization create greater choices, opportunities, and income for individuals (Wacquant, 2009).

The United States enacted neoliberal policies and pushed for neoliberal policies to be adopted in developing countries around the world such as Mexico. Unfortunately, neoliberal policies and the resulting globalization that followed have exacerbated poverty and income inequality in Mexico and the United States. The displacement of workers and increased poverty in Mexico caused a new wave of migration from Mexico to the United States and created a push for austerity measures to reduce funding for social welfare programs in the United States and limit immigrant access to social services. These measures have negatively impacted Mexican immigrants in the United States.

Neoliberal policies that impact poverty in Mexico and the United States

In Mexico and the United States the adoption of neoliberal policies of free trade and a deemphasized role of the federal government in social welfare programs increased immigration from Mexico to the United States and increased the vulnerability of Mexican immigrants living in the United States. Beginning in the early 1980s, Mexico adopted the neoliberal economic policies promoted by the United States, the World Bank, and the International Monetary Fund (IMF), but the adoption of neoliberal economic policies did not improve the Mexican economy. Instead Mexico reduced already sparse government programs and the country's economy nearly collapsed (Portes, 1997). At the same time, neoliberal economic policies were adopted in the United States which sought to significantly reduce the role of the government in providing social programs for those in poverty, especially among immigrant populations. In addition to Mexico, other Latin American countries began adopting neoliberal economic policies during the 1980s and as a result deregulated investments and price controls, privatized government services and programs, promoted trade through the reduction or elimination of tariffs, and attracted foreign investment by exempting foreign companies from taxes and labor codes and regulations (Haque, 1999).

Mexico and NAFTA

The post-revolution economy in Mexico relied heavily on government enterprises and protectionist trade policies. Mexico experienced an economic crisis that began in 1982 and lasted several years. Similar to the growth of neoliberal economic reform in the United States, the economic crisis in Mexico was viewed as a failure of the existing economic policies and allowed neoliberal policies to be adopted in Mexico (Thacker, 1999). The World Bank and the IMF pushed the Bank of Mexico to enact free trade policies, and in 1985 the President of Mexico, Miguel de la Madrid, introduced a reduction in trade barriers. This was the first step toward a free trade agreement with the United States. Negotiations for an official free trade agreement between Mexico, the United States, and Canada began in 1990.

The culmination of neoliberal economic policies for Mexico was the North American Free Trade Agreement (NAFTA) which took effect in 1994. NAFTA attempted to facilitate trade and economic development among the United States, Canada, and Mexico by eliminating tariffs and other barriers to trade (Burfisher et al., 2001). In order to accomplish this, Mexico privatized state owned and controlled industries and eliminated foreign entry restrictions for many industries including agriculture. Although touted as necessary for sustained economic growth and prosperity for all three countries, NAFTA had devastating effects on many segments of the Mexican economy and population (Otero, 2011).

NAFTA opened up the agricultural market in Mexico to competition and imports from the United States and, as a result, Mexico's agricultural industry could not compete with the United States. In a relatively short period of time, Mexico went from a food self-sufficient nation to a food-import dependent nation and employment in agriculture decreased by almost 25 percent (González Chávez and Macías Macías, 2007; Otero, 2011). Other sectors of the Mexican economy did not produce enough new jobs and this left hundreds of thousands of former agricultural workers without employment.

International migration is influenced by many factors and large-scale migration from Mexico to the United States has occurred for over one hundred years, but the displacement of agricultural workers in Mexico caused by NAFTA contributed to undocumented migration from Mexico to the United States (Otero, 2011). The low wages and scarcity of employment in Mexico combined with the demand for labor in the United States led millions of Mexican workers to migrate out of Mexico, mostly to the United States, in search of employment and a means to support their families. Unfortunately, although higher-paying employment was available in the United States, the neoliberal economic policies adopted by the United States would continue to negatively impact Mexican immigrants and their families once they arrived in the United States.

Policies that increase the vulnerability of Mexican immigrants in the United States

International neoliberal economic policies such as NAFTA, which contributed to undocumented immigration to the United States from Mexico, coincided with national neoliberal policies in the United States. There was a push since the 1980s to reduce the role of government in anti-poverty programs and promote work as an alternative to social welfare programs. Coburn (2004) states that neoliberal policies promote individualism over government action and therefore endorse economic inequalities because they motivate people to work and actively participate in the market economy. Conservatives in Congress advocated for a change in the welfare system of the United States to encourage people to work instead of being dependent on the government for assistance.

Welfare reform

The Personal Responsibility and Work Opportunity Reconciliation Act (PRWORA) of 1996 eliminated the Aid to Families with Dependent Children (AFDC) program which provided eligible families with cash assistance, and replaced it with the Temporary Assistance to Needy Families (TANF) program (Karger and Stoesz, 2006). Under the TANF program, recipients can only receive assistance for a maximum of 60 months and are required to participate in work or work-based activities in order to receive cash assistance.

PRWORA was consistent with neoliberal philosophies of a reduced role of the federal government in anti-poverty programs and the promotion of greater participation of individuals in poverty in the low-wage workforce (Coburn, 2004). PRWORA furthered the devolution of federal responsibility for anti-poverty programs by providing states with block grants which gave states more flexibility to develop TANF programs, but also created a system of TANF programs that varied from state to state in their eligibility requirements and level of assistance to TANF recipients (Soss et al., 2001). While the program was sold to the public as a program to educate and train TANF recipients to have the skills necessary to obtain employment in order to become self-sufficient, TANF recipients are actually pushed into the labor market as quickly as possible regardless of the type of job, the pay, or the hours of employment (Brown, 1997; Pavetti and Acs, 2001). The end result is that participants do not actually move out of poverty through employment—they simply are forced off of government assistance.

Neoliberal economic principles were used to create NAFTA in order to ensure free trade, but without the guarantee of free labor mobility, individuals living in poverty in Mexico and the United States were negatively impacted (Otero, 2011). NAFTA did not ease the restrictions placed on immigrant labor in the United States and a growing anti-immigrant sentiment combined with neoliberal anti-poverty programs such as PRWORA created a hostile environment for Mexican immigrants in the United States PRWORA impacted everyone living in poverty in the United States, but it contained a special provision, Title IV, aimed specifically at immigrants.

Consistent with the neoliberal approach which emphasized individualism and employment over government involvement in anti-poverty programs, members of Congress argued that immigrants should be expected to be self-sufficient and not rely on government assistance to live in the United States. Under the Title IV provisions of PRWORA eligibility for services was not solely based on income, but also determined by immigration status and date of arrival. Immigrants classified as Legal Permanent Residents (LPR) who arrived prior to August 22, 1996 were prohibited from receiving food stamps and Supplemental Security Income (SSI) benefits. Legal Permanent Residents who arrived after August 22, 1996 were also prohibited from receiving food stamps and SSI benefits and also from receiving Medicaid and TANF until they had lived in the United States for five years; even after the five years, eligibility for those programs was left to the discretion of each state (Fix and Passel, 2002; Kaushal and Kaestner, 2005; Kullgren, 2003).

In addition, under PRWORA undocumented immigrants were prohibited from accessing public services, such as TANF, food stamps, Medicaid, retirement, disability, and similar benefits by state or local governments (PRWORA; U.S. Public Law 104–193; Kullgren, 2003). PRWORA also created the new categories of "Unqualified Aliens" and "Qualified Aliens" to determine eligibility for federal and state social welfare benefits (Chang, 2005; Fix and Tumlin, 1997). "Unqualified Aliens" include all undocumented immigrants and are not eligible to receive any non-emergency federal benefits. "Qualified Aliens" or Legal Permanent Residents are those who are lawfully admitted for permanent residence in the United States. Prior to PRWORA, there was no eligibility distinction made for lawfully admitted immigrants (Chang, 2005; Fix and Tumlin, 1997). PRWORA's punitive measures restricting immigrant access to services allowed the United States to exploit undocumented immigrant labor which further exacerbated the negative effects of poverty among undocumented immigrants.

As a result of the adoption of neoliberal economic principles in the development of PRWORA, 935,000 Legal Permanent Residents lost their benefits (Fix and Passel, 2002). The implementation of PRWORA had a significant negative impact on unmarried immigrant women and their children. According to Kaushal and Kaestner (2005), PRWORA was associated with a significant increase in the proportion of uninsured single immigrant women. The negative effect of PRWORA was even greater in the proportion of uninsured children with immigrant mothers. This finding is especially significant because, as citizens, U.S.-born children are eligible to receive government services, but the fear of penalties for LPRs and possible deportation among undocumented immigrant mothers may cause them to avoid applying for services even for their eligible U.S.-born children (Kaushal and Kaestner, 2005). Many LPRs also avoid applying for social welfare benefits out of fear of being labeled a "public charge" that could affect their ability to become citizens or serve as sponsors to family members who want to immigrate to the United States (Dinan, 2005). A "public charge" is someone who relies on government assistance for support, and being labeled a "public charge" can be used to deny applications for permanent residency or citizenship. Although the federal government attempted to clarify the law in 1999 to indicate that the receipt of Medicaid, WIC, food stamps, and other non-cash benefits did not cause someone to be labeled a "public charge," the increase in anti-immigrant policies since 2001 has contributed to the continued fear and misunderstanding about the consequences of applying for and receiving government social welfare benefits (Dinan, 2005; Fremstad, 2000).

Many Latino immigrant families are also unable to afford health insurance or are ineligible for employer-provided health insurance (Cristancho et al., 2008; Pitkin Derose et al., 2009). The immigrant population without health insurance in 2009 was approximately two and a half times greater than that of individuals born in United States (DeNavas-Walt et al., 2011). Latinos have the lowest level of health insurance coverage in the United States and, among Latinos, 57% of Mexican immigrants lack health insurance (Saenz, 2010). As a result of policies restricting access to government services and a possible fear of deportation, immigrants tend to utilize medical and social services at lower rates than U.S.-born individuals (Kullgren, 2003; Vega et al., 1999).

In addition to the neoliberal foundations of PRWORA, the Title IV provisions restricting immigrant access to social welfare benefits were based on the belief that government welfare programs attracted immigrants to the United States and should therefore be eliminated. Despite studies that found immigrant families to be less dependent on welfare than U.S.-born families and that immigrants tend to contribute more to local, state, and federal budgets than they consume in services, rhetoric about the economic drain of immigrants in the United States has persisted (Becerra et al., 2012; Fix and Passel, 2002; Strayhorn, 2006).

Adopting neoliberal economic policies in the United States combined with the growing number of immigrants, and rising anti-immigrant sentiment, have created hardships for immigrant families living in the United States. There is a growing number of U.S.-born children with at least one immigrant parent. In 1990 the percentage of children with at least one immigrant parent was 13%, and by 2007 the percentage had increased to 23% (Fortuny et al., 2009). Of the approximately 17.2 million children of immigrant parents, an estimated 4.2 million of them live in poverty (Wight et al., 2011). In addition to U.S.-born children of immigrant parents, there are also approximately 1.6 million undocumented children in the United States (Dinan, 2005). Immigrant children tend to be at greater risk for academic, physical, and mental health issues compared to U.S.-born children (Tienda and Haskins, 2011). Over 38% of children with immigrant parents who are recent arrivals live in poverty compared with 27.2% of children from more established immigrant families; and children of undocumented immigrant parents have the highest rate of poverty (Wight et al., 2011).

Immigration and immigration enforcement

The demand for labor in the United States is a major factor in the migration of workers from Mexico to the United States. These immigrants fill the demand for labor in the United States and, despite free trade policies and globalization, anti-immigrant policies continue to be enacted at the federal and state levels to deter undocumented immigration. For example, several states have passed employer sanction laws which are intended to punish employers for hiring undocumented immigrants, but although workplace raids are conducted and undocumented workers are detained and deported, few businesses actually receive fines or sanctions for hiring undocumented workers (Hensley and Kiefer, 2009). E-verify is an automated system for employers to verify the work eligibility of potential employees in order to ensure that undocumented immigrants do not work in the United States (U.S. Citizenship and Immigration Services, 2010). These policies do not decrease the demand for low-wage workers and have had minimal impact on deterring undocumented immigration from Mexico. Instead, these policies force undocumented immigrants into isolated communities and they must resort to the unregulated cash economy for employment where they receive lower wages, no health benefits, and are at greater risk for exploitation.

Immigrant communities, especially composed of undocumented immigrants, tend to be socially, culturally, and often geographically isolated from mainstream American society and culture. Although these communities tend to be of lower socioeconomic status, immigrants often develop social structures and businesses that allow them to maintain their language, culture, and religion which may be helpful in the transition to a new country and a new language (Vega et al., 2011). Communities with a high percentage of undocumented immigrants may choose to remain isolated as a result of the fear of detection and deportation. Although there may be protective factors associated with these communities, the isolation and lack of contact with mainstream society and culture may inhibit immigrants' ability to integrate into society and improve their socioeconomic status (Vega et al., 2011).

Other extremely isolated and impoverished predominantly Mexican-American and Mexican immigrant communities along the United States–Mexico border, particularly in Texas, are known as colonias. These communities are unincorporated rural areas located outside of the official boundaries of cities and often are without electricity, paved roads, sewer systems, potable water, and access to quality education or health services (Ortiz et al., 2006). As a result, residents of colonias are often at risk for numerous health issues (Arcury and Quandt, 2003; Forster-Cox et al., 2007). Along the Texas–Mexico border there are an estimated 1,800 colonias with a combined population of approximately 500,000 residents, but there are also an estimated 1,000 colonias along the border in New Mexico, Arizona, and California (Davidhizar and Bechtel, 1999; Ortiz et al., 2006).

Colonias emerged as agricultural workers, primarily Mexican immigrants, were drawn to the United States–Mexico border region during the Bracero Program from 1942 to 1965, which brought Mexican laborers to the United States to fill the labor shortage as a result of World War II. Land developers and speculators who wanted to make money and exploit a vulnerable population realized that immigrants and farmworkers often could not qualify for conventional housing and subdivided unproductive land for sale with the promise that infrastructure for basic services would eventually be provided (Belden and Weiner, 1998; Gonzalez-Arizmendi and Ortiz, 2004).

Although the Bracero Program ended, the demand for labor remained. The continued demand for labor, along with the settlement in areas previously settled by other friends and family members, and the lack of affordable housing, caused immigrants to continue to settle in colonias along the border (Becerra et al., 2010; Davidhizar and Bechtel, 1999; Massey et al., 2002). As more residents moved into colonias, the plots of land were divided further and more housing was built on the land without permits or proper infrastructure (Coronado et al., 2006). More recently, the devastation of Mexico's agricultural economy, caused by NAFTA, forced displaced agricultural workers to move to the United States in search of work. Many of those immigrants settled in the colonias along the United States–Mexico border.

Following the neoliberal principles of shifting federal government power and control to state and local governments, there has been a devolution of the responsibility for immigration enforcement from the federal government to state and local authorities. Starting in 1996, not only did the federal government turn social welfare agencies into de-facto immigration enforcement officials by creating eligibility requirements based on immigration classifications, but also authorized state and local police forces to enforce immigration policies by signing a 287(g) Memorandum of Agreement (MOA) with federal immigration authorities (Varsanyi, 2011; Waslin, 2007). The 287(g) MOAs, which have been used increasingly since 2005, allow state and local law enforcement agencies to check the immigration status of everyone who is arrested and jailed (Coleman and Kocher, 2011; Varsanyi, 2011).

In 2010, Arizona used the 287(g) model to give state and local officials greater immigration enforcement authority and passed SB1070, which allows state and local police officers to check the immigration status of anyone they arrest or suspect is an undocumented immigrant (Pew Hispanic Center, 2010). SB1070 was used as a model for several other states such as Alabama, Indiana, Utah, and Georgia that wanted to enact anti-immigration state policies. Alabama's policy was even harsher than SB1070 because it barred undocumented children from attending public schools and made it a crime to transport or house undocumented immigrants, or for an undocumented immigrant to solicit work. Although the U.S. Supreme Court struck down three of the major provisions in SB1070 in 2012, the court upheld the "show me your papers requirement," that permits police officers to question people's immigration status, and workplace and community raids by county law enforcement continue in states such as Arizona. This recent anti-immigrant legislation in various states has only served to heighten fears and cause deleterious effects in Mexican immigrant communities. According to the Pew Hispanic Center (2010), six out of ten Latinos worry that they themselves, a family member, or close friend will be deported.

Workplace and community raids and deportations have a devastating impact on Mexican immigrant families in the United States. Since 2001, there has been an increase in immigration enforcement, including workplace raids by immigration and local authorities (Thronson, 2008). Deportations have hit record levels, with almost 400,000 immigrants deported during the first two years of the Obama administration (Pew Hispanic Center, 2012). These raids and the resulting deportation of hundreds of thousands of immigrants have produced fear among undocumented immigrants and their children, which can have lasting negative effects on the psychological well-being of children because of the trauma involved in the separation of families (Capps et al., 2007). The negative psychological impact of the workplace raids and deportation also extend to other members of immigrant communities. The same negative effects found in the children whose parents had been detained or deported have been reported in children who do not have parents or family members deported (Capps et al., 2007). Chaudry and colleagues (2010) found that these experiences can affect the mental health of children and lead to increased aggression, anxiety, excessive crying, and withdrawn behaviors, as well as changes to eating and sleeping patterns.

Conclusion

Neoliberal economic policies promised sustained economic growth and prosperity, but instead increased social, income, and health inequalities undermining the social programs that had helped to reduce poverty (Coburn, 2004). The United States encouraged developing nations to adopt neoliberal economic policies as a way to improve their economic conditions. Mexico experienced an economic crisis in the 1980s which prompted Mexico to adopt neoliberal economic policies that ultimately resulted in the passage of the North American Free Trade Agreement. NAFTA had a devastating impact on low-wage workers in Mexico, particularly in the agricultural sector. The combination of displaced workers in Mexico and a demand for low-wage workers in the United States contributed to an increase in migration from Mexico to the United States. Unfortunately for Mexican immigrants, the United States adopted the neoliberal philosophy that anti-poverty programs should have less government support and encourage work participation. The United States passed the PRWORA in 1996 which denied access to benefits for many immigrants.

The restrictive provisions against immigrants in PRWORA contributed to the narrative that immigrants are a drain to social services and the U.S. economy, which led to further anti-immigration policies. The adoption of neoliberal policies not only contributed to migration of Mexican workers to the United States, but also contributed to the adoption of policies in the United States that exploited Mexican immigrant labor, while denying Mexican immigrants access to health and social services, and forcing them into isolated communities for fear of deportation.

The economic crisis in the United States which began in 2007 may serve to highlight the failure of neoliberal economic policies to produce sustained economic growth and prosperity, but also the failure to protect oppressed and vulnerable populations. Recent events such as the implementation of the Deferred Action for Childhood Arrivals (DACA), which allows some young undocumented immigrants to apply for a two-year temporary work permit if they meet certain requirements, and the willingness by President Obama, Republicans, and Democrats to enact comprehensive immigration reform, may help the plight of millions of undocumented immigrants living in poverty in the United States. But it is important to remember that the negative effects of neoliberal and anti-immigrant policies will not be cured with the passage of immigration reform. It will take collaboration among immigrant communities, policy makers, law enforcement, educators, and health and social service workers to advocate for economic and social policies that better serve all segments of society and address the long-term negative effects that neoliberal and anti-immigrant policies have had on the Mexican immigrant population in the United States.

References

Arcury, T.A. and Quandt, S.A. (2003). Pesticides at work and at home: Exposure of migrant farmworkers. *Lancet*, 362, 2021.

Becerra, D., Androff, D., Ayón, C., and Castillo, J. (2012). Fear vs. facts: The economic impact of undocumented immigrants in the U.S. *Journal of Sociology and Social Welfare*, 39(4), 111–134.

Becerra, D., Gurrola, M., Ayón, C., Androff, D., Krysik, J., Gerdes, K., Moya-Salas, L., and Segal, E. (2010). Poverty and other factors affecting migration intentions among adolescents in Mexico. *Journal of Poverty*, 14(1), 1–16.

Belden, J. and Weiner, R. (1998). *Housing and rural America: Building affordable and inclusive communities*. Thousand Oaks, CA: Sage Publications.

Brown, A. (1997). *Work first: How to implement an employment-focused approach to welfare reform*. New York: Manpower Demonstration Research Corporation.

Burfisher, M.E., Robinson, S., and Thierfelder, K. (2001). The impact of NAFTA on the United States. *Journal of Economic Perspectives*, 15(1), 125–144.

Capps, R., Castaneda, R.M., Chaudry, A., and Santos, R. (2007). *Paying the price: The impact of immigration raids on America's children*. The Urban Institute, National Council of La Raza.

Chang, C. (2005). Health care for undocumented immigrant children: Special members of an underclass. *Washington University Law Review*, 83(4), 1271–1294.

Chaudry, A., Capps, R., Pedroza, J. M., Castañeda, R.M., Santos, R., and Scott, M.M. (2010). *Facing our future: Children in the aftermath of immigration enforcement*. Washington, DC: The Urban Institute.

Coburn, D. (2004). Beyond the income inequality hypothesis: Class, neoliberalism, and health inequalities. *Social Science and Medicine*, 58, 41–56.

Coleman, M. and Kocher, A. (2011). Detention, deportation, devolution, and immigrant incapacitation in the U.S. post 9/11. *The Geographical Journal*, 177(3), 228–237.

Coronado, G.D., Farias, A., Thompson, B., Godina, R., and Oderkirk, W. (2006). Attitudes and beliefs about colorectal cancer among Mexican American communities along the U.S.–Mexico border. *Ethnicity and Disease*, 16, 421–427.

Cristancho, S., Garces, D.M., Peters, K.E., and Mueller, B.C. (2008). Listening to rural Hispanic immigrants in the Midwest: A community-based participatory assessment of major barriers to health care access and use. *Qualitative Health Research*, 18(5), 633–646.

Davidhizar, R. and Bechtel, G.A. (1999). Health and quality of life within colonias settlements along the United States and Mexico border. *Public Health Nursing*, 16(4), 301–306.

DeNavas-Walt, C., Proctor, B.D., and Smith, J.C. (2011). *Income, poverty, and health insurance coverage in the United States: 2010*. Washington, DC: U.S. Census Bureau.

Dinan, K. (2005). *Children in low income immigrant families policy brief: Federal policies restrict immigrant children's access to key public benefits*. New York: National Center for Children in Poverty.

Fix, M.E. and Passel, J. (2002). *The scope and impact of welfare reform's immigrant provisions*. Washington, DC: The Urban Institute.

Fix, M.E. and Tumlin, K. (1997). *Welfare reform and the devolution of immigrant policy*. Washington, DC: The Urban Institute.

Forster-Cox, S.C., Mangadu, T., Jacquez, B., and Corona, A. (2007). The effectiveness of the promotora (community health worker) model of intervention for improving pesticide safety in U.S./Mexico border homes. *California Journal of Health Promotion*, 5(1), 62–75.

Fortuny, K., Capps, R., Simms, M., and Chaudry, A. (2009). *Children of immigrants: National and state characteristics*. Washington, DC: The Urban Institute.

Fremstad, S. (2000). *The INS public charge guidance: What does it mean for immigrants?* Washington, DC: Center on Budget and Policy Priorities.

Gonzalez-Arizmendi, L. and Ortiz, L. (2004). Neighborhood and community organizing in colonias: A case study in the development and use of promotoras. *Journal of Community Practice*, 12(1/2), 23–35.

González Chávez, H. and Macías Macías, A. (2007). Vulnerabilidad alimentaria y política agroalimentaria en México. *Desacatos: Revista de Antropología Social*, 25, 47–78.

Haque, M.S. (1999). The fate of sustainable development under neoliberal regimes in developing countries. *International Political Science Review*, 20(2), 197–218.

Hensley, J.J., and Kiefer, M. (2009). First firm punished under Arizona hiring law. *Arizona Republic*, December 18, B1, B8.

Karger, H.J. and Stoesz, D. (2006). *American social welfare policy: A pluralist approach* (5th ed.). Boston: Allyn and Bacon.

Kaushal, N. and Kaestner, R. (2005). Welfare reform and health insurance of immigrants. *Health Services Research*, 40(3), 697–722.

Kullgren, J.T. (2003). Restrictions on undocumented immigrants' access to health services: The public health implications of welfare reform. *American Journal of Public Health*, 93(10), 1630–1633.

Massey, D.S., Durand, J., and Malone, N.J. (2002). *Beyond smoke and mirrors: Mexican immigration in an era of economic integration*. New York: Russell Sage Foundation.

Ortiz, L., Arizmendi, L., and Cornelius, L.J. (2006). Access to health care among Latinos of Mexican descent in colonias in two Texas counties. *Journal of Rural Health*, 20(3), 246–252.

Ossei-Owusu, S. (2012). Decoding youth and neoliberalism: Pupils, precarity, and punishment. *Journal of Poverty*, 16(3), 196–307.

Otero, G. (2011). Neoliberal globalization, NAFTA, and migration: Mexico's loss of food sovereignty. *Journal of Poverty*, 15, 384–402.

Pavetti, L. and Acs, G. (2001). Moving up, moving out, or going nowhere? A study of the employment patterns of young women and the implications for welfare mothers. *Journal of Policy Analysis and Management*, 20(4), 721–736.

Personal Responsibility and Work Opportunity Reconciliation Act (PRWORA)(1996). U.S. Public Law 104–193.

Pew Hispanic Center. (2010). *Hispanics and Arizona's new immigration law*. Washington, DC.

Pew Hispanic Center. (2012). *Up to 1.4 million unauthorized immigrants could benefit from new deportation policy*. Washington, DC.

Pitkin Derose, K., Bahney, B.W., and Lurie, N. (2009). Immigrants and health care access, quality, and cost. *Medical Care Research and Review*, 66(4), 355–408.

Portes, A. (1997). Neoliberalism and sociology development: Emerging trends and unanticipated facts. *Population and Development Review*, 23(2), 229–259.

Saenz, R. (2010). *Latinos in America 2010: Population Bulletin Update*. Washington, DC: Population Reference Bureau.

Soss, J., Schram, S.F., Vartanian, T.P., and O'Brien, E. (2001). Setting the terms of relief: Explaining state policy choices in the devolution revolution. *American Journal of Political Science*, 45(2), 378–395.

Strayhorn, C. (2006). *Undocumented immigrants in Texas: A financial analysis of the impact to the State budget and economy*. Office of the Comptroller, Texas.

Thacker, S.C. (1999). NAFTA coalitions and political viability of neoliberalism in Mexico. *Journal of InterAmerican Studies and World Affairs*, 41(2), 57–89.

Thronson, D.B. (2008). Creating crisis: Immigration raids and the destabilization of immigrant families. *Wake Forest Law Review*, 43, 391–418.

Tienda, M. and Haskins, R. (2011). Immigrant children: Introducing the issue. *The Future of Children*, 21, (1), 3–18.

U.S. Citizenship and Immigration Services. (2010). *History and milestones*.

Varsanyi, M.W. (2011). Neoliberalism and nativism: Local anti-immigrant policy activism and an emerging politics of scale. *International Journal of Urban and Regional Research*, 35(2), 295–311.

Vega, W.A., Ang, A., Rodriguez, M.A., and Finch, B.K. (2011). Neighborhood protective effects on depression in Latinos. *American Journal of Community Psychology*, 47, 114–126.

Vega, W.A., Kolody, B., Aguilar-Gaxiola, S., and Catalano, R., (1999). Gaps in service utilization by Mexican Americans with mental health problems. *The American Journal of Psychiatry*, 156(6), 928–934.

Wacquant, L. (2009). *Punishing the poor: The neoliberal government of social insecurity*. Durham, NC: Duke University Press.

Waslin, M. (2007). Immigration enforcement by local and state police: The impact on Latinos. *Law Enforcement Executive Forum*, 7(7), 15–32.

Wight, V.R., Thampi, K., and Chau, M. (2011). *Poor children by parents' nativity: What do we know?* New York: National Center for Children in Poverty.

44

THE NEOLIBERAL DIET

Fattening profits and people

Gerardo Otero, Gabriela Pechlaner, and Efe Can Gürcan

The United States rose to world-power status partly thanks to modern industrial agriculture, and it boasts the most profitable and successful agribusiness of multinationals involved in the production and processing of agricultural and food products. But this system also exacerbates what we term the "neoliberal diet," which is largely composed of "energy-dense" foods with high contents of fat and empty calories. Foods that make up the neoliberal diet include those commonly called "junk food", since they contain low nutritional value (Drewnowski and Darmon, 2005; Drewnowski and Specter, 2004). This diet is strongly correlated with negative health impacts derived from being overweight and obese, such as diabetes, heart disease, and several types of cancer. According to the Institute of Medicine, the United States spends between $150 billion and $190 billion a year on obese-related illnesses (Howard, 2012: 13), which is clearly unsustainable. Indeed, the neoliberal diet could be chiefly responsible for the current trend that the present generation of children might be the first to have a lower life expectancy than their parents. Moreover, the neoliberal diet is not affecting U.S. citizens equally. Rather, while upper-income groups are seeing increasing access to higher-quality foods, including imported fruits, vegetables, wines, and other alcoholic beverages (Otero et al., 2013), the poor's diets are being increasingly narrowed to the nutritionally bereft "junk foods." The poor are thus also afflicted with a disproportionate amount of obesity and diet-related disease (Dixon, 2009; Drewnowski, 2009; Thirlaway and Upton, 2009).

This chapter outlines how diets have become increasingly differentiated by class and other socioeconomic strata in the United States. In the first section, we address the theoretical "structure" versus "agency" debate about obesity, contrasting the personal-responsibility perspective touted in Michael Pollan's highly celebrated *The Omnivore's Dilemma* (2006) against the more structural interpretations, such as that brought forth by Julie Guthman (2003, 2007a, 2007b, 2007c, 2011). The second section provides a statistical analysis of macro data from the United Nations' Food and Agriculture Organization (FAO, n.d.) on how the U.S. diet has evolved since the 1960s to a much greater emphasis on fats and high-caloric foods. Last, we connect inequality and diet as a means of linking the negative health impacts of the current food system to public policy.

Characterizing and resolving the problems of agri-industrialization

Michael Pollan's (2006) *The Omnivore's Dilemma* reached critical acclaim over his account of the negative implications of U.S. agri-industrialization and supermarketization of food.

In response to the dysfunctions of this system, Pollan argues that eating is not simply about sustenance or pleasure, but an agricultural, ecological, and political act (Pollan, 2006: 11). Hence he calls for us to "eat in full consciousness of everything involved in feeding" (2006: 9) and conduct ourselves accordingly. Pollan doesn't completely reject the industrial food system—which, despite its flaws, has provided us with abundant food—but he suggests that individuals must apply their greater consciousness of food production to finding a middle ground between the industrial, the organic, and the hunter-gatherer food systems. Without this consciousness, people have been vulnerable to the powerful manipulations of the agrifood industry, to their significant detriment.

To make his point, Pollan unravels the negative implications of various features of contemporary food systems, such as the prominence of corn. Corn's importance to the food industry is well documented, from its importance in feed for meat, dairy, and egg production, to its infinite flexibility as an ingredient as a starch, flour, oil, and sweetener. Given that we have limits on their capacities for consumption—no matter how one stretches it—agribusiness had to turn to processing as the means to maintain profit making. Processed food is highly profitable—as evidenced by the proliferation of fast food chains and sales of packaged food and soft drinks world-wide (Howard, 2012)—and corn in all its manifestations is an integral part of processed food:

> Corn is in the coffee whitener and Cheez Whiz, the frozen yogurt and TV dinner, the canned fruit and ketchup and candies, the soups and snacks and cake mixes, the frosting and gravy and frozen waffles, the syrups and hot sauces, the mayonnaise and mustard, the hot dogs and the bologna, the margarine and shortening, the salad dressings and the relishes and even the vitamins.
>
> (Pollan, 2006: 19)

Corn consequently constitutes one of the major sources of the obesity problem (Pollan, 2006: 101–103). Furthermore, this corn monoculture has not only been popularized by such agrifood monopolies as Cargill and ADM, but it has been enabled by a wide array of government subsidies and policy supports. It is through government intervention that corn sweeteners became less expensive than sugar, through mechanisms such as "investments in public research that raised yields for corn, sugar production allotments and trade restrictions, and subsidies for corn production" (Morrison et al., 2010: 17), with a dramatic increase in the availability of sweeteners (from 113.2 to 136.3 pounds per person between 1924 and 1974, excluding the war years). Not surprisingly, this has facilitated the production of cheap, sugar-based processed foods and beverages. Since the late 1970s, for example, the per capita availability of soft drinks has increased from 22 to 52 gallons (Ha et al., 2009: 50). Soft drinks are only the most blatant of a long range of sugar-based and sugar-enhanced processed foods.

Corn is one specific issue under the broader umbrella of what has been labeled the "nutritional transition" (Drewnowski and Popkin, 1997) which is marked by the greater availability of cheap vegetable oils and fats, on a global scale. At all points, this transition is not only driven by agrifood interests but finds significant government support. Even the "production and export of vegetable oils are promoted through direct subsidies, credit guarantees, food aid, and market development programs" (Drewnowski and Popkin, 1997: 34). Freeman (2007) argues that government supports play heavily in shoring up the profitability of the fast food industry, through mechanisms such as "subsidies for animal feed, sugar and fats," without which "the price of a typical fast food meal would triple" (Freeman, 2007: 2242, citing Sams, 2004: 43).

While Pollan provides a convincing critique of agrifood industrialization and supermarketization, his individualistic stance on resolving the food system's problems overemphasizes individual responsibility and underemphasizes structural fixes, such as the crucial role of state regulation. Pollan also neglects socioeconomic differences in the negative impacts of the modern food system which highlight the limitations of an individual-based resolution (Dixon, 2009; Guthman and DuPuis, 2006). This leads him to the naïve and anti-statist idea that the current agrifood regime can be altered individually "one meal at a time," which understates any collective efforts for genuine structural change (Guthman, 2007a: 78; Guthman, 2007b: 263–264).

Guthman's (2011) *Weighing In: Obesity, Food Justice, and the Limits of Capitalism* critiques Pollan's individualistic and consumer-centered account, emphasizing his failure to adequately address inequality in the food system (Guthman, 2011: 5, 9). Guthman makes a strong case that current problems in our food systems have to do with the nature of capitalism (Guthman, 2011: 16). While Pollan effectively identifies numerous problems with the modern agriculture and food system, this is only half the equation. His weakness is the second half—resolution. Guthman's analysis is more promising in this regard. For Guthman, neither buying organic produce to influence the market nor educating people to eat more fresh fruits, vegetables and organic produce will be sufficient to challenge powerful economic interests (Guthman, 2011: 5, 17).

According to Guthman, the powerful economic interests of capitalists in conjunction with government policy choices have transformed the food system into its current, socially problematic, form:

> ... fast and convenient food has been a triply good fix for American capitalism. It entails the super-exploitation of the labor force in its production, it provides cheap food to support the low wages of the food and other industries by feeding their low-wage workers, and it absorbs the surpluses of the agricultural economy, soaking up ... the excesses of overproduction to keep the farm sector marginally viable.
>
> (Guthman, 2011: 177)

Consequently, buying cheap fat- and oil-rich food cannot be reduced to a "lifestyle" choice, as this neglects the fact that the "current policy environment is a result of political choices, not consumption choices" (Guthman, 2011: 194). In fact, Guthman argues that the mainstream of the alternative food movement—of which Pollan is a major proponent—exhibits a colonial attitude with a "civilizing" mission to educate people on how to eat, without addressing the major negative effects of agrarian restructuring under neoliberalism. In contrast, Guthman demands active state intervention that targets not only inequalities in quality food access, but also broadly confronts capitalism, given that:

> The systematic production of inequality has taken place not only through farm and food policy but also through trade, labor, immigration, health care, economic development, taxation, and financial policy—in other words, just about all policies that have kept American capitalism (barely) afloat.
>
> (Guthman, 2011: 196)

This could occur, for example, through transparent public–private partnerships and radical governance mechanisms that would induce "more collectivist subjects," rather than mere atomized and disempowered consumers (Guthman, 2007c: 473–474; Guthman and DuPuis, 2006: 442).

Before we assess the disproportionate impacts of poverty on nutrition further, we will first turn to the historical transition of the American diet.

Evolution of caloric content in the U.S. diet, 1961–2009

Between 1961 and 2009, there has been a 28 percent increase in per capita food intake in the United States. A slight dip occurred starting in 2007, coinciding with the global food-inflation crisis. This crisis has made even the U.S. working classes vulnerable to the food insecurity that comes from food price fluctuations, although nothing comparable to that which occurred in developing countries.

Figure 44.1 depicts the relative rise/decline in the percentage contribution of the three main food sources to total daily per capita caloric intake in the United States. The absolute amounts of each component varied at different rates, with animal products remaining fairly stable throughout the period. Caloric contribution from cereals, however, increased from 627 kilocalories per capita per day in 1961 to 827 by 2009. While the percentage of cereals intake has remained roughly stable, absolute amounts of food intake have increased by 24 percent. Therefore, cereals, particularly the refined kind, have played a key role in the neoliberal diet (see Figure 44.2). Calories from refined flour are digested promptly, thus contributing to fat build-up in the body; while others coming from complex carbohydrates take longer to digest and are then eliminated via the small intestine (Howard, 2012: 7).

Figure 44.3 breaks down the percentage contribution to the food supply by each of the two main sources of fat—animal fat and vegetable oils—and shows a dramatic dietary change between 1961 and 2009. While animal fats used to make up about 7 percent of the U.S. total daily per capita caloric intake, this proportion had declined to 3 percent by 2009. Conversely, the contribution of vegetable oils spiked to almost twice, from 9.6 to 17.2 percent in the same period. Absolute amounts of food intake from these categories of fat followed similar trajectories. Animal fats declined from contributing 199 kilocalories per capita per day in 1961 to only 102 kilocalories by 2009. Conversely, the contribution by vegetable oils more than doubled from 276 kilocalories per capita per day in 1961 to 636 by 2009.

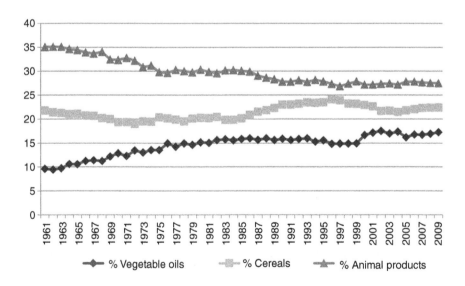

Figure 44.1 The percentage contribution of the three main food sources to total daily per capita caloric intake in the United States

Source: Constructed with data from FAOSTAT.

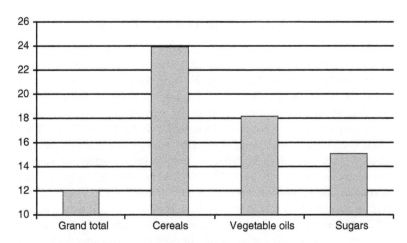

Figure 44.2 Percentage increases in U.S. food supply, 1985–2009

Source: Constructed with data from FAOSTAT.

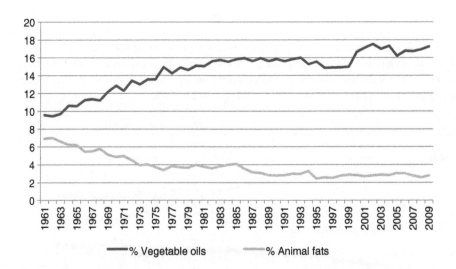

Figure 44.3 Percentage of vegetable oils and animal fats in U.S. food supply

Source: Constructed with data from FAOSTAT.

From the above we see that, in relative or percentage terms, only the increase of vegetable oils is dramatic in relation to total food intake. This is clear evidence of the "nutrition transition," i.e., a diet heavy on fats and calories, with added salt for enhanced taste.

Socioeconomic determinants of diet

In accordance with Guthman, we find that while heralding important issues with the modern food system, Pollan's individualistic approach neglects the fact that the current food regime is strongly marked by class differences. For example, while the wealthy access a rising organic sector that concentrates on providing them with luxury and anti-oxidant-rich "functional food" (Dixon, 2009), the poor are relegated to cheap, energy-dense "junk foods" associated with the proliferation of obesity. In short, access to specific foods tends to be closely related to people's class, race, and gender background (Guthman, 2011: 174, 177).

The social and economic stratification of diets argued by Guthman finds much resonance in the current literature on the topic, with significant scholarly support for the correlation between various socioeconomic-related variables and diet (Darmon and Drewnowski, 2008; Dixon, 2009; Drewnowski, 2009; Harrington et al., 2011; Lee, 2011, cited in Dean and Sharkey, 2011: 3; Thirlaway and Upton, 2009). Drawing on an extensive review of existing literature, Lee (2011), for example, concludes that social inequality is closely linked to the question of obesity in the United States at the individual, family, school, and neighborhood levels. While the reasons behind this socioeconomic class difference are less straightforward, a number of key variables have been identified, such as cost, education, and access.

Most notably, "junk food" is usually cheaper than fresh fruits and vegetables. Thus, "a person with a limited income will find it more cost effective to buy five packets of macaroni and cheese for five dollars versus one bag of organic mixed green salad at the same price" (Lee, 2011: 220). Simply stated, higher-calorie food provides a greater satiation "bang" for the buck. This simple economics stands even without the added issue of "stress-induced eating" by people in chronic poverty reacting to end-of-the-month-type food shortages: "when money runs out low-income individuals may restrict their food consumption and then binge on energy-dense food when money is available" (Lee, 2011: 220).

Good food not only costs more, but it also may be more difficult to access by the poor. A number of studies have shown poor neighborhoods are disproportionately less likely to have food outlets—such as supermarkets and chain stores—which stock affordable, healthy, food. Morland et al. (2002), for example, found that wealthier neighborhoods had three times as many supermarkets, and fewer neighborhood grocery and convenience stores (which are more likely to stock processed items), than lower-income neighborhoods (2002: 27). Rose and Richards (2004) concluded that neighborhood food availability, such as ease of access to supermarkets, was a significant factor in determining household fruit consumption in low-income populations in the United States.

There is also evidence that even the poor-quality food that is available in low-income neighborhoods actually costs more than it does in other neighborhoods. In part, this is a consequence of the lack of access to chain stores, indicated above. Chung and Myers (1999), for example, found the lack of large chain stores to be a significant factor in the higher grocery costs for those in poor neighborhoods. But it is not solely an access issue. There are also indications of racial disparities in access to good food (Block et al., 2004; Morland et al., 2002). Block et al. (2004), for example, found that "neighborhoods with 80% black residents had 2.4 fast food restaurants per square mile compared to 1.5 restaurants per square mile in neighborhoods with 20% black residents" (2004: 214). The percentage of black residents was an even more powerful predictor of fast food restaurants than median household income.

Another key factor is the concerted effort by processed-food companies to privilege taste over nutrition. In a seminal exposé, *New York Times* investigative reporter Michael Moss describes how the industry has used a "scientific" approach to optimize foods geared to reach a combination of the "bliss point" and "mouth feel" that creates addiction. "Don't talk to me about nutrition," said the CEO of General Mills. "Talk to me about taste, and if this stuff tastes better, don't run around trying to sell stuff that doesn't taste good" (Moss, 2013: 37). In the potato chip, for instance:

The coating of salt, the fat content that rewards the brain with instant feelings of pleasure, the sugar that exists not as an additive but in the starch of the potato itself—all of this combine to make it the perfect addictive food.

(47)

Moss consulted industry studies, some of them secret, that identified one particularly promising market: the "rapidly growing Hispanic and African-American communities" (2013: 38). It's never been about nutrition, but always about how to make people like the junk food to sell more.

These studies suggest significant evidence of diet as a social justice issue. In fact, there is so much evidence of the structural dietary difference that Andrea Freeman (2007) coined the term "food oppression," arguing that it indicates a "form of structural subordination" given that "government support of the fast food industry severely limits dietary choices for low-income, urban African Americans and Latinos" (Freeman, 2007: 2245). In the context of the structured nature of nutrition relations, it is hard to maintain support for Pollan's individualistic approach to dietary reform.

Conclusion: poverty and the future of nutrition

We have seen here a confirmation of the historical transition to a high fat, salt, and sugar diet in the United States, with strong support that this transition is subject to significant socioeconomic stratification, with substantial health repercussions enacted on the poor and minority populations of the nation. Without significant state intervention, all indications are that this trajectory is clearly on the increase. Any approach to reform the agrifood system that neglects this structural element is not only woefully inadequate, but also dangerously neglectful of significant social-justice issues.

Given the apparent synchronicity between government and industry economic goals, "food oppression" is very difficult to address (Freeman, 2007: 2245). Simply "encouraging low-income families to consume healthier but more costly foods" indeed seems like "an elitist approach to public health" (Drewnowski and Darmon, 2005: 265S). Even taxing unhealthy foods, as a disincentive to their purchase, in this context is equally regressive, although subsidizing healthy foods for the poor could be a more progressive means of achieving the same result. Whatever the tack, improvement clearly requires significant input from the same policy forces that helped to form the U.S. food system into its current, socially problematic state.

References

Block, Jason, Richard A. Scribner, and Karen B. DeSalvo. 2004. "Fast Food, Race/Ethnicity, and Income: A Geographic Analysis." *American Journal of Preventive Medicine* 27(3): 7.

Chung, C. and S.L. Myers. 1999. "Do the Poor Pay More for Food? An Analysis of Grocery Store Availability and Food Price Disparities." *Journal of Consumer Affairs* 33(2): 276–296.

Darmon, N. and A. Drewnowski. 2008. "Does Social Class Predict Diet Quality?" *American Journal of Clinical Nutrition* 87(5): 1107–1117.

Dean, W.R. and J.R. Sharkey. 2011. "Food Insecurity, Social Capital and Perceived Personal Disparity in a Predominantly Rural Region of Texas: An Individual-Level Analysis." *Social Science and Medicine* 72(9): 1454–1462. doi:10.1016/j.socscimed.2011.03.015.

Dixon, J. 2009. "From the Imperial to the Empty Calorie: How Nutrition Relations Underpin Food Regime Transitions." *Agriculture and Human Values* 26: 321–333.

Drewnowski, A. 2009. "Obesity, Diets and Social Inequality." *Nutrition Reviews* 67(Issue Supplement): S36–S39.

Drewnowski, A. and N. Darmon. 2005. "The Economics of Obesity: Dietary Energy Density and Energy Cost." *American Journal of Clinical Nutrition* 82(Supplement): 265S–273S.

Drewnowski, A. and B.M. Popkin. 1997. "The Nutrition Transition: New Trends in the Global Diet." *Nutrition Reviews* 55(2): 31–43.

Drewnowski, A. and S.E. Specter. 2004. "Poverty and Obesity: The Role of Energy Density and Energy Costs." *American Journal of Clinical Nutrition* 79: 6–16.

FAO. n.d. "Food Security Statistics." FAO, Official Website. Available at http://www.fao.org/economic/ess/ess-fs/en/ (accessed: February 16, 2012).

FAOSTAT n.d. General site. Available at http://faostat3.fao.org/faostat-gateway/go/to/home/E (accessed January 27, 2013).

Freeman, Andrea. 2007. "Fast Food: Oppression Through Poor Nutrition." *California Law Review*: 2221–2259.

Guthman, J. 2003. "Fast Food/Organic Food: Reflexive Tastes and the Making of 'Yuppie Chow.'" *Social and Cultural Geography* 4: 45–58.

Guthman, J. 2007a. "Can't Stomach It: How Michael Pollan et al. Made Me Want to Eat Cheetos." *Gastronomica* 7: 75–79.

Guthman, J. 2007b. "Commentary on Teaching Food: Why I Am Fed Up With Michael Pollan et al." *Agriculture and Human Values* 24: 261–264.

Guthman, J. 2007c. "The Polanyian Way? Voluntary Food Labels as Neoliberal Governance." *Antipode* 39: 456–478.

Guthman, J. 2011. *Weighing In: Obesity, Food Justice, and the Limits of Capitalism*. Berkeley: California University Press.

Guthman, J. and M. DuPuis. 2006. "Embodying Neoliberalism: Economy, Culture, and the Politics of Fat." *Environment and Planning D: Society and Space* 24: 427–448.

Ha, E.-J., N. Caine-Bish, C. Holloman, and K. Lowry-Gordon. 2009. "Evaluation of Effectiveness of Class-Based Nutrition Intervention on Changes in Soft Drink and Milk Consumption among Young Adults." *Nutrition Journal* 8: 50–55.

Harrington, J., A.P. Fitzgerald, R. Layte, J. Lutomski, and M. Molcho. 2011. "Sociodemographic, Health, and Lifestyle Predictors of Poor Diets." *Public Health Nutrition* 14(12): 2166–2175.

Howard, Charlotte. 2012. "The Big Picture." *The Economist*. Special Report on Obesity. December 15.

Lee, Hedwig. 2011. "Inequality as an Explanation for Obesity in the United States." *Sociology Compass* 5(3): 215–232.

Morland, Kimberly, Steve Wind, Ana Diez Roux, and Charles Poole. 2002. "Neighborhood Characteristics Associated with the Location of Food Stores and Food Service Places." *American Journal of Preventive Medicine* 22(1): 23–29.

Morrison, Rosanna M., Jean C. Buzby, and Hodan F. Wells. 2010. "Guess Who's Turning 100? Tracking a Century of American Eating." Economic Research Service, U.S. Department of Agriculture, Amber Waves 8(1). Available at http://www.ers.usda.gov/amber-waves/2010-march/guess-who%E2%80%99s-turning-100tracking-a-century-of-american-eating.aspx#.U-5dhrxdVeZ. (accessed August 15, 2014).

Moss, Michael. 2013. "(Salt + Fat²/Satisfying Crunch) × Pleasing Mouth Feel = A Food Designed to Addict." *New York Times Magazine*, February 24: 34–41, 46–48.

Otero, Gerardo, Gabriela Pechlaner, and Efe Can Gürcan. 2013. "Political Economy of 'Food Security' and Trade: Uneven and Combined Dependency." *Rural Sociology* 78(3): 263–289.

Pollan, M. 2006. *The omnivore's Dilemma: A Natural History of Four Meals*. New York: Penguin.

Rose, D. and R. Richards. (2004). "Food store access and household fruit and vegetable use among participants in the U.S. Food Stamp Program." *Public Health Nutrition*. 7(8): 1081–1088.

Sams, Craig. 2004. *The Little Food Book: You Are What You Eat*. New York: Disinformation Book Co.

Thirlaway, K. and D. Upton. 2009. *The Psychology of Lifestyle: Promoting Healthy Behaviour*. London and New York: Routledge.

45

GROUNDING GRANDMA

A qualitative discussion of home maintenance policies for aging in community

Lawren E. Bercaw

As of 2013, the population of older adults has grown at a faster rate than all other age groups combined, in part due to the aging Baby Boomer generation. Approximately one-in-five Americans is a Boomer, born between 1946 and 1964, and members of this largest generation are expected to live beyond age 80, longer than any prior generation. Growth in the population of older adults, coupled with increased longevity, creates a policy dilemma in meeting seniors' needs adequately. These needs include facilitating autonomy, as recent studies have shown that most older adults (88%) wish to remain independent in their homes for as long as they are able (AARP, 2000, 2010). This goal of living independently has given rise to aging in community, a phrase often used interchangeably with other terms including aging in place and healthy aging (Vasunilashorn et al., 2012).

First gaining prominence during the 1970s, aging in community is a process through which older adults opt to reside in their homes with community supports to meet their changing needs over time. Typically, these individuals remain in the same homes and neighborhoods where they lived prior to retirement, as opposed to relocating in later life to senior-specific housing, assisted living centers, or skilled nursing facilities. Though some seniors age in community while residing in rented properties, approximately 80% of Americans aged 65 and older own homes, and the majority of these homes are owner-occupied, indicating high rates of aging in community (Center for Housing Policy, 2012).

Historical background

Several federal policies have contributed to high rates of homeownership among American seniors. Since the first Homestead Act permitted Americans to apply for land grants in 1862, U.S. policies have marketed homeownership as a critical aspect of American identity. Homeownership represents an essential component of the American Dream and has been viewed as "good politics" and "an important goal of public policy" (Rohe and Watson, 2007, p. 5). This notion of "good politics" results from the idea that homeownership promotes wage labor, stimulates growth of economic markets, and expands social power (Kemeny, 1981; Ball, 1986; Berry, 1986; Marcuse, 1987; Ronald, 2008). The U.S. Department of Commerce (1921) even encouraged children to save money for future home purchase, marketing homeownership as "the stepping stone to advancement and happiness" (p. 9).

Historically, encouragement of widespread homeownership has addressed social problems unrelated to sheltering citizens (Marcuse, 1987; Bratt et al., 2006). Housing policies "were not the beginnings of a benevolent concern for housing the poor; they were a continuation of the use of state power to prevent any disturbance ... of the private conduct of economic affairs" (Marcuse, 1987, p. 252). Many early housing policies boosted national, state, and local economies by curtailing expenditures on health epidemics, fires, poor sanitation, and other effects of tenement overcrowding (Riis, 1903; Vale, 2007). In the wake of early twentieth-century tenement regulations, post-WWI and New Deal policies advanced private sector real estate development and mortgage lending to drive national economic growth. This housing-based economic stimulus persisted in popularity until the Second World War. During the early 1940s, homeownership rates stopped growing, as Americans focused attention and finances on supporting the war effort, but when the war drew to a close, homeownership surged. The 1944 GI Bill provided benefits to eight of every ten men born during the 1920s (Levitan and Cleary, 1973), including the opportunity to purchase homes with zero money down. Thus, this legislation allowed thousands of WWII soldiers to own homes (Collins, 2007).

Through the 1950s, additional policies offered mortgage subsidies to support new housing developments. These housing policies through the first half of the twentieth century fostered a national economy dependent on a growing housing market, rather than promoting a neoliberal focus on social justice or economic security. In turn, Americans became consumed by their desire for homeownership. Baby Boomers, many of whom were raised in homes purchased through the GI Bill, came of age during an era rooted in post-war American Dream ideologies of nuclear family homeownership. This generation was reared to view homeownership as a yardstick for prosperity and success. As a result, these Boomers perpetuated the focus on single-family homeownership from the 1970s through the early 2000s. Despite the 2007 recession and housing market failures, a recent report from the Joint Center for Housing Studies of Harvard University (2011) indicated that Boomers still prioritize homeownership; aging Baby Boomers are expected to increase homeownership rates among those aged 65 and older by 35% between 2010 and 2020.

Current environment

Although homeownership rates are highest among older adults, it is unclear how many senior homeowners are residing in structures that meet their needs effectively. Home structures must be (a) safe, meaning that homes are in good repair and without leaks or related structural concerns; and (b) adequate, meaning that homes meet residents' needs with features like accessible doorways, ramps, or other modifications. Because few federal U.S. policies address home maintenance, few researchers have considered the effects or benefits of home maintenance assistance on aging in community. However, one new study coupled home maintenance with occupational therapy and home healthcare, assigning various combinations of services to older adults (Szanton et al., 2011). For home maintenance, participants received an average of $1,285 in donated materials and labor, including "tightening or adding railings or banisters, gluing floor tiles to make floors flush, installing secure grab bars, repairing front stairs, and tightening carpeting" (p. 2318). Findings relied on self-reported data, but all participants said they benefitted from participation in the program. Unfortunately, decoupled results were unavailable, so data specific to home maintenance benefits were not reported. Still, this small study indicates that the need for home maintenance exists within the population of older adults. Failure to resolve home repair and modification concerns can lead to potential health and safety hazards, such as falls resulting from loose or uneven flooring and a lack of secure grab bars or railings.

Another study found that seniors who had used home maintenance services reported a lower likelihood (50%) of relocating compared to study respondents who had made no home repairs (Tang and Lee, 2010), suggesting that a well-maintained home environment facilitates aging in community. Likewise, a recent study conducted among seniors in five European Union nations evaluated the effects of home environment on aging in place, finding that "the home modification variable emerges as a significant predictor for aging-in-place" (Hwang et al., 2011, p. 253).

Accordingly, existing research highlights the benefits of aging in community for older adults, provided that their lived environments are safe and supportive. Yet, for older adults with fixed incomes, home maintenance costs to ensure structural safety and adequacy may pose an insurmountable financial burden. Gilderbloom and Markham (1996) found that costs of home repair can serve as a barrier to aging in community, resulting in possible relocation. Moreover, this finding suggests that all seniors have a choice in deciding to relocate. In reality, many seniors living in poverty cannot afford to invest in home maintenance, compensate movers, pay real estate professionals, or cover other moving expenses. These low-income seniors may feel trapped in homes that fail to meet their needs, without the option to relocate or improve their housing.

Poverty and federal policies for home maintenance

Current estimates indicate that one-in-six adults aged 65 and over lives in poverty (National Council on Aging, 2011). For many of these low-income seniors, owned homes represent a source of wealth through equity, regardless of whether housing meets older adults' needs as they age (Mitchell and Piggott, 2011). Accordingly, even when homes are inadequate or in need of costly repairs, senior homeowners may feel hesitant to sell their homes, as housing represents their only financial asset. Shapiro (2004) explained that for low-income senior homeowners who typically have no wage earnings and small fixed incomes, home equity represents huge potential to cover emergency costs or pass wealth to the next generation, noting, "Home equity accounts for roughly 44 percent of total measured net worth." In particular, low-income homeowners, including seniors with fixed incomes, may rely primarily on home equity as an emergency fund to cover unexpected costs or maintain a degree of financial security. This reliance on housing may be true particularly for minority and unmarried or nonpartnered seniors. These populations, especially older single women, have greater economic insecurity compared to their non-minority and married or partnered peers (Shapiro, 2004; Meschede et al., 2011a, 2011b). As a result, minority, female, and single older adults may have even greater struggles maintaining their living environments. For these groups, aging in community may become a sentence, rather than a choice or opportunity.

Despite this need for housing assistance to ensure well-maintained living environments, few federal policies or programs support the home maintenance needs of older adults. Among the programs that target home repairs or modifications, most fail to reach older adults, particularly seniors living in urban or suburban communities (Table 45.1).

Like federal homeownership policies, most modification programs historically have served as mechanisms for economic growth. In the early twentieth century, banks accepted the creation of federal homeownership programs, but lenders perceived home maintenance policies as an overstepping of government bounds. Harris (2009) writes of the earliest home maintenance program created in 1934: "[T]he American Bankers Association argued that the FHA [Federal Housing Administration] should get out of the [home] improvement business" (p. 414). Given this early opposition, federal lawmakers opted to focus policies on homeownership, resulting in very few national programs specific to home maintenance.

Table 45.1 Existing U.S. home maintenance policies and programs

Policy/program	Description	Target population	Accessibility
HUD Section 203(k) (created in 1934; revised in 1978)	Rehabilitation mortgage insurance offering better-than-market interest rates for additional financing to cover home repair costs; available for new or refinance loans	Low- and moderate-income homeowners seeking maximum loan amount of $35,000 above standard Federal Housing Administration (FHA) mortgage limit	Applications accepted only through FHA lenders; property value must meet local FHA limits (typically lower than area median prices)
USDA Section 504 (created in 1949)	Provides grants for small, rural home renovation projects and also offers small, low-interest loans for higher-cost projects	Low-wealth rural-dwelling homeowners aged 62 and older; repairs must remove health and safety hazards or modernize the home	Application process completed at local USDA office; USDA staff determine eligibility
USDA Section 502 (created in 1949)	Similar to Section 504 but available to a slightly less poor, rural population	Low- and moderate-wealth rural-dwelling homeowners of any age (income up to 115% of area median)	Application process completed at local USDA office; USDA office staff determine eligibility
USDA Section 533 (created in 1949)	Grants distributed to states, nonprofits, or tribal corporations for use by rural homeowners or rural rental property owners	Organizations obtaining funds must demonstrate how grants will assist rural low-income individuals and minorities; not age-specific	Entities must serve towns with fewer than 20,000 residents; individual access varies by locality
HUD community development block grants (created in 1974)	Flexible block grant program that awards funds to communities to address a variety of local needs	Localities choose their CDBG projects; some may relate to home repair or modification, but projects and target populations vary	Communities choose projects; if home repair funds are available, citizens apply through local HUD offices or partners
HUD home equity conversion mortgages (created in 1989)	Reverse mortgage for senior homeowners to borrow home equity; mortgage values based on borrower age, interest rate, and property value	Homeowners aged 62 and older who own and occupy their homes with little or no remaining mortgage debt; funds can be used for home repairs or anything else	Individuals must meet with a HUD counselor to apply; requirements mirror standard mortgage: fees, application, appraisals, and credit checks
HUD HOME investment partnerships (created in 1990)	Formula grant disbursed to localities to build, purchase, or rehab. affordable housing for rent/sale; 17% of HOME funds went to home rehab. projects from 1992 to 2008	States and localities apply for funds that can be used for loans, grants, or rental, assistance made to very low-income citizens (HUD income limits published annually); not age-specific	States and localities apply for funding; individuals apply through local HUD offices or partners, but application processes differ significantly across locations and programs

Source: GAO, 2005.

Of the seven policies described in Table 45.1, only two programs focus on meeting housing needs for older adults. One program provides assistance only to rural-dwelling senior home-owners, and the other extends mortgage reversion opportunities to older Americans. Reverse mortgages, available to any homeowner aged 62 or older, allow borrowers to take out loans against the equity of an owner-occupied home. Though reverse mortgages may present an opportunity to access wealth for seniors who have few other financial resources, existing adver-tisements and information concerning mortgage reversion can be vague and lacking sufficient details to help seniors make informed decisions (Bercaw, 2014). Accordingly, some older adults may enter into reverse mortgages without understanding the financial implications and hazards, particularly for those seniors living in poverty.

Although federal policies are few in number, some states, localities, and nonprofit organiza-tions offer home maintenance assistance, but as with national programs, these aid opportunities are limited. Homeowners must undergo complex application processes that hinder access, and even when applicants receive initial approval for aid, the months or years spent waiting for assistance may render initial acceptance moot. For certain populations, including low-income seniors who may need immediate aid, indefinite waiting periods may pose an insurmountable barrier to maintaining safe housing.

Local home maintenance assistance: a qualitative example

To explore the current home maintenance assistance opportunities available for seniors who are aging in community, this author completed a series of interviews among a sample of six state and local home maintenance assistance programs in a selected U.S. state.[1] Participants were individuals who provide home modifications and repairs through loans or grants made to homeowners. All interviewees were recruited via email, and additional interviewees were recruited through suggestions from other interviewees (i.e., snowball sampling). A series of broad questions were used to stimulate discussion, including asking what types of services were provided, how individuals participated, and what the overall process of obtaining a home repair or modification would be from start to finish. Other discussion topics focused on exemplar program recipients and problems with existing program designs.[2]

The findings across these six sample home maintenance programs indicated that access to apply for home maintenance assistance is open, though frequency of acceptance is much more limited. Some programs limit homeowners by age or income status, though most programs limit by specific geography, such that applicants must reside within the state, metropolitan area, or specific community to receive assistance. Programs offer either loans funded publicly through state and local appropriations or grants funded privately through charitable donations made to nonprofit providers (Table 45.2).

Organizations varied significantly in the breadth of repairs and modifications that were covered. One organization only administered home maintenance, while another entity offered certain hous-ing-related programs such as fuel assistance or lead abatement in addition to home repairs (Home Modifications Provider 3, 2012; Home Modifications Provider 5, 2012). Other interviewees described myriad tasks completed by their organizations including broad-based architectural design, policy and advocacy work, public housing voucher assistance, and senior services, such as congregate meals and elder transportation assistance (Home Modifications Provider 1, 2012; Home Modifications Provider 2, 2012; Home Modifications Provider 4, 2012; Home Modifications Provider 6, 2012). In sum, all organizations had the common goals of reaching local citizens for aid, but some interviewees described goals that related only to home maintenance and were only for seniors, while others detailed many types of services available to a broader selection of community members.

Table 45.2 A sample of existing local home maintenance policies and programs

Policy/ program	Description	Target population	Accessibility
Local Program 1	Publicly funded loans to make "access modifications" to homes (i.e., all changes must improve safety and accessibility)	All homeowners in the state who need to improve access to their homes to meet the needs of children or adult residents; multi-family and rental properties are not eligible	Applications are reviewed on a case-by-case basis; no-interest loans are available to low-income homeowners, and low-interest loans are available for higher-income homeowners
Local Program 2	Nonprofit organization that offers very small (<$1,000) grants to homeowners for minor repairs (e.g., replacement of a broken oven)	Low-income, senior homeowners residing in specific neighborhoods served by the local nonprofit organization; need determined case-by-case and based on availability of funding	Nonprofit uses donations to cover costs up-front; after work is completed, the organization requests city reimbursement through a separate grant
Local Program 3	Publicly funded loans distributed to individual homeowners on a case-by-case basis	Available to any single-family homeowner within one specific community; applicant must present income verification to determine eligibility for no-interest vs. low-interest loans	Individuals apply for assistance, and applications are reviewed, presented to a Board, and require property inspections before obtaining approval; on-site project management from funder also required; no-interest loans are available to low-income homeowners, and low-interest loans are available for higher incomes
Local Program 4	Publicly funded loans distributed to individual homeowners, but based on project types that specifically improve health and safety	All single-family homeowners in the state; applicant must present income verification to determine eligibility for no-interest vs. low-interest loans	Applications are determined based on type and purpose of home repair needed; no-interest loans are available to low-income homeowners, and low-interest loans are available for higher-income homeowners
Local Program 5	Nonprofit organization that provides grants for any type of home or office repair project	Low-income homeowners, homeowners with special needs, certain organizations that serve low-income or special needs individuals; all state residents eligible	Project applications require a lengthy review process that follows HUD guidelines, though not HUD-funded; if accepted, project completion is contingent on charitable donations, so repairs may take months or years
Local Program 6	Nonprofit organization that provides small grants and design assistance for projects that meet specific accessibility requirements (e.g., universal design)	All homeowners or rental property owners in the state may apply for design assistance; grants offered to only a few low-income homeowners	Grants are available on a case-by-case basis to homeowners with financial need, but organization staff can help with design ideas for any homeowner or rental property owner

Accordingly, annual assistance rates also varied from fewer than ten projects annually to more than 300, though no organization indicated it had completed more than 350 projects in the previous year. There appeared to be a correlation between smaller numbers of assistance recipients and funding volume, such that programs helping fewer individuals extended larger loans or grants. For example, the program that helped over 300 consumers capped its grants at no more than $1,000 per homeowner, while the organization that helped fewer than ten homeowners in the previous year extended loans of over $50,000 to each recipient (Home Modifications Provider 2, 2012; Home Modifications Provider 4, 2012).

These funding limitations also resulted in significant service provision delays; one interviewee said about the timeline for repairing a home, "It could be a month or two months; it could be a year, or it could be never" (Home Modifications Provider 5, 2012). Another interviewee explained that although an organization may have a prolonged process for providing home maintenance, the wait may be beneficial in the long-run, resulting in provision of more services: "We facilitate the entire rehab from beginning to end with the homeowner to ensure that compliance issues are met and oversight is there, so that the homeowner doesn't have to do it on their own" (Home Modifications Provider 3, 2012). This full-service format may be help-ful, especially for low-income seniors or others who have limited access to resources needed to ensure effective repairs. Yet, one must also question whether such homeowners have the awareness to ensure that their loan structures meet their short- and long-term needs.

In discussing lending practices with organizations that are loan-based, one interviewee was asked if these loans function in a way that is similar to reverse mortgages, allowing homeowners to bor-row against the existing equity in or value of their homes. The interviewee explained that a lien is placed on the home until the debt is repaid, similar to mortgage reversion. However, unlike reverse mortgages that require disclosure of financial records and home appraisals to evaluate loan eligibility, income is the only criterion used in determining eligibility for home maintenance assistance.

> We don't know what the equity is when we make the loan because we don't ask. We don't know what their credit score is. We do not have the same kind of financial scrutiny that any traditional loan would require from a bank. The only thing that we use to determine the type of loan that someone would be eligible for is their gross income. So yes, in some ways we are borrowing against the equity of the home, but we have no idea if they actually have equity.
>
> (Home Modifications Provider 4, 2012)

Another organization explained a similar process of ignoring home equity, home value, credit, or other typical means of determining loan eligibility. The interviewee said that the organiza-tion "documents income eligibility, that you're a homeowner, that you're the only person on the deed to the home, can't have a reverse mortgage, and can't have outstanding bills or taxes" (Home Modifications Provider 2, 2012). These interviewees added that default rates have been very low, but extending loans without knowledge of repayment ability or investment value seems like an unscrupulous practice for both lenders and borrowers. Particularly in the case of older homeowners aging in community, this lack of scrutiny could result in unpaid debts or loans that outlast homeowners, thus transferring liability to homeowners' surviving families and resulting in repossession of the home by the lending agency.

The future of aging in community

While this small sample of state and local home maintenance assistance programs certainly cannot encompass descriptions of policies and programs available nationwide, these interviews provide insight into the need for home repairs and modifications, particularly among low-income seniors who may be aging in community by necessity. Coupled with the narrow list of federal home maintenance policies and the growing population of seniors, the unmet need for home maintenance among older adults seems to be increasing. Assistance with other aspects of aging in community, such as transportation, healthcare, and civic engagement, have been and are being addressed through various federal, state, and local initiatives, yet housing has remained below the policy radar.

As Baby Boomers retire, development of more supports will be necessary to facilitate aging in community as a positive opportunity for seniors across wealth levels, rather than a choice for higher-income seniors and the only option for older adults living in poverty. In particular, more research is required to explore the current extent of need for home maintenance assistance among older homeowners, as well as projected repair and modification needs for the coming decades. Additional research will define the breadth and depth of need for home maintenance towards developing socially just and economically viable policies and programs that facilitate aging in community.

Notes

1 This research project was completed with guidance from Cornelia Kammerer, Ph.D.; exact locations, programs, organizations, and names for these 2012 interviews have been masked to ensure anonymity in compliance with research approval from the Institutional Review Board at Brandeis University.

2 Interviews were recorded with a digital audio recorder and were transcribed using a mixture of verbatim and thematic transcription methods. Riessman (2008) explains that a thematic analysis evaluates interviews as a whole to identify key ideas, rather than dissecting sentences or phrases to find meaning in their constituent parts. Accordingly, a process of thematic transcription and analyses was used for evaluating overall ideas and concepts across interviews.

References

American Association of Retired Persons (AARP). (2000). *Fixing to stay: A national survey on housing and home modification issues*. Washington, DC: AARP.

American Association of Retired Persons (AARP). (2010). *Home and community preferences of the 45+ population*. Washington, DC: AARP.

Ball, M. (1986). *Home ownership: A suitable case for reform*. London: Shelter.

Bercaw, L.E. (2014). From house to poorhouse: An analysis of reverse mortgage portrayal in selected media advertisements. *Journal of Poverty*, 18(2), 150–168.

Berry, M. (1986). Housing provision and class relations under capitalism. *Housing Studies*, 1(2), 109–121.

Bratt, R.G., Stone, M.E., and Hartman, C. (2006). Introduction. In R.G. Bratt, M.E. Stone, and C. Hartman (eds), *A right to housing: Foundation for a new social agenda* (pp. 279–295). Philadelphia, PA: Temple University Press.

Center for Housing Policy. (2012). *Housing an aging population: Are we prepared?* Washington, DC: National Housing Conference and Center for Housing Policy.

Collins, M. (2007). Federal policies promoting homeownership: Separating the accidental from the strategic. In W.M. Rohe and H.L. Watson (eds), *Chasing the American dream: New perspectives on affordable homeownership* (pp. 69–95). Ithaca, NY: Cornell University Press.

Gilderbloom, J.I. and Markham, J.P. (1996). Housing modification need of the disabled elderly: What really matters? *Environment and Behavior*, 28, 512–535.

Government Accountability Office (GAO). (2005, Feb. 14). *Elderly housing: Federal Housing programs that offer assistance to the elderly* (GAO-05-174). Retrieved November 10, 2012 from http://www.gao.gov/products/GAO-05-174.

Harris, R. (2009). A new form of credit: The state promotes home improvement, 1934–1954. *Journal of Policy History*, 21(4), 392–423.

Home Modifications Provider 1 (2012, January 10). Personal interview.

Home Modifications Provider 2 (2012, January 13). Personal interview.

Home Modifications Provider 3 (2012, January 13). Personal interview.

Home Modifications Provider 4 (2012, January 19). Personal interview.

Home Modifications Provider 5 (2012, February 3). Telephone interview.

Home Modifications Provider 6 (2012, February 13). Personal interview.

Hwang, E., Cummings, L., Sixsmith, A., and Sixsmith, J. (2011). Impacts of home modifications on aging-in-place. *Journal of Housing for the Elderly*, 25(3), 246–257.

Joint Center for Housing Studies of Harvard University (JCHS). (2011). *The state of the nation's housing, 2011.* Cambridge, MA: Harvard University.

Kemeny, J. (1981). *The myth of home ownership: Public versus private choices in housing tenure.* London: Routledge.

Levitan, S. and Cleary, K. (1973). *When old wars remain unfinished.* Baltimore, MD: Johns Hopkins University Press.

Marcuse, P. (1987). The other side of housing: Oppression and liberation. In B. Turner, J. Kemeny, and L. Lundqvist (eds), *Between states and markets: Housing in the post-industrial era* (pp. 232–270). Stockholm: Almqvist and Wiksell International.

Meschede, T., Cronin, M., Sullivan, L., and Shapiro, T. (2011a). *Rising economic insecurity among senior single women.* The Institute on Assets and Social Policy, Heller School, Brandeis University and Demos, New York.

Meschede, T., Cronin, M., Sullivan, L., and Shapiro, T. (2011b). *The crisis of economic insecurity for African-American and Latino seniors.* The Institute on Assets and Social Policy, Heller School, Brandeis University and Demos, New York.

Mitchell, O.S. and Piggott, J. (2011). Housing wealth among the elderly. In V.B. Bhuyan (ed.), *Reverse mortgages and linked securities: The complete guide to risk, pricing, and regulation* (pp. 149–160). Hoboken, NJ: John Wiley and Sons, Inc.

National Council on Aging (2011, January 24). *One in six seniors lives in poverty, new analysis finds.* Retrieved November 10, 2012 from http://www.ncoa.org/press-room/press-release/one-in-six-seniors-lives-in.html.

Riessman, C.K. (2008). *Narrative methods for the human sciences.* Thousand Oaks, CA: Sage Publications, Inc.

Riis, J. (1903). *The peril and the preservation of the home.* Philadelphia: George W. Jacobs, Co.

Rohe, W.M. and Watson, H.L. (2007). Introduction: Homeownership in American culture and public policy. In W.M. Rohe and H.L. Watson (eds), *Chasing the American dream: New perspectives on affordable homeownership* (pp. 1–14). Ithaca, NY: Cornell University Press.

Ronald, R. (2008). *The ideology of home ownership: Homeowner societies and the role of housing.* New York: Palgrave Macmillan.

Shapiro, T.M. (2004). *The hidden cost of being African American: How wealth perpetuates inequality.* New York: Oxford University Press.

Szanton, S.L., Thorpe, R.J., Boyd, C., Tanner, E.K., Leff, B., Agree, E., Xue, Q.L., Allen, J.K., Seplaki, C.L., Weiss, C.O., Guralnik, J.M., and Gitlin, L.N. (2011). Community aging in place, advancing better living for elders: A bio-behavioral-environmental intervention to improve function and health-related quality of life in disabled older adults. *Journal of the American Geriatrics Society*, 59(12), 2314–2320.

Tang, F. and Lee, Y. (2010). Home- and community-based services utilization and aging-in-place. *Home Health Care Services Quarterly*, 29(3), 138–154.

U.S. Department of Commerce. (1921). *Own your own home: A handbook for prospective home owners.* Washington, DC: Government Printing Office.

Vale, L.J. (2007). The ideological origins of affordable homeownership efforts. In W.M. Rohe and H.L. Watson (eds), *Chasing the American dream: New perspectives on affordable homeownership* (pp. 15–40). Ithaca, NY: Cornell University Press.

Vasunilashorn, S., Steinman, B.A., Liebig, P.S., and Pynoos, J. (2012). Aging in place: Evolution of a research topic whose time has come. *Journal of Aging Research*, 59(12), 2314–2320. Retrieved November 17, 2012 from http://www.hindawi.com/journals/jar/2012/120952/cta/.

46

POVERTY, HEALTH, AND ASIAN NON-LINEARITY

Shweta Singh, Shveta Kumaria, and Kathryn Berg

Introduction

Immigrants' health and access to services are submerged sometimes within the discussion on acculturation. Norms and practices and behavior patterns of groups and individuals influence immigrant health through myriad pathways that are difficult to predict because of the structural contexts of poverty and discrimination (Virvell-Fuentes et al., 2012). The focus on immigrants is compounded through questions that frame access and utilization of health services as a function of behavior, culture, and minority status. The limiting role of post-liberal economics in health processes and outcomes through its universal conceptualization of personhood and self-care remains underexplored. Additionally the cost-conscious health policy not only excludes the cultural ethos of construction of self but also conceptualizes health as a narrowly constructed idiom of absence of disease. In this way it contributes to defining health and health care in a disengagement of the self with services approach that reduces the consumption of health services.

This chapter explores the neoliberal economic policy as more than a source of income inequality and relative poverty in reference to the complex health care needs of Asian women in the diaspora. The first section theorizes on the conceptualization of health and personhood in liberal economic policy. The second section showcases the cultural roots of differences in women from Asia. The third section presents the limitations of the existing research embodying disconnect of concerns and the people. The fourth section discusses the access argument offered by neoliberal health planning and smaller models in the community that showcase that access issues can be addressed. The chapter concludes with identifying a need for health to be a social commitment rather than a liberal economics-defined privilege driven by an individual enterprise of self-care.

Conceptualizing health and personhood in liberal economic policy

The overtaking of political, social, and cultural decision-making by the market has been a transition from liberal to neoliberal economics. The market is no longer peripheral to our lives as a system of exchange of goods and services only; instead it serves as the locus, director, and the gate keeper of what ideas will find space as universally sound and which will be derided as cultural backwardness. Beyond the visible maintenance of law and order, everything else about a human life and capacity is now a decision made by the market and its needs; development has long been a euphemism for cost effectiveness and value-added paradigms that focus on building a better consumer. In this derivative, personhood is conceptualized as the informed, purchasing power-equipped consumer that supports the market and its productivity rather than the right to survive of all human beings. Instead of the philosophically oriented discussions on life, education, and social justice underlying health, the focus shifts to measurements and assessments of dollars spent in health care services provision. As community spirit and social care cost more than money, they take time away from a productivity-oriented individual and also distract from a consumer identity; these are vilified as traditionalist norms that subjugate individuality. The absence of community and limited and broken family structures result in mental distress and physical manifestations of poor health, but since health in neoliberal economics does not quantify happiness or enhanced wellbeing, it is not a problem till it intrudes on consumer identity that cannot retain a job or a home or a functional family. The neoliberal economist conceives a society of global communities that exist beyond boundaries through a universal thread of values that celebrate diversity and yet refuse to acknowledge its manifestations or its legitimacy to function as such.

Cultural variance

The commonality of values is presumed rather than explored even with evidence to the contrary. "Immigrant and refugee women are at risk for mental health problems due to their possible experiences of minority status, marginalization, intolerable memories, socio-economic disadvantage, poor physical health and difficulty adapting to host cultures" (O'Mahony and Donnelly, 2010, p. 919). This acculturation process exacerbates loss and grief related to the past and uncertainty about the future, leading to mental health issues like stress, anxiety, and depression (Dhooper and Tran, 1998). The idea of one Asian and its ethnocultural dimensions is perpetuated for neoliberal efficiency and justification of one-dimensional health information and health maintenance opportunities (Sadler et al., 2003, p. 1). Even the pathways and transition points within migration history and language competencies are disregarded. The existing research on immigrants fails to recognize the social and cultural context, the within group and across group difference, and the diverse social locations of ethnic minorities that creates variance in access to health care services and limits its outreach to immigrant Asian women. Bhattacharya (2004), in her study on health care seeking for HIV/AIDS among South Asians in the United States, outlines the importance of country of origin, degree of acculturation, immigration status, socio-economic level, and familial factors while developing effective interventions for and with South Asian immigrants.

These differences are most apparent in the construction of family itself as a complex institution of support and oppression that informs the South Asian identity. Within the diaspora, expectation from South Asian women is to conform to traditional roles, even more so than the women left behind in the subcontinent (Dasgupta, 1998). In Asian cultures, suffering as a part of human life and controlling excessive emotions are honored values (Dasgupta, 1998; Dhooper and Tran, 1998). This is truer in interpersonal conflict where cultural conceptions might inhibit sharing of incidence with people outside the family (for fear of bringing shame to the group). Lu et al. (2012) struggled to find participants for her study on reproductive health due to cultural taboos regarding sexual topics. Research by Spencer et al. (2010) found that East Asian Americans who perceived a need for mental health services were less likely to seek them, even when health insurance did not present a barrier. When diagnosed with a mental disorder by their primary health care physician, East Asians tend to avoid mental health services because of the stigma associated with mental illness and that emotional symptoms are considered a part of physical illness (Nguyen et al., 2012).

The data from the Centers for Disease Control and Prevention (CDC) highlights the differences in access and use of health services by women from Asia. Their marital status, employment status, and other variables are not clearly predictors of health choices and access to service choices. Cultural norms and community contexts are not given importance in planning, and these types of data remain under-studied.

Asian immigrant and health research

The disconnection between the specific health care needs of South Asian immigrants is reflected in the narrow focus of research. The limitations of sampling frameworks is compounded by missing theoretical foundations. The health concerns of majority populations are more marketable and have a wider consumer base, which explains the emphasis on breast cancer, polycystic ovary syndrome (PCOS), hypertension, coronary heart disease, osteoporosis, and HIV/AIDS. Whereas Frye (1995) discusses the "initial concerns" (p. 274) of South East Asian refugees as namely tuberculosis, anemia, and hepatitis B in health concerns, mental health issues like PTSD (posttraumatic stress disorder), depression, and anxiety are amongst those "emerging" but not adequately addressed. Derose et al. (2009) argue that "it is not surprising that these studies follow the patterns for health insurance and regular source of care" (p. 364). The research is not likely to be funded for study of immigrant diseases like tuberculosis as neoliberal economics prioritizes the advent of a healthy immigrant worker who can be productive, not one that needs treatment.

East Asian immigrants are not only underrepresented but also misrepresented in the literature on health concerns and access to health care. In framing research questions and designs, the ideal identity of the immigrant worker cannot be questioned, hence the discussion of this significant population remains hidden. Nguyen et al. (2012) note an underrepresentation of Asian Americans in clinical trials of psychotherapeutic interventions intended to represent the general population. This suggests negligence on the part of researchers in ensuring that empirically supported treatments reflect the interests of Asian consumers. Lin-Fu (1988) identified another oversight which has compromised literature about Americans of Asian heritage: a history of racial misclassification on death certificates. A study of California data revealed that both Japanese and Chinese infant mortality rates were misleadingly low as a consequence of this misclassification.

Some researchers have in the past clearly outlined specific health care needs for health care providers to know, in order to meet the needs of Asian American populations adequately. Lin-Fu (1988) noted that Asian Americans have a chronic carrier state for hepatitis B, which predisposes these populations to hepatoma and cirrhosis. The rate of Asian women having a Pap test within the past three years would be lower than all other racial ethnic groups in the United States (Yu et al., 2010). This is an issue of concern because although they have lower rates of breast cancer, the risk increases proportionate to their time spent in the United States (Sadler et al., 2003). There is variance in this pattern based on age and ethnicity, with Japanese Americans reporting the highest rate of annual mammography (72%) and Korean Americans the lowest rate (22%). In this instance, these two East Asian countries represent extreme differences in screening rates. Research on the determinants of this trend, in addition to Pap test use, could shed light on the reasons for the differential usage and therefore provide prevention strategies tailored to the specific ethnicities.

Issues in service access

The typical explanations for South Asian women's limited access, quality, and outcomes of health are explanations designed to blame the client groups. Similar to poverty sub-culture, these are compounded by a cultural mismatch argument that includes limited English proficiency and lack of familiarity with the U.S. health care system (Bhattacharya, 2004; Derose et al., 2009). Factors such as the impact of immigrant absorption in the low wage, unmonitored labor market and harmful conditions, in sectors that do not provide benefits like health insurance, remain outside the discussion regarding the access and use of health services. In particular the issue of legal identity and work authorization that puts immigrants from Latin America and South East Asia at risk (compared to U.S.-born and other immigrants) is often disregarded. Crucial factors of employment, migration, and nature of immigration (e.g., refugees, professionals, and spouses of professionals), the financial status of the family, and interactions of gender, socio-economics, and immigration status are not readily employed as control factors. This also adversely affected the development of informed policies with respect to immigrant women (Thurston et al., 2006). Many employed East Asian Americans do not have health insurance as compared to Americans in the United States (Kim and Keefe, 2010). For undocumented immigrants, an illegal status exacerbates health access issues by denying access to any form of health insurance.

For women, discrimination is experienced both institutionally as well as at home. Dhooper and Tran (1998) have classified the hurdles that immigrants face in accessing health care into patient-related factors (cultural), social environmental factors (economic), and the nature of the health care system in the host country. A recent study on metropolitan South Asian immigrant women in Toronto found that 75% of the women in the sample had a regular family physician, yet 85% had never had a screening mammogram (Ahmad et al., 2012). The cluster of barriers to screening mammography for this sample were: lack of knowledge (about breast cancer), fear of cancer, language and transportation, self-care, popular beliefs and practices, access to doctor, preferences, and systems, ease of access to mammogram centers, and dependence on family. The unique cluster of "dependence on family" brought out the issues of elderly, financially dependent immigrant women, who have language difficulties and a specific cultural nuance of "not wanting to be a burden on their children (so not accessing health services in spite of knowledge about the same)." This deep concern for others and spirit of "sacrifice" as a revered gender value in Asian cultures is recognized as a barrier to access. Health care is a collective decision rather than individual, and the role of the community and males of the family is important when planning outreach programs for South Asian women (Ahmad et al., 2012; Grewal et al., 2005). The family angle in health care is the least important in neoliberal economics as it requires facilitation of collectivist values that contradicts neoliberal thinking. The collectivism and family-oriented household model of economics contradicts the individualist mantra as a requirement of competitive human growth and progress. The household remains an uncharted territory for predicting wellbeing. For instance, additional obstacles arise when working with East Asian immigrants who are illiterate in their own language (Lin-Fu, 1988). This is addressed by placing a child in the position of making health care decisions and limits effective communications with health care providers (Kim and Keefe, 2010).

The stigmatization of mental illness and seeking of psychiatric help continues, and often the mental health of South Asian immigrants is "ill-identified" due to the unfamiliar cultural context. Informal social support from family members and close acquaintances is the first avenue for Asian communities instead of a trained health care worker. Many Asian Americans use alternative forms of health care that they turn to instead of medical care (Ye et al., 2012). In addition, they sometimes have erroneous information about diseases and low health literacy. The paradoxes of health research and the reality of Asians are apparent in the documented rates of mental health disorders. Nguyen et al. (2012) found that Asians have a lower presence of mental health disorders overall. However, adolescent females between the ages of 14 and 24 have the highest suicide rates in their age range, as do older women. The vulnerable women who accompany men from professional classes are treated as a liability by the market—therefore their access to employment, independence, and creating independent resources is blocked, not facilitated. The dependence, isolation, and resultant depression and anxiety are not studied, thus further reducing their access to specific intervention and support within health care systems.

Successful models in community health delivery

Low-cost examples of community-based models exist but are not replicated widely. When outreach and community-based efforts—including providing transport to and from the health centers; involving other members of the family; using link workers who can help with the language barriers; and providing translated literature—are used, health-related interventions for South Asian women have been found to be successful.

Immigrant women invited for breast cancer screening in inner city Cardiff responded positively to a multilingual information leaflet, translated screening invitation, and translated personalized GP endorsement letter. Provision of transport to and from the screening center was however under-utilized. Link workers and interpreters were an integral part of the process (Bell et al., 1999). Suthahar (2005) found higher acculturation levels had a positive effect on the recognition of mental illness by South Asian women and the identification of referral sources for those identified. "It also adds weight to the 'culture retentionist argument' by providing support for increased belief and reliance on religious and cultural values and the role of family and kin network for general support and sustenance" (Suthahar, 2005, p. 124).

A recent mixed-method study, using the community participatory approach, found many of the participants in their study on "barriers to mammography screenings" went for a screening mammogram after joining the study (Ahmad et al., 2012). One of the important findings of this study was that transport and language barriers, in the study's sample of women who were 50 years and above, was one of the predominant hurdles to accessing services. The collaborating agency in the study committed to addressing the transportation issue by launching a shuttle bus program after the study. The researchers advise "Future research should examine variations in the effectiveness of health promotion programs among recent and established immigrants whom may need different approaches for optimal success" (p. 248).

Ethnic matching between client and service provider can be beneficial. Nguyen et al. (2012) found that ethnic matching increases the retention of Asian American consumers. True (1990) recommends that Asian American female therapists can play a unique role for clients of the same gender and ethnicity, both by serving as a role model and by demonstrating strong sensitivity to their clients' experiences. Lu et al. (2012) also report that a combination of supports, including group education, assistance in scheduling, and culturally sensitive audiovisual materials, has successfully increased breast cancer screening rates among Korean Americans. In a large-scale study titled "The Asian Grocery Store-Based Cancer Education Program" (Sadler et al., 2003), the importance of culturally and linguistically relevant messages to each ethnic group (among Asians) was seen as the important factor in developing strategies to reduce health disparities and promote health equity. This study speaks to the assumption of homogeneity in the Pan Asian community, which disregards the dissimilarities among the cultural subgroups, contributing to health disparities within and among the subgroups.

Active engagement of family members is very important when planning outreach programs for South Asian women (Ahmad et al., 2012). Tanjasiri et al. (2007) found that involving men in breast cancer awareness workshops (held separately for both men and women) changed men's belief that they should support women's screening visits. Various approaches to wraparound services have also been successful in reaching East Asian American women. In

San Francisco's Chinatown, a drop-in child care program combined with services for parents (e.g., parent education, counseling, and support services) has been effective. It reaches mothers who need childcare and/or would find a mental health clinic unapproachable (True, 1990).

Shakil et al. (2010), in their study on screening for osteoporosis, blamed lack of health education for why South Asian women don't access health resources. Had the authors used a socio-economic explanation (e.g., 34% of the sample did not have any medical insurance) rather than cultural reductionism, it would have led to more insight on issues such as South Asian women and access to health care. The research, however, was a community-based intervention and, as a consequence of the education on osteoporosis, the sample showed a significant difference on a post-test rating after two weeks.

Conclusion

A lack of focus on the systemic and structural factors tends to result in blaming individual women (and their culture) for their own poor health, or for failing to take responsibility for prevention of illnesses (Habib, 2012). A focus on cultural barriers distracts from systemic and structural barriers in society. In conclusion, we can say that in a lot of studies on immigrant South Asian women the focus is on cultural explanations rather than it being one of the many contextual aspects that influences the lives of these women.

The argument between liberal and conservative care perspectives on health care dates back many years in the United States. The initiative of the Obama Government making health care a universal right and its provision as a government responsibility through the Patient Protection and Affordable Care Act of 2010 is applaudable. However, there remains room to identify health, health care, and health outcomes as beyond those of economic considerations and to explore the underlying cultural articulation of meanings of health and pathways and philosophies that increase access to services for this underserved group. The discussion of health care without discussion of social inequity is incomplete (Coburn, 2004). Market and global norms cannot be a good platform for developing health care and healthy individuals. Health needs to be framed as a right, and poverty seen as a deterrent to health. Without addressing the issues of poverty and marginalization from social institutions, the discussion of health remains unconvincing.

The neoliberal market has enhanced the life of people with resources through development of sophisticated technological advancements but reduced access to basic health and needs for the larger, poorer populations. By laying the responsibility of everything on the individua,l the market presumes a basic capacity in all people, and using the same logic it does not invest any resources in planning access to health. The marginalization of immigrant Asians from policy is ensured by their absence in research and the fact that their health concerns are not a part of problem definitions or service solutions. Just like the discussion on poverty is lost in market theory-based consumption and production patterns, the health argument is lost in discussions of disease. Health needs a definition from empirical and cultural and contextual dimensions.

References

Ahmad, F., Mahmood, S., Pietkiewicz, I., McDonald, L., and Ginsburg, O. (2012). Concept mapping with South Asian immigrant women: Barriers to mammography and solutions. *Journal of Immigrant Minority Health*, 14, 242–250.

Bell, T. S., Branston, L. K., Newcombe, R. G., and Barton, G. R. (1999). Interventions to improve the uptake of breast screening in inner city Cardiff general practices with ethnic minority lists. *Ethnicity and Health*, 4, 277–284.

Bhattacharya, G. (2004). Health care seeking for HIV/AIDS among South Asians in the United States. *Health and Social Work*, 29, 106–114.

Coburn, D. (2004). Beyond the income inequality hypothesis: Class, neo-liberalism, and health inequalities. *Social Science and Medicine*, 58, 41–56.

Dasgupta, S. (1998). *A Patchwork Shawl: Chronicles of South Asian Women in America*. New Brunswick, NJ: Rutgers University Press.

Derose, K. P., Bahney, B. W., Lurie, N., and Escarce, J. J. (2009). Review: Immigrants and health care access, quality, and cost. *Medical Care Research and Review*, 66, 355–408.

Dhooper, S. S., and Tran, T. V. (1998). Understanding and responding to the health and mental health needs of Asian refugees. *Social Work in Health Care*, 27, 65–82.

Fyre, B.A. (1995). Use of cultural themes in promoting health among Southeast Asian refugees. American *Journal of Health Promotion*, 9, 269–280.

Grewal, S., Bottor, J. L., and Hilton, A. B. (2005). The influence of family on immigrant South Asian women's health. *Journal of Family Nursing*, 11, 242–263.

Habib, S. Z. (2012). *South Asian immigrant women's access to and experiences with breast and cervical cancer screening services in Canada*. Unpublished doctoral thesis. The University of British Columbia, Canada.

Kim, W., and Keefe, R. H. (2010). Barriers to healthcare among Asian Americans. *Social Work in Public Health*, 25, 286–295.

Lin-Fu, J. S. (1988). Population characteristics and health care needs of Asian Pacific Americans. *Public Health Reports*, 18–26.

Lu, M., Moritz, S., Lorenzetti, D., Sykes, L., Straus, S., and Quan, H. (2012). A systematic review of interventions to increase breast and cervical screening uptake among Asian women. *BioMed Central Public Health*, 12, 413–428. http://www.biomedcentral.com/1471-2458/12/413.

Nguyen, D., Shibusawa, T., and Chen, M. T. (2012). The evolution of community mental health services in Asian American communities. *Clinical Social Work Journal*, 40, 134–143.

O'Mahony, J., and Donnelly, T. (2010). Immigrant and refugee women's post-partum depression help-seeking experiences and access to care: A review and analysis of the literature. *Journal of Psychiatric and Mental Health Nursing*, 17, 917–928.

Sadler, G. R., Ryujin, L., Nguyen, T., Oh, G., Paik, G., and Kustin, B. (2003). Heterogeneity within the Asian American community. *International Journal for Equity in Health*, 2, 12–29.

Shakil, A., Gimpel, N. E., Rizvi, H., Siddiqui, Z., Ohagi, E., Billmeier, T. M., and Foster, B. (2010). Awareness and prevention of osteoporosis among South Asian women. *Journal of Community Health*, 35, 392–397.

Spencer, M. S., Chen, J., Gee, G. C., Fabian, C. G., and Takeuchi, D. T. (2010). Discrimination and mental health-related service use in a national study of Asian Americans. *American Journal of Public Health*, 100, 2410–2417.

Suthahar, J. (2005). *Asian Indian women and their views on mental health*. Unpublished master's thesis. University of Nevada, Reno.

Tanjasari, S. P., Kawaga-Singer, M., Foo, M. A., Chao, M., Linayao-Putman, I., and Nguyen, T. (2007). Designing culturally and linguistically appropriate health interventions: The "life is precious" Hmong breast cancer study. *Health Education and Behavior*, 34, 140–153.

Thurston, W., Meadows, L., Este, D., and Eisner, A. (2006). The interplay of gender, migration, socio economics and health, PMC working paper series PCERII, Prairie Metropolitan Center. Retrieved August 19, 2014, from http://www.ualberta.ca/~pcerii/WorkingPapers/WP04-06.pdf.

True, R. H. (1990). Psychotherapeutic issues with Asian American women. *Sex Roles*, 22, 477–486.

Viruell-Fuentes, E. A., Miranda, P. A., and Abdulrahim, S. (2012). More than culture: Structural racism, intersectionality theory, and immigrant health. *Social Science and Medicine*, 75, 2099–2106.

Ye, J., Mack, D., Fry-Johnson, Y., and Parker, K. (2012). Health care access and utilization among U.S.-born and foreign-born Asian Americans. *Journal of Immigrant and Minority Health*, 14, 731–737.

Yu, T., Chou, C., Johnson, P. J., and Ward, A. (2010). Persistent disparities in Pap test use: Assessments and predictions for Asian women in the U.S., 1982–2010. *Journal of Immigrant and Minority Health*, 12, 445–453.

PART V

Organizing to resist neoliberal policies and poverty

Activism and advocacy

INTRODUCTION

Reuben Jonathan Miller and Jennifer Miller

> The great struggles of the twentieth century between liberty and totalitarianism ended with a decisive victory for the forces of freedom—a single sustainable model for national success: freedom, democracy and free enterprise.
>
> (President George Walker Bush, 2002)

> The most important—and unfortunately the least debated—issue in politics today is our society's steady drift toward a class-based system, the likes of which we have not seen since the 19th century.
>
> (Web, 2006)

In a forum on the Future of Black Politics (Dawson, 2011) Robin D.G. Kelley writes, "neoliberalism is a more powerful foe than just about anything we've seen before" (Kelley, 2012). Exhibiting its elusiveness and resistance to challenge, Kelley continues:

> The movements to which we often look for models enjoyed a kind of moral authority and operated at a time when the federal government at least pretended to bend toward social justice and enfranchisement ... [Even in the face of market failure] neoliberal ideology remains resilient, seeping into the collective unconscious of even those with good intentions.
>
> (Kelley, 2012)

These assertions are hard to dispute. As a "path dependent," "mongrel," and "promiscuous" concept used more among academics and activists than proponents of neoliberal social and economic policy (Peck, 2010), the neoliberal revolution is at once ubiquitous and invisible. It is envisioned by "neo-classical" economists as a return to free market rule and broad merit-based opportunity, and has risen, through contestation and redefinition, to become the dominant policy logic of the current age (Harvey, 2005; Klein, 2006; Peck, 2010). Neoliberalism has come to stand in as the dominant *mode of governance* thought to ensure market stability, even in the face of market failure due to its enactment, and a *policy logic* that frames nearly all forms of state intervention in light of what's best for the health of the market. It is at once a *policy program* that re-regulates the lives of the poorest and most marginalized denizens of the nation state, and the "new planetary vulgate," to borrow the term from Bourdieu and Wacquant (2001), that has redefined freedom, justifying "laissez faire" economic policies for the most privileged caste of the financialized economy.

As a technique of governance hostile toward collectivist action, neoliberalism is also a discursive strategy used to justify economic reform in ways that are resistant to coalition building. Thus, in "La Sociologie est un sport du combat" (Sociology is a Combat Sport), a popular documentary on his work, renowned sociologist Pierre Bourdieu remarked:

> I think the neoliberal revolution is a conservative revolution. It is a revolution which seems to return to the past and yet it dresses itself as progressive. Regression is turned into progress, so that those that fight this regression seem to be regressive themselves, [and] those who fight terror look themselves like terrorists.

Following this logic, we can see how through processes of neoliberalization the very field of political action has been redefined. Social actors who have historically resisted the "tyranny" of markets, and reimagined alternative, more egalitarian futures, are viewed as angry relics from a time of social unrest, who resist the progress of the period. The language of meritocracy and the logic of market rule has rendered human capital investment as the dominant community development strategy, while the "cultural trope of personal responsibility" associated with the ascendance of neoliberalism has taken the labor market itself off the table as a space of intervention, along with traditional strategies of resistance. Trading welfarist interventions that ensure the health and wellbeing of marginalized groups for the promise of broad-based prosperity through trickle-down economic policy, "identity politics" (based on race, religion, class, gender, sexuality, or some other category of difference) that once allowed for broad-based mobilization are re-cast in a regressive light (Duggan, 2005).

The poor are thought to be poor because of their choices, their irresponsibility, and their refusal to work or improve their lives. This is despite nearly a century of social scientific evidence that the poor overwhelmingly work and that systems that ensure the stability of others are simply inaccessible to them. In a free market economy thought to "lift all boats," even minimalist state intervention is believed to restrain the economy and harm the population as a whole. Given record income inequality and the condition of poor people in the United States highlighted in this Handbook, what, then, is to be done about the current state of affairs? How can impoverished communities resist the erosion of social citizenship in a world that is "post-civil rights," "post-welfare," "post-racial," and "post-identity"?

Political theorists consistently remind us that maintaining these "post" identifiers is key to effective resistance in this neoliberal moment, despite assertions otherwise. At the same time advocates must keep their eyes open for opportunities for broad-based coalition building. To this end, political scientist Lisa Duggan writes:

> Neoliberalism was constructed in and through cultural and identity politics and cannot be undone by a movement without constituencies and analysis that respond directly to that fact. Nor will it be possible to build a new social movement that might be strong, creative and diverse enough to engage the work of reinventing global politics for the new millennium as long as cultural and identity issues are separated, analytically and organizationally, from the political economy in which they are embedded.

(2005: 3)

Identity politics, to the extent they are crafted in the furnace of shared experience, are central to mobilization against neoliberal reform efforts. Thus the shared experiences of inequality, neglect,

surveillance, and shame may serve to reinforce poor people's position within the castaaway categories they have been ascribed to, or, as in previous poor people's movements, may act as a
catalyst for mobilization (Piven and Cloward, 1979). It is through mobilization that poor people
may change how they are viewed, and in some cases come to see themselves differently, pushing
back against not only the advance of harsh and punitive policies that exacerbate social inequalities,
but the logics and shaming practices that are used to justify them (Piven, 2011).

The contributions in this part highlight some of the ways in which poor people draw on
their shared experiences to resist the tyranny of neoliberalism, and together work toward the
re-imagination of alternative political, economic, and social realities. These efforts range widely
across sites of resistance and intervention strategies, demonstrating the power of poor people to
disrupt the encroachment of draconian policy reform from within and outside of state-sanctioned
institutions, mobilizing among themselves and enlisting the help of allies to resist neoliberal
reform. In "The Poverty of 'Poverty'" Gardner, Tovar-Murray, and Wilkerson highlight the
limitations of performance-based goal setting in education, challenging educators to move
beyond the marketized outputs currently associated with academic achievement. Graham's
chapter, "Legitimizing and Resisting Neoliberalism in U.S. Community Development," critically assesses contemporary community development initiatives, and demonstrates the problems
and possibilities of community development intermediaries in the promotion of and resistance
to neoliberal reform among poor people of color residing in marginalized spaces.

Turning our attention to human rights organizing, Jewell's chapter, "Too Legit to Quit," provides a case study of organizational change, documenting the shift of an organization from a welfare
rights to a human rights approach to advocacy. In the chapter, "Neoliberalism, State Projects, and
Migrant Organizing" Lesneiwski and Vonderlack-Navarro examine the organizing campaigns of
two migrant organizations in Chicago. They demonstrate how new, expanding forms of migrant
political activism emerge out of cross-border economic flows and interdependencies that interact
with various state initatives. Proweller and Monkman explore the world of youth initiatives to foster social change, exploring the ways in which youth are constituted through "youth leadership",
"student voice", and "civic engagement." Finally, in their chapter on "Migrant Civil Society",
Joassart-Marcelli and Martin discuss the role of Migrant Civil Society Organizations in the integration of immigrant communities, and the implications of these devolved practices for citizenship in
the United States. We see throughout these chapters an emphasis on the micro and macro politics
of identity and the mobilization of shared experiences to build coalitions among both institutional
and community based actors. These important contributions highlight the need to work within and
beyond helping organizations to resist the encroachment of neoliberal reform, and the work of poor
people and advocates for the poor to affect social change.

References

Bourdieu, P. and L.J.D. Wacquant. (2001). Neoliberal Newspeak: Notes on the New Planetary Vulgate.
    Radical Philosophy Review, 108: 2–5.
Bush, George. (2002). Bush's National Security Strategy. *The New York Times* (September 20).
Dawson, M. (2011). *Not in Our Lifetime: The Future of Black Politics*. Chicago: University of Chicago Press.
Duggan, L. (2005). *The Twilight of Inequality: Neoliberalism, Cultural Politics, and the Attack on Democracy*.
    Boston: Beacon Press.
Harvey, D. (2005). *A Brief History of Neoliberalism*. Oxford: Oxford University Press.
Kelley, R.D.G. (2012). *Neoliberalism's Challenge*. Boston: Boston Review.
Klein, N. (2006). *The Shock Doctrine: The Rise of Disaster Capitalism*. New York: Picador.
Peck, J. (2010). *Constructions of Neoliberal Reason*. Oxford: Oxford University Press.
Piven, F.F. (2011). *A Proud, Angry Poor: What the Occupy Movement Could Do for Poor People—and Vice
    Versa*. The Nation.

Piven, F.F. and R. Cloward. (1979). *Poor People's Movements: Why They Succeed, How They Fail.* New York: Vintage Books. Retrieved from http://www.thenation.com/article/165158/proud-angry-poor.

Web, J. (2006). Class Struggle: America's Workers Have a Chance to be Heard. *Wall Street Journal*, (November 15).

47

THE POVERTY OF "POVERTY"

Re-mapping conceptual terrain in education and counseling beyond a focus on economic output

Joby Gardner, Darrick Tovar-Murray, and Stanley Wilkerson

The social justice movement in counseling seeks to eliminate social illnesses caused by power, privilege, and oppression (Smith and Chen-Hayes, 2003; Smith et al., 2009) by placing issues of poverty, wealth, and growing economic disparities at the forefront of professional discourse (Hutchison, 2011). This movement coincided with concern among educational researchers about persistent and growing disparities in the quality of education available to wealthy and poor Americans (Darling-Hammond, 2010; Johnson, 2006), racial and economic resegregation (Kozol, 2005; Rothstein, 2004), and the concentration of disadvantage and social isolation of schools serving the poorest students (Bryk et al., 2010). Scholars in counseling and education are moving beyond simplistic discussions of poverty (often relying primarily on percentages of students receiving free or reduced-price lunches) to more nuanced discussions of social capital and community cohesion (e.g., Sampson, 2012), engagement with student and client cultural capitals (e.g., Carter, 2007), and how these factors can contribute to more adequate understandings of how individuals experience economic status (Liu, 2010a, 2010b). This recent shift in education and counseling literatures "can be attributed," in one recent formulation, "to [at least] three factors: (1) a lack of specificity when using terms connoting social status, (2) multiple perspectives on conceptualizing the construct of social class, and (3) an inherent difficulty operationalizing social status variables for research purposes" (Hutchison, 2011, p. 204). Although this shift has brought advances in how we counsel and educate the underprivileged, much work remains.

In what follows, we argue that "poverty" and "wealth" are often employed hastily in educational and counseling literatures without attending to their conceptual limitations. Policy makers, scholars, and practitioners tend to objectify a person's social status based on what are at best imperfect measures of economic circumstance "and from these indices place the person into a corresponding social class group" (Liu and Pope-Davis, 2003, p. 295), thus negating the variability that exists within social class groups (Liu, 2001, 2002). New approaches are necessary to move our professions beyond easy measures of poverty/wealth as "objective" indices of opportunity and to help us understand the complexities of human subjective experiences of opportunity (Liu, 2001, 2002). Below, we offer new models that allow us to focus on human potential and building on human strengths (Foss et al., 2011).

We also argue for a perspective on poverty that always, as a starting point, recognizes and seeks after the fundamentally human and humane possibility of cultural, spiritual, moral, empathic, and aesthetic "wealth" regardless of wealth/poverty and that understands education and counseling as fundamentally rooted in relationships, dialogue, and specific contexts. In making this argument, we are cognizant of the clinical/practical bind of navigating between pathology and romance when working with the poor. Thus, our intent is neither ascetic—to celebrate economic poverty as somehow liberating—nor is it etiological—to neglect people's basic humanity when attempting to educate, counsel, or work toward shared goals. Instead, we recognize the cycle of poverty as a complex interplay of relative economic opportunity, cultures, human suffering, the strength of interpersonal relationships, local histories, and the presence (or absence) of institutions and policies that nurture human potential (Liu, 2001; Myers and Gill, 2004).

Problems with "wealth"/"poverty" as guiding metaphors: ends and means

We see problems with "poverty" and "wealth" as organizing metaphors in education and counseling—problems of ends and problems of means. When a primary goal of education and counseling becomes economic growth, global competitiveness, and even national security (see, e.g., Darling-Hammond, 2010; Ravitch, 2012), we risk reducing the breadth of human potential to economic output alone and learning to that which can be easily measured. To be clear, we believe education and counseling provide valuable tools in the fight against poverty in general and, more specifically, our students' or clients' poverty. However, education/counseling for wealth accumulation promises a false existential panacea. In practical terms, we tell young people to do well in often under-funded schools so that they can go to college and get a well-paid job, as if work and wealth were universal tickets to happiness, and education the most efficient means to wealth. The logical contortions in these ideas are rarely critically scrutinized. This is striking given that education and counseling, even in their most exalted forms, do not provide clients and pupils with paying work and that schools and counselors cannot immediately enhance their students' or clients' wealth. Noddings (2003) points out some major flaws in these mantras of schooling: Our schools, at their best, touch obliquely on entire realms of human life, especially those realms like relationships, cultivation of personal passions, and family and home life, that, Noddings argues, can be sources of great satisfaction and happiness or, conversely, frustration and disappointment. Rather than helping us lead better lives, education and counseling, in these well-intended narratives, can become entirely means to a consumerist end.

Another problem with wealth/poverty as a guiding metaphor in education and counseling is a problem of means or what education and human services can offer *in the present*. Conceptualizing schooling or counseling as engines of (future) individual and national wealth generation raises questions about what, if anything, schooling and counseling—especially in economically impoverished schools or with clients facing severe poverty—offers students, clients, teachers, and counselors in the present. How does (or how can) the schooling we offer all students, especially those facing severe poverty, make our lives more humane right now? How can the day-to-day process of education—what we do and experience in schools and community organizations—foster connections, understanding, and compassion? How can schooling help us live and share across lines of perceived difference? How can education nurture imagination and spirit? Left out of our schooling or counseling as pathways-to-consumerist-ascendancy narratives, as critics like Banks (2006), Greene (2001), Hooks (1994), Meier and Wood (2004), Noddings (2003), and Payne (2008a) point out, is the breadth of our humanity that lies beyond wage labor and consumerism—including art, spirituality, compassion, humor, cross-cultural understanding, concern for justice and the environment, etc.

In short, we fear that these combined problems—a narrow focus on econometric ends combined with inattention to means or the impact of teaching/learning/counseling on those experiencing them—may contribute to alarming and well-documented attrition of both teachers and counselors (through burnout and leaving the profession; see, e.g., Borman and Dowling, 2008; Ingersoll, 2001) and students, particularly poor students and students of color (through dropout, pushout, exclusion, and incarceration; see, e.g., Orfield, 2004; Rumberger, 2011).

Pathology (and romance) as practical/conceptual pitfalls in working with poor students/clients

In a pathological view of poverty, poverty is simultaneously the cause and result of social problems. The poor become the social problems associated with (but not limited to) poverty—crime, violence, substance abuse, incarceration, etc. This conflation of the poor with social ills that, for a variety of reasons—including heightened scrutiny through racial and economic profiling and lack of buffering social institutions—may be most readily perceived among the poor, ignores the fact that social problems exist across the economic spectrum and likely define aspects of the human condition. That is, humans across time and cultures engage in destructive behaviors—these, along with more positive attributes like altruism, seem to define the range of humanity. A pathologizing perspective views poverty and attendant social ills as personal and moral failings (e.g., Thernstrom and Thernstrom, 2003). From this perspective, the most effective way to address problems like crime, violence, substance abuse, and despair among (some of) the poor is not by ending or mitigating their poverty, for example by providing access to education and jobs that respect basic human dignity, but by pursuing policies like ending welfare benefits, harsher criminal sentencing, and funding religious programs and schools that putatively strengthen the "moral fabric" of individuals and families. This is education and counseling as the imposition of worldview or normative and cultural schema rather than education and counseling as interactional and characterized by growth and transformation of both teacher/counselor and student/client. Its worst embodiments include avowedly paternalistic social and educational policies (see, e.g., Whitman, 2008), "values-imperialism" (for a critique, see Nussbaum, 2010, pp. 101–112), and policies aimed at "cultural assimilation" rather than multicultural competence (e.g., Spring, 2009). To be clear, avoiding pathologizing is not the same as ignoring pathology. That is, acknowledging that there are very real, very pernicious structural and institutional precipitants of destructive behaviors among the poor does not deny the agency of the poor—including the agency to screw up and make bad decisions (see, e.g., Payne 2008b, p. 199).

Conversely, romanticizing poverty is the ascetic celebration of poverty itself as somehow liberating or clarifying. One version is the belief that the condition of being economically poor somehow breaks the thrall of materialism, consumerism, and hyper-individualism with its attendant romantic celebration of the solidarity and collectivism that exist among some who are poor (as if solidarity and collectivism were caused by poverty). While there are those whose principled poverty—religious orders, some living on communes, ancient scholastics and ascetics—may prove at times intellectually or spiritually liberating, for the vast majority of the economically impoverished, poverty is just poverty—a constant struggle to meet life's basic necessities.

Toward new understandings of social class: the Social Class Worldview Model (SCWM)

In the fourth edition of the *Handbook of Counseling Psychology*, Liu and Ali (2008) argue that scholars continue to socially stratify poverty and wealth (Frable, 1997; Helms and Cook, 1999; Liu and Pope-Davis, 2003; Sue and Sue, 1999) and that the professional discourse surrounding understandings of the functionality of social class in the lives of students and clients is limited (Liu and Ali, 2008) and skewed by middle-class bias (Liu and Pope-Davis, 2003). Many scholars and policy makers describe social class as based on "objective"/easily measured aspects of life circumstances such as income (Liu and Ali, 2008), failing to address the subjective experience of social class (i.e., subjective cultural variables), the economic cultures related to a person's social class position (including the existence of varied forms of human, social, and cultural capitals), and the within-group variability in social class groups (Liu and Pope-Davis, 2003). Essentially, the problem with social stratification as it relates to social class is that we tend to group individuals based on limited measures and understandings of the availability of resources, easily identifiable lifestyle characteristics, income level, educational attainment, and occupational types (Liu, 2001, 2002; Liu and Pope-Davis, 2003).

In his efforts to ground social class in a more holistic approach, Liu (2001, 2002) developed the Social Class Worldview Model (SCWM) (Myers and Gill, 2004). The SCWM provides a theoretical base from which to understand poverty and wealth in terms of subjective experiences rather than as fixed, monolithic, objective, and objectifying traits or characteristics (Liu, 2001, 2002; Liu and Ali, 2008). Fundamental to the SCWM is that "1. Social class operates at an individual and subjective level in people's lives; 2. An individual's perceptions shape his or her reality; and 3. Individuals work toward homeostasis in their worldview" (Liu et al., 2004, pp. 102–103). The SCWM informs our understanding of poverty and wealth because it holds that social class is a "subjective experience that includes the individual's social class worldview and experiences with classism [and] that does not equate a person's objective life circumstance (i.e., income level) with a particular social class." Rather, Liu assumes that people "form self-perceptions that may be congruent or incongruent with their life situation, and that these self-perceptions do more to define their social class than the objective conditions in which they live" (Liu and Ali, 2008, p. 167).

An alternative to education and counseling focused on maximizing economic output: the Capabilities Approach

Martha Nussbaum opens her 2011 book, *Creating Capabilities: The Human Development Approach*, with the story of Vasanti, a slight 30-year-old woman in Gujarat state in northwest India who recently moved back into her parents' home to escape her alcoholic, abusive husband. While Nussbaum points out that Gujarat "has followed a[n economic] growth-oriented agenda," it has not "devot[ed] many resources to ... its poorest inhabitants" (Nussbaum, 2011, p. 3). Prospects for Vasanti—childless and with no formal education—are slim. To drive home her critique of approaches to human development that focus primarily or solely on economic growth metrics, Nussbaum asks her reader to consider:

> What does that figure [GDP], however glorious, mean to Vasanti? It doesn't reach her life and it doesn't solve her problems. [...] To her, hearing that GDP per capita has increased nicely [in Gujarat] is like being told that somewhere in Gujarat there is a beautiful painting, only she can't look at it, or a table set with delicious food, only she can't have any.
>
> (p. 13)

Thus, at the crux of the Human Development or Capabilities Approach, Nussbaum writes, are questions not just of freedom but freedom with real opportunities for individuals to make choices and enact their freedoms (after all, no law bars Vasanti from work or education, though patriarchy, social mores rooted in caste, and the virtual absence of schools or lenders to accommodate women render these "freedoms" next to meaningless). The Capabilities Approach, Nussbaum writes, "begins with a very simple question: What are people actually able to do and to be? What real opportunities are available to them?" (p. x). In Nussbaum's formulation, to ensure that people have real opportunities to "do and be" in dignified ways that respect their fundamental humanity, society must guarantee the threshold levels of ten "Central Capabilities." These include:

- Life
- Bodily health
- Bodily integrity
- Senses, imagination, and thought
- Emotions
- Practical reason
- Affiliation
- Other species
- Play
- Control over one's environment.

We find both Sen's (1999) and Nussbaum's (2011) work in this Human Development or Capabilities Approach to be a particularly promising alternative to economic and instrumentalist conceptualizations of education and human development. The work represents an important attempt to move beyond theories that equate development with economic development and focus primarily on GDP or poverty rates as proxies for human welfare. As in Vasanti's case, Nussbaum and Sen argue that measures of development primarily in terms of GDP can hide gross inequities in health and education and that GDP tells us little or nothing about any individual's ability to pursue choices or about their access to education, health care, personal safety and security, freedom to assemble, or other necessary criteria for dignity and freedom.

We appreciate the attention that Nussbaum, Sen, and other champions of the Capabilities Approach pay to education. We salute, for example, Nussbaum's assertion that education is a so-called "fertile functioning": something "at the heart of the Capabilities Approach," "pivotal to the development and exercise of many other human capabilities," and "of the highest importance in addressing disadvantage and inequality" (Nussbaum, 2011, pp. 152–153; see also Robeyns, 2005). We further appreciate that Nussbaum's is not a narrow or instrumentalist vision of education. Nussbaum argues both in *Creating Capabilities* and elsewhere (e.g., Nussbaum, 1997, 2010) that education to promote human development must go beyond "basic literacy and numeracy" to promote "skills associated with the humanities and the arts—critical thinking, the ability to imagine and to understand another person's situation from within, and a grasp of world history and the current global economic order" (Nussbaum, 2011, p. 155). In fact, Nussbaum even anticipates some of our criticisms of the Capabilities Approach as a model for educating and working with the economically poor—namely that it doesn't direct sufficient attention to the qualities necessary to sustain strong interpersonal relationships, trust, cross-cultural communication, and the rooting of education in specific community opportunities and problems.

We feel that the Human Development and Capabilities Approaches outlined by Nussbaum (2011) and Sen (1999) offer powerful, positive, and actionable alternatives to neo-liberal conceptualizations of education and human development that focus so much attention on test scores, measurement, competition, and education for the sake of economic growth. We particularly appreciate and applaud the emphasis on individual agency and on freedom to make choices. We see the great value in attending to positive and enabling freedoms (or an individual's ability to enact choices) over so-called "negative freedoms" or freedom from restrictions or prohibitions (in which a member of society may be [theoretically] free to pursue an education but practically unable to do so for reasons ranging from basic survival—health, safety, lack of adequate housing—to totally inadequate facilities, de-humanizing and humiliating treatment, etc.).

Questions and ways forward

As educators and counselors, we feel that additional attention must be paid to the foundation of all education and human services work in relationships and in the complexities and contradictions of individual lives. Our concern is that, as a framework, the Capabilities Approach focuses on social, political, economic, and social structural necessities and antecedents for freedom and agency but is less attentive to the necessities and antecedents for sustained dialogue, mutual recognition, and attention to individual histories and contexts that the SCWM can help us understand and that form the basis of the best education and human services work. While illuminating aspects of Vasanti's plight in ways that GDP and easy measurements of social class cannot, and despite Nussbaum's explicit mention of both pedagogy and content (see, e.g., Nussbaum, 1997, 2010), we read the Capabilities Approach and the SCWM as being relatively silent on how and about what we might educate or counsel Vasanti or anyone else. In other words, these approaches remain relatively quiet on the most fundamental questions of education and human development:

- What is the role(s) of a teacher or counselor? Facilitator, didact, guide, expert?
- What is or should be the source(s) and genesis of the curriculum or counseling plan—one that both includes the wishes of the student or client and ensures her/his growth beyond the current state?
- How should aims or goals that are potentially in tension (e.g., between education or human development for individual self-actualization and education or human development for political empowerment of the oppressed) be balanced?

As educators and counselors working primarily with impoverished and marginalized young people in the United States (incarcerated youth, LBGTQ youth, young people who have dropped or been kicked out of school, black and brown youth), our concerns with Nussbaum's work and Liu's models reflect our own positions. What attention can Nussbaum's discussion of human development in terms of national or constitutional protections or Liu's discussion of the subjective complexities of social class allow for issues especially germane to the young and marginalized: quality of teaching and counseling (not just access to these), ensuring opportunities for mutual recognition with, of, and by adults in positions of power, youth voice, youth agency, the protection, nurturing, and education of children, etc.? Does Nussbaum's (and others') focus on international development policy, especially as it plays out in India and other underdeveloped nations, take attention off the gross inequities (in incarceration rates, educational attainment, health, and wealth) that plague the United States? As a philosopher developing a corrective to (macro-)economic and political theories, does Nussbaum allow sufficient attention to dialogue and human interaction at the micro (interpersonal) and meso (institutional) levels? If we take seriously Liu's SCWM, what are the implications for clinical practice, beyond avoiding easy generalizations and further reifying existing social stratifications?

On issues like these we find additional inspiration in the work of adult and civil rights educators and activists like Paulo Freire and Myles Horton (e.g., Horton et al., 1990) who seek to bridge education, counseling, and community organizing (see also Ayers and Ford, 1996; Moses and Cobb, 2002; Payne, 2008a; Warren, 2001; Warren and Mapp, 2011). We do not mean to suggest that such work—i.e., rooting education and development work in abiding relationships of trust, based on familiarity with and appreciation of local circumstance and individual histories—supplants or obviates the need for a Capabilities Approach to development or a more nuanced SCWM of individual experiences of social class. It does not. We suggest, in a more limited way, that attending to education and human development work, as adult and civil rights educators like Freire and Horton (as well as those building on their legacies) suggest, provides a useful conceptual bridge between macro-social and political theory and more micro-level concerns about the hows, whens, whys, and with whoms of education and human development work. To draw the contrast even more sharply, where the Capabilities Approach would recognize and protect each individual's freedom (and ability) to choose participation in cultural and aesthetic pursuits and the SCWM would insist on the complexities of individual experiences over easy measures of life circumstance, an adult education/civil rights/community organizing approach would insist on getting to know (personally) and building from a particular individual's cultural history and the wealth of local experience to facilitate growth, interpersonal understanding, and collective action.

Conclusion

As Darling-Hammond (2010) points out in the context of a discussion of the tremendous inequalities that continue to plague public education in the United States, sometime in the early 1980s, educational and social policy attention in the United States began to shift from attention to opportunity and equity of inputs to focus on "outputs"—typically test scores, national rankings, projected GDP, and measures of earning potential. That is, at sometime in the recent past, our collective attention shifted from attention to the "opportunity gap" to the "achievement gap" which became synonymous with scores on high-stakes standardized tests (see also Carter and Welner, 2013). The result of this shift is that our work as educators and counselors has been reframed around us—from attempting to secure equity and opportunity for poor students/clients to attempting to ensure that students/clients score well on imperfect tests of a narrow range of human capability (in the hope that such achievement will promote future financial gain and economic ascendancy).

Our purpose here has been to shed light on the limitations of this reframing and to offer alternatives. This, we have argued, is far too atrophied a formulation of what education and human development should be about—and the acceptance of narrow, easily (though often not accurately) measured, and economic and nationalistic goals among educational and social policy makers has worked to our collective detriment. While damaging to all of us touched by it, the power of this constriction of education and counseling to a narrow focus on economic growth has had its most pernicious effects, we suggest, on the economically poor, desperate, and disenfranchised and on those of us who teach and counsel them. As educators and counselors, we find ourselves grasping at golden mirages and hollow promises. It's time we set our sights higher.

References

Ayers, W., and Ford, P. (1996). Afterword: Organizing and teaching. In W. Ayers and P. Ford (eds), *City kids, city teachers: Reports from the front row* (pp. 305–327). New York: The New Press.

Banks, J. A. (2006). Democracy, diversity, and social justice: Educating citizens for the public interest in a global age. In G. Ladson-Billings and W. F. Tate (eds), *Education research in the public interest: Social justice, action, and policy* (pp. 141–157). New York: Teachers College Press.

Borman, G. D., and Dowling, N. (2008). Teacher attrition and retention: A meta-analytic and narrative review of the research. *Review Of Educational Research*, 78(3), 367–409.

Bryk, A., Sebring, P., Allensworth, E., Luppescu, S., and Easton, J. (2010). *Organizing schools for improvement: Lessons from Chicago.* Chicago: University of Chicago Press.

Carter, P. L. (2007). *Keepin' it real: School success beyond black and white.* New York: Oxford University Press.

Carter, P. L., and Welner, K. G. (2013). *Closing the opportunity gap: What America must do to give every child an even chance.* New York: Oxford University Press.

Darling-Hammond, L. (2010). *The flat world and education: How America's commitment to equity will determine our future.* New York: Teachers College Press.

Foss, L. L., Generali, M. M., and Kress, V. F. (2011). Counseling people living in poverty: The CARE model. *Journal of Humanistic Counseling*, 50(2), 161–171.

Frable, D. E. S. (1997). Gender, racial, ethnic, sexual, and class identities. *Annual Review of Psychology*, 48, 139–162.

Greene, M. (2001). *Releasing the imagination: Essays on education, the arts, and social change.* San Francisco, CA: Jossey-Bass.

Helms, J. E., and Cook, D. A. (1999). *Using race and culture in counseling and psychotherapy: Theory and process.* Boston, MA: Allyn and Bacon.

Hooks, B. (1994). *Teaching to transgress: Education as the practice of freedom.* New York: Routledge.

Horton, M., Freire, P., Bell, B., Gaventa, J., and Peters, J. (1990). *We make the road by walking: Conversations on education and social change.* Philadelphia: Temple University Press.

Hutchison, B. (2011). The influence of perceived poverty and academic achievement on school counselor conceptualization. *Equity and Excellence in Education*, 44(2), 203–222.

Ingersoll, R. M. (2001). Teacher turnover and teacher shortages: An organizational analysis. *American Educational Research Journal*, 38(3), 499–534.

Johnson, H. (2006). *The American dream and the power of wealth: Choosing schools and inheriting inequality in the land of opportunity.* New York: Routledge.

Kozol, J. (2005). *Shame of the nation: The restoration of apartheid schooling in America.* New York: Crown Publishing.

Liu, W. M. (2001). Expanding our understanding of multiculturalism: Developing a social class worldview model. In D. B. Pope-Davis and H. L. K. Coleman (eds), *The intersection of race, class, and gender in counseling psychology* (pp. 127–170). Thousand Oaks, CA: Sage Publications.

Liu, W. M. (2002). The social class-related experiences of men: Integrating theory and practice. *Professional Psychology: Research and Practice*, 33, 355–360.

Liu, W. M. (ed.). (2010a). *Handbook of social class in counseling psychology.* New York: Oxford University Press.

Liu, W. M. (2010b). *Social class and classism in the helping professions: research, theory, and practice.* Thousand Oaks, CA: Sage Publications.

Liu, W. M., and Ali, S. R. (2008). Social class and classism: understanding the psychological impact of poverty and inequality. In S. Brown, and R. Lent, (eds), *Handbook of counseling psychology* (pp.159–175). New York: Wiley.

Liu, W. M., and Pope-Davis, D. B. (2003). Understanding classism to effect personal change. In T. B. Smith (ed.), *Practicing multiculturalism* (pp. 294–310). Needham Heights, MA: Allyn and Bacon Publishers.

Liu, W. M., Soleck, G., Hopps, J., Dunslon, K., and Pickett, T. (2004). A new framework to understand social class in counseling: The social class worldview and modern classism theory. *Journal of Multicultural Counseling and Development*, 32, 95–122.

Meier, D., and Wood, G. (2004). *Many children left behind: How the No Child Left Behind Act is damaging our children and our schools.* Boston: Beacon Press.

Moses, R., and Cobb, C. (2002). *Radical equations: Civil rights from Mississippi to The Algebra Project.* Boston: Beacon Press.

Myers, J. E., and Gill, C. G. (2004). Poor, rural, and female: Understudied, under-counseled, more at-risk. *Journal of Mental Health Counseling*, 26, 225–242.

Noddings, N. (2003). *Happiness and education.* New York: Cambridge University Press.

Nussbaum, M. C. (1997). *Cultivating humanity: A classical defense of reform in liberal education.* Cambridge, MA: Harvard University Press.

Nussbaum, M. C. (2010). *Not for profit: Why democracy needs the humanities*. Princeton, NJ: Princeton University Press.

Nussbaum, M. C. (2011). *Creating capabilities: The human development approach*. Cambridge, MA: Belknap Press of Harvard University.

Orfield, G. (2004). *Dropouts in America: Confronting the graduation rate crisis*. Cambridge, MA: Harvard Education Press.

Payne, C. (2008a). "Give light and the people will find a way": Ella Baker and teaching as politics. In C. Payne and C. S. Strickland (eds), *Teach freedom: Education for liberation in the African-American tradition* (pp. 56–66). New York: Teachers College Press.

Payne, C. (2008b). *So much reform, so little change: The persistence of failure in urban school reform*. Cambridge, MA: Harvard Education Press.

Ravitch, D. (2012). Do our public schools threaten national security? New York Review of Books, June 7. Retrieved from: http://www.nybooks.com/articles/archives/2012/jun/07/do-our-public-schools-threaten-national-security/ (accessed August 15, 2014).

Robeyns, I. (2005). The capability approach: A theoretical survey. *Journal of Human Development*, 6(1), 93–117.

Rothstein, R. (2004). *Class and schools: Using social, economic, and educational reform to close the black–white achievement gap*. New York: Economic Policy Institute and Teachers College Press.

Rumberger, R. W. (2011). *Dropping out: Why students drop out of high school and what can be done about it*. Cambridge, MA: Harvard University Press.

Sampson, R. (2012). *Great American city: Chicago and the enduring neighborhood effect*. Chicago: University of Chicago Press.

Sen, A. (1999). *Development as freedom*. New York: Anchor.

Smith, S. D., and Chen-Hayes, S. F. (2003). Leadership and advocacy for lesbian, bisexual, gay, transgendered, and questioning (LBGTQ) students: Academic, career, and interpersonal success strategies. In R. Perusse and G. E. Goodnough (eds), *Leadership, advocacy and direct service strategies for professional school counselors* (pp. 187–221). Belmont, CA: Brooks/Cole-Thomson.

Smith, S. D., Reynolds, C. A., and Rovnak, A. (2009). A critical analysis of the social advocacy movement in counseling. *Journal of Counseling and Development*, 87, 483–491.

Spring, J. (2009). *Deculturalization and the struggle for equality: A brief history of the education of dominated cultures in the United States*, 6th ed. New York: McGraw Hill.

Sue, D. W., and Sue, D. (1999). *Counseling the culturally different: Theory and practice*, 3rd ed. New York: John Wiley and Sons.

Thernstrom, A. M., and Thernstrom, S. (2003). *No excuses: Closing the racial gap in learning*. New York: Simon and Schuster.

Warren, M. (2001). *Dry bones rattling: Community building to revitalize American democracy*. Princeton, NJ: Princeton University Press.

Warren, M., and Mapp, K. (2011). *A match on dry grass: Community organizing as a catalyst for school reform*. New York: Oxford University Press.

Whitman, D. (2008). *Sweating the small stuff: Inner-city schools and the new paternalism*. Washington, DC: Thomas B. Fordham Institute.

48

LEGITIMIZING AND RESISTING NEOLIBERALISM IN U.S. COMMUNITY DEVELOPMENT

The influential role of community development intermediaries

Leigh Graham

Introduction

The U.S. community development field originated as a movement for the self-determination of urban poor Black and Puerto Rican communities, emerging from the social justice activism of the 1960s and 1970s. Political empowerment and economic autonomy was the means to transform "ghetto" circumstances and conditions into thriving, healthy, prosperous, and equitable environments for poor and segregated African-Americans and Latinos (Ferguson and Dickens, 1999; Goldsmith, 1974; Newman and Lake, 2006; Tabb, 1970). Key ingredients included "community organizing, political power, training, and participation" (Vietorisz and Harrison, 1971).

National and local funders initially supported community development's early emphasis on political organizing and fostering a proud collective identity for marginalized urban communities. Yet, as the political climate shifted rightward in the 1970s and into the early 1980s, funders began to pull out of this sector, citing a lack of measurable outcomes and responding to the increasingly conservative federal environment for urban low-income development. This retreat signaled the potential demise of the nascent sector.

Instead, the community development (CD) field grew and flourished in the subsequent decades, mainly due to its pragmatic embrace of federal devolution and privatization. Community development intermediaries, launched by Congress, foundations, and philanthropists between 1979 and 1982, played a particularly important role in rationalizing and professionalizing the field. This role of community development intermediaries is an important chapter in the evolution of U.S. anti-poverty practice and outcomes, and the focus of this analysis. Intermediaries are the key vehicle for institutionalizing market logics in the CD sector since former President Ronald Reagan's "privatization revolution" emphasized charity, voluntarism, and, critically, market efficiency in social welfare service delivery. Their creation, growth, and success in rationalizing the sector for financial investment and housing production has been described as the single most important story of the nonprofit development sector in the 1980s. Arguably, without this source of support for grassroots development activity, state and local governments would have displayed far less responsiveness to nonprofit developer needs over the decade.

(Liou and Stroh, 1998, p. 582)

Today, the CD sector sits within the larger Finance, Insurance, and Real Estate (FIRE) industry, a significantly structurally disadvantaged nonprofit component of the enormous, for-profit, private real estate and banking industry. The CD field is charged with the formidable task of developing affordable housing in low-income urban communities beset by processes of gentrification or chronic disinvestment. Bank legislation and profits continue to substantially fund the sector, alongside government funds, developer fees, and philanthropic contributions for programs and services. When banks rein in their profits, as occurred in the most recent global recession, affordable housing producers, their tenants, and their communities are hit especially hard. The commitments of local and national philanthropy, the private sector, and the national intermediaries make or break U.S. community development initiatives.

This chapter documents the role of community development intermediaries in institutionalizing and transforming the sector to one embracing market logics in the contemporary neoliberal economy. Yet, this narrative does not reach the often inexorable conclusion of neoliberalism as our only alternative. Instead, important opportunities exist within the field for reclaiming the community development movement's roots. The nagging tension within this newly mature field, almost 50 years young—of trying to honor enduring racial and economic justice goals within a framework emphasizing housing production and organizational efficiency—has opened up space for the field's founders and successors to challenge neoliberalism from within and without using equity, inclusion, and economic human rights-based frameworks.

I begin with the theoretical context of community development as a practice of urban entrepreneurialism within a "global political economy of place" (Fraser et al., 2003; Logan and Molotch, 1987). I then offer a detailed accounting of the role of CD intermediaries in shaping the contemporary CD field to survive in a neoliberal economy. I will conclude with an analysis of how intermediaries, their partners, and their challengers—especially since Hurricane Katrina in 2005—are confronting neoliberalism through movements for equity, inclusion, and economic human rights for U.S. urban poor communities of color.

Community development as urban entrepreneurialism

For the last four decades, cities have competed in what Fraser et al. (2003) describe as a "global political economy of place" (see also Logan and Molotch, 1987), forced through a trend of neoliberal globalization to become more entrepreneurial (Harvey, 1989), and to jockey for capital investment. Coming out of (a) the urban unrest of the late 1960s and 1970s, (b) the subsequent fiscal crises, (c) a rightward shift in politics, society, and governance that triumphantly holds that dependency prevailed in the war on poverty, (d) market liberalization and regulatory rollbacks that made capital increasingly flexible and globally consolidated, and (e) with little capacity to raise their own revenues, cities have come to over-rely on large-scale development projects to attract corporate capital or affluent taxpayers. U.S. public housing has been systematically demolished, tax credits finance the majority of affordable housing developed today, stadiums and entertainment districts and university expansions attract the middle class back to the city, and corporations receive enormous subsidies to site their headquarters and facilities in local economies. Labor and environmental regulations, development incentives, and social safety net policies have been modified to facilitate market-driven, private-sector growth and control over cities.

The market logics of competition, privatization, and ownership unfold on multiple scales in low-income communities and in CD practice, and attract a complicated network of actors that often clash with one another over how to respond to the chronic challenges present in low-income urban communities of color. At the neighborhood scale, poor communities have been defined as "markets" requiring private investment for revitalization, a frame that has attracted diverse interests such as "proponents of black nationalism, neoliberal economics, and postmodern micropolitics" (Cummings, 2001, p. 399). At the city-wide scale, low-income communities—especially those proximate to downtown development zones—are seen as drags on a municipality's attractiveness to private capital, and thus need to be revitalized to come in line with the city's overall marketing, development, and investment strategy to help it compete in the global political economy of place. Community development intermediaries play a central role in initiating and upholding these urban restructuring efforts.

Community development intermediaries: "Influential participant(s) in the global economy"[1]

Community development corporations (CDCs) originally were founded to build civic, political, and productive capacity in poor neighborhoods, to enable residents both to advocate for their own rights and to build viable economic and housing models. Yet, as the urban political economy evolved, CD funders and Congressional allies shifted their emphases to capture economic and political opportunity for low-income communities in this new, privatized, devolved environment. Taking a previously modest effort of providing financial intermediary support to nascent CDCs, Congress, The Ford Foundation, and other donors founded three national community development financial intermediaries (CDIs) between 1979 and 1982—the Neighborhood Reinvestment Corporation (d.b.a. NeighborWorks America), Local Initiatives Support Corporation (LISC), and The Enterprise Foundation (today Enterprise Community Partners). CDIs would "rationalize" the sector and minimize risk for urban investors. What followed was the growth, professionalization, bureaucratization, and de-politicization of the CD sector away from its confrontational, social justice, empowerment, and collective identity roots to a formalized practice of finance, land use planning, real estate development, and housing management to spur development in blighted, disinvested, low-income neighborhoods.

CDIs provide funds, technical assistance, and training to build the capacity of the CD field to develop new, affordable uses of land and housing (Liou and Stroh, 1998). Because the CD field has the social mission of providing housing and services for low-income communities, intermediaries are governed by a "social enterprise" ethos of making capital affordable and technical skills accessible for CDCs to deliver housing units and social services to their target communities. As such, CDIs have been dually characterized as "bankers" and "philanthropists" (Liou and Stroh, 1998).

One of CDIs' first successful efforts was lobbying for the Low-Income Housing Tax Credit (LIHTC) following the Savings and Loan scandal in the United States. The creation of the LIHTC in 1986 underwrote the growth of the CD sector. It is the major source of affordable rental housing production today (Roberts, 2008/2009), leading to the creation of more than 2M units.[2] Assembling affordable housing and tax credit deals is extremely complicated, time-consuming, and expensive; LISC and Enterprise have become the primary syndicators of tax credits today. Tax credit syndication is the bread and butter behind their capacity-building efforts and the environmental conditions they helped create for the proliferation of thousands of CDCs by the end of the 20th century. Sponsored research by CDIs shows that

supporting the construction and preservation of affordable housing—particularly housing financed by the federal Low-Income Housing Tax Credit (LIHTC) Program—has a
broad, positive effect in low-income communities that generates a significant return on
investment [including] family financial stability ... increased local purchasing power [and]
higher property values.

(Walker, 2010)

Yet there are two serious constraints to CD's overreliance on tax-credit financing for affordable housing. First, the value of tax credits is tied to the market. When the market collapses,
as we experienced with the recent and still devastating Great Recession, so does the value
of the tax credits. Instead of the CD sector, as an alleged part of the social welfare system in
the United States, running counter-cyclical to the market—ramping up affordable housing
access in times of economic hardship—the ability to produce much-needed shelter falls apart
along with the economy.

Second, the FIRE sector comprises 90% of LIHTC investors (Roberts, 2008/2009).
Along with federal Community Reinvestment Act (CRA) requirements and Community
Development Financial Institution (CDFI) legislation, the LIHTC acts as a key institutional
constraint situating the CD field in the FIRE industry. Financial firms, banks, insurance companies, and government-sponsored enterprises like Fannie Mae are the major investors of
affordable housing in the United States. Furthermore, the LIHTC, CRA, and CDFI are all
housed in the U.S. Department of the Treasury. Scholarship and practice situates affordable
housing and community development as the purview of the U.S. Department of Housing and
Urban Development (HUD), in part because of public housing, fair housing law, community
development block grants, and the general mission and aim of HUD. In actuality, CD practice
and policy arguably is a subsidiary policy aim of the U.S. Treasury, whose mission, "duties and
functions" include:

Maintain a strong economy and create economic and job opportunities ... enable economic growth and stability at home and abroad, strengthen national security by combating
threats and protecting the integrity of the financial system ... The Department of the
Treasury's mission highlights its role as ... an influential participant in the global economy
... the executive agency responsible for promoting economic prosperity and ensuring the
financial security of the United States.[3]

In contrast, HUD's mission is

to create strong, sustainable, inclusive communities and quality affordable homes for all.
HUD is working to strengthen the housing market to bolster the economy and protect
consumers; meet the need for quality affordable rental homes; utilize housing as a platform
for improving quality of life; build inclusive and sustainable communities free from discrimination; and transform the way HUD does business.[4]

So the mission of social inclusion and community sustainability based on stable affordable housing
is practically divorced from the production of the bulk of that affordable housing, which actually
fulfills a mission of economic growth and financial stability in a competitive global context. Thus,
critics of neoliberalism are absolutely correct in characterizing housing as a commodity produced
for profit and growth ends within a global economy (Marcuse, 1989; Marcuse and Keating, 2006;
Pow, 2009; Wu, 2005). As such, the production of affordable housing requires a set of rational,

efficient, low-risk, high-return, scalable mechanisms that constrains customization for local context. CDIs that syndicate tax credits thus drive the "mass customization" (Gilmore and Pine, 1997; Pine and Davis, 1993) of affordable rental housing nationwide, as specific design features and tenant mixes prove profitable, replicable, and scalable. This is why it is often so easy to recognize new mixed-income housing developments by their homogeneous New Urbanist design features. It is not just a design principle of walkability and community that drives this replication, but the cost effectiveness of reproducing it on a national scale by a small community of nonprofit and for-profit developers that can efficiently package tax credit deals, assemble multiple sources of financing, and deliver a number of affordable units for a set of low-income tenants using a limited number of design principles, with some modest tweaking to reflect local conditions.

CDIs as urban restructurers

The "realities of housing economics" (Dreier, 1997, p. 241) make it impossible to provide affordable housing for the poor, especially the extremely low income, without permanent subsidy. LIHTC projects do not target extremely low-income households, and must be affordable for 30 years. As the government has moved out of low-income housing provision and the LIHTC has taken over, the poorest in the nation are increasingly underserved in the affordable housing market. As developers and policymakers have focused on making mixed-income projects palatable to potential market rate tenants and to broader society in our uncritical zeal for poverty "deconcentration," low-income residents are ever more sidelined, including through toothless planning exercises (see, for example, Graham, 2010). Fraser and Kick (2007) find that for mixed-income housing to work, goal alignment between investors, the state, and nonprofits matters, whereas goal alignment with residents is irrelevant. Residents are "relatively underserved ... while other stakeholders realize a variety of benefits" (p. 2357).

Salamon (1993) describes this as a process of "marketization" in the social welfare sector, in which market logics of competition and efficiency shift emphases to a different set of skills, stakeholders, leaders, and metrics. In this vein, CD came to prioritize real estate finance acumen, quantifiable outcomes such as units produced, and donors and investors, guided by CDIs skilled at packaging complex housing deals. Concurrently, the sector shifted away from poor people's community organizing and political advocacy that might threaten relationships with the donors and investors funding housing production (Newman and Lake, 2006). Resident and "local" participation and self-direction is subordinated to the input and decisions of professionalized staff and a supra-local network of consultants, policymakers, funders, and technical assistance providers that determine the best practices and development priorities of municipalities and communities in today's global political economy of place. Graham (2010, 2012a) has described this as the "radicalization" of community organizing, building on Ferree's (2010) theories of "resonant" versus "radical" repertoires in "discursive [political] opportunity structures."

Although CDIs have used their substantial power to win important benefits for the CD field and to build 2M units of housing in the last 30 years, they have not reallocated that power to advocate for greater government responsibility for housing the poor—indeed, they have been structurally disinclined towards such activism. Their existence and success also obscures the reality that there is virtually no substitute for government subsidy for housing the poorest among us. Furthermore, their membership in the "dispersal consensus" (Imbroscio, 2008) has aided the federal government's aggressive efforts to privatize public housing in the United States, by intermediaries' ability and willingness and pride in redeveloping inarguably aged, underfunded, and physically declining public housing projects around the nation. As part of this wholesale privatization process, CDIs are key restructurers of the urban environment, central to the process of removing public access to land and housing from poor communities of color and regulating their continued presence in new privatized spaces. They are complicit in and constrained by the same "legislative and regulatory changes that implicitly seem to require [public housing authorities] to choose solvency over helping only the neediest" (Quercia and Galster, 1997, p. 566). In designing innovative new financing mechanisms for the production of affordable rental housing, intermediaries are part of the entrepreneurial regime that now governs and shapes cities. What is particularly alarming for local activists is intermediaries' national scale and their lack of rootedness to any particular locality. In this sense, they have the power to shape local places according to universal, replicable, anodyne norms that they helped design and disseminate.

Graham (2010) described the relative dominance of a culture of reform and caregiving in CD today. Practitioners work to mainstream the poor into middle-class society and the capitalist economy through rehabilitation and behavioral change. This is achieved by (a) mixing the poor with middle-class models of mainstream values and behaviors and (b) elevating the role of social service providers to meet the therapeutic needs of the urban poor. With the decline of public funding for community development, nonprofit housers, social service providers, and liberal philanthropists have taken on an outsized role in sheltering and ministering to the poor. They are empowered to speak for and act on behalf of the urban poor, who are recast as victims of poverty, in need of uplift and mainstream integration. That CDIs and their partners do so much of this CD work motivated by this moral, normative commitment to alleviating poverty and mainstreaming the poor obscures their direct role in the privatization and restructuring of urban space and the further marginalization of the poor.

Confronting neoliberalism from inside and out

This analysis has so far elided the agency of CDI leadership and their partners and allies to confront the market hegemony of the global neoliberal political economy. A defining characteristic of the CD field is that its leaders are former social movement entrepreneurs from black political mobilization of the 1960s and 1970s, and of workers' rights, immigrants' rights, and anti-poverty activism of the same period and early 1980s. These activists moved into CD practice and went on to professionalize the field, embracing the individual and collective political and economic power that came from private property ownership in low-income communities of color, as well as having a voice at the negotiating table for social welfare legislation. They became the executives of CDIs, labor unions, and legislative advocacy organizations, and professors in academia. Yet, despite their professional evolution, many of them are still guided by their movement histories, as Graham (2010) shows from working with a network of these activists-turned-executives in the aftermath of Hurricane Katrina. As a generational shift transforms the CD field, these leaders and their successors embody the tension within CD practice of surviving in the neoliberal economy while trying to fulfill the enduring goal of urban low-income community self-determination.

Hurricane Katrina's devastation of the Gulf Coast and especially New Orleans in 2005, and the nationwide economic fallout from the Great Recession beginning in 2008, are two key "focusing events" (Birkland, 1997) that have spurred a serious repositioning of CD leadership vis-à-vis neoliberal market logics and practices.[5] Urban political activism of the last decade reveals possibilities for CD practitioners and their social justice allies to confront the dominance of neoliberalism, from both inside and outside the system.

"Working the spaces of neoliberalism"

An edited collection by Laurie and Bondi (2005) demonstrates that neoliberalism has created a population of public and private sector professionals drawn up and out of grassroots groups, community-based organizations, and social justice activism who now straddle a strategic middle ground between government, the private sector, and civil society. They are in effect "strategic brokers" (Larner and Craig, 2005) sprinkled across the public and private sectors responsible for the institutionalization and execution of the neoliberal agenda, especially at state and local levels. Because of their grassroots or movement backgrounds, and their legitimated power working within the neoliberal political economic system, such professionals possess twin sources of knowledge and authority: historical–cultural knowledge of social inequality and change at the local scale as well as the technocratic knowledge of how to tackle problems of inequality, poverty, social exclusion, and economic decline. As such, they are positioned to challenge or resist neoliberalism by "working the spaces" within the system, "well aware" of the dichotomy of their roles versus being "naïve victims of neoliberalism" (Laurie and Bondi, 2005, pp. 6–7). Instead, these professionals use their privileged insider positions to contest neoliberalism, to transform it at "its core" (p. 6).

For example, leadership from LISC and Enterprise—with their labor, academic, and political advocacy partners—have launched a new democratic, green economic development initiative, the Emerald Cities Collaborative (ECC), that explicitly questions the utility and validity of "existing market-driven models of green retrofits," reflecting their painful lessons learned from leading housing and neighborhood recovery efforts in post-Katrina New Orleans.[6] The ECC model continues to use the insider-oriented political strategy of legislative advocacy, technical assistance, and public–private coalition-building, but it also uses an explicit equity and inclusion framework to turn what could be a narrowly tailored program of green building retrofits into a democratic movement for racial and economic justice with workforce and community development practices at its core.

Economic human rights and the right to the city

Urban activists critical of CDIs and the contemporary CD field's complicity in urban restructuring have in recent years clarified their opposition using an economic human rights repertoire in local, national, and global urban social movements. These repertoires demand the recognition and fulfillment of low-income residents' "right to the city" (Lefebvre, 1996) and the acknowledgement of these communities' positive contributions to the overall health of the city, rather than their treatment as a strain on society to be ameliorated. A notable example is the Right to the City Alliance, a grassroots, base-building "urban justice" movement launched in 2007 to resist neoliberalism and fight for poor people's right to the city, and their economic human rights, such as the right to housing and humane work.[7] Organizational members can point to specific instances of urban restructuring, such as the demolition of public housing and its redevelopment as mixed-income properties in post-Katrina New Orleans (Graham, 2012b), that led to their detailed critiques against neoliberalism, including in their expanded analysis and defense of public housing in the United States (Right to the City Alliance, 2010). Their critiques of neoliberal urban development practices include calling out CDIs for their participation in privatizing urban space and displacing or regulating the urban poor (e.g., Sinha, 2009), and re-positioning low-income communities as key spatial and cultural zones of contention against neoliberalism and for racial and economic justice movement building.

Conclusion

ECC is one example of the shift in community development practice from an individualized language of building "capacity" of poor urbanites and communities to a more righteous, justice-oriented, language of "equity" and "inclusion," reflecting a neighborhood's, household's, or person's right to a fair share of material, social, economic, or political capital and their right to fully participate in the processes that distribute this capital. Although this equity and inclusion language is milder in the U.S. political context than an explicit language of human rights, it is in a similar spirit of re-centering the voices of and power of urban poor communities of color in CD practice. Both frameworks are in stark contrast to the culture of poverty perspective and marketization zeal underpinning neoliberalism, in which concentrations of poor households caused subsequent patterns of crime, deviance, and blight in their neighborhoods, necessitating their dispersal and replacement with the financially and politically powerful middle class, often White but also Black (see Pattillo, 2007), as a means of resurrecting these pathologized, isolated, and disinvested neighborhood markets.

Instead, equity, inclusion, and economic human rights frameworks reclaim the power of these urban poor places, to recapture the "productive force" of urban space (Brenner, 2000) for and with the people who live in these neighborhoods. Urban space nonetheless remains "an object of political struggle" (Gotham, 2003) in neoliberal urban restructuring, but the equity, inclusion, and economic human rights-based movements that have arisen in response to neoliberal hegemony begin with the principle that urban poor communities have the right to their homes and neighborhoods; an expectation of social, political, and economic equity living in those places; and can provide benefits to the larger region on their own terms.

Notes

1 U.S. Department of the Treasury, *n.d.* "About." Retrieved from http://www.treasury.gov/about/role-of-treasury/Pages/default.aspx on January 31, 2013.
2 This has surpassed the number of public housing units (~1M), Housing Choice Vouchers (formerly Section 8) (~1M), and units built with HUD HOME funds (450,000 since 1990), another multi-billion dollar source of rental housing production for states, municipalities, and CBDOs.
3 U.S. Department of the Treasury, *n.d.* "About." Retrieved from http://www.treasury.gov/about/role-of-treasury/Pages/default.aspx on January 31, 2013.
4 U.S. Department of Housing and Urban Development, *n.d.* "Mission." Retrieved from http://portal.hud.gov/portal/page/portal/HUD/about/mission on January 31, 2013.
5 Powell (2007) described Katrina's aftermath as a "democratic moment still unfolding." The characterization holds today.
6 Emerald Cities Collaborative, *n.d.* "About." Retrieved from http://www.emeraldcities.org/?q=about on August 29, 2010.
7 Right to the City Alliance, *n.d.* "Mission and History." Retrieved from http://www.righttothecity.org/index.php/about/mission-history on January 31, 2013.

References

Birkland, T.A. (1997). *After disaster: Agenda setting, public policy, and focusing events*. Washington DC: Georgetown University Press.
Brenner, N. (2000). The urban question as a scale question: Reflections on Henri Lefebvre, urban theory and the politics of scale. *International Journal of Urban and Regional Research* 24(2), 361–378.
Cummings, S. (2001). Community economic development as progressive politics: Toward a grassroots movement for economic justice. *Stanford Law Review* 54, 399–493.

Dreier, P. (1997). Philanthropy and the housing crisis: The dilemmas of private charity and public policy. *Housing Policy Debate* 8(1), 235–293.

Ferguson, R.F. and Dickens, W.T. (1999). Introduction. In R.F. Ferguson and W.T. Dickens (eds), Urban *Problems and Community Development* (pp. 1–32). Washington, DC: The Brookings Institution.

Ferree, M.M. (2010). Resonance and radicalism: Feminist framing in the abortion debates of the United States and Germany. In D. McAdam and D.A. Snow (eds), *Readings on social movements: origins, dynamics and outcomes* (pp. 346–370). New York, NY: Oxford University Press.

Fraser, J.C. and Kick, E.L. (2007). The role of public, private, non-profit and community sectors in shaping mixed-income housing outcomes in the U.S. *Urban Studies* 44(12), 2357–2377.

Fraser, J.C., Lepofsky, J., Kick, E.L., and Williams, J.P. (2003). The construction of the local and the limits of contemporary community building in the United States. *Urban Affairs Review* 38(3), 417–445.

Gilmore, J.H. and Pine, B.J. (1997). The four faces of mass customization. *Harvard Business Review* 75(1), 91–101.

Goldsmith, W.W. (1974). The ghetto as a resource for black America. *Journal of the American Planning Association* 40(1), 17–30.

Gotham, K.F. (2003). Toward an understanding of the spatiality of urban poverty: The urban poor as spatial actors. *International Journal of Urban and Regional Research* 27(3), 723–737.

Graham, L. (2010). *Planning Tremé: The community development field in a post-Katrina world* (unpublished doctoral dissertation). Massachusetts Institute of Technology, Cambridge, MA.

Graham, L. (2012a). Advancing the human right to housing in post-Katrina New Orleans: Discursive opportunity structures in housing and community development. *Housing Policy Debate*, 22(1), 5–27.

Graham, L. (2012b). Razing Lafitte: Defending public housing from a hostile state. *Journal of the American Planning Association* 78(4), 466–480.

Harvey, D. (1989). From managerialism to entrepreneurialism: The transformation in urban governance in late capitalism. *Geografiska Annaler. Series B, Human Geography* 71(1), 3–17.

Imbroscio, D.L. (2008). [U]nited and actuated by some common impulse of passion: Challenging the dispersal consensus in American housing policy research. *Journal of Urban Affairs* 30(2), 111–130.

Larner, W. and Craig, D. (2005). After neoliberalism? Community activism and local partnerships in Aotearoa New Zealand. In N. Laurie and L. Bondi (eds), *Working the spaces of neoliberalism: activism, professionalisation, and incorporation* (pp. 9–31). Malden, MA: Blackwell Publishing.

Laurie, N. and Bondi, L. (2005). *Working the spaces of neoliberalism: activism, professionalisation, and incorporation*. Malden, MA: Blackwell Publishing.

Lefebvre, H. (1996). *Writings on cities*. Cambridge, MA: Blackwell.

Liou, Y.T. and Stroh, R.C. (1998). Community development intermediary systems in the United States: Origins, evolution, and functions. *Housing Policy Debate* 9(3), 573–594.

Logan, J. and Molotch, H. (1987). *Urban fortunes: The political economy of place*. Los Angeles, CA: University of California Press.

Marcuse, P. (1989). Gentrification, homelessness, and the work process: Housing markets and labour markets in the quartered city. *Housing Studies* 4(3), 211–220.

Marcuse, P. and Keating, W.D. (2006). The permanent housing crisis: The failures of conservatism and the limits of liberalism. In R. Bratt, M.E. Stone, and C. Hartman (eds), *A right to housing: Foundation for a new social agenda* (pp. 139–162). Philadelphia, PA: Temple University Press.

Newman, K. and Lake, R.W. (2006). Democracy, bureaucracy and difference in U.S. community development politics since 1968. *Progress in Human Geography* 30(1), 44–61.

Pattillo, M. (2007). *Black on the block: The politics of class and race in the city*. Chicago, IL: University of Chicago Press.

Pine, B. Joseph and Davis, Stan. 1993. *Mass customization: The new frontier in business competition*. Cambridge, MA: Harvard Business School Press.

Pow, C. (2009). Neoliberalism and the aestheticization of new middle-class landscapes. *Antipode* 41(2), 371–390.

Powell, L.N. (2007). What does American history tell us about Katrina and vice versa? *Journal of American History*, 94(3), 863–877.

Quercia, R.G. and Galster, G.C. (1997). The challenges facing public housing authorities in a brave new world. *Housing Policy Debate* 8(3), 535–569.

Right to the City Alliance. (2010). *We call these projects home: Solving the housing crisis from the ground up*. Retrieved from http://righttothecity.org/cause/we-call-these-projects-home/ on August 29, 2010.

Roberts, B. (2008/2009). Strengthening the low income housing tax credit investment market. *Community Investments* 21(3), 11–13, 39.

Salamon, L.M. (1993). The marketization of welfare: Changing nonprofit and for-profit roles in the American welfare state. *Social Science Review* 67(1), 16–39.

Sinha, A. (2009, May 11). Damaged roots in the fight for public housing? *San Francisco Bay View*. Retrieved from http://sfbayview.com/2009/damaged-roots-in-the-fight-for-public-housing/ on August 28, 2010.

Tabb, W.K. (1970). *The political economy of the black ghetto*. New York, NY: W.W. Norton and Company.

Vietorisz, T. and Harrison, B. (1971). Ghetto development, community corporations, and public policy. *The Review of Black Political Economy* 2(1), 28–43.

Walker, C. (2010). *Affordable housing for families and neighborhoods: The value of low-income housing tax credits in New York City*. Enterprise Community Partners, Inc. and Local Initiatives Support Corporation, Inc.

Wu, F. (2005). Rediscovering the "gate" under market transition: From work-unit compounds to commodity housing enclaves. *Housing Studies* 20(2), 239–258.

49

TOO LEGIT TO QUIT

Gaining legitimacy through human rights organizing

Jennifer R. Jewell

Introduction

Over the last century, the United States has been rife with groups and individuals organizing to create change by confronting systems of oppression. At no time was this more prevalent than during the 1960s and 1970s. The political culture during this time provided a supportive backdrop for a movement toward democratic participation from engaged citizens. The outrage of the people in disenfranchised communities and the political culture of this time provided a window of opportunity for the development of a wide-based civil rights movement to combat the oppression faced by many diverse groups in the United States. One of these organized communities consisted of welfare rights activists.

Yet, as the window of opportunity for social change started to close, some welfare rights activists began to embrace a human rights framework as their struggle for rights was "too legit to quit." The human rights lens, grounded in the United Nations' Declaration of Human Rights, is an internationally legitimate framework from which collective demands for basic human need can be drawn. This chapter charts this history and briefly highlights the transformation of one local organization as it reframed the struggle from welfare rights to human rights as a strategy to continue building personal and political power.

Women's way of organizing

Community organizing, as a method to gain both personal and political power, has the ability to challenge and transform oppressive systems. Exploring the ways in which women organize provides a basis for understanding the history of welfare rights organizing and the conflict that grew between various groups. For many poor and working-class women, the informal social ties formed in their daily lives help to provide the foundation for women's local community organization (Gittell et al., 2000; Haywoode, 1999). These informal ties are supported by the mutual trust and long-term interaction of women in the community. These informal networks serve a dual purpose. First, they provide for the exchange of resources such as information sharing, contacts for jobs, and emotional support, as well as concrete basic needs of food, clothing, housing, and childcare (Hardina, 2003; Haywoode, 1999). Second, these networks affirm the dignity and importance of all community members, which is empowering for oppressed groups, especially for welfare recipients who faced substantial backlash during the 1960s and 1970s. Through these networks, many working-class and poor women gain capacity to organize around issues impacting themselves and their communities (Haywoode, 1999). Whether loosely knit ties or a formal hierarchical structure, the development of these organizations is an indication of the growth or enhancement of a female consciousness (Kaplan, 1997).

A fairly new modern phenomenon, women's movements have increased over the last two centuries, particularly in the 20th century as women have become more engaged in the public sphere (Molyneux, 1998). Viewing their community work as an extension of their home and family life, the boundaries between women's public and private life often disappear as women organize to improve the standards of living for their families and communities (Abramovitz, 2001; Haywoode, 1999; Naples, 1998). Some use the term "neighborhood sphere" as an extension between the private and public sphere, to form connections between family and individual households to broader social and political groups and structures (Martin, 2002).

From the grassroots, women's activism often oscillates between concrete survival needs for their families and communities and broad demands for social justice (Molyneux, 1998). Women become more visible in movements in which they are demanding collective rights for their communities. Women often act collectively to preserve their families, class, ethnic groups, and communities, frequently ensuring their basic needs (Abramovitz, 2001; Bricker-Jenkins et al., 2007; Haywoode, 1999; Kaplan, 1997; Molyneux, 1998). Jewell (2008) argues that often poor women join the struggle to challenge authorities when society fails to ensure that women are able to provide housing and food for their families. A feminist model of organizing incorporates attention to process, shared decision making, holistic goals, humanistic values, the personal–political connection, consensus building, and an enabling role and facilitating style of the organizer (Joseph et al., 1991). But because of their organizational forms and leadership styles, women's activities have largely been ignored or underestimated (Haywoode, 1999; Kaplan, 1997; Mizrahi, 2007).

Women face particular challenges in community organization related to their subordinate position in society, particularly the balance between family and work and working within the dominant male culture of organizing (Abramovitz, 2001; Haywoode, 1999; Kaplan, 1997; Mizrahi, 2007). These struggles at times lead to marginalization of women and/or their style of community organizing, as was the case of some major welfare rights groups in the 1970s (Mizrahi, 2007). With women straddling both the public and private sphere, balancing work and family often inhibits or severely inhibits women from engaging in the community. These issues are often compounded by the overall decrease of community life already experienced by many in the United States. Despite gender as the common front, other factors, such as race, ethnicity, class, and religious concerns, often supersede gender (Mizrahi, 2007). It may be a combination or the intersectionality of these factors that helps to shape the perceptions of women organizing and thus their styles of organizing.

History of welfare rights organizing

Although the term welfare can refer to a broad range of government programs, such as social security and financial aid assistance, for the most part the term denotes the cash assistance provided to the poor (Nadasen, 2012). The first federal aid provided to poor mothers came through the program Aid to Families with Dependent Children (AFDC), Title IV of the Social Security Act of 1935, a means-tested cash assistance program. Amendments to the Social Security Act in 1939 allowed some widows and their children, who were considered "deserving," to transition to social security aid, which did not require a demonstration of economic need. Yet, only widows from certain occupations that tended to employ white workers were permitted this alternative to welfare, leaving a larger number of African American widows, divorced women, and unmarried mothers receiving public assistance (Neubeck and Cazenave, 2001).

Mounting criticism emerged during the 1950s and 1960s as the number of recipients grew and the face of welfare changed. A stereotypical image of a welfare recipient developed as an unmarried African American mother who was lazy and promiscuous. Welfare backlash grew and a war on welfare commenced through attempting to uncover welfare fraud, limiting eligibility, reducing the already meager payments, and pushing employment. Recipients were subjected to stringent and humiliating criteria, which required women to prove they were worthy of services (Kornbluh, 1997; Nadasen, 2012). In some states and cities, special departments formed to investigate if a recipient had a substitute parent living in the home. "Substitute father" or "man-in-the-house" rules denied women assistance if there was any evidence of a male residing in the home (Abramovitz, 2000; Nadasen, 2012; Neubeck and Cazenave, 2001). These units often used unannounced "midnight raids" to search recipients' homes, violating their privacy and stripping their dignity. The "suitable home" rule allowed caseworkers to deny aid to mothers who bore children out of wedlock or engaged in behavior that was deemed as immoral by the caseworker (Neubeck and Cazenave, 2001).

Although laws did not specifically restrict eligibility for women of color, countless African American women were denied aid, particularly in the South and in areas with a high African American population. Black women often were seen more as laborers than as mothers. One particular law that was primarily directed toward African American women, the Employable Mother law, helped to ensure a steady flow of workers into the labor force through the denial of assistance if the woman was able-bodied, even if employment was unavailable (Nadasen, 2012). For example, Louisiana implemented a policy requiring aid to be cut whenever mothers or children were needed to pick cotton (Neubeck and Cazenave, 2001). As these dehumanizing requirements, biased policies, and inflammatory rhetoric mounted, poor women became scapegoats for the many growing social problems.

Yet a shift in the response from these vulnerable women was looming, as overt opposition intensified as mothers redefined welfare as a right, rather than a privilege (Abramovitz, 2000). As the pain of punitive welfare policies was felt on the local level, many grassroots organizations sprouted up to confront unjust and racist rules and requirements. With local welfare organizing growing, national organizations were developed to organize a national agenda to address the experiences of welfare recipients. The National Welfare Rights Organization (NWRO) was one of the largest national organizations at the forefront of the welfare rights movement in the 1960s and 1970s.

In 1966, one welfare activist mother, Johnnie Tillmon from Watts, CA, attended a national convention on poverty and she, along with others, vehemently verbalized the problems experienced by poor people, which left the organizer of the event both embarrassed and inspired (Nadasen, 2012). Within a year, the NWRO was formed by George Wiley, the convention organizer, along with mostly male civil rights veterans. Wiley became the Executive Director and Tillmon, the outspoken welfare mother, served as the chairperson. NWRO's main goals were to improve public assistance and to establish a federally guaranteed income (Orleck, 2005). Membership expanded swiftly using a grassroots organizing strategy and, by 1969, membership reached 22,000. The local welfare rights organizations also saw rapid growth from 130 in 23 states in 1966 to 900 in 50 states in 1971 (Abramovitz, 2000).

Participation was twofold—one, to help transform the welfare system, and two, to empower those involved through participation (Nadasen, 2012; Orleck, 2005). With the increase of welfare rights organizing, on the micro level women questioned decisions made by their case workers and advocated for the services they knew were available as discovered through their social ties. Women, like these welfare activists, gain a sense of empowerment as they develop critical consciousness and self-efficacy skills. Self-advocacy for their communities becomes an extension of their duty to care for their families and communities (Jewell, 2008). On the macro level, using diverse and at times confrontational tactics, welfare activists secured changes from reluctant welfare administrators, demanded a role in policy development, increased democratic participation through serving on community boards and policymaking bodies, and engaged in campaigns to expand welfare and gain consumer credit (Kornbluh, 1997).

Fractures, along race, class, and gender lines, within NWRO, developed between recipients and staff of the organizations (Nadasen, 2012; Orleck, 2005). Brewing for some time, conflicts grew between the female recipients who volunteered their time and the mostly male organizers who were salaried employees. Often using a more Alinsky-style of organizing, staff members failed to honor women's ways of organizing. With less formal training, recipients' ways of organizing were rooted in their daily lives, with both a focus on the process and result. Through their personal experiences with poverty and as recipients gained knowledge and confidence about how systems functioned, clashes between staff and recipients grew (Nadasen, 2012).

Many welfare activist mothers believed that the stigma associated with cash assistance could be overcome by a moral argument. Although many well-meaning middle-class allies provided assistance, mothers wanted to speak for themselves because the stigma, isolation, and the demonization was as important to address as the provision of resources. Most wanted short-term concessions to address immediate needs but also saw the long-term value of transforming the public perceptions of welfare recipients and dismantling the structural nature of poverty that limits the choices and goals available to poor people to realize their rights (Nadasen, 2012). In the book, *Welfare mothers speak out: We ain't gonna shuffle anymore* (Milwaukee County Welfare Rights Organization, 1972), a welfare activist explains the rationale for the maintenance of stereotypes:

> Myths are needed to justify the welfare system, a system that cheats the very people it is supposed to help. Myths are needed to discourage eligible, low-paid workers from applying for aid. Myths are needed to divert taxpayer frustrations away from the country's big welfare recipients—the rich and the military—and onto the defenseless, powerless poor. In short, myths are needed to hide the real welfare crisis.
>
> (p. 72)

The divisions within the organizations were exacerbated by decreased funding, diminished liberal support, co-opted leadership, and an increased conservative political climate. In 1975, NWRO, one of the largest and most powerful welfare rights organizations, declared bankruptcy and closed its doors after years of discord (Abramovitz, 2000). The welfare rights movement did not disappear despite this significant blow. The work on the state and local level by groups such as Women's Economic Agenda Project (WEAP, Oakland), Justice, Economic Dignity, and Independence for Women (JEDI for Women, Salt Lake City), and Michigan Welfare Rights Union (MWRU, Detroit) continued to use creative and at times militant tactics to protest the dissolution of the safety net in the United States (Orleck, 2005).

Shifting framework for mass appeal

The social and political movements of the 1960s and early 1970s were quieted during the 1980s and, by the early 1990s, the political culture had shifted significantly, allowing room for a complete overhaul of welfare. In the United States, the poor, often labeled as lazy, dependent, and unworthy, are often scapegoated for the social ills of the country (Rehmann, 2011; Sidel, 2000). The harshest rhetoric is often reserved for poor women, typically poor women of color, which reveals the convergence of class, race, and gender oppression (Neubeck and Cazenave, 2001). Single mothers are blamed for numerous social ills, such as crime, drugs, poverty, illiteracy, and homelessness.

This othering or demonization of the poor provides fertile soil for the dismantling of the social welfare system, which was evident during the impassioned congressional debates surrounding "the end to welfare as we know it" in the 1990s (Sidel, 2000). The Personal Responsibility and Work Opportunity Reconciliation Act (PRWORA) of 1996 imposed work requirements and a five-year lifetime limit of assistance. No longer an entitlement program, Temporary Assistance to Needy Families (TANF) replaced AFDC as individuals were pushed into the private labor market as quickly as possible or risked the loss of benefits (Hays, 2003).

At the same time, the continued rise of neoliberalism and unbridled free enterprise created devastating economic and social consequences for many who felt they were insulated from poverty (Rehmann, 2011). With increasing unemployment and foreclosure rates, the transition to dire poverty is often one misstep away, increasing the "new poor." The growing number of middle-class people slipping down the economic ladder due to advances in technology and the number of working-class poor people who were shifted from welfare into low-wage jobs gave rise to a mounting force of people poised to take action against weakened trade unions, debilitating unemployment rates in some communities, skyrocketing foreclosure rates, and stagnant wages. As the culture was becoming less supportive for welfare rights organizing, a new organizing strategy emerged post-PRWORA, which focused on building a movement to end poverty through the leadership of the poor and, for some organizations, grounded in human rights (Neubeck, 2011).

The Universal Declaration of Human Rights (UDHR) outlines 30 non-binding directives (United Nations, 1948). Two covenants derived from the UDHR impose specific obligations. The International Covenant on Civil and Political Rights (ICCPR) and the International Covenant on Economic, Social, and Cultural Rights (ICESCR) provide the backing to enforce the provisions of human rights if a country signs and ratifies the instrument (Reichert, 2003). An ideological clash between the United States and the Soviet Union during the Cold War saw the United States support civil and political rights promoted by the ICCPR, while the Soviet Union garnered support for the economic and social rights outlined in the ICESCR. Many rights groups, primarily located in the United States and the global North, focused on the protection of civil and political rights and neglected economic and social rights because these rights were seen as controversial and unpopular. Since the early 1990s and following the collapse of the Soviet Union, human rights organizations have embraced economic and social rights- and other rights-based organizations, like certain welfare rights groups, have embraced human rights language (Nicholson and Chong, 2011).

Not without its shortcomings, the human rights lens offers a clear set of basic moral principles that are in opposition to inequality and injustice. Such instruments as the UDHR and its derivative treaties have legitimacy and a moral force in world opinion, which provides the moral authority for calls to action (Nicholson and Chong, 2011). Human rights are an internationally legitimated framework from which collective demands for basic needs can be made and unite often disparate and issue-based struggles (Caruso, 2011).

Creating a common vision, the use of a human rights framework draws in others who would be dismissive of a welfare rights agenda given the prevailing media images and predominant ideologies of poverty. Through more inclusive language, individuals are able to see similarities in their struggles and overcome race and class differences around common class concerns. Employing human rights opens up opportunities for social justice groups to connect to global human rights movements with similar activist groups, which are imperative given the rise of globalization (Smith, 2008).

Gaining legitimacy through human rights

Although employing human rights language has a long history in grassroots struggles, from such activists and intellects as W.E.B. DuBois, Malcolm X, and Martin Luther King, some organizations are renewing the human rights discourse (Caruso, 2011) and, specifically, urging for the acceptance of U.S. poverty to be recognized as a violation of human rights. Organizations like the Poor People's Economic Human Rights Campaign (PPEHRC) and Women in Transition (WIT) are building a movement to end poverty from the ranks of the poor to galvanize attention to the violation of economic human rights in the United States (Bricker-Jenkins et al., 2007; Jewell et al., 2009). Organizations like PPEHRC and WIT are adamant that poverty, along with the destruction of a safety net, is a violation of human rights (Neubeck, 2011).

Formed in 1998, PPEHRC's mission was a commitment "to uniting the poor across color lines as the leadership base for broad movement to abolish poverty" (http://www.economichumanrights.org). Members of Kensington Welfare Rights Union (KWRU), a Philadelphia-based welfare rights group, spearheaded the development of PPEHRC, an umbrella group of organizations addressing poverty-related concerns. KWRU realized that patchwork reforms in the welfare system were necessary but not sufficient to address growing inequality and, in order to build a social movement to end poverty, the scattered struggles of local groups must be united. PPEHRC crisscrossed the United States in the 1998 Freedom Bus Tour, meeting with organizations run by and for the poor and introducing the economic human rights framework as a method to unite these groups (Honkala et al., 1999). "The concepts and language of economic human rights provided key elements of the conceptual and strategic apparatus needed to move to the next phase—building a mass social movement to end poverty" (Bricker-Jenkins et al., 2007, p. 127). PPEHRC pointed to the articles in the UDHR that address economic human rights (Articles 23, 25, and 26) in calling for the abolition of poverty in the United States and stressed the contradictory stance the United States makes as an exemplar for human rights, yet refusing to sign the ICESCR (Neubeck, 2011).

In contrast to the NWRO, whose staff was largely middle class, white, and male, those who are directly impacted by poverty, welfare recipients, the unemployed, and homeless, form the leadership base and decision-making body of the organization. This notion is a fundamental factor in building a broad base to secure societal transformation, as historically significant social change requires those who are most directly affected to be at the forefront of change (Bricker-Jenkins et al., 2007; Jewell et al., 2009). PPEHRC's transnational linkages with other poor people's movements around the world, such as MST in Brazil and the Mothers of the Disappeared in Argentina, helped to strengthen an international movement of the poor to confront the persistent push toward neoliberalism, which has emphasized privatization, deregulation, and shrinking the public sector.

Women in Transition is a member of the network of organizations working to abolish poverty under the PPEHRC umbrella. Although WIT developed after the decline of the welfare rights movement, WIT started in response to changes in welfare policy under the Personal Responsibility and Work Opportunity Reconciliation Act of 1996, hence the organization started under a welfare rights frame. States were given two years to create and prepare for the implementation of new policies under PRWORA. In June of 1998, a group of welfare recipients, who were pursuing a post-secondary education, met to discuss these changes and develop strategies to comply with work requirements while completing their college education. From this formal meeting arranged by a local university in Louisville, these women decided to continue meeting, and Women in Transition was established.

As discussed earlier, informal social ties often provide the foundation for women's organizing and that was the case for the welfare mothers who formed WIT too. Through these social ties, WIT members provided significant mutual support and connections to much-needed resources. Whether through the sharing of food, passing down clothing, or babysitting while another member attended class, WIT members became a support system that helped to mitigate the impact of poverty on themselves and their families. Members became better equipped to advocate for services following information sharing and skill building. WIT members also developed a critical collective analysis of the systemic oppression propagated in the United States through consciousness-raising activities organized by the group and through increased involvement in other social justice organizations in Louisville. Like welfare activist mothers in the 1960s and 1970s, WIT identified the need to confront and transform the negative perceptions of welfare recipients through the development and facilitation of Dismantling Classism workshops that highlighted the interconnection between racism, classism, sexism, ableism, and other systems of oppression.

In the summer of 2003, PPEHRC organized the Poor People's March for Economic Human Rights from Selma to Washington to commemorate the 35th Anniversary of the 1968 Poor People's March, which was organized by Martin Luther King prior to his assassination (Bricker-Jenkins et al., 2007). During a stop in Louisville, PPEHRC met with the leadership of WIT and presented the human rights perspective as a conceptual framework in organizing a poor people's movement. WIT members were immediately sold on adopting the human rights lens and joining the ranks of PPEHRC.

Embracing a human rights framework rather than a welfare rights framework helped to strengthen the organization in multiple ways. A heightened sense of empowerment was developed by members, who no longer felt they were groveling for handouts but could make moral and legitimate claims to economic human rights as outlined in the UDHR (Jewell et al., 2009). Buying into the myth that the United States is the land of opportunity and when an individual works hard success is assured, WIT members often faltered with the language to discuss why providing for the poor was just. Members had to battle their own internalized classism that suggested the reason they were poor was simply based on their own shortcomings rather than systemic barriers that maintain stark differences between groups. The economic human rights language connoted legitimacy from which welfare mothers could argue that they deserved to live with dignity regardless of their participation in the waged labor market.

Becoming an affiliate of PPEHRC immediately connected WIT to over a hundred poor people's groups across the United States, which decreased isolation and increased exposure to others' organizing strategies. Members of WIT participated in events and direct actions throughout the United States and abroad. Through these experiences, the analysis deepened and new strategies developed. A single mother, who is a veteran, expressed:

> WIT is the first place in my life that I actually felt the words of liberation and dignity. Grassroots work is so important and I did not realize the power of it until I became a part of WIT, and how much it really had to do with me. I had never had the opportunity to participate in work that directly affected my life in a way that would be in pursuit of liberation for all oppressed people. I found a place, because of the human rights framework.

The language of human rights is more inclusive than welfare rights and, after a more thorough analysis, WIT expanded membership beyond welfare recipients to include men and people who identify as poor. The ranks of WIT grew as the unemployed, homeless, working poor, and allies joined to advance the broader mission of abolishing poverty. Although there were some unique issues experienced by welfare recipients, overall members understood the need to unite poor and working-class people for a broad-base group. For WIT, the adoption of the economic human rights framework bolstered their work in multiple ways, which strengthened the resolve of the members and organization.

Human rights is typically touted in the international arena, yet many grassroots groups in the United States, such as PPEHRC and WIT, use a human rights framework to secure much-needed provisions in the national and local arenas. In cities across the United States, groups are demanding "human rights in our own backyard" through local implementation (Armaline et al., 2011). Member organizations of PPEHRC, like WIT, participated and secured homes through housing takeovers, resisted foreclosures, prompted the passage of living-wage ordinances and funding for affordable housing, and challenged the stereotypes of poor people. PPEHRC brought international and national attention to the direct violation of economic human rights in the United States through large-scale and internationally publicized marches and tent cities and raised the question of poverty as a violation of human rights before the United Nations.

Despite facing mounting opposition to organizing for a more expansive welfare state, the struggle for survival and subsistence was one in which it was too legit to quit. Rather than bowing out as the window of opportunity closed on social change efforts in the 1970s, some welfare activists regrouped and embraced a framework that reinvigorated their legitimate and moral claims. Utilizing concepts and language from economic human rights and the human rights perspective has been shown to be an effective tool to increase legitimacy in society and confront the oppressive nature of neoliberal policies.

References

Abramovitz, M. (2000). *Under attack, fighting back.* New York: Monthly Review.

Abramovitz, M. (2001). Learning from the history of poor and working-class women's activism. *The Annals of the American Academy*, 577, 118–130.

Armaline, W.T., Glasberg, D.S., and Purkayastha, B. (eds). (2011). *Human rights in our own backyard: Injustice and resistance in the United States.* Philadelphia: University of Pennsylvania.

Bricker-Jenkins, M., Young, C., and Honkala, C. (2007). Using economic human rights in the movement to end poverty: The Kensington Welfare Rights Union and the Poor People's Economic Human Rights Campaign. In E. Reichert (ed.), *Challenges in human rights: A social work perspective* (pp. 122–137). New York: Columbia University.

Caruso, C. (2011). A case study on organizing: The struggle for water in postindustrial Detroit. In W. Baptist and J. Rehmann (eds), *Pedagogy of the poor: Building the movement to end poverty* (pp. 84–96). New York: Teachers College.

Gittell, M., Ortega-Bustamente, I., and Steffy, T. (2000). Social capital and social change: Women's community activism. *Urban Affairs Review*, 36, 123–147.

Hardina, D. (2003). Linking citizen participation to empowerment practice: A historical overview. *Journal of Community Practice*, 11(4), 11–38.

Hays, S. (2003). *Flat broke with children: Women in the age of welfare reform.* New York: Oxford University Press.

Haywoode, T.L. (1999). Working-class women and local politics: Styles of community organizing. *Research in Politics and Society*, 7, 111–134.

Honkala, C., Goldstein, R., Thul, E., Baptist, W., and Grugan, P. (1999). Globalisation and homelessness in the USA: Building a social movement to end poverty. *Development in Practice*, 9(5), 526–538.

Jewell, J.R. (2008). *The development of community organizations by poor women in China and the United States.* Unpublished doctoral dissertation, University of Louisville.

Jewell, J.R., Collins, K.V., Gargotto, L., and Dishon, A.J. (2009). Building the unsettling force: Social workers in the struggle for human rights. *Journal of Community Practice*, 17(3), 309–322.

Joseph, B., Lobo, S., McLaughlin, P., Mizrahi, T., Peterson, J., Rosenthal, B., and Sugarman, F. (1991). *A framework for feminist organizing: Values, goals, methods, strategies, and roles*. New York: Education Center for Community Organizing.

Kaplan, T. (1997). *Crazy for democracy: Women in grassroots movements*. New York: Routledge.

Kornbluh, F. (1997). To fulfill their "rightly needs": Consumerism and the National Welfare Rights Movement. *Radical History Review*, 69, 76–113.

Martin, D.G. (2002). Constructing the "neighborhood sphere": Gender and community organizing. *Gender, Place, and Culture*, 9(4), 333–350.

Milwaukee County Welfare Rights Organization. (1972). *Welfare mothers speak out: We ain't gonna shuffle anymore*. New York: Norton and Company.

Mizrahi, T. (2007). Women's ways of organizing. *Affilia: Journal of Women and Social Work*, 22(1), 39–55.

Molyneux, M. (1998). Analysing women's movements. *Development and Change*, 29, 219–245.

Nadasen, P. (2012). *Rethinking the welfare rights movement*. New York: Routledge.

Naples, N. (1998). *Grassroots warriors: Activist mothering, community work, and the War on Poverty*. New York: Routledge.

Neubeck, K.J. (2011). Human rights violations as obstacles to escaping poverty: The case of lone-mother-headed families. In S. Hertel and K. Libal (eds), *Human rights in the United States: Beyond exceptionalism* (pp. 234–254). New York: Cambridge.

Neubeck, K.J., and Cazenave, N.A. (2001). *Welfare racism: Playing the race card against America's poor*. New York: Routledge.

Nicholson, S., and Chong, D. (2011). Jumping on the human rights bandwagon: How rights-based linkages can refocus climate politics. *Global Environmental Politics*, 11(3), 121–136.

Orleck, A. (2005). *Storming Caesars Palace: How black mothers fought their own war on poverty*. Boston: Beacon.

Rehmann, J. (2011). Root causes of poverty: Neoliberalism, high-tech capitalism, and economic crisis. In W. Baptist and J. Rehmann (eds), *Pedagogy of the poor: Building the movement to end poverty* (pp. 49–68). New York: Teachers College.

Reichert, E. (2003). *Social work and human rights: A foundation for policy and practice*. New York: Columbia University.

Sidel, R. (2000). The enemy within: The demonization of poor women. *Journal of Sociology and Social Welfare*, 26(1), 73–84.

Smith, A. (2008). Human rights and social-justice organizing in the United States. *Radical History Review*, 101, 211–219.

United Nations. (1948). *Universal declaration of human rights*. Adopted December 10, 1948, GA Res. 217 AIII (Un. Doc. a/810).

50

NEOLIBERALISM, STATE PROJECTS, AND MIGRANT ORGANIZING

Jacob Lesniewski and Rebecca Vonderlack-Navarro

There is growing interest in emerging forms of migrant mobilization. Mexican immigrant mobilizing campaigns are especially pertinent given their dynamic organizing to counter economic, social, and political exclusion and to increase economic opportunity and alleviate poverty. The nature of community organizing has also shifted with the onset of neoliberal globalization. We argue that new forms of migrant political activism have emerged out of cross-border economic flows that interact with various state projects. The argument is supported by two Chicago-based case studies: migrant worker centers and immigrant hometown associations. The chapter aims to raise the profile and reinvigorate policy debate about various forms of migrant exclusion, the implications of global interconnectedness, and how community practice can advance social justice concerns and poverty reduction in migrant communities.

The changing landscape of migrant organizing

Treatments of new forms of migrant mobilization often miss contextual factors that influence organizing. The Fordist or New Deal Order, based on domestic-oriented economic and political strategies, provided an early context for migrant community organizing. Keynesian-inspired economic development initiatives, national mass-production industries, strong unionized labor, and broad welfare state interventions were important pillars of the model. Political and economic activities assumed an active and legitimate role of the state in economic affairs largely confined within national borders. Unions enforced adherence to workplace rules and standards, and relatively robust state and federal Departments of Labor provided a baseline level of protection for non-union workers. In addition, the political incorporation of migrants relied upon traditional notions of immigrant assimilation: a linear, evolutionary, and inevitable process whereby immigrants shed their allegiances from the old country and over time adopted those of the new host society (Sites et al., 2007).

Post-industrial globalization and resulting mass immigration significantly altered migrant community organizing and the living standards of migrants. The response to the international economic crises of the 1970s included: shifts from national to globalized production and service industries (deindustrialization), shifts to flexible and temporary labor, international economic development policies and unfettered capital mobility (free trade, eased foreign direct investment, privatization, deregulation), and welfare state retrenchment. Neoliberalization accelerated the weakening of unions and government regulatory agencies. New business models emphasize cost reductions (especially labor costs) as a key corporate goal. This reorganization of U.S. labor markets resulted in a highly polarized labor market for migrants in particular, who face shrinking middle-class job prospects and diminishing chances for economic mobility. This also created a situation in which low-wage migrant workers face substantially higher levels of workplace abuse (Bobo, 2009).

Additionally, nation states were no longer bounded entities. Immigrants' mobilizing and political allegiances can no longer be conceived as simply contained within one nation. Intensified market integration and porous nation-state boundaries contributed to the rise of what is termed as *transnational* activism, which highlights how factors of globalization have created new forms of political opportunities and alignments (Smith and Bandy, 2005). In regards to migrant campaigns, theories of globalization complicate classic assimilation models that assume a world in which immigrant national identity is singular or a linear progression from one country to another. And even if earlier waves of immigrants sustained a national pride from their sending country, recent advances in travel and technology facilitate immigrants and their organizations to maintain ties to the homeland with an unparalleled intensity and ease not possible for previous waves of newcomers (Smith and Bakker, 2008).

While theories of globalization and transnational migrant organizing are important, we caution against their tendency to downplay the continued importance of the host nation state in shaping immigrant politics and community responses. The state, in fact, has always played an active role in shaping immigration through labor-recruitment policies and guest worker initiatives. Even the immigration of asylum-seekers and refugees is a direct result of problems occurring during the maintenance or construction of nation states (Zolberg, 2006). The question for scholars and activists concerned with immigrant activism in this new global era is no longer *if* state projects influence immigrant activism, but rather *how* they shape activism.

In terms of the Mexico–United States relationship, advances in trade liberalization intensified the United States's economic integration with Mexico. This was accompanied by unevenly enforced immigration laws and the proliferation of low-end job opportunities for the large number of unauthorized migrant workers arriving in U.S. cities (Massey et al., 2002). The proliferation of low-wage job opportunities complicate the efforts of migrants to achieve economic stability through work alone. Politically, Mexican migrants have often been targets of blame for the country's economic struggles and, at the same time, seen as potential voting blocs by both Democratic and Republican strategists (Zolberg, 2006).

National immigration politics has fostered a complex terrain of strange-bedfellows in which some politicians in both parties have seen immigrants, especially Latino immigrants, as potential allies. American federalism complicates matters further as local political scenes differ dramatically in their treatment of newcomers, from nativist backlash in some areas to immigrant-dense cities which have witnessed significant efforts to expand migrant rights. Economic migrants confront labor market arrangements that echo the urban sweatshops of the early 20th century. Activism for migrant rights has increasingly taken on the world of employment and job quality issues to improve economic opportunity. We now examine two cases of emergent Mexican migrant organizing within Chicago to explore the various opportunities, threats, and tensions they encounter as they interact with various neoliberal state projects.

Arise Chicago Workers Center: rethinking labor organizing

Workers centers emerge as a response to the challenge of workplace abuse faced by low-wage migrants which robs migrant workers of income and the ability to rise out of poverty through work. Workers centers like Arise Chicago Workers Center develop a number of strategies to seek redress for the workplace abuses of migrant workers and fight for changes in working conditions. Arise Chicago, founded in 2002, "is a member-based program that serves as a community resource for workers, both immigrant and native born, to learn about their rights and join fellow workers to organize to improve workplace conditions" (http://arisechicago.org/worker-center). The center has approximately 250 members; the majority (75%) are Mexican immigrants. Most members experienced cases of workplace abuse they were unable to resolve through traditional channels, such as government agency complaints.

Arise Chicago's main intervention is the workplace justice campaign. The campaign applies community organizing principles to individual cases of workplace abuse and is responsive to the changing employment conditions of migrant workers, who primarily work in small, geographically scattered service sector firms (in contrast to large, geographically concentrated firms during the Fordist era). The campaign has a complex relationship with government regulatory agencies.

The campaign begins with a workers' rights workshop that highlights the absence of the state in regulatory enforcement, the importance of mutual aid and solidarity among migrant workers, and the necessity of direct action to change working conditions. Nelly (pseudonym), a 22-year-old single mother and undocumented Mexican migrant brought to the United States by her parents in childhood, worked at a bridal stand in a mall. For 12 months she received approximately $5.00 per hour, well below the state minimum wage of $8.25. Motivated by an Arise Chicago workers' rights workshop at the domestic violence shelter where she lived, she confronted her boss with the discrepancy. She was summarily fired. While the Illinois Department of Labor does have a wage and hour division charged to assist workers like Nelly, its effectiveness is limited. An investigative report unveiled:

> ... the department found wage-law violations an estimated 59.5% of the time, but only an estimated 28% of those cases led to verifiable full payments ... The remainder—an estimated 54.4%—were closed and filed away after being labeled as "assumed paid."
>
> (Zamudio, 2012)

Filing complaints entails a lengthy claim-process and requires documentation uncommon to contingent workplaces. When a worker manages to get an administrative judgment referring her case to the state's attorney for prosecution, the claim often languishes. Nelly did file a complaint with the Illinois Department of Labor—a move used to create leverage, since there is little hope of receiving redress through process. Arise Chicago claims that none of its complaints with the Illinois Department of Labor have ever resulted in a check for back wages in the hands of a worker. Since its inception in 2002, the center has recovered over $4.5 million in back wages, largely through direct action (where the worker and allies confront the accused employer). Nelly waited six months before receiving acknowledgement that her complaint had begun to be processed by the department.

The campaign proceeds by creating the conditions for the execution of a direct action. Nelly confronted her boss again. This time Arise Chicago organizers, members, and allies joined her to stage a mock wedding procession into the mall to demand payment of back wages. Most Arise Chicago direct actions, whether as dramatic as Nelly's or smaller, end with a worker receiving a check or promise of payment. Nelly's ended with the arrival of the police (called by the boss who accused the group of trespassing) and a court date for Nelly, accused by her boss of harassment. She was later cleared of charges and began to collect her back wages through a negotiated agreement between her, Arise Chicago, the boss, and the boss's attorney.

Mexican immigrant hometown associations: rethinking integration

In the midst of the rise of Mexican migration to Chicago, migrants began to organize into social support clubs. These *clubes de oriundos* or hometown associations were similar to earlier mutual aid societies: spaces to maintain cultural links to their homeland in an often unwelcoming land. Mexican immigrant hometown clubs in the Midwest (Illinois, Wisconsin, and Indiana) serve as a resource for new arrivals to celebrate hometown traditions, fight discrimination, and cultivate links with fellow *paisanos* (countrymen) in the United States. At times, the clubs would pool resources to support philanthropic projects back in their hometown villages, such as renovating a local church, paving a deteriorating road, or providing an ambulance to a local health clinic. Until the late 1980s, the clubs remained largely outside the purview of either Mexican or U.S. politics. Over the decades, however, Midwestern associations grew dramatically from 35 in 1995 to over 340 by 2008 (Chicago Mexican Consular materials, 2009) while simultaneously evolving into vehicles to fight for full citizenship and enhanced economic opportunities.

The expansion of the associations was due to growing Mexican governmental attention towards its diaspora. Mexican political elites became increasingly aware of the associations' growing economic clout through their remittance-based development efforts. By the late 1980s the Mexican government initiated outreach efforts through its consular offices to the associations to facilitate their growth, foster the formation of state-level federations, and multiply their economic development efforts within their Mexican *pueblos* (Goldring, 2002; Gomez, 2005).

Hometown associations are best known for their participation in Mexico's *tres-por-uno* (three-for-one) development program: for every dollar a club donates for development in their *pueblos*, a dollar match is contributed by the municipal, state, and national governments of Mexico. Chicago's 3x1 program began with an association from the Mexican state of Guerrero subsidizing Guerrero's social security program and aid families that had been deported. As a result of the significant public attention migrants were now garnering in their hometowns, many association cultural festivities began to take on political overtones as Mexican governmental elites often appeared championing emigrants for their continued devotion to Mexico (Gomez, 2005). Migrants, in turn, increased their political clout through negotiations with authorities over the implementation of development projects and becoming advocates for dual nationality and absentee voting rights in Mexico (Fitzgerald, 2006).

The significance of the remittances and organizations of emigrants to Mexican politics increased in the 2000s. Mexican President Vicente Fox (2000–2006) overhauled consular programming and nationalized outreach efforts to support the associations' growth and 3x1 programs (Fitzgerald, 2006). Hometown associations throughout the United States, in turn, began to receive political recognition due to their contributions towards development in Mexico (estimated at U.S. $30 million). Consequently, Chicago associations cultivated norms of political engagement, increased self-confidence, and demonstrated a level of negotiated political efficacy focused almost entirely on Mexico.

Even with organizations' intensifying connections to their homeland, they were not immune to the U.S. political climate. Following the terrorist attacks of September 11, 2001 and the beginning of the "war on terrorism," U.S. immigration increasingly became a national security concern. Chicago's associations, with support from the Mexican government, began to move into U.S.-centered financial service and political integration activities: support for the consulate's *matricula consular* documentation to provide undocumented members with formal identification and access to banking services; expanding organizational activities to include ESL classes, legal counseling, and scholarship activities; and joining the National Alliance of Latino and Caribbean Communities to support national pro-immigrant legislation. By 2003 eight

Midwestern federations and 175 associations coalesced into a unique Chicago-based confederation. A key driver of the confederation development from the state of Michoacán became Illinois Governor Blagojevich's director of the Office of New Americans Policy and Advocacy. This office worked to promote immigrant integration services in the state. While unique among federation leaders, this new connection to state government aroused further interest in domestic interest-group activity for some hometown leaders. In spite of these new activities, in 2005 Mexico still had primacy as the organizations battled for absentee voting rights in Mexico's 2006 presidential elections. This privilege was granted in early 2005 (although restrictions attached to the measure significantly reduced emigrant voter turnout) (Smith and Bakker, 2008, p. 133).

It would take a severe political threat to move U.S.-focused activity to the top of many hometown associations' agendas. House Judiciary Chair James Sensenbrenner introduced HR4437 (the Border Protection, Antiterrorism, and Illegal Immigration Control Act of 2005) which contained highly punitive provisions, including redefining any provision of support to unauthorized migrants as a criminal offense (Wayne, 2005). Insulted and frightened by the quick passage of the bill in December 2005 (with many leaders claiming as many as half of their members undocumented), association leaders gathered with other local immigrant activists to plan for the city's 2006 mass marches at the Michoacán federation headquarters. The Sensenbrenner bill played a critical role in catalyzing immigrants' collective resistance on March 10, 2006 with a mass march in Chicago, an effort that sparked mass protests throughout the country on May 1, 2006.

Soon after the mass marches of 2006, the associations were recognized by local politicians as a potential new voting constituency. From 2006 until the presidential elections of 2008, politicians in Illinois increasingly courted the associations as a voting bloc. While the associations continued their Mexico-focused activities, the organizations were also assuming activities focused on U.S. political integration: citizenship, lobbying, and voting drives. Some association leaders would come to resemble more of an interest group promoting voting campaigns over marching with an eye towards local political recognition. Other leaders, frustrated by failed immigration reform legislation and rising local repression, returned to traditional cultural- and identity-affirming activities.

Implications for community practice

Within neoliberalism the state is no longer simply the main channel for achieving integration and improved living standards. For hometown associations, various state actors on both sides of the Mexico–United States border at different times *facilitated* emerging political clout, *stymied* migrant political inclusion post-9/11, or, when useful, *co-opted* protest momentum into friendly voting blocs. This contradictory state activity, emblematic of neoliberalism, has important implications for conceptualizing migrant integration. One could argue that the trajectory of U.S. integration is no different from the mutual aid societies of the past: a space that celebrated homeland ties until the threat of Great Depression-era deportations instigated struggles for political inclusion (Innis-Jimenez, 2006). The critical difference in the context of neoliberalism is the role of the sending state and its enduring relationship with the diaspora. Mexico's contemporary state project is dependent on out-migration and return remittances, and this state–emigrant relationship is no better illustrated than by Mexico's outreach to hometown associations. The novel role of the sending state influences the associations' U.S. integration in significant ways: (1) early on Mexico purposefully emboldened the associations' political efficacy; (2) their political capital was transferable to U.S. politics (Smith, 2007); and (3) Mexico would back the associations' surge into U.S. protest and politics (not deter it) as it benefited from the diaspora's security and stability.

In Nelly's case, and in contrast to the Fordist era, state practices were also contradictory: at times *friendly*, at times *absent*, and at times a *punitive* force excluding workers from full economic and political citizenship and the ability to achieve economic stability through work. Traditional community and labor organizing emphasizes formal membership organizations that become strong political actors by taking their seat at the "table of democracy" (Alinsky, 1971; Smock, 2004). The largely undocumented migrant workforce that makes up the constituency of Arise Chicago, however, faces workplaces characterized by rampant abuse, low wages, and a lack of internal job markets. Achieving redress for workplace abuse often requires tactics outside of traditional community organizing models. The workplace justice campaign, an unconventional hybrid of organizing and individual case management, is arguably more effective than traditional models.

Attempts by Nelly and Arise Chicago organizers to engage agents of the state, specifically the Illinois Department of Labor's Wage and Hour division, were largely met with silence. The mere threat of state action, however ethereal, was something that Nelly's boss and her attorney admitted was what brought them to the negotiating table. Repressive state actions hindered a quick resolution of Nelly's campaign. Under Fordism, Nelly would have processed her claim through a union grievance procedure and been legally protected in her right to protest and picket her employer if the process failed. Arise Chicago, as a non-union, non-profit organization, is forced to use outsider tactics, often provoking punitive state responses, such as police threats of arrest for trespassing. Undocumented migrant workers often face bosses who threaten to call immigration authorities if workers complain about conditions or treatment. Regardless of whether the threat is legitimate, the fear it creates is illustrative of the chilling effects it can have on migrant activism.

Both case studies elucidate how inherited models of community practice fall short in this new context of neoliberalism. The changes facing migrants and their campaigns for political inclusion, improved working conditions, and economic opportunity demand new kinds of activism. Traditional community and labor organizing strategies are based on pluralist notions of a state willing to absorb new interest groups and new actors, not on the complex state practices of neoliberalism (Smock, 2004).

Hometown associations share the same challenge of other community groups faced with the challenging dilemma of political co-optation within pluralist politics as immigration reform failed to materialize, or marginality as the anti-immigrant climate heightened. A hopeful possibility is that the associations can productively cross what Sites et al. (2007) refer to as *"spatial/political* boundaries" where they can link local efforts with cross-border initiatives. This has begun in Chicago where the Midwestern confederation of hometown associations joined with the National Alliance of Latino and Caribbean Communities. The innovative alliance provides a way for local migrant communities to respond to multiple state projects. Its guiding principle promotes multi-national considerations for immigrant policies promoting advocacy in both countries of destination of migration and countries of origin. The alliance enhances the multi-scalar promise of hometown associations by offering important links to local, national, and transnational scales.

While workers centers such as Arise Chicago do not cross or even contemplate crossing national boundaries in their attempts to change the conditions of work for migrants in the United States, the notion of boundary crossing is still useful. Arise Chicago crosses "sectoral boundaries" (Sites et al., 2007: 536) by bringing together the traditionally discrete areas of labor and community as well as case management and organizing in ways that confront power relationships in the workplace. Workers centers have begun to leverage this boundary crossing to form "minority unions" of workers in various service sector industries (Fine, 2011). These nascent efforts attempt to amplify and concentrate worker center interventions within industries and attempt to overcome structural impediments to organizing small groups of workers working in small, geographically scattered firms. This strategy, which adapts the occupational union organizing strategies that proved effective for workers similarly marginalized under Fordist regimes, is one worth watching for its lessons for community practice.

Summary

The study of migrant campaigns is important because it shows the changing context facing community practice in the 21st century. The political and economic shifts of neoliberal transformation force migrants and organizers to develop new strategies, organizational forms, and tactics in their quest to promote migrant integration and economic opportunity in the United States. This chapter reveals the role of shifting state projects, cross-border interdependencies, and workplace regulatory regimes in shaping migrant activism and organizing. Effective community practice with other populations requires similar understandings of the context facing those groups as they seek to achieve their goals of human dignity and increased political and economic participation.

References

Alinsky, Saul D. (1971). *Rules for Radicals: A Pragmatic Primer for Realistic Radicals*. New York: Vintage Books.

Bobo, Kimberly. (2009). *Wage Theft in America: Why Millions of Working Americans Are Not Getting Paid—And What We Can Do About It*. New York: New Press.

Chicago Mexican Consular Materials. (2009). Miscellaneous documents related to Midwest Region HTAs. Retrieval date: May 9, 2010

Fine, Janice. (2011). "Worker Centers: Entering a New Stage of Growth and Development." *New Labor Forum* 20(3): 44–53.

Fitzgerald, David. (2006). "Inside the Sending State: The Politics of Mexican Emigration Control." *International Migration Review* 40(2): 259–293.

Goldring, Luin. (2002). "The Mexican State and Transmigrant Organizations: Negotiating the Boundaries of Membership and Participation." *Latin American Research Review* 37(3): 55–99.

Gomez, Dante. (2005). "Clubes mexicanos de oriundos." Archival material from the Chicago Mexican Consulate.

Innis-Jimenez, Michael. (2006). *Persisting in the Shadow of Steel: Community Formation and Survival in Mexican South Chicago, 1919–1939*. Dissertation available on ProQuest. Ann Arbor, MI.

Massey, Douglas S., Jorge Durand, and Nolan J. Malone. (2002). *Beyond Smoke and Mirrors: Mexican Immigration in an Era of Economic Integration*. New York: Russell Sage Foundation.

Sites, W., R. Chaskin, and V. Parks. (2007). "Reframing Community Practice for the 21st Century: Multiple Traditions, Multiple Challenges." *Journal of Urban Affairs* 29(5): 519–541.

Smith, J., and Joe Bandy. (2005). "Introduction: Cooperation and Conflict in Transnational Protest." In *Coalitions Across Borders: Transnational Protest and the Neoliberal Order*, edited by Joe Bandy and Jackie Smith. Lanham, MD: Rowman and Littlefield.

Smith, Michael Peter. (2007). "The Two Faces of Transnational Citizenship." *Ethnic and Racial Studies* 30(6): 1096–1116.

Smith, Michael Peter, and Matt Bakker. (2008). *Citizenship Across Borders: The Political Transnationalism of El Migrante*. Ithaca and London: Cornell University Press.

Smock, Kristina. (2004). *Democracy in Action: Community Organizing and Urban Change*. New York: Columbia University Press.

Wayne, Alex. (2005). "Views of Senate GOP, Bush Threaten Tighter Immigration." *CQ Weekly*, January 17.

Zamudio, M.I. (2012). "Waiting in Vain." *Chicago Reporter*, March/April 2012.

Zolberg, Aristide R. (2006). *A Nation by Design: Immigration Policy in the Fashioning of America*. Russell Sage Foundation. New York: Harvard University Press.

51

FROM THE SELF TO THE SOCIAL

Engaging urban youth in strategies for change

Amira Proweller and Karen Monkman

Introduction

The disproportionate number of children living in poverty in the United States is a constant reminder of the social inequities that loom large in this country. "Nationally, one-in-five children grow up poor, 9.2 million children currently lack health insurance, 3.9 million people are homeless (a number projected to increase 5% each year) and 1.3 million (or 39%) of them are children" (Leistyna, 2009, p. 52). Beyond the myriad of challenges that youth face in urban communities of poverty, many attend public schools caught in the cross hairs of a neoliberal assault, where escalating pressures for accountability, privatized reforms, and a growing emphasis on high-stakes testing predominate (Darling-Hammond, 2010; Kumashiro, 2012; Lipman, 2011). A heightened focus on techno-rational forms of instruction fail to provide youth with the knowledge and skills to understand and ultimately challenge profound social and economic inequalities that shape their daily lives (Giroux, 2009). These changes, along with others, are part of the neoliberal shift of the last several decades. "[N]eoliberal academic discourses and ideologies ... substitute cultural explanations of poverty for structural causes, pathologize people of color, and promote individual responsibility and market solutions" (Lipman, 2011, p. 89). In this context, the narrowing of school curriculum creates a space for the proliferation of programs of the types discussed herein. These initiatives are reliant on short-term funding acquired through market competition, thereby creating precarious conditions for their work and giving more power to funding sources to shape agendas. Increasingly targeted for societal and educational disinvestment, youth on the class and race periphery are marginalized and cast as social problems (Books, 2007). Despite notions of public schooling existing for and in the interests of all students (Smyth, 2012, p. 76), youth from urban communities of poverty find themselves academically disconnected and slowly disappear into the ravages of growing poverty in the United States (Darling-Hammond, 2010; Fine et al., 2004; Lipman, 2004).

There are, nonetheless, a variety of ways in which youth are involved in taking charge of and reshaping their lives. Typical of these opportunities in school settings are school governance and service learning courses, and, outside of school, there are programs within community-based organizations, church groups, and civic organizations, among others. Some ways of engaging, such as volunteering and community service, are either ancillary to or required by schools. A third space consists of after-school programs, which generally fall into two main camps:

childcare programs for school-aged youth, focused on providing a safe environment for youth to participate in unstructured activities, and youth development programs oriented toward the development of academic and socio-emotional competencies, skills, and commitments (Kahne et al., 2001; Riggs and Greenberg, 2004). In the main, this space acts as a bridge between school and community, serving the academic and social needs of low-income youth by minimizing or altogether eliminating the risks presented by unsupervised time while also providing opportunities to enhance youth development once the official school day is over (Borden and Serido, 2009; Dryfoos, 1999; Halpern, 2000, 2002; Halpern et al., 2000; Little et al., 2008; Mahoney et al., 2009; Witt, 2004).

In this chapter, we examine three common approaches that seek to engage youth as active participants in their own development and broader social change.[1] We focus on strategies that use the terminology of "youth leadership," "student voice," and "civic engagement." While these are only three of many kinds of initiatives (for example, empowerment, community service, youth organizing, and social entrepreneurship), we selected these three to examine given growing attention to them in both scholarship and programming and their explicit focus on engaging youth in social change processes. They can occur in school programs and after-school programs, or outside of school, although many are situated in after-school contexts. In this review of research, we look closely at how urban youth are understood and contextualized in each of these approaches, with explicit attention to youth in conditions of poverty.

Youth leadership

Youth development programs have tended to emphasize activities related to academics, arts, and sports, but they are increasingly directing their attention to youth leadership, leading Woyach (1991) to observe that "[y]outh leadership is big business in the United States" (as cited by Conner and Strobel, 2007, p. 276). Notwithstanding the proliferation of youth leadership initiatives in recent decades, there is no consensus as to the "definition of what leadership is, no dominant paradigms for studying it, and little agreement about the best strategies for developing and exercising it" (Hackman and Wageman, 2007, p. 43). In a general but vague sense, this literature tends to take up the role that youth leadership initiatives play in enhancing individual competencies for leading and, less salient, cultivating in youth the capacities for a broader societal critique along with taking action for social change. Moreover, little research explicitly engages leadership in relationship to youth from communities of poverty, in particular. Meaningful initiatives for this population would be built on a critical analysis of the realities that poor youth face in their day-to-day lives, but, in fact, leadership for whom, and to what end, remains murky.

While there is lack of consensus around a definition of leadership, several prevalent themes tend to surface in the literature, including an orientation favoring adult notions of leadership, an emphasis on developmentalist perspectives, and inconsistency in recognizing youth agency. Among them are theories of adult leadership that predominate in studies of youth leadership, which some researchers argue need to be conceptualized very differently and separate from theories of youth leadership (Conner and Strobel, 2007). Traditional models of adult leadership sometimes emphasize the idea of the single leader who embodies particular traits that are not learned and acquired over time but, rather, are inherent in and unique to the individual (MacNeil, 2006; Roach et al., 1999). These models focus on issues of authority— voice, influence, and decision-making in the models assumed for leadership—and speak to the authoritative ways that adults position themselves in facilitating youth leadership. Inherent in these models is the assumption that youth leadership development depends on adult guidance, rather than something that youth are able to cultivate either on their own or through intentional relationships with adults where each has the opportunity to learn from the other. In this framework, adults are positioned as experts with a singular vision of how best to shape youth into future leaders, which validates the notion that youth are not able to develop their own leadership identity through self-reflection and discovery (Wheeler and Edlebeck, 2006).

While consensus around a shared definition of leadership has eluded the scholarship on youth leadership, leadership experts, nonetheless, agree that leadership is a personal and developmental process aimed at enhancing individual competencies in communication, intrapersonal and interpersonal skills, critical reflection and decision-making, and positive community involvement (Mitra and Kirshner, 2012). More often than not, though, youth have been framed within these developmental models from a deficit rather than an asset-based perspective, vilified as dangerous problems requiring intervention rather than competent experts on their own lives with the capacity to engage in broader social change efforts (MacNeil, 2006). Youth leadership education devoid of opportunities that are connected to relevant issues in the lives of youth provides evidence of this. As Kress (2006) notes about this point,

> there is often a disconnect between efforts at youth leadership education and the needs of today's youth. Too frequently, didactic methods are employed to teach an assortment of skills related to leadership in isolation from an experience of real influence or without being cast within issues related to authentic youth concerns. The idea of leadership as a developmental, lifelong trait that transcends day-to-day achievements has been replaced with a set of abilities. When this happens, we relegate leadership to a position of commodity to be displayed rather than as the unique state of mind and being it really is.
>
> (pp. 51–52)

Leadership initiatives that are decontextualized and removed from the issues that concern youth deny them the opportunity to exercise their agency and undermine their sense of purpose. This is illustrated well in models of adult leadership that limit leadership development in youth to transactional activities that adults assign to youth rather than transformational tasks that the youth themselves determine and execute (Des Marais et al., 2000).

Traditional approaches to youth leadership development, however, have given way to "more complex and integrated forms of youth involvement" that include youth participating in research partnerships, grassroots movements for social change, and school reform efforts (O'Donoghue et al., 2006). Student voice is one such area of scholarship and practice.

Student voice

Student voice generally refers to initiatives that situate students or youth as active participants whose *voice* is part of dialogue, decision-making, and change processes on matters that primarily concern them, but can also impact school staff and the communities that schools serve (Fielding and McGregor, 2005, as cited in Cook-Sather, 2006, p. 362). Student voice initiatives have largely been discussed in relationship to school reform efforts, and scholarship has documented improved academic outcomes as a result of youth involvement in decision-making in their own schools and communities (Mitra, 2004; Mitra and Kirshner, 2012). Student voice initiatives enable youth to impact issues that are important to them, as active participants in their own classrooms and engaged problem-solvers, in close relationships with adults and peers, all of which contributes to an enhanced sense of their own agency (Mitra, 2004). Numerous benefits result for youth from this kind of integral involvement.

In its richest sense, *voice* is understood as having a legitimate presence and an active role in decision-making about policy and practice within schools and beyond. As such, *voice* is part of a dynamic that also includes agency and action. Having a voice means being able to speak about what one is thinking about but also being able to be heard in such a way that one's voice can affect a set of positive outcomes. However, the term *voice* is often used in a narrower sense about communicating one's point of view. Scholarship on student voice points out, though, that *voice* is not simply about just being heard, but about being an active participant in dialogue and decision-making, and engaging in activities for positive change. It challenges prevailing notions of the student as passive and silent. As Cook-Sather (2006) argues:

> ... voice is for some "synonymous with people simply expressing their point of view on a subject," but is for others "a much more involved act of participation where people engage with the organizations, structures, and communities that shape their lives" (Hadfield and Haw, 2001, p. 488) and "generate knowledge" that is both "valuable and might form a basis for action" (Atweh and Burton, 1995, p. 652).
>
> (Cook-Sather, 2006, p. 363)

Cook-Sather (2006) continues: "'Student voice,' in its most profound and radical form, calls for a cultural shift that opens up spaces and minds not only to the sound but also to the presence and power of students" (p. 363). The term "voice" alerts us that power dynamics and active forms of participation are central to student involvement.

The place of power, then, also signals a change in the relationship between youth and adults. Structural conditions need to change in order to support the active involvement of youth as equal partners with adults. For example, a student voice orientation invites teachers to reposition themselves as facilitating partners in the learning process (Cook-Sather, 2006, p. 376), "rather than keeping students in the role of recipient or victim of teachers' (and administrators' and policymakers') decision-making processes" (Cook-Sather, 2006, p. 376). When the power dynamics between adults and youth change, then the space is opened up for youth to speak out, and have what they say matter.

Beyond this social change orientation, scholarship has also documented a variety of positive outcomes for individual students, schools, and communities. Both O'Donoghue et al. (2006) and Mitra (2004, 2006; Mitra and Kirshner, 2012) argue that student voice initiatives result in enhanced student outcomes (e.g., effort, intrinsic interest in school, use of effective learning strategies, increase in school attachment, academic improvement, enhanced sense of one's abilities, awareness that students can impact change, stronger sense of ownership in their schools, students' improved understanding of how they learn). Furthermore, they see positive outcomes related to democratic habits (e.g., increased tolerance, engaging in constructive disagreement, self-expression, cooperation), school change (e.g., school reforms that benefit youth), meaningful community change, and changes in organizational climate (Mitra, 2004, 2006; Mitra and Kirshner, 2012; O'Donoghue et al., 2006).

While documenting the numerous benefits of student voice initiatives, the "voice" scholarship fails to unpack the role of context, namely the specific perspectives, realities, and experiences of youth that are typical in urban communities. Instead, the scholarship related to student voice tends to be reduced to a more general discussion of positive youth development especially as it pertains to student academic success. Like the youth leadership scholarship, lived experiences of youth in poverty are not fully integrated into this approach. While this is not unimportant, it does not fully recognize the salience of context, namely the multiple and situated voices of youth in communities of poverty. "We must recognize that students, like adults, are always speaking from complex positions—'not single but multiple … always located' (Kamler, 2001, p. 36) and always evolving" (Cook-Sather, 2006, p. 382).

Context, in these studies, is typically described as a backdrop—that is to say, the communities within which students live and go to school. Attention to context is implicit when researchers explain student voice experiences as being meaningful, particularly for youth who are identified as not being fully engaged in school, but context itself does not appear to be integral to the analyses of student voice. Within-school programs designed to provide students with opportunities to shape and exercise their voice have been studied in schools serving predominantly low-income youth of color (Mitra, 2004) and have made reference to the value of these programs for youth described as "urban," "at risk," and "troubled." However, explicit linkages between student voice approaches and the integral place of these efforts vis-à-vis the experiences of youth of color from communities of poverty are lacking (Nygreen et al., 2006). As such, the student voice literature doesn't completely flesh out why the conditions of poverty are critically important to a holistic understanding of youth as fully functioning agents of change in their own lives. Inequitable relations of power create and sustain conditions of poverty, and it is that structural analysis that is often missing (Anyon, 2005; Weis, 2007). While the socially situated nature of student voice approaches remains relatively underexplored, this body of scholarship, nonetheless, underscores that youth have perspectives that need to be heard, and that they have enormous capacity to enact their voices in highly intentional and participatory ways with profound impact.

Civic engagement

Civic engagement is related to democracy and its relationship to the individual. It is about teaching the next generation to be more civically minded and share democratic values, and about recognizing the importance of the active and participatory engagement of citizens in community and political life in ways that promote democratic practices and habits of mind. It encompasses activities as diverse as voting, volunteering, campaigning, tutoring, and service learning, as well as participating in community, civic, and youth organizations; religiously affiliated groups; school government, clubs, and extracurricular activities; and political and social movements. While society as a whole is invested with the responsibility of civic engagement, it usually falls to schools to carry this out (Youniss and Levine, 2009, p. 2). It is the case that schools and after-school programs encourage civic engagement for a variety of reasons that prioritize personal development and/or cultivate a sense of community or societal good.

Individual or personal perspectives are primarily related to the orientation of positive youth development. In that paradigm, civic engagement is seen as a means to foster developmental assets (Balsano, 2005; Nadeau et al., 2008). According to Balsano's (2005) review of scholarship in this area, civically engaged youth "tend to have an increased sense of their own competencies, be more internally driven to get involved in prosocial activities, and have higher self-esteem" (p. 188). Furthermore, they have a higher internal locus of control (Balsano, 2005), and increased confidence, inclusion, and empowerment (Nadeau et al., 2008). Youth civic engagement is understood as providing youth with opportunities to be actively engaged in their community while also learning skills, increasing their capacity to be employed, and to contribute to their broader personal development (Nadeau et al., 2008). This perspective emanates from a viewpoint that youth are resources that need to be developed by equipping them with positive attributes, skills, and competencies. As such, civic engagement is positioned as a strategy to promote positive youth development.

Other scholarship on civic engagement discursively centers on the politics of educating for democracy, often linked to discussions about citizenship education. Westheimer and Kahne

(2004) analyze different conceptions of citizen education for a democratic society, and the role that is played by civic engagement. Their model suggests "three kinds of citizens" (p. 239): the personally responsible citizen, the participatory citizen, and the justice-oriented citizen. In each, the characteristics of the citizen and forms of civic engagement will vary. As their model delineates, a responsible citizen is someone who has good character and is honest, responsible, and law-abiding. A participatory citizen is one who actively participates and takes a leadership role, generally within established community structures and organizations. Justice-oriented citizens "must question, debate, and change established systems and structures that reproduce patterns of injustice over time" (Westheimer and Kahne, 2004, p. 240). Examples of civic engagement as seen through this framework, as they explain, would identify a responsible citizen as collecting food for a food drive, a participatory citizen as helping to organize a food drive, and a justice-oriented citizen as investigating why people are hungry and take action to solve the structural, root causes of community hunger (p. 240). Specific strategies of civic engagement, then, are reflective of particular "political and ideological ... conceptions of citizenship [which] embody ... [particular] beliefs regarding the capacities and commitments that citizens need for democracy to flourish" (p. 263). This is one of several ways of situating civic engagement within a broader understanding of democracy (Banks, 2007, 2008; Youniss and Levine, 2009). This broader framing begs an analysis of who is involved and how.

Many civic engagement programs that involve youth take place in youth-centered environments (schools, youth groups, etc.) where adults are typically in positions of authority. In these contexts, youth are not often linked up with adults in collaborative cross-generational activity (Roholt et al., 2007; Wheeler and Edlebeck, 2006). Youth-only environments can enable youth to be actively engaged at all levels, that is, not relying on adults to lead the process, define the priorities, and establish goals. On the other hand, youth-centered environments do not often provide opportunities for collaborative work with adults, thereby developing the abilities and orientation toward seeing themselves as valuable collaborators in partnership with adults. Where youth are collaboratively engaged in reciprocal relationships with adults in their civic engagement activities, they have the opportunity to learn from adults and, inversely, adults can learn from them. Both youth-centered environments and those that are not youth-dominated can provide meaningful experiences, but can also be limiting. Paying attention to relations of power is critical; that is to say, strong programs strike a balance of power between youth and adults.

Of equal importance in this approach is attention to lived experience and social context. This is not unlike the points made above regarding youth leadership and student voice that assert that youth need to be positioned as experts on their own lives and given the tools to critique, challenge, and ultimately strategize for ways to change oppressive conditions. This points to Westheimer and Kahne's (2004) justice-oriented notion of citizen and Kirshner et al.'s (2003) notion of critical civic engagement, which allow for reflection on larger social issues and structures. "Such an approach may have particular resonance for youth who, by virtue of their ethnicity [and race] or socioeconomic status (or both), must cope with inequities or discrimination in their everyday lives" (Kirshner et al., 2003, p. 16).

In the civic engagement work framed within the democracy discourse, context is clearly present: democratic society is both the space within which civic engagement takes place, and is also the expected outcome of civic engagement practices. That being said, how one thinks about civic engagement is also conditioned by where youth are located. The less critical forms, i.e., personally responsible citizens (Westheimer and Kahne, 2004), tend to resonate with a more privileged situatedness, as manifested in contributing food in a food drive to others: the more privileged are being charitable to others who are deemed "less fortunate." As the beneficiaries of structural power, youth with social privilege have the ability to influence their world and, as such, don't see their own interests being served through a critical examination of structural advantage. Conversely, a more critical orientation toward civic engagement is more likely to resonate with youth in marginalized communities, as the critical analysis inherent in this approach will take up the underlying structural realities of inequity and discrimination that prevail in their everyday lives.

In all three approaches to working with youth toward meaningful social change, youth bring real differences, perspectives, and needs to the table and, as such, it is critical that scholarship does not deny their differences and the structural underpinnings that account for these differences.

Conclusion

It is critical that programs, whether focused on youth leadership, student voice, or civic engagement, move beyond a narrow focus on competencies to equipping students with the knowledge and skills to analyze and critique the socio-historical challenges facing them and their communities, enabling them to "disrupt dominant discourses and reframe" the social and educational issues important to them (Lipman, 2011, pp. 117–118). Without the ability to "analyze and critique root causes of social problems" (Westheimer and Kahne, 2004, p. 264), youth development initiatives unwittingly perpetuate the pathologization of youth in poverty, diverting attention away from a consideration of how youth living in communities of poverty can move from analysis, to critique, and finally to social action. Whether inside schools, in the community, or a combination of both, positive youth development opportunities are more important than ever, at a time when poor youth of color find themselves academically and socially disengaged, caught up in the vortex of neoliberal accountability and forcibly displaced from their communities. As such, youth organizations need to provide safe and engaging spaces for youth to explore their own identities, cultivating a critical understanding of the differences in opportunities and experiences that exist for youth in poverty, including the influence of neoliberalism. We must involve youth in meaningful activities that can impact change in school, and their communities, and reassert an ideology of democracy with concern for the common good.

Note

1 We use the term "social change" loosely in this chapter. In part we draw on Paulo Freire's (1993) ideas, namely that social change is a process that relies on a deep and critical understanding about the structural bases of inequalities, and subsequent collective action aimed at dislodging those underlying structures. We also use the term "social change" as it appears in the scholarship reviewed herein, although there it is rarely explicitly defined or problematized. A fuller engagement or critique of the notion of social change in this body of scholarship is beyond the scope of this chapter, and would require attention to how neoliberalism constrains possibilities for change. This would suggest that programs of the sorts discussed herein would more deliberately examine neoliberalism.

References

Anyon, J. (2005). What "counts" as educational policy? Notes toward a new paradigm. *Harvard Educational Review*, 75(1), 65–88.

Balsano, A. B. (2005). Youth civic engagement in the United States: Understanding and addressing the impact of social impediments on positive youth and community development. *Applied Developmental Science*, 9(4), 188–201.

Banks, J. A. (2007). *Diversity and citizenship education: Global perspectives*. San Francisco: Jossey-Bass.

Banks, J. A. (2008). Diversity group identity and citizenship education in a global age. *Educational Researcher*, 37(3), 128–129.

Books, S. (ed.). (2007). *Invisible children in the society and its schools*. Mahwah, NJ: Lawrence Erlbaum Associates.

Borden, L., and Serido, J. (2009). From program participant to engaged citizen: A developmental journey. *Journal of Community Psychology*, 37(4), 423–438.

Conner, J. O., and Strobel, K. (2007). Leadership development: An examination of individual and programmatic growth. *Journal of Adolescent Research*, 22(3), 275–297.

Cook-Sather, A. (2006). Sound, presence, and power: "Student voice" in educational research and reform. *Curriculum Inquiry*, 36(4), 359–390.

Darling-Hammond, L. (2010). *The flat world and education: How America's commitment to equity will determine our future*. New York: Teachers College Press.

Des Marais, J., Yang, Y., and Farzanehkia, F. (2000). Service-learning leadership development for youths. *Phi Delta Kappan*, 81(9), 678–680.

Dryfoos, J. G. (1999). The role of school in children's out-of-school time. *The Future of Children*, 9(2), 117–134.

Fine, M., Burns, A., and Payne, Y. (2004). Civics lessons: The color and class of betrayal. *Teachers College Record*, 106(11), 2193–2223.

Freire, P. (1993). *Pedagogy of the oppressed* (new revised 20th-anniversary edition). New York: Continuum.

Giroux, H.A. (2009). *Youth in a suspect society: Democracy or disposability?* New York: Palgrave Macmillan.

Hackman, J. R., and Wageman, R. (2007). Asking the right questions about leadership: Discussion and conclusions. *American Psychologist*, 62(1), 43–47.

Halpern, R. (2000). The promise of after-school programs for low-income children. *Early Childhood Research Quarterly*, 15(2), 185–214.

Halpern, R. (2002). A different kind of child development institution: The history of after-school programs for low-income children. *Teachers College Record*, 104(2), 178–211.

Halpern, R., Barker, G., and Mollard, W. (2000). Youth programs as alternative spaces to be: A study of neighborhood youth programs in Chicago's West Town. *Youth and Society*, 31(4), 469–506.

Kahne, J., Nagaoka, J., Brown, A., O'Brien, J., Quinn, T., and Thiede, K. (2001). Assessing after-school programs as contexts for youth development. *Youth and Society*, 32, 421–446.

Kirshner, B., Strobel, K., and Fernandez, M. (2003). Critical civic engagement among urban youth. *Penn GSE Perspectives on Urban Education*, 2(1), 1–20. http://www.urbanedjournal.org/archive/volume-2-issue-1-spring-2003/critical-civic-engagement-among-urban-youth. Accessed August 14, 2014.

Kress, C. (2006). Youth leadership and youth development: Connections and questions. *New Directions in Youth Development*, 109, 45–56.

Kumashiro, K. (2012). *Bad teacher! How blaming teachers distorts the bigger picture*. New York: Teachers College Press.

Leistyna, P. (2009). Preparing for public life: Education, critical theory, and social justice. In W. Ayers, T. Quinn, and D. Stovall (eds), *Handbook of social justice in education* (pp. 51–58). New York: Routledge.

Lipman, P. (2004). *High stakes education*. New York: RoutledgeFalmer.

Lipman, P. (2011). *The new political economy of urban education: Neoliberalism, race, and the right to the city*. New York: Routledge.

Little, P. M. D., Wimer, C., and Weiss, H. B. (2008). After school programs in the 21st century: Their potential and what it takes to achieve it. *Issues and Opportunities in Out-of-School Time Evaluation*, No. 10, February. Cambridge, MA: Harvard Family Research Project.

MacNeil, C. A. (2006). Bridging generations: Applying "adult" leadership theories to youth leadership development. *New Directions for Youth Development*, 109, 27–43.

Mahoney, J. L., Parente, M. E., and Zigler, E. F. (2009). Afterschool programs in America: Origins, growth, popularity, and politics. *Journal of Youth Development*, 4(3), 25–44.

Mitra, D. L. (2004). The significance of students: Can increasing "student voice" in schools lead to gains in youth development? *Teachers College Record*, 106(4), 651–688.

Mitra, D. L. (2006). Student voice from the inside and outside: The positioning of challengers. *International Journal of Leadership in Education: Theory and Practice*, 9(4), 315–328.

Mitra, D. L., and Kirshner, B. (2012). Insiders versus outsiders: Examining variability in student voice initiatives and their consequences for school change. In B. J. McMahon and J. P. Portelli (eds), *Student engagement in urban schools: Beyond neoliberal discourses* (pp. 49–72). Charlotte, NC: Information Age Publishers.

Nadeau, S., Cunningham, W., Lundberg, M. K. A., and McGinnis, L. (2008). Programs and policies that promote positive youth development and prevent risky behaviors: An international perspective. *New Directions for Child and Adolescent Development*, 122, 75–87.

Nygreen, K., Kwon, S. A., and Sanchez, P. (2006). Urban youth building community: Social change and participatory research in schools, homes, and community-based organizations. *Journal of Community Practice*, 14(1), 107–123.

O'Donoghue, J. L., Kirshner, B., and McLaughlin, M. (2006). Youth participation: From myths to effective practice. *The Prevention Researcher*, 13(1), 3–6.

Riggs, N., and Greenberg, M. (2004). After-school youth development programs: A developmental-ecological model of current research. *Clinical Child and Family Psychology Review*, 7(3), 177–190.

Roach, A., Wyman, L., Brookes, H., Chavez, C., Heath, S., and Valdes, G. (1999). Leadership giftedness: Models revisited. *Gifted Child Quarterly*, 43(1), 13–24.

Roholt, R. V., Hildreth, R. W., and Baizerman, M. (2007). The "youth" in youth civic engagement. *Child and Youth Services*, 29(3–4), 139–155.

Smyth, J. (2012). When students "speak back": Student engagement towards a socially just society. In B. J. McMahon and J. P. Portelli (eds), *Student engagement in urban schools: Beyond neoliberal discourses* (pp.73–90). Charlotte, NC: Information Age Publishing, Inc.

Weis, Lois (ed.). (2007). *The way class works: Readings on school, family, and the economy.* New York: Routledge.

Westheimer, J., and Kahne, J. (2004). What kind of citizen? The politics of educating for democracy. *American Educational Research Journal*, 41(2), 237–269.

Wheeler, W., and Edlebeck, C. (2006). Leading, learning, and unleashing potential: Youth leadership and civic engagement. *New Directions for Youth Development*, 109, 89–97.

Witt, P. A. (2004). Programs that work: Developing quality after-school programs. *Journal of Park and Recreation Administration*, 22(4), 103–126.

Youniss, J., and Levine, P. (eds). (2009). *Engaging young people in civic life.* Nashville: Vanderbilt University Press.

52

MIGRANT CIVIL SOCIETY

Shaping community and citizenship in a time of neoliberal reforms

Pascale Joassart-Marcelli and Nina Martin

Introduction

Since the 1980s, civil society organizations have become increasingly central actors in providing services to the poor. A succession of neoliberal policy initiatives and bureaucratic reforms over the last 30 years have shifted responsibility for the provision of social services for the poor from the state onto local nonprofit agencies, communities, and ultimately individuals. As welfare state programs have been dismantled, privatized, or come under increasing austerity pressures, nonprofits have become the principal providers of assistance to people in economic need.

Immigrants, for whom federally funded programs have historically been scarce and lacked broad political support, are particularly likely to access services and programming through the voluntary sector. New immigrants, who disproportionally come from the Global South, have considerable needs as they settle into their new place of residence. Those whose skills are limited and systematically devalued in the post-industrial economy often require assistance with employment placement, addressing legal issues, securing affordable housing and engaging in the many everyday activities that sustain life in a new place and create a sense of belonging. Migrant civil society organizations—community groups, faith-based organizations, nonprofits, and unions that provide services to, and in conjunction with, migrants—have become key players in shaping the integration of migrants into an increasingly polarized and spatially differentiated society. Yet, the lack of systematic public programs to assist immigrants in the United States and the growing reliance on nonprofits to address their multiple needs raise concerns regarding the ability of the current system to serve all immigrants equally and foster their integration into local economies and societies. In particular, recent research draws attention to the contradictory role of migrant nonprofit and voluntary organizations as they occupy a unique space at the intersection of the state and civil society.

In this chapter we focus on the tensions that civil society organizations face in serving immigrant needs. We begin by contextualizing the emergence of these organizations as key providers of services and advocacy work within two related trends: the globalization and marginalization of labor, and the introduction of neoliberal state reforms since the 1980s. We then provide an overview of the programs and strategies supported by the voluntary sector, paying particular attention to the relationship between nonprofit organizations and the state and emphasizing the geographic implications of a U.S. immigration system that depends heavily on migrant civil society. We end with a discussion of the impact of the re-scaling of immigrant assistance on communities and citizenship.

Globalization, neoliberalism, and the expansion of migrant civil society organizations

To better understand the causes and implications of the re-scaling of responsibility for immigrant service provision from the state to migrant civil society, it is important to situate it within the broader political and economic transformations that have affected the state and the economy in the past three decades. These can be summarized under the umbrella concepts of globalization and neoliberalism. While the former led to a restructuring of the economy associated with growing income polarization, an increasingly precarious low-wage labor force, and rising labor migration from the Global South, the latter contributed to welfare state retrenchment and the adoption of policies promoting the expansion of market-based modes of regulation. Together these trends have generated growing needs for migrant assistance that are no longer met by state programs.

Labor migration is a central feature of globalization. Between 1980 and 2010, the number of immigrants in the United States grew by 183 percent, from 14 to 40 million (U.S. Census, 1980, 2010). Today, approximately one in eight U.S. residents is foreign-born, with over 80 percent of immigrants born in Latin America or Asia (compared to 52 percent in 1980). Many scholars have linked this rise in migration from the Global South to macro-scale economic restructuring, which is threatening traditional livelihoods in developing countries while fueling a growing demand for low-wage, flexible, and contingent labor in the northern hemisphere and global cities (Samers, 2010). For millions, migration represents an attempt to escape poverty. However, economic advancement is not always forthcoming and, in the United States, according to the Census (2010), the poverty rate is higher for immigrants (19 percent), especially those from Mexico (28 percent) and Central America (21 percent), than for the native-born population (15 percent).

Simultaneously, neoliberal agendas began to drive economic policy, and the state's primary role became the enforcement of regulations facilitating market expansion. Welfare reforms in the 1980s and 1990s privatized or dismantled many state functions, calling for a greater role for nonprofits to provide social services to immigrants and other people in need (Kodras, 1997; Wolch, 1990). For instance, the 1996 welfare reform eliminated most federal programs for immigrant social services and shifted the responsibility to states to both define eligibility and provide services (Fix, 2011). As a result, many legal immigrants and their children lost access to Food Stamps and Medicaid (Cordero-Guzmán and Quiroz-Becerra, 2007). This devolution of responsibility has created fiscal tensions and prompted a race to the bottom in service delivery, making nonprofit and voluntary organizations the providers of last resort. Refugees are the only immigrants with a national program of assistance, although the majority of service programs are subcontracted to voluntary organizations (Jiménez, 2011). Thus, government contracts and grants support the re-scaling of service delivery by providing voluntary agencies with financial resources and mandates to carry out specific tasks. This is especially true in the areas of refugee assistance, workforce development, housing, and community development.

As a result of these reforms, the number of nonprofit organizations in the United States rose dramatically over the past three decades, with public charities growing by 87 percent between 1995 and 2012 to almost 1 million organizations (National Center for Charitable Statistics, 1995, 2012). Today, approximately 3,300 registered organizations claim to serve immigrants and refugees as their primary purpose (70 percent more than in 1995). Many more, however, provide assistance as unregistered organizations (including many faith-based organizations and smaller community groups) or as agencies involved in more broadly defined human service delivery.

Although the state's willingness to help immigrants adapt and integrate in the United States declined, it became increasingly concerned with policing immigration. Law enforcement has remained a high priority of the neoliberal state, which invested billions in border protection, incarceration, and deportation, effectively producing a class of vulnerable migrant workers, with very limited rights and prospect for well-paid employment (Hiemstra, 2010; Nevins, 2002; Theodore, 2007).

Together, these political reforms contributed to new forms of citizenships based on ideals of personal responsibility. For immigrants, especially those in poverty, this often translates into an expectation that they need to "prove their citizenship" by not becoming public burdens. In that context, migrant civil society became one of the primary mechanisms for immigrants to address unmet needs for services such as housing and employment assistance, while also providing opportunities for civic participation, political integration, and cultural adaptation (Mitchell, 2001; Staeheli, 2008; Trudeau, 2012).

Yet, because the rise in organized migrant civil society into nonprofits and voluntary organizations is a product of neoliberalism, there are reasons to be concerned about the ability of these institutions to challenge the relations that underscore the economic marginalization and social exclusion of migrant workers. Indeed, nonprofits and voluntary organizations may be in a difficult position to dispute state regulations when they themselves depend on the "generosity" of governments to function. The expansion of the nonprofit sector has also contributed to its professionalization and commercialization, both of which may impede its ability to address certain needs to the extent that activities are constrained by accountability and service contracts (Wolch, 1990) and are increasingly performed by paid and trained workers whose values and care ethics may differ from those of volunteers and activists (Cloke et al., 2007; Trudeau and Veronis, 2009). Furthermore, because this service model presumes the existence of organized "communities" that are able to articulate immigrants' needs and take advantage of resources available, it may exclude immigrants with less defined or active communities, including newer immigrants, those who may have limited financial resources and experience of civic participation, and those who reside in less-traditional destinations, away from urban centers and ethnic enclaves (Joassart-Marcelli, 2013). In addition to shaping immigrant integration through the location, type, and level of services they are able and willing to provide, migrant civil society organizations can also play a more indirect and less-studied role in the reproduction of neoliberal subjects by promoting ideals of work first and personal responsibility (Martin, 2010, 2011; Mitchell, 2001; Trudeau, 2012).

The capacities of migrant civil society to alleviate poverty and help immigrants, however, are not entirely determined by globalization and neoliberalism. The ways these trends play out and interact with local community resources and dynamics may be more complex than expected. Along with larger, corporatist "shadow state" organizations exist a host of smaller grassroots agencies, including labor unions, churches, and neighborhood-based and ethnic community organizations, that provide a wide range of services to immigrants in need and contest harmful and unfair policies and practices. Many of these organizations act as a platform for advancing the interests of immigrants, advocating for changes in programming and policies impacting immigrants.

The contradictory space of migrant-serving nonprofit and voluntary organizations

The benefits and services that nonprofit and voluntary organizations provide immigrants, and low-income people in general, can be divided into three broad categories. First, organizations are direct service providers, conducting a range of programming in such areas as health and wellness, housing and rental assistance, legal services, child and youth concerns, workforce training, employment assistance, and food pantries. Second, they aim to help immigrants with identity formation and social capital building. In a diverse society, where transnational ties have become increasingly common, immigrants often struggle to establish a sense of community and individual identity. By providing a place for immigrants to meet others and encouraging volunteering and civic participation, these organizations also contribute to the development of social capital, which has been shown to have a positive impact on economic integration and political incorporation. They can also actively foster a sense of community and social cohesion through culturally sensitive programming in realms as diverse as arts to entrepreneurship. And third, migrant civil society organizations conduct advocacy and educational outreach to promote the interests of immigrants to policy makers and society at large (Joassart-Marcelli, 2012; Theodore and Martin, 2007).

The capacity of nonprofits to offer these three types of services to immigrants is spatially shaped by their position within political geographies of social service delivery and intra-urban geographies of immigrant residential settlement. Indeed, nonprofit organizations occupy a unique political space at the intersection of the state and civil society (Trudeau, 2008), often mediating between these different spheres. Through their programming and activities, non-profit organizations can translate macro state policies into the everyday lives of the people they serve, while simultaneously contesting these policies and providing alternative approaches. As Trudeau and Veronis (2009) argue, it is within these organizations that neoliberal policies are enacted, performed, challenged, or transformed into particular actions that shape people's lives, including immigrant integration. State policies are often enacted in varying ways by organizations as they choose to apply for specific grants, participate in certain programs, or follow accountability procedures. The institutional history, organizational structure, primary purpose, and other attributes of these agencies are likely to influence their position within this contradictory political space and their role in shaping immigrants' lives. Organizations' ability to protect and advocate for immigrants is in constant tension with the neoliberal patterns of social welfare restructuring that shape the context of their work.

Because communities are characterized by different histories, social relations, financial resources, and geographic locations, the migrant civil society organizations they support are complex and diverse. While organizations may share a common goal of providing assistance to immigrants through some combination of the three categories of activities, migrant civil society is otherwise heterogeneous in its orientation to addressing social problems. Institutional characteristics influence the choice of activities and the philosophy of service provision within each organization. For example, larger, more established organizations are more likely to enact ideals of personal responsibility, assimilation, and work first, thereby being complicit in the neoliberalization of social policy. These organizations often have a closer relationship with government, and are therefore less likely to challenge government directives (Wolch, 1990). Smaller, newer organizations tend to be more activist in their orientation, engaging in political advocacy and seeking structural reforms.

The funding sources (for example, government agencies, foundations, grassroots fundraising, corporate gifts) of an organization can impact its operating style. Organizations that rely more heavily on grants from the government and from foundations have been shown to be less able to contest government policy, because their survival depends on maintaining a positive relationship with government agencies. In addition, these funders tend to demand accountability from agencies by subjecting them to various metrics of performance. While accountability is surely an important part of all organizations, it can create significant burdens. Staff can be diverted from providing services because of onerous accounting measures. This has led to the professionalization of staff at community development organizations. Professionalization requires a different orientation from staff and volunteers. Rather than valuing staff and volunteers based on their commitment to a neighborhood, a cause, or their local knowledge, expertise in law, accounting, or another relevant profession becomes prioritized. It is generally agreed that professionalization of community organizations can cause a loss of activism. For instance, organizations that focus on supporting financial independence and employment through job-placement, micro-lending, and training programs may be rewarded with state contracts and grants in a way that a group of immigrants organizing for better working conditions, working to improve their children's school environment, or fighting deportation may not. In some cases, organizations' work has been commercialized, with a growing share of their activities involving the marketing and sale of services or products to generate income. While this presumably helps finance their mission, it also takes resources and focus away from immigrants' pressing needs.

Despite these many challenges, migrant civil society can be credited with numerous wins in the policy and programming arenas affecting immigrants. In some cases, they have taken the lead in advocating for increased rights for immigrants at the federal, state, and local levels. For instance, nonprofit organizations have been active in demonstrating and lobbying in favor of immigration reforms, including the Dream Act. Others are involved in legal battles to help immigrants recover unpaid wages, reunite with family members, or contest deportation. But many more work in small and often unaccounted ways—at times challenging public mandates and regulations—to make immigrants' everyday life easier by finding housing, providing emergency child care, feeding families, giving a reference, and lending a "shoulder to cry on" and a "sympathetic ear."

Geographical impacts and implications

The intra-urban geography of immigrant nonprofit organizations also influences the role they play in people's lives and in the formation of communities. Most immigrant nonprofits remain located in traditional immigrant communities where there is a "critical mass" and a history of civic participation. While this helps serve a large number of immigrants, this also reproduces spatial segregation to the extent that it provides an incentive for immigrants with higher needs to reside in or near ethnic enclaves, where services are more readily available. In addition, research has also shown that the concentration of nonprofits in marginalized urban neighborhoods contributes to the reproduction of poverty and occupational segregation, since the resources and jobs available in these neighborhoods are often limited (Cope, 2001; Joassart-Marcelli and Wolch, 2003).

Recent changes in migrant settlement patterns have created new challenges for some organizations. Gentrification in immigrant neighborhoods in many cities across the United States has led to the displacement of immigrants out of traditional port-of-entry neighborhoods. The increasing suburbanization of the immigrant population (Singer et al., 2008) also means that the migrant population in many cities is more dispersed than before. Organizations are then sometimes left in neighborhoods with a reduced target population, and they struggle to provide services to a more dispersed population. Therefore, more dispersed and suburbanized immigrant groups, with a limited history of civic participation and a more fragile sense of community, are likely to be left out from the current system of immigrant service delivery (Joassart-Marcelli, 2013). Similarly, those within established ethnic communities but with limited economic resources are also facing obstacles in obtaining needed services. There lies the main problem of the current system; it promotes the idea of "communities" helping themselves, but fails to acknowledge the micro-politics of community, its contested and exclusionary nature, and its spatial unevenness.

Community and citizenship

The success of migrant civil society organizations in assisting immigrants rests on fragile assumptions regarding the existence of an "immigrant community" and its ability to support the work of nonprofit and voluntary organizations. This premise raises concerns regarding the equity of the current system of immigrant service delivery to the extent that it favors people and places that embody a certain ideal of community and citizenship.

As Staeheli (2003, 2008) argues, community has multiple meanings and can be used as a discursive category and a strategy to promote the devolution and privatization of public services. For instance, community has often been understood as a space of trust, mutual understanding, and social support, as well as a site of resistance to unfair laws and practices. But in the context of neoliberal politics, community is conceptualized more narrowly as an institutional structure and a source of social capital necessary for the implementation of policy. Values of accountability, responsibility, and assimilation are favored over messier values such as justice and fairness. Therefore, the sort of community associated with migrant civil society is likely to be shaped by the neoliberal principles that gave it a central role in the provision of immigrant services. Directors, staff, and volunteers of immigrant-serving organizations, who may have different understandings of community, have had to adapt their strategies to remain viable, shifting their grassroots and advocacy work off the books and at the margins of their work. Doing so often alienates these organizations from the very communities that support them and are in need of their services.

At the same time, the immigrant communities that are unable to organize and muster the resources needed to provide basic services to their members end up being left out. Their failure to fit a certain model of community—or worse, their presumed lack of community—defines them as unworthy of assistance.

The uneven distribution of services that results from this process is linked to a broader concern about citizenship and integration. Several scholars (Purcell, 2003; Sassen, 2005) have argued that citizenship is no longer defined primarily at the scale of nation states, but instead is increasingly shaped at both global and local scales, where communities of belonging exist. In particular, the downscaling of citizenship to cities and geographically defined communities is linked to changes in its interpretation from a set of rights to the responsibility to assimilate and contribute to society (Marston, 1995; Staeheli and Clarke, 2003). In that context, civic participation in community-based organizations is an avenue to become a valued member of society (Bloemraad, 2006; Wong, 2006), but also a way to distinguish between deserving and undeserving immigrants and regulate citizenship (Mitchell, 2001; Staeheli, 2011). To the extent that only certain types of immigrant communities are recognized and have the capacity to take advantage of state resources, there will remain differences in immigrants' ability to integrate, belong, and become citizens.

References

Bloemraad, I. (2006). *Becoming a citizen: Incorporating immigrants and refugees in the United States and Canada.* Berkeley, CA: University of California Press.

Cloke, P., Johnsen, S., and May, J. (2007). Ethical citizenship? Volunteers and the ethics of providing services for homeless people. *Geoforum*, 38, 1089–1101.

Cope, M. (2001). Between welfare and work: The roles of social service organizations in the social regulation of labor markets of the poor. *Urban Geography*, 22, 391–406.

Cordero-Guzmán, H. and Quiroz-Becerra, V. (2007). Cracking the safety net: Latina/o access to health and social programs in the post-welfare era. In M. Montero-Sieburth and E. Meléndez (eds), *Latinos in a changing society.* Westport, CT: Praeger.

Fix, M. (2011). *Immigrants and welfare: The impact of welfare reform on America's newcomers*. New York: Russell Sage Foundation.

Hiemstra, N. (2010). Immigrant "illegality" as neoliberal governmentality in Leadville, Colorado. *Antipode*, 42(1), 74–102.

Jiménez, T. R. (2011). *Migrants in the United States: How well are they integrating in society?* Washington, DC: Migration Policy Institute.

Joassart-Marcelli, P. (2012). For whom and for what? An investigation of the roles of nonprofits as providers to the neediest. In L. Salamon (ed.), *The state of nonprofit America*, 2nd edition. Washington, DC: Brookings Institution Press.

Joassart-Marcelli, P. (2013). Ethnic concentration and nonprofit organizations: The political and urban geography of immigrant services in Boston. *International Migration Review*, 47(3), 730–772.

Joassart-Marcelli, P. and Wolch, J. (2003). The intrametropolitan geography of poverty and the nonprofit sector in Southern California. *Nonprofit and Voluntary Sector Quarterly*, 32(1), 70–96.

Kodras, J. (1997). Restructuring the state: Devolution, privatization, and the geographic redistribution of power and capacity in governance. In L. Staeheli, J. Kodras, and C. Flint (eds), *State devolution in America: Implications for a diverse society*. Thousand Oaks, CA: Sage.

Marston, S. (1995). The private goes public: Citizenship and the new spaces of civil society. *Political Geography*, 14(2), 194–212.

Martin, N. (2010). The crisis of social reproduction among migrant workers: Interrogating the role of migrant civil society. *Antipode*, 41(1), 127–151.

Martin, N. (2011). Toward a new countermovement: A framework for interpreting the contradictory interventions of migrant civil society organizations in urban labor markets. *Environment and Planning A*, 43(12), 2934–2952.

Mitchell, K. (2001). Transnationalism, neo-liberalism, and the rise of the shadow state. *Economy and Society*, 30(2), 165–189.

National Center for Charitable Statistics. (1995 and 2012). Internal Revenue Service, *Exempt organizations business master files*. Washington, DC: The Urban Institute. Retrieved January 31, 2013 from http://nccsdataweb.urban.org/.

Nevins, J. (2002). *Operation gatekeeper: The rise of the "illegal alien" and the making of the U.S.–Mexico boundary*. New York: Routledge.

Purcell, M. (2003). Citizenship and the right to the global city: Reimagining the capitalist world order. *International Journal of Urban and Regional Research*, 27(3), 564–590.

Samers, M. (2010). *Migration*. New York: Routledge.

Sassen, S. (2005). The repositioning of citizenship and alienage: Emergent subjects and spaces for politics. *Globalizations*, 2(1), 79–94.

Singer, A., Wiley Hardwick, S., and Brettell, C. (2008). *Twenty-first century gateways: Immigrant incorporation in suburban America*. Washington, DC: Brookings Institution Press.

Staeheli, L. (2003). Women and the work of community. *Environment and Planning A*, 35, 815–831.

Staeheli, L. (2008). Citizenship and the problem of community. *Political Geography*, 27, 5–21.

Staeheli, L. (2011). Political geography: Where's citizenship? *Progress in Human Geography*, 35(3), 393–400.

Staeheli, L. and Clarke, S. E. (2003). The new politics of citizenship: Structuring participation by household, work, and identity. *Urban Geography*, 24(2), 103–26.

Theodore, N. (2007). Closed borders, open markets: Immigrant day laborers' struggle for economic rights. In H. Leitner, J. Peck, and E. S. Sheppard (eds), *Contesting neoliberalism: Urban frontiers*. New York: Guilford Press.

Theodore, N. and Martin, N. (2007). Migrant civil society: New voices in the struggle over community development. *Journal of Urban Affairs*, 29(3), 269–287.

Trudeau, D. (2008). Towards a relational view of the shadow state. *Political Geography*, 27(6), 669–690.

Trudeau, D. (2012). Constructing citizenship in the shadow state. *Geoforum*, 43, 442–452.

Trudeau, D. and Veronis, L. (2009). Enacting state restructuring: NGOs as translation mechanisms. *Environment and Planning D: Society and Space*, 27(6), 1117–1134.

U.S. Census. (1980 and 2010). *Census of population and housing*. Washington, DC: Department of Commerce.

Wolch, J. (1990). *The shadow state: Government and voluntary sector in transition*. New York: The Foundation Center.

Wong, J. (2006). *Democracy's promise: Immigrants and American civic institutions*. Ann Arbor: University of Michigan Press.

PART VI

Reframing poverty in the era of globalization

Alternatives to a neoliberal economic order

INTRODUCTION

Stephen Nathan Haymes and María Vidal de Haymes

The chapters in this part propose alternatives to the current neoliberal economic order by reframing poverty as a consequence of the values and practices of market fundamentalism, where all aspects of human life are reduced to exchange value and competitive individualism reigns supreme. David Harvey writes: "Neoliberalism is a theory of political economic practice, that proposes that human well-being can best be advanced by liberating individual entrepreneurial freedom and skills within an institutional framework characterized by strong private property rights, free markets, and free trade" (2005:3). Like so, the neoliberal state's function is not to intervene in markets but to create markets and guarantee their proper functioning, which according to Harvey is to promote the "process of neoliberalization." This is a process that, says Harvey, entails much "'creative destruction,' not only of prior institutional frameworks and powers but also of the division of labour, social relations, welfare provisions, technological mixtures, ways of life and thought, reproductive activities, attachments to the land and habits of heart" (2005:3). The values driving neoliberalism are market-driven ethics or, as Harvey points out, "neoliberalism values market exchange as an ethics in itself, capable of acting as a guide to all human action" (2005:3). Neoliberalization diminishes all human value to market exchange value, replacing previously held ethical beliefs and social relation with the contractual relations of the marketplace (2005:3). Harvey states, for example, that "[neoliberalization] holds that the social good will be maximized by maximizing the reach and frequency of market transactions, and it seeks to bring all human action into the domain of the market" (2005:3). In doing so, the market-driven ethics of neoliberalism undercut the nature of social obligation in civil society.

The neoliberal embedding of the market in everything, including the political power of the state, endorses a disregard for a wide array of human security concerns that span environmental, economic, political, and physical spheres, as a necessary condition for economic growth and material prosperity. The market ethics driving neoliberalism therefore promotes the view that, "the common good depends entirely on the uncontrolled egoism of the individual and especially, on the prosperity of transnational corporations" (Von Werlhof, 2008:96). Claudia Von Werlhof in this regard writes: "The allegedly necessary 'freedom' of the economy—which, paradoxically, only means the freedom of corporations—hence consists of a freedom from responsibility and commitment to society" (2008:96).

But growth under neoliberalism, and especially during its periods of economic crisis, as illustrated by the 2008 Great Recession in the United States, has come to mean record profits for corporations, increased poverty, inequality between the rich and non-rich, and vulnerability for everyone else, including the middle class.

In reaction to the growing vulnerability experienced by the majority of U.S. citizens, the authors in this part propose alternatives to the prevailing economic dominance of neoliberal market fundamentalism. In Chapter 53, "Creating a Sustainable Society: Human Rights in the U.S. Welfare State," Phyllis Jeroslow shows that in spite of the hegemonic dominance of neoliberal market fundamentalism most U.S. citizens continue to support "universal policies [e.g., Social Security and Medicare] that simultaneously improve well-being and enrich democratic freedoms." Part of what Jeroslow argues is that "[Western] capitalism cannot function without welfare state interventions." Jeroslow writes:

> [H]istory provides ample evidence of devastating episodes of market failure that necessitated state intervention in order to ensure human survival and revive the economy. The birth of the Western welfare state in the late nineteenth century is attributed to such a moment, charged with balancing economic growth with human need. As witnessed in the previous and current centuries, market failures continue to occur, requiring innovations in state intervention and new conceptions of social rights in order to sustain economic and social stability.
>
> (2014: p.559)

It is in the continuing context of market domination of U.S. society and its encroachment and reorganization of the welfare state, for example the privatization of public goods and stigmatization of the welfare state based on self-reliance ideology, that Jeroslow proposes a human rights approach that can strengthen the welfare rights claims of U.S. citizens as a response. In this regard, Jeroslow turns to Anthony Gidden's concept of the social investment state and Amartya Sen's capacities approach to human rights.

In Chapter 54, "Returning to the Collective: New Approaches to Alleviating Poverty," Susan Roll and Sue Steiner examine the role of grassroots community-based initiatives in addressing the economic well-being of people living in poverty. These initiatives are "community-based solutions that support people outside of the formal market-based system," which Roll and Steiner believe offer a "promising approach for low-income and low-asset families" (p. 567). The community-based approaches the authors focus on are "community currencies such as time banks, local economic trading systems, and complementary community currency systems" (p. 567). Roll and Steiner offer these approaches as "alternatives" which are the "antithesis of neoliberal global capitalism, [and that] move away from the global economy … into a very local economy." The community currencies approach is based on values that are radically different from those of neoliberal capitalism— "reciprocity, interdependence, fairness, and the centrality of social networks and strong communities" (p. 567).

In Chapter 55, "Why We Cannot All Be Middle Class in America," Lakshman Yapa argues that there are serious economic, ecological, and structural limits to expanding the middle class. For Yapa, expanding the "middle class [is] not only a discouraging task in futility, but also a misuse of resources … [and] nor a pathway out of poverty for millions" Instead, Yapa proposes a "post-capitalist politics" and what he calls a "Basic Needs Economy."

References

Harvey, David (2005) *A Brief History of Neoliberalism*, New York: Oxford University Press.
Von Werlhof, Claudia (2008) "The Globalization of Neoliberalism, its Consequences, and Some of its Basic Alternatives," *Capitalism Nature Socialism* 19(3), 94–117.

53

CREATING A SUSTAINABLE SOCIETY

Human rights in the U.S. welfare state

Phyllis Jeroslow

Introduction: crises and opportunities

Friedrich Hayek (1944) warned that socialism would lead society down the road to serfdom, robbing individuals of their freedom for self-determination, and subjecting them to domination by a centralized political and economic authority. Hayek succeeded in striking fear of socialism in the hearts of Americans, a concern that 65 years later dominated the debate regarding the provision of universal health care in the United States. Ironically, Americans have held dear their attachment to Social Security and Medicare benefits that provide quasi-universal protection for elderly citizens, even resisting the proposed privatization of social security investment accounts before the stock market plunge of 2008. The historical lesson is that initial resistance by Americans to universal protections may eventually give way to steadfast adherence to social rights. Additionally, the institution of social protections has not dismantled the capitalist enterprise. Apparent confusion in the American mind about the ability of socialist policies to co-exist with capitalism provides hope that, in the future, U.S. citizens could become more amenable to other universal policies that simultaneously improve well-being and enrich democratic freedoms.

From a theoretical perspective, the state, the market, and civil society form a triumvirate that provides order for supporting the economic and social fabric. Offe (1984) depicts these systems in a continual power struggle, not between classes as in Marxist analyses, nor between interest groups, as in pluralist conceptions of political and economic power, but among the very systems of the state, market, and family. The market reigns supreme, but the state and family are "flanking subsystems" that buttress the market while simultaneously constraining it (Keane, 1984, p. 13). As part of the triumvirate, capitalism cannot function without welfare state interventions, despite the friction between the two institutions. Indeed, history provides ample evidence of devastating episodes of market failure that necessitated state intervention in order to ensure human survival and revive the economy. The birth of the Western welfare state in the late nineteenth century is attributed to such a moment, charged with balancing economic growth with human need. As witnessed in the previous and current centuries, market failures continue to occur, requiring innovations in state intervention and new conceptions of social rights in order to sustain economic and social stability.

Polanyi (1944/2001) characterized the shift from agrarian to industrial economies as nothing short of a "great transformation," and North (1981) referred to the transition as the "second economic revolution," succeeding the progression from hunter and gatherer societies to agricultural civilizations. This author posits that the current period of economic and social internationalization spurred by advances in science and technology constitutes the third economic revolution and another great transformation with ramifications for humanity equally vast to those of previous eras. The transition during the twenty-first century will involve a re-examination and re-calibration of social rights conducive to a new balance of state, market, and civil society.

Marshall (1950/1992) describes how post-World War II economic growth resulted in a compression of the scale of the income distribution, such that people's standards of living were closely comparable to one another. Between 1945 and 1970, the years characterized as America's "Great Prosperity," the American economy provided the most dynamic and widely shared economic growth in world history (Reich, 2010, p. 48). Rising incomes conveyed a "universal right to real income" (Marshall, 1950/1992, p. 28). In the United States and Europe, a "golden era" of welfare state expansion prevailed.

After the mid-1970s, the boundaries of domestic economies began to dissolve into an internationalized economy, and capital and labor within countries were differentially affected. Capital could move easily across the globe, while labor could not. Capital could find cheap labor in less developed countries, putting people out of work and lowering wages in the industrialized welfare states. In the United States, new technologies required skilled labor by educated workers, and those with limited education became severely disadvantaged by the lack of job opportunities that remained after manufacturing jobs were off-shored (Yellen, 2006). Although U.S. jobs in the service sector grew, they paid poorly and afforded few if any benefits. The schism of inequality began to widen, and the American dream of upward mobility began to slip away.

Poverty and inequality in the United States are inextricably linked. Despite dramatic growth in the U.S. GDP per capita, disproportionate income gains for higher-income earners were accompanied by declines in real wages for less-skilled workers earning below the median wage, thus widening inequality between those at the top and bottom of the income distribution (Yellen, 2006; Kahne and Mabel, 2010). While a small percentage of citizens reaped unprecedented rewards from greater economic productivity, inequality widened to troubling proportions, with the United States leading this trend (Giddens, 2000; Stiglitz, 2012). Unlike the years of the "Great Prosperity" (Reich, 2010, p. 42) when economic growth lifted all boats, the economic rewards of globalization have been a boon for the wealthiest and a burden for the least fortunate.

The internationalization of contemporary economies now poses substantial challenges to Western welfare states, and to liberal welfare states in particular, due to their predominant reliance on the market for social provisioning. The need for social welfare endures through time and becomes most acute during historical transformations, pressuring political actors to take new actions that expand the influence of government relative to the market and civil society. The United States, along with other industrially advanced nations, now stands at a crossroads with the chance to choose a direction that could lead to more equitable social policies that uphold human rights to well-being.

Theoretical context

Although issues of jobs and economic growth currently captivate the American media and the public mind, the underlying social problems of poverty and inequality receive less attention. Theoretical orientations concerning political economy and the Western welfare state by Esping-Andersen (1990) and Marshall (1950/1992) shed light on the current inability of American social policy to treat the causes, rather than the symptoms, of poverty and inequality. Each author describes the adverse consequences of market domination over the state and civil spheres.

According to Esping-Andersen (1990), the configuration of state, market, and labor in Western welfare states is an instrument of social stratification. While the United States places far more rhetorical importance on equality of opportunity than on equality of outcomes, European social democracies are known for prioritizing a compressed range of social and economic outcomes aimed at minimizing inequality and increasing social cohesion.

The United States is a paragon of the "liberal" welfare state regime, exemplifying ethics of freedom, self-reliance, and industriousness in reaction to the stratification of social classes in Europe (Esping-Andersen, 1990, p. 42). The market is trusted to provide equal opportunity to all who are willing to work, and outcomes are based on competitive individualism in the marketplace. Equal outcomes are not promised, nor are they the goal of the system. Rather, unequal outcomes are acceptable, because they are assumed to reflect discrepancies in motivation and spur incentive (Esping-Andersen, 1990).

On the other hand, American citizenship provides some measure of political universality and equality. Individuals who cannot provide for themselves can access the modest benefits of the state's minimalistic safety net, but must endure social stigma associated with deficiencies in self-reliance. The United States does resort to universal solutions when the need for social insurance becomes inescapable (Esping-Andersen, 1990). Esping-Andersen depicts the social stratification in the liberal regime thusly: the group at the bottom relies on stigmatizing public relief; the middle relies on social insurance; and the privileged rely on market solutions.

Marshall (1950/1992) concludes that liberalism's valuing of equal opportunities over equal outcomes undermines the rights of citizenship. While capitalism and democracy co-developed across the centuries, Marshall explains that they arise from opposing principles. Democracy provides equal opportunity through the rights of citizenship, while capitalism is a "system of inequality" (p. 18) that produces unequal outcomes in the marketplace. The unequal outcomes of capitalism result in social classes structured by levels of wealth and privilege that, in effect, attenuate the expectations of equal rights through citizenship. Status differentials are produced through unequal access to education and occupation. In turn, stratification by education and occupation restricts equal access to future opportunities. For Marshall, rights to equality of opportunity and rights to equality of outcome cannot be separated. The greater the market inequality, the less meaning and power there is in citizenship rights. Substantial economic inequalities, such as currently exist in the United States, siphon power from the state and civil society to the market.

The reach of transnational capital compromises the ability of democratic governments to mediate the effects of the market on behalf of their citizens (Mishra, 1999; Reich, 2007). While the standard of living for workers declines, vast differences in wealth and power allow the privileged to overwhelm democracy by exerting their influence in various spheres of government (Reich, 2007). A highly unequal society also undermines social inclusion and cohesion (Giddens, 1998).

The capitalist road to serfdom

Despite the dramatic loss of well-paid manufacturing jobs in the United States and other negative consequences of global production and trade, the government did little to assist those left behind by the internationalized economy. Instead, social rights and entitlements came under siege through the resurgence of conservative ideologies which emphasized the responsibility to work over the receipt of entitlements. Rather than addressing the structural changes taking place in the workforce and world economy and attending to the economic implications of the rise of poor, female-headed households, the U.S. policy response became mired by rhetoric that anesthetized the American public with cultural and normative explanations for poverty. Public sympathy for the poor during the 1960s sparked by Michael Harrington's *The Other America* (1962), Edward R. Murrow's telecast *Harvest of Shame* (1960), and President Lyndon Johnson's "War on Poverty" morphed in the 1970s into resentment against the federal program "Aid to Families with Dependent Children" (AFDC), known simply as "welfare," which provided cash aid to poor single mothers without requiring work.

The welfare "backlash" that culminated in the passage of the Personal Responsibility and Work Opportunity Reconciliation Act of 1996 (PRWORA) serves as an example of a trend towards social responsibility and against entitlements (Gilbert, 2004). "Temporary Assistance for Needy Families" (TANF), the replacement for AFDC, embodies the primary markers of the new liberalization of social welfare. TANF increases the availability and attractiveness of work, while meting out financial penalties for those who refuse to work (Gilbert, 2004). A principal component of this much-touted welfare reform requires recipients of cash assistance to work, typically in low-wage jobs, or to enroll in training or education courses. Benefits are time-limited and capped over the lifespan. TANF ensures a subsistence standard of living for those who work through the assistance of tax programs, such as the Earned Income Tax Credit (EITC), that serve as wage subsidies to raise incomes close to the poverty line for families with children (Jeroslow, 2013). After the passage of PRWORA, exits from welfare increased and welfare entries decreased, but Acs and Loprest (2004) found that only 60% of welfare-leavers worked, and of this group, 85% still had incomes below twice the poverty threshold. Despite PRWORA's implementation, the proportion of families with incomes below 50% of the federal poverty threshold increased during the boom years of the 1990s (Zedlewski et al., 2002).

With President Clinton's announcement of the demise of AFDC in 1996 that "[ended] welfare as we used to know it," the EITC assumed a major role in reducing welfare entries and incentiviz-ing labor force participation among less-educated, single mothers (Grogger, 2004; Meyer, 2010). The EITC was first instituted in 1975, and is currently the largest American anti-poverty program for working families. In 2010, the EITC provided approximately $59.5 billion in tax rebates to 26.8 million families (IRS, 2014). The EITC operates via the federal tax code to redistribute tax revenues in the form of tax refunds that "make work pay" for low- and moderate-wage earners, primarily for those with children. Use of the tax code has been palatable politically because it eschews public discontent with more visible cash outlays that reward non-work (Ventry, 2000).

Despite the apparent success of the EITC, Hoffman and Seidman (2003) estimate that the program reduced overall poverty rates by only 0.2 to 0.4 percentage points in the 1980s, and by 1.0 to 1.5 percentage points in the 1990s. Since the EITC requires workforce participation, more than 60% of poor households are ineligible because they do not earn wages or do not have "qualified" children. Moreover, many beneficiaries of the EITC, including most former welfare recipients, have incomes that hover near or below the U.S. poverty threshold (Acs and Toder, 2007; Meyer, 2010). After more than 35 years of implementation and despite the EITC's achievement in increasing labor force attachment, the U.S. poverty rate for families with children has remained largely intractable since the inception of the EITC in 1975. Further, child poverty in the United States increased by 50% in the last quarter of the twentieth century (Rainwater and Smeeding, 2003), a time frame coincident with the enactment of the EITC and its subsequent expansions (Jeroslow, 2013).

Some analysts argue that the EITC has been more effective in its mission to increase the labor supply than in alleviating poverty (Grogger, 2004; Dowd and Horowitz, 2011). The EITC is viewed as a supplement for employers that institutionalizes low wages (Grover, 2005), while fail-ing to provide skill development or career advancement opportunities for workers (Dodson and Albelda, 2012). Hours may vary from week to week at an employer's discretion, and low-wage, dead-end jobs in the United States generally do not offer health insurance benefits, paid sick leave, or paid vacation time. Unlike other developed countries that offer universal entitlements to care for very young children, finding child care in the United States is a problem that must be solved by individual families, and quality child care is usually unaffordable for the working poor (Williams, 2010). With limited time and financial resources, many low-income parents are hard-pressed to meet their children's needs or promote their academic success (Dodson and Albelda, 2012).

While income transfers such as the EITC are helpful for meeting consumption needs in the short term, they do not enable poor families to raise their long-term productivity (Sachs, 2011). Contrary to the myth of the United States as the land of opportunity, a shockingly high correlation between the income and educational attainment of American parents and that of their children reveals that children from poor households are likely to be poor as adults (Sachs, 2011). As Sachs (2011) notes, the problem of poverty cannot be solved by modest income supports, such as those offered by the U.S. welfare state. Poverty eradication requires additional interventions that promote children's health and develop their human capital.

In a nation where the top 1% seized over 65% of the gain in total income between 2002 and 2007 (Stiglitz, 2012), 42% of American children two years hence resided in low-income families, split between 21% designated as near-poor (between one and two times the poverty line) and 21% below the poverty line (NCCP, 2012). For many observers, this situation is untenable for these children and for the nation (Sachs, 2011; Stiglitz, 2012). Hayek (1944) may have been fearful about socialism, but in the United States it is the increased power of market capitalism over the state and civil society that is producing "serfdom" jobs, and perpetuating "serfdom" across generations. Unlike the time of the "Great Prosperity" when the market lifted all boats, most American workers no longer benefit from economic growth, and many live in "serfdom," on the brink of hunger and homelessness, or trapped in low-wage jobs. A sustainable society will need to tame wanton market domination.

Two roads towards a "sustainable" society

Polanyi (1944/2001) observed that the ravages of unbridled capitalism were constrained by decommodifying labor through the institutionalization of social rights and protections in budding nineteenth-century welfare states. In contrast, solutions for market encroachment in twenty-first-century liberal welfare states will require a new paradigm that maintains labor attachment, while elevating social rights beyond mere subsistence to ensure human well-being. Giddens (1998) and Sen (1993, 1999), respectively, offer two possibilities for the forward march from social rights to human rights.

Several of Giddens's recommendations were adopted by Britain's New Labour Party in 1997, but their implementation lacked fidelity to Giddens's vision. This discussion will focus on Giddens's apparent intent.

Anthony Giddens: the social investment state

In *The Third Way*, Giddens (1998) advocates for a revival of social democracy that will rekindle the values of economic and social equality, in conjunction with state protections across the life cycle. The underlying principles of the "Third Way" are emblematic of changes being made across many Western welfare nations under the rubric of the "social investment state," adapted in varying degrees to existing welfare state configurations (Evers and Guillemard, 2013). A major goal of these reforms is to enhance citizens' capacities for coping with risky economic environments by shifting risk from the state to the individual (Bernstein, 2006). However, the social investment state extends far beyond basic security. It aims to expand opportunity throughout society by building human capital, increasing the integration and capacity of the public and private sectors to deliver services, and augmenting social capital through community organizations (Giddens, 1998).

The social investment state includes unemployment and pension insurances, but the emphasis is on a "redistribution of possibilities" that diminishes reliance on these benefits (Giddens, 1998, p. 101). Through ongoing education, training, and work opportunities, it is anticipated that people will remain productive throughout the life cycle, barring infirmities that preclude participation in the workforce (Giddens, 1998). Social inclusion and equality are sought through bolstering "people's life chances," rather than equalizing outcomes.

The catchphrase "*no rights without responsibilities*" is also a cornerstone of the "Third Way" (Giddens, 1998, p. 65, author's italics). Giddens makes clear that rights are no longer blanket entitlements, but are linked to work obligations. At the same time, Giddens (1998) adds that dead-end jobs will not suffice to combat social exclusion and inequality at the bottom. In the comprehensive social investment state, a new goal is to cultivate human potential to the point where it can nearly replace "after the event" redistribution (Giddens, 1998, p. 100).

Given the emphasis on social investment across the lifespan, Giddens (1998) describes social provisioning in the new language of "positive welfare" (p. 117). Positive welfare embraces wealth creation, and treats welfare less as an economic concept, and more as a gauge of psychic well-being (Giddens, 1998). In turn, positive welfare is viewed within the context of a "welfare society" that engages private, public, and community agencies in the project of "the active development of civil society" that embraces rich and poor alike (p. 118).

Amartya Sen: the "Capabilities Approach"

Over the course of several centuries, Hobbes's (1651/1994) quest for liberation and basic security and Smith's (1776/2004) faith in the freedoms afforded by the free market have evolved into the pursuit of human realization. Sen's "Capabilities Approach" (1993, 1999) marks the transition from a framework of social rights to one of human rights. Sen's (2010) conceptions of freedom, well-being, and human rights for the twenty-first century articulate an expanded vision for the fulfillment of human capabilities. In contrast to pre-capitalist social contracts, Sen's "Capabilities Approach" does not advance a theory of human nature. Instead, it is an ethical guide that identifies the conditions that national governments must meet in order to ensure human rights and dignity for all citizens (Nussbaum, 2011).

In Sen's theory, freedom is defined in relation to human capabilities to do and become. It is in the doing and becoming that the individual realizes her potential as a participating member of the social order. While the focus of Sen's (1999) "Capabilities Approach" is on individual freedom, such freedom rests on the opportunities that are made possible through a confluence of multiple sectors of society. Individual achievement is related to "economic opportunities, political liberties, social powers, and the enabling conditions of good health, basic education, and the encouragement and cultivation of initiatives" (Sen, 1999, p. 5).

While Sen's theory may be especially applicable to developing nations, it is no less relevant for advanced economies, particularly for those in which equality of opportunity has been substantially diminished. Inequalities between strata of society are not only created by vast differentials in earnings and wealth, but also by wide variations in the development of capabilities. Poverty is viewed not in monetary terms alone, but more expansively as a deprivation of opportunities.

In the "Capabilities Approach," the strength of a nation is defined more by its public expenditures for social investments than by the growth of its national product. An adequate program of social services, education, and health care is required to support the development of capacities that provide individual freedom. The conditions that allow freedom to develop are dependent upon institutional processes in civil, state, and market arenas, as well as individual endowments and initiative. The concept "Development as freedom" (Sen, 1999) implies that equalizing access to opportunities provided by social institutions, whether afforded by the market, state, or community, will diminish inequalities in outcomes.

"Development as freedom" posits freedom both as a means and as the end goal (Sen, 1999). Freedom rests on development, and development permits greater freedom. People are active agents in the formation of their destinies, helping themselves and others, and otherwise influencing the world by their actions. Sen's (1999) brand of freedom, like Giddens's social investment state, represents an advancement of rights that requires an extensive role for state and society.

Conclusion: comparing visions of the sustainable society

Giddens (1998) and Sen (1999) agree about the centrality of markets, but voice nuanced differences with respect to freedom and human capital development. Due to these distinctions, choosing one road over the other would result in differently constituted societies, although each is aimed at advancing the human project.

Both Giddens (2000) and Sen (1999) share a conviction that markets can do much to reduce inequality. At the same time, both caution that market efficiency alone cannot guarantee distributive equity, but must be supplemented by social goods and opportunities for achieving social equity. Chief among these are universal entitlements to health care and education (Sen, 1999). Sen (1999) avoids either defending or impugning the market institution, and Giddens (2000) similarly criticizes politically polarized views. The critical component is that the opportunities afforded by the market are widely accessible (Sen, 1999). Integration of economic, social, and political institutions is central to both Sen's "Capabilities Approach" and Giddens's (1998) "Third Way."

Where Sen and Giddens markedly differ is in the distinction between Sen's (1999) vision of human development and Giddens's (1998, 2000) reliance on building human capital. In the "Third Way," development is appraised according to its market value, and social investments are measured by their rates of return. While building human capital contributes to the development of the individual, its end goal is greater productivity. The capitalized individual becomes a means to that end, and individual freedom merely a by-product. In contrast, Sen (1999) sets "development as freedom" apart from human capital building. Development as freedom incorporates human capital building, but far exceeds limited market-oriented goals. Sen turns the human capital notion on its head. Freedoms and rights contribute to economic progress, but economic growth is a by-product of freedom. Sen concludes that human development is not a luxury, but an essential condition for economic improvement.

Giddens (1998) and Sen (1993) offer two conceptual foundations to enhance human well-being and productivity by rebalancing the relative power of the market, state, and civil society. It remains for political, economic, and civic leaders in the United States, with the support of the American people, to devise policies and programs that actualize Giddens's and Sen's visions of greater human rights and opportunities.

References

Acs, G., and Loprest, P. (2004). *Leaving welfare: Employment and well-being of families that left welfare in the post-entitlement era.* Kalamazoo, MI: The W. E. Upjohn Institute for Employment Research.

Acs, G., and Toder, E. (2007). Should we subsidize work? Welfare reform, the earned income tax credit and optimal transfers. *International Tax and Public Finance,* 14(3), 327–343.

Bernstein, J. (2006). *All together now: Common sense for a fair economy.* San Francisco, CA: Berrett-Koehler Publishers, Inc.

Dodson, L., and Albelda, R. (2012). *How youth are put at risk by parents' low-wage jobs.* Boston: University of Massachusetts Center for Social Policy.

Dowd, T., and Horowitz, J. B. (2011). Income mobility and the earned income tax credit: Short-term safety net or long-term income support. *Public Finance Review*, 39(5), 619–52.

Esping-Andersen, G. (1990). *The three worlds of welfare capitalism*. Princeton, NJ: Princeton University Press.

Evers, A., and Guillemard, A. (eds). (2013). *Social policy and citizenship: The changing landscape*. New York: Oxford University Press.

Giddens, A. (1998). *The Third Way: The renewal of social democracy*. Malden, MA: Blackwell Publishers Inc.

Giddens, A. (2000). *The Third Way and its critics*. Cambridge: Polity Press.

Gilbert, N. (2004). *Transformation of the welfare state: The silent surrender of public responsibility*. New York: Oxford University Press.

Grogger, J. (2004). Welfare transitions in the 1990s: The economy, welfare policy, and the EITC. *Journal of Policy Analysis and Management*, 23(4), 671–695.

Grover, C. (2005). Living wages and the "making work pay" strategy. *Critical Social Policy*, 25(5), 5–27.

Hayek, F. A. von (1944). *The road to serfdom*. Chicago: University of Chicago Press.

Hobbes, T. (1994). *Thomas Hobbes: Leviathan*. E. Curley (ed.). Indianapolis: Hackett Publishing Company, Inc. (Original work published 1651.)

Hoffman, S. D., and Seidman, L. S. (2003). *Helping working families: The earned income tax credit*. Kalamazoo, MI: Upjohn Institute for Employment Research.

Internal Revenue Service (IRS). (2014). EITC and other refundable credits: About EITC. http://www.eitc.irs.gov/EITC-Central/abouteitc

Jeroslow, P. (2013). The earned income tax credit as an anti-poverty programme: Palliative or cure? In G. Ramia, K. Farnsworth, and Z. Irving (Eds), *Social Policy Review 25: Analysis and debate in social policy*, 2013 (pp. 149–166). Bristol, UK: The Policy Press.

Kahne, H., and Mabel, Z. (2010). Single mothers and other low earners: Policy routes to adequate wages. *Poverty and Public Policy*, 2(3), article 7.

Keane, J. (1984). Introduction. In J. Keane (ed.), *Contradictions of the welfare state* (pp. 11–34). Cambridge, MA: The MIT Press.

Marshall, T. H. (1992). Citizenship and social class. In T. H. Marshall and T. Bottomore, *Citizenship and social class* (pp. 2–51). London: Pluto Press. (Original work published 1950.)

Meyer, B. D. (2010). The effects of the earned income tax credit and recent reforms. *Tax Policy and the Economy*, 24(1), 153–180.

Mishra, R. (1999). *Globalization and the welfare state*. Northampton, MA: Edward Elgar.

National Center for Children in Poverty (NCCP). (2012). Retrieved from http://nccp.org/publications/pub_975.html

North, D. C. (1981). *Structure and change in economic history*. New York: W. W. Norton and Company.

Nussbaum, M. C. (2011). *Creating capabilities: The human development approach*. Cambridge, MA: The Belknap Press of Harvard University Press.

Offe, C. (1984). *Contradictions of the welfare state*. J. Keane, (ed.). Cambridge, MA: The MIT Press.

Polanyi, K. (2001). *The great transformation*. Boston: Beacon Press. (Original work published 1944.)

Rainwater, L., and Smeeding, T. M. (2003). *Poor kids in a rich country: America's children in comparative perspective*. New York: Russell Sage.

Reich, R. (2007). *Supercapitalism*. New York: Alfred A. Knopf.

Reich, R. (2010). *Aftershock*. New York: Alfred A. Knopf.

Sachs, J. D. (2011). *The price of civilization: Reawakening American virtue and prosperity*. New York: Random House.

Sen, A. (1993). Capability and well-being. In M. Nussbaum and A. Sen (eds), *The quality of life* (pp. 30–53). Oxford: Clarendon Press.

Sen, A. (1999). *Development as freedom*. New York: Alfred A. Knopf.

Sen, A. (2010). *The idea of justice*. Cambridge, MA: The Belknap Press of Harvard University Press.

Smith, A. (2004). *The wealth of nations*. C. J. Bullock, (ed.). New York: Barnes and Noble. (Original work published 1776.)

Stiglitz, J. (2012). *The price of inequality*. New York: W. W. Norton and Company.

Ventry, D. J. (2000). The collision of tax and welfare politics: The political history of the earned income tax credit, 1969–99. *National Tax Journal*, 53(4), 983–1006.

Williams, J. (2010). *Reshaping the work–family debate*. Cambridge, MA: Harvard University Press.

Yellen, J. (2006). Economic inequality in the United States. *Federal Reserve Bank of San Francisco (FRBSF) Economic Letter*, 2006-33-34 (Dececember 1, 2006).

Zedlewski, S. R., Giannarelli, L., Morton, J., and Wheaton, L. (2002). Extreme poverty rising, existing government programs could do more. *Assessing New Federalism, Series B, No. B-045*. Washington, DC: The Urban Institute.

54

RETURNING TO THE COLLECTIVE

New approaches to alleviating poverty

Susan Roll and Sue Steiner

The inadequacy of income from low-wage work combined with minimal government benefits has become even more apparent in the recent recession. As hours and pay were cut back and government benefits began to diminish, families at the bottom could no longer meet their basic needs. This resulted in the loss of housing, limited ability to buy food and other necessities, inadequate or no child care options, and a significant reduction in medical care. To illustrate, in 2010 46.9 million individuals were living in poverty, up from 37.2 million prior to the recession in 2007. This represents the largest number of people in poverty since the United States began recording poverty rates in the late 1950s. Also in 2010, 17.2 million (one in seven) households experienced food insecurity, the highest number ever recorded in the United States (Coleman-Jensen et al., 2011). In that same year 25.6% of all Americans experienced at least one month without health insurance. In 2012, 27 states had waiting lists for child care vouchers for low-income families, and virtually every state had lowered the income threshold to qualify for these vouchers, making fewer people eligible (Schulman and Blank, 2012).

Research has shown that poor families use a combination of resources to make ends meet, which include income from low-wage work, government benefits, and social support networks. Given that work and benefits are often not adequate for some families to survive, much less thrive, social networks in many low-income communities allow different types of social and economic opportunities. Particularly for single women with children, the ability to swap or barter goods and services can make a substantial difference in the ability to sustain their families financially.

Creative, community-based solutions that support people outside of the formal market-based system offer a promising approach for low-income and low-asset families. Such approaches include community currencies such as time banks, local economic trading systems, and complementary community currency systems. These alternatives, which in many ways are the antithesis of neoliberal global capitalism, move away from the global economy, into a very local economy. They are based on a radically different set of values—reciprocity, interdependence, fairness, and the centrality of social networks and strong communities. As North (2005) notes, community currencies may offer a viable approach to reduce unemployment and social exclusion, recreate community, regulate the economy using a model embedded in moral and social values, and promote local, sustainable development.

Social supports

Research with financially vulnerable families suggests that their social relationships with others are a critical means of survival. Stack (1974), Wilson (1987), Dyke (1996), Edin and Lein (1997), Gilbert (1998) and Ehrenreich (2002) have all documented the stories of women who barter and exchange money, food stamps, child care, automobiles, job leads, and a host of other commodities necessary to meet the needs of daily living. To illustrate the level of sophistication in many communities, Wilson (1987) dispelled the myth that public housing communities were socially disorganized by illustrating an elaborate, well-organized economy that existed in the Chicago projects. Stack (1974) called the system that she found, in a predominantly African American community in the mid-west, *swapping*, as illustrated in the following quote: "That's just everyday life, swapping. You not really getting ahead of nobody, you just get better things as they go back and forth" (p. 34).

The concept of income packaging illustrates this well. Studies by Zippay (2002) and Hartmann et al. (2003) found that families make their decisions by considering their "income package," which is made up of three components: (1) government assistance, (2) wages, and (3) support from social networks such as family, friends, and local service providers. For low-wage workers, rarely are any of these components by themselves enough to sustain a family to be self-sufficient over time, but combined they do support families to get by (Hartmann et al., 2003).

Public policy has been a resource to address low wages and government-support benefits. Although the minimum wage and the availability of the safety net remain woefully inadequate for families, social welfare policy is a reasonable mechanism for addressing these two sources of income. The third source, social supports, is a far more nebulous concept to address in social policy and is virtually absent from discussions of how to support financially vulnerable families. In fact at times policy has actually worked against low-income families in their efforts to build a social support network. For example, in its attempt to de-concentrate poverty, housing policy has families transitioning to mixed-income communities. This approach may harm the natural networks that have long characterized public housing (Goetz, 2002; Clampet-Lundquist, 2004; Kleit and Manzo, 2006). There may be much to learn from this informal resource of social support. Unfortunately, the neoliberal economic agenda has worked against building communities in favor of rugged individualism. This is seen in both the tenets and results of globalization.

Globalization

The neoliberal agenda that has dominated American political thought since the Reagan administration suggests that less government interference in the marketplace and increased globalization will result in increased efficiency and an improved economy for all. Globalization here can be defined as the expansion of trade and multinational business activity. While certain regions of the world and some groups of individuals have benefited from this approach, many others have suffered. In the United States, globalism has resulted in well-paying manufacturing and lower-paying service jobs moving overseas. As Roberts notes, "[W]hat used to be U.S. GDP is now Chinese, Indian and other country GDP" (2010, p. 60). This has left entire communities in economic dire straits by contributing to stagnant wages and reduced benefits. It has also meant growing inequality as wealth is concentrated in fewer hands, with those at the top doing extremely well, while those in the middle and at the bottom are increasingly struggling (Congressional Budget Office, 2011). A primary cause of this is that, in a global economy, consumers have less power to influence hiring and wage policies of distantly owned corporations than they would with locally owned businesses.

The capitalist, consumerist economy ignores and marginalizes those who lack control over their own employment and do not have the money to consume. This has become a growing problem as globalization and neoliberal policies have resulted in the concentration of wealth and left increasing numbers of Americans with fewer resources. Presidential candidate Mitt Romney's statement about the 47% of Americans who give nothing and only want to take illustrates how non-consumers are viewed by some. This portrayal ignores the fact that most, if not all, Americans receive assistance from government in the form of infrastructure and education spending. But it also highlights a problem facing lower-income and lower-asset Americans who are seen as non-productive members of society, only takers and benefit recipients. In reality, the vast majority of the 47% are employees in service industries, caregivers, teachers, social workers, and others upon whom the economy relies to function.

Many of the poor who are seen as takers in the United States are part of what Edgar Cahn, the founder of TimeBanks USA, calls the "core service economy" (Cahn, 2004). The core service economy is based on the myriad unpaid and underpaid caregiving and service provision tasks provided by the working poor. According to a study by the National Center for Children in Poverty (Douglas-Hall and Chau, 2007), low-income parents are most likely to be employed in service occupations. These jobs are the least likely to offer livable wages, full-time hours, health insurance, and benefits, such as sick and vacation time. By way of example, according to the Bureau of Labor Statistics (2012), there were over 1.2 million people working as child care workers in 2010. The child care industry is expected to grow by 20% by 2020, one of the fastest-growing industries, yet workers can expect an average rate of pay at $9.28/hour.

The care and services provided by low-wage workers are essential for the maintenance of the society in which neoliberal global capitalism thrives. It is on the back of caregivers and service providers that the rich are able to acquire their wealth. People can engage in paid labor because someone else is taking care of their children and their homes, teaching their children, and working to address social problems to the degree necessary to maintain general calm in society. Cahn (2004) argues persuasively that if we require good parents and other care providers to thrive as a society, we should be prepared to compensate this segment of the economy. To effectively address poverty, it is important to consider approaches that help members of the core service economy receive more equitable treatment, more respect and value for their critical work, and the resources necessary to meet their needs.

Building on what we know about social support networks and the effects of globalization on low-income families, we suggest that there are innovative ways to address poverty that effectively help communities build social support networks to augment low wages and limited government benefits, and to help low-income people meet their economic needs. These innovations can also address some of the ills of globalization, reducing poverty and empowering people who are marginalized in the traditional economy. The alternative is the localism movement generally and the use of community currencies more specifically. Localism can be defined as the variety of efforts aimed at devolving power and control away from a central authority and reclaiming political and economic control by local regions. Localist efforts have a range of goals, including sustainability, reduced impact on the environment, community building, economic development, and the ability of local citizens to better meet their own needs (Hewison, 2000; Seyfang, 2006).

Community currencies

Community currencies, also known as alternative, complementary, or local currencies, offer an approach to meeting needs outside of the traditional capitalist and consumerist framework.

They can be defined as any currency that can be used to acquire goods or services without using the dominant, or fiat, form of national or multinational currency (Lietaer, 2001). The aim of most alternative currency systems is to increase economic and social capital in communities. Community currencies have existed for centuries and have been employed around the world. They offer individuals and communities a path to exchange goods and services without spending the official currency, which low-asset individuals and families may not be able to access. Community currencies can be developed and managed by individuals, organizations, corporations, or governments. They are usually limited to a specific geographic region and are utilized locally. They are not meant to completely replace traditional currencies, but to supplement them. Because they make currency more abundant, they are particularly important in geographical areas or among populations of people where there is not sufficient flow of cash (Seyfang, 2006).

Community currencies strengthen the local economy by providing access to resources for individuals and support to locally owned businesses. They shift the economic focus from global to local by requiring that all spending is done with local individuals or businesses. They provide important access to needed services and goods for individuals and families who do not have traditional currency. They allow people to receive child care, tutoring, transportation, elder care, home repair, food, and other necessities which keep families afloat. Additionally, several types of community currencies are reciprocal, meaning that people are not placed in the role of service recipient or client, but rather an interdependent position of both getting and giving. These types of currencies acknowledge that all people have something to contribute to the community. Because of this, participants are not viewed by themselves or others simply as takers.

Types of community currencies

There are a variety of approaches to categorizing community currencies. In general they can be grouped into three broad types: barter, complementary community currency systems, and mutual credit systems. Bartering refers to an exchange between two people, both of whom have something the other wants. Either goods or services can be offered in a barter exchange and there is no external or objective value placed on the items being traded. The parties involved determine the worth of the item or service and what would be a fair trade. In the United States the Internal Revenue Service considers barter exchanges to be taxable, and expects people to report them on their tax returns. There are several limitations with a barter system. First, there are only two people involved. If person A does not have anything that person B wants, then no barter will take place. Additionally, some items are indivisible: If someone wants an item that cannot be divided and is worth more than what they have to trade, the barter will not take place.

Mutual credit (MC) systems create a community-based credit economy (Seyfang and Pearson, 2000). They encourage empowerment by allowing communities to take on two roles traditionally held by banks: creating money and giving credit. Instead of using paper notes or coins, MC systems use credits and debits kept in a paper or online ledger system. The system facilitates the sharing of information and record keeping, recording credits earned and spent by each member. Systems call their credits by different names, adding ownership and a local or cultural connection. Members list services or goods they have to offer and what they want from others. Exchanges are recorded in the system, and people spend and earn credits as they would more traditional currency. MC systems allow members to accrue credit without paying interest, as credit that is given by others in the community is based on the trust that it will be repaid. A limit is usually placed on the amount of debt any member can accrue. MC systems address the primary challenge with barter systems, allowing people to exchange with many others in the system, removing the requirement for each person to have what the other needs.

Local Economic Trading Systems (LETS) and Time Banks are two of the most well-known MC systems. A LETS allows members to exchange both goods and services. Additionally, in a LETS, the valuation of the services or goods exchanged is set by those involved in the exchange. Individuals can negotiate what their goods and services are worth. A Time Bank operates similarly to a LETS, but only services are exchanged and all hours of service are valued the same. One hour is equal to one Time Dollar, thus valuing everyone's skills and contributions equally. Exchanges made in LETS are taxable, while those made in Time Banks are not (Collom, 2011). There are many resources available online to help communities decide what type of mutual credit system works best for them and begin the development and implementation process. Timebanks USA (timebanks.org) is a paid membership organization of Time Banks in the United States and ten other countries that provides support and an online management system. HOurworld (hourworld.org) is a national network of Time Banks that offers a free online management system and support. There are roughly 350 Time Banks that belong to the two organizations. The Dane County Time Bank in Madison, Wisconsin, is one of the largest in the United States. It has more than 2,000 members and has developed a variety of innovative programs to build community capacity and address community challenges (Dane County Time Bank, n.d.). They have developed a wellness project, a thrift store where people can buy goods with time dollars, and a youth court and community justice program. They are also working with a local food bank to help older adults and others in need in the community have access to quality, affordable food.

Complementary community currency (CCC) systems are created by individuals, groups, or governments who print currency that is used by people in the community and accepted at local businesses (North, 2006). The currency is given or sold to businesses and individuals in a variety of ways. Some CCC systems sell the currency at face value, while others sell them at a discounted rate. In some systems business members pay a fee to join, which is used to provide credits to non-profit organizations for their clients or individuals in need. Many use a combination of these approaches. Most link their currency to the national currency, though some are equated with other things, such as a basket of food. CCC credits are used to supplement the national currency, allowing members of the community to meet their basic needs and supporting local merchants. People who use the currency are only allowed to spend it at locally owned businesses and for local services, thus spurring local economic development. CCC systems' use of actual paper money alleviates the need for individual members or system staff or volunteers to keep track of hours, as is required in MC systems.

One long-standing and well-known CCC system is Ithaca Hours, begun in 1991. Businesses and individuals pay a small fee in U.S. currency to buy into the system, and get twice the amount back in Ithaca Hours bills. They can purchase additional Hours currency at many participating businesses. One Ithaca Hour is worth $10, which was the average hourly wage when the program began. There are currently five denominations of Hour notes. In its first 15 years of existence, several million dollars had been traded (Hermann, 2006). The Ithaca Hours Board gives grants to organizations, low-income people, and volunteers. People can negotiate the value of goods and services they purchase with Hours. BerkShares, another large CCC system, first issued notes in 2006. There were 2.5 million BerkShares in circulation in Western Massachusetts by 2010 (McKibben, 2010). Five community banks issue BerkShare notes. People pay $95 for $100 worth of currency, which is accepted at locally owned businesses throughout the area.

Growth and effectiveness of community currencies

Technology has facilitated the development and utilization of community currencies. Reaching potential members is easier via the Internet, and there are a number of online programs available to manage the systems. In part due to these technologies, estimates are that more than 4,000 community currencies are currently being employed worldwide, as compared to only about 100 in 1990 (Block, 2012).

Community currencies tend to thrive during difficult economic times. An economic crisis began in Argentina in the late 1990s, and the poverty rate reached 37.5% by 2001. In response to record unemployment and poverty rates, a large alternative currency system was developed based on a currency known as the Credito. People across the country joined "barter clubs" to trade their labor for goods and services. During the height of the country's economic challenges, more than 2.5 million members belonged to one of 4,500 clubs. Use of the Credito was the only thing that allowed thousands to survive (Ould-Ahmed, 2010).

Community currency systems have been expanding rapidly in the Eurozone during the recent economic crisis. They have become particularly prevalent in Spain and Greece, both of which have been suffering through very difficult economic times. Spain has been especially hard hit, with the highest unemployment rate in Europe. The number of Time Banks in Spain doubled to 291 in the past two years, and estimates are that tens of thousands of people are engaged in some type of alternative currency program (Moffett and Brat, 2012). There has also been a tremendous expansion of barter, LETS, and CCC networks.

Community currencies have been used for many years in the United States, expanding dramatically following the 1929 Wall Street Crash and into the 1930s. At that time municipal governments, merchant associations, and groups of citizens initiated barter networks and community currencies in cities and towns nationwide (Elvins, 2012). They allowed people to get their basic needs met before the federal government began to develop the New Deal programs. This movement has seen a significant resurgence recently. Estimates are that more than 150 alternative currency systems have been implemented in the United States in the past 20 years (Collom, 2008). According to the International Reciprocal Trade Association, roughly $12 billion worth of goods and services are exchanged annually in the United States without any national currency changing hands (Spitznagel, 2012).

The growth of community currencies makes logical sense given its great potential to reduce poverty. People who do not work or do not earn enough money frequently cannot purchase goods and services to meet their basic needs. Community currencies allow them to get needs met without an outlay of cash. Second, people who are not working may have time available to engage in LETS or Time Bank activities. Additionally, a goal of many community currency programs is an increased sense of community and social support. As noted previously, research indicates that this is important in reducing poverty. Finally, involvement in LETS and Time Bank programs has the potential to help participants gain employment skills and make new contacts that can help them find work.

While there has been limited research conducted on the effectiveness of community currencies in reducing poverty, what does exist suggests their promise. In research conducted on four different types of community currencies, North (2003) found that one of the major appeals of mutual credit systems is that they offer people a lifeline during times of economic crisis or disruption. However, he notes that need alone is not enough to allow the systems to thrive or even survive. There must also be positive reasons for their existence, such as increased community and an ideology of local production and consumption. Collom (2011) studied one of the oldest and largest Time Banks in the United States, receiving survey responses from 235 members. People primarily joined the Time Bank for economic and social reasons, and people with lower household incomes were most likely to have joined to get help meeting their basic needs. The study found that younger participants were most likely to gain employment experience or actual employment, unemployed members were most likely to have positive civic engagement outcomes, and low-income members were most likely to gain social outcomes. This latter fact is noteworthy given the importance of social capital in addressing poverty.

A study was conducted for the British Government to determine if participation in LETS provided a bridge to employment, self-employment, and exchange for needed items outside of employment (Williams et al., 2001). A multi-method approach was utilized, including contacting all 303 LETS programs in the United Kingdom and sending 2,515 questionnaires to members of 22 programs. Results suggest that experience gained by participating in the program directly assisted 4.9% of respondents in acquiring paid work. An additional 15% of respondents noted that LETS participation helped them gain new skills, that number increasing to 24% among unemployed members. While this had not led to direct employment yet, people believed that it could. Participation in the LETS also potentially contributed to employability by boosting self-confidence and self-esteem for 27% of respondents and 33% of unemployed respondents. A number of the unemployed noted that the formal economy did not value them, and their ability to "sell" their services in the LETS resulted in improved self-worth. Finally, 10.7% of LETS members stated that their participation helped them become self-employed by expanding their client base, easing cash flow in their businesses, and providing potential clients on whom to test their products or services on a smaller scale.

A final illustration is the Gorbals Time Bank in Glasgow, Scotland, that was established in a low-income section of the city. The membership of the Time Bank has a higher unemployment rate than the city average (20% vs. 6%), a high percentage of people receiving government poverty reduction assistance (50%), and high rates of single-parent families (46%) (Seyfang, 2004). Research suggests that the 22 organizational members of the Time Bank have been able to expand services and better meet community needs by using Time Bank members as volunteers. Similarly, the Time Bank has encouraged people who were not previously involved in their community to become involved, resulting in improved self-esteem, increased social support, new connections being made, and new skills being learned.

Conclusion

Fundamentally, our society needs to take a careful look at how we measure wealth and well-being. Is our most important measure GDP alone or do we also value non-commodified goods and services which enhance our quality of life? An Urban Institute synthesis of 28 reports on measures of economic well-being suggests that such indicators must include the economic value of caring and caregiving and a concerted effort to address the needs of marginalized communities (De Leon and Boris, 2010). Community currencies have the potential to support a revaluation of wealth, valuing caring and caregiving equally with other areas of production while addressing the needs of marginalized people.

In much of what was exemplified in the Occupy Movement, communities are asking for power to be brought back to the people. This can be done in local communities with the development of community currencies, giving people access to goods and services they might not otherwise afford. Additionally, community currencies have the potential to facilitate community building and essential social support. This combination of addressing unmet needs and development of strong community networks offers great potential for poverty reduction.

References

Block, B. (2012). Local Currencies Grow During Economic Recession. Worldwatch Institute: Vision for a Sustainable World. Retrieved January 10, 2014, from http://www.worldwatch.org/node/5978.

Bureau of Labor Statistics (2012). U.S. Department of Labor, Occupational Outlook Handbook, 2012–13 Edition. Retrieved November 14, 2012, from http://www.bls.gov/ooh/personal-care-and-service/childcare-workers.htm.

Cahn, E.S. (2004). *No More Throw-Away People: The Co-Production Imperative*, 2nd Edition. Washington, DC: Essential Books.

Clampet-Lundquist, S. (2004). Moving Over or Moving Up? Short-Term Gains and Losses for Relocated HOPE VI Families. *Journal of Policy Development and Research*, 7(1): 57–80.

Coleman-Jensen, A., Nord, M., Andrews, M., and Carlson, S. (2011). *Household Food Security in the United States in 2010*. ERR-125, U.S. Dept. of Agriculture, Econ. Res. Serv. Retrieved January 20, 2014, from http://www.ers.usda.gov/media/121076/err125_2_.pdf.

Collom, E. (2008). *Banking Time in an Alternative Market: A Quantitative Case Study of a Local Currency System*. Conference Papers—American Sociological Association, 1.

Collom, E. (2011). Motivations and Differential Participation in a Community Currency System: The Dynamics within a Local Social Movement Organization. *Sociological Forum*, 26(1): 144–168.

Congressional Budget Office (2011). *Trends in the Distribution of Household Income Between 1979 and 2007*. Washington, DC: Congressional Budget Office.

Dane County Time Bank (n.d.). Retrieved May 15, 2013, from danecountytimebank.org.

De Leon, E. and Boris, E. (2010). *The State of Society: Measuring Economic Success and Human Well-Being*. Washington, DC: The Urban Institute.

Douglas-Hall, A. and Chau, M. (2007). Most Low-Income Parents are Employed. Retrieved January 10, 2014, from http://www.nccp.org/publications/pub_784.html.

Dyke, I. (1996). Mother or Worker? Women's Support Networks, Local Knowledge, and Informal Child Care Strategies. In K. England (ed.), *Who Will Mind the Baby? Geographies of Child Care and Working Mothers* (pp. 123–140). New York: Routledge.

Edin, K. and Lein, L. (1997). *Making Ends Meet: How Single Mothers Survive Welfare and Low-Wage Work*. New York: Russell Sage Foundation.

Ehrenreich, B. (2002). *Nickel and Dimed: On (Not) Getting By in America*. New York: Metropolitan.

Elvins, S. (2012). Selling Scrip to America: Ideology, Self-Help and the Experiments of the Great Depression. *International Journal of Community Currency Research*, 16(D): 14–21.

Gilbert, M.R. (1998). "Race," Space and Power: The Survival Strategies of Working, Poor Women. *Annals of the Association of American Geographers*, 88: 595–621.

Goetz, E. (2002). Forced Relocation vs. Voluntary Mobility: The Effects of Dispersal Programmes on Households. *Housing Studies*, 17(1): 107–123.

Hartmann, H., Spalter-Roth, R., and Sills, M. (2003). *Survival at the Bottom: The Income Packages of Low-Income Families with Children*. Washington, DC: Institute for Women's Policy Research.

Hermann, G.M. (2006). Special Money: Ithaca Hours and Garage Sales. *Ethnology*, 2: 125–133.

Hewison, K. (2000). Resisting Globalization: A Study of Localism in Thailand. *Pacific Review*, 13: 279–296.

Kleit, R. and Manzo, L. (2006). To Move or Not To Move: Relationships to Place and Relocation Choices in HOPE VI. *Housing Policy Debate*, 17(2): 271–308.

Lietaer, B. (2001). *The Future of Money*. London: Random House.

McKibben, B. (2010). A Bang for Your Buck in the Berkshires. *Yankee*, 74: 93.

Moffett, M. and Brat, I. (2012, August 27). For Spain's Jobless, Time Equals Money. *Wall Street Journal—Eastern Editions*, pp. A1, A12.

North, P. (2003). Time Banks—Learning the Lessons from LETS? *Local Economy*, 18(3): 267–270.

North, P. (2005). Scaling Alternative Economic Practices? Some Lessons from Alternative Currencies. *Transactions of the Institute of British Geographers*, 30(2): 221–233.

North, P. (2006). *Alternative Currency Movements as a Challenge to Globalisation? A Case Study of Manchester's Local Currency Networks*. London: Ashgate Publishing Limited.

Ould-Ahmed, P. (2010). Can a Community Currency Be Independent of the State Currency? A Case Study of the Credito in Argentina (1995–2008). *Environment and Planning*, 42(6): 1346–1364.

Roberts, P.C. (2010). Death to Globalism. *International Economy*, 24: 59–61.

Schulman, K. and Blank, H. (2012). *Downward Slide: State Child Care Assistance Policies 2012*. Washington, DC: National Women's Law Center. Retrieved October 16, 2012, from http://www.nwlc.org/sites/default/files/pdfs/NWLC2012_StateChildCareAssistanceReport.pdf.

Seyfang, G. (2004). Consuming Values and Contested Cultures: A Critical Analysis of the UK Strategy for Sustainable Consumption and Production. *Review of Social Economy*, 62(3): 323–338.

Seyfang, G. (2006). Sustainable Consumption, The New Economics and Community Currencies: Developing New Institutions for Environmental Governance. *Regional Studies*, 40: 781–791.

Seyfang, G. and Pearson, R. (2000). Time for Change: International Experience in Community Currencies. *Development*, 43, 56–60.

Spitznagel, E. (2012). Rise of the Barter Economy. *Bloomberg Business Week*, 4277: 75–77.

Stack, C. (1974). *All Our Kin*. New York: Harper and Row.

Williams, C., Aldridge, T., Lee, R., Levishon, A., Thrift, N., and Tooke, J. (2001). Bridges into Work? An Evaluation of Local Exchange and Trading Schemes (LETS). *Policy Studies*, 22: 119–132.

Wilson, W.J. (1987). *The Truly Disadvantaged: The Inner City, the Underclass and Public Policy*. Chicago, IL: University of Chicago Press.

Zippay, A. (2002). The Dynamics of Income Packaging. *Social Work*, 47(3): 291–300.

55

WHY WE CANNOT ALL BE MIDDLE CLASS IN AMERICA

Lakshman Yapa

Many journalists, academics, and politicians from both sides of the aisle, including the White House, point to the decline of the American middle class in the last 30 years. Experience and data quite clearly support this conclusion. However, the seemingly common-sense conclusion drawn from this—that expanding the middle class is beneficial to America, and also a pathway out for the 48 million people living in poverty—is problematic. This chapter argues that there are serious economic, ecological, and structural limits that make the expansion of the middle class not only a discouraging task in futility, but also a misuse of resources despite well-intentioned efforts. Given that the project of expanding the middle class is neither possible on a large scale, nor a pathway out of poverty for millions, we need to envision an alternative framework which focuses on the lived experiences of poverty, rather than on increasing income and jobs. The first section of the chapter provides statistical evidence for the contraction of the middle class. The second section of the chapter describes the role of the middle class in a capitalist economy. The third section of the chapter delineates several structural limits to expanding the middle class. The fourth section of the chapter describes in brief a workable alternative to the vision of the American middle class—what I call the Basic Needs Economy.

The decline of the middle class

In 2009, when President Obama took office, he formed a White House Middle Class Task Force under the leadership of Vice President Joe Biden.[1] Its webpage states, "A strong middle class equals a strong America. We can't have one without the other." But who exactly is in the middle class? In 2011, the Tax Policy Center placed the median household income at $42,000; the Census Bureau placed it at $50,000 (Rampell, 2012). According to a 2012 Pew Research Center survey, people who call themselves middle class believe a family of four needs about $70,000 to maintain a middle-class lifestyle (Pew Research Center, 2012, p. 8).

Although there is no apparent consensus on who exactly is the middle class, let us use the 2012 Pew Report as a baseline. This report divided households into three income groups—the middle-income group consisted of households earning two-thirds to double the national median income. In 1970 this middle group received 62% of aggregate household income; in 2010, their share declined to 45%. The share of the lowest tier also declined, while the upper tier increased its share from 29% in 1970 to 46% in 2010.

When we consider lower- and middle-income households from the viewpoint of their net worth, the picture of inequality is even more striking. In 2010, 50% of the households in the United States accounted for only 1.1% of national household assets (Levine, 2012, p. 4).

Using data constructed from IRS tax records, Picketty and Saez (2006) report that in 1915 the top 1% of income earners in the United States had 18% of the nation's income.[2] Income inequality rose a bit during the Great Depression, then came down slightly during the War years, and continued to decline through the 1950s and 1960s, an era economic historians call the "Great Compression." Beginning in the 1980s, however, income inequality rose to levels not seen since the Great Depression, a trend that Paul Krugman (2007) called "The Great Divergence." Saez (2012) report that in 2010 the income share of the top 1% had grown to almost 24% and the share of the top 10% was nearly 50%.

Since 2000 there has been an explosion of books on the subject of income inequality and the decline of the middle class, some by academics and others by journalists. The decline of the middle class was a major theme of Paul Krugman's *Conscience of a Liberal* (2007), a topic he returned to in *End This Depression Now* (2012). President Clinton's former Secretary of Labor Robert Reich (2010) argued in his book *Aftershock* that the post-1980 concentration of income was an important factor in the decline of the middle class. These topics were also central to Joseph Stiglitz's *The Price of Inequality* (2012), wherein he relates increased income inequality and the decline of the middle class to the larger political economy of contemporary U.S. capitalism—monetary policy, fiscal policy, globalization, outsourcing, bank deregulation, and low corporate taxes, to name a few.

Among the many journalists who have commented extensively on the vanishing middle class there are: Ariana Huffington (2010), *Third World America*; James Carville and Stan Greenberg (2012), *It's the Middle Class, Stupid!* ; Timothy Noah (2012), *The Great Divergence*; Bill O'Reilly (2003), *Who's Looking Out for You?* ; and Lou Dobbs (2006), *War on the Middle Class.*

To take one example, in *Third World America*,[3] Huffington worries that with the disappearance of the middle class, America is in fact becoming more like a Third World nation. However, having invoked the First World/Third World comparison for her initial purpose, she quickly moves away from the binary, revealing that the term "America" was really a stand-in for the middle class. The term "middle class," however, does not yield an obvious binary because it represents a liminal state, something that stands in as a threshold or in the middle of another binary, in this case between rich and poor. The poor in America do not realistically aspire to be rich but rather to become middle class; in that sense the more useful binary here is the middle class vs. the poor. Huffington's fear seems to be that people who drop out of the middle class will become permanently poor.

Krugman, Reich, and Stiglitz, as well as Huffington, all make a convincing case for the decline of the middle class. The evidence is irrefutable. Yet they are all working within the paradigm of Keynesian economics, and implicitly share the belief that the solution to these problems is more economic growth, albeit of the sustainable and equitable variety. While we should remain critical of the global neo-liberal economic order, it is important to reflect that even during the Great Convergence from 1940 to 1980 poverty remained a serious problem in America. The postwar mass consumption boom did not extend to urban and rural blacks, rural whites in Appalachia, and Native Americans. Michael Harrington (1962) published his *The Other America* only four years after John Kenneth Galbraith (1958) wrote his *The Affluent Society* on the economics of opulence. Furthermore, while it is undeniably true that the middle class has declined in America since the 1980s, I find the seemingly common-place conclusion that the expansion of the middle class is both the solution for America and a pathway out of poverty extremely problematic and ultimately, for reasons

I shall detail, not of much use to either policy-makers or local change agents working in affected communities.

The role of the middle class in a capitalist economy

There is a remarkable congruence in the Marxian and Keynesian views of the role of the middle class in a capitalist economy. Imagine a simple model economy divided into firms and households and consider production and consumption relations between the two. Households supply labor to firms, and firms in turn pay wages to households; this is a production relation. Firms supply goods to households, for which households pay the firms; this is a consumption relation. Define the sum total of wages paid by firms (or capitalists) going to the households (or labor) as "The Wage Bill." We can proceed using the Marxian language of capital and labor or the Keynesian language of firms and households. First I shall present the Marxian argument. In *Grundrisse: Foundations of the Critique of Political Economy* (1973, p. 419) Marx said, "To each capitalist, the total mass of all workers, with the exception of his own workers, appear not as workers, but as consumers, possessors of exchange values (wages), money, which they exchange for his commodity." Wages are a cost of production to the capitalist which he would like to reduce so as to increase his surplus value. But if all capitalists did that it would be to the detriment of capitalists as a class because it is the total wage bill that determines the capitalists' capacity to realize surplus value from the sphere of circulation. So individual and class rationality are in conflict, giving rise to what can be called the contradiction of the wage bill.[4]

Next I revisit this idea using the Keynesian framework of firms and households. Firms typically try to lower wages because wages are costs. But if all firms lower costs, the total wage bill decreases, which reduces the capacity of the households to consume. That in turn reduces the total income going back to the firms, negatively impacting their capacity to invest, produce, and expand. Thus the individual interests of a firm do not coincide with the collective interests of all firms—what we called earlier the contradiction of the wage bill. In the Keynesian scheme the total national product Y is given by the following formula $Y = C + I + G + E$, where C = consumption or aggregate demand, I = capital investment, G = government expenditure, and E = income from exports. The term C or aggregate demand is related to what Keynes called the "paradox of thrift." Although individual saving is a virtuous habit, it is not beneficial to the economy as a whole because if all consumers save instead of spend, aggregate demand decreases and depresses the total national product Y. In a capitalist economy it is important for households to have enough income which they spend in consumption to keep aggregate demand high and the economy growing at a healthy clip. Much of Keynesian economics amounts to policy prescriptions to prevent the total wage bill from shrinking. Such measures include fiscal and monetary policy, minimum wages, unemployment compensation, welfare benefits, social security, and tax rebates. Henry Ford understood this mechanism well. In January 1914, he startled the world by announcing he would pay his workers $5 a day. The reason was simple enough: he wanted his workers to have enough money to buy his products. Showing Walter Reuther, the veteran leader of the United Automobile Workers, around a newly automated car plant, Henry Ford II is supposed to have said, "Walter, how are you going to get those robots to pay your union dues?" Without skipping a beat, Reuther replied, "Henry, how are you going to get them to buy your cars?" (*The Economist*, Nov. 4, 2011).[5] Maintaining aggregate demand is essential for the stable functioning of a capitalist economy. What we call "the middle class" is simply the cultural manifestation of this economic logic. It is not mere coincidence that the greatest expansion of the middle class in America was also the height of Keynesian economics in the United States. Or as Richard Nixon is supposed to have said, "We're all Keynesians now."

Structural limits to the expansion of the middle class

Krugman, Stiglitz, Reich, and Huffington all point to the neo-liberal economic order ushered in by President Reagan as a principal cause of the contraction of the middle class in the 1980s—a point I agree with in the main. However, I find problematic the implicit corollary: that the maintenance and expansion of the middle class is the answer to poverty, a position which as we saw is also advocated by the Obama White House Middle Class Task Force. As we shall see, there are numerous economic, ecological, structural, and global conditions which seriously limit the feasibility of this project.

Creating middle-class incomes. For the sake of argument consider $50,000 a year (the median household income in the United States) to be a reasonable middle-class income that would get a family out of poverty. Census income data from 2011 shows that if all the households below the median income were to receive $50,000 a year, the total income needed would exceed $1.5 trillion per year, about 11% of our national GDP. Given that levels of income inequality today are comparable to those seen during the Great Depression, it seems unlikely that even if that quantity of GDP were to be generated, the new money would go into the pocketbooks of the poor. Moreover, a massive transfer of income to the poor is highly unlikely in the political climate that has prevailed for decades. Most importantly, in a global economy of low wages, there is little prospect of creating enough jobs in the United States that pay $50,000 a year.

Creating jobs that pay middle-class wages. In 2011 the Bureau of Labor Statistics reported 12.3 million unemployed persons, involuntary part-time workers at 8.3 million, and those only marginally attached to the labor force at 2.4 million, all adding up to about 23 million people. In a globalized economy of very low wages, it is difficult to see how we can create 23 million jobs that pay $50,000 a year. There is a famous theorem in international economics called the Stolper-Samuelson theorem that says when a rich country like the United States trades with a poor, labor-abundant country such as China, wages in the rich country will fall and profits will increase. In the United States the neo-liberal agenda of the last three decades has created a "super-sized" global market for cheap labor—about 2 billion workers now compete with poor Americans for jobs (Palley, 2005).[6] It is also true that in the past few decades the fastest-growing sector of the U.S. economy has been the quaternary sector, which includes finance, real estate, communication, and the knowledge industries. Experience and data tell us that this is not a sector which typically employs the non-college educated poor.

The middle class and the permanent underclass. In my view the project to expand the middle class is a recipe for creating permanent inequality and perpetuating an underclass. A great danger in setting up goals that cannot be attained is that people soon become discouraged, disheartened, and angry. The desire to expand the middle class comes partly out of our sense of social justice and the valorization of equality. In her book *A Consumer's Republic*, Liz Cohen (2003) describes in some detail the powerful forces that have driven mass consumption in postwar America and why the middle class is such a dominant element of the American psyche. When we talk of expanding the middle class, the poor are invited (or expected) to join a class of consumers that they physically cannot; it is clear this drive for consumer equality is a prescription for creating permanent inequality because the poor will be judged by what they are not and never will be.

The middle class and ecological limits to growth. Expanding the middle class means, of course, also expanding consumption. Mass consumption by the middle class, however, happens inside the ecosystem, and expanding consumption quickly runs into three biophysical limits: finitude, entropy, and ecological interdependence, ideas that are clearly laid out by Herman Daly (1996) in his book *Beyond Growth*. An example of finitude is the concept of peak oil, in which the world production of petroleum is expected to peak around 2010 and then decline. The economic subsystem also depends on the ecosystem as a source for low-entropy inputs and as a depository for high-entropy industrial and consumer waste. The second law of thermodynamics states that, when energy is used, concentrated forms of energy are constantly being transformed into diffused heat unavailable for work—a process known as entropy. Increase in entropy (heat pollution and global warming are among the consequences) poses serious limiting conditions to economic growth. Examples of limits to consumption growth posed by ecological inter-dependence are legion, and they include pollution, global warming, pesticide contamination, eutrophication of lakes, loss of genetic diversity, and so on.

The middle class and the disarticulated economy. Earlier I presented a simple two-sector model of firms and households, and detailed the contradiction of the wage bill. Firms are interested in households not only for their labor but also for their purchasing power because households are both producers and consumers in the market for the commodities made by the firms. Historically, the tension between firms and households was absent in the developing world, giving rise to what can be called "disarticulated economies." The former colonies depended heavily on the export of one or two primary products such as cocoa, tea, bauxite, and diamonds. The workers were not in the market to consume such products, and so the firms, individually or as a group, had no built-in incentive to increase the wages of workers—the classic case of the "disarticulated economy." In contrast, we call an economy where this tension is present and well defined an articulated economy, as in the developed nations of the North. However, in a climate of economic globalization the U.S. economy has become increasingly disarticulated. In 2012 Apple employed 43,000 people in the United States, but created over 700,000 jobs overseas for workers making Apple products. According to Apple the reasons are not just cheap labor but the availability of far more sophisticated supply chains in places like Shenzhen, China. There is another fateful and seemingly contradictory shift to all this: U.S. businesses are now less dependent on a prosperous middle class at home. Markets and advertising are shifting towards production for the rich and emerging middle class overseas in BRIC countries (Brazil, Russia, India, and China) (Freeland, 2011 and Freeland, 2012, p. 285). The Henry Ford model of the articulated economy is being fast replaced by a disarticulated economy producing high-value products, including what are known as Veblen goods—that is, prestige commodities whose demand increases as their price increases (Veblen, 1994).

An alternative vision: the basic needs economy

It should be abundantly clear that not only are there unavoidable economic, ecological, and structural limits to the expansion of the middle class, but also that the expansion of the middle class is not a viable pathway to prosperity for the millions of poor in the United States. There are two serious defects in the vision for expanding the middle class in America. First, as I have shown in this chapter, expanding the middle class is an unattainable goal, one that has contributed significantly to many of the problems it purports to solve—inequality, poverty, a permanent underclass, exclusion, envy, resentment, large numbers of alienated youth, massive rates of incarceration, resources wars, and the ecological destruction of the planet. Second, the middle-class vision is so hegemonic that it has crowded out discussion of any serious alternative vision. The Republicans and the Democrats exhaust the range of political discourse, offering us their competing Tweedledee and Tweedledum vision of the middle class.

In this regard I would like to draw on the social theory that informed a 12-year project (1998–2010) that I directed in a poor neighborhood of West Philadelphia. It was offered as a Pennsylvania State University service learning course titled "Rethinking Urban Poverty: The Philadelphia Field Project." The guiding framework for the course was called "The Basic Needs Economy." Instead of asking whether we can increase the income of people (for which we have to increase the number of jobs that pay middle-class wages), we posed the question: Can we create spaces in the economy that meet people's basic needs while at the same time reduce their cost of living? That is to say, can we create economic spaces which address the lived experience of poverty, understood here not simply as the lack of income but as the scarcity of food, clothes, shelter, and security? This is what I call the Basic Needs Economy. Based on the 12-year experience of the Philadelphia Field Project I believe the answer to that question is a resounding "Yes, yes we can" (Yapa, 2009).[7] We now have enough knowledge in nutrition, urban agriculture, the elimination of chronic disease through diet and exercise, thermodynamic matching of energy sources to end-uses, the building of less auto-centered transport systems, and low-cost effective methods of education to create exactly such an economy. The literature is vast and too numerous for citation here, which frankly is a cause for celebration and hope. For example, urban farming, farmers' markets, and community-supported agriculture all make it possible to produce nutritious food in our cities at affordable prices. Highly regarded physicians claim that public health revolves around four themes—good nutrition, physical fitness, reduction of mental stress, and good social relationships; it is a fact that we now have the practical knowledge to achieve these at very low levels of capital investment. Similar arguments for improving the quality of life at very low levels of capital investment can be extended for transport and energy. Further elaboration of this argument is beyond the scope of this short chapter, but the larger point should be clear. We have not yet woven the extensive literature on food, health, energy, and transport into a coherent vision of an alternative to the consumerist middle-class dream.

The Basic Needs Economy is not an alternative to the existing market economy; it is simply a demand to create spaces within the larger economy where poor people are directly engaged in economic production for their own basic needs first. Some of our national problems—the contracting middle class, unemployment, and poverty—have no national solutions, but the same problems viewed locally are bursting with solutions. Once we begin to stop focusing on creating jobs and increasing incomes, we come to see that everyday people living their everyday routine lives can usefully engage the myriad sites at which scarcity is experienced and socially constructed. This is also the central theme of the book by two geographers, Kathy Gibson and the late Julie Graham. In *A Postcapitalist Politics* (2006), they argue that capitalism is not a total all-pervasive system; there are many other modes of production at work, particularly in the sphere of reproduction or the household economy. They point to several case studies of people and groups who have used their non-sovereign power to improve the quality of their life.[8] As they write:

> What if we were to accept that the goal of thinking is not to extend knowledge by confirming what we already know, that the world is a place of domination and oppression? What if instead we thought about openings and strategic possibilities in the cracks?"
>
> (Gibson-Graham, 2012)

I absolutely believe it is possible to create spaces that produce basic use values at costs affordable to the poor, even within the context of the larger market economy: first, we know how to reduce the cost of living for poor people, thus expanding the purchasing power of existing incomes; second, we know how to improve their quality of life while bringing down the cost of living; and third, there is a great potential to create jobs that pay modest wages—jobs that not only directly address the basic needs of households, but also cannot be outsourced.

While the contraction of the American middle class is undeniable, it does not necessarily follow that the expansion of the middle class is the panacea for America's economic ills. As I have argued here, there are serious economic, ecological, and structural limitations to the Keynesian growth theory of the expansion of the middle class. It is in fact not only an unattainable goal, but one not worth pursuing. I propose instead an alternative vision of post-capitalist politics, nonsovereign power, and community economies producing their basic needs first. The knowledge is already there—it is overwhelming and abundant in a multiplicity of fields, all of which directly relate to the lived experience of poverty—we have only to see this knowledge for what it is: a thousand and one opportunities to build new economies in the interstices of the old.

Notes

1 http://www.whitehouse.gov/strongmiddleclass
2 The data that Thomas Picketty and Emmanuel Saez constructed from Internal Revenue Service tax records goes all the way back to 1913 and is now publicly available online at http://elsa.berkeley.edu/~saez/TabFig2010.xls.
3 The title "Third World America" is an example of Derrida's notion of a privileged binary; other examples include "White/Black," "employed/on welfare," "rich/poor," and "First World/Third World." One term of the binary, the one on the left, is privileged, while the other is marginalized and becomes the lesser of the pair. We use attributes of the privileged term to judge the lesser by what it is not. Although Huffington collapses the two terms into a single title, the same logic is at work.
4 For an elaboration of this argument in the context of center–periphery relations in the world system see Alain de Janvry and Carlos Garramon (1977).
5 http://www.economist.com/blogs/babbage/2011/11/artificial-intelligence
6 http://www.hartford-hwp.com/archives/25/113.html
7 http://www.philadelphiafieldproject.com
8 http://www.communityeconomies.org/Home

References

Carville, J., and Greenberg, S. (2012). *It's the Middle Class, Stupid!* New York: Penguin.

Cohen, L. (2003). *A Consumer's Republic: The Politics of Mass Consumption in Postwar America*. New York: Random House.

Daly, H. (1996). *Beyond Growth*. Boston: Beacon Press.

de Janvry, A., and Garramon, C. (1977). Laws of Motion of Capital in the Center–Periphery Structure. *The Review of Radical Political Economics*, 9, 29–38.

Dobbs, L. (2006). *War on the Middle Class*. New York: Penguin.

Freeland, C. (2011, June 9). Getting by Without the Middle Class. *The New York Times*. Retrieved February 10, 2013 from http://www.nytimes.com/2011/06/10/us/10iht-letter10.html

Freeland, C. (2012). *Plutocrats: The Rise of the New Global Super-Rich and the Fall of Everyone Else*. New York: Penguin.

Galbraith, J.K. (1958). *The Affluent Society*. New York: Mentor Books.

Gibson-Graham, J.K. (2006). *A Postcapitalist Politics*. Minneapolis: University of Minnesota.

Gibson-Graham, J.K. (2012). *Virtual Issue—Imagining and Enacting Community Economies*. Retrieved March 11, 2013 from http://antipodefoundation.org/2012/06/20/virtual-issue-imagining-and-enacting-community-economies/

Harrington, M. (1962). *The Other America: Poverty in the United States*. New York: Penguin Books.

Huffington, A. (2010). *Third World America: How Our Politicians Are Abandoning the Middle Class and Betraying the American Dream*. New York: Crown Publishers.

Krugman, P. (2007). *The Conscience of a Liberal*. New York: W.W. Norton.

Krugman, P. (2012). *End This Depression Now*. New York: W.W. Norton.

Levine, L. (2012, July 17). *An Analysis of the Distribution of Wealth Across Households, 1989–2010.* Congressional Research Service 7-5700. Retrieved February 10, 2013 from http://www.fas.org/sgp/crs/misc/RL33433.pdf

Marx, K. (1973). *Grundrisse: Foundations of the Critique of Political Economy.* New York: Random House.

Noah, T. (2012). *The Great Divergence: America's Growing Inequality Crisis and What We Can Do About It.* New York: Bloomsbury Press.

O'Reilly, B. (2003). *Who's Looking Out for You?* New York: Random House.

Palley, T. (2005, September 29). *Super-Sized: What Happens when Two Billon Workers Join the Global Labor Market?* Retrieved February 20, 2013 from http://www.hartford-hwp.com/archives/25/113.html

Pew Research Center (2012, August 22). *The Lost Decade of the Middle Class.* Retrieved February 20, 2013 from http://www.pewsocialtrends.org/2012/08/22/the-lost-decade-of-the-middle-class/

Piketty, T., and Saez, E. (2006). *The Evolution of Top Incomes: A Historical and International Perspective, Working Paper 11955.* Retrieved February 20, 2013 from http://www.nber.org/papers/w11955

Rampell, C. (2012, September 14). Defining Middle Class. *The New York Times.* Retrieved February 20, 2013 from http://economix.blogs.nytimes.com/2012/09/14/defining-middle-class/

Reich, R. (2010). *Aftershock: The Next Economy and America's Future.* New York: Alfred A. Knopf.

Saez, E. (2012). *Striking it Richer: The Evolution of Top Incomes in the United States.* Retrieved February 1, 2013 from http://elsa.berkeley.edu/~saez/saez-UStopincomes-2010.pdf on 2013 Feb 1. Berkeley Libraries make the data on the Saez article no longer publicly available online.

Stiglitz, J. (2012). *The Price of Inequality.* New York: W.W. Norton.

The Economist (2011, November 4). *Difference Engine: Luddite Legacy.* Retrieved January 4, 2013 from http://www.economist.com/blogs/babbage/2011/11/artificial-intelligence

Veblen, T. (1994). *The Theory of the Leisure Class.* 1899. New York: Penguin Books.

Yapa, L. (2009). Transforming the University through Community Engagement. *Journal of Higher Education Outreach and Engagement,* 13, 131–146.

INDEX

"shock doctrine" 19; transnational capitalism 33–41; *see also* deindustrialization; deregulation

neoliberal education policy 12–15, 175–7, 218, 226–30, 409–10; and African Americans in higher education 179, 182–7; charter schools 19, 30, 193, 194, 196, 201, 229, 402; conditional cash transfers 208–14; and Latino students 218–24; limitations of performance based goal setting 503–9; online education 186, 199–206, 230; school privatization programs 19, 30, 193, 194, 229–30, 409; standardized testing 13, 194, 195–6, 229–30, 509; subversion of equality 190–7

neoliberal housing policy: community development 512–19; Housing Choice Voucher (HCV) program 269, 270, 275–8, 288, 289, 291, 292; low-income housing tax credit (LIHTC) 296–304, **302**, 514–15, 516; mixed-income housing programs 268–72, 275–6, 278–80, 285, 288–93, *291, 292*, 516, 568; privatization of housing safety net 285–93

neoliberal welfare policy 39, 176, 239–46, **242, 243**, 360–1, 388–9, 562–3; barriers discourse 143–58; and healthcare 330–9; and mental illness 363; and poverty reduction 259–64, **261,** *263*; and private emergency food networks 307–13; *see also* Personal Responsibility and Work Opportunity Reconciliation Act (1996)

New Deal 145–6, 286, 481, 531

New Hampshire, lotteries **65, 68**

New Jersey: Camden 26–31; lotteries **65, 68**; pawnshops 77

Newman, J. 21

Newman, K. 101

New Mexico: colonias 468; lotteries **65, 68**

New Orleans 19, 192, 193, 517, 518

newspapers: homelessness 456–7; and Occupy Wall Street movement 164, 165

New York: legal aid organizations 378, 380–1; lotteries 62, **65, 68**; pawnshops 77

New York Legal Aid Society (NYLAS) 378, 381

New York Shipbuilding 27, 28

New York Times 164, 477–8

Nguyen, D. 491, 492, 493

Nielsen, K.E. 448, 449, 450

Nixon, Richard 254

No Child Left Behind Act (2001) 196, 401–2, 409–10

Noddings, N. 504

Noguera, P.A. 220, 221

non-profit private universities 183, 184

Noordegraaf, M. 245

Nordic countries, universal provision 213, 214, 264

Nord, M. 307

North American Free Trade Agreement (NAFTA) 114, 464, 465

North Carolina, lotteries **65, 68**

North Carolina A and T 182

North Dakota, lotteries 62, **65, 68**

North, D.C. 559–60

North, P. 567, 572

Nussbaum, Martha 506–7, 508, 564

nutrition 472–8, *475, 476*

nutritional transition 473, 476

Nuzzi, Ellen 444

NWRO *see* National Welfare Rights Organization (NWRO)

Oakes, J. 220–1

Obama, Barack 196, 223, 226, 242, 282, 469, 494, 576, 579

obesity 472, 473, 477

Occupy Wall Street movement (OWS) 20, 22–3, 161, 162, 164–7

O'Donoghue, J.L. 541

Offe, C. 559

Ogbu, J.U. 185

Ohio: lotteries **65, 68**; low-income housing tax credit 299, 301–3, **302**

Oklahoma, lotteries **65, 68**

older people: debts 87; disparities in poverty 436–42, **437, 440, 441**; and homelessness 430, 431; home maintenance policies 480–7, **483, 485**; and material hardship measures 123, **124, 125**, 126, **127**; poverty rates *259*, 260, 436; welfare benefits 261, 330, 436

Ollmann, Bertell 230

Olympic Games, Atlanta 290

O'Mahony, J. 490

O'Malley, P. 390

one U.S. dollar per day discourse 106

Ong, A. 245

online education 186, 199–206, 230

Oportunidades program, Mexico 208, 210

Oral Roberts University 448

Oregon, lotteries **65, 68**

Orfield, Gary 196

organized crime 76

osteoporosis 494

Oster, E. 69

out-migration, Camden, NJ 28

out-of-wedlock births 249, 251, 253, 400, 402, 524

Owens, L.A. 451

OWS *see* Occupy Wall Street movement (OWS)

Ozawa, M.N. 254

paradox of thrift 578

parental home schooling 204, 205

PAS *see* Pennsylvania Abolition Society (PAS)

Passavant, Paul A. 353

paternity establishment 251, 388

pathologizing poverty 505